SMALL BUSINESS DESK REFERENCE

ALPHA

A MEMBER OF PENGUIN GROUP (USA) INC.

ALPHA BOOKS

Published by the Penguin Group

Penguin Group (USA) Inc., 375 Hudson Street, New York, New York 10014, U.S.A.

Penguin Group (Canada), 10 Alcorn Avenue, Toronto, Ontario, Canada M4V 3B2 (a division of Pearson Penguin Canada Inc.)

Penguin Books Ltd, 80 Strand, London WC2R 0RL, England

Penguin Ireland, 25 St Stephen's Green, Dublin 2, Ireland (a division of Penguin Books Ltd)

Penguin Group (Australia), 250 Camberwell Road, Camberwell, Victoria 3124, Australia (a division of Pearson Australia Group Pty Ltd)

Penguin Books India Pvt Ltd, 11 Community Centre, Panchsheel Park, New Delhi—110 017, India

Penguin Group (NZ), cnr Airborne and Rosedale Roads, Albany, Auckland #1310, New Zealand (a division of Pearson New Zealand Ltd)

Penguin Books (South Africa) (Pty) Ltd, 24 Sturdee Avenue, Rosebank, Johannesburg 2196, South Africa

Penguin Books Ltd, Registered Offices: 80 Strand, London WC2R 0RL, England

Copyright © 2004 by Penguin Group (USA) Inc.

All rights reserved. No part of this book shall be reproduced, stored in a retrieval system, or transmitted by any means, electronic, mechanical, photocopying, recording, or otherwise, without written permission from the publisher. No patent liability is assumed with respect to the use of the information contained herein. Although every precaution has been taken in the preparation of this book, the publisher and authors assume no responsibility for errors or omissions. Neither is any liability assumed for damages resulting from the use of information contained herein. For information, address Alpha Books, 800 East 96th Street, Indianapolis, IN 46240.

International Standard Book Number: 1-59257-295-2
Library of Congress Catalog Card Number: 2004111452

05   04   03   8   7   6   5   4   3   2   1

Interpretation of the printing code: The rightmost number of the first series of numbers is the year of the book's printing; the rightmost number of the second series of numbers is the number of the book's printing. For example, a printing code of 04-1 shows that the first printing occurred in 2004.

Printed in the United States of America

Note: This publication contains the opinions and ideas of its authors. It is intended to provide helpful and informative material on the subject matter covered. It is sold with the understanding that the authors and publisher are not engaged in rendering professional services in the book. If the reader requires personal assistance or advice, a competent professional should be consulted.

The authors and publisher specifically disclaim any responsibility for any liability, loss, or risk, personal or otherwise, which is incurred as a consequence, directly or indirectly, of the use and application of any of the contents of this book.

Most Alpha books are available at special quantity discounts for bulk purchases for sales promotions, premiums, fund-raising, or educational use. Special books, or book excerpts, can also be created to fit specific needs.

For details, write: Special Markets, Alpha Books, 375 Hudson Street, New York, NY 10014.

Publisher: *Marie Butler-Knight*
Product Manager: *Phil Kitchel*
Senior Managing Editor: *Jennifer Chisholm*
Senior Acquisitions Editor: *Renee Wilmeth*
Development Editor: *Ginny Bess Munroe*
Production Editor: *Megan Douglass*

Copy Editor: *Keith Cline*
Cover/Book Designer: *Trina Wurst*
Indexer: *Angie Bess*
Layout: *Becky Harmon*
Proofreading: *John Etchison*

Contents

Successful Selling   565

Keeping Your Customers Happy   615

Taxes   711

Insurance   745

Introduction

Are you running a small business or thinking of starting one? There's a lot you need to know. And if you're not careful, some of the things you do may come back to haunt you months or years later.

For example, Jim, a small business owner I know, entered into a partnership with two other guys and it's just not working out. Unfortunately, he didn't think about the implications when he signed the paperwork, and now he wishes he had read more about the subject. Another entrepreneur, Sharon, purchased a competitor's business but got stuck with some unforeseen liabilities. I've met numerous small business owners who have been sued for harassment, wasted money on poor marketing campaigns, or paid too much for their computer systems. And I'm certainly not immune—I chose the wrong type of health insurance for my company, and now I can't get out of the contract for another year!

Most small business owners aren't experts in writing contracts, analyzing financial statements, or knowing employment law. If you run your own shop, you probably don't buy and sell businesses on a daily basis. And I bet you aren't familiar with the nuances behind organizational structures. But I bet you'll agree on this—a little guidance will go a long way. If Jim had read about partnerships and corporations before relying on others, he might have had a little more to say about the arrangement. Or if Sharon had the chance to read a bit about acquisitions, she might have been much more alert about those unforeseen liabilities. I wish I had done a little more research on health insurance before jumping on the first plan that presented itself.

As a small business owner, you just don't have the time to do all the research you know you should be doing. And you're probably not thrilled about paying the fees required by those who are experts in the field. Of course, there's a lot of material in bookstores and on the Internet to read, but putting it all together in one place, or finding the exact information you're looking for is a formidable task.

A few months ago I was in the small business section at my local bookstore. I was amazed to find that there are no books about running a small business. Sure, there are plenty on how to start your own business. And there are lots of books about sales, marketing, accounting, management, even leadership. But what about the small business owner who needs help dealing with day-to-day issues specific to running a company? The management books I looked at seemed targeted to the corporate world. Running a small business presents an entirely different set of challenges. And yet there's no one source that I could go to for help. It was a frustrating experience, especially because I knew that I wasn't alone. I know lots of people that run their own companies, like Jim and Sharon. We're all looking for just a couple of good reference sources specifically designed for the small business owner. With a little help we can avoid a lot of minefields.

Are you starting up a new business and looking to set up your computer system? Or maybe you're running your own business and have a problem retaining good people. How do you find a good attorney? Are you looking at your financial statements the right way? What questions should you avoid asking when interviewing that prospective employee?

During the past 10 years of running my own small company, I've looked for a single source to get these answers and have never succeeded. For my marketing questions, I would pore through various marketing books, and for my personnel issues, I would seek advice from consultants. I've always wondered why there isn't one sole source, a reference book, that has the answers that small business owners need.

Now there is.

When I was asked to edit a book specifically targeted at small business owners like myself, I jumped at the opportunity. For one, I had the opportunity to put together a true reference guide that can be used by would-be entrepreneurs and small business owners alike. I almost fainted when I saw the amount of material that needed to be read and edited. But what great material there was!

This book is a collection of knowledge from fellow small business owners. They have all published advice and guidance in the past. But now these pearls of wisdom have been brought together in one place. Here you'll get educated about the tax system, how to assemble a great sales and marketing team, and what to look for when you attend a trade show. You'll also learn some lessons about extending credit or buying a franchise. You'll even be taught some estate planning and employment law. All in one book!

Like any reference material, this book is not designed to be read cover to cover. Rather, it's a book that should be referred to often, both by new and experienced small business owners alike. It's your starting point. Sure there are lots of books about customer service, but what are the basics that every small business owner should know? Check Part 13. Yes, you're going to want to consult your accountant and attorney before selling your business, but before you do make sure to read Part 18. What are some ways to keep your employees' productivity at its highest? Take a look at Part 17 about growing your business profitably.

This book is not just a bunch of advice from one person. It's a collection of intellectual property from a dozen different authors and sources. It represents hundreds of years of business experience and thousands of hours of writing effort. One person can't write the definitive reference book for small business owners. But a bunch of people can, as long as it's brought together in a readable manner. That's what the *Small Business Desk Reference* is all about. It's like having a dozen great consultants at your disposal … all in one place.

The *Small Business Desk Reference* is required reading for anyone running his or her own company. It is the first place to look whenever an issue arises—be it sales, marketing, employee-related, or financial.

What is a small business anyway? So many people try to come up with the definitive description. Some try to define a small business by the number of people they employ, or their revenues. Others look at their ability to go public on the stock market. But these definitions don't really matter. You're looking at this book because you know that you're running a small business, or thinking of starting one. You're not a specialist at any one thing, but you need to know more than the average bear, if only to stay ahead. You want advice on marketing, production, even writing up a legal contract. These are all things you can't (or won't) delegate to others.

And this reference book will always be by your side to help you succeed. Now you're armed to conquer the world.

EXTRAS

This book features a number of valuable sidebars that provide additional information in each section.

TIP

A handy piece of information or shortcut for success

PLAIN ENGLISH

A concise definition of a word or concept.

CAUTION

A warning showing what not to do.

TRADEMARKS

All terms mentioned in this book that are known to be or are suspected of being trademarks or service marks have been appropriately capitalized. Alpha Books and Penguin Group (USA) Inc. cannot attest to the accuracy of this information. Use of a term in this book should not be regarded as affecting the validity of any trademark or service mark.

Starting Your Business

Know What You Do Best and Do It

We all need to know what path we plan to take when we want to get from point A to point B. If you're making a life-changing decision such as going from being a hobbyist or employee to a part- or full-time businessperson, you'll need to take many factors into consideration. In this section, we help you explore what you know about yourself and learn how that translates into how you attain your goals.

Every action we take at every moment of every day, and even our inaction, involves making choices. Compromises are inevitable and can be beneficial—a growth experience. But compromising your soul or someone else's happiness to achieve your objective is too great a sacrifice. This section helps you define what your passion is, determine how to match your skills to that passion, and learn how to position yourself to accomplish your mission.

DEFINE YOUR DREAM

Of course we're happiest when we work at what we enjoy doing; it's most people's dream. But sometimes it's difficult to define exactly what work we want to do or to evaluate the skills we have and figure out how they can help us turn our dream into a new kind of life. Okay, so you've been thinking for a while about how to make money with a new business. Well, trust me on this: Until you formulate a plan and start putting that plan into action, nothing is going to happen!

If you're thinking of making the move from an employee to a business owner, make sure you're ready. Evaluate every factor: your interests, skills, time, money, family situation, and reason for wanting to do it. When you decide to start a business, it takes personal commitment and dedication to carry out the plan you've set in motion. If you think through all of your options before you act, you'll have a much greater chance of success.

TIP

To achieve your goals you need to ...

- Be clear about your purpose or mission in life.

- Live true to that purpose.

- Develop a purposeful compatibility in all areas of your life.

It's *Your* Life

Try to think of life as a journey leading you to your purpose. This journey is all about *you!* What will help you live more passionately every day and achieve your goals? Beneath the degrees, titles, or accomplishments, what is inside you to be discovered? What is your unique and special spark? Is it buried deep? Is it neglected? Or have you just chosen to ignore it? Have you been seeking to please whomever, drowning out the pure longings of *your* heart? Listen to the whispers from your spirit, the voice from deep within. *You* can claim it! It is *your* life! Set your goals, map out your plan, and then you can begin!

Your plan to make the transition from hobbyist or employee to businessperson has to be an extension of you, with your traits and your skills carefully applied to achieve your ultimate goals. Business success doesn't happen overnight, but each small step you take will move you closer to your goal.

Decisions, Decisions

Think for a moment about how many decisions you make every day. Isn't everything a decision? Do you get up as soon as the alarm goes off in the morning, or do you hit the snooze button? Do you wear your blue outfit today, or your green one? Will your day start with a purpose, or will you just go through the motions that are expected of you?

Every action or inaction we take, every moment of every day, involves making choices. What decisions are you making today? What will the combined impact of today's choices be on your tomorrow, your next month, or your next year? Regardless of how insignificant a decision may seem, think about it.

Remember, if you don't feel comfortable making a lot of decisions all the time, then running a small business may not be for you!

Choose It or Lose It

Starting today, when you're faced with a choice, consider it for an extra second and then take action to bring you closer to realizing your ideal life. Theodore Roosevelt said, "In any moment of decision, the best thing you can do is the right thing. The worst thing you can do is nothing." Deciding *not* to take action is like deciding to keep the door locked to your self-created prison. If your heart is racing, if you feel restless, if the feeling stirs you deep inside, the message to you is to make powerful choices. *Take action! Live your life as you were meant to live it!*

DISCOVER YOUR PASSION

The following quiz can help you discover your passion *only* if you take it, so please either take a moment now to grab a pad or notebook and something to write with or bookmark this page and promise yourself that you'll complete this exercise later. It's a look at your whole life history, so it may take you some thinking time to get it done.

Find Your Joy Factor

1. When did you experience the most sustained period of joy? What were you doing then? Where were you? Who were you with? How did it feel?

2. What are your three most favorite things to do? If you had a free day with no commitments, where would you be found? What would you be doing, and with whom would you be doing it?

3. In what area do you excel? (No modesty allowed here!) Truly, what are you complimented on a lot? It could be anything.

4. What do you most want to be remembered for? If you were designing your epitaph, what would you want it to say?

5. If you had a magic wand, what would you change about your life today? How would it look compared to how it looks now? Which aspects of your life are changeable, both short term and long term?

6. How does your joy factor overlap with your favorite activities and the areas you excel in? Does doing the things you do well bring you joy, or are they really for someone else? Do you see which activities are obvious joy matches and which aren't?

7. What is the first small step you can take to living out your passion as you defined it in Question 6? Take some time to really think this one through. Concentrate and focus before you respond.

TIP

After you discover your true passion and have taken time to understand who you are and where you want to go, you'll be focused on what will work for you. That's when you'll be able to set out in new directions, such as turning your hobby into a business.

In your response to Question 6, the activities that you thought of as overlapping with your joy factor, those that bring you the most joy are likely to be the things that will bring you into passionate purposeful living.

Now you'll be able to start the next step: building your overall business road map.

BUILDING THE ROADMAP

The following strategies helped one small business owner in her business venture and can help you start a business:

- **Pay attention to everything!** Do so even if it has nothing to do with anything you think you'd be interested in. This skill will enable you to know the right questions to ask and where to get the information. You'd be surprised how some of that information might help you in the future. Past employment experiences, conversations with people, and so forth are invaluable keys to the success of your future. You'd be amazed at the things you can learn throughout the years just through simple conversations with people, things that you would have never known to ask and that you may have never come across if you had not been paying attention. If you can continually collect and store information in your brain, it can be beneficial in helping you run a business.

- **Never be afraid to ask people questions!** No question is dumb—really!

- **Be willing to fail.** Recognize your failures and be able to learn from them. Failure is as good as success. It is a stepping-stone toward your goals. It can be a process that will enrich the outcome of your business.

THE 30-SECOND RECAP

- Before becoming a small business owner, evaluate your interests, skills, time, money family situation, and reasons for wanting to go out on your own.

- Your business will be your life, so make sure it fits in with your lifestyle.

- Decision making is a critical part of running a small business.

- Be passionate and enjoy what you do.

Tips for Choosing a Business

You've probably already identified some need in the market that's not being met, or you have a particular product line or service that you feel is right on target for the current marketplace. If so, you're ready to match your skills with those ideas. This section shows you how to choose a business that does makes you passionate and matches your skills.

MAKING YOUR LIST

Begin by listing what you enjoy doing, what your hobbies are, which skills you've acquired, what your work experiences have been, and what your plans are for your business. Making such a list right now may seem a little simplistic, but you'll be surprised at how much writing down your ideas will help you crystallize what you want from a small business. This exercise is just a starting point; nothing is carved in stone. As you learn more about the process of making the transition from a hobbyist to a businessperson, you'll evaluate and redefine your thinking until you have a plan that you're comfortable with and confident about.

Compare the list you've just made with your list of what the market wants. Do any obvious matches leap out at you? If not, don't give up.

Eliminate any of the businesses that you don't believe you'll really enjoy owning. As a small business owner, you'll be living, sleeping, and breathing your business—if you don't enjoy it, your chances for success are slim.

On the other hand, be wary of relying too heavily on your list of interests when making your choice. Don't forget that a lot of small business owners also spend time on tasks such as managing, marketing, haggling with suppliers, meeting with a lawyer or accountant, and so on. As a small business owner, you'll have to wear many hats in addition to being responsible for the design and production of your products or services.

Suppose that photography is your passion. If you open a store that sells photographic equipment, you'll have to pay rent, buy inventory, buy fixtures for the store, budget for all the other overhead, and possibly even have to consider hiring support staff. That'll cost you a lot up front, and you won't see any return on investment until you've made sufficient profits to recover your initial investment.

CAUTION

Don't get in over your head. If you don't have a lot of money to start with, look for a business in which you get paid up front and don't have a lot of start-up costs. Or consider starting on a part-time basis until you feel comfortable with taking it to a full-time business. Stay-at-home moms or people getting ready to retire in a few years often elect to start on a part-time basis. The goal is to get the business up and running and then build it into something that you can expand into a full-time operation when you're ready to make that commitment.

On the other hand, if you hire yourself out as a photographer, or if you sell your photography as prints, or perhaps if you use your photos as decoupage for wall décor or to create a stationery line, you can probably operate from home with few up-front costs. So your return on investment is a lot quicker.

REFINING YOUR BUSINESS FOCUS

You'll have many alternatives to consider and choices to make before you're ready to launch your business. Use the following list to be sure you cover all the bases:

- Consider businesses in which you'll have a lot of repeat customers, or create a product line or service that ensures that customers will continue to buy from you.

- Be realistic about your time and commitment to the venture, and whether it should be full time or part time.

- Consider the functional use of your products. Consumers tend to spend more money on products that serve a "useful" purpose while also being decorative so they can justify spending the money on them.

- Be realistic about your abilities and the time it will take to secure your market niche. Are you truly expert at what you do? Is the market large enough for your specialty?

- Avoid competing with discounters, mass merchandisers, or well-established local businesses—it will be just about impossible to rival their prices or range of merchandising. Instead, you'll want to compete in service and differentiate your business.

- Service businesses are obviously the easiest and cheapest to start because you don't have to buy a lot of equipment or produce and maintain a tangible inventory. If your goal is to someday sell the business and retire, however, be aware that service businesses are also often the hardest to find buyers for because their primary asset is often you, the owner (unless you've developed the business enough to have a trained staff).

- Look at the total picture—not just costs and potential income, but also how your decision fits with your lifestyle and family situation. Discuss your plans with those who will also be affected by the decision you make. Enlist their support and input so that as you set out to accomplish your plan, you have their understanding and willingness to see you through the process.

- Will this be a family affair or a partnership? If so, then you all have to participate equally in developing your plan together so that everyone is focused and in agreement on the objectives.

WHAT'S YOUR MISSION?

Before you can progress in business, you have to have some idea of where you're headed and how you plan to get there. It's called a mission statement, and you need to have one. This is a crucial step in planning your journey.

For instance, if you leave your house determined to find a new outfit for an important upcoming business function, your mission will be to make sure that you find just the right one before you return home. You must also develop a passion for your mission and be willing to stop short of nothing to accomplish what you've determined to do. That means that, not only will you buy that new outfit before you go home, you'll also drive a hundred miles to find just the right one!

You must decide what you hope to accomplish through your business. If you want to be known for providing the best-quality fabricated piping products, then that is your mission statement, plain and simple. By making it your mission, you obligate yourself to do exactly that: make every effort to provide the best-quality fabricated piping products. Your mission statement also gives you a place to start on a list, if you choose to, of how you plan to accomplish your mission.

Write down your mission statement. When you do, you'll be more apt to live by it. Think of it as key to your business success! Find an environment that is right for you to sit down and think. Put together notes and phrases as you capture your thoughts. Then combine your notes into a mission statement that adequately sums up what you want to accomplish.

TIP

Develop a product or service unique in design and creativity, something that others can't or don't offer. Create your own market position or niche to serve your target customers. For example the business owner who once specialized in "computers" now has honed his specialty to "networks" and "security." This has helped him become an expert in a specific niche of the computer industry.

After you decide what you want to accomplish through your business, determine what you must do to carry it out, propose what you're willing to do, and do it. Keep your mission statement close by, where you'll readily be able to see it when you need to remember why you're doing what you do. Think of it as more than a group of words written on a piece of paper—make it your passion, the driving force that becomes a pathway to your success!

THE 30-SECOND RECAP

- Before you decide on a business, you must define who you are and what you want to accomplish.

- Either live the life you were meant to live or survive in a life based on compromise—the choice is yours.

- Your enthusiasm for what you produce or provide makes it more attractive to the consumer.

- Before you launch your business, consider every way possible to refine your business focus.

- Write a mission statement, keep it nearby, and refer to it whenever you wonder what you're doing and why.

- The skills and experience that you bring to your business are a deciding factor in your success.

Wearing Different Hats

In the United States, it's estimated that only about 30 percent of all start-ups are still in business after 5 years. Many of us hear the call to ownership of a small business—complete freedom, unlimited opportunity, dreams realized— but of those who answer it, most do not succeed. Why? What separates those who succeed from those who fail? Knowledge of the business, sufficient capital, experience, and a unique idea at the right time are just some of the characteristics of a successful business owner. Although there isn't any way to guarantee that you'll become a successful business owner, you can greatly improve your odds by becoming well prepared for the task.

This section examines some of the unknowns or variables that you may want to consider in deciding what the direction should be for your new business.

HATS, HATS, HATS

We've all heard the stories of the corporate executive who moans about being overworked because he or she has to wear two or three hats. Well, most small business owners would give anything if they had to wear *only* two or three hats. If you're going to own a small business, some of the hats you'll be wearing are these:

- **Accountant/bookkeeper.** Even if you have an accountant, you'll need to know a little about accounting: which records to keep and how to keep them.

- **Advertising executive.** In addition to having to plan your advertising campaign, you may also write the advertising copy and design your brochures and related sales materials.

- **Business planner.** As the business owner, you'll inevitably want to make changes, perhaps to expand the business or add a new service or product line. If you want to make a change, it will be your responsibility to do it; you have to plan it and execute it. In making your decisions, you have to consider the outcomes that could result from them.

- **Buyer.** It will be your responsibility to locate wholesale suppliers for the equipment, supplies, and materials that you'll need to produce your products, offer your services, and run your business.

- **Clerk/receptionist/typist/secretary.** Even if you have some clerical help, you will inevitably do some filing, typing, and mailing, as well as some of your telephone answering. At a minimum, you'll have to know how to do it so you can teach your staff how you want it done.

- **Collector.** If you offer open account terms, when customers don't pay, it will be up to you to collect from them. You'll have to know what you can and can't do when collecting.

- **Human resources administrator.** If you have employees, you will be responsible for all human resources functions, including recruiting, hiring, firing, and keeping track of benefits information. You'll be the one filling out all the insurance forms, answering employee questions and complaints, and making the decisions that affect your employees.

- **Lawyer.** Even if you retain or hire a lawyer, you will have to know a little about the law. If you don't use a lawyer, you'll have to prepare all of your own forms, contracts, and agreements.

TIP

Operating a small business requires pitching in and doing whatever is necessary to get the job done, even if it means that the CEO has to sweep the floor and take out the trash.

- **Manager/supervisor.** The decisions are all yours, and along with that comes the responsibility of dealing with the effects that your decisions have on the success of your business.

- **Market researcher.** Before you start your business, you'll have to find out who your target customers are and where they're located. You may also have to conduct market research at various times during the course of your business, such as when you're considering introducing a new product or service.

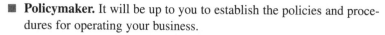

- **Policymaker.** It will be up to you to establish the policies and procedures for operating your business.
- **PR person.** Depending upon the type of business you own, you may have to join business groups; attend various breakfasts, lunches, and dinners; and just generally network with anyone who could help your business prosper.
- **Product developer.** It will be up to you to design your product line and packaging.
- **Product producer.** If you're producing products, you are responsible for the manufacture of your product line or, if you provide a service, the delivery of your service.
- **Sales/marketing executive.** In addition to having to plan your marketing or advertising campaign, you will have to carry it out. You may have do some preliminary market research, contact potential customers, and make sure that existing customers stay happy. You'll also have to sell your product or service directly.
- **Tax collector.** If you sell goods at the retail level, you're responsible for collecting and paying the sales tax. If you have employees, you're responsible for payroll taxes.
- **Technology expert.** As a small business owner, you will probably come to depend upon your computer. Unless you have a service contract with a computer technician, you'll have to solve problems, install upgrades, and load software. You'll also have to keep up-to-date on new software and hardware, and the latest changes in computer technology.
- **Trade show coordinator.** If you sell at art and craft or trade shows, you'll need to prepare for and attend these events.

You may not plan to start a business that will require employees or the subcontracting of any of the preceding responsibilities, but consider that, as your business grows and expands, you may eventually have to wear most of the described hats. You can reduce your business risk by recognizing that you may face many of these responsibilities at some time.

CAUTION

Not everyone is cut out to be an entrepreneur. It takes a special talent. Before you invest time, energy, money, and a piece of your heart, it's important to do some serious self-analysis.

Your Strengths and Weaknesses

Starting a business is risky, at best, but your chances of making it will be better if you understand the problems that you may encounter and have those problems worked out before you start up. The first question that you need to answer is about you: Do you have what it takes?

Strengths and Weaknesses Checklist

Following are some questions to help you evaluate whether you have what it takes to run a small business:

1. Are you a self-starter?

    ❐ I do things on my own. Nobody has to tell me to get going.

    ❐ If someone gets me started, I can keep going all right.

    ❐ Easy does it. I don't put myself out until I have to.

2. How do you feel about other people?

    ❐ I like people. I can get along with just about anyone.

    ❐ I have plenty of friends; I don't need anyone else.

    ❐ Most people irritate me.

3. Can you lead others?

    ❐ When I start something, I can get most people to go along.

    ❐ If someone tells me what we should do, I can give the orders.

    ❐ I let someone else get things moving; then I go along if I feel like it.

4. Can you take responsibility?

    ❐ I like to take charge of things and see them through.

    ❐ I'll take over if I have to, but I'd rather let someone else be responsible.

    ❐ There's always some eager beaver around wanting to show how smart he or she is. I say, go for it.

5. How good an organizer are you?

    ❐ I like to have a plan before I start. I'm usually the one to get things lined up when the group wants to do something.

    ❐ I do all right unless things get too confused; then I quit.

    ❐ I get all set, and then something comes along and presents too many problems, so I just take things as they come.

6. How good a worker are you?

☐ I can keep going as long as I need to. I don't mind working hard for something I want.

☐ I'll work hard for a while, but when I've had enough, that's it.

☐ I can't see that hard work gets you anywhere.

7. Are you comfortable making decisions?

☐ I can make up my mind in a hurry if I have to. It usually turns out okay, too.

☐ I can if I have plenty of time. If I have to make up my mind fast, later I think that I should have decided the other way.

☐ I don't like to be the one to decide things.

8. Can people trust what you say?

☐ You bet they can. I don't say things that I don't mean.

☐ I try to be on the level most of the time, but sometimes I just say what's easiest.

☐ Why bother if the other person doesn't know the difference?

9. Can you stick with it?

☐ If I make up my mind to do something, I don't let anything stop me.

☐ I usually finish what I start ... if it goes well.

☐ If it doesn't go right immediately, I quit. Why beat my brains out?

10. How good is your health?

☐ I never run down!

☐ I have enough energy for most things that I want to do.

☐ I run out of energy sooner than most of my friends.

Now total the checks that you made next to the first answer to each question, then the second answer, and then the third. If most of your checks were next to the first answers, you probably have what it takes to run a business. If not, you're likely to have more trouble than you can handle by yourself. Better find a partner who is strong in areas where you're weak. If many of your checks are next to the third answers, even a good partner may not be able to shore you up.

ARE YOU CUT OUT FOR ENTREPRENEURSHIP?

Being an entrepreneur takes a special talent. Some owners of small businesses have it, and some don't. The following are some more serious self-analysis questions that will help you assess your entrepreneurial abilities:

- Am I prepared to work hard and make sacrifices?
- Am I self-disciplined?
- Do I have management ability?
- Am I experienced enough in this field?
- What do I want out of life?
- Are my goals realistic and attainable?

Many studies have shown that entrepreneurs are persevering and not easily defeated. They thrive in a challenging environment and have a tremendous need to be in control. They turn diversity into opportunity. They are risk-takers. They welcome responsibility and are willing and able to make decisions.

Moreover, successful entrepreneurs are patient and able to wait out the sometimes-slow beginnings of a business. They are also able to learn from their mistakes, trust their own judgment, and maintain an optimistic outlook. It's obvious: You have to love your work. The key is to identify what you enjoy doing the most and then find a business opportunity that makes use of your skills and interests.

FOCUS ON WHAT YOU WANT

Goals are important because they will affect just about everything you do, from start-up to daily operations, to long-range planning. What do you want from your business? What does "succeeding" mean to you—and if you want to succeed, how will you know it when you get there?

Knowing what you want from your business, your goal, directs all of the other decisions that you'll have to make when you launch it. It will affect which business you choose, how you evaluate your chances for success, and how you determine whether you have the right skills.

How do your goals fit with your reasons for wanting to start a business? Your reasons are often the underlying guides to your goals. Your goals are not just the destinations you're headed toward—they're also the signposts along the way that will keep you on the right road. If you're still a little uncertain about goals and what they could mean to you, think of it this way: Goals won't just determine whether you start a small business; they'll also play a major role in just about every decision you make along the way, from how you structure your business to whether you hire employees, to how you plan to sell and market your products or services. It's not enough just to say, for example, that you want a change from working for someone else. You'll need to develop specific targets by quantifying your goals.

PLAIN ENGLISH

A **goal** is an end that one strives to attain. Short-term goals can help you achieve those small but important victories. Your short-term goals should be realistic and quickly achievable.

TIPS FOR GOAL-SETTING

Keep the following tips in mind as you go through the process of defining your goals:

- Make sure that the goal you're working for is something that you really want, not just something that sounds good. The important thing to remember here is that your goals must be consistent with your values.

- One goal should not contradict any of your other goals. For example, you can't buy a million-dollar house if your income goal is $50,000 per year.

- If you need help from someone in achieving your goal, will you have that person's cooperation? If you plan to open a business with a partner, but that person doesn't share your goal, then you both need to evaluate your goals to make sure they are compatible.

- Write down your goal in positive, not negative, language. Work for what you want, not for what you plan to leave behind.

- Write out your goal in complete detail. Instead of writing, "Open a new business," write "Start a part-time woodworking business out of my home making high-quality wood shelves and curio cabinets that I design and produce to sell at craft shows on weekends." The more detail, the better. It will help you picture your goal as real, which helps make it attainable.

- Make sure that your goal is high enough. Shoot for the moon! If you miss, you'll still be in the company of stars.

- Write out your goal as if you've already achieved it; this is vitally important. For example, "I own the state's largest graphic design company specializing in business logo designs."

YOUR GOALS ARE ON PAPER—NOW WHAT?

First of all, unless someone is critical to helping you achieve your goal(s), keep them to yourself. A negative attitude from friends, family, and neighbors can quickly drag you down. It can give you the negative, false belief that you're not capable of achieving your goals.

If you have a false belief that you're not artistic, create your own brand of artistry. You may not be a portrait painter, but you'll be able to craft something unique. Create your world as you would prefer it to be, instead of reacting to a world of someone else's creation.

It's very important that your self-talk (the thoughts in your head) remain positive. I call this *PMI,* for *positive mental image.* This is the process of seeing or visualizing yourself as having accomplished a goal.

Reviewing your goals daily is a crucial part of your success and must become part of your routine:

> Each morning when you wake up, read your goal list aloud. Visualize your goals as they appear on the list—achieved.
>
> Each night, right before you go to bed, repeat the process.
>
> Every time you make a decision during the day, ask yourself this question, "Does it take me closer to or further from my goal?" If the answer is "closer to," then you've made the right decision. If the answer is "further from," well, you know what to do.

This process will begin to replace any negative self-talk that you may have been carrying on with positive images of accomplished goals, and you will get started working toward them.

TIP

Successful small business owners have gone through many of the steps we've explored so far, taking each phase of building a business one step at a time. But most believe that one of the reasons for rising sales is enthusiasm, which shows in the quality of work.

QUANTIFY YOUR GOALS

Quantifying your goals can be a long process. You'll have to gather a lot more information before you're ready to set specific targets. Eventually, you'll probably want to shape your quantified goals into a business plan. Before we move on to the process of gathering information needed to quantify goals, here are some guidelines for quantifying them:

- **Be realistic.** Having high expectations is great, but make sure that you establish targets that are reasonable and potentially achievable. If you're opening a fast-food restaurant, saying that you want to be bigger than McDonald's or Burger King within six months is not realistic.

- **Be aggressive.** Don't set goals that are too easily achieved; set both short-term and long-term goals that are realistic and that still aim high. If after six months in business you accomplish all of your goals, then what? Don't sell yourself short: If you want to be bigger than McDonald's or Burger King within 20 years, go for it.

- **Set priorities and be consistent.** Beware of inadvertently setting inconsistent goals. For example, a goal of growing fast enough to have two or three employees within three years might be inconsistent with your net earnings goal if adding employees will lead to failing to meet your short-term net earnings target. There's nothing wrong with having both goals. Just be aware that the potential conflict exists; establish priorities among your goals, and have some flexibility in sorting out any conflicts.

- **Be specific.** Establish targets that can actually be measured, and use figures as targets whenever possible. For example, you may set a goal of selling your products or services via craft or trade shows, of having a certain number of products or services to offer when you open, or of reaching a certain dollar amount of sales. Tie those figures to specific time frames (within six months, within two years, within five years, and so on).

Some people have a hard time setting goals because they just don't know where or how to start. One way to get started is with an easily quantifiable goal. For example, start with the amount of money that you'll need to earn to cover your actual living expenses during the start-up phase of your business; no matter what, you'll need to make enough to make ends meet.

CAUTION

Owning a small business is not just another job. It's a totally different lifestyle. You need to make sure that your goals are compatible with your lifestyle. You have to ask yourself whether you're ready for a complete commitment to the success of your business.

Short-Term Goal-Setting

It'll be important psychologically in those first chaotic start-up months to be able to feel that you're making some progress. Short-term goals can help you achieve those small but important victories while you're working on long-term goals, such as getting the business running and helping it grow. Your short-term goals should be realistic and quickly achievable. Some short-term goals may be to ...

- Select and file a name for the business that reflects its nature and style.
- Obtain any business licenses required, or get your sales tax number.
- Set up the business bank account.
- Establish a merchant credit card account.
- Find a savvy small-business lawyer, accountant, and other professionals that you may need.

Keep Your Goals Flexible

If one important statement applied to all of us, it would be, "During the course of your life, the most constant thing you will experience is change." So your goals may have to shift. If they don't, perhaps you're not working on them, or they lack focus. Or perhaps you're so focused on a goal that you don't see other possibilities that can shift its original form. You may still hit the bull's eye, but it'll be on a different target.

Understand that a shift in your goal may not necessarily be negative, but a word of caution: I don't advocate changing your goals every other week or month. I merely point out that life circumstances and intense focus can attract possibilities not apparent at the time the original goal was defined.

Be flexible! And don't forget to celebrate achieving a goal with a *big* pat on the back for yourself.

Be the Master of Your Fate

The Great Houdini's contracts always specified that before he disappeared into the trunk or cell from which he planned to break out, he could kiss his wife. What no one knew was that, as their lips met, his wife secretly passed a small piece of wire from her mouth to his which he used to pick the locks.

At one of his most highly publicized performances, the wire didn't seem to be doing the trick. Houdini later wrote of the experience: "After one solid minute, I didn't hear any of the familiar clicking sounds. I thought, my gosh, this could ruin my career; I'm at the pinnacle of fame, and the press is all here. After two minutes, I was beginning to sweat profusely because I was not getting this lock picked. After three minutes of failure, with thirty seconds left I reached into my pocket to get a handkerchief and dry my hands and forehead, and when I did, I leaned against the vault door and it creaked open." And there you have it. The door was never locked!

TIP

As entrepreneurs, we can all be master magicians, the masters of our fate. All we have to do is face whatever barrier seems to be looming before us and then take the first step—give the door a shove. The biggest obstacles are the ones we create for ourselves in our own minds.

Harry Houdini believed the door was locked, so it may as well have been. It's the same way with all of us. The only lock is in our minds. Not only is the door not locked to us, but there may be no door at all—just the illusion of one. Give yourself permission to take a little risk. Take positive action, and unlock your mind to discover what possibilities could await you. What better road to follow as you start out on your path to making money with your hobby?

THE 30-SECOND RECAP

- As a business owner, you may have to deal with wearing many hats.
- Set your goals so that they are realistic and attainable, and that they can be actually measured so you can see the results.
- A positive attitude is crucial to achieving success.

Forming a Partnership

Now that you're heading down the road of entrepreneurship, you'll want to think about legally setting up your new venture. In this section we'll assume you're starting a business from scratch. If you've chosen to go into business with a friend or family member, then a partnership comes readily to mind. Two or more persons can establish a partnership. Usually, they sign a partnership agreement that specifies certain rights, such as profits, voting, and management. Each partner is personally liable for the business debts, and each partner is taxed on the partnership income. Is it the right choice? Please read on.

Choosing Among the Choices

You have a choice of partnership entities:

- Regular partnership
- Registered limited liability partnership (LLP)
- Limited partnership

The partnership and now its alternative choice, the registered limited liability partnership, is the choice of many professional firms, including doctors, lawyers, and accountants to name just a few. Limited partnerships have been frequently used as tax shelters for oil, gas, and coal operations, as well as real estate investments. Each of the three business entities has its advantages and disadvantages. Let's look at them one by one to see which type might work best for you.

Regular Partnership Is General

You can create an informal partnership with a simple handshake, but executing a *partnership* agreement is a much better way to begin business.

Your partnership begins with an agreement. Included in the terms of agreement should be an explanation of voting rights, profit and loss sharing, and admission of new partners. Each partner is personally liable for the debts of the partnership. The death or withdrawal of a partner may terminate the partnership, but this can be changed by the agreement. Each partner reports his or her share of the profit or loss on his or her individual tax return, whether distributed or not.

PLAIN ENGLISH

A **partnership** is an association of two or more persons who will act as co-owners of a business for profit. Individuals or business entities may form partnerships.

Most states don't require the partners to file anything with the secretary of state, unlike a corporation, which must file its articles of incorporation. If the partnership, like any entity, is doing business in another name, state law generally requires filing a "Doing Business As" certificate locally.

Drafting the Best Agreement for All

Partnerships are of this world, and as such depend on trust and a good partnership agreement. If you shake hands and proceed without an agreement, then the Uniform Partnership Act will provide the terms of your agreement as the default choice. For example, if there is no partnership agreement, the partners automatically share equally in the profits, losses, and votes.

If you decide to hammer out the terms and create an agreement (which I strongly suggest you do), you'll be trying to foresee typical challenges that you may face. Just this process of hammering out the terms is perhaps the best test of whether or not you and your partner or partners are compatible.

For example, two partners were going through the proposed agreement, but became stuck at the point of check authorization. One insisted that all checks over $5 be cosigned. In this situation, it seems that both parties should reconsider being partners. The trust level wasn't particularly high.

The following is a discussion of some of the terms that you and your partners should consider as you create your agreement:

- **Choosing your name.** The partners can choose to include their own names—such as Able, Baker, and Charlie—or any name not previously trademarked. Because a name may say it all, choose one that fits nicely into your business advertising.

- **Laying claim to a purpose.** Indicating your business purpose—what you intend to sell, provide, or trade in—in the agreement, is not necessary, but doing so will help you avoid future confusion if, say, one or more partners wants to go off in a direction different from what you anticipated when you signed up. Here's what can happen: My client originally established a partnership to sell wedding dresses and later discovered the other partner had decided to branch off into selling used cars. A more definite purpose statement would have required an amendment to the partnership agreement before one of the partners could start hawking cars instead of dresses.

- **Fixing the term.** Most partnerships continue until the partners retire or die, or until the business is no longer profitable. Few of the agreements specify a time limit. Because a partnership dissolves upon the death or retirement of a partner, the agreement should include a clause permitting the remaining partners to continue the partnership (and pay off the retiring partner or deceased partner's estate). For instance, one law firm had existed for several years. The partners never got around to executing a partnership agreement. Suddenly one of the younger partners died of a heart attack. The partnership dissolved and had to reform, at some cost and tax expense.

In addition to these terms, pay careful attention to financial terms. Each partner's initial capital contribution must be specified in the agreement. A prospective partner who has second thoughts about coming up with the money may have third thoughts when that partner is reminded of his or her legally binding promise. Capital contributions may be in the form of cash, property, or services to the partnership.

If contributions are property or services, the agreement should indicate how and by whom these contributions are to be valued. You should clearly indicate what property the partnership will own. For example, a partnership was about to break up, and the major dispute involved who owned what. The agreement specified that each partner's contribution of property was listed on attachment A. Unfortunately, no one had put together the attachment A, and memories of what was contributed considerably differed.

 CAUTION

Don't forget to have evidence of your debts to the partnership. The IRS may challenge a claim of debt without evidence of a promissory note and regular payments.

If a partner is to lend money to the partnership, clearly state the terms of the loan, including the rate of interest and payment due date. The partnership should execute a promissory note as evidence of the debt. The partnership may need additional capital contributions in the future, and you should provide for that contingency. Retaining some percentage of earnings or requiring additional capital contributions by the partners upon call of the partnership should be included in the agreement.

UNDERSTANDING PROFITS AND LOSSES

The partners can share profits and losses equally, in proportion to the capital contributions, according to the work performed, or any other way specified in the agreement. If there is no agreement, profits and losses are shared equally.

Determining profit and loss shares is never easy, and this can be further complicated if the partnership wants to distribute bonuses among the partners.

The partners may want to pay bonuses to one or more partners for superior performance. Beware that performance bonuses often engender resentment among those whose remuneration is not as generous. For example, a law partnership tried to allocate bonuses based on client revenue generated. This infuriated the partners with less-lucrative but important practices. Losses can be allocated differently than profits, but usually are the same, and income tax reporting usually follows the allocated share of profit and loss. Some partners are more effective workers than others are. A partner's income is limited to his or her share of the profits, unless the agreement specifies a salary.

In one company, for instance, one set of partners had other jobs, which meant that they provided limited partnership services while others were able or willing to work more for the firm. Nevertheless, all partners—underachievers and overachievers alike—received the same share of the profits. The partnership dissolved because of the resentment that built up between the two groups. A salary scheme would have solved this problem.

CREATING MANAGEMENT

Each partner has an equal vote in partnership business decisions, and a majority vote is usually required for approval. However, the partnership agreement may alter this equal vote and majority rule. For instance, partners could base voting rights upon the percentage of the profits or capital contribution. Other management concerns that you should specify in the agreement are quorum and notice requirements. For instance, your agreement should require periodic meetings, and minutes for each meeting should be kept. In fact, large partnerships often have a management committee elected by the partners to run the daily affairs. The agreement may want to designate a senior partner as the tiebreaker vote if there is a voting impasse.

DELINEATING PARTNER DUTIES

Partners owe a duty to properly attend to partnership business. But partners may have other jobs, particularly if they're just starting up a new company together. To avoid conflicts over work schedules, the partners may want to agree to a minimal amount of time that each partner must spend working for the partnership. Businesses vary, so no model provision specifying each partner's duties is appropriate. However, one partner may have expertise in marketing, another in accounting, and a third in management. An informal arrangement regarding these duties may be helpful.

TIP

If you began the business and the other partners joined later, you might want to consider retaining a majority of the votes to maintain your position as senior partner. Someone has to make the final decision.

If one or more partners end up working many more hours than the others work, the partners may want to pay the more dedicated partners more in salary or in profits. The thing to remember is that each partner owes his or her undivided loyalty to the partnership, called a *fiduciary* duty. This fiduciary duty requires every partner to eliminate any conflict of interest he or she may have and to keep his or her private business separate from the new partnership. For instance, you're not allowed to buy supplies for your new partnership concern from your personal business entity. Of course, a partner does not violate this duty if he or she discloses the potential conflict and receives partnership permission to proceed.

PLAIN ENGLISH

A **fiduciary** is a person who is bound to act with the utmost good faith in the management of property or affairs for the benefit of another. A partner is a fiduciary to the partnership.

MAKING CLEAR A PARTNER'S RIGHT TO ACCOUNTING

Each partner is entitled to review the financial records, but it is helpful to remind everyone of the law. The partner in charge of the accounting should readily respond to any partner's request for financial information. The agreement should specify at least quarterly profit-and-loss and balance-sheet financial information. Every partner should be aware of the partnership's financial situation. The books should be set up by an accountant, who then provides the quarterly and annual reports. Here's what happens when such a process is not established: In one company, the partners relied on one of the spouses to do the bookkeeping. Unfortunately, she had other demands on her time. Accounts receivable went uncollected and accounts payable went unpaid. No one knew whether they were making or losing money. They lost money and went out of business.

ADDING PARTNERS

The law requires unanimous acceptance of a new partner by all current partners unless the agreement states otherwise. Rejecting a potential partner may not be good business, so consider a majority or greater vote rather than a unanimous one. The partners should consider upon what terms a new partner is to be accepted, such as capital contribution, profit-and-loss share, voting rights, and so on.

WITHDRAWING PARTNERS

At the same time, keep in mind that the partnership will have to provide for any partner who retires. Usually, the remaining partners agree to purchase the retiring partner's interest based upon an appraisal and make a periodic payout over several years. The buyout is typically paid over several years to ease the impact on the partnership. The retiring partner usually has other sources of income, such as a new job or pension, so annual payments, rather than a lump sum, do not cause him or her a financial hardship.

Death can come to any partner, so your agreement should make provisions for that eventuality. One way to handle the payout to the deceased partner's estate might be through a term life insurance paid by the partnership. Because the partnership interest may be the most significant asset in the decedent's estate, the initial payment should be substantial. None of the deceased's family wants to wait around several years before the payments are finished.

APPRAISAL OF AN OWNERSHIP INTEREST

Appraisal of a going business is difficult at best. Your accountant should suggest several alternatives, one of which may be included in the agreement. Sometimes the best solution is to have an appraisal made at the appropriate time, with criteria established in the agreement. A departing partner may want to compete in business with your partnership. Your agreement can restrict the departing partner by prohibiting him or her from working in the same business for a reasonable time after departure. Courts will uphold this restrictive covenant as long as it is no more expansive than necessary to protect the partnership. For example, if the partner is a sales rep, the agreement may exclude him or her from working in his or her sales area for two years.

CAUTION

Payment to a retiring partner or partner's estate usually involves significant tax implications. Consult a tax accountant or lawyer to properly structure the payment for tax advantage to the departed and remaining partners.

EXPELLING A PARTNER

Clearly, there are some things a partner may do that require his or her removal. A law partner who is disbarred, for instance, is of little use to the partnership. A partner who lies, cheats, and steals cannot be tolerated. The partnership agreement should provide just cause for a partner's expulsion and a procedure by which the partner can be removed and repaid his or her capital contribution. The partnership may want to provide for a deduction of the partner's capital for the economic harm to the partnership. In one company, a partner was entrusted with client funds. Unfortunately, she stole the money to sustain her lifestyle and then the auditor caught her. The partners voted for her expulsion and denied her repayment of her capital, because the amount she had stolen was paid back by the partnership.

DISSOLUTION AND WINDING UP

It's difficult to consider shutting down when you're just beginning, but almost all goods things must come to an end. This section of the agreement should specify what dissolution requires, such as a majority vote of the partners, and the procedure involved. The agreement should specify who will be in charge of winding up the business. Either an individual partner or committee of partners is a viable choice.

Winding up involves completing work in progress, collecting accounts receivable, and paying creditors. The law requires that creditors be paid first. If the creditors do not receive payment, they may hold the partners personally liable for the unpaid debts. Because any partner may be liable for the entire partnership debt, it is important for all partners to make sure the business pays its creditors. If there are any contingent claims, the partnership may establish an account to handle the payments. After the business pays the creditors, the partners are entitled to any undistributed share of the retained earnings and capital contributions. The agreement specifies the method by which this is determined.

ARBITRATION

Inevitably, disputes arise within a new business partnership. Rather than storming off to court and paying enormous legal fees to resolve the problem, consider an alternative called arbitration. A knowledgeable expert, usually a lawyer experienced in partnership law, will provide an interpretation of the agreement in a timely and less expensive manner.

The arbitrator's decision may be binding, which means it limits review by the courts, or it may be subject to court review. Your agreement should specify which type of arbitration you prefer. All of the partners may split the costs or the agreement may state that the losing party must pay. In one company, the retiring partner was unhappy about the appraisal of his interest. Instead of a lawsuit, the retiring partner and the partnership presented written and oral evidence to the arbitrator, who then determined that the appraisal procedure was followed and ruled for the partnership.

TIP

Preparation is the key. If you go into arbitration, you need to prepare as much for that process as you would for a trial. A well-drawn agreement and detailed documentation of partnership decisions may settle a disputed point before it gets to arbitration.

In summary, the agreement requires you to make some difficult decisions. If you can't work them out, it is better to realize defeat now with a minimal investment, rather than wait for the anguish and anger that almost certainly occur when the unresolved issues arise.

CONTRACT LIABILITY

Each partner is considered an *agent* for the partnership. If a partner makes a contract with another party—a vendor or a client—the entire partnership is bound to abide by the terms of that agreement. There are some exceptions, but remembering this general rule is helpful. Likewise, if the partner is negligent while working and injures someone or damages property, the partnership is liable. You can see why choosing your partners wisely is important. But even then, negligence often just happens.

Partners should clearly understand the limits of their ability to bind the partnership to a contract. This understanding should be acknowledged in the partnership minutes or a memorandum. Then, a partner who violates this policy is on notice that he or she will be liable for any excess over the amount the partner is entitled to spend. Likewise, a partner's misconduct, such as negligence, can result in partnership liability for the negligence.

PLAIN ENGLISH

An **agent** acts on behalf of his or her principal and the principal is liable for his or her acts. A partner acts as an agent for the partnership when purchasing for the partnership.

However, this policy would not affect creditors who are not aware of the partnership's policy, which means that if creditors lend money to one partner—unaware that two partnerships are required—you would nevertheless be required to repay the debt. In fact, you might want to notify major creditors of the policy or state on any order form that a certain partner or partners must authorize every transaction involving a certain amount of money or term.

In one company, one of the law partners liked to spend money on research books. He contracted with a law book sales rep to purchase a set for $4,000. The others found out and were furious, but the partnership had to pay. The book rep had dealt with the partner concerning book purchases, and reasonably believed that the partner had the authority to bind the partnership.

TIP

Consider requiring two partners to cosign any contract over a certain amount (maybe $1,000), which can reduce your concern over an errant partner binding the partnership to a contract the majority does not want.

TORT LIABILITY

People do get careless, and although a negligent partner is liable for any actions performed during business hours, it's usually the partnership or the partnership's insurance company that pays. Here's an example: One partner did not timely file a client's tax return. The unforgiving IRS imposed penalty and interest on the client, who in turn insisted that the errant partner pay the tab. In the end, the partnership paid the penalty and interest because the amount was substantially more than the one partner, alone, could afford.

If the partner's misconduct is intentional—punching an irritating customer or stealing from customer accounts—the partnership will almost certainly be held liable. Just be aware of the risk and do what you can to protect yourself, such as purchasing a performance bond for the partner who handles the customer funds if you have even an inkling of impropriety.

WHOSE PROPERTY IS IT?

It's often difficult to discern the difference between partnership property and an individual partner's personal property. As previously indicated, make sure you designate any capital contribution of property as partnership property on your records. Any property a partner lends to the partnership should likewise be clearly designated as being that partner's property.

CAUTION

Tempers can be expensive. If a partner cannot keep his or hers, get that partner away from people or expel the partner from the partnership. A dog may be entitled to one bite before the owner is liable, but courts are less sympathetic to humans.

Property purchased with partnership funds is presumed to be partnership property, but make sure that title and records so indicate. For instance, a partner purchased a delivery truck with a partnership check, but put the title in his own name. Now the partner must prove that the truck is properly titled to retain his claimed ownership, because he bought the truck with partnership money. If the check represented a capital distribution to the partner, he would be able to keep the truck, but he has the burden of proof.

All of this information is important when it comes to taxes (who receives the depreciation), creditor's rights (an individual partner's creditor cannot attach partnership property), and distribution of partnership assets on dissolution of the partnership.

THE LLP (LIMITED LIABILITY PARTNERSHIP)

Partners are personally liable to partnership creditors. Each partner is liable for all of the debt, at least to the extent that other partners don't pay their fair share. Underpaying partners can be sued, but a judgment is only as good as its collection. In one company, the partnership went under, and the debts exceeded the assets. Two of the partners had substantial assets; the other two were mortgaged to the hilt. The partners with the money paid. The partners with no money filed bankruptcy and discharged their obligation to the partners who paid.

But wait! State legislatures have changed the rules of the game by creating a registered limited liability partnership (LLP). The change from a partnership to LLP is simple enough in most states. You must file a form with the secretary of state declaring the partnership to be LLP, and thereafter a partner is personally liable only for his or her own misdeeds, such as personal negligence, but not for the other partners' wrongdoing.

For example, under agency law, if one partner runs a red light and wipes out most of the pedestrians, the partnership is liable under agency law. In LLP, any excess liability beyond the LLP's assets would not be the liability of any partner other than the offending member.

Other than the change in liability, the LLP operates the same as a regular partnership.

CAUTION

Beware of the limited partnership: It shouldn't be the entity of choice for most businesses. The limited liability is available for all owners in the limited liability partnership or the limited liability company.

LIMITED PARTNERSHIP LIMITS

The *limited partnership* may be nearly extinct. Congress changed the tax code in 1986 to permit only certain tax losses to be taken by the partners, which denied considerable tax shelter advantages to the partners. Then came the limited liability company, and now the limited liability partnership, which provides the owner with limited personal liability for business debts but allows partnership tax treatment. But the old guy deserves some mention.

You can create a limited partnership by filing a certificate with the secretary of state. The certificate is usually an abbreviated limited partnership agreement. Here are terms that the partners need to include in the certificate:

■ **Name**. The limited partnership name must include its designation as a limited partnership or LP.

PLAIN ENGLISH

A **limited partnership** is a partnership formed with two or more persons as co-owners, which means that it has one or more general partners and one or more limited partners.

■ **Partners**. The certificate should identify each partner as either a general partner or as a limited partner. The general partner has sole management responsibility; limited partners have no management rights. The general partner is personally liable for the business debts; the limited partners risk only their capital investment. In essence, the limited partners are passive investors.

■ **Purpose**. In the past, limited partnerships usually involved investments that could generate a tax loss, such as real estate development and mineral extraction such as oil and gas. Because the limited partners have no management rights, a clear purpose statement is vital to their expectations.

■ **Term**. A time limit for its existence may be set. A general partner is required, so the death of the sole individual general partner would cause its dissolution. However, most limited partnerships permit the limited partners to elect a successor general partner.

TIP

A limited partnership may have a corporation as its general partner, thus avoiding co-owner personal liability for its debts.

■ **Capital contribution**. Each partner's capital contribution is recorded. The contribution may be in cash, property, or services. The value of the latter two should be clearly stated. Although the limited partner may request a return of his or her capital within six months of written notice, the law does not permit this distribution if it would impair creditor rights. Usually a limited partnership has borrowed heavily (to maximize the tax loss pass through to his or her own 1040), so the return of capital is highly unlikely.

- **Profits and losses**. The agreement specifies the shares allocated to each general and limited partner. Usually this is a specific percentage, although some partnership tax shelters have a reallocation formula.

- **Admission of new partners**. The agreement usually provides the method of admitting new general and limited partners. If nothing is specified, all the partners must consent. The interests of the limited partners are usually transferable without limitation, and the heirs of a deceased limited partner may inherit his or her interest.

- **Dissolution and liquidation**. The agreement may specify an event causing dissolution, such as the death of the general partner before the election of a replacement or a specific time for termination. The liquidation of the limited partnership requires supervision by the general partner. Creditors are paid first, then partners according to the agreement.

TAXES MATTER

Each partner, whether in a partnership, registered limited liability partnership, or limited partnership, reports his or her share of the distributable business income. The partnership reports the income and expenses on federal form 1065, and provides each partner with a form 1065 K-1. The K-1 specifies the amount and type of income the partner reports.

For example, if you are one of two equal partners and the partnership net income consists of $60,000 ordinary income and $40,000 capital gains, your K-1 will show $30,000 of ordinary income and $20,000 of capital gains. You'll report those amounts on Schedules E and D of your individual 1040, and so will your partner—even if you didn't actually receive it as income.

HELPFUL SOURCES

Almost all states have their laws available on their web page. You can download your state's *Uniform Partnership Act* and *Uniform Limited Partnership Act*. You may want to surf the web. Several law firms have websites that may provide specific information about partnership law in your state. In addition, several software companies, such as Quicken, sell business forms, which are available at many computer stores; I would use those forms with some caution and suggest a review of your draft by an attorney. Finally, your local library usually has books related to business formation, as well as the state code.

THE 30-SECOND RECAP

- Partnerships should have a detailed written agreement.
- Partners are personally liable for business debts, unless the partnership is a registered limited liability partnership.
- Partnerships are liable for the contracts and misconduct of the partners acting on its behalf.
- Each partner reports his or her share of the distributable partnership income.

Corporations and S Corporations

You, too, can be a corporation. Corporate status provides you with the protection of limited liability. You can choose between being taxed personally or having the corporation taxed on its business income. The corporation can exist in perpetuity, which may mean beyond the initial shareholders' lives. The corporation can have as many shareholders as it wishes. We will assume for this discussion that it's either just you or a few other shareholders, and in this section show you all you need to know to get started.

INCORPORATING YOUR BUSINESS FOR PROTECTION

Corporate organization is rather structured and, to become established, requires a number of documents, including the following:

- Articles of incorporation
- Bylaws
- Initial shareholder and board of directors minutes

When it comes to choosing what state in which to incorporate, you'll probably want to incorporate in the state where you'll conduct your business. By doing so, you'll avoid being treated as a foreign corporation in your own state. If you grow into a giant company, you may want to consider the state of Delaware, which is the happy home for many large corporations, because of its favorable corporation tax laws.

PLAIN ENGLISH

A **corporation** is an artificial "person" (in the form of a business) that is chartered by the state to conduct business. The state also charters not-for-profit, or charitable, corporations.

If you are going solo, you don't need what's known as a pre-incorporation agreement. With two or more shareholders, consider the pre-incorporation agreement to be a must-have document. Its primary purpose is to contractually bind all the potential investors/shareholders to their capital contributions. Many businesses fail because of insufficient initial capital, which is one good reason this contract is so important. The agreement can be as simple as including the following:

- Corporation name
- Amount of capital contribution
- Shares to be issued to each shareholder

Choose a name and reserve it with the secretary of state by filing a registration-of-name form. Avoid a name that's already trademarked (Coke, for example). Many states require the use of Corporation, Incorporated, or an abbreviation thereof in the name. If your chosen corporate name is too similar to an existing entity, the secretary of state will reject your choice.

If you are the sole shareholder, a bare-bones articles of incorporation is all that you need, and you can find the form on your secretary of state's web page. The articles usually contain the following information:

- **Name.** Widget Company, Inc.
- **Authorized shares.** One thousand shares of common stock.
- **Name and address of the registered agent.** Sam Service, 1 North Street, None, IN 46222.
- **Name and address of the incorporator.** Sam Service, 1 North Street, None, IN 46222.

You file the form with the secretary of state and pay a small fee. Congratulations, you have a new corporation!

CAUTION

Beware of hidden costs. Some states charge a significant fee or special franchise tax for incorporation in addition to an annual fee. Check with your state secretary of state for your state's fee schedule.

Stock issued to the initial investors in a small corporation will be common stock. If you realize your fantasies and your corporation sells its stock to the general public, you may want to create different classes of common or preferred stock. But by then you will have expensive lawyers, accountants, and brokers to shepherd you through the process.

The registered agent is the person designated to receive service of a summons should the corporation be sued. The incorporator (you or the person who filed with the state) signs the articles. After the articles of incorporation are filed, the shareholders, incorporator, and board of directors meet. The shareholders elect the board, and the board, in turn, elects the corporate officers. The board approves the bylaws, and receives the shareholders' payment for the stock. The board issues the corporate stock. If the corporation has numerous shareholders, things are more complex, so a more detailed articles of incorporation should be drafted. An attorney should be retained to prepare those articles.

The *bylaws* establish the procedure for the shareholder and board meetings, such as notice and quorum requirements. The bylaws provide a brief description of the duties of the officers.

PLAIN ENGLISH

Bylaws contain all provisions for managing the business and regulating the affairs of the corporation.

SHAREHOLDER AGREEMENTS TO AGREE

If your corporation has more than one shareholder, the shareholders should prepare a shareholders' stock purchase agreement. The agreement provides a method by which a retiring or deceased shareholder's stock may be purchased. Without this restriction, stock is freely transferable, meaning the stock can be sold to anyone. In a small corporation, shareholders are more like partners, so a new shareholder who is not approved by the other shareholders can cause problems if you don't have an agreement.

The shareholder agreement typically provides an option to purchase the stock of the retiring shareholder. The corporation and the shareholders have a right to purchase the stock by matching a price offered by an outsider. As an alternative, the agreement could determine the option price of the stock by an appraisal at its fair market value or at a fixed price previously established. A fixed price method is the least desirable because shareholders never seem to get around to adjusting the price as the business progresses.

For the shareholder who has died, the corporation and the shareholders agree to pay the estate for the stock. Usually the deceased's stock is appraised at its fair market value on the date of death.

TIP

Make sure your stock purchase agreement restricts transfer of the stock to only those approved by the other shareholders. This can avoid including the incompatible shareholder, but it can make selling the stock more difficult.

The option payment for the retiring shareholder typically is a structured pay-out that occurs over four or five years, whereas the estate payout may involve a significant down payment and periodic payments. Term life insurance on each shareholder's life can substantially fund the estate payment. Because the option payment comes directly from corporate funds or shareholder pockets, these payments will usually take longer (and the departing shareholder usually is earning other income during this time).

In addition, the shareholders may want to maintain the same percentage of share ownership among each other; they may agree to allow each shareholder an option to purchase his or her pro rata share of any new stock offering by the corporation.

Shareholders Share Almost Everything

Your percentage of stock ownership determines your share of the corporate profit, the distribution of which is a dividend, usually in the form of cash. Large corporations pay dividends quarterly. Most small corporations do so less frequently.

TIP

Establish the appraisal procedure in the stock purchase agreement. The corporation and the shareholder/estate may each appoint an appraiser. The appraisers will then select a third appraiser. This procedure should provide a fair means to determine value.

If the shareholders are also employees of the corporation, which is typical, most of their compensation comes from salary and fringe benefits. The choice of tax entity (*S corporation* or *C corporation,* discussed later in this section) may decide whether it is advantageous to declare dividends. The board of directors declares the dividends, usually from corporate profits.

Shareholders are not personally liable for corporate debts unless they personally guarantee a debt. Banks typically require shareholders to guarantee loans, but most individual creditors do not.

PLAIN ENGLISH

An **S corporation** or **C corporation** is a tax designation only. In an S corporation, the shareholders are taxed on the business income; whereas in a C corporation, the corporation itself is taxed.

Shareholders officially act in corporate meetings, and each shareholder is entitled to one vote for each share. Most states permit the meetings to be conducted by phone. As an alternative, shareholders may approve a corporate resolution without meeting with unanimous written consent.

The bylaws usually require a quorum (majority of the stock shares) and majority vote for the approval of a corporate resolution. Annual shareholder meetings are required. The president of the corporation or a majority of shareholders can call a special meeting for important business such as electing a new director.

BOARD OF DIRECTORS AND OFFICERS CONTROL

Directors are elected by the shareholders, usually for a one-year term, but may serve up to three years. They may be compensated for their services, and if they are, may set their own compensation and record it in the minutes. In a small corporation, the shareholders often are the directors. While the board sets corporate policy, its officers execute the board decisions.

TIP

Guarantee as little as possible. Usually banks will insist that all shareholders personally guarantee the loan. Some landlords may require a guaranty. The more you personally guarantee the more your own assets are at risk in case something goes south!

The directors serve at the pleasure of the shareholders and may be removed with or without cause by the shareholders in a meeting specifically called for that purpose.

For instance, in one corporation, shareholder/director Bob had a personality that allowed him to dominate the other shareholders. Finally the other two shareholders had enough. They sent proper notice and held a shareholder meeting. The other partners removed Bob as a director; because the bylaws so stated, they didn't need to state or prove a cause for Bob's dismissal.

THE ROLE OF THE BOARD OF DIRECTORS

The bylaws specify notice, quorum, and voting requirements of the corporation. Like the shareholders, the board of directors may meet by telephone or videoconference or may unanimously approve a written corporate resolution without any meeting at all. The board of directors must meet annually, but the bylaws may specify more frequent meeting and the president may call special meetings. Board functions include ...

- Approving/amending bylaws.
- Electing/removing officers.
- Establishing policy.
- Declaring dividends.

CAUTION

Don't neglect removal powers when you write your bylaws. Removal of a partner is always an acrimonious process and fraught with threats of litigation unless you carefully spell out the form of removal and the amount of notice required. Removing a partner is a powerful weapon and you may want to limit it in the bylaws by requiring a super-majority ($\frac{2}{3}$ or $\frac{3}{4}$) vote to enact it.

The board may remove an officer with or without cause in a meeting specifically called for that purpose. If an officer is also an employee, removal doesn't necessarily result in terminating employment.

The board acts to set policy and make major decisions, such as purchasing land or erecting an office building. The directors may also establish a personnel manual for employees, develop a business plan, and determine which offer has the authority to contract.

State law may restrict the board's authority to declare and pay a dividend. If a dividend is paid when corporate debts exceed assets, that may be an illegal dividend that the shareholders are required to return.

BREACH OF TRUST

Each board member has a duty of loyalty (fiduciary duty) to the corporation, so it's important that all board members avoid conflicts of interest. The board member who has a financial interest in the vote of a corporate resolution, for example, approving a contract between him- or herself and the corporation, must declare that interest and abstain from voting.

TIP

Talk to your accountant to make sure you don't establish an illegal dividend. In addition, because dividends may be taxable to the shareholder, consulting a tax advisor is important, particularly to the high-tax-bracket shareholder.

Board members are not usually liable if they make poor decisions; however, if they breach their fiduciary duty by self-dealing, or if their conduct lacks good faith and prudent care, they may be liable to the shareholders. Most statutes hold a director personally liable if the director's misconduct was reckless or willful. Some large corporations agree to purchase director and officer liability insurance to protect them from frivolous suits by disgruntled shareholders.

Here's a flagrant example of a fiduciary breach: A corporate director, who was secretly serving on a competitor's board, forwarded all the corporate plans to the other board. When the board discovered this double-dealing, it removed the director and sued him for the monetary damages suffered by corporation.

TIP

If you are buying corporate assets, hire a good accountant to allocate the asset purchase prices to maximize tax depreciation. If you are selling the business, insist on a premium to adjust for loss of the capital gain advantage.

THE ROLE OF THE OFFICERS

The board members also elect corporate officers. Corporations need a president and secretary who, in a sole shareholder corporation, may be the same person. In addition, the corporation usually has a vice president and treasurer. In a small corporation the officers often are the shareholders (and directors).

The bylaws describe officer duties, but the board may augment them. Officers execute policy and make decisions within the parameters set by the board. For example, the board may authorize the president to lease an office building or negotiate a loan. The officers run the daily operations and may delegate authority to others, such as supervisors, to contract for the corporation or to hire and fire employees.

TIP

If your corporation decides to employ an officer, consider drafting the officer's employment contract to allow termination as an employee if you terminate him or her as an officer. Disgruntled ex-officers don't make good employees.

Because officers are agents for the corporation, they have the same fiduciary loyalty to the corporation as do the directors. Officers are agents for the corporation, and they can bind the corporation to contracts made on its behalf. Also an officer's negligent conduct that harms another can result in a judgment against the corporation.

ACQUISITIONS AND DISSOLUTION MEAN CHANGE

In these heady days of mergers and acquisitions, anything is possible when it comes to the future of your corporation, so be prepared. The board and shareholders may one day be in a position to make decisions about a merger and dissolution of the corporation.

MERGER AND ACQUISITION

Merger is the purchase of Corporation A's stock by Corporation B, followed by A merging into B, and A going out of existence. Corporation B receives A's assets and is liable for A's debts.

The board and shareholders approve the merger, and then the articles of merger are filed with the secretary of state. If you are a shareholder in Corporation A, there may be an alternative to having your stock converted to Corporation B stock. If you voted against the merger, you can notify Corporation A that you want cash for your stock. State law establishes the procedure, as dissenter's rights. However, some states permit this right only if Corporation A's stock is not listed on a public exchange, such as NASDAQ or the New York Stock Exchange.

Corporations seem acquisitive of other corporations of late. Corporation A's stock may be acquired by Corporation B, but the two are not merged. This is referred to as a parent-subsidiary relationship. The two corporations are separate entities but the parent corporation (B) controls the subsidiary (A).

SALE OF ALL CORPORATE ASSETS

When the shareholders decide to sell the business, most small corporations end up selling their assets to the purchaser instead of the shareholders selling their stock. That's because the buyer wants the assets but not the corporation's liabilities (which it would be obligated to pay if there were a stock acquisition). Also there are tax advantages for the buyer to acquire the assets. Selling shareholders would prefer to sell their stock, because the capital gain from the sale of stock is taxed at a lower rate than the ordinary income resulting from the distribution of assets when the corporation is liquidated.

DISSOLUTION

Corporations can exist in perpetuity, but small corporations seldom last that long. When the time comes to sell the business assets or when the business goes under, the board and the shareholders must approve dissolution of the corporation. The articles of dissolution are then filed with the secretary of state. Upon dissolution, the debts (including the taxes) are paid first, and then the shareholders receive any remaining assets based on their percentage share of the stock.

DON'T FORGET UNCLE SAM

Corporate taxation may follow one of two paths: C or S. If you do not take an S corporation election by filing form 2553 with the IRS to tax shareholders directly on corporate income, the corporate tax status is as a C corporation. Simply put, the net income is taxed to the corporation. The tax rates progress depending on taxable income (gross income less deductible expenses). The federal tax is reported on form 1120, and the tax is paid by the corporation.

As a shareholder in a C corporation, you must report on your own 1040 any dividends the corporation distributes to you. In essence, if you're not careful, you'll end up paying double taxes (corporate and individual). To avoid this, some small corporations pay higher salaries and fringe benefits (tax deductible to the corporation) and little or no dividends. However, the IRS may audit your corporation and determine that this compensation is excessive and therefore not a legitimate deductible expense for the corporation. Consult your tax accountant or lawyer about this strategy.

Another tax alternative is to elect to be taxed as an S corporation. To qualify as an S corporation, your corporation must ...

- Be incorporated and organized in the United States.
- Have only one class of stock (common).
- Be limited to a maximum of 75 shareholders.
- Have only individuals, estates, and certain trusts as shareholders.
- Have no nonresident aliens as shareholders.

CAUTION

Avoiding dividend payment to avoid higher taxation is risky strategy. The IRS may impose additional taxes on the corporation if there is an unreasonable accumulation of retained earnings (insufficient dividend payments).

To be effective for the first year, you must file the election (form 2553) with the IRS before the fifteenth day of the third month from incorporation. If the election is later, it will be effective for all subsequent years after the year in which the election was made. All shareholders must consent to the election.

Here's an example: Corporation Alpha is a C corporation in 2004. The shareholders must file form 2553 no later than March 15, 2005 to convert to S status in 2005.

You'll report corporate income and expenses on the federal schedule 1120S, and then each shareholder will receive notice of his or her taxable income, which is allocated according to his or her percentage of stock ownership and reported on the 1120 K-1. The shareholder then reports this information on his or her 1040. The S corporation shareholder must report his or her share of the corporate income whether or not it is actually distributed to the shareholder.

For example, assume that you are one of two equal shareholders and the corporation has $100,000 of taxable income. The 1120S K-1 will report $50,000 income for each of you, which you must on Schedule E of your 1040. If the corporation later pays a dividend from the previously taxed income, such dividend is tax-free income to you (because you already paid the tax upon receiving the K-1).

TIP

As a shareholder of an S corporation, make sure your records are in proper order. The IRS will want to tax any dividends that shareholders receive unless the shareholders can clearly show that they have been previously taxed.

Note that some states do not recognize S corporation tax status for that state's income tax law, so that the corporation itself pays the tax on its income. This will not affect federal taxes, but you'll have to consider that fact when deciding whether to elect S status.

HELPFUL SOURCES

Before forming your company you may want to visit the Small Business Administration's website at www.sba.gov. Other good websites on this topic are www.allbusiness.com and www.entrepreneur.com.

Most state secretary of state websites contain all the corporate forms that you'll need to file with that agency. State websites contain the corporation code, and you may download it for your reading pleasure. Also some law firms in your state may have websites that discuss corporate formation and operation, as well as the tax elections. Local libraries, likewise, have books on incorporating.

The 30-Second Recap

■ Corporate shareholders are not liable for business debts unless the debts are personally guaranteed.

■ You can incorporate your business by filing articles of incorporation with the state secretary of state.

■ The board of directors elects the officers, establishes and amends the bylaws, and declares dividends.

■ A corporation may be taxed on its profits (C corporation), or the shareholders may be taxed on the corporation's profits (S corporation).

Limited Liability Companies

The limited liability company (LLC) is an alternative to a partnership or corporation. An LLC is an unincorporated association organized under state law, and the members of the association are the owners of the company. A member may be an individual or business entity. The members of the LLC are not liable for the business debts, which is a distinct advantage over the regular partnership (because, in such, the partners are personally liable for its debt); however, in the registered limited liability partnership (LLP) its partners are not liable for its debts. Each member reports his or her share of the business income (or loss). In this section, we discuss the pros and cons and ins and outs of the LLC business entity.

LLCs: The Basics

What are the advantages of an LLC as compared to partnerships and corporations? Well, partnerships tend to be quite flexible because the partnership agreement permits the partners to work out an arrangement that best suits their needs. However, the partnership's downside is personal liability for business debts and each partner must report his or her share of the partnership taxable income on the partner's 1040.

LLCs also have advantages over corporations, which tend to be more structured and require filings with the state secretary of state than do LLCs. In addition, LLC shareholders are not personally liable for the corporate debts. Any corporation with 75 or fewer shareholders can elect to have each shareholder report his or her share of the corporate taxable income on the shareholder's 1040. As an alternative, the corporation itself can be taxed on its profits. You may choose to convert your partnership into a limited liability company. The organization documents and steps are discussed in this section.

The conversion to the LLC should be tax free, but always use an accountant to prepare for the details making that possible. Your corporation may also convert to LLC, although this is less likely, because there is no personal liability for the owners of either entity, and the corporation can elect to have its shareholders taxed on its income.

YOUR ORGANIZING ARTICLES IS THE BEGINNING

The limited liability company (LLC) has the following features:

- Articles of organization filed with the secretary of state
- Operating agreement with flexible terms
- Member management or appointed managers
- Profit and loss determined by members as stated in the operating agreement
- Members are not liable for business debts
- Members may restrict transfer of ownership
- Existence as an LLC for 30 years or more
- Taxation as a partnership unless members elect corporate taxation

CAUTION

Members of the limited liability company are personally liable only for the business debts that they personally guarantee, such as a bank loan.

The articles of organization must be filed with the state secretary of state before the LLC may begin business. The articles may be fairly abbreviated, but must contain the following:

- **Name.** Able Limited Liability Co., LLC.
- **Registered agent and address.** Al Able, 1 South St., Somewhere, IN 46226. The registered agent accepts service of legal papers on the LLC.
- **Term of existence.** Perpetual. (The term may be less than perpetual, such as 30 years, but most LLCs use "perpetual.")
- **Management.** By members.

The articles of organization may be more detailed if the organizing members want it to be. If there is just one member (allowed in some states) or only a few, a bare-bones document is likely all that is needed. At least one of the organizing members must sign them; however, all members must sign the operating agreement. (The operating agreement is more significant and must be carefully drafted.) Many states have preprinted articles of organization, some of which can be downloaded from the secretary of state website.

OPERATING INSTRUCTIONS FOR THE BUSINESS

The operating agreement is the key LLC document and its terms are flexible enough to meet the needs of its members. To better acquaint you with LLC law, the following is a detailed discussion of the agreement.

TIP

You may want to reserve your name before filing the articles. Some states will charge you to reserve the name, and then hold it for a short period, such as 30 days. Remember not to use a trademarked name as part of your LLC name.

CHOOSING A NAME

The name of the limited liability company must include the words *limited liability company,* or more typically, an abbreviation, such as *LLC.* Because the name may appear in advertising, you may want to choose one that describes your business, such a Wedding Arrangements, LLC.

FORMATION AND COMPANY PURPOSE

The operating agreement formally states that the organizing members have acted to file the articles of organization and that the members will conduct business under the articles unless they create amendment.

Usually the purpose statement is broadly worded to include all activities authorized under state law. However, you might want to limit the purpose statement to include only those business activities that all of the members agree on conducting. Small businesses generally focus on just one or a few business activities. If the LLC is established to sell sporting goods and attire, for instance, just say so in the purpose clause. Later, you can add contract language to allow alternative activities as the members approve and amend the agreement.

MEMBERS AND THEIR CAPITAL CONTRIBUTIONS

The members' names and addresses must be listed, and each member's capital contribution must be recorded (usually as Exhibit A to the agreement). Keep in mind that a prospective member is not bound by an oral promise to make a capital contribution. Therefore, a preformation contribution agreement should be signed by each member to avoid undercapitalization.

The capital contribution can be in cash, property, or services. If the contribution is property or service, make sure they are properly valued and the property is transferred to the LLC. If the property has a title, such as the title to a motor vehicle, transfer the title to the LLC.

CAUTION

If you establish an LLC and offer memberships to outside investors, federal and state securities laws apply, and must be strictly adhered to if you are to avoid their violation. Consult an attorney experienced in securities laws.

Many small businesses underestimate their capital needs. If members can be required to make additional capital contributions, the procedure involved must be clearly spelled out. Capital contributions cannot be returned to a member if the distribution would impair creditors. The agreement should reiterate the law, and further specify when the members may permit a distribution when assets exceed liabilities.

Members are usually issued certificates (or shares) based upon their capital contribution. The number of shares may determine voting rights and profit/loss percentage, depending on the terms of the operating agreement.

Members may make loans to the LLC; however, the IRS may claim that the loan is a disguised capital contribution and deny the deduction of any payment of interest by the LLC. To avoid that problem, the LLC should execute a promissory note, have a reasonable rate of interest, and make timely payments to the member/creditor.

Members' Conduct

If the members collectively manage the LLC (and the finer points of management are discussed next), all the power to act on its behalf resides with them. Members are agents for the LLC (just as they are for a regular partnership) and can bind the company to contracts. Also the limited liability company may be liable for a member's misconduct. The member may abscond with client funds or negligently manage a client's affairs. For instance, one member of an LLC, let's call her Beth, was responsible for investing a client's funds. The client directed Beth to place her funds in a conservative investment portfolio. Instead, Beth speculated on the commodities futures market and lost heavily. Although the company is liable for Beth's negligence, it may choose to recoup its losses from Beth. However, if the losses were substantial, it's unlikely she would be able to pay. Members should be reminded that they owe utmost loyalty to the LLC and must avoid any conflicts of interests. If a conflict arises, as it may in a large LLC, the member should disclose the conflict and receive member approval to proceed, or desist if approval is denied.

CAUTION

Minutes or a formal resolution should specifically limit a member's contract authority by requiring at least one other member's signature. This may eliminate liability for a rogue member who tries to spend much more than authorized.

ACCOUNTING

Financial record-keeping is critical. Retain an accountant to set up the books and prepare at least an annual report. Large LLCs should have quarterly financial reports. Each member is entitled to review the records. Keep your financial records up-to-date and accurate so that even the most meticulous IRS auditor can't find a mistake.

PROFIT AND LOSS

Profits and losses are usually allocated according to the number of shares a member is issued. For instance, suppose Al owns 100 member shares and Betty owns 200 shares. If the LLC profits for the year are $90,000, Al is entitled to $30,000 and Betty to $60,000. The members determine whether profits are distributed or retained by the company and allocated to each member's profit account.

LOSS OF MEMBERS

Eventually a member will want to retire or will die. Some states specify that the LLC must dissolve when a member leaves or dies. To use the statutory language, this is called an act of disassociation. Unless the agreement specifies otherwise, some state laws permit the member to give notice 30 days prior to leaving. Actually, the agreement should specify a longer period, at least three to six months so that the LLC can make the necessary financial adjustments.

The agreement should permit the company to disassociate (expel) the member for wrongdoing, such as stealing client funds. Any financial loss should be deducted from the departing member's payment.

The agreement also should provide the terms by which the member's interest or the deceased's share is purchased. The LLC may purchase the interest based upon the member's capital and retained profit accounts, or upon a mutually agreed upon pre-established figure. When either one of these valuation methods is used, the member loses any goodwill generated by a going business— that is, neither method considers the value of the company name, reputation, etc. The LLC may purchase the interest based upon an appraisal of its fair market value. Any purchase should include a payout period that the company can afford, and the retiring member or the deceased's heirs can accept. Term life insurance can substantially fund a deceased member's buyout.

CAUTION

Don't skimp on the appraisal! Small businesses are notoriously hard to value. A business appraiser whose expertise involves your particular business activity is crucial so that everyone may be treated fairly.

ADDING A MEMBER AND MAKING AN AMENDMENT

If your corporation wants to add a member, it requires unanimous approval of the members, unless the agreement provides otherwise. You should consider a majority or super-majority (⅔ or ¾) vote to avoid the disgruntled member's blackball. The agreement must specify the means by which the members may amend it. Change happens.

TERMINATION OF THE LLC

If the LLC dissolves by member vote, bankruptcy, or other cause specified in the agreement, the members collectively, some appointed members, or the managers conclude the business, pay the creditors, and distribute the net assets to the members. The members are allocated the net assets according to their shares unless the agreement provides otherwise. Articles of dissolution are then filed with the secretary of state.

TIP

If you have drafted the operating agreement without consulting an attorney, be sure to have it reviewed by an attorney to ensure that it is complete and follows state law.

MANAGING THE LLC

And now for the most important, and complex, part of the operating agreement: The rules governing how you'll manage the LLC. You have several options every step of the way. The members may act as the LLC managers, as do partners in a regular partnership. Or the members may elect managers, which is similar to combining corporate directors and officers. Typically, small LLCs operate on the partnership model.

Large LLCs may require a manager, a chief operating officer, or several managers (an arrangement much like that of a corporation's board of directors and officers), and their duties must be clearly specified in the agreement. Often the equivalent of an abbreviated corporate bylaws is used. The members elect the manager or managers, and retain the power to remove them from office, with or without cause. It is especially important that any removal action fully comply with the procedural requirements (notice, quorum, etc.).

When the members manage, the agreement should specify ...

- That meetings be called by a certain percentage of the members.
- That notice be given of the date, time, and place of a meeting.
- The appointment of proxy to vote in behalf of a member.
- The voting rights of each member.
- The quorum and number of votes required to pass a resolution.
- Alternatives to meetings.

LLCs are be required to have annual meetings as do corporations; however, periodic meetings are also important to keep all members informed and to record decisions in the minutes. The agreement may permit any member or specify that a certain number of members may call a meeting. If there are five or fewer members, one should be allowed to call for a meeting. With a larger membership, one member's problem may not need much collective attention, so requiring a percentage of members makes more sense. Always follow the procedure requiring notice of a meeting, because a member who didn't know about the meeting and wasn't present could later claim no knowledge of a decision that binds him or her. As alternatives to formal meetings, the agreement could permit unanimous consent to a written resolution, or a telephone conference-call meeting.

Each member is entitled to vote according to terms of the agreement. The number of votes each member can cast is usually determined by his or her number of member shares (usually according to member's capital contribution). Alternatively, the agreement could specify equal voting rights among the members. Typically, LLC meetings require a quorum of 51 percent member voting shares, and resolutions require a majority of the share votes cast to pass. Members may be permitted by the agreement to delegate substitutes (*proxies*), but this is seldom practiced in small LLCs.

PLAIN ENGLISH

Proxy is the authority given by one person (for example, an LLC member) to another to serve as a substitute for a specified purpose, particularly voting.

Moving Forward

After the LLC is formed, you need to remember to operate according to the operating agreement. Perhaps this is self-evident, but more than one LLC has moved blithely forward, completely ignoring the dictates of the agreement.

If you are a single-member LLC, always separate your personal business from the LLC business. LLC creditors may attack your protected status (no personal liability) if they can demonstrate that you continually ignored the LLC as an entity when you conducted your business. To avoid this problem, you should ...

- Establish a bank account for the LLC.
- Ensure against obvious risks.
- Use the LLC name on all contracts.
- Document all important LLC transactions.
- Conduct all required meetings and prepare minutes as specified in the operating agreement.
- Keep good financial records.
- File any reports required with the secretary of state.
- Sign all contracts as "Ima Owner, member and agent, for None Company, LLC."

If you have a multimember LLC, never discount the importance of good minutes and financial records. Disgruntled members and disassociated members search for miscues.

Filing the annual reports with the secretary of state maintains your LLC status. Loss of that status can make you personally liable for business debts (same as a partner in a regular partnership).

Taxing LLCs

A limited liability company is not taxed, but simply files an informational return just as a partnership does. Each member is taxed on his or her share of the distributable LLC income, even if it's distributed. The share is determined by the operating agreement provisions regarding profit and loss. For instance, if an LLC has $90,000 in taxable income, and member Al owns 100 shares and member Betty owns 200 shares, Al reports $30,000 of income on his 1040, and Betty reports $60,000 on hers—whether or not the income is received.

A limited liability company can elect to be taxed as a C corporation by filing the form 8283 with the IRS; however, this is seldom done because the members want to be taxed personally.

Helpful Sources

Most state secretary of state websites contain the articles of organization. Books and software are available for drafting the operating agreement. You can also check out the Association of Limited Liability Companies website at www.llc-usa.com. Some state law firms have websites that discuss limited liability company formation and operation, as well as the tax elections. Your local library might have books on LLCs, too.

The 30-Second Recap

- Limited liability companies are formed by members.
- The LLC must file articles of organization with the secretary of state.
- The operating agreement specifies the members' capital contribution, voting, and profit share.
- Members are not personally liable for LLC debts.
- Each member is taxed on his or her allocated share of the LLC taxable income.

Buying a Business

What to Know Before You Buy

You may be a newcomer, eager to be self-employed and to be your own boss. Or you may already be in business and are looking to expand your current business, buy out a competitor, or diversify. You must examine your motivation to move from where you are now to the next phase. In this part, we'll discuss some things you'll need to consider before taking these crucial steps.

SELECTING THE RIGHT BUSINESS FOR YOU

If you're a newcomer, then like any novice, you need to spend a great deal of time (and some money) to determine if the new business you choose truly fits your personality and finances. You must examine in minute detail not only the target business but also its particular industry. For example, if you are considering the purchase of a small clothing store, check out the competition. An outlet mall just a few blocks away may mean a short-lived business for the small store.

If you are currently in the same business as the company you want to acquire, you're in very good position to judge the value of that company. You know the territory, so you need only examine this company and how it will fit into your current business.

If you want to diversify, however, you probably will be a novice at evaluating and running any new business. Your success in your current business doesn't always transfer to a new one. Many large businesses have diversified to their regret.

Before buying a different kind of company, find out the answers to these questions:

- Is the company in a good location for its market?
- Will the customers be there for you in the future?
- What reputation does the company have with its customers and suppliers?
- Are the company's physical and human assets sufficient?
- If this company is to join yours, how will it fit in?

This is not an exhaustive list, but it does ask crucial questions.

Realtors emphasize location, location, location, and for good reason. Although e-commerce sales are increasingly making the large brick-and-mortar business locations less important, most small businesses still sell to local customers. A good business corner where customer traffic is substantial does count for money in the cash register. Buy a fine restaurant in a deteriorating part of the city and you will not have many customers to serve.

You'll also have to earn customer loyalty on a continuing basis. Price may move them, or good service may keep them coming back for more. Visit the company as a customer and see how you're treated. If you're satisfied with how the company dealt with you, chances are that company's customers will likely stay. But if your visit was unpleasant, walk away—unless you consider yourself a turnaround expert—because there won't be many customers for you to count on when you take over.

The company's purchase price will consist of its physical assets and *goodwill.*

PLAIN ENGLISH

Goodwill is an intangible business asset that relates to the company's ability to generate income in excess of the normal rate of return for its physical assets due to superior management, marketing skill, and products.

A company's physical assets are relatively easy to value. Unfortunately, the employees you inherit are not. If your visit to the company as a customer uncovered poor management, but you buy the business anyway, you can hang out a sign proclaiming *Under New Management* to let customers know you're making changes. However, you may be pleasantly surprised at finding a well-run organization with good employees. Keeping them when you take over must be job one.

The business media often comments on the clash of corporate cultures that occur when two companies merge. One company may have casual dress every day, whereas the other requires its employees to wear business suits and dresses. Attire may seem a superficial criterion to make a judgment of corporate fit, but then, maybe not. If you own a fast-food restaurant, then acquiring another one should not cause much of a clash. But what if you decided to diversify into fine dining? Your experience in one business may not translate well into another.

Using a Business Acquisition Team

You better not enter the acquisition fray without a good supporting team. The members of your team should include ...

- A business broker.
- A certified public accountant.
- An attorney.
- A financial advisor.

If you know the company you want to buy and what to pay for it, then you don't need a business broker. However, if you're searching for the right business at the right price, and need someone to help you negotiate the deal, then consider a business broker. He or she will charge a fee, which may be a percentage of the purchase price, usually about 2 to 7 percent. You might find the house of your dreams by driving around the city or checking the ads, or you might not; just don't count on finding a business without a broker.

The business broker should be familiar with the type of business in which you're interested and be able to determine a fair price for the company.

It's your cash (or the bank's money that you must pay back) and you need to know what you're paying for. That means getting accurate financial information. Your accountant should be familiar with small businesses, and it would be a plus if he or she has some experience in the company's particular industry. Small businesses are notoriously bad at keeping good financial records, so an accountant who knows that and can make the adjustments necessary to give you an accurate picture is worth the fee.

TIP

Experience counts! Consult with bankers who have financed company purchases to see who they recommend as a business broker. Then ask the prospective broker for a list of previous clients, and discuss with them how effective the broker was in facilitating the purchase.

You provide your attorney with the price, payment terms, and other options, and your attorney should draft your contract to purchase the business. Make sure that you fully understand the contract. Have your attorney replace any legalese with real words.

Both the accountant and the attorney should be familiar with the tax laws regarding the purchase of the business. Even a straightforward purchase of the business assets requires tax allocations.

Your financial advisor can suggest ways to finance the purchase, and should be able to help you obtain the necessary funds at an affordable rate.

TIP

Once again, experience counts! Use a lawyer, accountant, broker, or financial advisor whose practice involves small businesses. Before hiring any professional, interview him or her. You are depending on the professional's sound advice.

EXAMINING THE FINANCIALS CLOSELY

You must fully understand the financial condition of the company you consider buying. The best financial information should include ...

- CPA-certified balance sheets for the current year and two prior years.
- CPA certified-income statements for the current year and two prior
  years.
- Federal and state income tax returns for the past three years.
- State sales tax reports for the past three years.

Because you have not yet made an offer, the prospective seller may be reluctant to disclose this information, especially if you're a potential competitor.
You may want to sign a statement affirming that the information is deemed
confidential and you will not disclose it to anyone or use it for any purpose
other than evaluating the company for possible acquisition. The accounting
and tax information should provide a more complete picture than just one or
the other.

The balance sheet lists the assets at their book value (purchase price) and
the liabilities; the information is stated as of a particular date: for example,
December 31, 2004. The income statement provides information about the
company's revenue and expenses for a stated period: for example, January 1
through December 31, 2004. Certified financial information means that a CPA
has prepared the information using generally accepted accounting practices,
and therefore should be reliable. However, many small businesses do not have
the reports certified, so your accountant should closely scrutinize them.

A business owner was interested in buying a tavern. He asked for the seller's
financial information and was offered three options: income tax returns on
which sales were underreported; his sales tax report, on which sales were
likewise underreported; or a "little black book," which was the true record of
sales. This is not the kind of company you want to buy! There is no guarantee
that the prospective seller is not cheating on his tax returns, but if he tells you
that his sales are $100,000, and he reported only $50,000 last year, then you
should walk, because he is either lying to you or to the IRS. If you buy the
corporate *stock*, you may inherit its tax problems.

PLAIN ENGLISH

Stock is the legal device used to determine ownership of a corporation. People or companies that own stock are called shareholders.

LOOKING FOR ANY LEGAL PROBLEMS THAT MAY ARISE

Before you sign on the dotted line of a purchase contract, find out everything you can about potential legal trouble that could end up costing you money down the road. There are a number of problems to look out for, from liens against the property to toxic-waste violations, from unpaid taxes to ongoing lawsuits. This section covers the kinds of problems to look out for.

CAUTION

Avoid buying the seller's stock. A stock sale benefits the seller, but at considerable risk to the buyer if unexpected or undisclosed seller debts appear after the closing when the seller is long gone. Stick to purchasing the company's assets only.

TITLES AND LIENS

The seller may tell you that he or she owns all assets free-and-clear. For any asset that has a title to it, such as real estate or motor vehicles, ask to see the title.

Search for mortgages on real estate or secured interests on personal property, including equipment, accounts receivable, inventory, and fixtures. Your attorney can order a title and lien search through a title insurance company to determine if the seller owns the real estate, and if there are any *mortgages,* mechanics' liens, or other encumbrances that would reduce the value of the property by the amount of the mortgage or lien.

Your attorney can order a search of the state secretary of state's files and the county recorder's files to see if any of the seller's personal property has been used as collateral (whether a financing statement was filed against the collateral), which would likewise reduce the value of the property.

PLAIN ENGLISH

A **mortgage** is placed on real estate for the property to serve as security for the payment of a debt. A financing statement records a debt against the personal property (collateral for a loan)..

COMPANY LEASES

The company may have leases for real estate and equipment that you could assume. Your attorney should determine if the leases can be assigned, and review the specific provisions so that you could discuss any unfavorable terms with the lessor in advance. The lease obligations become the new tenant's responsibility. If you're thinking about renting or leasing real property (such as an office), contact other tenants to determine if the landlord is responsive to their needs.

ZONING

Zoning laws may limit the business owner's use of his or her property. An individual wanted to purchase a store from a company; however, the property had never been rezoned from residential to commercial. The prospective seller assured him that rezoning would be no problem, so he conditioned the purchase on the rezoning at the seller's expense.

TOXIC WASTE

If you are buying real estate, remember three letters: EPA. Your prospective seller may own land contaminated with toxic wastes. If you buy that property, you run to risk of being responsible for any cleanup, possibly at the cost of several million dollars. Always have an environmental survey performed by an environmental engineering company to determine if there are toxic wastes. Most lenders require an environmental survey as a condition to obtaining a loan.

LAWSUITS

If you are buying the company's stock, rather than its assets, then you will inherit its liabilities, which could include outstanding lawsuits. Some lawsuits are frivolous and will go away; others, however, can end up costing a bundle. Therefore, insist that the present owner disclose all lawsuits and have your attorney review all pleadings, motions, and other related documents. Again, you must know what you are buying.

CAUTION

If the environmental survey turns up evidence of dangerous environmental wastes, do not buy the property, unless you're willing to risk the future of your business.

TAXES

Uncle Sam and his state nieces and nephews are a determined lot; they want to see the tax money. If the company you are buying is a taxpayer (C corporation, or any unincorporated association taxed similarly), you must have your tax advisor review its tax returns. If you buy the corporate stock, you get its tax liabilities, too.

WHEN TO KEEP CONTRACTS WITH SUPPLIERS AND EMPLOYEES

Contracts with suppliers, like leases, should be reviewed by your attorney to determine if they are assignable and for their important terms. If you buy just the company's assets, you probably will negotiate a new contract with the suppliers unless the old contract is particularly favorable.

You may want the company's employees to stay with you. Most employees are simply at-will, which means that they can be retained or terminated at any time. However, the company may have several employees with written contracts that last for several years. If you want to keep the employees under those terms, fine; but if not, then buy only the company's assets, or have the seller renegotiate the employee contracts.

SERVICE WARRANTIES AND TRADEMARKS

The retail business often provides its customers with service warranties. If you take over the business, you may be obligated to honor those warranties or face irate customers. The prospective seller should disclose this potential liability and adjust the purchase price accordingly.

Sometimes a name really does say it all. If your targeted company has an important trademarked name, make sure that the sale includes its assignment to you. Likewise, if there are patents, copyrights, or licenses that are essential to success of the business, ensure that they are assigned as part of the sale. If you're buying a tavern, for instance, you need the liquor license that goes along with it.

FRANCHISOR APPROVAL

If you are buying a business that is a franchisee, your lawyer should review its agreement, and your accountant should examine the financial arrangement. Franchises, as discussed shortly, are often very successful (fast-food restaurants, for example), but the franchise agreement may be long term, costly, and inflexible. The franchisor must approve the assignment of any franchise.

MAKING THE OFFER AND NEGOTIATING THE DEAL

If you are satisfied that there are no significant obstacles to making an offer, you might then want to send a nonbinding letter of intent to purchase to the seller. The letter should indicate your desire to make an offer and determine if the prospective seller is interested. The letter may contain ...

- A list of assets you want to buy and at what price.
- A list of licenses, permits, and so on that would be transferred.
- A list of documents your lawyer and accountant need to review.

The letter should clearly state that its purpose is to determine if the parties agree in principal on the sale, and that it is not a contract offer. Your lawyer would draft the contract offer after the seller has tentatively agreed to the deal.

TIP

Be thorough! Have your attorney draft the contract and be sure you include all those terms that are important to you, and to which the other party must react or accept. It is a fee worth paying.

After the parties have generally agreed, your attorney should draft the purchase agreement.

You must decide whether you are going to purchase ownership of the business, such as stock in the target corporation, or purchase the company's assets. Purchasing the stock in the corporation also buys its liabilities, so usually buying the business assets instead is preferable. The following discussion involves a contract to buy the assets and the terms that are usually included.

The purchase agreement to buy assets should usually contain the following terms:

- Assets being sold and the allocation of the purchase price
- Adjustment of sale price for contingencies
- Terms of payment
- Bulk sales law compliance
- Seller's representations
- Seller's covenant not to compete
- Conduct of business before closing
- Closing date

THE PURCHASE AGREEMENT

The purchase agreement should list the assets bought and allocate the purchase price for each asset according to its fair market value. The list includes real estate to be conveyed; tangible property, such as equipment, trade fixtures, and inventory; customer information and important records; any real estate or equipment leases or contracts to be assigned to the buyer; and intangible personal property, such as patents, copyrights, trademarks, and licenses.

You need to allocate the purchase price among the assets for tax purposes. As a buyer you want to allocate as much of the price as possible to depreciable assets, such as equipment and fixtures, and as little as necessary to property that cannot be depreciated, such as land and goodwill.

If you're buying inventory, the contract should have a tentative price, which then would be adjusted based on a complete inventory at some designated time prior to closing.

CAUTION

Be as accurate as possible! The IRS may review your purchase price allocation, so be prepared to demonstrate the fair market value for each item. You will need to report the allocation on IRS form 8594.

The purchase may be for a cash sum due at closing, which would be reduced by any earnest money you paid at the time of the offering. Or the agreement may permit you to make periodic payments over a specified term, with interest. It's recommended that you make at least two payments, even if you can pay the entire amount at closing. You might get hit with customer claims for refunds or warranties that you may feel obligated to honor, or creditor claims against inventory under the state bulk sales act. If by the second payment, perhaps in six months, a problem has arisen, then an adjustment in the payment would be required by the contract.

Under the state bulk sales act, a company selling all or most of its assets is required to notify its creditors before concluding the sale. The seller's creditors may proceed to collect before the seller trots off with the sale's proceeds. As the buyer, you should receive a list of the seller's creditors, and then notify each creditor of the impending sale. If you fail to comply with the law, the creditors not notified may assert a claim against the assets that you bought.

The seller should state in the purchase agreement that ...

■ The corporation (or other type of entity) is in good standing as a corporation, and its board and shareholder authorize the sale.

■ All assets are owned and conveyed free of liens.

■ All financial statements are accurate.

■ All leases and contracts are assignable.

■ There are no pending lawsuits.

■ All material facts have been disclosed to the buyer.

TIP

Know what you're buying. Seller representations are important and should be included in the contract, but you should rely on your own examination of the representations; for example, have your accountant review the financial information.

COVENANTS

You don't want to buy a retail store or restaurant from your seller, and then have the seller open a competing store in the same neighborhood. A covenant (promise) not to compete would eliminate this problem. If your customer base resides within a radius of 10 miles, you should prohibit the seller from opening a competing business within that radius for a reasonable time after the closing, such as three years. Courts will enforce the covenant if it is reasonable in time and distance.

The seller should agree to continue his or her same business practices until closing. You don't want the seller to make any detrimental changes, such as selling all the most marketable inventory, or issuing discount coupons that you would be forced to honor.

The closing date is stated to fix the time of payment and transfer of assets to the buyer.

If this is a new business that you are buying, you may want to have the seller stay on for a few months to help you. Include a provision in the agreement specifying the services to be rendered, and the compensation to be paid, for the period of time you need for the transition.

FINANCING THE PURCHASE

You need to come up with the money for the deal. Your current business retained earnings (undistributed profits) may be sufficient to fund the purchase, or your own personal assets, or you may be able to convince a bank to lend you the money. The seller may be willing to permit you to make monthly or annual payments, which may come partially from the income of your newly acquired business.

TAXING MATTERS

If you are buying the ownership of the company (corporate stock), you inherit all its tax attributes. The seller's depreciation schedules for its equipment and buildings are now your schedules. Its accounting method and elections are now yours, too. The tax status (S or C corporation) is now your status. And you guessed it, the corporation's tax liabilities are now your problem, too.

If your corporation is purchasing the stock of another corporation to merge or own the seller's corporation as a subsidiary, you have entered the tax world known as corporate reorganization. Its complexities are beyond the discussion of this book. Consult a tax advisor who is an expert in this arcane area of the law.

When you purchase the assets, you need to perform the price allocation, as previously discussed. The depreciable assets are then yours to write down, using the tax cost (*basis of property*) that you have determined. The IRS provides depreciation tables.

PLAIN ENGLISH

Basis of property is usually the acquisition cost; for depreciable assets, such as equipment, the basis is reduced by depreciation. Basis is used to determine gain or loss on the sale of property by subtracting the basis from the sale price.

CLOSING MEANS BEGINNING

The closing on the purchase of a business or business assets requires close attention to the following:

- Payment, which may be by cash for the total amount, or the initial payment for several installments
- Transfer of title to all titled assets (vehicles, for example)
- Bill of sale for nontitled assets (inventory, for example)
- Assignment of leases, and contracts
- Transfer of patents, copyrights, franchise documents, and so on
- Stock certificate transfer, if you are buying the business

If you're making periodic payments to the seller, the seller will probably insist on taking a mortgage on any real estate and a security interest against personal property, so you will sign documents related to that collateral. Likewise you will sign a promissory note for the debt.

HELPFUL SOURCES FOR BUYING A BUSINESS

Read *The Complete Idiot's Guide to Buying and Selling a Business* by Ed Paulson (Alpha Books, 1999). Several other excellent books on the market discuss business purchases and have forms for you to use as a guideline to help your attorney draft an agreement; several may be in your local library or can be purchased at a bookstore or on the web. Among these are *The Mergers and Acquisitions Handbook* by Milton Rock (McGraw Hill, 1994), *Selling Your Business: The Transition from Entrepreneur to Investor* by Louis Corsier (John Wiley & Sons, 2004) and *M&A: A Practical Guide to Doing The Deal* by Jeffrey Hooke (John Wiley & Sons, 1996). The IRS website (www.irs.ustreas. gov) provides the tax forms and related instructions for the asset allocation.

The 30-Second Recap

- Spend the time necessary to buy the right business for you.
- Use your accountant to examine the seller's financial statements.
- Search for liens against the assets to be purchased.
- Draft a contract that fully protects your interests.
- Allocate the purchase price to assets that you can write off.
- There is no single "right" way to arrange the financial aspects related to the purchase or sale of a company.

Assets, Stock, and Other Business Combinations

English is an incredible language. It has brought us Hemingway, Steinbeck, and Frost. It has also brought us tons of jargon, such as asset transfer, stock sale, merger, valuation, and buyout agreement. At some point, you are going to either make an offer to purchase another company or receive such an offer. This section presents the conceptual foundation upon which the offer's value assessment is based.

Differentiating Mergers and Other Purchase Agreements

It is possible for a company to be sold without it being a merger. A merger involves specific stock-related operations that are not involved when the company purchased is not a corporation.

In fact, there are specific reasons for a buyer not to completely merge with another company but instead acquire only a smaller subset of its total assets.

This brings us back to our old friends risk and reward. Remember that a buyer purchases future income benefits, and any associated risk factors tend to decrease the perceived value of the business being purchased. Also remember that any deal that becomes too complicated also acquires a risk factor of its own, which moves most business people toward transactions with minimal complexity.

Each type of sale/purchase arrangement has its own set of benefits and drawbacks. Which aspects are the most important to the transaction are truly based on the specific transaction and the people involved. Work your way through this section to understand these various sale/purchase arrangements.

ASSET PURCHASE: BUYING WHAT YOU WANT

A simple asset purchase is the least complicated of all purchase arrangements. The buyer designates the items that he or she wants to buy, and the seller agrees to sell them. The seller then passes the items along with their associated liabilities, such as outstanding loans on equipment, to the buyer who assumes their ownership.

Notice that this transaction involves no stock at all, unless the buyer offers stock instead of or in addition to cash as payment for the purchased items.

Notice that the buyer obtains the assets, which are typically equipment or other types of tangible property. It might also include customer lists, proprietary processes, special agreements that have value, performance contracts that can be transferred, copyrights, patents, and other intellectual property. The seller parts with these assets and relinquishes future rights to them in exchange for cash and/or other assets.

Notice that these assets have now been sold at a fair market value, which might be higher than their depreciated book value. Taxes should immediately spring to mind when you see words like that in the same sentence, and your instincts would be right.

This type of arrangement is often more beneficial to the buyer and less attractive to the seller than a standard stock sale.

TIP

Asset purchase plans are the only purchase method available when purchasing a noncorporate company such as a sole proprietorship or partnership, because only corporations can sell stock. The asset purchased might be the entire company for a single price, but the acquisition is still accomplished without any stock purchase.

Notice that the buyer has made no claim and assumed no liability for any other assets or liabilities associated with the selling company. The selling company is still a solvent, self-sustaining, legal entity that is responsible for its own bills and debts. If it just sold its primary means for earning a living and did not account for its debtors, the sale was shortsighted; it is not, however, the purchasing company's responsibility.

Notice also that this type of sale requires specific negotiations for each purchased asset—which takes time, money, and personnel—and it might cost the purchasing company more money in the long run.

STOCK PURCHASE: WHAT YOU DON'T SEE CAN HURT YOU

When a buyer purchases stock in a company, the buyer becomes a partial owner of that company. This applies to any stock purchase. When the buyer purchases all the stock in a company, he or she becomes its new owner. At that point, all company assets pass to the new owner along with all liens and liabilities.

Notice that this arrangement involves the word *all* and not specific items as seen with the asset purchase arrangement. *All* is not a scary word when dealing with items that you know about, but it can be frightening when dealing with items that you don't know about.

Let's face it, we all wish that the world was a completely honest place and that we knew everything that would happen at any point in time. But it just doesn't always work that way. The sellers might have neglected to tell you about pending actions against the company that had not yet materialized, or it might have underpaid its employment taxes for the past year, leaving a debt with the government. Then again, the owners simply might not have known that a prior action on the company's part would give rise to future claims against the company.

For example, there might be litigation against the company that has not yet been filed, and that the owners might not have even known about when you made your purchase. The point is that when you purchase the company's stock, you purchase its assets and its liabilities, along with its legal identity.

If you leave the company as a standalone company, the *parent company* will not generally be directly liable for any of these unforeseen occurrences. However, an unforeseen lawsuit or action by the IRS against the company certainly diminishes its future value, completely throwing your initial projections out the window.

PLAIN ENGLISH

A **parent company** is one that owns the majority, or all, of the stock in another company. For example, a company that purchases all the stock in another company would be the purchased company's parent company.

Notice that a stock purchase still keeps the purchased company and its stocks alive as a separate legal entity. This situation changes when two companies merge.

MERGERS: MAKING ONE OUT OF TWO

The American Heritage Dictionary defines *merge* as "to combine or unite," which is exactly what happens when the stocks of two companies are merged. One of the companies disappears and the stock of only one company remains.

A merger can involve large, medium, or small companies. A larger company can be merged into a smaller one, or vice versa.

For purposes of this discussion, the company being acquired is referred to as "target (B)" company, and the acquiring company as "buyer (A)."

There are various types of mergers, but the most likely types that you will encounter are the forward and reverse merger:

- A *forward merger* merges stock from (B) into (A), with only the stock from (A) remaining after the merger. Basically, the acquired company is merged into the buyer's company so that the purchased company essentially disappears.

- A *reverse merger* is just the opposite of a forward merger in that the stock from (A) is merged into (B). This means that the stock from the buyer is merged into the stock of the acquired company with only the acquired company's stock remaining after the merge.

A forward merger is pretty obvious, and intuitively it makes sense. The reverse merger, on the other hand, might take a little explaining. There could be any number of reasons for a reverse merger, and one reason is explained here.

CAUTION

Just because a person can talk fast with the jargon doesn't mean that he or she understands the mergers and acquisitions (M&A) process. Don't be afraid to ask a few more questions to ensure that this person can not only talk M&A talk but also walk the walk.

Assume that the buying company has a dubious reputation in the industry and is looking to continue its operation while not being hampered by its poor reputation. Purchasing a company with a solid reputation and performing a reverse merger allows the buyer to merge its operations into the purchased company, keeping its assets, employees, customers, and basic operation intact. At the same time, it can now function under the good name of the purchased company, which should reap benefits for it into the future.

Notice that if you are the seller in this situation, you want to make sure that you are well compensated for your good reputation because that is the primary asset purchased.

Mergers require a change in stock ownership, which means that a majority of the shareholders must approve the action. For a small, privately held corporation, this is generally not a problem because you are probably negotiating with the owners. For a larger company, which enters into complicated arrangements like *triangular mergers*, this might get complicated and take time. You should factor this consideration into the transaction expectations.

All assets and liabilities transfer from the seller to the buyer when the merger agreement is filed with the proper state authorities, such as the secretary of state's office. Notice that if the two companies reside in different states, you have to take certain legal actions to ensure that the desired level of corporate protection is retained within the involved states.

PLAIN ENGLISH

A **triangular merger** involves the target company and a subsidiary corporation of the buyer's corporation.

Shareholders in the target company are compensated with shares of stock in the buying company and possibly some cash. Before the merger can occur, both the buyer and seller must come to a valuation determination for each company. From that valuation, an agreement is reached regarding the number of shares of the buying company that will be traded for each share of the purchased company.

Take a look at this simple example as a starting point for understanding the merger-valuation process.

Assume that the buying company (A) has a stock market value of $5 per share and the target company (B) has a stock value of $10 per share. This means that trading two shares of the buying company (A) for every one share of the target company (B) adequately compensates the shareholders for their ownership interest. They previously owned $10 in a corporation before in the form of one share of (B). After the merger they own $10 of corporate stock in the form of two shares of (A).

The shareholders should be happy with the arrangement because the merged company should have brighter future prospects than (B) had previously on its own, or the merger would not have been desirable to either (A) or (B).

This example is highly simplified, and it won't make you an expert. It is only for you to understand some of the considerations involved when looking at a merger situation.

A LITTLE CASH AND A LITTLE STOCK

Transactions need not be all cash or all stock. They can also be a combination of the two, which can be beneficial for both parties.

Assume that a company is purchased for $1.5 million and that the purchasing company does not have adequate cash on hand to pay the entire amount. It might, instead, offer $500,000 in cash and $1 million in the buying company's stock.

TIP

Stock ownership offers can appear pretty attractive at first and indeed might turn out to be great investment decisions. But never forget that stock is only worth what someone else is willing, and able, to pay for it. This means that the other person must value the stock at the same general value you expect and you must be able to sell the stock.

The seller frees himself or herself from the operation of the company along with any cosigning liabilities that might have been assumed over the years of ownership. He or she also walks away with $500,000 in cash and ownership in a company that both the seller and the buyer hope will be stronger as a result of the acquisition. The future prospects for the stock are bright, making the buyer and seller happy. Furthermore, the buyer avoids a $1 million cash payment and the seller gets to add a substantial amount of money ($500,000) to his or her retirement fund. This is a good deal overall, as long as the stock performs up to expectations, which becomes the seller's primary future concern. You should consult your attorney for more information.

Tax implications may be involved with this transaction that affect the net payment received by the seller.

CONSOLIDATING FOR SOMETHING NEW AND DIFFERENT

Assume that both the buyer (A) and the seller (B) decide to combine forces as a completely new company. In this case, the stock of (A) and (B) would disappear, and a new stock, (C), would be created in the form of a new corporation that represents the combined interests of shareholders from both (A) and (B).

This type of arrangement is called a *consolidation* in that the two share types are consolidated to create a third.

Shareholders in (A) and (B) are compensated by stock in (C) in a ratio determined in a fashion similar to that discussed in mergers. The transactions could involve all stock, all cash, or some combination of the two.

For example, assume that (A) is cash rich, whereas (B) is cash poor but has tremendous technological advantages. Shareholders in (A) might feel that their ready cash reserves, which have no future risk associated with them at all, warrant some type of immediate cash distribution to them as part of the consolidation. (B)'s shareholders are compensated by the shares in (C), but might not deserve the cash distribution simply because they brought little cash to the transaction in the first place.

BOARD OF DIRECTOR OBLIGATIONS

All corporations have a board of directors. This board might consist of a single person for a small corporation, or in the case of a company like General Motors, a large number of high-powered executives. The role of the board of directors in general, and its member(s) in particular, is to monitor the overall operation of the organization to ensure that the shareholders' asset value (their underlying share worth) is invested in the best possible way.

Common industry terminology talks about the creation of *shareholder wealth,* and it is the board's job to optimize shareholder wealth creation.

PLAIN ENGLISH

Shareholder wealth is the underlying value of a share of stock as determined by its assessed market value. Actions that increase market value increase shareholder wealth.

Should the shareholders determine that their stock value is not being optimized because of board decisions, the stockholders can take certain steps to remedy the situation. They can vote in a new board of directors for a start. This does not correct past losses, but it does ensure that future losses are minimized by preventing poor decisions by the same board members. They can also file suit against the board members, which gets a board member into a tricky situation.

Assume for a moment that you are a board member of publicly traded corporation. Also assume that two different companies have made offers to purchase your stock. Company (A) is a trustworthy company with a solid reputation and proven track record of taking good care of acquired company assets, personnel, vendors, and customers. Company (A) offers $10 per share for your stock, which the going price for your company the week before the offer was made.

Company (B) offers $12 per share, which is the price per share after the offer became public knowledge. You also know that (B) has never left one of its acquired companies intact, and has indeed sold off the assets and fired the employees from its past two acquisitions.

Which company do you choose? The short-term best answer is (B) because it offers the shareholders $2 more per share, or 20 percent more, than the (A) offer which you and all other board members agree offers better long-term investment returns. Which one optimizes shareholder wealth? It is all a matter of perspective, and the short-term perspective is the safest legal route for shareholders to take. There is little doubt that $12 is larger than $10 and that the shareholders would make more money from the (B) offer. There is risk with the longer-term perspective associated with (A).

Which is the right approach? The board of directors exists to make these determinations, and only later can we assess whether they made the decision that optimized shareholder wealth. The business judgment rule protects board members who choose the more risky option as long as they truly believe that it is the overall best option (in their business judgment) for the shareholders.

MANAGEMENT AGREEMENTS AND WHY THEY SHOULD BE AVOIDED

Have you ever heard of people who purchase a house with a "lease-option" arrangement whereby they lease the house, while retaining the option to purchase at a future date? Management agreements are essentially the same thing.

CAUTION

It is almost impossible to set up a useful management agreement without risk to the seller. When the buying personnel become involved in your daily operations, they will definitely learn information about customers, processes, and finances that otherwise would be confidential. If they choose not to purchase at the end of the agreement period, you could have revealed your company secrets and received nothing in return.

When a management agreement is set up, the purchasing company retains the right to purchase the selling company at a future date, but opts to manage the company for a while before actually making the purchase. As the buyer, this provides an opportunity to verify that you are indeed buying what you think you are buying—kind of like test driving a car for a month before purchasing it.

The bad news from a seller's perspective is that you can definitely assume that the buyers will find things out about the company during the course of the agreement that they did not know before it started—and you can almost guarantee that the things they discover will decrease the value of the company, and the purchase price. They might even find out things that cause them to reconsider, or back out of, the complete purchase.

For this reason, it is usually a good idea to avoid management agreements altogether if possible. For the buyers, they also pose the dilemma of sitting on the fence and not simply choosing one side or the other. It ties up your personnel with management activities. Intercompany operations are put into a limbo state because you haven't really made the purchase. Money is also in limbo in that it is both allocated and not allocated at the same time.

Indecision is often detrimental to a business's operation, and management agreements put the purchase into indecision until the period of the agreement expires. For these reason, it is best to avoid them.

On the other hand, if you are a seller with nothing to hide trying to convince a hesitant buyer of your honesty, a management agreement might be the only way to close the deal. As always, you are the only one who can make that determination.

KEEPING THE FOUNDERS AROUND FOR A WHILE

As a buyer and as a seller, you have an interest in promoting the future financial prosperity of the company. With smaller companies, the reputation, name, and "goodwill" of the company might be intimately tied with the founders. Larger companies have more employees over which to spread responsibility, meaning that each employee has a smaller impact on the overall business operation. Company goodwill is not usually tied to a particular employee except under very unique circumstances.

TIP

If you think about it for a moment, larger companies are typically organized and operated with organizational chart slots with requirements that are filled by people. The people fill slots that are relatively independent of the person filling that slot as long as the basic qualifications are intact. Impersonal, but true.

Smaller companies, on the other hand, are often organized around the people involved because there usually aren't that many people. The organizational chart slots are tailored to match the skills of the people involved.

For example, General Motors might have a position open for an electrical engineer. The company puts an ad in the paper, interviews candidates, and eventually hires someone with the skills needed to fill the position. This person might be one of hundreds of engineers in a given department and, based on that person's specific knowledge, typically can make minimal direct impact on the overall company's performance. As an employee moves higher in the organization or moves into strategic positions within the company, his or her impact is more profoundly felt, but the mainstream employee works within this diffused framework. If you don't believe this, simply note the popularity of the *Dilbert* cartoon strip!

Smaller companies have few employees, which makes the impact of each employee more profound. Each employee in a 20-person company comprises 5 percent of the personnel and is typically involved in a much higher level of management decision making than would be possible with a larger company. This is naturally based on the person's specific job responsibility.

Let's now extend this small company scenario to the founders. These are the people who initially created the company and, through their work, dedication, and reputation, grew the company to the point that it can support a 20-person payroll. Their credibility is highly linked to the credibility of the company unless they have specifically worked at hiring excellent employees to whom they have turned over much of the daily operation. This does happen, but it is rare with smaller companies simply because the owners have nurtured their company since day one and they have evolved the operation around their involvement.

There is nothing insidious or wrong with this approach, and it doesn't reflect a conscious scheme on the founders' part to maintain control. It is just a natural evolution for a successful smaller company.

Now you, the buyer, come along and want to purchase the company. Note that negotiations will probably be made with the founders, who might be completely unaware of their importance to the company. The founders might even downplay their importance. Just know that the likelihood of their being crucial to operations is most often the case. If you let them leave when you purchase the company, it might put you in the position of owning a company that just lost its most important assets, the founders.

TIP

Arranging for a portion of a purchase package to include future stock incentives for the selling company's founders is a proven method for keeping their attention in the future. Otherwise, as with most entrepreneurs, their attention will wander on to newer, more exciting pastures.

For this reason, it is usually best to keep the founders around for a while, and purchase agreements try to keep the founders with some stock in the new company. This keeps the founders with an incentive to work for the prosperity of the buying company. These seller-retention agreements, sometimes called employment contracts, are usually for two or three years. And they put the selling founders into strategic roles that promote the success of their former company and also optimize their overall contribution to the buying organization.

There are, on the other hand, times when you would want the founders completely out of the picture. If the founder is a strong personality who keeps a lock on the company operations, which might cause substantial conflicts with the management and culture of the buying company, it might be in the buyer's best interest to specifically get the founder out of the picture.

There are also times where your due diligence reveals that customers are not working as fully as possible with the purchased company because of a lack of trust in the current management. This opens opportunities to the buying company because getting rid of the management might increase sales.

THE 30-SECOND RECAP

■ Only corporations can perform a stock merger because only corporations are based on shares of stock.

■ Buyer and seller company valuation is the basis for determining the stock basis during mergers.

■ Management agreements might be attractive to the buyer but generally work to the detriment of the seller.

■ The method of transaction financing affects the taxes associated with the transaction.

■ The advantages and disadvantages of retaining the founders of the purchased company need to be determined on a case-by-case basis.

Franchising for Success

Every Saturday morning, children across America spend their TV time watching cartoons sponsored by fast-food chains. Most American children can probably even spot a McDonald's among the urban clutter of buildings from the family car. You may be interested in joining thousands of businesspersons who become franchisees in a variety of businesses, such as learning centers, office and home cleaning, and convenience stores, and make a good living in the process.

Franchising has become an extremely popular for would-be entrepreneurs to start up their own businesses. There are many benefits and pitfalls to consider when entering the franchise world. This section will help you understand the basics of starting up a franchise.

AN OVERVIEW OF FRANCHISING LAWS

A franchise is a contract arrangement giving the franchisee the right to use the franchisor's trademark, logo, goodwill, and marketing expertise to sell goods or services. Franchises fit into two basic forms:

1. An entire business franchise
2. A product distribution arrangement

If you want to become a fast-food restaurant owner, for example, your franchise agreement will be just one entity in the entire business franchise. You'll have one product to sell under the franchisor's trademark.

If you're in a retail business that sells several product lines, it's possible to have a franchise distribution arrangement with one or more major dealers to sell their products in a specified market. For example, you might own a bicycle shop that sells several competing brands for which you've become a local franchisee. Many auto dealers are also franchisees.

As the franchisee, you own your own business and therefore can decide what form of business organization to operate under, including as a corporation or limited liability company. In addition, you would operate according to the franchise agreement, which can be expensive and restrictive.

A good franchise offers you not only a recognizable name to operate under, but also a proven plan to run the business and help from the franchisor if you have problems. Your company will run the same operation as several hundred other franchisees. For instance, a Subway in Indianapolis, Indiana, runs similar to a Subway in Seattle, Washington.

CAUTION

If you crave freedom, and don't want big brother (franchisor) looking over your shoulder, a franchise is probably not for you. Deviation from the standard practices is not usually encouraged in franchises because similarity and standardization provide customers with confidence in the product offered.

The cost of your new franchise may be an important consideration. The franchise fee, which may be a substantial advance, could range from as little as $500 to as much as $45,000 or more. National franchises, for instance, usually command a significant initial fee. In addition, the franchisor will be entitled to a percentage of your gross sales, and may require you to purchase its equipment, goods, and supplies.

Many franchisors do not require that you have prior experience in the business, and will train you and your employees, but this, too, usually comes at a price to you. You may also have to pay a fee for national or local advertising, and you'll probably be restricted in the merchandise you can sell. Fast-food restaurants sell the franchisor's food, period.

The franchisee, like any business owner, bears the risk of loss in the business; in a franchise, however, this risk is often reduced by the sale of a known product or service that generates sales by the name alone. On the downside, you are limited to operating in a particular area and may not be allowed to move without the franchisor's permission. Also you may not be able to transfer your business to anyone other than the franchisor or someone approved by the franchisor.

CHOOSING THE RIGHT FRANCHISE

Before you sign a franchise agreement or pay any money, ask yourself the following questions:

- Am I suited for this type of business?
- Am I compatible with the franchisor?
- Does the franchisor have strong name recognition?
- Does the business have strong growth possibilities?
- Will the franchisor find me a suitable business location?
- Will the franchisor help with financing?
- Does the franchisor have a good record of successful franchisees?
- Is the franchisor selective in awarding franchises?
- Have I understood all the fees and costs?
- Does the franchisor have an excellent training program?
- Has the franchisor disclosed everything required by law?
- Is the franchise agreement fair?
- Has the franchisor answered all my questions?

It's your money and future, so it's important to thoroughly investigate the franchise. Unpleasant surprises can cost you a bundle.

TIP

You should follow the adage *Know thyself.* Only you can determine whether the franchise business is the type of business that you truly will enjoy. However, enthusiasm will not conquer all, so you need to take inventory of your skills and personality. If you are not a people person and the franchise is service oriented, consider hiring someone who revels in customer contact, or look elsewhere for a business that requires less interaction by you with the public.

KNOW WHO YOU'RE DEALING WITH

You and the franchisor will be partners—not legally, but operationally. You must be able to work effectively with the franchisor. If at the initial stages of your discussions you have to fight through the franchisor's bureaucracy to get answers or your calls aren't returned for several days, don't buy into the franchise. Can you trust their word? What is their business background? And obtain all the franchisor's audited financial information. Avoid a financially weak franchisor. You need to believe in your franchisor and its vision for its (and your) future.

The franchise's name need not be a household word, but it helps. You are going to invest a lot of money to use the franchise's trademark, so it should be well established and have an excellent reputation for quality products and services. In this instance, the advice to invest in what you know and like is sound.

TIP

Comparison shop for financing. Closely scrutinize the terms. Be skeptical of any lender who seems overly eager to lend you money.

RELY ON THE FRANCHISOR'S EXPERTISE

The franchisor should share with you its plan for business development, nationally and locally. Franchisor growth and market share are important to your success. If you are going to be one of the first franchisees in your area, you need to know that others will follow, not as competitors, but for increased name recognition.

Location, location, and location. The good convenience store franchisors, for instance, know where to locate their stores for the maximum of traffic and sales. Your franchisor should help you select an appropriate site or may already have a location in mind. Carefully consider the franchisor's advice.

You need a good financial plan. The franchisor has experience with determining a franchisee's financial needs, and you should insist that it provide you with a typical franchisee budget. If money is in short supply, the franchisor may be willing to lend you some of the money up front.

REPUTATION AND COOPERATION COUNT

Insist that the franchisor provide you with a complete list of franchisees in your area, and be sure to contact them. Think of them as the franchisor's customers—if they are well satisfied and successful, it's likely that you will be, too. Don't forget to ask the franchisees if the franchisor has been responsive to their business challenges. If the franchisor hasn't helped when financial, customer, or other problems have arisen, don't invest in that franchise.

In addition, if the franchisor isn't very selective in awarding franchises, the quality of the total franchise will suffer. Just as your reputation will depend on the quality of your employees, the franchise's reputation will be enhanced by its selectivity. The franchisor should thoroughly examine your credentials, and, if it doesn't, then reconsider.

CAUTION

You should thoroughly understand all the fees and costs associated with the franchise. Do a reality check with other franchisees to compare the franchisor's claims. You don't need any surprises on what you owe the franchisor, because money will be tight for some time after you begin.

Many franchisors assume that you have no prior business experience, so they will train you in general business matters as well as the specific franchise business. Contact other franchisees to see whether they received the help that they needed. If there were any deficiencies, the franchisor should readily agree to improve the training. The franchisor should have a strong commitment to continued training and education. The franchisor should be willing to at least bear part of this cost.

You are making a substantial investment, so the franchisor should disclose as much about itself as required by law, and readily do so. If you don't receive this information, avoid this franchisor. Federal and state law disclosure requirements are discussed below.

READ THE FINE PRINT

The franchisor's attorneys draft the franchise agreement. The franchisor has developed the business that you want to join, so it's understandable that the franchisor wants to protect itself and control the arrangement. However, its terms should not be oppressive. Equally as important is the operating relationship between the franchisor and franchisees. The franchisees should tell you if the franchisor always insists on the letter of the contract rather than the spirit. A franchisor that always insists on its rights to the detriment of an embattled franchisee should be avoided.

After you have read all the franchisor's information and discussed with the franchisees all your concerns, you should have several questions for the franchisor. Don't hesitate to ask, and follow up with other questions until you fully understand everything about the arrangement. The franchisor's answers should be straightforward and responsive. Walk away if they are evasive.

THE FRANCHISE DISCLOSURES DULY NOTED

Most franchise arrangements come within the dictates of the Federal Trade Commission (FTC) disclosure requirements. If you are a prospective franchisee, the franchisor must give you an offering circular (disclosures) at the earliest of your first in-person meeting, or 10 working days before you sign a contract or pay money to the franchisor. Several states also regulate franchise arrangements, and the franchisor that makes an offer in those states has to comply with state law as well.

■ **Experience and history.** You need to know as much about the franchisor as possible. Examine its business history and finances. If the franchisor has a short history in the business or has a long history of rocky finances, then beware, because you will be in the same boat with the franchisor as captain. Get to know its major players; if you have doubts about its honesty or the franchisor seems to talk a better game than it plays, keep your money and run to the nearest exit. Check out its business plan and confer with franchisees to confirm that the plan is being followed.

■ **Current and past litigation.** If the franchisor is knee-deep in litigation, particularly with several franchisees, then, likewise, depart. However, most large franchisors get sued for a lot of reasons, some of which are not important. Your attorney can help sort out the legitimate claims from the frivolous ones. If the franchisor is in bankruptcy, however, definitely have your attorney investigate the filing. Some times a bad market glitch causes a temporary problem that bankruptcy reorganization and time can resolve, but maybe not.

■ **Fees, fees, fees.** Franchise fees and other costs must be detailed in a financial statement, and you need to check with other franchisees to see whether this statement reflects their experience. This is particularly true for the franchisor's estimate of your initial investment beyond the fees paid to it. Costs vary from city to city. What you would pay for rent and employees in New York City will be more than what you'd pay in Indianapolis.

TIP

When it comes to negotiating fees, err on the side of a conservative budget, because running a business almost always costs more than you predict.

■ **Understanding your restrictions.** You may be closely tied to the franchisor's products and services. The franchisee is often obligated to buy its equipment from the franchisor and use the franchisor's services.

■ **Territorial and product limits.** You may be restricted to selling only the franchisor's products or have a limited sales territory. Talk with other franchisees about these limits. If they receive shoddy products or inefficient services from the franchisor, or the franchisor's merchandise is poor quality, you will not be successful. If your sales territory is not exclusive, another competing franchisee can take away customers. And know the territory—another bicycle sales store at a busy intersection may be one too many.

- **Obligations.** The disclosure circular lists the franchisee's obligations, but don't rely on this list. Always read the contract and fully understand your obligations, because any contract you sign is binding. Likewise the disclosure circular lists the franchisor's obligations. This list is only as good as the franchisor who follows it (and the contract). The only realistic way to determine if the franchisor meets its obligations is to confirm it with the franchisees. For example, if you are obligated to pay an advertising fee, which often you are, then ask the franchisees if the advertising has been effective.

- **All necessary financing.** If the franchisor offers you financing, the circular will disclose its terms and conditions. This will enable you to compare the franchisor's terms with other sources of financing. Check with other franchisees to find out how they financed their investment and operations.

- **Trademarks and confidential information.** You are going to use the franchisor's *trademark* (or service mark). Check with the U.S. Trademark Office in Washington, D.C., to determine whether the mark has been registered. If not, it's possible you may not be protected in using the mark in your state. Do your own quick market survey with friends and acquaintances to find out if they have heard of the company's name. This may not be scientific, but it can tell you if the name is recognized. If not, then count on a ton of advertising dollars to gain that recognition.

PLAIN ENGLISH

A **trademark** is a word, name, or symbol used in commerce to identify a product. Pepsi and McDonald's are trademarked and cannot be used without the owner's permission. The franchisor's trademark is licensed to the franchisee for use during the period of the franchise agreement.

- **Franchisee participation.** If you bought this book, you are unlikely to be a passive investor in the franchise. Be aware, however, that most franchise arrangements will require you to be an active manager, completely involved in the business. So if your role is largely passive, you better ensure that hiring a manager will do.

■ **Details on resolutions.** You want to control the destiny of your franchise business, so examine very closely any restrictions on your ability to do the following: renew the franchise for additional periods at minimal cost; terminate the franchise upon *just cause* (make sure the franchisor can terminate only under just cause); resolve disputes with expedition and minimal costs; and freely transfer your franchise to a business successor or buyer.

PLAIN ENGLISH

Just cause means good cause. The franchisor would be required to prove that the termination of the agreement was reasonable due to franchisee misconduct.

■ **Celebrity promotions.** Famous people endorse many products, from autos to shoes, and do so for a sizeable fee. They also endorse franchises. The FTC requires these celebrities to disclose their compensation and the extent to which they are involved in management or control of the franchise, as well as any money they have invested in the business. Your hero or heroine may just have lent his or her name, so be a little skeptical about these endorsements.

■ **Claiming what you've earned.** Most franchisors do not make earnings claims. If the franchisor does make claims about your potential earnings, however, the FTC requires the offering circular to disclose the factual basis and assumptions made. Compare this claim with the experiences of other franchisees who operate under circumstances similar to yours. A self-laundry outlet may do very well near several apartments, but less well in an affluent neighborhood. Remember, the franchisor wants to sell you the franchise, so expect a little exaggeration.

■ **List of outlets.** The franchisor must list all operating franchisees, as well as those that are nearly ready to open for business. The franchisor who has several operating franchisees in your area has developed a track record that you can check. Use this list to contact franchisees in your state. Even a simple "How are things working out?" can help you decide to go ahead or to look elsewhere. The franchisor must also include a list of canceled or terminated franchises that occurred within the last three years. Too many of these should provide sufficient warning.

■ **Financial statements.** The franchisor is required to provide you with two years of audited balance sheets and stockholders' equity, as well as the cash flows for the last three years. Although the FTC doesn't require a specific franchisor net worth, your accountant should be able to advise you as to its adequacy. And although the FTC requires all this to be disclosed, it does not verify the information. That is your number-one job.

- **Keeping copies.** The FTC circular requires the franchisor to provide you with copies of all contracts you are expected to sign. Turn these over to your attorney for his or her review.

TIP

Share all information with your business advisors. Hire an attorney who is familiar with franchise arrangements and an accountant who is properly skeptical of earnings claims. Fraud occurs in franchise arrangements just like it does in stock offerings.

YOUR FRANCHISE AGREEMENT

Expect your franchise agreement to run more than 50 pages. The franchise's attorney drafts the agreement in the franchisor's best interests, so hire an attorney who is well versed in franchise law and sufficiently aggressive to negotiate a more favorable agreement. Your franchisor may tell you to sign the contract, or walk. This may be an effective way of getting what it wants from you—your signature on the contract. Some well-established franchisors can dictate the contract, but others sometimes are more flexible.

Study the proposed agreement in conjunction with the FTC offering circular; if the contract has terms that conflict with the FTC requirement, make sure the contract is corrected. Although it's impossible in this discussion to cover each and every provision you'll find in a franchise agreement, here are some of the most common ones.

CAUTION

Don't confuse sales with profit. You may sell a lot, and pay the franchisor based on this figure, whereas your profit is what remains after all your costs (including what you should be paying yourself as an employee and investor).

- **Fees, payment schedule, and advertising.** What you owe and when it has to be paid should be at the top of your list of things to review. The initial fee is just that. Your ongoing fees (royalties) may be based on gross revenues, not your profit.

Advertising should help you in your market. The advertising may be directed to a majority of franchises in other markets, yet you are paying a fee; your agreement should allow you to use a portion of your fees specifically as you desire in your market.

■ **Audits.** Because the franchisor will receive a percentage of your gross revenue, you will be expected to provide sales information. The franchisor will want the right to audit your books. If an audit occurs, it should be at the franchisor's expense unless there is a substantial difference between what you report and what your records show. Likewise the franchisor must agree to keep your financial information confidential.

■ **Purchase requirements.** You may be locked into buying the franchisor's goods and services. Consider requiring the franchisor to warrant the quality of the merchandise and agree to sell at a fair market price. You should get what you paid for at a fair price.

■ **Sales territory.** If you're locked into a sales territory, make sure that its market is not oversaturated with other franchisees. And ensure that the franchisor cannot unilaterally reduce your territory. Likewise the franchisor should be precluded from establishing a franchisor-owned company in your territory to compete against you.

■ **Consents by the franchisor and obligations.** Several provisions of the agreement may require the franchisor's consent. Add a provision that would require the consent not be unreasonably withheld or delayed. Time is of the essence.

Understand both your obligations and rights as a franchisee. Make sure that there are no ambiguous or vague terms that could later come back to haunt you. Try to visualize how each of your duties or your rights will affect your business. If you are not satisfied with certain provisions, propose changes. Reasonable requests to remove onerous terms should be honored.

TIP

Note the words *may*, which is permissible or discretionary, and *shall*, which is mandatory. These words do make a difference.

■ **Trademark usage.** You must be given (licensed) the right to use the franchisor's trademark or service mark. You are paying to operate under that name. The franchisor should warrant its ownership and its federal registration and should indemnify you for your damages and related costs if a third party sues you for trademark infringement.

■ **Default.** The agreement will specify numerous ways it is possible for you to default (breach the agreement), but list very few franchisor defaults. Make sure that only the most serious defaults by you—such as defrauding the franchisor—permit automatic termination. Lesser defaults, such as a failure to provide timely financial information, should permit you a period of time to cure (fix) the wrong before termination. For franchisor defaults, consult with other franchisees to determine what continual problems they have, then specify that, in your case, the franchisor must cure such defaults within 30 days, or you have the option to terminate the agreement.

■ **Term and renewal.** The agreement will specify the duration of the franchise, such as 5 or 10 years. Negotiate a provision giving you the right to renew the franchise for an unlimited number of times so long as you are not in default. This may come at a modest fee, which should be negotiable.

■ **Arbitration.** You don't want to litigate every substantial disagreement. Consider a clause requiring the parties to submit their disputes to an independent arbitrator, who has the experience in franchise law to interpret the agreement. The arbitration should occur in your city, use impartial arbitrators, and provide a method of assessing costs.

■ **Termination.** The franchisor should not be able to terminate the arrangement except for just cause. You should be given adequate time to cure any defaults, except perhaps the most serious ones. Usually the franchisor will insist on its right to terminate if you fail to operate the business, understate gross revenues, don't pay the royalties and fees, or compete with the franchisor.

■ **Covenants not to compete.** If the franchise is terminated or not renewed, the franchisor may want you to stop operating your business altogether and not continue under another name. The agreement may, therefore, contain a *covenant not to compete.* Understandably, the former franchisor would not want you, by then a former franchisee, to compete with a new franchisee. You, on the other hand, want to keep the option open and delete the covenant.

■ **Transfer.** The franchise is usually not freely transferred (assigned) by you to another franchisee. The agreement will require the franchisor's approval or, at least, the franchisor's first option to buy back the franchise. If approval is required, you should include language to the effect that it "would not be unreasonably withheld." If the franchisor has first option, require that it be exercised in a timely manner. Your transferee will be required to assume the existing franchise agreement or the latest version and payment of a transfer fee. You should include a provision permitting your spouse or heirs to operate the franchise if you die or are disabled.

■ **Entire agreement.** The agreement may conclude with a provision stating that it contains all the contract terms between the franchisor and franchisee. This clause excludes all separate oral or written terms. If the franchisor has made any promises or claims, insist that they be included in the agreement or an addendum thereto. Otherwise, these side agreements are not enforceable in court.

SOLUTIONS TO FRANCHISOR PROBLEMS THAT CAN ARISE

Problems occur in all relationships. Good communications between the franchisor and you are vital to maintaining a productive relationship. If you have a problem, contact the franchisor and explain your difficulty. Emphasize that it is a mutual problem because anything that affects your sales reduces the franchisor's income and diminishes its reputation.

On the other hand, don't blow up and threaten a lawsuit unless the franchisor has clearly violated the agreement and you have totally exhausted attempts to get the franchisor to correct the problem. A lawsuit is expensive and may destroy your business. It should be the last resort.

Consult with other franchisees—your problems may be theirs, too. Negotiating with the franchisor can be enhanced if more of you speak out. If the franchisor is faced with several common concerns, it is more likely to respond to a group of franchisees than it might to a single franchisee's complaint.

Finally, heeding the old adage *Disagree without being disagreeable* will go a long way in helping you to resolve problems. Light, not heat, is better.

FRANCHISE RESOURCES

Visit the Federal Trade Commission website (www.ftc.gov) for franchise disclosure requirements. Most states have websites with the state franchising laws. You can find a number of books and magazines on franchising available at your bookstore or library. You may want to contact the American Association of Franchisees and Dealers at PO Box 81887, San Diego, CA 92138, or the Association of Small Business Development Centers, 3108 Columbia Pike, Suite 300, Arlington, VA 22204.

THE 30-SECOND RECAP

- The franchise is a contractual arrangement for the franchisee to sell goods and services using the franchisor's name.

- You must take the initiative to thoroughly investigate the franchisor's business.

- Federal and many states laws require the franchisor to disclose significant information to you before you sign the contract.

- Your franchise attorney should review the agreement and negotiate more favorable terms for you.

- Join or create an association of other franchisees for mutual support.

Your Business Plan

Analyzing Your Proposed Venture

There is a point in any new venture when you have to move your investigation to the next level of detail. Your initial survey identified this venture as viable, but your early information is almost never enough to cover everything involved.

Obtaining this detailed information is as much an art as a business science, and the best approaches blend the two. Much of the public information can be obtained by extrapolating what is known about an industry into the unknown areas in question. Obtaining the specifics of your proposed venture can be an art form, where the beauty is in the style, manner, and credibility of the plan. You must obtain this information from the buyer, purchase the information from a third party, or find other methods of determination. Otherwise, any future financial projections will be based on unsubstantiated conjecture as opposed to educated guesses. Which would you prefer?

WHAT WILL THE COMPANY SELL?

Buyer beware is good advice for any consumer, and it is particularly sound when it comes to starting a business. The reality is that you will not know everything there is to know about the company you are starting.

Oddly enough, companies often do not see their own operation as well as an outsider might see it. Any consultant will tell you the same thing. This is the essence of the justification for using consulting services instead of using internal people to help you analyze a proposed venture.

Think about a bookstore, for example. With large bookstores dominating the market, the small bookstore must stay on its toes to stay in business.

TIP

The success or failure of a company is usually based on a combination of unique things that make this company different from all others. Investigate the pieces, but always keep your eye on the unique combinations that might spell success.

If a local bookstore sees itself primarily as a provider of books, it will probably struggle to maintain a consistent clientele. If, on the other hand, the store sees itself as a bookstore/social center where local people can congregate to catch up with each other and talk about their latest reading find, you have a recipe for repeat client visits. Clearly, the books must be there, but books without atmosphere might not be enough.

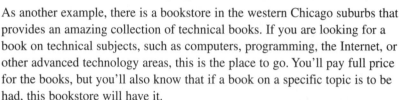

So what does this bookstore sell? Books or a total literary experience? Many people believe that the more successful bookstores provide some special products or services that cater to the people who live in the local community.

As another example, there is a bookstore in the western Chicago suburbs that provides an amazing collection of technical books. If you are looking for a book on technical subjects, such as computers, programming, the Internet, or other advanced technology areas, this is the place to go. You'll pay full price for the books, but you'll also know that if a book on a specific topic is to be had, this bookstore will have it.

It turns out that this bookstore has a dedicated clientele that attend workshops, author signings, and other special events. They even communicate with each other about projects, jobs, fairs, and other human-interest subjects. Clearly, this bookstore provides more than just books.

If you were to buy this business and shift the focus from technical books to general-topic books, there is a reasonable likelihood that you would lose a percentage of your existing clientele. Customers are a business's most important asset, and shifting a business's focus without paying close attention to the aspects perceived as valuable to the customers could cost you in the long run.

Notice that this discussion deals with more than the assets of the company, such as inventory, products, equipment, and buildings. It deals with the intangible aspects of the company that might be the difference between this company and others, which are comparably equipped, but don't thrive as well. A careful review of your proposed company's operation is needed to fully understand what you are starting. Is it over and above those things that will be listed on the balance sheet.

FINANCIAL ASPECTS TO CONSIDER?

When analyzing your proposed venture, keep these financial facts in mind:

- A growing company needs an adequate financial capacity to pay for that growth. Growth is not free, and rapid growth has put more than one company out of business.

- A shrinking company might deplete its cash reserves in a short period of time. Make sure that any financial assessments you make today incorporate projected negative cash flows into the future, up to the point of purchase.

CAUTION

Don't take one expert's version of what makes a company successful at face value. The expert (your CPA or attorney, for instance) might not necessarily know the unique combination of people, products, luck, timing, or other characteristics that truly make a business a success. Get a bunch of opinions!

- Shrinking companies also borrow to fund their operation through the lean times. Make sure that your company won't be borrowing itself into an unrecoverable position.

- In essence, whether in a growing or shrinking marketplace, you want to make sure that you either have adequate cash reserves on hand or have access to credit. Cash is like oxygen to a business, and without cash the business won't last for long. Is this part of your plan?

Amazing as this might sound to many of you, and contrary to the advice of some accountants, the value of a company is not based solely on its financial statements. A company's value should be heavily based on its perceived future performance levels, which are far less certain. Taking the time to determine required cash levels forces you to project the future, which in turn requires you to perform a reality check on your proposed company. If it passes the cash requirement test, you just might have a company worth pursuing. If not, make sure that your are taking into consideration the additional risk that you will be assuming.

Your starting point is always the financial projections.

CAUTION

If you do not properly assess the risks associated with an investment, you will have a difficult time properly assessing the financial return required to make the venture viable.

Prepare financial projections for the next five years so that you can determine either positive or negative trends.

WHO WILL REALLY OWN YOUR COMPANY?

Make sure that you determine the legal structure of the company. This means determining if the company is a sole proprietorship, partnership, C corporation, or S corporation, among others. In addition, determine your home state for the corporation, and determine who is the registered agent of the corporation. This information will be on public record for any potential investors or creditors to see.

TIP

If the company is registered as an S corporation, it can have no more than 75 shareholders.

WHAT IS YOUR PROPOSED COMPANY'S INTELLECTUAL CAPITAL?

Intellectual capital is a particularly important area of consideration, especially in today's high-technology business environment. *Intellectual capital* (property) might include software programs, Internet website locations, trademarks, business processes, certifications, special processes, and other nontangible items that are of value to the company.

Placing a value on trademarks, copyrights, and patents is an interesting topic that is beyond the scope of this section. The intention here is to ensure that you consider these types of items when creating your company. A few questions regarding intellectual property items might open a completely new perspective to the company that you are looking to start.

PLAIN ENGLISH

Intellectual property (capital) asset are items owned by a company that are not tangible in nature, such as equipment, but still have commercial value. Typically these properties involve legal protections, such as seen with patents, trademarks, and copyrights.

Make sure that intellectual capital items are truly owned by your company and that they can legally be transferred with the sale. Also verify their remaining useful life. This section won't make you an intellectual property attorney, but it will provide you with a basic understanding of intellectual property protection.

IMPORTANT TRADEMARK HIGHLIGHTS

A trademark is the name of a product or service that is sold by a particular company. For example, anything with Ford on it is associated with the automobile manufacturer and, by association, receives all the positive and negative points associated with Ford. Ford is a registered trademark of the Ford Motor Company, and any other company who tries to transact business using Ford as part of its product name might very well find itself being sued by Ford Motor Company. Just having the name Ford associated with a product or service provides credibility that, unless authorized by Ford Motor Company, might represent an unfair usage by a non-Ford company. And if that company does a poor job of designing its products or services, Ford Motor Company might be negatively impacted, which could hurt them as a whole.

For this reason, large companies dedicate entire departments to monitoring, preserving, and enhancing *brand equity*.

For example, Pepsi has teams that travel to Pepsi suppliers who sell only Pepsi and not Coke. These people then place an order for something like a "hot dog and a Coke." If the counter person simply takes the order and provides a Pepsi instead of a Coke, without letting the customer know that it is Pepsi and not Coke, the retailer can lose its license to sell Pepsi.

If you think about it from Pepsi's perspective, their brand name is being diminished because their product is being sold as a Coke product. The counterperson must say something like "Is Pepsi okay?" to remain in compliance with the Pepsi requirements.

There are complexities associated with determining when legal trademark ownership starts, but the most definite proof of ownership is to have a trademark registration with the United States Patent and Trademark Office. A formal registration procedure is required to register a trademark, but from the point of registration forward, you, the owner, have the legal right to stop others from using the trademark and can recover damages in a lawsuit.

PLAIN ENGLISH

Brand equity is the asset value associated with a particular trademarked name, such as Ford, Coca-Cola, Yahoo!, or Kleenex. Increasing the perceived market value of products bearing the brand name increases its brand equity.

Once again, go to one of the federal repositories for details associated with trademark registration, but make sure that you verify ownership with the target company's management or you might not be purchasing the expected level of legal trademark protection.

IMPORTANT COPYRIGHT HIGHLIGHTS

A copyright is used to protect the expression of something such as a book, magazine article, screenplay, or advertising. Assume, for example, that the target company has a specific trademark that is widely know as associated with the company. The company might have produced a manual that provides general brand equity management tips along with specific instructions on using the company's brand itself.

Note that the trademark is protected under its trademark registration, and the manual, as a written expression of company policy, is protected under copyright law. If a company uses a particular trademark in conjunction with specific associated text, both trademark and copyright protection law are involved.

Copyrights obtained by persons after 1977 are protected for 50 years past the life of the author. For employees of companies that perform the copyrighted activity on behalf of their employer, the copyright lasts for 75 years from the date of publication or 100 years from the date of creation, whichever comes first.

In general, however, as soon as something is published, it is copyrighted whether a formal copyright has been recorded or not. To protect your litigation rights, the work should always be formally copyrighted with the United States Copyright Office. The procedure is simple and inexpensive.

Verifying the formal copyrights of the targeted company to any works included in the sale is an important process. Once again, check with any federal repository for additional information and the required forms.

TIP

It is a good idea to talk to a copyright attorney when determining the effective date at which something is really copyrighted, because the details often get confusing.

IMPORTANT PATENT HIGHLIGHTS

Patents are obtained by people or companies that have a better device, design, or process that is substantially unique enough to be considered novel or nonobvious.

Patents are expensive and time-consuming animals that many smaller companies do not pursue, often to their own regret. A typical patent might cost $20,000 or more and take several years to record. In addition, from the point that the patent is recorded, it becomes public knowledge, meaning that all your competitors also know what you know about your patented product or process. For this reason alone, many companies do not pursue a patent.

On the other hand, if another company produces a product similar, or even identical, to yours and you do not have legal protection, the winner will be determined by the marketplace and not in the courtroom.

Patents are issued by the United States Patent and Trademark Office, and have terms of 17 years, after which the idea becomes unprotected. That might seem like a long time, but more than one company has been successful for 17 years based on patent protection only to find its own success used against it as others copied the idea and competed at a lower price.

THE 30-SECOND RECAP

- A company's value should be heavily based on its perceived future performance levels, which are far less certain.

- Make sure that you determine the legal structure of the company. This means determining if the company is a sole proprietorship, partnership, C corporation, or S corporation, among others.

- Make sure that intellectual capital items are truly owned by your company and that they can legally be transferred with the sale.

Make Contact: Doing Your Market Research

If you've assessed your strengths and weaknesses and then defined your mission and goals, you now need to find out whether your venture is as suitable for the marketplace as you think it is. You also need to concentrate on finding your specific target or niche market and sorting who, what, when, where, and why information to design and market your products or services down the line. The way to gain perspective and insight in all these areas is by collecting data, information that will enable you to make informed decisions based on your findings—in other words, market research.

WHAT IS MARKET RESEARCH?

Market research is the collection and analysis of data about your target market, competition, and/or environment, with the objective of gaining an increased understanding of your potential market. Market research is not an activity that you conduct only once; it is an ongoing process to help you build a successful business.

TIP

Your environment includes the economic and political circumstances that can influence your productivity and operations. Through the market research process, you can take data, a variety of related or unrelated facts, and create useful information to guide your business decisions.

How Market Research Helps

Information gained through market research isn't just "neat stuff" to know. It is a collection of basic, solid facts that can guide your most important strategic business decisions.

Market research is effective when the findings or conclusions you reach have a value that exceeds the cost of the research itself. For example, if you spend $500 on market research activities that yield information leading to a revenue increase of $5,000, the research was well worth it!

Market research is a good thing to do because it ...

- **Minimizes the risk of doing business.** The results of some market research may do more than identify opportunities—it may indicate a planned course of action that you should *not* pursue. For example, marketing information may indicate that a specific marketplace is saturated with the type of product or service that you plan to offer. This may cause you to alter your product or service offering or to choose an alternative location for distribution, where your product or service may be needed.

- **Uncovers and identifies potential problems.** Suppose that a retail outlet is thriving at its location on the main road through town. Through research, you learn that in two years, the city is planning an alternate route to bypass the main road to ease the town's traffic congestion. You've identified a potential problem! Early detection provides you with vital time to work on a countermeasure.

- **Helps you track your progress.** It's important to know, for later comparisons, the condition of your business at particular moments in time. Ongoing market research allows you to make comparisons against your previous research. For example, you might establish a benchmark measurement of your target market demographics and learn that 60 percent of your customers are women between the ages of 35 and 55. One year later, you again survey your customers and learn that this age group now represents 75 percent of your customer base. You're tracking a trend in your customer demographics, and you can respond to it immediately and appropriately.

- **Helps you evaluate your success.** Information gathered through market research helps you determine whether you're reaching your goals. In the preceding example, if your product's target market is women between the ages of 35 and 55, you're making progress toward your goal. If not, this information can indicate a needed change in marketing strategy!

WHAT MARKET RESEARCH CAN TELL YOU

Market research data becomes information when it can *tell* you something:

- **Information about your customers.** What characteristics are shared by your customers? Market research answers questions such as these: Who are my customers? What is the size of their population? What percentage is female? What are their ages, races, and income and education levels? What are their occupations, skills, interests, and hobbies? How many children do they have? Do they have pets? Where do they live and work? What is their purchasing power, and what are their buying habits? What is their current usage of my services? When do they purchase? Where do they shop? Why do they decide to buy? How often do they buy? How much do they buy at a time? Do they own or rent their homes? How do they typically spend their disposable income? What methods of payment do they use? Who in the family or company makes the decisions to buy? What are the deciding factors in making a purchase? Do they want only the best for their family? Are they looking for convenience and time-saving devices? Are they concerned with how they are perceived by others? What are their unmet needs? Do they demand intensive customer service? Are they only concerned with the lowest price? What media magazines, radio, television, newspapers, Internet providers, and so on are they exposed to?

TIP

Doing market research on your venture will disclose what the market trends are for your product or service. It should tell you whether the industry is growing, is at a plateau, or is declining.

- **Marketplace competition.** This is information about the other companies in your type of business. Research answers these questions: Who are my primary competitors in the market? How do they compete with me? In what ways do they not compete with me? What are their strengths and weaknesses? Are there profitable opportunities based upon their weaknesses? What is their market niche? What makes my business unique compared with the others? How do my competitors position themselves? How do they communicate their services to the market? Who are their customers? How are they perceived by the market? Who are the industry leaders? What is their sales volume? Where are they located? Are they profitable?

- **Environmental factors.** This information uncovers economic and political circumstances that can influence your productivity and operations. Questions to be answered include these: What are the current and future population trends? What are the current and future socioeconomic trends? What effects do economic and political policies have on my target market or my industry? What are the growth expectations for my market? What outside factors influence the industry's performance? What are the trends for this market and for the economy? Is the industry growing, at a plateau, or declining?

MARKET RESEARCH TYPES, METHODS, AND TECHNIQUES

Two types of research exist: *primary research,* or original information gathered for a specific purpose; and *secondary research,* or information that already exists somewhere. Both types of research have a range of activities and methods for conducting the research associated with them. Secondary research is usually faster and less expensive to obtain than primary research. Gathering secondary research may be as simple as browsing the Internet or making a trip to your local library; or to an art, craft, or trade show; or to a business information center.

SECONDARY RESEARCH

Because secondary research is usually the easiest and least expensive, we'll take a look at it first. Secondary research may be a study, a group of articles on a topic, or demographic or statistical data gathered by someone else. For example, if you need demographic data about homeowners in your area, your chamber of commerce or the local board of realtors has already gathered it for you! Gathering secondary research data on your target markets is basically a process of reviewing and analyzing what's been published (in magazines, books, research studies, government publications, and so forth) or reported in other media.

Simply find reliable sources such as the following, and don't forget to check out the websites that many of them have.

The basic sources of secondary research information are ...

- **Libraries and other public information centers.** There are many free resources available at public and university libraries. There are also many specialty libraries for law, science, business that can be used by the general public. Other public information centers include business organizations, private foundations, and not-for-profit societies.

■ **Books and business publications.** Many books have been written on specific industries and markets. Check out *Urlich's Directory of Serials* to see whether anyone publishes a trade journal in your specific area.

■ **Magazines and newspapers.** Each and every day, studies and survey results make news. So do environmental factors, such as the leading economic indicators, housing starts, or political elections.

■ **Trade associations.** Most associations publish reports on the industry they serve, the standards they operate under, and the leaders in their industry. They may have industry figures that you can use as benchmarks to compare with your results. Many even conduct educational seminars on trends and other issues.

Two great ways to find the right association are *Gale's Directory of Associations* and the *National Trade and Professional Associations* directory, both available in your library.

■ **Local college marketing departments.** What successful college marketing student hasn't conducted a research project? Ask for access to data that has been collected through special research projects. Sometimes you may even be able to have students help you with your research.

■ **Chambers of commerce.** Your local chamber of commerce is a terrific resource for area maps and information on the community that you hope to serve and its businesses. You can also learn from other members at networking events.

■ **Banks, real estate brokers, and insurance companies.** They may have information and statistics on the communities they serve.

■ **Wholesalers and manufacturers.** Contact manufacturers and wholesalers of your type of product or service for information on industry standards, customers, costs, distribution, and potential problems. The *Thomas Register* is a listing of manufacturers grouped by industry and product. You can find it online at www.thomasregister.com and in your public library.

■ **Federal government resources.** The government provides extensive demographic data on population, markets, and the economy. Two resources from the U.S. Department of Commerce include the "U.S. Industrial Outlook," published annually and categorized by *SIC* code (Standard Industrial Classification) and U.S. Census Bureau statistics.

■ **Regional planning organizations.** Local governments have historical and current data on community growth trends. Many offices also have forecasted future demographic statistics for the area.

PLAIN ENGLISH

The **SIC** code stands for Standard Industrial Classification. This is a standard system of coding businesses by numerical category, set up by the Small Business Administration (SBA).

- **Media representatives.** Advertising salespeople at television, radio, and print media outlets compile studies and reports on their audience to target potential advertisers. If you call and ask for a media kit, you'll usually get some very valuable demographic information on the area they serve.
- **Competitive businesses.** Ask your competitors for company brochures, lists of products and services, prices, annual reports, and so forth. Hint: It helps to disguise yourself as a potential customer!
- **Business Information Centers (BICs).** These are area offices of the U.S. SBA. Most BICs have collections of books, publications, videos, CDs, and other sources of information exclusively for small business owners.

PRIMARY RESEARCH

Sometimes the information you need just doesn't exist—anywhere! You searched the Internet, and you scoured the library, the journals, and the databases—all to no avail. That's when you may need to conduct primary research, or original research conducted for a specific purpose.

Primary research activities include conducting surveys to create market data or using other research instruments, such as questionnaires, focus groups, and interviews. Each method uses some form of "sampling," which allows the researcher to reach conclusions about a population within a certain degree of accuracy without having to survey everyone. Under the direction of experienced researchers, samples as small as 1 percent of a target market can often provide reliable results.

Primary research can be either qualitative or quantitative. *Qualitative research* provides definitive market information regarding the opinions and behaviors of the subjects in the market research study. *Quantitative research* is used to achieve a variety of objectives.

Qualitative research is used for the following purposes:

- To obtain helpful background information on a market segment
- To explore concepts and positioning of a business or product
- To identify attitudes, opinions, and behaviors shared by a target market
- To prioritize variables for further study

- To fully define problems
- To provide direction for the development of questionnaires

PLAIN ENGLISH

Qualitative research relates the opinions and behaviors of the subjects in a market research study to the likelihood that specific products or services can be marketed to them. **Quantitative research** creates statistically valid market information that can be used in any number of ways.

Personal interviews and focus groups are the most common methods of qualitative market research.

Generally, no more than 50 interviews are conducted on a one-on-one basis (usually recorded on audiotape), most often using an unstructured survey and open-ended probing questions. Focus groups are groups of 8 to 12 people led by a moderator who follows a script.

Quantitative research creates statistically valid market information typically used …

- To substantiate a hypothesis or prove a theory.
- To minimize risk, or to obtain reliable samples for projecting trends.

Personal, telephone, and mail surveys are the most common quantitative techniques.

The advantages of personal surveys include …

- The interviewer can observe reactions, probe, and clarify answers.
- The technique usually nets a high percentage of completed surveys.
- The interviewer has flexibility with locations and schedules.
- The interviewer can use visual displays.
- Under controlled conditions, interviewing allows good sampling.

The disadvantages include …

- Interviewing is costly and time-consuming.
- Results may contain interviewer biases.

Telephone surveys have some advantages:

- They are faster and lower cost than personal surveys.
- They have a lower response bias than personal surveys.
- They have a wide geographic reach compared to personal surveys.

TIP

You can personally conduct simple market research, such as asking customers to complete a questionnaire while visiting your booth at an art, craft, or trade show, or by posting it on your website.

The disadvantages are that …

■ The survey length is limited, and it is difficult to reach busy people.

■ It is difficult to discuss certain topics, and it can be expensive compared to mail surveys.

Mail surveys have some advantages, such as …

■ Wide distribution and low cost.

■ No interviewer bias is present.

■ Respondents remain anonymous.

■ Respondents can answer at their leisure.

The disadvantages are …

■ Obtaining accurate mailing lists is difficult.

■ Respondents are not necessarily representative of the target population.

■ The survey is limited by its length.

■ Survey questions are not timely.

■ Probing questions and clarifying answers are not possible.

■ A specific total sample cannot be guaranteed.

Whatever research method you select, the key thing to remember is that, first, you must define your specific objective or exact goal. Then you can select the most effective research method to accomplish the task.

GETTING STARTED ON MARKET RESEARCH

Like other components of marketing, such as advertising, market research can be quite simple or very complex. An example of some simple market research that you might conduct is gathering demographic information about your customers by asking those who visit your booth at an arts, craft, or trade show to complete a questionnaire. On the more complex side, you might engage a professional market research firm to conduct primary research to aid you in developing a marketing strategy for launching a new product.

Regardless of the simplicity or complexity of your marketing research project, you'll benefit by reviewing the following steps in the market research process:

1. **Define marketing problems and opportunities.** The market research process begins with identifying and defining the problems and opportunities that exist for your business—opportunities such as launching a new product or service, and problems such as low awareness of your company and its products or services, or underutilization of your company's products or services (the market is familiar with your company but is not doing business with you), a poor company image and/or reputation, or problems with distribution (your goods and services are not reaching the buying public in a timely manner).

 CAUTION

Existing small business owners often establish a marketing budget by allocating about 2 percent of their most recent annual gross sales. A new business, however, may want to allocate as much as 10 percent of estimated gross sales for marketing.

2. **Develop objectives, budget, and a timetable.**

   a. **Objectives.** With a marketing problem or opportunity defined, the next step is to set objectives for your market research. Your objective may be to explore the nature of a problem so that you may further define it. Or perhaps it is to determine how many people will buy your product if it's packaged in a certain way and offered at a certain price.

   b. **Budget your research.** How much money are you willing to invest in your market research? How much can you afford? Your market research budget is a portion of your overall marketing budget. One popular method that small business owners use to establish an overall marketing budget is to allocate to it a small percentage of gross sales for the most recent year. This usually amounts to about 2 percent for an existing business. Other methods used by small businesses include analyzing and estimating the competition's budget, and calculating its cost of marketing per sale.

   c. **Prepare a timetable.** Prepare a detailed, realistic time frame for completing all steps of the market research process. If your business operates in cycles, establish target dates that will allow the best accessibility to your market. For example, a holiday greeting card business may want to conduct research before or around the holiday buying period, when customers are most likely to be thinking about their purchases.

3. **Select research types, methods, and techniques.** Refer to the market research types, methods, and techniques in the preceding sections on primary and secondary research.

4. **Design research instruments.** The most common research instrument is the questionnaire. When you're designing a questionnaire for your market research, keep these tips in mind: First, keep it simple! Include instructions for answering all questions on the survey. Second, begin the survey with general questions, and then move toward more specific ones. Third, keep questions brief. Fourth, remember to design a questionnaire that is graphically pleasing and easy to read. Finally, before taking the survey to the printer, ask a few people for feedback on its style, its user-friendliness, and what they perceive as its purpose.

   Vary the formats of the questions: Use scales, rankings, open-ended questions, and closed-ended questions for different sections of the questionnaire. The format may influence the responses. Basically, there are two question formats: *closed-ended* and *open-ended.*

   a. **Closed-ended questions.** Respondents choose from possible answers included on the questionnaire. Types of closed-ended questions include multiple choice, which offer respondents the ability to answer yes or no, or to choose from a list of several answer choices. Scales refer to questions that ask respondents to rank their answers or measure their answers on a scale.

   b. **Open-ended questions.** Respondents answer questions in their own words. Completely unstructured questions allow respondents to answer any way they choose. Types of open-ended questions include word-association questions; and sentence, story, or picture completion questions such as, "I commute by _____ (mode of transportation)."

PLAIN ENGLISH

With **closed-ended questions**, respondents choose from possible answers included on the questionnaire. Respondents answer **open-ended questions** in their own words.

5. **Collect data.** Unless you conduct the research yourself, train and educate any research staff before beginning the collection of data. An untrained staff person conducting primary research will lead to interviewer bias.

6. **Organize and analyze data.** After your data has been collected, it needs to be "cleaned." Cleaning research data involves editing, coding, and tabulating results. To make this step easier, start with a simply designed research instrument or questionnaire. Some helpful tips for organizing and analyzing your data are listed here. Look for relevant data that focuses on your immediate market needs. Rely on subjective information only as support for more general findings of objective research.

   a. **Analyze for consistency.** Compare the results of different methods of your data collection.

   b. **Quantify your results.** Look for common opinions that may be counted together. Read between the lines. For example, combine U.S. Census Bureau statistics on median income levels for a given location with the number of homeowners versus renters in the area.

TIP

A questionnaire should be simple and should include instructions for answering all questions. Keep questions brief, and begin with general questions before moving toward more specific ones.

7. **Present and use market research findings.** After marketing information about your target market, competition, and environment has been collected and analyzed, present it in an organized manner to everyone working with you in the business venture.

In summary, the market research information that you create is to help guide you through your business decisions, from deciding what business to start, to initiating your start-up, to evaluating the products or services that you plan to market, to gathering the continuous informational support that you'll need as you continue to build your enterprise.

Market research is something you really need to do if you're serious about making money with your new venture.

The 30-Second Recap

- You need market research to define your target market so that you can focus your marketing efforts in the right direction.
- Market research can tell you about your customers, your competition, and your potential market.

- Primary market research is gathering original information, and secondary research is using existing market data.

- Secondary market research is less expensive than primary market research, is usually easier to obtain, and is probably all that a small business needs to do.

The Elements of the Plan

Being an entrepreneur differs sharply from being an administrator. An administrator assumes responsibility for an established department or function within a larger organization. An entrepreneur must create a business from scratch and with very limited resources. Although MBA stands for Master of Business Administration, most business schools have established or expanded their course offerings for those who want to become entrepreneurs. This recognizes that many students would rather start a company or join a small company than work for a large corporation. They would rather be entrepreneurs than administrators.

However, it also recognizes that many large companies want to hire people capable of managing entrepreneurially. These companies realize that sometimes they can compete in a market only by starting a totally new business, apart from or within the larger organization. They have also learned that developing these new businesses calls for approaches different from those required to manage their traditional, established businesses. Therefore they seek entrepreneurial managers for certain areas of the business.

This section examines the process of building a business plan.

BIG PLANS

The *entrepreneur* faces three broad tasks. He or she must finance the business, produce the product or service, and bring it to market. Clearly, there are other tasks, such as finding suppliers and setting up an accounting system; however, financing, producing, and marketing the product are the big ones.

These tasks are also linked in chicken-and-egg fashion. How do you market a product if you haven't produced it? How do you produce a product if you don't have much money? How do you raise money if you don't have a proven product?

The business plan answers these questions. A business plan describes the product or service, its market and its production and distribution requirements, the background and qualifications of the entrepreneurs, and the amount of money that the business will require.

PLAIN ENGLISH

An **entrepreneur** organizes resources into an enterprise that brings a product or service to people who need it, while making a profit for him- or herself and the investors. A **start-up** is a new business created to bring a product or service to market. Most start-ups begin with one product or service, or an idea for one.

The business plan is a blueprint for the business as well as a sales tool. (The business may be either a *start-up* or an existing operation, but the discussion here focuses on plans for start-ups.) As a blueprint, a business plan guides the entrepreneurs through the steps necessary to get the business up and running. Therefore, the business plan must be complete and realistic. As a sales tool it tells potential investors and lenders about the company's business, prospects, and financial requirements. Therefore, it must also be positive and optimistic.

ANALYZING YOUR BUSINESS

One of the first steps you're going to have to take before putting together your business plan is to analyze your proposed venture. You'll need to ask yourself many questions and prepare many financial projections. You'll want to think about your proposed company's products, marketplace, ownership structure, and other important matters.

PREPARING THE PLAN

Although the exact section titles and their order may vary, every business plan must include the following information:

- Table of Contents
- Executive Summary
- Business, Products, and Services
- Market Analysis
- Management Team
- Operations
- Financial Projections

A business plan should be written in plain English and answer the major questions that prospective investors, lenders, employees, and suppliers have about the enterprise:

- What is the product?
- How large and needy is the market?
- Who are the managers of the business?
- Can this business make and sell the product?
- What are the potential sales and earnings?

Do not load up the main sections of the plan with too much detail. That material should go into appendixes. The outline presented here would work for a proprietorship, partnership, or corporation, but assumes that the business is a corporation seeking equity investors.

Describe the Business, Products, and Services

Describe the location, nature, industry, and history of the business, and its current products and services and those in development. Mention brand names, trademarks, *service marks*, and patents, as well as any licensing arrangements, alliances, or joint ventures. Although financial information is covered later, it's good to note sales and profits, and the proportion of sales and profits derived from key products and services, in this section. Also note any trends and government regulations affecting the business.

PLAIN ENGLISH

Service mark is similar to a trademark except related to a service procedure instead of a particular product. This term is commonly used by service organizations, such as consulting, accounting, and training companies.

Particularly if the only products are still in development, briefly describe the underlying technology and the functions it performs and customer needs that it meets. Note the stage of development. For example, is there a prototype? Has it been tested? How will the product be produced, packaged, distributed, serviced, and maintained?

This section is also where basic data on the company such as year founded, locations, facilities, number of employees, and so on should go.

ANALYZE THE MARKET

Market analysis is a key section of the plan and one of the hardest to write for a business with no track record. In those cases, the analysis will depend almost solely on market research, which should be conducted in each major target market.

It is not enough to determine that a good portion of the respondents say they "like" the product concept or are "likely to purchase" it. Survey respondents often give positive answers just to be agreeable. Therefore, the research must ascertain how and how often they would use the product, how they are currently addressing the need the product addresses, and how much money they would make or save by using the product. These questions prompt respondents to relate their needs and behavior to the product.

Market research can also bolster the case for products already in the marketplace. In those instances, the research should substantiate that there is still a large, untapped market for the product even though it is already available.

Finally, the market analysis should describe existing and potential competitors and substitute products. Take care with this section and never assume that your business will face no competition. Even if it has no competition in the beginning, if the business succeeds it soon will have plenty.

TIP

Research is not necessarily the last word on a product's feasibility. When a product or service is totally new, a company may just have to launch it to build a market. For example, Citibank developed and introduced the ATM (automated teller machine) even though survey respondents said they would never use it. People said they needed a live teller, they wouldn't trust a machine, and they feared being robbed. Today, however, most people could barely get along without ATMs.

Note, however, that although Citibank acted in a highly entrepreneurial manner, it was at the time the largest bank in New York. Its branch network and its base of accounts positioned it to win over customers to the new technology.

MARKETING AND SALES STRATEGY

Many start-up companies fail not because they have a poor product, but because they cannot sell it or get it distributed. The business plan must therefore present realistic marketing, sales, and distribution strategies. Also mention any firm orders you have for your products or services and the expected delivery date.

INTRODUCE THE MANAGEMENT TEAM

Investors and lenders must know the qualifications and track records of the business's senior managers. If the product or service depends on technology, they need the same information on the key technical people.

At a minimum, the business needs an experienced general manager, a sales or marketing professional who can close sales, a production manager, a manager of information systems, and an office manager. Perhaps one person can cover two of these functions, but attempting to attract financing without the right people on board is foolhardy.

The plan should include the resumés of key employees and emphasize each individual's qualifications for his or her role. If any key positions have not yet been filled, mention that and specify a time frame for filling them.

DESCRIBE THE OPERATION

The plan must describe how the company's products will be produced and how its services will be delivered. When and how will the production facilities be built, leased, or purchased? What equipment will be necessary and will it be leased or purchased? If production will be done by a *contract manufacturer,* describe the outfit. What are its capabilities? What is its track record? Mention any details, such as packaging, shelf life, and other product characteristics, that affect production, distribution, and storage. Also identify major suppliers and their record of quality and reliability.

PLAIN ENGLISH

A **contract manufacturer** produces products to the specifications of another company, which has designed the product and handles the marketing, sales, and distribution. This allows the entrepreneur to minimize his investment in productive plant and equipment.

Discuss the staffing requirements in the various operating functions and the qualifications and sources of any highly specialized personnel (for instance, software engineers).

Other questions to address at this point include the following:

- Which distribution channels will be used for the product? Who are the wholesalers, retail chains, or other middlemen involved in the process?
- What are the product's transportation and storage requirements?
- Are there seasonal variances in the sales and production cycles of the business?
- What are the anticipated needs for facilities, equipment, staff, and distribution?

ANALYZE THE FINANCIAL NEEDS AND POTENTIAL RETURNS

For an established business, the plan should include historical financial statements for the past five years through the most recent quarter. It should also include *pro forma* statements for the next five years. Present monthly projections for the next two years and quarterly projections for following three years.

If the company has not yet opened for business, only pro forma statements can be presented. However, an accounting of the money invested so far by the founders and other investors should be presented. How much has been invested and raised? How has it been used? How much cash is on hand? Mention other investors who have backed the business or made firm commitments to back it. Note the current distribution of the company's stock and the effect that new investors will have on that distribution.

PLAIN ENGLISH

Pro forma financial statements project the values for the various accounts on the balance sheet, income statement, and cash-flow statement. Underlying pro forma statements are assumptions about future sales growth, financial requirements, and other factors. Therefore the believability of the pro forma statements depends on the believability of the assumptions, which should be included as footnotes to the statements.

The financial section should also include the owners' compensation plan and benefit plan (if any) and those of other employees. Most important, this section must explicitly state how much money you are trying to raise and the uses to which that money will be put.

KEEP IT SHORT AND SUBSTANTIVE

Some business plans are long on sales pitches and short on substance. Although many insubstantial plans did raise money in the 1990s, today's business plans must be true plans rather than sales pitches. That does not, however, mean that a plan should bury the reader in information. Investors "get it" very quickly and can decide whether they are interested on the basis of the two-page executive summary. If they are interested, they will want to meet with you and will request more detailed information.

Incidentally, the planning process may reveal that the business would not, in fact, become successful. If that happens, that's good. You have just saved yourself (and others) huge amounts of time, energy, and money by avoiding a situation that was destined to fail.

PLANNING YOUR GROWTH

No matter how well a business has been planned, things rarely proceed according to that plan. After the business begins operating, entrepreneurs generally face one of two problems: growing too slowly or growing too quickly. This must all be considered as part of your business plan.

If the business is growing too slowly, some of the steps you would need to consider are as follows.

- Evaluate your salespeople and sales process to ensure that both are able to close sales rather than just generate interest. New businesses need "missionaries" and "rainmakers," enthusiastic people who can close sales. Is this part of your plan?

- Adjust your marketing message. Does your plan have alternative marketing messages?

- If you have a new product, be sure you've identified and reached the relevant innovators and early adopters.

- Find out, through informal and formal research, why customers are not buying or not buying repeatedly and address those issues.

- Learn whether the company is delivering as promised. Great sales efforts must be backed up by great products and service. Early customers will tolerate a few glitches from a new company with a new product. But sloppy service or unsolved problems will inevitably generate bad word of mouth. You will need to think about these matters in the planning stage.

- Obtain the resources needed to grow the business. If the business could grow more quickly with more money, people, and other resources, work hard to get them. What is your plan to do this?

In some cases, patience and persistence are the keys to surviving a slow start. However, your plan must take into consideration the reasons why things start too slowly and think of solutions to remedy the situation.

If the business starts growing too quickly, you will have another set of problems. You may be thinking, "We should all have such problems," but business history is filled with companies that grew too fast and flamed out as a result. If you expect fast growth, your plan must take into consideration certain factors.

If the business is growing too fast, you may have to …

- Exercise leadership to motivate people through the long hours and high demands that growth imposes on a rapidly growing company. Let them share in the rewards of growth (for example, through bonuses). Have you considered these rewards in your plan?

- Collect your accounts receivable as quickly as possible. Booking sales without collecting the cash will not enable you to pay your employees and suppliers. Your plan may need to consider using the receivables to secure a loan or line of credit in order to speed up your cash flow.

- Do all you can to expand production without compromising quality. Make and ship products as fast as you can; when quality problems arise, however, fix them fast, even if it costs a lot. A disappointed customer particularly a large disappointed customer can quickly spread the word that you don't have your act together.

- If you become strapped for resources, you may need to outsource some of the production, installation, and even customer service, instead of expanding permanently and increasing your fixed costs.

- Keep your investors informed about your success and your problems. They may well be willing to invest more money in what now looks like a success if that money will help you grow. This would also be a good time to meet with your banker about a loan or line of credit. Is this part of your timeline?

- Get all the advice you can from your board of directors, network of advisers, and your accountant, suppliers, and industry association.

- If production, quality, delivery, or financial problems overwhelm the company, seriously consider hiring a competent operating executive to put the right management systems and controls in place.

Never underestimate the power of systems and controls, which are necessary in every company. Consider these in the business plan, too. Management systems provide vital information on the needs and performance of the business for instance, on sales, expenses, inventory, time usage, customers, transactions, and other aspects of the business. Controls involve understanding the contribution that each activity makes to the business and creating policies and procedures that cut less-productive activities and increase the more-productive ones.

Systems and controls also send employees, customers, investors, and other stakeholders the message that this is a true business rather than a fly-by-night operation. Most of all, systems and controls, especially financial controls, keep management in touch with reality.

TIP

Data must be developed into information by cross-referencing, examining trends, and identifying patterns. For example, data on customers—who they are, where they are, how much they spend on which of your products, how they heard about your company, their creditworthiness, and so on—can be used to develop customer profiles.

A customer profile can enable marketing to target and tailor your company's message to the most promising prospects. It can also help sales understand how best to close deals with them. And this is just one type of information that can be developed from the data generated by good systems.

Policies and procedures distinguish a well-managed business from a seat-of-the-pants outfit. A business plan needs to address policies and procedures that will guide people in areas such as accepting deliveries, using overnight delivery, purchasing materials, handling customer complaints, and responding to emergencies to name a few.

This means that in the midst of all the production and sales activity, someone must see to the administrative side of the business. In the early stages, the business may get by with an office manager, a bookkeeper, and a sales assistant, and perhaps with a few people performing multiple functions. However, as the company grows, it will need specialists and even more sophisticated systems. Have you projected these costs?

For instance, when enough money is flowing through the business (the amount varies by industry and company size), an on-staff accountant or controller becomes necessary. In many jurisdictions, after a business has a certain number of employees, it must begin complying with a new level of regulation and perhaps institute an employee benefits plan. At that point, a knowledgeable head of human resources may become necessary. To get to "the next level," a company may need a seasoned vice president of marketing or sales, or even a new CEO. Many companies flounder when an entrepreneur can't let go of the company he or she founded even though he or she is not equal to the managerial demands.

Financing Growth

As the saying goes, it takes money to make money. Start-up capital is only the beginning. Your plan will need to address how your venture will finance its growth. It takes money to grow a business, and that money can come from only two places: inside the company or outside the company.

Internally generated funds, the earnings generated by the business, are the cheapest source of growth capital. They carry no interest rate and no promise of future dividends. Internally generated funds also enable the founders to maintain the most control over the company.

Yet insisting that the business stick to self-funding may hamper its growth. If the company is growing or is positioned to grow faster than it can fund itself, it's quite likely that external financing will be necessary to bring the company to its greatest potential.

To finance growth, the business must usually locate additional financing from the original investors, new investors, or one or more banks. At a certain point, most truly successful companies at least consider in their business plans the ultimate step in gaining access to capital: going public.

THE IPO

A successful initial public offering (IPO) will provide long-term capital at a lower cost than borrowing. An IPO also usually enables the early investors in the company management, angels, venture capitalists, and so on to reap huge profits.

An IPO comprises a series of steps, which include working up in-depth information on the business and its history and plans (in the form of a prospectus), notifying the Securities and Exchange Commission (SEC) of the owners' intention to sell stock to the public, registering the securities with the SEC, setting a price, and deciding how the stock will be sold and distributed.

An investment bank usually guides the owners through this process. Aside from providing the legal and financial expertise to make the IPO happen, the investment bank has the distribution network needed to sell the stock to investors. The investment bank is compensated with a fee, at least some of which is tied to the amount of money raised by the IPO.

A successful IPO, meaning one that raises the targeted amount of capital or close to it, often identifies the issuer as a growth company in the minds of investors. As noted in Part 4, these investors expect any profits to be reinvested in the business to finance its growth. For that reason, and for the ability to raise additional capital in the public markets if necessary, going public is the ultimate in financing strategies.

BUYING A BUSINESS

Although the image of the entrepreneur starting on his or her kitchen table or garage and going public several years later may be the popular one, many entrepreneurs prefer to buy a business. It may take a bit more creativity to start a business from scratch than it does to buy a going concern, but the business challenges are quite similar.

Anyone buying a business, whether it's a small retail store or a division of a large company, must understand its products and services, market and customers, facilities and operations, and financial history and prospects.

Understanding the impact of current legal actions, tax matters, and regulatory issues on the company is also part of the *due diligence* required when you purchase a business. Rather than deal only with the owners or brokers of the business, speak to key employees, customers, suppliers, and lenders about their history with the business and their role in its future.

PLAIN ENGLISH

Due diligence refers to the process of discovering and understanding all aspects of the business and all the factors that could affect the prospects of the business. Due diligence must be undertaken by brokers representing securities for sale, managers, and investment bankers involved in a merger or acquisition, and anyone buying a business.

In addition to the sources of financing already mentioned in this chapter, the buyers of the business may be able to use a leveraged buyout to raise some or most of the funding. In a leveraged buyout, or LBO, the new owners use the assets of the company to finance the purchase of the company. The borrowings are then repaid out of the company's future cash flow. If the current managers of a company are buying the business from the owners, the transaction is often referred to as a management buyout.

TIP

Leveraged buyouts can be used to take a public company private. The company's senior managers (or other purchasers of the company) pledge the company's assets as collateral for the loans to finance the purchase of the stock. Then they use the proceeds of the loan to buy the stock from the existing shareholders, usually at a premium over the current market price.

However they finance the purchase, people buying a company must understand the business, develop a plan to keep the company growing or to boost its growth, and avoid paying too high a price. Any key employees, and for that matter the former owners, should be available in at least a consulting capacity to see that the new owners get off to a good start. This is particularly important for buyers of a service business, where the relationships and skills of the former owners probably played a big role in the success of the business.

As always, *caveat emptor* (buyer beware) are the watchwords. It is easy for a buyer to overpay for a successful business. Savvy founders are motivated to sell when the value of the company has peaked. They may know that competitors are entering the market, that the company's technology is about to be superceded, or that the fad that drove their success is about to end. It's difficult to know these things if you're not in the industry. In other words, there is almost no way to overdo due diligence.

TIP

If your business plan includes the prospect of buying a business, try to structure the deal so that part of the purchase price depends on the future earnings of the company. This can be tough to do, because the seller (a) wants his or her money, and (b) doesn't want his or her payments to depend on your competence. Yet to the extent that at least some of the price can be linked to certain contingencies (for example, continuance of a contract with a major account), you as a buyer have some protection.

CORPORATE VENTURES

Many major companies understand the value of entrepreneurial behavior and realize that their organizations are too large and rigid to encourage such behavior. Although these companies need the creativity, drive, and willingness to take risks of the entrepreneur, most true entrepreneurs do not want to work for them. The standard salary structures and bonus policies of most large companies don't offer the entrepreneur the earnings potential of starting a company, particularly one that might go public. Bureaucracy stifles entrepreneurs; and entrepreneurs often lack the patience to sit through unproductive meetings, deal with the chain of command, and have their ideas reviewed, altered, and, perhaps, killed.

Recognizing this, a number of large companies have launched efforts, called corporate venture programs, to find and tap into entrepreneurial businesses in their industry. Others try to give their "home-grown entrepreneurs" the environment and compensation they need to act like entrepreneurs.

A corporate venture program looks for new businesses, solicits and reviews business plans, and provides financial, distribution, and other resources needed by a small company. As noted, the deals may range from distribution or licensing agreements to direct investment in the smaller company.

Efforts to grow in-house entrepreneurs are often related to product development, research and development (R&D), or business-development efforts. The company will form a small team under the leadership of a creative executive with both technical and business skills and give it a mission. Ideally, the team is cut off geographically from the rest of the company, provided with extra financial incentives, and given funding, a goal, and freedom to find ways of reaching that goal.

However, true entrepreneurs put their own capital at risk and want complete autonomy. Therefore, it is difficult for a large company to create and hold on to true entrepreneurs, because that element of risk (and extraordinary reward) cannot really be duplicated in a large, relatively secure organization. Large companies can encourage a certain amount of entrepreneurial behavior, however, and some have had some success in doing so.

ENTREPRENEUR AWAY

Not everyone is suited to the entrepreneurial way of work. It takes dedication, high energy, risk tolerance, a willingness to fail, and the ability to form relationships and get things done with minimal organizational structure. That last item is key. Many of us spend most of our early years in structured environments: family, school, scout troop, baseball or soccer team, band or debating squad, and military service. In contrast, entrepreneurs must function with very little structure. They make it up as they go along.

When you create your business plan, keep all of this in mind.

That ability to improvise to make it up as they go along and to do it productively and profitably may be the signal characteristic of true entrepreneurs. That is a difficult thing to learn. But many entrepreneurs have learned how to improvise, if only because they had to in response to the demands of the market and their business. Moreover, very few entrepreneurs would change their way of working. Most people who "go out on their own" never regret it, and that even includes the ones who fail.

THE 30-SECOND RECAP

- An entrepreneur identifies a need and organizes the financial, productive, human, and other resources required to fill that need, and then, if he or she succeeds, fills it profitably.

- Entrepreneurs either buy a business or start their own. The latter is the more challenging undertaking, but both require a true entrepreneurial approach.

- Successful start-up companies are built around a product or service that meets a genuine need by founders with management skills, access to financing, and the means to make, market, deliver, and distribute the product or service.

■ A business plan is the sales tool for the entrepreneur seeking investors.

■ Sources of financing include the founders themselves, individual investors (or "angels"), large companies, venture capital firms, and sometimes banks.

■ Large companies that have tried to encourage entrepreneurial behavior have a mixed record, but those that have succeeded have reaped rewards.

Financing Your Business

Things to Consider Before You Look for Cash

You've looked at your personal bank account and (after you stopped crying) have decided you just don't have what you need to get your business started. You may have to look to family, friends, or outsiders for help. If you discount robbing your bank or winning the lottery, there are really only two prime strategies for raising money: Borrow it or bring in investors. Borrowing money is called debt; investment in your business by investors is called equity.

There are sound reasons why one strategy may be better for you than the other.

In this section, you learn the pros and cons of raising money with a loan. You'll also find out about the consequences of bringing in investors. You'll discover other sources of financing that you might not have considered. Finally you'll learn which type of financing strategy is best for you.

FIGURING OUT HOW MUCH YOU NEED

No book can tell you how much money you'll need to start and run your business. You have to determine that with the help of your accountant and business advisors.

Your business plan can be as detailed as you desire. Consider it your blueprint for building and operating your business. Begin by creating an accurate business plan, which should include the following:

- A description of your business
- A marketing plan
- A financial plan
- A management plan

Although business plans have been discussed earlier, some of this information is worth repeating here.

The nonfinancial sections of the plan should describe your company and what it intends to sell or service, and how you intend on becoming successful. Several books can help you develop the plan, such as *The Complete Idiot's Guide to Starting Your Own Business, Fourth Edition* (Alpha Books, 2004), by Edward Paulson.

The financial section of the plan should contain the following:

- Current and projected sources of funding
- A start-up budget
- An operating budget
- An equipment and supply list
- A balance sheet
- A profit-and-loss statement
- A cash-flow projection

CAUTION

Plan for the worst and hope for the best, at least when it comes to finances. Remember: Everything always costs more than you plan, and income is usually less than you expect.

When starting a business, the sources for this financial information are accountants familiar with your particular business, other small business owners who have the experience, or a franchisor who can provide a model budget for the franchisee.

Your start-up budget should include costs you'll incur before opening, such as legal and accounting fees, licenses, equipment, insurance, supplies, advertising, initial payroll, and advanced rent. Your operating budget should include all ongoing expenses, including payroll, insurance, rent, utilities, loan payments, advertising, supplies, fees, and maintenance.

The cash-flow projection should pinpoint those months of slow sales or higher expenses, so that you can plan accordingly. You might want to cover these periodic cash deficits with a line of credit from a bank.

Now you are ready to determine how to best finance your initial and working capital requirements.

DETERMINING YOUR ASSETS

Your business will require an investment of your assets. Lenders may lend, and investors may invest—as long as you, too, have a financial stake in your business. For your investment capital, you may look to the following:

- Personal savings
- Equity in your home
- Whole life insurance

- Retirement savings
- Salary

You may have certificates of deposit, savings bonds, savings accounts, stocks, bonds, and mutual funds, all of which you carefully invested in over the years. Each provides a return and a safety net, so you may be reluctant to risk your savings on this new adventure, and it is not suggested that you must. In fact, most experts recommend that you keep something in reserve for your personal or family needs, and a little for future investment in the business should it run into cash-flow problems. However, if you use most of your current investments to start up your business, you'll be apt to gain a much greater return, both financially and psychologically. If you own your home, you may be able to obtain a home equity loan at a favorable rate of interest from a bank. Many lenders will lend up to 80 percent or more of the value of your home.

Your equity in the house is the difference between its current value and any mortgage on it. You may want to ...

- **Refinance and obtain a new mortgage.** If your current mortgage interest rate is higher than the going rate, refinancing is probably to your advantage, particularly if the closing costs are no greater than they are for getting a second mortgage or a line of credit. Part of the loan will repay the current mortgage, and the rest of the equity loan proceeds can be used to invest in your business.

- **Obtain a loan for a second mortgage.** If your current mortgage rate is better than the going rate, keep the current mortgage and take out a second mortgage to cover your equity. You may need to use all of the loan proceeds from the second mortgage, or you may need only a portion of it now. If the latter applies, a line of credit loan should be your choice. You will be charged interest on the amount borrowed.

- **Obtain a line of credit for a second mortgage.** A line of credit is a loan that entitles you to borrow up to the amount of the loan; you may not need all of the loan proceeds at first. Compare lender rates. Your local banks, savings and loans, and credit unions may be in competition for your loan business. E-lenders are also now advertising. Have your attorney review all loan documents.

You can get a whole life insurance policy with a loan option. Part of each premium that you pay builds up a cash surrender value. If you have owned the policy for several years, the loan amount may be used for whatever purpose you want and the interest rate is usually low. If the loan is not repaid and you keep the policy, the loan amount and accumulated interest will be deducted from the proceeds paid at death. Consult your insurance agent about this option.

Retirement savings in individual retirement accounts (IRAs) and defined contribution pension plans, such as 401(k), may represent another source of investment funds. You can withdraw some or all of your savings after you reach age 59½, without premature-withdrawal tax penalty. However, any amount that has been tax-deferred income will be taxed when you withdraw it, and for almost all 401(k) plans and many IRAs, all of it will be taxed. If you are under age 59½, consult with your plan administrator, because the law severely restricts borrowing against your account.

CAUTION

Mortgages have to be paid or you can lose your house. Enough said.

If you run the business part time, you may be able to allocate part of your current salary as partial funding for the initial and operating budget. Starting small and working out of your home may make this a viable option.

BORROWING MONEY

Okay, a quick course called Borrowing Money 101. When your business borrows money that has to be paid back along with interest, this is called a loan. If you borrow from Citibank or another financial institution, you're dealing with a commercial loan. If you borrow from your mother-in-law or best friend, you have a private loan.

CAUTION

Loan brokers can help you find a loan. But some loan brokers operate scams. Check out any ads offering loans to individuals based on their "credit worthiness." If you have any doubts, check with your Better Business Bureau.

Loans have a language of their own. You (or the business) are the borrower, or debtor. The bank or other lending source is the lender, or creditor. The time during which you have the use of the money you borrow is called the term or period of the loan. This is also called the loan's maturity. The amount you borrow from the lender is called principal. (You'll be talking like a loan officer in no time!)

You get a loan by making a loan application. Because you're looking for money for your business, you'll probably be asked to show your business plan. The loan application process varies considerably, depending on the type of loan you're going for. Some applications are as brief as a page and don't go into great detail. Others are much longer and ask many of the questions you already answered in your business plan.

As fascinating as your business is, the lender is not really interested in the intricacies of the product you sell or the service you provide. The main thing a lender wants to know is, will he get his money back? The lender doesn't benefit from your profits (beyond money used to pay back the loan). The lender doesn't own any part of your business. (Of course if you fail to repay the loan, the lender may be able to take your house or car, but let's not even go there.)

CAUTION

The owner of a corporation can be personally liable for a loan to the business because almost all lenders will require the owner to give her personal guarantee for the loan. Incorporation doesn't protect the personal assets of an owner who personally guarantees a loan to the business.

While you look for a loan for your business, the lender looks as closely at you as he is at the business. The reason? As the owner of a small business, you'll be asked to cosign or guarantee the loan. In other words, the cash will go to the business, but if the business goes under, your friendly bank manager will come knocking on your front door for repayment. Therefore, your personal credit history will affect whether you can get a business loan.

The time between making the application and hearing the happy news that you've been approved can also vary a great deal. It can be as short as a few days, but usually is a lot longer. For business loans, depending on the loan program involved, it may be several months before you learn whether you'll get the money.

CONSEQUENCES OF BORROWING

Like casual dating, borrowing means that you have a limited relationship with the lender. You make a loan application and, if it's approved, your contact with the lender is basically one of making monthly payments. Some banks are more aggressive in providing counsel and advice to businesses. Some bankers, for example, may try to establish a more personal relationship with lenders and help them to make contacts in the community.

At the end of the loan term, when you've paid off your debt, the relationship ends. You may, of course, renew the relationship by taking out another loan with the same lender, but it's not like feelings will be hurt if you go down the street to another bank for the next loan.

Borrowing does mean that you have to come up with the cash each month to pay off the debt, plus a little (or a lot) in interest. Sometimes the loan can be set up as a balloon loan. Although balloons may conjure up a day at the zoo, this is a little less fun. The balloon is a great big payment, usually at the end of the loan. Instead of paying back a part of the money you borrowed in monthly installments, you simply pay interest each month. At the end of the term of the loan, you must pay all of what you borrowed in one lump sum.

TIP

A balloon loan may be a good way to borrow if it's an option. It lets you make smaller payments up front while you're getting started. But don't let your balloon burst. Be sure to put aside enough money to pay off the principal when it comes due.

How Long Will It Last?

Business loans generally fall into two main categories: short term and long term. In banking lingo, a short-term loan is one that will be paid back in less than one year. Examples of short-term business loans include the following:

- Working capital loans
- Accounts receivable loans
- Lines of credit (or revolving lines of credit)

Long-term loans are loans that (you guessed it) the borrower takes a while to pay back. The loans typically have a payback period of at least one year. Generally, long-term loans don't run longer than seven years. Typically, long-term loans are used for major business undertakings like expansion or the purchase of equipment or real estate.

Loans for start-up capital generally fall in the long-term loan category. So you can anticipate repaying a loan and saying a fond farewell to the lender in three to seven years.

Where can you look for loans? Try the Quicken Business Cash Finder, which provides one-stop shopping for small business cash needs at www.cashfinder. com. Also look for banks already proven to be small-business friendly and willing to loan money. These banks are in the Small Business Administration's Directory of Small Business Lending at www.sba.gov/ADVO/stats.

Borrowing from Family and Friends

When depressed Dane Hamlet said, "Neither a borrower, nor a lender be; for loan oft loses both itself and friend," Shakespeare's character was giving sound advice for any entrepreneur who is contemplating borrowing from family or friends. Your relationship changes to debtor-creditor, no matter what is said. But if you must borrow, do so from someone who doesn't need the money, and may be very tolerant about your potential inability to timely repay the loan. If you do borrow, prepare a promissory note and a repayment schedule (and adhere to it).

Better yet, your grandmother (or some other benevolent loved one) may be willing to *give* you the money, perhaps as an advance toward your inheritance. He or she can have the joy of seeing you succeed in business and reduce estate taxes all at the same time; there will be no federal gift tax on a gift to you of $11,000 (subject to annual indexing) or less in any one year.

If you don't want to (or can't) get a commercial loan, consider a private loan from family or friends. The good news here is that the process can be very informal. After all, the lender knows you, probably quite well. You may not even need to show him your business plan.

CAUTION

If you borrow from your friends or relatives, make sure you explain the risk they're taking. You don't want to borrow from someone who will end up in the poorhouse if you can't repay the money.

Of course, the main drawback to borrowing from family and friends is what can happen to relationships if the business doesn't fly. If you can't repay the loan, you might lose a friend, or run the risk of never being invited to the family reunion again.

TIP

It doesn't matter that you're borrowing from Uncle Charlie, always put it in writing. In a private loan situation, drawing up a formal agreement is more for the protection of the lender than for you. If you have a written loan agreement stating the amount borrowed, the rate of interest charged, and the terms of repayment, Uncle Charlie will be in a better position to write off the loan on his tax return if you skip town. Without a loan agreement, the IRS may disallow the write-off, claiming that the loan was really a gift to his favorite nephew.

THE 30-SECOND RECAP

- Your business plan is your blueprint for building and operating your business.
- You will need to create a start-up budget and a cash flow projection.
- Try to use your assets to start up a business rather than incurring significant debt.
- Debt financing is the most common source of funds for the start-up entrepreneur.

Your Banker

Okay, so you're not a Rockefeller flush with cash. You've decided you just don't have the personal resources to get the business started on your own and so you have to look to Chase, Citibank, and other commercial loan sources for help. You might be able to borrow from these banks, even getting favorable terms under special loan programs sponsored by the Small Business Administration (SBA). There are also organizations that make loans just to small businesses.

In this section, you'll learn about the difference between a personal loan and a business loan. You'll learn how to do the application two-step to get a commercial business loan. And you'll understand what it means to get a handout from Uncle Sam in the form of an SBA loan and find out about special SBA loan programs, one of which might just be right for you.

GETTING A LOAN: PERSONALIZE IT

Your house is already mortgaged to the hilt, your credit cards are tapped out, and your selfish spouse isn't willing to work four jobs just so you can start your business. Don't get discouraged. Although banks are usually for standing in line and getting dinged with bounced-check charges, maybe in this case your friendly banker can actually help. Think about going for a personal loan to start your business.

A bank looks for two things when it makes a personal loan:

- A good personal credit rating.
- The ability to repay the loan. If you continue working at your job but want the loan to start a sideline business, your salary may be enough to convince a bank to give you a loan to start up.

Both commercial banks and savings and loan associations make personal loans. To get the personal loan paperwork in gear, ask your local bank or credit union for an application. Generally they'll ask you to list your assets and work history. You have to state the purpose for the loan—to buy a franchise, for example. The lender generally doesn't need to know that you have a Ph.D. in baking and great ideas about opening up a gourmet bread franchise. The lender doesn't need to see your business plan (though this shouldn't stop you from making one). And the lender doesn't need to see proof of how you spent the money.

CAUTION

If you don't repay the loan, the lender can sue you and get your personal assets (if you have any) to satisfy the loan. If you don't have enough assets to pay off the debt, the lender can use a judgment against you to garnish your salary if you have a job. It's basically a way to grab your paycheck out of your hands. The judgment can stay on your credit history for a very long time.

Here's the bad news: Interest on a personal loan is higher than the interest rate charged on home mortgages (or even car loans). That's because the loan is *unsecured.* You're not putting up your little split-level home so the banker can easily take it out from under you to get his money back. The lender is advancing you the money based only on your promise to pay (and what it considers your ability to do so).

PLAIN ENGLISH

An **unsecured loan** is one in which you don't have to put up your car or other property as collateral (security for the loan) that the lender can keep if you don't keep your promise to repay the loan on time.

Now that you know all about a personal loan, do you still want to consider it? You're probably better off with a business loan because it offers lower rates and the business repays it (as you'll see in a minute).

But having said all that, many individuals apply for personal loans because they're too darn lazy or uninformed to write a business plan and convince a loan officer they've got a great idea. Also some individuals are more comfortable dealing with their local savings and loan than with a big commercial bank. But now that you've read all the sage advice in this book, you won't be lazy or uninformed. You've got what it takes to get comfortable with the bank that can really help you.

THE COST OF BANK BORROWING

Banks are the money stores. They have it and you need it. Banks may be a little more willing to lend today than they were years ago, but many are still reluctant to lend to small businesses. You have to convince your banker that you are creditworthy. The banker will want to examine your business plan, particularly other capital sources, budgets, and cash flow. He or she will also want an appraisal of all property to be used for collateral and a lien search to ensure that the bank will be the first creditor.

You can expect a bank loan to involve the following provisions:

- **Amount to borrow.** The amount you want to borrow and the amount the bank is willing to lend may differ. You need to convince the bank that you can pay the loan back on time, and if you can't, the collateral is sufficient to cover the loan, interest, and cost of collection. If you have a bank loan officer who understands small businesses, this job will be much easier.

- **Interest rate.** The interest rate on your loan is usually pegged to one or more points above the prime rate offered to top commercial customers. For example, the current prime rate may be 8 percent, and your loan will be two points above that, or 10 percent. As prime rate varies during the term of the loan, so will your rate.

- **Payment schedule.** The bank may want to test you by offering only a short-term loan, perhaps six months, particularly if you are not putting up much collateral. After you establish that you pay your debts on time, the bank may be willing to extend the loan. Set the payment dates to conform to your cash flow; if money isn't there at the first of each month, agree to make payments by the tenth.

- **Loan fees.** Discuss the lender's loan processing fees before you commit to the loan. The lender may be flexible about these fees, particularly if you have investigated competitors who charge less.

- **Prepayment.** You should insist on the right to prepay the loan without any penalties. You may find an alternative source of financing that is more attractive.

CAUTION

Negotiate what collateral is required for the loan. The lender doesn't need to be over-collateralized. You may need to retain some assets free of a lien for other loans.

■ **Default.** The lender is likely to insist on a variety of events that can cause you to be in default on the loan. If you fail to make your payments on time, if you file bankruptcy (personal or business), or if collateral value falls below a set amount (or other enumerated breaches), the bank can call the entire loan in default and immediately due. There may not be much room to negotiate about the causes of default.

■ **Collateral.** Lenders want collateral—and the more, the merrier. The collateral may be your personal assets, including but not limited to your home or other real estate; motor vehicles; household goods; and stock and bond portfolio. The lender might also consider your business assets, including the building, fixtures, accounts receivable, equipment, and inventory. The lender will obtain appraisals for all the collateral (at your expense), and then conduct a lien search to ensure that it will be protected from other creditors' claims against the assets.

Upon loan closing you will execute a mortgage against the real estate and a security interest (lien) against your personal property (assets other than land and buildings). The mortgage and security interest will be released when the loan is repaid. Obviously, this collateral will not be available as security for other loans.

■ **Cosigners and guarantors.** Your signature alone on the promissory note may not be enough. If you are borrowing as a corporation, the bank will insist on your personal guaranty, because shareholders are not otherwise personally liable for corporate debts. The lender may require your spouse to cosign the loan, which may be difficult to get if he or she has concerns about the marriage lasting. The cosigner or guarantor runs the risk that his or her personal assets could be liable for repayment of the loan.

After you pay off the promissory note, the bank will return it. Keep the original. Burn a photocopy of the note; its smell is better than incense.

I have used the generic *bank* to include all lenders, but don't overlook the following:

■ Credit unions
■ Savings and loans
■ Commercial finance companies

Credit unions usually offer personal loans to members at favorable rates. Savings and loans traditionally have been restricted to mortgage loans. Commercial finance companies provide consumer and business loans. However, all these distinctions have become less rigid in the past few years.

Let Your Business Do the Borrowing

The business of banks is lending money. Whether you need just a few thousand dollars or tens of thousands of dollars to get your business started, you might just want to think about a commercial loan. It's important that you apply for a loan with the bank that you have the best chance of getting a loan from. Take a moment to think about which kind of bank is your perfect match.

TIP

Joe's Bank for Savings doesn't make commercial loans. So the savings and loan association that's holding the mortgage on your home or the one where you have your personal checking account isn't the one to look to for a business loan. The same is true of credit unions, which don't make commercial loans.

Commercial banks make commercial loans; it's just that simple. You can easily locate a commercial bank in your area, if you don't already know one, by looking in the Yellow Pages under the heading "Banks" and steering clear of any listing in which the word *savings* appears. Major commercial banks include Bank of America, Chase, Citibank, and Wells Fargo.

Commercial banks make money by lending it out to businesses and receiving interest on their money. So, in theory, commercial banks should be more motivated to make loans to businesses, right? Well in practice, they may not be motivated to help you. The reason is the cost involved in processing loans. It's expensive for a bank to review your loan application. In years past if you only wanted to borrow a small amount, say $5,000, it simply didn't pay for most banks to even consider your application. The lender may have been interested only in making loans of $50,000 and more.

But times are changing. Some lenders are now offering loans to the same small businesses they used to turn their noses up at, and other commercial lenders are expected to follow suit. Here are some ways to quickly learn which bank may be receptive to your application:

- ■ **Ask around.** Ask other small business owners in your area which bank they've borrowed from.
- ■ **Check out the SBA's Small Business Development Center for a referral to a lender in your area willing to make small loans for starting up a business.** To find the center nearest you, call 1-800-U-ASK-SBA or click on www.sba.gov.

- **Look for loan offers.** Wells Fargo has aggressively sought small business loans by offering lines of credit as small as $5,000. It has sent out thousands of invitations to small business owners explaining its one-page application that cuts preparation time to as short as 15 minutes.
- **Talk to your chamber of commerce.** Ask for advice on where your best chances of getting a loan in your area might be.
- **Surf the web.** Look for loan sources online. For example, a number of institutions list their lending information on the Quicken Business Cash Finder at www.quicken.com/banking_and_credit.

PLODDING THROUGH THE PAPERWORK

You think it took paperwork to get your home mortgage? You ain't seen nothin' yet! Be prepared for paperwork like you've never seen before. The bank wants to know everything about your business and you. You'll have to supply this information as well as contracts, sales agreements, and other documents they ask for. Understanding what's in store for you means you're prepared, which, in turn, should help make the process go more smoothly.

STEP 1: PREPARE THE PAPERWORK

The first thing to do in applying for a commercial loan is to get all necessary papers to the bank. For this you may need a shopping cart.

- **Loan application.** This form, which you get from the bank, asks basic information about the business and its owner: you. The length of the application, one page to many pages, varies from bank to bank.
- **Loan proposal.** The bank wants to know why you want the loan. You have to explain the type of loan you're asking for and the reason you want it. For instance, you want a line of credit (type of loan) to start up your business (reason for the loan).
- **Business plan.** You generally have to attach your business plan to the loan application. The plan describes your business and outlines your strategy for the next several years.
- **Repayment plan.** It's not that it doesn't trust you, but the bank has this tendency to want to know how and when it's going to be repaid. If the business plan projects significant profits—more than enough to cover loan repayment—the lender may be satisfied. You may not need a separate repayment plan. But if your business will take some time to get rolling, you may have to give a separate explanation of how you intend to repay the bank until the business can make the payments.

- **Personal profile.** Apply for a loan and suddenly you're fascinating: The bank wants to know as much about you as it does about the business. Your business background, as well as your personal financial picture, all can make or break getting a loan for your business. Your business background may be explained in the business plan. Your personal finances aren't, so you need to get that together. The bank might ask questions about your personal finances on the loan application, or you may have to provide an additional statement to go with the application.

- **Other documents.** You might be asked to give supporting documents, such as letters of reference, contracts, or vendor quotes.

- **Collateral.** Gone are the days when you could use your good name to guarantee a loan: The bank wants to have something concrete to repossess if you can't repay the loan. The bank holds stocks, bonds, or equipment as collateral until you pay off the loan. Sometimes you're allowed to hold the collateral but you can't sell it without the bank's okay. When the loan is paid off, the collateral is returned to you (if it was held by the bank).

TIP

Before you prepare your application, ask what supporting documents the bank wants you to provide. They won't even begin processing your loan until every scrap of paper is in. Giving them everything at once will save you time. But don't give them more than what they want because it may delay the process, or worse, divulge information that may hurt your application.

STEP 2: FOLLOW UP

Okay, you spent your summer vacation collecting enough paper and filling out enough forms to sink the *Titanic*. What's next? The bank will review the papers you've submitted. They will probably want to talk to you—in person or over the phone—about certain things like, you know, that time back in 1977 when you were three days late paying a credit card bill. Be prepared to answer questions about the information you've included in your papers.

STEP 3: APPROVAL OR REJECTION

The *Equal Credit Opportunity Act* states a bank has to give a small business (start-ups and existing companies with revenues of $1 million or less) an answer to a loan application within 30 days. They can call you on the phone or write you a letter, but however they do it, you must get an answer—yes or no.

The 30 days start from the day on which you finally submit the last piece of information the bank asks for.

If you don't get loan approval, find out why. The bank has to state in writing the reason for rejecting your loan. The reason may be anything from a bad credit history to not enough collateral. (It cannot be just because they don't like your face.)

But as with folks who don't pass their driver's license test the first time, you can go back as many times as you like until you get approved. The bank keeps the application and other documents on file for one year. During this time, you can try to correct the reason for the loan rejection and win approval of a reapplication.

If you're rejected by one bank, this doesn't mean you can't get a loan. Different banks have different standards. Your failure to get a loan from one bank doesn't prevent you from going to another and meeting its standards. Don't get discouraged. Rob, a persistent entrepreneur, got a loan for his diet supplements business after four tries with four different banks.

TIP

If you were turned down for a loan and believe it was because of your sex, race, national origin, or marital status, you can get help from the federal agency that supervises the bank you dealt with. If you sue because of discrimination and win, you can get money for damages, including punitive damages against the lender, attorney fees, and court costs.

If you're rejected for a commercial loan, the bank may advise you to reapply under an SBA program discussed later in this section.

You're on the Hook, Too

If you get the loan, you'll be asked to give your personal guarantee for repayment. This means you get to sign the loan application on two separate dotted lines—once as the business owner on behalf of the business and again as an individual cosigning the loan.

Getting Investors

Instead of borrowing money, which you have to pay back with interest, you may want to bring in an investor. With an investor, you share the ownership of your business with someone else. If you have an idea for a business and start it on your own, you own 100 percent of the business. If you bring in an investor, your 100 percent is reduced.

The amount of the business you give away depends on how much money the investor brings to you, how much that money is worth to you at the time, and how much the investor's willing to settle for. For example, $10,000 to get your business off the ground may be the difference between getting started and not getting started, so it's very significant to you. You might be willing to give up 2 percent, 10 percent, 20 percent, or even more of the ownership to the investor.

Of course, the investor may have other ideas. Paul was trying to raise money to buy more inventory for his foot-cream business. One investor was anxious to help—in exchange for a majority interest in the business. Paul may have been needy but he wasn't crazy enough to hand over his business. Instead, he kept looking for the money he needed and found it with another investor who wasn't greedy.

In deciding how much ownership you're willing to exchange for the cash, weigh the possible return to the investor (what you think that share may be worth a few years down the road when your business is profitable) against your current level of desperation (how badly you need the money). A $300,000-a-year business is going to return tens of thousands of dollars a year to a 20 percent investor, who may have put up only $5,000 up front. Is her investment really worth it?

Here's the real payoff with an investor: When she puts money into your business, you don't have to pay anything back—nada, nothing, zip. You don't have to make monthly payments of interest and principal. This is a big plus because the money that you would have used to make loan repayments can be used to help your business. The investor benefits from her cash contribution only if the business makes it and becomes profitable.

TIP
You may want to give up part ownership to bring in needed capital even though you give up some control. After all, it might be better to have a smaller percentage of something than 100 percent of nothing (what you could wind up with if you can't get the money you need to start up).

As a rule of thumb, a private investor (other than perhaps a relative or a friend) is looking for a high return on investment (as much as 25 percent or more) in a relatively short time (usually less than five years). When Aunt Lottie invests in your company, her expectations might be quite different. She might not be looking for quick profit as much as she's looking to help you out. (Of course, she doesn't want to lose her shirt, either.)

Because you don't have to pay anything back, the investor is less interested in your credit history, and more in the business itself. Is this the best idea since sliced bread? Is it practical? And, most important, will it make money so she's not flushing her money away? The answer to this last question, which the investor must answer for herself, is often the reason she decides to ante up.

Like having a baby, when you take on an investor she is going to be around for a long time. When you bring an investor into your business, it's important that you understand you're beginning a long-term relationship. Just like being a parent, there's no set time for this kid to move out (although it's certainly possible to disown her if you come to a mutual parting of the ways).

When you look for investors, there's no formal or established process like filling out a loan application. However, most prospective investors (outside of your family) will insist on seeing your business plan. If that sparks any interest, then the investor will meet with you before deciding to go any further.

Getting investors interested in your business to the point where they're willing to put up cash may take weeks or even months. Then you generally involve attorneys in the process to formalize your arrangements. This, again, will take time.

INVESTORS COME IN ALL SIZES

Just because you take on an investor, you don't have to give up total control of your business. Investor arrangements are not all the same. There are various ways to set them up:

- **Partners.** If you bring in someone to work with you on the business and you're not incorporated, you two become a partnership. You don't have to be equal partners—a 50/50 split makes you equal partners— you might prefer something like a 60/40 or 75/25 split of the business (and hence the profits).

  A partnership arrangement is the closest thing in the business world to a marriage. Partners must get along and be able to agree on most issues that come up.

  There's a benefit to bringing in a partner in addition to the money it means for the business. A partner can bring not only additional capital but also additional talent to the business. You may be a whiz with numbers while your partner is great at sales, for example. Partnerships are discussed further in Part 1.

- **Limited partners.** You can share the ownership of the business with a partner without giving up any of the control over day-to-day activities by forming a limited partnership. The limited partner puts in money but is only entitled to receive a share of the profits. He can't tell you how to run the business.

- **Members.** You can form your business as a limited liability company and bring in members who will contribute needed cash. You can define the role of a new member either as a general partner or a limited partner. Make sure that the investor understands whether he will have a say in how the business is run.

- **Shareholders.** If you have incorporated your business and find an investor willing to put money into it, you can sell stock (shares) in the corporation to investors. Investors then become shareholders (or stockholders; the words are interchangeable). How does this affect your ownership interest? This is a little complicated, but bear with me for a moment.

   Here's an example: Suppose your corporation is formed with 200 shares of stock. You issue 10 shares of stock to yourself. You own 100 percent of the corporation. You want to bring in an investor and decide that the investor should have a 10 percent ownership interest. You can do this by selling the investor 1 of your 10 shares of stock. You now own 9 of the 10 outstanding shares, or 90 percent of the company; the investor owns 1 of the 10 outstanding shares, or 10 percent of the company. Alternatively, the investor can buy 1 share of stock directly from the corporation. In that case, you own 90.9 percent of the company (10 of 11 outstanding shares); the investor owns 9.1 percent of the company (1 of 11 outstanding shares). Get it?

An investor who owns shares in the corporation may or may not have a say in the business. As a minority shareholder, there's not much an investor can do to tell you how to design your widgets or sell your skin cream. However, as a practical matter, you may want to work with the investor to start up and grow the business, taking his counsel and advice.

You might begin with co-owners who pool their investments with your own, so that partners, limited liability company members, and stockholders increase the available business capital. Each co-owner usually receives an ownership interest equal to his or her percentage of the total capital contribution. Co-owners may be required to make additional capital contributions, as the business requires, or permit the business to retain a share of their earnings. Co-owners are not a likely source if you need a substantial infusion of new capital.

Outside investors include the following:

- **Private-placement investors**. Private-placement investors may be looking at your company as an alternative to the stock market, because their ownership interest will likely require you to listen closely to their suggestions. They may have other investments that generate a tax loss that cannot be used without a similar investment that produces a tax gain.

- **Venture capitalists**. Venture capitalists usually invest in high-growth companies, such as dot.coms. These investors expect to receive a substantial equity interest and may insist on a significant voice in management decisions.

- **Strategic partners**. Another company may be willing to develop a strategic alliance with your company, and provide financing in exchange for equity. The strategic partner may be one of your suppliers or customers.

- **Public stock market investors**. The stock market might welcome your public offering. You retain a substantial block of the stock and the rest goes on the market. If your capital demands run in the millions of dollars, this may be your only recourse. However, this book won't go there, because this is a book for small business owners.

FEDERAL SECURITIES LAWS

Anytime you offer to sell an investment interest in your business, assume that federal securities laws apply. For example, if you advertise in your local newspaper that you are selling stock in your company, this activity may be an investment "offering" and regulated by federal law. This section will not make you a securities lawyer, but it will alert you to certain dangers that could result in civil and criminal suits against you.

A brief excursion into the arcane rules of the Securities Act of 1933 and the role of the Securities and Exchange Commission (SEC) is important. The SEC has several functions that may relate to your small business offering, including the following:

- Requiring substantial disclosure for securities offerings
- Regulating the securities market
- Investigating securities fraud

The SEC protects investors by requiring registration of a securities offering, unless there is an exemption from registration. Even if an offering is exempt, such as a sale to a current officer or director, the offeror cannot defraud the investor by making materially misleading representations.

The statute broadly defines security to include virtually any investment where the investor is not actively involved in the management of the business. Investments covered by the act include the following:

- **Common and preferred stock.** If the corporation issues only one form of stock, it's common stock; more than one form of stock may be another type of common stock or *preferred stock;* the corporation's articles of incorporation specifies the rights of the various forms of stock.

- **Stock warrants and options.** Stock warrants and options permit the holder to convert them into corporate stock. Warrants may be issued to permit a holder to buy stock at a stated price, say $25. If the stock is worth $50, the warrant to buy it at $25 is valuable. A company frequently grants stock options to its valuable employees as an incentive. The stock works in a similar way to a warrant.

- **Limited partnership units.** Limited partners don't participate in management, so they are passive investors, and need the protection of the securities act.

- **Investment contracts.** Investment contract is a generic term, which encompasses any investment offer that involves investment of money, with a common enterprise or business activity, and the expectation of profits, solely from the efforts of others.

PLAIN ENGLISH

Preferred stock is stock that gives holders priority over the common shareholders in corporate dividends and liquidation. The corporation's articles of incorporation details all of the preferred shareholders' rights.

INVESTORS AND SECURITIES LAWS

You may have to raise money by selling equity (ownership) in your company. If you choose this option, you'll have no lenders to pay back, but you will owe stockholders dividends on any profits your company makes. However, you may have to relinquish some of your control over the company. Certainly never sell more than a 49 percent interest; if you own a majority interest, you can have the final say.

Several years ago, there was a case in which individuals invested $25,000 in so-called mortgage-backed securities. The seller promised a 12 percent annual return and claimed that the individuals' investment was completely secure because real estate was its collateral. These investors were impressed enough to give him more than $3 million, which promptly disappeared. The seller violated both the registration and antifraud provisions of the 1933 Securities Act.

Start with the rule that you must register each security offering with the SEC, and then look for exemptions for registration. You don't want to spend the enormous time and substantial costs to register unless you are going public.

If you want to raise capital from a few private investors, several Securities Act exemptions are available under SEC Regulation D:

- **Rule 504** permits you to sell up to $1 million of securities within a 12-month period to any investor; form D must be filed with the SEC.

- **Rule 505** permits you to sell up to $5 million of securities within a 12-month period; there cannot be more than 35 unaccredited investors; no general solicitation is permitted; and form D must be filed with the SEC; this form discloses certain financial, historical, and other information about the offeror.

- **Rule 506** permits you to sell an unlimited dollar amount of securities; there cannot be more than 35 unaccredited investors; the offeror must reasonably believe that each prospective investor (alone or with an investment advisor) has such knowledge and experience in financial and business matters that the investor is capable of evaluating the merits and risks of the investment; form D must be filed with the SEC.

- **Section 4(6)** permits you to sell up to $5 million of securities to accredited investors only, not to unaccredited investors; SEC must be notified of all sales.

- **Rule 147** permits you to sell unregistered securities to legal residents of your home state; no resale of the securities may occur for at least nine months after the last security is sold. This exemption is for purely local securities offerings. Because this offers no protection to investors, the courts don't favor it.

Disclosure is the operative word under securities law. Typically, you would use the exemption under Rule 506 or Section 4(6). You need to prepare a private placement memorandum for each offeree. More precisely, your attorney must draft this document, but it requires significant input from you. This memorandum should contain the following details:

- Description of the rights of the securities purchaser
- Disclosure of the use for the proceeds of the offering
- History of company; its products and services
- Balance sheet and profit-and-loss statement
- Description of company management and their holdings and compensation
- Description of pending lawsuits

CAUTION

Never assume that you have an exemption from federal registration. Always consult an attorney who specializes in securities law before you make any offer.

Verify all statements because the antifraud rules apply even if your offering is exempt from federal registration. Don't make any separate oral or written statements that may be misleading. Clearly specify all potential risks. Require each recipient of the memorandum to acknowledge receiving it.

 CAUTION

Get all the facts, especially if you're relying on an offeree's claim to be an accredited investor. Make sure you obtain the offeree's financial statement and investment history.

Don't take any shortcuts. If you did not follow the exemption requirements, the investor can sue for a refund of the investment. Likewise, there may be a criminal case filed against you by the U.S. attorney, particularly if there are allegations of securities fraud.

STATE SECURITIES LAWS

All states have their own securities laws (known as blue sky laws) that regulate the offer and sale of securities within individual state borders. You must comply with any state securities law where you make an offering. Federal exemption from registration does not exempt your offering from state registration.

Many state securities laws are patterned after the Securities Act of 1933, with disclosure and antifraud provisions. State registration is usually made through the state securities commissioner (often part of the secretary of state's office). State exemptions vary too much to be detailed in this book.

VENTURE CAPITALISTS

Some of you might be saying, "Hey, I've read about venture capital firms that invest in new companies; why not mine?" True. But venture capital isn't all that easy to come by. A venture capital firm is a company of savvy investors who are in business solely to find profitable ventures, invest, and reap (they hope) huge profits.

As a practical matter, your gift-basket business, or small businesses for that matter, aren't attractive to venture capitalists, who are generally looking for the latest technology or the hottest new product. If you're the next Bill Gates developing a new software technology in your garage or have ideas about a biotechnology product, you may interest a venture capital firm (which you can find through a directory of venture capital firms in the reference section of your local library). Otherwise, don't waste your time or theirs. Even if you have the right product, most venture capitalists are interested only in existing businesses that are already profitable, which leaves out start-ups.

Although you may not be able to entice a venture capital firm to join with you, it's possible to find *angels* interested in backing you. Just as venture capital firms take an ownership interest in your business, angels also become co-owners as the price for investing in you. Like angels who underwrite Broadway shows, they're willing to gamble on the chance for success.

PLAIN ENGLISH

Angels are independently wealthy businesspeople who are willing to invest in private companies for a piece of the action. Heaven sent? Well, it depends on the terms they're offering in exchange for the money.

FREE MONEY: OPTIONS FOR FINDING START-UP CASH

Instead of borrowing from a lender or giving up part of your ownership interest in exchange for an investment in your business, you may be able to find free money. Although money still doesn't grow on trees, grants and awards provide money that doesn't have to be repaid. It's like a prize. There are a variety of grants and awards given to businesses.

If you're lucky enough to get a grant, you'll have a continuing relationship with the grantmaker for the term of the grant. You'll generally have to do a certain amount of paperwork, sending in interim reports telling the grantmaker how things are going and that you're using the money the way you said you would. At the end of the grant term you also have to write a final report. The grantmaker will also audit your books to make sure you haven't spent the money on a vacation home in the Bahamas.

CAUTION

Although a grant is desirable because it doesn't get repaid, it's perhaps the most difficult kind of money to get. You're at the mercy of the people making the grants. They have special interests and you have to fit their mold if you want the money. And even if you find a grant you may be suited for, you have to overcome stiff competition to get it.

GETTING MONEY FROM UNCLE SAM: GOVERNMENT GRANTS

Although you may think of the government as taking money rather than giving it back, the government does make grants to businesses in certain industries. There are grants designed for small businesses, but typically they're not suitable for start-ups. There may, however, be exceptions for special businesses. For example, Ramona, a retired teacher, was one home-based business owner who saw an opportunity in government funding. She applied for a government grant designed to provide tutoring services to inner-city children. Because the government often supports economic development for depressed areas, this was a great match.

There may be grants for special business owners—women, minorities, or people with disabilities. Home-based business owners can also apply for these grants.

FOUNDATION GRANTS

Grants and awards are also made by foundations. Foundations are basically charitable organizations set up to fund projects they're interested in. Some foundations give out seed money, which can be used to start up a business. Generally, however, like government grants, foundation money is designed to go to businesses that already have a track record.

TIP

Look for grants for seed money in the "bible" for grants called *Awards, Honors and Prizes* (published by Gale Research), which you can probably find in your local library.

GRANTING YOUR BUSINESS WISH

You start the grant process by finding a specific grant you think you might be eligible for. Once you've found the right match, you can begin the application process.

Start by sending the government agency or foundation making the grant a letter of intent. This letter informs the grantmaker that you want to submit a formal proposal, which is just another word for an application. The letter should contain a brief outline of your project—which may be simply to start up a business. Describe your business, your background, and any other key people you work with. Specify how much grant money you're looking for and how the money will be used.

Sometimes your letter of intent will be answered with encouragement to continue and submit a formal application. Other times you might get word not to bother going any further. Still other times you might hear nothing at all and have to forge ahead with no inkling of whether there's a chance for success.

CAUTION

Watch out for deadlines. Some grants can be submitted anytime and will be considered when received. Other grants have an application deadline that's as sacrosanct as April 15 is for the IRS.

Remember, the government agency or foundation making the grant doesn't know you exist. Your job is to make yourself sound fascinating and convince them that the grant should be given to you over thousands of other applicants.

WHAT TYPE OF FINANCING IS BEST FOR YOU?

Many factors influence your pursuit of financing. In fact, there's nothing preventing you, other than the time and effort required, from exploring all avenues at the same time. Friends thought Jim was nuts when he described his efforts to get the money he needed for his software development business. These included loan applications to Citibank; calls to Arty, his college roommate; begging for cash; and even a grant proposal to a foundation. But he didn't seem so crazy when the bank loan came through and his college roommate Arty anteed up. Jim had enough money to start developments on two projects at the same time!

The following table provides a checklist for some things to consider when deciding how to raise money for your start-up. Weigh the plusses and minuses of each type of funding.

Selecting a Form of Financing

Factors to Consider	Debt	Equity	Grant
Limit on funds available	Yes	No	Yes
Application process	Complex	Informal	Complex
Obligation to repay	Yes	No	No
Loss of control	No	Yes	No
Impact of your credit history	Yes	No	No
Applicable for start-ups	Yes	Yes	Limited
Open to home-based business	Yes	Yes	Yes

Notice that this table indicates a limit on funds available through a loan. Although there might be high limits on loans available, the amount you can qualify for is limited by your personal financial situation.

THE 30-SECOND RECAP

- Borrowing means you have to pay back the cash in monthly installments over a set time with interest.

- Borrowing from friends or family may take less effort, but it can take a toll on your relationship if things don't go right.

- Bringing in investors allows you to have more cash for use in the business.

- Venture capital generally is not suited for home business start-ups.

- Free money for start-ups is very hard to come by, but might be worth exploring.

- One type of financing may be better for you than another.

Other Venues for Raising Cash

Believe it or not, you may not need to look beyond your own front door to find the money to get your business off the ground. You may be sitting on a pile of cash you can use to start your business even if you don't know it yet.

In this section, you'll learn how to recognize the personal resources you may already have that can be used to start your business. You'll see that it's easy and quick to tap into each of your personal sources of funding. But before you mortgage the farm, it's also important to weigh the pros and cons.

BE YOUR OWN BANKER

In the best of all possible worlds, you'd be independently wealthy and wouldn't need anyone's help to start your business. You wouldn't have to borrow or share your ownership or look to outsiders in any way. If you didn't have to borrow, you wouldn't have to make monthly payments and you'd save on interest expenses. If you didn't have to bring in investors, you'd keep full control and enjoy all of that lovely money from your business for your own selfish pleasures.

Yeah, right. Now let's get real. Most of us aren't independently wealthy. But most of us do have resources we might not have thought of to finance our own businesses. Using those resources keeps control of your business in your own hands, even if you aren't a Rockefeller. So let's look at what you have that you can borrow against or turn into cash for your business.

EMPTYING OUT THE CHRISTMAS FUND

With personal savings there's no process at all. It's right at your fingertips. So the best-case scenario is to be your own banker and rely on your own savings to get your business started.

TIP

According to the SBA, almost 80 percent of all new business owners don't use commercial loans to get started. More likely, they're relying on personal resources to get their businesses going. Take a good inventory of your assets.

Okay, be brave. Open your savings passbook. Do you have enough cash on hand to pay for the things you figure you need to get started? Maybe you're one of those farsighted people who had the idea to start up a business when you were 10. Maybe you had enough foresight and discipline to save your pennies for your goal. (Or maybe, like Howard, a computer technician downsized by IBM, you can use a juicy severance package to start your business. He used his to start a catering business from home.)

But back to reality. We all know how difficult it is to save, and only a select few find themselves in the enviable position of having a bank account flush with enough cash to start a business. Still, there might be a way to build personal savings for a business start-up that you just haven't thought about.

SAVE AS YOU GO

If you keep your day job and start up your home-based business on a part-time basis, you can use part of each paycheck from your job to pay for your business. Say you normally put some of your paycheck into a savings account each month. Use that money to pay for an extra phone line, business insurance, stamps, paper clips, or other business expenses.

GO "ON MARGIN" AGAINST YOUR INVESTMENTS

You may not have your savings sitting in cash. Maybe you went the Wall Street route and bought stocks or bonds. Or maybe you were lucky enough to inherit them from Aunt Adelaide. That stash can be turned into cash for your business; you just have to know how to get at it.

Suppose you have 100 shares of Boeing. Sure, you can sell the stock and use the $10,000 or so you'd get to help your business. But remember, not all of that money is yours. First, there are selling expenses—commissions to sell the securities. And don't forget federal (and, in some cases, state) income tax on any profit from the sale. In tax parlance, profit is called gain. Your gain is essentially the difference between what you paid for the stock and what you got for it when you sold it (less any selling expenses). Uncle Sam eats gain for breakfast.

TIP

If you incorporate your business, be sure to keep track of all the savings you put into your business. That way you can see whether you're making any money on your investment. Also, for tax purposes, your contributions to the business are added to the cost basis of your stock. That means you reduce your gain if you sell off some of your stock or sell the business entirely.

Instead of selling the stock, why not simply borrow against it? If you let a brokerage firm hold the stock in street name (the name of the brokerage firm), you can go on margin. "On margin" is just a fancy Wall Street term for borrowing, with your stock used as collateral for the loan.

You go on margin (get your loan) simply by signing a margin agreement. The margin agreement details the terms of the loan (the interest rate and so on). You can usually borrow up to 50 percent of the value of your stocks and up to 90 percent of government securities. For example, say you own $30,000 of treasury bonds and $20,000 worth of stock that's held in your brokerage account. Your maximum margin loan is $37,000 ($27,000 [90 percent of $30,000], plus $10,000 [50 percent of $20,000]). After the papers are signed, the money's yours when you want it, even the same day!

So it's easy to go on margin, but is it a good idea? Here are a couple of points to keep in mind:

- **You can get a favorable interest rate for the loan.** In many firms, you're charged only a small percentage historically 1.5 percent higher than the broker call rate (an index created by the major brokerage firms that's similar to the prime rate). Some firms may even offer rates below the broker call rate.

- **You don't have to pay the loan back at any set time.** You don't have to make monthly payments of either interest or principal. Each month the interest is added to your outstanding debt. The interest continues to be figured on the outstanding balance of the loan. As you pay it back, your interest payments shrink (assuming the interest rate remains the same). If you have the money, you can repay the loan all at once. Or you can pay it back in any kind of installments you want.

Although these are good reasons for using a margin loan (as opposed to another type of loan), there's also a downside:

- If you don't make payments, you'll begin to pay interest on the interest.
- The interest rate can bounce around like a little metal ball in a pinball machine. In times of low interest, the interest on your margin loan is also low. But as the prime rate rises, the interest on your margin loan can be adjusted each month, or even several times in the same month. Although the past several years have seen relatively stable interest rates (rises of no more than a point or two), those who remember way back to the 1970s and 1980s recall interest rates zooming into double digits practically overnight. Other types of loans allow you to lock into an interest rate at the start so you know exactly what interest rate you're paying for the privilege of borrowing money, but not when you borrow on margin.

TIP

Because there are almost as many margin rates as there are brokerage firms and because those rates are at the mercy of rising and falling interest rates, be sure to check with your broker if you're considering a margin loan. Your margin interest rate is posted on your monthly brokerage statement.

- If the value of the securities you borrowed against falls, you may be subject to an unpleasant little thing called a margin call. When that happens, you might be forced to sell some of your holdings or come up with outside cash to bring the value of your account up to what it was to keep the loan going.

Let's take the same facts as before for an example. If the value of the stock drops from $20,000 to $15,000 and you borrowed the maximum margin loan you could, you'd have to sell enough to pay off $2,500, the part of the loan no longer supported by the value of the stock ($5,000 drop in value multiplied by 50 percent, because it takes $2 of stock for each $1 of margin debt). Or you'd have to put $5,000 into the account from outside sources to bring its value up to the previous level.

In some years you may experience a continually rising stock market, and the values of many stocks will climb. But remember, even where the stock market rises, the value of individual stocks can fall.

If nothing else, you can see that this is not a game for amateurs. The discussion of margin loans here covers just the basics. (For example, there are other complications, such as house calls when your holdings are sold to cover a margin loan when the value of the holdings dip below margin requirements.) Just keep in mind that you should discuss margin loans with your stockbroker if you think they're the way to go.

CREDIT CARDS FOR CASH

A tempting source of cash for your business may be those lovely little slivers of plastic in your wallet. Just go to an ATM, slide your credit card in, punch a few buttons, and the cash is yours. For small business owners it's become an all-too-easy source of cash. According to one source, about 70 percent of small businesses are funded using credit cards and personal loans. is it a good idea? In most cases, it's about as good an idea as sticking your arm in a buzz saw.

Sure, credit card borrowing is easy. There are no forms to fill out, and the cash is yours instantly. But the price you pay for the privilege of borrowing against your credit cards is high. Interest can run around 18 percent a year, maybe even higher. (If the statement says you're paying 1.5 percent per month, this translates into 18 percent a year.) Credit card borrowing is just about the most expensive way there is (short of going to a loan shark!) to raise money.

CAUTION

Use credit card borrowing only as a last resort because of the high interest rates you'll pay. Then try to pay off the debt as quickly as possible. You may be able to pay off credit card debt with some other type of loan once your business gets rolling.

Despite the high interest rate, credit card borrowing can be useful for limited purposes. If you need a computer for your business, you may want to charge it as a way to finance your purchase. If your business earns money (or you have extra cash), you can pay off the credit card immediately, getting rid of any interest charges. If you can't pay the balance in full, you can pay the computer off over time. Just remember: The longer you take to pay off the charge, the higher your interest costs will be.

USE THE NEST EGG YOU LIVE IN

When I needed money to put an extension on my home for my office, I didn't have to look farther than my own front door. If you own your own home, you're probably sitting on a nest egg you never thought about. This particular nest egg is called *equity in your home.* You can take out the equity and use it in your business.

PLAIN ENGLISH

Equity in your home is the amount you'd be able to put in your pocket if you were to sell your house today after paying off any mortgages you already have on your home.

You can tap into this equity without selling your home. You do this by taking out a second mortgage or a home equity line of credit.

HOME EQUITY LOAN PROCESS

How much can you borrow? As a rule of thumb, figure that you can borrow up to 75 percent of the equity in your home (though some lenders will go as high as 100 percent or even higher).

Let's say your home is worth $150,000 and you already have a mortgage with a balance of $100,000. Your equity is $50,000. You can't borrow more than 75 percent of the value of your home, which comes to $112,500. Because you have an existing mortgage of $100,000, the limit on a second mortgage or home equity line is $12,500.

The interest rate you pay on a home loan is usually lower than the rate you'd pay on commercial loans. However, rates vary from lender to lender. You can get fixed-rate loans where the interest rate is set from the start. Or you can get a variable-rate loan, also called an adjustable-rate mortgage (ARM), where the interest rate goes up or down, according to a prefixed index and at preset intervals.

TIP

If you're planning to leave your job to run your business full-time from home, it's a good idea to apply for the loan before you quit your job. Self-employed people have a harder time borrowing money (even a home mortgage) than employees do. So limit the paperwork and hassle by coordinating your job departure with your loan application.

You usually repay home loans by writing a check every month. The repayment period is long term, running up to 15 years. The longer you stretch out the payments, the more each monthly payment shrinks. But, remember, the longer you take to pay off the loan the more interest you pay over the life of the loan.

To get a home equity loan, you make an application to the bank or other lender. The process is just about the same as getting a first mortgage on your home (and you remember what fun that was).

DRAWBACKS TO BORROWING AGAINST YOUR HOME

Although there are a number of good reasons to use a home equity loan over other borrowing options, you should know about some important drawbacks. You can expect to wait more than a month after submitting a wheelbarrow full of paperwork to get approval for a second mortgage on your home. Then get ready to sit through a closing and, depending on state law, to wait three days after the closing to get your money. If you used a mortgage to buy your home, you've probably experienced this.

Getting a second mortgage or a home equity loan is usually no easier than it was to get your first mortgage. You complete a lengthy application form. The lender does a credit check on you. But even if you have a less-than-perfect credit history, you'll be able to get a mortgage. That's because the lender is protected if you don't repay the loan: He can just sell your home out from under you and pocket what he's owed. Your credit history may, however, affect the interest rate you'd have to pay.

It may be weeks or even longer before you can close (finalize the loan) and get your money.

You may also be charged points on the amount you borrow. Points, which are a percentage of the loan, are, in effect, additional interest that you're paying up front for the privilege of borrowing money. If you're charged one point on a $100,000 mortgage, you'll pay $1,000. In addition to points, there may be closing costs. These can be modest or quite steep, depending on the lender and the loan program involved. But adding up the points and other closing costs, the fact remains that it's going to cost you money to borrow money.

But let's say the paperwork doesn't get you and you're willing to pay the piper to get the loan. The fact remains that borrowing against the equity in your home puts your home at risk. If you invest money in your business and don't succeed, you still have to pay off the home loan because it's your personal debt. Even if you incorporate your business, you remain personally liable for your home equity debt.

TIP

If you already have a mortgage on your home you don't have to go to the same lender for the home equity loan. Shop around for the best loan possible, comparing interest rates, repayment terms, closing costs, and other loan features.

TAKE A LOAN FROM YOUR LIFE INSURANCE

Remember Jimmy Stewart's character in the movie *It's A Wonderful Life?* He needed money for a business debt and decided to jump off a bridge so his life insurance could pay for it. Good news. You don't have to do anything that drastic to tap into insurance money. If you own a permanent life insurance policy (a whole life policy or a universal life policy), you may have another source of ready cash. As long as you've owned the policy for several years, you may have equity in the policy. Equity in a life insurance policy is called *cash surrender value.*

PLAIN ENGLISH

Cash surrender value is the amount of money you'd receive if you turned in your policy to the insurance company for cancellation.

Of course, you can simply choose to cash in your policy and use your cash surrender value without arranging for a loan. But in that case you lose your insurance protection. What's more, if you later decide to get a new policy, you have to undergo a new insurance physical and pay higher premiums (because odds are you're older and the premiums are fixed by your age when you take out the policy). Or you might even find yourself uninsurable because of recent high blood pressure or another condition uncovered during a physical.

TIP

If you own a term policy, which is the least expensive kind of life insurance to own when you're young, you don't build up any cash value in the policy. All of your premiums go to pay the death benefit under the policy (what your beneficiaries get when you kick the bucket) plus the fees of the insurance company (which are built in to the policy). Bottom line: Don't look to term insurance (which doesn't build up a cash surrender value) as a source of financing.

There are a lot of reasons why a life insurance loan can look good to you. First, it's very easy to arrange. You don't have to fill out any request forms or loan applications. You just call your life insurance agent or the insurance company that issued your policy and ask for a loan. It can be handled over the telephone (although you'll be asked to sign a loan form that will be sent to you). Getting the loan doesn't depend on your credit rating or what you plan to do with the money. The life insurance company doesn't ask any of these questions. Because the cash surrender value is really your money, the insurance company makes it easy for you to borrow it. You may be able to get your money in a matter of days.

Another good reason for life insurance loans to finance your business is that you get a favorable interest rate. This rate is much lower than the rate you'd pay on a commercial loan.

Need more reasons? You don't have to pay the money back at any special time. Although you can't simply withdraw the cash surrender value from the policy—it has to be treated as a loan—in effect it's a withdrawal at your option because you don't ever have to pay it back. If you want to pay it back (and stop the interest meter from running), you can do it any time you want and in any size payments. You can pay it back all at once or a little at a time.

CAUTION

Although you have the flexibility of repaying the loan when you can afford to, delaying the repayment can have negative results. If you die before you pay back the loan, the insurance company simply subtracts the outstanding debt against the death benefit it will pay your beneficiaries. Of course, you won't be around to care, but you're reducing the protection you originally planned for your family.

USE YOUR RETIREMENT PLAN FOR A LOAN

For many people today, especially those who've stayed in the same job for a long time, retirement plans are a big chunk of their savings. If you or your employer have been contributing to your retirement account, you can tap into this resource without having to pay any current income tax on the retirement benefits. But the tax law has strict limits on loans from retirement plans, so be sure that you know the rules and follow them. If you don't keep the loan within these limits, you'll have to pay tax that you could have avoided.

Ken ran an antique business on a part-time basis while working full time in a Fortune 500 company. He started his business by taking a $60,000 loan from his company's 401(k) plan. Wouldn't you know, he was downsized out of a job just a few months after taking out the loan. To avoid immediate tax on the funds, he had to put the outstanding amount back into the 401(k) plan. To do this, he had to sell off some of his antique bric-a-brac at a serious loss.

If a retirement plan loan fits your situation, ask your plan administrator what your vested benefits in the plan are. Basically, vesting is a sly form of inden-tured servitude: The longer you stay in your job, the more of your own money you can have. Vested benefits are yours now; you wouldn't lose them if you left your job today. Your vested benefits affect the dollar amount you can borrow. The limit is 50 percent of your vested benefits or $50,000, whichever is less. Of course, any loans you've already taken from the plan and haven't repaid reduce the $50,000 limit.

Getting a loan from your plan is easy. All you have to do is ask the plan administrator (if you can find her between meetings). You don't have to complete any lengthy application forms or even tell your company you're taking the money to get out of their lousy job down the road. You just have to sign a loan agreement.

The interest rate on a retirement plan loan is usually low (lower than rates charged on commercial loans). What's more, you're really paying the interest back to yourself. So if you borrow $10,000 from your 401(k) plan to start a sideline business from home and pay 7 percent interest on the loan, the interest, along with your principal repayment, goes back into your own account.

CAUTION

You can only use a 401(k) loan if you continue to work for the same employer. The reason? If you leave your job, you have to pay off the loan. If you don't pay the loan, the money is a taxable distribution and, if you're less than 59½ years old, you'll also pay a 10 percent premature distribution penalty in addition to income tax on the distribution. If you hope to grow your sideline business into a full-time job, look for other ways to raise money to start your business.

You have to repay the loan in level amounts over a term of not more than five years. But, as you continue to build up money in your retirement plan (through additional contributions by you or your employer on your behalf), you can take additional loans (subject to the dollar limit explained earlier). This could go on for years, as long as you have the stamina to do two jobs!

The biggest reason not to take a loan from your retirement plan to start a sideline business is the fact that you'll be reducing that little retirement nest egg that was growing on a tax-deferred basis. Remember, you don't pay any current income tax on contributions to the plan. And earnings on those contributions are also tax deferred. But if you borrow those funds, there's less in the plan to earn income on. Your retirement plan account will be smaller at retirement time when you'd hoped to move to Florida and golf all day.

TIP

If you have a traditional IRA, you can't borrow from your account. A loan is treated like a distribution and you have to pay tax on it. But there's a way to use money in your IRA on a temporary basis without Uncle Sam biting you in the shorts. You can withdraw the funds and use them any way you want. However, there's a Cinderella clause: You have to put the money back into the IRA within 60 days or the distribution becomes taxable and you turn into a pumpkin. Still, this source of "borrowing" can be helpful in stopgap situations.

IS THIS LOAN DEDUCTIBLE?

If you borrow large sums, you're going to be paying high interest expenses. Are your interest payments deductible? You may already know that you can't deduct personal or consumer interest other than home mortgage interest (within limits). But just because you borrow from personal resources doesn't make the loan a personal loan. Interest is deductible if you use the money for business or investment. Here's how to test your loan for interest deductibility:

- **Business loans.** Interest is fully deductible. A business loan is one that you make only if you're protecting a trade or business. This can include the trade or business of being an employee of your company. So if you make a loan to your business primarily to protect your salary (your only source of income), interest on the loan is fully deductible as business interest.

- **Investment loans.** Interest is deductible up to the amount of your dividends, interest, and other investment income. Generally, loans to start a business are viewed as investment loans, not business loans. This is because you don't yet have a salary from the business that's worth protecting compared with the cash investment you've made.

- **Passive activity loans.** Interest is deductible only to the extent of passive activity income (income from other passive activities). Passive activities, in general terms, are businesses in which you don't participate on a day-to-day basis but, rather, are a silent partner. So this rule would limit interest deductions for any silent partner you bring in.

- **Retirement-plan loans.** Interest on a loan taken from your 401(k) or other retirement plan to invest in your business may not be deductible. The loan is treated like an investment loan so that interest is deductible only to the extent you have investment income, such as dividends and interest. (Even this break doesn't apply to key employees who borrow from their retirement plans.)

CAUTION

If you "borrow" from your IRA and fail to repay the funds within 60 days, you're taxed on all of it. If you're under the age of 59½, you're also gonna get hit with a 10 percent premature-distribution penalty.

WEIGHING YOUR OPTIONS

You don't have to pick one source for finding cash to start your business. You can take a little here, a little there, to put together the funds you need. The more planning you put into this process, the easier it will be to find the cash. You'll have the time to save at least some money so you won't have to borrow everything.

THE 30-SECOND RECAP

- Personal savings is the best kind of money to use.
- Borrow against your securities instead of selling them to raise cash.
- Credit card borrowing is the most expensive form of financing.
- Use your home equity for your business.
- Borrow from your retirement plan only if you're starting a sideline business.
- Interest on loans from your personal resources may be fully deductible, partially deductible, or not deductible at all.

Government Programs

Although it may not always seem that way, the government supports business. To do that, it's created a federal agency that's in the business of small business: the Small Business Administration (SBA). This section describes some of your options for obtaining funds from the government.

CAUTION

Your home and other property are at risk when you give your personal guarantee. If the business can't pay off the loan, the bank can sue you personally and try to get the money back from your personal assets.

FINDING AN SBA LOAN PROGRAM YOU CAN LOVE

The SBA has a variety of loan programs for small businesses. You may qualify for an SBA-guaranteed loan from a bank. One such program, called the LowDoc program (and for which the paperwork is minimal) may guarantee up to 80 percent of a loan of $100,000. Under other SBA programs, you may be able to obtain an SBA-guaranteed loan up to $500,000. Check out the SBA website at www.sba.gov for a more complete discussion of its loan programs and requirements to qualify.

You can't exactly get an SBA loan. That's because the SBA doesn't make loans. It sponsors loan programs. The loan programs work like this: Chase makes a loan, and the SBA guarantees a portion of that loan. The SBA guarantee for small loans (up to $100,000) is generally 80 percent of the loan. The percentage is 75 percent on larger loans and even less on some other loan programs. This means that the lender can't lose more than a small percentage of the money it has loaned out under the SBA loan program, so it's more generous with its money.

The SBA is constantly changing its loan programs and adding ones that are more helpful to current business needs. Here's a rundown of the SBA programs open to small businesses right now, which comes right from the sources at the SBA:

- **Basic 7(a) Loan Guaranty.** This program serves as the SBA's primary business loan program to help qualified small businesses obtain financing when they might not be eligible for business loans through normal lending channels. It is also the agency's most flexible business loan program, since financing under this program can be guaranteed for a variety of general business purposes.

    Loan proceeds can be used for most sound business purposes including working capital, machinery and equipment, furniture and fixtures, land and building (including purchase, renovation and new construction), leasehold improvements, and debt refinancing (under special conditions). Loan maturity is up to 10 years for working capital and generally up to 25 years for fixed assets.

    Typical customers are start-ups and existing small businesses. This program is delivered through commercial lending institutions.

- **Certified Development Company (CDC), a 504 Loan Program.** This program provides long-term, fixed-rate financing to small businesses to acquire real estate or machinery or equipment for expansion or modernization. Typically a 504 project includes a loan secured from a private-sector lender with a senior lien, a loan secured from a CDC (funded by a 100 percent SBA-guaranteed debenture) with a junior lien covering up to 40 percent of the total cost, and a contribution of at least 10 percent equity from the borrower. The maximum SBA debenture generally is $1 million (and up to $1.3 million in some cases).

Typical customers are small businesses requiring "brick and mortar" financing. These loans are delivered through Certified development companies (private, nonprofit corporations set up to contribute to the economic development of their communities or regions).

■ **Microloan, a 7(m) Loan Program.** This program provides short-term loans of up to $35,000 to small businesses and not-for-profit child-care centers for working capital or the purchase of inventory, supplies, furniture, fixtures, machinery and/or equipment. Proceeds cannot be used to pay existing debts or to purchase real estate. The SBA makes or guarantees a loan to an intermediary, who in turn, makes the microloan to the applicant. These organizations also provide management and technical assistance. The loans are not guaranteed by the SBA. The microloan program is available in selected locations in most states.

Typical customers are small businesses and not-for-profit child-care centers needing small-scale financing and technical assistance for start-up or expansion. This program is delivered through specially designated intermediary lenders (nonprofit organizations with experience in lending and in technical assistance).

■ **Loan Prequalification.** This program allows business applicants to have their loan applications for $250,000 or less analyzed and potentially sanctioned by the SBA before they are taken to lenders for consideration. The program focuses on the applicant's character, credit, experience and reliability rather than assets. An SBA-designated intermediary works with the business owner to review and strengthen the loan application. The review is based on key financial ratios, credit and business history, and the loan-request terms. The program is administered by the SBA's Office of Field Operations and SBA district offices.

Typical customers are designated small businesses and the program is delivered through nonprofit intermediaries such as small business development centers and certified development companies operating in specific geographic areas.

TIP

Find the right SBA loan program for you by calling the SBA at 1-800-827-5722. Also get loan program information on the Internet at www.sba.gov.

KNOWING WHEN YOU'RE SPECIAL

In addition to commercial banks that make loans under SBA-sponsored programs, there are special programs to explore. Small Business Investment Companies (SBICs) are privately managed firms licensed by the SBA to make loans to small businesses. Instead of straight loans where you pay back the money, these lending programs generally give the SBIC firms options to buy stock in your company. They may also involve something called convertible debentures—bonds that can be changed into stock under certain conditions.

TIP

To find one of the 175 SBICs across the country, contact the National Association of Small Business Investment Companies at 202-628-5055 or at www.nasbic.org, or through the SBA at www.sbaonline.sba.gov/INV. To find an SSBIC (also discussed in this section), call the National Association of Investment Companies (NAIC) at 202-204-3001 or at www.naicvc.com.

And if you're not confused by all these options yet, Specialized Small Business Investment Companies (SSBICs), also licensed by the SBA, make loans to businesses that are mostly owned by socially or economically disadvantaged individuals. Financing under the SSBICs generally involves only equity arrangements (you take them in as a partner); there are no straight loans.

SBA LOANS: CAN YOU MAKE THE GRADE?

Want an SBA loan? Here's what's required:

- **A "reasonable stake" in your business.** This is kind of a "hey, you first" approach: The SBA doesn't want to stand behind a loan to you if you haven't first put your own money into the business. You must have already invested between 25 percent and 50 percent of the amount you want to borrow. So, if you want to borrow $30,000, you have to sink between $7,500 and $15,000 into your business (depending on the lender and the loan program you want).

- **A good business plan.** Didn't I tell you a business plan was important? The SBA wants to be sure that you understand the business you're in and have thought things through so your business will succeed (and you'll repay the loan).

- **A good personal credit rating.** Because you have to give your personal guarantee for an SBA loan, you have to show that you aren't a deadbeat. The bank will run a credit report on you and include this information in your file for the SBA. The SBA may also look at your work history and even ask for letters of recommendation to back up your personal standing.

■ **A plan to repay the loan.** Just like any commercial loan, you have to show how you plan to repay the money you borrow. Your business plan should show that the business will have enough cash flow to make the monthly loan repayments.

GETTING A BREAK: WOMEN, MINORITIES, AND PEOPLE WITH DISABILITIES

Most bankers want you to fit a cookie-cutter mold, but here's where it pays to be different. A number of private loan programs are designed to encourage business ownership by women, minorities, and people with disabilities—groups that, until recently, were underrepresented in the business world. For example, in the past the National Association of Women Business Owners (NAWBO) joined with Wells Fargo Bank to offer loans to existing women-owned businesses that want money to expand. (For information, call 1-800-55-NAWBO or click on www.nawbo.org.)

The SBA used to have special loan programs for women, minorities, and people with disabilities, but it eliminated them several years ago. However, the SBA has an Office of Women's Business Ownership (www.sba.gov/womeninbusiness/index.html) that oversees more than 80 Women's Business Centers and the Online Women's Business Center (www.onlinewbc.gov).

THE 30-SECOND RECAP

■ Using a personal loan for your business is a less-complicated process than going for a commercial loan, but it's not necessarily the best loan for you.

■ Go to commercial banks that are eager to make small business loans.

■ Master the commercial loan application process so things will go smoothly for you.

■ The SBA doesn't make loans directly, but sponsors many different loan programs.

■ Some SBA-sponsored loans have easy applications and quick approval for small business.

Accounting and Finance Matters

Accounting 101

This section will help you understand the nitty-gritty of financial records and accounting methods—the kinds of records you need to keep and why. To accomplish this, we briefly cover some basic accounting principals and related terminology that you will be working with in your business. Think of accounting as a tool that you will use to determine the financial health of your business. Even if you plan to have an accountant take care of your books, no matter how large or small your business is, you still need to have a basic working knowledge of accounting—the terms, the process, and what the figures mean. It's the only way you'll be able to manage effectively and plan for continued growth and expansion.

Most businesses typically use one of two basic accounting methods in their bookkeeping systems: the cash method or the accrual method. Although most businesses use the accrual method, the best method for your company depends on your sales volume, whether you sell on credit, whether you have inventory, and what your business structure is. The following list summarizes the two systems and their differences:

- **The cash method.** This is the simplest of the two methods because the accounting is based on the actual flow of cash in and out of the business. Income is recorded when it is received, and expenses are recorded when they are actually paid. Many sole proprietors and businesses with no inventory use the cash method. From a tax standpoint, it is sometimes advantageous for a new business to use the cash method so that recording income can be put off until the next tax year, whereas expenses can be counted right away. That way, less income and more expenses can be reported at the end of your fiscal year, which means that your tax payment will be less.

- **The accrual method.** With the accrual method, income and expenses are recorded as transactions occur, whether or not cash has actually changed hands. An excellent example is a sale on credit. The sale is entered in the books when the invoice is generated rather than when the cash is collected. Likewise, an expense occurs when materials are ordered, not when the check is actually written. The downside of this method is that you pay income taxes on revenue before you have actually received it.

CAUTION

If you have inventory, you operate as a corporation, or your annual sales exceed $5 million, you are required to use the accrual method of accounting.

The accrual method is required if your business has inventory, if your annual sales exceed $5 million, or if you are structured as a corporation. It is also highly recommended for any business that sells on credit because it more accurately matches income and expenses during a given period.

SETTING UP AN ACCOUNTING SYSTEM

Whether you use the cash method or the accrual method of accounting, you must set up a system for keeping your financial records. Space allows only a brief summary of the basics. Debits, credits, and double-entry bookkeeping all are demystified in this handy guide. Included in this book are the steps for setting up a company's books the right way the first time, monitoring expenditures, creating budgets, paying taxes, and managing precious cash.

- **Chart of accounts.** To get started, you need to set up a chart of accounts. This is simply a list of the accounts that you want to track. Whether you decide to use a manual system or a software program, you can customize the chart of accounts to your business.

- **General ledger.** In the general ledger, you sum up all your business transactions. Every account that is on your chart of accounts will be included in your general ledger. The system used in recording entries on a general ledger is called a system of *debits and credits*.

PLAIN ENGLISH

Debit is a record of an indebtedness; specifically: an entry on the left-hand side of an account constituting an addition to an expense or asset account or a deduction from a revenue, net worth, or liability account.

All general ledger entries are double entries; the amount involved in every financial transaction (whether it's cash or a commitment) goes from one place to another. When you write a check to pay for materials, for example, the money flows out of your account (cash) into the hands of your supplier (an expense). When you sell goods on account, you record a sale (income), but you must have a journal entry to make sure that you collect that account later (an account receivable).

PLAIN ENGLISH

A **credit**, in accounting, is an accounting entry system that either decreases assets or increases liabilities.

- **Accounts receivable.** Money owed to you is recorded in *accounts receivable* and is tracked through an accounts receivable ledger. If you plan to sell goods or services on account, you will need a method of tracking what is owed you, by whom, how much is owed, and when it's due. This is where the accounts receivable come in. If you'll be accepting credit cards, the accounts receivable ledger is where you would record the amounts due from those credit card sales.

- **Accounts payable.** Money that you owe to others is tracked through the *accounts payable* ledger. Accounts payable is similar to that used to track accounts receivable. The difference is that accounts payable occur when you purchase inventory or other assets from a supplier. It's important to track accounts payable in a timely manner to ensure that you know how much you owe each supplier and when payment is due.

- **Fixed assets.** How much are your business's assets worth? Fixed assets are items that will be used in your business over the long term, generally five years or more. They are not bought and sold in the normal course of business operations. Fixed assets include vehicles, land, buildings, leasehold improvements, machinery, and equipment. The value of a fixed asset is based on the original purchase price minus *depreciation* (the decrease in value that occurs as the asset ages). The balance left is referred to as the *book value.*

PLAIN ENGLISH

Book value is an accounting term which usually refers to a business' historical cost of assets less liabilities. The book value of a stock is determined from a company's records by adding all assets (generally excluding such intangibles as goodwill), then deducting all debts and other liabilities, plus the liquidation price of any preferred stock issued. The sum arrived at is divided by the number of common shares outstanding and the result is the book value per common share. Book value of the assets of a company may have little or no significant relationship to market value.

- **Liquid assets.** Liquid assets include cash, stocks, bonds, inventory, or any other asset that can be converted into cash quickly.

- **Liabilities.** These are unpaid amounts of money that you owe. They are also referred to as accounts payable. Liabilities are usually broken down into either *short-term* liabilities (due within 12 months) or *long-term* liabilities (payable over several years or more).

- **Depreciation.** In an accrual system of accounting, fixed assets are not recorded when they're purchased; they're expensed over a period of time that coincides with the useful life of the item (the amount of time that the asset is expected to last). This process is known as *depreciation.*

In most cases, depreciation is easy to compute. The cost of the asset is divided by its useful life. For instance, a $50,000 piece of equipment with a 5-year useful life would be depreciated at a rate of $10,000 per year. This is known as straight-line depreciation.

Other more complicated methods of fixed-asset depreciation allow for accelerated depreciation on the front end, which is advantageous from a tax standpoint. You should seek the advice of your accountant before setting up depreciation schedules for fixed-asset purchases.

INVENTORY

Are you selling products? Then you'll need to keep track of inventory. Unless you're starting a service business, good inventory control will be a vital part of your bookkeeping system. If you are going to be producing (manufacturing) products, you must break inventory into categories.

TRACKING YOUR INVENTORY

You should establish separate inventory records for each of these categories: raw materials, works in process, and finished goods.

Whether you're a wholesaler or a retailer, you'll be selling many different types of inventory, and you'll need an effective system to track each inventory item offered for sale.

THE IMPORTANCE OF INVENTORY CONTROL

An up-to-date inventory control system will provide you with the following vital management information:

- Which items sell well, and which items are slow moving
- When to order more raw materials or more items
- Where in the warehouse the inventory is stored
- Length of time in the production process for each item
- A typical order by key customers
- Minimum inventory level needed to meet daily orders
- Cost of goods sold

A key reason to track inventory very closely is its direct relationship to the cost of goods sold. Because nearly all businesses that stock inventory are required to use the accrual method for accounting, accurate inventory records are a must for tracking the materials cost-associated with each item sold.

PAYROLL ACCOUNTING

If you have employees, you have to get a handle on payroll. Payroll accounting can be quite a challenge for the new business owner. Many federal and state laws regulate what you have to track related to payroll. Failure to do so could result in heavy fines, or worse. Many small business owners use outside payroll services that guarantee compliance with all applicable laws. If you choose to do your own payroll, it is highly recommended that you purchase an automated payroll system. Even if the rest of your books are done manually, an automated payroll system will help considerably with compliance. There is not a lot of margin for error when dealing with the federal government!

INCOME AND EXPENSES: PROFIT AND LOSS

Monitoring your income *and* expenses is vital to the growth of your business. Obviously, if income is not sufficient to cover expenses, unless the business owner injects new cash or borrows money, the business cannot continue to operate.

- **Income.** Income is money received from the sale of your products or services. Income is broken down into *unearned income* and *earned income.* The money received before the customer has taken full possession of the item purchased—for example, deposits for special orders—is *unearned income.* When the product or service has been delivered to the customer, income is then called *earned income* because the sale is now completed.

- **Cost of sales.** Cost-of-sales expenses are the costs directly linked to the production or sale of a product or service (raw materials, labor, packaging, and any other related expenses).

- **Gross profit.** This is the amount of money left after you cover your cost of sales. Income – Cost of sales = Gross profit. Out of the gross profit, you pay your operating expenses.

- **Operating expenses.** These are the expenses associated with running your company (utilities, rent, telephone, office supplies, wages, and so on).

- **Net profit (also called net income).** This is money left after all the operating expenses have been paid out of the gross profit, but before state or federal taxes have been paid (also called net *profit before taxes*).

TIP

Accounting periods are measurements of time, such as months, quarters, or years, that allow you to compare your company's financial reports from one period to another. For example, the first quarter of last year compared to the first quarter of this year will allow you to compare your company's performance for the first quarter period.

- **Net profit after taxes.** This is the "bottom-line" earnings of the business. It is computed by subtracting taxes paid from net profit.

- **Owner's equity.** This is the amount left when you subtract your liabilities from your assets.

- **Other income and expenses.** Other income and expenses represent those items that do not occur during the normal course of operation. For instance, a pottery maker does not normally earn income from rental property or interest on investments, so these income sources are accounted for separately. Interest expense on debt is also included in this category. A net figure is computed by subtracting other expenses from other income.

THE 30-SECOND RECAP

- Most businesses typically use one of two basic accounting methods in their bookkeeping systems: the cash method or the accrual method.

- Whether you use the cash method or the accrual method of accounting, you must set up a system for keeping your financial records.

- Unless you're starting a service business, good inventory control will be a vital part of your bookkeeping system.

- Monitoring your income *and* expenses is vital to the growth of your business.

Your Financial Statements

Financial statements give an indication of how financially healthy a business may be at one given moment in time.

The key to analyzing financial statements is to identify trends and find reasons behind the numbers. The secret to determining whether a business is healthy is to analyze several periods (years, if possible) to determine trends.

Trends tell the true financial picture behind every business entity. Companies that are particularly well run will possess an upward sloping trend line that rises with the economic health of the country. Businesses that are facing financial problems will have a downward sloping trend line that shows a performance that is less than the current economic condition would indicate.

Because every business can be faced with an adverse situation at any particular time, it is important to get as much historical information as possible on an entity. To do this, every manager needs to possess a basic understanding of financial statements and the direction these statements show that the business is headed.

RECORD-KEEPING AND REPORTING

The main financial statements that every business owner should monitor on a regular basis are the income statement, the balance sheet, and the cash-flow analysis statement. These three statements will provide you with all the vital financial information you need to make good management decisions.

TIP
You'll find the cash-flow statement to be an invaluable tool in understanding the how and why of cash flowing into and out of your business. For more information and examples of the financial statements mentioned, read *The Complete Idiot's Guide to Starting Your Own Business, Fourth Edition*, by Ed Paulson (Alpha Books, 2004).

Financial statements simply help you monitor your financial resources—to ensure that you are making more money than you are spending. They are a critical component in your decision-making process.

Financial statements use a system called double-entry bookkeeping. This system requires the use of accounts called debits and credits. A debit is an item that is placed on the left-hand side of an account. A credit is placed on the right-hand side of an account. Every time a debit is recorded on a set of financial statements, a corresponding credit must be recorded for the same amount on the financial statement. By following this procedure, the corporate books are said to be in balance because debits must always equal credits.

There are four primary financial statements:

- The balance sheet
- The income statement
- The cash-flow statement
- The statement of changes in stockholders' equity

THE BALANCE SHEET

The balance sheet provides information concerning your company's assets, liabilities, and owner's equity. A typical balance sheet will have assets on the left side and liabilities and owner's equity on the right. Assets are accounts that list what is owned by the business. These accounts are broken down into short-term assets and long-term assets. Short-term assets are assets that can be converted to cash in less than one year's time. Long-term assets are assets that have an expected life greater than one year. An example of a long-term asset would be a building. Buildings are constructed to last for many years, and, therefore, the benefit of the building will continue for years into the future.

TIP

The common-size balance sheet is a valuable tool for financial analysis. The total assets are set equal to 100 percent with all assets listed as a percentage of these total assets. On the right side of the balance sheet, the account labeled "Total Liabilities and Equity" is set equal to 100 percent. All liability and equity accounts are then represented as the appropriate percent of the total liabilities and equity. This statement helps analyze the distribution of various accounts on the balance sheet. Of particular interest on the asset side are the percentages of total assets comprised by cash, inventory, and accounts receivable.

Liabilities are obligations to creditors that the company has acquired throughout the normal course of business. Like assets, they can be broken down to short- and long-term obligations. Typical short-term obligations would be acquiring goods or services on credit. Businesses are generally extended credit terms that provide 30 days or more to pay for current obligations. This type of credit is normally listed on the balance sheet as an account payable.

Companies are also granted credit for more than one year if the credit is being used to finance an item that may last for more than one year. If a company takes out a mortgage to finance a building, this loan would normally be granted for a number of years because the underlying asset being financed has a life expectancy of more than one year (similar to an individual purchasing a home).

Owner's equity is the final group of accounts on the balance sheet. As the title indicates, these are accounts that deal with the net worth of a business. This net worth is the difference between the assets and liabilities of a company and shows how much of the assets are being financed by the owners as opposed to how much is financed by the creditors (liabilities).

The balance sheet is a snapshot in time. This provides a picture of the company's financial position on the date stated. Balance sheets contain all the company's permanent accounts. Unlike income statements these account balances are carried from period to period and year to year. The balance sheet is generated by a business at least once a month. Many of the accounts on the balance sheet are reviewed and analyzed more than once a month because of their vital importance to running a business.

Current assets include the following:

- Cash
- Accounts receivable
- Inventory
- Prepaid expenses

TIP

Remember that you can read the footnotes in financial statements to get clarification of the firm's numbers.

Long-term assets include the following:

- Plant and equipment
- Land and buildings
- Accumulated depreciation

Cash is the first asset listed on the balance sheet. It is the most vital component on the company's balance sheet because it is the means by which a company can pay for supplies, meet its payroll, and invest in assets that can help the company generate income.

The designers of financial statements constructed all statements to list and group accounts by order of liquidity. Cash is the most liquid asset because it is already in a medium of exchange that is widely accepted. After a company's cash accounts are listed on its balance sheet, the next item in order of liquidity would be accounts receivables. These are obligations owed to the firm by individuals or companies that have been extended credit on account.

All assets are listed on a balance sheet at historic or purchase price value unless the asset has been *impaired*. Inventory is an example of an asset that can be impaired. Because inventory is acquired and then stored until consumed or sold, you run the risk that it may become damaged or obsolete. Under current accounting rules when this happens the asset must be recorded at the lower cost or market price. In other words, if the cost for an inventory item is $10 and subsequent to use or sale it has been determined that it is only worth $5, this item must be reduced to the lower value on the balance sheet.

Short-term liabilities include the following:

- Accounts payable
- Accrued expenses
- Short-term debt
- Income tax payable

Long-term liabilities include the following:

- Mortgage payable
- Long-term debt

Short-term liabilities are obligations that the company must repay in less than one year's time. Often times these liabilities are due in 30 days or less. Accrued expenses are expenses the business has incurred but has not yet been presented with an invoice to pay. A company wants to make sure all its known liabilities have been recorded as quickly as possible. By doing this, it is able to show a clearer picture of its financial health sooner to internal management, creditors, and owners of the business.

Stockholders' equity includes the following:

- Capital stock
- Additional paid in capital
- Retained earnings

Capital stock is the face value of the number of shares of company stock the company has outstanding multiplied times the par or stated value of the stock. Normally when you review a financial statement this shows up as a very small number because the stock may have a value of one dollar per share or one cent per share. However, one of the most common ways stock is shown on a financial statement is at no par value. By doing this, the company is saying they have not assigned any monetary value to their stock. When they receive money for their outstanding stock they list only a small portion of this money being paid for the stock and the remainder of this money is recorded as *additional paid-in capital.* Additional paid-in capital is the difference between the face value of a share of stock and the price a buyer actually pays for the stock from the company.

TIP

Flash reports can be helpful in making operational decisions. These are quick internal reports. Many companies use them to report sales on a daily basis, cash in the bank, or inventory positions. They should be used in combination with financial statements because the flash reports are not as accurate.

Retained earnings are prior earnings the company has generated that they have decided to retain in the business to help it grow. Often a portion of a company's earnings is returned to the stockholders in the form of a dividend. Companies that pay a dividend generally distribute these dividends quarterly.

To completely understand the balance sheet, you must understand the basic formula. This formula is as follows:

Assets = Liabilities + Net worth

THE INCOME STATEMENT

The income statement provides a picture of the company's financial performance over a specified period of time. This statement depicts the income generated and the expenses incurred by the firm during this period—painting a picture of how the company got to the point of the balance sheet. This cycle, which is one year in length, can follow a calendar year or use another yearly time period (which is referred to as a *fiscal year*). An example of a fiscal period would be February 1 to January 31 of each year.

PLAIN ENGLISH

Fiscal year is the declared accounting year for a company, but it is not necessarily in conformance to a calendar year (January through December). However, it does cover twelve months, 52 weeks, 365 days. The U.S. Government fiscal year ends September 30, for example. October 1 through September 30 is their fiscal or accounting year.

Bottom line: The income statement tells you if there is a profit or loss as a result of the year's operations. Net income (commonly referred to as a profit) occurs when revenue exceeds expenses. There is a net loss when the expenses exceed the revenue.

The cash accounting method does not recognize items that are prepaid or accrued. Revenues are reported in the period in which they are paid. For example, sales made in March but paid for in May would be reported as revenue in May in the cash accounting method.

The same is true of expenses. They are reported in the accounting period in which they are actually paid. For example, if you bought a copy machine for your department in October, but it was not paid for until December, the expense would not be booked until December under the cash accounting method.

Accrual accounting records income and expenses when they occur. The accounting principle this follows is called the matching principle. The matching principle requires expenses to be matched or recorded against the revenue the expenses helped to generate. By recording these accruals at that time, a clearer picture of the profitability can be shown to internal and external users of the financial statements.

Most larger companies use the accrual method. Small businesses generally opt for the cash accounting method because they usually do not have many significant deferred or accrued items to materially impact their financial statements.

The three choices when accounting for inventory are as follows:

- **LIFO (Last In, First Out).** The principal behind LIFO is that the last items going into inventory will be the first items sold out of inventory. This method came about when inflation was running at very high levels. By matching the last items into inventory against the selling price, less profit was recorded during inflation; therefore, less tax was being paid. LIFO will also better reflect replacement cost for inventory.
- **FIFO (First In, First Out).** This method states that the first items into inventory will be the first items out of inventory. This method is more widely accepted than the LIFO method.
- **Weighted average.** This method does not look at the time the inventory was received. It looks at the total value of the inventory and determines an average price based upon all the items in the current inventory.

During periods of rising prices, LIFO offers a tax advantage to its users. LIFO assigns the most recently purchased items to cost of goods sold (which impacts profit and loss). The weighted average inventory method would be used when price levels are stable and you are trying to use a more uniform price for your cost of goods sold.

TIP

Improved efficiency in managing inventory can positively impact the company's cash position. Lower inventory levels mean less cash is invested in inventory. Yet care must be taken to ensure that sufficient inventory levels are on hand to meet customer needs. Just-in-time (JIT) inventory methods have helped to better manage inventory levels by ensuring that appropriate amounts are on hand when needed. A JIT supplier is responsible for delivering goods just when they are needed and in the amounts in which they are needed. This reduces inventory-carrying costs for the firm, because they are getting the goods exactly when they want to use them and do not have to store the goods.

THE CASH-FLOW STATEMENT

The cash-flow statement reflects the cash position of the firm. It starts by listing cash at the beginning of the fiscal period, and then shows how cash was generated and used by a business. That is, this statement details the sources and uses of cash.

The general formula utilized in the cash-flow statement is this:

Cash inflows – Cash outflows = Net change in cash

The terminology *cash sources* (inflows) and *cash uses* (outflows) may be used in this statement. Sources of cash include noncash expenses such as *depreciation* and *amortization*. Depreciation and amortization are expenses booked against current operations that have been paid for in a prior period. Other sources of cash are net profits, positive changes in assets and liabilities, and company borrowings. Uses of cash include purchases of long-term assets, net losses, loan paybacks, and dividends paid to stockholders.

PLAIN ENGLISH

Depreciation is the amount of expense charged against earnings by a company to write off the cost of a plant or machine over its useful live, giving consideration to wear and tear, obsolescence, and salvage value.

The cash-flow statement was not standard accounting practice until the 1980s. As companies began to realize the importance of cash, the cash-flow statement kept growing to greater value by people reading financial statements. Financial statement users quickly realized that a company that could not internally generate enough cash to fund operations would have to look to outside sources to keep itself running. Realizing that capital markets and lenders can be fickle caused the truly wise investor to focus in on the cash-generating operations of the business.

PLAIN ENGLISH

Amortization is the process of spreading the cost of an intangible asset over the expected useful life of the asset. For example: a company pays $100,000 for a patent, they amortize the cost over the 16 year useful life of the patent.

The Statement of Changes in Stockholders' Equity

The statement of changes in stockholders' equity reconciles the net worth of the business and provides an analysis of the change in that net worth. This statement tracks the net worth of the owners of the business beginning with their initial investments and adjusting for changes to these investments.

Items recorded on this statement would be net profit or net loss, the company selling additional shares of its stock to investors, and repurchases by the company of its own stock. (These transactions are called treasury stock transactions.) Dividends would also be recorded on this statement.

TIP

If you were a potential investor, the statement of changes in stockholders' equity would be a good place to look. It would provide an insight into the changes to your investment over time.

Financial Ratios

Financial ratios are used to provide insight into how effectively the company is being managed. Financial ratios measure the relationship of one item to another in a mathematical expression. For the ratio to have any significance, a relationship must exist between the two figures you are measuring. Even after you have determined that a relationship exists, you must still do further analysis to determine the full impact of this relationship and how it hurts or helps your company.

A number of different types of ratios are utilized to examine different components of the financial statements.

CAUTION

Using any one financial ratio as an indicator is insufficient in painting a picture of the company's financial position. One ratio tells you very little. You need to use these ratios in combination with others.

Liquidity ratios provide an indication of the company's ability to pay its short-term debts. They examine the relationship of current assets to current liabilities.

The *current ratio* is one of the most popular ratios that companies use. This is the ratio of current assets to current liabilities. If the current ratio is 1:1, there is $1 in assets existing to pay $1 in debt.

This ratio should be at least 2:1 for a comfortable level. When the current ratio is less than one, the business cannot generate enough cash flow to meet its current obligations. This is obviously a dangerous position for the company to be in.

This ratio does have a major disadvantage to be considered. This number is generated with no regard to the timing of current assets. It may, therefore, distort the financial position of the firm.

The *quick ratio* uses "quick assets" as opposed to all current assets in the current ratio. The ratio specifically excludes inventories. The quick ratio is generated as follows:

Cash + Accounts receivables = Current liabilities

TIP

Inventories are excluded from the quick assets because turning over inventory quickly would mean making significant price concessions that would negatively impact the financial position of the firm.

This ratio provides an indication of the company's ability to quickly pay their bills. A 1:1 ratio is considered good for most firms.

Receivables turn is the speed at which receivables are collected; the ratio is generated by dividing sales by accounts receivables. This provides the number of times that accounts receivables are turned in a specified period of time. Ideally, you want a faster turn to make cash available more quickly.

Payables turn is the speed at which the business is paying its bills; it's generated by dividing the cost of goods sold by the accounts payables.

Debt to equity is simply the ratio of the firm's debt to equity. That is, the ratio of the company funds from owners to those from lenders. The range considered good is between 1:1 and 4:1. The larger ratios indicate greater risk to those lending money to the business. Greater risk to a lender will lead to a firm paying more for the credit it is extended.

THE IMPORTANCE OF BUDGETING

Budgeting is a tool used to control the business. This involves measuring the firm's actual performance against the expected performance. Generally, the current period's actual performance is compared against last year's actual performance and the current period's budget.

TIP

Zero-based budgeting (ZBB) begins the budgeting process at zero and builds each line item from this point. In ZBB, it is not acceptable to use last year's figures and add a predetermined amount.

The budgeting process is important for every size organization—no matter how small or large. Budgeting runs the gamut from simple to complicated. The budget is a powerful tool (if used appropriately) in the planning function. Budgeting makes sure that you are moving toward your plan. It is a check, if you will, that you are moving in the right direction.

The same accounting systems that provide the information to generate financial statements provide the information for the budgeting process. The budgets determine what financial resources you have at your disposal.

The budgeting process is identified as a "game" in American business. Just as in the game of chess, there are some standard "moves." The most common tactic is to pad expenses (with more than you really need) to ensure coming in under budget. This can be varied to ask for more line items than you really want (so you can "sacrifice" some and be seen as a good guy).

Historical data is usually the starting point for your projections. You must take the past into consideration when making decisions about the future. To smooth the way for the budgeting process, consider these tips:

- Solicit input from your employees.
- Review past budgets and actual performance trends.
- Use your discretion to fine-tune the numbers.
- Review a draft to ensure it makes sense and is complete.

CAUTION

It is important to consider GIGO when developing budgets. That is, garbage in, garbage out. The quality of information you use for input will impact the quality of your budget. Take care to use the best data possible.

Monitoring your budget enables you to identify variances and then take corrective action. This can make the difference between having a good reputation (and recognition) and a bad reputation. When there are early signs that your budget is getting out of line, you may need to take some actions, such as watching your discretionary expenses, freezing new hires or delaying any noncritical projects.

OPEN-BOOK MANAGEMENT

Open-book management has become more popular in the last decade. This is the process of opening up the operating numbers to the employees of the company. Although some companies tend to shroud the financial performance of the firm in secrecy, those using open-book management keep their employees informed. They try to expand the stake of the employees in the business.

This ownership culture is an attempt to assist the employees in understanding the performance of the firm.

The basic foundation of the effective use of open-book management is to ensure that employees and managers see themselves as playing on the same team in a cooperative relationship—versus an adversarial relationship.

Only by understanding the financial position of the company can employees make better decisions concerning their contributions to the company's profitability. Secrecy concerning financial performance makes it more difficult for employees to make this connection to better contribute.

But just providing information is not enough. Employees must be taught how to read and use this information. The tools for understanding the information they are being provided are essential. An internal training program is a key component of effective open-book management.

All bonus systems should be tied directly to the financials. This is even more of an incentive for employees to learn what the numbers mean and how they are read.

You have a big role in open-book management. You must let go and empower employees to act—giving them opportunities to improve their area's financial performance. But accountability must accompany this empowerment. Employees are accountable for their performance and should also be included, therefore, in the development of forecasts (or projections).

Part of open-book management is displaying results and openly sharing this information. As good performance is widely publicized and celebrated; poor performance should be addressed jointly (by management and employees) to develop a plan for corrective action.

TIP

Many companies are using scoreboards to monitor the progress of units toward their goals. Specific measures are selected and then posted to keep employees aware of progress. Typical goals include monthly units sold, days without an accident, number of shipments per week, etc.

Open-book management doesn't necessarily mean that all financial data must be disclosed to employees. There are degrees of disclosure that can still be successful in getting employees onboard. The key is to begin to divulge some financial information and then educate employees as to what this information means.

THE 30-SECOND RECAP

- The key to analyzing financial statements is to identify trends and find reasons behind the numbers.
- Even if an accountant handles your books, no matter how large or small your company is, your business will run better if you understand its accounting system.
- One of many good reasons to track inventory very closely is that it can tell you the cost of goods sold.
- For efficient management and planning, the three key financial statements that you need to review carefully are the income statement (P&L), the balance sheet, and the cash-flow statement.
- The balance sheet lists assets on the left and liabilities and owner's equity on the right.
- The income statement depicts the income generated, the expenses incurred, and provides a picture of the company's financial performance over a specified period of time.
- The cash-flow statement reflects the cash position of the firm.
- The current ratio is a liquidity ratio that examines the relationship between current assets and current liabilities.
- Open-book management opens up the financial books of the firm to expand the stake of the employees in the business.

Hiring Your Advisors

Business is a team sport, so begin yours with a strong, supportive team of advisors. Some of the team members will be paid, whereas others will provide solid advice for free.

Your team will be made up of men and women with expertise in different aspects of business and tax law. Their knowledge and guidance can be invaluable. However, do not forget for one moment that you are in charge. No one on your team should tell you what to do. People on your team can offer options and discuss consequences, but only you can determine what your best business decision is. So you will have to do some homework to be as competent as possible in taking charge.

This section examines how to put together a good team and what kind of experts you should sign on. Here are the possible team members you may need to recruit, perhaps not all at once, but at some point along the way: lawyer, accountant, insurance broker, real estate or leasing broker, computer consultant, financial planner, and other business owners.

SELECTING THE RIGHT ACCOUNTING SERVICES

First we look at some of the differences in accounting services, which will help you select the right one—maybe even at the right price. Remember, accountants are not bookkeepers. You have to supply them with all the figures that they need to prepare financial statements and tax returns. If they do offer bookkeeping services, they charge accordingly.

An accountant can help you understand your total financial picture. A professional can assist you in your business planning by helping you understand such things as the tax implications of the type of business structure you select, and whether you should buy or lease a vehicle, a computer, or other business equipment.

If you require business financing, your accountant can prepare the financial statements and support documentation required by your bank. Accountants can be invaluable in helping you structure your business to take advantage of all the possible tax benefits.

Most small and home-based businesses do not require the full-time services of an accountant, and owners find that their accountants are best used (after assisting with the business start-up) to help them take steps to minimize their tax bills and to prepare their tax returns.

What Accounting Services Are Available?

You must have an accountant because you must have a clear picture of your business financial position—and a bookkeeper can't do more than provide bare numbers.

Here is a brief list of accountant services:

- Set up the books
- Provide monthly, quarterly, and annual financial statements
- Project future earnings
- Suggest cost savings
- Prepare the tax forms and suggest tax deductions and credits
- File a protest for property tax valuations

CAUTION

Any accountant who has been suspended for misconduct in the past may have reformed, but you should probably look elsewhere.

Several levels and types of accounting services are available, including these:

- **Certified public accountants (CPAs).** These accountants are licensed by the state, have a four-year college degree, and, as a result, usually charge more. Most CPAs tend to specialize in corporate work, so be careful—they may not be the best choice for a small or home-based business. A CPA can prepare your financial statements, produce your quarterly reports, do your taxes, and assist in your business financial and tax planning.
- **Public accountants.** These pros offer the same services as a CPA. They usually charge less and offer a full range of accounting and tax services.
- **IRS enrolled agents (EAs).** EAs are licensed by the Treasury Department. They are qualified to handle complex tax issues, prepare annual tax returns, and represent you before the IRS (the same as a CPA can). They may be the best choice for your annual tax filing. EAs cost less than other accountants but are probably the most educated in the complex tax rules and regulations that a business has to deal with. You can get a list of EAs for your area by calling 1-800-424-4339.
- **Tax preparers.** These experts are best used for personal income tax returns only. You need to seek out the most qualified tax specialist possible to make sure that you take full advantage of the tax deductions available to you under the law.

■ **Payroll services.** These companies handle all your payroll record-keeping, prepare all the reports in a timely manner, and send them to you ready to sign and send in.

■ **Bookkeeping services.** These services are available for small businesses to track where your money is coming from and going to, and to get all the numbers plugged into the right accounts with the proper values. They also offer payroll services and your choice of quarterly or annual financial statements.

TIP

Visit the American Accounting Association website at www.rutgers. edu/Accounting/raw/aaa/index.html. You can use this site to locate the regional group serving your area, and then contact the group if you need a referral.

■ **CPA Finder: www.cpafinder.com.** This service focuses on connecting businesses with accountants, utilizing a database categorized by state.

CUTTING ACCOUNTING COSTS

The big question is this (and now you have to be truly honest): Are you the type of person who will take charge of your accounting and keep good, up-to-date records, or is a shoebox stuffed with receipts and invoices more your style? When was the last time you did your personal bank statement reconciliation? Have you ever bothered to prepare a family budget to track where all your money goes? Okay, you get the idea.

If you know deep down that crunching numbers is not your forte, you should plan to hire someone to take care of that responsibility. This is an area that, if left unattended, will certainly spell disaster for your plan to develop a successful business.

If you opt to keep track of your own financial records, doing it with a computer and accounting software is the way to go. In that case, you may need only the services of a good tax accountant, so you'll spend less. But whether doing your own accounting or spending the money makes sense for you as an individual is your decision to make.

TIP

Accountants specialize just as attorneys do. Accounting firms may have one partner who provides your financial reports, whereas another may prepare small business tax returns.

What is in the past (financially speaking) may be prologue to the future (financial success). If your financial records are properly set up, you will have a firm base to project future growth. Your accountant should be able to advise you on the financial aspects of business proposals. If you want to expand into another market, product, or service line, the project revenue must at least meet projected costs. Nothing is certain, but sound financial planning is a must.

Business taxes seem to come in incessant and innumerable forms. We often focus on federal income taxes, which do snatch too much of our business profits. If you have an accountant prepare your business (and personal) returns, he or she can spot tax savings hiding in the labyrinth of the Internal Revenue code. Large companies hire accountants to discover the breaks and keep Uncle's share down. You should do likewise.

If your business owns inventory, equipment, or real estate, the state or local assessor will hit you with a property tax. If your accountant doesn't advise on these taxes, ask him or her to suggest someone who does. Your accountant may suggest that you protest the valuation, or show you deductions not previously taken. If your accountant's fee is less than the taxes saved, you're ahead (and the fees are deductible).

Small accounting firms may fit your needs better than the larger, more expensive firms, but the big four (or whatever mergers have reduced them to) are catering more to small businesses. Check with other small business owners to find out who they use, or if you are a member of a business association, choose an accountant it recommends. If you have a specialized business, such as construction or a restaurant, choose an accountant who is familiar with your business.

INSURING AGAINST THE RISKS

Your business may be underinsured, and most certainly you have less life insurance than you need. Risks are part of life and business; some just have to be endured, like a tax increase, whereas others may be insured against, like fire or casualty.

Your insurance agent or underwriter can advise you on policies for …

- Medical and dental health for you and your employees
- Disability
- Death
- Property damage
- Liability
- Workers' compensation
- Business continuation

Most employers provide some health insurance for their employees (and the self-employed). Costs are high and coverage varies considerably. You need to find an insurance company that you can trust to pay the medical expenses. Compare costs. Consult your business association to see if it participates in a plan that is available to member companies.

If you or an employee becomes physically disabled, you don't want to rely solely on Social Security. Consider disability insurance to protect future earnings. Finding an affordable policy is the key, so consult with a good insurance broker who will suggest options that are affordable.

Group term life insurance should be part of any employee fringe benefit. The cost is relatively low; the premiums paid by the employer are a deductible expense, and coverage up to $50,000 is not taxable to the employee. If there are business co-owners, you should have a life insurance policy to fund the business buy-sell agreement.

Fire, theft, tornado, and assorted calamities could strike with unerring accuracy. You can't afford not to protect yourself. You need an affordable policy for the reasonable risks, and an insurance agent who will ensure that all of your assets are continually reviewed to assess their value. Insuring a building at its original cost, not for its replacement cost, may be a fatal mistake.

And don't forget to discuss business-continuation insurance with your underwriter. While the destroyed building is being rebuilt, probably very little business can be conducted. To cover this forced inactivity, consider purchasing business continuation insurance to replace some of the revenue lost and enable you to continue paying key employees.

Employees do the darndest things, like running red lights and smashing into another car, or slipping on the shop floor and breaking a leg. Your company may be liable in either event. The law requires the employer to be financially responsible for employee negligence while on the job. Likewise, the workers' compensation laws make the employer liable for workplace injuries, even if the employee or fellow employee's negligence caused the injury.

The insurance agent who takes care of your personal insurance (such as auto and life insurance) may be just the person for you, but not the one for your business. Shop around. Check with other small business owners or your business association. Insurance premiums can be a huge expense, so choose wisely.

TIP

Use an insurance agent who is familiar with the needs of a small business and is prompt in attending to those needs. Personal attention is critical when you need a check to replace your burnt inventory.

BANKING ON YOU TO SUCCEED

Your business probably will need to borrow money, and bankers (or other lending institutions) have the line of credit that may tide you over when there are cash-flow dams.

Unfortunately, many bankers view you as the supplicant, risking their money on a speculative adventure. Contrast this attitude with bank credit cards. Credit worthy or not, credit card companies are ready to let you realize your every desire with plastic.

Find a banker who specializes in small business loans, and has been with the bank for some time. And find a bank that wants your business. After all, you are paying interest for the privilege of using the money, and probably putting up collateral, and personally guaranteeing the loan. Your banker should be more than a cash machine. The banker should work with your accountant to determine your cash needs, for now and in the expandable future when you double or treble your business. Part 4 discusses how to select the right banker in greater detail.

BROKERING THE REALTY

If you work out of your house and intend to continue with your home office, you need read no further. However, for the rest of you who are planning to work in a different location, consider hiring a commercial real estate broker to help you purchase or lease your business home.

The commercial real estate broker can assist you in ...

- Finding the building and negotiating a purchase agreement.
- Finding the right location and negotiating a favorable lease.

Buying a building for your business is a huge investment. You need to determine if it is in the right location and if it can be bought at the right price. Negotiating over the price and terms of the contract may be difficult. Some of us are blessed with the ability to cut a great deal; others shy away from confrontation. Certainly if you are the latter, consider hiring a real estate broker to help you.

The broker should know the going price of property. You could save more than the broker's fee if you obtain a price that is considerably less than the initial listing. The broker will help you draft a contract that is favorable to you. For example, it may be typical that the buyer pay the second half of the semiannual installment of property taxes after the closing; your broker may convince the seller that the best way to close the deal is to pay the entire year's property taxes. Or the broker may convince the seller to reduce the price because you will need to extensively remodel the building, and you have only so much money.

TIP

You might want to ask your banker for a recommendation of an attorney or accountant. Particularly in smaller communities, the bankers get to know who works and who doesn't.

If you think you might want to lease, keep in mind that the rent per square foot may be just part of the cost of leasing. The landlord might want additional rent as a percentage of your gross sales. Negotiating that percentage downward can mean a great savings on future revenue. If the landlord is eager to have you as a tenant, the landlord might be willing to foot some of the renovation costs. The landlord's lease was no doubt drafted by the landlord's attorney. Even so, your broker should be able to negotiate more favorable terms for you. For example, the landlord might exclude all its liability for *anything* that goes wrong in the building after you occupy it. However, your broker would probably insist that the landlord be liable for its own negligence, so if its employee causes a power outage, the landlord would be responsible for your lost sales.

You and the real estate broker will enter into a contract, which will specify the broker's duties and fee. Check with other business owners or bankers to see whether the fee is reasonable and the broker is reliable.

Computer Sourcing

This book was written on a computer, and was edited through e-mail attachments. Some of us can use word processing and that's about all, whereas others are maestros at the computer. If you lean toward the former, or are in the middle of the computer pack, consider seeking advice from a computer expert.

You need computers to run your business, from writing business letters to controlling inventory, and from sending e-mail to conducting e-commerce. Unless you have a talented computer whiz on staff, and can keep that whiz kid challenged, consider hiring a computer consultant. The changes in hardware and software are rapid and mind-boggling. You have a business to run, so let an expert advise you on obtaining the best computer equipment and software, at a favorable price, that fits your needs.

TIP

Computer consultants often speak a variant of English that is understood only by other consultants. If your consultant is one of this breed, avoid him or her. You must know what you are getting for your money and how it will be integrated into your business.

Running a website is common for many businesses, and you, too, may need one to gain new customers and retain old ones. E-commerce changes the marketing and selling of goods and services, and you can't ride its wave unless you have expert advice. The website must be easily accessed, attractive, and functional. A site must be interesting, which means more than a listing of your products and services, but too many pictures make downloading a chore. If the customer is going to buy from you, the sales process must be quick and painless, and the merchandise must be what the customer wants. Moreover, the site must be updated frequently.

Seek referrals from other business owners who have used a computer consultant they believe is really good. Bugs are inevitable in any system, so find out if the consultant who is recommended stayed around to squash the bugs as they appeared. Advice is what you are buying from the consultant, and the other business owners will tell you whether they got their money's worth. Heed their advice.

Investing the Cash

You need to plan for your success. Then, when you succeed and start showing a profit beyond what you ever expected, you should start success planning. The money you have made should be working as hard as you are. Here's where a financial planner can help.

A financial planner should help you with the following:

- Investing your spare cash
- Reviewing current and projected future financial needs
- Recommending estate planning

Most banks aren't generous with their interest on savings accounts or CDs. Some stocks have spectacular ascents, and often, equally dramatic descents. You run a business that requires your full attention, so let an expert advise you on the best way to use your money. But set guidelines. If you just want a reasonable return, not a killing in the market, make that clear to your investment advisor, and put it in writing.

The financial planner should examine your income and expenses and suggest ways to increase the former, and decrease the latter. You may have a spouse, several children, and a few pets who depend on you. If you have dependents, the advisor should suggest life insurance to protect them from your loss. An Individual Retirement Account (IRA) or pension contribution should be part of any financial plan; the sooner you begin, the more money will be available upon retirement.

Years have a way of moving into decades, and we get older a lot quicker than we thought possible. Most of us don't even have a Last Will and Testament. The financial planner won't draft your will or living trust, but he or she will suggest you see a lawyer, and do it now. If you have not properly planned your estate, the state will dictate who gets what. Enough said.

Virtually anyone can be a financial planner, so beware of labels. Your attorney may be able to suggest a planner that he or she has worked with, or another business owner may be able to refer you to one. Discuss the planner's fee. If it is based upon other products or services you buy, go elsewhere because he or she is selling, not advising.

RETIRED PROS PLAYING FOR YOU

Small business owners who have retired are often eager to impart their wisdom to beginners. They have been through the good times and bad. Business war stories can be more than just reminiscing; they can contain valuable advice. In the computer age, we often look down on those who relied on the typewriter. But technology isn't everything—people problems really haven't changed all that much, and selling still requires getting the interest of a buyer.

Retired businesspersons are in your neighborhood, often sitting next to you in your house of worship, or are members of a local civic organization. There may be a local association of retired business executives that you can contact for their services. Get to know them, and don't be hesitant to talk business. Your problem may be one that they can solve.

You may receive some excellent advice for free, which is always the right price. But consider paying a modest retainer. That will make you feel better about asking the person for help. Or, if the person will not take a fee, suggest making a contribution to his or her favorite charity.

HELPFUL SOURCES

You can obtain a great deal of valuable information on your own. The federal government's websites are good sources. For example, the Small Business Administration (www.sba.gov) provides various pamphlets related to starting and operating a business. The Equal Employment Opportunity Commission (www.eeoc.gov) is an excellent site for employment law guidelines. Tax information is readily available from the IRS (www.irs.ustreas.gov). If you want to trademark your product, visit the Trademark Office (www.pto.gov). State and local governments have websites that you can visit to look up a law or municipal code, or find the appropriate forms and related instructions you need to obtain a license.

Many law firms, accounting firms, insurance companies, and real estate brokers have websites that can help you. Several companies have developed software that you can use to develop business plans, design websites, and manage your finances.

And don't forget your local library. Books can advise you for no cost but the time invested to read them.

THE 30-SECOND RECAP

- An accountant should set up your books and provide periodic financial statements.

- Protect your assets with adequate casualty and liability insurance.

- Computer consultants can improve your bottom line.

- Seek the advice of retired business owners who have the experience.

- Two methods of accounting exist: the cash basis and the accrual method; the accrual method is required if your business has inventory, if your annual sales exceed $5 million, or if you're structured as a corporation.

Extending Credit and Collecting from a Reluctant Customer

This section could have been titled "Creditor's Rights." If you extend credit, your risks and rights are important to your business success. Accounts receivable receipts don't mean much until they are turned into cash. We'll also look at the downside—your debtor's bankruptcy and see whether anything can be collected from the bankrupt. This section also explores the ins and outs of credit as it applies to your small business.

GETTING PAID: THE OPTIONS

Getting paid for your work or selling your goods is always a supremely gratifying moment. Your customer may hand you several portraits of Andy Jackson, General Grant, or Ben Franklin. Or you may get plastic in the form of a credit or debit card. Sometimes, your customer will have the bank electronically transfer the money.

CASH

Cash is good. But our currency isn't copy-proof, so you may want to use one of those handy devices, such as a special pen, to determine the real from the fake. If you get a stack of hundreds from a customer and it totals more than $10,000, under federal law you must report this transaction to the IRS on Form 8300. The feds have suspicious minds.

CREDIT CARDS

MasterCard, Visa, and the rest charge you for the privilege of allowing your customers to use their cards. The charge may range from 3 percent to 5 percent of the sale. You must follow the credit card issuer's rules, such as checking the expiration date of every card and getting approval for certain purchases. In most cases, even if the cardholder doesn't pay his or her bill, you'll still get your money, (which is why you're willing to pay the fee to the credit card company). However, if the customer claims your merchandise was defective and refuses to pay on that basis, you'll be the one who'll have to answer that charge directly.

If you're opening a physical retail store or will sell on the Internet or by mail order, you need to be able to accept credit card payments. Not being able to take payments by phone, fax, e-mail, web page forms, or regular mail will hinder your business. Even if you plan to sell at art and craft shows, or wholesale only, the value of offering your customers the opportunity and convenience of using credit cards will greatly improve your sales. Without a merchant account, businesses cannot accept credit cards, and according to what the experts say, those businesses may miss out on more than 60 percent of their sales opportunities.

TIP

The National Craft Association offers its members complete merchant credit card programs at very competitive rates for both traditional and online businesses. Call the NCA at 1-800-715-9594, or visit the website at www.craftassoc.com for more information.

CHECKS

Taking personal checks is always risky business. The customer may have insufficient funds to cover the check, the account may be closed, or someone, other than the customer, with the proper authority to do so might have to sign the check. You might want to take the following precautions:

- Accept only local checks.
- Accept only checks that display the preprinted customer name and address.
- Require that customers sign personal checks in your or your clerk's presence.
- Confirm all business checks with business owners if you don't know who has the authority to sign.
- Don't accept checks larger than the purchase price and give cash back.
- Don't give a cash refund until the bank has cleared the check and you've received the money in your account.
- Verify large checks with the bank.
- Ask to see photo identification.
- Stamp the back of the checks "for deposit only" and promptly deposit them.

Do you want to charge a customer whose check bounces? If you do, *the law states that the customer must be notified* of this and of the amount of the fee before that person writes the check to you.

CAUTION

If a customer's check bounces, before you redeposit it, call the customer to be sure that sufficient funds are in his or her account. Otherwise, if the check bounces a second time, your bank will charge you another fee.

If you decide to charge customers fees for bounced checks, you must post a sign that is clearly visible to customers making payments. If you have a store, or if you sell at a booth in a show, the sign must be posted near the checkout area. If you sell by mail or on the Internet, your policy must be stated on your order form. Almost all businesses have a bounced check charge to offset bank charges that they must pay when a customer's check bounces. Bank fees usually start at around $20, and a lot of businesses simply charge the customer double their bank charge.

How will you handle a bad check from a customer who ignores your polite efforts to collect on one returned to you for nonsufficient funds (NSF)? You can ask your bank to collect it for you. You fill out a "protest check form" at the bank and pay a fee (usually around $15 to $20). Then your bank will instruct the bank that the check was drawn on to pay the check as soon as funds are available in the account. Banks will usually hold the check for payment for one month, so if funds are deposited into the customer's account during the holding period, you'll get paid; if not, you won't.

If a customer's check is returned marked "account closed" or "no account," it may be evidence of fraud. You can send a copy of the returned check, along with documentation about what efforts you made to collect the money, to the district attorney's office. It is a crime to write a bad check, and if it's an out-of-state check for $250 or more, that makes it a felony instead of a misdemeanor. You could also consider using small claims court to collect the check.

Evaluate how much time and expense you're willing to commit to collecting on a bad check, based on the amount of the check. The number of bad checks given to vendors who sell at art and craft events seems to run way below the retail store averages. Most artisans report that they have very few problems in this area, and that if they do get an occasional bad check they can usually just resolve it with a phone call to the customer. Nevertheless, it's good to have a plan for dealing with a serious collection problem.

Despite your precautions, bad checks may bounce up. If so, check first with the bank to see whether the customer now has a balance sufficient to honor the check. If the customer does, run—don't walk—to the bank and cash the check. Second, call your customer and give him or her the chance to correct what may well have been a simple mistake. If you don't succeed at this point, write your customer a brief letter requesting payment and suggesting a lawsuit if prompt payment doesn't occur. Finally, if you still don't receive valid payment, file a lawsuit in small claims court. Many state laws permit damages of three times the amount of the check, plus court costs and attorneys' fees. Or turn the check over to a collection agency and let them have a go at it.

TIP

Get two signatures on an unknown customer's check. If you don't know the customer but do know someone with whom he or she's shopping, have the known customer endorse the check as well. That way the companion would be secondarily liable if the customer's check bounces.

You can request prosecution, but unless the bad-check writer is a notorious crook, the police may decide they have more important priorities.

Keep in mind that the customer may have stopped payment on the check, causing it to bounce. If that's the case, try to determine the problem and resolve it. For example, the customer may have changed his or her mind about buying the merchandise. The simplest resolution may be for you to ask for its return.

Another alternative you should consider, particularly for checks involving significant amounts, is to require a cashier's check issued by a bank, or have the customer get his or her check certified by a bank. In certifying a check, the bank is guaranteeing that the funds are on deposit, and your risk is shifted to the bank.

PROMISSORY NOTES

Cash, checks, and credit cards are the most common ways consumers pay for the goods they buy. An alternative is a promissory note. By accepting an I.O.U., you are, in effect, financing the customer's purchase. In return, your customer agrees to pay you on or before its due date, with interest, according to the terms of the note you both sign. The promissory note is typically used by the businessperson who sells on credit, such as for large equipment; the businessperson may want to sell the note at a discount to a finance company.

The customer, known as the maker of the promissory note, is primarily liable for the note. If you sell the note to a bank or finance company (usually at a discount of its face value), you, as endorser of the note, will be secondarily liable; you pay the bank or the finance company if the maker does not.

If one maker is good, a co-maker (cosigner) may be better, because you would then have two persons who are primarily liable. Remember that the *Equal Credit Opportunity Act* prohibits discrimination based on race, gender, and so on, so don't insist as a matter of practice, for example, that all wives get husbands to cosign.

SECURING THE LOAN WITH COLLATERAL

A promissory note is just a promise to pay. The maker's word may be good, but better yet is the maker putting up some collateral you can seize if the maker defaults on the loan.

STATUTORY LIENS

State law may protect creditors in certain transactions by creating a statutory lien, which is a claim or right against certain property, and which may be satisfied from the proceeds of the sale of the property. The statutory lien is different than a mortgage lien, which the mortgagor and mortgage company agree to. The two most typical liens involve property improvements: mechanic's lien against real estate and an artisan's lien for repairs to personal property.

If your company installs a roof, constructs an addition to a house, repaves a driveway, or otherwise improves real estate, you may be entitled to a mechanic's lien against the property if your customer doesn't pay you. You must file the lien in a timely manner and the law may require you to foreclose the lien within a year of filing. Most states require the filing within 60 to 120 days from completion of the work. Usually, the homeowner, developer, or business that you file against will pay after receiving notice. If not, your recovery in the foreclosure can include attorney fees and court costs.

For example, if an artisan repairs personal property and the computer repair company or the auto service station has a possessory lien against the customer's property for work performed, the customer must pay for the services rendered before receiving her property. The lien is terminated when the repairperson voluntarily returns the property to the owner.

MORTGAGE

A *mortgage* is a lien on real estate created because of a loan. The property owner (mortgagor) borrows money from and executes a mortgage to the lender (mortgagee). The mortgage is then recorded in the county recorder's office where the real estate is located. The real estate becomes a form of collateral for the lender. If the borrower breaches the terms of the loan, the lender can sue to foreclose on the mortgage and have the property sold.

If you're providing services or selling property to a customer who will sign a promissory note, you may want to take a mortgage on business or personal real estate as collateral. The customer may already have a first mortgage, so make sure there is enough equity (value about the first mortgage) to cover his or her debt to you. You must have a title search done, usually by a title insurance company, which would disclose ownership and any liens. If the information is satisfactory, have the customer sign the mortgage and promptly record it with the county recorder. Retain the mortgage (promissory) note in your files.

SECURITY INTEREST IN PERSONAL PROPERTY

A security interest on tangible and intangible personal property is similar to a mortgage on real estate—the creditor wants protection against default. If you are a creditor, you'll want to look at the value of the debtor's business assets, take the appropriate steps to include some of those assets as collateral for the loan or credit sale. Collateral typically includes equipment, machinery, inventory, fixtures, accounts receivable, and notes receivable. The *Uniform Commercial Code (UCC)*, Article 9, Secured Transactions, is the state statute that covers security interests; many states have a slightly different version of this article.

As a creditor you take the following steps to create and perfect (file) a security interest:

- Appraise collateral to determine its value.
- Search the *UCC* files at the secretary of state or county recorder.

- Prepare a security agreement, which the debtor signs.
- Prepare a financing statement, which the debtor signs.
- File a financing statement with the secretary of state or county recorder.
- Prepare a promissory note, which the debtor signs.

CAUTION

Choose with care the collateral you accept against debts owed to you. If the proposed collateral has a prior filed financing statement, yours would be second in line; use other collateral that is not covered because two financing statement is one too many.

You should search the office where another creditor might have filed a financing statement against your proposed collateral. Where you search depends on how the collateral is being used by the debtor. Financing statements against equipment, machinery, inventory, and accounts receivable are filed with the secretary of state in most states; however, financing statements filed against farm assets may be filed with the county recorder. Financing statements against fixtures, such as shelving or lighting, are usually filed with the county recorder. If your search shows no financing statements exist, you proceed to the next step.

THE SECURITY AGREEMENT

The security agreement is the contract between the debtor and the creditor. The debtor conveys a security interest in the collateral to the creditor (secured party). The security interest is like a lien against the collateral, and the security agreement provides the remedies available to the secured party if the debtor doesn't repay the loan. The security agreement usually contains the following terms:

- A list of all the collateral
- The transfer of security interest
- The written permission required to move the collateral, if the debtor wants to move it to a different store
- A provision requiring the debtor to maintain the good condition of collateral, and pay insurance premiums, and taxes on it
- A clause describing repossession rights and other remedies for breach

Some types of collateral may be listed generically (all the inventory located at 1 North South Street, Notown, IN) or by specific identification (motor ID number). Inventory should include the proceeds from its sale, and any purchased after the security agreement is in effect, often referred to as a floating lien.

If the collateral decreases in value, the secured party loses some of its protection; therefore, the agreement will require the debtor to maintain the collateral, as well as pay for its insurance coverage. When the collateral is mobile, the secured party doesn't want to chase after it if repossession is necessary, thus the requirement of written permission to move it.

The security agreement provides terms for default by the debtor. Typically, the secured party is permitted to repossess the collateral even if it is necessary to go on the debtor's property to do so. The repossession may not use or threaten physical violence.

The agreement usually gives the secured party the option of retaining the collateral (and extinguishing the debt) or selling it in a public or private sale. If the collateral is sold and its proceeds are less than the debt (and cost of collection), the secured party is entitled to the difference. Therefore the secured party can still collect the difference from the debtor.

After both parties sign the security agreement, the secured party will require the business debtor to sign a financing statement. A consumer who buys merchandise will just sign the retail installment agreement, which contains the security agreement.

The financing statement will be filed with the secretary of state or the county recorder, which is called perfecting the security interest. Depending on the debtor's use of the collateral, you'll file either with the secretary of state or the county recorder. (Review the prior discussion about a *UCC* search, which would be conducted at the secretary of state's office or county recorder's office prior to granting the loan.)

CAUTION

Don't procrastinate! Timely filing of the financing statement is crucial, because the first secured party to file generally has first right to the collateral.

MEANS OF PERFECTION

The *UCC* provides two other means of perfection along with filing the financing statement with the secretary of state or county recorder: possession of the collateral and attachment of consumer goods, or automatic perfection.

The pawnbroker is a typical example of perfection by possession; this is often referred to as a pledge. The pledged goods have a perfected security interest as long as the secured party retains possession. If the collateral is a promissory note or certificate of deposit, possession is the means of perfection.

When a consumer buys merchandise on installment, the agreement will create a purchase money security interest, which is automatically perfected. Few consumer credit sales involve perfection by filing a financing statement.

After the secured interest in the collateral is perfected, the secured party usually has a prior claim to any subsequent creditors or buyers. There are two significant exceptions. When a secured party has a security interest in inventory, a consumer purchasing merchandise in a retail store takes free of the security interest. If the security agreement included proceeds from the sale of the inventory, the proceeds become the collateral. In addition, debtors who have purchased consumer goods might sell them to a neighbor; the neighbor who is unaware of the security interest takes the merchandise free of the interest. In neither instance is the debtor released from the debt because of the sale.

TIP

If collateral is moved to another state, the secured party needs to perfect in the new state, generally within four months of arrival.

Collection Process: Letter to Collecting the Judgment

Bad debts occur despite your best efforts. Some debtors may not be worth pursuing, others may justify your time and trouble. Sometimes just a little extra effort may reward you with at least a partial payment of the debt.

Collecting Without Suing

An ounce of prevention—a credit check performed in advance of delivery of the merchandise or services—may help avoid the problem of collection, but it will not eliminate it entirely. You should send a follow-up bill, if the first one hasn't been paid promptly. Customers do lose statements or procrastinate. You may want to follow this with a telephone call after sufficient time has elapsed, but this may be more confrontational than you want.

TIP

Get it in writing! When a customer places an order, you should have an agreement that clearly specifies a rate of interest for overdue amounts and the right to charge collection costs, including court costs and attorney fees; the latter is generally not allowed unless specified in the contract between the parties.

Sending out a collection letter may be the next step. Although the *Fair Debt Collection Practices Act* does not apply to small businesses that collect their own debts, you should follow the basic philosophy imbedded in the statute—do not harass the debtor. Your letters should be firm and perhaps suggest a compromise if appropriate, but should not contain any threats of criminal prosecution, communication with the customer's employer, or public disclosure. You may indicate that nonpayment may result in turning over the debt to a collection agency or a lawsuit.

A collection agency may be feasible if the collection process becomes too time-consuming. Obviously, the collection agency will charge you, usually a percentage of the amount collected, but 50 percent is better than 0 percent. You might want to consider hiring an attorney just to write a collection letter; sometimes the lawyer's letterhead, alone, may say enough to get you paid.

JUDGMENT AND COLLECTION

Unless you have a right to repossess the collateral under a security agreement, you probably will not be able to convince a court to allow a prejudgment (before the verdict) seizure of the debtor's property.

After you obtain a judgment, you may proceed through the court to collect on it. One method is to obtain a writ (order) of execution against the debtor's non-exempt assets, have the sheriff seize the assets, and sell them at a public sale. With many consumers this may not be feasible because the exempt assets may be the only assets the debtor owns. Exemptions vary from state to state, and generally are described in the next section. For example, if the debtor owns a few household goods and a very used car, the writ of execution will not be productive.

Another method you might consider is a *garnishment* order against the debtor's wages or money in a bank account. The garnishment order is served upon the debtor's employer or bank. However, federal law generally restricts all garnishment orders of an employee's wage to 25 percent of disposable earnings per week.

PLAIN ENGLISH

Garnishment is a court order directed against the debtor's assets held by a third party (garnishee) to turn over the property to the court.

DEBTOR BANKRUPTCY

There are some notices you just don't like to receive. One is a notice from the bankruptcy court in which a debtor has listed you as a creditor. If you are an unsecured creditor, and a consumer debtor has filed under the liquidation chapter, your outlook for repayment is bleak.

The main bankruptcy code chapters for our discussion are ...

- Chapter 12 bankruptcy, liquidation for individuals and businesses.
- Chapter 11 bankruptcy, business reorganization.
- Chapter 13 bankruptcy, wage-earner plan.

PETITION, STAY ORDER, AND INITIAL PROCEEDINGS

Bankruptcy law has two goals: to protect the debtor by giving him or her a fresh start free from creditor claims, and to ensure that the bankrupt's creditors are treated fairly in receiving the debtor's nonexempt property in settlement of their claims.

A bankruptcy filing under Chapter 7 may be voluntary (initiated by the debtor) or involuntary (initiated by creditors); involuntary personal bankruptcies are rare. The debtor must initiate Chapter 13, which means that no creditor can bring a bankruptcy action under Chapter 13. The bankruptcy petition is filed with the U.S. district court where the debtor resides, and is assigned to a bankruptcy court. The petition triggers a stay (an order to stop) on all of the debtor's creditor collection efforts; this stay usually applies to creditors who are suing, collecting on a judgment, repossessing, or foreclosing against the debtor. For example, if you are suing the debtor on a breach of contract, all action in the case stops from the moment the petition is filed. Creditors can apply to the court for relief from the stay.

TIP

When the debtor owes you a bundle, consider retaining an attorney to review the petition and determine whether the debtor is worth pursuing through bankruptcy. A small debt is probably not worth the effort and expense of professional advice.

The voluntary personal bankruptcy petition and supplemental forms will contain the following information about the debtor:

- A list of assets
- Identification of property claimed as exempt
- A list of secured and unsecured creditors
- Current income and expense

When the voluntary petition for personal bankruptcy is filed, the court will enter an order for relief, and the clerk will mail notices to all listed creditors, indicating the time of the creditors'/debtor's meeting, and deadline for filing creditor claims and objections.

Creditors can object to the bankruptcy discharge if the debtor's petition is fraudulent, willfully conceals assets, or a discharge has previously been granted within six years of filing.

Most personal bankruptcies are no-asset estates (all exempt property), so the trustee's function is fairly minimal, because the listed debts are discharged and the bankrupt person keeps the property claimed as exempt; the trustee is appointed by the bankruptcy court. If there are significant nonexempt assets, the trustee collects this property, liquidates it, and pays the creditors according to the priority established in the code.

Exempt Property, Distribution, and Discharge

The bankrupt person's estate consists of all of his or her property wherever it's located. If the bankrupt party has made a gift of property to a friend or relative within a year, or if within 90 days of the petition a creditor has been paid more that it would have received in the liquidation, those assets may be included.

Federal law permits the bankrupt to keep some of his or her property in a Chapter 7 liquidation. You should consult with a bankruptcy attorney to determine the current exemptions allowed.

 CAUTION

A bankruptcy trustee may require a creditor to repay to the trustee any money received from the bankrupt within 90 days of the petition.

Many states have opted out of the federal exemptions, so check your state law.

After the exempt property is successfully claimed, the trustee may distribute any remaining property of the bankrupt party according to a stated priority. The order of distribution is as follows:

- Administrative expenses—court costs, trustee and attorney fees
- Paternity, alimony, maintenance, and support obligations
- Taxes
- Unsecured creditors

Secured creditors may be able to repossess the collateral through the bankruptcy court or have the bankrupt party pay the secured party. A creditor is a secured party only to the value of the collateral. For example, if the debt is $10,000, and the collateral is worth $5,000, the security interest is limited to $5,000, and the rest of the debt is unsecured.

Creditors can object to the discharge, which is a court order wiping out the debt. But certain debts are not dischargeable, such as three years back federal income taxes, property or credit obtained through fraud, alimony, and child support. Claims based on willful misconduct (such as a battery judgment) government fines, certain consumer loans, luxury items of $1,075 obtained within 60 days of the order for relief, and certain student loans are also not dischargeable.

If a debt is discharged, a creditor can no longer collect it. However, the debtor can reaffirm a debt before discharge. The reaffirmation agreement must be filed and approved by the court and clearly state that the reaffirmation is not required.

BANKRUPTCY CHAPTER 13

Wage earners only need apply for Chapter 13. This chapter permits the bankrupt to partially pay creditors over a period of three to five years, and thereafter the debts are discharged.

CAUTION

Don't assume that bankruptcy laws don't change. Congress is currently considering bankruptcy amendments that would limit Chapter 7 personal bankruptcy. Consult with your attorney about any changes.

Any individual who has regular income and owes fixed unsecured debts of less than $269,250, or owes fixed secured debts of less than $807,750, may petition. The bankrupt person's plan of payment is submitted to the court (creditors may object), and if approved, the bankrupt person will turn over his or her disposable income to the trustee who then will pay the creditors. Disposable income is defined as income not reasonably necessary for the maintenance and support of the debtor and dependents. Failure of the debtor to make timely payments may result in conversion to Chapter 7 liquidation.

HELPFUL SOURCES ON BANKRUPTCY

Cornell University's website has a discussion of bankruptcy and creditor's rights laws: www.law.cornell.edu. The American Bankruptcy Institute website is another source: www.abiworld.org. Finally, use the bankruptcy lawfinder:

www.agin.com/lawfind. Many trade organizations provide useful suggestions about collecting debts.

THE 30-SECOND RECAP

- Have the debtor's check certified by the bank if you have doubts.
- A security interest in the debtor's collateral may protect you in the event of a default.
- Send a collection letter before filing a lawsuit.
- You may be able to collect a judgment against the debtor by garnishing his or her wages or executing against his or her nonexempt property.
- Unsecured creditors in a personal bankruptcy liquidation can expect very little.

Paying the Bills While Paying Your Dues

Running a business means paying your bills each month. To do this you need to know what you can expect. First, there are costs you'll encounter in your start-up phase. That generally carries you for about the first three months. After that, you need to learn how much it's going to cost you each month to stay in business.

In this section, you see the types of costs you might have when you're just getting started. Then you'll learn to estimate your personal living expenses. After all, you have to eat while your business gets off the ground. You'll also find out how to make an operating budget.

HOW YOUR START-UP COSTS STACK UP

No more theory or generalities about what it's going to cost you. The time has come to get specific. Like a Boy Scout, you've got to be prepared—prepared for expenses you may face during your start-up phase, typically the first three months of operation.

Start-up costs are different from the costs you'll be paying month in and month out. Start-up costs involve one-time expenses, such as legal fees to have your lawyer review your franchise agreement or deposits you'll have to make on phone lines or storage space outside your home.

Close your eyes and picture your office and what it will take to get it ready for you to begin. Need furniture? A computer? Stationery? Paper clips? Permits and licenses? Maybe you already have a setup that's usable for a time. Or maybe you have an empty room that you have to fill up with the things you need for your business.

If you're selling specific items, you'll have to estimate what you need to get started. Don't order more than you'll sell in the first few months because your money's tight. But don't order too little either. You don't want orders to go unfilled. And you don't want to miss out on better prices that buying larger quantities may give you.

TIP

Don't go overboard ordering stationery, invoices, and business cards. Get just enough to get you started in case the information about your business changes. You may add a second phone, incorporate, or get an e-mail address that you'll need to include.

Make your own grocery list of expenses you'll have to pay to get going. Here are some to get you started:

Professional Fees

Legal

Business purchase	$_____
Franchise purchase	$_____
Incorporation	$_____
Partnership agreement	$_____
Business name search	$_____
Zoning variance	$_____

Accounting

Advice on business structure	$_____
Selection filing	$_____
Setting up the books	$_____

Insurance

Health	$_____
Disability	$_____
Liability	$_____
Property	$_____

Materials

    Equipment

    Computer, printer, etc. $_____

    Copier/fax $_____

    Furniture $_____

    Specialized tools $_____

    Other equipment $_____

    Car/truck $_____

Supplies

    Stationery $_____

    Business cards $_____

    Office supplies $_____

    Postage $_____

Inventory

    Inventory $_____

Office Space

    Remodeling costs $_____

    Connection fees and deposits on utilities $_____

    Deposits on storage space $_____

Marketing

    Company brochure $_____

    Yellow Pages ad $_____

    Web page design $_____

    Business opening announcement $_____

PERSONAL EXPENSES

Starting a business takes time. It may be many months before the business generates enough money for you to begin taking a salary or otherwise tap into the cash. Think about how you're going to put food on the table in the meantime.

How to Eat While Feeding Your Business

If you're working on your business on a full-time basis, you need to plan so you have money for things like your rent or mortgage and utilities. (Remember, your business is only taking up a portion of your home. The cost of running the other part of your home is not a business expense.) You need money to eat, pay for flu shots, put gas in your car, and even to go out to the movies occasionally.

You have a few options to help you survive while you feed your budding business:

- **Live off your savings.** If you've put aside a nest egg, you may be able to use it now for your personal expenses while your business gets started. In this case, you don't have to budget for personal living expenses in your start-up costs.

   Some people begin their own business as a result of an unexpected windfall. For example, a corporate executive who was laid off in a wave of downsizing got a generous severance package that continued his wages for nine months. He decided to start a home business using marketing skills he learned in the corporate world. He used his windfall salary to pay the mortgage and put shoes on the kids' feet. With careful budgeting, that nine-month severance package carried him more than a year!

   If you plan to use your nest egg to buy the business, or to purchase needed equipment, you have to be realistic: Is your nest egg a robin's egg or a dinosaur egg? Your nest egg may not be big enough to cover both business start-up costs and your personal expenses. You may have to borrow additional money.

- **Rely on your spouse.** If you have a working spouse whose income can cover your personal living expenses, you don't have to budget for them in your start-up costs. Sometimes, however, a spouse's income may only cover so much. Be sure to include any other money you need to cover your personal living expenses in your start-up budget.

TIP

Figure your personal living expenses for at least six months. Then make a plan for how you'll pay these expenses while your business gets up and running.

KEEP YOUR DAY JOB

You don't have to burn all your bridges to start a new business. Many people start a small business on a part-time basis. By moonlighting, they can continue to earn a salary and benefits. The salary from their day job covers personal living expenses. If you're still employed, you may want to try this approach when starting your business.

In deciding whether to begin part time, take into account the all-important exhaustion factor. If you work all day, you only have nights and weekends to devote to starting up your business. You may be shortchanging yourself. There may not be enough hours in the day to work your day job and spend the time your business needs to succeed. Or you may just be too pooped to do a good job in your own business.

TIP

Keeping an outside job while starting up a small business may be a good idea because you won't need to have it become successful overnight because you're not relying on it for a living.

Don't ignore the impact your decision will have on your family. If you're working day and night, there's little time for anything else, like going to Johnny's soccer game or doing the housework. This work arrangement may be fine for a short while, but it probably won't work indefinitely.

There are pros and cons to both starting a business part-time and taking the full-time plunge. In making this choice, ask yourself these questions before you quit your job:

- **Will you be able to pay your bills if you quit?** Be sure to include the cost of health care in your plans if you're not covered under a spouse's plan. When you leave your job you're entitled under a federal law—COBRA—to continue the same health coverage for 18 months. But you, not your former employer, have to pay the cost!
- **What happens if the business doesn't work out?** Will you be able to go back to your old job or get a new one?
- **Can your ego handle the drop in income?** Are you comfortable relying on your spouse for support?

JUST WHAT THE DOCTOR ORDERED: OPERATING EXPENSES

You've learned about preparing a start-up budget. Now you have to make an operating budget. But how do you know when a business passes the start-up phase and enters the operating phase? There's no magic number. As a rule of thumb it's helpful to look at your start-up budget to carry you through the first three months of business. The operating budget should be designed to carry you for the next three months of business. Some experts suggest you budget for at least the first year.

Many of the items you budgeted for in the start-up phase won't go away in the next phase of your business—the next three months of operations. Let's say you planned for advertising costs in the start-up phase. You have to continue or even accelerate your advertising campaign as you nurture your business. Be sure to budget for expanding your operations.

You'll be glad to hear, however, that some of your start-up costs disappear as you move forward. You don't need to plan for occupancy costs in the operating budget. After you've put in the new phone and wiring in your office, you don't have to budget for them in the operating budget. These are one-time costs.

Some items may have been more heavily budgeted in the start-up phase. For example, professional fees might be a big bite when you're buying a business and working out the legal stuff. But you might still have ongoing professional fees throughout the life of your business. So if you pay an accountant to do your books and tax returns, you should budget for this service.

However, it's not all good news: There are several new items to include in your operating budget that weren't necessarily there at start-up. These items include payroll, *debt service,* taxes, dues and subscriptions, Internet-related costs, and repairs and maintenance.

PLAIN ENGLISH

Debt service is a term used to describe the repayment of a loan. It includes the repayment of principal as well as interest on the loan.

PAYROLL

Payroll is usually one of the most significant operating expenses for any business. That's because it's people that get the job done! But along with people come people-related expenses. These costs generally fall into the following categories:

- **Wages.** Include the amount of wages you expect to pay. If you're an employee of your own business (your business is incorporated), you can include your own salary in this category. If the business is not in-corporated, don't include payments to yourself here. (You'll account for the payments in your personal living costs.) If you contract out your work, you're not talking about wages, but you'll have to pay a similar amount to get the work done.

■ **Other benefits.** During the start-up phase of your business you probably won't be providing any fancy fringe benefits, such as retirement plan contributions, for yourself or your employees. However, there may be some additional benefits—car fare when your employee works late, for example—that you want to plan for.

■ **Workers' compensation and disability.** By law you're required to provide workers' compensation and disability for employees. These expenses may have already been included in your insurance costs. If not, be sure to add them into your payroll costs.

CAUTION

If you're self-employed (haven't incorporated your business), Uncle Sam has a nasty surprise for you: You can't get workers' compensation and unemployment insurance for yourself. You can't even choose to be covered by these government benefits. If you're injured on the job or your business fails, you have no government protection, so don't budget for it.

■ **Unemployment insurance.** You may pay state and/or federal unemployment insurance to cover workers if they're laid off or fired (unless, of course, they walked off with the company petty cash). The amount of unemployment insurance you pay depends on the size of your payroll and your unemployment experience. A business with high unemployment experience—people coming and going like a turnover revolving door—will pay higher unemployment insurance than a company that keeps its people around, even though both have the same number of employees.

■ **FICA.** You've seen this little fella on your pay stubs: An employer must pay Social Security and Medicare taxes on employee wages. Social Security and Medicare taxes are called FICA. As an employer you have to withhold a matching amount of FICA from employee wages—the employee's share—and pay this to the IRS along with your employer's share. However, because the employee's share is subtracted from wages, it's not an additional cost for you.

There's definitely more to payroll than writing out the checks. Complete this worksheet for figuring your payroll costs. Later in the section you'll transfer the total from this worksheet to another one, so keep it handy.

Worksheet for Payroll Costs

Payroll Cost	Total Cost
Wages	$_____
Health insurance, vacation pay	$_____
Workers' compensation and disability	$_____
Unemployment insurance (FUTA)	$_____
FICA	$_____
Total	$_____

SERVICING YOUR DEBT SERVICE

If you're one of the fortunate ones who has not borrowed any money to get your business started, you can skip this section and go get a cup of coffee. But if you have taken a loan to help you get going, you have to plan for paying it back.

Not all loans are equal. You may, for example, have a loan that doesn't call for any immediate repayment of principal. In that case, you include only your interest payments for the second three months that you're in business.

If you have a loan with an interest rate tied to the prime rate or some other rate that moves around more than a rock band on tour, it may be more difficult to budget for your interest payments. Will interest rates rise? Will interest rates fall? If droves of economists with Ph.D.s can't predict this, how can you? If you want to make a conservative budget you may want to include some rise in interest to cover yourself. However, as a rule of thumb, just use the initial interest rate when making your budget.

TAXES, TAXES, TAXES

Here's an understatement: There are a number of different kinds of taxes. In fact, people get postgraduate degrees in this topic, write whole books on it, and go crazy trying to keep up with the constant changes. You've already seen payroll taxes on wages. Here's the gist of some other taxes.

For the purposes of budgeting your operating expenses, the most common type of tax your business may face is sales tax. This is a tax you collect from your clients and customers on the product or service you provide—you know, the 27 cents you add to the price of a pen at Kmart. If you're unlucky enough to live in a state with a sales tax, check with your state to find out about your sales tax requirements. Some states might exempt certain goods and services from tax, whereas others might not.

And lest we forget, if you're fortunate enough to have your business be profitable from the start, you must also consider income taxes on your profits.

Taxes are further discussed in Part 14.

DUES AND SUBSCRIPTIONS

As you begin to run your business you might want to join local business groups or trade associations. Despite popular belief, the purpose of these memberships is not to eat a lot of rubber-chicken lunches every month (although you will). These memberships help you network your business with other business owners, learn what's happening in your business community, and deal with some of the cabin fever you may suffer when working alone in a home office.

Check out the cost of membership. Become a member of the groups you can afford to join that will give you the greatest business benefit or personal enjoyment for your buck.

Business newspapers, magazines, and trade journals can also help you stay current and, maybe, even one step ahead of your competitors. You may also want to sign on to the Internet with an online service provider. Investigate your monthly costs for these services.

 TIP

According to a survey of business owners who succeeded and those who failed, those in the success column overwhelmingly kept up on developments affecting their business and their industry. You want to stay abreast of not only the latest developments in your industry but also developments affecting business in general (taxes, insurance, technology). To do this you need to read, read, read.

REPAIRS AND MAINTENANCE

It's Murphy's law: If you use equipment of any kind in your business, even a simple copier, you can bet that sometime, somewhere, something will break. It is hoped this won't happen too often, especially if you buy or lease new equipment. But when something does break, you need to get it fixed. Be sure to plan for repair costs.

Even if nothing breaks, you'll save money in the long run if you follow a routine service program and have checkups for your equipment. Most service contracts for your equipment offer an annual or more frequent checkup or service call.

TALLYING YOUR OPERATING EXPENSES

After you make educated estimates, transfer the total of all of the items in this section and other costs you think of to the operating budget work sheet that follows. In entering your items, you may be confused about where to list them. For example, where do you put your Internet-related costs, such as your service provider, if you expect to have them? You might list them with utilities or with advertising. The category you choose isn't important; what matters is that you've taken the costs into account.

Worksheet for Projecting Operating Costs for a Small Business

Item	Estimated Cost
Payroll	$_____
Debt service	$_____
Taxes	$_____
Dues and subscriptions	$_____
Repairs and maintenance	$_____
Equipment	$_____
Inventory (for product-oriented businesses)	$_____
Supplies	$_____
Legal, accounting, other professional fees	$_____
Insurance	$_____
Licences/permits	$_____
Utilities	$_____
Advertising and promotion	$_____
Miscellaneous and unanticipated expenses	$_____
Personal living costs	$_____
Total Operating Cost	$_____

THE 30-SECOND RECAP

- Cover the costs of getting started by budgeting for them.
- Be sure that you plan for your personal expenses in addition to your business needs.
- Consider moonlighting so that your day job pays your personal bills while you start up your business at night and on weekends.
- Your operating budget should carry you for the second three months you are in business.

Understanding the Value of Your Time and Paying Yourself

Henry David Thoreau said, "What is once done well is done forever." This is particularly true when you think of your time as money. If you squander your time in useless or meaningless ways, it is gone, wasted, lost forever. As a business owner, wasting time could have serious consequences. After you realize the real dollar value of your time, you'll probably think twice about how you spend it. This section shows you how to determine your actual hourly wage and price your products accordingly, and examines ways to use your time to maximize your business's potential.

HOW MUCH ARE YOU WORTH PER HOUR?

First, think about how much an hour you need to make. It doesn't matter whether you plan to operate your business full or part time, and we're not considering your business expenses or the cost of materials. The following exercise is for arriving at a dollar figure for your time—an hourly labor rate, or what you would pay yourself as a reasonable salary that you could afford to live on. Before you do the exercise, estimate your hourly rate here: $_____.

Now let's determine the actual value of your time. Just follow along and fill in the questions to arrive at your estimated hourly rate:

Part 1: Estimated Salary

What do you want to make as an annual salary?	$_____
Add 30 percent to cover health insurance and retirement benefits	$_____
Total Estimated Salary	$_____

Part 2: Billable Days

Next, using the 365-day year, subtract the number of days that you normally use as days off and days to do indirect labor. Indirect labor is the time that you spend on administrative or marketing tasks (nonproduct production work time). Most artisans estimate that indirect labor accounts for 20 to 40 percent of their time.

Number of sick and personal days per year	_____
Number of official holidays per year (about 10)	_____
Desired number of vacation days per year	_____

Desired number of days off per year (days per week × 52)   _____

Number of days spent on indirect labor   _____

Billable Days (subtract total from 365)   _____

Part 3: Hourly Rate

Divide the total salary that you calculated in Part 1 by the billable days from Part 2 _____. This is your rate per day.

Divide your rate per day by the number of hours worked per day—say, 8.

Your hourly rate would equal: $_____

How does this number compare with your original estimate? If you had assigned yourself, say, $40,000 yearly and added the 30 percent to cover health and retirement benefits, you need to earn $52,000. If you worked five days a week (260) and gave yourself 10 sick days, 10 holidays, and a two-week vacation (10), and if you then spent one day a week (50) for indirect labor, you would have 180 billable days left in the year.

Divide your salary ($52,000) by the number of billable days (180) to determine the amount that you need to earn per day ($288.88). Divide this number by the number of hours that you plan to work each day (8 hours) for your hourly rate. Using this example, your hourly rate would be $36.11 per hour. Remember that you will have to pay taxes too, your net rate will be lower.

YOUR PRODUCT'S REAL COST AND PRICING

Now that you know what your fair hourly wage is, you can determine the real cost of your product. If it took you 15 minutes to make an item, add $9 ($36 per hour, divided by 4) for labor to the item's cost—say, $6. To be paid fairly, you need to charge $15 per item—its *real* cost.

The dilemma of what to charge for products or services has been experienced by most, if not all, new business owners. The following few comments reflect what many artisans have to say about pricing:

CAUTION

Most artisans don't make enough income because they make the common mistake of underestimating the value of their time. If you want to make money with your hobby, the first step is to account for all the time that you spend operating your business to see what you're actually being paid. Then be sure to include a fair rate of pay for your time in your business budget.

What to Charge for Freelance Work

The field of commercial freelance writing and graphics contains a lot of mixed theories as to what ought to be charged because there are no fixed guidelines, restrictions, or standards to setting fees. There are only scattered pieces of information that hint about what should be charged. Because of the freedom in setting your own fees, it's common to hear about one freelance writer getting paid $850 to write a brochure and another freelancer getting paid $400 to write a similar brochure. Some charge by the hour; others charge by the project. Why is one freelancer paid higher than the other?

- **Level of experience.** A freelancer who has more experience obviously is in a position to charge more. A beginner might not have the clout or the samples to command higher pay or to attract the type of clients that would pay the big bucks.

- **Type of industry.** Corporations pay writers higher than most other industries. The difference in pay between writing a brochure for a corporation and writing one for a small business can be hundreds of dollars.

- **What others are charging.** Understand what other businesses are willing to pay you and what others are charging, to help you price your services competitively.

- **Type of work involved.** Not every project or assignment is the same. Using the example of a how-to booklet, one freelancer may have been required to do additional research or was required to attend a seminar (which means more billable hours and, therefore, higher pay). Another freelancer may have had the information already at hand to write the booklet in less time.

- **Type of economic conditions.** Regional economic conditions can affect what businesses are willing to pay you, as well as how much work is available in your area.

- **Type of employer.** Some companies are better managed and more desirable to work for. Your rate may reflect this.

Research Tips

If you plan to self-publish informational books, newsletters, or perhaps hobby guides based on your specific specialty, this type of material is usually priced by the cost of comparable products or services, or what the market will bear (the amount the customer will pay).

Because there are no hard-and-fast rules, of course, you will have to find out what the going market rates are for the type of freelance work that you want to do. To get started, get a current edition of *Writer's Market* (www.writersmarket. com/index_ns.asp), published yearly by F&W Publications. It provides a handful of pages on what commercial freelance writers should be charging for assignments and projects.

In addition, the *Guide to Freelance Rates and Standard Practice,* published by the National Writer's Union (www.nwu.org/), provides some information on commercial freelance writing fees.

A book worth reading is Robert W. Bly's, *Secrets of a Freelance Writer: How to Make $85,000 a Year,* which includes freelance rates. Or contact the National Writers Association, 1450 S. Havana, Suite 424, Aurora, CO 80012; phone: 303-841-0246 or at www.nationalwriters.com; fax: 303-751-8593. This association also publishes a bimonthly magazine called *Authorship.*

ONLINE RESOURCES

Author Link marketplace (www.authorlink.com/) is where editors and agents buy and sell rights to unpublished and published manuscripts and screenplays. Industry news and information also is available.

Writers Digest (www.writersdigest.com/) also offers tips and workshops for beginning writers and a guide to the life of writing. This site offers links to some of the best information resources for writers as well.

MAXIMIZING YOUR TIME

Now that you're aware of the real value of your time, let's explore some ways to invest it wisely in running your business. Most new business owners start feeling as if there's always far too much to be accomplished in a given period than is feasible to get done. The key is to maximize the value of your time by setting priorities and focusing on strategies that produce positive results.

Develop a true customer focus. Understand that customers always go where they get good value and go where they are treated well. When the value isn't clear or the level of service slips, they slip away. Take some time to identify your target customer; the more you know about your customers, the easier it is to serve them well and to provide goods or services that they want so that your time is well spent.

- **Gather and analyze management information regularly.** You need strategic information on your own business to know what's really going on and to make wise decisions based on accurate, timely information. Use the following four areas: financial, customer, industry information, and market trends.

■ **Increase the customer's perception of value.** Value is not the same as price. If you position your marketing on value it saves time because you are also building the products image. It also includes considerations of quality (are your products better?) and quantity (do you offer more than others do?). However, most customers are somewhat price-sensitive. Instead of across-the-board markup, consider variable pricing strategies to broaden your market share.

The "value-added" approach to presenting your product or service is very important to increasing your customers' perceived view of your product. It doesn't take much time or work to produce a hang tag with the subtle value-added statement such as "since 1975," which tells the customer that you are established and builds credibility. "100 Percent Satisfaction Guaranteed" says you stand behind your work no matter what—a value-added guarantee. "Each Piece Dated and Signed" hints at collectible status, which translates into substantiating the item's value. "Lead Free, Dishwasher Safe, Microwave-Proof" adds dollar value to the quality. "Your Design or Ours" offers custom design work, another value-added benefit of doing business with this company.

In addition, of course, is the big hook—"Free Personalization." Is this a value-added benefit or what? As you can see, the product hang tag is a *silent salesperson* for the product. It very carefully builds and adds value to the way customers perceive the product and ultimately to the value that they get for the price.

TIP

Develop a true customer focus. The more you know about your customers, the easier it is to provide the products and services that they want. Stay on top of the current trends, colors, styles, designs, textures, or whatever drives your product line.

■ **Position the business uniquely.** You aren't one of the big guys, so don't try to be like them. It is a waste of time. Position yourself in areas where big business can't compete with you, such as friendliness, customer bonding, special orders, original designs, special services, personalization of items, and so forth. Where can you say, "We're better because ..." or "We're unique because ..."? Handcrafted products usually have one major advantage: *They are your own unique design!* That's right, *your product is exclusive*—a product line to which only you have the exclusive distribution rights. You're in a unique position—play it to the hilt!

TIP

You have to put a hang tag or a label on your product anyway. Isn't it better to use it as a sales tool than as just a decoration with your contact information?

■ **Eliminate extra steps.** Time is money, and eliminating time wasters saves you money. Look for areas where you may be duplicating efforts, or where you could streamline the operation; perhaps cut some steps out of your order entry process or your shipping methods. It's just human nature to keep doing things the same way. Every once in a while, you have to stand back and take a hard look.

SERVICE BUSINESSES: THE NEED TO PLEASE

If you plan to provide a service-based business, be forewarned that there is a very serious bug going around that many new business owners catch. It's called "the need to please."

CAUTION

When you operate a service business, your time is your income. If you waste it on non-income-producing tasks, how will you make any money or achieve your goals? Do what you agreed to do for a customer, and make sure that any additional services are billable.

You catch the bug from your own misguided sense that when you spend too much time with a needy customer, you're doing a good thing, when the only good thing you may really be doing is feeding your own desire to feel needed and good about yourself. The "need to please" bug slows you way down and causes you to waste valuable time that you should be spending productively. It makes you a slave to people who learn to prey on your good nature and willingness to please your customers, taking advantage of you perhaps without even realizing that they're doing it.

The "need to please" bug has nothing to do with your providing the best service possible, as you contracted to do. But if you have the bug, you do volumes of work for the same initial payment simply because it's demanded of you. You start out doing it to provide good customer service—maybe you even think that it will get you additional referral business. But in the end, overservicing demanding customers is to your detriment: It means the loss of your valuable income-producing time.

It is important to learn the skill of spotting particularly needy customers early on and to deal with the situation up front. The fact is that only a small percentage of people will latch onto you, thinking that by hiring you, they own you body and soul. But beware—they are out there!

The next time you feel the urge to hand over all the fish to feed the multitude, take out a fishing pole and teach your demanding customers how to fish. They may not be happy with you initially, but they may learn something; more important, you'll have more time to nurture your growing business.

THE 30-SECOND RECAP

- Establish a fair rate for your time, and add your hourly wage to the cost of the items that you sell. Don't sell yourself short; charge what your work is worth.

- Freelance rates need to be researched and compared to the going market rates for the particular job that you're doing.

- Always try to maximize your time by looking for ways to improve your efficiency.

- Learn to recognize and restrain the "need to please" urge; it will rob you of time that you should be spending on your business.

Legal Issues 101

Finding a Good Attorney

Most business start-ups will need some professional advice to get up and running. While the business owner focuses on the demands of a new business's start-up, legal issues are best left to the professionals. As the business grows, you will face new issues that are even more complicated.

There are quite a few self-help books, computer programs, and preprinted forms for the new business owner, but they should not be relied on exclusively. The law can be complicated, and mistakes can be costly. Legal professionals often point out potential problems that you may not have anticipated and give you guidance in additional ways. Enlisting the help of legal professionals can improve your competitive edge. This section will explain how you can find the right legal professional for your business.

YOUR LAWYER'S ASSISTANCE

You need a lawyer on call. You are operating in a business system that is dominated by the law.

Here's a brief list of legal services you should consider:

What a Lawyer Can Do	Example
Draft organization documents	Articles of incorporation
Prepare business documents	Buy-sell agreement
Advise on tax decisions	S vs. C corporate tax status
Write contracts	Purchase agreements
Draft employment documents	Employee handbook
Advise and litigate	Sue deadbeat debtors
Plan your estate	Last will and testament and living trust

You can do it yourself, if you choose. Drafting a contract or setting up your corporation saves you the legal fees, which may be a considerable sum for a tight budget. However, the money you save does come at a cost. Time is money, and your time may be better spent on running your business. Plus, there is a risk that your legal document may be insufficient if challenged. The contract that you draft may have dozens of loopholes.

TIP

You may want to draft a contract or other legal document by using a standard form or legal software and then have the draft reviewed by a lawyer. You put in the terms most important to you and the lawyer makes sure that the document is legally sufficient. And you save legal fees!

Your attorney should be willing to take calls from you without exorbitant fees. Often you just need to know whether legal services are necessary. If in doubt, call. Reliable attorneys will frequently suggest a solution that you can implement without an attorney. The best legal advice is always practical, and frequently costs very little.

FINDING THE ATTORNEY YOU NEED

Like selecting a doctor, finding the right attorney is not easy. As with any business decision, you must weigh the time and cost of selecting and hiring professionals against the benefits of the advice and other services that they can provide.

It can seem like quite a challenge to find the right group of professionals to meet your specific business needs, but it's really a research process that includes getting references from friends, relatives, local professional associations, the chamber of commerce, and other professionals and business owners. There are plenty of places to look for a qualified attorney. For example:

- Local community groups and universities may also provide good leads.
- Professionals who specialize in helping start-ups often attend local entrepreneur conventions and meetings.
- Local colleges and trade schools offering business programs often feature attorneys, accountants, insurance consultants, and business consultants as guest speakers.

That notwithstanding, you can find a lawyer in the Yellow Pages where you'll see dozens of attorney listings. Lawyers often list their primary areas of practice, such as business, employment, or tax matters, for example. If you choose this route, ask the lawyer for a reference of three or four business clients to contact. Then call the references to confirm the lawyer's expertise, billing practice, and timely service.

It's a good idea to discuss your selection with your other advisors, because they often have experience using attorneys and know the ones who best suit your needs.

Check with the state and county bar association or licensing agency to determine whether any justifiable complaints have been filed against your prospective attorney.

The following sections give you some guidelines to help you evaluate your needs and make sound decisions about the attorneys' help that you enlist.

SELECTING AN ATTORNEY

Although any attorney can probably fulfill an entrepreneur's legal requirements, only a small fraction will have the expertise and experience to meet the entrepreneur's specific small business requirements. Would you go to a foot doctor to find out why you have a sore throat? It is just as important to match the attorney that you decide to hire with your specific type of business.

FINDING ATTORNEYS TO CONSIDER

In addition to identifying attorneys that you want to consider by getting references from people you know and by attending events where you can see local lawyers in action, you can do some research online at the following websites:

- **Attorney Find: www.attorneyfind.net.** Here you can sort possible choices of lawyers by location and specialty.
- **Lawyers.com: www.lawyers.com.** This site offers a wealth of legal information to help individuals better understand the law, make more informed legal choices, and identify high-quality legal representation. From Martindale-Hubbell, this site carries more than 420,000 listings of attorney firms worldwide.
- **Business Law Lounge: www.lectlaw.com/bus.html.** This site, the 'Lectric Law Library, is primarily for legal research, but it could help you find out more about attorneys that you're considering.

There is no single way to find a lawyer who is right for your business. One way to start the process is to call several lawyers you've been referred to. Some offer free consultations so you can get an initial feel for the individual and exchange information.

After you set up appointments to meet the attorneys you want to consider hiring, find out everything you need to know to make a fully informed choice. Keep the following list of questions in mind so that you can get the most from your meetings:

1. What is your experience in the area of legal matters specific to my type of business?

2. What percentage of your practice is devoted to my type of business? (For example, as a business owner, you may want an attorney who devotes the majority of his or her time to small business and contract law.)

3. What are your hourly rates?

4. How many attorneys are in your firm? Is it a full-service firm, do any of you specialize in small business legal matters?

5. Does the firm provide tax return preparation, or tax or estate planning?

6. Are you familiar with the following areas of federal and state law: income/estate taxation, corporations, contracts, partnerships, securities, antitrust, product liability, or the Uniform Commercial Code (UCC)?

7. Do you have knowledge about and experience in such nonlegal areas as business finance, financial accounting, management techniques, and ways to work with bankers, brokers, insurers, zoning boards, or industrial development agencies?

TIP

Your questions should be unique, based on your business's particular needs, so use this list as a guide.

After your interviews, review your notes and examine the strengths and weaknesses of each lawyer. No single factor will decide which lawyer to hire; you will need to weigh many factors to determine which is the "best fit" for you and your business needs.

FACTORS TO CONSIDER

Some of the factors to consider in weighing your choice of an attorney are listed here:

- **Availability.** Can the lawyer work with you immediately? Will other lawyers in the firm also work on your legal matters?

- **Comfort.** Do you feel comfortable with the lawyer? Do you trust the lawyer not to discuss private matters? Does the lawyer really listen to you?

- **Cost.** Do you feel comfortable and informed about the way you'll be charged for the legal services rendered?

- **Experience.** Does the lawyer have the necessary experience for your type of business?
- **Skills.** Does the lawyer know your specific industry and have connections that will save you time and money?

In the end, you'll have to decide which of these or any other factors are the most important to you. Most of the sites on the internet do not recommend or monitor attorneys because the perception of one attorney's competence is a unique judgment.

WHEN TO CALL IN AN ATTORNEY

The following list contains some of the situations in which complications are more than likely to arise will give you an idea of when you should call in an attorney:

- **Business start-up.** An attorney can assist you when you start up a business by clarifying your business objectives and analyzing your business proposal. Your attorney can evaluate the soundness of your business plan, research, and risk analysis. The attorney should also be able to recommend bankers, accountants, insurance professionals, government officials, and financial planners.
- **Business structure.** When you're considering setting up any form of corporation, partnership, or limited liability company (LLC), an attorney will steer you through all the legal documentation that is required and advise you on the differences between these structures so that you can make an informed decision.
- **Contracts.** Consult an attorney *before* you sign a contract, not afterward. Contracts should be drafted in writing to avoid possible misunderstandings. Seek your lawyer's advice before you sign contracts. Of course, your lawyer can also help you draw up contracts too!
- **Estate planning.** Attorneys can provide guidance concerning wills; trusts; estates, gifts, and income taxes; S corporations; powers of attorney; family partnerships; health-care proxies; living wills; and guardianships.
- **Formal written opinions.** When a business is sold or borrows money, opinions are often requested relating to specific regulatory problems, the priority of liens, absence of defaults, and other matters. A bank or purchaser of the business may request a formal written opinion from your business's lawyer.

- **Litigation.** An attorney can help you avoid lawsuits and legal hassles. If your business is incorporated, you must engage an attorney to represent it whenever it sues or is sued. An attorney is needed in areas of labor and management disputes; debt collection; buying, selling, or merging a business; licensing, copyrights, trademarks, and patents; bankruptcy and reorganization; or criminal matters to name a few.
- **Real estate.** An attorney should be consulted before a purchase contract or lease is signed. Consult an attorney regarding local codes; environmental concerns; zoning regulations; assessments against the property; liens that may have been placed on the real estate; the existence, validity, and terms of any leases; tenant and landlord agreements; the purchaser's right to assume existing mortgages; and services that must be provided by the landlord.

HOW MUCH WILL IT COST?

Hiring an attorney may not be as expensive as you may think. Attorneys charge for their services using one or a combination of these three methods:

- **Flat fees.** They are predisclosed amounts usually charged for basic legal matters, incorporation of a small business, real estate closings, basic wills, and bankruptcy.
- **Contingent fees.** In the contingent fee arrangement, you pay the attorney a certain percentage of your recovery through a suit if and only if you win, but the attorney cannot guarantee the result. If you sue for $1 million and you recover only $99 after trial or settlement, and there is a one third contingency fee arrangement, the attorney's fee will be $33.
- **Hourly fees.** Generally charged for all other types of cases, including estate planning and defense of lawsuits. Some companies retain an attorney on a monthly basis, whereby the attorney is paid a specified monthly retainer fee regardless of the amount of time spent on the client's matters.

You can do a lot to keep your expenses for legal work and advice under control by following these tips:

- **Be organized, prepared, and proactive.** Business owners can use an attorney more efficiently and save money, too. For example, if you need a contract drawn up, before you meet with the attorney, draw up a rough draft of all the key points that you want covered. With the draft done, the attorney can go over it quickly with you and just add the necessary legal language to protect your interests.

■ **Standardize your employment forms, contracts, noncompete or nondisclosure agreements, and any legal forms that your business may frequently use.** This way you pay for only the original legal drafting of the document once, rather than having an original document drawn up each time you have a need for one.

CAUTION

When you are not clear on what a legal term or contract clause means, ask! You are responsible for every agreement that you sign, so be sure that it's worded the way you intended it to be.

■ **Take initiative.** Keep the attorney informed of important business and legal issues that may have seemingly insignificant legal consequences that the attorney may spot. More important, the attorney will have your business at the forefront of his or her thoughts if any relevant legal issues occur.

Whatever the fee structure is, the client must pay for all disbursements, such as process service fees, investigations, court costs, travel expenses, long-distance calls, expert testimony, medical reports, appraisals, and all other out-of-pocket expenses.

After you've decided on fee terms, ask for a written fee agreement that sets forth the services to be performed by the attorney, the amount of the legal fee (hourly rate, contingent, or flat), and the anticipated amount of disbursements.

WORKING WITH YOUR ATTORNEY

You need to understand some factors about your working relationship with your attorney. The major ones are covered in the following sections.

ATTORNEY-CLIENT PRIVILEGE

It is of primary importance to define the boundaries of your attorney-client privilege, as outlined in the following list:

■ **A lawyer employed or retained by a corporation or similar entity owes allegiance to the entity.** Allegiance is not owed to a shareholder, director, officer, employee, representative, or other person connected with the entity. Occasionally, a lawyer for an entity is asked to represent a person connected with the entity in an individual capacity. In such cases, the lawyer may serve the individual only if the lawyer is convinced that differing interests are not present.

■ **When hiring an attorney, clarify whom the attorney represents.**
The attorney-client privilege does not protect communications with a lawyer unless the person making the communication is a client. If the client is a corporation, privilege will protect communications made by any company employee to the attorney, if the communications relate to the employee's duties and are made at the direction of a corporate superior. Although the company founders may initially be the only representatives of the company, they are usually not considered the client. Thus, if the board of directors later decides to fire the founder, the attorney cannot represent both the founder and the company. Additionally, any communications between the attorney and the founder would not be privileged.

CAUTION

Attorney-client privilege does not extend to business advice. In addition, the privilege is lost by the client if any communication with the attorney is intended to further a crime or an illegal act, or if any communication is shared with others or is witnessed by outsiders.

THE 30-SECOND RECAP

■ Referrals are often the best way to find attorneys, accountants, and other professionals to help you with your business.

■ You can do a lot to keep your expenses for legal work and advice under control.

■ Research and interview professionals who you're considering, and select those who are knowledgeable about your specific type of business.

Protecting Your Trade Secrets

A rose by any other name may be trademarked. Write, and it shall be copyrighted. Invent a better mousetrap and file a patent. All these go under the label of intellectual property. Your business plan may be a better-kept trade secret than our top-secret nuclear files. This section explores the world of trademarks (and its cousin the service mark), copyrights, and patents so that you can hang on to your trade secrets.

MAKING YOUR MARK

Your company name is important to your business because, with any luck, customers will identify with it. If you have any doubt about its importance, think about the most identifiable names and symbols in this country. There may be some isolated soul in this world who hasn't heard of Coca-Cola, but it's doubtful. Although the name and symbol of your small business may not ever gain worldwide recognition, you do want to make sure that it's all yours to do with as you please.

TRADEMARK AND SERVICE MARK

Federal and state laws permit you to trademark your products and service mark your services. Your business can continue without a trademark, but if you want to expand, especially through Internet sales, then consider a trademark.

A trademark (or service mark) is a word, phrase, symbol, or design (or combination of words, phrases, symbols, and designs) that identifies and distinguishes one from another the source of the goods or services. To simplify things a little, in our discussions in this section, I'll use trademark and service mark interchangeably. For example, McDonald's trademarks virtually all its "Mc" products. Nike trademarks its swoosh. Mr. Peanut is a trademarked figure to identify Planters brand peanuts. "Winston tastes good like a cigarette should" was a popular trademarked slogan from the 1950s.

A trademark must be distinctive enough to enable consumers to identify the manufacturer of the product easily and to differentiate among competitive merchandise. Trademarks may fall into these categories:

- Independent marks
- Secondary meaning
- Trade dress

Invented *trade names* may become powerful trademarks, such as Xerox, Kodak, and Pepsi. Consumers can easily identify these brands because they have become strong marks without describing any particular product. Keep in mind, though, that you can't trademark general terms, geographic terms, or personal names—unless you can give them what's known as a "secondary meaning." Steven Jobs couldn't trademark the apples he could grow in an orchard, but he could trademark the apple as a symbol for the computers he invented.

PLAIN ENGLISH

The term **trade name** indicates a business name, and may be protected as a trademark if it's the same as the company's product.

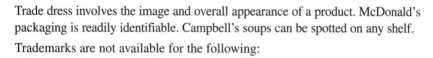

Trade dress involves the image and overall appearance of a product. McDonald's packaging is readily identifiable. Campbell's soups can be spotted on any shelf.

Trademarks are not available for the following:

- An image of a living person without consent
- Material that is immoral, deceptive, or scandalous
- Disparagement of persons, institutions, beliefs, and symbols
- Anything similar to a current trademark if likely to deceive

CREATING THE TRADEMARK AND SERVICE MARK

The trademark or service mark may be established by using the mark in commerce or registering the mark with the U.S. Patent and Trademark Office (PTO). Many states have their own trademark offices. After the mark is used for goods or services, it exists and may be protected by law, unless it conflicts with an existing mark.

Federal registration provides the broadest protection and is recommended if you are going to conduct your business in more than one state. Registration gives nationwide notice that the trademark belongs exclusively to you and cannot be used without your permission. You use the symbol ® as public notice of the federal registration. The application form and instructions can be obtained from the PTO website: www.uspto.gov.

TIP

Take advantage of the most up-to-date search engines. The PTO is continuing to develop its electronic search capacity, so check with its website before proceeding with the application.

After you apply, the PTO publishes your application; if there is no objection, the office issues you a certificate of registration. To determine whether there is a conflict between two marks, the PTO looks at the likelihood of confusion, that is, whether consumers would be likely to associate the goods or services of one party with those of another party. For example, another soup company using the distinctive red and white Campbell's label would confuse grocery shoppers—but not if the label were on a can of paint. You should renew your federal registration every 10 years.

PROTECTING THE MARK

Make sure that you document and substantiate when you first used your trademark, perhaps with a dated invoice that displays the trademark. Continue to use the trademark on your advertising, letterhead, and invoices, and note whether it is a registered trademark or state protected, by using the trademark or service mark symbol (™ or ˢᴹ) next to it. If you don't use it, you could lose it.

Vigorously enforce your trademark rights. If you discover another company using the mark, or infringing on your copyright, send the company a letter demanding it refrain from future use. If the company continues to infringe, then you may have to sue. If you win the lawsuit, you could receive an injunction against the defendant and damages.

CAUTION

A word of warning: Aspirin was once trademarked, but it became used so generically that it went into the public domain, and was no longer protected. You must rigorously enforce the trademark by demanding that any infringer stop using your mark, or you will sue.

The PTO has recently issued an Examination Guide to deal with trademarks, service marks, and domain names.

COPYRIGHTING PRINTED OR RECORDED WORK

Suppose you create a model business plan that could be sold to others. Or your advertising materials are unique and creative, but you want to add one superstar, say, Snoopy. On a personal level, you enjoy downloading music from the Internet. Before you do anything, think copyright.

CREATING COPYRIGHT MATERIAL

Federal copyright law protects the creator of literary or artistic works. When the work is in a fixed form—such as a manuscript or piece of sheet music— there exists an automatic and immediate copyright. Copyright protection exists at the moment of creation, even if the work is never published. The creator doesn't have to affix the copyright notice to the work, although doing so and filing with the Copyright Office provides some legal advantages that we'll discuss later in this section.

For example, just by typing up your business plan, you've copyrighted it. It is yours and no one else has the right to publish it or use it.

To be copyrighted, a work must be original and fall within one of these categories:

- Literary works
- Musical works
- Dramatic works
- Pantomimes and choreographic works
- Pictorial, graphic, and sculptural works
- Motion pictures and audiovisual works
- Sound recordings
- Architectural works

All kinds of work may be copyrighted, including some that is slightly less than completely original, such as a compilation of short stories—the compiler would hold the copyright to that collection, as long as he or she received permission to collect the works from the original authors.

The copyright law specifically does not offer protection for an idea, procedure, process, system, method of operation, concept, principle, or discovery. For example, you may have a great idea for communicating to customers through the Internet, but you can't copyright it. However, if you write an article describing the idea, the article itself is copyrighted. Mystery writers constantly seek new ways to kill victims; writers can freely borrow the idea from others without violating copyright law. But if one writer used the words and characters of another, he or she would be infringing on the copyright and could be liable for damages.

TIP

If you create a computer program, copyright it! The Copyright Office has accepted software registration for several years.

All works created are protected for the life of the author plus 70 years; then, unless the author's estate extends the copyright, the work reverts to the public domain.

After the copyright material has been created, the owner has the exclusive right to do, or to authorize others to do, the following:

- Reproduce the work
- Prepare derivative works based upon the work
- Distribute copies of the work
- Perform or display the work publicly

TIP

If you hire someone to create a business plan or brochure for you, make sure that your contract is "work for hire." This type of contract allows you to own the copyright to the material the work-for-hire writer creates.

PROTECTING THE COPYRIGHT

Although the copyright is secured immediately upon creation, registration with the U.S. Copyright Office is recommended. Whether you register or not, affix the copyright notice upon the work using a line like, "Copyright 2000 Stephen M. Maple." The notice informs the public that the work is copyrighted. If someone uses the work without the copyright owner's permission, the infringer may be liable for damages.

Although informal copyright has legal force, registration with the Copyright Office has certain advantages, including ...

- Creating a public record of the copyright.
- Providing the necessary prerequisite to filing an *infringement* lawsuit.

PLAIN ENGLISH

An **infringement** is the improper use of a patent, writing, graphic, or trademark without permission, without notice, and especially without contracting for payment of a royalty. Even though the infringement may be accidental (an inventor thinks he is the first to develop the widget although someone else has a patent), the party infringing is responsible to pay the original patent or copyright owner substantial damages, which can be the normal royalty or as much as the infringers' accumulated gross profits.

■ Entitlement to statutory damages and attorney fees if the copyright is found to be infringed upon.

Registration is a rather simple process: Complete the application form, enclose the fee, and send it back along with a copy of the work. Registration is effective as soon as you meet the requirements.

TIP

If your business operates on an international basis, make sure to ask the Copyright Office for a pamphlet that defines your right of copyright in that venue.

INFRINGEMENT AND FAIR USE

Anyone who violates the exclusive rights of the copyright owner is liable to the owner for infringement. This includes engaging in authorized reproduction, adaptation, public distribution, public performance, public display, and importation. If someone has infringed on your copyrighted work, you may sue in federal court. Typically, you will ask the court to issue an injunction prohibiting future infringement, and allowing for you to receive money damages and recoup attorneys' fees. A prerequisite for the lawsuit is registration of the copyright. Actual damages are based on the harm caused to the copyright holder by the infringement. As an alternative to actual damages, the owner can elect to recover statutory damages from $500 to $20,000, or up to $100,000 if the infringement is willful.

Copyright law does provide a limited exception to infringement, referred to as fair use. Clearly, this exception is very limited. The law permits such use for purposes of literary criticism, comment, news reporting, teaching, scholarship, and research.

Factors considered under fair use include the following:

■ The purpose and character of the use, including whether it's used for commercial or nonprofit use.
■ The nature of copyrighted work.
■ The amount and substantiality of the portion used in relation to the whole work.
■ The effect of use upon the potential market for the work.

Get permission for any commercial use of copyrighted material. Even one picture of Snoopy in a an ad could violate the law. However, if you're using two pages out of a large manual for internal training purposes only, this would likely be fair use.

PATENTS FOR USEFUL THINGS

A patent for an invention is the grant of a property right to the inventor, issued by the U.S. Patent and Trademark Office. The grant of a patent involves the right to exclude others from making, using, or offering for sale the invention.

CREATING A PATENT

Patent law recognizes two kinds of patents: a utility patent and a design patent. Any person who invents or discovers any new and useful process, machine, manufacture or composition of matter, or any new and useful improvement can be granted a utility patent. For example, if your company invents a new chemical compound, you can get a utility patent on it.

A utility patent is appropriate for inventions that are new, useful, and nonobvious. For an invention to be nonobvious, a person with ordinary skill in the technology involved would be able to see a significant difference between the new invention and those similar to it created in the past. This test precludes a patent for minor tinkering on a previously patented invention.

A design patent covers an object's novel nonfunctional visual and tactile characteristics, including the shape of a product and the way that it is decorated.

The inventor must apply to the U.S. Patent and Trademark Office (PTO) for a patent. Usually a business hires a patent attorney or agent to perform a patent search before the application. The search will help identify any prior patents that may conflict with the applicant's claim. The patent application must include the following:

- A specified patentable claim
- A summary of the invention
- Drawings showing each feature to the invention

TIP

Make sure you get your employees who invent for you to sign an agreement requiring them to assign any patents to the employer. Although the so-called "shop right" may give an employer the implied right to an assignment, it is better to make the assignment explicit.

The description must be specific enough to distinguish it from other inventions. If the invention is an improvement on another product, the specification must point out the part of the original product to which the improvement relates.

After the patent has been applied for the inventor may attach the notice "Patent Pending." The PTO assigns the application to an examiner who searches for U.S. and foreign patents to determine whether the applicant's invention is new, useful, and nonobvious. The PTO keeps the information on the application strictly confidential. After the examiner is satisfied, the PTO issues the patent.

However, if the PTO denies the patent application, the examiner will issue a formal action giving specific reasons why the claims on the application are defective or are not patentable in light of prior inventions. If the patent is denied, the applicant may request reconsideration and reply to all of the examiner's objections. If there is a final rejection, the applicant can request review by the Board of Patent Appeals; if further denied, the applicant can appeal to the federal court of appeals or sue the commissioner in the District Court of the District of Columbia.

PROTECTING THE PATENT

The patentee (owner) has a grant that confers the right to exclude others from making, using, selling, and so on, the invention for a period of 20 years (14 years for a design patent).

A violation of the owner's exclusive right is called an infringement. The owner can sue for the infringement in federal court, and the owner has the burden of proof and must show how the defendant's device or process infringes on the patent. The defendant is liable even though he or she made a trivial change or slight improvement.

If the court finds an infringement has been found, it will likely issue an injunction. The court may also award damages adequate to compensate for the infringement, such as a reasonable royalty fee for the use by the infringer. The owner's lost profits, including sales that went to the infringer, may be a good measure of damages. If the violation was willful, the court could triple the damages as well as award attorney fees.

TIP

Consult your state department of commerce and industry about helping you develop and market your invention.

TRADE SECRETS KEPT

You may have a business process or information that cannot be patented, copyrighted, or trademarked, but is important to your business success. There is no federal law that protects trade secrets, but most states have a statute that protects your secrets.

Trade secrets can include such things as the following:

- Business plans and marketing strategies
- Customer lists not generally available
- Databases
- Computer programs
- Product specifications
- Recipes
- Employee handbooks

Thus trade secrets apply to both ideas and the expression of those ideas.

The subject matter of the trade secret must be kept secret, and the owner must take reasonable efforts to maintain secrecy. In addition to asking employees and customers to sign contracts saying they agree not to disclose trade secrets, you may want to keep trade secret documents apart from ordinary files, label the materials as confidential, and have a sign-out policy. The secret must have actual or potential independent economic value, such as a market survey or a recipe for special barbeque sauce.

TIP

Require employees who have access to trade secrets to sign an agreement not to disclose the confidential information. Likewise, your customers who have access to trade secrets should sign a nondisclosure agreement. Emphasize that this provision is important and will be strictly enforced. Indicate in the agreements what information is considered a trade secret.

State statutes impose liability only if there is a misappropriation of the trade secret. For example, if a competitor hires away one of your employees and obtains the secret information, the competitor has violated the statute. Of course, if you voluntarily disclose this information to the public, it's no longer a trade secret and anyone can use it. Likewise, if the information becomes dated, such as a customer list that is several years old, it is no longer trade secret information.

The owner of the trade secret can sue in state court (or federal court if there is diversity jurisdiction) for an injunction prohibiting its use, and for damages. For example, if the competitor used your secret customer list to lure your customers away, you may sue for lost profits or for whatever the misappropriator gained (such as savings due to the efficient use of your databases).

HELPFUL SOURCES ABOUT PATENTS AND TRADEMARKS

The PTO website provides very useful information for patents and trademarks: www.uspto.gov; the Copyright Office website is www.loc.gov. Information on intellectual property is available at www.legal.net. Cornell University website is informative: www.law.cornell.edu. Check out www.findlaw.com. State websites may contain information about state registered trademarks, and contain the trade secret statute. Check with your state and local governments to obtain assistance on promoting your inventions.

THE 30-SECOND RECAP

- Register your product name with the U.S. Patent and Trademark Office.
- Copyright protection begins when the written work is finished, but may be registered with the U.S. Copyright Office.
- Patents for inventions are protected for 20 years.
- Confidential information may be protected under state trade secret statute.
- Online trademark searches are becoming a reality.

Government Regulation of What You Produce

As the manufacturer (producer) of products or services, some regulations or laws at one governmental level or another will probably affect you. Which ones you must comply with are usually determined by the products or services that you plan to sell.

Generally, these laws relate to the safety, health, and general well-being of the consumer, and were written to ensure that manufacturers use proper labels, adhere to health or safety standards, and make disclosures to protect the consumer in all of these areas.

There are thousands of products you could create, many more than we can cover in the scope of this book. The information contained in this section is simply provided to help point you in the right direction. If you think that your product(s) may fall into any of the categories described, be sure to contact the government agency responsible for the regulation to get compliance details. If you are not quite sure about how certain laws affect your products, get some legal advice before you start selling them.

THE CONSUMER PRODUCT SAFETY ACT

The Consumer Product Safety Commission (CPSC) oversees the *Consumer Product Safety Act,* which protects the public against unreasonable risks of injury associated with consumer products. CPSC (www.cpsc.gov) has a toll-free hotline, 1-800-638-2772, with a menu from which you can select publications, report problems with purchased products, or connect with the Small Business Ombudsman department, which offers information to help business owners comply with CPSC regulations or solve problems related to them.

CAUTION

Consumer lawsuits are common these days, so make sure that you know what safety laws are associated with your product line. See to it that all your products comply with the applicable laws before you start selling them.

The CPSC is very active in the area of consumer products and toys designed for children. If you make any toys, be extra careful about the materials that you plan to use, and be sure to meet all the guidelines required for safety.

SUGGESTED SAFETY GUIDELINES FOR MAKING TOYS

The CPSC's guidelines for making toys follow:

- Materials used must be nontoxic, nonflammable, and nonpoisonous.
- Items must be too large to be swallowed.
- Items must have no sharp edges or points.
- Items must not break easily or be apt to leave sharp or jagged edges if broken.
- Items must not be put together where nails, pins, or wires could be easily exposed.
- Use only paints, varnishes, and other finishes that are labeled *nontoxic* (lead-free).

TIP

If your business makes collectible items such as dolls, teddy bears, antique toy replicas, or other items that might look like toys but that are not intended for children, protect yourself by adding a label or a hang tag to them with the proper disclosure ("Not recommended for children under the age of three," for example).

PAINTS AND SURFACE COATINGS

Paints and surface coatings (varnish, lacquer, shellac, and other finishes) sold for household use must meet the *Consumer Product Safety Act's (CPSA)* requirements for minimum amounts of lead. The CPSA has banned paints and finishes that contain more than .06 percent lead by weight. Acrylics and other water-based paints are nontoxic. As a precaution, always check to make sure that the label shows that the product is nontoxic.

Specialty paints must have a warning on the label about the lead content. However, beware: "Artist's paints" are not required to have a warning label of any kind because they are exempt from the CPSC's lead-in-paint ban, so be sure to check all the paints, varnishes, or finishing coat materials used on your products with a lead-testing kit (available in paint stores), especially if they are intended for use in children's toys or furnishings.

The *Federal Hazardous Substances Act* deals with products that are toxic or corrosive, that are irritants, or that are strong sensitizers, like lye. If you're making products that may use such substances, double-check to make sure you're in compliance with all the applicable regulations or laws.

LEAD TESTING FOR FOOD OR DRINK CONTAINERS

If you are planning to make ceramic, pottery, or porcelain items that could be used for food or drink containers, be sure you lead-test them before you sell them. The Food and Drug Administration (FDA) regularly makes random lead tests of food container products being shipped in interstate commerce, and often works in conjunction with your state's department of health. The FDA is empowered to confiscate any products that fail to meet the lead release guideline of less than 0.5 parts per million.

If making your products "food safe" is a concern, start by designing a product line based on decorative ware, and label all food or drink style pieces as "to be used for decorative purposes only," or make them unusable by drilling a hole in the bottom of each piece. For your safety, do not forget that your kiln should have a hood-exhaust system that vents to the outdoors and is positioned so it will not vent into an area where people or animals will be exposed to lead fumes.

LABELS FOR TEXTILES, FABRICS, FIBERS, AND YARN OR WOOL PRODUCTS

The *Federal Fair Packaging and Labeling Act* requires that a label identify the product. The label must show the name of the manufacturer or distributor, and the net quantity of the contents. You can get a copy of this law from the Federal Trade Commission (FTC), Washington, D.C. 20580 (www.FTC.gov/).

The law requires labels if you produce products using textiles, fabrics, fibers, yarn, or wool to make wearing apparel, household furnishings, decorative accessories, or soft toys. Some state and federal government agencies require the attachment of a variety of different tags or labels to products sold in the consumer marketplace, as described in the following sections.

CONTENT LABELING LAW

The Content Labeling Law is part of the *Textile Fiber Productions Identification Act,* monitored by both the Bureau of Consumer Protection and the Federal Trade Commission (FTC). It covers what is in a product and who makes it.

The law requires that a special label or hang tag be attached to all textile wearing apparel and household furnishings (except wall hangings) that are made of any fabric, fiber, or yarn. This includes wearing apparel and accessories, decorative accessories, quilts, pillows, comforters, table linens, stuffed toys, floor cloths, rugs, and so forth. The tag or label must include the name of the manufacturer, and the generic name and percentages of all fibers in the product that amount to 5 percent or more, listed in order of predominance by weight content. For example: cotton 50 percent, polyester 35 percent, nylon 15 percent.

CARE LABELING LAW

The Care Labeling Law, also part of the *Textile Fiber Productions Identification Act,* covers how to care for products. Wearing apparel and household furnishings of any kind made from textiles (any fabric, yarn, or fiber), including suede and leather, must have a "permanent care" label explaining how to take care of the product. For detailed information about permanent care labeling, go to the FTC website at www.FTC.gov/, or write to the Consumer Response Center, Room 130, Federal Trade Commission, 600 Pennsylvania Avenue, NW; Washington, DC 20580.

If you're already aware of the details of the Care Labeling Rule (16 CFR Part 423), be sure that you're up-to-date on the Amended Care Labeling Rule. The two amendments concern clarification of cleaning instructions and revision of the water temperature definitions.

For complete details on the Amended Care Labeling Rule, see www.FTC.gov/os/2000/07/carelabelingrule.html, or write to the FTC at the address in the preceding section.

WOOL CONTENT LABEL LAW

The FTC requires products made with any wool content to have an additional label. *The Wool Products Labeling Act of 1939* requires the labels of all wool or textile products to clearly indicate when imported fibers are used. For example, a sweater knitted in the United States but made from wool yarn imported from Scotland would read, "Made in the USA from imported products" (or similar wording). If the wool yarn was spun in the United States, a wool product label could be as simple as, "Made in the USA."

STATE BEDDING AND UPHOLSTERED FURNITURE LAWS

State labeling laws affect sellers of items that have "concealed filling," such as dolls, teddy bears and critters, stuffed toys, pillows, quilts, comforters, soft picture frames, soft or padded books, and even scrapbooks or album covers. Contact your state's consumer protection agency, department of health, or department of commerce and industry standards to find out if your state has a bedding and upholstered furniture law, and where to get information about it.

The law makes no distinction between large manufacturers and those who just make a few handmade items, so a small producer is just as liable for infractions as a large manufacturing company.

CAUTION

If you produce a product that contains "concealed filling" (stuffing), be sure to check with your state officials before you start to sell it.

If you plan to sell wholesale or via shops, take every precaution possible to make sure you have the proper labels on all your products. You may be required to purchase a license and your merchandise will have to have tags imprinted with your special registry number. NCA has learned that another possible solution is to use the fiber-fill manufacturer's information and license number (from the bulk packaging or poly bag the fill arrives in) to label products you produce using that manufacturer's fiber fill.

Before you take this alternative, however, it is strongly suggested that you check with the manufacturer you purchase your fill contents from to be sure such labeling complies with this law.

THE FLAMMABLE FABRICS ACT

The Flammable Fabrics Act, regulated by the CPSC, pertains to manufacturers who sell products made of fabric, particularly products for children manufacturers and especially those who sell products wholesale or to shops. This act prohibits the movement in interstate commerce of articles of wearing apparel and fabrics that are so highly flammable they are dangerous when worn or used for other purposes.

Most fabrics are in compliance with this act, but if you make children's clothes or toys, you'll want to make doubly sure the fabrics you use are safe. Be sure your fabric supplier is in compliance with *The Flammable Fabrics Act.* The guarantee of compliance is often stated on the supplier's invoice; if it isn't, ask the supplier for a written guarantee, or check with the CPSC to find out if the supplier or manufacturer has filed for a continuing guarantee. For more details on this act, see www.cpsc.gov/businfo/ffa.pdf.

OTHER PRODUCTS THAT MAY REQUIRE LABELING

To find out whether products you're producing may require labeling, check the following FTC web pages, or write to the address in the preceding section, "Content Labeling Law."

- Advertising and labeling of feather and down products: www.FTC.gov/bcp/conline/pubs/buspubs/down.htm
- Fur Product Labeling Act: www.FTC.gov/os/statutes/textile/furact.htm
- Wedding gown labels: www.FTC.gov/bcp/conline/pubs/buspubs/wedgown.htm
- Labeling and advertising cotton products: www.FTC.gov/bcp/conline/pubs/buspubs/cotton.htm
- FTC/U.S. Customs Service regarding textile country of origin marking: www.FTC.gov/be/v980034.htm

TIP

You can comply with CPSC as well as local fire-safety regulations by asking the supplier or manufacturer of a product to supply compliance documentation.

MAKING THE REQUIRED LABELS

Many small business owners make whatever tags or labels are required and affix them in the manner specified by the law. With a computer and the wide array of software available, making your own labels is a very practical option. Of course, you can opt to order them from companies that specialize in tags and labels. They offer stock labels and custom designs to meet specific needs. Label supply sources include ...

- **Name Maker Inc.,** website: www.namemaker.com.
- **Sterling Name Tape Company,** website: www.sterlingtape.com/.
- **Widby Fabric Label Company,** website: www.widbylabel.com/.

FOOD AND THE GIFT-BASKET INDUSTRY

A majority of gift-basket makers use food as a staple in the contents of their arrangements. So if your business is in this industry, you have to find out what your state laws are for the handling and preparation of food items sold to consumers. The safest way to protect yourself and your clients is to purchase and use only prepackaged foods, snacks, and beverages. That means that items are in ready-to-use size units, packed in cellophane, boxes, or bags so that your hands have no direct contact with the food products.

CAUTION

Is including alcohol in your gift baskets worth the licensing expense, and the risk, for example, that a minor might accept delivery and drink the alcohol?

When you check with your health department, find out:

- If they restrict certain types of businesses from buying prepackaged food for resale in baskets.
- If an inspection of your premises is required.
- If a permit or health department certification is required.
- What, if any, fees are involved.

In many states a health department license is required if you prepare or wrap food, but is not if you use only prepackaged food items. Be sure to check your state and local regulations governing gift baskets produced by home-based businesses.

COMMERCIAL-USE ISSUES

Many fabrics, images, and likenesses have restrictions on their commercial use. Two areas commonly related to products produced from fabrics are outlined in the following sections.

COMMERCIAL USE OF DESIGNER FABRICS AND LOGOS

Just because you can buy designer fabrics from a wholesaler or a manufacturer does not mean you have unlimited commercial use of it. Always ask the fabric distributor if there are any restrictions on its commercial use, or contact the copyright owner or manufacturer to be sure.

On fabrics purchased at retail shops, check the salvage edge for warnings. If there is a notice such as "This fabric is for individual consumption (or use) only," or if there's a copyright notice with a designer's name, *do not use it to make your products.* For example, you must avoid any use of designs made by Disney, copyrighted cartoon characters, or sports logos such as the NFL's.

TIP

If you do want to use a particular team's sports logo or a famous cartoon, for example, you'll most likely have to pay a licensing fee and a percentage of your sales to the copyright holder for the right to use it. To find out the cost and details, call the company and ask for the licensing department. Of course, the more recognizable the property, the more you can expect to pay for the licensing rights.

CELEBRITY RIGHTS ACT

The Celebrity Rights Act is a special law that protects the rights of deceased personalities. You cannot produce a product, advertise a product, or provide a service that in any way utilizes the name, photograph, likeness, voice, or signature of a deceased person for a period lasting 50 years after that person's death unless you have a license or special permission. Manufacturers, distributors, and retailers caught selling unlicensed products can be sued, so forget about using Elvis in a design for your new line of wall hangings.

TIP

If you want to find out who handles the estate of a celebrity, you can contact the Academy of Motion Picture Arts, at www.oscar.org/, or the Screen Actor's Guild, at www.sag.org/.

PERSONAL CARE PRODUCTS AND HERBAL REMEDIES (OR AROMATHERAPY)

The FDA statute defines cosmetics as "articles intended to be rubbed ... or otherwise applied to the human body ... for cleaning ... except that the term cosmetics shall *not include soap,*" unless the soap claims to have certain cosmetic properties.

SANITARY PRODUCTION OF COSMETICS

If federal law classifies your product as a cosmetic, you must manufacture and store it under sanitary conditions and avoid contamination with filth. This is a standard of cleanliness that small businesses are hard pressed to meet. Sanitized equipment, gloves, hairnets, confirmation of weights and measures by a second person, sampling, water testing, and absence of tobacco products are just a few of the Good Manufacturing Practice Guidelines that cosmetic manufacturers are measured against.

SOAP LABELING

Whether or not your soap is considered a cosmetic under FDA rules, the label must contain several things:

- The weight must always be expressed in ounces (you may also include metric units).
- The name and complete address of the manufacturer must be listed. (The street address may be omitted only if the company is listed in a current telephone directory.)
- If under FDA regulations your soap is classified as a cosmetic, you must list all *ingredients* in the order of their predominance. Color additives and ingredients of less than 1 percent may be listed without regard for predominance.

PLAIN ENGLISH

Ingredients as defined by the FDA means "any single chemical entity or mixture used as a component in the making of any cosmetic product." This definition clearly disputes the erroneous impression, which some soap makers have, that a chemical is not an ingredient if it reacts with other chemicals and thus is no longer present in the final product.

- Some ingredients are exempt from disclosure regulations and may be referred to as "and other ingredients."

- Listed ingredients must be identified by the names established or adopted by regulation. The list of ingredients must be conspicuously placed on the product label so that it is likely to be read by the purchaser.

- If the safety of your materials has not been substantiated—for instance, if you used a color additive not tested and approved by the FDA (a natural colorant, for example, such as rose hips or brazilwood)—your label may have to carry a conspicuous warning: "Warning: The safety of this product has not been determined." That is why many soap makers prefer to work with soap base and commercial melt-and-pour products—to avoid having their product classified as a cosmetic.

A good book to read on this subject is *The Soapmaker's Companion* (Storey Books, 1977), by Susan Miller Cavtich.

HERBAL REMEDIES: AROMATHERAPY

Currently, alternative remedies can fall under food or drug regulations, depending on their ingredients and the claims being made about them. Remedies that are governed by food regulations are not required to meet any standards in terms of efficacy or patient information. Those that are deemed to be drugs are few and far between, partly because of the expense involved (considered prohibitive by the many small producers of alternative remedies) and partly because the scientific testing applied to mainstream, single active-ingredient synthetic drugs cannot be transferred to most alternative remedies.

By law, drug labels must provide essential information, but herbal remedies are being marketed as "dietary supplements" with little of the type of information needed to enable people to use these products properly. The herbal industry blames current regulatory policies for some of these problems. The FDA is bound by law to regulate products that make medical claims as drugs. Be sure to contact the FDA and visit the website www.fda.gov/comments.html to get a clear understanding of the rules and regulations before selling your products.

FOOD PRODUCTS FOR RESALE OR CATERING

The state health departments under the guidance of the FDA regulations require licenses for and inspection of the facilities where food products are made. The regulations are known in the business as the "commercial kitchen laws."

In most cases, the regulations governing the preparation of food products for resale require a kitchen, utensils, a food storage area, and appliances that are separate from those for your personal or family use. The food products prepared for resale also cannot be commingled with the food used for your family.

Strict sanitary guidelines are enforced, even more rigidly than those required for the cosmetics industry; in many states, it is almost impossibly costly to set up a food-related home-based business. However, enterprising individuals have found that renting time-sharing space in a commercial kitchen (using a restaurant kitchen during off-hours, for example) or the facilities at churches or private clubs is a way to get around the problem.

THE FEDERAL TRADE COMMISSION AND MAIL ORDERS

FTC rules apply to all businesses and cover a broad range of categories, such as trade practices, truth in advertising, unfair methods of competition, product labeling, unfair or deceptive acts and practices, and mail-order marketing. For example, the word *new* can be used to describe a product only for the first six months of its life. To use it afterward is in violation of FTC rules. The FTC offers free booklets on these categories. Every new business should order a set and get up-to-speed on these regulations.

TIP

To obtain pamphlets on FTC rules, go to www.FTC.gov, or write to the Consumer Response Center, Room 130, Federal Trade Commission, 600 Pennsylvania Avenue, NW, Washington, DC 20580.

If you take orders through the mail, you need to become familiar with the FTC's Rule Concerning Mail-Order Merchandise (16 CFR 435). The rule is explained in an easy-to-read booklet, "A Business Guide to the Federal Trade Commission's Mail Order Rule." Some of its basic features are summarized here:

■ You must ship the merchandise within 30 days after you receive a properly completed order and payment, unless your ad clearly states that it will take longer. This rule is strictly enforced, with possible fines of up to $10,000 for each violation.

■ If there will be a delay, you must notify the customer in writing. You must give the customer the option of a new shipment date (if known) or the opportunity to cancel the order and receive a full refund. You must give the customer a postage-free way to reply. You may assume that a customer who does not reply has agreed to the delay.

CAUTION

If your ad clearly states that it will take longer than 30 days to ship your merchandise, it's important to put a notice on your order form stating that "orders are shipped within six to eight weeks," for example. You may not need to take that long, but this allows a cushion for unforeseen delays.

- If the customer cancels, you must refund the customer's money within seven days of receiving the canceled order. If the customer used a credit card, you must issue the credit within one billing cycle.
- A customer who consents to an indefinite delay can still cancel the order at any time before its shipment.
- A customer who cancels or never receives the ordered merchandise does not have to accept a store credit in place of a refund, but that customer is entitled to a cash refund or a credit on the charge card used.

The mail-order rule does not cover mail-order photo finishing; spaced deliveries, such as magazines (except for the first shipment); sales of seeds and growing plants; COD orders; or orders made by telephone and charged to a credit card account.

THE VALUE OF DISCLAIMERS

A final precaution: The liberal use of disclaimers is strongly recommended. A few little words, such as "Not recommended for children under five years old," or "This item is not a toy" can mean so much. A disclaimer serves as a warning to the buyer, but much more than that, it may save you from being dragged into court for a product liability claim. The disclaimer should be printed on a label or a hang tag attached to the product.

A good rule of thumb for disclaimers is that if you have even the slightest question of whether you should use one, *use it.* It's a pretty cheap way to have a little extra insurance and peace of mind.

THE 30-SECOND RECAP

- The consumer product safety rules will affect your business, especially if you make products for children.
- You must get written permission to use designer fabrics, logos, and celebrity-related images or words for your product or service.

- If you use any textiles or fabrics in your products, you must comply with content and care labeling laws.

- Personal care and aromatherapy products that make any medical claims are regulated by the FDA.

- Liberally use disclaimers to protect yourself, and attach them to your products.

Employment Law 1: Having the Right Documentation

Decisions. You have hired your employees and established their compensation, but now for the really difficult task—management. You need to develop an employee handbook to guide employee conduct and specify employee benefits. You need to avoid violating antidiscrimination statutes when you discharge or discipline an employee. That's what is discussed in this section.

PUT IT IN WRITING

"Put it in writing" is especially good advice for employers. Every employer should have an employee handbook, which is a handy reference for employment policies and employee benefits. Most small businesses do not have written contracts for their employees; the employees are at-will and may be terminated at any time for any legal reason, which you should state in the employee handbook.

EMPLOYEE HANDBOOKS

Prepare an employee handbook, and then give it to each new employee. The handbook communicates your employment rules and the employee's benefits. You can prepare a draft of the handbook, and then have it reviewed by your employment attorney. The handbook should be well-written and concise. It is suggested that the handbook include the following:

- **An introduction.** The introduction should include a brief history of your business and its products and services. You should also welcome your new employee as a member of your team.

- **Hours.** Your handbook should define normal business hours and include a reminder that employees may be requested to work overtime (for which they will be compensated at one and one half their hourly pay for any hours over 40 in a week), as required by the *Fair Labor Standards Act.*

■ **Pay.** Explain how the criteria for an employee's initial pay is established. Then discuss the procedure involved in receiving raises, including performance reviews. Because you are a small business, pay increases usually depend on business success and you need to emphasize the correlation between an employee's efforts and company success. If you intend to offer bonuses, explain how you'll determine who gets them and how much they'll be.

■ **Benefits.** List and explain all the employee fringe benefits you provide, such as paid vacations, paid holidays, medical insurance, group term life insurance, pensions, unpaid leaves, and others that you intend to make available. Indicate what is required to qualify for each benefit, such as one year of service before participation in the pension plan. Any benefit mandated by law, such as the *Family and Medical Leave Act,* should be clearly explained.

TIP

Benefits, particularly medical insurance, can be costly. The handbook should state that you, as the employer, may modify these benefits at any time, so you won't be tied to a disastrously expensive plan.

■ **Policies.** Periodically review your employee's performance for purposes of retention, promotion, and wage increases; that evaluation permits the employer and employee to discuss successes and problems and construct goals. Address any absence and tardiness issues. Prohibit the use of alcohol and illegal drugs at work; you may offer a substance abuse treatment program to help your employees if it seems to be a pervasive problem. You may have a smoke-free workplace (or specify smoking areas). Clearly state that sexual harassment will not be tolerated and may be a cause for dismissal; the handbook should specify the procedure in making sexual harassment complaints, usually through the immediate supervisor or director of human relations (or to you, the owner).

■ **Grievance procedure.** An employee may have a compliant, legitimate or not, and should have a procedure beyond talking to his or her immediate supervisor to help resolve this grievance. This process permits an airing before the complaint festers into a disciplinary problem or legal action. If your business is large enough, you may want to establish a director of human resources to resolve all grievances.

■ **Discipline and discharge.** Specify the kind of conduct that may result in discipline and discharge. The list should be representative and not exhaustive, such as making a false statement on the employment application, theft, excessive absences or tardiness, fighting, sexual harassment, insubordination, unauthorized release of confidential information, use of drugs or alcohol at work, and incompetence.

CAUTION

Clearly state in the handbook that an employee is employed at will, and termination may occur with or without cause. You don't want to be sued for a failure to prove the termination was with cause, so a broad employer's right-to-terminate clause is important.

The handbook should clearly state that you, as the employer, may amend it at any time and thus the handbook is not an employment contract. Emphasize the point by including a clause to that effect on a receipt the employee signs for the handbook.

EMPLOYEE CONTRACT

If your company does not have a written contract for your employees, you may want to consider providing written contracts, at least to your key employees. This is particularly important if you want to protect confidential information and prohibit the employee from competing with you when he or she leaves.

A simple employment contract should include the following:

■ **An introduction.** This should indicate the parties to the contract (company and employee), when and where you execute the contract, and should specify that it is an employment contract.

■ **Period of employment.** If the employee is a new hire, the period of employment should be relatively brief, for example six months to one year; however, the period may be longer for a valued employee. This clause provides a degree of employment stability; however, the period of employment would be subject to early termination under its contract provision.

■ **Pay.** You may specify pay based on a salary or hourly wage. You can refer the employee to the employee handbook for the fringe benefits. If the employee is to receive a fringe benefit beyond what he or she would receive under the handbook—such as the use of a company car—specify this additional fringe in the contract.

■ **Employee duties.** Specify the job and general duties for the employee. Because small businesses often have employees with overlapping duties, use a generic job description, followed by the phrase "and other duties assigned by the president or employee supervisor."

■ **Confidential information.** Your business has customer lists, business plans, financial data, pricing lists, and trade secrets that must be protected. The employee should agree to refrain from disclosing this information to any outside person while employed and for a reasonable time thereafter.

■ **Covenant not to compete.** The employee should agree not to work for any competitor during employment with your company. Further, the employee should agree not to work for any competitor for a specific period after the employment contract terminates. Courts will enforce this covenant if it is reasonable in time and distance. For instance, most courts will accept a two- or three-year covenant. Courts will allow the covenant to extend to any territory reasonably necessary to protect the employer, while not unduly interfering with the employee's reemployment. For example, if you have a salesperson whose territory is the southern part of Indiana, the covenant for that territory can be enforced, but not one for all of Indiana.

■ **Termination.** You may want to include the termination language from your employee handbook in the contract, listing various causes for termination, such as sexual harassment. Rather than litigate the issue of discharge for cause, you could provide for arbitration by an independent third party empowered to determine the facts and render a decision.

Needless to say, have your employment attorney review any employment contract you draft before you or your employees sign it.

REVIEW PERFORMANCE PERIODICALLY

You, or your supervisors, should conduct a performance review of each employee every year. You and your employee should use this as an opportunity to communicate mutual expectations. Although the written evaluation can be useful to justify discipline or discharge, this should not be the primary purpose. Both the supervisor and employee should discuss improving the latter's performance, and how they each can best accomplish this goal.

Standard performance evaluation forms include documentation of the following:

- **Quality of work.** You know quality work when you see it (or if you don't, your business will surely fail). Each employee should know what is expected and then respond accordingly. Your sales employee should generate repeat customers eager to buy from you. Your service employee should make your customer feel that your employee will drop everything to provide excellent and timely service. Your employee must know what is to be done and how it's done—then do it. This is the heart of your business. All else is really incidental.

- **Dependability.** *Dependable* is a rather old-fashioned word, but carries a message about the employee. Can you count on the employee to be there and on time? Does the employee follow instructions? Is the employee willing and able to work independently without constant supervision? Has the employee met his or her deadlines?

- **Attitude.** Customers and other employees appreciate genuine enthusiasm. Each employee is a team member, and the team is most successful when all have a caring attitude. The lack of these attributes can quickly poison your business.

- **Organizational skills.** If your employee approaches his or her work in a haphazard way, throwing everything together at the last minute, he or she needs guidance in developing organizational skills. Your employee should be able to effectively plan his or her workload to complete the task.

- **Relating to others. No man (or woman) is an island. Especially in the business world.** An employee who is successful in completing a task relies on other employees. If your employee can't enlist that help, you need to examine the cause of this reluctance. The employee should be able to deal with confrontations when they occur and manage them diplomatically and successfully.

- **Communication skills.** "What we have is a failure to communicate" can apply to any business. The employee should have good oral and written communication skills. No one can effectively manage by mumbling.

The evaluation form should also include a way for your employee to respond. Your employee should be able to include a self-evaluation of his or her performance: the employee's strengths and weaknesses, and what the employee needs to do to improve, and what the supervisor or you can do to help. The employee must be permitted to write a response to the evaluation, particularly if the performance was rated as unsatisfactory. Some forms use an alpha or numeric rating system for each category. Many believe a narrative format is more helpful for most small businesses. A letter or number grade is much less informative.

EMPLOYEE FILES

You must create a file for each employee, the contents of which should include his or her ...

- Job application.
- Employee contract (if any), confidentiality agreement, and covenant not to compete (if any).
- INS I-9 form for immigrants.
- IRS W-4 for tax withholding.
- Employee handbook receipt.
- Employee benefits.
- Performance evaluations.
- Compliments and complaints.
- Awards.
- Disciplinary actions.
- Attendance record.

CAUTION

Don't gloss over a bad employee performance on an evaluation form. If you then later fire the employee, you can be sure that the employee's lawyer will introduce the "good" evaluation in a wrongful-termination lawsuit.

Two words—*document* and *facts*—should guide you in maintaining an employee's file.

Document the good with the bad—just be fair. If an employee's misconduct warrants a written reprimand, put a copy in the file. Nothing will lose a wrongful discharge case quicker than contending the employee deserved to be fired and then not providing the court with any evidence of poor performance or disciplinary infractions.

Include facts only, not conjectures or allegations, in the file. A note from a supervisor alleging that the employee appeared to be intoxicated better have enough detail to warrant that conclusion, such as smelling alcohol on the employee's breath. Otherwise, if the employee proves he or she was under the influence of prescribed medication, you may be liable for defamation of character (slander or libel).

Keep the employee's file confidential. Assign someone to maintain the file, and then limit access to those persons who need to know (the business owner or employee's supervisor). In many states, employees have a right to review their files; if your state permits this and the employee wants a copy of a particular item, make a copy for the employee—keep the original. No one else should have access to the file, except by court order.

CAUTION

Among other laws, the *Americans with Disabilities Act* limits what you can do with medical information and the files are strictly confidential. Keep the medical files you have on these employees separate from personnel files, and limit access to a designated person in the company.

THE 30-SECOND RECAP

- Employee handbooks are a great way to document your company's policies and procedures.
- You should have written employment contracts that clearly spell out mutual responsibilities.
- Written performance reviews are important as a learning tool and as a protection against any potential future legal claims.

Employment Law 2: Terminating an Employee

Some employees need closer supervision than others. An employee may be chronically tardy or rude to customers or co-workers. An employee may have substance-abuse or anger-control problems. An employee may be incompetent. All these problems are your problems, and they usually won't go away. This section offers important considerations for when you must terminate an employee.

DISCIPLINE

Your employee handbook will state particular causes for discipline. If an employee hits a co-worker or customer, steals, uses illegal drugs at work, or commits sexual harassment, this would result in immediate discharge. The handbook could include a provision for progressive discipline for less-serious misconduct.

TIP

The employee handbook should contain several references to employment at-will. You may want to add the following language: "The employee and the company may terminate employment at any time. The employee should give the employer two weeks notice prior to termination."

The progressive discipline process involves, usually in this order:

1. Oral warning
2. Written warning
3. Suspension without pay
4. Termination

The handbook should emphasize that this procedure is optional, and the company reserves the right to skip one or more steps, or discharge an employee. Emphasize that this is a process to help the employee improve his or her conduct and retain employment with the company.

Progressive discipline isn't required, because most employees are employed at-will, but it may be useful as evidence in a subsequent wrongful termination case. You can demonstrate your willingness to help the employee improve, and the employee's inability or obstinate refusal to change.

CAUTION

Don't fire an employee because he or she files a complaint. If the employee has previously filed a workers' compensation claim, OSHA complaint, EEOC complaint, or FLSA overtime charge, federal and state laws prohibit employer retaliation. Those agencies take the retaliatory charges very seriously.

DISCHARGE

You should have a sense of failure, even if the employee proved incompetent, although a sense of relief can easily be imagined. But there may be more to the drama. The employee may turn around and file a complaint with the EEOC or state civil rights commission, or sue for wrongful termination.

It is suggested that you treat every termination as a potential lawsuit. Your documentation of misconduct or incompetence in the employee's file will help convince the EEOC or a court that the firing was justified. Your evaluations should reflect poor performance, if that was the cause for the discharge. If you wait until the lawsuit is filed to prepare your case, then you're too late.

Any time you discharge an employee, briefly review the anti-discrimination employment laws. For example, if the employee is disabled and unable to perform the work with reasonable accommodation, make sure that you document your efforts to make those accommodations. If the employee is discharged for sexual harassment, prepare an investigative file with signed statements from the complainant and witnesses.

If the employee has an employment contract and you terminate it prematurely, consult your lawyer to determine whether you are breaching the contract. A well-drafted contract will allow you latitude in terminating the contract for just cause as specified in the contract, such as making false statements, misappropriation of company funds, sexual harassment, disclosure of confidential information, and so on. You must prove your termination was justified by producing appropriate evidence, such as fraudulent sales reports prepared by the discharged employee.

Many states prohibit employee discharge for certain public policy reasons, such as when the employer retaliates against employees who filed a complaint with an agency over alleged public safety violations. For example, if your employee filed a charge with the Food and Drug Administration that your pharmaceutical company has allegedly falsified reports, and you fire that employee, you can count on a wrongful discharge lawsuit.

If you decide to fire an employee, prepare a termination letter. The letter enumerates any compensation owed to the employee, health continuation benefits under federal law, and any severance package you offer. The severance package, which is optional (unless required by the employment contract), may include additional pay or continued payment of health insurance premiums for a period after termination, and an agreement not to contest any employee application for unemployment compensation. In return for the severance package, you may want to have the employee release any claims regarding employment and termination, including the claim of employment discrimination in violation of the *Age Discrimination Act,* Title VII, or other employment laws. Carefully draft this waiver (or have your attorney do so). You may want to use language similar to *ADEA waivers* for early retirement. As you recall, by signing the waiver the employee agrees not to later file an ADEA complaint against the employer.

PLAIN ENGLISH

The **ADEA waiver** permits employees upon retirement to waive any alleged ADEA violations, but the employee must be advised to consult an attorney, allowed at least 21 days to consider the agreement, and permitted to revoke within 7 days after execution of the agreement.

THE RIGHTS OF EX-EMPLOYEES

Your ex-employee and dependents may be entitled to continued health-care insurance under your company policy according to the *Consolidated Omnibus Budget Reconciliation Act,* more understandably referred to as COBRA. The length of coverage varies from 18 to 36 months, depending upon the cause of the termination. The employee must pay all the premiums for this coverage.

Your ex-employee may be entitled to state unemployment compensation. The employee files a claim and the agency determines whether he or she is eligible. The determination may be appealed within the agency and a hearing held. Unless the employee committed a serious violation, such as sexual harassment or theft, the law typically permits the ex-employee to receive the compensation. Your unemployment tax rate probably will be increased only slightly, at the worst, so fighting the claim may not be worth the time and cost involved.

To soften the blow of a discharge, you might suggest to the employee that he or she resign. If possible, you could offer to help the employee find a new job, and provide a favorable reference. Sometimes employees who don't succeed for you may be very successful in a different environment.

THE 30-SECOND RECAP

- Your employee handbook should state specific causes for discipline.
- You should treat every termination as a potential lawsuit.
- Ex-employees are entitled to certain rights, such as health benefits, under law.

Employment Law 3: Sexual Harassment and Other Legal Matters

Your company must have a written policy against sexual harassment and then enforce it, even if federal law does not cover you because you have fewer than 15 employees. This section covers sexual harassment and other legal matters.

SEXUAL HARASSMENT

Sexual harassment violates Title VII of the *Civil Rights Act of 1964*. Sexual harassment can involve a request for sexual favors or creating a hostile workplace environment. The EEOC and courts will find sexual harassment exits if ...

- The conduct is gender related.
- The victim has not consented to sexual advances nor participated in perpetuating a hostile work environment.
- The conduct has affected the victim's job.

Sexual harassment is actionable whether the harasser is of the opposite sex or the same sex; both males and females can bring sexual harassment charges.

Sexual harassment exists if an employee is threatened with adverse employment consequences, including the prospect of being fired or demoted if he or she doesn't perform sexual favors; or if the employee is offered job benefits in return for sexual favors. The latter form of sexual harassment is referred to as *quid pro quo* ("something for something"). Usually it is the employee's supervisor who commits this form of harassment, but courts will hold the company liable for any adverse employment effect on the victim.

The hostile workplace environment exists when verbal or physical conduct of a sexual nature has the purpose or effect of creating an intimidating, hostile, or offensive environment at work. This may include unwanted and offensive sexual contact, solicitation, or innuendoes. The employer will be liable if it knew of the offensive conduct and tolerated it, or should have known (complaints were lodged with supervisors and nothing was done to correct the hostile environment).

Your sexual harassment policy should contain ...

- A statement prohibiting sexual harassment.
- A procedure to file complaints.
- Discipline procedures for the harasser.

The employee handbook should inform a harassment victim that he or she can complain to the supervisor or another designated person within the company. This alternative allows the alleged victim to choose, which is important if the supervisor or designated person is the harasser.

CAUTION

Thoroughly investigate any claim of sexual harassment. If harassment if found, the harasser should be punished; if no harassment is discovered, the alleged harasser should be clearly exonerated in your findings.

The employee handbook should let the harasser know that misconduct could result in discipline or discharge.

Consider training your employees to be aware of how their conduct may affect others. What may seem like a cute off-color story or a funny racial joke to some people may be deeply offensive to others.

SAFETY ON THE JOB

You want a safe environment for your employees, so the workplace should be free of physical danger. But injuries do occur, and the injured employee may be entitled to compensation.

TIP

If your company handles toxic chemicals or workers are exposed to certain hazards, such as noise or air pollution, your workers' compensation insurance carrier should suggest ways to conform to the OSHA regulations and make the environment safer.

OCCUPATIONAL SAFETY AND HEALTH ACT (OSHA)

OSHA was enacted to reduce workplace injuries by creating a safer environment. OSHA requires employers to eliminate hazards likely to cause death or serious injury. For example, consider one individual who was employed to rewire a steel plant; the employer permitted high voltage wire to be strung everywhere, including bare wire across water puddles—an electrocution waiting to happen. OSHA has established safety standards for certain work environments or industries. You can visit the OSHA website (www.dol.gov) to view some of these standards.

Usually, OSHA will not inspect your business unless an employee has complained, there has been a serious injury or death, or the workplace is inherently dangerous (for example, produces toxic chemicals). If OSHA cites your company for a violation, you may contest the citation with OSHA, and that decision is subject to court review.

WORKERS' COMPENSATION

Workers' compensation is a state law that provides income and medical expenses for employees who are injured or develop illnesses that are work related. For example, if your employee slips on a wet floor at work, or drills a hole in his or her hand rather than the metal, or suffers a respiratory illness because of poor ventilation, the employee is eligible for workman's compensation.

TIP

Insist that your workers' comp insurance carrier inspect your business and suggest ways to reduce risks of employee injury; then follow its advice. You will save money on the premiums and make the workplace safer.

Most small businesses buy workers' compensation insurance to cover their potential liability, although state law may allow your company to be self-insured; however self-insurance is too risky for anyone except large companies. If your employee is injured at work, your company is strictly liable and the employee will be compensated according to a fixed state schedule of benefits. For example, if your employee negligently cuts off his little finger on the left hand, the schedule will indicate the money benefit for that specific injury. The employee's or fellow employee's negligence is not a defense to liability; however, if the injured employee was intoxicated or deliberately inflicted the injury, the company may use that as a defense.

Your injured employee cannot successfully sue your company or another employee who caused the injury; the sole remedy is the benefit from workers' compensation.

WORKERS WITH DISABILITIES

Congress passed the *Americans with Disabilities Act (ADA)* to prohibit discrimination against persons with disabilities. Employers violate the ADA if they discriminate in employment practices based upon a person's disability. This includes all employment decisions, such as hiring, firing, discipline, compensation, and promotion. A person is considered disabled under the ADA, if he or she ...

- Has a physical or mental impairment that substantially limits one or more major life activities; or
- Has a record of being disabled; or
- Is regarded as being disabled.

Disability is broadly defined. Examples of life activities covered by the ADA include walking, talking, seeing, hearing, breathing, and learning. Mental and psychological disorders are also considered disabilities. AIDS is covered by the act, too. A temporary condition, such as a pulled back muscle, would not be covered, but a severe and permanent back injury that limits the employee's activities would be. If the person has a record of a disability, such as a persistent mental illness, he or she is covered. Likewise, a person who the employer perceives as disabled is covered. For example, a salesclerk who was disfigured by an automobile accident may be regarded as impaired if customers refused to buy from that clerk.

Disability under the ADA does not include the illegal use of drugs, homosexuality, sexual behavior disorders, or compulsive gambling.

ADA requires the employer to make reasonable accommodations to enable the disabled to work. This may include making the workplace accessible, modifying equipment, and changing work schedules. For example, you may have to redesign the computer workstation to accommodate a wheelchair-bound employee.

The disabled person with reasonable accommodation must be able to perform the essential functions of the job, but the employer does not have to restructure the job. For example, if the dockworker is required to lift packages on to a conveyor belt, and that is an essential job function, you don't have to eliminate the task even though it would exclude a disabled person from getting the job.

Further, the employer is not required to accommodate a disabled person if it would place an undue hardship on the employer. For example, if your software development business is located on the second floor of an older building with no elevator, you may assert that the substantial cost of installing an elevator would be an undue hardship (excessive cost) to your small business. Obviously, General Motors could not claim undue hardship in a similar situation.

TIP

Federal tax law may allow an employer certain tax credits for hiring disabled workers and tax deductions for removing barriers to access. For example, if a company removes a physical barrier in accordance with its reasonable accommodation obligation under the ADA, and if the barrier removal meets the ADA Accessibility Guidelines, the company is eligible for a tax credit on its next tax return for a portion of the cost of this removal.

LABOR UNIONS

Most small businesses are not the target of union organizing attempts, but you should know the rudiments of the *National Labor Relations Act (NLRA)* just in case.

The NLRA gives employees the right to act together to form or join a union, present employees' grievances, bargain for a labor agreement, go on strike and picket the employer. Employees protected by the act are most nonmanagement personnel, usually hourly employees.

If 30 percent of the employees file union election authorization cards with the National Labor Relations Board (NLRB), the agency will conduct a secret ballot election. Meanwhile, you can voice your position: You may oppose the election, for example, and contest union organizer claims of low pay or poor working conditions by favorably comparing their jobs with those of your competitors. You may point out that unions control employee grievances and employees may have to pay substantial dues. What you may not do is one of the following:

- Fire or discipline employees for organizing.
- Increase or decrease compensation during the election period.
- Ask individual employees how he or she will vote.
- Threaten to move the company if the union wins.

These illegal acts are called unfair labor practices. If your company violates the law and the union loses the election, the NLRB may order another election, or if there has been serious employer misconduct, certify the union as the exclusive bargaining representative for your employees.

If the union wins and is certified, you have to bargain with it for a labor agreement. After the union is in, obviously you lose some control over employment decisions. The best way to avoid unionizing is to treat your employees fairly and respond immediately to workplace complaints. Arbitrary conduct is an invitation to a union.

THE 30-SECOND RECAP

- Every employer must have a policy prohibiting sexual harassment.
- Employers are strictly liable for employee workplace injuries.

Your Estate Plan and Your Business

Procrastinate long enough and you won't need a last will and testament. Your state has its own plan for your estate if you don't have a will. The IRS and your state department of revenue will likely receive more than their fair share of your estate if you don't properly plan your estate. This section discusses estate planning from A to Z.

BUSINESS AND OTHER ASSETS

Are you as prepared with your estate plan as you think you are? Let's start with a brief checklist (circle the applicable answer):

Yes	**No**	My spouse and I have current wills.
Yes	**No**	My spouse and I have recently consulted an estate-planning professional.
Yes	**No**	I have reviewed the value and ownership of all my assets and liabilities.
Yes	**No**	My spouse has reviewed the value and ownership of all his or her assets and liabilities.
Yes	**No**	I have reviewed all my business ownership agreements.
Yes	**No**	I have reviewed my life insurance needs.
Yes	**No**	I have a pension or 401(k) plan.
Yes	**No**	My estate will have sufficient cash to pay the debts and taxes, with enough left over for my family.
Yes	**No**	I have designated someone to handle my affairs when I am no longer capable of doing so.
Yes	**No**	I have taken sufficient steps to reduce my income taxes now, and the death taxes against my estate.

If you've answered "no" to even a few of these statements, you've got some work to do!

YOUR PERSONAL ASSETS

You must inventory your assets to determine their value and ownership forms, such as property that is solely owned, jointly owned, or co-owned with a spouse.

Solely owned property is distributed to the beneficiaries named in your last will and testament. For example, if you own corporate stock solely in your own name, the stock ownership is transferred to the person(s) named in your will upon death. If you have no will, the state *intestate* law transfers it to the heirs whom the state designates.

PLAIN ENGLISH

Intestate simply means dying without a will. If a spouse survives a decedent and children, under state law those survivors may be required to divide the solely owned property.

You may own a bank account, certificate of deposit, stocks and bonds, real estate, and miscellaneous other property as joint tenants with right of survivorship. This means that if you or your spouse dies, the other automatically owns the property. The decedent's will has no effect on jointly owned property, unless both die simultaneously.

The bank account card you signed with the bank usually will have the phrase "joint with right of survivorship" on it if co-owned; CD, stocks, and bonds will have the phrase on its face; the real estate deed will include this phrase after the grantees' (owners') names.

Or you could co-own property as *tenants in common*. This form of ownership may occur when siblings inherit property together, such as when two sisters inherit the family farm. Or two nonrelated persons may invest in property together. When one co-owner dies, his or her heirs or beneficiaries of the will receive it.

Tenancy by entirety and *community property* are spousal co-ownership rights. Spouses may also own property as joint tenants; many states limit tenancy by entirety to spousal co-ownership in real estate. For example, if a husband and wife co-own their home as tenants by entirety (on the deed), and one dies, the surviving spouse owns the house; the decedent's will has no effect. In the community property states, the surviving spouse owns his or her half, and the other.

PLAIN ENGLISH

Community property states include Arizona, California, Idaho, Louisiana, Nevada, New Mexico, Texas, Washington, and Wisconsin. Puerto Rico allows community property. Each state has slight differences in their community property laws.

Life insurance proceeds are paid to the beneficiary named in the policy regardless of any different stipulations that might appear in the decedent's will. If there is no designated beneficiary in the policy, the will distributes the life insurance proceeds to its beneficiaries, or if there's no will, the heirs receive their share.

Pensions have a designated beneficiary who will receive the balance of the pension upon the owner's death. If married, the owner usually designates the spouse. In fact, the spouse is entitled to his or her share of the other spouse's pension unless the spouse waives it in writing. Annuities, likewise, usually have a surviving annuiant (beneficiary) named. If no surviving pensioner or annuiant is designated, the balance is distributed as if it were solely owned property.

A person may have placed his or her property into a living trust. The trust itself designates to whom the property is transferred upon the owner's death.

BUSINESS ASSETS

You will likely be operating your business under one of these forms: sole proprietor, partnership, limited liability company, or corporation.

If you are a sole proprietor, each business asset is solely owned property, and title to all your business property is in your own name. If you have a will, the will distributes the business assets, or if there is no will, your intestate heirs get the property.

The sole shareholder and the sole member of a limited liability company own the corporate stock or LLC membership, whereas the entity itself owns its business assets. Upon the owner's death, his or her corporate stock or limited liability company membership is distributed like any other solely owned property.

If you are a partner in a partnership, limited liability partnership, or limited partnership, or are a member among several members of a limited liability company, or are one shareholder among several corporate shareholders, the disposition of your interest may be controlled by the agreement that you signed. A well-drafted partnership agreement, limited liability operating agreement, or corporate stock purchase agreement will specify the rights of a deceased's partner's (or member's or shareholder's) estate to his or her interest and the corresponding duties of the surviving partners (or members or shareholders).

Usually this takes the form of a mandatory purchase of the interest by the survivors, and a mandatory sale by the personal representative of the deceased's estate, which receives the proceeds, often over several years. However, if there is no buy-sell provision, the deceased partner's, member's, or shareholder's interest becomes part of the estate and is distributed by the will, or in its absence, to the heirs.

AVOIDING PROBATE

There are many horror stories about *probate*. The squabbling heirs, the innumerable court appearances, and the greedy lawyers are part of the tale. This happens most frequently when the deceased failed to properly plan his or her estate. There is no magic formula for trouble-free probate, but here are some valuable suggestions.

PROBATE OR NO PROBATE

First, what *probate* is, then what it is not. A person's estate *is* subject to probate if he or she ...

- Solely owns property.
- Co-owns property as tenants in common.
- Shares in community property (in some states).
- Owns a pension, annuity, or life insurance with *no* named beneficiary.

PLAIN ENGLISH

Probate is the court supervision of the distribution of a decedent's estate. State laws somewhat vary on their probate procedure.

Conversely, property is *not* subject to probate if she or he ...

- Co-owns property jointly with a survivor.
- Co-owns property with a surviving spouse as tenants by entirety.
- Owns a pension, annuity, or life insurance with a named beneficiary.
- Has property in trust.
- Owns a life estate in property, such as a mother who would deed her house to a daughter, but retain for her life the right to use the house rent-free.

The majority of the estates will not require probate because the decedent co-owned property jointly with survivorship, tenants by entirety, or owned life insurance with a specified beneficiary. In addition, some states provide a simple transfer of property by affidavit (sworn statement) if the solely owned asset's value is under a specified amount, such as $25,000.

PROBATE PROCEDURE

Probate may not always be avoided, so you need to know the basics of the process.

The estate is opened by filing a petition with the probate court in the county where the decedent resided. Usually the person named in the decedent's will as the personal representative (executor) files the petition, but any beneficiary in the will could also file. If there is no will, typically an heir files the probate petition.

Many states have two different forms of probate: supervised and unsupervised. The latter typically involves opening the estate, filing an inventory (list of assets), and closing the estate with only minimal court involvement. Supervised administration requires court approval for virtually everything. Usually all the beneficiaries of an estate must agree to use unsupervised administration, because it typically does not require probate court approval for the personal representative's acts.

The petitioner requests the court to admit the will, and to appoint the person named in the will as the personal representative. After the court does so, the newly appointed personal representative notifies all the beneficiaries listed in the decedent's will and any known creditors. Most states also require a local newspaper to publish a notice to the creditors and other interested parties of the probate. The court may require the personal representative to obtain a performance bond to protect the estate from any wrongdoing by the personal representative.

If the decedent died without a will, the state statute usually provides a priority for a near relative (spouse or children) to serve as a personal representative; the rest of the procedure is the same.

The personal representative is responsible for collecting the decedent's probate assets, and then listing those assets on an inventory filed with the court. The personal representative is also responsible for paying the estate debts and taxes from its assets. Many of these debts are relatively straightforward, such as utility bills, credit card debts, medical bills, and funeral expenses. A creditor's claim may be contested, and the result determined by the court.

If the estate is unsupervised—usually unadviseable—the court is not involved in the personal representative's acts. However, if the estate is supervised, the court must approve any sale of assets and distribution of the net assets to the beneficiaries of the will or the heirs. In addition, the court must approve an accounting of all assets received and expenses paid; in unsupervised probate, the personal representative just accounts to the beneficiaries or heirs.

PLANNING TO AVOID PROBATE

There clearly are some advantages to avoiding probate, including the following:

- No court costs
- No probate attorney fees
- Quicker distribution of the decedent's assets
- No will contest, because the will is irrelevant
- Possible death tax savings

Court costs are usually in the $100 to $250 range. Attorney fees may be considerable, often around 5 percent of the estate. Jointly owned and tenancy by entirety property become the survivor's property upon the co-owner's death. The pension, annuity, and life insurance are distributed according to the terms of their contracts. Likewise, the trust distributes its asset or pays its income according to its terms. If a decedent had a life estate, the remainder owner becomes the sole owner. For example, a widow may deed her house to her daughter (who becomes the remainder owner), retaining a life estate in it; when the widow dies, the daughter owns the house because the mother's life estate is extinguished at her death.

Will contests can be messy affairs. If there is no probate, the will has no assets to distribute, and no disgruntled heirs to attack it.

Planning, such as giving appropriate gifts during your lifetime, may avoid tax and probate. Likewise, property held jointly with a spouse is free of federal estate tax at one spouse's death.

What are some things you can do to avoid probate? Many experts suggest the following:

- Create joint ownership bank accounts with the persons who you want to own the accounts at your death; the creation of the accounts will not in itself trigger a gift tax; only the withdrawal by the noncontributors will do that.
- Put your spouse's name as co-owner on all your property; there is no gift tax for transfers to a spouse; however, if your estate is $1 million or more, a wholesale transfer may cause substantial estate taxes upon the death of the last to survive.
- Make sure that all of your pension plans, annuities, and life insurance policies have named beneficiaries.
- Consider using a trust to transfer your assets at death, rather than a will (or in addition to a will).

CAUTION

An unhappy heir may challenge the creation of a living trust by alleging the person establishing it was mentally incompetent, defrauded, or subject to undue influence. Likewise, a transfer by gift or creating a joint account can be contested on these grounds. Proof of mental incompetence in challenging a living trust is usually more difficult than for a will contest.

A word of caution is in order. Avoiding probate may be a laudable goal but, like most things, it does have its tradeoffs. Any time joint ownership is created from solely owned property there may be a potential gift-tax problem. Also if you create a joint account with only one of several children, the surviving child takes the entire account—a result that you may not intend. Therefore, carefully plan with your estate-planning professionals.

TIP

An alternative to joint ownership may be to designate persons to which a bank account is paid on death (POD). This makes the beneficiary clear and can avoid future lawsuits.

ESTATE AND GIFT TAXES FOR LIFE PLANNING

Federal tax folks are very demanding. You give property away, and you pay a gift tax. You die and your heirs inherit, they pay an estate tax. And the state revenue department wants its share, too. It's a nuisance. Fortunately, these pesky taxes do have exemptions.

You can give away up to $11,000 per person each year (subject to indexing) with no federal gift tax; this amount is doubled if your spouse joins in making the gift. In addition, in 2005 up to $1.5 million lifetime or estate transfers are free of federal gift and estate taxes; this figure gradually increases to $3.5 million in 2009 and disappears completely in 2010. And you can give or leave to your spouse an unlimited amount free of either tax.

The following sections discuss the federal estate and gift taxes. State gift taxes are not discussed here; however, you should know that there are a few states that do tax certain substantial nonspousal gifts. State death taxes are also not covered; almost all states either follow the federal estate tax (at a much, much lower rate) or have an inheritance tax on the beneficiaries (at a fairly modest rate with near relatives generally taxed less).

FEDERAL ESTATE TAX

Any property a decedent solely owned, co-owned, or substantially controlled is part of what is known as the gross estate. If a surviving spouse co-owned property, only one half of its value is included, and the other half is usually a marital deduction, resulting in no spousal property being taxed. Other co-owned property is included to the extent the decedent had an interest in the property.

Revocable living trusts, which were created by the decedent for the decedent or others, are included in the gross estate. Likewise, life insurance proceeds from a policy the decedent owned are in the gross estate. If the decedent transferred property and retained a life estate (deeded the house to the children and kept the right to live in the house), that is included. Pensions and annuities may be included in the gross estate. There are other less typical inclusions, but this constitutes the vast majority of property included in the gross estate.

CAUTION

An issue with the IRS is the value of property; if there is any doubt and big bucks are involved, use an appraiser who has been successful in similar estate situations. The IRS almost always will challenge small business evaluations. Your accountant may be acquainted with an appraiser.

Any debts owed by the deceased are deductible from the gross estate, including mortgage and credit card debt. Casualty losses that occur during probate are deductible. Probate fees are deductible, as are transfers to charity. Transfers to the deceased's spouse either as surviving co-owner or through inheritance can be deducted; certain transfers in trust to the spouse also count.

Property received by a surviving spouse outright from the deceased spouse qualifies for a martial deduction from the gross estate. The law permits one spouse to establish for the other spouse a certain type of trust, called a *qualified terminable interest property (QTIP),* which will also qualify for the marital deduction. This trust is often used to protect the surviving spouse from unwise decisions about his or her inherited money.

PLAIN ENGLISH

A **spousal trust,** called **qualified terminable interest property** or **QTIP,** qualifies for a marital deduction when the spouse receives the annual income and the property is included in the spouse's estate at death; children are often the beneficiaries after the spouse's death.

The federal estate tax return must be filed within nine months of the decedent's death. The personal representative files the required Form 706. The time for filing state death tax returns varies with the state, so consult your state department of revenue.

FEDERAL GIFT TAX

Giving your property away can avoid the federal estate tax, but don't get carried away, particularly if Congress increases the exemption.

Gifts to your spouse or charity are tax-free. Immediate transfers to an ex-spouse in a divorce settlement are not subject to the tax. Gifts to your children or others are subject to the tax only if the gift is over $11,000 per year ($22,000 if the spouse joins in the gift).

A loan to a child at less than the going rate of interest is considered a gift of the foregone interest. For example, if you lent your child $50,000 at 0 percent interest and the federal fund rate was 10 percent, you gave your child $5,000, which is clearly within the $10,000 exemption; however, a larger gift loan or other gifts may exceed the exemption.

Congress did not repeal the federal gift tax, although it raised the lifetime exemption and lowered the maximum tax rate. The lifetime gift tax exemption has gone up to $1 million and will stay there (unlike the estate tax exemption). That means you will be able to make a total of $1 million of taxable gifts over your lifetime before owing any federal gift tax. In addition, you can make an unlimited number of $11,000 gifts (to different recipients) of cash or other property each calendar year, completely tax-free.

The downside is that those gifts that exceed the annual exemption reduce your exemption amount (actually for computation purposes it reduces your tax credit) for future gifts or for the estate tax.

WILLS AND TRUSTS AND YOUR BUSINESS

You need a last will and testament because no estate plan is complete without a will. No matter how much you plan to avoid probate, things often change before you get around to making a change. A lucky lottery number or an unexpected gift or inheritance may be in your future. A trust is certainly something that you should consider.

DYING WITHOUT A WILL

Many people do procrastinate about making a will, and because we are still alive, everything's okay; tomorrow is soon enough. Unfortunately, tomorrow may not come for some of us. Dying can be a tragedy; dying without a will is a complication. If you don't have a will, your heirs will be specified by state statute, so property may be inherited by someone you wouldn't want to leave a dime to. Probate will be more time-consuming and expensive. There may be more death taxes, too.

State statutes vary about an heir's rights, but the spouse and children usually share equally in a decedent's probate estate where there is no will; however, a second or later spouse who did not have a child with the decedent may receive less. If there are no children (or grandchildren), the spouse and the decedent's parents may share in the estate, with the surviving spouse receiving the greater portion. If there is no spouse, the children receive the entire estate. Beyond this your heirs include your parents and siblings. Close friends, stepchildren, and in-laws are not your heirs.

If you are not satisfied with the state distribution, create a no-probate estate, or make a will.

Your Last Will and Testament

A typical will has three major sections: beneficiary *(devisee)*, personal representative (executor), and guardian.

PLAIN ENGLISH

Devisee is the modern term for a person who receives property from the will. Heir is more commonly used for a person who receives the decedent's property through intestate distribution.

You can name anyone as devisee in your will. However, if a spouse is excluded (or given less than he or she would receive in an intestate distribution), the spouse can elect against the will and receive the intestate share (usually one half of the probate estate).

You can divide up your estate in any manner that you choose. For example, you could give one half to your spouse, one fourth to your children, and one fourth to a charity. You can also make specific devises, for instance, "I devise my collection of 1961 New York Yankee baseball cards to John Smith."

Choose a personal representative who has good common sense; because you have a business that may be part of your estate, the person should be someone who has some business experience. The personal representative is responsible for moving the estate through the court, so he or she should be well organized. The estate's attorney will provide the personal representative with legal advice so an attorney as executor is not necessary. For many uncomplicated estates, the spouse serves as the primary personal representative and one or two of the adult children as an alternative.

TIP

Choose your children's guardians with care. If managing money is not a guardian's strong point, you could name a bank as guardian of the property, or set up a trust to manage the children's money.

If you have a minor child (under age 18) or a mentally or physically disabled adult child who is not capable of managing his or her affairs, a court will appoint a guardian for the child when you and your spouse are no longer living. You should name a person(s) to serve should that happen. It is suggested that a person or couple who is compatible with your age and lifestyle—someone who you would want to rear your children.

The court appoints the guardian, based upon what is best for the children, but usually honors the nomination in a parent's will. The guardian is responsible for rearing the children and managing their money. The guardian will make financial reports to the court every one or two years. The guardianship terminates when the child reaches age 18, unless the child has an incapacitating disability; then the guardianship may continue for a lifetime.

You shouldn't be tempted simply to prepare and sign your own will, thus saving legal fees. This may be a false savings if the will is not properly executed or confusingly written. There is certainly more of an incentive to contest a will if the probate estate is ample. Some attorneys charge between $150 and $300 for a simple will.

After you have a will, review it every three or four years to make sure that it meets your current needs. If you marry, divorce, add children, retire, sell your business, or hit the lottery, review the will to determine whether changes are warranted. Don't make any written changes on the will itself, because this may invalidate it.

Most states require at least two witnesses to the will. The person making the will signs and the witnesses sign, all in each other's presence. The witnesses are told that they are signing a will, but they need not see its contents. The will does not have to be notarized.

If you want to make any minor changes, such as naming a different personal representative, prepare a codicil—an amendment to a will. The codicil is executed in the same formal manner as the will. If you have any substantial changes, such as changes in beneficiaries, execute a new will.

TRUSTS

A trust is an estate-planning document that permits a trustee to administer the assets of the grantor who establishes the trust. The trust may be established during the grantor's life, which is called a living or *inter vivos* trust. Or the trust may be established through a will upon the grantor's death, which is called a testamentary trust. The living trust may be revocable or *irrevocable*.

PLAIN ENGLISH

An **irrevocable living trust** usually involves children or even grandchildren as its main beneficiaries. The grantors have no power to change the trust terms after it is created. The federal gift tax may apply because the creation of the trust is a gift to a third party.

The essential contents of a trust are ...

- Grantor (settlor) establishes the trust.
- Trustee administers the trust.
- Principal (corpus) is property transferred to the trust.
- Income beneficiary receives trust income during life.
- Remainderman beneficiary receives trust property at termination.

If you want to avoid probate yet want to control your assets during your life, the revocable living trust may be for you. You (and your spouse) may establish the trust as grantor by executing the trust document and depositing a minimum of one dollar in the trust, which is the principal or corpus of the trust. Virtually any property can be transferred to the trust.

For example, the grantor(s) may put some or all of their liquid assets into a trust, including stocks, mutual funds, CDs, and so on, by simply changing the owner from their names as individuals to their names as trustees. A residence or other real estate can be transferred to a trust by executing a new deed to the trustee.

The grantors are usually the trustees unless both are incapable of managing the trust. The trust is revocable so that the trustees can add or withdraw principal. The grantors are the income beneficiaries, so they retain all the income from their investments; the tax effect remains unchanged in the grantor trust— the grantors are taxed on the income. The typically revocable trust provides for the distribution of its principal after the death of the last surviving spouse, usually to the children.

The revocable trust usually provides for successor trustees if the grantors or trustees are no longer capable of managing the trust. Frequently the successor is one of the children, but it can be a bank or other institutional trustee; the latter, of course, would charge a fee but does provide professional management.

If you have young children, consider a trust for them to protect them if something happens to you and your spouse. The trust may be an unfunded revocable living trust, which later could be funded by the proceeds of a life insurance policy on the parents' lives and from the probate estate. The alternative is a testamentary trust for each parent, which becomes effective upon death.

In either event, the children's property is held in trust until they reach a mature age. The income and the principal would be used to pay for their expenses, including college costs. The trust allows the children to be more mature when they receive their inheritance. In most states, when a child becomes 18, he or she is free of a guardianship and entitled to any inheritance.

POWER OF ATTORNEY AND LIVING WILL

If a person becomes incapable of managing his or her financial or personal affairs, a guardian may be appointed to do so. The guardianship is supervised by the court, so everything is public, and the guardianship costs money to administer. A trust created before a person becomes incompetent is a viable alternative.

Another possibility is a durable power of attorney. The power of attorney is given to another person, typically a spouse or child. Usually, the authority under the power cannot be exercised until the grantor becomes incompetent. The power of attorney continues until death or revocation by the grantor.

A living will is a legal form directing that the declarant's life not be artificially prolonged if he or she is in a terminal condition. The living will is chosen by some to allow themselves death with dignity. If you chose to execute a living will, give copies to your physician and to your local hospital to be included in your medical records.

MARRIAGE AND DIVORCE HAS ITS EFFECT

Marriage and divorce may seem unusual topics to cover in a book for small businesses. But read on.

MARRIAGE

If you are a single businessperson contemplating marriage, you may want to consider a *prenuptial agreement*.

Let's say a businesswoman wants to keep total ownership of her property in her name. In that case, her husband-to-be must sign a prenuptial agreement, which would waive any right to claim the business as a marital asset subject to court division. Whether the agreement provides a waiver of her husband's claim upon the death of the business owner may depend if this is a second marriage and her children are her first priority as her heirs.

PLAIN ENGLISH

A **prenuptial agreement,** signed by both of the future spouses, spells out any aspects of property ownership during the marriage that the two can think of, and it is a legally binding. The prenuptial agreement may specify what property is to remain the separate property of each party, and what property will be marital property. The agreement usually indicates who gets what in the event of a divorce or death; typically, this involves a waiver of any claim to certain property.

Although the courts usually enforce prenuptial agreements, each party should have an attorney, or at least be advised to get one, and completely disclose the premarital assets. This will deter a later claim of fraud or undue influence that could render the contract voidable. The prenuptial agreement should have a signature block for both attorneys and an attachment for each party's financial disclosures.

DIVORCE

If a businessperson has a prenuptial agreement, all may be well for keeping the business, and keeping the court from considering it as an asset for which the other spouse should be compensated. If there is no prenup, expect to pay to keep the business.

No-fault divorces are the norm, so the issues that arise are usually child custody, child support, ex-spousal support, and (relevant in this instance) property distribution. Most courts will divide the marital property fairly evenly, maybe not 50-50 but close to it. If the business owner in my example wants to keep her business, her spouse will get the equivalent in cash or other marital property. If there is not enough other property, that may be a big problem. However, if the marriage was relatively brief, the court could consider the business as separate property, with little or no compensation going to her husband.

Alimony may not be a favorite word, but it has a place in divorces, particularly in property settlements. The advantage to the payor is a tax deduction from gross income; conversely, the payee has to report it as income. This continues to apply until the final payment is made, with one exception—if most of the alimony is paid in the first three years, the payor may have to report some of the previous deductions as income—a penalty for front-loading the alimony.

CAUTION

Take care with your pension during a divorce. If there is a pension involved, the spouse releasing his or her right to the pension must execute a form with the pension company; a clause in the divorce decree or property settlement agreement is insufficient.

The amount of the alimony is obviously negotiable. The payor may have to pay a bit more to compensate for tax to the payee. If there are children, perhaps there could be some minor reduction in child support, which is not deductible for the payor, and an increase in the alimony, which is deductible.

BUSINESS-SUCCESSOR PLANNING

You may have been in business for many years and it may be time to consider a successor when you retire. If the business is all yours, you may want to sell it or turn it over to your children. If the business is co-owned, the other owners may be willing to buy you out.

Think about the following:

- Analyze the current status of the business.
- Consider the cash value of the business.
- Review any buy-sell agreements with co-owners.
- Ponder which child could take over, or perhaps which employee.

Most businesses have a life cycle. The beginning involves struggle and little value other than potential, then the company turns the corner and becomes profitable, and finally it reaches a point where success mandates expansion and change. If you are in the last stage, it's your call about moving up or moving on. The point is—think about the business in your future.

If your business has been successful, it may be an attractive purchase for someone. You may realize its greatest potential for growth when the business is at the point of change—to expand or regress. If your business is worth so much because you are there, the purchaser may want you to stay on as manager, at least for a brief period.

You may want to pull out your buy-sell agreement and reread it to see what you agreed to those many years ago. Then put the pencil to the paper to see how much you would get if you left right now. If you intend to stay a bit longer, this may provoke some thinking, particularly if your share wouldn't reflect what the company's worth. You may want to amend the agreement.

A family business may have an appointed successor. Everyone gets used to this succession, and responsibilities can increase with experience and success. If there is no apparent successor, it's time to groom one. You are there to delegate and advise. Do so before it's too late.

If there is no natural successor, perhaps a key employee might be interested in buying you out. If that is a future prospect, consider offering the employee an equity interest in the business.

For example, you may offer some minority share, such as 10 percent of the common stock. Consider a contract that would require the employee to successfully serve for a period of time, say two years, before receiving the stock. The tax law refers to this as a restricted property transaction, and the employee reports the fair market value of the stock as income when the restriction expires, or can elect to report it as income when the contract is executed. The election may be a better choice if the company's value, and thus the stock, substantially appreciates in value.

HELPFUL SOURCES FOR ESTATE AND GIFT TAX PLANNING

Many banks and trust departments have excellent pamphlets on estate planning. Life insurance companies will do a thorough analysis of your estate. The library will have several books on estate planning. The Senior Law website is www.seniorlaw.com, and the AARP website is www.aarp.org. Other good sites are www.aboutlivingtrusts.com and http://law.freeadvice.com/tax_law. Many law firms that specialize in estate planning have valuable websites. Your state website likely will include its probate code.

THE 30-SECOND RECAP

- Start your estate planning by reviewing your current finances.
- Jointly owned property with right of survivorship avoids probate.
- Probate is the process of administering the decedent's assets that pass through the will, or go to the heirs if there is no will.
- A revocable living trust avoids probate and may avoid a guardianship.
- A prenuptial agreement may allow the business owner to keep the business after a divorce.
- If retirement is in the near future, plan now for a business successor.

Personnel Considerations

Discrimination and Compensation Laws You Need to Know

In most cases, your business will require other people—employees—to make it go. You select, train, and pay your employees, and, sometimes, have to discipline or discharge a few. All of these employment decisions must be made within the context of federal and state employment laws. Some of the laws are fairly obvious, including the one that disallows the hiring, promoting, compensating, and firing on the basis of skin color. Other laws are more complicated, including those that require you to make reasonable accommodation for disabled employees. This section takes you through the hiring process.

ALL THE MAJOR EMPLOYMENT LAWS

What follows is a very brief summary of each law and a discussion of each one in the context of your employment decisions, such as hiring employees.

ILLEGAL DISCRIMINATION

Congress and the states have enacted several laws that prohibit employment discrimination, among these are the following:

- **Title VII of the *Civil Rights Act of 1964*.** This act prohibits discrimination by employers on the basis of race, color, religion, sex, or national origin. Employers are not permitted to discriminate against any persons in these so-called protected classifications when making employment decisions, such as hiring, firing, promotion, and compensation. Under this act, almost all employees fall into one or more classifications. Title VII applies to any business with 15 or more employees.

- **Section 1981, *Civil Rights Act of 1866*.** This act prohibits discrimination on the basis of race in contracts, which includes the implicit or explicit employment contract you make with any and all employees. Courts have broadly interpreted this law to include racial or ethnic discrimination. For example, an employer cannot refuse to hire a person from the Middle East because of his or her national ancestry.

- ***Equal Pay Act*.** This act prohibits discrimination in compensation based on gender. An employer must compensate men and women with equal rates of pay for equal work. The real issue is the question of what is equal work. For example, an employer cannot pay a male sales clerk more than a female sales clerk performing the exact same tasks, unless he has seniority and is paid for his years of service.

- *Age Discrimination in Employment Act (ADEA).* This act covers any business with 20 or more employees and prohibits discrimination against employees or potential employees 40 years old or older. Any employer decision made solely on the basis of this age category violates the law. For example, an employer cannot force an employee to retire at age 65 based on age alone; however, if the employee cannot perform the work, that may be a valid basis for retirement.

- *Americans with Disabilities Act (ADA).* This act prohibits discrimination against qualified employees who have mental or physical disabilities. The law broadly defines disability to include any impairment that substantially limits a major life activity. Employers must provide reasonable accommodation to a disabled employee who is qualified to perform the job. For example, an employer cannot refuse to hire a visually impaired person whose job would include using a computer; a reasonable accommodation might be to provide a special computer monitor for the disabled person. A business with 15 or more employees is covered by this act.

- *National Labor Relations Act (NLRA).* This act permits employees to organize a labor union, collectively bargain, and engage in economic strikes. Employees have the right to elect a union to represent them and bargain with an employer over compensation and other contract terms, and, if the bargaining is unsuccessful, conduct a strike. An employer cannot discriminate against an employee because of his or her membership in a union. For example, an employer cannot refuse to hire an employee who strongly supports unionizing the company.

- *Immigration Reform and Control Act.* This act makes it illegal for employers to hire undocumented aliens. Each employee is required to complete an INS form I-9 to ensure that the employee can work legally in the United States. The act prohibits discrimination for national origin or for citizenship when the latter is an alien *lawfully* admitted for permanent residence. For example, an employer violates the law by refusing to hire any permanent resident alien.

- **State and local civil rights laws.** Almost every state has laws that parallel the federal antidiscrimination laws. Some states and local governments may have more inclusive categories, such as marital and sexual-orientation discrimination.

The Equal Employment Opportunity Commission (EEOC) administers the federal antidiscrimination laws, with the exception of the *National Labor Relations Act,* which is administered by the National Labor Relations Board (NLRB).

COMPENSATION

The following is a list and brief discussion of each law governing how you must pay your employees:

■ *Fair Labor Standards Act (FLSA).* This act requires the employer to pay a minimum wage ($5.15 in year 2000) and overtime (one and one half times regular pay) for any hours over 40 hours per week. Some employees, such as executives and supervisors, are exempt from coverage under this act. The Labor Department administers the FLSA. For example, if an employee is regularly paid $8 per hour, and works 41 hours in a week, the company must pay the employee $12 for the forty-first hour.

■ *Family and Medical Leave Act (FMLA).* Employees who have worked for an employer for at least 12 months are entitled to up to 12 weeks of *unpaid* leave during any one year period because of the birth or adoption of a child, because of the need to care for a spouse, child, or parent, or because of the employee's health condition which makes the employee unable to work. For example, Jane gives birth and requests 12 weeks maternity leave, which she is permitted under FMLA. A business with 50 or more employees is covered by the act.

■ **Unemployment compensation.** Employees who are terminated because of employee reductions or fired because they are not compatible with their jobs are usually entitled to unemployment compensation under state law. For example, if an employer reduces the number of employees to cut costs, an employee given the pink slip can file with his or her state unemployment compensation agency for benefits. Employees who are fired for serious misconduct, such as stealing or assault, or employees who voluntarily leave their jobs without good cause are not entitled to unemployment compensation.

■ *Employment Retirement Income Security Act (ERISA).* This act regulates employee benefit and pension plans. An employee pension plan must not discriminate in favor of highly compensated employees, have substantial employee participation, provide for employee nonforfeitable rights in the pension, and require distribution not later than when the employee reaches age 70½. Qualified plans must conform to IRS and Department of Labor regulations.

HEALTH AND SAFETY

The following is a brief discussion of the health and safety laws; later each law is discussed in the context of employment decisions:

- *Occupational Safety and Health Act (OSHA).* This act was designed to reduce workplace hazards and improve employee health and safety. Employers are required to provide a workplace free of physical dangers and meet specific health and safety standards. For example, if an employer permits employees to handle toxic materials without proper safeguards, the employer violates the law.

- **Workers' compensation.** Employees who are injured on the job may be entitled to state workers' compensation. The employer is usually held strictly liable for the injury, even if the employee or fellow employee is at fault. For example, if employee Jim was a little careless at work and a machine severed his finger, state law determines the amount the employer pays for the lost digit. The amount of the compensation depends on the seriousness of the injury. Each state establishes its own payment schedule.

LEGAL CONSIDERATIONS WHEN RECRUITING AND HIRING

Finding and then hiring a good employee has become more complex. There are laws to make sure that potential employees do not suffer from discrimination. What follows are some basic guidelines that you should follow to stay out of trouble.

TIP

An excellent introduction to recruiting new employees is the EEOC's *Uniform Guidelines on Employee Selection Procedures (1978)*, which can be found in the Regulations section of the EEOC website (www.eeoc.gov). Although somewhat dated, the regulations are a useful checklist for hiring employees.

JOB DESCRIPTIONS

Write a job description that provides objective criteria to measure which job applicants are most qualified. Ask your employees to help you prepare the description—they should know what the job requires. Include in the description the following:

- **Essential job functions.** You need to list the core functions of the job. Ask yourself: What must be done by this employee? If you're hiring a shipping clerk, will the job require lifting and carrying boxes, and what would the typical box weigh? If you're filling a filing clerk position, does that job require typing or answering the telephone? By focusing on the functions, you can avoid the trap of excluding women as shipping clerks because they are not as strong as men or denying a person with a disability the job because he or she can't perform some nonessential function.

- **Qualifications required for the job.** After you decide on the job functions, determine what qualifications are necessary for the job. Skills: Does the job require excellent typing skills? Education: Does the job require a college degree in accounting? Experience: Does the job require previous sales experience? You are looking for the best match of qualifications to essential job functions.

- **Nonessential job functions.** After you've determined the essential job functions, consider related functions that would be desirable but not necessary. If your shipping clerk makes occasional deliveries, you might want to list a driver's license as a preference. Because this skill is not required, you wouldn't exclude a disabled person from the job because he or she could not drive.

Job Advertisements

Your advertisement should follow these general rules:

- Briefly describe the essential job functions.
- Indicate necessary job qualifications.
- Don't use phrases that could be discriminatory.
- Include the phrase *equal opportunity employer.*

You've determined what the essential job duties are, so put those in the advertisement in abbreviated language. For example, if you are hiring a secretary, you indicate that position, then state the duties: answering customer inquires over the telephone, taking dictation, and typing.

Rather than state that the job requires someone with a high school or college degree, specify what the duties of your accounting position entail, such as preparing profit-and-loss statements and corporate income tax returns. The reader should infer from the duties listed that the position requires substantial accounting knowledge; beginners need not apply.

Don't use the following words and phrases:

- **Young** indicates that persons age 40 or older are not desired, which violates the *Age Discrimination Act.*

- **Retiree preferred** may indicate that persons age 40 to 65 are excluded, which could violate the *Age Discrimination Act.*

- **Healthy** implies that disabled persons will not be considered, in violation of the *Americans with Disabilities Act.*

- **Salesman** should be replaced with *salesperson,* so that you would not be accused of gender discrimination in violation of Title VII.

- **Christian** suggests that you would not hire a person of another faith, a violation of religious discrimination provisions of Title VII; however, there may be an exception if you run a Christian school.

- **Single** may violate some state or local laws, and may also imply to the applicant that women with children need not apply, violating Title VII.

- **Fluent in English** may discriminate against persons because of their national origin, violating Title VII, Section 1981, and the Immigration law; however, if this is an essential job skill (proofreading manuscripts written in English), there may be an exception.

Do use the phrase *equal opportunity employer.* The reader gets the message that you do not intend to violate the law with your hiring practices.

Also consider where to place the advertisements. You want to broaden your pool of potential applicants. Use a city newspaper or radio station that is read or heard by a large audience. Advertising cost is a factor, but most want ads are not expensive. You can obtain a diverse workforce by extending the advertisements beyond the suburban papers.

CAUTION

If an employer's workforce is made up entirely of one race, the EEOC takes the position that employee recruiting must extend to other races through the media that they read, watch, or listen to.

JOB APPLICATION FORM

The job application form you ask potential employees to fill out should include the following:

- **List essential job functions and qualifications.** The list of job requirements should clearly communicate your expectations, so no applicant can later successfully claim that you misrepresented the position.

■ **Obtain basic applicant information.** The application form should ask for the applicant's name, address, telephone number, and require the information necessary to decide whether the applicant is the best person for the job. The application should list the position applied for, the education of the applicant along with any special skills, employment history, special training, entitlement to work in the United States if the applicant is not a U.S. citizen, and starting date.

■ **Consent to background investigation and reference check.** This is to avoid any claim that the applicant's privacy was invaded, because he or she voluntarily consented. The former employers will be more candid if the applicant has consented to the reference check.

Note what you should *not* ask: age, health, number of children, marital status, race, religion, national origin, or gender.

BEFORE YOU HIRE

When you have the job applications in hand, you begin the process of interviewing potential candidates, and then double-check the information that they provide.

INTERVIEWING

You must prepare for the interview by reviewing the job requirements. Develop questions that focus on the applicant's ability to perform the duties, for example ...

■ What were your duties in your previous secretarial position?

■ Why should we hire you for this job?

■ How have you handled unhappy customers in your prior job?

■ How have you motivated people in your other jobs?

 CAUTION

Resumé inflation, or padding a resumé with false achievements and awards, is unfortunately all too prevalent. If the applicant's resumé looks too good, you'd better confirm every claim.

These open-ended questions permit a broader, more informative discussion than simple yes-no questions.

Just as your application form should not ask discriminatory questions, your interview should be free of these unlawful inquiries, too. A few illegal questions include the following:

- Are you pregnant?
- Do you have small children at home?
- How old are you really?
- What country are you from?
- Are you on any medication?
- Have you ever been arrested?
- Are you near retirement?

INVESTIGATING THE APPLICANTS

What you don't know about an applicant may hurt you—or one of your employees or customers. Be skeptical. Before you hire a person, check him or her out thoroughly. To avoid a claim by the applicant that you are invading his or her privacy, get a signed consent specifically permitting you to contact former employers, schools, references, and law enforcement agencies.

CAUTION

One question you may want to ask—and that is legal for you to ask—is, "Have you ever been convicted of a felony?" The answer to this question is particularly important if the felony were theft (and the job involved handling money), or rape (especially when you have female employees), or child molestation (especially when the applicant may be in contact with young people).

Former employers may be reluctant to give you more than the employment dates. They may fear a lawsuit for slander if they say something negative about their ex-employee. Perhaps the best approach is to simply ask them if they would hire the person for the type of job sought with your firm. If the answer is "no," or if it's evasive, you have your answer.

If education is an important job qualification, request that the applicant provide official transcripts from the universities attended and graduated. If you require accounting skills, you want to see the accounting courses that the applicant successfully completed. Don't be surprised if some applicants claim a Harvard degree when the closest they came to that college was wearing its sweatshirt.

References may vary from former teachers to clergy. You assume that these people would make favorable comments, but that is not always the case. Your state may permit you to obtain an applicant's criminal record, and it may be prudent to do so. Because violence in the workplace really happens, you want to know whether the applicant has been convicted of a violent crime. A conviction for drunk driving is relevant if the job includes driving.

TESTING AND PASSING

You may be interested in testing for skills or medical and drug abuse. Approach either category of tests with caution.

SKILLS TESTS

You may want to go beyond the application and interview to determine whether the employee has the skills and knowledge to perform the job; testing may be your answer. Thirty or so years ago, standard employee written tests were in vogue. Courts determined that many of these written generic tests were discriminatory, because the courts determined that they had a racial and ethnic bias. Truth is, these tests weren't particularly helpful anyway because they were pseudo-IQ tests and not related to job performance potential.

If you want to test a future employee, focus on the essential job functions and determine what skills and knowledge the job requires, test accordingly. Depending on the job requirement, here are some skills you might test for:

- Speed and accuracy of typing
- Software manipulation
- Driving
- Engine repair
- Math
- Writing
- Proofreading

CAUTION

Lie-detector tests are illegal in almost all situations under the *Employee Polygraph Protection Act*. Written honesty tests also are of dubious value.

You want to test for relevant skills or knowledge. A writing sample may not be appropriate for a mechanic, but it would be for a newspaper reporter. A driving test is important for a person making deliveries, but not for an editorial position, although proofreading may be essential for the latter job. Both the typing and software tests may be important for the secretary.

There are personality tests from commercial vendors, but use these with extreme care, particularly if they ask about religious belief, sexual preference, politics, and other touchy subjects. You may want to contact a human resource director with a larger company to see what tests they use.

MEDICAL AND DRUG TESTING

Don't require medical examinations of prospective employees because they violate the *Americans with Disabilities Act (ADA)*. If you require a medical examination of all employees, you may make the medical exam a condition of employment *after* you make the job offer. For example, if the job requires extensive night driving, you would want to know whether the applicant's sight is uncorrectable and he or she has poor night vision. The conditional hire cannot reasonably perform and he or she does not get the job. Remember, the ADA only requires *reasonable* accommodation for a disability.

You are entitled to maintain a drug-free workplace. State laws vary on your right to conduct drug testing, however, so consult with your employment lawyer. If the job involves public safety, such as driving a delivery truck, you may be able to test for illegal drugs after you make the job offer. Condition the offer on the drug test, and obtain the applicant's consent for the test. Also hand each applicant your antidrug policy statement.

HIRING THE BEST THAT YOU CAN GET

When you're ready to hire the applicant, here are some final reminders:

- Don't make employment promises that you can't keep.
- Make sure that the INS Form I-9 is completed for immigrants.
- Comply with state law regarding hours for under-18-year-olds.
- Assess applicants only on objective job-related criteria.
- Consider using a written contract.
- Give each employee your employee handbook and benefits book.
- Make sure that all tax-withholding forms are complete.

INDEPENDENT CONTRACTOR RULES

Independent contractors supply your company with services under contract. They are not your employees even though they might perform services that an employee could provide. Typically, they are temporary workers, contracted for a limited time or task. These contractors have worked for other companies in the past and will do so in the future. The independent contractor is employed by some other company, which supplies the person's services to you, or the independent contractor is his or her own independent agent.

The advantages of using an independent contractor include not having to be concerned about ...

- Tax withholding.
- FICA payments.
- Health insurance or other fringe benefits.
- Paid vacations or sick leave.
- Overtime pay.
- Workers' compensation or unemployment tax.
- Antidiscrimination employment laws.

CAUTION

Do not promise any job security to the employee. All your employment documents should state employment is at-will, which means that the employee can be terminated at any time. However, if you intend employment for a specific period, such as one year, provide for termination for cause or changed business conditions.

There are disadvantages, such as lack of control over the independent contractor's time or means of accomplishing the job. The independent contractor may increase his or her charge for services to cover the absence of fringe benefits. And there is the risk that the IRS, Labor Department, or other agency may insist on back taxes or penalties for the erroneous claim of independent contractor status, some of which, such as overtime pay, are the employer's responsibility to pay.

The IRS wants you to collect its withholding and FICA, so it prefers employment status. You need to carefully structure the contract to clearly demonstrate an independent contractor relationship.

Typically, the IRS will contend that there is an employment relationship if you ...

- Control the time and manner of completing the task.
- Can terminate the relationship without legal liability.

- Furnish the tools or a place to work.
- Pay according to time spent on the job, not task performed.

CAUTION

Temps may claim employment status. In the recent Microsoft case, temps claimed that they were really employees for purposes of participating with regular employees in stock bonus plans, because the two categories had virtually indistinguishable job descriptions. This should be a cautionary tale.

If you exercise substantial control over when the person does the work and how he or she does it, you've effectively hired that person, and any independent contract you've both signed won't be worth the paper it's written on. So how do you avoid this improper employee classification? Specify in the contract what services the person is to perform, but not how he or she performs it. You can set performance deadlines, but don't require office hours. Contract payment is based upon satisfactory performance of the tasks, not on time spent. And you sign the contract along with the independent contractor.

HELPFUL SOURCES REGARDING DISCRIMINATION AND EMPLOYMENT LAW

A wealth of employment information is available on federal websites. The EEOC site is www.eeoc.gov, the Department of Labor's is www.dol.gov, the IRS site is www.irs.ustreas.gov, the National Labor Relations Board's is www.nlrb.gov, and the Department of Justice site is www.doj.gov. Many of the websites provide downloadable pamphlets. Also visit your state civil rights and department of labor websites for state laws and regulations. Cornell University has a good employment law website: www.law.cornell.edu. There is software available with employment forms and checklists, and your bookstore and library have recent books on employment law.

THE 30-SECOND RECAP

- Use the federal and state antidiscrimination laws as a checklist of what not to do.
- Employee recruiting should focus on the essential job functions.
- Independent contractors can save you money, but you must design the relationship to demonstrate independence from your control over the time and means of accomplishing the task.

What to Know When Screening Candidates

As a result of your recruiting efforts, you've received a number of resumés. Your next job is to determine which applicants are worth interviewing. In this section, you learn how to pick the candidates whose backgrounds appear to be closest to those required for the open job, to prepare carefully for the interview, and to conduct it effectively.

THE FIRST STEP: SCREENING THE RESUMÉS

Always remember that the resumé is a promotional piece written by the applicant to persuade you why he or she should be hired. It is not necessarily an objective recap of qualifications. Your job is to find among those glowing words, what the applicant has really done in his or her past jobs and schooling.

TIPS ON RAPID SCREENING

You may receive hundreds of resumés in response to an ad. It can take hours and hours of your time to read them and make your preliminary judgments. You can save time and uncover hidden problems in the resumés by following these guidelines:

- Establish some "knockout factors." These are job requirements that are absolutely essential to performing the job. They include necessary educational qualifications and/or licenses, for example, a degree in electronics, certification as a plumber, or a pilot's license.

  TIP

  Show some flexibility in using "knockout factors." For example, unless a specific degree is needed for legal or professional reasons, a person who lacks the degree but has extensive experience in a field may be better qualified than a person with a degree and less experience.

- Select key components of the job and screen for them. When you have many applicants for a position, you can narrow the field by looking for experience in those key aspects. For example, if one of the major requirements for success on a job is experience in marketing to major food chains, by scanning resumés for this experience, you will focus on qualified applicants.

- Look for gaps in dates. Some people who have had short duration jobs omit them from their resumés.

- Watch for candidates who give more space on the resumé to past positions than current ones. This may be due to the applicant just updating an old resumé instead of creating a new one. This could be a sign of laziness, or it may just mean that the more recent jobs were less pertinent than previous ones.

- Keep an eye out for overemphasis on education for experienced applicants. If a person is out of school five or more years, the resumé should primarily cover work experience. What was done in high school or college is secondary to what has been accomplished on the job. For such applicants, information about education should be limited to degrees and specialized programs completed.

- As you read the resumés, check to see whether a significant amount of education and experience the applicant specifies includes the key factors the applicant must have to qualify.

- If these factors are mentioned, determine whether this experience or training has been acquired in a setting comparable to that of your organization. (For example, cost accounting experience in a chemical company may not be of much value to an automobile parts company as the cost systems are entirely different.)

- Determine whether the applicant has enough depth of experience to meet your requirements.

CAUTION

Resumés are only pieces of paper, which cannot possibly describe the whole person. If you choose not to see an applicant based on the resumé, you will lose this prospect—perhaps the best candidate—forever. If you have any doubts, before placing it in the reject file, telephone the candidate to obtain more information.

None of these is necessarily a knockout factor. They simply suggest further exploration in the interview.

THE APPLICATION FORM

In addition to requesting resumés, some companies also require all candidates to fill out an application form. This form serves several purposes. It's a rapid means of providing the interviewer with the basic information about the applicant. It alleviates the need for the interviewer to take time asking for this routine information. It provides legal protection. It makes it easy to compare candidates. The following is a prototype application form, which you can adapt to your own particular needs.

Application for Employment

Date: _____

Name: _____   Social Security number: _____

Address: _____

City, State, ZIP: _____Phone: _____

Position sought: _____   Salary
                                             desired: _____

EDUCATION

Level: _____   School/Location: _____

Course: _____

Number of years: _____   Degree or diploma: _____

College: _____

Other: _____

_____

_____

EMPLOYMENT RECORD

1. Company/Address: _____

   Dates: _____ Salary: _____ Supervisor: _____

   Duties: _____

   _____

   _____

2. Company/Address: _____

   Dates: _____ Salary: _____ Supervisor: _____

   Duties: _____

   _____

   _____

3. Company/Address: _____

   Dates: _____ Salary: _____ Supervisor: _____

   Duties: _____

   _____

   _____

   How were you referred to this company? _____

   Are you 18 years of age or older? _____

   If you're hired, can you provide written evidence that you are authorized
   to work in the United States? _____

   Is there any other name under which you have worked that we would
   need in order to check your work record (if so, please provide):

   _____

   APPLICANT'S STATEMENT

   I understand that the employer follows an "employment-at-will" policy,
   in that I or the employer may terminate my employment at any time or
   for any reason consistent with applicable federal and state laws. This
   employment-at-will policy cannot be changed verbally or in writing
   unless authorized specifically by the president or executive vice president of this company. I understand that this application is not a contract
   of employment. I understand that the federal government prohibits the
   employment of unauthorized aliens; all persons hired must provide satisfactory proof of employment authorization and identity. Failure to submit such proof will result in denial of employment.

   I understand that the employer may investigate my work and personal
   history and verify all information given on this application, on related
   papers, and in interviews. I hereby authorize all individuals, schools,
   and firms named therein, except my current employer (if so noted), to
   provide any information requested about me and hereby release them
   from all liability for damage in providing this information.

   I certify that all the statements in this form and other information provided by me in applying for this position are true and understand that
   any falsification or willful omission shall be sufficient cause for dismissal or refusal of employment.

   Signed: _____

ALL APPLICANTS *MUST* FILL OUT THE FORM

Some candidates may be reluctant to complete an application. They might tell you that all of that information is in the resumé. And sometimes it is. But, as was pointed out earlier in this part, a resumé is designed to play up the strengths of the applicant—sometimes to cover up negative factors. If your company requires that candidates complete the form to be considered for the job, stick to this policy.

CAUTION

"I don't have to fill out the application. I have a resumé." This is not a good argument. If an applicant doesn't want to take the time to complete your application form, he or she may be hiding something—or it may be an indicator of laziness or unwilling-ness to follow instructions.

THE FORM PROVIDES INFORMATION YOU NEED

It's convenient to have essential information in one easy to find place. The form provides name, address, phone number, Social Security number, and educational background. Most useful is the work history with dates of employment, positions, companies, and a brief description of duties and responsibilities. Usually it includes salary, reason for leaving, and the name of a person in the company who can provide information about the applicant.

It gives you enough basic information to determine whether or not the prospect is worthy of further consideration. Although most forms don't have enough space to give details about a person's activities, actions, and accomplishments, it provides, along with the applicant's resumé, adequate data to make preliminary judgments.

YOU CAN COMPARE CANDIDATES

Whereas resumés are written in a variety of styles, applications for jobs in a company are all formatted in the same way. This makes it easy to compare applicants. Placing application forms side by side, you can immediately measure the education and experience of each candidate against the others. You can compare duration and types of experience and note salary variations.

TIP

Impressive resumés might make a candidate stand out, but when the resumé and application together are considered, you might find that the applicant with a less-impressive looking resumé actually has a better background.

APPLICATION CLAUSES TO PROTECT YOU

In addition to being a selection tool, the application form is a contract. Of course, it's a one-sided contract in that it's written to protect the employer. Courtrooms have been filled with lawsuits against companies by job applicants who have claimed that companies discriminated against them in the hiring process. Others have claimed that companies jeopardized their current job by calling their employer for a reference, or that their privacy was invaded by having their backgrounds investigated.

Properly designed application forms can protect companies. For example, if no questions on your application request age or related information, applicants will have a tough time proving that a company discriminated against them because of age. If the application form requests permission to contact current employers or to perform background checks, companies are protected on that front.

TIP

Before reprinting your application form each time more copies are needed, have your legal counsel review it to ensure it's in compliance with the latest laws and regulations.

Attorneys strongly recommend some important clauses be included in this document. You will find suggested wording in the sample application form in this part, but it is always advisable to consult your attorney, because wording may have to be adapted to union contracts, local laws, and court rulings.

PERMISSION TO INVESTIGATE BACKGROUND

A background check covers two different types of investigation: checking references and using an investigative service to look into the applicant's background.

- **Reference checks.** Because of their concerns about litigation, many companies refuse to give information about former or current employees. By getting a release from the applicant authorizing the employer to provide information, you obviate this concern. Many companies have a clause to cover this on their application form; some have this on a separate document.

  See the sample application form in this section for an example of such a clause.

TIP

Some lawyers suggest that even if a release clause is incorporated in the application form, a separate form should be signed for each school and employer to be contacted.

■ **Investigative reports.** Under the *Fair Credit Reporting Act,* a federal law, if you consider using the services of an outside credit or investigative reporting agency, you must provide the applicant with a written notification stating that such a report may be ordered. The applicant must be advised that he or she has the right to request a copy of such a report from the agency that conducts the investigation and that the name of such agency will be provided on request. If you plan to use this type service on a regular basis, this clause should be printed on the application form in print that is no smaller than the rest of the application and should have a space for the signature of the applicant and of a witness. If you use investigative reports for only a few positions, rather than print it on the application, develop a separate form to use when appropriate.

EMPLOYMENT AT WILL

Unless an employee is protected by an individual contract with the employer, a negotiated contract between the employer and a labor union, or is civil service employee, that person falls under the employment-at-will status. This means that the employer has the right to terminate the services of that employee at any time, for any reason, or for no reason at all so long as it complies with applicable laws such as the civil rights laws. Most employees in American companies fall in this category. However, to ensure that new employees are aware of this, it should be indicated on the application form. By having the applicant sign the application form, he or she acknowledges understanding and acceptance of "employment at will".

CERTIFICATION OF TRUTH

If after you hire a person, you find out that he or she had lied in his or her application or resumé about an important factor, you should have the option to take immediate action to terminate that person.

Have your company's legal advisors word the certification of truth clause to meet all appropriate laws.

SURVIVING THE INTERVIEW PROCESS

After you've sifted through all the applications and/or resumés and put together a stack of likely candidates, it's time to pick up the telephone. Probably the most frequently used screening tool is the telephone. In a relatively brief telephone interview, you can acquire a lot more information about a candidate than can be obtained from the application and/or resumé.

It's not a good idea to call the applicant at his or her place of work to discuss your job opening. This is not only unethical, but it puts the applicant in an awkward position as other people may be nearby who can hear the conversation. Instead, call the applicant at home in the evening. This may mean you have to make these calls from your home or work late at the office. It's just one of the sacrifices that recruiters and managers have to make to get the people they want.

Plan the phone call as carefully as an in-person interview. Read the application and/or resumé carefully and note the areas that require elaboration. Don't be afraid to ask hard questions, such as why the applicant wants to leave his or her current position, why the candidate was unemployed for lengthy periods of time, what his or her relations with superiors were like, and specific details about work or educational background. Suggestions on how to conduct an interview are covered later in this section—adapt these techniques to the telephone interview.

TAKE NOTES

In a telephone interview, it's even more important than in a personal interview to note the answers to your questions. It's not a distraction to the interviewee as it might be in a face-to-face interview, so you have more freedom to be thorough in your note taking. We tend to remember people and what they tell us more easily when we see them in person than when we just hear them over the phone.

CLOSING THE TELEPHONE INTERVIEW

In closing the interview, review your notes to ensure that you have all the information you need. If you're sure you want to extend the invitation, do so. If you have some reservations or want to discuss your reaction with others in your organization, tell the applicant you'll be in touch with him or her. Give a specific time when your next contact should be expected, and be sure to keep your promise. If you have decided to reject the applicant, either say so immediately or notify the applicant in a reasonably short time after the phone call.

IT'S SHOW TIME

You've done the preparatory work. You've studied application forms and resumés and completed a preliminary phone interview. Now you're ready to see the applicant. Interviewing is both an art and a science. It's a science because it can be structured to bring out the information desired. It's an art because the interviewer must be able to tailor the questions and interpret the responses.

Interviews are more than just pleasant conversations between you and the applicant. How the interviewing process is planned and followed can make the difference between hiring the best candidate and just selecting one by instinct.

PREPARING FOR THE INTERVIEW

Before an applicant enters the interviewing room, study the application and resumé. Note any areas that require more information or are indicators of strengths or weaknesses so that you will remember to ask questions about them.

TIP

Although many well-known organizations have developed sophisticated selection tools, including structured interviews, psychological evaluations, and multiple assessments, the great percentage of companies relies on informal interviews by supervisors and managers as their primary selection method.

Keep in mind the objectives of the interview: first, to determine whether the candidate has the technical qualifications needed for the position; second, to find out whether the applicant has the personality traits needed to be successful in the job.

PLAN YOUR QUESTIONS

Well-designed questions based on the job specs can help determine skill qualifications. Personality qualifications are much more difficult to measure. Some of these intangibles may be listed in the job specs. For example, "must be able to work under pressure," or "should be able to present public speeches." It's not easy to reduce personality factors to a simple statement. The interviewer's knowledge of the job, the people with whom the applicant will have to work, and the company culture must be taken into consideration.

Some interviewers sit down with the applicant with only a general idea of what questions they plan to ask. They may start with a general question such as "Tell me about yourself." From the response, they then pick aspects of the background to explore. This may be okay for an experienced interviewer who just uses that question as an opening device and has thought out what added questions to ask. However, the danger here is that the applicant may tell you only what he or she wants you to hear and you may never get around to asking about areas not mentioned.

MAKE A LIST OF KEY QUESTIONS

In planning for the interview, develop a list of questions you plan to ask. An effective interview is well planned. The interviewer doesn't ad lib questions.

Some interviewers write down the questions they plan to ask and refer to it during the interview. Others make notes on the applicant's application form to remind them about areas they wish to explore. Still other interviewers depend on their knowledge of the field to develop questions as they move along in the process. Later in this chapter, you'll find a structured interview form listing questions that are effective in obtaining good information.

CAUTION

It's important to prepare questions to ask an applicant at the interview. However, don't limit yourself to asking just those questions. Be alert to responses and ask additional questions based on answers received.

THE STRUCTURED INTERVIEW

Most good interviews have some kind of structure. If not, they result in a chaotic exchange of questions and answers with little possibility of making reasonable decisions. However, some companies use specially prepared *structured interview* forms, which interviewers must follow virtually line by line.

PLAIN ENGLISH

Structured interviews are conducted using a list of questions that must be asked in exactly the same way in exactly the same order. They are also called *patterned interviews, diagnostic interviews,* and *guided interviews.*

ADVANTAGES OF USING A STRUCTURED INTERVIEW

Some labor lawyers argue that asking each applicant exactly the same questions in exactly the same order will be a defense against charges of discrimination. Some psychologists have designed structured interviews with the objective of uncovering patterns of behavior. Others use structured interviews simply to make the interview process as easy as possible. Whether the reason is legal, psychological, or just pragmatic, there are some advantages to using some form of structured interview.

By asking questions from a printed list, you won't miss asking an important question. In addition, structured interview forms provide space next to the questions to record answers. This helps the interviewer remember the responses. In addition, as all applicants are asked the same questions, it makes it easy to compare applicants when making the final decision.

CONSIDER THE DOWNSIDE

The negative side of a formal structured interview is that it stifles creativity and flexibility. In the formal structured interview, you are not allowed to deviate from the form. Both those forms developed for legal reasons and those with psychological implication require strict adherence to the structure.

Sometimes an applicant's answer to one question may make it advisable for you to depart from the structure and follow-up to obtain more or better information.

USING A LESS-FORMAL STRUCTURE

The structured interview should be used only as a guide. This cannot be done if the format you use is one in which the psychologist requires the interviewer to phrase questions exactly as printed or if you're company requires strict adherence. However, most structured interviews are not of this nature, and variations and flexibility can be built in to them.

The following is an example of a modified structured interview form. It is designed to serve as a guide and gives the interviewer freedom to be flexible. You may adapt this for your own use. Follow the instructions at the beginning of the form.

CAUTION

When using a structured interview form, don't fall into the trap of reading the question as if it were a questionnaire. Present the questions in a conversational tone and rephrase where necessary to put the question into the context of the conversation.

To use this system effectively, it must be personalized for each specific job and for each applicant. The suggested questions are to be used only as guidelines. They might or might not be asked of each applicant depending upon pertinence.

Most important: Specific questions relating to job requirements should be developed for each job based on *your* job description, company needs, and interviewer's follow-up to responses given by the applicant.

STRUCTURED INTERVIEW QUESTIONS

(Complete this section before the interview begins.)

Name of applicant: _____

Address: _____

_____

Telephone/fax/e-mail: _____

_____

Position: _____

Department: _____

Interviewed by: _____

Date: _____

Note: In designing the form to use in your company, leave spaces between questions to note answers.

EDUCATION

Ask questions in Part A of applicants who did not attend college. Use questions in Part B for college graduates or those who have had same college. For applicants who have been out of college five years or more, omit A or B and ask only questions in Part C.

A. For Applicants Who Did Not Attend College:

1. What was your highest level of schooling completed?
2. Why did you decide not to continue your formal education?
3. How were your overall grades?
4. What extracurricular activities did you participate in?
5. If you worked during school, how many hours per week? Summers? What kind of jobs?
6. What steps have you taken to acquire additional education since leaving school?
7. What training have you had in high or other schools that helped in your career?
8. What was the first significant job you held after leaving high school?
9. How did this lead to your present career?

B. For College Graduates or Those with Some College:

1. I see that you attended (name of college). Why did you select that school?
2. What was your major? Why did you choose it?
3. What were your overall college grades? How did they compare with your high school grades?
4. What courses did you start in college and later drop? Why?
5. In what types of extracurricular activities did you participate in college? What offices did you hold?
6. How did you finance your college education?
7. If you worked in high school or college, how many hours per week? Summers? Kind of jobs?
8. What were your vocational plans when you were in college?
9. If your vocational plans are different now, when did you change your thinking? Why?
10. What additional education have you had since college?
11. How do you think college contributed to your career?
12. (If college was not completed.) When did you leave college? Why? Do you plan to complete your degree? (If so, ask about plans.)
13. What was the first significant job you held after leaving (graduating from) college?
14. How did this lead to your current career?

C. For Persons Out of School Five Years or Longer:

1. What educational background have you had that has contributed to success in your career?
2. What courses or seminars have you taken recently? (If job-related, how did you apply them to your job?)
3. What are you doing now to keep up with the state of the art in your field?
4. What magazines and types of books do you read regularly?

WORK EXPERIENCE

Ask these questions for *each* job held:

1. On your application you indicated you worked for (name of company) Are you still there? (Or: When were you there?)

2. Describe your duties and responsibilities in each of your assignments with this company?

3. What were some of the things you particularly enjoyed about that job?

4. What were some of the things you least enjoyed in that position?

5. What do you consider your major accomplishment in that assignment?

6. Tell me about some of your disappointments or setbacks in that job.

7. Tell me about the progress you made in that company.

8. If progress was significant, ask: To what do you attribute this fine progress? If not, ask: Were you satisfied with this progress? If not satisfied, ask: How did you attempt to overcome this?

9. Why did you leave (or: why do you want to leave) that company?

Specific Questions

On a separate sheet of paper, list specific questions to be asked—based on the job description. (See the section immediately following this form.)

Intangible Factors

In addition to the questions on job qualifications, ask some questions to elicit information about the applicant as a person:

1. What are you seeking in this job that you are not getting in your present job?

2. Tell me about your short- and long-term career goals.

3. In what way could a job with our company meet your career objectives?

4. If you had to do it over again, what changes would you make in your life and your career?

5. Think of a supervisor you particularly respected. Describe his/her management style? Describe your least effective supervisor?

6. What have supervisors complimented you for? What have they criticized you for?

7. Tell me about some of the significant problems encountered? How did you solve them?

8. If hired for this position, what can you bring to it that will make you productive right away?

9. In what areas could we help you become even more productive?

PREPARING SPECIFIC JOB-RELATED QUESTIONS

The responses to the general questions in your interview will give you enough information to determine whether the candidate is basically qualified for your job. However, there are in every job certain very specific areas of knowledge, experience, and expertise that the applicant must demonstrate to be capable of becoming productive rapidly. To determine this, also prepare a list of questions that will probe for these details.

TIP

Read your job specs carefully. Discuss the job with the department head or team leader. Frame questions that will enable you to get the information needed to determine whether this applicant is best for the open position.

As the questions differ from job to job—even jobs with the same or similar titles may require different specific factors—you must develop appropriate questions for each job.

To do this, study not just the job specification, which lists the qualifications required, but also the job description, which gives details of job functions.

For example, if your opening is for a medical technician, prepare questions about the types of medical equipment the applicant has learned to operate in school, his or her experience in operating the equipment, and the venues in which the person worked (hospital? clinic? physician's office?). If you are not fully knowledgeable about the job, have the person to whom the person would report design these questions for you—and, of course, the appropriate answers.

TIP

Lists of specific questions to ask applicants for more than 70 different jobs can be found in *Be a Better Employment Interviewer*, by Dr. Arthur R. Pell. It sells for $14.95 and can be ordered from Personnel Publications, PO Box 301, Huntington, NY 11745.

GETTING STARTED

To obtain the best results from an interview, the interviewer must put the applicant at ease. To do this takes a little time, but even in a brief interview is well worth it.

ESTABLISH RAPPORT

To make the applicant feel at ease, the interviewer must be at ease and feel comfortable about the interviewing process. An ideal setting for an interview is a private room, comfortably furnished with a minimum of distracting papers on the desk. To avoid telephone interruptions, turn on your voicemail or have somebody else answer your phone.

It's much better to personally go to the reception area than to send a secretary to fetch him or her. So get up from your chair and get out there. Introduce yourself and escort the applicant to the interviewing room.

When greeting the applicant, use his or her full name. "David Livingston. Hi, I'm Henry Stanley." This makes the applicant feel that you identify him or her as an individual, not just another candidate. Dale Carnegie put it best when he said, "Remember, a person's name is to that person the sweetest and most important sound in any language."

By using both the first and the last name in addressing the applicant and in introducing yourself, you are putting both of you on equal footing. If you call yourself Mr. or Ms., and call the applicant "Dave" it sounds condescending.

The opening should be related to the interview, but should not make the applicant defensive or upset. Don't start with such questions as "What makes you think that you could handle this job?" or "Why were you fired from your last job?"

A better approach would be to select an innocuous area from the application and comment on it. It may be based on something in the background that you relate to. For example, "I see you went to Lincoln High School. Did you know Mr. Salkin, the drama teacher?" or "I see you live in Chelsea. That neighborhood is growing rapidly."

GUIDELINES FOR BETTER INTERVIEWING

To get the most out of the interview, here are some guidelines to follow when asking questions:

- Don't ask questions that can be answered with a simple "yes" or "no." This stifles information. Instead of asking, "Have you any experience in budgeting?" ask, "Tell me about your experience in budgeting?"

- Don't put words in the applicant's mouth. Instead of asking, "You've called on discount stores, haven't you?" ask, "What discount stores have you called on?"

- Don't ask questions that are unrelated to your objectives. It might be interesting to follow up on certain tidbits of gossip the applicant volunteers, but it rarely leads to pertinent information.

■ Do ask questions that develop information as to the applicant's *experience* ("What were your responsibilities regarding the purchasing of equipment?"), *knowledge* ("How did you, or would you cope with this problem?"), and *attitudes* ("How do you feel about heavy travel?" Or "Why do you wish to change jobs now?").

TIP

An important objective of the interview is to create a favorable image of the company in the eyes of the applicant. The reputation of the firm may be improved or harmed by the manner in which applicants are treated. You want your top candidate to accept a job offer and who knows, even rejected applicants may be potential customers.

An effective way of probing for full information is to use the "W" questions: "What," "When," "Where," "Who," and "Why." With the addition of "How," you can draw out most of the information needed. For example:

"What computer software was used?"

"When did you design that program?"

"Where was the program installed?"

"Who was responsible for supervising that project?"

"Why did you make that decision?"

"How did you implement the new system?"

TIP

Glib applicants may come up with high-sounding solutions to situations, but they may not be really practical. Follow through by asking what problems might be encountered if the idea were implemented.

ASK SITUATIONAL QUESTIONS

Give the applicant a hypothetical situation and ask how he or she would handle it. The situations should be reasonably close to actual problems found on the job. Judge the response by knowledge of the subject, approach to the solution, value of the suggestions, and clarity in communicating the answer.

SUMMARY QUESTIONS

After you have asked the applicant about a phase of his or her background, ask another question that will summarize what has been presented. For example "You certainly have extensive background in quality control, briefly summarize what you can contribute to make our company more effective in that area."

USING NONDIRECTIVE TECHNIQUES

It's not always possible to obtain necessary information by direct questioning. Nondirective approaches may help in these cases. Nondirective questioning uses open-end questions such as "Tell me about ..." The applicant then tells whatever he or she feels is important. Instead of commenting about the response, you nod your head and say "uh-huh," "yes," "I see." This encourages the applicant to keep talking without your giving any hint as to what you are seeking.

TIP

Try this: After the applicant responds to your question, count to five slowly (to yourself, of course) before asking the next question. By waiting five seconds, you'll be surprised how often an applicant adds something—positive or negative—to the response to the previous question.

In this way, the applicant may talk about problems, personality factors, attitudes, or weaknesses that might not have been uncovered directly. On the other hand, it may bring out some positive factors and strengths that were missed by direct questioning.

Another way of using the nondirective approach is to be silent. Most people can't tolerate silence. If you don't respond instantly, the applicant is likely to keep talking.

GIVING INFORMATION TO THE APPLICANT

An important part of the interview is giving the applicant information about the company and the job. All the work and expense undertaken to get good employees is lost if the applicants you want don't accept your offer. By giving them a positive picture of the job at the interview, you're more likely to have a higher rate of acceptances.

WHEN AND WHAT TO TELL ABOUT THE JOB

Some interviewers start the interview by describing the job duties. Some give the applicant a copy of the job description in advance of the interview. *This is a serious error.* If an applicant knows too much about a job too soon, he or she is likely to tailor the answers to all of your questions to fit the job.

For example, suppose you tell a prospect that the job calls for selling to department store chains. Even if the applicant has only limited experience in this area, when you ask, "What types of markets did you call on?" guess which one will be emphasized?

The best way to give information about duties and responsibilities is to feed it to the applicant throughout the interview—*after* you have ascertained the background of the applicant in that phase of the work. For the sales job that involves calling on department store chains, you might first ask the candidate to state the types of markets he or she called on.

You should then ask specific questions about the applicant's experience in each of these markets. If the department store background is satisfactory, you might then say, "I'm glad you have such a fine background in dealing with department store chains as they represent about 40 percent of our customer list. If you're hired, you'd be working closely with those chains."

If the background in this area was weak, you might say, "As a great deal of our business is with department store chains, if we hire you, we would have to give you added training in this area."

At the end of the first interview, the interviewer should have a fairly complete knowledge of the applicant's background and the applicant should have a good idea of the nature of the job. At subsequent interviews, the emphasis will be on obtaining more specific details about the applicant and giving the applicant more specific data about the job.

ANSWERING APPLICANTS' QUESTIONS

Most interviewers give the applicant an opportunity to ask questions about the job and the company at some point (usually at the end) of the interview. The questions asked can give some insight into the applicant's personality and help you in your evaluation.

Are the questions primarily of a personal nature? (Such as vacations, time off, raises, and similar queries), or are they about the job? People who are only concerned about personal aspects are less likely to be as highly motivated as job-oriented applicants. Their questions can also be clues to their real interest in the job. If you feel, from these questions that a prospective candidate might not be too enthusiastic about the job, it gives you another chance to sell the prospect on the advantages of joining your company.

You are always "selling" when you interview. It's important that you present your company and the job in a positive and enthusiastic manner. This doesn't mean that you should exaggerate or mislead the applicant. Tell the applicant the negatives at the interview, but show how the positive aspects outweigh them. Remember that you, the interviewer, will be working with this candidate. An honest interview discussing positive and negative aspects helps to build trust.

CAUTION

Every job has its negative aspects, and if you hide them, the applicant will find out sooner or later. This could lead to rejection of the job offer, or worse, acceptance and early resignation.

CLOSING THE INTERVIEW

When you have all the information you need, and you've told the applicant about the job and given him or her an opportunity to ask questions, it's time to bring the interview to a close.

END ON A POSITIVE NOTE

All interviews should end on a positive note. The applicant should be told what the next step would be: Another interview? Testing? A final decision?

INFORMING THE APPLICANT OF YOUR DECISION

If, on the basis of the interview, you have decided not to hire the candidate, it's only fair to tell him or her. In most cases, the reason may be obvious. During the interview, it became clear to both of you that the applicant was not qualified. Just say, "As you don't have experience in area X and Y, which are essential to being able to do this job, we cannot consider you for it."

TIP

Don't keep applicants on a string waiting to hear from you. If you are not interested in a candidate, write or phone him or her no later than a week after the interview. If the applicant is still being considered, but the decision is delayed, keep the applicant advised of the status.

If the reason is not directly job related, such as lacking personal characteristics or your reaction to the applicant, rather than reject him or her outright, say, "We have several more applicants to interview. After we've seen them all, we'll make a decision." Then, after a reasonable period, let them know they were rejected.

Remembering the Applicant

You've seen a dozen applicants for the open position. Unless you take notes, it's unlikely to remember what each one has told you and your reaction to them.

Good Notes Keep You Out of Trouble

If you've kept good records of the interviews, it's easier to compare candidates. By rereading your notes rather than depending on your memory, you are more likely to make sounder judgments. When several people interview the same candidate, a consistent system of recording information will facilitate an in-depth analysis of the applicant's qualifications.

Good records also come in handy if you face legal problems. In case of an investigation by government agencies such as the EEOC or state civil rights divisions, good records of the interview can be your most important defense. Where no records or inadequate records have been kept, the opinion of the hearing officer is dependent on the company's word against the applicant's. Good, consistent records provide solid evidence.

Taking Notes

Taking notes often has a negative effect on applicants. Some get very nervous when they see you write down everything they say. They may be inhibited from talking freely and hold back on important matters.

Taking notes also may have a negative effect on you, the interviewer. You're so busy writing what the applicant just said, that you don't listen to what is now being said.

Write brief notes during the interview. Immediately after the interview review them and write a summary, while the interview is still fresh in your mind.

List the reasons for accepting or rejecting each candidate. Succinctly stating a reason helps overcome intuitive decisions based on some vague like or dislike. Don't forget that the EEOC or other agencies may challenge the reasons.

Some companies have special forms designed for interview record keeping. Others suggest you make notes on the application form or on a paper to attach to the form after the interview. In any case, a summary form should be completed *immediately* after the close of the interview.

The 30-Second Recap

■ Before evaluating resumés, set up a series of knockout factors. Unless the applicant meets these specs, there's no point arranging for an interview.

- Don't take a resumé at face value. Read between the lines. Look for hidden negative factors.
- Before conducting an interview, review the job specs and description application as well as the applicant's resumé and application form.
- Prepare a list of key questions.
- A good interview should be structured, but flexible enough so that follow-up questions can be asked.
- Telephone interviews can provide enough information to determine whether it's worthwhile to invite the applicant for a face-to-face meeting.
- Put the applicant at ease by asking nonthreatening questions at the start of the interview.
- To get full information, use the "W" questions: "What," "When," "Where," "Who," and "Why." With the addition of "How," you can draw out most of the information needed.
- Use nondirective approaches to elicit additional information about candidates.

Team Interviewing

An interview is one of the primary tools for choosing new employees, but it's not the only one. After all, an interview is, by its very nature, subjective.

To supplement your reaction to applicants, it's a good idea to have other managers or staff members interview them. Because each person tends to look for different facets of an applicant's background, if several people do the interviewing, you will uncover much more about a candidate than any one interviewer can find. In a team setup, it's particularly helpful for team members to interview people who may join their team. Other techniques for obtaining information about prospective employees are to check their references and, in some cases, have them undergo testing.

This section discusses these and other approaches to learning as much as possible about applicants before making your hiring decision.

MULTIPLE INTERVIEWS

Hiring an employee can be the most important decision you make as a manager. The people who comprise your staff can make or break your endeavors. No matter how good you may be as an interviewer, it's a good idea to seek the reaction of others before making a final decision.

TIP

Before making a hiring decision, have an applicant interviewed by other people who will work closely with the candidate should she be hired.

In larger companies, a member of the human resources department usually conducts preliminary interviews with applicants. Only people who meet basic job requirements are referred to the manager.

If HR isn't involved in the interview process, it's still a good idea to have the applicant interviewed by at least one other person. You may have missed important facts or been overly influenced by one factor or another.

The person (or persons) you ask to be the other interviewer should have the appropriate type of job and level of responsibility. To interview for jobs of a technical or specialized nature, a person with expertise in that area is the best choice. If a new employee will work closely with another department, the opinion of the manager of that department will be meaningful. Many companies require finalists to be interviewed by the manager at the next higher level (your boss).

WHEN YOU WORK IN TEAMS

Because the team concept involves every member of a team, the process of choosing members for the team should be a team activity. The danger is that interviewing takes time: If every team member interviews every applicant, other work will suffer.

It's not necessary for every team member to conduct a full interview. Each team member should concentrate on the part of an applicant's background in which she or he has the greatest knowledge. All team members will have the opportunity to size up an applicant, and to share their evaluations with the rest of the team. It also gives a candidate a chance to meet the people with whom he or she will be working, and can help the candidate make the best decision as to whether to join your team.

Have each interviewer fill out an interview summary sheet so that evaluations can be compared more easily.

EMPLOYMENT TESTS: A PANACEA OR A WASTE OF TIME?

Do tests help in choosing employees? Some companies swear by testing; others swear at them. In companies in which tests are used extensively as part of the screening process, the HR department or an independent testing organization does the testing. Except for performance tests (discussed later in this chapter), it's unlikely that you will have to administer tests.

Let's look at the most frequently used pre-employment tests.

INTELLIGENCE TESTS

Like the IQ tests used in schools, these tests measure the ability to learn. They vary from simple exercises (such as the Wunderlic tests) that can be administered by people with a minimum of training, to highly sophisticated tests that must be administered by specialists with a Ph.D. in psychology.

The major flaw in using general intelligence tests is that two individuals who receive the same score can earn it in very different ways. One may be high in reasoning, low in numerical skills, and average in verbal skills. The other may be high in numerical skills, low in reasoning, and high in verbal skills. They display entirely different intelligence profiles. Judging them by the total score can be misleading. To get the true picture, the test has to be evaluated by the scores of its components.

Tests often create other problems, too. For instance, some people believe that highly creative people score lower on standardized exams.

Another problem is that some tests violate the equal opportunity laws. To ensure that a test is in compliance, it must be validated to be free from cultural bias, and the score on the test must be directly related to the ability to do the job. Most test publishers have taken steps to eliminate cultural bias, but it is up to the company itself to prove that the test does have relevance to job success. For example, a test may contain questions about Greek mythology—a subject biased against minorities who come from cultures where this subject is less likely to be studied—and such questions are not relevant to ability to learn the job. The Equal Employment Opportunity Commission has issued guidelines on validation of tests, which can be obtained directly from its office in your area.

APTITUDE TESTS

These tests are designed to determine the potential of candidates in specific areas such as mechanical ability, clerical skills, and sales potential. Such tests are helpful in screening inexperienced people to determine whether they have the aptitude in the type of work you plan to train them for.

PERFORMANCE TESTS

These tests measure how well applicants can do the job. Examples include operating a piece of machinery, entering data into a computer, writing advertising copy, or proofreading manuscripts. Such tests are usually not controversial, and in most instances give the employer a realistic way of determining the ability of the applicant to do the job.

Designing performance tests for more complex jobs isn't easy. There are no performance tests for managerial ability or for most advanced jobs. Some companies, as part of the screening process, have asked applicants for such jobs to develop programs or projects for them. This makes sense. Asking an applicant for a marketing position to develop a marketing program for a new product can provide insight into his or her methods of operation, creativity, and practicality. However, such tests can be carried too far. One company asked an applicant for a training director's position to create a leadership-training program for team leaders. He worked on it for several days and submitted it, but didn't get the job. Some months later, he learned that the company was using his plan to train team leaders. He billed the company for providing consulting services. When the company ignored his bill, he sued and won the case.

CAUTION

If performance tests are used, the exact same test, under the same circumstances, must be used for all applicants. For example, in a recent case a company testing applicants for a clerical job gave each candidate a spelling test. However, African American applicants were given words that were much more difficult than those in the test given Caucasian applicants.

PERSONALITY TESTS

Personality tests are designed to identify personality characteristics. They vary from quickie questionnaires to highly sophisticated psychological evaluations. A great deal of controversy exists over the value of these types of tests. Supervisors and team leaders are cautioned not to make decisions based on the results of personality tests unless experts make the full implications clear to them.

Selecting tests or similar assessment tools must be done very carefully. In buying a published test, ascertain the legitimacy of the publisher and the test by checking with the American Psychological Association and by contacting current and, if possible, past users of the test for their opinions.

TIP

A large number of personality tests are available. You can obtain information about approved tests from the American Psychological Association, 1010 Vermont Ave, Washington, DC 20005-4907. Phone: (202) 783-2077. Website: www.psychologicalscience.org.

Managers should always remember that the administration of one or more personality tests is not the same thing as a comprehensive pre-employment assessment by an industrial psychologist. Such assessments include ability and personality measures, plus an extensive interview. These assessments typically cost in the neighborhood of $500 to $1,000 per candidate, and are usually based on an hourly rate charged by the psychologist.

Are these tests worth the cost? It depends on whom you speak to. Most of the companies that use some form of testing report mixed results. However, as many factors—not just the test results—are considered before making the hiring decision, it's difficult to determine just how valuable the tests are.

Who Uses Employment Tests?

The American Management Association (AMA) administered a survey about workplace testing to nearly 1,100 human resources managers. Because AMA corporate members are mostly midsize and large companies, the data does not reflect the policies and practices of the U.S. economy as a whole, where small firms predominate. Nevertheless, 48 percent of respondents say they use some form of psychological testing to assess abilities and behaviors for applicants as well as employees. Tests measured cognitive ability, interests/career paths, managerial abilities, personality, and simulated job tasks/physical ability.

Despite the advances in computerized psychological testing, face-to-face interviews or interpersonal exchanges designed to create a psychological profile remain the most frequent types of such tests used (43 percent of respondents test applicants this way.)

Nearly 65 percent of surveyed employers test applicants' job skills. This includes skill tests such as typing, computing, or specific professional proficiencies (for example, accounting, engineering, or marketing).

Making Meaningful Reference Checks

Applicants can tell you anything they want about their experiences. How do you know whether they're telling the truth? A reference check is one of the oldest approaches to verifying a background, but is it reliable? Former employers unfortunately don't always tell the whole truth about candidates.

They may be reluctant to make negative statements, either because they don't want to prevent the person from working—as long it's not for them—or they fear that they might be sued. Still, a reference check is virtually your only source of verification.

TIP

To make reference checks more successful, talk to an applicant's supervisor, not to a member of the HR staff. Prepare good questions. Begin with verification questions. Advance to detailed questions about job duties, and comment on responses. Then ask for opinions about performance, attitudes, and so on.

You have more insight into your staffing needs and can ask follow-up questions that will help you determine whether the applicant's background fits your needs. Be careful to follow the same guidelines in asking questions of the reference as you do in interviewing applicants. Just as you can't ask an applicant whether she has young children, for example, you can't attempt to get this type of information from the reference.

Getting Useful Information from a Reference

Most reference checks are made by telephone. To make the best of a difficult situation, you must carefully plan the reference check and use diplomacy in conducting it.

The following list provides some tips for making a reference check:

- **Call an applicant's immediate supervisor.** Try to avoid speaking to the company's HR staff members. The only information they usually have is what's on file. An immediate supervisor can give you details about exactly how that person worked, in addition to his or her personality factors and other significant traits.

- **Begin your conversation with a friendly greeting.** Then ask whether the employer can verify some information about the applicant. Most people don't mind verifying data. Ask a few verification questions about date of employment, job title, and other items from the application.

- **Diplomatically shift to a question that requires a substantive answer, but not one that calls for opinion.** Respond with a comment about the answer, as in this example:

  You: Tell me about her duties in dealing with customers.

  Supervisor: [Gives details of the applicant's work.]

  You: That's very important in the job she is seeking because she'll be on the phone with customers much of the time.

CAUTION

Never tell an applicant that he or she is hired "subject to a reference check." If the references are good but you choose another candidate, an applicant will assume that you received a poor reference. Also never tell a person that the reason for rejection is a poor reference. Reference information should be treated as confidential.

By commenting about what you have learned, you make the interchange a conversation—not an interrogation. You're making telephone friends with the former supervisor. You're building up a relationship that will make him or her more likely to give opinions about an applicant's work performance, attitudes, and other valuable information.

"ALL I CAN TELL YOU IS THAT SHE WORKED HERE"

If a former employer refuses outright to answer a question, don't push. Point out that you understand any reluctance. Make the comment, "I'm sure that you would want to have as much information as possible about a candidate if you were considering someone." Then ask another question (but don't repeat the same one). If the responses begin coming more freely, return to the original question, preferably using different words.

One of the great paradoxes in reference checking is that companies want full information about prospective employees from former employers, but because of their fear of being sued for defamation, when asked for information about their former employees, they give little more than basic information—dates of employment and job title.

What happens if you believe that the person you're speaking to is holding something back? What if you sense from the person's voice that he or she is hesitating in providing answers or you detect a vagueness that says you're not getting the full story? Here's one way to handle this situation:

> Mr. Controller, I appreciate your taking the time to talk to me about Alice Accountant. The job we have is very important to our firm, and we cannot afford to make a mistake. Are there any special problems we might face if we hire Alice?

Here's another approach:

> Ivan will need some special training for this job. Can you point out any areas to which we should give particular attention?

From the answer you receive, you may pick up some information about Ivan's weaknesses.

DEALING WITH POOR REFERENCES

Suppose everything about Carlos seems fine, and in your judgment he's just right for the job. When you call his previous employer, however, you get a bad reference. What do you do?

If you have received good reports from Carlos's other references, it's likely that the poor reference was based on a personality conflict or some other factor unrelated to his work. Contact other people in the company who are familiar with his work and get their input.

Maybe Carlos's previous boss tells you that he was a sloppy worker. Check it out some more. The ex-boss may have been a perfectionist who isn't satisfied with anyone.

Perhaps you hear a diatribe about how awful Carlos was. However, you notice that he had held that job for eight years. If he had been that bad, how come he worked there for such a long time? Maybe his ex-boss resents his leaving and is taking revenge.

KNOWING WHEN TO CHECK REFERENCES

Check references after you believe that an applicant has a reasonable chance of being hired. If you have more than one finalist, check references for each one before making a final decision. A reference check may turn up information that suggests a need for additional inquiry. Arrange another interview to explore it.

DETERMINING WHETHER AN APPLICANT CAN DO THE JOB

When the time to make a decision comes, all of those under consideration are basically qualified to do the job. Your responsibility is to select the best one.

FINAL CONSIDERATIONS BEFORE HIRING

Although all the surviving applicants meet the basic specs, they all offer different degrees of expertise in the key areas as well as additional qualifications. For example, Betty and Sue both have been operating room nurses. Betty's experience has been in a hospital in a small community. She hasn't worked with the sophisticated equipment that Sue, who worked in a large hospital, has. Your hospital doesn't have this equipment at this time, but is planning to install it. Your decision between Betty and Sue would depend on their total backgrounds. Sue's experience is an asset, but perhaps Betty is a better overall candidate with the potential to learn to use the new equipment when it is installed.

Do They Have Those Critical Intangibles?

Meeting the job specs is just part of the decision-making process. Equally important is having those intangible factors that make the difference between just doing a job and doing it well. Let's look at a few of these factors and how to evaluate it when interviewing the candidates:

- **Self-confidence.** When Jeremy was interviewed he exuded self-confidence. He wasn't afraid to talk about his failures and didn't brag about his accomplishments. Jeremy was matter-of-fact about his successes. He projected an image of being totally secure in his feelings about his capabilities. It is likely that Jeremy will manifest this self-confidence on the job, enabling him to adapt readily to the new situation.

- **Fluency of expression.** Laura was able to discuss her background easily and fluently. She didn't hesitate or grasp for words. When the interviewer probed for details, she was ready with statistics, examples, and specific applications. Not only does this indicate her expertise, but her ability to communicate.

TIP

Some applicants can talk a good game, but can they perform? To determine whether an applicant is a talker but not a doer, ask depth questions and probe for specific examples of his or her work. Glib phonies cannot come up with meaningful answers.

- **Maturity.** Maturity cannot be measured by the chronological age of a person. Young people can be very mature and older people may still manifest childlike emotions. Mature applicants are not hostile or defensive. They do not interpret questions as barbs by a "prosecutor out to catch them." They don't show self-pity or have excuses for all of their past failures or inadequacies. They can discuss their weaknesses as readily as their strengths.

- **Intelligence.** Although some aspects of intelligence may be measured by tests, you can pick up a great deal about the type of intelligence a person has at an interview. If the job calls for rapid reaction to situations as they develop (such as a sales rep), a person who responds to questions rapidly and sensibly has the kind of intelligence needed for the job. However, if the person is applying for a job where it is important to ponder over a question before coming up with an answer (such as a research engineer), a slow, but well thought out response may be indicative of the type of intelligence required.

CHOOSING AMONG SEVERAL TOP-LEVEL APPLICANTS

In a tight job market, you may have only one viable candidate. Your choice now is easy. Hire or don't hire. However, in most cases, you have several good people from which to make your final selection.

THE FINAL SELECTION

To systematize making the decision, compare applicants by placing their backgrounds side by side. One way of doing this is to create a worksheet such as the following:

FINAL SELECTION WORKSHEET

Job Specs

	Education	Experience	Intangibles	Other (specify)
Applicant 1 Name:				
Applicant 2 Name:				
Applicant 3 Name:				
Applicant 4 Name:				

INTUITION OR GUT FEELINGS

Often candidates are very close in their qualifications for the job. You have to make a choice among relatively equally competent people. Now it is a matter of your judgment. Choosing a candidate purely on gut feeling without systematically analyzing each prospect's background in relation to the job specs is a mistake. When the decision is choosing the best among equals, you have to trust your gut feelings on which one to pick. As we said, hiring is both a science and an art. When you've exhausted the "science"—the systematic comparison of candidates—then the "art"—your gut feelings—takes over.

AVOIDING DECISION-MAKING BLUNDERS

In making a hiring decision, avoid letting irrelevant or insignificant factors influence you. These factors include the following:

■ **Overemphasizing appearance.** Although neatness and grooming are good indicators of personal work habits, good looks are too often overemphasized in employment. This bias has resulted in companies rejecting well-qualified men and women in favor or their more physically attractive competitors.

■ **Giving preference to people like you.** You may subconsciously favor people who attended the same school you did, who come from similar ethnic backgrounds, or who travel in the same circles as you.

■ **Succumbing to the "halo effect."** Because one quality of an applicant is outstanding, you overlook that person's faults or attribute unwarranted assets to him or her. For example, Sheila's test score in computer know-how is the highest you've ever seen so you offer her a job, only later to learn that she doesn't qualify in several other key aspects of the job.

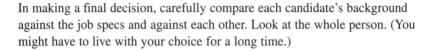

In making a final decision, carefully compare each candidate's background against the job specs and against each other. Look at the whole person. (You might have to live with your choice for a long time.)

MAKING THE OFFER

After you've decided which candidate you want to hire, you are ready to make a job offer.

REVIEW THE JOB SPECS

Don't take anything for granted. During the entire process, the candidate has been enthusiastic about the job, has expressed sincere interest, and seems anxious to start work. Before making the offer, it's important to review the job and make sure that both you and the applicant are on the same track.

TIP

Don't make a job offer unless you are sure that you and the candidate know exactly what the job entails and that the applicant not only is qualified for it, but the job fits his or her career goals.

Go over the job description point by point. Although the candidate may have read it already, most job descriptions are not comprehensive, and there are many facets not specified. Discuss each aspect of the job to ensure that it is what the applicant has understood.

What the Company Expects

In addition to the job duties expected of a staff member, most companies have policies and practices that should be made clear to an applicant before making a job offer. As noted previously, if the job requires travel, overtime work, work on weekends, or unusual working conditions, this should be made clear to the applicant. Indeed, this should have been brought up early in the process, so if there is a problem in complying, the applicant could withdraw before reaching this point.

"Sell" the Job

In today's competitive market, applicants often have to be sold on accepting job offers. Salary and the entire compensation package are important, and these are discussed in the next section. Often it isn't money that will make the difference between acceptance and rejection of a job offer by the person you really want. Learn about the applicant's goals, aspirations, special needs, and anything else that may affect his or her job satisfaction.

The Compensation Package

Most companies have a clearly defined compensation program. Before making an offer, check all the arrangements with your boss to avoid misunderstandings.

In negotiating salary, keep in mind what you pay currently employed people for doing similar work. Offering a new person considerably more than that amount can cause serious morale problems. There are exceptions to this rule, of course. Some applicants have capabilities that you believe would be of great value to your company, and to attract these people, you may have to pay considerably more than your current top rate. Some companies create special job categories to accommodate this situation. Others pay only what they must and hope it won't lead to lower morale.

TIP

Even when the salary you offer is less than an applicant wants, you may persuade that person to take your offer by pointing out how the job will enable him or her to use creativity, engage in work of special interest, and help reach career goals.

Salary alone isn't a total compensation package. It includes vacations, benefits, frequency of salary reviews, and incentive programs. All these items should be clearly explained.

CAUTION

Don't let your anxiety over losing a desirable candidate tempt you to make an informal offer—promising a higher salary or other condition of employment that hasn't been approved—with the hope that you can persuade management to agree to it. Failure to get this agreement will not only cause the applicant to reject the offer but can also lead to legal action against your company.

OVERCOMING OBSTACLES

What do you do if at the time you make the offer, the applicant brings up new objections? Just as a salesperson must be prepared to overcome last-minute reservations to buy a product, you must be ready to face and overcome these objections. What follows in the next sections are some common problems.

THE SALARY IS TOO LOW

Your first choice is Hillary. Early in the interview process, you explored her salary requirements, and your offer is in line. At least that's what you thought. Now Hillary demurs. "If I stay where I am, I'll get a raise in a few months that will bring me above that salary. You'll have to do better."

Having received approval of the hire at the salary offered, you have to either reject her, persuade her to take the job by selling her on other advantages, or consider a higher rate. What you do depends on many factors. Do you have other viable candidates for the job? If not, how urgent is it to fill the job? Determine whether you can legitimately offer other benefits, such as a salary review in six months, opportunity for special training in an area in which she is particularly interested, or other perks. Think over the situation carefully and discuss it with others.

If you think Hillary should still be considered for the position, determine how much above your original offer you're willing to pay and what else you can offer. With this in mind, you can negotiate with her and try to reach an acceptable arrangement. If this new negotiation doesn't lead to agreement, discontinue the discussion and seek another candidate. Continuing to haggle over terms of employment is not advisable.

I NEED FLEXIBLE HOURS

Some companies have an established policy on flextime. If the job for which the candidate is being considered falls into this policy, there's no problem. All that has to be worked out are the hours. However, if there is no policy, whether to grant this request depends on a variety of circumstances. If you give a new employee flexible hours, will the current staff also want their hours changed?

There are some jobs in which flexible hours are more appropriate than in others. Is filling this job so difficult that it pays to bend the rules?

WHAT ARE MY OPPORTUNITIES FOR ADVANCEMENT?

Of course, you can't promise automatic advancement in most jobs. Employees have to earn promotions. Point out that the company conducts periodic performance reviews and that advancement is based on these reviews. If the company has a career-pathing program, take this opportunity to describe how it works.

I'M CONSIDERING OTHER OFFERS

It's not unusual for a good applicant to be looking at several possibilities. All through the interviewing process, you should be feeling the applicant out to determine what he or she is really seeking in the new job. Keep a record of this. Does he seek rapid advancement? Does she want special training? Has he commented on a particular type of job interest? Has she expressed concern about health benefits? Here is where you can use that information to persuade the candidate you want to accept your offer.

One way to counteract other offers is to ask the prospect to list all the advantages of joining the other company or staying on the present job. Then you list all the advantages of joining your team. Be prepared to show how your job— which may even pay less or have fewer benefits than other offers—is still the best bet. Use all the information gleaned at the interviews about what the candidate desires, and show how your job will help the prospect meet the goals he or she has set for the future. If this prospect is the one you really think will be the best for your team, it's well worthwhile to make this effort.

COUNTERING THE COUNTEROFFER

You've knocked yourself out reading resumés, interviewing applicants, and comparing candidates. You make the decision that you'll hire Barbara, and she accepts your offer. A week later she calls to tell you that she has changed her mind: When she told her boss that she was leaving, her boss made a counteroffer.

Frustrating? You bet. To minimize the possibility of a counteroffer, assume that any currently employed candidate will get one. At the time you make your offer, bring it up and make these points:

- ▪ You know that she has done a great job in her present company. You also realize that when she notifies her company that she's planning to leave, it will undoubtedly make a counteroffer. Why? Because they need her now.

- If the company truly appreciated her work, it wouldn't have waited until she got another job offer to give her a raise. It would have given it to her long ago.

- Many people who have accepted counteroffers from a current employer find out that, after the pressure is off the company, it will train or hire someone else and let her go.

- From now on, she will always be looked on as a disloyal person who threatened to leave just to get more money.

- When the time for a raise comes around again, guess whose salary has already been "adjusted"?

When these arguments are used, the number of people who accept counteroffers decreases significantly.

ARRANGING FOR MEDICAL EXAMS

Many companies require applicants to take a medical exam before they can be put on the payroll. You cannot reject an applicant on the basis of a medical exam, however, unless you can show that the reason for the rejection is job related. If a job calls for heavy lifting, for example, and the candidate has a heart condition that could be aggravated by that task, it's a legitimate reason for rejection. On the other hand, rejecting an applicant, not because of the work, but because it will increase your insurance premiums, isn't acceptable.

TIP

The *Americans with Disabilities Act (ADA)* requires that a medical exam be given only after the decision to hire is made. The exam cannot be used as a reason for rejection unless a person's physical condition is a job-related issue and your company cannot make accommodations for it.

Most companies arrange for a medical exam close to a person's starting date. They tell applicants that they are hired subject to passing a physical exam. If this is your policy, caution applicants not to give notice to a current employer until after examination results have been received.

CONGRATULATIONS—YOU MADE AN OFFER!

Although most companies make job offers orally (no letter and no written agreement), an oral offer is just as binding as a written one. Some companies supplement an oral offer with a letter of confirmation so that there are no misunderstandings about the terms.

CAUTION

When you make a job offer, the salary should be stated by pay period—not on an annual basis. Rather than specify $30,000 per year, specify $1,250 per half-month. Why? Because some courts have ruled that if you quote a salary on an annual basis, you're guaranteeing the job for one year.

A job offer letter should contain these elements:

- Title of job (a copy of the job description should be attached)
- Starting date
- Salary, including an explanation of incentive programs
- Benefits (may be in the form of a brochure given to all new employees)
- Working hours, location of job, and other working conditions
- If pertinent, deadline for acceptance of offer

Employment Contracts—Yes or No?

In some situations, the employer and employee sign a formal contract. These contracts are often used with senior management people and key professional, sales, or technical personnel. Although it's rare, some organizations require all salaried employees to sign a contract—often little more than a formalized letter of agreement concerning conditions of employment. In many cases, they're designed for the benefit of the company, and the employee has little room for negotiation.

One of the most controversial areas covered in contracts is the so-called "restrictive covenant," which prohibits employees who leave the company from working for a competitor for a specified period of time. Although these types of contracts have been challenged, they're usually enforceable if they're limited in scope. Prohibiting a person from working for a competitor for a limited period of time, for example, is more likely to be upheld than prohibiting that type of employment forever.

Senior managers and other employees who hold critical positions in a company and applicants who have skills that are in great demand have the clout to negotiate personal contracts with the company. Any contract, whether it's generic or a negotiated special agreement, should be drawn up by a qualified attorney.

REJECTING THE ALSO-RANS

Some companies just assume that if applicants don't get an offer, they will realize that they were rejected. It's not only courteous but also good business practice to notify the men and women you have interviewed that the job has been filled.

TIP

Don't notify unsuccessful applicants until shortly after your new employee starts work. If, for some reason, the chosen candidate changes his or her mind and doesn't start, you can go back to some of the others without having them feel that they were a second choice.

You don't have to tell applicants why they didn't get the job. Explanations can lead to misunderstandings and even litigation. The most diplomatic approach is just to state that the background of another candidate was closer to your needs.

THE 30-SECOND RECAP

- All candidates should be interviewed by more than one manager and/or staff member.
- Tests can be a helpful screening tool, but use them as an aid, not as the chief source, for making your decision.
- Whenever possible, check the references of a prospective employee by speaking to the person to whom he or she reported, not to the HR department.
- When you compare candidates, consider the whole person, not just one aspect of his or her background.
- In making a job offer, make sure that the candidate fully understands the nature of the job, the salary and benefits, and other conditions of employment.

Getting Started on the Right Foot

You've done everything right in attracting, screening, and finally hiring some-one for the open job. A starting date has been set, and at last, the new employee reports to work. What you do those first few days may determine whether that person becomes a loyal, dedicated, enthusiastic staff member or a half-hearted worker already on the way to disillusionment and potential problems. This sec-tion offers advice for getting started on the right foot.

THE FIRST CRITICAL DAYS

Most larger companies have some type of orientation program for new employ-ees. The human resources department usually conducts the program on the first day the new employees report to work, before they are sent to the depart-ment they will work in. They may be shown videos, be given a tour of the facilities, receive literature, or attend a lecture. They learn the history of the organization, further details about their benefits, and the company's rules and regulations. This is a good start, but it's not enough.

CAUTION

Recent studies have shown that one of the key reasons a whop-ping 55 percent of newly hired employees fail or voluntarily leave their new organizations within the first two years is due to a failure to properly introduce and assimilate them into the new culture.

The team leader or supervisor must augment this with an orientation to the team or department. This should include a detailed discussion of the nature of the specific job the new worker will be performing and an understanding of what the supervisor plans to do to train the employee and help him or her to become productive.

ON-BOARDING

A relatively new approach companies are using is known as *on-boarding*. This process supplements and makes more effective the traditional orientation pro-gram. Originally designed to bring newly hired executives into the mainstream rapidly and thoroughly, it is now being extended to technical, professional, and administrative personnel, and in some companies, to all new hires.

PLAIN ENGLISH

On-boarding is a systematized approach to orienting a new employee to the company, the department or team, and the job.

Here's how a successful on-boarding process works.

THE DEVELOPMENT OF A PLAN

The single most important aspect of successful on-boarding is the development of a comprehensive plan to shepherd the new employee through the first several months. Unfortunately, most organizations are not very good in doing this, and few that have a plan rarely take the time to describe it in writing.

The best plans contain the following elements:

1. A Very Clear Sense of What They're Trying to Accomplish

All of the best plans and on-boarding strategies contain a *statement of purpose.* Obviously, this is very important in helping bring focus to the on-boarding effort, and as insurance against some future misunderstanding. In many cases, the purpose statement is no more than a sentence or two, but the effect is always the same: *To make clear the reason a successful on-boarding effort is important to both the company and to the new employee.* Rather than using a boilerplate plan for all new employees, the most effective on-boarding plans are tailored to the special needs of the new employee and the organization.

2. An Honest, Objective Assessment of the Current Environment

A careful assessment of the current environment is a particularly important element of a good on-boarding plan. Every company culture has positive and negative qualities, and every new employee is likely to experience both. The best, most successful on-boarding plans carefully evaluate both the forces that tend to work in favor of a new employee to increase the likelihood of a successful introduction, and those that work against it. Being sure which is which, and to what extent, can have as much to do with success and failure as anything else.

During the on-boarding process, the new employee should be given a full and honest assessment of the situation that he or she will face. For example, Jason expected to take over an ongoing collections program that "needed a little sharpening up." When he started the job, he found that the system was in shambles and collections were well behind schedule. Had he been given the true picture, he would have been far better prepared for the work he had to do.

3. Key Critical Objectives

One of the biggest contributors to failed on-boarding attempts is taking on too much too soon. It's not at all unusual for new employees to feel as though they're "in the spotlight" for some period of time. People are watching and they're forming impressions—and making judgments. It's important that the first few months of a new employee's tenure be orchestrated, at least to some appropriate extent. One of the best strategies in this regard is identifying and clarifying the three or four (seldom more) key objectives that are critical to the success of the new employee in those first months of the job.

4. Short-Term, Intermediate, and Long-Term Goals with Timetables

In addition to identifying key critical objectives, good on-boarding plans also specify a series of key goals, and the dates by which they should be achieved.

5. Mentor

One very important step in successfully on-boarding a new employee is the selecting of a mentor. Obviously, it's important that this person be intimately familiar with the internal workings in the firm.

Mentors provide important advice for new employees on a range of topics. Their overall mission is to "pave the way" for the new person, make sure they're introduced to the right people, and run interference should the going get tough. Later in this section, the use of mentors is covered in more detail.

SOME ADDITIONAL SUCCESSFUL ON-BOARDING PRACTICES

When a person starts a new job, he or she is naturally ill at ease. They don't know their new colleagues, they are unfamiliar with the company culture, and they are anxious to make a good start. As a manager, you want that person to begin producing rapidly and become successful. Here are some suggestions for easing this transition:

- ■ **Arrange for some early successes.** One of the biggest problems new employees face in assimilating to the culture of a new company is a lack of initial focus. One way organizations have found that helps a new hire get off on the right foot is to enable them to achieve some significant successes during the first couple of weeks on the job.

    Let's see how this worked with one company. As part of the on-boarding process for Ben, an assistant marketing manager, he was given an assignment to study the possibility of using e-marketing outlets for the company's products. As Ben had worked with e-markets in his previous job, he had a good deal of knowledge in this area. By enabling him to use his expertise immediately, the company gave him the opportunity to demonstrate his value to the organization early on.

This not only was a benefit to the company, but also made Ben feel like part of a winning team from the beginning. It also enabled his colleagues and teammates to observe their new team member at his very best—ensuring his acceptance by the group.

TIP

Give new employees a chance to show early successes by assigning projects in which they can utilize their expertise.

- **Develop a job description, with clear performance standards.** Few things are more helpful to a new employee—and contribute more to a successful assimilation—than the development of a well-conceived job description, which focuses on the results expected and how they will be measured.

- **Give new employees at all levels ample time to learn, study, and plan before assuming any major responsibilities.** Successful companies often give new employees, particularly in the management and technical areas, up to three months (and even more in some instances) to settle into their jobs and "learn the ropes" before they assume major responsibilities.

- **Overcome resentment of "bypassed" employees.** When outsiders are hired for higher-level jobs, it's not uncommon for it to lead to jealousy or resentment of the new hire by a current employee or group of employees. They may feel they were unfairly "overlooked" for the job. In some cases, it may lead to flagrant attempts to undermine the new person through whispering campaigns, unjustified criticisms, rumor-mongering, and subtle refusals to cooperate, and a general lowering of morale in the department and perhaps the company itself.

Companies must prepare to cope with these and other major internal obstacles to success, and to swiftly minimize their impact.

CAUTION

Don't expect immediate results from new people. No matter how experienced they may be, they need time to adapt to your company's culture and style of work. Providing the new employee with full support, training, and encouragement over the first few months will maximize the chances of developing a productive and loyal staff member.

■ **Provide unwavering support.** Unless you seriously doubt your new hire's ability to do the job, there seems to be little question that the single most valuable contribution company executives can make to the assimilation of a new hire is the offering of unwavering support. Too many organizations badly underestimate the importance of this, and as a result, begin encouraging, however unintentionally, subtle challenges to their decisions.

TRAINING AND MENTORING

In most organizations, training is done on the job by supervisors and team leaders—not professional trainers. Training is not an innate talent, but it can be learned. No company is too small to train new employees.

THE FOUR CS OF SKILL TRAINING

Training cannot be a haphazard process. It must be planned and systemized. An effective and simple training program consists of four steps: conditioning, communication, conduct, and conclusion.

CONDITIONING

To condition the trainee to learn and to accept what is being taught, tell a trainee, before the training begins, what will be taught, why it's performed, and how it fits into the overall picture. When people can see the entire picture, not just their small part in it, they learn faster and understand more clearly, and they're more likely to remember what they've been taught.

COMMUNICATION

You can't say to a trainee, "Just watch me, and do what I do." It's not that simple. Work is much too complex to learn just by observation. The following four steps can guide you in showing someone how to perform a task:

1. Describe what you're going to do.
2. Demonstrate step by step. As you demonstrate, explain each step and explain why it's done. (For example, "Notice that I entered the order number on the top-right side of the form to make it easy to locate.")
3. Have the trainee perform the task and explain to you the method and reason for each step.
4. If the trainee doesn't perform to your satisfaction, have him or her repeat the task. If he or she performs well, reinforce the behavior with praise or positive comments. All employees are "on probation"

officially or unofficially for the first few months on any job. Make every effort to help that person succeed, but if he or she just can't do the job, it's best to transfer them to a job for which they are better qualified or just let them go.

CONDUCT THE WORK

After you're satisfied that a trainee can do a job, leave him or her alone, and let the trainee do it. The trainee needs an opportunity to try out what he or she has learned. They will probably make some mistakes, but that's to be expected. From time to time, check out how things are going and make necessary corrections.

CONCLUSION

The final step is important because people tend to change what they have been taught. Careless people may skip some steps in a procedure, causing errors or complications. Smart people may make changes that they believe are better than what they were taught. Although you should encourage your employees to try to find more effective approaches to their job, caution them not to make any changes until they have discussed them with you. They often may not be aware of the ramifications of their suggested changes.

Schedule concluding discussions of new assignments three to four weeks after the conduct step. At that time, review what the associate has been doing, and, if changes have been made intentionally or inadvertently, bring the person back on track.

WHO SHOULD DO THE TRAINING?

Usually the supervisor does the training, but this isn't always the case. Some organizations encourage an entire team to participate in the task of training new members; others assign one person to act as a mentor.

Whether you are team based or not, it may be advisable to assign somebody other than the supervisor to do or assist in the training. Determining who will train new members or be assigned to retrain others depends on what people are being trained to do. *Caution:* A person who knows the job best isn't always the most qualified person to train others. It takes more than job knowledge to be an effective trainer.

Job know-how *is* essential for the person who will do the training, but it's only part of the picture. Look for these additional factors:

■ **Personal characteristics.** Patience, empathy, and flexibility are good qualities to look for.

TIP

Practice does not make perfect. If people practice doing things wrong, they become perfect in doing things wrong. Practice makes permanent. When you train associates, periodically check out what they're doing. If it's wrong, correct it immediately, before it becomes permanently ingrained as a bad habit.

- **Knowledge of training techniques.** If a team member has the right personal characteristics, he can learn the training techniques. Some companies provide "Train the Trainer" programs to build up the communications skills of people who will do training.
- **A strong, positive attitude toward the job and the company.** If you assign a disgruntled person to do your training, that person might infect the trainee with the virus of discontent.

TRAINING TOOLS AND TECHNIQUES

Today's leaders have a variety of aids and techniques available to them to facilitate their training efforts. Some have been around for years; others were developed more recently.

TRAINING MANUALS THAT REALLY TRAIN

Training manuals, or "do it by the numbers" handbooks, are helpful for teaching routine tasks. They make the training process easy for both the trainer and the trainees; you can always refer to them when you're in doubt about what to do.

TIP

Make sure any training manual you write or approve is written to the level of the trainees and is clear, concise, and complete.

Unfortunately, training manuals can be poorly written and confusing; some are laced with technical terminology intelligible only to the engineers who wrote them.

Because jobs today are becoming less and less routine, training manuals are often inadequate—to the point that they even stifle creativity. Don't rely on a book because it's easy; rather, think out new and possibly better approaches to training.

INTERACTIVE COMPUTER TRAINING

Many companies develop or purchase a variety of interactive computer programs to train employees. Such programs were initially designed for use in schools to enable students to learn at their own pace. Slower learners could take their time and repeat sections until they understood them. Fast learners or students who had more background could move ahead quickly, and students could test themselves as they progressed.

Because most companies have their own ways of doing things, generic programs, such as the ones used by schools, haven't been of much value. However, there are generic programs, such as those that teach basic accounting skills and various computer operations, which can be an asset to any organization. Check software catalogs to determine which programs might be valuable to you.

Walk into any computer store and you'll find a variety of standard courses on CD-ROM. You'll find courses in all types of computer functions, typing, general office skills, accounting, marketing, business planning, and general management. These can be used at the workplace or given to employees to use at home.

THE INTERNET—THE SCHOOL OF THE FUTURE

Computers have moved training from the classroom to the desk, the kitchen table, and even the lap of each individual.

Universities and private organizations offer courses and individual study programs on hundreds of subjects. You can study a foreign language, learn basic or advanced math, acquire technical know-how, and even obtain a college degree. The Internet makes it possible for students to engage in classroom interaction, even when they're participating from home.

TELECONFERENCING

Sometimes the most effective way to train or retrain staff members is to hold classes that bring together employees from several locations. This is a common practice among national and global organizations. It's also one of the most expensive ways to train. Not only do the participants take time off from their regular work, but they also spend additional time getting to and from the training site. Travel, hotel, meals, and often the cost of renting the training facility (for example, a conference center) add to the expense.

One way to reduce the cost and time involved is teleconferencing. Using specially designed computer and TV equipment, participants can see, hear, and interact with the instructor and each other without going far from their base. Larger organizations may have teleconferencing technology available on-site.

Smaller companies can use the services of teleconferencing firms that can set up such conferences wherever needed.

At the University of Notre Dame, for example, executive MBA courses are held simultaneously via satellite at three corporate facilities: Ameritech, Carrier Corporation, and Owens-Illinois.

CASE STUDIES

A *case study* is a description of a real or simulated business situation presented to trainees for analysis, discussion, and solution.

Case studies are used in graduate schools, seminars, and corporate training programs to enable trainees to work on the types of problems they're most likely to encounter on the job. The studies are often drawn from the experiences of real companies. The experience of working out these types of problems in a classroom instead of learning by trial and error on the job pays off in fewer trials and less-costly errors.

TIP

To make case solving most effective, design cases that are related to the job. Make them complex and challenging, and make their solutions necessitate collaboration and teamwork.

A significant advantage of using case studies in management development is that trainees work on the case collaboratively. They learn how to organize and use teams to solve cases.

ROLE PLAYING

In today's companies, most jobs require interaction with other people. Perhaps the best way to train people for this type of interaction is through role playing.

As in case studies, role playing should be based on realistic situations a trainee may face on the job: dealing with a customer, resolving a dispute among team members, or conducting a performance review. Role playing should be fun, but if it's only fun and not a learning experience, you're wasting your time.

Effective role playing must be carefully structured. Participants should be briefed on the goals of the exercise, and each participant should be given a specific part to play. Don't give people scripts—improvisation makes the exercise more spontaneous and allows for flexibility. Just make sure you establish limits, so participants don't stray from the goal of the exercise.

To get everyone—not just the players—involved, give each role to a group of people. Have the group study and discuss how the role should be played. Appoint one member of the group to play the role and have the other group members step in to supplement the primary player. For example, if the person playing the role of a personnel interviewer fails to ask a key question, one of the members of that group can intervene and ask the question.

After the role playing is completed, have all the group critique what has transpired and discuss what they've learned from the experience.

USING VIDEO

Videotapes, like training manuals, are most appropriate for training people to do routine jobs. For example, you can purchase videos for training people in basic computer skills, accounting, and other general subjects. For situations in which flexibility and initiative are necessary, tapes can impede creativity. In such cases, customizing videotapes to meet your own needs is a more effective option. This list describes some ways to use customized video to enhance the effectiveness of your training programs:

- **Tape demonstrations.** For work of a physical nature (most factory or maintenance jobs and some clerical jobs), a good demonstration is an important part of the training. You can tape yourself or one of the best workers performing the job. Show the tape in real time to demonstrate the pace at which a job should be carried out. Use slow motion to better explain each step of the task. After you have a good demonstration on tape, you can show it to any of your trainees at any time.

- **Tape job performance.** One of the best ways to help people recognize exactly what they're doing on the job is to videotape them at work. Rather than trying to verbally describe a person's strengths and weaknesses, let her review the tape and see for herself.

- **Tape team meetings.** Here's an example of how taping a team or group meeting can lead to improvement. When Diane studied the tapes of meetings she had participated in, she noticed that she tended to dominate group discussions. She pushed her ideas across, shut off opposing arguments, and was sometimes rude to other participants. She told her team leader that although she knew she was an assertive person, until she saw the tape she didn't realize the way she came across to others and agreed to attend a human relations training course.

- **Tape role playing.** Role playing is an excellent way to develop interpersonal relations. By videotaping role playing and reviewing the tapes, role playing becomes an even more effective training tool.

■ **Tape presentations.** If you're required to make presentations at internal meetings or outside functions, there's no better way to improve your oratory skills than to study videos of your practice deliveries.

USING AUDIO

One of the best ways to train people whose jobs require lots of telephone use—telemarketers, customer service representatives, order clerks, credit checkers—is to record telephone conversations.

You can purchase a component that connects the telephone to a voice-activated tape recorder. Some voicemail and answering machines have this capability built in.

CAUTION

In some states, taping telephone conversations is illegal without the consent of the party being recorded. Check your state laws.

Tape several conversations, and then review them with the trainee. Listen to what is said and how it's said. Pay close attention to the way the trainee reacts to what the other party says—and how that person reacts to him or her.

CROSS-TRAINING

When teams are the operating units in an organization, it's helpful for everyone on a team to be able to perform the work of any other member. The whining comment "It's not my job" is no longer valid.

You cannot always expect a team of people from various disciplines to be able to do work in other areas: A multidepartmental team consisting of people from marketing, engineering, and finance doesn't easily lend itself to cross-training.

Most teams, however, are made up of people who do similar work. One sales support team consists of order clerks, customer service representatives, and computer operators. All are trained in every aspect of the team's work and can move from job to job as necessary.

Although that team's order clerks spend most of their time processing orders and the customer service reps are almost always on the phone, if the pressure is on processing orders, customer service reps can work on order processing between calls. If a customer service rep is out of the office, any team member can fill in at a moment's notice.

PREPARING FOR ADVANCEMENT

Training isn't limited to teaching job skills. Training team members to become team leaders or rank-and-file employees to become supervisors is an important aspect of organizational development.

THE CADET CORPS

For many years, training for management positions was limited to people who were on a special management track. They usually were hired as management trainees after graduating from college and went through a series of management training programs within an organization, often supplemented by seminars, courses, and residencies at universities or special training schools.

One of the most commonly used cadet programs was job rotation. After basic orientation, trainees were assigned to work for a short period in each of several departments. The objective was to give them an overview of the company so that when they moved into regular positions, they would have a good concept of the entire operation.

Makes sense? Sometimes. In many companies, the time spent in each training assignment was not long enough to give the trainees any more than a superficial knowledge. They never really got their feet wet. They wasted the time of the department heads, which had to divert their energies from working with their own teams. The regular team members, knowing that the trainees would be gone shortly, often resented their intrusion. Resentment was compounded by people's feelings that these cadets were of a privileged class and would someday be their bosses without having worked their way up.

EVERYBODY IS A POTENTIAL MANAGER

In recent years, the special management track has been supplanted by employee development, in which training for management is open to any employee. And why not? Even the military has learned that graduation from military academies isn't essential to be a top leader. Companies have recognized that latent leadership talent exists in most people and can be developed in them.

MENTOR, MENTOR—WHERE IS MY MENTOR?

Earlier in this section, *mentors* were mentioned as a key factor in on-boarding. However, the role of the mentor is much broader. It's a well-known fact that when a high-ranking manager takes a younger employee under his or her wing—becomes that person's mentor—the protégé not only has a head start for advancement, but will acquire more know-how about the work, the workings of the company, and the "tricks of the trade" than others.

PLAIN ENGLISH

A **mentor** is a team member assigned to act as counselor, trainer, and "big brother" or "big sister" to a new member.

Why shouldn't everybody have a mentor? Why leave it to chance that some senior managers choose a protégé while others don't? Why not make mentoring a job requirement—not only for senior executives, but for all experienced staff members? By structuring a mentoring program and assigning the best people on your team the responsibility of mentoring a new member, you take a giant step forward in encouraging productivity and growth in the newcomer.

A structured mentoring program requires that chosen mentors be willing to take on the job. Compelling someone to be a mentor is self-defeating. Not everybody is interested in or qualified for this assignment. New mentors should be trained in the art of mentoring by experienced people.

TIP

Both the mentor and the mentored benefit from the process of mentoring. Those who are mentored learn the new skills while mentors sharpen their skills in order to pass them on. It heightens the mentor's sense of responsibility as he or she guides his or her protégé through the maze of company policies and politics. It also makes the mentor more effective in his interpersonal relationships.

TEN TIPS FOR NEW MENTORS

If you're a first-time mentor, you're probably unsure of how to deal with this new responsibility. If you have had your own successful experience with a mentor, use that as a guide.

In any case, here are 10 tips to start you on the right track:

1. Know your work. Review the basics. Think back on the problems you've faced and how you dealt with them. Be prepared to answer questions about every aspect of the job.

2. Know your company. One of the main functions of a mentor is to help the trainee overcome the hurdles of unfamiliar company policies and practices. Just because you own the business doesn't mean you know everything going on.

3. Get to know your protégé/new hire. To be an effective mentor, take the time to learn as much as you can about the person you are mentoring. Learn about his or her education, previous work experience, current job, and more. Learn his or her goals, ambitions, and outside interests. Observe personality traits. Get accustomed to his or her ways of communicating in writing, verbally, and, most important, nonverbally.

4. Learn to teach. If you have minimal experience in teaching, pick up pointers on teaching methods from the best trainers you know. Read articles and books on training techniques.

5. Learn to learn. It is essential that you keep learning—not only the latest techniques in your own field, but developments in your industry, in the business community, and in the overall field of management.

6. Be patient. The person you are mentoring may not pick up what you teach as rapidly as you would like. Patience is key for successful mentoring.

7. Be tactful. You are not a drill sergeant training a rookie in how to survive in combat. Be kind. Be courteous. Be gentle—but be firm and let the trainee know you expect the best.

8. Don't be afraid to take risks. Give your protégé assignments that will challenge his or her capabilities. Let the person know that he or she won't succeed in all the assignments, but that the best way to grow is to take on tough jobs. We learn through failure, after all.

9. Celebrate successes. Let the trainee know you are proud of the accomplishments and progress he or she makes.

10. Encourage the person you are mentoring to become a mentor.

LAYING THE FOUNDATION FOR SELF-TRAINING

It wasn't long ago that when you were trained for a job, you were considered fully trained after you mastered the skills and functions of the job. This training was augmented by occasional technology updates. Now, just a few years later, many formerly routine and highly structured jobs are dynamic and flexible.

Look at the position of "secretary." It used to connote a woman taking dictation, making appointments for her boss, answering the phone, filing papers, and acting as a gofer. Today that secretary is more of an executive assistant. She or he may prepare the agenda for a meeting, supervise clerks, compile information and write reports, and make important business decisions. It's a considerably different job. Traditional secretarial training isn't adequate preparation for this type of work.

Training must be replaced by *learning.* The difference between training and learning is that training is a one-way transfer of information from trainer to trainee. Learning involves not only absorbing information but also knowing how to identify potential problems, seeking the knowledge and information that are necessary to solve problems, and creating new concepts. This process is the focus of modern training and development.

TIP

Training people is often a one-way process. The teacher presents information; the student absorbs it (you hope). When training is replaced by learning, the emphasis shifts to developing the trainee's ability to identify and solve problems, seek knowledge, and take the initiative to continue self-development.

THE 30-SECOND RECAP

- Start the new employee using a well-designed on-boarding program.
- Use the Four Cs (condition, communicate, conduct, conclude) to train skills.
- Incorporate into your training program techniques such as case studies, role playing, interactive computer programs, and audio- or videotaping to make the training experience more exciting, more meaningful, and more productive.
- Encourage experienced employees to become mentors for new employees, and experienced managers to mentor potential team leaders.
- Redesign your training programs to meet today's challenges. Emphasize problem solving and creative thinking and help participants become self-learners.

Keeping Employee Compensation Competitive

You do get what you pay for, and employees are no exception to that rule. But you have choices in the way you structure your company's compensation that will benefit the employee at the expense of the IRS and allow you to exist and thrive at the same time. You'll also find that you must comply with certain antidiscriminatory laws. Furthermore, tax law and employment laws are intertwined, sometimes with straightforward rules, other times with confusion and complexity.

COMPENSATION OVERVIEW

Money, in the form of salaries and wages, matters. Your employee usually looks first to his or her take-home pay. With any luck, this check pays the bills and allows for a little savings. Although each employee also wants the maximum of medical insurance coverage at the minimum of cost to him- or herself, as well as a myriad of other benefits, the one overriding employee question is "How much am I making?" One of your tasks as an employer is to redirect this thinking a bit, so the employee does focus on what you pay for medical coverage, group term life insurance, education reimbursement, and pension contributions. It is your cost and the employee's benefit.

In structuring a compensation package for your employees (and yourself), consider ...

- **Salary and wages.** Each employee receives an hourly wage or salary, but this figure doesn't include the FICA (Social Security and Medicare) portion you pay, nor does it include the *FUTA (Federal Unemployment Tax)*, nor the workers' compensation premium (covers workplace injuries). All of which add up.

- **Medical insurance.** Medical insurance appears to be on an ever-increasing upward cost spiral. Containing costs while maintaining sufficient coverage has to be one of your top priorities. Employees usually take coverage for granted in large companies. Many small businesses cannot afford such generous coverage. As a small business owner, you know that this cost could almost literally drive you out of business if you didn't contain it. If your employees complain, remind your employees that the coverage the employer pays for comes tax-free to them.

PLAIN ENGLISH

FUTA tax provides funds that the states use to administer unemployment benefits. States may reduce the unemployment tax on employers who experience stable employment.

■ **Other fringe benefits.** *Fringe benefits* is really an odd phrase to represent a number of employee benefits. Some, like paid vacations and holidays are pretty much expected, and group term life insurance is frequently provided, too. You could also provide your employees with free or reimbursed parking, discounts on the purchase of your products, subsidized eating facilities, dependent care, educational assistance, or moving expenses. These, too, come at a cost. However, many are tax-free to the employee.

■ **Pension plans and ERISA provisions.** Many small businesses provide some pension benefit. Often the business will provide a 401(k) plan, to which the employee contributes a percentage of his or her salary, such as 4 percent, which the employer then matches. The employer contribution is tax deferred (meaning the employee doesn't need to pay tax on it right away), and the employee's salary is reduced by his or her contribution, thus reducing the employee's income tax. The challenge is not just to come up with the money, but to comply with the pension laws, collectively known as ERISA *(Employment Retirement Income Security Act)*. Congress, in its infinite wisdom, requires both the IRS and Labor Department to establish ERISA regulations.

■ **Employment antidiscrimination laws.** You must observe federal and state antidiscrimination laws. Some are more obvious than others. For instance, you can't pay a man more than a woman for the same job if they both have the same employment background. And you can't discriminate in pay or in hiring because of race, religion, national origin, age, or disability. Other employment laws are more difficult to discern. For example, you must continue health-insurance coverage for an employee who is on a medical leave.

MINIMUM WAGE AND OVERTIME REQUIRES PUNCHING THE CLOCK

When the labor market is tight, you probably won't have to worry about complying with the minimum wage law. Unfortunately for your bottom line, you'll pay more to attract your employees, even those who work part time in your fast-food restaurant or as a custodian in your clothing store, typically low-paying jobs. The minimum wage for the beginning of the year 2004 is $5.15 per hour, but it will increase, because Congress periodically revises it.

COVERAGE

In the 1930s, Congress enacted the *Fair Labor Standards Act (FLSA),* which requires most employers to pay minimum wage set by law, and overtime for all work over 40 hours per week. The Wage and Hour Division of the U.S. Department of Labor administers this law.

There are some exceptions to FLSA coverage for your small business and its employees. Although the law states that a business is not to be covered by FLSA if its sales are less than $500,000, it extends coverage to all employees involved in interstate commerce. Because your business likely receives mail, makes telephone calls, or handles goods moving from one state to another, your business is likely covered by the act.

However, certain employees may be exempt from coverage:

- Executives and certain managers
- Professionals
- Outside salespersons
- Certain computer-related employees

Minimum wage is not the issue for these employees; it's overtime. You and your executives may work as many hours as you mutually agree upon without receiving overtime pay. If your lower-level managers spend about 80 percent of their week administering their department, supervising two or more workers, making personnel decisions about the employees, such as hiring, firing, or promotion, and you pay them at least $250 per week, they are not covered by the overtime law. However, describing an employee as a "manager" without the supervisory authority and pay described in the prior sentence will not exempt that employee from the FLSA overtime provisions.

Professionals, such as accountants, lawyers, and doctors, whose primary duties include work requiring advanced education, are also not covered by the FLSA overtime provisions.

CAUTION

Don't underpay! Your state may have a minimum wage law that requires a higher minimum wage and provides greater employee coverage than the FLSA. You must check with your state department of labor for this information.

If you employ outside sales personnel who regularly work away from your place of business while making sales or taking orders, and who spend no more than 20 percent of their time doing work other than selling, the overtime provisions don't apply to them, either. Usually you'll pay outside salespersons by commission, and commission work for these employees has no minimum wage requirement.

The FLSA exempts computer system analysts, programmers, and software engineers who earn at least $27.63 per hour.

OVERTIME

If your employee is covered by the overtime provisions, as are most clerical and factory workers, you must keep an accurate record of the time each employee works. The FLSA requires you to pay a nonexempt employee at least one and one half times his or her regular wage for all hours worked over 40 hours in one week. A week is generally defined at any seven-day period, and each workweek stands alone. For example, if Frank Factory worked 45 hours in week one, and 35 hours in week two, you would pay Frank for the 5 extra hours in week one. You are not required to pay overtime for any hours worked over 8 in a single day, or for weekend work, unless the total hours for the week exceed 40.

Employee work time includes any time that you control the employee's activities. If your employee agrees to come in early or stay late to finish work, the employee is on the clock, even if not literally so. Generally, the time employees spend changing clothes before or after work, eating a meal, or commuting to work is not covered; however, there are exceptions. For example, if you require an employee to come in after work hours to repair faulty equipment, the commuting time would be part of his or her work time.

An employer cannot avoid paying overtime by providing an employee hour-for-hour compensatory time off for previous overtime work. However, an employer may rearrange a particular workweek, for example, 10 hours per day for 4 days. Also an employer may be able to arrange for comp time in a single pay period. For example, Jane gets paid every two weeks; she works 44 hours the first week, and works 34 hours the second week. The employee is given an hour and one half of time off for each hour of overtime worked.

CAUTION

You must keep accurate records to show the Wage and Hour Division. If an employee claims he or she worked overtime and was not paid for this work, you hold the burden of proof to prove him or her wrong.

PAY PRACTICES TO AVOID LAWSUITS

Federal and state laws prohibit pay discrimination when not based on valid criteria. For example, you cannot pay a Catholic less than a Methodist, or an African American less than Caucasian just because they are who and what they are. However, you can pay more for an employee who is more efficient than other employees, or holds a graduate degree.

Pay for purposes of the antidiscrimination laws include all forms of compensation.

- **Wages.** If the hourly wages of your female clerks are typically less than the males, you must be able to justify each employee's differential or you may be violating Title VII of the *Civil Rights Act of 1964* and the *Equal Pay Act.* It would be difficult to show that all of the females were less efficient or less educated, but you may be able to prove that all the men were hired before the women. Be careful, however; hiring discrimination may be the cause of this discrepancy.

- **Fringe benefits.** Review your medical insurance plan. The *Pregnancy Discrimination Act* (amending Title VII) requires that pregnancy-related conditions must be covered on terms equal to nonpregnancy-related conditions. Or your medical-insurance policy may not be able to exclude HIV-infected employees, because the *Americans with Disabilities Act* covers that illness. Your pension plan can't require women to contribute more than men simply because they are going to live longer, statistically speaking. ERISA has certain nondiscriminatory provisions to protect low-paid employees. Even paid holidays may need to be reviewed; not everyone celebrates Good Friday.

YOUR PAY PACKAGE: SALARY AND FRINGES

Your pay package is important to every one of your employees, and to you. You need to review your options.

SALARIES

Each employee may be paying a lot of his or her salary to the IRS, which Uncle Sam surely must appreciate. The employee can reduce the tax bite somewhat by contributing to a 401(k), which reduces the salary by the contribution. However using a deferred compensation plan would be better. Deferred gratification can save taxes, which to many of us is supremely gratifying.

For instance, if your employee is in the higher marginal tax bracket, perhaps offering a deferred compensation package is the way to go. For example, Hal Highbracket enters into an employment contract that provides an annual salary of $120,000; $100,000 is to be paid each year and $20,000 in annual installments paid after Hal retires, when he is in a lower tax bracket.

The deferred compensation plan would not be currently funded (no money deposited in the plan) because it would be immediately taxed to the employee; therefore, there is a risk of nonpayment by the employer. However, under limited circumstances, the plan could be funded without immediate tax to the employee, if the money were held by a third party and if it were subject to forfeiture, such as if the employee breaches the employment contract. Professional athletes often use deferred compensation to reduce their tax burden.

FRINGE BENEFITS PLANS

Congress wants to encourage you to provide fringe benefits to your employees, so it has made your costs tax deductible and your employees' benefits excludable from their gross income for their tax purposes.

These benefits do cost you; and a few, such as medical insurance, cost a great deal. And some fringes benefit certain employees more than others. Some of your employees would prefer cash to any fringe benefits, and the tax law permits you to give employees a choice.

If you adopt what's known as a cafeteria plan, your employees may choose between cash and nontaxable benefits. Cafeteria plans provide the flexibility to allow each employee to tailor his or her pay package to fit individual needs. For example, if you have a plan that costs, per employee, $200 for group term life insurance, $2,000 for medical insurance, and $300 for dental insurance, the employee can choose to use those benefits or take the cash they're worth instead. A married employee who's covered by her husband's medical insurance might take the $2,000, instead, but she has to remember that the cash is taxable.

Employee flexible spending plans are a variant of the cafeteria plan. The employee agrees to a reduction in salary to cover expenses, such as dental, that the employer can pay without the employee recognizing it as gross income. In essence, the employer pays or reimburses the employee for the nontaxed benefits up to the amount of the salary reduction. Use it or lose it. If the employee doesn't spend all of the money, the employer retains it. You can't include long-term care insurance benefits in either the cafeteria plan or the flexible spending plan, but you can provide it separately.

FRINGE BENEFITS

Typical nontaxed employee fringe benefits include the following:

- Medical and dental insurance
- Long-term care insurance
- Group term life insurance
- Child or dependent care
- Educational assistance payments
- Employee discounts
- Moving-expense reimbursement

The following sections take a closer look at each of these fringe benefits and how they impact both you and your employees.

HEALTH INSURANCE

Most employers who provide medical or dental insurance pay for a portion of the cost and the employee pays the rest. For example, if the employee's premium is $2,400 annually, and your company pays 50 percent of the premium, the $1,200 paid on the employee's behalf is not taxed to the employee; the employee pays $1,200, which he or she might be able to deduct from his or her own tax return as an itemized deduction (Schedule A, 1040).

Small businesses with 50 or fewer employees often establish a medical-reimbursement plan. Your company would purchase medical insurance with a high deductible, perhaps as much as $2,000, which means the employee would be liable for the first $2,000 of his or her medical expenses. Then you would make a contribution to each employee's medical savings account (MSA) that the employee could use to reimburse him- or herself for medical expenses. The employee does not pay taxes on your company's contribution to the MSA.

Your older employees may be interested in insurance for long-term care. The insurance covers the retired employee's expenses in a nursing home. Your company payment of the premium (or a portion) is not taxable to the employee. If the employee enters a nursing home, not all financial benefits paid by the insurance may be excluded from his or her gross income. There is a maximum benefit exclusion for each day the employee receives long-term care.

GROUP TERM LIFE INSURANCE

Most of your employees need more life insurance. An inexpensive way to increase coverage is to provide group term life insurance. Your company can provide coverage up to $50,000 of group term life insurance without the employee having to pay any taxes on the premium. For each $1,000 of coverage in excess of $50,000, however, the employee must include an IRS-determined amount in his or her gross income.

For example, if your company provides an executive aged 40 with $100,000 of coverage, the first $50,000 coverage is tax-free; the next $50,000 of coverage has a formula for inclusion: $.10 per $1,000 coverage per month, or $50,000 ÷ $1,000 × $.10 × 12 (months) = $60, which is reported as income by your employee.

CAUTION

Watch your tax bottom line! Business owners are not considered as employees for the tax exclusion of fringe benefits unless the entity is a C corporation. For example, any fringe benefit payment to a partner or to a 2 percent or greater shareholder/employee of an S corporation is nondeductible to the business and is taxable to the owner.

CHILD AND DEPENDENT CARE

Your company can provide child and dependent care to enable your employee to work. The value of such services paid for by the employer can be excluded from the employee's gross income up to $5,000, or a lesser amount if a spouse earns less than this amount. On-site child-care facilities may be important to your employees.

TIP

Your employee's out-of-pocket child-care expenses may qualify for a child-care tax credit. The amount of the credit depends on employee's adjusted gross income and number of children in childcare.

EDUCATIONAL ASSISTANCE

Your company may provide each employee up to $5,250 for undergraduate education tuition, fees, books, and supplies. Usually, undergraduate expenses paid by the employee are not deductible for the employee. For example, if your company pays the tuition of $500 for an undergraduate accounting course, the employee does not have to include this as gross income; however, if you had no such plan and the employee paid his or her own tuition, this would be a non-tax-deductible expense. An educational assistance plan is a way to improve your employees' skills at no tax cost to the employee.

EMPLOYEE DISCOUNTS

Your company may sell its products or services at a discount to your employees. The discount may be tax-free if the discount is ...

- No greater than the gross profit for sale of a product.
- No greater than 20 percent of the customer price for services.

For example, your store sells an employee a refrigerator for $700, the customer price is $800, and your markup, or gross profit, is $150. The employee's discount is $100, which is less than the $150 gross profit, so the discount is not taxable to the employee. If the employee purchases a service contract for $80 and the customer pays $100, the discount is 20 percent and, therefore, also not taxable to the employee. Any discount in excess of the qualifying amounts means that the employee must pay taxes on the excess, because it is considered income. Your company could also provide a no-additional-cost service form of fringe benefit to its employees. For example, if you operate a hotel and permit employees to stay without charges when there is an available room, the value of the hotel room is received tax-free by your employee.

TIP

Your employee may be entitled to either a Hope scholarship credit or a lifetime learning credit. Either tax credit is available to low- and middle-income individuals for higher education expense. For example, the Hope credit may be up to $1,500 per year for the first two years of postsecondary education. You can obtain information about these credits at the IRS website.

MOVING EXPENSES

You may pay for or reimburse your employee for his or her job-related moving expenses, and the payment is tax-free to the employee. Moving expenses include moving household goods, personal effects, and employee and family member travel expenses to the new residence (lodging and mileage, but not for meals). If the employee incurs greater expense than your reimbursement for these moving expenses, the excess is a deduction from the employee's gross income (Schedule 3903, Form 1040).

OTHER FRINGES

This discussion of fringe benefits isn't exhaustive by any means. In fact, here's another list of possible "extras" you can offer your employees:

- Lodging and meals furnished for the employer's convenience
- Employee achievement awards
- Athletic facilities provided to employees
- Employee transportation to work
- Child adoption expense

PENSIONS AND DEFERRED COMPENSATION TO DELAY TAXES

Social Security may be there for your employees, but they won't be happy existing just on what it will pay them after retirement. Nor can they count on saving for retirement, because most of us spend up to our income (or beyond with the help of plastic). That leaves the pension as a significant source of retirement income. Fortunately, the tax code permits the employee to defer paying taxes on your company's pension contribution until he or she withdraws it. Your company deducts the contribution as you pay it into the pension plan.

PLAN TYPES

The two typical pension plans are ...

- Defined benefit plan.
- Defined contribution plan.

The defined benefit plan was typical for large industries. Joe or Jane would work for General Motors for 40 years, then would receive a stated benefit for the rest of his or her life (or the spouse's life). They could count on the check arriving each month, and could budget accordingly. GMC had its actuarial staff compute the payments over the recipient's retirement, then fund part of the payment and pay the balance from a portion of each new car it sold. Your business probably won't use a defined benefit pension plan.

The defined contribution plan specifies the amount that your company and the employee will contribute. A separate account is maintained for each employee, and benefits are based upon the amounts contributed and income that accrues in the employee's account. The 401(k) plan is a defined contribution plan, as is a profit-sharing plan (such as a Single Employer Plan, or SEP), stock bonus plan, and employee stock ownership plan (ESOP).

PLAN REQUIREMENTS

To be a qualified plan, and thus tax-deferred, the plan must meet certain requirements. Hire a plan administrator, such as an insurance company, to set it up for you. This is only a cursory treatment of this complex law. Basically, you'll have to concentrate on the following aspects of the plan:

- **Nondiscriminatory.** The plan may not discriminate in favor of a company's highly compensated employees, but may determine contributions proportional to pay.

- **Participation and coverage.** All employees who are age 21 and have worked for the company for one year are eligible to participate in the plan. The plan generally must cover at least 70 percent of your employees.

- **Vesting.** The employee is always *vested* in his or her contributions, which means he or she has a right to that money when he or she decides to withdraw it. He or she also must be vested in the company contributions according to certain requirements, say 100 percent after five years of service or a set percentage after three years and 100 percent at seven years of service.

PLAIN ENGLISH

Vesting in a defined contribution pension means that the employee has a nonforfeitable right to the amount of the contribution. For example, if the employer's contribution has been $10,000 and the employee is 60 percent vested after five years service, $6,000 is his or her vested portion.

- **Distribution.** Each employee must withdraw a minimum distribution amount (set by the IRS) when he or she attains age 70½ (and may begin withdrawal at age 59½). Any tax-deferred amount (and accrued income) is taxable to the employee when withdrawn.

Contributions to the employee's defined contribution plan cannot exceed either $40,000 or 100 percent of the employee's total compensation, whichever is less. Check with the IRS, because this money limit is adjusted to the consumer price index changes, and, therefore, will increase.

The 401(k) plan is typically used by small businesses. In 2004, The employee may elect to receive up to a maximum $11,000 (plus an additional $1,000 if the employee is aged fifty or older) in cash, which is taxed as salary or wages, or to have the employer contribute up to that amount in a defined contribution pension plan. The plan may also permit the employee to reduce his or her salary (taxable income) with his or her own contribution. For example, your company agrees to match your employee's contribution up to 5 percent of his or her salary, which is $40,000; each of you contributes $2,000 to the 401(k) plan, and each contribution is tax-deferred until withdrawn. Under the employee's salary reduction agreement, his or her salary is reduced to $38,000.

An option for employers with 100 or fewer employees is a Savings Incentive Match Plan for Employees (SIMPLE), which can be in the form of a 401(k) plan. Or an employer may contribute to an employee Individual Retirement Account (IRA) in an amount equal to the lesser of $30,000, or 15 percent of the employee's earned income; this is known as a Single Employer Pension Plan (SEP). More information on SEPs can be found at www.irs.gov/retirement.

HELPFUL SOURCES FOR EMPLOYMENT PLANS

Visit your government websites. The Department of Labor (www.dol.gov) provides information about the *Fair Labor Standards Act* and ERISA. The Equal Employment Opportunity Commission at www.eeoc.gov discusses various antidiscrimination laws. Tax law is covered at the IRS website: www.irs.ustreas.gov. For Social Security benefits, go to www.ssa.gov. Financial planning websites are a useful source of retirement and employee benefit information. Check out your state department of labor website. Your bookstore and library have numerous publications explaining employee benefits.

THE 30-SECOND RECAP

- *The Fair Labor Standards Act* requires a minimum wage of $5.15 per hour (as of 2004), and one and one half times regular pay for each hour worked over 40 hours per week.
- An employer cannot discriminate in compensation based on gender, race, religion, national origin, age (40 and over), and disability.
- Medical insurance premiums paid by the employer are tax-free to the employee.
- Employer pension contributions to a qualified plan are tax-deferred to the employee, who is taxed upon withdrawal.

Working at Home

Working at Home with Your Disability

Anyone can achieve the financial and personal rewards that working from home can provide. If you're blind, confined to a wheelchair, or have some other disability that prevents or severely limits your access to traditional workplaces, then working from home may be the best alternative for you to earn money and maintain your independence.

In this section, you'll learn that the laws designed to protect you in the workplace aren't really doing their job. You'll see how you can modify your home or use special tools to accommodate your needs. You'll find out how technology now affords you new ways to become profitable from your own home. And you'll learn about special government programs to support your entrepreneurial efforts.

LIMITED ACCESS OUTSIDE DOESN'T LIMIT A HOME BUSINESS

Anyone in a wheelchair who's faced a flight of stairs at the entrance to an office knows the outside world can be a challenging place. Just getting to and from work each day can be a job in itself. (Although public transportation is supposed to have handicapped access, such access is still very limited.) Under the *Americans with Disabilities Act (ADA)*, a federal law requiring employers to reasonably accommodate workers' disabilities by modifying space, providing help for the hearing impaired, and giving other types of assistance, the workplace is supposed to be more user-friendly. Unfortunately, statistics from the National Organization on Disability show that employment rates for the approximately 17 million Americans with less-severe disabilities has decreased in spite of laws designed to encourage their employment (at a time when the overall employment rate in the United States has increased).

PLAIN ENGLISH

The *Americans with Disabilities Act (ADA)* is intended to protect people who suffer a physical or mental impairment that substantially limits one or more of their major life activities. The ADA applies only to employers who regularly employ at least 15 workers, so small companies don't even have to comply. And it just so happens that the majority of employers are small businesses that may be exempt from ADA requirements.

Even where buildings have been made accessible, office space modified to accommodate the disabled, and bathrooms changed for the physically challenged, it doesn't mean the outside workplace will welcome you with open arms. A television investigative report that aired in 1999 showed that employers tend to hire someone who's not in a wheelchair over someone who is, even though both have similar qualifications. (This is so even if the chair-bound person is better qualified!)

If you aren't being accommodated in your current place of employment, or if you're tired of being turned down for work you know you're qualified to do, you have two choices: You can sue for discrimination under federal and state laws designed to protect you. (You may be able to recover damages by filing a complaint with the U.S. Equal Employment Opportunity Commission.) Or you can thumb your nose at the establishment, take the bit in your teeth, and start your own business right from your home.

HAVE IT YOUR WAY

You may not be able to move your wheelchair through the bathroom stall in an office building downtown, but you can certainly get into the bathroom in your own home. You've probably already modified your home environment to accommodate your personal disability.

CAUTION

There have not been any cases or rulings so far that specifically allow these tax breaks for home offices, so claiming a write-off may invite IRS scrutiny. But there's no logical reason why they shouldn't apply in the right situation. These tax write-offs are discussed in IRS Publication 334, "Tax Guide for Small Business," which you can get by calling 1-800-829-1040 or downloading it from www.irs.gov.

Why not make the changes necessary to let you work from home? You can put a desk and materials in locations most convenient for you. If you haven't already done so, you can modify door openings to your office, move light switches and electrical outlets, or make other necessary changes to accommodate your limitations. Uncle Sam may even help you pay for construction costs to a space in your home that you treat as a home office (assuming you own your home) in the form of a tax write-off:

- You can claim a tax credit for a portion of such costs up to $10,000 (for a top credit of $5,000).
- You can elect to deduct such costs (up to a limit) instead of depreciating them over a number of years.

After you've got the space the way you want it, furnish it with the things to help you work effectively. Get the technological alternatives that will allow you to operate a computer and other office machines despite your disability. A listing of some gadgets or other aids may be found at the end of this section.

TIP

Think you can't afford special equipment? You may be able to get special loans to buy the equipment you need to accommodate your disability. You'll find a discussion of special programs that can help you get the equipment you need later in this section.

HIGH-TECH (AND LOW-TECH) OPPORTUNITIES

Having a disability limits your business opportunities only as far as your imagination can stretch. Down's syndrome didn't stop one talented young woman from starting a greeting card business. Her simple yet charming drawings put her business in the black. Another fellow with a mental disability who'd been in the "system" for more than 20 years started a stuffed-animal business and, for the first time in his adult life, became self-sufficient.

But craft-related businesses aren't the only avenue to starting a home-based business for someone with a disability. Today technology has made it even easier for the disabled to create their own businesses. There are two good reasons for this. First, technology has provided machines and equipment to help the disabled function despite their limitations. For example, a person whose disability prevents her from typing on a computer can now use voice-recognition technology or other means to enter data into a computer.

Second, technology has provided a new avenue for businesses that can easily be run from home with the help of a computer. By establishing your business online, you don't ever have to meet face to face or even talk with a customer; the computer is your means of communication with the outside world. One young man with cerebral palsy started an online cleaning-supply company that's doing great. His speech limitations didn't limit his online business.

Here are two types of businesses that can easily be run from home regardless of disability:

- **Retail sales.** With virtual malls and online auctions, you can sell your wares around the world.
- **Web businesses.** Web page design is one of the hottest (and a highly lucrative) types of business around today. Find your niche (perhaps servicing other home businesses or those with disabled owners), and your customers will find you.

TIP

Can't get out to mail your products? Call FedEx, UPS, or other private carriers, and they'll arrange pickups right from your home. There's no extra charge for pickups. Even the U.S. Postal Service has free pickup service for certain types of mailings.

Can't get the things you need from Uncle Sam? If you can afford it, there are plenty of commercially available gadgets and whatnots to help the disabled deal with technology. For example, there's speech-recognition software for hands-free access to computers and speaker phones and cordlesses that respond to voice commands for easy phoning. Special mouse options enable those with impaired motor skills to work a keyboard with not only fingers, but feet, nose, or a mouth-held stick. Quadriplegics can operate a computer with eye, facial muscle, or even brain activity signals.

Here are some resources that help the disabled get online.

Online Technology Aids

Company	Product	Website
Able-Phone	Speaker phones/ cordlesses	www.ablephone.com
Adaptive Computer Empowerment Services	Various	www.adaptive.org
Assis-Tech Inc.	Various	www.assis-tech.com
The Boulevard	Various	www.blvd.com
Dragon Systems	Voice-activated software	www.naturalspeech. com
IBM	Talking web browser for the visually impaired	www.ibm.com/sns
IntelliKeys	Keyboards operated with feet, nose, etc.	www.keytools.com
Logitech	TrackMan Marble FX for special PC mouses	www.logitech.com
Microsoft	Accessibility site	www.microsoft.com/ enable

continues

Online Technology Aids   *(continued)*

Company	Product	Website
Leapfrog Technologies	MindMouse (facial muscle-activated PC controls)	www.mindmouse.com
Pitney Bowes	Universal Access Copier System for speech-activated photocopying	www.pitneybowes.com

DISABLED DOESN'T MEAN LACKING BUSINESS ABILITY

It may be hard to get around because of your wheelchair or sight impairment, but that doesn't mean you can't use what you can do to start your own business. Working from home eliminates one of the hassles that some disabled people face: Just getting to work.

As a disabled person, you may be able to tap special resources to help you get up and running. For example, you can get help in putting your ideas together and in raising the capital you need to go forward.

HELP TO MAKE YOUR DREAMS COME TRUE

It's hard enough for anyone to start a business. But when you add a disability into the mix, the challenge may seem overwhelming. Well, you're not alone. Government agencies, nonprofit organizations, and private groups can come in handy when it comes to starting your own business.

There are government programs you can use to get your business up and running. These programs help you formulate your business plan, taking your disability into account. For example, there are a number of programs designed to foster *supported self-employment* or *supported entrepreneurial employment.*

As any start-up entrepreneur knows, finding seed money is one of the greatest challenges you face in getting started. For the disabled, it may be even harder to find the money. You may have relied on Social Security benefits for many years and have been unable to save any seed money. Or there may be subtle or even overt discrimination in obtaining commercial loans. Government sources can help, as you'll see in a moment.

PLAIN ENGLISH

Supported self-employment means you start and run your own business, but you have the ongoing help of special programs to back you up. Although not fully independent, you're interdependent on these programs to succeed. (**Supported entrepreneurial employment** is a fancy way of saying assistance with consulting work.)

There are also programs you can use to receive special equipment to accommodate your disability and let you operate to the best of your ability, which you'll learn about shortly.

To find out more about business start-up help for the disabled, check out the National Organization of the Disabled website at www.nod.org. Also look at Trail to Success for ideas and support in launching a home-based business (www.trailtosuccess.org).

SPECIAL HELP FROM UNCLE SAM AND OTHERS

What's it going to take to get started? Like any other entrepreneur, many costs are involved in just getting started. In addition, be sure to add the cost of special equipment or other costs needed to accommodate your disability—structural modifications to your home office, a personal assistant, or special computer equipment to let you work. The price tag for this equipment may be steep.

Fortunately, the government recognizes your special needs and has several sources you can use to find the money you need to start your business. In New York, for example, the Office of Vocational and Educational Services for Individuals with Disabilities (VESID) has a self-employment counseling program to help the disabled create their own successful businesses. To find programs in your state, check with your state department of labor.

The Social Security Administration (SSA) has a program called Plans for Achieving Self-Support (PASS) to help individuals get off supplemental security income (SSI). The Social Security Administration can be reached at 1-800-772-1213 or at your local office. They also post information on their website at www.ssa.gov.

The Labor Department also has training programs under its *Job Training Partnership Act*. Although this training is geared toward work as an employee, you can translate the skills you learn into self-employment. Again, check the information listed at www.dol.gov.

There may also be special loan programs geared toward underwriting self-employment for the disabled. In the past there were programs restricted to the disabled. Now programs are open to all individuals, with the following programs most useful to the disabled.

■ **Prequalification pilot loan program.** Just a few years ago, the Small Business Administration (SBA) used to provide special loan programs for the disabled. It no longer has any funding for this help. However, there's one SBA-sponsored loan that may be of special interest for a business owner who's disabled. Under a pilot program, small business development centers and certain nonprofit organizations can help you develop your loan application package. You can then submit it to the SBA for qualification. When you receive this qualification, you can shop around for the best terms for a loan of up to $250,000. Qualification under this program is based on your character, credit history, and reliability rather than on your assets. The term of the loan is up to seven years, with interest rates pegged to the prime rate. (The amount over prime depends on the size of the loan.)

■ **Microloan programs.** These programs (typically sponsored by states, cities, and community-development corporations, or a combination of these groups) may provide loans ranging between $100 and $50,000 to start or expand a business. The program may give special consideration to "high-risk" borrowers—those with poor credit ratings.

Equipment Assistance to Level the Playing Field

An individual runs a messenger delivery business from a spare bedroom in his home. On the phone, no one would know he uses special computer equipment to let him read the screen on which his runs display. (Diabetes left him legally blind.) The cost for this special equipment: one year for free, with special assistance to buy it after that.

Every state has an agency that provides assistant technology to accommodate certain disabilities. Each agency can provide training in the use of the equipment, free equipment, or loan programs for the purchase of equipment not otherwise provided to you.

The 30-Second Recap

■ You can't rely on the law to make employers welcome you in the outside world.

■ The cost of modifying your home or buying special equipment to permit you to work may be cheap in the long run.

■ Technology may present you with a business solution to making a living.

■ Government, nonprofit, and private programs can help you start your business.

Advice for Separating Business from Pleasure

One of the things that makes working from home so great—having family and business all in one place—is also the very thing that makes a home-based business so difficult to run. Your personal life spills over into your business and vice versa.

This scenario is all too common: A suburbanite with two small children dreams of starting her own business. Her dream turns into a nightmare when she can't figure out how to run her business in between her children's naps, school bus schedules, and other family demands. Then there's the young professional couple who end up at the marriage counselor because the workaholic husband won't stop answering his business calls in the home office at all hours. There's no such thing as getting away from the office anymore. A home businessperson who doesn't learn how to separate business from family life often can't make the business succeed (or may lose the family along the way while trying to make the business succeed).

In this section, you'll learn to identify some key personal issues you'll have to sort out to be able to run your business from home. As you'll see, there are many different solutions. You can probably think of your own solutions—if you know what to look for.

WORKING JUST ENOUGH, OR NOT TOO MUCH

How much time do you want to spend each day on your home-based business? This may seem like a simple question, but you may surprise yourself by not knowing the answer.

You may just say, "I'll spend as much time as I can." If you do, you'll find that there's no time; all of your time is eaten up by looking after your children, doing laundry, grocery shopping, making trips to the cleaners, or just talking to neighbors. Or maybe you're the type who finds you can't remember your kids' names and you've forgotten that Sunday is supposed to be a day of rest. Many home businesspeople work 12 hours, 7 days a week without even realizing it.

You need structure. You need to be able to rise above the barking dogs and crying babies and get down to work. But you also need to know when to turn off the light and stop working.

CAUTION

Even if you work full-time, you'll still have to learn to say no to demands made on your time (demands not placed on those who work away from home). Because you work from home, some people simply don't take you seriously.

SET A SCHEDULE TO GET WORK DONE

One of the joys of working from home is that you can do what you want, when you want to. However, if you don't fix a schedule, you may never find the time to do any work. Flexibility means taking responsibility for setting up a work schedule. This schedule doesn't have to be rigid, but you have to set priorities. When you need to return a client's call, you may have to put off starting dinner.

Make a tentative work schedule to get you going. In blocking out your time, set specific times for the personal things you have to do, like picking up your child from school or driving your spouse to the train station. In scheduling, you may need to adjust for the seasons. If your children are small and off for the summer, you may not be able to put in as many hours as you'd like to for business during that time. Don't try to schedule work when, as a practical matter, you know you won't be able to get to it.

TIP

Dressing up like you're going for work may be a good psychological tool for you to get used to your routine. Eventually you can drop the dressing up for something more comfortable.

Also block out the time you think you'll have to spend on personal matters. If your children are young but in school, maybe you'll work only during their school hours and be with them after they get home. Or maybe you'll find you can squeeze in extra hours after they've gone to sleep.

Use the worksheet below to plan your work schedule. It may be a good idea to use a pencil rather than a pen because your schedule's bound to change. You may be able to spend some time on the weekends with your business. If you do—as is the case with nearly 35 percent of all home-based business owners, according to an AT&T Home Business Resource study—then add Saturday and Sunday to your schedule.

Work Schedule

	Monday	Tuesday	Wednesday	Thursday	Friday
7 A.M.	_____	_____	_____	_____	_____
8 A.M.	_____	_____	_____	_____	_____
9 A.M.	_____	_____	_____	_____	_____
10 A.M.	_____	_____	_____	_____	_____
11 A.M.	_____	_____	_____	_____	_____
Noon	_____	_____	_____	_____	_____
1 P.M.	_____	_____	_____	_____	_____
2 P.M.	_____	_____	_____	_____	_____
3 P.M.	_____	_____	_____	_____	_____
4 P.M.	_____	_____	_____	_____	_____
5 P.M.	_____	_____	_____	_____	_____
6 P.M.	_____	_____	_____	_____	_____
7 P.M.	_____	_____	_____	_____	_____
8 P.M.	_____	_____	_____	_____	_____
9 P.M.	_____	_____	_____	_____	_____

Of course, what you start with may not be what you end with. As your business grows, it may take up more of your time—something you'll just have to work into a new schedule.

WHEN TO CALL IT A DAY

Those same souls who used to come home late from the office can now be seen in their home office late into the night. After all, they now live in their office. Work becomes the prime focus of their day—and night.

When you work at home, there's no division between the office and home, so there's a tendency to work just about all the time. Home-based business workaholics have to learn when to quit.

Even if you're not a type A personality who loves to work all the time, you may have a realistic belief that you can't afford to turn down any work that comes your way. You don't yet have the security of a well-established business to say no, even if it means working longer hours than you'd like to.

TIP

In setting up a schedule, be sure to take your personal work habits into account. If you're a morning person, don't plan to work late into the night, because you'll never do it or you won't do it well. Know your personal preference and schedule your work accordingly.

This pattern of working all the time isn't good. First of all, it's generally not healthy to work so many hours. Second, if you're working all the time, you're not taking care of your personal responsibilities. And third, and most important, your family may resent all the attention you're giving to your business at their expense. They may be able to understand 9 to 5, Monday through Friday. But 7 to 7, seven days a week may be a little hard to swallow. Oddly enough, the answer to overwork is the same as the answer to procrastination, with slight twists: Set a schedule, and keep to it.

If you have a tendency to go overboard in your work hours, having a fixed schedule will help you set limits. Planning your personal activities—scheduling them in much the same way as you would your business tasks—will also help limit your work hours. Each week, make a list of the personal things you want to accomplish and then schedule them into your weekly appointment book or other planner.

Maybe you don't need someone to tell you how to spend your leisure time. But work is like a magnet, drawing you in. You'll need to schedule time off. Use some of the personal activities listed here to give you ideas of what you might want to plan for.

Personal Goals for the Week

Read a book   _____

Exercise three times
(30 minutes each time)   _____

Do volunteer work   _____

Visit a friend or neighbor   _____

Go shopping   _____

Hear a lecture or seminar   _____

See a movie or show   _____

Sleep (naps or extra hours)   _____

TIP

In running a business you have to keep appointments, return phone calls, and more. You can't afford to overlook things. You won't if you write it all down. Use a daily organizer by Franklin Planners (www.franklincovey.com), Daytimers (www.daytimer.com), or Filofax (www.filofax.com); a contact management program (like GoldMine or ACT!), a PDA (a personal data assistant); or even just a calendar on your desktop computer to keep track of your appointments and other time commitments.

As you begin to work at home, some of these planning tips may become second nature. After a while you won't formally have to set aside time for your personal life; it'll become automatic. In the beginning, however, the exercise of planning for personal time may be important so that you'll have the confidence that you'll be able to fit everything in.

CREATING MORE TIME

Whether you find it hard to get to work or hard to extinguish the midnight oil, you could probably do with more time. Sure, there are only 24 hours in a day, but you can convert more of those hours for business if you need to and know how:

- **Hire help.** The days of trying to be Superman or Superwoman are over. Accept it. You can't do it all yourself. You may need help—in your personal life or in your business. Hire someone to clean your house (a job you'd normally do) so that you can spend more time on your business. The same is true for help in your business. Consider hiring clerical help or farming out work to contractors to create more time for you. Even your childcare responsibility may have to be delegated. If your children are small and can't be left on their own, you may want to hire a babysitter or ask a willing relative for help.

  When Denise started out at home, she thought she'd be able to care for her one-year-old while running her business. After only a few days it became apparent to her that her child's irregular nap schedules simply didn't give her enough time for business. She had to take her daughter to a neighbor's home for a few hours each day to give her the time she needed to concentrate only on work. As her daughter got older and didn't need constant supervision, she didn't need the outside childcare.

- **Use machines and technology.** One of the key benefits to technology is saving time. Machines can do the work faster than it takes to do it by hand. If you usually keep your books by hand, automate. Putting your financial information on the computer may save you hours and hours over the course of a year—time you can better use for something else.

KEEPING THE FAMILY AND BUSINESS SEPARATE

With your family and your business under the same roof, your family life can easily spill over into your business operations. How do you set boundaries—both psychological and physical? You don't have to build a brick wall between your office and your kitchen; there are less-drastic measures you can take.

TEACH YOUR FAMILY AND FRIENDS RESTRAINT

If you live alone, there's no one at home to barge in on you. If you have a spouse, a significant other, children, or a roommate, however, telling them not to interrupt you is like telling someone not to think of an elephant. Suddenly they're inventing reasons why they've just got to walk in on you. Don't be too hard on them; they probably just miss you. After you've decided you want to work between the hours of 1 and 5, you've got to stick to your guns. You have to train them to leave you alone for four hours.

Sound simple? Well, it's not. It means telling them over and over again to hold their questions and solve their own problems while you're working. You'll probably find it's easier to get your kids to keep quiet than to get your spouse to leave you alone. After all, the kids are used to being disciplined, but your poor spouse thinks he has a say in what goes on under your roof.

Will a closed door stop people from bothering you? Probably not. Will a *Do Not Disturb* sign on the door keep your family out? And although heavy artillery might work, it's probably out of the question. In short, it's up to you to adapt. You have to be the one to set the limits—but be ready to smile when your family crosses the line.

TIP

Keep your sense of humor. No matter how hard you try, it may be impossible to bar your family from your office without a steel door. So when they barge in and interrupt, gently remind them that you need to be left alone—and laugh it off.

People in your home aren't your only problem. Friends who were used to having their morning coffee with you before you started your business also have to be taught about limits. Tell them that coffee's out and that they have to call after business hours to chat because you don't want to be interrupted during your work time. Of course, you'd probably like an occasional call to break up your business routine. Better that you're the one who makes it when it's convenient for you to talk.

SEPARATE BUSINESS FROM PLEASURE—PHYSICALLY

Just as Virginia Woolf needed a room of her own to write, in the best of all possible home-based business situations you get a separate room with a door. But that's not always possible. You may be forced to share space with your family. When you work on the kitchen table and your son wants to make a peanut butter sandwich there, it's hard to go on working. There's only so much space.

But space isn't your only problem. There are also the psychological intrusions on your concentration. Working in the kitchen, for example, may be a constant reminder of the fancy dinners you're no longer preparing.

It's a good idea to set aside a separate space for business if you can—one that won't be used by your family for other things. If you use part of a family room as your office, try to put your desk in a corner of the room that's away from toys and TV. Keep your supplies close at hand and separate from your family's games and baseball gloves. You don't want your kids poking around your paper clips, looking for the pieces to their Monopoly board.

TAKING TIME FOR TIME OFF

Remember those days when you got paid for a two-week vacation? Certainly it was one of the perks of a job. Now you can take all the time off you want— or can you? One of the hardest things for many home-based business owners to do is to leave the office for vacation. There's no one telling you that you can't. But there's concern about what'll happen to the business while you're away. Still, even a home-based business owner needs time off once in a while. Here are some ideas for fitting a vacation into your busy schedule:

- **Schedule vacations for your slow season.** As your business develops, you'll be able to see what times of the year are busier than others. Hannah, a financial writer, found out after observing her writing assignments for several years that she was busiest in the summer and fall, slower in the spring, and slowest in the winter. It was clear that migrating to Florida in January was the way to go.

- **Take long weekends.** If a week away would undermine your business, what about a three- or four-day weekend once in a while? Clients and customers are out of communication with you for no more than a day or two instead of a full week.

- **Hire help to watch the office.** While you're away, you can have someone else look after your business. You don't necessarily need someone to run your business as you would; you only need someone to field calls, schedule appointments, and handle simple problems that may come up with customers, clients, or suppliers.

TIP

Hiring someone to look after your home-based business while you're away on vacation can have added benefits besides those to your business. Having someone else in your home every day is a deterrent to robbers. Hiring someone to look after your business and your home will give you peace of mind while you're away.

The 30-Second Recap

- It takes planning to make sure that business responsibilities aren't overshadowed by your personal life.
- Make time for personal things so that your in-office time doesn't become all-consuming.
- Create more business hours in your day by hiring help and using machines and technology.
- Don't fail to schedule vacations away from home and your home office.

How to Look Bigger Than You Are to the Rest of the World

In planning a wedding, you would probably decide to use professional photographers. Whatever kind of business you own, the public wants to deal with a professional. They want to know they're in good hands and can trust your work or your product.

Working at home poses unique problems in presenting a professional image to the public. Barking dogs, crying children, or the churning washing machine aren't exactly conducive to the aura of a conventional office. And, as with any business, you face the problem of physical dishevelment: mounds of paper, stacks of samples, and overflowing wastebaskets. This is an issue more critical to the home-based business owner because of your space limitations: You don't have a conference room to entertain clients away from the clutter of day-to-day work.

In this section, you'll learn how to get organized. And you'll discover ways in which you can create a unique and professional image for your business.

Getting Your Act Together

Some people fold towels and straighten pictures like demons; they can't help themselves. Others are more like Charles Schultz's cartoon character Pigpen. They have to make a conscious effort just to stay visible under the papers that pile up around them. Organization is important in presenting a businesslike image to the public. Just because you work from home, you still don't want to have to tell a client who calls to "wait a minute while I find a pen and paper"—a statement that typically isn't heard in a conventional office where pens and paper are as ubiquitous as stale coffee.

One good reason to get organized is to be able to put your hands on information and materials when you need them. If your desk looks like a junkyard on speed, for example, you'll waste time trying to put your hands on correspondence or other papers that you need.

CAUTION

Estimates show that the average person (which includes those who work both in or out of the home) spends as much as six weeks out of every year searching for papers that have been mislaid, misfiled, or buried under other papers. Wouldn't you rather spend those six weeks lying on a beach somewhere?

What needs to be organized? Everything. You should organize your time, which you've already seen how to do. But you should also organize your files and your supplies.

BECOME A PAPER PUSHER

Remember just a decade ago, when the personal computer came into its own, there was a prediction about a "paperless society"? Well, they also predicted zero national debt, and you know what became of that. Today we handle more paper than ever. But where do you put it all when you work from a home office?

There are only three places where your papers belong—your desk, your files, and the garbage. You have to learn to process mail and the documents you create—getting it all from your desk into your files. And, most important, you need to be able to trash unnecessary papers.

- **Your desk.** Set up a priority system for your desk. Use the three-tray method to process your papers. When mail comes in, it goes into your "in" tray or basket. From here there are only two places for mail to go—into your next tray, "pending," or into the garbage can. Your "pending" tray or basket should be used for mail you have to answer or act on. After you've done what you have to do, the completed papers should be placed in your third tray or basket, marked "out." The "out" tray is only a temporary holding pen for papers that will be saved permanently in your files.

TIP

Before you throw out paper, consider recycling. If you use mounds of computer paper for drafts of proposals or letters, recycle the paper as drawing material for your children. Or cut the paper up and use the reverse side for sketching rough drafts and as scrap paper for notes. And before you dispose of paper, check with your city or town's recycling rules. Many towns now require "office paper" to be disposed of separately from household garbage or newspapers.

■ **Your files.** Set up a file system. Most people need at least two types of files—current files and dead files. Current files contain papers relating to projects you're working on now. These files can also contain materials relating to current projects (such as reference materials or brochures). These files should be close at hand—in or on your desk. Dead files are just that: storage for projects you've completed and other material you want to save but won't need to look at for some time, if ever. You should keep all tax-related records and receipts in your dead files to back up tax deductions for past years.

Label your files so you (or whoever works for you) can find them easily. How you label your files is an individual choice. You may want to create major categories and then use subcategories for separate files. Try using color-coded labels to quickly identify the categories in which the individual files belong.

PUT IN TIME TO ORGANIZE

Organization takes time. Crazy as it sounds, you need to schedule time in order to save time. Develop a daily routine to process your paperwork—read your mail, answer letters, throw away unnecessary paper, and file papers you want to save.

Setting up a routine will let you do several things:

■ **Avoid procrastination.** Processing papers can be boring, and many people understandably put off unpleasant tasks. But procrastination in this case just leads to more paperwork buildup, making the job that much more unpleasant. By having a set time each day to tackle the necessary but unpleasant job of going through papers, you can be sure the job will get done.

■ **Stay on top of your work.** By setting a daily time to dive into paperwork, you can make sure that important matters will get the immediate attention they deserve. Not answering that letter from your major client because it got lost in a pile could cost you big-time.

TIP

As your dead files grow, you may run out of space to store them in your home office, attic, or garage. Consider storing your dead files off the premises—in a warehouse or Aunt Maisie's basement— to save space.

■ **Change your habits.** You can do away with some paper and the need to file it if you change your work habits. Instead of printing everything from your computer, simply save it to your hard drive or a floppy. If you have an internal fax, you don't have to print out messages before you send them—just send them (with the messages stored on your hard drive).

CAUTION

Don't let your computer's hard drive become another place for clutter. Regularly delete unneeded material, such as old e-mail messages or faxes, from your computer. If you don't you'll only slow down your machine's operating efficiency.

■ **Read your reading matter.** If you take the time to read up on trends or news affecting your business in trade publications, magazines, and newspapers—something that's certainly a good idea to do—be sure you don't simply collect the articles and never read them. Plan a time each day or each week when you go through your collection of reading matter. Kathy, a real estate agent, reads her stack of magazines each day while walking on the treadmill at the health club. You may find it helpful to clip out articles of interest and discard the rest of the publication. If you want to save any articles for future reference, be sure to file them away in appropriately labeled files.

TIP

Use the Internet to catch up on your reading. Instead of saving articles in your file cabinet, you'll save space by jotting down only the name of the article and the magazine it appears in. Then track it down on the Internet when you're ready to read it.

The Supply Cabinet Is Full

Paper clips, rubber bands, and staples—you can always find room for these supplies. If your business uses a lot of paper, however, like mine, decide where you're going to put it all.

If your business uses more than just office supplies—cleaning supplies for your cleaning business or electrical supplies for your electrical contracting business, for example—storage can become even more of a problem. Put in shelves in your garage or basement to store your supplies. Make sure that the spot you've picked won't drip oil on your Lysol or melt your electrical cables.

TIP

Where space is limited, store only one extra copier toner, printer ribbon, and carton of paper. When you use your extra toner, it's time to order a replacement. With Staples and many other office-supply stores offering overnight delivery, there's no need to over-stock your supply cabinet.

Creating a Professional Image

Just because you work from home doesn't mean you're a slouch. You're just as professional as a business owner who pays rent on an outside office. But you need to let your customers, suppliers, and everybody else know it.

A professional image is part of your marketing—it establishes confidence in you and your business. Everything your business does—the letters it sends, the business cards you pass out at a party—reflects on you. Sloppy typing may make people think that your business operations are sloppy, too. Smartly styled materials say, "I'm a professional, I pay attention to details, and I can handle your job."

You want your professional image to be apart of every aspect of your business, from your office décor to how you answer the telephone. You don't want background noise from a crying baby to spoil that image.

What's Your Business Personality?

How do you want the public to see you—conservative, creative, high-powered? You can be informal without being unprofessional. Whatever characteristic you choose, it's your business personality. It should shine through in everything you do—your attitude and your written communications.

■ **Create something that can be identified with you and you alone.**
All the big companies do it. "Big Blue" is a well-known alter ego of
IBM. Everybody recognizes the red Coca-Cola logo. Use a consistent
logo or color on all your written material—letterheads, business cards,
envelopes, invoices. You can use inexpensive software, such as *The
Complete Idiot's Business Card and Stationery Maker, The Complete
Idiot's Marketing Materials Maker,* and *The Complete Idiot's Business
Forms Maker* (each under $20) to give a unified look to your printer
materials.

CAUTION

Keep your children's toys and homework out of your office (or at
least out of view) if outsiders come to visit. These personal items
may give the wrong impression about your professionalism.

■ **Answer the phone in a consistent way.** Decide how you want to
impress the caller. Some choose to answer with the number to let the
caller know she has reached the right place. Or you may want to
answer with the name of your company. Remember that the phone
can be the first impression of you for many clients or customers, so
make it a good one.

■ **Decorate your office for success.** If you regularly bring clients or
customers to your home office, make sure it conveys the impression
you're trying to establish—professional and businesslike. Hannah, an
art appraiser, spent big bucks decorating her home office, with its
adjoining powder room, in rich wood built-ins, expensive carpeting,
shades, and wallpaper. Because she regularly dealt with a wealthy
clientele, she needed a place to match her business. But even if you
don't spend big bucks, a simple bunch of flowers from your super-
market or backyard can spruce up the place.

SCREENING OUT BARKING DOGS, CRYING BABIES, AND OTHER BACKGROUND NOISES

Working from home has distractions (to you and your clients) that aren't ordi-
narily found in offices. Barking dogs, the patter of little feet, the guy running a
lawnmower next door, or other noises may be heard by clients or customers
over the telephone. Depending on the nature of your business, these noises can
be, at best, a real disturbance. At worst, they'll be a serious annoyance to the
guy at the other end of the line.

Figure out how you plan to handle these noises. It may be as easy as closing a door. Or you may find that you want to limit your telephone hours to times when these noises are at a minimum in your home—when your children are at school and the neighbor is taking a break from cutting his grass.

A related issue is the question of who picks up your telephone. If you use a personal phone line for business and your spouse and children have access to it, your family may rub verbal shoulders with your clients, customers, and suppliers. In many cases, this is not a problem. For example, you may regularly deal with a few different customers for many years, and you may let your children take messages from them. Your customers may come to know your children well, and this is fine.

For some businesses, however, this casual interaction between family and business may be disastrous. In this case, it's important to separate your family life from your business communications. Limit business calls (in and out) to a separate phone line.

WHEN IS A HOME BUSINESS NOT A HOME BUSINESS?

In the not-too-distant past, many home-based business owners tried to camouflage the fact that they didn't have fancy offices at posh addresses. They never divulged the fact that they worked from home. Today, with the growing acceptance of home-based business, this dodge is, by and large, no longer necessary. On the contrary, having a home-based business is a thing to be proud of.

Still, there are circumstances in which you may need or want to take your business out of the house to function efficiently. You may want to take advantage of a "front" office, a business address other than your own home, for several important reasons.

CREATING A "FRONT" OFFICE

You may live in Podunk, Massachusetts, and think a Boston address would be classier. If you want to use an address that has more national recognition, there are companies that can provide you with an address. Louis sold a beauty cream of his own formula from his home, which was located in a less-than-desirable neighborhood. He wanted to put a glamorous face on the business for marketing purposes. He decided to use an address of Mail Boxes Etc. in a well-known major business area to create the impression of a prosperous business. He even got a suite number so it looked to outsiders like he had a business located in an office building. When he had to meet with business contacts, he met at local restaurants over breakfast or lunch. Customers and suppliers never had reason to come to his home.

One of the problems that some small business owners face is a prejudice against one-person operations. Clients or customers may not feel secure that there's any backup for you in case of emergency. (And there may not be, but you don't want them thinking that!) It may be necessary to create the appearance that there are others working with you who can fill in for you. It's not a question of lying to clients and customers about your business. Rather it's a matter of creating the confidence in them that you've got things covered. You can do this, for example, with automated telephone messaging that identifies separate departments in your business (shipping, marketing, and so on).

TIP

Need conference space for that special meeting and don't want to use your dining room table? Consider renting by the hour office space from such companies as Executive Office Club Inc. (www.houroffice.com) and Office Suites Plus (www.officesuites-plus.com). There are thousands of executive suites nationwide, some of which rent for under $10 an hour.

Ding-Dong: UPS!

If you get an occasional delivery, it's easy to arrange to be home to receive it. You might even be able to make arrangements with neighbors to help. Depending on where you live, you don't even have to be home to get deliveries— packages can simply be left on your doorstep (if you know they're safe). Leave instructions for FedEx to leave packages without your signature.

But a home-based business may be no place to send and receive a lot of packages on a regular basis. If you run an inventory business, frequent deliveries may pose a problem. Neighbors may object to the constant UPS trucks or other delivery services at your door. You may find that using a mail-receiving service (check your Yellow Pages under this listing) can simplify this aspect of your business as it has for many home-based business owners. You don't have to be home to receive deliveries.

You can also take advantage of other services at a mail receiving service. For example, Mail Boxes Etc. offers packaging and shipping. Alternatively, you can use a post office box number for receiving deliveries. A local mail-receiving service may have better hours for you than the post office. For example, many Mail Boxes Etc. locations are open until 9 P.M. six days a week. And the private boxes can receive express deliveries from UPS and FedEx, whereas boxes in the post office cannot.

Another option for some types of inventory-based businesses concerned with both incoming and outgoing packages is to use a *fulfillment company.*

PLAIN ENGLISH

A **fulfillment company** is a business that takes and processes orders for you. For a flat fee (a charge per item), it takes an order and sends out the merchandise to the customer. It generally can accept payment via charge cards.

A fulfillment company was the right solution for Eddie, a home-based business owner who wanted to broaden his market to sell a pain-relieving cream to Hispanic customers. Eddie couldn't even order food in a Mexican restaurant, but he was able to find a fulfillment company with Spanish-speaking operators who could take and process orders. Because of his foreign language limitations, he would have been unable to tap this segment of the market without the fulfillment company. And his merchandise was shipped from his supplier directly to the fulfillment company. This eliminated the need to store the cartons of cream in his home.

THE 30-SECOND RECAP

- Organize your paperwork to save time and to help create a professional image.
- Keep your personal background noise out of earshot from your business telephone line.
- Create a professional identity with your attitude, stationery, and office appearance.
- Use off-site locations to enhance your business operations.

Working Alone Without Getting Lonely

For most home-based business owners, working at home means working all alone. If you used to have a job in corporate America, working alone at home is quite a change for you in many ways. Besides the nature of your work, your working social life just shrunk by about 100 percent. There may be no one to talk to, face to face. The only sound of a human voice you hear all day may be your three-year-old. You may actually begin to miss those meetings you always complained about.

But working alone doesn't have to be lonely. There are many ways to connect to the outside world. You may even come to love the solitude and increased productivity that working alone can give you.

In this section, you'll see how to handle being alone all day. You'll see how you can connect with other people in your area—many of whom may be working out of their homes just like you. And you'll find out about joining trade associations to benefit you and your business in many ways.

WHEN YOU'RE THE ONLY ONE AT THE WATER COOLER

If you used to work at a job in an office or some other place out of your home, you may think back fondly on meeting other people at the water cooler and swapping company gossip. You just can't do this when you work alone in your home. (Well, you can, but talking to yourself by a water cooler is a sure sign of mental weakness.)

Some people enjoy the peace and quiet in the home office when the rest of the family has left for the day. There are no human distractions to keep you from getting down to business. And there's more time because you're not wasting it socializing. You may be surprised at how much work you can get done every day. You can use these extra minutes for your business. Or you can use your extra time for errands, shopping, and watching *Oprah.*

But some people don't like being isolated. They get cabin fever, feeling confined to the house day in and day out. They miss the social opportunities working an outside job gave them.

Some home-based business owners are cooped up all day with young children. They don't have any adults around, and when they begin talking in single syllables, they realize they need to get with grown-ups—fast.

You have to determine your own comfort level. If you like being alone and find it helps you do your work, you don't have to find ways to get out and connect. If you're the type who needs to bump up against people during the day, however, there are many ways you can do it while working from home.

TELEPHONE TALK

You knew this as a teenager, but you may have forgotten it: Talking on the telephone is an important way to stay in touch. You've seen how you can use your phone for business. But don't forget you can also use it for social contact throughout the day.

Of course, it goes without saying that you need to balance your personal telephone time with your business needs. Tempting as it may be to talk to a good friend about her vacation in Aruba for three hours, you need to set priorities so that your most productive time is not spent socializing. Make personal calls on breaks you schedule between business tasks you need to get done. For example, if you normally spend the first hour of every day going through mail and answering correspondence, slot in a personal call after you've finished your business letters.

INTERACT WITH THE INTERNET

Today more and more people are socializing long-distance without ever speaking into a telephone. Instead of meeting face to face, they are talking through a computer. The Internet and commercial online services such as America Online allow you to meet people who may have interests similar to yours without ever leaving your home office. You simply call them up on your computer.

You can stay in touch with e-mail. Although it's a one-way conversation, it lets you get your thoughts across to another party without interrupting your work. What's more, if you want you can take the time to carefully compose what you want to say (and keep a written record of it for your files).

You can enter *chat rooms* devoted to business topics or you can keep them strictly personal. For example, you can exchange ideas about your home office with others at Home Office Computing's website (www.smalloffice.com), which America Online subscribers can access directly (keyword: soho). Or you can get into chat rooms about personal issues, such as gardening, tattoos, or religion.

PLAIN ENGLISH

Chat rooms are online areas you can visit to interact with others on a topic of mutual interest. In chat rooms you can just eavesdrop on the conversations of others or you can jump right in and participate.

There are also bulletin boards where you can post your ideas or messages and get feedback. For example, if you're a woman looking for loan sources strictly for women, post your question on the bulletin board at iVillage (www.ivillage.com).

GET OUT AND ABOUT

You're not the Prisoner of Zenda. Just because you work in a home office doesn't mean you have to stay there. Depending on the type of work you do and where you live, you may find that you spend a good deal of time out of the office on business. You may be visiting clients or customers, meeting with suppliers, or working trade or other business shows.

Janet is an estate planner. When she does estate planning, she usually meets with clients in their homes instead of having them come to her home office. The arrangement gets her out of the house, and it also has extra benefits. The clients view her visits as an additional service. (Because many of her clients are elderly, they don't like to travel.) What's more, the arrangement is more efficient because clients have all their records and documents in their home. Meeting there saves them from having to schlep all their papers to her office.

Even if you don't have a business reason to get out of the office, you may find that you have the time to get out for personal reasons. Since you don't spend time commuting to work and since you don't spend time socializing at the office, you have more time for yourself. And you can spend this free time any way you want.

TIP

According to one survey, home-based business owners have a lot more "extra" time than they used to when they worked in an office. They use this extra time to exercise, follow up on family activities, do volunteer work, simply run errands, or even do housework.

You can also schedule time away from the office. Once in a while, try to arrange personal or business lunches with your friends or business associates.

Connect Through Networking

Networking has been around forever. The "old-boy" network allowed prep-schoolers-turned-Ivy-Leaguers to make important contacts that they used in business for the rest of their lives. The old-boy network is still around today, but it's not the only network in operation. Formal networking groups started in the early 1980s, initially to give women the advantages the old boys had. These networking avenues soon expanded to include both men and women looking for business contacts.

PLAIN ENGLISH

Networking is word-of-mouth marketing in which contacts are made for the purpose of transacting business together.

Today networking is an important way for all types of business owners to interact with others of their breed. It allows you to swap stories and stay up to speed with your type of business and your business community.

But for a home-based business owner, networking is even more important than for business owners working outside of their homes. Networking is not only a vital marketing tool, it's also a way to break the cabin fever and socialize. Attending a meeting of an organization gives you the chance to get out of your home and mingle with other businesspeople, some of whom may also be home-based.

There are places where you can network with other business people. Almost every time you talk with someone, it presents a networking opportunity to explain your business. Here are some organizations you can use to network:

- **Become a Lion, Elk, or other networking animal.** Networking has long been done indirectly through Rotary, Lions, and chamber of commerce meetings. Luncheons and working together on special projects allow you to get to know other businesspeople on a personal level. Business connections typically are made after personal relationships have been forged.

- **Join professional associations.** If there's an association for your business, it may give you a chance to network. For example, if you're a home-based lawyer you could belong to a county bar association where you could meet with other attorneys to learn about developments affecting the law. There's also a time and place to make friendships through these associations that go beyond business.

TIP

You can locate a network organization by word of mouth. (Ask other businesspeople where they network.) You can also find a listing of network organizations in local newspapers. Check under "Community News" or call your local newspaper and ask where network organizations are listed.

- **Networking organizations.** Today there are also special clubs and associations designed especially for networking. You may find networking organizations in your community that meet for breakfast, lunch, dinner, or after dinner most any day of the week (they're a hungry lot) for the sole purpose of exchanging business cards and making contacts. You can choose the meeting that fits best within your schedule. Some of these organizations are open forums; others limit participation to members. Where membership is limited, you might want to join one that restricts the number of members from a certain type of business. Cynthia, an interior designer, didn't want to join a network that had wall-to-wall interior designers. She shopped around and found another group to join.

START YOUR OWN NETWORK

If there's no network organization in your community (or if existing ones don't meet your needs), you may just want to start your own. Decide on your format—open or by invitation only. Fix the time and date for meetings (say, a breakfast meeting at 7 A.M. on the second Tuesday of each month).

Let other businesspeople in your area know about your new organization. If you don't have enough people to invite to your first meeting, place an ad in your local newspaper or get the word out to business owners you know in the area about your new network organization. A local restaurant, community center, or even the public library might be the perfect spot for your new organization to assemble.

NON-NETWORKING FOR CONNECTIONS

Perhaps the most effective way to network is to "non-network." No, you're not hearing things. Getting involved in your community without necessarily identifying your business can lead to positive network results for you and your business. People in your community get to know you and, it is hoped, trust and respect you. This trust and respect carries over to your business. People want to know what you do and, in an informal setting, hear about your business.

CAUTION

It may take time and money to get a group started. Be prepared to give it several months before the group is firmly established. Also be prepared to pay the costs of getting going (advertising, room rental in excess of money collected from attendees). After all your efforts, the group may never get off the ground and you may have to just walk away.

Non-networking can take the form of membership in your local political club, health club, university alumni association, PTA, or Boy or Girl Scouts, or it can be volunteering for the United Way. Some people coach Little League or soccer; others join the board of their local library.

You pick your area of interest and then jump in. One home-based business owner became a volunteer firefighter. This community service has given him not only a personal challenge and satisfaction but also the opportunity to market his services. He also is able to find out about the services that others in his community have to offer.

JOIN A TRADE ASSOCIATION

As a home-based business owner, you may feel like a small fish, isolated from the information and buying opportunities that large companies enjoy. You don't have to feel this way any longer. Many trade associations are geared specifically to home-based or small business owners. These trade associations let you act like you're a big shot when buying insurance, booking hotel rooms, lobbying for legislative changes, and more.

Trade association membership, which may cost less than $50 annually, offers you a lot:

- **Business and personal insurance.** Being a member allows you to buy your own insurance at group rates. The types of insurance include medical and dental coverage, special home office business insurance, life insurance, and even car insurance.

- **Financial services.** As a member you may be able to get merchant authorization so you can accept credit cards from your customers (something that's difficult to do as a home-based business owner). You may also be able to get legal and tax assistance on your business questions. You may even be able to take advantage of mutual funds and other investments.

- **Communications.** Membership entitles you to special rates with some long-distance carriers. You may be able to get inexpensive online access to the Internet, e-mail, and other computer-based communications services. Each trade association also has its own newsletter giving you regular news affecting home-based or small businesses.

- **Products and services.** You may enjoy special rates on travel, car rentals, dining, and even relocation counseling. You can buy fax machines, schedule planners, and many other products for your business at discount prices. You may get discounts on overnight delivery and copying services. You may be able to attend local educational seminars geared to small or home-based businesses.

- **Legislative clout.** Trade associations may act as lobbying groups to press Congress for changes that will benefit home-based and small businesses. Trade associations for home-based businesses participated in the White House Small Business Conference in June 1995 and were instrumental in pushing the home business agenda. As a result, tax rules for home office write-offs have been liberalized.

The following table shows some trade associations you might want to check into.

Association	Phone	Website
American Association of Home Based Business	1-800-447-9710	www.aahbb.org
American Home Business Association	1-800-664-2422	222.homebusiness.com
Home Based Business Association	302-656-2926	www.hbba.org
Home Based Working Moms	512-266-0900	www.hbwm.com
Home Office Association of America (HOAA)	1-800-809-4622	www.hoaa.com
Mother's Home Business Network	516-997-7394	www.homeworkingmom.com
National Association for the Self-Employed (NASE)	1-800-232-NASE	www.nase.org
National Association of Home Based Business (HAHBB)	410-581-0071	www.usahomebusiness.com
Small Office Home Office Association (SOHOA)	1-800-969-7646	www.soho.org

TIP

The Home Office Association of America (HOAA) has created its own bill of rights that it hopes will be adopted at the local level to: (1) limit zoning restrictions to activities that change the residential character of a neighborhood; (2) ease up on licensing bureaucracy and fees; (3) avoid arbitrary limits on the number of employees permitted in a home-based business; (4) avoid arbitrary limits on customer access to home-based business; and (5) reconsider all the rules imposed on home-based business.

THE 30-SECOND RECAP

- Working alone at home doesn't have to be lonely.
- You can use the telephone or the Internet to connect with people without leaving home.
- Networking gives you business contacts and social opportunities.
- Trade associations give you buying clout and other benefits once limited to major corporations, and they lobby for legislative changes favorable to home businesses.

When You Know It's Time to Leave the Nest

Some people, like me, start a business in a home office and work there happily ever after. But for others, a home office is only an incubator—a place to nurture an idea and let it grow. At some point, the business starts busting out of the home office in several directions at once. More space is needed and, if you don't want to add a new wing to the house, it's time to move out into the world again.

Space isn't the only force that can drive you from your home office. You may need to hire people to help and zoning laws just won't allow you to keep them in your den.

In this section, you'll see the warning signs of a home business ready to leave the nest. You'll discover ways to stay at home as long as possible if that's your choice. You'll find out how to choose the best location for your new office and how to make a smooth transition to a commercial space.

WARNING SIGNS THAT IT'S TIME TO LEAVE

If you're a consultant or a one-person operation, you may never have to leave home again.

But not all businesses are the same. Your business may have gotten off to a great start in your home, but you may reach a point when it's time to cut the apron strings. Staying put may stifle further growth of your business.

Sure, after all your efforts to get comfortable in your home office, you're probably cozy there. You love all the positives about working from home—no commute, low overhead, great flexibility, and slouching around in sweatpants all day. If you've been successful and your business has expanded, however, it may no longer make sense to stay at home. Recognize the signs that it's time to move on so you can make a smooth transition.

TAKING ON EMPLOYEES

Zoning restrictions may prevent you from hiring additional employees needed to staff your growing business. Depending on where you live, you may be allowed no more than one employee who isn't a member of your household. Recheck your local zoning rules to find the limits on employees. The zoning rules may have changed since the time you first started your home-based business.

If you need more employees and want to postpone the move, try some of these stop-gap measures. In some cases they may help you avoid the need to ever leave the nest:

- **Use independent contractors.** Farm out some of your work to people with their own businesses. Suppose, for example, you think you need a full-time bookkeeper. Instead of hiring one, you may want to use a bookkeeper who's an independent contractor. The bookkeeper has his own business of providing bookkeeping services to a number of clients.

  Home construction contractors routinely use independent contractors for different parts of the job. Instead of having a plumber as an employee, the contractor just subcontracts the plumbing work to a plumber with her own plumbing business.

  ### TIP
  Using independent contractors to handle different aspects of your business not only saves space in your home office, it also cuts down on your employer's payroll taxes. Just be careful you follow the (very strict) IRS guidelines for independent contractors!

- **Use employees who work from their homes.** If you need someone to devote all of his time to your business and you control how and when the work gets done, you need an employee. (You can't just label the worker an independent contractor.) But your employee doesn't have to work in your home. You may let the employee work out of his own home. Today there are more than 7 million employees working for large corporations who telecommute. If it's good enough for AT&T, why not you?

TIP

Want to offer an employee a fringe benefit that doesn't cost you a thing? You can offer a tax incentive to an employee you want to hire to work from his home. Joe or Sally can deduct his or her own home office expenses if use of the home office is for the convenience of the employer (that's you). Because you can't and don't provide them with work space in your home office, the arrangement should satisfy tax law requirements for claiming home office deductions.

You can also maximize communication with your employee if both of you have computers with modems. This way, material on one computer can be easily and quickly sent across the street or even to the next town.

If neither independent contractors nor employees working from their own homes is the answer for you, the warning light should go on. It's time to relocate to a regular office in a commercial area.

CRAMPED QUARTERS

Your home just may not be big enough for your family and your business. If you're a graphic designer, for example, as you get more projects and store more artwork, you may need larger studio space than your home can provide.

Before you move your business out of your home office, however, look into some ways to stay put, if you want to:

- **Clean up your act.** Maybe the reason you're feeling pressed for space is because there's just too much paper around. You're a pack rat; you save everything, even a 1985 directory to your Lion's Club. Learn to clear the decks and make space. Do a spring cleaning on your files. Aim for a paperless office: Don't save paper if the information is saved on your computer (if you have a backup system, such as saving info to floppies).

- **Hire professional designers.** There are professionals who design interior space. Logically enough, they're called interior designers. They look at the space you've got and the space you need and try to make a fit. For instance, putting in overhead storage space (much like kitchen cabinets) can free up floor space for another desk. These professionals (and the suggestions they give to make your space work) don't come cheap. But their bill may be less than it would cost you to move from home and pay office rent each month.

■ **Move a wall, add a room.** If you love working from home but just don't have the space anymore, you may want to remodel your home to make it work. Of course, if you rent your home, your landlord might frown on moving walls willy-nilly. If you own your home, however, you can make changes. If you have two small bedrooms, you may want to break down a wall to create one large office. James started in a small office, just 8 feet by 8 feet, off his living room. After two years and not enough bookshelves, it was build or move. The old office was torn down and a new office, 12 feet by 25 feet, with plenty of bookshelves, went up in its place.

Structural changes are a big commitment on your part. They can cost thousands of dollars (and you have to live through the aggravation and mess of construction). But the price may be worth it to you. It means you can stay where you are rather than moving to a commercial office. And it may increase the value of your home.

TIP

You can share the cost of construction with Uncle Sam. If you own your home and make structural changes, you may be able to write off your cash outlays on your tax return through depreciation. (The taxes you save by deducting your costs means, in effect, that the government has shouldered a part of the cost.) Check to see whether you qualify for home office deductions.

If you've evaluated your space needs and just can't adapt your home office to meet those needs, the warning sign should flash. You've got no choice but to move out.

WHERE TO WAREHOUSE

Consultants and other service businesses usually have more modest space requirements. If you sell a product, however, storing the inventory can be a real problem for a home office. Maybe you haven't parked a car in your garage for years because of the cartons of Mama's Homemade Croutons, and still your space is running short. What's an entrepreneur to do?

■ **Take warehouse space.** You may find a local warehouse in which you can store some of your products. Of course this costs money, but if your business has grown so that you need to stock so much product, you can probably afford the warehouse rent.

CAUTION

You may be tempted to solve your storage problems with makeshift sheds, carports, or other buildings that are not part of your house. This isn't a good idea. You may expose your products to water damage, theft, or other problems that can be costly to you in the long run.

- **Reevaluate your business.** Maybe the way you've been operating can be changed so that you don't have to store cartons in your living room. You may, for example, be able to use a fulfillment company to handle your orders. You can have your products delivered directly ("drop shipped") to the fulfillment company instead of to your home. The fulfillment company, not you, has to worry about storage space.

Storage may not be your only problem. If the UPS or FedEx truck is always at your door, your neighbors may start to complain. You may have zoning issues to deal with. Before you move on account of pick-up and delivery, however, see if you can't make other arrangements with carriers to cut down on the traffic.

If you can't use warehouse space because you don't want to split your business (you're in one place, and your products are in another), you can't use a fulfillment company, or you can't solve your delivery problems, again, read the writing on the wall. It's time to move out into more suitable space.

Can You Afford to Move?

You may be cramped where you are and want to move. But can you afford to do it? Make an educated guess about the cost of moving your office from your home to a commercial site. Write down the things you'd need to buy or pay for if you move, using this worksheet as a guide.

Expenses to Move

Expense	Amount
Getting New Office Ready	
Wiring	$_____
Decorating	$_____
Phone installation costs	$_____
New furniture	$_____

Expense	Amount
Moving Company	
Packing	$_____
Moving office equipment and furniture	$_____
Printing Costs	
New stationery	$_____
Business cards	$_____
Bank checks	$_____
New location announcements	$_____
Total	**$_____**

Moving is only the first cost you face in running your business from a commercial space. Be sure you know what you're getting into after you unpack the boxes. Use this next worksheet to make an educated guess about the monthly costs you'll have running your business from leased commercial space that you didn't have in your home.

Monthly Expenses of Operating from Commercial Space

Expense	Amount
Personal Costs	
Commuting	$_____
Eating out	$_____
Special clothing	$_____
Rent	$_____
Parking fees	$_____
Utilities	$_____
Extra phone lines	$_____
Cleaning services	$_____
Miscellaneous	
Answering service	$_____
Secretarial staff	$_____
Total	**$_____**

Add up the amounts you must pay just to make the move. Then add in what you'll be paying each month to run your business from outside your home. Make sure your business can survive the move before you make it. Of course, you may be as lucky as Rita, who found that the move of her electrolysis business from her basement to a small office building down the street was just what it took to find new customers. The income from her greatly expanded clientele more than paid for her office rental costs each month.

TIP

In figuring your moving costs, be sure to get three estimates from moving companies so you'll know that the price you're paying is reasonable. Get the estimates in writing, along with their guarantees in case of damage or loss of your property. You may want to use a moving company that specializes in office moves, even if they charge you more than household movers. These companies are experienced in moving computers and other electronic equipment.

RELOCATION RULES

So you've tried everything but you just can't stay in your home office. You've tallied the numbers of a move and faced the fact that it's time to call the moving company. But where will you go and how will you make it happen?

You want to make a smooth transition to new quarters so that you don't disrupt your work and lose business because of it. You want to find a new office that's convenient to you and your clients and within your budget. And you want to keep your sanity in the process.

KEEP YOUR HEAD WHEN YOU MAKE YOUR MOVE

Remember, you're moving because you've made it. Your business has prospered and you need more space. That's great. But don't get in over your head when you make your move.

- **Keep commuting in mind.** As a home-based business owner you've been spoiled by not having to commute. Now things will change. Unless you live above a storefront or office, you'll have to spend time getting to your new place of business. In choosing an office, keep the commute in mind. Maybe you'll be able to recoup your commuting time with added productivity. (Maybe you won't spend as much time watching TV or playing with the dog.)

- **Keep clients and customers in mind.** Your existing client/customer base was used to your home office. Getting them geared to a new location may not be so easy. The closer you stay to your home, the easier it may be for them to reorient themselves to your new office. And you don't want them to start to use someone else's services because you moved out of convenient range.

- **Keep costs in mind.** Just because you've succeeded to the point of moving doesn't mean you can stop counting pennies. After all, it was cost consciousness that helped you become successful. Figure out how much space you need on a square-footage basis. Check out commercial rents (which are generally quoted on a square-footage basis).

In deciding where to move, there are some things you should avoid. Review this list of don'ts for relocating:

- **Don't rent more space than you need now (or can reasonably expect to need in the near future).** You'll only be throwing rent money away. If there's an opportunity to rent more space than you currently need at a great price, you may be able to sublease the unused part. That extra space may come in handy in the future should your business continue to expand.

- **Don't pay for fancy space if you don't plan to bring in clients or customers (for example, you're strictly mail order).** It may be great for your ego but hard on your pocketbook.

- **Don't ignore traffic if you're taking retail space.** You want to be where people are drawn to, such as a popular shopping area. The cheap rent for a store on a quiet block is cheap for a reason.

- **Don't forget to check on the location of your competitors.** You don't want to be next door to your biggest rival.

- **Don't overlook parking availability.** Neither you nor your clients or customers want to have to park blocks away or pay for expensive parking garages.

You may be able to find a special rental situation that's halfway between your home office and regular commercial space. There are special office suite arrangements in which you get your own office but share common spaces, such as a reception area, copying room, and conference room. These special rental setups generally are less expensive than individual office space—and you get the benefit of sharing a copier and some other equipment as well as a receptionist.

Last-Minute Reminders for a Smooth Transition

Moving a business, like moving your home, requires more planning than D-day. The more you plan, the fewer surprises you'll face. For example, you may want to schedule the move on a weekend so that you don't miss a beat in your business. Of course, there are bound to be snags. But here are some things you can do to make the move go as smoothly as possible:

- **Telephones.** Make sure the phone lines for your new office are in place. If you're moving to an office that's close to your home, you may be able to keep your same phone numbers. If not, be sure that the phone company message on your disconnected line tells the new number to those who call. Keep in mind that your Yellow Pages listings may be several months behind your new location.

- **Computer lines.** Have your electrical wiring completed before you move in your computer and other equipment. Make sure the wiring is adequate for your needs. Be clear with your landlord on who's responsible for the cost of wiring.

- **Announcements.** Let your clients, customers, and suppliers know about your new location. Send out announcements, giving your new address and phone number.

- **Stationery, business cards, and so on.** Make sure that your new address appears on all your correspondence, including your invoices and statements. You may also have to change your address on your bank checks. Getting all this printed might take several weeks or more.

TIP

Send announcements not only to your current mailing list but also to former clients and customers. Your new location, which may show that you've come up in the world, can inspire former clients or customers to renew their business relationship with you. If nothing else, it gives you an excuse to remind them of your existence.

Before you move out, take out the yellow pad. Draw a line down the middle of the page. On one side list the reasons for moving your business out of your home. On the other side list the reasons for staying. Now add up the entries on each side of the page (giving extra points to entries that may be more important to you than others, such cost or convenience). Maybe you're not ready to go yet. But maybe you are.

THE 30-SECOND RECAP

- Think of moving to commercial space when you need more employees than your zoning laws enable you to have at home.
- Think of moving to commercial space when you can't fit your files, employees, or inventory into your home office.
- Before deciding on a move, figure the cost of the move and the ongoing cost of renting commercial space.
- Make your move a smooth one with good planning.

Location, Location, Location

Real Estate 101

With low interest rates and real estate being a potentially lucrative investment, some believe it is the business to be in. Regardless of whether or not you want to go into real estate, you might want to purchase real estate for your business. This section explains why you may decide to purchase property for your small business or even rent this property out.

There are different types of property and property ownership you should know about. Understanding these differences can help you in the long run.

THE MANY CHARACTERISTICS OF REAL ESTATE

Real estate is made up of both physical and economic characteristics. You should be aware of these characteristics because understanding them will help you determine how the real estate market in a specific area will perform. This information is important to you not only while investigating property for purchase but also for the life of your ownership. Understanding the local real estate market will help you determine whether a property is rentable and at what price, as well as whether a property is saleable and at what price. This is all good stuff to know.

LET'S GET PHYSICAL

Here are the main physical characteristics that determine real estate property value:

- **Immobility.** Everything on top of land can be moved by actions of nature and people, but the geographic location of land will never change.
- **Lack of standardization.** No two pieces of land are exactly the same. Location, location, and location are the three big Ls of real estate and possibly its biggest characteristic. Even two pieces of land right next to each other will be different because of their locations. The lack of standardization is what affects value of real estate. Zoning restrictions and other encumbrances also add to the differences of real estate and affect the value of property.
- **Long life.** Land can have a lifespan of hundreds of years before a change is made in property lines or ownership.
- **Indestructibility.** Land is known to be durable and a relatively stable investment. Don't misunderstand us. Value can be destroyed, but the land will still remain.

THE ECO-DYNAMICS

When looking for real estate property, take note of these economic distinctions:

- **Scarcity.** Land in very desirable areas will become scarce or very valuable. There is, of course, plenty of land available that can be purchased for low prices, but land in specific areas and for specific uses often is insufficient and does not meet demand.

- **Fixed investment.** Most improvements such as buildings, to land cannot be easily moved, and it may take 20 or 30 years to repay the investment, so the investment is known to be long lasting. As an investor, try to determine how long a property's usefulness will last before purchasing or improving it.

- **Location.** Just as location plays a physical role, it also affects the economic aspects of land. Desirability, climate, and population shifts can increase the value of land in one location, whereas the value of similar land in other areas may decline.

- **Improvements.** Land has the capability to be modified or improved. Buildings, fences, and other things added to the land will directly impact its value.

MOST COMMON TYPES OF REAL ESTATE

There are different classifications for *improved property:* residential, commercial, industrial, farm, recreational, and government. Even though you may only be concerned with owning property that would meet one or two of these improved property classifications, you still should know what the other classifications represent:

- **Residential.** Residential property includes any type of structure designed for personal living. A wide range of properties are included in the residential categorization of property. In addition to single-family homes, there are apartments, town houses, row houses, condominiums, cooperatives, and mobile homes.

PLAIN ENGLISH
Improved property simply means land that contains structures.

- **Commercial.** Commercial property represents any property designed for retail or wholesale services, financial services, office space, and shopping centers. Buildings with storefronts and apartment units are also considered commercial. Usually, this type of property is acquired for investment purposes only.

■ **Industrial.** Industrial property is improved land intended to be used for manufacturing and warehousing of industrial and consumer products. Factories, warehouses, and utility companies are just some examples of industrial property.

■ **Farm.** Farm property, sometimes referred to as rural property, is usually used for agricultural purposes. Farmland, ranches, orchards, and pastures all fall under this classification.

■ **Recreation.** Recreational property is improved land used for leisure activities and vacations. Mountain- or ocean-side resorts, golf courses, and city parks are examples of recreational property. Many times, real estate developers set aside land solely to be used for recreational purposes.

■ **Government.** Government surplus land is property used and owned by the government. Much of this type of land is designated as public areas. The government, through its many agencies, owns approximately one third of all the land in the United States.

MOST COMMON TYPES OF RENTAL PROPERTY

With the exception of government land currently being used for some governmental capacity, all the other types of property have the potential of being purchased for investment purposes. And sometimes the government has been known to sell land that is no longer needed. Many industrial properties are rented as warehouse space for big industrial companies, just as there are instances in which farms and recreational property have been purchased by investors for rental income.

However, the most common types of real estate that are bought as investment property are residential and commercial properties. These categories of real estate start to take on new definitions when considered as rental real estate. The classifications technically remain the same; your local Uncle Sam figured out how to tax property differently based on the sizes and uses of properties.

Residential property is still classified as property designed for living in, but for it to be considered residential for tax purposes, there must be no more than four rental units in a building. So a five-family apartment house is still a residential property, but it is not taxed at a residential rate. Instead, this same five-family building is taxed at a commercial rate because it is now considered commercial property. Try to remember that this change in the definition of residential property relates only to tax issues. Residential property is considered one to four units regardless of whether the owner resides at the property.

There are also differences between residential and commercial property when it comes to operating these types of rental properties. There are rules that deal not only with how to use property but also how to manage it. The Laundromat is handled much differently than the cottage at the lake. The law treats commercial property and residential property differently. Landlord and tenant responsibilities and liabilities will differ as will eviction procedures and office policies.

THE BUNDLE OF RIGHTS

Any professors who teach real estate know about the *bundle of rights*. The bundle of rights refers to the belief that, when you purchase real estate, you also purchase certain individual rights that are inherited with the ownership and use of the land and/or property.

PLAIN ENGLISH

Picture the **bundle of rights** as a bundle of sticks with each stick representing a specific right you have in the property. If you sell a stick, the bundle gets smaller and you lose a right. Zoning laws and market conditions in an area will determine how big that bundle can be.

If you already own rental property, you might be wondering, "What rights?" It can be, and very often is, debated that property rights are fewer with each passing year. Regardless of personal opinion, the basic definition of real estate includes land, every interest and estate in land, and any permanent improvements on the land.

Real estate combines a physical element as well as the element of ownership. The land and everything permanently affixed to it are the physical portion. The ownership element refers to the nature, extent, amount, and quality of rights that a person or persons can possess in land. The basic concept of ownership is defined as the right to control, possess, enjoy, and dispose of property in a manner allowed by law. Some of the rights that relate to the physical aspects of the property may include mineral rights, air rights, and water rights. Other inherited rights of ownership are the rights to use, occupy, sell, and of course, rent.

WHO OWNS WHAT?

You think you're ready to take the plunge into the world of owning investment property? Well, before you find yourself up to your neck in shark-infested waters, you need to carefully plan how you will own your investment. You might be thinking, "What do you mean *how?*" There have been many before you who have not considered the extent of the liability associated with rental property, who did not plan accordingly, and who lost not only the investment but also much more.

So you thought you would just buy a rental property the same way you and your spouse bought your personal home. It is important for you as a new investor to recognize the different types of ownership that exist because selecting one or the other may award certain benefits and protection. A landlord today has a lot of liability, and the assets of the landlord need to be protected. Careful planning is necessary before investing in any venture, especially rental property. The same care should be taken before owning rental property as before investing in the stock market or starting a business. As a smart investor, you need to try to structure a plan that will successfully protect your assets from harsh liabilities and expensive taxes.

WHAT'S ALL THIS LIABILITY STUFF?

Along with the prestige of ownership comes the liability of ownership. Lawsuits are very popular in today's world, and a landlord must take the proper steps to insure and protect his or her investment. Remember that operating rental property is not just an investment but also a business. Accidents happen and the results can be damaging. The old "slip and fall" or unfortunate discoveries of environmental hazards such as lead paint are just a couple examples of an owner's liability. It's impossible to guarantee that no such hazard will occur or to watch over your property 24 hours a day. It also is not healthy to live in constant fear of these or other possible dangers. Therefore, you should examine and consider the different types of ownership and see if one will allow you to operate your property with peace of mind.

THE 30-SECOND RECAP

- Real estate has many physical and economic characteristics that affect its value.
- Several different classifications define real estate by type.
- Before you invest in rental real estate, research the many different types of real estate ownership available to you.
- With the help of professionals, careful research, and financial planning, you can help deter possible claims against you for liability and maybe help protect your personal assets.

How to Lease Office Space

To be or not to be, that you've already decided. To rent or to own, that's the question. Either rent or mortgage payments represents a significant business cost. The right choice can save you money. And the ins and out of renting a space for your new business are what is discussed in this section.

USING A BROKER TO FIND THE RIGHT PLACE

If you're in the retail or food service business, you know that customers have to find you, so the right location can add thousands of dollars to your sales. On the other hand, if your business doesn't require a high volume of customer traffic, the specific location may not matter nearly as much; for example, visibility isn't important for a market research company.

Searching for just the right place may be time-consuming. If you've ever bought a house on your own, you may recall driving around a lot and flipping through seemingly endless for rent/for sale ads in the newspaper. To avoid this situation, you may want to hire a real estate broker to help you find your location and then assist in negotiating the lease or the purchase agreement. The broker can tap into a multitude of sources to find out what properties are currently available. To maximize his or her utility to you, use a commercial broker familiar with your type of business. A broker who locates office space, for instance, may not be particularly helpful if you are looking for a shop to sell sports apparel.

The commercial real estate broker should help you determine ...

- What location best suits your business.
- Space requirements now and in the near future.
- Rental period and terms or purchase contract terms.
- Affordable rent or a reasonable purchase price.

TIP

The landlord or seller may pay the broker's fee. If a seller has employed a broker, your broker may split that one fee. The landlord who is eager to rent may be willing to pick up your broker's fee; after all, the broker put you two together.

For instance, Sharon, an architect, wanted to relocate to an office downtown. She hired a broker who found an excellent location, reviewed the lease, and suggested changes. The landlord agreed to remodel the office to meet her specifications and provide a moving allowance. The landlord even paid Sharon's broker's fee.

THE WAY TO RENT

A lease, also known as a rental agreement, is a contract between the landlord and tenant. The lease can be for month-to-month, one year, or several years; it may be renewed, or the property purchased. The lease terms are negotiable, but some landlords are more pliable than others; a prime location commands prime rent and not much negotiation over the lease terms. An eager landlord may be willing to negotiate virtually everything.

The landlord will provide you with a proposed lease, which should act as the starting point for your negotiations. If you have a broker, he or she should review the lease and advise you. Have an attorney who is familiar with commercial leases review it, too, and make suggestions. This may seem like considerable trouble and expense, but it may save you dollars and avoid disputes with the landlord.

Your lease will contain a number of stipulations that you'll need to understand before you sign on the dotted line. Be sure to read through this section to pick up the important points to consider. Your lawyer will point out the rest.

THE RENTAL PERIOD

You want the lease period to be long enough to accommodate your current space needs. If you're beginning in business, talk with your advisors, especially about future growth and expanding space requirements. However, if you have been in business for a while, you should have a fairly good idea of your current space needs; then add a little for possible expansion.

Request the right to renewal for an additional period(s) at your option. The landlord will want to increase rent for the additional periods, so rely on your broker to suggest what would be a reasonable adjustment. Remind the landlord that your renewal will save him or her the time and expense of finding a new tenant.

The beginning date may not be a problem for most landlords, but if your building is under construction, the landlord's date may be optimistic. If you are moving out of your old rental or advertising a date when you will be open for business, adherence to the beginning date is critical. The landlord should pay you a *per diem* (per day) amount for each day you cannot occupy the premises; this amount should also cover any moving and storage costs occasioned by the delay.

RENT MONEY

Your rent is usually a stated amount per month, such as $1,000 payable on the first of each month. In shopping center leases, there is a base rent per month plus an additional rent determined by a percentage of your gross sales. That may be all you pay to the landlord, but there may be more, maybe much more, including ...

- **Utilities.** You expect to pay for your utilities (telephone, electricity, heating, and cooling). But you may be required to pay for a portion of the common area utilities, particularly if you are located in a shopping mall. Have your utilities separately metered. These pass-through costs are usually allocated to the tenants for them to pay on the basis of the portion of space each occupies.

- **Real estate taxes.** The landlord pays the real estate taxes, but the lease may permit the landlord to pass on your portion to you. Property taxes vary considerably, even in the same city. Review the landlord's tax statements to determine what you will be paying. Remember, property taxes never go down.

- **Insurance.** You will be required to pay for your own insurance, and the landlord may pass on the cost of his or her casualty and liability insurance. Review the landlord's insurance premiums. And remember that insurance premiums always increase.

- **Repairs and maintenance.** Your building, its heating and cooling, and its parking lot require maintenance and periodic repairs. The larger the complex, the greater the costs. If you are renting an older building, count on considerable repair costs. If the parking lot needs resurfacing, the lease may require you to pay your share. These are called CAM costs (common area maintenance costs). Your broker should walk through the premises to get some idea of potential problems. Check with other tenants to see what costs they have incurred.

- **Advertising.** If you're renting in a shopping center, count on the mall's advertising expense to be passed on. The landlord will argue that you are the beneficiary, not the landlord, but that is only a part truth if he or she gets a percentage of your gross sales. Discuss the advertising costs with the landlord, and then compare what you hear with the tenant's experience. If you are the most significant tenant, also known as the *anchor tenant,* insist on input in any advertising campaign your landlord undertakes.

TIP
Require your landlord to estimate other costs in addition to rent, and check with other tenants for their experience. Without this, you cannot prepare an accurate budget.

- **Security deposit.** Your landlord will require a security deposit, usually an amount equal to the first and last month's rent. The deposit is to protect the landlord should you breach the lease by moving out early or damage the premises (more than ordinary wear and tear). The lease should require the landlord to return the deposit within 30 days after you leave, and detail all landlord expenses that reduce the return of the entire amount. You may ask the landlord to keep the deposit in a separate interest-bearing account for you.

THE SPACE

If you are renting a portion of the building, the lease should specify your space, such as Suite 5, and include a copy of its floor plan. The base rent may be determined by the square footage (for example, $10 per square foot), so double-check the landlord's calculation.

You may share space with other tenants, including restrooms, storage, and parking. Make sure that the lease specifies your rights to use each area. If parking spaces are critical to your business, put your requirements in the lease.

Consider the possibility of future expansion. You may want to specify in your lease that you have an option to rent adjacent space, if available, or move to a larger location in the building.

CONDITION OF THE PREMISES

Your broker should inspect the premises (or hire someone to do so). Everything should be in good working order when you occupy it. Avoid later disputes with the landlord over what needed repair by providing a list of repairs the landlord must make before occupancy, and make sure that the landlord agrees to the items and follows up by getting the work done. If the premises were damaged prior to your occupancy, make sure that your landlord knows of the damage; you don't want to have your security deposit reduced for damages you did not cause.

Usually the lease will require you to leave the premises in the same condition as you rented it, with consideration for normal wear and tear. What is normal depends on the business. If you operate a restaurant, the carpet is going to have constant use and will be well worn—expected wear and tear that you should not have to pay for when you depart.

ROOM FOR IMPROVEMENT

You may be renting space that is merely a shell, waiting for the tenant's special requirements. The landlord and you will negotiate what needs doing and at whose expense. If this is your first business, consult with experts to lay out the rental space to meet your business requirements. An office rental should be designed for efficiency; a retail rental should be designed to maximize customer service. If your office will rely heavily on computers, ensure that there is proper wiring.

TIP

Insist that all improvements be specified in the lease or an attachment thereto. Include drawings and detailed specifications, and insist that an architect or construction expert prepare and supervise the construction.

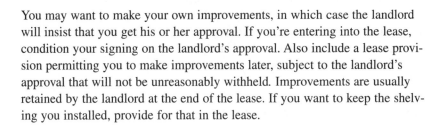

You may want to make your own improvements, in which case the landlord will insist that you get his or her approval. If you're entering into the lease, condition your signing on the landlord's approval. Also include a lease provision permitting you to make improvements later, subject to the landlord's approval that will not be unreasonably withheld. Improvements are usually retained by the landlord at the end of the lease. If you want to keep the shelving you installed, provide for that in the lease.

TENANT'S USE OF THE PROPERTY

In the absence of a lease provision restricting use, you may use the property for any legal purpose consistent with that type of property. Usually the lease will specify your use and limit it to that activity, such as serving food in a restaurant, providing insurance to customers in an office, and so on. You don't want the use clause to be too restrictive, however. For instance, if you think you might want to open a clothing store later, don't limit yourself in the lease to a sporting goods store. In a shopping center, the landlord may insist that your store not compete with other tenants. For example, if you sell office supplies, your lease may not allow you to sell computer software if someone else in the center already does.

Your landlord may insist on having the right to periodically inspect the premises, or enter to make repairs. The lease should specify that this occurs at reasonable times, upon notice, and will not interfere with your business activities. Insist that the landlord include a *covenant of quiet enjoyment* in the lease.

PLAIN ENGLISH

A **covenant of quiet enjoyment** is a binding promise by the landlord that he or she will not disturb the tenant's occupancy of the premises.

COVERING YOUR LIABILITY BASES

Your landlord will require you to carry insurance to cover any damage done to the premises by you or your customers. (Your cook catches the kitchen on fire, for instance.) The landlord will also want you to obtain casualty insurance. (A customer slips on the wet floor and sues you and landlord, for instance.) The landlord might set specific amounts of coverage. If so, review the requirements with your insurance agent to see whether you may be able to convince the landlord to reduce the coverage and save you money.

Your landlord may also want to include a provision that excuses him or her for *any* damage to the premises. Consider this scenario under such a provision: Your landlord's employee negligently repaired your wiring and caused severe damage to your computers; the landlord would not be liable. The clause should be revised to read: "Landlord will be liable for its employees' negligent and intentional misconduct." More advice about your legal contracts can be found in Appendix C.

COMPLYING WITH THE AMERICANS WITH DISABILITIES ACT

You and the landlord are required under the *Americans with Disabilities Act (ADA)* to make the premises accessible to disabled persons (with few statutory exceptions). Your lease should include a provision stating that your premises and the common areas comply with the ADA, and that all improvements will comply with the ADA. You, or your expert, should review the ADA survey of your premises.

Subleasing

If you want more space than your current premises affords and you know someone who will move in, you want to be able to assign the lease to the new tenant and leave with no further liability to the landlord. If you want to sublet part of the premises because you have the room and could use the extra income, the lease usually requires the landlord's written permission. Try to convince the landlord to at least accept additional language to permit an assignment or sublease, which would read "Consent of the landlord will not be unreasonably withheld."

The Sign of Your Business

If you want customers to find your shop, make sure that the lease permits adequate signage. You need a sign outside your shop, and, if you are in a shopping center, signs on the landlord's signs. The landlord may require approval, so attach a drawing of the proposed sign to the lease.

CAUTION

Don't create signage before you check with your city planning office. City ordinances may restrict the type of signs you can install.

The End of the Line

Usually you cannot cancel your lease before it ends; however, try to include specific provisions that would allow you to do so, for example ...

- The premises are damaged and a portion is unusable.
- The premises are in a substantial state of disrepair.
- Road repairs make a retail store virtually inaccessible.
- Expected income was not reached within the stated period.

Admittedly, some of these clauses will meet with adamant refusal by the landlord. However, if fire or wind have seriously damaged the premises, you should insist that the landlord immediately begin repairs and set a time by which the repairs must be completed.

Your premises should be habitable (fit for occupancy), and be sure to include that clause in your lease. The clause should permit you to notify the landlord of a problem that causes substantial interference with your business; the landlord should be required to promptly make the necessary repairs.

Road repair is the bane of retail stores. You might try including a clause permitting you to terminate the lease, or at least reduce the rent during the repairs, if your income is substantially reduced.

If the landlord enticed you to rent based on projections of income, the landlord should be willing to consider permitting you to terminate the lease, or at least reduce the rent, if your sales fall short.

TIP
You should have business-continuation insurance to replace income lost during casualty repairs.

BREACH OF PROMISE

The lease itself should specify the remedies available if the landlord *breaches* the lease. You may want to include a provision in the lease permitting you to contract for the repairs not performed by the landlord and reduce the rent accordingly. You may also want to specify that, if the landlord's breach is substantial, you can terminate the lease. For example, if you operate a restaurant and the landlord allows rats to roam the premises, causing health code citations or a shutdown, this should permit you to terminate the lease. In addition, you may sue for money damages for the harm done to your business.

PLAIN ENGLISH
Even if you **breach** the lease, the landlord may have a duty to mitigate damages by making a reasonable effort to re-let the premises.

The lease also should specify the landlord's remedies if you are in breach of the lease. For example, one tardy rent payment may not justify your eviction, but several may. If rent is computed on a percentage of the revenue and you misrepresent gross revenue to the landlord, the landlord could specify that he or she is entitled to the difference plus the accounting fees for the audit. The lease could also specify that, if you are seriously behind in your rent, become bankrupt, or significantly damage the premises, then the landlord will go to court to have the lease terminated and you evicted. In addition, the landlord may be entitled to money damages for past due rent and rent due for the rest of the lease period, as well as any physical damage to the property. If the tenant is evicted because of a breach of the lease, the landlord has a duty to *mitigate* or lessen money damages for the breach.

LANDLORD PROBLEMS TO AVOID

It is almost inevitable that you and the landlord will have problems. The disputes may be fairly trivial, such as parking in someone else's spot, or serious, such as needed repairs aren't being made. A good lease may reduce the conflicts, but probably not totally eliminate them. Keep in mind the following:

■ Know your lease.

■ Put your complaints in writing.

■ Insist on a timely response.

■ Threaten a lawsuit only as a last resort.

Don't complain until you are sure that you have the right to do so under the lease. What you believe should have been in there may not be, and the landlord will tell you so. If you are in the right, put your complaint in writing; be firm but diplomatic. A written complaint will put the landlord on written notice and will be helpful if you need to sue. Insist that the landlord timely fix the problem and set a reasonable deadline. Finally, don't threaten a lawsuit unless you intend to file; idle threats just escalate tempers.

THE 30-SECOND RECAP

■ You may want to hire a real estate broker to help you find your location and then assist in negotiating the lease or the purchase agreement.

■ The landlord will provide you with a proposed lease which is usually open for negotiation.

■ A typical lease will cover rent period, rent money, space, condition of premises, room for improvement, tenant's use of property, mutual liabilities, disability considerations, subleasing, termination, and breach.

The Basics of Buying an Office

You really need a broker to buy real estate, and that means your broker, not the seller's broker who will not have your best interests at heart. There are so many things that can go wrong when you buy real estate, even if it's just vacant land on which you will build.

You should rent the movie The Money Pit, *which may be all too real for many of us who bought a house without a proper pre-offer inspection. It is also a cautionary tale for anyone who buys business real estate. You've learned about how the broker will help you find property; in this section, you will see what else the broker can help you with once you've found a place for your business.*

MORTGAGE FINANCING

Before you make an offer to buy real estate, line up your financing. Mortgage terms vary, so your broker and accountant should advise you as to the most suitable for your income. The mortgage rates vary from fixed (same rate over the life of the mortgage, such as 10 percent for 20 years) to variable (such as beginning at 7 percent, then adjusted based on a prime interest rate for commercial customers). The mortgage and mortgage note terms are usually not negotiable, but your attorney should still review them for such terms as late payment fees, prepayment penalties, and assumability of the mortgage, so you're not caught off guard later.

GET THE BUILDING INSPECTED

Ask your broker to recommend a building inspector and be sure you have an inspection conducted. Obtaining a termite report is just a beginning. You'll want to know about every loose nail and leaky pipe. Some problems may require minor repairs; others, like a collapsing roof or an inefficient heating or cooling system, may mean major dollars. You need to know just what you are buying and the inspection report should tell you. Environment and zoning problems are discussed later in the section.

FIND A TITLE INSURANCE COMPANY

Your broker can help you find a title insurance company whose job it is to examine the real estate records for your real estate and insure against any defects of record. For example, if the seller has a mortgage on the property or if there is an easement for utilities, the policy will list those items. If the policy fails to disclose a defect in title, such as a judgment lien, the title company is required to reimburse you for your loss, including paying off the lien to clear title. When you buy real estate and purchase title insurance, you pay a one-time premium based on the gross sales price. The policy will list exceptions that the title company will not insure, such as delinquent real estate taxes. Your real estate attorney should review any such exceptions before you close on the sale to determine if they are acceptable and won't diminish your marketable title. The attorney should attend closing and insist the policy be updated to the closing to ensure that no liens have been filed subsequent to the original title search. *Mechanics' liens,* liens used to pay those supplying labor or materials to improve a property, have a way of suddenly appearing at the last minute. For example, the roofer hasn't been paid for the new roof and filed a lien against the property to collect the debt.

PLAIN ENGLISH

A **mechanic's lien** is a lien against real estate to secure payment to those supplying work, labor, and materials to improve the property.

RECOMMEND A REAL ESTATE ATTORNEY

A broker and a real estate attorney have different functions. An attorney must handle any title issues and must examine the title and is authorized to issue title insurance through a title insurance company. The broker may negotiate the deal and bring the buyer and seller together, but the attorney actually handles the settlement and all related tasks. Everyone needs an attorney for the purchase of real property.

PURCHASE AGREEMENT TERMS THAT BENEFIT YOU

You may want to outline the contract provisions that will be in your offer, and have your real estate attorney draft the final copy. If your offer is accepted, it becomes the purchase agreement. All the terms of your offer should be in writing, and it should include at least the following:

- **Offer.** When you make the written offer for the real estate, the seller may accept your offer, reject it, or make a counteroffer. You set the specific date and time for the seller's written acceptance, such as before 1 P.M. April 1, 2004. If the seller does not accept by that time, the offer expires.

- **Purchase price and earnest money.** Your offer includes the price that you are willing to pay. If the seller has a broker, your broker should be willing to suggest a price that is somewhat less than the listed price, because the list price is typically higher than what the seller expects to receive. The buyer usually includes earnest money with the offer, which can amount to anywhere from $500 to $5,000, depending on the sales price. If you breach the agreement, the seller is allowed to keep the earnest money, or the deposit you provide to hold the offer open.

- **Closing and possession.** The closing date and the date of possession are stated in the offer. There should be a *per diem* penalty if the seller delays your possession. At closing, the seller is required to deliver a fully executed general warranty deed conveying marketable title free of any liens or encumbrances, except those disclosed in your title insurance policy. Each state differs on what other closing documents are required; the attorney will list those in the agreement.

■ **Taxes and assessments.** The contract will specify when you become responsible for the real estate taxes. States differ on the tax lien and payment due dates. You might have to pay the next installment, or the taxes might be prorated from time of closing. How and when taxes are allocated is important if you deduct the real estate taxes on your income tax return. Special assessments are typically imposed by your city for property improvements, such as sidewalks and sewers, and are paid for over several years. If such assessments were made on the property you're buying, the seller can provide you with the tax and assessment information, and the latter could be addressed in the contract.

■ **Property lines and zoning requirements.** Any building and property improvements must not encroach on the neighbor's land. A property line survey, preferably one for which the surveyor actually pounds stakes in the ground, should be required. The seller should pay for the survey.

The real estate that you are buying must be properly zoned for your business. If you're buying a building to use for an insurance office, its zoning will be different from that of a retail store. The contract should specify your zoning requirements, and you should confirm the zoning classification with the local planning board. Likewise if the building is under construction or renovation, the planning commission will require permits, which the seller should have obtained, and you must confirm. If you are buying a tavern, the building should be licensed for that purpose. Carefully check your zoning ordinances.

■ **Title insurance.** Title insurance was discussed earlier; the seller should pay for it. There are two types of title insurance: owner's and lender's. Lender's is required; owner's is optional, but recommended. They serve basically the same function, but lender's protects the lender and owner's protects the owner. Also lender's coverage will expire when the loan is paid off. Owner's overage lasts for the length of time the owner owns the property.

■ **Environmental survey.** You must insist on an environmental survey. Federal and state environment laws make the owner of the real estate responsible for any toxic-waste cleanup expenses. Consider this scenario: Toxic materials may have been buried, or containers allowed to rust and leak, on the property you're buying. Your worst nightmare is to have your property declared a Super-Fund site by the Environmental

Protection Agency. An environmental engineer's report may be expensive, and you may have to pay for part of its cost, but that is money well spent.

■ **Inspection.** Always have the building thoroughly inspected. If the inspection reports serious problems, the contract should permit you to cancel it and receive your earnest money. If the building is significantly damaged and cannot be repaired before closing, or if the state has begun condemnation proceedings to take all or an important part of the property, the contract should permit cancellation. A feasibility study to determine the feasibility of the property for the buyer's intended use includes all of the above items (environmental survey, inspection, title examination, etc.) and a specified period of time the buyer has to perform these tests (30, 60, or 90 days). In the event any of the tests are unfavorable making the feasibility of the property questionable, the buyer can get out the contract and the seller must return the buyer's deposit and each is released from any further liability relating to the contract.

■ **Nonperformance.** If the seller doesn't fulfill the conditions of the contract, such as providing a satisfactory environmental report, you should be able to cancel the contract and the seller must return your earnest money. You may waive one or more of the conditions, such as minor problems in the inspection report, but do so only on the advice of your attorney.

■ **Contract breach and remedies.** If either party breaches the contract—if the seller can't convey marketable title or you changed your mind about buying the property, for instance—then the nonbreaching party may sue for money damages. The nonbreaching party may also sue for specific performance; this remedy permits the court to order the seller who breaches to execute the warranty deed, or the court orders the breaching buyer to make payment.

If all goes well, you and the seller will close on the sale, and you will own the real estate. Congratulations!

HELPFUL SOURCES ON THE WEB

The federal government has several useful websites:

■ Environmental Protection Agency (www.epa.gov)—this site will help you identify potential environmental issues that you should consider for the property you're buying or renting;

- Small Business Administration (www.sba.gov)—the definitive website for small businesses, with lots of tips about property ownership, etc.
- Equal Employment Opportunity Commission (www.eeoc.gov).for *Americans with Disabilities Act (ADA)* compliance

Your local planning commission may have a website for zoning information. Title insurance companies and brokerages have brochures to help you. State statutes and some local ordinances may be on the web or in your library. Your library and bookstores will also have several books on leasing and buying real estate, and several have forms you can use to help you prepare a preliminary draft of the lease or purchase agreement. Likewise several software companies provide forms.

THE 30-SECOND RECAP

- Use a broker to find the right location to lease or buy.
- Don't just sign a standard landlord-written lease; negotiate terms to protect your interests.
- The base rent may be only part of your rental costs.
- Put all your lease problems in writing and respectfully request a prompt response from the landlord.
- Require a satisfactory physical inspection of the property for any real estate you buy.
- Your real estate attorney should review the title insurance policy and draft all contracts.

Setting Up Your New Office

In a corporate, middle-size, or even small company, you'll find that everyone has a job to do. The bookkeeper keeps the books, the office manager manages the office, the middlemen and -women keep the papers shuffled in the right places, and the president tells everyone what to do. For a small business, the level of corporate management is simple. The business owner is the book-keeper, the office manager, the sales staff, the mail clerk, the receptionist, and the cleanup crew, just to name a few. You also are president, of course, and being president means you get to tell yourself what to do. That's what being in business for yourself is all about!

Being in business for yourself also means you need to learn how to run your operation smoothly. As your business grows, so will your need for organization and efficiency. If you're just starting out, you might be able to get by without a computer because your paper load will be minimal. As your business grows, however, you will acquire more of a workload. Keeping track of everything from your customers to paying your bills will seem time-consuming and costly, but not keeping ahead may cost you the business.

OFFICE SETUP

When starting up, you need the basic supplies. Among the usual suspects of a stapler, a phone, pens, file folders, and a desk to put them on are other basic and not-so-basic supplies that will make your office run smoothly. But this is only the tip of the iceberg. To properly go to war you'll need to be equipped with the best weapons. Here are some of the essentials you'll need.

PAPER CLIPS AND THEN SOME

If you think you can run a business without the basic supplies, think again. While you're picking up your desk lamp and paper clips, include the following on your office-supply shopping list:

- **Business phone with speaker feature.** Having your hands free while you're on hold and handling a few things at once will save you money on physical therapy bills for neck strains. If you're running a home office and want a home life, a separate phone line is your best bet.

- **Answering machine or voicemail.** You will get calls 24/7. If people can't leave a message, count on them not calling back or calling back angry. Get a good answering machine, one that saves the date and time of your messages, or sign up for voicemail through your local phone company. Voicemail messages also are easy to retrieve and save from wherever you are. This is especially handy if you work from home and live with others who will be occupying the phone. You can get voicemail through your local phone company, and it usually costs less than $10 per month.

- **Fax machine.** You will need to receive credit reports and other info over the fax, and you will need to fax out info as well. You may also want to consider signing up for one of the many internet fax services. These services allow people to fax their documents to a toll free number where the document is automatically scanned and forwarded to you as an e-mail attachment.

TIP

Voicemail can be a great option. Calls are never missed because, whether you're on the phone or away from the office, messages are left with the voicemail service.

■ **Photocopier.** They're not as expensive as you might think, and you will use this constantly. In the long run, it's less expensive than getting 5¢ copies at the gas station. And it's time-saving.

TIP

Consider a cell phone. After you have a cell phone, you won't know what you did without one. Checking and returning messages from your cell phone will save time. You can have tenants use the main office number to leave messages, and you can choose to whom you give the cell number.

■ **Printing calculator.** For accounting reasons, there's no sense in getting a calculator that doesn't.

■ **File cabinets and plenty of file folders.** Stacks of files on the floor get lost and coffee-stained. There are a lot of cheap file cabinets out there now—plastic, on wheels, and your standard gray metal.

■ **Paper shredder.** We'll presume you're not re-creating Watergate, but it's still a good idea to get rid of unwanted documents this way.

■ **Mail drop slot.** Just in case customers drop by after hours to make payments you want to give them the facility to do so.

■ **Cork and marker boards.** "Out of sight, out of mind" really applies to office organization. Whichever system works best for you, be sure to post the important things: open orders, back logs, vacation schedules, a calendar for showings, or anything that you'll need to refer to often.

■ **Store it.** Set aside room on your property for storing your tools, plumbing and electrical parts, smoke detectors, mailboxes, toilet seats, light bulbs, trash bags, and cleanup supplies.

ENTER THE TWENTY-FIRST CENTURY

There's no doubt about it these days, getting the right computer and software will organize things you didn't even know needed organizing. As your business grows, everything from finances to eviction notices will seem like a breeze when you have a machine to take care of it. For accounting purposes, a computer can't be beat. Think of tax time. What's easier, rummaging through shoeboxes of receipts to calculate what you've earned and spent over the year or printing out a report from your computer?

If you currently own only one or two properties, you can get by without a computer. Keeping records by hand or by typewriter probably won't be that cumbersome. On the flip side, this might be the perfect time to get technical, especially if you are computer illiterate. If you wait until your business grows even more before purchasing a computer, you will have to stop and set aside even more time to transfer the piles of growing files on to your new machine. Not to mention learning how to work the thing in the first place. The bottom line is: Don't be afraid; user-friendly computers do exist, and they will help in your quest to run an efficient business.

If you don't already own a personal computer, check around before leaping at the first one you see. Ask your fellow entrepreneurs and friends what they have. Go to their offices or houses and test drive some of their computers and software. Now that computers are a common home office tool, there are bargains to be had. There are also a lot of bad deals out there, so beware of the slick computer salesperson. Everyone's needs are different, but make sure you choose a computer with a good amount of memory (128 megabytes of RAM or more), modem speed (56K or more), and the right software, including a good word processing program, an easy-to-use accounting program such as Quicken or Microsoft Money, and Internet software.

TIP

E-mail is becoming a necessity. The Internet and e-mail are great ways to get connected with other people, provided you have a computer to get connected in the first place. Nowadays, not having an e-mail address can put you at a huge disadvantage.

Whatever configuration of wires and plastic you invest in, it will be worth your money when it gets the job done. Be sure, however, not to rely solely on the machine. Back up all your files and print hard copies of all accounting reports, forms, and anything else you create on the computer. Home computers these days are pretty reliable, but they're not always a sure bet. Always have a backup when it comes to computer files.

MAKING CONNECTIONS

When setting up your office, make your presence known. Call the building inspector and fire marshal to introduce yourself. Get references from other tenants as to which electrician, plumber, roofer, sider, lawn care, and snow removal contractors have the best reputations. Print up business cards.

You may think that networking is not really a necessity. Just stick to taking care of your business, right? Networking can only help your business. People talk and, especially in smaller communities, reputations get around fast. If people in town get to know you and know you are looking to increase your business, you will get ahead.

THE DAILY GRIND: PRIORITIZE, PRIORITIZE, PRIORITIZE

It's Monday. You've just come back from a quiet and restful weekend with no emergencies and lots of time doing nothing. Your answering machine is blinking—you have 42 messages. You've got bills to pay and customers to chase down. What do you do first? First you take a deep breath and make a cup of tea. In any business, time management—known technically as "what the heck do I do first?"—is important.

Keep it in perspective, though, and try not to let managing your time take over your time. If you have hired office staff, you should all be working together to divvy up the responsibilities. If you're on your own, then managing your time the right way will make all the difference in getting the job done.

MANAGING YOUR TIME

Let's go back to Monday and the 42 callbacks to make, half-dozen bills to pay, and half-dozen more customers to track down. Checking your messages is priority one. Emergency situations should be taken care of right away. Calling back prospective customers who are looking to buy is also a top concern. Paying your bills heads the list, too. What the heck do you do first?

After you get all your messages from the answering machine or voicemail and have checked the fax machine, you're ready to set your priorities. Don't start making callbacks until you've organized what you'll do first. If you try to call back all 42 people, including your Aunt Frieda who just called to say hi, pretty soon it will be lunchtime, and some priorities that should have been taken care of in the morning have gone right out the window.

When organizing your to-do list, make two categories:

- **Category 1, a.k.a., The Now Category.** Emergencies and time-sensitive projects need to be addressed first. Anything else is Category 2.
- **Category 2, a.k.a., Pencil It In.** Don't just list everything else that needs to get done, schedule a time for getting it done. Your bills can be taken care of during quiet times such as late afternoon when it's difficult to get people on the phone. Other things may be more pressing.

The trick to time management is not to overmanage. Write things down on a to-do list, your calendar, or whatever system you've created, and just do them. If you're not careful, you might spend too much time scheduling everything, and then you'll have to move it around again when it doesn't get done because you've spent too much time scheduling. Things will come up during the day that you haven't planned for—that's a certainty.

Being a small business owner is not your ordinary desk job, that's for sure. You will probably spend less time at your desk than you even imagined. Make the most of the time you do spend at your desk and plan your day as best you can. You can't beat the clock and build Rome in a day; know your limits. You can work out a schedule that uses your time wisely and that wrestles the concept of time into submission. At least for the time being.

STICK IT ON THE WALL

Files are great for filing things that have been completed, but they're not the best for staying on top of things. If something is out of sight, it will be out of mind. The best thing to do when you need to refer to something often is to stick it on the wall. Put it in plain view and it will stay fresh in your mind.

KEEP IT SAFE: STASH YOUR CASH

If you have a cash-based business, you need to take extra caution. Follow these guidelines:

- If you have to chase customers down for payments and they pay in cash, try to bring someone with you.
- If you're collecting a lot of cash at once, try to vary the route from month to month.
- If possible, try not to carry a lot of cash on you at once. Break up the cash collecting by bringing back cash to the office.
- If you collect a lot of cash, deposit the money quickly.
- If you find that you cannot get to the bank quick enough, consider buying a safe. Get one that either bolts down or is ironclad heavy.

KEEPING RECORDS

Although you will use your computer to create records needed in daily operations, you won't have everything on the computer. Probably the most important thing you can do to run a tight ship is to keep thorough and efficient records. Realistically, it is nearly impossible to keep track of every single possible thing you do in a day. And every single thing doesn't need to be recorded. Just every single important thing such as conversations with customers, conversations with their references, credit checks, copies of key agreements, money exchanges, and expenses and. Keep a copy of anything you give to a customer including his or her contracts, receipts, credit checks, and any correspondence or letters sent to the customer.

TIP

Banking on the Internet is becoming increasingly popular. You can also set up bill payments online. Some bill-paying sites and banks have features that allow you to see what is being paid before the money gets removed. Before signing on, make sure you know where and when your money is taken out of your hands.

HERE'S YOUR RECEIPT

Always give out receipts and keep a copy for yourself when receiving payment for anything. You can pick up an inexpensive carbon-copy receipt book at any office-supply store. When you fill out a receipt for payment, make sure you include the date, the amount, what the payment is for, who it's from, and any balance due. Always remember to sign your receipts.

CUSTOMER LOGGING

Have a separate notebook, binder, or computer file to record each customer's history. Be sure to include key contact information.

Make sure you also have a place to record any conversations, and services performed. Anything that will help protect against claims of noncompliance or retaliation or that will help in a dispute should be written down. Better to take a few minutes to record an issue than to try and defend yourself in court without any proof.

In addition to a log book (or instead of, whichever works better for you), keep a separate file folder for each customer. In the folder, keep a copy of key contracts and agreements, credit-check report, and all info to come.

THE 30-SECOND RECAP

- Acquire the basic supplies and more, such as a speakerphone, record-keeping files, and an easy-to-use computer, for an efficient office.
- The trick to time management is not to overmanage. Write things down on a to-do list, your calendar, or whatever system you've created, and just do them.
- Keep important records that pertain to your tenants, repairs, and anything that will protect you in court or from going to court. Keeping efficient accounting records will make tax time easier.

Zoning, Permits, and Other Regulations to Consider

Market research reported by Link Resources Corporation shows that more than 32 million people run either full-time or part-time businesses from their homes. Most of them require only a local business license or permit. They are easy to obtain, normally entailing a short visit to the local courthouse. Fees, if any, are minimal. It's easy to determine what your local licensing requirements are; simply call or visit your city or county government offices for information.

It may be inconceivable to you that your home-based consulting service or needlework business would have to comply with any of the numerous local, state, and federal regulations, but in all likelihood, it will. A word of caution: Avoid the temptation to ignore regulatory details; you may avert some red tape in the short term, but you could encounter obstacles as your business grows. Taking the time to research the applicable regulations, which we look at in this section, is as important as knowing your marketing strategy.

THE ZONING LAWS

Zoning requirements are those laws that regulate how property can be used and, in some cases, certain activities that may not be permitted. If you intend to operate a business from your home, be sure to check local zoning requirements as well as any property covenants before you apply for any permit or license.

Zoning ordinances may be one of the biggest obstacles you'll face if you plan to operate your business from your home. Restrictive zoning in most residential areas is designed to prevent business activity that may create noise, pollution, and traffic; add commercial vehicle traffic; or bring to the residential zone other activities normally associated with commercial or industrial zones.

Many residential zones do allow professional and service businesses to operate, along with other types of business that do not interfere with a clean and quiet environment. In some residentially zoned areas that permit such businesses, however, you may be prohibited from displaying a business sign of any kind.

The purpose of zoning ordinances is to designate specific areas (zones) within municipalities and counties for specific types of activities such as residential-only, agricultural, industrial, light industrial, heavy industrial, or in some cases, a mix of residential and commercial zones. The more populated an area is, the more likely it is that you'll find stricter regulations and enforcement of the zoning laws.

TIP

Agricultural, industrial, and commercial-residential areas should not pose a problem in setting up your new business. If you rent, even if you are in a nonrestricted area, be sure to check your lease. Some leases have clauses preventing tenants from operating a business; to do so would be in violation of your lease.

Some "residential-only" zoned areas are so restricted that no business activity whatsoever is allowed, but this is very rare. In most cases, there are provisions for residential business situations. This option is becoming more prevalent with the tremendous growth in the home-based business market. Worst-case scenario: You live in a residential-only area. What do you do? Ignore the zoning and go ahead anyway? Think again. What if a jealous rival or neighbor reports you? The authorities investigate you and send one of those dreaded "cease-and-desist" letters. (People are rarely fined unless they continue operating after an official warning.) Don't do it: Instead, think positively and be proactive.

DEALING WITH LOCAL BUILDING AND ZONING OFFICIALS

There's a certain amount of administrative discretion under building codes and zoning ordinances—enough, certainly, that it can help greatly to have the administrators on your side. Here are some ideas for accomplishing this:

- Call or visit the zoning department. Get all the details on your zoning regulations. Treat it as one of the things you have to do to before you start your business. Make sure that you understand everything—if you don't, get answers.
- Find out what the procedure is for pursuing a change.
- Find out if a lawyer is needed to present your case to the zoning board.
- Find out how long the time is from petition to decision.
- Do some homework. Find out if other home businesses operate in your area—if so, enlist their support. Speak with the SBA, your local chamber of commerce, or local business organizations to enlist as much support as possible.
- Plan your strategy. Use the codes to your advantage. Let's say that your business will provide sales tax revenue, but you will not have retail customers coming to your house. You won't add noise or traffic congestion to the neighborhood, or cause pollution or damage, and there will be no visible changes to your property that in any way indicate that it houses a home-based business. Explain that you are doing the same thing you always did when it was just a hobby; the only difference is

that now you'll be taking orders for your work, packing up your products, and taking them to the post office. If possible, get nearby neighbors to write letters supporting you, and agreeing that your business will not be a nuisance or destroy the quality of life on your block. Act now to avoid any delays in the time schedule for opening your business.

THE DECISION IS NOT NECESSARILY FINAL

If you get an adverse decision from the local planning commission, for example, don't give up. You may be able to have a board of zoning adjustment or have a board of appeals interpret the zoning ordinance in a way that's favorable to you. Alternatively, you may be able to obtain a variance (a special exception to a zoning law) if a strict interpretation of the ordinance causes a hardship. In some cases, you can get a conditional use permit, which lets you use the property in question for your kind of business as long as you meet certain conditions set down by the administrative panel.

TIP

There's a certain amount of administrative discretion under building codes and zoning ordinances—enough, certainly, that it can help greatly to have the administrators on your side. "No" is not always the final answer.

In dealing with administrators, and especially with appeals boards, it is important to have the support of neighbors and others in your community. A favorable petition signed by most other businesses in your immediate area, or oral expressions of support from half a dozen neighbors can make the difference between success and failure at an administrative hearing.

CERTIFICATE OF OCCUPANCY

If you're planning to occupy a building for a new business, you may have to apply for a Certificate of Occupancy (commonly called a CO or a C of O) from a city or county zoning department. For more information, contact the county or city office in your area. You may also try going to your state home page, at www.sba.gov/world/states.html. When you open the page, just select your state; then locate its search feature and type in "certificate of occupancy" or "county information."

BE PREPARED FOR OBSTACLES

In some communities, you must get a zoning-compliance permit before you start your business at a given location. Other communities simply wait for someone to complain before zoning compliance gets looked at.

> **CAUTION**
>
> Keep in mind that by applying for a construction permit for remodeling, or by filing for a tax ID or a business license with your municipality, you may trigger an investigation of zoning compliance.

Applying for a tax number can trigger obstacles. Some entrepreneurs suggest getting a post office box in a commercially zoned area before applying for tax numbers, permits, or licenses, and then using it as your legal business address.

In addition to zoning laws that regulate traffic, environmental factors, and the placement of signs, there are historic district restrictions in some communities. They may keep you from modifying the exterior of a building or even changing the paint color without permission from a board of administrators. Years ago, people tried to argue in court that such regulation of aesthetics wasn't a proper governmental function, in that it wasn't related to the protection of the public health and safety. However, carefully drawn ordinances seeking to preserve the special appeal of historic districts have tended to survive such legal challenges.

BUILDING CODES

For anything but the most minor renovation (such as putting in track lighting or installing shelves), you're likely to need a permit—maybe several—from the building and safety department that enforces building ordinances and codes. Often, separate permits are issued for separate parts of a construction or remodeling project, including permits for electrical, plumbing, and mechanical (heating and ventilating) work. If you don't have experience in these areas, you may need a licensed contractor to help you discover the requirements for your construction or remodeling project. Building codes are amended frequently, and each revision seems to put new restrictions and requirements on the building owners.

PERMITS AND LICENSES

There are licensing and permit requirements at all levels of government: federal, state, regional, county, and city. It is not always easy to discover exactly what licenses and permits you'll need, but it's very important. Thoroughly research this issue before you start a new business, complete the purchase of a business, change locations, or remodel or expand your operation. If you do not, you may face expenses and hassles that you had not anticipated.

You'll probably need a basic license or permit for your business, and you may need one or more specialized licenses. This is especially likely if you serve or sell food, liquor, or firearms; work with hazardous materials; or discharge any materials into the air or water.

CAUTION

For most small businesses, permits are a regulatory fact of life. From a basic business license to a toxic-waste disposal permit, businesses must know which license or permit to apply for and how to navigate the sometimes complex application process.

Each state has its own system of licensing, as does each unit of local government. Obviously, it is impossible to provide a comprehensive list of every permit and license in the United States. Fortunately, there are some general principles to help you learn about and comply with the licensing or regulation requirements that may affect your business.

Your business may be required to have one or more of the following licenses or permits:

- **Business license.** Check with the city and county governments to determine which business licenses are required.

- **Health, fire, and other special permits.** Any business that processes or sells food to the public must have a health department permit. Businesses that handle flammable materials or have large numbers of people on their premises may also be required to have a fire department permit. If you expect to discharge any substance into the air, sewer system, or local waterways, you may have to obtain a special permit from agencies controlling pollution and environmental health.

- **Occupational permit.** Most states require special licensing, which may entail a written or oral examination for businesses in certain categories, such as occupations that involve direct physical contact with customers (hairdressing, massage, or medical treatment are examples), or businesses that involve special technical expertise that may be related to consumer safety or health (plumbing, electrical work, auto repairs, pest control, engineering, and dry cleaning are examples). This also applies to agencies involved in real estate, insurance, and collections.

- **Sales tax permit.** Those who sell products directly to consumers must usually collect a sales tax. (Food products are exempt from a sales tax in some states.) If you sell products only to wholesalers, retailers, or other middlemen, you usually do not have to collect a sales tax, but you must maintain tax-exemption forms. Some states require those who sell services to collect sales taxes. Many states require that you pay a bond or an advance deposit against sales taxes to be collected when you first apply for a sales tax number.

- **Federal tax ID.** Form SS-4 is the application for an employer identification number (EIN), which should be filed by every business. If you are a sole proprietor, you may use your own Social Security number rather than a separate employer identification number, but it is generally recommended that even sole proprietors obtain an EIN, especially if they plan to hire employees or retain independent contractors. This is one good way to keep your business and your personal affairs separate.

- **Federal licensing.** This is required for gun dealers, security and investment brokers and advisers, radio and television stations, and drug manufacturers.

- **Licensing based on products sold.** Some licenses for businesses are based on the products sold. For example, there often are special licenses for businesses that sell liquor, food, lottery tickets, gasoline, or firearms.

GOVERNMENT REGULATIONS AND YOUR BUSINESS

Bear in mind that regulations vary by industry. If you're in the food service business, for example, you'll have to deal with the health department. If you use chemical solvents, you'll have environmental compliance to meet. Carefully investigate the regulations that affect your industry. Being out of compliance could leave you legally unprotected, may lead to expensive penalties, and could jeopardize your business.

Double-check license and permit rules. When you investigate the type of licenses and permits that you need for your business, check directly with the appropriate governmental agencies. Never rely on the fact that an existing business similar to yours did not need a license or had to meet only minimal building code requirements. Laws and ordinances are amended frequently, generally to impose more stringent requirements. Often an existing business is allowed to continue under the old rules, but new businesses must meet the higher standards.

For obvious reasons, do not rely on the advice of real estate agents, business brokers, the seller of a business, or anyone else with a financial interest in having a deal go through.

WHAT'S THE WORST THAT COULD HAPPEN?

In a worst-case scenario, if you fail to meet government regulations, you could be prevented from operating your planned business at a particular location but still be obligated to pay rent or make mortgage payments. For example, what if you sign a five-year lease for business space and then discover that the location is not zoned properly for your type of business? What if you start a catering business and find out that you can't get a liquor license? Or suppose that you rent or buy business space thinking that you can afford to remodel or expand it, without realizing that remodeling means you must comply with all current ordinances? You may have to pay for $10,000 worth of improvements to comply with the federal *Americans with Disabilities Act,* or $5,000 for a state-of-the-art waste-disposal system.

If you lease in a plaza or a mall, in most cases, you'll be paying for all the improvements, repairs, and maintenance, so check your lease carefully before you sign.

In short, license and permit requirements can affect where you locate your business, how much you'll have to spend for remodeling, and whether you'll have to provide off-street parking. If zoning requirements are too restrictive, you may even decide to avoid the hassle and move somewhere where you don't have to fight city hall—literally—for the right to do business. Similarly, if building codes require extensive and expensive remodeling to bring an older building up to current standards, you may want to look for newer space that already complies with building and safety laws.

TIP

The Consumer Information Center (www.pueblo.gsa.gov) has pamphlets such as "Americans with Disabilities Act: Guide for Small Businesses," "General Information Concerning Patents," "Guide to Business Credit for Women, Minorities, and Small Businesses," "Resource Directory for Small Business Management," "Running a Small Business," "Selling a Business," and "Starting a Business."

CHECK YOUR STATE BUSINESS LICENSES

Many types of licenses exist. You need one to operate legally almost everywhere. If your business is located within incorporated city limits, you must obtain a license from the city; if you're outside the city limits, you must obtain a license from the county. For more information, contact the county or city office in your area, or visit your state home page, at www.sba.gov/world/states.html, using keywords "business license" or "county information."

PROTECT YOUR SAFETY

To protect the safety of your employees, customers, and community, note the following:

- Beware of hazards in your industry.
- Implement safety procedures.
- Regularly and thoroughly maintain equipment and machinery.
- Use and maintain safety equipment.
- Be alert for fire hazards.
- Keep a first-aid kit in your work area.
- Think safety. Train yourself to monitor safety conditions in your work areas.

Don't think you're exempt; even the most experienced people have accidents! John, a wood crafter, worked for 32 years in his shop. One day while rushing to get some orders finished, he cut off three fingers on a table saw. Why? Because he didn't take the time to engage his safety shield; after all, he just had one more board to cut. Debra, a 10-year veteran candle-maker had another preventable accident. She had a 12-quart kettle of hot wax that she wanted to remove from the stove, so she put on big oven mitts that had large rings sewn into them for hanging. As she picked up the kettle, one of the rings caught on the stove gas grate and caused her to spill hot wax on one of her arms and her chest. What was as painful as the burns was the fact that it had happened before (without injury). She had meant to cut those rings off the mitts, but she just hadn't stopped long enough to do it!

OCCUPATIONAL SAFETY AND HEALTH ACT RULES AND REGULATIONS

As an employer, you are responsible under the *Occupational Safety and Health Act (OSHA)* to provide a workplace free from recognized hazards that are causing or are likely to cause death or serious physical harm to your employees. You must comply with standards, rules, and regulations issued by OSHA under the act. You must be familiar with the standards and must make copies available to employees for review upon their request.

Most employers of 11 or more employees are required to maintain records of occupational injuries and illnesses as they occur. Employers with 10 or fewer employees, and employers in certain industries, regardless of size, are exempt from keeping such records unless they are selected by the Bureau of Labor Statistics (BLS) to participate in the Annual Survey of Occupational Injuries and Illnesses.

TIP

OSHA record-keeping is not required for employers in the retail trade or in the finance, insurance, real estate, or service industries (Standard Industrial Classification [SIC] 522-89). The exceptions are building material and garden supplies (SIC 52), general merchandise and food stores (SIC 53 and 54), hotels and other lodging places (SIC 70), repair services (SIC 75 and 76), amusement and recreation services (SIC 79), and health services (SIC 80).

OSHA's SMALL BUSINESS SAFETY MANAGEMENT SERIES

Even if you do not have employees, OSHA may be able to provide you with valuable tips to help you design a safe work environment for your business. Perhaps you work with chemicals or paints that require proper ventilation. What about safety glasses, if you use a grinder or a sander, or if you work with caustic materials? What fire safety measures do you have in place if you work with torches, hot plates, or gas burners? The flyer for small business employers "Keeping Your Workplace Safe: Q's & A's for Small Business Employers" provides an overview of OSHA services and can be downloaded from OSHA at www.osha-slc.gov/OshDoc/Additional.html.

THE 30-SECOND RECAP

- Wherever you decide to locate your business, you must first check the zoning laws to be sure that it will be allowed.

- Zoning regulations can be amended, so don't accept "no" without pursuing the matter further.

- Your business probably will need a license or a permit, and possibly several of them, so be sure to find out exactly what's required before you proceed.

Technology Considerations

Selecting a Computer System and Office Equipment

Naturally, some businesses are completely dependent on computers—not only computer consultants, but also writers, graphic designers, stock analysts, and newsletter publishers. Even if your business isn't tied into technology, you may find it difficult, if not impossible, to run your business without one. Today the computer is used for most mainstream business-type stuff: keeping books and records, printing out invoices, writing correspondence, faxing, and even sending and receiving e-mail.

The computer isn't the only piece of equipment you may want or need for your line of work. There may be other high-tech items to help you run your office efficiently, like a fax machine or a super-high-speed copier. In this section, you learn about the computer and what model is right for you. You'll also see whether it pays to buy or lease a computer or other equipment.

WHICH COMPUTER'S FOR YOU?

Buying a computer is like buying a car—you have to think about how much you'll use it and for what kinds of things before you make the purchase. Do you need a rugged, expensive pickup truck for a small construction business or a used motorcycle for an around-the-town courier service? Does your computer run your business or just spit out six invoices at the end of every month? Whatever the focus of your business is, you'll probably need a computer if you don't already have one. According to a study by the National Foundation for Women Business Owners (NFWBO), 73 percent of home businesses use computers.

You may be a business owner who's completely dependent on a computer—it's the heart and soul of your business. Or you may use a computer only as a tool to help you with billing, writing letters, and bookkeeping. What you want your computer to do for you will affect, to some extent, the type of machine you get.

If your business is focused on the computer, you want to get the best machine you can for your money. Judy, who puts out a monthly newsletter, needs a computer that has enough memory to support her desktop publishing software. Don is an economic forecaster who runs his business from home. He needs to continually crunch numbers, which requires both memory and speed. His computer has to be top of the line.

TIP

If you already own a computer that you've been using to balance your checkbook and play solitaire, you don't need to buy a new one for business. Just "convert" your computer to business use, upgrading its memory and processing speed to handle more work if necessary. But if your mate and/or kids regularly use the computer, you may want a separate computer for your business. That way you'll always have access to it (and the kids, while playing Intergalactic Space Nerds, won't accidentally trash that 50-page report you just finished).

On the other hand, Jane uses the computer to do only a few everyday clerical things (for bookkeeping or letter writing); she can get by with a slower, less-expensive model. Someone like Jane might be able to buy a used computer for her home-based business. Used machines can cost only a few hundred dollars, much less than the thousand or more it costs for a new computer. You can even buy used computers from a reputable dealer and get a warranty.

COMPUTERS MADE SIMPLE

Fifth graders today can sit down at a computer and whip through some new program they've found in two seconds flat. Some people—especially kids who've grown up in the computer age—are very good with computers. You may be one, and if you are, you certainly don't need to read this section to tell you about the ins and outs of computers.

But if you're just starting up a home-based business and you've never worked with a computer, you probably need a lesson to brush up on your skills. If you don't have a clue about how to work a computer and what it can do for you, you need to learn so you can make an informed decision on the model you buy or lease.

If you're shopping now for a computer, decide in advance what you expect to use it for and how much you expect to use it. If you think you'll be doing a lot of number crunching or heavy word processing, the PC-type of computer (the Dells, Gateways, HPs, IBMs) are probably for you. If you're doing graphic design or publishing, however, the Macs from Apple may be a better choice. Then rank how great your demand will be for speed and storage, and use one of these sample hardware scenarios as you wander the store aisles. Don't let some computer store clerk intimidate you: Pick the type of computer system and the level of computer you need, and then hand the guy this book and point to one of the PCs below:

- **High usage.** A Pentium 4 processor, 3.6-GHz machine with a built-in CD-ROM or DVD drive, fax/modem of at least 56 bps, 512 MB of RAM, and a 400-gigabyte hard drive. Expect to pay around $2,500 for this baby.

- **Medium usage.** A Pentium 4 processor, 3.4-GHz processor with a built-in CD-ROM or DVD drive, fax/modem of at least 56 bps, 256 MB of RAM, and at least a 400-gigabyte hard drive. You might find one of these for less than $1,500.

- **Low usage.** At least a Pentium 4 processor with 2.8-GHz processor, external CD-ROM drive if needed, fax/modem of 56 bps, 256 MB of RAM, and 250 MB of hard drive memory. You will pay around $500 for this model.

For the Macs, you'll want to look at eMacs and iMacs. Comparable models to the above will run you about the same prices.

How do you know whether the computer you're thinking about is going to keep your business humming? Make your computer decision by first looking at what you need to do and the software programs you'll need to run to do those things. Then pick out a computer with enough space and power to do them.

CAUTION

If you already own an older Mac or other Apple computer, be aware that upgrading isn't all that easy. Your old files aren't easily understood by a new machine and your old add-ons, like a modem, may be incompatible with the Mac G5.

You wouldn't buy a car without reviewing *Consumer Reports* and checking out the list of features on the sticker, so get educated before you choose your computer, too. You can learn about computers by visiting computer superstores and asking questions. You can read up on computers in books and magazines. And you can ask other people who already own computers and use them for business what they like and don't like. Or you can go to the real experts: Ask your kids!

Buy or Lease?

Don't feel like laying out thousands of dollars at the moment? Relax, you don't have to buy your computer. You can lease one. There are compelling reasons to go one way or the other:

TIP

There's not much difference in terms of total dollars between buying the computer over time (financing the purchase) and leasing it. The monthly payments are about the same (although the lease alternative may be slightly higher). This is because the life of a computer is rather short. So your cash flow can be helped by either buying over time or leasing.

■ **Buying.** If you buy a computer, you own it. You can purchase the computer with one payment or finance all or part of it. Obviously, with financing, the interest you pay raises the total price of the computer. After you've paid off what you've financed, the machine is yours free and clear. Dream systems, with all the features you could want, run upward of $3,000; budget systems that perform adequately are less than $1,000.

You can ease the sticker shock if you buy used equipment. There's an increasing market for pre-owned computers. In fact, today 1 in 10 home office businesspeople buy used systems. The reason for this is simple: cost. The cost of reconditioned computers is about 40 percent less than the cost of new ones. Most pre-owned computers bought from companies that recondition them come with a warranty ranging from 60 to 90 days, including parts and labor. Almost-new may be good for a second system (for use if something goes wrong with your new computer or if you have an employee who needs a computer to work on occasionally).

TIP

Using more than two computers in your home (with you in one room and your spouse or kids in another)? Think "network." This allows you to effectively join the computers together so you can easily pass information from one machine to the other. As an added bonus, you only need one printer. To network, you'll need special software, so do your homework before you join your computer forces.

■ **Leasing.** Most small business owners consider leasing when multiple computers or servers are being purchased at the same time. If you lease a computer, you have the right to use it for the period or term of the lease. At the end of the lease, it's bye-bye computer (unless you exercise your right to buy it at that time at a fixed price). With leasing, you generally don't have to pay much up front (just a deposit of a month or two). Your monthly cost (depending, of course, on the system you select) can be less than $100. So cost is the main attraction of leasing. The cash you don't have to put into the computer when you lease it (as opposed to buying it) is available for other business needs—advertising or payroll, for example.

Remember that current tax laws allow qualifying small businesses to deduct capital expenditures, which include the cost of computer equipment, in the year they are purchased. There is an annual limitation to this deduction so check with your accountant. The savings from this incentive may significantly factor your decision whether to buy or lease.

TIP

It's a good idea to take a service contract for repairs and maintenance on your computer. It's pretty cheap. (Dell offers one on its computers for less than $100 for on-site—in home—service for three years.) And you know you'll get quick service—an essential because a computer that's down can mean you're out of business until it's repaired.

Leasing equipment doesn't let you off the hook for keeping it in good repair. You also have to take out insurance to cover the cost of the computer in case it's damaged or stolen. If you have any questions about a lease, it's a good idea to have an attorney look it over for you.

TIP

Computers go out of date faster than shoe styles. According to some statistics, businesses should expect to replace their computers every 27 months. This is because technology's been moving so fast that older computers become almost obsolete in no time. Businesses that want to keep up with the Joneses (and be able to handle new software applications) must replace old computers with faster and better ones.

LEASING MADE EASY

If you've ever tried to read the fine print on a car lease, you know they're written by and for lawyers. The same is true of leases for computers. If you know what you're looking for, however, it can help you get the best lease terms and not get trapped by the fine print.

- **Lease term.** Typically, computer leases are for three- to five-year terms, but you may be able to negotiate for shorter or longer leases. Because a computer becomes "old" in less than three years, don't take a lease for any longer than that.

CAUTION

Signing a lease is like signing a pact with Lucifer—it can't be canceled or shortened once it starts. If you want to pay off the lease early, there may be prepayment penalties. If you go bust, you're still responsible for paying off the lease. Even if your business is incorporated, you may be personally responsible for payments on the lease. Most companies won't lease equipment to a small business unless you, the owner, cosign or guarantee the lease payments.

- **Documentation fees.** They get you coming and going. There are fees to write up the lease and then there are fees to wind up the lease. These can be as modest as $50 or a whopping 2 percent of the lease itself.
- **Security deposit.** To make sure that you make the lease payments on time, the company giving you the lease will usually require a security deposit. Typically, this deposit covers two months of the lease. (Some may only require a one-month deposit.)
- **Buy-out option.** Most leases give you the chance to buy the computer at the end of the lease. Your buy-out price is set in the lease, but you may still be able to negotiate a lower price when it comes time to make the decision at the end of the lease.

SOFTWARE: IT MAKES YOUR COMPUTER GO

A computer's only a machine. The thing that makes all this hardware work is software. There is operating system software such as Windows or Linux that basically tells your computer how to wake up in the morning, buzz, and whir; then there is software you use to get things done, such as word processing or spreadsheet programs. The operating system software is probably already on your computer when you buy it and you don't have to worry about it; when it comes to the other kind of software, you've got some decisions to make.

TIP

When you buy a computer today, you usually get the computer operating system, such as Windows XP, and a software package, such as Microsoft Office, factory installed so you have everything you need to get started.

Which software you get depends on your business needs. Today, several "office packages," called software suites, include word processors, spreadsheets, and more. Microsoft MS Office Professional includes Word (a powerful word processing program), Excel (a spreadsheet application), PowerPoint (a business presentation application), and Access (a database program); Corel's WordPerfect suite includes WordPerfect (another word processing program), QuattroPro (a spreadsheet application), and Corel Presentations. Although these office suites don't come cheap, they're integrated, meaning you can easily take files from one application and use them in another.

You can put together your own software package by buying separate products to meet your needs as they arise. For example, you can get Microsoft Word for your word processing and add Intuit's QuickBooks for your accounting software to keep track of your invoicing, bill paying, receivables, and payables.

CAUTION

Don't copy software from your next-door neighbor just to save a few bucks. Not only is it illegal (it's called copyright violation), your computer might catch a nasty virus.

WHO YOU GONNA CALL?

Computers, like any other machinery, can have problems and will eventually break down. But unlike the broken faucet in the bathroom, you may not have the tools or knowledge to repair them. You may have to rely on experts to service your computer.

Be sure you understand what you've got coming to you in the way of service when you buy or lease a computer. Will the store stand behind it and provide technical support? For how long? If you buy your machine through mail order, what recourse do you have? Will you have to go back to the manufacturer for help?

TIP

The stuff you put into your computer is vital to your business. Protect it by backing up files. Store your backup in a safe place. Use a fireproof safe in your home office or store your backup off-site (such as in a bank safe-deposit box).

Many computer problems can be handled over the telephone. More often than not, the problems stem from software. Sometimes the way the computer is configured (that just means the settings you use to make it run) is the problem. These things can be tweaked to correct the problem, and a phone conversation might do the trick.

Most computer manufacturers have technical support over the telephone. Software companies also provide telephone support to handle problems in their software. In the past, telephone support was typically a toll-free number, but now you'll find that you usually have to pay for it. What's more, if you're put on hold (a common occurrence), the cost of the call and the waiting time can be expensive. But the phone cost is certainly less than the cost of a house call by a technician you find in the Yellow Pages or through a referral from your local computer store who may charge $60 an hour or more. Even if you've paid for an on-site service contract, the tech won't come until after you've gone the telephone support route.

PERIPHERALS R US

Just when you think you've got it all in hand—the computer and the software—there's more. There are peripherals, which include all computer-related equipment except the guts of the computer—the processor, and the memory. All computers need some peripherals to operate them—a mouse, cables, and a keyboard, for example. Other peripherals are pretty essential: It's hard to live without surge protectors (gizmos to keep electrical surges in the line from damaging your computer) and a printer.

As for other peripherals—scanners or back-up drives—it's your call. What does your business need? What can you afford to buy?

PRETTY IN PRINT

A printer can cost as little as a few hundred dollars or as much as several thousand dollars, depending on quality, speed, and other considerations.

Laser printers are the Mercedes Benz of printers. They have speed and the best quality reproduction of images on the page. They're also very quiet when they're running. Like Mercedes, laser printers cost the most because you get the most in terms of reproduction. If you print a newsletter with a lot of graphic images and embossed text effects, you need a laser printer. The same is true if you print pictures that demand good resolution. There are color laser printers, but their high price tag (around $3,000) makes them worthwhile only if your business is printing color brochures or other color graphics.

TIP

Should you go for a color printer or the standard black-and-white printer? Letters and invoices don't require color. Only businesses that regularly produce brochures, reports, proposals, and newsletters need to consider color—a feature that raises the cost of the printer. And the ink cartridges on the color printer will cost you more in the long run.

Inkjet (also called deskjet) printers are the next best thing to laser printers. They also have a fairly high quality of reproduction. They print in color. They don't run as fast as a laser printer and their quality isn't as good, but they cost less (as low as $250).

The Yugos of printers are dot matrix. If you still own a black-and-white TV or a rotary phone, you'll love these. Of the three types of printers, this is the noisiest, slowest, and has the poorest output quality. However, it's also the cheapest (around $150). If you're only printing out invoices, a dot matrix may do. But for the money, an extra hundred bucks to spring for a deskjet is a good investment in your business image.

WHAT A GREAT PICTURE!

Monitors come in black-and-white and color, although all computers but low-end laptops now use color monitors. Like TVs, monitors come in all sizes, from as small as 13-inch screens to 17-inch screens or even larger. If you're doing desktop publishing and use your screen to get a good look at a design layout, you want as large a screen as you can afford (which is up to 21 inches).

Monitors also use different resolutions, which is a fancy word for how clear the image is. Consider looking into flat-screen monitors, which cut down on glare (but usually cost a bit more).

Cost depends on the quality of the monitor, resolution, and size. The better the quality, and the larger the screen—you guessed it—the higher the cost.

The newest type of screen is the LCD. It takes up a lot less desk space and looks great, but you sacrifice some resolution. Of course, as technology improves, expect resolution of LCD monitors to get better.

Back Me Up!

You'll never realize the significance of maintaining a good back-up system until you lose data. Backing up is always an afterthought until there's a problem. Then it becomes the most important thing in the world! Having a reliable back-up system is absolutely required for a small business.

There are several ways to back up (keep a separate record of) the data in your computer:

- **You can save your files on disks.** With high-density disks, you can now store a lot of information on a single disk. For example, all the words in this book were saved on just one disk! But if you have big files, especially graphics, storage on disks might not be for you. Fewer people backup to disk now, as the storage space is minimal, and often disks go corrupt, get lost or get broken.

- **You can use a memory key.** A backup method that's really becoming popular is the memory key. Just plug this keychain size device into the back of your computer or laptop and you can instantly copy megabytes of data to it. Then unplug it and carry it around in your pocket if you like. The device can work with any computer that has a USB port, which is very standard nowadays.

- **You can get a special peripheral called a tape backup, which allows you to record your computer's information on tape.** Relied on for many years, this method is the least expensive alternative and still very popular.

- **You can back up your computer data onto another drive.** The information is recorded on a disk that looks a lot like a floppy disk in a thicker plastic box—this is commonly called a "zip" drive. There are also other ways to store data, such as on Flash USB drives (they're the size of a keychain and plug into the back of your computer) or an external hard drive that also connects into the back of your computer. Some of these drives can hold gigabytes of data. Remember that another drive can also be another computer's hard drive on your network too!

- **You can back up your computer data onto CDs and DVDs.** CDs and DVDs have become very inexpensive to buy. "Burning" files to this media has become an extremely popular way to back up data. All you need to make sure is that your computer has a "read/write" CD or DVD drive and includes software to copy the files.

CD-ROM AND DVD

Not all software comes on a floppy disk. Most now comes on a compact disc that looks like an audio CD. CD-ROMs can contain a vast amount of information—the contents of an entire encyclopedia can fit on a single CD!

A CD-R disk means that, once recorded, it can never be re-recorded. The data can only be read for it, not written to it. A CD-RW disk allows you to read and write repeatedly to the same disk. What you see is all you get. As mentioned previously, however, much of today's software is now on CD-ROM. For instance, if you want to use a program to prepare your tax return, you'll probably use CD-ROM–based software.

CD-ROM software requires a special CD player (typically installed inside the computer). CD-ROM players are described by speed: 2X (two-speed), 4X (four-speed), 8X (eight-speed), and 12X (12-speed).

DVDs are devices that let you not only run programs but also play music and view DVD movies when you're on your coffee break.

MUSIC AND PICTURES

Any software programs that contain sound as well as visual effects, whether on CD, DVD, or a floppy, require a sound card in your computer to translate the sound information. There are different sound cards (with different prices). And on top of that, you'll need speakers to hear the sound.

If you want to play the neatest video game or watch the latest box-office release, you also need a video card to handle all those pretty pictures. New computers will all come with a built-in sound and video card and the software (called drivers) to run them.

FAXES AND MODEMS KEEP YOU IN TOUCH

Communication from a home office to the outside world is essential for running most businesses. To stay in contact, you need to be able to communicate with other computers as well as with other people. Two ways to communicate are via fax and via e-mail.

A fax lets you send images to another fax machine over telephone lines. The fax mechanism can be internal to your computer, in which case it sends the fax using your computer's modem. A software program lets your computer act as a fax machine to transmit information. Standalone fax machines are discussed later in this chapter.

A modem lets your computer communicate with another computer not only to send faxes, but also to get online. Today, a modem is becoming an essential piece of equipment because you need it to access the Internet. As discussed later in this section, small businesses can use the Internet to get information, buy and sell goods and services, and communicate with other business owners. You can also use e-mail to leave messages for clients, customers, and suppliers.

A modem can be either internal or external. An external modem takes up a little more desk space but can be used with your next computer when you upgrade your equipment. Of course, the modem may also become dated because newer models have faster speeds. Currently, the newest models have speeds of 56 KB. The faster you can upload and download files, the less time you're online, saving you online charges if you pay by the minute.

Depending on where you live, you may also be able to use a cable modem to connect to the Internet and gain access through such companies as Verizon or Comcast.

If you opt for high-speed Internet connections, such as ISDN (Integrated Services Digital Network) or DSL (Digital Subscriber Line), your phone company will provide you with the necessary equipment as part of its connection package. ISDN and DSL are known as broadband services that allow you to be connected to the Internet at all times while still having access to your telephone or fax machine.

Scanning Your Way to Fame

Remember that flier some guy left on your windshield last Tuesday? It had a couple of photographs mixed in with the text. How did he do it? With a scanner. This is a machine that's connected to your computer by a cable. It transmits any image into your computer. After that image is in your computer, if you have software that can handle it, you can work with it like any other computer file, making changes, resizing the image, and so on.

Scanners can also digitize text—words on a page—into a computer file to save you typing it all in again. But to read the words, you need a special program, called OCR (optical character recognition), which lets you edit the text you've scanned into the computer. Do you need all this? If you're not a graphic designer or marketing type, probably not. But at least now you know what it is! Another great use of scanners is to store checks, bills, and other business documents. This way you can use your computer as an electronic filing cabinet!

Digital cameras may also be helpful for your business. These cameras let you input photos into your computer. (There's no developing necessary and scanning isn't required.) With models starting out at just over $100, you may not be able to afford not to buy one. If you sell antiques or want to easily put photos into your written materials, a digital camera may be ideal for you. Scanners are also great for real estate and website pictures, too!

OFFICE EQUIPMENT YOU CAN'T DO WITHOUT

Today a well-equipped home office has just about the same type of equipment as any office at General Motors. In addition to a computer, your home office should also have a copier and a fax machine (if you don't have one in your computer). There are also great online fax services, such as efax.com which can send and receive faxes for you via e-mail.

COPIERS

How did businesses operate before there were photocopiers? The type of copier you get depends on the number of copies you expect to make each month. If you don't plan to make many copies, you can get by with a personal copier. If you expect to make a lot of copies each month, you'll want to look at a more sophisticated model.

Like computers, you can buy or lease. The same benefits and cautions discussed earlier for buying or leasing computers also apply to copiers.

The price of copiers runs all over the place, depending on the complexity of the machine. A simple, personal-type copier is only a few hundred dollars. The bigger and better ones can run several thousand dollars.

TIP

Whether you buy or lease your copier, check out whether you're covered for servicing of the machine. Copiers—especially the more complex ones—notoriously break down and need servicing, usually when you've got a serious deadline staring you in the face.

MACHINES THAT WEAR MANY HATS

Today you can buy all-in-one machines that act as a fax, a copier, a scanner, and a printer. The upside to getting this type of machine is saving money. The cost of one multifunction machine is less than the total cost of three separate single-function machines. It also saves space.

The downside to getting a multifunction machine is total dependency on just one piece of equipment. If something goes wrong—say, for example, the fax portion of the machine malfunctions—you can be out of business until it's repaired. Forget copying or printing anything until the service guy shows up.

Because these tools are the foundation of your business, you don't want to cut corners here. Expect considerable wear and tear on your tools, and buy the best you can afford to get the longest use possible.

Extend the life of your equipment by keeping it in good condition. Set up regular service schedules to keep your machines in good repair.

TIP

There is good news: The cost of buying your office equipment can be offset by some tax savings. For example, you can deduct the cost of the equipment you buy up to a certain dollar limit each year.

THE 30-SECOND RECAP

- Almost all home-based businesses need a computer and other equipment to run professionally and efficiently.

- The computer you use for your business depends on the type of business you're in and on what you can afford.

- You can buy or lease most of your office equipment.

- Lining up service support for your computer, copier, and other equipment will let your business run smoothly even if you run into mechanical problems.

- The peripherals you select depend on the type of work you do in your office.

Selecting the Right Software for Your Business

Now that you've purchased the right equipment you're going to need the best software tools to help you do things quicker and better. In this section, we'll discuss the various business software applications available for your company.

ACCOUNTING SOFTWARE

Every small business needs to have accounting software. Even if you're not generating financial statements on a regular basis, you're still going to need to write checks, print out invoices, and keep track of your cash somewhere. And at the end of the year, your accountant will need to prepare your tax returns and will expect to receive your financial information in some readable form. Shoeboxes are becoming less and less acceptable.

A lot of great small business accounting software products can be purchased for less than $250 for a single user. The most popular accounting applications are QuickBooks (by the makers of Quicken, the personal financial software) and Peachtree. Other well-known applications include One-Write and MYOB.

All of these products have been on the marketplace for many years. Although they look somewhat different from each other, they basically all cover the same tasks that are essential for small business accounting. Make sure your application generates acceptable-looking documents, like checks and invoices, and can be customized.

CAUTION

Buying an accounting application is a very important purchase. You'll live with this system for a long time! Make sure you take the time to evaluate all your options and don't rush the process. Allow yourself the time to properly parallel your existing system. Make sure you get good references from the vendor.

These products can be purchased at most computer and office-supply stores, as well as online. Installing the products is quite easy on a single computer, and there are lots of local computer shops that can help you if you need. Involve your accountant when setting up your general ledger and transferring beginning balances. Take the time to set up a simple balance sheet and income statement so that you can start analyzing how your business is doing!

For small businesses that outgrow these entry-level products, there's plenty to choose from on the next "tier." A larger version of QuickBooks, called QuickBooks Enterprise, is available. In addition, Microsoft offers a product called Small Business Manager, and Best Software offers a product line called MAS90 or MAS200.

A great site to help you select your accounting software is www.findaccountingsoftware.com. This is a free service—you answer questions online and over the phone with a consultant, and they'll put your confidential information on their dealer network to accept proposals from their partners. Then you can sit back and wait for the software people to call you!

WORD PROCESSING AND ANALYSIS

You're going to need to generate letters, proposals, faxes, and analysis. To do this, you'll need a good word processor and spreadsheet. Microsoft Office dominates the marketplace. The full package of Microsoft Office retails for around $600. It includes Microsoft Word for word processing, Microsoft Excel for spreadsheet, Microsoft Outlook for e-mail (discussed shortly), Microsoft

PowerPoint for presentations, Microsoft Access for databases, and other modules. As of this writing, the most recent version of this product is Microsoft Office 2003.

Other competing office applications are available—for example, Corel's WordPerfect suite and Sun's StarOffice.

Make sure you get the licensing right. Microsoft Office requires a license for each installation. So if you have a small office of four people, you will need four licenses of Office to be in compliance.

Most small companies normally use a small percentage of the actual functionality of these products. It's very worthwhile to invest in a few days of training to make sure you know every feature available to you and how you can make your people more productive using these tools.

COMMUNICATIONS

Nowadays most companies have e-mail. You should, too. Your Internet service provider can provide you with e-mail accounts, but you're going to need e-mail software to retrieve, store, manage, and send messages. Microsoft Outlook is an e-mail application and comes as part of Microsoft Office. It's hugely popular. When you install Microsoft Outlook, it asks you some basic information about where to retrieve and send your e-mail. You may need to ask for help from an IT consultant to make sure these configurations are initially set up properly.

Besides Microsoft Outlook, there are other good e-mail applications, too, among them Eudora, Netscape, and Lotus Notes. There are also many free e-mail applications to choose from on the Internet. Quite a few Internet service providers also make web-based e-mail available to their customers, negating the need for any local e-mail software at all. Look into these options and match them with how you best work. In addition, some contact managers (discussed shortly) have their own built-in e-mail applications.

In addition to e-mail, Instant Messaging (IM) is becoming very popular. IM software can be downloaded for free from Yahoo, AOL, and MSN. After you set up an IM identity, you can chat, in real time, with other IM users. It's a quick way to communicate with others in your office as well as customers and vendors.

CONTACT MANAGEMENT

To manage all the people who come in contact with your business, buy contact-management software. The most popular applications available are ACT!, GoldMine, and Microsoft Outlook/Exchange.

With a contact manager, you can build a centralized database of customers, vendors, and other people who do business with you. This database can store fields of information about them, such as what products they buy or how many children they have. Workgroup contact managers, such as GoldMine or Outlook/Exchange, can then support calendars for you and your employees so that you can each know what the other is doing. A history of your activities can be stored for each contact, too.

Taking things to the next level, you can use your contact-management database to send mass mailings and e-mailings to selected groups. Applications such as GoldMine accept information from the Internet automatically and enable you to build automated processes to check up on customers and prospects without being told. There are even sales-forecasting and quoting tools available.

Contact-management software can be purchased at most office-supply stores or online. To make the best use of these products, you will probably need to have a consultant help you set up the database and provide some training.

REMOTE ACCESS

You and your employees probably want to work when you're at home, or on the road, too. You may have traveling sales people or a part-time workers who live far from the office. There's plenty of great technology available to help you do this.

When you want to set up a remote-access system, the first thing you'll need to establish is a virtual private network or VPN. You'll need to hire a network person to help you do this. A VPN is your own private slice of the Internet, fully encrypted and protected with your company's security policy. This helps ensure that no one else, besides your employees, gains unauthorized access to your network. After the VPN is set up, the remote user must log in to your network from his or her remote location.

Next there's remote-control software. Products such as gotomypc, PCAnywhere, and Laplink will allow your people to remotely connect to a PC in your office, right over the Internet, and take control of it. After a connection is established, it's as if the employee is sitting right there in the office. You can even watch what he or she is doing (kind of like one of those old-time pianos that play by themselves). Products such as gotomypc cost less than $20/month per user, and the other products are only a few hundred dollars to purchase outright. The downside to these products is that after a remote user "takes control" of a PC, no one else can exclusively use the PC until the remote user logs off.

Many small companies like to set up "thin client" access. This allows multiple remote users to access one PC or server at the company at the same time, without the other users noticing that they're there. Using a thin client, the remote users first log on to the VPN, then open up their web browser, type in the address of the thin client server, and then log on again. Another browser window will open with their own "virtual desktop" of icons for programs. Another benefit of using thin client technology is that nothing has to be installed on the remote user's computer. Popular thin client programs are Windows Terminal Server and Citrix.

If you're going to remotely access your business applications you'll need to setup a Virtual Private Network (VPN) to make sure that access is secure and encrypted.

SPECIALIZED APPLICATIONS

In addition to the software noted above, many small businesses purchase specialized applications for their company. Some examples are outlined in the following sections.

FAX SOFTWARE

Maybe you want to send faxes right from your desk and receive faxes right into your computer system? Fax software will help you do this. The most popular applications available are Winfax (www.symantec.com), OmniRush (www.omnirush.com), and Rightfax (www.rightfax.com). These programs also integrate directly with word processing and contact-management software programs, too.

UTILITIES

No system is complete without certain necessary utilities. You will need antivirus software to protect against malicious files. You'll also want to set up a good firewall to stop people from gaining unauthorized access to your system. Different from anti-virus software, which guards a computer against naughty files that may destroy data, a firewall is either hardware or software that prevents someone from the outside getting unauthorized access to your system. In addition, other utilities will help your system run faster and smoother. A good place to start your search for utilities is at www.buy.com

VERTICAL APPLICATIONS

You may not want to purchase a generic application and instead desire something that is really tailored for your industry. Chances are there's a vertical application out there to suit your needs. A vertical application is an application built specifically for an industry and usually includes an accounting interface, too. These applications are generally more expensive than off-the-shelf solutions and are sometimes made by small developers that offer fewer support resources, so be careful. Popular vertical applications include Top Producer (a contact management for the real estate industry), TimeSlips (a time and billing software for service companies), and Jobboss (a suite of manufacturing modules for the small and medium sized business).

CUSTOM APPLICATIONS

Sometimes you can't find exactly the business system you need. You may have to build one yourself. Many small business owners build their own system using database programs such as Microsoft Access or FoxPro. Building your own system is not for the faint of heart. You will probably want to get a programmer involved.

THE 30-SECOND RECAP

- There are many great accounting applications to choose from to help you run your business. These applications have been around a long time and are reliable.
- Contact management and communication software are quickly becoming required tools for today's business and should be considered as part of your overall system.
- Setting up remote access for you and your employees is not very difficult and a common practice.
- Other applications and custom solutions may need to be considered if you can't find the right answer off the shelf.

Lines of Communication

As a home-based business owner, the telephone is nothing less than your lifeline to the world. There's no way around it: It's an essential piece of equipment, and you can't do business without it, regardless of whether you sell a product or provide a service.

When you establish your home office, you need to pay special attention to your telephone setup because the way you receive and handle phone calls is a key part of your business image. You have a number of options that can add to your effectiveness. But of course, these options cost money.

In this section, you learn about your phone options. You'll also find out how to stay in touch with your office, your clients, your customers, and other business resources when you're away from home with technology like paging and e-mail. And you'll see what services from the phone company can let you connect to the Internet more efficiently.

WHAT'S MY (PHONE) LINE?

Whether you're writing a cyberspace newsletter, sending out a mail-order catalog of educational toys, selling super vitamins direct under a network marketing arrangement, or tutoring acting students in your home, your telephone is perhaps the single most important piece of equipment for your business.

Gone are the days when a single phone line could meet the needs of even the typical family, let alone one with a small business. If you're a home-based business, odds are the existing phone line to your home may not be enough (especially if there's a teenager around the house). You may need additional lines or special services.

There are several alternatives, and no single solution is best for every business. The way you set up your phones depends on things like the nature of your business.

TIP

In the future, you'll be able to have full-service communications via your cable lines. You'll get tele(vision) phones, with both local and long-distance service, more rapid Internet access, and traditional cable service from the same company. You may want to investigate.

KEEP IT PERSONAL

Obviously, adapting your personal phone service to business use is the least costly way to go. However, this option works best if your business doesn't involve a lot of phone contact.

You can convert your personal phone line into a faux second line by getting call waiting, a special service provided by the phone company for a flat monthly fee in addition to your regular bill. Call waiting lets you know when there's another call coming in (you'll hear a beep). Instead of getting a busy signal—the last thing you want to have a business contact hear—the caller gets through to you. You have to put your first caller on hold while you attend to the second caller. You can make arrangements to call one of them back or juggle two conversations by going back and forth.

TIP

If you haven't already done so, be sure your plan includes un-limited local calls for a fixed price. This type of phone service is, in almost all cases, most economical for home-based business owners.

BITE THE BULLET AND ADD A BUSINESS LINE

If you use your phone regularly and continuously for business, one line just won't do. You may have no choice but to bring in a second phone line despite the added cost. Your new line is strictly business; your old line is for you and your family to use.

There's an important advantage to having a phone line just for business. You can get a listing in the classified section of your Yellow Pages, so potential customers can let their fingers do the walking to your home-based business. With a single personal line, you can't advertise your business in this easy and familiar way.

You also gain the tax advantage of being able to deduct all of the costs of the business line. What's more, having a business line doesn't prevent you from deducting any business calls you make on your personal line. You can get a separate telephone for the business line. Or you can get a two-line phone to handle your personal line and business line.

CAUTION

If you have only one phone line in your home office, you can't deduct the basic monthly costs of service. You can, however, deduct your long-distance charges for business calls and the business portion of the cost of any special services (such as call forwarding or call waiting).

Bringing in a second line involves not one, but three separate costs:

- **Telephone equipment.** You need to have a new phone for your business line. This can be a second one-line phone, or you can get a two-line phone for your business and personal lines.

- **Telephone installation charges.** You have to pay the telephone company for running a second line to your location. If you have the business line run to more than one room, your installation charges are even higher. Be sure to keep in mind that the phone company charges higher installation fees for business lines even though there's no additional work involved. Why? Because they can.

■ **Telephone monthly charges.** The monthly costs of a business line run higher than comparable service for a personal line. Although this may make sense only to the phone company, you just have to write it off as one of life's little injustices.

TIP

Having a two-line phone in a home office may be something you need. It saves space. It may also make sense to have another two-line phone installed in a room like the kitchen.

In looking at the cost of the monthly charges, don't ignore the separate cost of long-distance charges (if you use them in your business). Having a business line means lining up a long-distance carrier. These carriers have different pricing structures. Forget the 10-10 numbers you see advertised on TV. You probably won't make the type of calls that would qualify for any savings. But many long-distance carriers offer special deals for small businesses. And trade and professional associations offer special discounts to members for some long-distance carriers. Check around before selecting the carrier for your business line. Don't hesitate to switch carriers if a better offer comes along (and believe me, they will, usually around dinnertime every other evening).

HOW MANY LINES ARE ENOUGH?

Believe it or not, one separate business line may not be enough for you to run your business efficiently. You might need a third or even a fourth line.

If you have a fax or modem, you may want to have a dedicated line—one used exclusively for online stuff. All large companies do it, and maybe you should, too. If you run your Internet connection and fax on the phone line you use to talk to clients, customers, or suppliers, you'll have telephone logjams when calls and equipment compete for the line. You have to stop your telephone conversation every time you want to receive or send a fax.

You also can't talk and use your computer's modem at the same time, so your clients might get that lethal busy signal when you're online. The cost of a dedicated line for your fax or modem can be less than $15 a month.

If your business is heavy on phone calls, you may also want extra lines. This becomes very important if you have an employee or two who work from your office. They may need separate lines to use the phone for business if you, too, are using the phone for business.

If you're on the road a lot, it might be better to have a second line that's wireless. Cell phones let you take your telephone number with you virtually anywhere. You're always in touch. You'll learn about cell phones later in this section.

PAYING THE TOLL: 800 NUMBERS

Do you need to have a toll-free number for clients and customers to reach you? Again, the type of business you run will provide the answer. If you have a mail-order business that invites customers to place orders by phone, for example, you may have no choice but to offer a toll-free number (if you want to be competitive). It costs to provide one, but that cost can easily be repaid by increased orders. And you don't need a separate phone line. The 800 calls can come into the same line as your regular phone. It's only the billing—toll calls and regular calls—that's separate.

Toll-free numbers are offered by long-distance carriers. Phone numbers starting with 800/888/877 are called "toll free," but this is only half true. The calls are toll free to the caller, but you, the receiver, pay for them. The cost of having these numbers varies from one carrier to another. Here are the two types of charges you should ask about when investigating a toll-free number:

- **Monthly fee.** You pay a flat monthly fee for the privilege of having a toll-free number.

- **Per-call charges.** You're charged a set amount per minute for all calls made to you via your 800/888/877 number, even wrong numbers and crank calls. Some carriers offer a single per-minute charge. Others have different charges for in-state versus out-of-state and for regional calling.

BE IN WHEN YOU'RE OUT

The telephone can be used to connect you to the outside world even when you're not at home. And even if you're in the office, there are times when you just may not be taking calls. Still, you don't want your business callers to get turned off by busy signals or a phone that rings and rings. The good news is you can easily stay in touch even when you're not available to answer the phone.

AN OLD-FASHIONED ANSWERING MACHINE

The simplest and least expensive way to be sure to get phone calls when you're unavailable is to hook up an answering machine to your telephone.

Any decent answering machine allows you to get your messages when you're out of the office. These machines have a unique remote-access number. When you call in and press that access number, the machine plays back any messages.

The cost of a good answering machine—one that records the time and date of calls, displays the number of messages, and allows you to access your messages from an outside line—can be well under $100.

VOICEMAIL

Want a solution to allow your business callers to leave recorded messages without ever getting a busy signal? Consider a messaging service. This is a service you can get through your local telephone company. Thus, even if you're on the phone, your second or third caller can leave a voice message for you. You can then access your messages at any time, 7 days a week, 24 hours a day. Voicemail is rapidly becoming the messaging alternative of choice.

You can choose from numerous add-ons (special features) to enhance voicemail. These include the ability to leave automated information messages for your callers, signals to your personal pager (discussed later in this section), and more. Donna, who ran a one-person cleaning company from her home, appeared to outside callers as a large operation. The reason: She had a feature called Multiple Mailboxes. When one of her accounts called in, the customer heard a message that said "To speak to the billing department, press 1 now. To schedule a cleaning, press 2," and so on. Her customers assumed the company had a dozen departments when, in fact, Donna was a one-woman wonder.

CAUTION

Currently, voicemail might be limited to those who live in urban areas. If you live outside of a metropolitan area, you may not have easy access to voicemail at this time. For an alternative, consider an old-fashioned answering service.

You can also use voicemail to take messages for you if you're in the office using your phone line for an Internet connection. Having only one line for both talking on the phone and surfing the web won't prevent the public contacting you by phone.

The cost of voicemail can be rather modest. You must figure in the cost of your local calls to access your messages, unless you pay for unlimited local calls. Most of the major phone carriers offer voicemail services.

ANSWERING SERVICES COULD BE YOUR ANSWER

In ancient times, before answering machines and computer-based messages, an answering service was the only way someone could get messages when he or she was not in. You can set up your phone calls to "roll over" to the answering service. Answering services are still around today. For some businesses, they still make sense.

An answering service gives the caller the opportunity to speak to a human being and leave a personal message. The answering service can respond to the caller's needs more personally, saying things like, "Mr. Smith will be right back," or, "Mr. Smith will be out of the office all day but will be calling in for messages; is this an emergency?" Of course, the service has probably never even met Mr. Smith and may have no idea what kind of business he runs, but his customer doesn't know this.

An answering service also gives the business a veneer of professionalism. The caller doesn't have to know that she is speaking to a service. Instead, the caller can believe that she has reached your office and is speaking to your incredibly efficient staff.

E-MAIL YOUR WAY TO SUCCESS

Welcome to cyberspace! An increasingly popular alternative to phone calls is to stay connected to business contacts via your computer. Instead of calling up on the telephone, you use your computer to receive and send messages with e-mail (electronic mail).

To use e-mail, you need certain equipment—a computer, a modem (or broad-band access, which is discussed shortly), and an online provider (such as America Online, MSN, or a local Internet provider). However, it takes two to e-mail: Even if you have what it takes for e-mail, it will do you no good if the other person doesn't have e-mail, too.

There are several advantages to e-mail:

- **Convenience.** You can leave detailed messages of virtually any length when it's convenient for you, and your contact will get them the first time, instead of leaving a trail of voice messages to call each other back. One entrepreneur, based in New York City, has customers in California. E-mail means he can leave lengthy messages for his customer at 6 A.M. that he picks up when he gets in the office, three hours later.

- **Cost.** E-mail is a lot cheaper than long-distance calls. If you regularly speak with business contacts long distance, whichever long-distance carrier you use, you still pay for long-distance service. With e-mail, however, your online provider is generally only a local call away. Thus, even if the guy you're e-mailing is in another state or even another country, you pay only for the local call to your online provider. Of course, getting messages from e-mail means you have to place another phone call via your computer to access them, but it's still a local call. You also have to pay a monthly fee to your provider, which may or may not include unlimited online time (depending upon your service provider).

- **Time savings.** E-mail is a serious time-saver. You avoid the personal, but time-consuming, aspects of calling and just get down to business. You can send the same message to numerous people with ease (and with a time savings to you). Although e-mail may at first seem cold and impersonal, your business contacts will also appreciate the time savings.

- **Written and electronic record.** Unlike phone calls, which don't leave a trace of their contents, you get a record of your communications with e-mail. You can print your e-mail messages and keep them on hand for future reference. Most e-mail programs have a "search" feature that allows users to search their messages (sent or received) by subject line of within the text itself. This is a great way to find a specific piece of correspondence.

The chief downside to e-mail for some people is that they feel it's too impersonal. You can't pick up cues from body language or tone of voice as you go. A lot of people prefer to speak directly to another person and don't like the more formal, correspondence feel of e-mail, even when it's tempered with "emoticons" (those annoying little smiley symbols, the Hallmark cards of computer speak).

CELLULAR PHONES FOR EVERYONE

Walking on the street, sitting in the train, or driving on the highway, you're bound to see someone with a phone glued to his ear. Cell (cellular) phones have gone mainstream, with the guy in front of you in line at the bank, the lady in the next booth at the IHOP, and even the kid in your neighbor's sandbox all sporting cell phones. You can carry a cell phone with you just about anywhere. It's a convenience because it means you don't have to find a telephone booth or other phone line to place or receive your calls. You can stay in touch with your home office and it can stay in touch with you.

Before you decide to affix a cell phone to your ear, beware: Cellular phones are generally more expensive to operate than those that are wired up. (For example, a service plan may charge a $30 monthly minimum whether you make any calls or not. This minimum may cover only 30 minutes of phone time; you'll pay more for additional use.) They are helpful primarily to business owners who need to stay in phone contact with business callers when they're out of the office. They may not make sense, from a cost perspective, for business owners who make only occasional portable calls.

In figuring what you'll pay a month, think about the options you need. Cell phones let you receive voicemail, forward calls, and even access the Internet so you can check your e-mail. You get what you pay for, so don't pay for what you don't need.

CAUTION

Tax law limits your depreciation deductions for the cost of a cellular phone if you use it both for business and personal purposes. You must use the phone more than 50 percent for business if you want to deduct accelerated (rapid) depreciation. If your business use is less, your deduction is limited.

PAGERS FIND YOU ANYWHERE

If you're out in the field a lot, you may need to stay connected to your home office in a more immediate way. Business clients, customers, or others may need to contact you *now;* they can't wait until you choose to retrieve messages from voicemail or an answering machine. For these impatient callers, you have two choices: a cell phone or a simpler, less-costly solution, a personal pager, or "beeper."

Here's how it works. You give John Customer the telephone number for your pager. When John needs to speak to you, he calls that number and keys in his phone number. Your pager beeps (or vibrates or whistles the "Star Spangled Banner") to let you know that a call has come in. Your pager displays John's phone number and you return the call.

The cost of using a pager includes the cost of the pager itself (a modest expense whether you buy or lease the pager) and the cost of the monthly monitoring company (about $20 per month).

Some pagers have become highly sophisticated. They're no longer just numeric, displaying simply a phone number and the time of the page. Instead, they're alphanumeric, capable of displaying short, or in some cases, even lengthy, written messages. Older pagers just showed you your caller's phone number (like you have all your customers' numbers memorized and know who the heck you're calling back). Nowadays, a pager can also display your caller's name and other information.

Many pagers also now have text messaging. With text messaging you can receive and send messages right from your pagers. It's a great way to instantly communicate with the office.

TIP

Although there are now more than 2,000 monitoring services nationwide, they're not the same. There are local, regional, and national services. Some have 24-hour-a-day, 365-day-a-year service, whereas others keep bankers' hours. Of course, you get what you pay for, so if your business is entirely local, why pay for regional or national service? You may be able to get temporary national service at a small cost if you travel.

CONNECTIONS TO CYBERSPACE

If you use your computer for more than just printing invoices, you'll probably want to connect to the Internet. Whatever your reasons for going online, you'll need to explore connection alternatives.

Modems allow your computer to dial up through your phone lines to the Internet. The speed at which you can receive information or send it depends on your modem and your phone company lines.

Your kids may be happy to connect to their favorite chat room using a modem that connects at 28 or 56 kbps, but this may not be fast enough for your business. Depending on where you live, your local phone company may offer ISDN or DSL connections enabling you to send or receive information at speeds that can dazzle you. In addition to phone companies, some private corporations offer these options to small businesses.

TIP

Broadband services, which run in the background so your computer can be on even if you're talking on the same phone line, is currently being offered as ISDN (Integrated Services Digital Network) or the even faster DSL (Digital Subscriber Line). These run at 3 to more than 100 times the rate of the conventional 56 kbps modem (depending upon the type of service you get).

The plus side to ISDN/DSL connections is that they enable you to run more than one operation through the same phone line. So, for example, you can receive faxes at your fax machine while you surf the Net. The downside is the added cost each month. Expect to pay between $20 and $400 a month, depending on the speed you select. And there's another catch: The service may not be available in all areas at the present time.

In or out of your home office, you can connect to the public, and let it connect to you, in many different ways. Take advantage of changing technologies for optimum connections. But don't overlook cost. The more you get, the more you pay for. Decide what you really need and what you can use to meet that need in the most cost-effective way.

THE 30-SECOND RECAP

- The telephone is probably the most important piece of equipment for a home-based business.
- Using your personal phone line for business saves money but may not be right for your business needs.
- You may need a dedicated phone line for a fax or modem.
- A toll-free number may be necessary for some types of businesses.
- A cell phone or pager can help you stay in touch with your office and business contacts when you're out in the field.
- Connections to the Internet through your telephone line may be vital or merely helpful to your business.

Ins and Outs of a Successful Website

Your website serves as the central hub for your Internet initiatives. Because a well-designed website is so important to your marketing and communication efforts, this section will help you increase the chances that your website will contribute to your business.

This section explains what your website needs to accomplish to contribute to your overall business. The characteristics of good websites are also discussed.

After that, you learn about some of the nuts and bolts of setting up and maintaining a website. Website design has a significant technical side, Although it's useful to understand the technology side of websites, it isn't absolutely necessary.

WHAT YOUR WEBSITE NEEDS TO ACCOMPLISH

Most businesses understand they should have a website but have only a superficial idea of what the website is there for. And many small businesses don't really have a good grasp of the details. To build a successful site requires that you have a clear sense of what you want to accomplish with your website. Your goals should be as follows:

- Create a positive professional image
- Create a sense that you value the welfare of visitors and clients
- Expose your services to the largest audience possible
- Provide easy and fast access to information
- Bring in business

The following sections describe these five goals of a good site.

CAUTION

Most websites run by small business owners are a complete waste of space. They accomplish almost nothing because they are poorly thought out, and the owners are not clear about what the website is for. Hundreds of thousands of websites have virtually no visitors and not much to offer the few visitors they attract.

CREATE A POSITIVE PROFESSIONAL IMAGE

Your website needs to enhance your image. Visitors (prospective and current clients) should come away with the impression that you are reputable, trustworthy, and professional. In that sense, a website is no different from any written material you produce. For example, you wouldn't produce a sales brochure full of spelling errors. You wouldn't include an adult-oriented ad in a print newsletter related to your consulting business. It's the same for websites.

CREATE A SENSE THAT YOU VALUE THE WELFARE OF VISITORS AND CLIENTS

One golden rule to remember is to place the welfare of clients above your own. Your website is an opportunity to send this message to clients and customers.

A website that is simply an online sales brochure is going to be perceived as an indicator that you are less interested in your customers' welfare and more interested in taking their money. A website that provides information and tools useful to visitors will be perceived much more positively.

EXPOSE YOUR SERVICES TO THE LARGEST AUDIENCE POSSIBLE

The more people who know about you and what you do, the better chance you have for increased business. One of the great things about having a website is that there is potential to reach a lot of prospective clients.

But it's not just a question of volume. Let's say you are a management or health-industry consultant. Does it help you if your site is visited by children? No, of course not. You must reach decision makers, people in positions to hire you. So, although you want volume, or a high level of traffic to your site, you really need to have a specific kind of traffic.

Targeted traffic refers to visitors to your site who are in positions to benefit your business. You need the right kinds of visitors.

PLAIN ENGLISH

Targeted traffic is traffic that comes from people who are in positions to help your business or purchase what you provide. In other words, you want traffic from decision makers or people in positions to advise decision makers.

PROVIDE EASY AND FAST ACCESS TO INFORMATION

The attention span of web surfers is notoriously short. Typically visitors will come to your site, take a quick look at the page they land on, and determine within 20 seconds whether they can find what they are looking for. If they don't see what they want, or an obvious way to get what they want, they go elsewhere. You've lost them.

So whatever information you provide must be front and center, and easy to find. Above all, visitors must be provided with what they want without hassle. And fast.

AND THE BOTTOM LINE ... BUSINESS

Of course, the bottom line is that your website must bring in business. It so happens that the things described so far will help you bring in business, but let's not forget that business is the underlying goal of all the other issues. Your website is not just a free public service. Thus, while we talk about image, speed, and provision of value to visitors, we are doing so with the assumption that accomplishing these goals creates more business.

CHARACTERISTICS OF SUCCESSFUL CONSULTING WEBSITES

How do you create a website that will achieve these goals? That's a question and a half. In fact, that's a book in itself. Still, we can look at the most important characteristics of successful websites:

- Content (what's on your site)
- Design (what your site looks like)
- Search-engine friendly

Content (What's on Your Site)

What's the most common mistake made by small business owners with respect to their websites? It's using websites as sales brochures. Entrepreneurs who use their sites as brochures may end up with very attractive sites that have almost no visitors. Why? The site is of no value to its visitors.

TIP

Don't think of your site as a brochure. Think of it as a television show that has content (programs), with ads embedded in the content. Your content or program attracts people to the site. Then you expose them to your products and services. Not the other way around.

So what should be on your site? The content should fall into one of two categories: free, high-value content; and clear, fast-to-access, and highly visible content related to your products and services.

Free, High-Value Content

What free, high-value content can you provide? Obviously it depends on your specialization. It also depends on what will be valued and useful to the decision makers (targeted traffic) you want to attract to your site. Let's work through an example related to John's website.

John is a human resources consultant. One of his targeted markets includes human resources professionals, because they are often in positions to hire him or make recommendations to hire him. John's first task was to determine what kind of content they might value in a website. Information, right? Information about legal issues, downsizing, interviewing, and so on. Because he had a fair number of articles "on tap" that he had written, he put those relevant articles on his site. On the page where each articles appeared, he put information about services he provides that might be of interest to this group.

TIP

To provide value to visitors, you need to know your market and know the needs of the decision makers you want to attract. That's why having experience in your field is so important. When thinking about free, high-value content, ask yourself, "What do my prospective clients look for and need?" Then fulfill that need.

John didn't stop there. He also knew that human resources professionals look for forms and other tools specific to the profession. So he provided access to this kind of material. Because he doesn't develop such things, he linked to material developed by others, to provide his visitors with quick access.

Getting the picture? If you run a fitness center, you'd want hints, tips, and articles related to physical fitness. Maybe some pictures of exercises. If you own a graphic design firm, you might provide some free, high-quality images or artwork that can be used in things like newsletters.

FAST INFORMATION ABOUT YOUR SERVICES

There's a second type of content information about your products and services. You need to let people know how you can help them. Notice the phrasing. As with other forms of promotional material, you don't provide information only about your services. You slant that information to focus on how those services can benefit your prospective clients.

What kind of content fits here? Consider the following:

- Benefits to customers
- Specifics of products and services
- How to get more information
- Your company's experience and success delivering its products and services
- Qualifications to deliver these products and services

Should you post your prices on the website? The answer depends on your business. Your prices may depend on the nature of the services as negotiated on a case-by-case basis. Thus, any figures you quote on a website may actually be misleading to prospective visitors. At this point in the marketing process, you don't want to focus on price. You want to focus on how your company can help and the value you provide.

Before moving on to website design, here's a key principle: The information about your products and services and the value you can provide should be interwoven with the free, high-value content on your site, just like television programming and ads.

WEBSITE DESIGN

It's easy to design a website. That is, if you don't care much about website success. Actually, it's easy to build an unsuccessful website, and it's not that difficult to build a serviceable website. However, it's exceedingly difficult to develop an excellent website that will build your consulting practice.

But it's worth it. You may need to enlist some expert help to get a decent website design. That's for two reasons. First, the actual design and the coding of your website require some specialized skills, skills most people don't have or don't want to learn. Second, web development is time-consuming.

Regardless of whether you decide to build the website yourself or hire someone on a consulting basis, or even a bit of both, you need to be actively involved. You can hire someone to do the coding of your site or to develop the look and appeal of your site, but you are the one responsible for the content decisions and for deciding how best to meet the needs of your website visitors. The more you know about web design, the better off you are.

There are three areas of concern in website design: the appearance of your site, the ease of navigation (moving around the site), and the degree to which your site is search-engine friendly. This will be explained shortly.

APPEARANCES ARE IMPORTANT

Appearances are important. If your website is cluttered, uses ugly color schemes, and is hard to read, people won't stay more than a few seconds. Here are some guidelines:

- **Incorporate lots of "white space."** There's a tendency to crowd as much as possible into the available space. White space (space that's not used for anything) actually makes the content on each page stand out to the viewer.

- **Use shorter pages rather than longer ones.** Each page should have a unique narrow focus or theme and should be compact. This helps the pages load more quickly, so the page appears faster to the visitor.

- **Avoid using a lot of pictures or graphics.** Use only graphics that are absolutely essential. This also speeds up page loads.

- **Keep the color scheme simple.** It is recommended you use no more than three or four main colors. Never use black as a background.

- **Incorporate good security.** Implementing logins and secure processing where necessary to give the users comfort that their private or financial information is being handled discreetly.

TIP

Should you design and code your website yourself? It depends. If you have the skills and programs to do so, and if you enjoy the challenge and process, go for it. If not, you may want to get help. You may want to check out *The Complete Idiot's Guide to Creating a Web Page, Fifth Edition,* by Paul McFedries (2002).

- **Use a readable font size.** The size of the print on the screen should not be too small. Keep in mind that different users have different kinds of display monitors. Something that looks fine on one monitor may be much too small to read on another.

- **Keep the variety of fonts to a minimum.** There is rarely a reason to have more than two different fonts on a page. Specifically, use standard fonts like Arial, Times Roman, and Verdana. All computer systems can display these properly.

These ideas about web design can get you started. However, there are many more design principles. You may want to read a good book on web design principles.

NAVIGATION AND HOW PEOPLE GET AROUND

Navigation refers to how visitors get from one page of your website to another. Suppose your site has 20 or 30 different pages. Is it easy for a visitor to get from one to the other? Can a visitor see almost instantly what's on the other pages of your site? These questions reflect the two most important aspects of navigation design: the ease of use and the ability to see what's on the site.

Normally every page should have a navigation bar (also called a menu). The *navigation bar* is a small part of the page that shows the major sections of your website. It is usually placed at the top of each page or on the left side. For example, it might contain the following links:

- About Us
- Contact Us
- How We Can Help You
- Free Resources

For a small site, your navigation bar may contain more specific links to other pages. On a large site, you'll be limited to the major categories of information on your site. That's because the navigation bar can hold only so much information. You can get around this limitation by having navigation bars or menus that expand when clicked. However, there are some drawbacks to this. For the moment, think simple.

The key things, again, are that the visitor be able to see what is available on your site and be able to access the content quickly. Therefore, your navigation bar should be prominent, use a different color than the other parts of your page, and be visible as soon as the visitor arrives. In other words, it should stand out.

SEARCH-ENGINE FRIENDLY? WHAT THE HECK IS THAT?

Is your website search-engine friendly? We've come to one of the most complex parts of website success. You'll see why in a moment. Think about this. After your site is up and running, looks great, and navigates well, how in heck do you let people know it's there? With millions of sites out there, people aren't likely to stumble upon you.

Of course, you are going to promote your website in your print material and via discussion lists. But people must also be able to find you via the major search engines on the Internet.

Don't know what a *search engine* is? It's simply a website that indexes web pages. A person looking for something can go to one of these sites and type in a few words, and the search engine will return a list of sites that it thinks the visitor is looking for.

TIP

Originally, web pages needed to be coded by hand, and that required knowledge of the programming language (HTML). Now it's much easier. You can purchase web-development programs that work like desktop publishing programs and don't require in-depth knowledge of HTML. Programs like Microsoft FrontPage and Macromedia Dreamweaver make web development much easier.

There are about 10 major search engines or directories. The main ones include Yahoo!, Google, Altavista, Excite, and Open Directory Project. Some, like Yahoo!, charge a fee for including your site in their systems; others include your site for free.

Here's why search-engine listings are so complex. Each one works differently and applies different rules. And these rules are changing as you read this (well almost) as search-engine companies work to defeat those trying to beat the system.

Basically, you want your site to come up high on a search result list when your prospective customers type in search terms to try to find information you have.

Are these easy answers? Yes and no. Some basic rules tend to be important over time and have to do with the design of your page.

Each page of your site should have a different and distinct title and file name that reflect what's on that page. The title and name should contain the words you think your visitors might use in search engines (those are called *keywords*). For example, a page on performance appraisal could have the following title

"Performance Appraisal Free Help." The file name might be performance-appraisal.html. Notice The key terms *performance* and *appraisal* have been included in both the title and the file name.

Each page of your site should include your targeted keywords within the text of the page and also in the first 200 words on your page, reading top to bottom and left to right. The keywords should appear several times in the text. The longer the page, the more times they should appear.

TIP

Want to learn more about how search engines work? Try searchenginewatch.com. You'll find information for the beginner and the more advanced user.

Each web page has what are called *meta-tags*. They include information like the title of your page and also a list of keywords to help some search engines know what your page is about. Each page should have a different title and keywords that apply specifically to that page. Do not use the same keywords for each page. Also note that meta-tags are becoming less important, and some search engines don't pay any attention to them.

Never try to trick search engines to get a higher ranking. Site owners attempt a number of methods to try to trick search engines into thinking their sites should come up more often. Trying to trick the search engines is likely to result in none of your pages making it into the search engine.

In terms of search engines, you have one more option. Several companies like goto.com and findwhat.com use a system in which you pay for each click or person they send to your site. You bid on specific search terms related to your website. The higher the bid, the more likely people will visit. I'll leave you to explore this possibility by visiting these sites, but it's worth considering, because the investment can be small (but may not be).

Unfortunately this discussion is only able to scratch the surface. It is suggested that you read as much as possible about websites and web designs. Now let's move on to a few other web-related topics.

SOME OTHER WEBSITE ISSUES

Most people contemplating the development of a website have common questions. A few of the questions are addressed here.

Do I Need a Web Host?

First, what's a web host? The files for your site have to "live" somewhere. A *web host* is a company that provides a residence for your files and website. So, yes, you need a home for your site. However, you may already have one available. Some companies that connect people to the Internet allow their customers to build their websites on their computers. Check with the company that you use to connect to the Internet. However, keep in mind that "homes" provided by these companies may be limited in size and features.

There's another alternative. Some companies offer free website homes. In return, they usually place ads on your website. Don't use these kinds of websites for professional purposes. First, they don't do much for your professional image. In fact, if you use a free website, your visitors may see you as unprofessional. Second, you don't have complete control over your website, and the features are limited. Third, these companies are suffering financially, and there is no guarantee your website will be available if the company changes policies or goes bankrupt.

So what should you do? Pay for a reputable web-hosting company. Talk to friends and colleagues to get recommendations. Don't base your decision solely on price. To repeat: Don't go just by price. Lower-priced deals tend to be available from companies that provide somewhat less-reliable service. There's no point having a website if visitors can't get to it due to technical difficulties 10 percent of the time, or if the pages load too slowly. Visitors give up easily.

CAUTION

Many neophyte web owners sign on with companies promising all kinds of things for a few dollars a month, only to discover that there's no help and no customer support, and that lots of times their sites aren't available. In fact, there's some research to suggest that web owners go through at least three Internet hosts before they find the one that works for them. Do some research, don't rely on sale hype, and pay a little more for quality.

Do I Need My Own Domain Name?

Don't know what a domain name is? It's simple. Each page or website has an address. That's the information a person types into the browser to get to a site. A *domain name* is the "house address" of your site, just like the address of your house. Your site may have different pages (like rooms), but each page is part of your domain.

There are different types of addresses. One, for example, looks like this: http://www. escape.ca/test. Escape happens to be the company that connects you to the Internet, and it hosts a website called test. Every person at Escape who runs a website, and has not purchased his or her own personal domain name, has an address that includes the www.escape.ca part.

The problem is that these kinds of names are long, and not very distinctive. The other option is to obtain your very own unique domain name. That would look like this: http://www.marksgroup.net.

This address is shorter and easy to remember. There's another important reason why you must have your own domain name. Your domain name follows you around. If you have your site on Company A, and need or want to move it to Company B, people will still be able to find it under your original name. You own the name, and you decide where you want that name to point.

There are probably about a dozen other reasons to have your own domain name. It's fairly cheap, no more than $35 a year, and often less.

You need to register your name and pay for it. Companies that allow you to do this are called "registrars" or "domain registrars." Alternatively, your web host may be able to help you with the process. Do it.

THE 30-SECOND RECAP

- Your website is much more than an electronic brochure. You need to provide reasons for people to visit it.

- It's easy to design a poor website, but very difficult to design one that works well.

- Determine what your prospective consulting customers are looking for on the Internet, and do your best to provide them with free high-value information.

- At minimum it's worth paying for a good-quality web host and your own distinctive domain name.

Smart Marketing

The "Four P's" of Marketing, Plus One

The "four P's" (place, product, price, and promotion), and the all-important "fifth P" (people), are at the heart of creating those exchanges that get your offerings to customers and their money to you.

Marketing professors have been using the four P's for 50-plus years, and yet look around. The world of products and services has gotten much more sophisticated. Whereas half a dozen hair-coloring products from two main suppliers once served a mass market, we now have many more hair-care companies offering dozens of different versions of their products.

So why study a model built to describe one mass market when most of us are engaged in much more targeted activities? Because it still works.

This section updates the old four P's where there's a need. Place these days can include the Internet. Product is more likely to be about services. Price hasn't changed much, but promotions has grown some online avenues. And then there's that important new P, people—the customers, competitors, employees, and suppliers who inhabit the world described by the four P's. People are integral to the activity of marketing, a fact we should never forget. That's why people are the unofficial fifth P.

FOUR INGREDIENTS MAKE UP THE MARKETING MIX

The four P's make up the *marketing mix,* the components of marketing that are under your (the marketer's) control. You can't do a thing about the weather, but you can control the four P's.

PLAIN ENGLISH

The **marketing mix** is the combination of activities that make up your approach to your marketing. It is a blend of strategies regarding the four P's of products, places, prices, and promotions. These four elements are under a marketer's control. Marketers have begun to include "people" in the marketing mix because customer behavior is also a key element of marketing strategy.

Kalika is a good small business owner to demonstrate the marketing mix. Kalika has developed a product line (fruit juices) and offers them at a price she establishes by balancing greed and reason. She chooses a place for distributing the product (the college commons) and promotes her line in a few simple ways, like signage and a cheerful selling technique. Her presence in the cart keeps her close to the people she serves. That's how she's chosen to mix the elements of marketing strategy.

WHAT IS YOUR PRODUCT?

The word *product* covers a lot more than the obvious tangible, physical articles available for sale. A product can be a service, like dry cleaning or management consulting. A product can also be a concept you would like an audience to believe. You might be selling support for a person, place, event, organization, or idea.

Your product will most likely be a combination of tangible items, services, and beliefs. That is why many like to use the word *offering*. What you offer customers will almost certainly contain elements of each. A haircut is a product, but it results from the service of cutting hair. A political candidate is in many ways a product, promising to function in a way that solves problems for you if you elect him or her to office. Nonprofit agencies sell feelings, asking us to support activities that make us feel good about doing good. Each of these examples represents a different offering someone is asking an audience to buy or buy into.

The product also includes its packaging and the customer service policies that back it up. For retailers, choice of product is key in creating an appealing merchandise assortment. For all businesses, product life cycles must be taken into account.

PLAIN ENGLISH

The *product life cycle* begins with Introduction (the product launch) and moves on to a Growth phase if the Introduction was successful. A growing product will reach a Mature phase that can end in months or endure for decades. Most products will eventually enter a final stage of Decline. At this stage there's a risk that unless the product is phased out or rejuvenated, it will sap resources.

"TURN, TURN, TURN": THE PRODUCT LIFE CYCLE

As a small business owner and marketer, you must understand something about the life cycle of your products. Most products (and product categories) will pass from Introduction through Growth, Maturity, and Decline. Marketers cannot ignore this. You need products in different phases of the *product life cycle* to ensure against one product going bad and turning your whole operation sour. If one product is slipping in popularity, you need to have something else in the pipeline.

Sometimes a declining product can be reintroduced and enjoy a second go-round. In Malcolm Gladwell's *The Tipping Point* (2000, Little, Brown and Co.), he describes an unexpected product rebirth. As he tells it, sales of Hush Puppies shoes were down to 30,000 pairs a year in 1994. In 1995, 430,000 pairs were sold. Why the increase? Hip young New Yorkers began wearing the shoes to trendy youth clubs in Manhattan. In 1996, the company sold more than 1.7 million pairs of Hush Puppies. Good thing the company hadn't followed through on plans to "kill the puppies" back in 1994!

How do you develop new products? Are there innovations you can bring to current products to make them "new and improved"?

NEW AND IMPROVED! SOME PRODUCT STRATEGIES

Following are just a few of the issues that can affect product strategies.

- **Improve functionality.** What features of your product do your customers find important? How does your offering compare to your competitors'? Maybe there are features you can add to products that will transfer into real customer benefit. The manufacturer who developed the self-cleaning kitty litter box broke new ground with new product features.

- **Add convenience.** What specifics do you know about the demographics and lifestyles of your customers? Tailor products to fit them better. This can be as simple as selling soup in individual-serving cans for singles or toilet paper in six-roll packs for big families.

  Think about these three issues: improved functionality, convenience, and expanded uses in relation to your current products. Do you see opportunities for new or improved product offerings?

- **Find new uses.** There's one thing that never changes in marketing—you always have to adapt to change! Try finding new uses for old products, like the guy who thought of marketing Arm and Hammer baking soda as a refrigerator deodorizer.

PRODUCT STRATEGIES IN ACTION

How do product strategies affect small businesses? Kai Miaka deals with product issues each time his band releases a new CD and a new package must be designed for it. A Life of Faith Dolls and Bob's Bottomless Boats are both adding new products to their merchandise assortments with every new season. By doing so, they keep current customers coming back to see what's new ... and making purchases as a result. New products almost always require some advertising support. If you emphasize new products in your marketing mix, be sure to put some money in your promotions budget to get the word out.

TIP

Never forget the first rule of marketing: People don't buy products; they buy solutions to problems. If your product offering fails to evolve, solving customer needs as those needs evolve, you put your business at risk. Carefully consider the product life cycle of your offerings. For those that are mature, look for ways to freshen or improve them to stave off decline.

WHAT'S PRICE GOT TO DO WITH IT?

Price is the amount of money or other consideration that is exchanged for a product offering. Price is a quantifiable way of measuring the value customers place on the product. For effective marketing, you need more than a price on your product. You need a pricing strategy.

Some people don't believe price is a marketing issue. They believe price is a result of accounting for the cost of materials, overhead, and profit goals slated for a particular product. These people are wrong. Pricing policies that don't take market realities into consideration can lead to disaster.

The price you ask exerts an influence over your whole operation, from your customers' perception of your value to the amount you take home in your check. An effective pricing strategy is the result of good strategic thinking.

Value is the key to pricing, not just what the product costs to make, but also what quality is delivered at what cost. The price you ask affects the image of the product. Underpricing a product that delivers premium value can be as destructive as overpricing a low-value item. You have to communicate value to your audience so strongly that price seems reasonable in relation to the product.

Pricing for profit is a big facet of your business, one of the most critical decisions you'll ever make, and make, and make again.

A Life of Faith Dolls uses pricing to establish the value of the dolls and accessories they offer. By setting their prices near that of comparable American Girls dolls, they persuade potential buyers that these dolls are of comparable quality and desirability.

WHEN IS "PLACE" NOT A PLACE?

Place can mean a lot of things to a marketer: location, or distribution, or virtual sites in cyberspace. If you're a retailer, place might really mean "place" to you. Is your store located in a convenient, attractive location? Are you open the hours customers like to shop? If so, you've got *place strategy* under control.

PLAIN ENGLISH

A **place strategy** to a marketer means getting the right goods in
the right quantity to the right place, at the lowest possible cost,
without sacrificing customer service. Place can mean a retail
location, a distribution system, or an online presence—or all of
the above.

Very few of us, however, actually do business through one location. Even
small retailers have websites that expand their reach beyond their storefronts.
If you're a consultant, perhaps your work takes place at your clients' offices
rather than your own. If you run a pizza delivery service, your "place of business" is customers' doorways. When we talk about place, we're really talking
about all the aspects of getting products to end users.

A successful place strategy satisfies each of these requirements:

- Products are stored in the right quantity at the right place. This is an
  operational issue affected by how well you can predict demand and
  get inventory to where that demand is.

- You are achieving the lowest possible cost because of the efficiency
  and effectiveness in how you actually move products from your place
  to your customers.

- Your place is convenient to the customer. If the place where customers can take possession of the offering is out of the way or complicated, you have negatively affected the value of your offering.

UP AND DOWN THE DISTRIBUTION CHANNELS

For most businesses, the *P* in *place* is actually a *D* for *distribution*. In this situation, a place strategy will concern what market area you're willing to serve,
how you dispatch your resources to serve it, or how you make use of others to
create a *distribution channel*.

A distribution channel is just a fancy name for the way in which a product or
service gets from its point of origin to its final destination, the person or business that uses it. Typically a product moves from manufacturer to wholesaler
to retailer to consumer. You might be involved in any of these stages, and you
could certainly be involved in more than one.

A business can *pull* a product through the distribution channel by creating
demand at the end-user level, or it can *push* a product through by giving wholesalers and retailers special incentives to sell that product or service. Both
strategies focus on leveraging distribution as the place *P* in the marketing mix.

A company that uses home sales, like Tupperware or Creative Memories, is combining wholesaler and retailer into one independent sales agent. They've taken the place aspect right into America's homes, shortening the distribution channel and increasing price efficiencies by cutting out middlemen.

Everyone downstream from you in your distribution channel is your customer. To get a product successfully from factory floor to end user, a lot of people along the way have to believe in its merits. No matter whom you're talking to, wherever he might be in the channel, he's looking for solutions to problems. Offer them, and you've got the start of a mutually beneficial relationship.

TIP

A survey by Jupiter Research in early 2003 predicted that retail spending online would grow at a rate of 21 percent each year through 2007 and found that nearly a third of all retail spending is influenced by the Internet. What are your online plans?

PLACE STRATEGIES IN ACTION

For a business with lots of customers, like University Credit Union (a credit union that serves college students and staff), convenient locations offer a chance to stand out from competitors. The credit union adds several branches each year, following trends among their members carefully to figure out where new branches should go.

Life History Services is a different story. This unique service records a transcript of a customer's life through interviews and other means, and then turns that transcript into a written, living history of that person. Life History Services is by its nature a "Flying Dutchman" of a business. It doesn't matter where its owner, Anita, lives because she travels nationally to deliver her service. Anita's early projects for families in far-flung locations have led through word of mouth to more business in those and other cities. She travels several months of the year to conduct interviews where her clients are most comfortable … in their homes. Her business place strategy involves trying to schedule work trips for maximum productivity and to get her out of her Wisconsin home base in winter.

For University Credit Union and Life History Services, place is about delivering the offering at a location that meets customers' needs for convenience.

PROMOTE THE DAMN THING!

Your marketing mix won't add up to much if it doesn't include some good old-fashioned promotions. If you're going to develop a product, put a price on it, and bring it to market, you'd better put some work into promoting the damn thing.

Promotions in this context means more than the contests and giveaways you probably think of when that word is used. To a marketer, the promotion *P* includes all aspects of marketing communications, from planning the advertising campaign to training the sales staff to designing the gimmicks and giveaways that boost sluggish customers' desire to buy. It's all aimed at helping the prospect realize a need and then triumphing over other similar offerings when the prospect goes out to fill that need.

PROMOTION'S "THREE-LEGGED STOOL"

Three classifications of activities come under the heading of promotion: advertising, selling, and sales promotions. Think of it as the three-legged stool that promotions sit on.

Advertising, the first leg of that stool, encompasses the planning and development of advertising strategies and then the creation and placement of the advertising messages themselves. Advertising is a way of mass selling. It's only useful if you have a large enough market wanting to hear about your offering, and if there are *media outlets* (i.e., newspapers, television stations, radio, and so on) available that reach the market.

PLAIN ENGLISH

Media outlets are the newspapers, magazines, billboards, television stations, and other vehicles available for you to purchase commercial space or time.

Advertising doesn't work alone. It is only one part of the promotional process, creating the environment in which more targeted selling can take place. Advertising contributes to the success of sales people, developing prospects and creating awareness and interest. It works both early in the sales process by helping to stimulate desire, and at the end of the process by helping the purchaser feel happy about his choice.

TIP

The key to getting good publicity is to find something about your business and the product or service it offers that is truly newsworthy and then find the right media to tell your story. Print and television editors are always on the lookout for newsworthy stories that will interest their readers or viewers.

Selling makes up the second leg of that stool. Advertising brings in prospects. Salespeople use their skills to turn prospects into trial buyers and trial buyers into repeat customers. There are a number of skills involved in sales, from understanding human behavior and the selling process to knowing how to motivate yourself when you'd rather be out fishing. If you're smart, your promotional strategy will include plans for developing these skills in yourself and your staff. The third leg of the stool under promotions is *sales promotions.* Sales promotions are the short-term strategies marketers come up with to give customers incentives to buy. When you use coupons from your local quick-lube station or dry cleaner, or you drop your business card in a bowl to enter a drawing, you're responding to a sales promotion.

Sales promotions are tools that produce results quickly but without lasting impact. When the promotion ends, its effect tapers off quickly and sales will return to previous expectations. Sales promotions are common in some industries and rare in others. Professional service providers, such as lawyers or accountants, are not likely to engage in two-for-one offers or business card drawings. Retailers, on the other hand, are likely to use sales promotions often.

PROMOTIONS IN ACTION

For University Credit Union and Bob's Bottomless Boats, promotions are a dominant part of the marketing mix. That's because these businesses have an ongoing need to communicate with their audiences (because competition is intense) and because those audiences can be reached efficiently through local newspapers and local television (because both appeal to a broad consumer audience in a relatively confined geographic area). Don't be surprised to find more about these businesses when we take up the topic of advertising.

TIP

There are three good reasons to engage in a sales promotion: to temporarily increase sales, to create a sense of urgency, and to produce temporary excitement. Resist the temptation to use promotions for other reasons, such as to hurt a competitor.

IT'S THE PEOPLE, PERIOD

Marketing is psychology applied to the arena of business. For that reason, psychology, an understanding of people and why they do what they do, is critical to anyone who wants to be a success in marketing. Or to succeed in the world, for that matter. Want to be happier? Less stressed? Better able to influence others, more savvy about their influence on you? Get more money, friends, power? Study psychology, baby. Only through understanding human behavior can we hope to meet the marketplace and have a clue what's going on.

In the world of the marketer, people fall into four groups:

- Your staff team
- Your suppliers
- Your customers
- Your competitors

Obviously, customers are the group of most interest to marketers. But the other groups are key as well. If the staff aren't persuaded of the benefits of a product, or aren't informed of a promotional campaign underway, they can unintentionally undermine your best efforts. Suppliers and competitors can cause you hell if you don't understand what they're doing and what motivates their actions. As marketers, we must be close students of the people all around us.

There's a dark side to this. We study, we gain knowledge, and we gain expertise at using it. Marketers use psychology to manipulate people to produce behaviors, like purchasing a specific brand or voting for a specific candidate.

With our knowledge of persuasive techniques, we have power that we can use for good or for evil.

TIP

Adhere to a simple, two-part moral formula and you should be okay. First, cause no harm; and second, do nothing you wouldn't want to tell your mother.

"People" is where the new thinking in marketing is happening these days. Theories and techniques are growing around concepts like one-to-one marketing and permission selling. The rise of management practices such as customer relationship management (CRM) reflects the importance of people in the marketing process.

In any of our example businesses, there would be no business without people! No music students for Kai, no boaters for Bob. No people to tell their life stories to Anita, nobody to log on to University Credit Union's online services, no grandmas to buy dolls from A Life of Faith for little girls who'll someday study music, buy a boat, or join a credit union.

Right now, use the following worksheet to record your thoughts about the four P's plus one in your marketing mix. Jot down any strengths and weaknesses that come to mind as you think about each *P* in the mix. Then rank each item in order of its significance to your current situation.

P	Strength	Ranking	Weakness	Ranking
Product	_____	_____	_____	_____
Price	_____	_____	_____	_____
Place	_____	_____	_____	_____
Promotions	_____	_____	_____	_____
People	_____	_____	_____	_____

THE 30-SECOND RECAP

- Product, price, place, and promotion are the four elements of the marketing mix that combine to attract and sell offerings to customers.

- To maximize your product strategy, think about your products' place in their life cycle, the benefits each segment of users receives from the offering, and what innovations might keep your offering "new and improved."

- Your prices should be based on more than just costs plus profit margin.

- The successful place strategy will get the right goods, in the right quantity, to the right place, for the lowest possible cost, without sacrificing customer service.

- Promotional activities include advertising, personal selling, and sales promotions (short-term incentives).

- People, including staff, suppliers, customers, and competitors, are critical to good marketing and deserve study so that you can understand and influence their behavior.

Playing the Pricing Game

It goes without saying that the goal of any business start-up is profit. If you don't make a profit, you won't be in business for very long. Making a profit is simple, really; you just have to make more than you spend. The trick is to know how much more. To guarantee profits, accurate pricing is absolutely critical. Your prices must be high enough to cover all costs and enable you to earn a reasonable return, but low enough to remain attractive to potential customers. This section describes a variety of pricing methods and guidelines to help you decide which pricing method best suits your particular business.

PRICING STRATEGIES

New entrepreneurs often have difficulty pricing the value of their time and expertise. Some say that they can work cheap because they're fast, so they'll fill in with low-paying jobs between more lucrative opportunities. For this group, the mind-set seems to be that any work is better than no work; this may seem reasonable when you first start out and want to make your mark, but the downside of this short-sighted approach is that customers will think of your business as "cheap"—even after it has become established.

Another group of entrepreneurs takes the approach from the outset that they're worth top dollar. They demand fair pricing for the value they provide, and they won't accept anything less. This group seems to be more successful in the long run. They get off to a slow start, but by setting their standards high to begin with, when their business does become established, it usually has a favorable image and a firm foundation.

Setting prices for products and services is a challenging task for small and home-based business owners. The *best price* is not necessarily the one that will create the most business. The selling price must take cost, market conditions, and perceived value into account. For a business to make money, it must deal with hard economic facts.

Some major considerations in setting prices include these:

- Direct costs (materials and supplies)
- Indirect costs (overhead)
- Adequate salary for the owner
- Markup for profit
- Prices of comparable products or services, and what the market will bear (the amount the customer is willing to pay)

To begin the process of establishing the best prices for your business offerings, answer the following questions:

- How much does it cost to produce your product?
- What are all of the costs involved in operating your business?
- How much profit do you want to make?
- Can you afford to sell this product for that price?
- Will the customer buy your product at this price?
- Does your price reflect the business image you want to create?
- Are there federal, state, and local laws that regulate pricing of your product?

PLAIN ENGLISH

The best price is the market price at which the customer is willing to buy and the seller is willing to sell.

Begin the pricing process by determining the top price (ceiling price) and the bottom price (floor price) that a customer will pay for your product or service. Considering your target customer, your competition, your business image, and information from trade and professional organizations will help you determine your ceiling and floor prices.

CAUTION

If you exceed the ceiling price by too much, you may lose sales by being over the average market price. On the other hand, if your prices are too low, you may *cheapen the value of the item* from the consumers' point of view because they've probably seen your competitors' similar products at a higher price.

The market determines your ceiling price. Your bottom price, or price floor, is determined by all your costs of doing business, the price below which you *cannot sell and make a profit.* If you want to sell to stores, you need to consider whether your floor price would allow the store to double your price and still stay within the average market price for the item.

The price of your product or service needs to include all the costs of operating your business and the amount of profit you desire. Your ability to earn a profit will determine whether you remain in business and bring your dream to reality. You may make a quarter of a million dollars, but if your costs are greater than that, you're losing money.

PRICING POLICY

There are several approaches to establishing a *pricing policy:*

PLAIN ENGLISH

Pricing policy (or pricing strategy) is the method you use to determine the prices for your products and services. It needs to be continually reviewed and updated to be sure you're always positioned for sufficient profit to build your business.

- **Value pricing.** The uniqueness of your product and your ability to customize and provide special services will allow you to charge more for your goods. If your customers perceive your product to be excellent, and if you are reliable or are highly regarded in your field, this approach can allow for maximum profits. Value pricing is best used when there is little or no competition. If there is competition, you periodically review your market position, and maintain and lower prices—or perhaps even increase them accordingly.

- **Competitive pricing.** If your product is the same or similar to what is being offered by others, you may want to use a competitive pricing approach; that is, price your product in the same price range as the competition. This approach serves to attract and maintain customers. Another way to meet and beat competitive pricing is to offer package pricing to customers. If you produce household accessories, you may offer a lamp and a companion vase at a lower price if purchased together than if purchased separately, or special discounts for buying several mix-and-match pieces. A service business could offer something free that would normally be billable, such as a bonus when certain services are purchased, or that business could package some services together, offering a saving over buying them separately.

- **Cost pricing.** Cost pricing is one of the most commonly used approaches. It figures the cost of goods sold times three, or the cost of goods sold plus a predetermined markup of 25 to 50 percent. Be careful if you choose to use this approach: It often overlooks the effects of competition, changes in costs of overhead and materials, and current trends in the market, so it may not provide you with a maximum profit.

Unit Cost Per Item

To arrive at the unit cost per item, you have to establish the total cost for the *labor and materials used to make one item.* Do not include your labor in your calculations for designing the prototype (first one), because designing the prototype will take much longer to produce than the final product; instead, use the average time it takes to make the product after you've made four to six of them. If your work is always one of a kind, however, such as the work of a painter, sculptor, woodcarver, or other artist, then, of course, use the actual time that it takes to make the original piece.

TIP

An easy way to have your material costs ready for unit pricing is to figure them out as each new shipment arrives. Break down the bulk purchase into measurements used for that type of material. For instance, if you buy a spool of ribbon that is 25 yards, add the freight and then divide the total by 25 to arrive at the cost per yard.

There are two methods for figuring unit cost per item:

■ **Time log.** You need a method of keeping track of production time. It can be as simple as a notepad in which you jot down each start and stop time, and then add up the totals to arrive at the actual amount of time that it took to make each item. Some like to use an electric clock, the type with hands. When they start an item, they set it at 12:00 and then unplug it when they stop. By doing this each time they start and stop, if the clock says 6:00 when they finish the item, for example, they know that it took six hours. Even with this method, you should keep a written log of the total time used to produce each item.

■ **Materials log.** There are two ways to track materials used for each item: Write down exactly what you used in each item, or do an estimate based on the cost of the materials divided by the number of items you can make. The advantage to this method is that it includes waste. Either method will give you accurate unit costs. Experiment to see what works best for you.

Costing Terms

Become familiar with terms used in costing a product. Knowing what costs are included in the terms can help you better understand pricing formulas.

DIRECT COSTS

Production costs figured in direct costs include ...

- **In a wholesale operation.** This cost includes the materials and supplies for production, labor for production, and any incoming shipping fees. (If you are the production unit of your business, the labor is your time in the actual production.) Labor costs should include salary and related expenses.
- **In a retail operation.** The cost of goods includes the wholesale cost of the product, plus the shipping and handling costs.

INDIRECT COSTS = OVERHEAD

Include the costs (overhead) of running the business, *excluding* the cost of goods sold. If you produce several different products, you will want to distribute indirect costs to all of them. The easiest way for you to do this is to divide your total indirect costs by the total number of units produced. This will give you your indirect cost per item.

Indirect costs include both fixed and variable costs:

- **Fixed costs.** Those costs that remain the same during the month or year, regardless of the number of units produced or sold. These costs include items such as the following:
  - Allowance for the space used in your home, or rent, or other cost of your work space
  - Labor cost for administrative duties
  - Equipment payments, auto payments, interest, and bank fees
  - Accounting, insurance, and legal costs
  - Utility payments, telephone bill, water bill, and laundry expenses
  - Business licenses, membership dues, and subscriptions for trade publications and magazines

TIP

As a home-based or small business owner, you will probably fill many roles: designer, producer, administrator, and so on. Each role requires different talents and tasks, so each could be figured at a different wage rate. For example, when you are in the designer role, you may charge $50 an hour for your expertise; in your roles as production worker or office staffer, however, you may want to calculate your salary at a lower rate.

■ **Variable costs.** The costs that vary during the month or year depending on goods produced or goods sold. These costs include items such as these:

- ■ Office and shipping supplies
- ■ Business travel (to customer locations, trade shows, buying trips, and so forth)
- ■ Advertising or promotion, and photography
- ■ Merchant account fees, bad debts, or other losses
- ■ Shipping and handling

DETERMINING COSTS

To determine a price, you need to figure the cost of your materials, the amount of time needed to make the item, the amount of money needed to pay for the time (direct costs), and the operation expenses necessary to run your business (indirect costs or overhead). Be realistic! If the business uses materials, there has to be some waste. Failure to allow for waste will reduce your profit.

Your direct and indirect costs can be recorded on a break-even analysis worksheet. Your total direct and indirect costs are used to figure your *break-even point.*

The break-even point can give you a realistic picture of the financial aspect of your business offering, and it must be considered before you set your price. When they start out, so many artisans feel uncomfortable charging as much as everyone else. Don't let your lack of self-confidence fool you into settling for a lower income. Take the time to figure out exactly what it costs you *to produce a piece and sell it.* Avoid the mistake of making a product just because you like it, or like to make it, if the numbers don't work. Make that favorite item in your spare time instead, for fun.

PLAIN ENGLISH

The **break-even point** is the point at which you will neither lose money nor make money.

MARKET-BASED PRICING

This type of pricing is based on a price comparison of similar products or services using the current selling prices for a specific market area. This method assumes that a competitive market exists! Prices are set by market activity, not by a particular vendor or group. Terms and discounts in the market, the degree of competition, and many other factors should be taken into consideration. Be alert to where in the life cycle a product may be in your price comparison. This method requires knowledge of the current market conditions and the ability to accurately compare same or similar items.

Start by carrying out a competitive analysis. Find out how your product compares with your competitors' on the basis not only of price, but also of costs. If you were going to source this information by approaching competitors directly, a word of caution—don't. It could be considered an attempt at *price fixing.*

CAUTION

The Sherman Act in the United States (and similar legislation in many other jurisdictions) prohibits businesses of any size from entering "contracts, combinations, or conspiracies" in restraint of trade. Making deals with competitors about what price you'll charge—in other words, price fixing—is illegal. This is one area where you just don't want to give even the whiff of an impression of doing anything along those lines.

Instead, to keep tabs on what your competition is up to, read their ads, talk to their suppliers, engage mystery shoppers in conversation about your competitors, or play consumer and ask them to send their brochures and price lists (to your cousin, of course). Also check retail prices for similar items in stores and galleries. (You can usually assume that the wholesale price is half of the asking price.)

When you've completed your research on the competition, analyze your competitive advantages and disadvantages. If you learn that you have an advantage over your competition, this advantage is something that your customers will likely pay more for. Adjust your prices accordingly.

PRODUCT PRICING FORMULAS

There is a variety of formulas for pricing. You may want to examine several of them before you select one. You may also find that you will need to use more than one pricing formula.

As you use these formulas, keep in mind that *the easiest formula to use may not always be the best.* Pricing formulas serve as guides for you to make a fair profit. Then whatever final price you arrive at will need to be compared with the going market price. If you cannot realize a profit after you've factored in labor and materials and overhead (direct and indirect costs) and added a percentage for profit, consider dropping that particular item, or find a way to cut the expenses or reduce the production time for it.

You can use several basic methods or formulas to determine the wholesale price of your product. Work through the formulas with your own facts and figures. Remember that no single formula will work for all products or ensure maximum profit. Putting your data into these formulas should enable you to compare the different ways to price your product.

If you don't know what your overhead is because you're just starting out, you can figure that, as a general rule, it should be 20 to 25 percent of your labor and materials.

The following example illustrates the use of each of the formulas:

An artisan manufactures lamps and wants to work 40 hours per week operating the business. Twenty lamps can be produced in 40 hours. The indirect costs have been figured at $40 per week, and the materials to manufacture the lamps cost $40 per week. The business owner wants to make $12 per hour, or at least $480 per week in wages (labor). A $40 profit per week is needed for inflation, business expansion, and investment.

Formula 1

Materials + labor = $_____ ÷ number of units = $_____: wholesale selling price per unit

Example: ($40 + $480 = $520) ÷ 20 units = $26 per item. This pricing method is frequently used, but there is no allowance for overhead costs, inflation, or profits.

Formula 2

Materials × 3 = $_____ ÷ number of units = $_____: wholesale selling price per unit

Example: $40 × 3 = $120 ÷ 20 = $6 per item. This formula is easy to calculate, but profit margin is slim or nil unless production time is very efficient and materials are relatively inexpensive and readily available.

Formula 3

Materials + indirect costs + production time × hourly wage = $_____ ÷ number of units = $_____: wholesale selling price per unit

Example: $40 + $40 + (40 hours × $12 = $480) = $560 ÷ 20 = $28 per item. This approach does not include a profit factor.

Formula 4

Materials + indirect costs + desired weekly wage + profit = $_____ ÷ number of units = $_____: wholesale selling price per unit

Example: $40 + $40 + $480 + $40 ÷ 20 = $30 per item. This is the most individualized method because you are deciding on the wage you want and the amount of time you spend earning that wage.

Formula 5

Materials + labor + (50 percent of materials and labor) = $_____ ÷ number of units = $_____: wholesale selling price per unit

Example: $40 + $480 + (.50 × 480 = $240) = $760 ÷ 20 = $38 per item. This direct cost approach depends on establishing a contribution percentage that will cover (contribute to) all your overhead expenses plus your profit. This example is figured on direct costs (materials and labor) but can also be figured per labor hours, per pound of raw materials, or per machine hours.

TIP

When you use any of these formulas, you will arrive at the wholesale price per item. See the "Retail Pricing" section that follows to calculate the price for selling at the retail level.

Formula 6

Labor + materials + overhead = $ _____ (subtotal here) + profit (take 20 percent of the subtotal to arrive at the profit figure) = $_____: wholesale price

Example: $480 + $40 + $40 = $560 ($560 × 20% = $112) + $112 = $672 ÷ 20 = $33.60 per item. This formula is very accurate because it contains all the actual costs and provides a 20 percent profit allowance as a constant factor.

Formula 7 (Percentage Markup Basis)

This is calculated by dividing the original cost into the amount of markup and then multiplying the result times 100. The amount of money that a business adds into a product's price, over and above the cost of the product, is expressed as a percent. A piece of candy costing $.05 to produce that has a markup of $.10 (meaning that the price to the consumer is $.15) has a percentage markup of 200 percent.

RETAIL PRICING

If you decide to sell your product at retail, you must first establish the wholesale price and then establish a retail price. You can use two basic methods to price for retail, the keystone method and the dollar markup method:

- **Keystone method.** Assumes that you will double the wholesale price of the product to obtain a retail price. Formula: Wholesale price × 2 = retail price.

- **Dollar markup method.** Begins when you determine the markup in dollars needed to cover your operating expenses and provide your business with a profit. Formula: Wholesale price + dollar markup = retail price.

The following example illustrates how to determine a retail price using these methods:

A manufacturing business decides to retail its teddy bears through craft shows. Using one of the previously illustrated pricing formulas, the owner has figured the wholesale price (cost) of one of the bears to be $21. The owner needs to recover costs associated with attending the craft show (booth rent, travel, retail license, lodging, and so on). The owner needs to achieve at least a $19 markup on each bear sold. Use these figures to compare the two methods.

Keystone Method	
Wholesale price × 2 = retail price	$21 × 2 = $42

Dollar Markup Method	
Wholesale price + dollar markup = retail price	$21 + $19 = $40

It's important to keep your own retail prices the same whether you sell at trade shows, on the phone, via sales reps, on the Internet, or at your own facility. Wholesale buyers need to feel assured that you will not undercut their efforts to sell your work. Undercutting is a quick way to create a negative business image and destroy the business relationships that you're working hard to build.

CAUTION

The easiest price formula to use may not always be the best. Price formulas serve as guides to what an item should be priced at for you to make a reasonable profit. To realize a profit, you need to include labor, materials, and overhead (direct and indirect costs), and add a percentage for profit. Then compare the final price with the going market price.

Test each of these formulas using a piece of your work. Ask yourself whether you think you can sell the item at that price. If you can't, where can you cut some of the costs? Do you think that you can sell it for more based on the average market-based price? The most important consideration is to make sure that you're charging enough for each item you make so that you can earn a livable wage and stay in business. The fastest way to go out of business is to sell a lot of work but lose money on every sale.

DECEPTIVE PRICING

The Federal Trade Commission (FTC) has jurisdiction over deceptive pricing practices. At the state level, it's usually the attorney general's office or, in bigger cities, the district attorney's consumer fraud unit that enforces laws dealing with deceptive trade practices. The two biggest problems that enforcers encounter concern merchants' incorrect price comparisons with prices of other merchants or with their own regular prices, and merchants who offer something advertised as free but that has a hidden cost.

PRICE COMPARISONS

Offering a reduction from your usual selling price is a common and powerful sales technique. To satisfy legal requirements, however, it's essential that the former price be the actual, bona-fide price at which you offered the article. Otherwise, the pricing is misleading.

> **Example:** Woodworks, Inc. produces design software and announces a new product for $129. The company sells the product to wholesalers as if it were a $79 product and similarly discounts it to direct customers. The $129 price has never really existed except as a device to mislead customers into thinking that they were receiving a discount.

Price comparisons often use words such as *regularly, usually,* or *reduced.* For example, it's common to see a price tag that says, "Regularly $200. Now $150." On the other hand, sometimes a sign says "40% off our regular price." These comparisons are fine, legally, if you in fact offered the sale merchandise at the old price for a reasonable length of time. They're not okay if you've bought or produced a special batch of merchandise just for the sale and created a fictional "regular" price or one that you adhered to for only a day or two.

If your ad compares your price with what other merchants are charging for the same product, be sure of two things: that the other merchants are selling the identical product, and that there were a sufficient number of sales at the higher price in your area to make your offer a legitimate bargain. In other words, make sure that the higher comparison price isn't an isolated or unrepresentative price.

FREE OFFERS

If you say that goods or services are "free" or "without charge," be sure that there are no unstated terms or conditions qualifying the offer. If there are any limits, state them clearly and conspicuously. Assume, for example, that you offer a free paintbrush to anyone who buys your kit, "How to Paint Natural Roses," for $8.95, and you describe the kind of brush. Because you're disclosing the terms and conditions of your offer, you're in good shape so far. But there are pitfalls to avoid. If the $8.95 is more than you usually charge for this kind of kit, the brush clearly isn't free. You can offer free products or services, *as long as there are no strings attached.*

As you can see, setting the *right price* for your products and services is absolutely crucial to the profitability of your business. With careful calculations and a methodical approach, you should be able to arrive at fair prices without too much difficulty. But don't stop there: Your prices operate within a constantly changing environment, and you need to be ever vigilant to ensure that your prices remain at their best competitive position.

One final piece of advice: If you're in doubt, price high rather than low. It is much easier to reduce prices than it is to increase them.

THE 30-SECOND RECAP

- Your pricing strategy should include consideration of the perceived value and the going market rate as well as the product cost.
- Market-based pricing is determined by how much the customer is willing to pay for a particular product or service.
- Usually more than one pricing strategy is used because no single strategy is appropriate for all products or services.
- The retail price is usually figured by doubling the wholesale price.
- When in doubt, price higher; it's easier to reduce prices than to raise them.

Understanding Advertising

Advertising is everywhere. None of us can escape it, even if we want to—and many of us do. Yet despite criticism, which has been around as long as advertising itself, the volume of ads in any medium continually increases over the long term.

Why?

Because it works. That is, advertising works enough to encourage companies to keep doing it.

This section provides a general overview of what makes advertising work and why so many companies use it in so many different forms. You'll also learn a bit about public relations, another method of business communication.

WHAT IS ADVERTISING AND WHAT DOES IT DO?

Advertising is a positive message about a product, service, or organization in a communication medium that is paid to carry the message. In any advertisement, the sender of the message is identified. (Note that the sender does not have to be a business. Many nonbusiness outfits, including the military and nonprofit organizations such as the American Heart Association, use advertising, as do individuals, such as political candidates and people selling their cars in the classified ads of a newspaper.)

Since the rise of television advertising in the 1950s, critics have said that advertising manipulates people.

The manipulation allegedly takes the form of using constant repetition, over-promising benefits, hiding products' disadvantages, and, in the minds of some critics, even hiding subconscious messages that in effect "hypnotize" people into buying. Other criticism states that advertising uses constant intrusion, bad grammar, and, worst of all, bad taste to appeal to the lowest common denominator. Finally, some people oppose advertising on the grounds that it needlessly raises the price of the products being advertised.

TIP

Advertising Age and *Adweek* are weekly publications that cover trends and issues in the advertising industry. If you are interested in influencing your company's advertising strategy, they may be worth a look. They're available at large newsstands, by subscription, and at many libraries.

Defenders of advertising point out that consumers realize advertising is self-serving, so they view it skeptically. Defenders also believe that people's purchase decisions are influenced by many factors besides advertising: recommendations from friends; their own experiences and observations; and elements such as salespeople, service, warranties, financing, and, of course, price. Although a lot of advertising deserves criticism, no one has proven that it forces people to buy products.

Advertising's place in the marketing mix is simple: It is part of promotion, the fifth P as previously discussed. It plays a role in establishing and reinforcing the product's positioning. As a marketing tool, advertising supports the sales force.

Advertising, and any advertising campaign, works with the other elements in the mix to present the product to prospects, along with reasons to buy. Advertising cannot make up for failings in the product or in other parts of the marketing mix.

COMPONENTS OF ADVERTISING

Many questions arise in any advertising decision. The major ones center on ...

- **Message.** What should you say in advertisements?
- **Money.** How much should you spend on advertising?
- **Media.** Where should you run the advertisements?

AD MESSAGES: SAY WHAT?

There are three types of advertising messages: creative messages, selling messages, and those that that try to sell creatively.

A creative message tries to capture the audience's attention by standing out from the clutter (advertising overload). Advertisements that rely on humor are good examples of creative messages. So are most MTV-influenced television ads, such as those for Levi's jeans, soft drinks, and some luxury cars.

These approaches are often called image advertising, because they aim to create a mood, a feeling, and an image around the product rather than to sell it on its features, benefits, or competitive merits. Jeans could be sold on their merits. In fact, Levi's once were, showing their durability with a picture of two mules trying to pull the pants apart. Soft drinks and luxury cars could also be sold on features and benefits, and sometimes are. But creative messages tend to ignore standard descriptions of features and benefits, and instead focus on getting attention and generating an attractive product image.

Selling messages are more matter-of-fact in their approach and oriented toward features, benefits, and requests for action ("Buy now and save up to 30 percent on any Black and Decker power tool").

Slice-of-life commercials for detergents, cleaners, headache and indigestion remedies, and diet products are good examples of selling messages. You know the kind: A woman suffering from a cold can't get to sleep. She gets out of bed, goes to the medicine cabinet, opens it, and takes some NyQuil. Next, she is sleeping soundly. This is straightforward and, for these kinds of products, effective advertising.

The best advertising aims to combine the factual information of a selling message with the humor or visual appeal of a creative message. This is extremely hard to do. The Energizer Bunny ad campaign was a great example of a creative (and funny) ad that constantly sold the main feature of the battery: long life. People even started referring to their most energetic co-workers or tireless friends as "Energizer bunnies." This kind of advertising is the exception rather than the rule.

Most advertisers want either image-oriented ads that create an ambiance of luxury or "hipness," or reality-based pitches that tout a benefit ("Get better checkups with Crest") or incite customers to action ("Only three days left in the Toyota sell-a-thon"). At the same time, a major goal of almost all advertising is to establish or reinforce a *brand.*

PLAIN ENGLISH

A **brand** is a company name (Levi's, Chevrolet) or product name (501 jeans, Corvette), together with its logo (that is, a distinctive graphic associated with the name) and any other identifiers, which can even include the shape of a bottle (as for Perrier water).

HOT COPY

The kind of message you use depends on your product, its positioning, the audience, and the medium you are using. So does the content of your message. Various guidelines developed over the years offer hints on developing *ad copy.* Two of the most famous, which are useful, are the AIDA formula and the Unique Selling Proposition.

The AIDA formula helps you remember the four key things that good copy must do: get Attention, capture Interest, create Desire, and request Action.

- Getting *attention* is essential because people are busy, clutter is everywhere, and you can't sell to people until you have their focus. Humor, color, movement, design, offbeat situations, and astonishingly attractive models are major tools for getting attention.

- After the audience notices the ad, you have to get them *interested* in it. Copy that starts with a provocative question ("Can you afford to die?") or statement ("Don't throw money away") are trusty tactics. Others include dramatizing a problem, offering an escape, or using a celebrity endorsement, which can also get attention.

PLAIN ENGLISH

Copy narrowly refers to the text in a print ad or the words read by an announcer. More broadly, it means the total ad as presented to the audience. This includes not only the text, but also the color, graphics, photos, video, and so on. Copy strategy refers to all the choices you have to make in developing an ad.

- A good ad must create desire for the product. Appeal to the heart, the head, the stomach, the wallet, the whatever. Tell customers about the money they'll save, the fun they'll have, or the affection they'll win with your product. Show the luscious turkey, the happy family, the headache-free worker, the beautiful lawn—whatever your product or service offers. Make them want it.

- Then you ask for *action*. Tell your customers what they have to do to quench this flaming desire you have created. Sample actions you can suggest include these: Call now. For a limited time only. Send no money. Operators are standing by. Be the first on your block. Saturday only. Don't let this once-in-a-lifetime opportunity slip through your fingers.

Another excellent concept for developing a message, or a theme for an entire campaign, is the Unique Selling Proposition (or USP). The USP is, as the name indicates, the unique thing about your product or service that provides a motivation for people to buy it.

This can be something real, such as Federal Express's "Guaranteed overnight delivery," or something made up, such as "Wonder Bread builds strong bodies 12 ways."

A really great USP is not just a memorable tag line, like Sprite's "Obey your thirst." Instead, it's something unique about the product that provides motivation to buy. The USP can begin in the product-development process. "Guaranteed overnight delivery" is a feature, benefit, product, and selling proposition—all in one. And when FedEx started, it was unique.

If you can't create a USP around a wonderful and intrinsic feature of your product, you have to come up with something almost as good. "You deserve a break today" is great because it reminds people who are too tired and overworked to cook that there's a fast way to get a tasty meal. It's not in itself unique (any fast-food outfit can make that claim), but through advertising it became unique because it was McDonald's message.

MONEY: YOUR ADVERTISING BUDGET

The advertising budget is part of the marketing budget. It's the amount the company will spend on paid messages in the media. This will include any ad agency fees as well as money spent on the media itself. If your account is large enough, the advertising agency works for 15 percent of the bill for *media buys*. If not, the agency bills you directly for its services.

PLAIN ENGLISH

A **media buy** is the purchase of space (in print media) or time (in broadcast media) for running your advertisement.

The advertising budget can include the direct-mail budget, because technically direct mail is an advertising medium.

There are several ways of setting your advertising budget. One easy way is just to set the amount of the ad budget as some percentage of sales. If you do well spending 5 percent of total sales on advertising, do that. Or move it higher. Or lower. This method has the advantage of tying this cost to revenues, but it does little else.

TIP

If you are shopping for advertising or are curious about a particular media's demographics and audience, call and ask for a rate card, which details the prices for various ads. Most media sales departments can also send you a media kit that provides even more information, including demographics.

Other approaches are to just pick a number (yes, this is done), or to spend the industry average, or to spend a bit above or below the industry average. Many advertisers fall into habits, believing that because they've always advertised in certain media, they should continue to do so. Habit is a bad way to budget.

There is a more thoughtful approach: Decide what you want to achieve, and then see how much you must spend on advertising to get there. This could result in your spending either more or less than you did as a percentage of sales last year or compared with the industry average. However, it ties the expenditures to what you're trying to accomplish. You may not have the money to do all you would like to do, but at least you can then back off the "ideal" number and spend where you believe it will do the most good.

There's an element of risk in advertising expenditures. Advertising is an inexact medium in that no message is guaranteed to work and the correlation between expenditures can vary. There is also the issue of luck. A massive distraction, such as a natural disaster, snowstorm, or major trial on television, can distract people or even keep them from buying. For instance, warm winters hurt ski resorts even though they can make snow and usually have temperatures cold enough to ski. It is just that people don't think about skiing as much during a warm winter.

If you've hired an advertising agency to handle your advertising budget, a media planner in the agency will determine the best use of your money. He or she will calculate the cost per thousand. That is, the cost of reaching 1,000 people for the media being considered. Cost per thousand (or CPM) places the costs of various media on an equal basis.

Cost per thousand enables you to compare the costs of media that deliver different-size audiences at different prices. Be careful, however. A low CPM is of no value unless the audience being delivered is *your* audience.

MEDIA: WHO'S WATCHING?

As you develop your advertising message, you have to consider which media you will use to deliver that message to your target audience. The major media you have to choose from are print and broadcast. More specifically, they include the following:

- Magazines
- Newspapers
- Broadcast television
- Cable television
- Radio

Other media include these:

- Direct mail
- Outdoor advertising (billboards, posters)
- Internet

Different media have varying potential for displaying your product, explaining its uses, and dramatizing the satisfaction customers will get from it. Some products, such as exercise machines, benefit from live demonstration, which television provides. Others, such as mutual funds, benefit from printed charts and graphs, and newspapers and magazines work well for that. Still others

benefit from a quick reminder to customers that you're always available. A
billboard can generate that kind of *awareness.*

PLAIN ENGLISH

Awareness is a major goal in advertising. On one level, it means
that people know your product exists. On another, it means they
think of your product when making a purchase. (This is called
top-of-mind awareness.) On another, very specific level, awareness means that people recall seeing your ad. Market research
can measure these kinds of awareness.

Before you choose the media in which to run your ad, you have to decide what
you're trying to do with your ad. Are you demonstrating? Dramatizing?
Explaining? Displaying? Motivating an immediate purchase? Then you must
consider the media's ability to help you do that.

Consider the Demographics

The demographics of a medium are the demographics of the audience that the
medium delivers to the advertiser. The desirability of a medium's demographics depends on your target market or markets. In other words, it depends on
what you are selling and to whom you are selling it.

It's no coincidence that you'll find rock 'n' roll CDs advertised in *Rolling Stone*
and investment CDs in *Money.* Movies are advertised during television shows
for 18- to 34-year-olds because they are the most frequent moviegoers. Products
for babies and the elderly are advertised during soap operas because mothers
with young children and housebound elderly people tend to watch those shows.
(In fact, soap operas got their name because detergents were originally the
most heavily advertised products on daytime dramas.)

These examples may lead you to believe that choosing the right media for
your target market is a no-brainer. It often isn't. First, there's the issue of cost:
Getting your ad in a major national magazine or during prime-time TV can be
expensive. Second, the psychographics can be impossible to determine. Third,
there's the chance that your target audience will not even see the ad due to
clutter (too many ads competing for attention) or "channel surfing."

As a new medium, the World Wide Web is carving out a role among the "old
media" of print (magazines and newspapers), television, radio, and outdoor
platforms (billboards and posters). But as of this writing, marketers are questioning the effectiveness of web-based advertising. This is to be expected,
given the number of dot.com failures in recent years and the recession-related
downturn in ad spending.

Measures of web-based advertising's reach, frequency, and impact are being developed because metrics such as hits and click-throughs have proven inadequate. Moreover, most users ignore banner ads and see pop-up ads as intrusive (or infuriating). Yet readers ignore magazine ads and hate television commercials, too.

As a new medium, the web is still evolving, and so is its role in marketing. The novelty has worn off for most users, who now turn to the web for information more than entertainment. Given this, marketers must carefully tailor their messages and offers to fit their product and audience. For instance, compare several sites for prescription medications and universities with those for resorts and music CDs to see how information-rich sites (for the medications and schools) differ from those geared more toward "straight selling."

OTHER MEDIA CHARACTERISTICS

When deciding where to place your ad, you must also consider some other, somewhat technical media characteristics:

- **Reach** is an inexact number that attempts to quantify how many people or households have been exposed once to a single ad. Reach calculates the number of people using the media (that is, the number who read a publication, watch a particular television show, or listen to a particular radio station at a certain time of day) when the ad ran in that media. Reach tells you the number of people who were *potentially* exposed to the ad, not the number who actually saw it or can recall it.

- **Frequency** is the number of times these people will see or hear the advertisement. There's a way to measure frequency. Let's say a monthly magazine has 500,000 readers. Suppose that in a month, 200,000 will see the ad once, 200,000 will see the ad twice, and 100,000 will see it three times. The ad's frequency would equal 1.8, as calculated here:

  $(200,000 \times 1) + (200,000 \times 2) + (100,000 \times 3) = 900,000 \div 500,000 = 1.8$

  This number, which is more precise than the value for reach or measures of impact, can be compared with the frequencies of other media to evaluate them as potential advertising venues. In general, the higher the frequency, the better.

- **Impact** determines whether the advertisement is remembered and communicates what it's supposed to. Ultimately, impact should be evident in increased sales. However, the connection between advertising and sales can be fuzzy because factors other than advertising, including the competition and even social trends, can affect sales.

Impact can be assessed by market research designed to measure ad recall and even purchase behavior after recall.

Before choosing the correct media for your ad campaign, you must compare media on reach, frequency, and impact, as well as on cost and demographics. Then choose. After that, await the market's response.

PROMOTIONAL TOOLS

Promotional items have their place: You've probably got several corporate coffee mugs in your cabinet, or T-shirts and tote bags emblazoned with company logos in your closet. These and similar *premiums* carrying the name of your company or product should be part of an advertising or marketing campaign—but just a part.

Other tools of promotion include the following:

- Discounts
- Coupons
- Incentives and rebates
- Free samples and demonstration models
- Contests
- Special events

PLAIN ENGLISH

A **premium** is a token item such as a coffee mug or tote bag that features the company name and logo. Premiums are given away either free or with a purchase. The goal of a free premium is to get your company name out there.

Briefly, discounts, coupons, incentives, and rebates all have one goal: to get people to buy your product. A discount, coupon, or rebate reduces the price, usually for a limited time. Technically, incentives are any inducement to buy, but more narrowly include items such as optional features, related products, or special services offered for a limited time.

Free samples can be very effective with consumer packaged goods such as cereals, snack foods, mouthwash, and candy. Demonstration models (demos), such as a test drive for a car or a "demo disc" for a video game, let people try a product when free samples are impossible.

Contests work in three ways: First, they attract attention and associate your product with an exciting experience. (A chance to win concert tickets if you buy a CD is one example.) Second, those who enter the contest become more bonded with your product by having taken the trouble to enter. Third, by collecting entry forms, you are getting the names of potential prospects.

Sponsoring special events can take many forms. These include sporting events or teams, racing cars, marathons, or parts of an event (such as the Miller Half-Time Report for NBA games) or even the stadiums themselves (such as the Fleet Center in Boston, sponsored by Fleet Financial Services). These are not incentives to buy, but rather a means of advertising and associating the product or company and the event in the minds of the target market.

Of course, these promotional tools should reinforce one another and your advertising. For instance, a promotional tie-in with a movie combines premium items (figures of the characters), a special event (the release of the movie), and advertising (for the movie and the promotional item).

PUBLIC RELATIONS PROGRAMS

Public relations (PR), broadly defined, includes nonadvertising communications aimed at the company's existing and potential customers and shareholders, and at the general public. In many businesses, especially consulting, financial services, and health care, PR aims to establish the company's people as experts whom the media can call for interviews. These spokespeople boost the name recognition of the organization and represent the interests of the company and its industry to the public.

More narrowly, public relations focuses on developing article ideas for editors of print media and ideas for segments for producers of broadcast and cable media. These should, of course, place the company, its products, and its people in a positive light.

Public relations services also include writing speeches and press releases. Another key service is assisting executives in dealing with reporters and interviewers, especially in times of a company crisis.

Depending on your industry, good PR can be more powerful than advertising. People realize that an advertisement is a paid announcement intended to sell. But a positive story about your company or its people or products is generally viewed as fact, and therefore builds credibility in a way that is close to impossible with advertising.

In the early 1980s, a public panic ensued when poison was found in some Tylenol capsules. This could have led to a full-fledged public relations nightmare, but Johnson & Johnson, the manufacturer of Tylenol, acted instantly. First, the company immediately pulled all existing product off the shelves.

Then the CEO quickly addressed the media to discuss the manufacturing process, the investigation of how the poison got there, and the development of tamperproof packaging. The company also explained the situation in newspaper ads.

Johnson & Johnson's open, intelligent approach to this crisis is widely credited with earning back the public's trust in the product and regaining Tylenol sales.

On the other hand, in August 2000, the U.S. government began investigating deaths related to Ford Explorers and Firestone tires. Firestone recalled more than 6.5 million tires, about two thirds of which were on Ford SUVs and trucks. Initially, the companies supported one another in their public communications. Yet before the month was over, Ford released documents showing that Firestone had received complaints about tires in 1997. Firestone, of course, became defensive and cited problems with Ford's SUVs. Congressional hearings worsened the strain, and both companies wound up publicly brawling and blaming one another, to the detriment of both their images.

THE 30-SECOND RECAP

- Advertising is a paid-for, positive message in a communication medium. The sender of the message is identified. Advertising doesn't force anyone to buy a product, although getting people to buy is its ultimate goal.

- The best way to set the advertising budget is to decide what you want to achieve, then see how much you must spend on advertising to achieve it, and then look to your costs and your competition to reach a final figure.

- Ad copy must get attention, capture interest, create desire, and request action.

- Advertising media can be viewed in terms of reach, frequency, and impact. These three measures, plus cost per thousand and demographics, enable you to use similar measures to compare different media.

- Various promotional tools can reinforce advertising and help prompt people to buy. Public relations can build credibility in a way that advertising cannot, and good PR is essential during a company crisis.

Using Customer Information

Over in the conference room at University Credit Union, the marketing people are sitting across the table from the "IT" guy. He's the one from Information Technology, the one they go to for a mailing list of members living near the newest branch or a count of students using the online-banking website. Marketing and IT have faced off over this conference table before. The relationship is sometimes an uneasy one. After all, from the IT guy's point of view, his job is to support the people in operations by tracking member account data. "It's nice that member data is useful to Marketing," the IT guy thinks, "but that's not what we're here for."

For Cary, UCU's marketing director, IT's perception of marketing has got to change. So once again, she launches into her explanation of the importance of customer information to the marketing function.

It goes like this: It's a proven fact that it is cheaper and easier to sell new offerings to current customers than it is to recruit new customers. Sales to current customers are more profitable because it takes less money and time to reach them than to reach strangers in hopes of making a sale. To get those increased profits, to experience that reduced cost and effort of selling, you need one thing: customer information.

In this section, we discuss how using information about your current customers can help you generate significant more business for your company.

CUSTOMER INFORMATION IS KEY

With customer information you can differentiate your customers on the basis of their purchasing behavior, as well as other traits such as their demographic attributes and their life stages. This serves you well in that it helps you perform market research to predict their likely purchase needs, and it helps you predict and analyze trends. But it also serves your audience well. You provide better customer service when you have accurate information available to you at every customer *touch point.* By focusing on touch points, you influence your audience's perceptions of your business.

PLAIN ENGLISH

Touch points are the moments when an individual has a personal interaction with someone or something representing your business. When someone stops by your trade show booth, that's a touch point. When someone dials your phone number and reaches an automated voice response system, that's one, too. A touch point is an opportunity to either delight or disappoint an individual.

Accurate information lets you use what you know about certain customers who show potential to become better customers. You can flag them for special follow-up or target special offerings to them based on the products or services they're using now.

How marketers market has been changing over the past few years, and the big change is this: leveraging the value of customer information.

TIP

If you have only a few dollars to spend on marketing, concentrate your efforts on current customers. Because customers who use more of your products or services tend to build strong relationships with you, it makes sense to devote your resources to converting low-volume purchasers into loyal high-volume purchasers who either buy more frequently or buy more of different items you offer.

New buzzwords have sprung up to describe this big marketing idea. We now throw around phrases like touch points, one-to-one marketing, permission-based marketing, and customer relationship management (CRM). You'll be familiar with these terms and hopefully sold on using these techniques by the time you finish reading this section.

Big Idea: The Goal Is Share of Customer

In 1993, Don Peppers and Martha Rogers wrote a book that broke new ground in the field of marketing. That book, *The One to One Future,* presented a manifesto for how companies can increase profits by selling more things to fewer people. Their key insight? Instead of concentrating on how to reach an ever-larger number of new customers, the focus should be on keeping customers longer and getting more transactions from each of them over time.

The thinking behind their book, and their one-to-one marketing strategy, is straightforward, and it led directly to this moment, with Cary and the IT guy squaring off across the table. To emphasize her point, Cary asks everyone at the table to envision a customer's lifetime stream of needs from their credit union.

Members typically enroll in University Credit Union when they arrive on campus as freshmen. Their needs are for checking accounts, credit cards, and student loans. For some, there will be auto loans as well.

Then the students graduate and move into the working world. If the credit union can keep these customers, there will come a string of mortgages and lines of credit. These members start families and begin savings programs for their children's education. They take out loans for bigger houses and bigger cars. Many begin saving for retirement.

As life's parade passes the teller windows, the credit union's members will be met with the products and services they need from cradle to retirement condo. That, in a nutshell, is the *share-of-customer* approach to marketing.

PLAIN ENGLISH

The **share-of-customer** approach to marketing means that you don't focus on a single offering and try to sell it to as many customers as possible—you focus on addressing a larger share of each customer's needs over the long term.

Cary wants to launch a new marketing program aimed at increasing share of customer. To her, this is more than just a new ad campaign. It's a whole new philosophy, recognizing that members enrolled as students can and should be members for life. Her goal in calling this meeting between the Marketing and IT departments is to gain the cooperation she needs, so she can steer her marketing efforts in this new direction: building share of customer with one-to-one marketing. But Cary's success relies on more than just getting access to the customer information. One-to-one marketing can only be truly effective if it takes into account two things:

- We must consider each customer as an individual with a lifetime stream of needs and desires.
- We must collaborate with that customer if we are going to participate in that lifetime stream of purchases.

Collaborating with the customer has become a technique, and it's been given a name: *permission marketing.*

PERMISSION MARKETING

Peppers and Rogers's one-to-one marketing strategy led to subsequent eye-opening observations, including Seth Godin's popular book, *Permission Marketing: Turning Strangers into Friends, and Friends into Customers.* The basic idea of *permission marketing* is very simple. Consumers are constantly filtering out most marketing messages, but are actively looking for others related to their needs and desires of the moment. As marketers, we seek not to intrude on individuals with unwanted messages, but to engage in a dialogue with consumers who give us permission. If what we offer matches reasonably well with what's on their "wish lists," that dialogue develops into a relationship that grows stronger over time.

Permission marketing implies directing messages to those who are open to them and leaving the rest of the world in peace. Permission marketing absolutely requires getting and maintaining permission to exchange messages with potential customers, one to one. "You can't build a one-to-one relationship with a customer unless the customer explicitly agrees to the process," says Godin.

PLAIN ENGLISH

Permission marketing means obtaining permission from a prospect or customer before directing marketing efforts toward that person. Permission, properly gained and used, benefits both the consumer and the marketer.

Permission marketing benefits both the consumer and the marketer. Consumers get the information they need to make purchase decisions, and marketers get the efficiency of directing their efforts toward those most likely to buy.

The goal of permission marketing is to move those who've consented to the process along a continuum from strangers to friends to customers. To do this you engage in learning about each other. You don't spew information at a prospect; like any good relationship, you let the give and take of your conversations guide you. As a marketer, you need to have a "curriculum" ready to teach your prospects about you and your offerings, as their curiosity draws them closer to you. But you don't force that curriculum on your new friends. You respond to each offered permission with another lesson in the benefits of your offering.

Moments of contact, whether initiated by the prospective customer or by the marketer, are the touch points in the customer relationship. Each is an opportunity to strengthen that individual's feelings of trust, comfort, and loyalty in relation to the offering and the institution that offers it.

TIP

The goal of permission marketing is to get invited to engage in learning about each other. If the marketing messages you send have been invited, if they are relevant and personal, they will cut through the clutter and increase the recipient's knowledge about you and the benefits of your products or services.

At University Credit Union, Cary's got plans that make the cooperation of the IT guy a must. She wants to analyze current account information to create profiles of graduating students' typical needs. She then plans to solicit permission from individuals in highly defined target segments, to offer them messages about products or services that her analysis indicates they're likely to want.

That means capturing each response to the survey and then tracking every subsequent customer touch point, record by record. That's a lot of demand on the database.

Back in that meeting, Cary's practically pounding the table with her shoe as she makes her case. Accurate information tracking is necessary if she's going to know the permission or "opt-in" status of any one individual customer or prospect at any given moment. Accurate customer records will drive every step of the marketing approach that Cary envisions. With IT's help, she can do it.

EVERY TOUCH POINT IS AN OPPORTUNITY TO GAIN OR LOSE PERMISSION

Every touch point is a moment of truth. Handle it skillfully, and that customer interaction becomes an opportunity for personal follow-up, or to make a recommendation based on products and services that individual is using now. You can use customer touch points to cross-sell, to reward loyalty, and to stave off buyer's remorse with a well-chosen word in praise of a purchase decision.

Cross-selling is a useful technique to increase share of customer. At UCU, Cary's marketing plans include training the tellers and customer service representatives in cross-selling techniques. With customer information at their fingertips, they can easily see what products and services a customer isn't using but could be, judging by life stage and demographics.

How can you use touch points to increase your share of customer? Educate customers about the wide range of products and services beyond those they already use. You can mix techniques like sales promotions and personal selling to keep your customers learning the curriculum you've designed for them. Use each touch point to share information about different products and services, to the extent you have been given permission!

TIP

Permission marketing, when conducted online, is called "opt-in" marketing. An opt-in is a very basic level of permission, gained when a website visitor clicks a selection box to indicate willingness to receive messages on specified topics. But too many marketers run too far too fast with opt-ins. Permission is not flexible. It's too easy to misjudge a prospect's interests, attitudes, or perceived relationship with you. Using opt-in status to send a message like "Because you like X, you'll probably be interested in Y" is not permission marketing!

Every time you (or anyone associated with your operation, right down to the delivery driver) have contact with a customer, it's an opportunity to make that relationship warmer or colder. The bookstore that delivers orders in person presents an example of maintaining a warm relationship by maximizing customer touch points. You can call it a bold new technique or a back-to-basics movement—just don't call it late for dinner. Make the most of every customer touch point as an opportunity to learn and to share.

WHAT IS CUSTOMER RELATIONSHIP MANAGEMENT (CRM) AND WHAT DO I DO WITH IT?

Customer relationship management (most often just called CRM) is a straight-forward idea: Put together what you know about your customers and use it. For some, CRM is a way to market to customers more efficiently. For others, it is a way of automating the operational functions of sales, marketing, and customer service. It's a no-brainer that customer data can be used to retain customers and increase profits. The question is really, how? In the bad old days, businesses used file cards. Now, spreadsheets and databases automate customer record-keeping. Dedicated *CRM software* has emerged that reaches far beyond what those record-keeping methods can do.

PLAIN ENGLISH

CRM software functions as a central location for all of your customer data—sales records, contact information, prospect lists, and more. CRM can improve operations by helping to predict demand for certain products. CRM can help marketers time promotions and customer touch points to arrive just as customers are likely to buy again.

CRM can be looked at two different ways: through marketing or operations.

MARKETING-ORIENTED CRM

If your business is like many, you have data about your customers scattered across your company. Some information is in the billing software, whereas other information is in salespeople's contact management systems. Some important information may be stored nowhere other than in key individual's brains. The point of CRM is to get that data together, and then to get it "speaking" to you.

Jim Novo, in his book *Drilling Down,* says, "Marketing with customer data is a highly evolved and valuable conversation." He explains that customer data "speaks" by sharing three key facts:

- Who purchased *recently*
- Who purchased *frequently*
- Who has spent the most *money* in total

These three keys add up to a powerful model for predicting who will be your best customers in the future. Your primary goal is to monitor recency of purchases, frequency of purchases, and money spent. As a marketer, you need access to the data that will support that goal.

The basic customer information you're tracking (recency, frequency, monetary value) provides the foundation for a marketing approach built on CRM. What you build on that foundation can be a cottage or a castle.

All the customers who score high on recency, frequency, and monetary value are by definition your best customers. Now, let's mine that data to describe a best customer profile. Do these purchasers have other traits in common? What are they?

Try pinpointing your customers on a map. Do they share geographic characteristics? Try grouping them by age, gender, income level, or life stage. Do clusters appear? Look at the purchase habits within those clusters. Are patterns taking shape?

This type of customer-profile analysis generates insights that are invaluable to a marketer. You can use this information to make your marketing tactics more successful. You can purchase better direct mail lists, choose more efficient media buys, or decide where to locate your next store. Whatever your marketing challenges, a foundation of customer information leads to better strategic choices.

Marketing-oriented CRM seeks to make the most of the potential in customer touch points. Touch points are often initiated by the customer. The touch point can arise at any moment, without notice. Anyone providing customer service should have immediate access to accurate information about each previous communication with any individual customer. The data brought together by a CRM database is just the tool a customer service provider needs to turn touch points into successful long-term customer relationships.

TIP

When is CRM not CRM? Depends on who's talking. To a marketer, CRM generally means the whole philosophical approach of managing relationships customer by customer—one-to-one marketing, in other words. To a technical type, CRM more often refers to the software that supports the marketer's idea of CRM. When you get in a conversation about CRM, make sure you're all talking about the same thing!

Hearthstone Book Company provides an example. Hearthstone's owner, Katy, likes to take new books to her customers. She reviews each customer's profile before leaving the office. If the opportunity arises, she makes suggestions about other books the customer might enjoy. Just like Amazon.com, but pleasantly personal! It's thorough tracking of customer data that allows this business's marketers to manage the complex mix of customers and prospects for the bookstore, the inn, and the café.

To summarize—the point of CRM from a marketing perspective, is to ...

- Help you draw best-customer profiles, to guide marketing tactics.
- To make detailed customer information available to anyone who needs it, at any customer touch point.

OPERATIONS-ORIENTED CRM

Small businesses have a distinct advantage when it comes to implementing CRM. There's been a lot of grumbling from large enterprises over CRM, and it all boils down to "It cost us a fortune, and now we can't get people to use it." The biggest challenges for larger businesses are integration of "legacy data" (the records in the billing software, or on the file cards, or whatever) and low adoption rates by the people expected to use the system.

With smaller businesses, both issues are less problematic. In a small business, there is simply less legacy data to bring into the new system. It's easier to upgrade 200 records than 20,000. Plus, in smaller workplaces there tends to be a different attitude toward change. Small businesses tend to run lean and mean, with the result that individuals are generally more eager for changes that allow them to do their work more efficiently.

Does your operation justify a full-blown CRM software installation? Many businesses don't. Kalika's juice cart has no need to track who purchased recently or frequently or spent a lot of money in total. When hunger and hot sun combine, smoothies sell themselves.

TIP

Does a very small business need a CRM system? Maybe yes, maybe no. A micro-retailer like Kalika with her juice cart has very little need for the operational benefits of CRM. She doesn't use marketing tactics that require customer profiling, and she manages her customer touch points just fine by simply using her head. If you serve a fairly small customer base and see your customers nearly every day, you can probably do without CRM.

For many businesses, a database and a spreadsheet program can do the job of CRM software—that is, if the marketer knows how to use both and takes the time to do it!

Kai Miaka (the musician) and Anita (Life History Services) use simple contact-manager software to approximate CRM. A Life of Faith Dolls uses a system designed for mail-order businesses. University Credit Union will make the leap to CRM software when the dust settles from that meeting between Marketing and IT. Bob's Bottomless Boats has been using CRM software for years.

Do you need CRM? You need the approach, whether or not you need the software. If you are looking to goose your business into a growth phase, implementing CRM and the software to support it is a good way to go. To find systems suited to your needs, you could start with "CRM" and a search engine. But that may be a little too much like diving in among sharks for your tastes. Ask around among your business associates. What software do they use to perform CRM? Expect to hear names like GoldMine and Salesforce.com. Microsoft has a product designed for smaller businesses named Microsoft CRM. You might start out reading about these, if you're heading toward CRM.

USING CUSTOMER INFORMATION MEANS USING TECHNOLOGY

CRM is in many ways an old idea in new clothing—database marketing. Often it seems the excitement in marketing work comes from reaching new markets and getting new customers. But great profit potential can be found by turning to your existing customers. The people in your database have an awareness of your offerings, a positive (hopefully) perception of your business, and a potentially loyal relationship with you.

You know more about these people than you do about the general public you reach through mass marketing. With your knowledge of them and their knowledge of you, it only makes sense to focus on them.

Each business faces a decision whether it makes sense to allocate part of its marketing budget to creating, maintaining, and using a customer database for one-to-one marketing. As long as you're committed to technology to support that database, why not see how far you can take the computer as your partner in CRM?

Online marketing lends itself to automated solutions. In the online world, an opt-in equals permission to share a relationship. Computer scripts can take it from there.

One example of one-to-one marketing based on permissions is the *cascading response sequence,* a series of touches triggered by customer-driven events. The cascading response sequence can be driven entirely automatically, using e-mail autoresponders.

TIP

Sophisticated database functions make one-to-one marketing possible. You can sort that database and use specialized printing to deliver mail pieces that are customized right down to the individual recipient, a technique called variable printing.

If there's one message you should've gotten by now, it's this: You've got to have some technology in place to manage customer information. You can't use the information you've got if you don't have it stored where you can get to it, in the right format, when and where you need it. The flaw with the old box of file cards was the format. You can't automate a search and sort routine on a box of papers. You can't drive autoresponders with a few sheets of address label masters.

Customer data must be kept in a format that's sophisticated enough to support two activities: sifting that data for insight, and making the relevant data available to stimulate and respond to customer touch points.

THE 30-SECOND RECAP

- One-to-one marketing shifts the focus from mass-market share to share of individual customers over their lifetimes.
- The tools of one-to-one marketing are permissions and touch points.
- Customer relationship management (CRM) is a marketing approach and a software solution.
- Using customer information requires technology; this can be as simple as a spreadsheet and a database, or as complex as an enterprise-wide dedicated CRM software application.

Marketing a Service

Kalika is an immigrant to this country who runs a juice cart on a college campus. From her cart, she dispenses a variety of freshly squeezed juices, blended "smoothie" drinks.

Is she selling a product or a service? Both.

The clue to the service component of her business lies in the phrase "freshly squeezed." She brings you the product, peaches and raspberries, but she adds value by processing those raw materials into the form you like, a delectable juice drink.

Restaurants (and that's what Kalika's cart really is) make an excellent example of an offering halfway down the continuum from pure product to pure service. Restaurants provide a tangible product. But the services they provide, from food preparation to serving at table, add the value that distinguishes one restaurant from the next. At the far end of the spectrum are services that leave no trace, the intangible services like pumping out your septic system or defending you at trial.

This section takes a look at that continuum and what makes a service different from a product.

WHAT MAKES A SERVICE UNIQUE?

Pop Quiz

Question: What's the first law of marketing?

Answer: People don't buy products; they buy solutions to problems. Looked at this way, there is no difference between a product and a service. Both are simply vehicles for delivering solutions.

But anybody can tell you a service is not the same as a product. When you buy a service, you don't get to take something home in a box. And that fact of life brings with it a host of issues for marketers.

SHADES OF GRAY: HOW TO TELL PRODUCTS FROM SERVICES

Services have characteristics that set them apart from products:

■ **Products are tangible; services are intangible.** Buyers can't see, feel, smell, hear, or taste a service before they agree to buy it. When they purchase services, they have to purchase a promise of satisfaction, and that requires a leap of faith that purchasing a product does not.

■ **Services can't be separated from their providers.** This fact affects you in fundamental ways. Most services are delivered by people. To buy a service, you must come in contact with the one who provides it— you watch Kalika as she spins the blender to make your smoothie; you make small talk in the chair while the stylist cuts your hair. Naturally, you come to believe that that person brings something special to the process. A smoothie from another cart might taste a little different. A haircut by someone else might ruin the next month of your life.

■ **Services are perishable.** Services provided by people can't be stored. Suppose you're a dentist, and you're expecting a patient at 10 A.M. When that patient blows you off, it's too late to sell 10 A.M. to someone else. When the plane takes off with empty seats, they can never be sold again. Your service is not like a product that will sit on the shelf waiting for a buyer.

There are several strategies for dealing with perishability. You might perfect your ability to forecast demand (booking appointments well in advance) or use tiered pricing strategies such as early-reservation discounts or a no-show charge.

THE MARKETING MIX FOR SERVICES

How can you use the tools at your disposal, your product (actually your service), your place, your price, and your promotions to cope with the unique situation facing you as a marketer of services?

TIP

Price discounts are great for some businesses, but not for professional services! In some fields, consumers rely on price as an indication of quality. If you're in a consulting field, like law and accounting, for example, don't use promotions that offer discounts. When price is the main indicator of quality, price discounts send the wrong message.

To deal with intangibility, use a product strategy. Try designing your offering to include satisfaction guarantees. You can plan your promotional strategy to make service seem tangible, too. Your promotions can feature testimonials and demonstrations—these give customers a chance to encounter the service before they purchase. Promotions help you to drum up demand.

The inseparability of service and provider is a tough riddle to solve. Some respond by attempting to make the service uniform, so that anyone can step into the role of service provider and deliver the same outcome. When Kalika needs help at her cart, she trains her helpers in the art of making smoothies "Kalika-style."

Others customize. If each offering is completely tailored to a customer's needs, the contribution of the individual providing the service has less impact on the service delivered. After all, the customers are defining the service they seek. Of course, if you do a terrific job of executing that service, you score a lot of points with each customer you serve. Either standardizing or customizing could be a potential strategy for marketing your services. But, right now, who are you serving? Where will you set up camp in the landscape of service possibilities?

EXPLORING THE LANDSCAPE OF SERVICE PROVIDERS

How you sell your services is, of course, dependent on who you are selling to. Advertisers use different styles and approaches depending on whether they are selling products or services to consumers or to businesses. Consumers can use a lot more emotional and psychological appeals than businesses. If you're selling services to business, you're going to have to be more direct and more practical. In both cases you're still selling solutions, but the benefits are different. Let's look at both.

SERVING CONSUMERS: WHEN A SERVICE IS LIKE A PRODUCT

Service retailers sell directly to end users. Kalika and your hair stylist are in retail. The person who pinstripes your Corvette (okay, Ford Taurus) is also in retail. Your plumber serves both consumers and businesses, and you can bet he sells different services in a different style to each. If a business person is buying for himself, he is just another consumer, although he could be a big one.

For retailers, big and small, it makes sense to understand the following categories. Those categories apply to consumer services as easily as products: They are *convenience, shopping,* and *specialty.*

Services, like products, can be divided into three types: *convenience* (an inexpensive recurring need), *shopping* (a service that requires evaluation before purchase), and *specialty* (rarely purchased, and usually expensive). A convenience service calls for a different marketing strategy than a shopping service or a specialty service.

What makes a service a convenience? Just like a convenience product, a convenience service is typically inexpensive, the need recurs on a regular basis, and you don't care much where you buy it. A car wash is a convenience service. So is a shoeshine.

Shopping services require more involvement than convenience services. As a shopper, you do care where you get them. You want to be able to compare price, style, and value. Hiring a maid service for monthly housecleaning qualifies as a shopping service. You care about finding a reputable firm; you want the job done well; you want to pay a fair price and not more. You would probably interview several potential firms before you chose one for this personal service.

Specialty services, like specialty products, are rarely purchased, are expensive, and require a high degree of consumer involvement. The person you hire to put a new roof on your house is offering a specialty service. The architect you hire for your new custom-built home is even more so.

Most home repair services begin as either a shopping or a specialty service. After you choose a shopping service, like your maids or even your plumber, it can become a convenience service if you are satisfied with how the job was done. Plumbing problems may not happen every day, but they happen often enough to make a reliable plumber a convenience. Specialty services are too rare to move into the convenience category. Even if you are wildly happy with your roofer, you won't need that service again for, hopefully, 20 to 30 years.

Does one of these categories describe your business? Determining which one will directly affect how you assemble your marketing mix. Obviously, a car wash uses different strategies to price and promote than an architect.

SERVING RETAILERS: WHEN A SERVICE HAS A FEEDER FUNCTION

Retailers need a very special kind of service. They need to get their merchandise selection from distributors. You may or may not want to become a distributor, but if you sell a service other than consulting you need to know what services a distributor can provide.

Pure distribution consists of breaking bulk, assembling lots, and creating assortments. You wouldn't believe how much actual service is coiled in these functions. Retailers could be product poor without the services of distributors, and consumers could be deprived of lots of variety.

Given that the distributor is actually buying the product he distributes from the manufacturer, it may surprise you to be told that the manufacturer is also buying a service from the distributor. How's that? Think of it this way. The distributor's service relieves the manufacturer of the headache of trucking the goods around the nation and relieves the retailer of spending time hunting merchandise.

Take, for example, Ron Essex, of Essex Sportswear. This is a company that distributes imprintable sportswear (that's T-shirts and sweat pants) to the screen-printing and embroidery trades.

First, the bulk-breaking function: This company buys truckloads of products from manufacturers. Semi loads from Fruit of the Loom and others show up every day and are emptied into a vast warehouse. From that stockpile, smaller quantities are picked to fill orders for cases of sweatshirts, dozens of T-shirts, and even single units. To perform this function, the distributor takes ownership and assumes the risks, such as spoilage, storage cost, and prediction of demand. In return, he earns the right to charge retailers a higher price than he pays the manufacturers for the goods.

Distributors make it possible for their customers (often end users or retailers) to have products they want, when and where they want them. But distributors are middlemen. If they cease to provide a real economic value, they are soon squeezed out by the intense competition around them. Keeping everyone happy can be a challenge for a distributor.

The second function is assembling lots. When the Green Bay Packers won Super Bowl XXXI, T-shirt printers all over the Midwest wanted green and gold active wear by the gross. Even the big retail chains got in on the action, placing orders for hundreds of thousands of Packer-imprinted green and gold shirts. Ron rose to the challenge! He met the demand by working with manufacturers and other distributors from coast to coast.

The distributor's third function is creating assortments. Let's say it's early August. A screen printer has taken in orders this week for three cases of orange T's (assorted sizes) for a Halloween fun-run, 36 red-and-black windbreakers for the new high school football team, and 200 polo shirts for the employees of a restaurant chain. He faxes the distributor his order, and Ron pulls and ships the required merchandise from his warehouse full of goods.

That's breaking bulk, assembling lots, and creating assortments—distribution in a nutshell. The other services that businesses buy are lumped under the heading of "consulting."

SERVING AS A CONSULTANT: WHEN SERVICE WEARS A WHITE HAT

Consultants don't always come to the rescue in the nick of time, but they are individuals or firms who offer expertise that a client needs now, but only for a specific project or for a limited time. If they needed these services on a continual basis, they'd create a staff position instead. But they don't, so they hire consultants to deliver those services. Repair services fall in this category whether they sell to consumers or businesses.

Remember, we buy solutions to problems. Solutions are what consultants provide, and they provide them in four general areas: finances, operations, marketing, and personnel. A temporary help agency provides bodies to help a client cope while staff are on vacation. A human resources consultant helps the personnel department write a new manual. A graphic designer helps marketing make a new brochure. A consulting engineer helps reduce workplace injuries by redesigning the assembly line, thereby improving operations. An electrician repairs a faulty circuit breaker. An accountant helps find the bookkeeper who embezzles—and a lawyer helps prosecute him. These are all consultants providing services that help solve customers' problems.

Does one of these categories describe your business? Whether you are a retailer, distributor, or consultant will have an impact on your marketing activities. Retailers, for example, have to keep themselves in the public eye, using the media as often as they can afford to. Because distributors are closely tied to the world of products, they can rely on a range of product-oriented marketing tools, such as catalogs, to make their activities profitable. Consultants walk a narrower line. What they sell comes by the hour in hours billed to the client. Marketing consulting services can't be done with a catalog! A much more customized marketing mix is needed.

A map has been created, helping you see where you fit into the landscape of service providers. Now it's time to start talking about directions. How do you start from where you are and get where you want to go? That's the next subject we'll take up.

THE 30-SECOND RECAP

- Most offerings are neither purely product nor completely service in nature, but some combination of both.

- Services are intangible, perishable, and inseparable from the person providing the service.

Analyzing Your Service Offering

Job one is to develop your service offering for maximum profit potential. To do this, you need to analyze your offering, examining it from the perspectives of both your existing and your potential clients.

This section discusses various ways of analyzing your service to make sure you're truly addressing market needs.

Examine the Three Aspects of Service

Just as with products, every service has three aspects to it: its core value, the basic solution it offers; its expanded service, the added values that enhance the core value; and its service concept, the big picture surrounding that service's development, marketing, price point, style of delivery, and long-range place in the company's overall objectives.

You are going to want to ask yourself how well your service does in providing a core value to your clients, what you do for each client to enhance that value, and how completely you have planned to make your offering profitable.

Let's go down to Barney's Car Wash for an example. Barney has three or four of these establishments and a customer visits them because they have a core value that is important to her. She drives a vintage car, and it demands a brushless car wash to keep its fragile paint looking spiffy. Only Barney's offers the brushless wash, so she goes to Barney's.

Once there, she chooses from a variety of packages available. In the winter, she goes for the extra polish coat and the anti–road salt undercarriage flush. In the summer, she skips those preventatives, but maybe she splurges on one of the detailing packages, like hand-polishing her chrome. She and her baby like to look good on our Sunday drives! Barney has assembled these packages of extended services to enhance his core value, meet this customer's varying needs, and tempt her into purchasing more than the core service.

Barney saw a niche in the car-care market, a need for higher-quality cleaning than the coin-op and gas station car washes were offering. He responded by assembling a variety of services that fit his concept of a premium car-care provider. He tailors them to the needs of special clients, like corporate fleets and rental companies, as well as the various consumer niches like vintage cars and sport vehicles. (He even has a Sunday night mud-off special for weekend cowboys.) These offerings illustrate Barney's service concept.

TIP

Manage the physical evidence of your service to your advantage. Give it form in a way that supports your brand. Create a "service identity plan" that isolates the something extra you provide to make your service unique. Then turn that into a promotional position. Barney's Car Wash could offer "the car-lover's choice." Pros use every opportunity to give their service an identity that helps communicate what makes it special.

To achieve your greatest potential, analyze your service offering from each of these angles and make changes where necessary, focusing core services to meet defined needs, adding value with such things as timing, and monitoring the success of your service concept.

While you're at it, consider other aspects of your offering, such as the people who participate in delivering your service and the process of delivery. These, too, contribute to what your service is and how it sells.

PAY ATTENTION TO THE SERVICE ENCOUNTER: "WHERE RUBBER MEETS ROAD"

When the consumer interacts with the service provider, that's the *service encounter.* If you're in the rental car business, it's not enough that the car works when the driver gets in. The process of getting the car has to be satisfactory as well. If your customer had to wait too long or put up with an inexperienced clerk, you're failing at managing the service encounter.

There may be one or many encounters in the delivery of a service, depending on the nature of your business. In some businesses the service encounter makes up the entire delivery of the service, and in others there is much work done between encounters.

A barber giving a haircut is performing a one-encounter service, with no behind-the-scenes activity, unless you count sweeping up between customers. A graphic designer producing a brochure has several encounters with the client, and considerable work goes on behind the scenes between visits.

PLAIN ENGLISH

Service encounter is a very important concept. It's the customer touch points on steroids. It refers to the quality of the interaction between the customer and the person providing the service.

Failure in the service encounter can ruin a client relationship as easily as failing to deliver good service. If the barber tells off-color jokes, the customer may not return even if the cut was acceptable. If the designer is always late or disorganized, her firm will not get additional work from this client even if the creativity of the brochure was top-notch. Get the picture? You can't just deliver a good service; you have to deliver it well.

"YES SIR!" ARE YOU MANAGING YOUR CUSTOMER TOUCH POINTS?

The quality of the contact between you as service provider and your customer gives you an opportunity to sharpen your competitive edge. If you're in a law firm, the personality of your receptionist is as much a part of your product as your senior partner's legal ability. What do you do about it?

For some, standardization is the answer. Standardizing services is possible if you run a car wash or juice cart, but nearly impossible if the service bought is, say, dentistry. Even so, you can instill in everyone who has contact with customers the manner you'd like them to project. A print shop or fast-food restaurant trains customer service personnel to project a friendly demeanor. If you can, standardize elements of the service-delivery process so new employees can be trained to deliver just like the old hands. Consistency improves customers' perception of service quality.

Another strategy for managing service quality is customization. In some circumstances, a service is truly individualized to each customer. A chartered plane flies to whatever destination the customer chooses. "Know your customer" is the guiding rule. Find out what they will perceive as service quality— then deliver it. If they want champagne instead of chardonnay in flight, get champagne.

The very nature of Anita Hecht's Life History Services requires customization. Each family she serves has a choice of avenues to explore and a choice of ways to present the results of those explorations. Anita has to be a master at quickly grasping what her customers want.

One thing to remember when we're talking about service quality: It's very much a matter of perception. You can believe you're delivering a high level of service quality and find out that your customers disagree. What you do about that is called "managing the gap."

If you have direct front-line contact with customers, you're probably in the know about what they expect. But if you're not, you may be suffering from a *negative gap*.

PLAIN ENGLISH

A **negative gap** is when customers have complaints about your service that you aren't aware of, or when you don't know exactly what they want. If you surprise them with better service than they expect, that's a *positive gap*.

But gaps can be *positive* as well. A young man celebrated his birthday by taking his mother to a fancy restaurant. He was tactfully asked for his ID when he ordered a bottle of wine. A bit disgruntled, he presented his driver's license and was served, but he overheard the waiter say "We'll have to do something about this." What was the problem? Nothing, as he discovered when complimentary desserts were brought after the meal. The waiter, noticing his birth date on the license, took the occasion to offer more service than expected. The young man and his mother were delighted and impressed. Will he go back there? You bet! Will he tell others how great that place is? You bet, again. Can you buy those kind of endorsements? No. But you can earn them, and that's one of the secrets to success in the service business.

Look for the negative gaps that may be undercutting your efforts to deliver service quality—and fix them. Look for the opportunities to create positive gaps and encourage your staff to exploit them.

LOOK FOR NEW SERVICES YOU CAN SUPPLY

Whether you have a new idea for your existing business or your first idea that could lead to a new business, it pays to keep a lookout to see whether you can supply a service that others will pay for. Here are a couple places you can look.

A NEW SERVICE FOR EXISTING CUSTOMERS

The good news about service businesses: You have such close contact with customers that you're well prepared for brainstorming successful new service offerings. The seeds your customers plant with you will grow into your new profit centers, if you nurture them.

Two trends—the changing ethnicity of American people and the aging of baby boomers—are fueling the development of new services and products.

Trend forecasters are predicting extensive growth potential in five areas. They predict there will be increased demand for services related to education, health, finances, home, and leisure.

The thing you must be sure of, as you develop new services, is that they work for you—not just for your customers.

A boarding kennel sent an announcement of a new service: home visits, allowing your pet to stay at home while you're away. This may seem odd, because what they previously sold, lodging for pets, involved physical resources amounting to a considerable investment. What was the reason for the new strategy? Why not build new kennels if they wanted more business?

Not only does this allow them to serve more people without a capital invest-ment, it brings them into a slightly different market as well. Cats are the usual recipients of the at-home service, whereas dogs are more likely to be kenneled than left at home unsupervised. (It's a litter-box thing.)

Their boarding business, having cornered as much of the kenneling market as they could expect, chose to add the home-visit service as a way to grow into a new market. So it works hand in hand (paw in paw?) with their current operations.

A Service to Fill an Unrecognized Need

Maybe you've been itching to sell your talent as a problem-solver, but you haven't defined which problem people need solved so much that they'll pay for your service. It becomes vague in your mind and you end up thinking about needs that others are already filling. But that's not what you want. Let's think now ... something new?

Irene and Michael Tobis, a couple of Ph.D.s, did some powerful thinking about what they'd observed and what they could offer, and they came up with a great idea: People need organization. Irene is a psychologist, and Michael is a systems engineer. They created a consulting business called Ducks In A Row. They tar-geted entrepreneurs, professionals, collaborative teams, and busy people. They offered services to help individuals achieve their goals by developing skills, strategies, and tools to handle information, space, and time.

The Ducks service could be delivered in your home, your office, your company— anywhere you need to get organized. But they don't just organize you; they aid your psyche. They help you overcome obstacles, develop strengths, and handle your organizational problems for yourself.

Next time you're poking around in the messy closet of your mind, remember the Ducks and figure out what you can offer that lots of people need.

You could have a talent that others need. You never know what service would make life happier, easier, or more functional for people. So think about talents you have that can fill an unrecognized need people have. Dog-walking services had to start with someone who knew people were getting busier and could use relief from some of their daily chores. Hmmm? Wouldn't it be nice if you could be someone's eating service? Oh well, keep thinking.

Check Out Offering Online Services

Online service is primarily a new method for purchase and delivery of prod-ucts, or a form of advertising through a home page, or an information provider. It also provides a tool for collaboration over long distances. Offering new ser-vices online is still a possibility—it's a competitive field, but who can stop you when you have your thinking cap on? There's a business that sells demographic reports via the World Wide Web. There are desktop publishers, transcription-ists, web designers, and researchers who provide their service and deliver the end results entirely through the web. You might have an idea that could lead to a website offering information-based services for a fee.

Many online services, like those provided by web designers, transcriptionists, and researchers, work well as home-based businesses. Broadband Internet connections and the reliability of the PDF (Portable Document Format) have made it possible for workers separated by space to collaborate just as if they were working next door to each other in the "cube farm." If you're interested in a home business, check out online service offerings—and if you're skilled at a service that can be delivered over the web, check out your home office options!

NONPROFITS DON'T MARKET! (YES, THEY DO.)

Most nonprofit organizations market services or intangibles like good health, so let's talk about them. They have different marketing objectives because success can't be measured by the same financial statements as a for-profit business uses. Instead, success is measured against general goals—like changes in atti-tude, behavior, and social norms—or measurable goals, like numbers of clients served, total funds raised and distributed, lower crime rates, fewer heart attacks, and higher school grades.

Most nonprofit organizations serve two different publics: the people who enable them to serve and the people they actually serve. Depending on your niche, you might call the first group donors, patrons, friends, or contributors. Their objective is to help your organization deliver services, rather than to receive those services personally (though they might be on the receiving end—at least partially—if the organization is a church, for example).

The other group, who actually receive services, might be called recipients, clients, constituents, patients, or members, depending on what you do. In a for-profit situation these people would be called customers. They are con-sumers of the services provided.

When you market to donors, you are actually fundraising. Although fundraising uses many marketing tools, it is itself a separate activity with its own rules and principles of behavior. You may want to get a specialty book on fundraising.

THE 30-SECOND RECAP

- Analyze your offering to ensure you deliver a high quality of service and a pleasant service encounter.
- Look for new services you can supply by following demographic and technological shifts.
- Nonprofit organizations serve two audiences, donors and recipients, who are best served through target marketing.

Developing Your Positioning Strategy Through Branding

One summer not too long ago, the new-product folks at Coleman (the camping equipment company) cooked up a strange idea: Let's create a gas grill for the (gasp!) backyard. Coleman had a successful brand built over its 100-year history, but the company had never produced a product that wasn't camping gear.

The product-development team researched what, exactly, the Coleman identity meant in consumers' perception. And they found? That Coleman products are perceived as reliable, durable, and above all—green.

So how to bring this heritage into a new product category? By leveraging the "Coleman green" brand. At the end of its development process, the company produced not the most advanced grill on the market, but one that had the company's signature hefty feel and green paint job. This is branding in action. By building on long-established elements of the company's brand, Coleman has ensured that, when you see this grill in a store, you know instantly, "That's a Coleman."

Branding will drive your strategic use of positioning—and in turn, positioning will guide your development of a creative approach, which you'll then use to develop specific advertising messages. In this section, we'll figure out what a brand is and what a branding strategy can do for you.

BRANDING: WHAT IT IS (AND ISN'T)

At the core of a brand lies the question: With our [product or service], how do we make our customers feel? Making customers feel good about your product or service is the key to breaking through the cluttered marketplace of products and messages. Branding helps customers build loyalty to your company and its offerings. A strong brand, consistently communicated, creates a relationship between a company and a consumer that grows in value over time.

TIP

Even if you sell only one product branding is still important. When you introduce the next product you'll be able to give it a push with your current brand's good reputation as Coleman did.

A brand is much more than just a trademark or slogan. A brand is made up of a complex mix of components. These can include the following:

- Logo or symbol
- Name
- Slogans and taglines
- Musical signature or "jingle"
- Color scheme
- Packaging designs
- Staff phone demeanor
- Uniform or dress code

Each of these components contributes to the feeling that is your brand, but none by itself creates a brand. The brand is the result of consumers' accumulated experiences with and perceptions about your company, its people, and its products.

Branding works for services as well as for products. Branding can be created around ingredients or around whole companies and even geographic regions. Examples? Think about the "I (Heart) New York" logo, originally designed to promote tourism. Think about California marketing boards' campaigns for raisins ("Heard it through the grapevine") and milk ("Got Milk?"). The power of branding turned these farm commodities into cultural icons. Consider the ingredient-branding strategy in BASF's long-running slogan "We don't make a lot of the products you buy. We make a lot of the products you buy better." These examples prove that a branding strategy works for a wide range of offerings.

WHY BRANDING WORKS: A LITTLE COGNITIVE SCIENCE

One of the ways the human mind handles the barrage of advertising it receives is to pick something to believe and then hold that notion until forced to change. Snap judgments become permanent beliefs, because it is uncomfortable and difficult to change convictions once formed. The mind tends to filter out new information that doesn't support already-held beliefs. This attribute of the mind explains why branding is an effective strategy.

Branding works because it gives the mind something to hang on to. Several aspects of cognitive behavior explain why branding has become a key component of marketing strategy:

- **Looking for "good enough."** In the search for products and services to fulfill their desires or solve their problems, people are looking for "good enough." In an uncertain world, we value consistency over quality, predictability over risk. Most of us are satisfied if we avoid making a bad choice. The brand purveys a promise of reliability.

- **The halo effect.** The mind works by associations. For example, we tend to believe attractive people are smarter than less-attractive ones, even though we know that one trait has nothing to do with the other. Our minds associate many positive traits with each other. Through "halo effect," a product and company become associated with positive attributes conveyed by the brand's advertising.

- **Anchoring.** The mind doesn't simply form impressions; it becomes anchored in them. Our first snap judgments are apt to become our enduring beliefs. The brand communicates directly at the "feelings" level, and thus is easily anchored as a core belief.

TIP

There was a time when products had real differences. Today just about everything is good enough. Cheap junk seldom makes it to market, and when it does, it won't survive long in competition with better alternatives. When everything is good enough, what's a marketer to do? Turn to a branding strategy to make your offering stand out from the crowd.

WHEN ALL PRODUCTS ARE "GOOD ENOUGH," BRANDING MAKES THE DIFFERENCE

Once upon a time, products had real differences. For example, the first running shoes on the market were a remarkable improvement over the old sneaker. A vast array of features, from heel stabilizers to shock absorbers, made it clear why a consumer might choose the new shoes over the old. It was easy to create advertising that persuaded people to buy the new shoes, just by explaining their benefits.

But soon the market was crowded with parity products. Before long, running shoes from different manufacturers all met the consumers' baseline needs for comfort, style, and function. Now how do you persuade consumers they need your brand above others? By selling the emotional bond that purchase creates. By choosing Nikes, the consumer projects a "Just do it" attitude. Adidas projects a more "hip" image, whereas New Balance proclaims that its wearer is more interested in quality than fashion. By choosing Keds over more high-tech shoes, a customer displays a different attitude, cheeky or just cheap. Branding lifts a simple offering into the realm of feeling and self-expression.

In a world of product parity, it's crucial that you leverage consumer emotions in your favor.

TIP

Branding and product development need to be closely tied at all levels in your company, from long-range strategy to day-to-day operations. Keep thinking about your products as you develop your understanding of branding.

Consider University Credit Union's situation. All financial services are pretty much the same; if you peek behind the fancy lobbies and the glossy racks of brochures, you find all the players are competing to sell you access to *their* money (loans) or storage of *your* money (deposits). To stand out from the crowd, University Credit Union exploits two angles: the fact that it is cooperative-owned, and the natural loyalty people feel toward their alma mater. A branding strategy that emphasizes the slight price advantage of credit unions and the warm fuzzy feeling of allegiance to the old school helps UCU rise above "product parity."

Help potential buyers see that your offering is "good enough" by showing how your offering is similar to other offerings. Then help potential buyers see that "this is better" by communicating the differences only you can claim. A Life of Faith Dolls first establishes that its products are similar to American Girls Dolls, and then communicates its dolls are different and better, through the focus on religious faith. Bob's Bottomless Boats establishes parity and difference through its claim to have "bottomless inventory." It promises you'll find at Bob's every product you might find in competitors' stores—and more.

BUILDING BRAND EQUITY

Marketing activity builds a brand's equity, if done well. You invest advertising dollars to build awareness and to form positive associations in the minds of your targeted audience. These are banked over time and converted to profits when brand-loyal consumers purchase your offering. Coleman had banked enough good feelings over its 100 years to enter a new product category with ease.

Every marketing activity your strategy calls for should be carefully chosen to support your brand. Your advertising campaigns, sales promotions, special events, and team or event sponsorships must reinforce the brand.

 TIP

Keep in mind—even if your business model is business to business—the person who cuts a purchase order for your product is just that: a person. Look for what stirs feelings and connections in the hearts and minds of these individuals. Build your brand identity around that.

The brand is, at its heart, a promise. It warrants that the product or service carrying that brand will live up to its name. The value of that brand rises or falls with the integrity of the people behind it. The ultimate authority for managing the brand lies with the highest officers in the company. The "principles of the principals" make or break a brand.

MANAGING THE BRAND

Branding is not an activity you can accomplish overnight or purchase ready-made from a consultant or advertising agency. A successful brand is built over time from the hundreds of little things you do right.

When most people speak of branding, they are referring to its external components—the elements consumers experience directly, like your advertising jingles and the logos painted on the company fleet. But there are internal components to branding, and these must be managed as well. Internal branding reflects the efforts you aim at people inside the company, so that they can help you project a consistent image for the brand. To fully benefit from the power of branding, it is important to take a 360-degree view of branding in your company.

Successful brand managers learn how to turn every customer touch point into a "moment of truth" that reinforces positive aspects of the brand. Bob's Bottomless Boats hires passionate paddlers to work the kayak kiosk because he wants every customer touch point to build the "Bob's" brand.

TIP

Does your offering need a brand name? Yes! People need labels to help them identify things. Brand names provide labels for individual offerings and for product/service lines. Consider the handy taxonomy of "Stouffer's Lean Cuisine Thai-Style Chicken Entrée." It communicates a brand, a product line, and a specific product. The name you choose should project your brand image, identify the function of your product, and lend itself to memorable advertising.

Measuring the Brand

Over the life of your brand, you will need to measure its performance. You can study how your marketing initiatives are creating or shifting brand awareness using techniques like focus groups, quantitative surveys, comparison of sales volumes, and internal review of customer accounts.

To measure a brand, you want to answer the following questions:

- Is the desired audience aware of you?
- What attributes do they associate with you?

Before you deploy a branding strategy, use research to probe perceptions regarding your company and its offerings. Based on that knowledge, you can build a brand that plays to your strengths.

Then just ask these questions again over time to measure change. As you implement your branding strategy, you repeat the research process to track changes. You'll learn more about the weaknesses or strengths in your branding strategy. Adjust your advertising and other marketing strategies to counter the weaknesses or leverage the strengths revealed by research.

Putting Branding to Work

Putting branding to work for you is not difficult—in fact, because of the way human minds work, it will happen whether or not you are controlling the process. To use branding strategically, integrate branding into every aspect of your business, from top-level corporate strategy to the last detail of packaging and display. Your branding strategy will make you stand out from the crowd.

Branding is closely tied to the next concept we're going to talk about: positioning. Branding and positioning go together like graham crackers and a glass of milk. Positioning helps the brand go down.

Positioning occurs as the brand takes shape in the audience's hearts and minds. Positioning connects your overall brand strategy to your specific advertising campaigns and sales promotions.

Cognitive behavior is shaping how your audience perceives your brand, whether you are aware of it or not. Even if you are not consciously pursuing a branding strategy, prospective customers are still associating positive or negative traits with your company and anchoring on those first judgments. If your company is a new entrant in the market, be very careful! Like the new kid at school, others' snap judgments made on first impressions are going to follow you for a very long time.

THE 30-SECOND RECAP

- Brands help differentiate your offering from competitors' by leveraging the way the mind works.
- A brand's value builds over time; brand equity must be managed and measured like any other business asset.

Positioning Your Product for Success

If someone walked up to you in a mall and asked you to name the top three local shoe stores, the one you mention first has top-of-mind awareness with you. Top-of-mind awareness is one of those fun marketing phrases. It means that a particular product, business, or service comes first in the mind of a customer—ahead of the competition.

If you're asked why you rank it tops, you'll probably be able to respond because of its large selection, cutting-edge styles, or low prices. What you're describing is that store's positioning, and the fact that you know it is a reflection of its positioning strategy. You can bet the store has spent good marketing money to deliver that positioning message to you.

In this section, we'll discuss various ways you can question you product to achieve success.

Positioning gives your offering a unique place, or position, in the minds of your prospective customers. There's a fundamental law of physics that says no two objects can occupy the same space at the same time. That law is true in marketing as well. In consumer perception, no two shoe stores can have the lowest prices, or the best selection, or whatever. One store leads the competition in any dimension you care to measure.

PLAIN ENGLISH

Positioning is the way you present your product or service that helps you stand out from the competition. It's about how you want your customers to remember you. It's been said that "positioning is the art of sacrifice." Positioning requires focusing on only one or two dimensions of competition in which you can claim to be "first and best."

IT'S BETTER TO BE FIRST THAN BEST

The easiest way into a person's top-of-mind awareness is to be first. In the mind, second is not a unique position—it's merely the start of "the rest of the pack." The mind can remember some levels beyond "first" and "other," but divisions quickly become fuzzy among the also-rans.

Because of the "anchoring" tendency, being first is better, even if being first is not logically important. Developing your positioning strategy is the art of choosing and communicating a dimension in which you can make a compelling claim to be first—and therefore, in the marvelously illogical mind, best.

Choosing a position usually means finding a "hole" in the marketplace that you can fill. That position takes into account not only your company's strengths but competitors' weaknesses as well. Think about those cognitive behaviors—the halo effect and anchoring. We remember firsts and, given the right encouragement, associate positive traits with them. As you work out your positioning strategy, consider—where do you come in first?

TIP

Experience proves that we remember firsts but not also-rans. Who was the first person to fly across the Atlantic Ocean? Who was the first woman appointed to the Supreme Court? Charles Lindbergh and Sandra Day O'Connor, respectively. Now try to name the seconds in these categories. The lesson for marketers: It's easier to gain a first position by opening new territory than it is to knock somebody out of an already-established category.

DIMENSIONS OF COMPETITION

Each *dimension of competition* is an area where you might be able to drop anchor and claim your first. In deciding whether to shop with you or the competition, what influences customers the most? Certain dimensions are going to be more important than others to any given market segment. Some customers care more about price, still others might care about selection, whereas others care about convenience. And that's just a few of the many dimensions that come into play.

Here's a partial list:

- Image (style/fashion)
- Innovation
- Geographic location
- Customer service
- Performance (the form/function utility)
- Selection
- Distribution (time/place and ease-of-possession utilities)
- Convenience
- Price

TIP

Don't forget: You care about your potential customers' perceptions, not your own. It doesn't matter how you think you rate on these various dimensions of competition. It matters what they think. If you can't get into the minds of your customers, it's time for research.

In most situations, no more than two *dimensions of competition* are duking it out in prospective customers' minds. This is because Western philosophy, with its bias toward dichotomy, has groomed modern consumers to process either/or decisions. As a result of that influence, we prefer decisions that are presented to us that way.

PLAIN ENGLISH

Dimensions of competition are areas in which you can claim a memorable point of difference, some aspect in which you are *first* or *better* than similar offerings.

You can probably name the beer that used the slogan "Tastes great. Less filling." That slogan is a classic demonstration of two dimensions of competition. The marketers addressed two concerns of a niche market of beer drinkers. Dieters who didn't want to give up drinking beer couldn't find a low-calorie beer that tasted good. By convincing that target group that this particular light beer tasted better, marketers solved a consumer problem and increased the brand's sales.

What's your position in the marketplace now? Don't say you don't have one. Everyone does, from the day we open our doors. What do customers think about your business? On what dimension would they rank you first?

SAMPLE POSITIONING STRATEGIES

Here are a few popular positioning strategies now playing in a marketplace near you. As you read these examples, you might recognize yourself in one or more situations. But how do you translate this into relevant advice for your situation? Let's try. Follow along as Bob's Bottomless Boats tries on each for size:

- **Product's superior attributes.** Positioning on superior product attributes is an obvious choice if your product has features (benefits) that show innovation or are a breakthrough in some way. Because Bob sells basically the same boats as his competitors, this strategy doesn't hold much promise for the business as a whole. For introducing a superior new kayak to its target market, however, this strategy may be right on the money.

CAUTION

Be wary if the unique quality of your product or service is easy to duplicate! When a laundry detergent entered the market in a disposable paper carton, it positioned itself on a superior attribute. But other detergents rushed to duplicate that feature, and the first entrant lost the advantage fairly quickly.

TIP

Many political campaigns feature particularly nasty against-the-competitor positioning. Avoid playing dirty if you choose this approach! You might be voted right off the shelves for poor sportsmanship.

- **Price/quality/value equation.** Consumers tend to let price be an indicator of quality. In most cases it is true that what you pay a little more for comes with benefits that make it worth the price. Value is whether those benefits are important to you. Because of his depth of inventory and his buying clout, Bob is able to offer an excellent value on lower-priced but still reasonable-quality watercraft. Here he has an advantage he can claim and live up to.

- **Against a competitor.** "We're Number Two. We try harder." You knew that was Avis talking, didn't you? Even though that campaign hasn't run in years, it still stands as one of the best examples of against-the-competitor positioning. Because people remember firsts, this strategy leverages others' investment in their position and exploits it in your favor. This strategy is usually chosen by a late-entrant competitor who wants to overtake the number-one player. Market leaders usually refuse to acknowledge that other competitors even exist. Bob is the "Hertz" of the boating market, so this strategy doesn't hold water for him.

- **Specific uses.** One good way to encourage people to remember your product is to give them clues about when and where to use it. The plethora of nutrition products for athletes, such as Power Bars and Gatorade, are examples of otherwise ordinary food products positioned for specific uses.

  Bob's market is broad, covering everyone from kayakers to pontoon boat purchasers, so this approach is a sloppy fit at best. This approach would work better if Bob could target specific uses, like paddle sports, exclusively.

- **Response to customers' needs.** Find a problem that your competitors' product has failed to address, and engineer a solution to it. Now let the world know, and presto! You have a successful "response to customers' needs" strategy. Bob's Bottomless Boats is basically a distributor of products, so innovation and responsiveness are not subject to his control the way they should be to choose this positioning strategy. Again, this might work in relation to a new product launch, like the new Kaya Canoe Bob's brother has designed.

- **Product users.** If the "80/20" rule of thumb holds true, it's likely that 80 percent of your business comes from the 20 percent who are your best customers. What are these people like? Dramatize their loyalty to your offering, and you will attract others like them. The most obvious example of "product user" positioning is the celebrity endorser. From "I liked it so much I bought the company," to

"Choosy mothers choose Jif," we've seen pitchmen and -women encourage us to affiliate with certain products just because they've set the example. This works, especially in categories that are essentially commodities, with little real difference between one product offering and another.

This positioning seems best for Bob's Bottomless Boats. One can see a bottomless supply of humorous TV spots with fishermen, kayakers, and water skiers demonstrating the fun life a Bob's boat bestows. If local celebrities like the football coach or the mayor have boats from Bob's, we've got a great local product user opportunity.

So Bob's positioning strategy is looking like either the price/value leader or some variation on product users. How he chooses to express those strategies will result in a catchy tagline and a creative advertising strategy. How do you select a positioning strategy for your offering? Start here, with Bob's Bottomless Boats. Just think about your situation, and try the different possibilities on for size.

There are more than six possible positioning strategies, of course. How will you discover the other variations and permutations of positioning? Read up on it. A good book is *Differentiate or Die: Survival in Our Era of Killer Competition,* by Jack Trout.

Remember, positioning demands sacrifice. You can't be all things to all people; choosing one of these positioning strategies will help you choose what to be and whom to be that to.

In short: Target your market. Develop a brand personality to please them. Choose a positioning strategy and work it to communicate your brand in a clear and focused way. That's all there is to it!

Use this worksheet to jot down some thoughts about you and your toughest competitor's branding and positioning strategies.

My Branding and Positioning Notes

Brand Components

Describe how (or if) you/your competitor are currently using each component to communicate brand identity.

Strategy	Me	My Toughest Competitor
Logo or symbol	_____	_____
	_____	_____
	_____	_____

Strategy	Me	My Toughest Competitor
Name	_____	_____
	_____	_____
	_____	_____
Slogans and taglines	_____	_____
	_____	_____
	_____	_____
Musical signature or "jingle"	_____	_____
	_____	_____
	_____	_____
Color scheme	_____	_____
	_____	_____
	_____	_____
Packaging designs	_____	_____
	_____	_____
	_____	_____
Staff phone demeanor	_____	_____
	_____	_____
	_____	_____
Uniform or dress code	_____	_____
	_____	_____
	_____	_____
Image (style/ fashion)	_____	_____
	_____	_____
	_____	_____
Innovation	_____	_____
Geographic location	_____	_____
	_____	_____
	_____	_____
Customer service	_____	_____
	_____	_____
	_____	_____
Performance (the form/ function utility)	_____	_____
	_____	_____
	_____	_____
	_____	_____
Selection	_____	_____
	_____	_____
	_____	_____

continues

My Branding and Positioning Notes   *(continued)*

Brand Components

Describe how (or if) you/your competitor are currently using each component to communicate brand identity.

Strategy	Me	My Toughest Competitor
Distribution (time/place and ease-of-possession utilities)	_____ _____ _____ _____	_____ _____ _____ _____
Convenience	_____ _____ _____	_____ _____ _____
Price	_____ _____ _____	_____ _____ _____

Audition These Sample Strategies

Jot down a few notes as you consider how each strategy might apply in your situation. Are any of these strategies being used by your competitor?

Strategy	Me	My Toughest Competitor
Product's superior attributes	_____ _____ _____	_____ _____ _____
Price/quality/ value equation	_____ _____ _____	_____ _____ _____
Against a competitor	_____ _____ _____	_____ _____ _____
Specific uses	_____ _____ _____	_____ _____ _____
Response to customers' needs	_____ _____ _____	_____ _____ _____
Product users	_____ _____ _____	_____ _____ _____

THE 30-SECOND RECAP

- Positioning requires knowledge of the dimensions of competition that are top concerns to your target market, such as price or styling.
- To find your position, try different strategies, starting with the samples listed in this section.

Exhibits and Expositions

A successful exhibit trade show means meeting the right buyers and the right sellers together in the same room. Are they worth attending?

In this section, we will walk you through these issues. We'll discuss the various things you need to know before investing your time and money in attending or exhibiting at a trade show.

EXPOSITION OR TRADE SHOW

An exposition is a show that's open to the public, whereas a trade show is open to members of the meeting's organization.

Every year, in many cities across the country, local builders and remodelers have home-remodeling shows. These expositions are open to the public, and you pay a fee at the door. This is different from a trade show that's only open to registered attendees. This section is about attending trade shows and does not deal with the issues of public shows.

CONFUSING CONSIDERATIONS

So someone suggests you need to exhibit at a trade show. Before jumping on the bandwagon, ask yourself the following questions:

- Why is it beneficial to have this exhibit?
- When will the attendees have time to look at them?
- Will they be several hours long or one or more days?
- Will they be scheduled in parallel with other sessions?
- What is the value to your business?
- Is there sufficient space for you?
- What is a reasonable fee to exhibit?

■ What impact will exhibits have on your budget (both income and expense)?

■ Will you receive a return on your investment?

Exhibiting in a trade show can cost thousands of dollars. Costs include the booth and materials (and shipping them), travel expenses, promotional brochures and giveaways, time out of the office for one or more people, and booth registration fees. You need to show a return on your investment to make this worthwhile.

Trade shows should be considered only if both your attendees and exhibitors will really benefit from them. Refer to your meeting's goals and objectives. (This is a perfect example of why you need them.) How does a trade show fit into the scheme of things? Does it make sense?

LOCATION, LOCATION, LOCATION (AGAIN)

Convention centers are specifically designed to hold expositions and trade shows, but in some cases, hotels are used. (Conference centers are not used for trade shows or exhibits. Their size and purpose differ from convention centers.) It's really an issue of space availability and the complexity of your show that determines your location decision.

Here are some other considerations:

■ Will you have easy access to the show?

■ Can you move in easily?

■ What additional fees will you be charged by the facility?

■ Can you plug in your own electrical cords, or are there union restrictions?

■ Is there an open-dock policy, or do you have to hire someone to carry your exhibit material in for you?

■ Can you exhibit what you want to? For example, if you are an equipment manufacturer, can you display your equipment?

■ What are the building policies on it?

■ What is the floor load capacity? Will your exhibit be too heavy?

HOW TO BUY SPACE FROM THE ORGANIZER

You usually buy booths in a booth package. Typically a booth includes an 8-foot pipe and drape back wall, 3-foot-high side rails, a table, and two chairs. Anything else is extra and is paid for by you. The trade show organizer will have a package according to the trade show needs.

In addition to buying a booth, many organizers will offer to sell you ad space in the program and sponsorship opportunities. Some charge a premium for the best booth locations—corners, near food stations, in front of the main door—island booths, and other unique configurations.

EXHIBITOR PROSPECTUS

An exhibitor prospectus and application form contains all the information you would need to know to make an informed decision about exhibiting. These can be two different documents or sometimes they're incorporated into one. Here are some things to look for in the prospectus:

- Information about the show's location
- The dates of the show including move-in/move-out and exhibit hours
- Why you should exhibit
- An attendee profile
- Rules and regulations
- A floor plan (draft)
- Statistics on last year's show if available (number of attendees, testimonials, and success stories)
- How booth assignments are made (first-come, first-served; random; or lottery)
- The booth fee and when deposit/payment is due
- The cancellation policy
- Exhibitor services contractor information
- Music licensing information

Here are some things that are included on the application:

1. The organization's name
2. A contact name/title/address/phone/fax/e-mail for correspondence and the program
3. Exhibitor names for name badges (state how many are included) and if you are a full conference or exhibit only registration
4. A statement to sign saying that you understand the show rules and regulations and will abide by them
5. Booth number and location preference (you may be asked for your top three, if applicable)

6. How the booth sign should read— note how many characters and spaces are allowed

7. What products and services are being exhibited by you

8. When and where to return the application

9. Twenty-five words or less about the product or service (this information may be needed for the attendee program)

10. Liability waiver

11. Insurance statement (you need to have insurance)

Rules and Regs

Every show must have rules and regulations. The organizer will communicate with you regarding move-in procedures, move-out procedures, security information, liability waiver, insurance requirements, shipping and storage, booth construction and obstructions, the booth-assignment procedure, and the procedure for enforcement of rules and regulations. Each trade show will have rules that pertain to its specific industry. For example, a food show may require that visqueen (plastic sheeting) be laid on top of carpet if cooking is done in the booth. You get the idea. The booth-assignment procedure can be first-come, first-served or at the organizer's discretion. The organizer usually reserves the right to reassign booth space if necessary and (hopefully) pays attention to competitors. In certain industries, you may be asked whether there is any organization you do not want to be near on the floor.

TIP

Most booth packages include two or three complimentary registrations. Sometimes exhibitors are invited to all meal functions, and in other cases they are not. Pay attention to these differences.

Issues Onsite

Sometimes the meeting host places a registration table next to the exhibitor services company on the show floor so that the exhibitors can check in with both at the same time.

Move-In

Moving in can be a lengthy affair depending on the facility and the number of exhibitors. Most organizers publish specific move-in hours that must be adhered to. Depending on the facility, only so many exhibitors can use the loading dock at the same time. Sometimes exhibitors are allowed to "carry in" their stuff through the front doors as long as they do not need carts and other assistance. Other times, they are required to use the loading dock. Ask the organizer about these rules.

When a loading dock is very busy, some facilities require a *marshalling yard*. This is an area away from the facility where exhibitors wait to be called to the dock in an orderly fashion. Unless the show is really big, this probably isn't applicable. But now at least you know what one is.

PLAIN ENGLISH

A **marshalling yard** is an area away from the facility where exhibitors wait to be called to the dock for unloading. It is "take a number" and wait.

THE HOOK

Some organizations create games that offer prizes for attending booths in the exhibit area. For one show, an Exhibit Passport Getaway was created. Attendees had to find the six different booths with special stamps and get their passports stamped. After they did that, they placed their passports in a raffle drum, and they were eligible for drawings at the end of the day. The prizes were hotel and restaurant certificates.

There are a number of neat ideas like this that organizers use to provide incentive to attendees. You may be asked in advance to provide prizes.

MOVE-OUT

What goes in must come out. Make sure you check the rules regarding when teardown can begin.

The rules that applied for bringing stuff in still apply when taking it out. Before the show is over, the organizer will have instructed the exhibitors how to get their boxes shipped out. You can even hire the exposition services contractor to tear down, pack, and ship the items for you.

THE 30-SECOND RECAP

- Have valid reasons and plenty of market research to support exhibiting at a trade show.

- The exhibitor prospectus contains all the details of the trade show, including who the audience is, why exhibitors should participate, the dates and times of the show, rules and regulations, and other details.

- Tabletop shows are smaller. They are great if you do not have a budget to attend a full-fledged trade show.

How To Be a Publicity Hound

You know how movie stars always end up being interviewed in the press or on the talk shows just when they have a movie coming out? That's not a coincidence. They have press agents at work getting them out in the public eye. It gets attention for the movie, TV show, book, or whatever. Now you may not be able to afford a press agent, but you can use some of their techniques to get your name in the local news in a way that brings some positive notoriety to your business.

For some businesses, like Anita Hecht's Life History Service, sustained effort at positive publicity is the main marketing activity.

It's not hard to be a publicity hound, if you have dogged determination. This section looks at ways to become a publicity hound.

Publicity? It Couldn't Hurt and It Might Help

There are two different things people can mean when they recommend you go after some *publicity*. The first is that you should encourage the media to write or air news about you. The second is that you should get yourself known in the community by other means. They might mean networking, doing charitable work, or hosting special events. Publicity is anything you do that keeps your name (or your business's name) coming up in conversation.

PLAIN ENGLISH

Publicity involves the actions you take—not including your paid advertising—to let others know something about you and your business.

There's another reason having a handle on publicity is important to you. Sometimes bad things happen to good people. When bad things happen to you, the press will come calling. You need to have a disaster plan already in mind, or at least have a clue how to get the media to tell your side of the story.

By the way, people often use "publicity" and "public relations" as if they mean the same thing. They almost do, but not quite. Publicity is just one part of the larger activity of public relations, which includes a broader scope of communications activities, like customer relations and quality control.

HOW TO SNIFF OUT YOUR BEST PUBLICITY OPPORTUNITIES

It's possible to get publicity through a number of avenues, including the following:

- Word of mouth
- Communications to employees
- Special events
- Charity sponsorship
- Relationships with the news media

The last one comes to mind the most often when we think about publicity, but it can be the hardest and least controllable way to get your message out. Take some time to consider other avenues before you decide you are finished with this subject. Some obvious ones can be productive. A garage owner located near a university campus became a public radio sponsor. His business was thanked every day at drive time. He calls it one of his best publicity investments.

PUBLICITY'S PLACE IN YOUR MARKETING

Everything you plan to do with your advertising and marketing has its publicity impact. The reverse is also true: Your publicity efforts have an impact on the success of your marketing. Suppose you're planning an advertising campaign that features an innovative technique, such as the billboards put up by a telephone company. When the company changed its name, lifelike "worker" mannequins appeared in front of billboards, painting over the old logotype with the new one. The company received numerous phone calls, including some from people concerned that the "employees" were working such long hours. The company saw the publicity potential in that and called the local media. The result was *good ink*—positive mentions of the company both in the print media and on local radio and television.

PLAIN ENGLISH

Good ink is what you're looking for with publicity. It's an insider's term meaning that you or your company got into the news and the stories were positive.

The moral of the story: Whatever you are doing, publicity can amplify its effect. A corporate name change, a new product line, an innovative management decision—any and all can present opportunities for the media to look your way.

Don't think for a minute that publicity is a dance in which you lead. You can offer stories to the press, but you can't control the content or the timing of the coverage you receive. The wrong reaction can lead to long-lasting damage. Play publicity like a contact sport. Keep an offensive and a defensive strategy in mind.

If you are a solo home business, getting publicity is even more difficult. You might find it more useful to start an e-mail newsletter (where you are your own news outlet) or to use postcards to make the announcements and offers that keep your name in front of clients and prospects. If you find the right opportunity, the right story angle, however, you might still get yourself noticed by the press, especially if you can claim expertise in an area that is newsworthy.

If you have trouble picturing yourself pursuing publicity on your own, take note of Anita Hecht's approach. She invested her energy in helping the Association of Personal Historians (APH) become established. One of the main functions of this professional organization is to help members market their services. Publicity is a key marketing tool for all APH's 300-plus members. APH provides members with tools for generating publicity on a local level and also pays for a publicity agent to work at placing stories in national media. The group's marketing committee has created template press releases and suggests occasions for publicity like "May Is Personal History Month" so that members can time their efforts to build on each others' work.

FINDING OPPORTUNITIES AND STORY ANGLES

If you want to see stories about you in the press, send them the news you want to see. How do you do that effectively? By understanding the gatekeepers of the news—editors who make decisions about what stories will run and why.

First, understand their job. Each idea that crosses their desks has to pass this test: "Is this of interest or service to my audience (readers, viewers, or listeners)?" If the answer is yes and your idea is presented with a strong *story angle*, you're on your way.

TIP

Good reporters will try to present a balanced view. Chances are, they will fill out their stories by interviewing another authority who might not agree with your statements. Prepare ahead of time what you will say if you are challenged. A good response begins with something like, "I'm glad you asked that."

What's a story angle? It's the approach you choose that sells the editor on the merits of your story. Here are some tried-and-true story angles:

- **News announcements.** Information or events of potential interest to the public are opportunities for a news announcement. Introducing a new product, changing location, breaking ground on a new building, or sponsoring a workshop are all worthy of an announcement. Profit growth, with a dose of optimism about the economy, can get an editor's attention. Even the routine happenings in your business are worth a shot. Personnel promotions and new hires deserve a news announcement. If someone receives advanced training, a professional certification, or an award, send an announcement. These may not be high-priority news, but editors usually have a bit of space in the business section reserved for these morsels. Be sure to try trade journals as well as local newspapers.

- **Features.** A feature story explores a subject that informs or interests the public but is less tied to a point in time. Ask yourself: What do you know well, that the public would find interesting? The beauty of this type of publicity is the positive light it shines on you, the expert informant.

  For example, a dry cleaner followed this advice. When a national story came in about the ecological perils of dry-cleaning processes, he was able to give the press a local spin by describing the measures his business had already taken to offset those dangers. The story ran as a local good news piece, rather than the usual hair-raising report of dangers. Our man came across as a proactive businessman who makes his community's safety a priority.

  Features can be fillers, too—light news items that might appear as the last segment of a news broadcast. When a feature has no timeliness to it, publicity people will refer to it as an "evergreen."

TIP

If you want to provide a story idea for a local, state, or regional trade magazine, ask the editors for their editorial calendar. This will tell you what topics each issue will cover for a one-year period. Find a category that fits your business and tailor your story idea to fit the magazine's calendar.

- **Opinion.** Wherever a controversy exists, the media will be interested in communicating the opposing sides' points of view. Build a leadership image for yourself in your community by letting the media know where you stand on issues on which you have authoritative views.

Write a letter to the editor, or explain your point of view and submit it as a story idea. Even if members of the public disagree with your position, you have established yourself as a person willing to take a stand and speak your mind.

Use this test: Is my position fair to all concerned and based in solid facts? Is my desire to express it coming not from my own ego but from a desire to help my fellow citizens? If you can answer yes, you can expect positive outcomes from expressing your opinions.

Create a list of the media you want to target, and then create publicity releases using your different story angles. You'll quickly learn what sorts of stories the different editors are looking for. Feed them newsworthy material on a regular basis, and you'll soon build solid relationships. Before you know it, they'll be turning to you for the local angle, even on national stories that touch your area of expertise.

A story can be presented in one of two ways. You can send a news release informing the outlet of an item to write about, or you can actually write the story and submit it, leaving it to the editor to go with the piece as is or to rewrite it. Which you choose depends partly on your skill as a writer but also on the story angle and the type of media you're approaching. For example, daily newspapers prefer to write their own news, whereas the overworked staff at a trade journal will appreciate your writing assistance.

WORKING WITH THE MEDIA: WHAT DO THEY WANT?

Reporters and editors for the news media are some of the most hard-working, idealistic people you'll meet. They want to get the story right, and they have to get it on time. What they want—deep inside—is help! When you write a press release, tailor it to the exact needs of each specific contact. A feature editor will want a more chatty story than the general news desk; a business writer will want facts and figures; a lifestyle editor will want to hear the stories behind the numbers. So the most helpful thing you can do is to bring them the news they want, packaged in the style they need.

Here are some other tips to help you help them do their jobs:

- **Be a good assistant.** If you don't know the facts, offer to find out and follow up. Always keep your word. If you tell a reporter that a story is exclusive, don't break that promise by discussing the story with other journalists.

■ **Be quotable.** When a reporter calls, package your answers in concise *sound bites.* Start with the important items and keep your statements simple and direct. Here's a suggestion from the pros—restate the question in your answer. That makes it even easier to edit for concise reportage.

PLAIN ENGLISH

A **sound bite** is a nugget of newsworthiness, a morsel of meaning, chopped out of the context of an interview and served up like a news canapé. Short attention spans and quick-cut visual styles have made the media more and more reliant on sound-bite reporting.

■ **Use colorful descriptions.** Don't say, "We have 5 million cubic feet of storage in our new facility." Instead say, "All the water in Lake Watoosie wouldn't fill our storage facility." Colorful comparisons are more entertaining than straight statistics.

■ **Be available whenever you're needed.** When a reporter calls, chances are she's on a deadline. Drop whatever you're doing to take her call.

■ **Have one designated person talk to the media.** There should be a policy that employees to not talk to the media. Only a specific (and experienced) PR person should represent the company in the press. This will avoid confusion and miscommunication.

USING SPECIAL EVENTS TO GET PUBLICITY

"There's just no news," you say. "Nothing good has happened, and nothing bad either." You should make an event that makes news.

You can create a newsworthy event by sponsoring a seminar, inviting a celebrity to appear on your behalf, or hosting an open house or plant tour. Your possibilities are limited only by your creativity. A planned event gives you a timely opportunity for a news announcement. Work hard at getting reporters and photographers to come to the event. Show them a good time and you're likely to see a positive write-up afterward. For several years, Ducks In A Row hosted an "office holiday party" for the self-employed; the event was colorful and original enough to attract positive mentions in the business press.

To your friends in the media, the invitation, the event, and the results (new sales goals met, contest winners, and so on) all constitute news. It may not make the paper if there's a fire at the wiener factory on the same day, but it's just the kind of filler that most editors need on a regular basis.

WHAT TO DO WHEN BAD THINGS HAPPEN

Some people are only happy when it rains, and some editors love bad stories best of all. Still others follow the maxim "If it bleeds, it leads." The media won't limit themselves to reporting only good news. If you have adverse news, you can lay as low as you like, but the reporters may still come calling. How do you cope?

The most important strategy is to plan ahead. Just as you practice fire drills with your children (you do, don't you?), your business needs "publicity fire drills" as well. The place to start is with your press kit, which will be described a little later in this section. Keep up to date, and store copies of it at home as well. Decide who on your staff should and shouldn't talk to the media, and keep them briefed on the message you want to communicate. Follow this advice for best results:

- **Be honest at all times.** You don't need to tell all you know, but never tell a lie.

- **Do not repeat a reporter's incorrect statement,** as in "Are you saying I stole the money?" You might unwittingly give a sound bite that places you in a negative light. You never know how your comments will be edited.

- **Never try to kill a story.** You're more likely to increase interest in the news, or worse yet, you'll draw attention to your desire to withhold information.

- **Allow only PR specialists to talk to the media**. When it comes to crisis (or even general public relations), you should enforce the policy that only PR reps talk to the media. Employees should not talk to the media, and they should be told that it goes against company policy.

The University Credit Union (UCU) had to handle one of those bad things that happen through almost no fault of their own. It's a classic case of a tough decision. Here's what happened. After the popular polar bear in the local zoo died, UCU arranged to have two polar cubs shipped to the zoo from Alaska. The cubs needed a home, so the cost of the donation was low. To get some publicity for the donation, UCU decided to hold a "name the cubs" contest. The cubs already had names, but UCU had been told they were just paperwork names. Unfortunately, news reporters from Alaska released a different story, which led locals to believe the cubs had been named by children in Alaska, so they flooded the papers and UCU with letters of protest.

The truth of the matter was that the names actually were given by the news writers themselves. But the UCU, with help from consultants, decided the truth would sound like an after-the-fact fiction. So UCU decided not to tell a lie, but also not to tell all. They admitted a mistake and enlisted their members to make suggestions on how to handle the contest already launched. In the end, popular opinion called for keeping the cubs' original names and donating the promised prize money to the local children's museum. The result was positive for UCU. Townspeople congratulated them on their openness to collaboration. Admitting a mistake (which they did make by not double-checking the original story) and sitting on the whole truth got UCU better publicity than the contest would have. The moral: Once again, even with publicity, you have to know your audience.

TIP

Don't be afraid to mix business with pleasure. First, you should balance your community involvement between business-related professional groups and the community service activities that interest you. When you've chosen what you'll participate in, then give yourself fully and don't hide who you are. Talk about your business and let people see your enthusiasm.

COMMUNITY INVOLVEMENT: EFFECTIVE MARKETING ON HALF A SHOESTRING

There's a side to publicity that has nothing to do with news releases and making friends with the media. It is about getting yourself known in the community. It's a solid publicity strategy, and a lot of successful people take a very planned approach to it. They network (and not in that boring business-card-shuffle way), participate in charitable activities, serve on boards, and coach little league. All are activities that keep their names (and hopefully their businesses' names) in circulation.

Many professional service providers find advertising, and even publicity activities, too self-promotional for comfort. Some, like lawyers and doctors, are so recently arrived in the world of marketing that community involvement is the only avenue they feel comfortable pursuing.

SELLING YOUR STORY USING A PRESS KIT

Whether you go looking for news or news comes looking for you, it helps to be prepared. That's where your press kit comes in. A press kit can be as simple as a set of stapled press releases, or it can be an elaborate folder with glossy photos and company literature included. It can be a generic description of your company and your products, or it can be dedicated to a specific topic, like your new product or a special event.

A press kit might include any or all of these components:

- Press release
- Photos
- Fact sheets about the company and its offering
- Personnel statements with credentials, education, and achievements
- Video or audio press releases
- Company literature (annual reports, brochures, and so on)

A PRESS RELEASE FOR EVERY OCCASION

The press release, or news release, is the meat of the press kit. It's the story presented in a way the editor can run as written, or use as the basis for her own report. You don't know which way she'll go, so you write it as follows, to cover all your bases.

The generally accepted format for a press release is ...

NEWS RELEASE

Contact:

Bob Waterman
Bob's Bottomless Boats
3800 Riverview Parkway
123-456-7890 ext. 1

For Immediate Release

Headline: WHAT IS A KAYA CANOE? ASK AT BOB'S BOTTOM-LESS BOATS

Bob's Bottomless Boats on Riverview Parkway has launched the flagship of a new product line, a lightweight hybrid combining the sporty maneuverability of a kayak with the more comfortable ergonomics of a canoe.

Bob's Bottomless Boats has developed the new design with the help of experts in sports medicine from University Hospital. The forward-thinking kaya canoe positions the knees, hips, and spine for maximum comfort and power in motion. "Our goal is to ease the discomfort a body feels when it tries to participate in a demanding sport," said the boat's designer, Bill Waterman.

The new boat is a lightweight one-person craft with a unique new seat. The boat combines the comfort of canoeing with the mobility only kayaks have delivered. Because of their stability, kaya canoes are excellent for bird watching, fishing, and nature photography.

Weighing in at about 35 pounds, the boats are easy to maneuver both in and out of the water.

By introducing a boat that's affordable, comfortable, and fun, Bob's Bottomless Boats once again demonstrates its leadership in all things boating in the Lake City region.

-30-

Contact:

Bob Waterman
Bob's Bottomless Boats
3800 Riverview Parkway
123-456-7890 ext. 1

TIP

Editors edit. More often than not, they will modify your release. At a minimum, they will shorten it, but they may also leave out critical statements so that the meaning of the release is changed somewhat. Editors on tight deadlines might get confused by what you have included in a release. Concise writing on your part is critical.

Every press release should begin with a header section, with the word *NEWS* first, followed by a release date or "for immediate release." Give your contact information, even if the release is on your company letterhead.

Next comes the body of your release. Start with a headline that demonstrates your most newsworthy element. Go on to a lead paragraph that gets attention and then tells your story. The whole story must be summarized in this lead paragraph. If the editor doesn't cut the story down to this, the average reader probably will. Writing the lead is the most difficult part of the press release.

Everything following the lead paragraph expands on what was introduced. Use quotes to keep the copy personal. Use subheads if they help you introduce points.

If your release is several pages long, write "more" at the foot of each page. Start each subsequent page with a two- or three-word *slug* for your story followed by the page number.

PLAIN ENGLISH

Slug is one of those charming terms left over from the hot-lead days in the newsroom. The slug is a topic word or three at the top of manuscript to identify the story, author, draft version, page, and more.

To close the press release, use the notation -30- to indicate the story's end. (This is a long-standing tradition with newsroom editors and typesetters.)

List any enclosures or available materials, like photos or videotapes. Repeat your contact information from the header section.

PHOTOGRAPHS: WORTH A THOUSAND WORDS

If at all possible, include a photo with your press release. Have high-quality professional pictures taken that go with your story. Good photos can serve many purposes beyond publicity. Your effort here can cross over to brochures, advertisements, and other applications. One day spent shooting pictures around your business can provide resource material for the future. When you include photos with your press kit, always attach a caption.

MANAGING PR: YOUR ACTION PLAN

Publicity activity takes a commitment. You have to exert energy consistently over time if you're going to see results. You must make time and a place for it in your work activities so you can stay on task.

Develop a calendar outlining the upcoming year's activity. This is the most important aspect of your publicity plan—it's what connects thought to action. Be sure to note when newsworthy events will take place, when advance work should begin, when follow-up is due, and when to begin future planning activities.

Your calendar should include a newsworthy event for each quarter of the year. It could be a personnel change, an anniversary, a special event, or a professional recognition. It's up to you to find the appropriate stories for your situation.

Plan your publicity strategy by defining the message to be communicated. Double-check that this message is consistent with the positioning and advertising messages you've developed. Then develop an implementation strategy to get that message out. Keep track of the media contacts who will help you do this.

SUCCESS IS IN THE FOLLOW-THROUGH

So you plan your activity, develop your messages, send out your releases, and wait for the stories to appear. What to do if nobody bites? Don't panic. Most stories you see about businesses—unless there's skullduggery afoot—are the result of months of follow-through by someone to get that story placed.

TIP

The most important PR activity you can undertake is to get to know your local reporters by their beats, their styles, and their bosses. Take notes on who writes what about whom. Over time, your dossier will grow until you develop a sixth sense for whom to call with what type of story. Then tailor your communications to each individual's needs. Your efforts will pay off in good ink.

Most publicity work is done on the phone and supported by e-mail, faxes, and the mail. You send out your press releases and press kits. You develop story angles and pitch them to your media contacts. If you're lucky, eventually they bite, and your phone rings. (Most interviews are done over the phone; the deadlines are too tight for reporters to go running around.) If you've done your homework, you're ready with the facts at your fingertips. Handle the phone call with aplomb, and the story that appears will be accurate and flattering. Congratulations! You've mastered another angle of the marketing job.

THE 30-SECOND RECAP

- Use publicity to amplify whatever you're doing in your business. Your expansions, personnel changes, and innovative management solutions all present opportunities for good publicity.

- Whatever you propose must have news value. Ask yourself, "Is this of interest or service to this medium's audience (readers, viewers, or listeners)?" If so, pursue the story. If not, look harder for a newsworthy angle.

- When you start feeling like "nothing ever happens around here," stir up some excitement with a special event. Your sales contest, seminar, or visit from an industry leader constitutes news, if nothing better comes along.

- Community involvement, such as public speaking, writing and placing articles, and volunteerism, helps keep your name in front of your audience.

- Develop a professional-looking press kit, with press releases, background information, and photographs. Make yourself easy to report on, and you'll see your name in the news more often.

- Be a good assistant to your media contacts. Be available, prepared, and quotable. Follow through when you say you will.

Successful Selling

The Skills You Need to Sell

Nothing happens until somebody makes a sale. Maybe you've heard that saying. The sales transaction gives a purpose to your business; without it, you're out of business. That said, here's something else to ponder: Nobody ever sells anything to anybody.

Do those statements sound contradictory? Well, here's the point: You don't really sell things to other people. What you do is help people sell things to themselves. As a good salesperson, you facilitate that process. That's really what selling is all about—helping people understand why what you offer is going to fulfill a need or solve a problem. When you do a good job of that, transactions happen. If you want to know how to help people sell themselves whatever it is you offer, read on.

MARKETING ISN'T NECESSARILY SELLING

Many people use the words *marketing* and *sales* as if they mean the same thing. They don't. In fact, understanding of the difference between the two is essential to success.

Marketing consists of getting a mutually beneficial exchange to take place between a buyer and a seller. Marketing sees the big picture.

But marketing activity doesn't put money in the cash register. Sales activity does.

PLAIN ENGLISH

Marketing and **sales:** two halves of a tough nut to crack! Marketing means planning and executing the pricing, promotion, and distribution of an offering so that a mutually beneficial exchange can take place. Sales means the personal effort of individuals who work to complete that exchange.

Sales is the personal side of marketing. Sales activity focuses on how people handle the buying exchange. It can be as simple as taking quarters at a lemonade stand or as complicated as writing an order for a custom computer program that hasn't been developed yet.

Sales and marketing are more than a little related, of course. Good marketing is important if you expect good sales results. Marketing activities provide the base on which you build sales activities.

Have you ever worked in sales? Then you know how important it is to have the right product at the right price and with the right promotional programs in place to help you get your message across. Each element of the marketing mix contributes to the success or failure of the sales force.

People in sales rely on marketing and advertising to bring in well-qualified leads. When you play the sales role, you appreciate having a good place to start—a list of people who have expressed interest or are predisposed to buy. Almost as important as good leads are good brochures to leave behind and persuasive sales presentation tools. It's the job of marketing and advertising to provide these.

With leads, advertising, and sales support materials in place, you can consider how to sell. So let's take a look at the tools you can use for your selling approach, the selling process itself, and the skills you will need to succeed.

CHOOSE YOUR SELLING APPROACH TOOLS

How do you get in touch with your potential customer? You can use any or all of these *selling approach tools:*

- Cold-calling
- Personal letters
- Telemarketing
- In-person sales

Your choice will depend on several factors. First, there are probably norms for your industry. What do other people like you do? Then, there is your personality and what feels most comfortable to you. Let's look at an example.

PLAIN ENGLISH

Selling approach tools are the methods you can use to approach your customers. The tools are cold-calling, personal letters, telemarketing, and in-person sales. In most cases, your sales approach will use a combination of these tools.

Rich is a sales rep for a photography studio that specializes in catalog shooting. His customers are production managers and art directors. They might work at catalog houses, or they might work for the agencies hired to produce the catalogs. These are busy people, and they can be tough gatekeepers.

So the question is, how does Rich use his selling approach tools to build a relationship—to go from total stranger to valued consultant?

It starts with cold-calling. Rich digs everywhere, from the Internet to the pages of *Catalog Age* to the local printers' client lists to create his prospect list. Then he cold-calls to prequalify the list, finding out as much as he can about each company he's targeted.

Because the product he sells is visual, Rich relies heavily on a variation of the personal letter approach. Three or four times a year, he produces a postcard showcasing some recent work by the studio. These mailings act as a reminder and also provide an expanding collection of samples that art directors can keep and refer to when shopping for ideas.

Rich makes sure to spend a portion of his time on telemarketing as well. How is that different from cold-calling? Cold-calling gathers information to facilitate approaching a prospect. It can turn into telemarketing, or it can lead to other selling approaches.

TIP

There are ways to make your cold-calls warmer. Read job promotions and trade journals, and pay attention to local gossip to build your house prospect list. The first time you pick up the phone, make it purely a fact-finding mission. Then when you make that sales call, you know they need what you sell.

Telemarketing is the specific activity of calling someone on the phone and asking for a sale. For Rich, this means keeping in touch with good prospects with regular phone contact. (Like most successful sales people, Rich uses contact-manager software, like GoldMine or ACT!, to maintain detailed records of his customer touch points.) He'll call to ask whether there's anything coming up that he can bid on, whether a recent proposal is still active, or whether samples are back from the printer on the last job. It doesn't matter so much what he's calling about, but that he calls. In some industries, and this is one of them, buyers like to feel sought after. When you're spending thousands of dollars for something, you want to be treated like you matter.

That's one reason Rich spends a portion of his time on in-person sales as well. He knows the importance of "face time." Sometimes the reason for the visit is to show the work—to demonstrate a new technical capability, for example, or a new photographer's unique style. Other times the reason is a mix of business and pleasure—a lunch to brainstorm about a new project, or just to keep in touch. In-person sales offer Rich the opportunity to practice *collaborative selling,* pursuing genuine dialogue with his customers to make them partners in the selling process.

PLAIN ENGLISH

Collaborative selling means selling like a consultant—not a sales-person. It means building a relationship of trust with your prospect. The prospect shares with you the details of his needs and trusts you to bring to his attention products or services that meet those needs—not waste time bringing those that don't.

Rich's selling approach includes a little of everything. His success lies in the way he tailors the approach to each client's needs. Although cold-calling helps bring in new business, letters asking key business associates for referrals are very effective, too. A combination of phone, e-mail, and in-person contact helps Rich reach his goals. Certainly a different marketer on a different mission would mix the ingredients differently.

THE SELLING PROCESS: THINK BIG

The art of selling varies dramatically depending on the situation you find yourself in. A distributor selling business to business finds himself in a very different world than a retail store selling to local customers. Professionals selling their services experience a different climate. The advice that follows in this section is more appropriate to the retail situation, although many techniques and concepts cross over.

The selling process begins with image, and image begins when you first make contact with your prospect. Your advertising should reflect your image. In fact, you should project a consistent personality (brand identity) through all your contacts, ads, stores, vehicles, and staff. It's a cliché that happens to be true: You never get a second chance to make a first impression. Control your image so that the first impression prospects form is a good one.

ADVERTISE FOR LEADS

Your advertising should contain enough hard information about your product or service to bring in well-qualified prospects. This is one of the strongest arguments in favor of long copy in ads. If the product you sell is complex or expensive, buyers will want information they can refer to for comparison shopping.

If your ads are not especially informative, make sure you have a brochure that spells out the facts. You'll waste less time explaining widgets to people looking for whatsits.

First Contact: Show, Tell, and Question

Okay, let's practice that image-establishing first contact. A prospect has turned herself in: She's called or come to your store. Now you can learn about each other to see whether the relationship should go forward. The prospect wants information about the product or service. Give it to her. That's your opening— use it to determine as quickly as possible whether to work with this prospect or gently move on to one with greater potential.

What do you say to the customer who's out shopping and just walked into your store? Make a helpful, friendly greeting, and then watch and wait. That's not always easy! Don't hover, but don't disappear. When the customer seems comfortable, begin the selling conversation. Use this formula: Show, tell, and question.

"I see you're looking at coffee makers. This one is particularly nice—it has a neat gizmo for mounting under a kitchen cabinet, which really saves space. How are you currently making coffee?" The answer will guide you to what benefits matter to this prospect and help you find out her personality style, too, if you listen carefully.

Present the widget, describe a benefit, and then ask a probing question. This simple formula works like magic. You can use it for any situation where you have a prospect's attention.

Build a Platform for Your Skills

You will need to base your skills on a couple of necessities: product knowledge and a persuasive personality. Now don't start shuffling your feet. First of all, anyone can apply themselves to learn their products well enough to know everything prospects might ask. And yes, the sales personality thing is harder, unless you just naturally have it. If you ground yourself in product knowledge and practice the skills that sales professionals use, however, you may just find yourself blooming into a sales charmer.

Base Your Skills on Product Knowledge

Make yourself an expert on the products you sell. Knowledge like this gives customers confidence both in you and in the product you know so much about. It makes you part of the value you offer and can give you a real edge over your competition.

How do you get product knowledge?

- **Ask your customers.** If they're using your products, they know what they like and don't like about them. Next time you see the coffee-maker lady, ask her how her purchase is working out. If she says, "It saves space, but it drips all over the place," you've learned something important.

- ■ **Ask your suppliers.** Study the printed literature your suppliers provide. Probe your sales reps for information. Listen to the language they use to sell these items to you. The same phrases will help you sell to your customers.
- ■ **Study your trade sources.** Attend trade shows, join your trade association, subscribe to your industry's journals. Product knowledge is one of the main assets they have to offer.

All across America, from grocery stores to bookstores to hardware stores, small business people are facing competition from major chains and discount stores that offer low prices. They fight back with product knowledge and personal service.

Your job is to become the ultimate know-it-all where your products and services are concerned.

TIP

There is a right way and a wrong way to show off a product. To demonstrate a product effectively, handle it frequently and treat it like a star. Be an actor—project how much you like and want the product, and your audience will adopt the same attitude.

TIP

Whatever you do, don't abuse the product. It used to be popular to demonstrate durability with rough treatment, but this often backfires. You don't want to leave an impression the product is of little value.

BECOME PERSONALLY PERSUASIVE

You can be a highly motivated person who believes in your product or service and still stink as a salesperson. Some people are born with persuasive sales ability. You probably remember them from your high school class—the people who were able to get their way about anything they wanted. Well, those people might very well be pursuing successful sales careers today. But what about you? Maybe you were a late bloomer? Or maybe you're one of those self-effacing types who feel uncomfortable praising yourself or voicing a strong opinion. Do a little personality weightlifting. Practice the skills top sales professionals use. You can bet a lot of them felt they couldn't sell when they started out.

DEVELOP THE SKILLS PROFESSIONALS USE

When you're buying something, you don't want to deal with salespeople who don't have your needs in mind, and neither do your customers. When you understand what it is they're looking for, you're not going to waste their time and you're not going to waste your time either. So develop the skill of "reading" your prospects.

SELL THE WAY PEOPLE BUY: MATCH YOUR STYLE TO THEIRS

Have you ever worked with someone who, no matter how hard you tried, just could never understand your approach to things or agree with you without a fight? You probably had mismatched personality styles. This can be worse for a salesperson than mismatched socks.

Researchers in human behavior have identified ways people act that actually create barriers to communication. You can reach across these barriers if you learn to identify other people's personality styles. Then you can choose successful ways to get your ideas across. In a management situation, this can lead to a smoother workplace. In sales, it leads to sales.

Your personality characteristics tell where you belong on this grid. Of course, not everyone is an extreme example.

Can you find yourself on the following table?

Personality Styles Matrix	
Task Oriented	Detail Oriented
Idea Oriented	People Oriented

Personality styles matrix.

Personality Styles—Attributes

	Task-Oriented	Detail-Oriented	People-Oriented	Idea-Oriented
Your conversation is:	Straight to the point	Full of background	About feelings	Full of compliments
You make decisions:	Quickly	Never enough information	Consensus	Intuitive (flash)
Your strengths:	Dependable	Thorough	Team builder	Visionary
Your weaknesses:	Inflexible	Perfectionist	Never finished	Impractical

How do you find out the style of others? First, take a good look around his or her office. Look for clues like these.

Personality Styles—Décor

	Task-Oriented	Detail-Oriented	People-Oriented	Idea-Oriented
Décor:	Calendar, bulletin board	Piles: Everything is in sight	Homey: pictures, candy dish	Cluttered, especially with awards (likes recognition)

Then mine for information that will let you place your prospects on this grid. Questions about families, hobbies, or recent changes in their business can bring out clues. When you have a fix on the prospect, tailor your communication to their needs. This may require bending who *you* are quite a bit. Learn to be an actor—a good one. Phony salespeople are a plague on humanity.

A people person will appreciate your "just in the neighborhood" visits or an occasional invitation to lunch. Task-oriented people will appreciate it if you leave them alone but respond like lightning when they need price quotes. Even if your style makes it hard for you, adjust your approach accordingly.

TIP

Knowledge of effective interpersonal communication will greatly improve your skills as a salesperson. Look for books on the subject or seminars you can attend.

Phrase your benefits in a way your prospects can relate to if you want to persuade them to buy what you're offering, be it a mail-order book or a creative idea. A detail-oriented person will be interested in dollars saved—and don't round the cents. A people-oriented person will enjoy hearing testimonial stories and will probably want to check references. An idea person will want to hear about new opportunities that this purchase will create. A task-oriented person will respond to hearing how this offering solves a problem.

PRACTICE ACTIVE LISTENING

You should employ active-listening techniques. Focus with empathy on your prospects' words. Ask open-ended questions, and really listen to the answers. To train yourself in this, repeat back what you are hearing, in your own words. If your prospect is saying, "I wish my copier didn't break down so often," you could say, "So you're looking for a copier that performs reliably." You are showing you understand his or her situation; you are building a bond of affirmation between you.

MAKE USE OF PEOPLE'S MOTIVATION TO BUY

People make purchases when they perceive a need, have the ability to buy, and find a product that suits their expectations of function and value.

Are you selling features instead of benefits? Tape your next selling conversation and study it. Have you fallen into the habit of talking about features, rather than probing for problems and offering solutions? Are you saying your widget features "dual wobbles" instead of saying your widget will make the sound fuller and clearer? If you want to increase your sales, focus on talking about benefits instead. Remember, this person is buying a solution to a problem—not just a product!

Sometimes you'll find buyers using rational reasons to cover basically illogical motivations to buy. "Because I like it," sounds so empty (although it's not) that many times we make up reasons to justify our actions. A woman choosing the pricier suit in a department store might insist it's because it goes with other clothes she owns—not just because she likes it. There's often a little guilt that goes with a purchase. A good salesperson will help people ease that guilt by helping them come up with good reasons this purchase is justified, such as "Because it's so well made, it will last longer."

NOW YOU ARE READY FOR ADVANCED SKILLS

Okay, you know your product. You're a practiced listener and you know how to read your prospects. Confidence brims. So plunge into the heart of the sales transaction: handling objections and closing the sale.

OVERCOME OBJECTIONS

First, realize that not every question is an objection. On the other hand, treat each objection as a question that still hasn't been effectively addressed.

Learn to distinguish the two types of objections: product-knowledge questions and barrier-to-sale questions. The product-knowledge ones are your cue to explain features and describe their related benefits. These questions are a valuable assist from your prospect and will help you make the sale.

Barrier-to-sale questions are the objections and hesitations your prospects raise. Real objections are the most interesting part of the sales process, if you're truly a motivated salesperson. Here's advice from the pros on handling objections:

- **Don't get angry.** You'll never make up the lost ground if you lose empathy with your customer.

- **Actively listen to the customer's question or concern.** Show it: Nod your head and use phrases like, "I see your point of view."

- **Clarify with questions.** Probe for the real reasons behind a customer's resistance. Break general statements into specifics that you can answer one by one.

Plenty of times in your sales career, you'll come up against tough customers—the skeptics who are never convinced or the moving targets whose needs you can never pin down. Know when to cut your losses, and end the conversation gracefully. Make sure this person walks away with a good impression of you and your offering.

TIP

The objection you're probably most worried about facing is price. When someone says, "It's just too expensive," or "I don't have that kind of money to spend," what can you say? The last thing you should do is lower your price at that moment. Instead respond by demonstrating the value delivered at that price. Explain payment terms or return on investment over the life of the product. If the price objection remains, offer a different product at lesser price. Never cut price on the original product. Even if you are selling services, offer a different package. Don't simply say you'll do the job for less. Once word gets out that you're negotiable on price, you'll never get top dollar again.

CLOSING TECHNIQUES YOU'LL TAKE TO THE BANK

You don't want to waste your time selling to people who will not buy. We sometimes forget that the purchase exchange goes both ways: There has to be something beneficial for you in the deal, as well as something for your prospect. Answer these four questions as early as you can in the sales process. Gracefully shut the process down and get on with your life if the answer to any one question is "no."

- **Does your prospect need what you have to offer?** You can sell something for which there is no need, but later, at least one of that "committee of six" is going to be disappointed, and that will reflect on you. It is better for your long-term health not to press for this sale.

- **Is he or she the decision maker?** You can sell to non-decision makers, but you can't close. They can say "no," but they can't say "yes." Find out the decision process you're up against, and press for a meeting with the ones who can say "yes."

- **Does he or she have money budgeted for this purchase?** If no money is available, you're being used. Someone is wishing for what you have but they're not going to say "yes" no matter what you do. Find out when money will be available—maybe next fiscal year.

- **Is he or she politically able to buy from you?** Often a deal will look good, but then at the last minute, you find out there's no hope for you.

If you've ascertained that the prospect meets these four criteria, you know it's worth your effort to work at *closing* this sale.

PLAIN ENGLISH

Closing means asking for a specific action on your customer's part. There are small closes, when the customer agrees with you on specific sales points, and there is the ultimate close, when the customer agrees to the purchase.

Closing a sale is the real test of your skill as a salesperson. To choose the right moment and the right words to say, you must be perfectly attuned to the state of mind of your customer. You must have perfect self-confidence, or the fear of failure will stop you from taking the risk. Sales requires a relentlessly positive state of mind and superb customer knowledge.

Here's how to close: Watch for the prospect to communicate strong interest through posture, facial expression, or gestures. Listen to the tone of voice in which questions are asked. Listen to the content of questions. Is the customer asking about delivery and installation? Then he has already made the purchase in his mind.

When the prospect shows signs of being ready to buy, make your move. Ask for the sale—directly or indirectly. Be very open to what happens next. If the customer raises an objection, return to your active-listening mode until you've removed that concern. Then try to close again.

Here are seven tried-and-true closing techniques. Think about how these questions could be rephrased to fit your selling situation.

1. **Close on a small choice.** "Would you like that in peach or teal?" or "Would you like those by the dozen or by the case?"

2. **Close via small affirmations.** "Would you like to see a size larger? Isn't that more comfortable? Isn't the fit flattering? Would you like me to wrap it for you?"

TIP

Still not confident about closing the sale? Put the shoe on the other foot. Study the selling situations next time you go out to buy something. Analyze how salespeople lead you through the process. Learn from their examples, good or bad.

3. **Close on a bargain opportunity.** "They're selling fast—we won't have them long at this price."

4. **Close on joining the club.** "We're selling a lot of these to people like yourself."

5. **Close on a method of payment.** "Will that be cash or charge?"

6. **Close on approval.** "Would you like to take this home and try it? We guarantee satisfaction or your money back."

7. **Close by asking for the order.** "We can begin work as soon as you sign here on the contract."

Try different closes, to see which work in your situation. It really helps to role-play with a friend or business associate. You may even want to write and rehearse a script that takes you through active listening, demonstrating the product, handling objections, and closing the sale. Not that you'll stick to the script in live selling situations, but the practice will make appropriate phrases come to mind when the situation arises.

TIP

If you don't follow up on a sale to make sure your customer is satisfied, you're in trouble. One small business owner said, "I just send the boxes out the door and hope they don't explode." Heaven knows printing—a custom manufacturing process—is particularly prone to post-sale disappointment. But his approach was dead wrong, and he's not in the business today.

Support After the Sale

After a sale, contact the decision maker and make sure everything is okay. This may be one of the toughest pieces of advice in this section. You absolutely have to make that post-sale satisfaction call. Resolve any doubts or misgivings if you can. Even after the sale takes place, there are still concerns for you as the salesperson. Remember the "committee of six" involved in the purchase! Two remain to be satisfied after the sale: the consumer (the one who uses the product) and the evaluator (the one who is able to say later whether the product satisfied the need).

Let's look at the lady who bought the coffee maker that saved space but leaked on her counter. As a consumer she's less than happy, and as an evaluator she's likely to point out the product's deficiencies to others, maybe even suggesting that your deficiency in product knowledge led to her bad purchase.

What should you do about it? Everything you can. Handle it like a complaint, and take action to make it work for you instead of against. Call your supplier and see whether you can get some kind of "make good" for the defective coffee maker. Maybe a replacement, maybe an offer of free repair, or maybe a free supply of special coffee filters. Your effort will make the buyer feel better about you. Employ your empathy to make customers feel heard even if there's nothing you can do to resolve their complaints. Given what it costs to advertise and bring in new customers, you should realize what a valuable asset your current customers are. Your support after the sale is your insurance policy on that asset.

Remember, every company makes an occasional mistake. If your company does, admit it and then go all out to make it right. Over the long run, some of your most loyal customers are likely to be those with whom a mistake was made initially and then was corrected quickly and fairly.

How to Sell Services

When someone comes to you for your expertise and experience, he needs to believe that the result of your work together will be the solution for whatever problem motivated him to seek you out. To give him that belief, you need to focus on two things: the process by which you'll solve his problem and the results of that work, as tangible as you can make them.

TIP

When you sell a custom product or service, you must define what will be delivered on each and every job. This definition of processes and outputs is called the scope of work. Once defined, it gives both client and service provider a means of verifying what's been done, what remains, and what the agreed-on budget is supposed to cover.

Explain the Process

Your best approach is to demystify the process by which you do your work. When people can envision what you do (and what a pain it would be to do it themselves), they can place value on what you do.

Jeremy, who owned his own graphic design firm, would break the project down into steps: information gathering, concept development, and execution. He defined what inputs he would need—existing photographs, interviews with key management, or whatever. He would describe the process that would take place at each step. He would define the final deliverables of his work: a printed box of brochures, a graphic standards manual, or an electronic template for a catalog. Taken together, this description made up the scope of work to be performed, and that's the basis on which a customer contracted with him. This outline makes sense for any type of service. It will help you define inputs, describe processes, and list outputs.

Promise Tangible Results

If you understand your customers' problems, you should have no trouble phrasing tangible results you will deliver that will solve those problems. It's particularly important to be precise about what you promise to deliver. Don't get in trouble saying you would "edit copy to client's satisfaction." You should probably say that you will "provide one draft plus two editorial revisions."

You'll find the contracting process, and the job itself, will go much smoother if you describe any milestones, such as key approval and delivery deadlines, so that clients can tell when the work is finished. Specific language is the key to this stage of the sale. Use language to keep the prospect focused on tangible benefits.

Unlike retail selling, where hundreds of transactions might take place each day in your store, selling professional services requires pacing the prospect through several rounds of meetings and proposals and finally negotiating a contract.

THE 30-SECOND RECAP

- Develop the selling approach tools (printed literature, telemarketing scripts, and so on) that you will need to get your sales work underway.

- Your success in sales will be based on your ability to balance product knowledge, empathy, and selling skills.

- Choose the right mix of selling approaches, and then tailor your activities to the personality styles of those you sell to.

- Study, practice, and rehearse your way through the selling process, from first contact to closing to support after the sale.

The Difference Between Marketing and Sales

A company's financial health starts with sales. Every company must sell its products or services to make money to pay its bills and earn a profit.

This makes marketing and sales two of the most important functions in a company. Their job is finding people to buy what the company sells. In most businesses, this isn't easy. When it is easy, it doesn't stay that way because competitors quickly come along. So marketing and sales offer some of the most challenging work in business. But it's some of the most satisfying and financially rewarding work as well.

In this section, marketing and sales and how they serve the company and its customers are examined. Basic marketing and sales concepts are also covered.

WHAT DRIVES THE COMPANY?

A market-driven company looks to the market (to groups of customers) to learn what it should be doing. A market-driven company listens to customers to learn why and how customers use what they sell. A market-driven firm watches trends in the marketplace in technology, pricing, packaging, and distribution (where and how it sells its products). It also watches competitors.

A customer-focused company also listens to customers for cues on what it should do. However, the term *customer-focused* emphasizes an effort to make each customer's experience satisfying. A customer-focused company believes that every customer is important and tries to ensure that each customer is treated as an individual. These companies tend to be very accommodating when they face customer requests, taking a "can-do" approach. Many companies say they're customer-focused, but few truly are.

Sales-driven companies are focused on the top line. They want sales. It's not that they ignore their markets and customers. No company can do that. It's just that those are not the main priorities. Increasing sales is the main priority.

Many insurance and securities firms are sales-driven. They often hire salespeople focused on "making the numbers." This works because many prospects can't distinguish among financial services firms and the product is intangible, so the outfit that pushes hardest can often close the sale.

Of course, all companies want increasing sales. But sales-driven companies take a very direct route to this goal. They hire salespeople who "push product" rather than discover and satisfy needs. They take a "get-the-money" approach to customers, which can close sales but fail to win long-term customers.

Think of marketing as selling to groups of people, whereas selling is done one on one. Marketing raises people's awareness of a product and generates interest in buying it. However, it takes selling to get an individual to hand over money or a check.

Advertising and direct mail are great examples of "selling to groups." But marketing goes beyond advertising and direct mail to include many other activities.

Selling means getting a person or a company (a customer) to pay for your product or service. But selling goes beyond "pitch the product" and "ask for an order."

In most organizations, marketing exists to support the salespeople. That's good, because selling is the toughest job in business. Most people will not part with their money, or their organization's money, without a good reason. The marketing and sales departments are there to supply those reasons.

Marketing is a staff activity, usually located at the company's headquarters. Selling is a line activity, and salespeople are said to work "in the field."

Marketing also tends to be *strategic*, whereas sales tends to be *tactical*. This flows from the idea that marketing supports sales. That support often takes the form of planning and guidance. For example, marketing identifies groups that appear to need the company's products. Then salespeople go to individuals within those groups to try to meet those needs with the company's product.

PLAIN ENGLISH

Strategic initiatives operate on a larger scale than **tactical** initiatives. Managers craft a strategy to achieve a goal. For instance, to achieve the goal of increased sales, management may adopt a strategy of pursuing a new market. To implement that strategy, the company will have to develop the right tactics, which might include developing new products. In general, tactics implement strategy.

People in marketing and sales approach business a bit differently. Marketing people tend to view their work in more intellectual and abstract terms than salespeople. The issue of "selling to groups" insulates marketing people from the hurly-burly of face-to-face selling. A marketing person researching product features faces less difficulty than the salesperson phoning busy people for appointments or trying to persuade a reluctant buyer.

There is often some tension between marketing and sales. Marketing can view salespeople as mere tools in its grand strategy, people who exist simply to execute the wonderful plans that marketing geniuses hatch. Meanwhile, sales can view marketers as hopelessly out-of-touch "staff-types" who would starve to death if they had to actually make sales.

People in marketing and sales must either eliminate this tension by fostering mutual respect, or at least manage it creatively.

TIP

To get marketing and salespeople to understand one another, force them to work together. Be sure marketing includes salespeople in its planning process and decisions. Be sure salespeople tell marketing about competitors and problems they face in the field. Get salespeople to take marketing people along on sales calls now and then, just so they can observe the process. Get marketing people to solicit ideas from the salespeople about how marketing can best support them.

COMMERCIAL VERSUS CONSUMER SALES

In business, there's a distinction between consumer and commercial or business-to-business marketing and sales.

If the person is buying the product or service for himself or herself as an individual, we're talking about *consumer sales*. If he or she is buying it for his or her organization, we are talking about *commercial, corporate, industrial,* or *business-to-business sales,* which all mean the same thing.

The product or service usually dictates the type of sales. For example, breakfast cereal and toothpaste are sold to consumers. (In fact, they're in a category known as consumer packaged goods.) Meanwhile, factory supplies and photocopiers are business-to-business items.

PLAIN ENGLISH

In **consumer sales,** the customers buy the product or service with their own money for their own personal use. In **commercial sales** (also called **corporate, industrial,** or **business-to-business**), the customers buy the product or service with their organization's money for professional use by themselves or others on the job.

But it gets tricky. For example, the 1990s boom in home-based businesses created a whole new market for personal computers, fax machines, and office supplies. This market has characteristics of both the commercial market and the consumer market.

Each type of sale (consumer and commercial) presents its own challenges, which we examine as they arise in the following sections.

FIRST MARKETING, THEN SALES

Companies compete largely on price and quality. Basically, a company can deliver either high quality at a high price (like Mercedes Benz) or lower quality at a low price (like Hyundai). The economics of our planet will not allow a company to manufacture a car with the quality of a Mercedes for the price of a Hyundai.

So the first strategic decision for a company is to choose the basis on which it will compete: price or quality. Then marketing delivers that message to the marketplace. John's Bargain Store says, "Come here if you want to pay a low price and get commonplace goods." Neiman Marcus says, "Come here if you can pay top dollar for the very best."

CAUTION

It's hard to find customer-focused employees in the United States because many people see being of service as somehow beneath them. (This is recognized as a major problem in the retail business.) This makes building a company culture that values customer service challenging. But when companies do manage to make service a priority (FedEx, Disney), the results can be spectacular.

There's another dimension: service. Here service means everything not included in price and quality—selection, post-purchase support, warranties, and so on. In some businesses and markets, service can be as important as price and quality. And there are other elements such as novelty, design, prestige, ease of use, and technical sophistication.

Of course, things have been simplified considerably, but essentially the goal of marketing strategy is to have a competitive advantage and to get word of that advantage out to the marketplace.

A sales call is a visit or phone call a salesperson makes to a customer or prospect to sell something.

TRANSLATING YOUR MARKETING PLANS INTO SALES GOALS

Every company wants to grow, which means that the dollar volume of sales must always be higher next year. There are several ways to achieve a sales increase:

- Increase your prices
- Sell more existing products to current customers
- Sell new products to current customers
- Sell existing products to new customers
- Sell new products to new customers

Let's briefly look at each of these strategies.

INCREASE YOUR PRICES

A price increase would seem to be the simplest way to increase your sales. All you have to do is raise your prices 5 percent, then sell the same amount of product next year as you did this year, and your sales increase by 5 percent. Great, huh?

There's only one problem: *price resistance*. That's MBA-ese for customers not wanting to pay a higher price. When they see higher prices for the same products, they look for other places to buy or they try to get along with less of it, or without it. They'll also bargain harder with your salespeople.

PLAIN ENGLISH

Price resistance refers to the fact that customers who face high or increasing prices for a product or service will generally seek cheaper alternative products or services, try to get a lower price from the seller, or go to a different seller with lower prices.

If you have the market power—that is, if you face few competitors and your customers have no options—your price increase may stick. However, it's not a strategy you can count on for long. A product that commands constantly increasing prices will quickly attract competition. Also customers often learn to live without companies they see gouging them.

The other four goals all involve selling more units of product, rather than selling the same amount of product at a higher price.

SELL MORE EXISTING PRODUCTS TO CURRENT CUSTOMERS

This comes down to "pushing product," and it can work. It is based on the reasonable idea that your best prospects are your current customers.

This strategy can work if your current customers are underserved or your product line is broad, or both. If you have only scratched the surface of your current customers and you have a broad product line to sell, you have ample opportunity to *cross-sell* them—that is, sell them other products that you offer.

PLAIN ENGLISH

Cross-selling means going to a customer who is buying one kind of product from you and selling him another kind, too. The question "Would you like fries with that?" is surely the most common example of cross-selling.

You can also offer volume discounts and find ways of binding the customers closer to you, perhaps by setting them up on an electronic system for automatic purchasing and billing. Anything you can do to make doing business with your company easier can help.

SELL NEW PRODUCTS TO CURRENT CUSTOMERS

New products are extremely vital. Even if you have what you think are satisfied customers, someone is out there working on ways to satisfy them even better or more cheaply. So you must always be improving your current products and developing new ones to meet your customers' needs.

Current customers can be your best prospects for new products, particularly products that solve problems you learned about when selling them old products.

SELL EXISTING PRODUCTS TO NEW CUSTOMERS

Some companies get into a rut by just serving the same old set of customers. When you have a successful product or service, constantly ask yourself: "Who else might buy this? Who else can use this?"

The search for new customers should never stop. Even the most successful companies lose at least some customers each year. Even your best accounts may leave you, for any number of reasons—a better product or price from a competitor, a snafu with a salesperson, or a simple desire for change.

Also any potential customer that you don't approach is one that a competitor will probably win. Why give away business without a fight?

TIP

New markets for existing products can even give rise to entirely new businesses. For example, the office-supply retailers Staples and Office Depot did not exist before the home-office boom. But then the need arose.

Companies selling office supplies commercially were not about to start calling on consumers. However, consumers, who are used to going to a store when they need something, have no problem going to one for paper, toner, or folders.

SELL NEW PRODUCTS TO NEW CUSTOMERS

When sales of your product begin to slope off (often in the phase of market *maturity* or *saturation*), you have three choices: (1) Close up shop or sell the business, (2) try to survive on repeat and replacement business, or (3) sell new products to new customers. The third choice is the best, provided you want a growing business. But don't make the mistake of waiting until your markets are saturated with your old products before developing new ones.

PLAIN ENGLISH

Market maturity means that the product has achieved wide acceptance and that growth in sales has leveled off. **Saturation** means that every potential customer who wants, needs, and can pay for your product already has one. It can be hard to know when your product has saturated its markets, because it depends on the true market potential for the product.

Selling new products to new customers can be the most powerful of the five growth strategies.

However, new products for new markets can be the hardest to develop. Even if you stay close to your main business (and generally you should), it's tough to come up with something new for a new market. That's why companies usually develop new products for their current markets, even when they enter a new business. For example, Disney entered theme parks in the 1950s. That was different from films, but Disney was already established in family entertainment. Nike, Adidas, and Reebok now offer active wear, but their target customers were already buying their athletic shoes.

Most business owners think constantly about ways to increase sales. These five strategies can move those thoughts in practical directions.

DIFFERENTIATING YOUR PRODUCT

Product differentiation means making your product different from the others like it. Successful products offer customers a difference, something better. Even products that compete mainly on price should offer some difference.

Marketing plays a big role in making and highlighting product differences. The following sections examine proven ways of achieving product differentiation.

IMPROVED PERFORMANCE

Performance improvements actually make the product better. The Japanese challenge to U.S. automakers in the 1970s was one of improved performance. Gas mileage, durability, and value for the price improved dramatically in Japanese cars during this decade.

Improved performance may strike you as a manufacturing issue rather than a marketing issue. But product improvements must be announced and "made real" in the marketplace, and that's a marketing challenge. It's not enough to build a better mousetrap. You have to show and tell people that it's better.

A company can decide to improve the performance of its product in various ways, including ease of use, durability, freedom from maintenance, economy of operation, and characteristics such as speed, weight, or water resistance.

One caution: Worthwhile performance improvements are those that people want and will pay for. If you make improvements that customers don't care about, you're not differentiating your product in a meaningful way. The result is often "a gold-plated crowbar." You get nothing but added production costs, which are the last thing you need.

IMPROVED APPEARANCE

Modern society is visually oriented. Today the appearance of a product can be as important as its performance. Therefore, design, the blend of form and function that dictates the appearance of a product, is now a powerful product differentiator.

IMPROVED IMAGE

In our society, many people define themselves at least partly by what they buy and use. Thanks to advertising, television, and movies, products convey certain images, both to ourselves and others. These images involve wealth, youth, status, sophistication, sexuality, health, caring, environmental consciousness, power, and danger (and in some cases, a social critic would surely add, stupidity).

Product images pervade our culture. Consider the various images cultivated by products as diverse as Marlboro cigarettes (rugged and manly), Chivas Regal scotch (smooth and sophisticated), Sears Kenmore appliances (sensible and reliable), Campbell's soups (wholesome and comforting), Kellogg's corn flakes (pure and simple), *New Yorker* magazine (urbane and literary), Harley-Davidson motorcycles (big and American), and the MGM Grand Hotel in Las Vegas (entertaining and swingin').

These images often go beyond mere product qualities. They attempt to create an experience for the customer that says, "When I buy this product, I am saying that I value these qualities, and that I have them myself."

THE PRODUCT ADOPTION CURVE

The product adoption curve states that a successful new product will be adopted by various categories of buyers in a predictable order. That's because not all buyers are willing to try something new. Many people need to see other, more innovative buyers adopt the product first.

The product adoption curve and the categories of buyers are shown in the following figure.

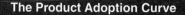

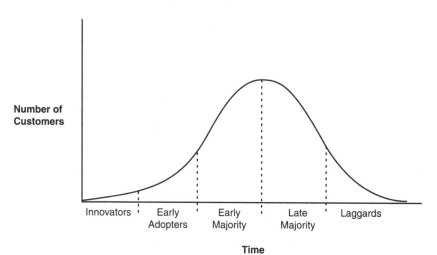

The product adoption curve.

By definition, the following percentages apply to each category of buyer:

Innovators	=	The first 2½ percent of buyers
Early adopters	=	The next 13½ percent
Early majority	=	The next 34 percent
Late majority	=	The next 34 percent
Laggards	=	The final 16 percent

These categories present different marketing and sales challenges. Innovators have to be located, which can take some doing, and then persuaded to try something new and unproven. Early adopters present similar challenges, but at least you have some earlier customers to point to as success stories.

You have to get to the early majority quickly, because you're soon going to face competitors if the product is successful. You may have to broaden your marketing effort and increase the size of the sales force. The late majority will probably require discounts and other inducements, such as service plans. At this stage you're in a battle for market share. You'll also be trying to find completely new markets for the product, perhaps overseas.

TIP
Different types of customers respond differently to different marketing messages and sales approaches. For example, innovators and early adopters get excited when they hear that something is new and different. In contrast, you have to sell the late majority on the reliability and wide acceptance of the product.

By the time you're selling a product to the laggards, the challenge has shifted to controlling your sales and manufacturing costs to squeeze all the profitability you can from the product while it's still alive.

The product adoption curve is also called the technology adoption curve because it applies to a technology (such as the VCR or personal computer) as well as to new products.

THE PRODUCT LIFE CYCLE

Like people and organizations, products have lives. They are conceived, they are born, they grow, they have a period of maturity, and they go into decline. The product life cycle was developed in the 1960s to describe the predictable phases in the life of a product. Those phases are as follows:

- Introduction
- Growth
- Maturity
- Decline

Usually these phases are shown on a curve that plots sales over time, as shown in the following figure.

Each phase presents a different marketing and sales challenge. In the introductory phase, the challenge is "missionary work"—spreading word of the new product and finding the first customers. During growth, the challenge is to beat competitors, who introduce similar products when they see one that makes money, and win as many customers as possible. In maturity, the challenge becomes controlling sales costs, fighting for market share, and developing variations of the product. In decline, the challenge is deciding what to do with the product: Can it be revitalized? Is it still profitable enough for you to sell?

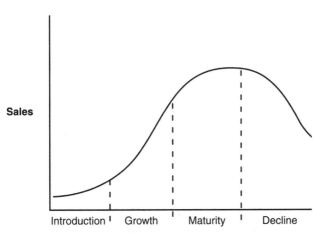

The Product Life Cycle Curve

Sales

Introduction | Growth | Maturity | Decline

Time

The product life cycle curve.

TIP

Few things in business are predictable, but the product life cycle is one of them. Unfortunately, the timing of the phases is not very predictable. The key thing to watch is the sales trend. When sales are slow early in the product's life, it is in the introductory phase. When sales rise sharply, it is in the growth phase. When sales growth levels off for an extended time, it is in maturity. And when sales decrease, it is in decline.

The length of any particular phase can vary for different products. A fad item such as Tamaguchis ("virtual pets") can have a life of a couple of years, with phases measured in months. A car brand like the Ford Mustang can take off rapidly, moving quickly from introduction to rapid growth, and then enjoy a long maturity and gentle decline with periods of revitalization. The product life cycle can be applied to entire product categories such as healthy frozen dinners (now in maturity) or steam locomotives (now defunct).

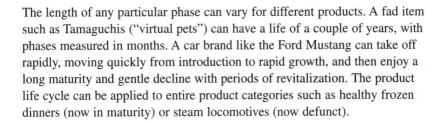

Occasionally a product or category can go into decline, and then stage a comeback. Large-engine, gas-guzzling cars and vans bounced back from their 1970s decline with the economic boom of the 1990s. Sales of fur coats also rose in 1997 after several years in decline due to antifur activism.

By the way, the product life cycle applies only to successful products. Those that don't make it past the introductory phase are product failures (products that are introduced but do not win market acceptance). Such failures are more common than most nonbusinesspeople realize. "New" Coke, Microsoft's Bob software and the Betamax come to mind!

THE 30-SECOND RECAP

- Think of marketing as selling to groups, whereas sales is done one on one. Marketing, which tends to be strategic, exists to support sales, which tends to be more tactical.

- Because companies basically compete on price and quality, a company must first decide where it wants to be in terms of price and quality. Then it must establish and reinforce that position through its products and marketing message.

- There are several ways to increase sales: increase prices, sell more existing products to current customers, sell new products to current customers, sell existing products to new customers, or sell new products to new customers.

- To differentiate your products, you can improve their performance, appearance, or image relative to competitive products.

- Successful products go through a life cycle from introduction, to growth, to maturity, to decline. Each phase of the life cycle presents a different marketing and sales challenge.

- A product will usually be adopted, either rapidly or gradually, first by innovators, then by early adopters, then by the early majority, followed by the late majority, and finally the laggards.

Types of Sales

Salespeople play several crucial roles in a company. First, they are the primary source of revenue. Second, salespeople are the link between the company and its customers. Finally, the sales force represents the company's frontline offense and defense. They are directly exposed to the pressures of finding prospects, solving problems, making deals, handling complaints, and beating competitors.

Given these critical roles, a company must do all it can to develop and support the best possible sales force. This section will show you how to do that.

TYPES OF SALES

Sales can be characterized in several ways, which will be discussed over the following pages. Here are a few:

- Order taking occurs at a movie theater or sporting event. The customer asks for a ticket and the vendor sells one. It occurs when a delivery person (for example, for a brewery or bakery) takes the order for the next delivery from a restaurant or store. In order taking, the customer either approaches the company or is purchasing a steady stream of product on a schedule.

- Active selling, on the other hand, involves prospecting, presentation, problem solving, and persuasion. In active selling (the focus of this section), the salesperson approaches the customer, and to some degree the customer resists purchasing. Thus, active selling involves overcoming *sales resistance.*

  You'll sometimes hear a salesperson mocked as an "order taker." This means that the salesperson is supposed to be actively selling, but isn't. Instead he or she is getting by on current accounts, going for easy sales, and avoiding the hard work of prospecting and persuasion.

PLAIN ENGLISH

Sales resistance takes various forms, including delay, evasiveness, indecisiveness, budgetary excuses, and simple reluctance, plus, in commercial sales, bureaucracy.

- Inside sales refers to selling done mainly by telephone. This may include telemarketing, but also allows for situations in which the customer comes to the salesperson's place of business. Inside sales usually does not mean retail sales, which is yet another type of selling.

- Outside sales involves going to the customer, and starts with getting appointments to meet with businesspeople or to see consumers in their homes.

ORGANIZING A SALES FORCE

The two major issues in organizing a sales force are ...

- Size of the sales force.
- Alignment of the sales force.

WHEN IS BIGGER BETTER?

Remember the law of diminishing returns? It says that more of a good thing is good, but only up to a point ... the point of diminishing returns. So one way to get the right-size sales force is to add salespeople until the last one does not produce more in sales than he or she earns. In other words, add salespeople as long as they profitably add sales. This is actually one sensible method of sizing the sales force.

There is, however, another consideration: the proper workload.

The average salesperson's workload should also guide decisions about the size of the sales force. You have to think about this carefully, because sometimes small accounts require more sales effort than large ones. Large accounts are often large because they routinely place an order every month.

The sales force has to be large enough so that each prospect and customer receives adequate *coverage* (communication and attention). Management, even the sales manager, can quickly lose track of how well accounts are being serviced, especially if the poor coverage is masked by growing sales. Poor coverage is an open invitation to competitors.

PLAIN ENGLISH

Coverage means regular sales calls and other forms of communication, and enough service to keep the account from ever feeling neglected.

To judge the workload properly, the sales manager must carefully analyze how many tasks the salesperson must complete to cover his or her accounts, prospect properly, and solve the inevitable problems that arise every week or month. Then the manager must examine the number of working hours in the week or month, and adjust the number of salespeople accordingly.

SALES-FORCE ALIGNMENT: THREE CHOICES

The alignment of the sales force refers to the way in which the sales force is organized in relation to who and what it is selling. There are three ways of aligning the sales force:

- **Alignment by territory** divides the company's market into geographical areas. For a regional company, this might mean by cities. For a national company, it might mean by states. An international company may divide its markets by countries.

  However it's done, alignment by territory has the advantage of simplicity. A salesperson or sales team sells all the company's products to consumers or companies in their territory. The disadvantage is that a company with lots of product lines may find that *product knowledge* suffers. The next type of organization addresses that issue.

PLAIN ENGLISH

Product knowledge includes everything the salesperson has to know about the product. First-rate salespeople can answer virtually every question about the product they sell: its construction, use, installation, and maintenance. They will also know how their product differs from competitive products. In some businesses, especially high tech, this is too much to ask of a salesperson, so the salesperson teams with a technician who has complete product knowledge.

- **Alignment by product** means that each salesperson or sales team specializes in a product or product line. For example, an office-supply company might have one sales group for computers and related equipment, another for general office equipment, and another for furniture and fixtures.

  The advantage of this arrangement is that each salesperson offers deep product knowledge and total coverage of each customer. The disadvantages are a potentially too-large sales force and numerous salespeople calling on the same customer.

  The best way to handle this may be to have an overall account manager who then calls in a product manager or a brand manager for a particular product line.

■ **Alignment by customers** calls for coverage of certain types of customers by certain salespeople. Alignment by the customer's industry is quite common. Many commercial banks have account teams for specific industries, such as consumer-packaged goods, telecommunications, high technology, and so on. This reflects the customer's desire for account managers who "understand my business."

Customer characteristics other than industry can also be used: a common one is size. Many banks have special account reps for "high-net-worth individuals" in their retail (that is, consumer) divisions. In commercial sales, various levels of sales volume will move an account to a different sales team. And many companies have national account reps who sell to corporate customers with nationwide operations.

Companies often use more than one of these methods of aligning their sales forces. A company can even combine all three methods, having sales teams for different product lines covering different-size customers by geographical territory. The idea is to get the best alignment for both the company and the customer.

COMPENSATING AND MOTIVATING YOUR SALES FORCE

We look at the issues of compensating and motivating salespeople together because most salespeople are heavily motivated by money. Their compensation has to reflect this.

Salespeople can be compensated by straight commission, straight salary, or salary plus commission.

■ Salespeople on straight commission are paid a percentage of the amount of each sale they make. They are paid only their commission. They get no salary, although they may receive a draw (advance against future sales), or benefits, or both.

■ Salespeople on straight salary receive a salary, but no additional commission based on sales.

■ Salespeople on salary plus commission get paid a base salary (also called the "base") plus some percentage of the sale.

Benefits as well as bonuses can be added to any of these compensation systems as well.

Commission plans are often structured so that the salesperson makes a certain percentage on the first, say, $100,000 of business he or she sells, then a higher percentage on the next $100,000, and then an even higher percentage on sales above that.

The big advantage of a commission plan, particularly straight commission, is that it ties pay directly to performance. It also ties sales costs to sales. What's more, commissions can be tweaked in various ways to focus the sales force on particular goals. For instance, many firms pay a higher commission on new business than on repeat business. Some outfits pay higher rates on sales of new products.

There are also disadvantages to commission compensation. First, these systems can be complex and costly to administer. Second, some salespeople get so focused on selling that they resent anything that cuts into selling time and any initiative they see as "fiddling with their income." Third, if sales decrease (which may or may not be their fault), they may become depressed or desperate when their incomes dwindle. Finally, whereas most people are honest, there is greater temptation to abuse a commission system.

When their incomes depend on how much they sell, some people resort to an aggressive hard sell that can alienate customers. Salespeople may also be more prone to dishonestly report sales in ways that generate higher commissions. One way this is done is to report sales they'll make in January as December sales to pump up the current year's revenue.

It gets worse. Sales teams have moved business around among salespeople to manipulate commissions, and then shared the artificially high payments. There are also illegal "kickbacks"—bribes paid by dishonest salespeople to dishonest customers out of their commissions.

Straight salary is easy to administer and not prone to abuse, but most salespeople do not find it very motivating. Most companies shoot for the best of both worlds: a base salary plus a commission on sales.

Surveys have shown that money is the biggest motivator for most salespeople. There are, however, other ways of motivating salespeople, some of which relate to money, some of which do not.

Sales quotas (the amount of revenue an individual salesperson or team is budgeted to bring in) tend to work, provided they are neither too high nor too low. They work because financial rewards such as higher commissions and most bonuses are tied to quotas. If they're too high, they frustrate and anger the salesperson. If they're too low, the company will overpay for the amount of sales it gets. That's because commissions are usually based on the salesperson making his quota and then exceeding it by various amounts. Quotas have another built-in advantage: You can terminate salespeople who consistently fail to meet their quotas.

TIP

A good portion (say, 30 to 50 percent) of a salesperson's salary should be in commissions or bonuses. This is critical for small firms, which really can't afford to pay nonproducers.

Sales meetings, particularly off-site meetings that include golf, tennis, and banquets (and, yes, cocktails), are popular with salespeople and build camaraderie (to put it mildly).

Sales contests work for many companies, even companies that think they might be "too sophisticated" for them. The winners usually must beat their quotas significantly and are ranked by performance for the grand prize—usually a vacation at a nice resort on company time or a cash payment, and subsidiary prizes. Structuring these contests takes skill. For example, there can be monthly winners and various ways of qualifying for the grand prize to keep the sales force pumped up for the entire year.

Some relatively inexpensive (and less impressive) motivators include plaques, awards, membership in the "CEO's Roundtable," and so on. Access to senior management in meetings or special luncheons and inclusion on special task forces are useful, inexpensive rewards that are generally underused.

Finally, the opportunity for advancement can be a powerful motivator. But watch out. Many a first-rate salesperson has found managing others, not to mention meetings and paperwork, boring and worse than what he or she was doing before. A few salespeople promoted to sales manager or product manager have been known to yell, "Give me a bag and put me back on the road!" after two months.

SUPPORTING A SALES FORCE

Salespeople are "out there," exposed, competing, and facing daily rejection. To do their job, they need the best support a company can give them.

This support starts with the best products, service, and marketing that the company can deliver. The products have to be the best in their class and price range. The service has to have one goal: total customer satisfaction. The marketing has to be connected with the real world of customers and their problems and buying motives.

Support also means a sensible and (key point) consistent credit policy and good credit management. Having a salesperson break his or her neck to make a sale only to have it killed by the credit department makes no sense. It helps if the credit policy is predictable and if salespeople can get an early reading on a prospect's creditworthiness, with a call to the credit department, for example.

Support includes good management. Unfortunately, some sales managers believe fear and threats are motivational. Maybe firing the three lowest producers is a good idea, but doing it publicly is not. Salespeople, like everyone, need trust and the authority to make decisions. And more than most people, they need minimal paperwork and bureaucracy and the freedom to manage their own time.

Finally, rapid resolution of customer complaints about quality, defects, and delivery is essential. That's where a good customer service department comes in handy.

TRAINING YOUR SALESPEOPLE THROUGH CUSTOMER SERVICE

Many companies of all types have customer service departments separate from the sales function. They usually report to sales or to marketing (the best ones work closely with sales). They deal mainly with customers (people who have purchased the company's products), but some also answer inquiries from prospects.

Customer service has two goals: to keep customers happy (or make them happy if they aren't) and to do it without burdening the salespeople.

That second function is essential. Everyone in a company wants the customer to be happy, especially the salespeople. But the time that salespeople must spend resolving disputes, answering routine questions, and fielding requests for price lists and product literature erodes selling time.

TIP

Be sure to give your customer service people the authority they need to resolve problems. Customers find it extremely irritating to deal with people who can't help them. Some companies get customer service right, whereas others seem to use it as an obstacle to service. Hire good people for this function and let them do their jobs. Dissatisfied customers can hurt your company far worse than competitors.

So customer service should be staffed with individuals who have people skills (including patience), product knowledge, and an understanding of what can be done operationally, procedurally, and legally to resolve customer complaints.

Customer service can be a great training ground for future salespeople. In fact, if they develop leads that later become customers, they should get some kind of compensation or recognition. It's a small price to pay to someone with the sales orientation that keeps a company growing. Customer service is discussed in more detail in Chapter 13.

A Few Other Words on Sales Training

Too often new salespeople are given a bunch of product literature to read, taken on a couple of sales calls, and then given a desk, phone, and phone book. Some outfits view salespeople as cannon fodder and hire 10 for every 1 they figure will make the grade.

Smart companies take a different approach. They do their best to hire smart. When they seek experienced people, they take the time to locate good performers who will fit in well. When they seek entry-level people, they hire just as carefully and train them in sales. They also train everyone, new or seasoned, in the company's products and procedures.

General sales training can be valuable, and any good-size city has firms that provide it. But it is believed that the training will help only those people who have that special motivation that real salespeople have: They are competitors. When they sell, they win—and they hate to lose. More than being outgoing or gregarious or "a people person," that motivation, plus an interest in solving customers' problems, makes a true salesperson.

The 30-Second Recap

- Salespeople are a company's source of revenue, link to customers, and frontline offense and defense. They find prospects, solve problems, make deals, handle complaints, and fight competitors, so they need lots of support.

- The major parts of the sales process are prospecting, problem solving and presenting the product, and persuading prospects to purchase.

- When figuring the best size for a sales force, consider the added sales of each additional salesperson as well as workload per salesperson. A sales force can be aligned by territories, products, or customers ... or all three.

- In most businesses, salary plus commission is the best way to compensate salespeople.

- A customer service department can make life easier for salespeople while perhaps delivering better service than a busy salesperson might. It can also generate leads and be a training ground for future salespeople.

Channels of Distribution: Selling Through Retailers, Wholesalers, and Agents

If you're in business, you've got a distribution function. There's no way around that. From Kalika driving her juice cart down to the college campus to Bob's Bottomless Boats accepting another shipment from Chris-Craft, there's a whole lot of distribution going on. Unfortunately, distribution can be a big pain. Goods get lost or broken. Customers get the wrong shipments and get upset. Wholesalers go behind your back and sell direct to your customers.

How do you manage a function that by its very nature leaves you so vulnerable? Very carefully. Let's do a little problem analysis. There are two halves to the problem of distribution: the "who" and the "how."

We're going to look at the players in the distribution game first, examining both the channel sellers and the physical product deliverers. Then we'll examine how the distribution process works, and finally some potential strategies for making distribution decisions. The goal is to arm you with the knowledge you need to improve your distribution function. But first, let's take a look at the big picture.

DISTRIBUTION'S PLACE IN THE SCHEME OF THINGS

As discussed in a previous section, the "four P's" (place, product, price, and promotion) and the all-important "fifth P" (people) are at the heart of creating those exchanges that get your offerings to customers and their money to you.

Distribution is all about the concept of place. The basic question asked by the marketing term *place* is "How do I get what I sell to the buyers?" It's really a question of distribution, but the term got its start from the place (the pushcart, the store, the shop) where a seller or "maker" exchanged with a buyer. It starts out simple, but as a business comes into being, the distribution or movement of goods and services from the maker/producer to the buyer gets more complicated.

Let's immerse ourselves in the place issue by taking a dip in the river that marketers call the *channel of distribution*. Like most rivers, this one doesn't flow straight from its source to the sea—it wanders in all directions, reflecting the landscape around it.

PLAIN ENGLISH

A **channel of distribution** is the complete sequence involved in bringing a finished product from its producer to its ultimate consumer.

Distribution channels are made up of a sequence of transactions between business partners: manufacturers, wholesalers, retailers, and all kinds of agents and dealers' representatives in between.

A short channel might flow like a spring on a mountainside plunging into a lake, with no intermediaries—just one straight rush from producer to end user. A longer channel might involve many twists, turns, and side branches.

In almost all cases, you won't be able to get the offering you produce directly into your buyer's hands in a timely and convenient way. You'd have to be running all over the place, or getting your customers to come to you, which isn't always convenient.

You need to distribute your offering through a strategically chosen channel. Your distribution channel will add the time and place utilities to your offering. They'll reduce the distance between buyer and seller, making your offering available at more times and in more places. When a product is located near the people who want it and is available at a time convenient to these folks, they are happier. That's why when you need a gallon of milk, you don't go to the farm or even to the dairy. You hit the convenience store down the street. Now, let's look at the potential players in the distribution channel.

WHO'S WHO IN YOUR CHANNEL

Kalika, with her juice cart, handles distribution when she sells a freshly made banana-kiwi smoothie to her end user. In her distribution channel, one person assumes the roles of manufacturer, distributor, and retailer.

Not all producers can distribute their products so easily. Most have to choose one or more of the available distribution channels. Dozens of intermediaries can be involved in the movement of goods from producers to end users. Call them wholesalers, distributors, retailers, agents, and middlemen—they're the people who provide various services to help keep products and services flowing to buyers. It's a good idea to keep your channel short.

HOW THE RETAILER WORKS

Your first stop in looking for a distributor could be a retailer. If you can get a retail distributor who you deal with directly, you'll shorten the channel and reduce the number of possible glitches and costs. If Kalika decides to spend her time creating and bottling her smoothies, she might look for a retailer to sell them for her. Most retailers are not producers of the goods they sell. Most concentrate on core retailing functions, such as choosing a market niche and selecting the mix of products and services that niche will buy. If you're looking for a retailer as your distributor, your first step is to search out retailers whose mix of products and services would accommodate your offering.

The word *retail* can cover every kind of store, from a shop specializing in light bulbs to a giant warehouse store with something for everyone. Picture these two on a continuum from high markup and high service to low markup and low service. Along the way, you would find wholesale clubs, discounters, department stores, and many others.

Each retailer, no matter where he or she falls on the continuum, is faced with the challenge of creating the right merchandise assortment. How does a retailer decide what to carry? The process begins, of course, when she chooses the location and market niche she'll serve.

TIP

What a retailer decides to carry in her store is called her "merchandise assortment," and it's the difference between success and failure for many merchants—as important as "location, location, location."

It wouldn't hurt to interview buyers for stores whose assortments impress you. You can also make a point of bringing some evidence to retailers that your offering is something their customers would like to see them carry!

To create her merchandise selection and keep it lively as the seasons go by, a florist friend of mine follows suggestions from channel members upstream—distributors, wholesalers, and manufacturers. She reads trade magazines. She follows the local newspapers, talks to customers, and visits stores in other cities. She sniffs out trends wherever the clues can be found. She never visits another city without stopping in at local flower shops, browsing the selection, chatting with the merchants, and studying their display techniques. She—like many other retailers—is very willing to hear proposals for new offerings. So if you're just getting your feet wet, try talking to some relevant retailers.

Of course, location is important to the retailer, and important to you when you're looking to hook up with a retailer.

What the Distributors/Wholesalers Do

Retailers don't just wait for merchandise to show up. Our florist friend assembles her eclectic merchandise from a number of sources. She's a channel-of-distribution case study. Picture her near the end of the stream, turning around and looking back up to see sources for merchandise she can sell. She is now in the role of a customer. She pursues every possible source, from mainline distributors to growing her own.

Intermediary distributors are essential for makers, manufacturers, small entrepreneurs like our friend, and all her peers up and down our Main Streets and shopping malls. As you'll see, distributors as intermediaries assume the risks and tackle the chores of distribution. Channel members upstream and down—like you, the manufacturer, or the retailer—would have to take on those functions. In such a world, only the large would survive.

To a great extent, distributors expedite the purchasing function, making ease of possession a reality. They'll take a quantity of your offering—a bulk lot—and break it into smaller lots, or assemble large lots from small ones. Then they deliver your offering to the retailer, sorted into the desired quantities and varieties, and the retailer "delivers" it to the end user. Because the distributor performs this sorting and delivering function, our florist friend can plan and order the quantity and variety she needs.

Distributors also finance customer purchases over 30, 60, and even 90 days, providing credit services more flexible than a bank's. Further, they provide the all-important function of taking risks, assuming the responsibility for problems such as spoilage, storage, and uncertain demand. They are responsible for the physical safety of their products, accepting the risk of fire or damage in transit or loss in any other way.

Finally, distributors play a big role in facilitating the flow of information between manufacturer and retailer. In return for all this, the distributor earns the right to charge his customers a higher price than he paid the manufacturer for the goods.

Bring In the Specialists: Using Agents and Independent Reps

Okay, let's say Kalika has bottled her smoothies. Her demand is steady, and she turns her cart over to a trained employee. Then she contracts to provide a specific quantity to Natalie, an alternative beverage sales rep from a nearby city. Natalie begins selling smoothies in her "territory." She sells other drinks as well as Kalika's, but she is now a fixture in Kalika's distribution channel. She's not on staff. She either buys Kalika's offerings outright or works on percentages.

Agents frequently operate on commission; the manufacturer has no obligation to pay the agent if the product doesn't sell. That's an advantage over hiring a staff person to sell for you. Agents also typically cover large geographic territories, stretching your reach to places where thin demand wouldn't justify having your own sales force.

Now the question you want to ask is "How do you know when you need a sales agent or rep?" After all, you could do without a sales rep and still sell in other territories than the one you live in. Take, for example, the shoe dealer who designs her own children's shoes, has them manufactured in Spain, imports the finished products, and then gets in her car and travels the country selling that year's models. She's a pro at the process. Of course, if you want to expand to another city and don't want to travel as part of your business, an agent would be a good idea.

TIP

A good rule of thumb for making the decision about sales agents is this: The less you know, the more you need to work with those who do. This is particularly true when it comes to working with agents. Agents know the territory. Think of them as guides you share profits with. They bring insider knowledge, a familiarity with who wants what and who can provide it. They know who's tried what and whether it did or didn't work.

Some go-betweens receive their remuneration from the buyer in the deal; others are paid by the seller. You should "follow the money," as the saying goes. Make sure you have a general understanding of how your agent or rep is being rewarded for her trouble before you get in too deep. A good agent makes deals that are good for all parties. Don't be afraid to lean on your agent for help.

The bottom line: When you know nothing, you hire people for their expertise. When you've learned what you can from them, you can decide whether to assume the job yourself.

Physical Distribution: The Wheel Dimension

Okay, so Kalika is now selling her offering in several geographical territories. Her new company, Smoothies for the People, has to send 20 cases of orange-kumquat-banana smoothies to one place, 40 cases of carrot-peach-guava smoothies to another, and so on. Selling is no longer the issue. Now, Kalika faces physical distribution concerns—what shippers, warehouses, and packaging are needed for her cases to make the trip to the purchaser on time, in good repair, and at reasonable cost.

Physical distribution introduces a lot of opportunities—and some of the deepest pitfalls you'll encounter. You will always be balancing the desire to keep costs down against the desire to give your customers the best possible service. Sacrifice one and you'll lose your customers—sacrifice the other and you'll lose your shirt! Excel at either, and you will find your reward in your improved bottom line.

PHYSICAL DISTRIBUTION ISSUES

You'll have to do more than consider what packaging, warehouses, and shippers are needed to get your offering on the road and into the right hands. Who sees to it that it arrives safely on time and at a reasonable cost? That's the job of physical distribution.

The goal of physical distribution is to minimize cost while ensuring that your delivery mechanism provides maximum customer value and service. Unfortunately, these are often contradictory goals. A customer would like you to drop everything to drive over, deliver and, perhaps, install the new Jacuzzi. But instant service would add an unacceptable cost, because you'd need to have workers standing by around the clock. So you and the customer arrive at a mutually beneficial compromise. The Jacuzzi comes next Tuesday, and the customer pays what he perceives to be a fair price for installation.

TIP

Place (distribution) is the slowest to change of the original four P's. You can change prices overnight, and your product and its promotion usually can be changed in a few months. But building a solid distribution channel can take years.

Because the challenge is to minimize cost while delivering maximum customer service, planning and coordination are essential. Make sure these ingredients are in your distribution planning mix:

- Authority and responsibilities are clearly defined and clearly assigned.
- There is a structure for communication between each functional area that touches distribution: marketing, operations, finance, and personnel.
- Each channel member has access to the information he needs to do his job; each member's input is listened to; each receives feedback on how well he is performing and how he can improve.
- A distribution manager is in charge, and this position is filled by a person with strong leadership ability.

DISTRIBUTION STRATEGIES

The key to your physical distribution strategy is understanding customers. If you know their priorities and your own, you can perform the right balancing act between cost control and service.

Of course, you'll want to choose a channel of distribution that will work to your satisfaction. Two factors influence your choice of distribution channel: your marketing mix (the influence of the other P's on this P) and the environment, the sea you swim in.

Your strategies regarding price, the characteristics you've designed into your product, and the degree and nature of the promotions you've committed to will all influence your distribution strategy. If you're committed to being the low-cost leader, you can't afford a long channel with lots of markups to pay along the way. You'll have to look at direct marketing and other cost-efficient ways of getting the product from producer to consumer.

What characteristics does the market display? What is the projected number of customers, where are they located, and what is the average size of their purchase? If the buyers are few but large, that lends itself to a short channel. If the market is made up of many small customers, more complex channels are likely to develop.

What intermediaries are available to your market? In some geographic areas, there may not be an intermediary suitable to your needs. That's why Sears and Roebuck started a catalog operation all those years ago—the frontier stores were too few and far between.

HOW MANY OUTLETS?

One, two, three, or many? Distribution can range from exclusive, where only one outlet in an area is allowed to sell a product, to intensive, where that product is placed as widely as possible. To determine what approach is right for you, consider the nature of the purchase. Is this offering a convenience, shopping, or specialty product or service?

A convenience product is typically inexpensive, the need for it recurs frequently, and purchasers would rather settle for another brand than go out of their way to find the original. This situation calls for an intensive distribution strategy to get your product placed wherever the consumer might look for it.

TIP

Well-established relationships are the key to successful channels of distribution. Unless you're in a completely unworkable mess, stick with what you're doing now, and look for ways to make it better.

If you sell a convenience product, distribution is the key to a healthy business. Anything you can do to make your product available in more places, at more times of day, will increase your sales.

Specialty products are the seldom-purchased items that require a significant investment. These typically require a more aggressive degree of sales and often some after-market service. An exclusive distribution strategy gives only one retailer in an area the option to sell a product and protects him from direct price competition. That motivates the retailer to provide the sales and support effort this product needs.

TIP

The World Wide Web combined with the convenience of electronic data transfer presents a technological advantage for products that can be distributed electronically. These include numerical- or text-based products like data or white papers, and electronic graphics products like type fonts and stock photos.

In between these two extremes is selling the "shopping product," which calls for a selective distribution strategy. A shopping product requires more involvement on the consumers' part than convenience products. These items have recognizable product differences, and often where they're purchased has an impact on their desirability. Makeup purchased at Marshall Field's makes the wearer feel different than makeup from Wal-Mart, although the difference may not be perceivable to a casual observer. A selective distribution strategy limits the number of outlets where your product is available. This protects the cachet of your product or service and gives you more control over marketing strategy.

Remember, the strategy you choose has to mesh with the rest of your marketing mix. Convenience items need maximum distribution. Shopping items that project a prestige image must arrive looking prestigious, not bashed-about or shop-worn. A specialty product that took months to sell had better not be delayed too long in delivery, or buyer's remorse may set in.

PUSH AND PULL STRATEGIES

There are really three strategies here, because you can opt for push, pull, or a combination of both.

In a push strategy, the manufacturer concentrates on wooing channel members and then using them to push products to the consumer. Wooing channel members means offering incentives that encourage middlemen to carry the goods. Your goal is to get those channel members fired up about moving your product. If that takes offering a Caribbean cruise, do it.

A push strategy fits when the product is in the mature phase of its life cycle. Essentially, you're recruiting your distribution channel members to help you stimulate consumer demand. This is easier than using a pull strategy, especially when the product lacks "new and improved" features to generate consumer excitement.

In a pull strategy, the manufacturer concentrates on reaching and persuading potential consumers, stimulating demand. These consumers go to the middlemen in the channel and demand the product, in essence pulling it down the channel.

When a new product creates a new product niche, sometimes a pull strategy is the only option you have. Distribution channel members have no motivation to take risks on untried products. Why would they? Creating consumer demand is the fastest way to show them you've got a viable product offering.

 TIP

Although customer focus is critical, so is company focus. Keep your company's strategic goals in mind as you develop distribution strategies. There's no point in serving customers if you aren't serving yourself as well.

In a combination strategy, the manufacturer tries a little of both. Warning: This takes money! You will need to design promotions and devote marketing energy to each segment, and that means spending more money.

The most important rule of thumb you can follow in distribution is to maintain your customer focus. If you pick a target market and then orchestrate the channel members and physical distribution strategies to serve that market's needs, you'll stick to the right track.

A Life of Faith Dolls provides a tidy example of using push, pull, and combination strategies. The doll line was launched using a pull strategy. The company mailed catalogs to several thousand families who had registered at the website promoting the Elsie Dinsmore books. That mailing brought a 14 percent response—extremely good for direct mail. Then the company developed attractive in-store display units that presented the entire line of dolls, books, and accessories, and displayed the line at a major Christian booksellers' convention. The owner, Robin, and her team used the success of the earlier direct-mail shot to demonstrate demand to the Christian retailers. The retailers responded positively, and a whopping 17 stores signed up to carry the dolls—three times the number A Life of Faith hoped to gain from that show. The catalogs pull consumers toward the product, while the in-store display units push product toward the consumer.

Then A Life of Faith moved into a combination strategy, using the catalog in areas where Christian booksellers are scarce, but using retailer promotions in areas where the dolls are available in stores.

SELECT YOUR CHANNEL MEMBERS

So you've decided which strategy fits your situation. Perhaps it involves your channel members or a change in your channel lineup. How will you go about choosing your business partners?

This checklist will help. Ask yourself, does this organization ...

- ❒ Have the right people in place in management?
- ❒ Display the right attitude of cooperation?
- ❒ Carry other lines that are compatible with yours?
- ❒ Have the talents and skills to advertise and promote the product?
- ❒ Have a strong financial track record?
- ❒ Have the necessary services available to its customers?
- ❒ Have a good reputation in the industry?

You can't really decide whether this player is right for your team until you know what your strategy is for the game. A pull strategy requires different characteristics in the channel than a push strategy does.

CUTTING COSTS

Cost is the main reason you care about physical distribution. If you can reduce cost in this area, you can claim a serious competitive advantage. A few pennies saved on freight, packaging, or storage go straight to your bottom line.

Customers care about getting their goods; they don't care about how. That's your business. So if you can reduce costs through a change in operations, and that change is invisible to the customer (or perceived as a benefit), you're doing the right thing.

How do costs add up in the distribution channel? There are handling costs at each step, transportation from manufacturer to wholesaler/distributor, wholesaler/distributor to retailer, and retailer to buyer (if delivery or installation is required). There are costs associated with storage at each step as well, real estate costs for warehousing, insurance costs, and less-obvious costs for products lost to damage or obsolescence.

How can you cut those costs? Advanced technology is the first place to look. Computers reduce errors and save labor costs associated with order processing, inventory management, and billing. Other cost-reduction strategies result from changes in warehouse location, increased automation, and use of lower-cost freight carriers (land instead of air, for example).

SHIPPING OUT! TRANSPORTATION DECISIONS

Now we'll talk about the actual movement of your offerings from one place to another. Your decisions will involve what routes products take to market, who carries them there, and how much this process costs you. Let's look closer at each of the components of the transportation question.

USING SHIPPERS

Most of us will use shippers of various sorts to meet our physical distribution needs. In many instances, distribution will involve a mix of shipping modes. A truck may ride piggyback on a railroad car. A package may be transferred from package service (taxi) to air freight (Federal Express) and back on its way from producer to end user. For information businesses, distribution has become increasingly electronic. When online data transfer became reliable enough, products like stock photos and type fonts began traveling by modem rather than CD-ROM.

CAUTION

Changes in energy costs often affect shipping decisions. A temporary spike in gas costs may cause surcharges from over-the-road haulers as they struggle to protect their profit margins.

Each mode has its advantages and disadvantages; each has its part to play in the balancing act between customer service and cost control. If they needed it yesterday, the customer will pay for air freight. If they need it next year, water transport will probably do.

PAYING THE FARE

The main factor affecting which shipper you choose will be cost. What is the lowest possible expense that will meet your customer's need for timeliness? The main factor affecting the cost of the various options is that carrier's energy cost. It obviously costs more to fuel an airplane than to keep a freighter floating in the right direction. Keep an eye on energy costs and let increases be your cue to reexamine your transportation strategies.

INVENTORY AND WAREHOUSED PRODUCTS

Goods often have to be housed for the time between their production and their consumption by the end user. Bulk lots are often broken down in the warehousing phase of distribution. For you to buy a stuffed bunny at the toy store, a toy distributor buys a pallet of bunnies from the factory, a chain buyer takes a case of 12 dozen bunnies, and each of his stores gets a bag of a dozen and breaks that open to sell one.

At any of those stops along the way, that bunny was vulnerable to damage by fire, water, theft, or accident. If you need to consider warehousing as part of your distribution strategy, here are some things to think about.

INVENTORY CONTROL

How many stuffed bunnies is enough? That's the fundamental question of inventory control. The ideal level of inventory is the one that keeps your costs low and at the same time provides the service customers want. (There's that balancing act again.)

Your only hope of answering the question of "how many" is to make accurate *sales forecasts*. If you were able to sell 144,000 bunnies last year, your projections will start with 144,000 bunnies for this year. You can adjust that by any factors you see affecting you.

PLAIN ENGLISH

A **sales forecast** is a projection of future demand expressed in terms of dollars and units sold. A survey is sometimes useful for projecting demand in dollars for many products and services.

MATERIALS HANDLING

Boxes of bunnies have to hop off the trucks from the manufacturer, on to and off of the storage shelves, through the picking and packing process, and back out the door. That process is called materials handling. People and machines are necessary to unload, identify, package, and reload the goods. Check to see if the warehouse your distributor uses has automated systems. Automation can reduce risk and cut costs.

ORDER PROCESSING

Closely related to materials handling is the processing of orders that goes along with it. For each quantity of bunnies shipped, there's also a bunny order form, a choreography of picking from the shelves and packing for delivery, and with that an invoice.

Packaging for Shipping

Packaging for shipping is of vital importance. Your product must be protected during both storage and transportation. Packaging has to be strong enough for stacking and secure enough to prevent mildew, dirt, or insect invasions. Packaging can also improve order-processing accuracy if you use color-coding or other labeling to allow boxes to proclaim their contents.

Warehouse Cost Control

Each of the issues of warehousing—inventory control, materials handling, order processing, and packaging—represent opportunities to increase or reduce costs, depending on the balancing act you perform between customer service and cost control. Technology is an excellent tool to reduce those costs. Another way is to stock no more units than necessary.

Just-in-Time (JIT) Delivery

Just-in-time delivery is an excellent choice for cost control. It involves having the raw materials and parts arrive just in time for assembly, and then feeding the finished product into the distribution channel just in time for final purchase. Money is saved all along the channel. *JIT* attempts to reduce shortages or surpluses anywhere along the way. As well as controlling costs, it helps avoid disappointing customers. Dell Computer uses this strategy, and look where it's gotten them.

PLAIN ENGLISH

Just-in-time (JIT) delivery means reducing problems of warehousing by having materials and products arrive just in time for use. In this way, the cost to store them and the potential for damage while in storage is reduced or eliminated.

Clearly, you need to make some strategic decisions about warehousing as well as decisions about distributors, retailers, and other actors in your channel of distribution. Some distributors find that having one central warehouse works best, and others deploy dozens of warehouses across the country and swear by that system. What works best for you depends on your strategic objectives.

The 30-Second Recap

■ A channel of distribution is an interdependent system of manufacturer, wholesaler, distributor, and retailer.

- Distributors provide services, such as flexible financing, risk taking, and assuming the tasks of physical distribution, earning them the right to charge a markup on the products they carry.

- Physical distribution is about balancing desire to minimize cost with desire to deliver maximum customer service.

- Successful physical distribution involves getting your product to market—deciding what routes your products will take, who will carry them, and how much this will cost—and making sure this strategy meshes with the rest of your marketing mix.

- Understanding transportation and warehousing operations will help you discover ways to contain costs throughout the distribution process.

- Cost is the main reason you care about physical distribution. If you can reduce cost in this area, you can claim a serious competitive advantage.

- In many instances, distribution will involve a mix of shipping modes.

- The ideal level of inventory is the one that keeps your costs low and at the same time provides the service customers want.

Keeping Your Customers Happy

Customer Service: What's It All About?

In this section, you learn about basic customer service principles that are true in any situation, and about customer service myths that prevent some companies from enjoying the success that could be theirs.

THE IMPORTANCE OF CUSTOMER SERVICE

In their book *Built from Scratch,* Home Depot founders Bernie Marcus and Arthur Blank discuss at length how they built their $30 billion business on an absolute commitment to customer service. Home Depot currently operates more than 800 stores and is growing by more than 20 percent each year.

The Disney Company is arguably one of the most admired companies in America. For years, Disney's commitment to customer service has enabled it to grow by leaps and bounds. New employees are required to attend several days of customer service training before they start work, and ongoing customer service training is mandatory for everyone. The result of Disney's emphasis on customer service is customer satisfaction and customer loyalty.

But in spite of the obvious success that an unyielding commitment to customer service has brought to these companies and others like them, customer service remains the single most overlooked and underutilized weapon in the strategic arsenal of business in the twenty-first century. In fact, in America, customer service at most firms, especially small firms, is appalling.

A few years ago, The Research Institute of America conducted a study for the White House Office of Consumer Affairs. The results of that study demonstrate just how costly it is for a business to be apathetic toward customer service. Here are just some of their findings:

- The average business will hear nothing from 96 percent of unhappy customers who receive rude or discourteous treatment.

- Ninety percent of customers who are dissatisfied with the service they receive will not come back or buy again from the offending organization.

- Each unhappy customer tells his or her story to an average of nine other people.

- Only 4 percent of unhappy customers ever bother to complain. For every complaint brought to the attention of a company, 24 others go unreported to the company—but are indeed reported to other potential customers.

■ Of the customers who register a complaint, between 54 percent and 70 percent will do business again with the organization if their complaint is resolved. That figure rises to 95 percent if the customer feels that the complaint was resolved quickly.

■ Sixty-eight percent of customers who quit doing business with an organization do so because of company indifference. It takes 12 positive incidents to make up for 1 negative incident in the eyes of customers.

CUSTOMER SERVICE: WHAT IS IT?

Customer service is the art of serving a customer. It is by far the most important marketing strategy a business can use in its quest to capture and retain market share.

PLAIN ENGLISH

Customer service is a way of life that involves putting the customer first in every aspect of the business. It is characterized by an obsession to achieve complete customer satisfaction in each and every encounter. It is an obsession that is shared by everyone in the company from the chairman of the board on down.

The objective of customer service is to understand and meet the needs of customers, whatever those needs may be. Its importance stems from an understanding of one of the basic tenants of free enterprise so simply stated by the late Sam Walton: "There is only one boss: the customer. And he can fire everybody in the company from the chairman on down, simply by spending his money somewhere else."

Customer service isn't the product of "smile training"; it isn't a scripted, predetermined response to a menu of anticipated customer complaints; it isn't a magical transformation that occurs as a result of a one-shot corporate training program; and it doesn't happen because of corporate lip service, or directives and mandates from upper management demanding that customers be treated with respect and dignity.

Customer service is a way of doing business that is born out of genuine concern for the customer, and it involves every person in the company, from the chairman of the board to the custodian. It's not just a way of doing business; it's a way of life.

IT's a Culture, Not a Program!

Effective customer service begins with an understanding and commitment by you, the business owner. You must get directly involved in hands-on customer service activities. It's one thing to demand that your employees attend customer service workshops; it's another when you attend and actively participate in the training! When a company's top boss lives and breathes customer service, the rest of the firm is inspired to do the same. Conversely, most customer service programs fizzle because either the owner doesn't understand his value or he's just too busy to roll up his shirtsleeves and get involved.

But that's not the case at Southwest Airlines. Here's what Herb Kelleher, the company's chief executive officer, has to say about the value of a customer service culture:

> The culture of Southwest is probably its major competitive advantage. The intangibles are more important than the tangibles because you can always initiate the tangibles; you can buy the airplane, you can rent the ticket counter space. But the hardest thing for someone to emulate is the spirit of your people.

The customer service culture at Southwest Airlines has had a major influence on the company's performance record. Consider this: Southwest is the fourth-largest carrier of passengers in the United States; the company has shown a profit over the past 27 years; it is significantly more profitable than most of its bigger and better-known competition; its record of on-time service is one of the best in the industry; and the company has never experienced a strike.

Small businesses that have developed outstanding customer service cultures share some important characteristics:

- The owner defines customer service as job number one and is actively involved in customer service activities.
- Managers are thoroughly trained in quality customer service techniques and serve as coaches and trainers to those who report to them.
- Every employee understands that, first and foremost, he or she is in the service business.
- Customer service training activities are ongoing, and everyone participates.
- Employees are valued, and important customer service accomplishments are recognized in meaningful ways.
- Employees are empowered to solve customer service problems on the spot, with some companies authorizing employees to spend as much as $2,500 to resolve problems quickly or prevent repeat occurrences.

- Measurements of customer service outcomes, in which customer opinions are solicited (both formally and informally), are regularly used to monitor quality and make adjustments as needed.

THE QUALITY OF CUSTOMER SERVICE

The customer is the final arbiter in all matters involving customer service. It is the customer who will ultimately judge the quality of an organization's customer service efforts, and that judgment is based solely on the customer's perception, regardless of the facts.

Whenever customers become involved with an organization, even if only peripherally, they quickly perceive the quality of the service they are receiving and, based upon that perception, they judge the organization and its products. This means that *quality of service* is a moving target that can, and will, be uniquely defined by each and every customer.

PLAIN ENGLISH

Quality of service is the customer's perception of the service that an organization provides. It is a perception that is reevaluated by the customer with each succeeding contact, wherever in the organization those contacts occur, from the executive level to the loading dock.

INFERIOR QUALITY

Inferior customer service always produces dissatisfied customers. These feelings of dissatisfaction lead customers to react in ways that have harmful long-term effects on the organization.

You can bet that your organization has customer service problems if …

- Customers are often hostile and threatening to representatives of the company.
- Supervisors regularly spend an inordinate amount of their time "stomping out fires," attempting to resolve highly charged disputes between customers and the company.
- Employee productivity is low because employees are spending too much time trying to resolve problems.
- Customer loyalty is low.
- Managers spend little or no time training employees in the area of customer service.

- The business budgets very little time and money for ensuring customer satisfaction and instead commits more of its resources to providing a steady stream of new customers.
- The work environment has become unusually stressful and negative.
- Employee turnover is high.
- The business lacks credibility in the marketplace—and employees begin to notice that the company seems to be advertising its shortcomings.

CAUTION

Whenever you spot customer service problems, regardless how minor they may appear, act immediately to correct the problem. Major customer service problems are often those that originally appeared insignificant. Treat every customer service problem with a sense of urgency.

From the customer's perspective, an organization's reputation for customer service is determined in two ways: from the customer's own firsthand experience and from comments heard from others. A customer who has heard negative things about an organization's products or services is likely to be negatively predisposed to the organization. What's more, negative predispositions are just as damaging (and just as costly) as firsthand negative experiences. Conversely, a customer who has heard positive remarks about a company is often positively predisposed to it, resulting in a significant payoff for the organization.

TIP

According to studies conducted by the United States Office of Consumer Affairs, it costs seven times more to acquire a new customer than to keep an existing one. A solid customer service program within any organization is simply good business practice.

CAUTION

Be sure of the accuracy of your company's claims to excellence. Customer service excellence shouldn't be emphasized in an aggressive advertising campaign unless fundamental changes have been made that ensure service excellence. Companies that make claims about something that doesn't exist do irreparable damage to their reputations in the marketplace.

MEDIOCRE QUALITY

I mention the mediocre category of customer service only because so many companies seem to believe it exists. They're wrong. In customer service, you either do it right or you do it wrong; there's no middle ground.

HIGH QUALITY

Organizations that routinely provide high-quality customer service have an important edge in today's competitive global marketplace. That edge can easily make the difference between success and failure. It's a fact: Exceptional customer service results in positive customer perceptions, customer satisfaction, and customer loyalty—and that's the stuff success is made of.

But make no mistake: High-quality customer service involves more than merely hiring good people; it requires more than offering a training session now and then.

Businesses that are serious about developing ongoing high-quality customer service must make a major commitment to shape and mold a culture in which customer-oriented values and beliefs are supported by the entire organization. A business owner needs to become so obsessed with high-quality customer service that the customer becomes the heart of every operational policy, procedure, and process.

In a high-quality customer service culture, everyone—from the janitor to the owner of the company—has a clear understanding of the importance of the customer to the success of the enterprise. At every level of the organization there is an appreciation of the requirements and needs of the customer.

TIP

Employees who make it a practice to meet the needs of customers are generally happier and more productive, and enjoy a greater sense of fulfillment in their jobs. That's because employees who make customer service a top priority are often the beneficiaries of the thanks and praise of satisfied customers. Employees, like customers, have a basic need to be appreciated and valued by others. One of the effects of customer service training is higher employee morale.

A high-quality customer service culture has the following characteristics:

- Company representatives at all levels maintain a courteous and responsive attitude toward customers and want to be of real assistance to them.

- The owner of the company is fully committed to maintaining a program of high-quality customer service (and the commitment is real, not just lip service).

- All persons in the company know that they are in the service business—not the manufacturing business, the banking business, the insurance business, the real estate business, or anything else.

- Every manager knows exactly what the customer expects and has developed the systems and processes necessary to meet those expectations (as well as established measurements of customer outcomes to monitor employee performance).

- There's substantial flexibility in meeting the needs of customers.

- Employees treat customers as "partners" rather than adversaries.

- The product or service is continuously improved to meet the changing needs of the customer.

- Prevention-based, or proactive, management has replaced reactionary, after-the-fact management.

- Corporate leadership relies on customer satisfaction, market share, and long-term profitability as measures of performance instead of immediate bottom-line financial results and quick return on investment.

- Quality of products or services is defined in terms of the customer's requirements and needs rather than the organization's standards.

- Important decisions are customer-driven instead of product-driven.

- Employees are involved in ongoing customer service training that introduces new ways of helping customers, and at the same time repeats and reinforces basic principles.

SOME COMMON CUSTOMER SERVICE MYTHS

Here are five of the most common myths about customer service, along with the facts that dispel them:

1. **Myth:** The only effective customer service happens when you're in a position to say "yes" to every customer request. For those organizations that can't always say "yes," high-quality customer service is just a pipe dream.

   Fact: There are few, if any, organizations that are always able to say "yes" to every customer request. High-quality customer service can take place even when you have to say "no" to a customer—as long as saying "no" is done in a manner that preserves the dignity of the customer.

In such situations, providing optional solutions helps customers feel respected and in control. High-quality customer service means providing the best service possible. It doesn't mean customers always get what they want.

2. **Myth:** Some employees feel that they don't have to be concerned with customer service because they don't deal with the customers of their company.

   Fact: Regardless of the kind of work an employee performs within an organization, you have customers who need to be satisfied: those who depend on them. Your organization will never be able to meet the needs of its external customers until the needs of its internal customers are met.

3. **Myth:** Our organization provides excellent customer service, but the perception in the field is that we don't. That's just the way it is.

   Fact: If the perception of the customer is that your organization's customer service is poor, you need to take a hard look at what you're doing, and not doing, to satisfy customer needs. Remember that it is the customer who defines the quality of your customer service efforts. If the customer says they're poor, they're poor.

4. **Myth:** Customer service in our organization is better than that of any of our competitors. If our customers don't like what we offer by way of customer service, let them try our competitors. They'll be back.

   Fact: Don't count on it. Maybe one of your competitors has read this book and has already made a commitment to improve customer service. But the real problem behind this particular myth is a "take it or leave it" attitude. Organizations that have that kind of attitude toward their customers will sooner or later either change their attitude or be left in the dust. Another problem with this myth is that it's based upon an erroneous comparison. How an organization's customer service quality compares with that of its competitors' means nothing; how it is perceived by the customer means everything.

5. **Myth:** Our organization can't afford to offer high-quality customer service to our customers. We'd go broke.

   Fact: It's more likely that you'll go broke if you continue to ignore the value of high-quality customer service. According to the U.S. Department of Commerce, the average American business loses half of its customer base every five years, 60 percent of whom leave because of poor customer service. The same government agency has determined that it costs seven times more to acquire a new customer than to keep an existing one. Your organization, regardless of the

products or services it sells, can't afford to ignore the financial benefits that result from offering high-quality customer service.

THE 30-SECOND RECAP

- Most business firms don't understand the value of quality customer service.

- The customer, not the company, defines the quality of an organization's customer service.

- Mediocre customer service (service that's just so-so) doesn't exist—you're either doing it right, or your customers are looking elsewhere.

- Highly successful enterprises recognize that they are in the service business, not the manufacturing business, the insurance business, the banking business, or the real estate business.

- Customer service is a culture, not a program—it's a way of life.

- Superior customer service provides a significant competitive edge to those firms that achieve it.

Who Are Your Customers and What Do They Want?

In this section, you learn to identify three levels of customers, and you see how each affects the success of the company. You also learn about the most common customer complaints and the six basic wants of customers everywhere.

WHO'S THE CUSTOMER?

Perhaps the broad definition of the term *customer* as any person or group who receives the work output of another surprises you. Most business people who talk about customer service initially have a much narrower definition in mind—one that includes only those who finally purchase their product or service.

PLAIN ENGLISH

The **customer** is any person or group who receives the work output (product or service) of another.

There are, however, three levels of "customer" in the typical organization, and each level is important to the success of the enterprise. To develop the kind of customer service that puts wheels under your company and wings alongside it, the needs, wants, and priorities of customers at each level cannot be ignored; they need to be defined and incorporated into the business strategies of the organization.

THE EMPLOYEE-CUSTOMER

In the first act of *Hamlet,* William Shakespeare wrote: "This above all: to thine own self be true." Those words had special meaning in Shakespeare's play, and they have special meaning in the world of customer service.

The first level of customer is the *employee-customer* who participates in the research and development, manufacturing, or sale of a company's product or service. Each first-level customer has ownership of a process for which he or she is responsible. These *process owners* are motivated by a desire for excellence and are satisfied with their work only when the product or service is of such quality that it evokes a sense of personal pride.

Characteristics of the employee-customer include a positive attitude about the product or service, an obsession with quality and self-inspection, a preoccupation with personal performance, and a commitment to personal improvement.

PLAIN ENGLISH

Process owners are employees, or groups of employees, who are responsible for a specific aspect of the finished product or service of an organization.

THE INTERNAL CUSTOMER

Internal customers are those who receive work output (product) from internal process owners. For example, the Boeing Company has a large plant that manufactures airplane wings. This particular plant is the internal customer of several other Boeing facilities that manufacture the parts needed for the construction of airplane wings. At the same time, the wing-manufacturing facility is also a process owner whose internal customer is another Boeing facility that assembles airplanes for delivery to customers worldwide.

The primary objective of each process owner is to satisfy its internal customers by providing top-quality products and services. Product quality, timeliness of delivery, and cost are among the most important factors influencing internal customer satisfaction.

Excellence in internal customer service is reflected in the quality of the finished product; the better the internal customer service quality, the higher the product quality.

It's also true that if internal customers are dissatisfied, the final customer—the one who purchases the product—will be dissatisfied, too. Use *prevention-based management* to ensure customer satisfaction throughout the entire process.

PLAIN ENGLISH

Prevention-based management is the supervision and control of those systems and processes designed to prevent customer dissatisfaction. It also concerns itself with the need for service recovery, which is the organization's attempt to make things right. Prevention-based management is proactive and attempts to identify problems before they affect customer perception.

THE EXTERNAL CUSTOMER

The *external customer* is the ultimate recipient of the finished product or service. He or she is the final arbiter of quality, value, excellence, and *service*. More than any other single factor, the judgment of the external customer determines the success or failure of the enterprise.

CAUTION

Take every possible step to ensure customer satisfaction up front and to avoid negative perceptions. Although changing the public's perception of a company's product or service is possible, the effort often involves significant public relations and advertising expenditures and requires years to accomplish. Where customer satisfaction is concerned, proactive prevention-based management is the key.

PLAIN ENGLISH

Any product-based interaction between a customer and a company is **service.** Service requires genuine concern for the customer by a representative of the organization who is technically capable of offering assistance. Service requires that the company representative possess both the desire and the ability to treat each individual's problem as unique, even though the representative may have dealt with the same problem on countless other occasions.

MOST COMMON CUSTOMER COMPLAINTS

Whether you sell widgets or washing machines, when something goes wrong, customers have a right to expect someone from the company to demonstrate appropriate concern and solve the problem immediately. Unfortunately, that doesn't always happen.

Here's a list of common customer complaints:

1. **There seems to be a total lack of interest in the customer's problem.** This is without a doubt the number-one complaint in the field of customer service. "The company representative as much as told me that he just didn't care!" When your company lacks real interest in customers' problems, employees verbally and nonverbally communicate an attitude of indifference, even contempt. A customer has a right to expect that the same company that sold the product will be genuinely interested in doing whatever it takes to make sure the product does what it's supposed to do. Nothing will irritate a customer quicker than an attitude of "I don't care, it's not my problem."

2. **No one wants to "own" the problem (otherwise known as the "custom**er service shuffle," previously known as "passing the buck"). A customer with a problem is told, "I'm sorry, I don't deal with those matters. That's just not my area of responsibility. You'll have to talk with Mr. Jones about that." A high-tech version of this same problem occurs when a customer who needs help phones a company and is immediately confronted with voicemail and a seemingly endless series of menu options—which may or may not lead to a human being. Voicemail systems may be efficient and effective in some ways, but from a customer service perspective they're public enemy number one.

3. **The company representative uses condescending language that patronizes or belittles.** Have you ever experienced difficulty with a product and then contacted the company's customer service center, only to find yourself being talked to like a nine-year-old? No one likes to be patronized. It's demeaning and embarrassing. But it's one of the most common complaints of customers, who understandably like to be regarded with dignity and respect.

4. **The company is unresponsive to the customer.** Some companies have the mistaken idea that if you ignore the problem, it'll go away. The truth is that if you ignore the problem, your customer will go away—for good! Customers want a response to their problem, and they want it immediately. And if a commitment is made to a customer, it should be considered a sacred obligation. Putting people off with promises of future service may solve an immediate problem, but it creates an even worse problem if those promises aren't kept.

5. **The company provides the customer with wrong or inaccurate information.** No one likes to look stupid. But the fact is, none of us is able to provide the right answer every time. We all encounter problems that we simply don't know how to solve. When that happens, some representatives elect to provide the customer with wrong or incomplete information rather than admit they aren't sure and call for assistance. Only one thing is worse than providing a customer with no information, and that's giving him the wrong information.

6. **The company treats the customer rudely.** Customers will not allow you to treat them rudely for any length of time. Company representatives who treat customers rudely cost their companies an incredible amount of money per hour. (The higher the profit margin, the more they cost.) Most people simply refuse to be treated in this manner. Most of us consider rudeness a personal invitation to immediately stop doing business with a company and never return.

7. **The representative uses company policy and procedure as an excuse for not providing service.** It's amazing how frequently customers make this complaint—and rightfully so! To succeed in today's competitive business environment, companies need to be driven by customer needs and wants, not by internal policy and procedure. Companies who think of customers as anything but the most important people in the company need to make a paradigm shift before it's too late.

PHRASES THAT AROUSE ANGER

There are numerous phrases that exasperate customers. If you're interested in resolving problems and satisfying customers, you'll avoid these phrases:

- You're going to have to ....
- What did you do?
- It's company policy that ....
- You can't ....
- You'll have to talk with ....
- Why are you talking to me about ...?
- I'm new here.
- That's really not my department.
- We can't do that!
- You should have ....
- You must have ....
- That's not my problem!

When internal customers encounter service-related problems, the result is anxiety, tension, a breakdown in morale, and a final product that is of diminished quality. In the words of world-renowned management consultant Tom Peters: "I can think of no successful company that has found a way to look after external customers while abusing internal customers. The process of meeting customer needs begins internally."

By the time customer service problems affect external customers, the company is in real trouble. We live in a global business environment that is filled with competitive entrepreneurs, many of whom have a keen understanding of the value of customers and know how to provide the service they need.

To be successful in business today, you need a real sense of commitment to the customer at every level. You need to practice proactive management to prevent internal and external customer service problems whenever possible, and you need to quickly and aggressively solve the problems that occur in spite of your best efforts.

THE MCDONALD'S ATTITUDE

Ray Kroc, founder of McDonald's, built his multi-billion-dollar company with customer service as a primary value. Long ago, McDonald's developed "10 commandments" for customer treatment. The customer service commitment expressed by these commandments remains at the heart of the company's day-to-day operation.

1. The Customer is the most important person in our business.
2. The Customer is not dependent on us—we are dependent on the Customer.
3. The Customer is not an interruption of our work, but the purpose of it.
4. The Customer does us an honor when calling on us. We are not doing the Customer a favor by serving him or her.
5. The Customer is part of our business, not an outsider.
6. The Customer is not a cold statistic, but flesh and blood: a human being with feelings and emotions like our own.
7. The Customer is not someone to argue with or match wits with.
8. The Customer is deserving of the most courteous and attentive treatment we can provide.
9. The Customer is one who brings us his/her wants. Our job is to fill them.
10. The Customer has the right to expect an employee to present a neat, clean appearance.

McDonald's commitment to customer service made the company one of the genuine success stories of the twentieth century. Theirs is a model well worth emulating.

WHAT YOUR CUSTOMERS WANT

Excellence in customer service translates into significant sales and significant growth. Before you can deliver consistently excellent customer service, you must first understand what your customers want.

CAUTION

Some companies confuse advertising with a commitment to excellence in customer service. Don't embark on expensive advertising campaigns that tout your exceptional service until you've committed yourself to developing a customer service culture and have initiated the processes that ensure excellent performance. Don't promote what you don't have. False claims in advertising undermine trust and can do your company irreparable harm.

Here are six qualities that customers want and expect in organizations with which they do business:

- **Respectful treatment.** A good rule of thumb is: Do for your customer what you would want done if you were the customer. Treating customers with respect and dignity is where customer satisfaction and customer loyalty begins.

- **Responsiveness.** Customers want your immediate attention. They want you to be receptive to them and empathetic about their needs or problems, whatever they may be.

- **Technical excellence.** Customers expect company representatives to be knowledgeable about the company's product or service—in other words, to know what they're doing. Few experiences are as frustrating as talking to someone about a customer service matter only to learn, late in the conversation, that the person has absolutely no idea what you're talking about. Employees who represent a company with customers should not be newcomers to the organization, nor should they lack the experience and skills necessary to fully represent the products sold by the company. In fact, they should be among the friendliest and most knowledgeable people in your company.

- **Focus on problem solving.** When there's a problem, customers want it solved—fast! They expect the person helping them to remain totally solution-focused. Nothing intensifies a service problem faster than a representative who finds reason after reason for the company's inability to solve the problem immediately.

- **Flexibility.** Customers with a problem want to deal with someone who can be flexible and creative in finding solutions. A "one-size-fits-all" approach to customer service is a design for disaster. Customers expect you to be able to overcome roadblocks and cut through whatever red tape exists so that their problem can be solved without further hassle.

- **Prompt recovery.** When mistakes happen, customers expect prompt *recovery.* They're not interested in knowing who or what is to blame. They don't want long, drawn-out explanations about why the mistake occurred. What they do want is an acknowledgment of the mistake, an apology, a resolution of the problem, and an assurance that it won't happen again. More on recovery is discussed later in this chapter.

PLAIN ENGLISH

Recovery is the process used by a company with its customer to rectify a mistake or solve a problem caused by the company. The goal of recovery is complete customer satisfaction.

IGNORE THE BASICS, PAY THE PRICE

There are many examples of companies that have ignored the basics of customer service and paid the price for their ignorance. The following story is just one example for you to consider.

A few years ago, *USA Today* ran a story titled "Bank Gets Million Dollar Lesson." It began when John Barrier went to Old National Bank in Spokane, Washington, to cash a $100 check.

When Barrier attempted to get his parking ticket validated (to save 60 cents), a bank receptionist refused to validate it because he hadn't conducted a transaction that qualified. "You have to make a deposit if you want us to validate your ticket," the receptionist told him. "That's the bank's rule and I'm not permitted to waive it."

Barrier told the receptionist that he was a "substantial depositor" with the bank. Nevertheless, that fact made no difference to the receptionist and he was told, "Rules are rules."

Barrier asked to see the bank manager, but the manager stood by the bank's rule that prohibited validating a parking ticket unless a deposit was made.

The next day, Barrier went to the bank headquarters determined to withdraw his $2 million-plus unless the manager apologized for the error and made things right. He was told that the manager was actually just doing his job; that it was fiscally responsible to control these kinds of bank expenditures.

"So the next day I went over and the first amount I took out was $1 million. But if you have $100 in a bank or $1 million," he said, "I think they owe you the courtesy of stamping your parking ticket."

THE 30-SECOND RECAP

- There are three levels of customer: the employee-customer, the internal customer, and the external customer.

- To improve customer service immediately, begin by eliminating those situations that consistently incur customer complaints, and train employees to avoid phrases that arouse customer anger, such as those outlined in this chapter.

- Make sure that you and your employees know what a customer wants and expects from your company.

- Whatever you do, don't ignore or underestimate the value of customer service to the success of your company. Remember: Regardless of what you sell, you're really in the service business!

Your Only Competitive Advantage

In this section, you learn what the fundamental values of excellent customer service are and how to design an effective customer service delivery system— one that will transform customer service into the most powerful marketing tool your company will ever discover.

GAINING THE COMPETITIVE EDGE

There was a time when the life of a businessperson was simple. Sales of products or services were generated by salespeople or through various forms of advertising, and advantage over one's competitors was gained with the right combination of price and product quality.

Business has become much more complex. In today's global marketplace, competitive pricing and high-quality products or services are no longer enough to win customers over—they're just the price of entry for companies seeking to join the game of earning customer loyalty. Today, if you want to gain a competitive edge over your competition, excellence in customer service is an absolute requirement.

Providing top-notch customer service is the key to finding and keeping customers. And providing service that's better than the competition is what keeps the profits rolling in.

CAUTION

Even though pricing and product quality are no longer enough to win the competitive war, they remain important to the overall effort. High-quality products that are competitively priced, together with top-notch service quality, are the recipe for success in today's global marketplace.

THE FINANCIAL VALUE OF A CUSTOMER

In case you're wondering whether you're doing everything necessary to develop a customer service culture in your company, consider the following scenario.

Store A sells a widget to Customer A for $100. The profit margin for widgets is 40 percent, or $40, on the sale.

The typical customer buys 10 widgets a year. This means that if Store A offers excellence in customer service, the customer is likely to buy 9 more widgets from Store A during the year, bringing in another $360 in profit, for a total annual profit of $400. That's the annual value of one typical widget customer. Over a 5-year period, the value of Customer A is $2,000.

If Customer A tells 10 friends how satisfied he or she is with Store A's widgets and service, and each of the 10 friends in turn buys 10 widgets a year from Store A, over 5 years the value of Customer A becomes $22,000.

Whatever amount of effort and money your company invests in customer service, you can be sure that it will bring an excellent return. Conversely, failing to invest in customer service can mean the loss of significant profits over time.

AMAZON.COM AND CUSTOMER SERVICE

A few years ago, Jeff Bezos enrolled in an introductory course in book-selling offered by the American Booksellers Association. He was captivated by a customer service story told by his instructor, who owned a small bookstore in Mississippi.

The instructor recounted an incident in which one of his customers became upset and angry when dirt from a second-story flowerpot was accidentally spilled onto her car, which was parked outside his store. To solve the problem, the instructor rolled up his sleeves and personally washed the customer's car. The customer was so impressed by this gesture of goodwill that she returned to buy numerous books and told all her friends to do the same.

That kind of commitment to excellence in customer service is what Bezos insisted be the guiding principle of his company, Amazon.com. Last year, Amazon.com had sales of $1.6 billion dollars, representing 15.4 percent of all commerce conducted over the Internet.

The three keys to Amazon's success are competitive pricing, quality of product, and excellence in customer service.

PLAIN ENGLISH

Customer service occurs when you meet the needs and expectations of the customer as defined by the customer.

THE FOUNDATIONS OF EXCELLENCE

There's a principle of successful living that is so simple that many people seem to miss it altogether. It's this: You get back from life what you put into it!

We see that principle at work every day of our lives. People who skim by, who do only what's absolutely necessary and no more, and who settle for less than they are capable of usually receive very little from life in return. They often end up feeling that life has somehow shortchanged them.

On the other hand, people who always give 110 percent of themselves to everything they're involved in seem to get much more out of living. The casual observer may be tempted to attribute these people's zest for living to "good fortune" or "luck," when the truth is they're just reaping what they've sown; their investment in life continues to bring them the best that life can offer.

This particular principle isn't true only in the lives of people; it's also true in the lives of corporations and other forms of organized business.

When a business attempts to do as little as possible to ensure customer satisfaction, and worries more about profits, it rarely rises above the level of mediocrity. That's true even if the business spends a fortune on advertising and has products that are of high quality and are competitively priced.

Excellence in customer service requires five important core values to which everyone in the company must genuinely strive to adhere:

- Commitment to building a culture
- Willingness to pay the price
- Desire to exceed customer expectations
- Obsession for excellence
- Eternal vigilance

COMMITMENT TO BUILDING A CULTURE

Famed Green Bay Packers coach Vince Lombardi once said, "The quality of a person's life is in direct proportion to their commitment to excellence, regardless of their chosen field of endeavor." Excellence in customer service has its roots in an unyielding commitment by top management to create a culture of customer service in which every facet of the business is customer-driven.

WILLINGNESS TO PAY THE PRICE

Excellence in any endeavor is not automatic. Excellence in customer service is no exception. As Dr. Stephen Covey, author of *The Seven Habits of Highly Effective People,* says, "Real excellence does not come cheaply. A certain price must be paid in terms of practice, patience, and persistence."

Building a culture of customer service requires patience over time. And persistence is necessary to continue moving forward toward excellence in customer service, even when it would be less time-consuming, less demanding, and less costly to be less than excellent. Once established, successful customer service techniques must be practiced both internally and externally—and everyone in the organization needs to be involved.

DESIRE TO EXCEED CUSTOMER EXPECTATIONS

Consistently exceeding customer expectations is a challenge to go a step beyond the usual. It involves giving a little more than is required or expected. It's not necessarily doing an extraordinary thing; rather, it's doing an ordinary thing extraordinarily well.

Smuckers, the jam and jelly maker, has a policy of filling its containers with a bit more product than the official weight indicates. Most customers never weigh the jar and consequently are never aware of the bonus. But giving the customer more than is expected is part of the Smuckers service to its customers. It's their practice, whether people are watching or not. Is it any wonder that Smuckers has captured a huge share of the jam and jelly market?

OBSESSION FOR EXCELLENCE

Winston Churchill once said, "I am easily satisfied with the very best." Your customers are, too. When companies consider their customer service efforts "good enough," the reality is that their service is usually somewhere between mediocre and horrible.

The definition of a company's customer service quality will ultimately become the definition of the company itself. Hallmark cares enough to send "the very best." How do you know? The quality of their product says so.

ETERNAL VIGILANCE

If you're serious about wanting to provide *excellence in customer service,* and thereby maintain your competitive edge in the marketplace, the price you must be willing to pay is eternal vigilance.

L.L. Bean president Leon Gorman has defined customer service as "just a day-in, day-out, ongoing, never-ending, unremitting, persevering, compassionate type of activity." But however you define it, customer service is always a journey, not a destination.

PLAIN ENGLISH

Excellence in customer service is a way of doing business that involves going beyond the call of duty, stretching perceived limits, and empowering everyone in the organization to maintain the highest standards, pay attention to details, and go the extra mile. Take a lesson from Mother Goose: "Good, better, best; never rest till 'good' is 'better' and 'better' is 'best.'"

YOUR SERVICE DELIVERY SYSTEM

John Goodman, president of TARP, Inc., once said, "Eighty percent of customers' problems are caused by bad systems, not by bad people." He's right. Most of the service problems your customers encounter in trying to do business with you occur because your *service delivery systems* (the systems you rely on to serve customers) are either antiquated, too complex, or just plain unfriendly.

PLAIN ENGLISH

Service delivery systems are the means, methods, and procedures used to provide a product or service to the public and to
provide other customer assistance as deemed necessary by the
customer.

For example, most dysfunctional systems include telephone technology that
features such customer "displeasers" as call director or voicemail systems
with frustratingly lengthy menu options, or caller-hold features that entertain
callers with annoying elevator music from the *Twilight Zone*. (Some organizations even dare to interrupt the entertainment with an occasional commercial
message.)

To add insult to injury, when a customer finally reaches a real person, too
often that person has little knowledge of the company's products and no
power to solve the customer's problem or fix what's wrong. Such telephone
technology costs companies millions in lost customers.

SEVEN CHARACTERISTICS OF EFFECTIVE DELIVERY SYSTEMS

It's true that each company's customer service delivery system is somewhat
unique. But among highly functional systems, there are seven identical characteristics.

To be world class and capable of achieving customer service excellence, your
service delivery system needs to be …

■ **Customer-driven.** Your customer service delivery system should be
   designed as a partnership with the customer. Remember, the purpose
   of your company is to satisfy the needs of your customers and potential customers; never make the mistake of thinking that your company exists simply to produce and sell goods or services. So think of
   your customer as a partner. Take a walk in your customer's shoes.
   What kind of service delivery system would please you?

■ **Available.** Open the way for customers to do business with you.
   Make it easy for customers to purchase your goods or services.
   When you encounter obstacles that prevent your customers from easily and conveniently doing business with you, make it a priority to
   remove those obstacles. If you're going to succeed, you need to be
   available to your customers.

■ **Responsive.** Design a service delivery system that gets you up-close-
   and-personal with your customers. Know your customers' needs,
   desires, and expectations; and make them the standard against which
   you monitor your organization's efforts. Companies that make it a

practice to know their customers as if they were family members are companies that are responsive to their customers. Customer loyalty rises or falls based on your ability to respond appropriately to their needs, desires, and expectations.

■ **Correct.** Customer service delivery systems should consistently provide customers with accurate information. This is particularly true when it comes to technical aspects of products and information about warranties, price, delivery, billings, and so on. Customers are quick to perceive when the person helping them knows less about a product than they do.

■ **Integrated.** Customers should be able to obtain all of the information they need from one source within your company. It is unnecessarily frustrating when customers are asked to obtain service in a piecemeal fashion by talking with several people in your company.

■ **User-friendly.** The process that the customer uses to access your company's services should be friendly, uncomplicated, and accessible. Avoid using voicemail whenever possible.

■ **Fast.** Customer service delivery systems should provide assistance to customers quickly. Customers perceive speedy help as excellence.

CAUTION

Remember that customer service doesn't just belong to the "customer service department." It's everyone's business. In developing a customer service culture, it's absolutely necessary to involve everyone in the company. Customer service isn't a job title; it's a way of life for everyone in your company from the chief executive officer to the part-time window washer. It's an all-or-nothing proposition.

THREE KEYS TO EXCELLENCE

In addition to building a firm foundation of *customer-centered* core values and designing a customer delivery system that makes doing business with your company convenient and easy, you need good people to make it all work. Excellence in customer service doesn't just happen because our hearts are right and our program design is good; it happens because good people working in *customer-centric* environments make it happen.

PLAIN ENGLISH

Anything that is centered entirely on the customer is **customer-centric**. The more "customer-centric" an organization becomes, the more it is aligned with the needs, wants, and desires of the customer.

Let's focus our attention on three specific characteristics of highly effective customer service staff:

- Technical quality
- Human interaction
- Empowerment

These are the keys to excellence in customer service, and they will give your company the competitive advantage it desires.

TECHNICAL QUALITY

Technical quality is what enables you to compete in the marketplace. Your *frontline employees*—those in your company who directly interact with customers—must be able to provide assistance in ways that demonstrate a high degree of technical competence.

PLAIN ENGLISH

Frontline employees are those who deal directly with the customer—the purchaser of the product or service.

Excellence in customer service not only requires a top-notch product, but also requires that those serving the customer be knowledgeable about the company, its products, and their applications—or that they know where to go to find the necessary answers. Customer satisfaction soars when employees know what they're doing, *like* what they're doing, and are entirely absorbed with the company's purpose and mission.

Here are a few of the most important characteristics of employees who strongly influence a customer's assessment of technical quality. Excellence is conveyed by employees who ...

- Consistently provide customers with accurate information about the company and the product it sells.
- Know the internal processes required to resolve customer problems or complaints (and how to cut through the red tape whenever necessary).

- Understand the way in which the company's products are used by customers and know how potential problems associated with the product can be avoided.
- Are effective problem solvers—they know what to do.
- Can solve a customer problem, or resolve a complaint, quickly and efficiently.

HUMAN INTERACTION

There's a human side to the customer service equation, and it's important. People want to be treated as human beings, as unique and important people who deserve the very best you and your company have to offer.

In any type of enterprise, human interaction is what separates the excellent from the good. And it's human interaction that wins customers and keeps them over time.

Here are some examples of ways in which human interaction can be used to create excellence in customer service:

- Customers are greeted politely and courteously. Service representatives are courteous even when customers aren't, and they remain calm in the face of anger and chaos.
- An atmosphere of friendliness prevails throughout each customer interaction. Friendliness is not just a slogan; it's a way of doing business.
- By their words and body language, your staff conveys a deep respect for customers and demonstrates that respect with warmth in each interaction regardless of type (telephone calls, walk-in visitors, letters, sales contacts).
- Empathy and understanding for a customer with a problem or complaint is communicated in genuine ways that are not judgmental or critical but that demonstrate acknowledgment and appreciation of the customer's feelings.
- Information—even of a technical nature—is communicated in understandable ways without making the customer feel ignorant or put down in any way.
- Customers are treated fairly in every interaction with the company.

EMPOWERMENT

Dr. Benjamin Schneider, professor of psychology at the University of Maryland, is credited with this wise observation: "Treat your people like gold—or dirt—and they'll treat your customers accordingly." An empowered employee is an important key to providing excellence in customer service.

Empowered employees are authorized to solve customer problems on the spot in predetermined ways. For example, Horst Schulze, president of the Ritz-Carlton Hotel Company, allows any employee working on a customer service issue to spend up to $2,500 to resolve the matter and to prevent a repeat occurrence. According to a recent J. D. Power survey, 94 percent of Ritz-Carlton customers report that they are well satisfied; the Ritz-Carlton's best competitor for the same period received only a 57 percent rating.

Empowering your employees to meet the needs of customers is not just a good idea, it's absolutely necessary if your goal is excellence in customer service. An empowered employee …

- Solves customer problems quickly and efficiently.
- Builds partnerships with customers that are based on mutual understanding and respect.
- Speaks volumes about the entire company's commitment to excellence in customer service.
- Provides an atmosphere of high morale in which employees take ownership of outcomes and customers are "treated like gold."

THE 30-SECOND RECAP

- The true financial value of a customer cannot be measured in terms of one sale, but rather in terms of the purchases the customer is likely to make over time.
- In today's global marketplace, the three keys to success are competitive pricing, quality of product, and excellence in customer service.
- For excellence in customer service, everyone in the company must share five core values: commitment to building the culture, a willingness to pay the price, a desire to exceed customer expectations, an obsession for excellence, and eternal vigilance.
- Develop customer service delivery systems that make it easy for people to do business with your company.
- The three keys that unlock the potential of your company's frontline customer service staff are technical quality, human interaction, and empowerment.

Hiring a Service-Oriented Attitude

In this section, you learn the importance of people in creating and maintaining a customer service culture. You also learn which specific qualities to look for in candidates and how to use behavioral interviewing techniques to discover whether candidates can succeed in a customer service environment.

WINNING THE WAR

When David Frost interviewed Gen. Norman Schwarzkopf, commander of the Allied Forces in the Gulf War, he asked the general, "What's the greatest lesson you've learned out of all of this?"

The heroic general replied, "I think that there is one really fundamental military truth. And that's that you can add up the correlation of forces, you can look at the number of tanks, you can look at the number of airplanes, you can look at all these factors of military might and put them together. But unless the soldier on the ground, or the airman in the air, has the will to win, has the strength of character to go into battle, believes that his cause is just, and has the support of his country, all the rest of that stuff is irrelevant."

Technologies, systems, protocols, procedures, processes, strategies, and plans all provide the means. But only individuals, properly supported, well trained, and motivated by the mission, win the war.

That statement is also true in modern business, where the battlefield is the global marketplace, the battle objective is to gain market share, and victory is profitability. It takes the combined effort of top-quality people who are thoroughly trained, properly motivated, and continuously supported to achieve that victory.

HIRING QUALITY PEOPLE

J. W. "Bill" Marriott Jr., chairman and CEO of the Marriott Corporation, puts it like this: "You start with good people, you train and motivate them, you give them an opportunity to advance, then the organization succeeds."

Building and maintaining a winning customer service culture in your company begins with hiring good people who can build positive relationships with customers. The success of your organization depends on your ability to hire well.

MISTAKES ARE COSTLY

Hiring mistakes can be very costly to your organization. In fact, some studies have shown that the direct costs alone can equal as much as four times the annual salary for the position.

But the indirect costs of hiring mistakes can be even more staggering. In addition to lost productivity, the drain on management, and the harm done to employee morale, the wrong employee can alienate some customers and substantially damage customer relations in general.

If we again consider the example of Customer A from before, who buys 10 widgets a year, each of which produces $40 in profit to Company A, then losing Customer A would produce an annual loss of profit to the company of $400. Over a 5-year period, the loss of profit would amount to $2,000. And if Customer A tells 10 friends—each of whom also buys 10 widgets a year—how badly he or she was treated by Company A, the potential loss to the company over a 5-year period is $22,000.

If 10 customers are alienated, and each customer tells 10 others, the potential profit loss now grows to $222,000! And that's if you're selling widgets. Imagine what the loss would be if the products were cars, construction equipment, computers, or other widely purchased products.

Hiring the right person for the job is critically important to the future of your company.

DON'T SETTLE FOR A "WARM BODY"

Finding the right person for the job takes time and effort. Unfortunately, most businesses today spend more time buying a new copy machine than they do choosing the right employee. And, too often, jobs that involve dealing directly with customers are given to the first "warm body" that promises to show up for eight hours each day of the workweek. The results are predictably disastrous.

Companies that consistently outperform their competition in quality of product and service delivery never settle for warm bodies. They know the value of hiring top-quality people. And they never allow the process of finding and hiring the right people to be rushed.

Several years ago, Seattle-based retailer Nordstrom opened its first store on the East Coast, in McLean, Virginia. To adequately staff the new operation, Nordstrom needed to hire 400 employees to serve in frontline positions. According to a story in the March 4, 1988, edition of *USA Today,* more than 3,000 people were screened and interviewed to find the 400 who would complement the Nordstrom customer service culture. Nordstrom values its customers—and its employees. No wonder it's one of the most successful retailers in America.

THE HIRING PROCESS

Hiring is a process that involves ...

- Analyzing the job opening to determine *mandatory success factors.*
- Recruiting candidates internally and externally who possess the desired qualifications.
- Screening resumés for further consideration.
- Checking references.
- Developing appropriate interview questions.
- Conducting interviews.
- Selecting the best candidate for the job.

PLAIN ENGLISH

Mandatory success factors are the specific competencies and skills that are absolutely essential to successful job performance. They are determined by thoroughly analyzing the job and by providing profiles of the job and the ideal candidate.

ANALYZING THE JOB

What skills or competencies are required to be successful in the job? That's an important question. Unless you know exactly what it takes to succeed in the job, it's impossible to know what to look for in job applicants.

Here are some typical questions to ask as you analyze the open position:

- What *functional skills* are required to do this job well?
- What technical competencies (degrees, certifications, licenses, and so on) are necessary?
- What *self-management skills* are needed?
- What *interpersonal skills* are required?
- What are the requirements of the corporate culture?

PLAIN ENGLISH

Functional skills are skills that help people function effectively on the job. They include the ability to communicate, to listen, to lead, and to be flexible.

Self-management skills are personal characteristics that help people do the job successfully. Included are such skills as creativity, honesty, competence, appearance, and helpfulness.

Interpersonal skills are the "people skills." Such skills are particularly important to consider when interviewing for frontline positions. Good interpersonal skills include the ability to respect others, to be empathetic and caring, to listen attentively and respond accordingly, and to maintain objectivity and refrain from emotionalism.

CAUTION

Attitudes that reflect a genuine love of people and a burning desire to be helpful to others are particularly important for frontline staff. People can be trained to be proficient in most of the areas necessary for successful job performance, but attitudes are difficult to change. The attitude you hire is usually the attitude you'll have to live with during the tenure of the employee. Be careful.

A thorough analysis of the open position will result in a clear profile of both the job and the ideal candidate. When you know what you're looking for, you're ready to start your search.

RECRUITING CANDIDATES INTERNALLY

Now that you know exactly what you're looking for, begin your search by making existing staff aware of the position and the qualifications being sought. Asking existing employees for referrals and recruiting within the organization by posting the job are cost-efficient ways to fill vacancies.

Seeking applicants from within has another important advantage: It tends to build morale. Employees appreciate knowing that their employer values them, and nothing communicates that message more clearly than offering to existing staff the first new opportunities.

RECRUITING CANDIDATES EXTERNALLY

There was a time when the chief means of locating candidates for employment outside the organization involved placing a "help wanted" advertisement in the local newspaper. Most major employers today do not rely on single-source recruiting efforts. Instead they solicit applicants from a number of sources, such as ...

- Newspaper advertising.
- Advertising on the company web page.

- Internet job search services.
- Employment or recruitment agencies.
- College-graduate placement services.
- Public job services.

Successful candidates can come from many different sources. It's a good idea to communicate the job opening to a lot of sources simultaneously for maximum results.

TIP

Be sure to offer candidates several options for submitting their resumés (in person, mail, e-mail, fax). Some organizations even allow applicants to apply online at the company's website. Make it easy for prospective candidates to send you their applications.

SCREENING RESUMÉS

The objective in screening resumés is to select applicants for further consideration. You want to narrow the field of applicants to those whose education and experience appear to fit the identified mandatory success factors.

It's a good idea to ask others to help you screen the resumés that you've received for an open position. Develop and use a standardized evaluation tool so that each resumé can be rated against specific criteria.

After the screening process is complete, notify by letter those who have been disqualified from further consideration. Be sure to thank them for applying for the job, and encourage them to apply for future openings with your company.

CAUTION

Resumés rejected by evaluators should be kept on file, along with accompanying notes and evaluations. To defend yourself against possible litigation, it's important that your reasons for rejecting an applicant be firmly rooted in the requirements of the job, not in anything extraneous. Your documentation should clearly identify job-related reasons for screening out the applicant from further consideration.

CHECKING REFERENCES

After you've narrowed the field of candidates, it's a good idea to check references. Reference checks *before* the interview? Why would you want to do that?

For two important reasons: First, the process of checking references helps employers gain a better understanding of the candidates under consideration—and that's an important objective of the evaluation process. Second, during the reference checks, employers often discover areas of special concern that require further exploration during the interview.

But whether you check references before the interview or after, be sure to check them. Some business journals have estimated that the references of as many as 70 percent of all new hires are never checked. That's asking for trouble.

CAUTION

After the interview and reference-check stages, have successful applicants complete a company application that contains broad written permission allowing you to talk with those who have first-hand knowledge of their abilities and experience. Many experts advise considering a "hold harmless" clause that prevents former employers from being sued by an applicant as a result of what they divulge. Consult your attorney about the company's employment application.

DEVELOPING APPROPRIATE INTERVIEW QUESTIONS

Developing interview questions that elicit specific information related to one of the mandatory success factors is a critical part of the selection process. The trouble is, the questions that are asked during most interviews don't yield the information needed to make a reasonable hiring decision. In fact, the number-one "question" asked in interviews today is "Tell us a little bit about yourself." Ninety-five percent of all interviews begin this way.

In developing interview questions, consider using structured behavioral interviewing techniques that will provide you with evidence of a candidate's ability in a specific area. *Behavioral interviewing* is based upon the behavioral consistency principle that the best predictor of future behavior is past behavior under similar circumstances.

Developing questions that are behavioral in nature will give you the information you need to make an informed decision about a candidate. And employing behavioral interviewing techniques will significantly improve your chances of hiring successfully.

General interviewing techniques are more fully explored in Chapter 7. The following is an example that demonstrates the difference between a standard question and a behavioral question in a job interview. Assume that the objective of the interviewer is to learn more about the candidate's attitude toward customer service. Which of these two types of interview questions do you think is more effective?

Standard Interview Question

In a standard interview, an interviewer seeking information about a candidate's customer service attitude might ask: "How do you feel about customer service?"

The question might produce some interesting commentary that may, or may not, reveal the level of hands-on experience a candidate has with customer service. In the course of answering the question, if the candidate describes his or her own involvement in actual customer service situations, this may reveal the candidate's attitude toward customer service.

Behavioral Interview Question

In a behavioral interview format, however, the candidate is asked to provide behavioral evidence that substantiates his or her claim of possessing the skills identified as mandatory for job success. An interviewer seeking information about a candidate's attitude toward customer service might ask the following behavioral question: "Tell me about the most difficult customer service problem you have ever encountered. What was involved? What did you do?" The candidate's response to the question will tell you about his or her attitude toward customer service in general and will give you a glimpse of his or her level of skill in handling difficult customer service situations.

The behavioral interview question will elicit real-life information about "the most difficult customer service problem" ever faced by the candidate. By listening closely to the answer and probing for additional information, not only will you gain important insights about the candidate's attitude toward customer service, you'll also be given a firsthand view of how well the candidate is able to translate attitude into action.

Conducting Interviews

After you've formulated your interview questions, you're ready to begin interviewing candidates. You should invite others who are stakeholders in the final hiring decision to also participate in the interviews.

Plan your interviews to have an opening, an information exchange, and a closing. The *opening* is the time you use to put the candidate at ease. Tell the candidate what to expect during the interview and provide some idea of the time required. The opening is also a good time to ask any specific questions about the applicant's education or experience that remain unanswered.

During the *information exchange,* ask the candidate your planned behavioral questions (each candidate is asked the same questions) related to specific mandatory success factors. Take all the time you need with each question. Probe whenever you feel the need to explore further.

The *closing* of the interview should include a company "sales pitch" delivered by one of the members of the interview team. Whether or not the candidate will be the one selected for the position is irrelevant; your objective should be for each candidate to leave the interview with the understanding that yours is a great company to be part of.

The closing of the interview is also the time for you to explain to the candidate what happens next—when a decision will be made and how he or she will be notified. It's also the time to ask whether the candidate has any unanswered questions about the job or the company.

SELECTING THE BEST CANDIDATE FOR THE JOB

Before you begin selecting the best candidate for the job, develop a candidate-evaluation tool so that you will be evaluating each candidate on the same factors. Immediately after each interview, have each member of the interview team complete an evaluation.

The hiring decision should ultimately be based upon the evaluations of the candidate. Unless there is very good reason to do otherwise, the candidate who receives the highest ratings by evaluators should be offered the position.

The successful candidate is usually notified by telephone, but be sure to follow up with a letter confirming the details of the offer. Be sure also to write each of the remaining candidates to let them know that a decision has been made and to encourage them to apply again in the future.

THE 30-SECOND RECAP

- Employees are vital to the success of any enterprise. Top-quality people produce top-quality results.

- Hiring mistakes are costly—they hinder your company's quest to develop the kind of customer service culture that will cause phenomenal growth and success.

- Develop and maintain a hiring process that identifies the mandatory success factors of a position and helps to select candidates who possess the requisite skills and competencies.

- Each new employee changes your corporate culture for better or for worse. Take as much time as you need to do a thorough job of selecting.

Keeping a Service-Oriented Attitude

In this section, you learn how to retain top-quality employees and how to use high-quality, ongoing training as a guarantee that your employees remain committed to providing the very best in customer service.

THE MICROSOFT EXAMPLE

Then there's the story of Microsoft. Bill Gates and Paul Allen started their business a number of years ago in the Gates family garage. The company grew so fast and became so successful that Gates had to drop out of Harvard to devote all of his time to it. Today Microsoft is one of the largest publicly held companies in America, with gross revenues exceeding those of many governments throughout the world.

One major contributor to Microsoft's success has been its understanding of the importance of customer service. However, at the heart of Microsoft's philosophy of customer service is another very important business truth: its treatment of employees.

Microsoft makes it a practice to treat its employees the same way it expects its employees to treat customers. The result: The company experiences high *employee retention* and high levels of employee and customer satisfaction. Employees are treated very well. They, in turn, pass that treatment on to customers. It's a win-win proposition. Learn from Microsoft.

PLAIN ENGLISH

Employee retention is an integrated process, not a series of isolated events or programs. The process of retention (keeping top-notch employees from going elsewhere) begins at the time of recruitment and is embedded in employment policies and practices that affect the employee throughout his or her career.

RETAINING TOP TALENT

But what does it take to retain good customer service people? More than you might think.

When a company recognizes that there is a direct correlation between losing good employees and losing customers, it gets serious about employee retention. Creating a customer service culture in which good employees are highly valued assets is a fine beginning. But retaining good people and helping them achieve corporate service objectives also means making some basic management decisions that will keep them from leaving for the competition.

Following are a few areas that managers need to consider with regard to customer service employees.

SALARY AND BENEFIT PACKAGES

Never let it be said that money solves the entire problem of employee retention; it solves only a substantial part of it. Although money isn't a good substitute for major deficiencies in the company (bad reputation, inferior product quality, poor management, and so on), it is an important consideration in hiring and keeping good people.

Competition for good people in the new world order of the twenty-first century is fierce. Many small businesses today offer prospective employees a financial package that combines an excellent salary with such perks as 401(k) plans, profit sharing, health care, cars, and so on.

If you want to attract and keep good people who, in turn, will be profit generators, it's essential to offer a compensation package that expresses your estimate of their worth.

Some companies claim that money and benefit packages aren't all that important to employees. They're wrong.

FAVORABLE WORK ENVIRONMENT

One of the most important factors in retaining good people is a favorable work environment. And nothing is more conducive to a favorable work environment than owners who value their employees.

One of the most common reasons people leave their jobs for greener pastures is that they have somehow become disconnected from their bosses as well as from the work itself. Good bosses—those who embody the company's vision and who consider employee satisfaction to be a priority—make a big difference in employee retention.

Companies that are serious about retaining good workers need to be careful about whom they select and train to be supervisors and managers. Good people won't continue to work for a jerk.

And here's the real payoff: Study after study has shown a direct relationship between employee job satisfaction and customer service satisfaction.

TIP

Some companies have found that turnover is reduced when a portion of a manager's pay is tied to retention. When managers are rewarded for good retention stats, and penalized for high turnover, they develop innovative strategies designed to keep people happy in their work.

CHALLENGING WORK ASSIGNMENTS

To keep good employees, it's important that assignments be challenging, rewarding, and motivating. However, over time any job can become stagnant and boring. That's why, even in the best work environments, people sometimes need to change jobs.

Companies with the best records of retention have developed programs that allow employees to move laterally. Lateral movements often involve temporary or developmental job assignments that allow the employee to become revitalized. These opportunities not only offer new challenges, but also allow employees to gain a fresh perspective on the organization's mission.

Experiencing different positions within the company also affords employees an opportunity to explore their strengths and interests. Finding a job that best suits each employee is a key factor in retaining them, and lateral movement within the company fosters that kind of exploration.

REWARDS AND RECOGNITION

Recognition and reward are two powerful motivators for inspiring job excellence. Some studies have demonstrated that these two factors are even more important to job satisfaction than salary and benefits.

When you formally recognize employees for good work, you publicly acknowledge their value to the company and you demonstrate that their efforts have not gone unnoticed. People tend to stay in situations that provide ample amounts of personal satisfaction.

CAUTION

Managing is much like parenting: Be careful what actions you praise or reward, because you're sure to get a lot more of the same.

TIP

Be sure to recognize people for work accomplishments, not just for their longevity with the company. Recognition for real work accomplishments is rewarding to the employees being recognized and is motivational to others.

EMPOWERMENT

Empowerment means encouraging employees to take ownership of their jobs and to use creativity in meeting performance objectives and solving problems along the way. And employees who take ownership of their jobs are much more likely to remain with the company.

But empowerment doesn't just happen because you want it to. Empowerment requires companies to invest time and money in meaningful training activities that teach employees about the mission of the company and provide them with technical information about the company's product or service. Empowerment also requires that employees have the right tools to perform their jobs well and that they know how to use those tools.

Empowered employees not only are likely to remain with a company long term, but will have a major effect on customer service as well. Empowered employees feel that customer satisfaction is a personal responsibility and will resolve customer issues on the spot.

TRAINING AND RETENTION

Training is a lifelong experience. In his book *Life on the Mississippi,* Mark Twain wrote, "Two things seemed pretty apparent to me. One was that in order to be a Mississippi River pilot, a man has got to learn more than any one man ought to be allowed to know; and the other was that he must learn it all over again in a different way every 24 hours."

PLAIN ENGLISH

Training is a lifelong experience that has three primary objectives: to give employees a basic understanding of their job and a vision of the mission of the company, to provide the skills and tools necessary to perform the tasks of the job correctly and efficiently, and to keep people functioning at high levels throughout their careers.

The need for training never ends. Evolving technology, developing markets with special needs, continually improving methods of ensuring quality and service, and the frequent introduction of new products and services make training in the twenty-first century of absolute importance. Time spent in meaningful training activities is profitable for the employee and the company alike.

POOR TRAINING MEANS POOR PERFORMANCE

It's sad but true that the primary reason for poor employee performance is lack of basic training. The next time you're faced with a poor-performance problem, ask yourself whether specific kinds of training may be needed. By answering the following simple questions, supervisors and managers can quickly diagnose whether additional training will solve the problem:

- Does the employee know the primary purpose of his or her job? (For example, the primary purpose of a hotel doorkeeper is to assist customers who are arriving or leaving the hotel; it's not simply to call for cabs.)

- Does the employee understand the process—that is, the steps required to do the job well? (When people don't understand what they are supposed to do, they can never meet expectation levels. People need to understand the process required to do their jobs successfully.)

- Does the employee possess the necessary technical skills to perform each required task? (For example, a grocery store clerk may understand the entire process of assisting customers at checkout; but unless the clerk understands how to find the price of an item that won't scan, he or she is not well trained.)

CAUTION

Don't make the mistake of using training as a punishment. Training should never be used in a negative way. Send people to training to help them grow and develop as employees and as people.

TRAINING SHAPES ATTITUDE

There's an important link between training and employee retention. Employees who are involved in ongoing training that is focused on helping them do their jobs better are more satisfied, and therefore more likely to remain with the company.

Training shapes employee attitude and behavior, and motivates workers to provide the very best in customer service. Training is the catalyst for positive change in any company; it is far and away the most powerful culture-building tool you have.

Developing and maintaining a positive service culture in which employees thrive and turnover rates are low depends to a great extent on the quality of training you provide. All training—even technical training—should be delivered from a customer service perspective and have clear behavioral objectives relating to internal and external customers.

All training should result in ...

- An understanding by employees that their number-one responsibility is serving customers (internal or external).

- Inspiring employees to aim beyond customer satisfaction—causing customers to say "Wow!" in response to the quality of service received.

- Learning specific problem-solving techniques that help satisfy the needs of customers and that effectively and quickly handle customer problems.

- A better understanding of the corporate vision and the individual mission of the employee.

- Enhanced internal cooperation and a better appreciation of teamwork.

- A more customer-centric organization.

- Greater employee empowerment to serve the customer better.

TIP

Consider creating a company library consisting of books, video-tapes, and audiotapes on subjects of interest to your employees. Topics of special interest would include communication, customer satisfaction, conflict resolution, assisting the difficult customer, problem solving, negotiating, and quality management.

Don't underestimate the power of customer service training that includes ongoing mentoring and coaching by supervisors and managers. Your company's customer focus, or lack of it, will determine the degree to which your company ultimately succeeds. Training that helps employees serve customers better also helps reduce employee turnover by making jobs more satisfying and rewarding.

Investing in customer-focused training is just good business.

THE 30-SECOND RECAP

■ Retaining service-oriented people and retaining customers go hand in hand.

■ Retaining good employees requires a substantial commitment from management to provide the kind of environment that encourages people to stay.

■ Ongoing training is an important key to developing and retaining service-oriented employees.

What's Your Vision?

In this section, you learn the importance of developing an inspirational, customer-centered vision for your business. You also learn how to communicate your vision in ways that cause employees to approach their jobs with enthusiasm and a sense of adventure.

ESTABLISHING THE VISION

The first step in developing a customer service culture in which customer satisfaction is valued above everything else is to establish a *customer-centered vision* for your company. This vision is what you want your company to become. It is customer-focused and customer-directed.

PLAIN ENGLISH

Customer-centered vision is a clear picture of how your business will serve the needs of customers in the future. According to Richard Whiteley of the Forum Corporation, such a vision is an ambitious, desirable future state that is connected to the customer and is better in some important way than the current state.

THE CARLSON COMPANIES

The Carlson Companies, whose owner, Curt Carlson, started the business in 1938 with a $55 loan, is a great example of a company with an ambitious customer-centered vision.

To help other companies maintain customer loyalty, Carlson introduced the concept of trading stamps. In the 1960s and 1970s, Carlson branched into the hospitality industry by buying and expanding the Radisson Hotel chain, and later added other hospitality companies to his holdings, such as T.G.I. Friday's, Mr. Foster Travel Agencies, and Country Kitchen Restaurants.

Today, the Carlson Companies is one of the largest travel and hospitality companies in the world. It is also one of the most successful privately held corporations in America, with operations in more than 140 countries and 188,000 employees. In 1999, the combined sales of all the Carlson subsidiaries amounted to $31.4 billion.

Carlson's business philosophy was simple: "Whatever you do, do with integrity; wherever you go, go as a leader; whomever you serve, serve with caring; whenever you dream, dream with your all; and never, ever give up."

Curt Carlson, who died in 1999, attributed his success to his ability to envision how things can be without being distracted by how things are. And his visions, inspired and directed by customers and potential customers, always involved ways of serving people better.

FEDERAL EXPRESS

In the early 1970s, Fred Smith wrote a paper for his economics class at Yale University. The paper discussed Fred's vision of creating an air-express delivery system that would be capable of transporting urgent packages overnight anywhere in America. His professor considered the subject of the paper to be impractical and awarded him a *C* for the effort. The paper outlined what would ultimately become Federal Express.

Smith's business philosophy is simple, clear, and customer-oriented:

> We will produce outstanding financial returns by providing totally reliable, competitively superior global air-ground transportation of high-priority goods and documents that require rapid, time-sensitive delivery. Control of each package will be maintained utilizing real-time electronic tracking and tracing systems. A complete record of each shipment and delivery will be presented with our request for payment. We will be helpful, courteous, to each other (internal customers) and to the public (external customers). We will strive to have a completely satisfied customer at the end of each transaction.

Today, Federal Express is one of the most successful companies in the world. It is also consistently ranked among the best places to work in America. And it all started with a vision of providing a service to customers throughout America.

The spectacular success of this outstanding company has everything to do with its customer-centered and customer-directed strategies. Achieving total customer satisfaction by finding new and better ways to serve customers continues to be the vision of Federal Express.

THE PURPOSE OF A CUSTOMER-CENTERED VISION

Your customer-centered vision is not just a clear picture of how you will serve your customer's needs in the future, but an image of what your organization will eventually become. Your customer-centered vision serves two important purposes:

- It's a source of inspiration.
- It's a guide for decision making.

INSPIRATION

People today are in search of purpose. Your employees are, too. They want to know that their job is important and relevant, more than just a way to earn a paycheck. For most people, work is tied to their identity, self-image, and sense of worth.

Your company's customer-centered vision should inspire your employees to action. Employees should see themselves as important stakeholders in the development of your company. Inspiration occurs when employees are involved as owners of a customer-centered vision and are empowered to do whatever it takes to move from vision to reality.

Employees who are inspired by your company's customer-centered vision will be energized, motivated, and challenged to excellence by its power. The vision will also provide a single unifying purpose that will help develop a sense of teamwork.

DECISION MAKING

Important decisions affecting the company's future are sometimes difficult to make. Having a clear customer-centered vision of the future helps to provide a context. Everyone benefits when important individual and corporate decisions are made with the company's customer-centered vision guiding the way.

A well-defined customer-centered vision also acts like an organizational constitution. It guides the organization and unifies its functions to conform to a single goal. It becomes the point of reference by which everything else in the organization is ultimately evaluated. During times of conflict, it is the highest authority and becomes the final judge.

SCANDINAVIAN AIRLINE SYSTEMS

In 1981, Jan Carlzon became president of Scandinavian Airline Systems and within one year turned a $17 million loss into a $54 million profit. He transformed the airline by creating a customer-centered vision that made customer satisfaction a top priority.

"The only thing that counts in the new Scandinavian Airline Systems," said Carlzon, "is a satisfied customer. We are going to be the best airline in the world, and that means putting the customer first in everything we do."

The vision was preached, taught, and lived by airline executives and managers. Before long, every airline employee had caught the vision and knew exactly where the company was headed.

The vision became a guide and a rule for all decision making. Employees were encouraged, empowered, and excited by a vision that became their own. The result was one of the most successful turnaround stories in the annals of modern business.

Great customer-centered visions have tremendous power for change.

TIP

It's important to appreciate the difference between strategy and vision. Strategy is like a blueprint: It provides builders with a detailed description of each component of a project. Vision deals with a future in which important goals and objectives have been met, resulting in success for the company and opportunity for everyone involved. By its very nature, strategy can be uninspiring to some people. But great customer-centered visions are charged with excitement and result in inspiration and enthusiasm among workers.

DEVELOPING A CUSTOMER-CENTERED VISION STATEMENT

Developing a customer-centered *vision statement* isn't as difficult as it might seem. The objective isn't to create an impressive document that will wind up gathering dust on your managers' shelves. Customer-centered vision statements need to inspire, excite, and mobilize your entire workforce.

PLAIN ENGLISH

Vision statements are statements that briefly describe a company's commitment to customer service. They communicate, in a few well-chosen words, important company philosophy that undergirds practice.

Effective customer-centered vision statements are down-to-earth and easy to understand. Take a look at six of the most successful customer-centered vision statements ever produced:

- Quality Is Job One! (Ford Motor Company)
- Sell good merchandise at a reasonable profit, treat your customers like human beings, and they'll always come back for more. (L.L. Bean Company)
- Quality, Service, Cleanliness, Value. (McDonald's)
- Putting People First. (British Airways)
- Kyakka shoko (Best service). (Nippon Telephone)
- I have one, and only one, ambition for Chrysler; to be the best. What else is there? (Lee Iacocca, Chrysler Motor Company)

TIP

Consider creating a special work group to draft a customer-centered vision statement for approval by management. In preparing the statement, encourage the work group to talk with employees, supervisors, managers, and especially customers.

To develop an effective customer-centered vision of your own, begin by talking with customers to get their ideas on what your organization should look like in the future. What will they need from you? How could you serve them better? What could be done to make doing business with you easier and more efficient?

Then sit down with your management team and ask the following questions:

- What kind of company do we want to build? (Describe in as detailed a manner as possible what you want the company to look like in the future—in 1 year, 5 years, 10 years, etc.)
- How will our customers view us when we've achieved our vision? (In what ways will we serve them better? How easy will it be for them to do business with us? In what ways will we outperform the competition in terms of customer service?)
- How do we want to be known? (When people hear our company name, how do we want them to think of us?)
- What will our customers need from us in the future? (How will we meet those needs?)

■ What do we value most? (What do we really care about? How will our vision for the future affect each of these values? How do these values relate to the needs of our customers?)

■ How will our customer-centered vision change the way we operate internally? (How will our vision affect our practices?)

■ Does everyone in the company have a part to play in the future vision of the company? (What will we do to motivate employees to help achieve the vision? How will we keep the momentum going?)

Remember that you're not attempting to write a book, just a customer-centered vision statement that will encompass your company's customer-centered vision for the future. Keep your statement clear, concise, and meaningful to everyone in the company.

CAUTION

Examine your present mission statements and slogans to make sure that they are consistent with your customer-centered vision for the future. Are they aligned with your company's values and linked to the needs of your customers? If your present statements and slogans no longer fit, replace them with something fresh that communicates an exciting, meaningful vision for the future.

ARTICULATING THE VISION

After you've developed your customer-centered vision, impart it to management and staff. Your objective is to articulate the vision in a way that results in a shared commitment by everyone.

Commitment to the vision requires two important and ongoing functions:

■ Communication

■ Training

COMMUNICATION

Now that your customer-centered vision is developed, the most important thing you can do as a leader is to talk about it and encourage your managers to do the same. Call a general staff meeting and tell your employees about the company's vision that many of them helped produce; write about it in official company newsletters, brochures, or other periodicals. Don't let a day go by without communicating the vision.

As you begin to formulate a strategy, set challenging goals and objectives that will help achieve the vision. Communicate those goals and objectives in ways that demonstrate how every employee is an important contributor. Emphasize the vision, and make it real.

Celebrate milestones on your way to achieving the vision. Reward exceptional effort on the part of individuals and teams, and do it publicly. Make each celebration a time of renewal of individual commitments to the vision. Communicate over and over the idea that the success of the company, and the success of each employee, depends on achieving the vision.

And most important, communicate commitment to the vision by your personal actions and those of your managers and supervisors. Walk the walk; don't just talk the talk. Communicate by your actions that things really are going to be different from now on.

Do you really mean what you say? Seeing is believing.

TRAINING

To achieve your customer-centered vision, your managers and staff will need training—lots of it. In fact, every formal or semiformal gathering of employees should include some form of training that relates directly to the customer-centered vision. Unit meetings, departmental meetings, general staff meetings, all present important opportunities for training.

Here are some of the best topics included in most successful ongoing customer-centered training programs:

- Product knowledge (including customer applications)
- Telephone skills and etiquette
- Helping the difficult customer
- Expressing empathy
- Achieving mutual agreement in problem solving
- De-escalation techniques in dealing with angry customers
- Active problem solving
- Assertiveness training
- Managing conflict with co-workers
- Promises and follow-up
- Selling with service
- What you can do when you can't say "yes"
- Saying "no" without offending the customer
- Teamwork

Of course, there are many more topics that can be used in customer-focused training. Search them out and use them.

When your employees know what's expected (through training), why it's expected (to achieve the vision), and what their reward will be for achievement (company and individual success), they are much more likely to see themselves as key players. That's what it takes to achieve their commitment.

TIP

Consider selecting a team made up of employees and managers to formulate training activities over the period of a year or two. Make sure that employees have direct input into the planning process to avoid having the plan labeled "the boss's."

Devote whatever time it takes to develop, communicate, and reinforce your company's customer-centered vision. A company's success in the marketplace is in almost direct proportion to its ability to define itself internally and externally by a well-crafted, customer-centered vision statement.

THE 30-SECOND RECAP

- Every great company started with a great company vision.
- Your company's vision should be customer-centered and specific about how the company will outperform the competition in the area of customer service.
- Your company's customer-centered vision will inspire and guide you every step of the way.
- After your company's customer-centered vision is developed, you need to preach it, teach it, and practice it publicly.

What's Your Business?

In this section, you learn how to gain an advantage over the competition by recognizing that service is the real product of your business. You also learn 10 common ways in which companies tell their customers they're not important.

EXCEPTIONAL SERVICE IS THE KEY

Knapp's Restaurant is an institution in the city of Tacoma, Washington. Getting a table sometimes means waiting in line for 10 minutes or more. And Knapp's is always busy, no matter what time of day or night you arrive.

Over the years, Knapp's Restaurant has gained an outstanding reputation for excellent food, generous portions, and prices that are among the lowest in the area. But the real secret of their success is that years ago Knapp's recognized that they weren't in the food and beverage business—they were in the service business! Excellent food and low prices were just a couple of the ways they could serve their customers, means to an end. Knapp's learned early on that their principal product was service, and this understanding has made all the difference. It's the very heart of their success and is the reason their customers walk away thinking "Wow!"

Whatever your business—banking, manufacturing, investments, travel—it's critical to your success to understand that, first and foremost, you're in the service business. And when you provide excellence in service, sales results inevitably follow. Exceptional service creates increases in sales, and sales result in growth for your business.

DEVELOPING EXCEPTIONAL SERVICE

Developing exceptional customer service in your business isn't difficult. It doesn't require a knowledge of advanced business principles, nor does it demand the use of complex and sophisticated formulas and planning mechanisms.

CAUTION

Resist the idea that customer service is a "job function" or "department" within the company. The development of exceptional customer service in your company requires a real commitment on the part of everyone to make service your company's principal product.

What it does require is the completion of three important tasks:

- Knowing "why"
- Managing customer impressions
- Knocking down the barriers

Coupling these three tasks with a commitment to reorient your thinking and that of your employees to the idea that service is your principal product will lead your organization to customer service excellence.

Knowing "Why"

Have you ever noticed that people never make real changes in their lives until they have a personal investment in making a change?

People need compelling reasons to make significant changes—and those reasons need to have personal meaning for them. That's why most people think about dieting when spring and summer months approach. Why? Because most people want to look good in bathing suits and in other summer fashions. Looking good is a compelling reason to endure the difficulties that come with dieting.

Exceptional customer service means that you and your employees are going to have to work harder and do more to please your customers. Everyone must go beyond the call of duty to ensure that customers are pleased enough to say "Wow!"

What are the compelling reasons for your employees to perform in this manner? What are the personal benefits attached? Why should they do the things that will cause customers to remain loyal and tell others about your business?

Give your employees the "why" for exceptional customer service by rewarding them and recognizing them accordingly. Behavior that is rewarded is repeated. Think about featuring a customer service employee of the month in your company newsletter. Tell your people exactly what special customer service the employee provided to receive the honor. Provide that person with a dinner for two, or a special parking slot for the month, or some other tangible expression of your appreciation. And don't forget to include an employee's customer service skills in regular employee evaluations. Make it clear that there is a direct relationship between customer service excellence and raises or promotions with your company.

Managing Customer Impressions

Customer impressions of your company are important. The customer service goal of every company should be to favorably impress a customer every time he or she comes into contact with any aspect of the company, regardless of how seemingly insignificant or remote. And this goal should apply to both internal and external customers.

Managing customer impressions means identifying *moments of truth*—potential points of customer contact—and identifying ways to favorably impress the customer at each of those points.

Moments of truth can occur anytime and anywhere customers, or potential customers, have contact with a representative of your company. When a potential customer asks a financial advisor what's involved in an IRA rollover, that's a moment of truth for the company that stockbroker represents. When an irate customer arrives at your company's doorstep, there's a moment of truth that begins with the first individual he or she meets.

Each moment of truth involves a very short period of time (40 seconds or less) during which a customer forms an impression of the quality of service provided by your company. This impression governs the remainder of the customer contact. What's more, studies have shown that it takes as long as two years before people forget the impression formed by their first moment of truth with a company.

PLAIN ENGLISH

Moment of truth is a customer service term created by Jan Carlzon of Scandinavian Airlines. Carlzon defined a moment of truth as "an episode in which a customer comes in contact with any aspect of the company, however remote, and thereby has an opportunity to form an impression."

Considering each moment of truth in your business, what does it take to make your customers say "Wow!"? What would it take to ensure that this level of service would be consistently offered? What are you willing to do by way of providing reward and recognition for this level of customer service?

TIP

Why not ask your employees to help define what it takes to favorably impress customers at each moment of truth? Make your employees a real part of designing exceptional strategies for customer service.

KNOCKING DOWN THE BARRIERS

In your quest to develop exceptional customer service, you will inevitably encounter barriers along the way. Don't panic, and, whatever you do, don't let barriers discourage you. The only path that has no barriers is the path that leads nowhere.

You may encounter three kinds of barriers:

- People
- Policy
- Process

PEOPLE

It's unfortunate, but true, that some people in your organization will resist becoming more service-oriented in their thinking and work. These are the same people who will not favor the creation of a customer service culture, and who may even work to undermine the customer-centric efforts of the company.

When these people make themselves known, you should probably encourage them to find employment elsewhere. Their attitude toward the company's customer service efforts will be the attitude they show your customers. This kind of employee is too costly to keep.

Make sure your employees understand that your new approach to customer service isn't just a flash in the pan, that it's more than just another new program designed to make them work harder and longer. It's vital that employees recognize the real commitment on the part of management to create a customer-centered and -driven organization. And make sure that your employees understand that the company's success, as well as their personal success with the company, depends upon how well customers are treated.

TIP

Involve your employees in helping to identify barriers to exceptional customer service within your organization. When the barriers are identified, ask employees to suggest ways to overcome them.

POLICY

If yours is the kind of business governed by formal policies, review them. Oftentimes, formal policy statements interfere with providing exceptional customer service. Be particularly mindful of policies that disempower employees, inflexible policies that prevent efficient customer service, and policies requiring numerous approval points that create a restrictive bureaucracy frustrating to employees and customers alike.

When you encounter policies that restrict the ability of your employees to provide exceptional customer service, eliminate those policies. If a policy can't be eliminated, change it so that it's no longer in opposition to your customer service objectives.

Remember: Your most important policy is to provide the customer with exceptional service. Every other policy in your organization must conform itself accordingly.

PROCESS

How easy is it for customers to do business with you—before, during, and after the sale? That's an important question and one you'll need to answer if your goal is to provide exceptional customer service.

Examine your company's processes that directly involve customers. Are they customer-friendly? Do they involve miles of red tape? Are they unnecessarily complex? Do they help, or hinder, your efforts to provide exceptional customer service?

Don't do what James, the owner of a small, not-for-profit community organization used to do. He offered members of various community groups the opportunity to bring their problems and concerns directly to him. That sounded great, but the truth of the matter was that it was nearly impossible to reach him by phone. So he instructed his staff to redirect callers to the appropriate people, depending upon the nature of the call.

James had attempted to improve customer service by offering an "open door" to anyone with a problem. What he ended up creating was a customer service nightmare. People who had been promised direct access to the boss were shuffled off to underlings, and were offended by that kind of treatment.

The matter was finally resolved when James's staff provided him with a brochure listing each department head, together with a description of the services they provide and their phone numbers. He could still promise that problems would be resolved quickly, but instead of directing people to himself he sent them to the people who needed to get involved.

Reengineer and retool every process that complicates life for your customers and hinders the resolution of their problems quickly and efficiently. Make your processes work for you by designing them with your customer in mind. Design the kind of processes that cause your customers to say "Wow!"

WAL-MART'S COMMITMENT TO EXCEPTIONAL CUSTOMER SERVICE

In 1962, when Sam Walton opened his first store in Rogers, Arkansas, he never dreamed that his company would become one of the largest corporations in America. But that's exactly what happened.

Walton's business philosophy was simple: If you structure a retail sales organization around the customer by providing top-quality merchandise at low everyday prices, with unquestionable customer service, the company is bound to succeed. And it is this same wise customer-centered business philosophy that continues to guide and propel Wal-Mart into the twenty-first century.

Wal-Mart's commitment to customer service is more than just lip service or ad copy. This company really understands that service is their chief product. And Wal-Mart goes out of its way to ensure that its service to customers is exceptional beyond measure.

Consider the depth of Wal-Mart's customer service commitment. To provide customers with quality merchandise and the best possible price, Wal-Mart gets deeply involved with its more than 65,000 suppliers, helping them to stream-line their operations and cut costs. Wal-Mart examines every penny that their suppliers spend. Lee Scott, Wal-Mart's chief executive officer, says he is com-mitted to "driving unnecessary costs out of businesses."

The result: Wal-Mart's suppliers benefit from the management expertise of America's premier retailer; Wal-Mart benefits because it's able to offer prod-ucts at the best possible prices; and customers (most of whom never even real-ize the effort Wal-Mart has made in their behalf) benefit from the savings. Everybody wins.

With that kind of customer-centered commitment, it's no wonder that Wal-Mart is America's top retailer. Service really is their principal product.

TEN WAYS TO TELL YOUR CUSTOMER "WE DON'T CARE!"

Wal-Mart's situation also happens in reverse: Many companies started with the idea of becoming one of the largest corporations in America but ended up falling flat on their corporate posteriors. They were long on dreams but short on real customer-centered focus and commitment. What's worse, most of them, in one way or another, told their customers "We don't care!"

Here are 10 common ways that companies tell their customers "We don't care":

1. **They take their customers for granted.** Even simple courtesies like saying "Good morning," "Let me know if I can be of help," or even "Thank you! We appreciate your business" are absent. Customers interpret the lack of these niceties to mean that the company has come to expect their business or doesn't need it. The message is clear: "We don't care!" Stop showing your customers that you appre-ciate and care about them, and they'll go away in droves.

2. **They make it difficult for customers to do business with them.** You don't have to look far to find an abundance of companies that have acquired real skill in this regard. Sam, a small business owner, wanted to secure a second business line for his consulting practice. He phoned his service provider and was greeted by an automated telephone routing system that had him on the line for more than 20 minutes. When he finally reached the end of their annoying list of

menu options ("Press 1 if you're still there"), he received a recorded announcement telling him that the office had closed 10 minutes earlier and would he please call back tomorrow. Their message to him was clear: "We don't care!" He never ordered that second line.

3. **They don't listen to their customers.** Customers are told what they should want and why they should want it. Customers are never asked for feedback, and only rarely are they consulted about what they really want. Customers will tell you how to please them if you just let them do so. But you'll never hear what a customer wants unless you're willing to listen. When you fail to listen to your customer, your message is clear: "We don't care!"

4. **They run ads that say customer service is their strength, but the reality is something else.** This becomes evident to a customer almost immediately. The message is as insulting as it is ludicrous: "We don't care about what you think—we can buy a reputation for customer service excellence." But that strategy always fails. An abundance of companies in the boneyard of broken dreams have learned that lesson the hard way.

5. **They depend heavily on voicemail.** Humans don't answer the phone—at least, not most of the time. Customers leave messages and never receive timely calls back. A voicemail system is one of the most expensive pieces of equipment a company can own. The vast majority of customers hate it! Customers are given the impression that they're not important enough to be put in contact with a "real person." The message is "We don't care!"

CAUTION

If you use a voicemail system, be sure to monitor how it's being used by employees. Phones that aren't answered by the third ring, systems in which talking with a live person isn't an option, complaints from customers indicating that phone messages aren't being answered—all are red flags that should prompt further investigation.

6. **They treat customers with disrespect.** Disrespectful staff can cost your business everything. Whenever a customer leaves an encounter with your business without his or her dignity intact, the likelihood of that person remaining your customer is slim. Even when customers are obviously wrong, they deserve to be treated with respect. Arguing with a customer is a fatal error. You can win the argument, but you

will lose the customer. Not much of a win. Showing disrespect for a customer is saying "We don't care!"

7. **They judge customers based on their perceived importance.** Nothing tells a customer that you don't really care faster than the second-best treatment. Instead of making every customer feel special and important, some companies cater to a particular market—for example, the extremely wealthy—and make everyone else feel inferior. Their message is clear: "We don't care!"

8. **They aren't proactive about problem solving.** Customers want you to care about them. When you discover a problem that you know will affect them, they expect you to take the initiative and notify them of it. When that doesn't happen, and customers find out you knew about the problem, the message is clear: "We don't care!" A few years ago, Firestone tires used on Ford Explorers were in the news. Not only did the tire have a long history of failing, especially in warm climates, evidence then surfaced that the manufacturer knew about the flaw for years and chose to do nothing. It will be a long while before the public forgets the message conveyed by Firestone's actions.

9. **They don't train their staff.** Staff who don't understand the product and haven't been trained to serve customers can do serious damage. When you don't train staff, you set them up for failure—and set your customer up for substantial irritation. Untrained staff send a clear message: "We don't care!"

10. **They allow staff to serve the customers while ignoring them.** Customers changed grocery stores simply because the checkout clerk insisted on carrying on a conversation with a fellow employee while scanning an order. That's inappropriate and rude. Customers deserve the full attention of the person serving them. When that doesn't happen, the message is unmistakable: "We don't care!"

Be conscious of the underlying message you're giving your customers. Make sure that it represents the way you really feel about them.

THE 30-SECOND RECAP

- Regardless of what business you're in, service is your principal product.
- Developing exceptional customer service requires a paradigm shift in which you redefine your business as a service business.
- Knowing why changes should be made, managing customer impressions, and knocking down barriers are tasks that lead to exceptional customer service.

■ Be careful of the underlying message your company is sending to customers. Make sure the message is "We really care about you. You're the most important person in our company!"

Meeting (and Exceeding) Customer Expectations

In this section, you learn the importance of communicating with your customers, and the six steps for turning complaints into opportunities that can strengthen your relationship with customers.

LEARNING FROM CUSTOMERS

What do your customers think about your product or service? You'll never know until you ask them. Learning how customers and potential customers feel about your product is where your quest for exceptional customer service begins.

HARLEY-DAVIDSON

Some years ago, the Harley-Davidson Company was experiencing a severe drop in sales. In spite of the quality of their motorcycles, people weren't buying them. Management was baffled.

Vaughn Beals, Harley-Davidson CEO, decided to find out why the company's motorcycles were no longer selling. Beals asked his senior management team to dress like bikers and join him on the road. Their journey took them to biker rallies and other events where they talked with customers and potential customers about what people really want in a motorcycle.

When the executives returned home, they had an abundance of fresh new ideas that were based on the expectations of bikers from coast to coast. Willie G. Davidson, vice president of styling, selected the best of those ideas and incorporated them into a plan for redesign. Some of the changes that would be made included more chrome, a shorter chassis, and sculpted gas tanks.

By learning exactly what bikers wanted, and by adapting the product to meet their expectations, executives turned around sales of Harley-Davidson motorcycles. Before long, the company had secured 60 percent of the domestic motorcycle market. It's no accident that today the name Harley-Davidson is synonymous with "exceptional quality" and "fine workmanship."

DISCOVERING WHAT CUSTOMERS EXPECT

If you don't know what your customers expect of your organization and its products, you'll never be able to give it to them. Meeting customer expectations—and exceeding them when possible—is what enables your organization not only to survive but to prosper.

Your customers are your best source of ideas and suggestions for improving product and service quality. They will tell you how you're doing as a company, about what works and what doesn't, about how their needs are changing and what your company can do to meet those changing needs, and about who in your company is "doing it right" and who needs additional training. Think of your customers as a source of guidance that will help you direct the future of your company.

There are several ways to determine what your customers expect: surveys, focus groups, advisory boards, conversations, and complaints. You may choose to use any of these methods or, better still, several methods simultaneously. How you tune in to your customers isn't what's important. Listening to what they have to tell you is.

SURVEYS

Surveys can be a useful source of customer service information. If they are administered correctly, they can help you monitor the pulse of your company. But unless you have staff with advanced degrees in statistical analysis, consider engaging the services of a professional marketing company.

Here are some important questions you need to answer before you can develop a survey that will yield worthwhile data:

- **What do I want to measure?** For example, if you want to gauge *customer satisfaction,* construct a survey that compares your customer's opinion of how well you performed with the customer's predictive expectations. If you want to measure *perceived quality,* construct a survey that compares your customer's perception of what happened with his or her ideal expectations (what should have happened).

PLAIN ENGLISH

A **customer satisfaction** survey is a construct that compares what actually takes place in a given situation with what a customer thought would happen. Typical customer responses include comments like, "What I received was not what I expected to receive"; "I can always count on your company to do what's right"; "Your product didn't do for me what your advertisements said it would." The purpose is to determine whether your product or service met your customer's expectations.

PLAIN ENGLISH

Perceived quality is a survey construct that attempts to compare the customer's perception of what happened with what the customer feels should have happened ideally. Customers express perceived quality with statements like, "Ideally, you should have ..."; "When I booked my meeting at your five-star hotel, I expected ..."; "I expected more from a company considered the best in the business." The purpose of the construct is to determine whether your product or service meets your customer's ideal expectations.

- **Whom do I survey?** Some companies limit survey activity to external customers only. However, many more have learned the value of including internal staff in customer service surveys. The reason is simple: Employees who feel they are treated well by their employers will usually treat customers in the same manner.

- **What kind of survey do I want to conduct?** There are many types of surveys that your company may want to consider: *customer exit* surveys that focus on asking customers questions as they leave your premises; *targeted* surveys that measure specific types of accounts; *random* customer surveys in which randomly selected customers are asked to respond; *internal attitude* surveys that provide a measurement of internal satisfaction among employees; and *lost-account* surveys directed to customers who no longer do business with your firm.

- **Which method should I use?** There are several possibilities: *face-to-face interviews* (excellent, but costly); *telephone interviews* (not quite as costly, but time-consuming); *questionnaires* by mail (the least costly, but response rates can be problematic). Alternatively, some companies have found that the best results are achieved when a number of survey methods are used simultaneously.

- **Who should administer the survey?** This is the most important question of all, and one you should consider carefully. Unless you have staff who are trained in the science of constructing and conducting surveys, consider using a consultant or marketing firm. It's true that doing so increases the cost of surveying, but the quality and reliability of the information you obtain will usually be worth the cost. Remember that information obtained from a professionally conducted survey is critical to the future of your business. View this expense as an investment in your company's future.

Focus Groups

Focus groups usually consist of a small number of customers (8 to 10) who participate in a roundtable discussion about specific service-related issues. The company is represented by one or two managers who act as moderators for the session. Discussions normally continue for a predetermined length of time, rarely extending beyond two hours.

Focus groups work best when they are held off-site. Participants always seem more at ease in hotel meeting rooms or other neutral locations. Be sure to have plenty of refreshments on hand, and consider including a breakfast or lunch with your meeting. Combining a meal with your focus group meeting is a great way to thank participants. Most hotels offer meeting space at no cost to groups that include a meal function.

If you hire a consulting or marketing firm to gather information from customers, be sure to include a representative of that firm in every focus group meeting. Ask the consultant to suggest questions that will help you assess the level of customer satisfaction while exploring ideas for improvement and growth.

TIP

Employee focus groups are also beneficial. Product- or service-related questions and problems are identified and discussed, together with other issues affecting the workplace. Employee focus groups are especially effective when they are part of an ongoing staff survey project that seeks to keep a finger on the company's pulse, both internal and external.

Advisory Boards

Advisory boards offer the company a unique and powerful way to communicate with customers. These boards are made up of selected customers who regularly meet with company representatives to identify and resolve service-related problems. Advisory boards often become sounding boards for the company and unofficial (but powerful) advocates for all customers doing business with a company.

Conversations

Knowing what's important to customers in general is vital to the success of your business. But knowing the details about a specific customer's needs, wants, and desires gives you the ability to provide exceptional service. One-on-one conversations are the best way to discover those important details.

Ichiorou Suzuki, the chief engineer in charge of designing the Lexus for Toyota, understood the value of one-on-one customer conversations. Suzuki insisted that, as an integral part of the design process, several weeks needed to be spent talking with the company's customers in the United States.

Suzuki wasn't attempting to determine the level of customer satisfaction with Toyota. Instead, he wanted to learn some personal information about his U.S. customers: what they liked and disliked, what their hobbies were, what they valued, and so on. Based on the information he obtained through those conversations, Suzuki concluded that the American consumer was more hard-working and conservative than the company had believed. As a result, he designed the interior of the Lexus to provide a soft and comfortable environment.

Lexus understands the value of one-on-one contact. In fact, maintaining one-on-one communication with its customers is so important that Lexus requires each of its U.S. employees to talk with at least one Lexus owner each week. The information obtained from customers as a result of these calls helps Lexus to continually improve its product.

The Ritz-Carlton Hotel chain is another company that prides itself on one-on-one customer contact. Every employee of the hotel is asked to document the unique requirements and special requests of each guest. This information is entered into the hotel chain's computer system and is accessible by every Ritz-Carlton hotel throughout the world.

As a result of the Ritz-Carlton's one-on-one dialogue with guests, service can be tailored and personalized to meet the specific needs of each customer. As the guest's needs change, those changes are input into the system for future reference by other hotels in the chain.

It's no accident that the Ritz-Carlton is a winner of the prestigious Baldrige Award for world-class service. The organization prides itself on building and maintaining relationships with its customers through ongoing one-on-one dialogue. Five-star customer service is the result.

COMPLAINTS

Complaints are misunderstood by many businesses today. Instead of considering a complaint as an opportunity to engage in meaningful dialogue with a customer, many companies view it as a menace to be avoided at all costs. That kind of thinking is not just unfortunate, it's more costly than the average company realizes.

A few years ago, the Travelers Insurance Company conducted an in-depth study of customer complaints. The study concluded that only 9 percent of those who did not complain about a defective product or service costing $100 or more would ever do business with the company again. But 82 percent of those who complained, and whose complaints were dealt with quickly and satisfactorily, would continue to patronize the business.

What does this mean? It means that complaints are unmistakably an opportunity that needs to be understood and exploited.

Complaints not only offer an opportunity to engage in meaningful dialogue with a customer, but also provide the company with valuable information about its products and services. Complaints signal the need to refine a product or develop something new. They also furnish insight about service-related difficulties that need to be corrected.

Well-managed companies today do more than welcome complaints; they invest in them. They understand that for every customer who complains there are approximately 26 who don't, most of whom will never do business with the company again. As a result, these companies actively solicit customer complaints and make it easy for customers to be heard.

Some companies install dedicated toll-free telephone lines to help customers complain. Others solicit complaints by phoning customers to ask whether they're having problems with the company's products or services. These companies have learned that investing in customer complaints is good business.

General Electric has been a pioneer in soliciting customer complaints. Every General Electric appliance now comes with a service manual that lists a toll-free number to call if customers have questions or need help with any kind of problem. Not only has this effort resulted in significant goodwill, but the company has benefited from warranty savings as well. What's more, callers frequently purchase additional products as a result of information provided during their conversation with the company.

General Electric estimates that each toll-free call costs between $2.50 and $4.50. But savings in service calls and profits from new sales generated as a result of the program offset the costs involved and provide an additional center of profit.

When complaints are handled expeditiously and with skill, most customers will be satisfied and remain loyal. That's important because, according to a study done by the U.S. Office of Consumer Affairs, it costs seven times more to acquire a new customer than it does to keep an existing one. What's more, according to a multi-industry study conducted by Harvard Business School, increasing a company's customer retention rate by as little as 5 percent can boost company profits by as much as 85 to 100 percent!

YOUR CUSTOMERS' EXPECTATIONS FOR RECOVERY

When things go wrong, your customers have expectations about what you need to do to recover. How you recover when a mistake has been made is vital to your company's future.

Service recovery is so important that every frontline employee should be thoroughly trained in it. Furthermore, given the importance of recovery to your company, recovery procedures should be reviewed and reinforced often.

When mistakes are made or when customer feedback indicates that a problem has been experienced with your product or service, the manner in which you respond can turn a negative situation into a positive one. Turning disappointment into customer satisfaction is what service recovery is all about.

SIX STEPS TO EFFECTIVE RECOVERY

An effective and customer-satisfying service recovery involves six steps:

1. **Listen empathetically and actively.** The key word is *listen.* Step out of your role as a company representative and view the problem from the customer's standpoint. Be nonjudgmental—don't talk about what the customer should have done to avoid the problem. Practice *active-listening* skills, and ask *open questions* that encourage the customer to talk. Be understanding and compassionate; demonstrate that you care about making things right. Allowing customers to vent their frustrations is a vital part of recovery.

PLAIN ENGLISH

Open questions are questions that can't be answered with a simple "yes" or "no." They often begin with phrases such as "Tell me about ..." or "Describe what happened when ...." The purpose of open questions is to obtain the information necessary to solve a customer problem by encouraging the customer to talk freely.

PLAIN ENGLISH

Active listening is a technique with origins in the field of psychotherapy that helps assure customers you're listening to them intently. Active listening means encouraging customers to talk freely by reflecting back to them the meaning of their communication, both verbal and nonverbal, in ways that promote further exploration and awareness. For example, "You're upset because our product doesn't seem to work properly when installed with your system." There's more on active listening later in this chapter.

2. **Apologize to the customer.** Someone once said, "Eating crow isn't pleasant, no matter how much mustard and ketchup you put on it. But the sooner you eat it, the less unpleasant it is to the taste." Tell the customer you're sorry for whatever mistake has been made. By saying "I'm sorry," you acknowledge responsibility and support the customer, two critical steps in recovery.

3. **Fix the problem.** After you've listened to your customer's explanation of the problem, allowed him or her to vent frustrations, and apologized, it's time to fix what went wrong. Let your customer tell you what it will take to make things right. Tell your customer, "We value your business and want to keep you as a customer. What can we do to solve the problem and make things right?" Then quickly resolve the problem in a way that satisfies your customer. Remember that the more quickly you resolve the matter, the more likely you'll keep your customer.

4. **Offer a value-added atonement.** In addition to fixing the problem, give your customer something. Even if your value-added gift is more symbolic than valuable, it's important. The customer will remember your extra consideration, no matter what it is, long after the problem has been forgotten. Exceeding a customer's expectations communicates a message that you value the customer and want to do what's right.

CAUTION

It's important that frontline people who deal with customer complaints have broad authority to resolve problems on the spot. Review your company's policies and procedures and eliminate as much red tape as possible.

5. **Keep your promises.** When promises are made to customers, they must be kept. Making promises that can't be kept not only adds fuel to the fire, but also wipes out your other efforts to resolve the issue and causes your customer to defect. Make absolutely sure that your employees understand what they can and cannot deliver.

6. **Follow up.** Nothing demonstrates concern and commitment more than a follow-up contact after the problem has been resolved. A simple phone call to the customer, checking to see that a problem has been resolved to his or her satisfaction, is impressive. Unfortunately, follow-up contacts are often viewed as optional—a nice thing to do if time permits. Big mistake. A short follow-up call is an important part of the recovery process and should never be neglected.

Remember that in the eyes of the customer, you and your business are only as good as your last interaction. Your company may have provided exceptional service in the past; however, if the most recent interaction was negative, your customer will think of your business in negative terms.

Mistakes do happen. But when they do, you have the ability to manage your company's recovery. Exceed your customer's expectations by following the steps in this section, and show that you really care. That's how to turn a negative situation into a positive encounter.

THE 30-SECOND RECAP

- Discovering what your customers expect is the first step in developing products and services that they want.

- Maintaining a dialogue with your customers is the best way to keep abreast of potential service problems and to learn about changing needs in the marketplace.

- No matter how diligent your efforts, mistakes will occasionally happen. But when they do, it's imperative that the company recover quickly and professionally.

- There are six steps to recovery that will ensure exceptional customer service.

Keeping Your Customers in the Driver's Seat: Part 1

In this section, you learn how to design a down-to-earth service delivery process that is totally customer-centric. You also learn about 10 tools for building intimate, mutually beneficial, long-term customer relationships.

RESPONDING TO CUSTOMER NEEDS

A few years ago, the national news carried a story about a little-known crate-and-barrel manufacturer from Connecticut that was closing its doors after having been in business for more than 100 years. In its heyday, this manufacturer was considered a major employer in the state in which it operated. Now, the payroll had shrunk to only eight people, each of whom was an old-world–style craftsperson. Most had started with the company as apprentices and were now nearly ready to retire.

At one time, the company was busy meeting the needs of its customers. Customers had to place their orders with the company well in advance to ensure an adequate supply of packaging materials, and for years the demand exceeded supply and the business thrived.

But as the years went by, fewer and fewer companies used wooden crates and barrels for packaging. Reinforced cardboard had gradually absorbed the market once controlled by the manufacturers of wooden crates and barrels.

The company responded to its dwindling market by downsizing through attrition—not replacing workers who retired or who left for other reasons. But finally, in late 1999, it became clear that the day of the wooden crate and barrel had passed into history. It was time to close shop.

The needs of customers who once packaged their products in wooden crates and barrels had changed, but the crate-and-barrel maker hadn't changed along with them. In the final year of the twentieth century, this company was still committed to nineteenth-century business practices. The failure of the enterprise was inevitable; even a casual observer could have predicted it many years before.

Responding to the changing needs of customers is essential to the survival of any enterprise. *Putting customers in the driver's seat*—letting their changing needs dictate the future of your company—is just good business!

THE 30-SECOND RECAP

- The needs of your customers change over time. Successful companies respond to those changing needs by providing quality products and services that are competitively priced.

- An effective service delivery process requires an understanding of the role of customer perception and a commitment to helping each customer achieve a positive experience.

- Perception defines your customers' experience with your company, and there are specific ways to ensure that the customers' perception is positive.

- Remember the value of empathizing with your customers, partnering with your customers, and recovering with style.

Keeping Your Customers in the Driver's Seat: Part 2

In this section, you learn about customer feedback and measurement strategies for evaluating your company's services, and about the value of benchmarking.

WORLD-CLASS DELIVERY

Keeping your customers in the driver's seat requires management strategies that will ensure the proper functioning of your service delivery systems. Management models for world-class service delivery include:

- Methods of gathering specific information about the quality of service delivery, including both customer feedback and objective measurement

- Measurement results that are compared against established benchmarks

- Results that are scoreboarded (made visible to every employee of your organization) so that every internal stakeholder has an opportunity to evaluate his or her performance and correct deficiencies

- Opportunities to learn from your customers what you need to improve on

- A means of identifying and solving problems, concerns, weaknesses, and deficiencies on an ongoing basis

Remember that the delivery management process is ongoing. A process of ongoing measurement, evaluation, learning, and adjustment will keep your customers in the driver's seat and provide you with the information you need to respond to service delivery problems or changes in your customer needs.

CUSTOMER FEEDBACK AND MEASUREMENT

The first step in an effective delivery management process is actively soliciting customer feedback. Feedback enables you to develop *customer-focused measurements* and standards that let you know exactly how you're doing. Feedback is not a one-time or every-now-and-then exercise, but an ongoing process. Here's why:

Only 4 percent of customers who experience service problems with your company will tell you about them. That means that 96 percent of your dissatisfied customers will suffer in silence as far as you're concerned. However, it doesn't mean they won't tell others.

PLAIN ENGLISH

Customer-focused measurement is the comparison of customer expectations with actual company performance. For example, if customers expect deliveries within 24 hours of purchase, that number is compared with the actual delivery time and a determination is made of the number of times that the 24-hour expectation was actually met.

Research has repeatedly demonstrated that this dissatisfied group of customers tells an average of nine other people about the "horrible" service they experienced the last time they did business with your company. And those nine people will each tell another five people about the "horrors" of doing business with your company.

I shudder to think of the numbers of people who will eventually share the "nightmare" with others—and how the "hellish experience" will grow in negativity along the way.

CAUTION

Here's one of the most important principles of customer service: If a customer thinks there's a problem, there's a problem. Learn this principle, understand it, and teach it to every employee in your organization. And remember that problems are a matter of customer perception. You may or may not agree with your customer's perception.

Too often, problems perceived by a customer go unresolved simply because no one in the company knew they existed. The customer said nothing, but stopped doing business with your firm. Unresolved customer problems result in more and more of your customers being lost to the competition.

To avoid losing customers because of unresolved service problems, it's important to develop both formal and informal ways of soliciting and encouraging customer feedback. Although research shows that most customers who experience service problems will defect rather than complain, it also demonstrates that companies who solicit feedback from customers break down the barrier of silence. When problems identified in this manner are resolved quickly and fairly, customers remain loyal.

USE FORMAL FEEDBACK METHODS

It's a fact that you get what you inspect, not always what you expect. Measurement is a means of inspection. It is a method of feedback that helps you determine whether your organization is doing the things that will meet customer expectations.

Measurement is also an effective way to determine what your customers think about the service you provide. It also provides an opportunity for customers to let you know whether there's a problem. Measurement is an intelligence-gathering mechanism that helps your company stay on track.

It's important to formally and continually measure key performance factors and compare them to the customer-focused standards set by the company. For example, if your company has established the standard of answering the telephone by the third ring, a measurement should be established that monitors the standard.

Customer-focused standards are established by the company to ensure excellence in the treatment of its customers. Responding to mail from customers within 36 hours is a customer-focused standard, and one that is monitored by logs of incoming and outgoing customer mail.

Transactional standards are equally important but much more difficult to measure because they involve the face-to-face dimensions of customer contact and include such aspects as being friendly and helpful, being empathetic, using active-listening methods, and so on. Transactional standards are often measured via supervisory observation ("Your call may be monitored for customer service purposes").

Outcome standards are objective and easily measurable. They can be measured quantitatively (using numbers) and qualitatively (using subjective opinion and perception).

PLAIN ENGLISH

Customer-focused standards are the internal regulations that govern how a job is done. **Transactional standards** deal with customer interaction and are often expressed in such guidelines as "Reassure the customer that the problem will be resolved" or "Be friendly and courteous." **Outcome standards** focus on outcomes: "The customer complaint can be considered resolved only when;" "Twenty-four-hour delivery means that our product is actually in the hands of the customer within 24 hours."

TWO AREAS OF QUALITY MEASUREMENT

There are two general areas of measurement that help organizations monitor their quality of customer service: systems quality measurements, and customer quality measurements. Both types of measurement should be ongoing.

CAUTION

Many companies have elaborate systems quality measurements but few, if any, customer quality measurements. Although systems measurements are important indicators of how internal procedures and processes are functioning, they provide no information on customer perception. And it's the customer's perception about your service quality that determines your company's destiny. Internal systems should be defined by the needs of your customers and should support your efforts to satisfy customers.

Systems quality measurements help ensure that established processes continue to work effectively. They should be used in conjunction with customer quality measurements. Systems quality measurements are internal and seek information such as ...

- Was the customer's call answered on the first ring, the second ring, or the third ring?
- Was the item ready for shipment within four hours of taking the order? Was it shipped within eight hours of taking the order?
- What was the total turnaround time on the order?

Customer quality measurements relate directly to how well your company is meeting the expectations of its customers. Such measurements provide vital intelligence for corporate growth and development. These measurements are used to measure the quality of performance in areas defined by the customer as being essential, and to seek answers to questions such as ...

- How easy was it for the customer to do business with us? What obstacles made doing business with our organization difficult for the customer?

- Did the customer receive the product within 24 hours of taking the order?
- Was a shipment tracking number given to the customer along with verbal confirmation of the order?
- Was the billing presented in an understandable manner?
- Was the product well packaged for shipment?

BENCHMARKING

We live in a rapidly changing business environment. Never in the history of modern business has change occurred so rapidly.

With continuous change in the marketplace comes continuous change in operating practices. Companies desiring to become leaders in their industry can no longer afford to think they have all the answers, nor that they're capable of inventing the solutions necessary to meet marketplace challenges.

PLAIN ENGLISH

Benchmarking is an ongoing process of investigating and studying practices that produce exceptional results. Often, the task of benchmarking involves the careful examination of competitor practices.

In today's high-velocity marketplace, it's suicidal to attempt to reinvent what others have already learned to do. Leadership in the marketplace requires companies to "Adopt, adapt, and advance"—and to do so creatively!

Benchmarking studies the practices of other companies, including competitors, that have discovered how to perform a critical task in some manner that is qualitatively different and better than the way your organization performs the same task. When you've discovered a practice that will help you improve your product or service, borrow it and adapt it to fit your purposes. Benchmarking is a way to find new ideas to serve your customer better.

Benchmarking is the managerial tool that facilitates "creative adaptation." It's a catalyst that enables an enterprise to learn and improve quickly.

In some companies, benchmarking teams actively search for better operating systems that are targeted to specific critical functions such as billing, order entry and fulfillment, distribution, and the like. Benchmarking is also an advanced business concept with applications for high-level functions such as restructuring, financial management, and joint-venture management.

If you're not using benchmarking in your business, you're missing a powerful management tool that can help you achieve breakthrough performance improvements. You keep your customers in the forefront by providing them with the best of the best.

Benchmarking is a highly practical tool that is easily taught and easily grasped. It doesn't deal with abstract suppositions and concepts but focuses on finding real-world solutions to everyday business problems.

Here's an example of how benchmarking has been used:

In his book *Made in America,* Sam Walton wrote about the part that benchmarking played in the formation of Wal-Mart:

> The discount idea was in the future. We had only two choices: stay in the variety store business and be hit hard by the discounting wave, or open a discount store. So I started running all over the country, studying the concept, from the mill stores in the East to California, where Sol Price had started his Fed-Mart in 1955. I liked Sol's Fed-Mart name, so I latched right on to Wal-Mart. On July 2, 1962, we opened Wal-Mart No. 1 in Rogers, Arkansas, right down the road from Bentonville. We did a million dollars in a year.

Performance management is the process of managing and improving operations and involves both benchmarking and benchmarks. Benchmarking seeks new and better ways to serve your customer; benchmarks measure the performance of specific practices or systems. Top-performing companies rely on both benchmarking and benchmarks.

BENCHMARKS

Benchmarks are the operating measurements by which two or more systems or functions are compared and evaluated. Performance benchmarks involve comparison at several levels. Here are a few of the most common levels of comparison:

- Best-in-world
- Best-in-country
- Industry leader
- Industry norm
- Industry standard
- Best-in-company

PLAIN ENGLISH

An operating measurement that defines the level of performance of any given practice or system is a **benchmark.** Benchmarks can help identify hidden opportunities to innovate and improve performance.

The most critical functions to benchmark are those core functions that are of the highest strategic importance to the company. These benchmarks reflect best-in-class performance (best-in-industry, best-in-country, best-in-world, depending upon whether the business competes in national or global markets). Federal Express, for example, has identified 12 core functions that, according to their customer research, are of the utmost strategic importance. The company developed a measurement system based on these 12 functions, which it calls its Service Quality Indicator (SQI). Those measurements are watched very closely by managers at every level to ensure total customer satisfaction.

Other functions that are less strategically significant may also be benchmarked, but the benchmark level is usually less (best-in-company, industry standard, or norm). Benchmarks for support functions not critical to an organization's strategic advantage are often just internal measurements.

MEASURE WHAT'S CRITICAL TO SUCCESS

You can't measure every aspect of your business, but it's important to measure the aspect that is critical to the success of your business. For example, at Starbucks Coffee, management recognizes that inconsistent product quality and slow service are the two operating failures that could destroy their business. Starbucks, therefore, diligently measures and monitors these two significant performance factors.

What are the most important operating functions of your business? Why not establish appropriate benchmarks for those processes, systems, or functions? Then monitor and measure actual performance against established benchmarks.

Here are some helpful examples of critical performance benchmarks for customer service:

- Customer retention rates
- Customer repurchase rates
- Customer defection rates
- Customer satisfaction/dissatisfaction measures
- Customer ratings of sales and service personnel
- Customer ratings of delivery timeliness
- Customer ratings of product quality
- Customer ratings indicating the ease of doing business with the company

TIP

Through a program of ongoing measurement, you will identify those people who are doing an outstanding job of serving customers. Be sure to formally recognize those people in some meaningful way. Performance that's rewarded is repeated.

SCOREBOARDING

Scoreboarding is not just keeping score; it's broadcasting results so that everyone concerned is aware of what took place.

Make critical customer performance measurements available to everyone in your company. Whenever possible, break down these measurements into meaningful levels. For example, critical measurements will have special interest to company management, but you need to make them meaningful to the line worker as well. Therefore, in addition to measurements reflecting overall company performance in critical areas, let each division, section, and unit know how it measured up as well. For example, when Federal Express breaks down its late-delivery numbers to the various workgroups directly involved, it gives line staff and managers the information they need to make necessary improvements.

When important measurements are scoreboarded by operational unit, employees are given the chance to take ownership of the results. By directly observing his or her contribution, an employee can help maintain present levels of functioning or assist in correcting deficiencies. This kind of scoreboarding also can result in competition for excellence among operating units, which will help achieve even better results.

LEARNING

Managing the service delivery process involves a commitment to continuous learning. As a result of customer feedback and formal measurement, your customers will tell you what it is they want and whether you're providing it; they'll tell you what needs to be continued and what needs improvement; they'll tell you who is doing a good job and who isn't; and they'll tell you what you need to know to plan for the future.

Learning is a never-ending process. To achieve success today and in the future, you need to learn all you can about your customers and how your products or services can be modified to meet their changing needs. You need to learn about your competition—in depth—so that you know how they respond to the needs of customers and what they do to meet the same problems and challenges you encounter.

CONTINUOUS IMPROVEMENT—MAKING THE NECESSARY ADJUSTMENTS

Competing, surviving, and winning in the competitive business economy of the twenty-first century require an absolute commitment to continuous improvement. This commitment must come from top management and from every employee of the company.

Continuous improvement is not just a buzzword or a fad. It's a way of thinking, planning, working, and striving for excellence in every aspect of the business. It's a way of life.

Continually improving is like running a race with no finish line. It's an adventure that is both demanding and satisfying. It's demanding because it's a never-ending journey; it's satisfying because through each journey you discover new and innovative methods to enhance skills, processes, systems, procedures, and technologies, all of which ultimately enable you to serve your customer better, improve your market share, reduce cost, and improve your effectiveness.

Serve, measure, scoreboard, learn, and improve. This is the formula to successful customer service management—and the way to ensure that your customers remain in the driver's seat of your enterprise.

THE 30-SECOND RECAP

- Ninety-six percent of your dissatisfied customers will never tell you about their dissatisfaction, but they will tell an average of nine people about it—and those nine people will tell an average of five others.

- Develop a process for managing customer service delivery that ensures quality customer service by establishing methods of customer feedback and measurement.

- An effective model for managing service delivery includes ongoing measurement of core functions, benchmarking for best practices and benchmarks that provide target operational objectives, scoreboarding to communicate results, learning, and continuous improvement.

Participative Management

World-class businesses recognize the importance of exceptional customer service. They also understand that to provide exceptional service, everyone in the company needs to realize the importance of the customer and share in the commitment to excellence.

The Wal-Mart Company makes sure that new employees clearly understand the importance of customer service and that they share in Wal-Mart's commitment to excellence. Whether they've been hired as a store manager or a stock clerk, each new employee makes the following pledge:

> *From this day forward, I solemnly promise and declare that whenever a customer comes within 10 feet of me, I will smile, look them in the eye, and greet them, so help me Sam.*

New employees are then reminded of the immortal words of Sam Walton, the founder of Wal-Mart: "Remember, a promise we make is a promise we keep."

In this section, you learn that exceptional customer service is everyone's job—from the owner to the frontline worker—and that participative management techniques can promote a strong customer service culture.

Everyone's Responsibility

Achieving excellence in customer service doesn't happen by itself. It requires planning, training, and effort. But more than anything, it requires everyone in the organization working together to achieve the common goal of total customer satisfaction.

Exceptional customer service can't be achieved without teamwork, employee commitment and involvement, a sense of ownership in the final product, and a healthy working relationship between management and employees. Participative management is the key.

What Is Participative Management?

Participative management is a process in which managers and employees work together as peers to produce exceptional products and services that exceed customer expectations.

Participative management eschews typical lines of authority and enables employees to make decisions that affect the product purchased by the customer. Participative management stimulates productivity and innovation, and increases employee commitment to customer service throughout the organization. It also encourages employees to modify the functions of their work units to allow them to perform better for the sake of the final output. The result is a happier work force producing a better product, and improved customer service to boot.

PLAIN ENGLISH

Participative management is a process in which managers and employees work together as peers to produce exceptional products and services that exceed customer expectations.

Customer Service and Participative Management Techniques

Establishing a customer service culture that involves everyone in the company means a significant change will take place in your organization. Change is always difficult.

Most people want to feel in control of their environment. They will resist change unless they understand what is being changed and why, and have some input in the change process.

Informing employees of your intent and commitment to enhance the customer service emphasis of the organization is important. Basic education and training about the impact of customer service on the future of the company and its employees sets the stage.

Here are some important participative management techniques that will help bring about change in your organization:

■ Communicate, communicate, and communicate. Hold all-staff meetings to talk about customers and their role in determining the future of the company and its workers. Make sure these are dialogues in which everyone has an opportunity to share ideas and thoughts. Make sure that customer service is on the agenda every time there's a scheduled unit, departmental, or section meeting. Use every opportunity to talk about the importance of exceeding customer expectations.

■ Although everyone in your organization is responsible for exceptional customer service, frontline employees will be most affected by any change in customer service philosophy. Make them part of the changes by including them in every aspect of the process.

■ Form a customer service management team made up of frontline employees and representatives from management. Give the team the responsibility for recommending process changes to help the company achieve its customer service objectives. Sponsor training events for employees, and keep customer service matters paramount in the minds of employees.

■ Empower frontline workers to solve customer problems quickly and effectively. Empower supervisors to recognize and reward exceptional customer service and to address problems effectively and promptly. Make it a point to "catch people doing something right," and reward them accordingly.

In addition to the preceding techniques, a business owner has some special tasks to perform to promote a customer service culture. You need to …

■ Articulate its absolute commitment to building a customer-focused organization. Management needs to communicate levels of expectation and give overall direction to the effort.

- Communicate its vision for the future with its new emphasis on customer service. Talk about what that change will mean for the company and each of its employees. Demonstrate to employees why becoming a customer-driven company is important.

- Measure your organization's progress. Monitor results of your enhanced customer service efforts by using appropriate benchmarks. Make the results visually available to your entire organization (scoreboarding).

- Make adjustments or corrections when they're needed. Use benchmarking techniques to constantly be on the lookout for new and better practices that bring higher degrees of customer satisfaction.

- Motivate employees by focusing on job enrichment, empowerment, and decision making, and foster a participative environment in which innovation and creativity flourish.

- Provide everyone with the tools and skill-building training needed to do the job. Positive change will not occur unless those who must make the change are well equipped and properly prepared. Remember, too, that training for enhanced customer service shouldn't be viewed as a "one-shot" experience, but as an ongoing one. Companies should consider spending 10 percent of their annual advertising budget on customer service training.

- Inform your service providers of your customer service expectations. Tell them that you intend to hold them accountable for the outcomes outlined in your contracts with them. Develop a mechanism for monitoring the compliance of your service providers to ensure they're meeting your standards and outcomes are being met.

- Publicly reward those who do the job well. Take appropriate corrective action when necessary.

- Demonstrate your commitment to customer service in ways that are worthy of employee emulation.

- Establish a working environment in which communication is unrestricted. Actively listen to others' concerns and ideas about any aspect of the business. Empathize with the feelings, suggestions, and requests of others.

- Care about your employees by providing the necessary support mechanisms. For example, when it becomes obvious that employees need to improve performance, provide the necessary counseling, training, and feedback to correct the situation. Employees should be selected for specific jobs on the basis of skill and past performance; employees who are given jobs beyond their present skill levels are set up for failure. Employees desiring to advance should be offered job rotations along with classroom and on-the-job training, and mentoring and coaching from more experienced workers.

Be kind. Work with your people. Understand that a change of this magnitude isn't made overnight. Understand also that every employee will have a different rate of acceptance. The common psychological stages of change are fear, anxiety, confusion, acceptance, and energy. And it takes some people longer than others to move from fear to energy.

THE TEAMWORK ADVANTAGE

In developing a customer service culture within your company, take advantage of the special benefits that come with teamwork. Teamwork not only assists in the process of change, but also provides an immediate vehicle for improved customer service.

Customer service, after all, works best as a team activity. Teamwork fosters interdependence and interaction with others who are working to achieve the same goal. Through team participation, everyone in the company can have a role in providing exceptional service.

TIP

Management studies have consistently shown that the optimum number of participants for effective teamwork is between five and seven.

Here are some special advantages that teamwork offers:

- Teams tend to unify people, helping them to share common goals, objectives, values, and vision.
- Teamwork helps break down the barriers that sometimes exist between work units (sections, divisions, departments, etc.). Teams provide an opportunity for people throughout the company to work together to achieve a common objective.
- Teams provide a sense of direction—where the organization is going and what part each employee has along the way.
- Teams are fertile ground for new ideas and provide a fresh perspective on existing problems.
- Teamwork gives the customer a perception of good service. The organization appears well organized and completely able to meet the customer's expectations.

■ As stakeholders in outcomes, team members share responsibility and accountability for the tasks assigned to each, thereby helping to ensure the success of the effort.

TIP

Teams tend to spend more time planning than implementing what's been planned. That's because less time is needed to introduce change, because team participants are already in agreement. Change that occurs without teams usually requires less time in the planning stage, but more time is needed for implementation.

■ Teams offer a venue for effective delegation of work assignments and for monitoring the progress of work underway.

■ Regular team meetings and the distribution of team minutes offer an opportunity for increased communication with all employees.

■ Teams make better decisions than individuals because there is more reliance on innovative and *proactive problem solving.*

PLAIN ENGLISH

Proactive problem solving anticipates problems and obstacles associated with a particular task and solves them before they're actually encountered.

EFFECTIVE TEAMS

Here are some important characteristics of effective teams:

■ Effective teams know what their mission is and are committed to achieving it; team members—regardless of positions held in the organization—are regarded by one another as peers who share responsibilities and team roles.

■ Effective teams are empowered by the company to complete an assigned mission; members are empowering to one another and to others within the company with whom they have contact.

■ Effective teams operate in ways that are informal and people-friendly.

■ Effective teams always encourage open and spontaneous communication among members; there is no fear of reprisal.

- Effective teams seek win-win solutions to problems.
- Effective teams welcome an opportunity to explore new ideas that initially present themselves as conflicts or differences of opinion.
- Effective teams have a leader, a secretary, a facilitator, and a timekeeper, and these roles are rotated among team members to avoid domination of the team.
- Effective teams make decisions by *consensus* of the members.

PLAIN ENGLISH

Consensus occurs when after deliberating on every viable alternative, all team members agree on a specific course of action. Although each member may not prefer the course of action, each supports it.

THE 30-SECOND RECAP

- Providing exceptional customer service is the responsibility of everyone in your organization—from the CEO to the frontline worker.
- Participative management techniques help to establish and promote a customer service culture in which the needs of the customer are paramount.
- Team participation is a good way to involve both management and line staff in service-related tasks and projects.

Service Delivery Skills and Techniques

Service delivery skills and techniques are what make exceptional employees exceptional. They are the little things that together persuade your customers to think well of your entire organization.

Most of these time-tested skills and techniques are easy to learn and use. Each should be included in your training menu for frontline workers. Consistently using these skills and techniques will pay off tremendously for your company in the form of customer satisfaction.

In this section, you learn important techniques and skills for improving the interaction between yourself and your customer.

COMMUNICATION

Communication is one of the most powerful tools available for providing exceptional customer service. It's a skill that is perfected by training and practice.

Your employees' ability to successfully interact with your customers is vitally important to the future growth and development of your business. And it's your employees' ability to communicate that determines the quality of customer interaction.

Communication doesn't just involve talking or writing; it's much more than simply sending a message. In fact, talking and writing constitute only one third of the process. Listening and understanding are equally important in the process of creating a shared meaning—a message held in common.

PLAIN ENGLISH

Communication comes from the Latin root *commune,* which means "something held in common." In the context of customer service, communication is a process of sharing information with a customer in such a way that you understand what the customer is saying, and the customer understands you.

The typical customer forms a lasting impression of your company's quality of service in 40 seconds or less. That impression governs the remainder of the customer's contact. If the "moment of truth" is mostly positive, chances are good that the customer will have a favorable impression of your organization; if it's mostly negative, that impression will likewise be negative.

Your employees' ability to communicate effectively with your customers will generate positive "moments of truth" and will help the customer form a positive perception of your organization. That's worthwhile!

Here are some ways to improve one-to-one communication with your customers:

- **Use your customer's name.** Don't take this suggestion for granted. Customers like being referred to by name. Why? Because calling someone by name is a way of demonstrating that you care about him or her as a person. When you address a customer by using his or her name, you start things off on the right foot—your "moment of truth" begins with a positive!

- **Smile sincerely.** Customers perceive someone who smiles sincerely, and often, to be friendly, approachable, and capable. Words spoken by someone who smiles are much more likely to be perceived as beneficial and helpful. A sincere smile will have a major positive impact on every "moment of truth."

■ **Look them in the eye.** It's been said, "If someone can't look you in the eye, they're not to be trusted." Most people still feel that way, especially when they're making a purchase or attempting to deal with a problem. When you're talking with customers, look them in the eye whenever possible. But never stare at customers. Staring causes feelings of intimidation and anxiety in the customer.

■ **Don't cross your arms.** Crossing your arms sends a message to your customers that your mind is closed and that you are unapproachable. Even when your verbal message is friendly, warm, and helpful, if your body language sends a conflicting message your customer will be confused and will be less likely to perceive the experience in positive terms.

■ **Respect your customer's personal space.** No one wants his or her personal space invaded. Personal space may be defined in various ways, but a good rule of thumb is one arm's length in all directions. People feel intimidated—even threatened—when their personal space is violated.

■ **Lean forward when listening.** This is a simple, but powerful, nonverbal technique that tells your customer that you're really interested in what he or she is saying. And if there's one thing that's important to your customer, it's assurance that you're listening!

■ **Show agreement with your customer.** Whenever possible, indicate your agreement both verbally and nonverbally with your customer. A good nonverbal method of showing agreement is by nodding. Nodding indicates that you've been listening to what the customer has said and that you agree.

■ **Watch your appearance.** What they see is what they think they'll get. When you're dealing with customers, what you say will be filtered by how you look. Employees who look like they spent the night in jail won't inspire confidence in their customers. Appearance may not be everything, but it has an important role in creating a positive perception in the minds of customers.

ACTIVE-LISTENING SKILLS

As discussed earlier, active-listening skills are among the most important customer service tools available. Helping customers to talk openly and freely about their needs, expectations, problems, and concerns is where real customer service begins. Active listening promotes warmth and honesty in communication.

Here are some active-listening techniques that can help you help your customer:

- **Tune in to the customer.** Be genuinely curious about what the customer says. Make a conscious decision to listen intently to what your customer tells you. Tune out everything else. Concentrate on what your customer is telling you verbally and through body language.

- **Be nonjudgmental.** Deliberately suspend your internal self-talk. Allow your customer's message to sink in without making decisions about it. Don't jump to conclusions about what your customer is telling you.

- **Resist distractions.** Don't allow external or internal distractions to disturb your focus on what the customer is saying.

- **Wait to respond.** Be sure your customer has finished talking before responding to what he or she has said. And avoid superficial responses—they will only frustrate your customer further.

TIP

As your customer is speaking, mentally repeat to yourself those words that the customer uses to describe feelings and facts. This will help you stay focused on what the customer is saying and prevent your mind from wandering. Asking questions to clarify feelings and facts will further help define the problem.

- **Reflect content.** Listen for feelings and facts; then reflect back to the customer what you hear him or her saying. For example, "You're angry because you paid extra for overnight delivery, but your item was sent parcel post." This technique communicates understanding (or offers an opportunity to correct misunderstanding).

- **Provide supportive cues.** Supportive cues are nonverbal ways of communicating support. Good eye contact and an occasional nod of the head demonstrate that you understand what the customer is telling you.

- **Listen for solutions.** When customers are allowed to express the facts and feelings that surround a problem, they will also tell you what they expect you to do to resolve it. Use direct questions to ask customers what they would like you to do to make things right.

- **Confirm the solution.** When your customer has finished explaining the problem and defined what he or she expects to be done, restate the proposed solution so that there's no misunderstanding.

Remember that listening is an important part of communication. Active listening enhances communication by demonstrating to customers that they not only have been heard, but have been understood.

CUSTOMER HOT BUTTONS

We all have *hot buttons*—words, attitudes, phrases, or comments that set us off. Whenever one of these hot buttons is pushed, especially when we suspect that it's been done deliberately, we react in negative, nonproductive ways that usually make a bad situation worse.

PLAIN ENGLISH

Hot buttons are those words, attitudes, phrases, or comments that cause us to react in an unhealthy and nonproductive manner, usually with anger.

A customer also has hot buttons, and they're particularly easy to push when something has gone wrong and the customer is already upset. Be aware of the danger that hot buttons represent, and be sensitive to your customer's level of anxiety when problems have occurred.

Here are a few suggestions that will help:

- Empathize with your customer; don't force the customer to see the problem from your perspective.
- Don't finger-point. Telling a customer that the problem is really his or her own fault is a sure way to add insult to injury.
- Don't scold, insult, or call the customer names. Encourage employees who habitually relate to customers in this way to seek other employment.
- Be careful of the phrases you use. Statements like "I'm sorry, but it's against our policy to ...," "I'll have to check with my supervisor and I'll give you a call when I know more," or "That's not my job" are sure to push your customer's hot buttons. Avoid them.

CAUTION

You also have hot buttons. What are the customer words, phrases, attitudes, or actions that set you off? Be aware of your emotions during customer encounters and purposely avoid allowing a customer to push your hot buttons. Remember that even if a customer is angry, how you react is a choice that only you can make. Remain focused on resolving the problem, nothing more.

HANDLING CUSTOMER REQUESTS

Responding to customers who request information is an important part of serving them. Handling customer requests requires knowledge of the company's products and services as well as the ability to skillfully interact with customers.

Here are the steps involved in responding to customers with requests:

- **Understand what's being asked.** Use your active-listening skills to fully understand what a customer is requesting. Restating the request to the customer sometimes prevents misunderstandings.

- **Don't guess when answering customer questions.** If you don't know the answer to questions asked by the customer, say so. Immediately attempt to bring a supervisor or some other knowledgeable employee into the conversation so that the customer's questions can be answered. But whatever you do, don't guess at answers to customer questions. You run the very real risk of turning a bad situation into a disaster.

- **Provide accurate and current information.** This means that you must thoroughly know your company's products and services. Again, if you don't know, immediately find someone who does and bring that person into your conversation with the customer.

- **"A promise we make is a promise we keep."** Everyone who deals directly with customers should echo those words, originally spoken by Sam Walton. If you promise something, deliver on the promise. If there's any doubt about being able to deliver, don't promise it!

- **Learn how to say "no" in a customer-friendly manner.** That's not as difficult as it might seem. Sometimes you have no choice; you must say "no." But saying "no" doesn't have to be a negative situation. Begin by empathizing with the customer and demonstrating that you understand the problem. Tell the customer why you aren't able to do what he or she is asking. Then offer alternatives—give your customer some choices of things that you *can* do.

- **Sometimes it's okay to say "maybe."** Customers may sometimes ask for things that may or may not be possible. If you aren't sure, say so, but reiterate what it is you can do. Say, "Here is what we can do immediately. We may be able to do something different in your case, and if you'd like me to do so, I'll pursue it further." This gives the customer an immediate answer while demonstrating a willingness to serve the customer further by advocating on his or her behalf.

Underpromise and Overdeliver

Underpromising and overdelivering is arguably the world's greatest technique for ensuring customer satisfaction. Make it a regular part of your company's customer service practice.

The 30-Second Recap

- Communication is the most powerful customer service tool that exists.
- Communication is not just talking; it also involves listening and understanding.
- Moments of truth are effected positively or negatively, depending on your organization's ability to communicate effectively.
- Active listening helps to isolate the facts of a situation as well as what will satisfy the customer.
- Beware of your customer's "hot buttons" as well as your own.
- Saying "no" can be done in a customer-friendly manner.
- Underpromising and overdelivering should be an objective in every customer service situation.

Handling Difficult Customers

In this section, you learn the importance of handling angry customers with confidence and professionalism.

The Angry Customer

We've all dealt with customers who are angry, demanding, and sometimes downright nasty. Such customers sometimes even engage in personal attacks against the company representative trying to help them. Assisting these kinds of customers is a situation that requires skill, ability, and a cool head.

Your goal in handling difficult customers is to turn a potentially negative interaction into a positive one by solving whatever problems are presented and making sure your customer is satisfied. That's not always an easy task.

Serving the Angry Customer

Most anger begins when a person feels hurt and disappointed by the actions of another. Instead of admitting the hurt and doing something to correct the situation, some people keep it inside. If anger continues to grow, it ultimately leads to acts of revenge—sometimes overt, as when angry customers verbally attack anyone attempting to help; sometimes covert, as when customers don't tell the company what happened but make it a point to tell everyone else. In rare instances, revenge can even take the form of destructive criminal actions.

How you choose to react to angry customers will determine whether the situation will be resolved or whether it will escalate. If your goal is to provide the kind of exceptional customer service that turns an angry customer into a happy and satisfied one, you'll have to possess the requisite skills.

Here are a few important facts you need to know about serving angry customers:

- Conflict and disagreement are part of life. They cannot be avoided.
- Customers who engage in personal verbal attacks are angry with the company, not the person attempting to help them.
- Irate customers can't be helped until they calm down.
- Communication is the key—helping customers to express what they feel, what they want, and what they think is the pathway to resolving the problem.

CAUTION

Unfortunately, a few people seem to enjoy being angry. For whatever reason, these people thrive on what they consider unsolvable problems and have no real desire to find resolution. When you encounter this type of customer, simply do your best to solve his or her problem. Exceptional customer service doesn't always result in the customer getting what he or she wants, but it should always involve the obligation to give the best service possible.

THE LARSON APPROACH

Following is a successful technique for handling angry customers. It's called the LARSON approach, with each letter representing an important step of the technique.

L = LISTEN

Listen to your customer. Let him or her vent. Practice active listening, *empathizing* with the customer often. When you speak, use words and phrases that reassure the customer that you hear what's being said and that you want to help. Listen to your customer in the same way you would want to be listened to if you were in the customer's position. While you're listening, take notes of important facts. Note-taking helps you remain focused on what the customer is saying, and observing you take notes helps the customer focus on the facts of the situation, not just the emotion surrounding it.

PLAIN ENGLISH

Empathy is the ability to walk around in the shoes of a customer in order to know how he or she feels in them; it's the process of attempting to understand, from the customer's point of view, the thoughts and feelings he or she has about something of personal importance.

Sympathy occurs when one becomes so associated with another individual that he or she reacts or responds to a situation in much the same manner. Sympathy usually results from becoming so enmeshed with another person that objectivity and reason no longer play a functional role in problem solving.

A = AGREEMENT

Find areas of agreement. "I certainly have to agree with you, Mr. Smith; we really blew it this time!" When you agree with an angry customer, you begin to defuse the anger as well as any form of verbal revenge. Remember, the irate customer expects you to engage in a power struggle of sorts (which would only escalate the problem). When you voice your agreement with some of the customer's accusations, his or her perception of you immediately changes from that of an enemy to a possible friend who can help.

TIP

If a customer yells at you, respond by talking softly. Use words that are kind and considerate as you talk in a voice that is soft, but not so soft that the customer can't hear what you're saying. This is one of the most effective techniques I've found for defusing angry situations.

Empathize with your customer. Say something like, "You've got every right to be angry, Mr. Smith. I'm really sorry that this happened to you. I can certainly understand why you'd think that no one from XYZ Corporation cares about you. I'm so sorry that happened; we can't afford to offend good customers like you." Try it—it works wonders.

TIP

Remember that there's a big difference between empathy and sympathy. Empathy means seeing a situation from the customer's standpoint. Sympathy means becoming overly enmeshed in the customer's situation. Empathy is objective and positive, and fosters solutions to problems; sympathy skews objectivity and can be extremely nonproductive.

R = Repeat, Restate

Using the words of your customer, repeat what he or she perceives to be the problem. Be as accurate as possible. Ask your customer to correct you if you state something that's wrong. Repeating and restating communicates to your customer that you are listening intently to what he or she is saying and that you're committed to solving the problem, whatever it may be.

TIP

Correcting misunderstandings and answering customer objections are situations that require special handling. Correct customer misunderstandings by offering the correct information. Answer customer objections by offering proof. In dealing with irate customers, be sure that you have sufficiently de-escalated the customer's anger before attempting either technique.

S = Seek Resolution

When your customer is sufficiently calm and focused, ask what he or she would like you to do to solve the problem. When you seek resolution, you communicate your desire to act in the customer's behalf. That goes a long way toward defusing anger. Say something like, "Now that you've helped me understand the problem, tell me what you'd like me to do to solve it for you." Or say, "I'm very sorry that this happened to you. I can certainly understand why you're upset. Here's what I can do right now ...."

O = Offer a Sincere Apology

Offering an apology is another act that defuses anger. By offering an apology, you communicate that you've accepted blame for the situation. Apologies should not be partial ("I'm sorry for whatever part we played in creating the problem"), nor should they be conditional ("If you can show me that we caused the problem, we will certainly accept responsibility and do whatever it takes to correct the situation"). Many times, a sincere apology is what really turns the tide; it's a very powerful tool.

A second offering should be made to compensate the customer for all of his or her trouble. This offering can take many different forms (a discount on a future purchase, a dinner for two at a special restaurant, the gift of a product). Your offering of something tangible makes your apology much more meaningful.

N = Now!

Take action now! After you've defined what needs to be done to solve the problem, and you've offered a sincere apology to the customer, take whatever action is necessary to solve the problem—and do it immediately!

Your ability to turn a negative situation into one that's positive depends on your ability to solve the problem that has upset your customer. Frontline employees should be empowered to solve problems on the spot, without having to obtain administrative approval. In instances where the entire problem cannot be remedied immediately, they should be empowered to solve as much of it as they can on the spot and seek a supervisor's assistance to solve the rest.

Solving major customer problems is a bit like triage at a busy urban hospital emergency room: It's not always possible to cure the problem immediately, but it's important to stop the bleeding without delay.

SOME IMPORTANT CAVEATS

The LARSON technique for handling irate customers works well. But as with all techniques, there are some caveats to keep in mind:

- Never allow yourself to be drawn into the customer's negativity. When this occurs, you lose any hope of effectively correcting the situation.
- Never argue with the customer or engage in power struggles. These will only escalate the customer's anger and diminish your chances of coming to a resolution. Remember, you're not engaged in a contest with the customer; your job is to help solve a problem to your customer's satisfaction.
- Never blame the customer for any part of the problem. ("This would never have happened if you hadn't ....")
- Never use sarcasm with a customer. Sarcasm has a way of creating ill will faster than anything else. And when it's used with irate customers, it's akin to pouring gasoline on a bonfire.
- Never get caught up in the emotionalism of the encounter. Your job is to listen to the customer and to solve the problem. Stay focused on problems and potential solutions.

■ Never personalize the situation. ("If you would just calm down, we could make some progress" or "If you would stop calling me names, maybe I could find a way to help you.")

■ Never continue working with a customer if he or she threatens physical violence. In these situations, instruct your employees to disengage with the customer immediately and report the incident to you. If the customer, in turn, threatens you with physical violence, call the police. ("Excuse me, but I don't think we can continue working on this problem today. I'd really like to help you at a time when we could discuss the situation without resorting to threats.") Threats of physical violence should be taken seriously.

FOLLOW UP WITH YOUR CUSTOMER

Be sure to follow up with your customer. Your customer will be positively impressed if you take the time to phone a few days later to ask whether he or she has any further concerns.

Some people think of following up as "looking for trouble." That's nonsense. Exceptional customer service includes contacting customers who have experienced problems to make sure you've satisfied them.

USING THE LARSON TECHNIQUE

For years, Joe has owned a bookstore that specializes in rare and vintage books. It's not at all uncommon for a first edition of a classic title to sell for $1,000 or more. Some of the store's customers are established book collectors who know the true worth of a rare book based on its condition and the "points" that make it a true first edition. But many of the store's customers are new collectors who may be well-read, but who lack knowledge about rare books.

A few months ago, a customer purchased a first edition of *A Farewell to Arms,* by Ernest Hemingway. The book was in very good condition, but lacked a dust jacket. Nevertheless, the selling price was $575. The customer was delighted with his purchase.

A few days later, however, he returned the book and demanded a refund. He was livid. He accused everyone involved of "conspiring" against him and perpetrating a fraud. "How dare you take advantage of people like this! What kind of people are you anyway? I trusted you and you deceived me."

THE TECHNIQUE IN ACTION

Employing the LARSON technique in working through the problem, Joe's first objective was simply to *listen.* As difficult as it was to be the subject of insults and accusations, it was more important to allow the customer an opportunity to vent his concerns and frustrations.

Joe used active listening techniques to help the customer get to the heart of the matter. "You feel that we cheated you by selling you a book that is not a true first edition?" The customer replied, "That's right! I took this book to my wife's brother, who really knows his books, and he told me that this is definitely not a first edition; that a true first edition has a disclaimer by the publisher printed on one of the first pages of the book! I didn't know that, and you took advantage of me for not knowing! My wife wasn't happy about me spending $575 on a book in the first place. And now that her brother has told her that I was cheated, my life at home is a living hell!" Allowing a customer to vent serves a two-fold purpose: It de-escalates the situation and enables you, through the application of active listening techniques, to discover the source of the customer's concern.

The second step in the LARSON technique involves *agreement* with the customer. This can sometimes prove challenging, especially when (as in this case) the customer's complaint is founded on poor information. It's important to remember that the irate customer expects you to engage in an argument or a power struggle with him or her. Instead, if you're following the LARSON technique, you will listen, clarify, and agree with the customer in some meaningful way. Here's what Joe said to show agreement with the customer: "I can understand why you're angry with us, Mr. Jones. Collecting rare books is an expensive hobby, and it's important to be able to trust those with whom you do business." Soft-spoken and friendly statements of agreement spoken with sincerity normally result in the complete de-escalation of an irate customer.

The third step in the LARSON technique is to *repeat* or *restate* the primary complaint of the customer that you discovered in Step 1. Repeating or restating the problem is a further attempt to clarify it in terms that both you and your customer understand and agree with. Joe in this situation attempted to clarify by saying, "So if I understand you correctly, Mr. Jones, you are angry with us because you believe that the book you purchased was not the first edition of the work that we claimed it to be. Is that correct?" Mr. Jones agreed; the real problem behind all the anger and the accusations was clear: His wife's brother (a would-be rare-book expert) had given our customer some bad information. Joe's customer had accepted his advice at face value and concluded that he had cheated him, and his anger with Joe was fueled by an angry wife.

Because the customer's complaint involved a *misunderstanding,* Joe needed to correct that matter before going further. The customer believed, based on erroneous information, that a true first edition of the famous Hemingway novel contains a disclaimer. That's untrue—in fact, the disclaimer didn't appear until the second printing of the book. "Let me review the points to look for in a true first edition of *A Farewell to Arms,*" Joe told Mr. Jones. "First, the first edition was published by Charles Scribner's Sons and has a black cloth cover with gold printed paper labels on both the front cover and the spine; the copyright date is 1929, and the Scribner's seal is included on the copyright page; there are 355 pages; and there is no disclaimer included as a preface to the book."

Immediately, the customer raised an *objection.* "My brother-in-law has been collecting books for some time and he knows what he's doing. He insists that the disclaimer must be present in order for the book to be considered a true first edition!" Objections require proof, so Joe retrieved the store's copy of *Book Collecting 2000: A Comprehensive Guide,* by Allen Ahearn and Patricia Ahearn (Putnam Publishing Group), explaining to his customer that the book is used by book sellers and buyers worldwide to identify and value rare books. The guide recited each of the first edition points our representative had explained to the customer.

When the customer was finished reading the information, Joe made a copy of the page for him so that he could correct his brother-in-law. With his objection answered, the customer was satisfied and even apologetic. Joe assured him that he was happy to have been of service and invited him to consult with him whenever he had a question concerning a rare book—even if he was considering purchasing it from someone else.

CORRECTING MISTAKES

If Joe had unknowingly misrepresented a book to a customer, however, he would have proceeded using the LARSON technique. His next step would have been to *seek resolution* to the situation by asking, "What can we do to solve the problem?" Customers usually know what it takes to resolve the matter. If he had sold the disclaimer version of *A Farewell to Arms* as a first edition, for example, he would have said, "I'm sorry this happened to you; it's clearly our mistake. I can certainly understand why you're angry. What would you like me to do to make things right?" The customer could ask for a refund, or may want to keep the book at a reduced price (one that is fair for a second printing of the work). By seeking resolution, you refocus the customer's attention to the solution rather than the problem. It also provides the customer with a strong signal that you're really on his or her side.

The *O* in the LARSON technique stands for your *offer* of a sincere apology for a situation that should not have occurred. Saying "I'm sorry" may sound trite, but to a customer who has been offended by something your organization said or did, those words are like sweet music. Had Joe's little store misrepresented a book, he would have sincerely apologized and offered a special customer discount certificate (50 percent off the next purchase) as evidence of his sorrow over the matter and as a token of his appreciation for the customer.

The final step in the LARSON technique is to resolve the situation by taking action *now*. Be sure that your employees have the authority to properly handle customer problems and complaints. From your customer's standpoint, there's nothing worse than to fully explain the nature of a grievance to a company representative only to be told, "I'm sorry, but you'll just have to come back tomorrow when the owner will be here." Solving problems immediately is an important key to exceptional customer service.

THE 30-SECOND RECAP

- Angry customers deserve to be treated with respect and understanding.
- In dealing with angry customers, your objective is to determine what happened and to fix it in a way that meets the customer's needs.
- Use the LARSON technique to deal with angry customers.
- Make sure that you understand which tactics you should avoid during an encounter with an angry customer.
- Follow up with the customer after the problem has been solved to ensure that he or she is satisfied.

Taxes

What Tax Entity Is Right for You?

If you're sole owner of a business, your choices of an entity are sole proprietorship, corporation, or limited liability company.

If you are one of several co-owners, your choices include partnership, registered limited liability partnership, limited partnership, corporation, or limited liability company.

This section further describes these entities.

SOLE PROPRIETOR

A sole proprietorship is a business owned and operated by one person for profit. If you're a sole proprietor, you just fill out Schedule C (self-employed business) and Schedule SE (self-employment tax, which includes Social Security and Medicare) and attach it to your personal 1040. All your business income and expenses are reported on Schedule C, and then the net income or loss is carried forward to your 1040.

You have some ability to manipulate income and expense if you report on the cash method of accounting (income reported when received and expenses deducted when paid). Delay sending out your December customer bills until January, and pay your own January bills in December.

It is suggested that you use Schedule C as a checklist of possible deductions. Your tax advisor may happily surprise you with a few more.

PARTNERSHIPS AND LLCS

A partnership can be a business entity in which two or more individuals carry on a continuing business for profit as co-owners. Legally, a partnership is regarded as a group of individuals rather than as a single entity, although each of the partners files their share of the profits on their individual tax returns. Another type of partnership can be an agreement between businesses to pursue some objective jointly. Usually, such partnerships are a joint venture or strategic alliance. A legal entity that has the option of being taxed like a partnership, but shields personal assets from business debt like a corporation is a limited liability corporation or LLC.

Your partnership, limited partnership, or limited liability company reports its income and expenses on its Form 1065. You receive a Form K-1, which specifies what your distributable share of each item of income is. You record the income on your own 1040 and pay whatever tax is due; the entity just files an informational return.

Take this example: Al Able and Betty Blue are equal partners in a two-person law firm. The partnership reports ordinary income of $200,000 and capital gains of $20,000. Al's (and Betty's) K-1 records $100,000 of ordinary income and $10,000 of capital gain income. In other words, each partner reports his or her share, whether or not it is actually received.

CORPORATION C OR S

A corporation is a legal entity that has rights usually only reserved for individuals. The primary advantage of a corporation is that it provides its shareholders with a right to participate in the profits without any personal liability.

Small corporations (75 or fewer shareholders) may elect S corporation tax status. The corporation files an information return (1120S) and sends each shareholder a K-1. Shareholders pay the tax on the distributable income just as partners do in a partnership. There are minor differences between partnership and S corporation tax.

Any corporation is taxed on its own income as a C corporation. If the corporation doesn't qualify for S status (it has more than 75 shareholders) or the shareholders don't elect S status, the corporation is taxed under C status. The corporation files a Form 1120 and reports and pays the tax on its taxable income. If the corporation pays dividends, its shareholders report the dividends received as taxable income.

The previous sections briefly outlined the three general types of business entities and their tax matters. More detailed information follows.

ALL IN THE FAMILY

The family partnership is frequently suggested as a tax shelter, spreading the income among all members, including those dependents in the lowest tax bracket. Tax law does not permit a family member to be recognized as a partner unless the member either …

- Made a significant capital contribution from his or her own funds.
- Materially contributes his or her services to the partnership.

CAUTION

Be cautious of forming a partnership with a family member. The IRS scrutinizes all family partnerships, so be forewarned and clearly comply with the law.

Think of it this way: Your daughter has just graduated from college and wants to work in the family partnership business. If she works for the company and significantly contributes to the business, she can be treated as a partner. However, if you transfer a partnership interest to your preteen who neither pays for it nor works in the business, forget treating her as a partner for tax purposes.

THE 30-SECOND RECAP

- If you're sole owner of a business, your choices of an entity are sole proprietorship, corporation, or limited liability company.
- If you are one of several co-owners, your choices include partnership, registered limited liability partnership, limited partnership, corporation, or limited liability company.

Tax Considerations Before You Start Your Business

This section discusses some of the tax elements you should consider as you form your new small business.

OWNERSHIP CONSIDERATIONS

Partnerships must have two or more owners. The limited liability company (LLC) may have one member (taxed as a sole proprietor) or several members (taxed as partners are).

The S corporation must have no more than 75 shareholders and is limited to individuals, estates, and certain trusts and must have only one class of stock; the shareholders must all elect to be taxed under S status. The C corporation may have one or more shareholders and different stock classes.

CHOICE OF TAX YEAR

Partnerships and LLCs have the same tax year as the majority of partners or members. If the partners (members) are individuals, the partnership or LLC tax year is a calendar year, just like the individual partners.

The S corporation is restricted to a calendar year, unless the IRS approves a different year for business purposes. Some S corporations created before mid-1980 have noncalendar (fiscal) years. The C corporation is not restricted to a calendar year, and its choice of fiscal or calendar year is selected when its first return is filed.

CONTRIBUTION OF PROPERTY TO ENTITY

Generally, a partner's or member's capital contribution of property is not taxable to the contributor (nor the entity) when contributed. If you contribute land to the partnership for an interest in the entity, you will not be taxed; there are some exceptions to this, including the situation where the mortgage on the land exceeds your tax investment (basis), which is usually your initial cost less any depreciation. Please consult a tax advisor before contributing property.

CAUTION

If you contribute services for a partnership interest (or membership) or share of stock, you will be taxed on the fair market value of the interest or stock you received.

Shareholders who contribute property (other than cash) are at risk for being taxed on their contributions. So never do this without talking to a good tax advisor. To avoid taxation, the law requires the contributing shareholder(s) receive stock in the exchange and control 80 percent of the stock after the transfer. For example, shareholders Al and Betty contribute debt-free land in forming the corporation, and each receives 50 percent of the common stock in return. No tax would result from that transfer, because both transferors received in return at least 80 percent of the stock. However, if shareholder Charlie later transferred property for 10 percent of the stock, he would be taxed, because he did not own 80 percent of the stock after his transfer. However, the corporation is not taxed on receipt of the contribution.

ORGANIZATIONAL COSTS

The start-up expenses of any entity must be amortized over 60 months. For instance, corporation Alpha incurs legal costs, accounting expenses, and filing fees in forming the corporation; these expenses can be deducted at $\frac{1}{60}$ per month.

THE 30-SECOND RECAP

- Ownership, tax year, contribution of property and organizational costs will all impact your tax liability.

How Your Profits Are Taxed

After you get your business up and running, you have to consider certain operational aspects that can impact your tax profile. Taxes are paid on profits, so every deduction you can find saves you money. In this section, we'll discuss how owners get taxed, when taxation occurs, how income is allocated, what defines income, why some deductions are limited and other facts that will affect your tax liabilities.

TAXATION OF OWNERS

Each partner, LLC member, and S corporation shareholder reports his or her share the entity's distributable taxable income (1065 K-1 or 1120S K-1) on his or her 1040. However, an S corporation that had previously been a C corporation may incur a tax in very limited circumstances. Personal tax rates are progressive.

A C corporation pays the tax on its income. C corporation shareholders pay a tax only on dividends received.

TIMING OF TAXATION

A partner or LLC member reports his or her share of the taxable income in the same year in which the entity's tax year ends. If the partnership or LLC has a calendar year, then the owner reports the distributable taxable income from that year. For example, Alpha LLC has taxable income of $100,000 in 2004. Member Al reports his distributable share of the income in 2004.

S corporation shareholders usually have the same calendar tax year as the entity; therefore, the income is reported in that year. For example, Alpha Corporation has taxable income of $100,000 in 2004. Shareholder Al reports his distributable share of the income in 2004.

C corporation reports its income according to its tax year (calendar or fiscal); shareholders report dividends in the tax year received.

ALLOCATING INCOME AMONG OWNERS

Here is how the different entities allocate income to their owners:

- **Partnership.** Allocates profits and losses to the partners according to the partnership agreement.
- **LLC.** Allocates profits and losses among its members according to its operating agreement.

- **S corporation.** Allocates its profits and losses according to each stockholder's pro rata shares owned.

- **C corporation.** Shareholder reports income only when he or she receives a dividend.

Consult your tax advisor about the effect of your entity choice on your personal taxes.

LIMITATION ON DEDUCTIBLE LOSSES

A partner or LLC member is allowed to deduct his or her allocated entity loss up to the amount of his or her capital investment (and for a partner, up to his or her share of a regular partnership's debt). For example, partner Pete has invested cash of $20,000, and his share of the partnership debt is $10,000; he may deduct a partnership loss of $30,000. But please read further in this section.

TIP

An owner who wants to take his or her entire share of the tax loss should consider an additional capital contribution. This would increase the owner's investment and potential deductible loss.

An S corporation shareholder may deduct his or her share of the corporation's loss up to the amount of his or her investment and his or her personal loan to the corporation. For example, Alpha, Inc. shareholder Al invested $20,000 in the corporation and lent it $10,000. Al may deduct a corporation loss of up to $30,000. But please read further in this section.

What the tax code giveth, the tax code taketh away. Under the tax law at-risk rules, any tax loss that exceeds the owner's investment may not be deducted. In the two prior examples, the owner can deduct up to his or her investment ($20,000); any loss not taken in a year may be carried forward for future years.

With the enactment of passive-loss rules applicable to partners, members, and S corporation shareholders, tax loss deductions were further limited.

Even if you pass the at-risk rules, the tax code will not allow you to deduct the loss against any other income except income from another partnership, LLC, or S corporation. For example, shareholder Al can take up to his $20,000 deductible loss in a year if he has passive income from a similar entity (such as distributable income from a partnership, LLC, or S corporation).

FRINGE BENEFITS

Medical and dental insurance, term life insurance, and child-care reimbursement are fringes that are usually excluded from the employee's taxable income. Unfortunately, partners, LLC members, and S corporation shareholders who are also employees cannot exclude such fringe benefits; however, an S corporation shareholder/employee who owns 2 percent or less of the stock is entitled to an exclusion. C corporation shareholders who are also employees can exclude fringe benefits, too.

SALE OF OWNERSHIP INTEREST

If a partner or LLC member sells his or her interest, the gain may be taxable partially as ordinary income and partially as capital gain, usually according to the entity's capital and ordinary income assets. Taxing as a capital gain is preferable because of the lower marginal rate. Loss is determined by the same procedure. You should use an accountant to figure what part is ordinary income and what is capital gain. There is no way to explain the tax result in less than one section. However, the shareholder who sells his or her stock at a gain will receive capital gain treatment on the entire gain.

THE 30-SECOND RECAP

- A partner, LLC member, or S shareholder is taxed on his or her share of the entity's distributable income.
- A C corporation shareholder is taxed on dividends received.
- Tax-free fringe benefits are available to C corporation shareholders only if they are also employees.

What To Do If You Get Audited

Suppose you receive an audit notice from the IRS. Revulsion and fear set in. The IRS is like the police officer driving behind you in traffic; you may not be speeding, but you still know the cop is there. In this section, we'll discuss how to prepare for your audit.

BEING PREPARED

The grand inquisitor is ready for you, so be thoroughly prepared to win your case by following these simple tips:

- Make certain that you and the auditor agree on the issues to be resolved in the audit.
- Know all the facts and bring all the proper documents and records.
- Research the relevant tax law (or have an advisor do it for you).
- Prepare a list of points that support your case.
- Understand what points the auditor may use against your case.
- Prepare for the tax consequences of each point at issue.
- Determine where the auditor might compromise rather than litigate.

The IRS spends most of its audit time on large businesses and businesses that operate primarily with cash transactions, because that is where the tax under-reporting occurs.

The audit process begins with the ill fortune of your return being chosen. The IRS might simply send you a letter detailing the proposed corrections, and seek your agreement. If your math skills resulted in an error, by all means check the IRS calculations, and if they're correct, agree with the IRS. Be sure to promptly pay any deficiency because interest stops accumulating as soon as your payment clears. If you disagree with the IRS, provide a detailed list of your reasons and the records to support your position (or the law, if that is at issue).

If the IRS requests an interview, prepare for the interview using the list given earlier. After the interview, you will receive their findings. If you agree, arrange for payment and move on. If you disagree, you'll receive a 30-day notice letter to request an appeal conference, whether or not you later decide to go to court. The initial auditor has little authority to settle legal issues, so an appeal will be necessary for those cases. (If you do not respond, the IRS will send you a formal notice of deficiency.)

The appeals conference is typically held at the IRS office. The appeals officer is highly trained, has several years of IRS experience, and holds a CPA. Most appeals require you to prepare a letter stating the facts, issues, and your legal authority. If the tax controversy involves several hundred or thousands of dollars, use a tax accountant or tax lawyer to prepare the letter. The appeals officer has considerable latitude in settling any issue, and will certainly consider whether the case is worth pursuing in court.

If you settle every issue at appeals, you don't need to do anything further, other than pay up if that's the agreement you made. However, if there are unresolved issues, the IRS will send you a deficiency notice (90-day letter). At this point you definitely need a lawyer, because a lawsuit is in your future.

You have the right within 90 days of receiving the deficiency notice to petition the tax court. The tax court will set a hearing in a large city near your home. The trial is by judge alone. If you lose, you must pay any tax plus accumulated interest. You are entitled to appeal this ruling to the federal circuit court if you believe the decision is wrong.

If you do not choose the tax court route, then, in order to take your case to court, you must pay the tax and file for a refund. After the refund is denied by the IRS, you may sue the IRS for the tax in your local U.S. District Court or the Court of Federal Claims (in Washington, D.C.). The District Court case is heard by a jury, whereas the Federal Claims Court trial is heard by a judge alone. If you win, celebrate, for justice has been done! If you lose, you may appeal the ruling to the Federal Circuit Court.

THE 30-SECOND RECAP

■ An audit can happen to anyone, so you must be thoroughly prepared.

■ There is a detailed appeals process in place to protect the taxpayer.

States and Cities Want Their Share, Too

Uncle Sam may grab the most taxes, but his progeny are not far behind. State and city income taxes, sales and use taxes, and personal and real property taxes all do their damage to your bottom line. In this section, we'll discuss the various state and local taxes that will affect your business.

STATE INCOME TAXES

State laws vary so much that it is difficult to generalize. Most states tax the business income at about the same rate and in the same manner as the federal government does, with some notable exceptions. Not all states apply the tax on taxable income (gross income less deductible expenses). Some states tax the gross income, or have a variant of net income tax. And not all states recognize S corporation tax status. To find out about taxation in your state, go to your state's website for the department of revenue or equivalent agency; most states now have their forms and pamphlets online for you to download. But it is strongly suggested you consult your tax advisor—you will be money ahead.

CAUTION

Don't neglect to check the laws in every state in which you conduct business because each state might lay claim to your income
(at least the portion generated in that state). Just advertising in
a state will not require payment, but having a physical presence
(an office with employees) will be a sufficient connection for an
income tax.

Some cities also tax business income (including the self-employed).

STATE SALES AND USE TAXES

Forty-five states and the District of Columbia have a sales tax on retail sales to
consumers. The use tax is imposed as a complement to the sales tax. If a consumer purchased goods outside his or her home state for use at home, the consumer owes a use tax to the state where he or she lives. Some states require its
taxpayers to report out-of-state purchases and compute the use tax on the income
tax form. For instance, if you live in Indiana and buy your car in Kentucky,
you might owe Indiana a use tax payment.

Retailers are required to collect the tax and forward the proceeds to the state
department of revenue. The current controversy involves collecting the sales
tax on e-commerce retail sales. As of this writing, there is a moratorium on
collection. Stay tuned for future developments.

You may be able to apply for a state sales tax exemption to be used when you
purchase your business supplies. Consult your state department of revenue.

More on state sales and use taxes is included in the next section.

LOCAL PROPERTY TAXES

Local governments tax business inventory and equipment (personal property
tax), and land/buildings (real property tax). The taxes are based on the value
of the property to be taxed. Numerous exceptions and exemptions often make
property taxes baffling to the small business owner. Scrutinize your tax bill,
then consult someone who specializes in property tax appeals. Many appeals
are successful in reducing the tax. Most large companies routinely protest
their property tax, so go ye and do likewise.

STATE TAX CODE SOURCES

Go to your state website where you'll find most tax forms as well as the state
tax code. Other helpful sites include the IRS website at www.irs.ustreas.gov,
the Government Printing Office (where you'll find tax laws) at

www.access.gpo.gov, links to other tax sites at www.taxsites.com, and a CPA tax site at www.aicpa.org. Remember that websites do change. Many local law and accounting firms also have websites, and your local library has tax books (but some of them may be dated because tax laws can change quickly).

THE 30-SECOND RECAP

- Check with your state and local governments for taxes that may apply to your business.
- The web provides a wealth of tax information.

Sales Tax Considerations

It is very possible that your products will be subject to sales taxes. This section discusses certain considerations you should bear in mind regarding your sales tax liabilities.

TAXABLE PRODUCTS

Most products or services that you sell are taxable, so you need to obtain a sales tax number (or vendor number) from your state department of revenue or state department of taxation. The number is used for reporting the sales tax collected from your customers.

Your tax number is also used when you buy supplies. You're exempt from tax when you purchase materials or supplies that will be a component part of your product. Tax is paid when the "end user" takes possession of the product—that is, it is added to the price of the final finished item when the purchaser pays for it.

TIP

The main office for each state tax office is listed on the U.S. Small Business Administration website (at www.business.gov or www.sba.gov/), which offers a link to each state's home page. Just select your state, and then search your state's site for sales tax information.

To find out if your product line or service is taxable, call your state tax office. If it is, request the proper forms, and file them to be issued a tax ID number.

If you sell retail to consumers, you're responsible for collecting and paying the sales tax. Your state sales tax department will send you forms to complete and return with the total amount of taxes you have collected for the period. If you sell wholesale, you're required to obtain and keep on file a resale certificate for each customer. This is your proof that you were not required to collect tax from that customer. If you're buying for resale, you must supply the company you're purchasing from a completed resale certificate.

CAUTION

Sales tax reporting and payment is easier to do if you keep a separate bank account for the sales taxes you collect. This way, the tax money is always on hand when it's due. If you commingle sales tax dollars with your general business money, it's too easy to inadvertently use some of the funds to pay other expenses.

You can obtain a copy of a resale certificate from your state tax department. Most business owners fill out an original resale certificate with their company information and leave the portion blank that refers to the vendor they are sending it to. They make copies of the form and keep them on hand to complete and send to new suppliers whenever required. Some wholesale suppliers won't even send you a catalog until they receive a copy of your resale certificate. They want to know that you're a viable business that may become a customer before they invest in you by sending a catalog.

SALES TAX TIPS

Chances are, you'll run into one or more of the following situations. Here's how to handle them:

- If you plan to sell at trade shows in states other than the one in which you operate your business, you're required to obtain a sales tax number for *each state* that you do business in. Most states offer temporary (if you plan to sell at only a few) or one-time sales tax permits to cover this situation.

- If you sell via mail order or on the Internet, you're required to collect sales tax only from residents of the states in which you have a *physical* business location. (Lawmakers are currently trying to close this loophole.) So if you operate a home business in New York State, only New York State residents who are buying retail products or services from you are required to pay sales tax. This includes sales via the Internet or by phone, fax, mail, or e-mail. All of these sales are considered mail orders and are covered by the laws that presently govern mail-order sales. This will probably change in the near future if the law-makers get their way; at present, however, apply this rule for collecting tax from retail customers.

TIP

If you sell via mail order or on the Internet, you're required to collect sales tax only from residents of the states where you have a physical business location. The sales transaction is considered as having originated at your place of business.

■ If you do sell wholesale, you need to get a completed, signed copy of a resale certificate from your customers, with their valid tax ID number. Keep this on file as proof that you did not have to collect sales tax from this customer. This is very important documentation to have if you're ever subject to a sales tax audit. It's proof that you made a valid nontaxable sale. Without this proof, you could be subject to paying the sales tax yourself, even though you did not collect it. Keeping good records for tax purposes is very important. It can save you a lot of headaches in the future.

The 30-Second Recap

■ Most products or services that you sell are taxable.

■ Make sure you obtain a sales tax number or identification from your state.

■ There are special sales tax considerations if you're selling a trade show, by mail order, or over the Internet.

The Deal on Business Deductions

Deductions on your tax return reduce your taxable income and thereby your tax liability. Taking full advantage of legal deductions will save you a significant amount of money. In this section, we'll discuss tax deductions, including considerations about when a business is a hobby, what's allowable as a deduction and specific expenses that may or may not be deductible.

TIP

Read IRS Publication 334, "Tax Guide for Small Businesses." This publication provides overviews of the tax rules. It is a must-read guide for small businesses.

HOBBY OR BUSINESS?—THE IRS VIEW

Whether you're engaged in a hobby or a for-profit business is a critical distinction. If you have a sideline business, be it designing wearing apparel, producing woodcrafts, or making soaps and toiletries, *any income that it generates is subject to tax.* The good news is that you're entitled to deduct your sideline business's expenses. How much you can deduct depends on whether your sales of products or services is deemed by the IRS to be a hobby or a profit-motivated business. If it's considered a hobby, your expenses are deductible only to the extent of income generated by the sideline during the year. For example, if you sell $500 in wooden shelves, only $500 in expenses qualifies for a deduction, even if you spent three or four times that amount on advertising, craft show fees, and the like. Beyond that, you may not even be able to deduct the $500 because hobby expenses can be claimed only as a "miscellaneous" itemized deduction. Miscellaneous expenses, which include job, investment, and tax-related expenses, are deductible only to the extent that they exceed 2 percent of your adjusted gross income.

CAUTION

If you sell your work, whatever it may be—decorative painting, wearing apparel, florals, woodcrafts, or soaps and toiletries—any income that it generates is subject to tax.

The 2 percent floor means that you may have to resign yourself to the fact that you won't receive much, if any, tax benefit from your hobby. When you spend money on your hobby, simply keep in mind that the federal government will provide little, if any, help in subsidizing the costs. Just consider your hobby a pleasurable diversion, and enjoy it.

AVOIDING RESTRICTIONS ON DEDUCTIBLE EXPENSES

If your sideline business is more than a hobby, you may be able to avoid the tight restrictions on hobby expenses. If you can prove that your sideline is a profit-motivated business, you won't be hampered by the 2 percent floor on miscellaneous deductions. You'll be able to deduct all your expenses, even if they surpass the income generated from the business, on Schedule C, where business income and expenses are reported, and you'll be able to claim your deductions whether or not you itemize. But to do all this, you'll need to make sure that your sideline measures up to IRS standards.

As you might expect, the best way to demonstrate that your sideline is a profit-motivated business is to make the operation profitable. The IRS will automatically presume that it is if it has made a profit in at least three of the past five years (two of seven years for breeding, training, showing, or racing horses). If you can't turn a profit that often, you won't automatically lose the right to deduct expenses in excess of income. The tax law does recognize that in the real world, even the most profit-minded businesspeople sometimes have trouble turning a profit in most years—particularly in the early years of a new enterprise.

If you don't meet the three-of-five-year profit test, you can still try to convince the IRS that your sideline is more than a hobby by offering evidence that your enterprise is being run in a businesslike manner and that you're working hard to make it profitable. It's not always an easy case to make, especially if your sideline is the sort of thing that hobbyists tend to do, such as sewing, writing, stamp collecting, or breeding dogs. That's why tax advisers tell their clients to try hard to meet the three-of-five-year-profit test. If you don't meet the three-of-five-year profit test and you want to present a strong case to the IRS, make sure that you document all your business activities, save your records, and keep your business and personal finances and records separate.

WHAT IS DEDUCTIBLE?

To be deductible, a business expense must be ordinary and necessary. An *ordinary expense* is one that is common and accepted in your type of business operation. A *necessary expense* is one that is helpful and appropriate for your type of business. An expense does not have to be indispensable to be considered necessary.

PLAIN ENGLISH

Ordinary expenses are common to your type of business. **Necessary expenses** are appropriate and don't have to be indispensable. The rule of thumb to determine the cost of goods sold is to include all expenses that are required to produce your product.

THE COST OF GOODS SOLD

If your business manufactures or purchases products for resale, some of your expenses include the cost of making or preparing the product that you sell. You use these expenses to figure your cost of goods sold during the year. Deduct these costs from your gross receipts to figure your gross profits for the year.

You must maintain inventory records to determine your *cost of goods sold.* The same costs cannot be deducted again as business expenses. The typical expenses included in the cost of goods sold are these:

- The cost of products or raw materials, plus any shipping that you paid to obtain them
- The cost of storing your products
- Direct labor costs (including contributions to pension or annuity plans for workers who produce the products)
- The overhead to maintain your studio, workshop, or the area where production is done
- Product packing materials
- Packing and handling costs

TIP

It's important to separate your business and your personal expenses. Keep separate bank accounts, and keep copies of invoices and receipts for all your business expenses. If you ever need to make a case for deducting expenses to the IRS, it will be a lot easier.

CAUTION

Do not confuse or duplicate deductions for business expenses with deductions for your cost of goods sold. See IRS Publication 538, "Inventories."

CAPITAL EXPENSES

You must capitalize some expenses rather than deduct them. These costs are considered your part of your own investment in your business. In general, there are three major capital expenses:

- The cost of going into business
- Business assets
- Improvements

These expenses are handled by a method of either depreciation, amortization, or depletion, all of which allow you to deduct a portion of the expense each year over a number of years. This is an area that you'll want to discuss with your accountant because various business operations may require different applications under the law.

PERSONAL EXPENSES

If you have expenses that are partly business and partly personal, you must separate the personal part from the business part and keep reasonable records to support your deductions. For example, if you have a business in your home, you may qualify to deduct a percentage of your total personal household expenses (rent, utilities, insurance, water, and taxes) equal to the actual amount of designated space that your business occupies within your home. If you're able to qualify, the deductions can bring lucrative tax savings. Fortunately, more home-based workers should now be able to qualify for home office deductions as a result of the *Taxpayer Relief Act of 1997*.

BUSINESS USE OF YOUR HOME

Congress has relaxed the eligibility guidelines for workers who base their businesses at home but tend to perform their services away from home (as is often the case for outside salespersons, plumbers, interior decorators, artisans who consistently sell at retail or wholesale trade shows, contractors, caterers, and so forth). Under the new law, such workers will be allowed to claim home office deductions as long as their home office is regularly used to perform administrative or managerial tasks, and so long as there is no other fixed location where they conduct "substantial administrative or managerial activities."

If your home office is used for more than one business, each business use must qualify for home office deductions as a separate entity. If no business use qualifies, you won't be eligible to claim any home office deductions. IRS Publication 587, "Business Use of Your Home," is a must-read for anyone planning a home-based business. Be aware that, if you've taken the home office deductions, there also may be tax consequences when you sell your home. Be sure to read the IRS rules on selling your home in Publications 523 and 544, which cover this topic in depth.

CAUTION

To make informed decisions, check out the IRS rules on selling your home in Publications 523 and 544, which cover other assets.

Home Office Storage Areas

Home office deductions may be claimed for a space in the home used to store product samples or inventory. People who sell products out of their homes may be able to claim some extra home office deductions on their income tax returns, even if the storage area is sometimes used for other purposes. Storage areas are exempt from the "exclusive-use" requirement.

To qualify for storage deductions, you must be in the business of selling products, and your home must be the *only fixed location* of your business.

TIP

As a general rule, if the expense is a result of the operation of the business, it's a business expense and a viable deduction.

Business Deductions

Most people have a pretty good idea of what business expense deductions are allowed. As a general rule, if the expense is a result of the operation of the business, it's a viable deduction.

Business deductions are pretty straightforward, but be careful; some deductions do have specific qualifications, as you'll see in the following sections.

Business Use of a Vehicle

The IRS standard mileage rate is the simplest way to deduct business use, but it's not always the best option.

When writing off business use of a car, you generally have the option to deduct actual expenses or to claim the IRS standard mileage rate plus parking and tolls. The IRS mileage rate changes just about every year.

The mileage rate used to be allowed only for cars you owned, but beginning with 1998 returns, the IRS allowed the mileage rate to be used for leased cars. That should be welcome news to the growing number of drivers who lease their cars and are tired of the record-keeping burden of computing actual expenses.

If you're not going to keep the records needed to compute actual expenses, the simpler mileage rate is the way to go. However, if you do hang on to your receipts, you'll sometimes find that, if you use your own car, adding up your actual expenses will produce a bigger deduction. (Actual expenses include not just gas and oil, but depreciation or lease payments, insurance, automobile club memberships, license fees, car washes, repairs, maintenance, and more.) Which method will produce the bigger deduction depends on how many miles you drive and how expensive your car is to maintain. If you're traveling every weekend, selling at craft or trade shows, you'll definitely want to evaluate which method gives you the best deduction. The difference between the two methods tends to be greater for leased cars. You'll probably get a larger deduction on a leased car if you use actual expenses.

To use the standard mileage rate for a car you own, you must choose it for the first year you use the car for business. In future years, you'll have the option to choose either method. If you want to use the standard mileage rate for a leased car, you must use it for the entire lease period.

Business Equipment

When you write off business equipment, be it a computer, a fax machine, a file cabinet, a table saw, a sewing machine, or a canopy, you'll generally find the best option to be the "first-year expensing" method. This special depreciation method, which is referred to as Section 179 on IRS tax forms, was intended to give smaller businesses a simple and fast way to write off their business equipment.

TIP

For more information on business use of a vehicle, read IRS Publication 463, "Travel, Entertainment, Gift, and Car Expenses."

Instead of having to depreciate the equipment's cost over a period of years, the expensing method allows you to fully write off the equipment you purchase up to a specified ceiling.

Among other restrictions, *write-offs under the expensing method are generally limited to the amount of taxable income you have from your business.* But there is an exception if you have income from another job. The IRS allows employees with sideline businesses to count salary that they earn from their regular job as business income when figuring their limit on expensing deductions for the sideline.

Special restrictions also apply to personal computers, cellular phones, and certain other equipment that's used partly for personal purposes. To qualify for expensing, these items must be used more than 50 percent of the time for business.

For more detailed information, read IRS Publication 946, "How to Depreciate Property."

Entertainment Expenses

Taking a client or customer out to lunch or for a round of golf or a night on the town often makes good business sense. Such outings can provide the social lubrication needed to grease relationships in the business world. In many cases, not a word of business needs to be uttered to produce results. There is much to be said for meeting business associates in a setting away from your business base. It's more relaxed and offers a great opportunity to network, cement your business relationships, and build new ones.

CAUTION

Keep in mind that business meal and entertainment expenses are only 50 percent deductible. The cost of getting to the restaurant or entertainment event, however, is 100 percent deductible.

So if you take a client to lunch and hope to deduct the cost, you need to talk some bona-fide business and keep a written note of the nature of the discussion in case the IRS later questions the deduction.

The deductible limit on business gifts is $25 a year to any one individual. You can't circumvent the $25 limitation by making separate gifts to family members of the customer. Nor can you exceed the limit by also having your spouse make a gift to the same customer—even if your spouse has a separate business relationship with the customer.

However, you can deduct a few incidental expenses beyond the $25: the cost of engraving, wrapping, and mailing the gifts, and the cost of promotional gift items, such as pens or calendars on which your name is imprinted and which cost no more than $4 each. So you can buy a customer a gift that costs $25, spend an extra $4 to wrap and mail it, and then give the same customer a $3 pen with your company's name on it. You'll then be eligible to deduct a total of $32 as a business expense on your tax return.

Membership Dues

Although the law itself seems to apply the ban broadly, the IRS carved out some major exceptions.

Under IRS regulations, the deduction ban is limited to country clubs, business luncheon clubs, airline lounge clubs, hotel clubs, athletic clubs, and other organizations whose principal purpose is to provide entertainment facilities or activities for members and their guests. But the IRS lists several types of membership organizations for which business deductions for dues are still generally allowed. They include professional organizations (such as bar associations and medical associations), civic or public service organizations (such as Kiwanis and Rotary), and business trade groups (such as chambers of commerce and your business-related trade associations).

WRITE-OFFS FOR HOME PHONES

No matter how much a home phone may be used for business calls, the tax law doesn't permit deductions for any part of the basic monthly service charge for the first telephone line into a residence. However, that prohibition does not apply to optional services on your first line. Therefore, charges for such options as caller ID, call waiting, extra directory listings, and equipment rental can be deducted in proportion to your business use.

If you have a second phone line at home, both basic and optional service charges on the second line can be deducted in proportion to your business usage.

TIP

You should obtain a separate business telephone line rather than take business calls on your home telephone line. The phone line and all business-related charges can be deducted in full.

If you intend to present a professional business image, most experts will strongly suggest that you have a separate business phone line. It should never be answered by anyone incapable of handling a business call in a professional, knowledge-able way. Use an answering machine or voicemail to cover the line when you're not available, and return your calls promptly. This will go a long way in help-ing you build strong customer relations.

For more tax deduction information, read IRS Publication 529, "Miscellaneous Deductions."

BUSINESS TRIP MEALS

Instead of having to total up all your receipts for meals you've had while trav-eling, you can take the IRS option of using a fixed-rate allowance, ranging from $30 to $46 a day, depending on the destination. (The allowance covers food and certain incidentals, including tips and dry cleaning.)

If you claim the IRS "standard meal allowance," you won't need any receipts to substantiate your meal expenses, although you still need to keep a record of the time, place, and business purpose of your travel.

TIP

If you need any IRS forms, you can now get them online in several formats. Just go to www.business.gov/ or www.sba.gov/. You can download or print any of the forms you select.

Be aware that if you use the IRS meal allowance for any business trip, there are, as they say in the restaurant business, no substitutions. You have to use the same method for computing meal expenses for all your business travel during the year. In other words, you can't compute actual expenses for your business trip to New York when you went on a fine-restaurant binge and then use the standard meal allowance for your business trip to South Dakota, where you dined at only fast-food restaurants or truck stops.

KEEPING RECORDS

When you start your business, set up a simple record-keeping system—or, better yet, use a computer. Try to total your financial information at least once a month, with quarterly subtotals. Then tax time will not become your worst nightmare. More important, you'll have some real information to help you gauge how your business is doing. That way, you'll be able to spot trouble right away and take steps to correct it before it becomes a major stumbling block to growth and expansion.

The financial information in this section should be used as only a guideline to help you understand business expense deductions. Always seek the help of a qualified professional before making any financial or tax-related business decisions.

THE 30-SECOND RECAP

- You must be able to prove that your venture is profit-motivated to be recognized as a business by the IRS and to get the appropriate business deductions.

- Most ordinary business operating expenses are tax-deductible, subject to the tax rules that apply to each category.

Your Home Office Tax Shelter

There are many aspects of running a home-based business that we discuss in Chapter 8 of this book. We briefly discussed home office deductions earlier in this section, but there is a lot more to tell. Whether you rent your home or own it, part of the housing expenses you're already paying may be deductible.

Running your business from home doesn't automatically mean write-offs for a portion of your rent or depreciation on the home you own. Tax law is very strict about which businesses can claim a deduction for certain expenses of operating from home. These tax rules are called home office deduction rules, but they apply to any business you run from home—electrical contracting, potter's studio, or catering service.

In this section, you'll learn about the tax rules for deducting the things that are unique to working from home. You'll see these rules aren't always fair— and often aren't even clear—but you need to understand them if you want to claim deductions.

THE HOME OFFICE DEDUCTION TWO-STEP

Everyone knows that tax law's complicated. Part of its bad reputation comes from the home office deduction rules. To be blunt, they're as clear as mud and as simple as quantum physics.

You're already paying for your home—whether you run a business there or not. But it's possible to be able to treat some of your personal expenses for the home as a business write-off. This special tax break is called a home office deduction. To fall under the home office rules, you'll have to meet two separate tests. If you fail the first test, don't bother looking at the second because you're out of luck and can't deduct your home office expenses.

TEST 1

Test 1 has just one question, but it's a deal-maker or -breaker: What kind of business do you run? The answer affects whether you pass or fail the test.

The home office must be your principal place of business. Your home office is treated as your principal place of business if it's the place where you conduct your business. It can be your prime activity or a sideline business. As long as it's the main location for the business, it's your principal place of business. This test's easy for some people. Writers, no problem. Day-care providers, no problem.

Even if your work takes you all around town, however, you may still qualify your home office as your the principal place of business. Under a law that went into effect on January 1, 1999, a home office is treated as a principal place of business if it's used for substantial administrative or management activities and there's no other fixed location, like a storefront, for doing such activities. So if you're a home contractor, you do the contracting work at the customers' homes and your administrative work in your home office, you can treat the office as your principal place of business assuming you don't have another office somewhere.

What's a substantial administrative or management activity? The IRS says it includes billing customers, clients, and patients, forwarding orders, keeping books and records, ordering supplies, reading professional or trade journals and papers, scheduling appointments, and writing reports.

In a fix about your fixed location? Don't be. Just because you do some work in your car, like scheduling your appointments, or in a motel room when you're on the road, doesn't mean you have another fixed location. Neither the car nor the motel room are treated as a fixed location, so don't worry.

Do you bring home a briefcase full of work from your day job on a regular basis? If you run more than one business from a home office, each business has to meet the home office requirements in order to deduct any home office expenses. So if you have a full-time day job but run a sideline business from your home office, make sure that if you do any work for your day job in your home office, your employer wants you to do it at home (and you're not doing it there just for your own convenience).

Did you build a nice little office over the toolshed? There's a special rule for a separate structure (that isn't attached to your house or residence) that you use in connection with your business. If you have a separate, freestanding structure on your property, you can treat it as a home office if you use it exclusively and regularly for your home office activity even if it's not your principal place of business. A separate structure may be a garage, a studio, a greenhouse, or even a barn.

Let's assume you have a separate structure. It doesn't have to be an actual office for you to deduct home office expenses. The separate structure doesn't even have to be the principal place of your business activity. It only has to be used in connection with your business.

For example, Angelo owns a landscaping business and uses his home office to schedule appointments and make up his monthly bills. The home office isn't his principal place of business because the most important activity of the business—mowing lawns and landscaping—is done at the customers' locations. But if he used a freestanding greenhouse on his property to grow flowers that he plants at his customers' locations, he could deduct the expenses of the greenhouse as a home office deduction. Or if he put up a freestanding garage to house his truck, mowers, and other equipment, Angelo could deduct the expenses of the garage.

TEST 2

Take a deep breath. You've passed the first test. Now let's see if you can pass the second.

In this test you must show that you use your home office exclusively and regularly for business. Exclusive use of a home office means that it's used only for your business and not for personal purposes. So if you equip a spare bedroom or a den with a computer, telephone, and perhaps a fax/modem for your business, you won't meet the exclusive use test if you also let your family use that room in the evenings to watch TV.

The exclusive use test doesn't mean you have to set aside an entire room for business. You can meet the exclusive use test as long as you clearly delineate a part of a room for business. It must be a separately identifiable space, but you don't have to build a wall around it. In one actual case a court allowed a piano teacher who used part of her living room for giving lessons on her grand piano to deduct the expenses related to that part of her living room. (That part of her living room was a home office.)

There are two important exceptions to the exclusive use requirement: day-care businesses (explained later) and storage space for inventory or samples for a retail or wholesale business run from the home. If you use a portion of your home for either of these purposes, you can claim deductions even though you don't meet the exclusive use test.

DEDUCTING WHAT YOU'RE ALREADY PAYING FOR

Congratulations. You've passed the tests and can now figure your write-offs.

Figuring what you can write off isn't easy to do, mainly because it involves one of those notoriously well-written IRS forms. You figure your deductions on IRS Form 8829.

If you follow the line-by-line instructions on the form, you'll come up with your home office deduction. All the separate deductible expenses are added together and subtracted from your business income as one deduction called a home office deduction.

DEDUCTIONS: ONE AT A TIME

What expenses does having a home office entitle you to deduct? As you'll see from the form, the tax law separates expenses into two categories: *direct expenses* (fully deductible) and *indirect expenses* (partly deductible).

Just to give you some idea of what indirect expenses you can have, here's a list:

- Deductible mortgage interest
- Real estate taxes
- Casualty and theft losses
- Depreciation
- Rent
- Utilities
- Insurance
- General repairs to the home (such as painting the outside of the house)
- Security systems
- Snow removal
- Cleaning

PLAIN ENGLISH

Direct expenses relate solely to the home office, such as wall-papering the office.

Indirect expenses relate to the entire home, such as your monthly rent.

All of your direct expenses are deductible, but indirect expenses have a different rule. Only the part related to the business use of your home is deductible. How do you decide what this part is? You have to make something called an allocation. Technically, this allocation can be made on any reasonable basis. Usually, though, you make an allocation on a square footage basis, using this formula:

Take an example. Say your home's 2,000 square feet. Your home office is 10 feet by 20 feet, or 200 square feet. Your home office use is 10 percent (200 square feet ÷ 2,000 square feet).

If the rooms in your home are about the same size, you're allowed to allocate indirect expenses as a percentage of the number of rooms.

Example: You have five rooms in your home, all of which are about the same size. You use one room for business. You can allocate one fifth of your expenses, or 20 percent, for business.

After you determine your business percentage, you can apply this percentage against each indirect expense. So if your business percentage is 10 percent and your real estate taxes for the year are $5,000, you treat $500 ($5,000 × 10 percent) as part of your home office deduction. The balance of your real estate taxes ($4,500) is claimed as a personal itemized deduction if you itemize your deductions.

Casualty losses can be either an indirect or direct expense, depending upon the property that's damaged or destroyed by a fire or storm. So if just your home office is damaged in a hurricane and your insurance doesn't cover all of your loss, you can claim the entire loss as a direct expense. If you have flooding throughout the first floor (which includes your home office), however, you treat the part of the loss relating to your business use of the home as an indirect expense.

If you rent rather than own your home, you can deduct the business portion of rent as an indirect expense. If you own your home, you can't deduct a fictitious rental amount (what you think someone would pay to rent your home office). Instead, you're allowed to claim *depreciation* on your home office.

PLAIN ENGLISH

Depreciation is a deduction that allows you to write off the cost of property over a period of time related to the life of the property. In theory, the property's worn out or used up over the time it's depreciated. (Because land doesn't get used up or worn out like a building, land can't be depreciated.) In practice, property may even increase in value over the same period of time, but you're still allowed to depreciate it.

In figuring depreciation, the deduction's based on either the *fair market value* of the home at the time you first began to use a home office or the original price of the home, whichever is lower. You subtract the value of the land when you figure depreciation on your home because land is viewed as property that never wears out. The rules for figuring depreciation on your home office are explained later in this section.

PLAIN ENGLISH

Fair market value is how much a willing buyer would pay and a willing seller would accept if each knew all the facts and neither had a gun to his head (neither being under any compulsion to act, to you lawyers).

In most cases, utility expenses for electricity, gas, oil, water, trash removal, and cleaning services are treated as indirect expenses. The business portion of these expenses is part of your home office deduction. You can't deduct the nonbusiness part of utilities. However, you may be able to deduct a greater share of a utility expense if your business use warrants it. Frank's home is heated by oil, but his home office, a later extension, has electric heat. He uses a lot of electricity in the winter to heat the office. He's in for 10 or more hours each day, so he can deduct that additional amount as a direct expense.

The business portion of your homeowner's insurance policy is an indirect expense. If you also carry extra coverage under your homeowner's insurance just for your home office, however, you can write off the additional coverage as a direct expense. Ask your insurance agent for a breakdown of what your premiums cover. You may carry special coverage for the computer or other equipment in your home office. Or suppose you add a personal liability rider to your homeowner's policy to cover you if a client takes a dive on your front steps. These additional types of coverage are deductible as direct expenses.

Repairs can be direct or indirect expenses. The cost of repairing the boiler for your home is an indirect expense. If you repair a window in your home office, it's a direct expense.

A home security system for your entire home generally involves two types of costs. There's the cost of the system itself. You may be able to depreciate the cost of the system related to your home office. And there are also the monthly monitoring fees. A portion of these fees is an indirect expense.

Special rules apply to deductions for your office telephones. Telephone expenses aren't part of your home office deduction. The cost of business phone use is separately deductible. But tax law doesn't let you deduct the basic monthly service charge for the first telephone line to your home as a business expense. You can deduct business-related long-distance calls or call answering, call waiting, call forwarding, or any other special services. You can also deduct the entire phone bill of a second phone line you use just for business, including dedicated fax or modem lines.

Certain expenses can't be deducted even though they relate to your home office. Tax law doesn't let you deduct a portion of the cost of landscaping and lawn care as an indirect expense even though it enhances the appearance of your home and home office.

SPECIAL RULES FOR DAY-CARE BUSINESSES

If you're in the business of watching children, the elderly, or people with disabilities in your home, you figure your home office deductions differently from all other businesses. Even the IRS realizes that once you let small kids into a building, they're everywhere; you can't confine them to one corner of one room any more than you can make them eat Brussels sprouts. You don't have to meet the exclusive use test described earlier.

This isn't child's play. It's very complicated to figure your deduction. The best thing to do is follow the line-by-line instructions for Form 8829.

Just to give you an idea of the calculations you'll have to make, here's what you've got to do. Allocate the expenses of using your home for business (between business and personal use) by using two special formulas:

Formula number 1:   Total square footage used regularly for day-care use ÷ Total square footage of your home

Formula number 2:   Total hours you run your business ÷ 8,760 hours (total hours in the year)

Here's an example for direct expenses (and you'll use only formula number 2). You run a day-care center in your basement, which is 1,500 square feet. Your entire home is 3,000 square feet. You run your business 12 hours each day, 5 days a week all year (except you take 2 weeks off for vacation if you're lucky). For purposes of deducting your direct expenses, apply formula number 2 to your total costs. In your case, the total hours you run your business is 3,000 (12 hours × 250 days [5 days/week × 50 weeks]). Dividing this by the total hours in the year, 8,760, means that you use your space 34.25 percent of the time for business. So you deduct 34.25 percent of your direct expenses.

CAUTION

To be treated as a day-care business, you must meet state licensing requirements. If you haven't already gotten one, apply for a license, certificate, registration, or approval as a day-care center or as a family group day-care home (whatever the law in your state requires).

Here's an example for indirect expenses (and you'll use both formulas). Applying formula number 1, you figure that you use 50 percent of your home for business (1,500 square feet used for day care divided by 3,000 square feet). So 50 percent of 34.25 percent, or 17.13 percent, of indirect expenses are deductible.

It's obvious that you can use a family room, living room, or basement area for your business. But sometimes you might also use other parts of your home for business. Maybe you've got a laundry room that you use to wash sheets or children's clothes as part of your business. Maybe you have a storage area or garage where you keep toys and equipment. Remember to add in these areas when you figure your write-offs.

DEDUCTIONS: THEY'RE NOT FOR EVERYBODY

By now, you've met the home office deduction tests and have figured out your write-offs. Now you have to see if there's any limit that may keep you from using your deduction.

Yes, even though you paid for a legitimate home office expense, you may not get any benefit from it for tax purposes. This is because the home office deductions you claim can't be more than your *gross income* from the home office activity.

If you run your primary business from home and earn a living from it, this gross income limit is probably no problem. As long as the business makes money, deductions are fine with Uncle Sam. If you have a bad year, however, just when you need your deductions, they may be limited. The same is true if you're just starting out in business or if your home-based business is only a sideline.

If you earn less (gross income) from your home office business activity than you spent (your total business expenses), your home office deduction is limited for the year. You can deduct the business portion of the expenses you would have deducted without a home office—mortgage interest, real estate taxes, and casualty and theft losses—regardless of the amount of your business income. But insurance, utilities, repairs, and depreciation, items that wouldn't be deductible if you weren't in business, can only be claimed if you have gross income from your business to offset it.

PLAIN ENGLISH

Gross income for purposes of your home office deduction means revenues from your business reduced by expenses that are not attributable to business use of your home, such as salary of an employee or office supplies.

Head spinning? Well, there's good news. As a practical matter, you don't really have to understand this gross income limitation. It's all worked out for you on IRS Form 8829. (Use this form if you're self-employed or the IRS worksheet that's virtually identical to the form if you're a partner in a partnership.) When you go through each line of the form, the limitation is automatically applied for you.

If you made too little this year to offset all your home office deductions, you don't lose them entirely. Instead you can carry forward the unused portion. The carryforward can be deducted down the road if your same home business has gross income to offset it.

There's more good news. There's no time limit on the carryforward. You can claim the carryforward even if you move to another state, as long as there's gross income from the same activity to offset the deduction. Be sure to keep great records to back up your carryforward deduction.

CAUTION

If you've incorporated your business and you lease part of your home to your corporation, your corporation can deduct the cost of the lease. But you can't deduct any expenses related to the home office other than your typical homeowner expenses—mortgage interest and real estate taxes (if you itemize deductions). And you have to report the rent you receive on your personal tax return.

ADDING ON SPACE, TAKING OFF DEPRECIATION

Suppose you own your home but your existing space just isn't big enough for a family and a budding business? Maybe, if you have the money or can borrow it, you can remodel—converting a garage or unfinished basement or attic into the perfect home office. Or maybe you decide to enclose a screened-in porch and make it into your headquarters. Or maybe you expand an existing room for your entrepreneurial endeavors. If you do undertake these construction projects, you can't just deduct your costs in the year you pay them. You can only write off your costs (recover them) through depreciation.

APPRECIATING DEPRECIATION

Figuring depreciation on your home office involves several steps:

1. Start with your home's *basis* for depreciation. This is the lower of your *adjusted basis* or the fair market value of the home on the date you start to use your home office.

2. Subtract the value of the land on which the home sits.

PLAIN ENGLISH

Basis is how much you paid for property (called cost basis), or some other amount viewed as your investment in the property.

Adjusted basis is your original basis increased by permanent additions or improvements to the property and decreased by depreciation you've already taken.

3. Apply the home office percentage representing the part of the business use of your home. This is the percentage you used earlier to figure the deductible part of indirect expenses. This will give you the depreciation basis.

4. Apply the depreciation percentage from the following table. Take the percentage for the month that you begin to use your home for business.

   Example: You own a condo that cost you $200,000. In October 2003, you began to use 10 percent of the space for business. On this date your home was worth $225,000. (Assume the value of the land is zero.) You start with the lower of your cost or fair market value. Here your cost ($200,000) is less than the home's value ($225,000). Because 10 percent of the home is used for business, 10 percent of $200,000, or $20,000, is your depreciation basis. Apply the depreciation percentage from the following table. Because the home began to be used for business in October, 1.177 percent of $20,000, or $235.40, was your depreciation deduction for 2003. In 2004 and every year after that until the home office is fully depreciated (it takes 39 more years for this), the annual depreciation deduction is $512.80 ($20,000 × 2.564 percent taken from the following table). A final write-off applies in the fortieth year.

CAUTION

Depreciating your home office can come back to haunt you when you sell your home. If you've used your home office for more than three years before you sell, the home office portion of your home won't qualify for the home sale exclusion that allows for tax-free profits of $250,000, or $500,000 on a joint return. Instead, you'll have to figure your profit or loss on your home office.

Special Breaks for Helping Special People

Having people come to your home for business creates potential liability for you. What if they fall on your steps or slip in your hallway? Insurance can protect you, but why not avoid the hazards in the first place and add to your customers' convenience by making your home safer? If you put in ramps or handrails or make other modifications to your home so that business visitors who are elderly or have disabilities have an easier time of it, you can recoup your costs more quickly than using normal depreciation. You have two choices:

- You can deduct up to $15,000 when you make changes in your business that will help out the elderly or people with disabilities.

■ As a small business owner, if you spend at least $250 (but not more than $10,250) you can claim a *tax credit* of 50 percent of your costs.

PLAIN ENGLISH

Tax credit is a reduction of your income taxes on a dollar-for-dollar basis. Unlike a deduction, which reduces your income before you figure your tax, you take the credit after figuring your tax.

THE 30-SECOND RECAP

■ Make sure you meet the tax law tests for a home office before you deduct your office expenses.

■ Special tax rules apply to day-care businesses.

■ You can claim depreciation for adding on to your home for business.

■ There are special tax breaks for making your home more accessible to the elderly and people with disabilities.

Insurance

Protect Thyself: Insurance

If you operate a business out of your home, you may be surprised to learn that many homeowners' and renters' policies do not cover losses from business activities. Actually, many homeowners' and renters' policies specifically exclude losses from business activities. A small business cannot operate without insurance; it allows owners to minimize the risk of loss from circumstances beyond their control.

The first step in choosing types of coverage for your business is to identify the particular risks associated with the kind of business you're operating and to determine the largest amount that each loss could cost you. The amount of property or liability insurance you need and what kind of health coverage you choose will be based on your individual circumstances. Every business has different insurance needs. After you calculate your coverage needs, the right amount of insurance for you will depend on how much the business can afford on an annual basis and what other financial reserves you could tap if you had a major loss.

WHY YOU NEED INSURANCE

You need insurance to cover the danger zones in your business, the areas in which a loss could be so great it could create a serious business disruption—or, worse yet, make it impossible for you to continue to operate. Don't buy insurance for small exposures; the cost of premiums probably would outweigh the value of what you cover and would waste dollars you'll need to buy coverage for your major exposures.

After you've determined that you do need insurance and have decided what you should cover and how much you can afford to spend on premiums, don't rush to your insurance agent's office. First see if you can do the following:

- Eliminate or reduce your risk by properly managing maintenance, repairs, training, and safety programs.
- Assume some of the risk yourself by buying policies with high deductibles and having the business pay for small losses.

Then transfer the risk to your insurer by buying an appropriate amount of insurance tailored to your specific needs.

CAUSE-OF-LOSS INSURANCE

The cause-of-loss form insures your property against all risk of direct physical loss, including fire; volcanic action; smoke; sprinkler leakage; sinkhole collapse;

explosion; vandalism; riot or civil commotion; lightning; windstorm or hail; aircraft or vehicles; glass breakage; damage from falling objects on the building exterior; damage to building walls or the roof from the weight of snow, ice, or sleet; water damage caused by accidental discharge or leakage from a plumbing, heating, or air-conditioning system or domestic appliance; and the collapse of building walls or the roof.

TIP

Property insurance is most commonly needed to defend against fire and smoke damage. Small businesses should also consider the possibility of losses from floods, hurricanes, or other severe storms; earthquakes; building collapses; or other unusual events based on your location and the probability of such an occurrence in your particular area.

The cause-of-loss form excludes these losses: mysterious disappearance of property; damage done to property being worked upon; artificially generated electrical currents; wear, tear, marring, or scratching; insects or vermin; dampness or dryness of the atmosphere; changes in temperature; rust or corrosion; theft from an unattended or unlocked auto; fidelity of an employee or officer of the bank; damage done by rain, snow, or sleet to property in the open; earthquake; flood (surface waters or water that backs up through sewers or drains); water below the surface of the ground, including that which exerts pressure or flows, seeps, or leaks through sidewalks, driveways, foundations, walls, basement floors, or any opening; and the explosion of steam boilers and steam pipes.

Be sure you know what is and is not covered by basic insurance, and buy extra insurance that you think you need for losses not protected in the basic policy by adding special endorsements to it. Basic property insurance includes coverage for fire, sprinkler damage, and lightning, for example; but you may want to add endorsements to cover such losses from earthquakes or infestation of insects or vermin. Cost, not whether the coverage is available, is often the major factor in deciding what to include in a property insurance policy.

Coverage for loss is usually provided on the basis of full replacement costs of the items destroyed, without deduction for depreciation. Replacement costs fluctuate, so you should constantly check your insurable values to make sure that you have adequate coverage. Most insurance policies have a deductible, the amount you pay out of pocket off the top of the claim. So if you have an insurance claim approved for $1,500 and your policy has a $250 deductible, the insurance company pays you the net total due of $1,250.

TIP

Insurance for losses covers both the property damage itself and the extra costs after the loss, such as out-of-pocket expenses for cleaning up and removing debris, unexpected storage costs, or temporary rentals and repairs. Another important kind of extra cost is business interruption loss if the business has to shut down for a period after the damage. Customers may be lost, and money may be owed to suppliers.

BUSINESS INCOME INSURANCE

The purpose of business income insurance is to replace the operating income of your business when damage to your premises or other property prevents you from earning income. If your business suffers a business interruption and has to close for several months, or if it has to operate at a reduced pace because of fire or another peril covered by this form of insurance, your operating income will remain the same.

Business income insurance covers the actual loss sustained by the insured that results directly from the necessary interruption of business caused by damage or destruction of real or personal property.

Other specific policies cover other kinds of property. Boiler and machinery policies cover a variety of business equipment, including computers, furnaces and coolers, telephone systems, and manufacturing equipment. Crime policies cover losses from vandalism or theft, by either employees or outsiders. Special insurance is also available for cash, securities, and other valuable items.

WORKERS' COMPENSATION AND EMPLOYERS' LIABILITY

Workers' compensation coverage pays benefits required under workers' compensation laws, and employers' liability pays employees not covered by workers' compensation laws. If you subcontract certain operations, workers' compensation laws state that the principal contractor is responsible for compensating employees of uninsured subcontractors. In determining compensation premiums, you will be charged a premium for coverage in connection with employees of subcontractors unless the subcontractors have insured this obligation and have furnished satisfactory evidence of such insurance. *You should always obtain certificates of insurance from all subcontractors working for you.*

LIABILITY INSURANCE

In any small business, many unforeseen events can require *casualty,* or *liability,* insurance. (The terms have the same meaning.) A customer might be injured in a fall in a store and might sue for damages related to the injury. An engineer might be sued for the design of a walkway that had to be repaired at great expense to the business owner. Every small business should be covered for liabilities.

Many art and craft or trade shows now require the artisan to have liability insurance and provide proof of it before participating in the show. This is especially true of shows held in government-owned facilities, such as fairgrounds, or in parks or on public streets. When you rent a booth at a show, that booth space becomes your "store." This makes you responsible for covering your liability exposure, just as if you were operating your own retail store.

Liability insurance covers the personal injury losses involved in the liability claims, such as medical expenses after an injury, and related compensatory damages.

Another major type of liability loss is property loss, such as damage to a car resulting from the collapse of an awning in front of a retail store.

Liability insurance also covers the legal fees required to defend against lawsuits filed against a business. Often the insurance company will hire lawyers to defend the business to avoid having to pay out the loss claim.

 CAUTION

You are just as liable for injuries to your customers in your show booth as you would be in a retail store. For example, a customer could trip over an extension cord in your booth and suffer injuries from a fall, a child could be hurt by toppling a display, or a sign could fall and hit someone. That's why it's essential to have liability insurance.

Remember that the insurance choices you make for your business (in consultation with an insurance expert) will be based on the fundamental nature of the business, environmental factors, your state's liability legislation and typical litigation outcomes, and the amount of financial reserves that you have and could tap if you had a major loss.

In property liability, risk is always a factor, but the risks are different for each business owner. For example, a small chemical manufacturer may face higher liability losses because of the possibility of toxic chemicals escaping into the environment than would an engineering firm specializing in parking lot construction. The amount of inventory carried also plays a role; for example, a business that has $5,000 in basic inventory would pay less for property insurance than one that averages $25,000 in inventory.

Many forms of liability insurance exist, and there's much to say about them. Unfortunately, space does not allow more than a brief review of the most common liability insurance types. The Insurance Information Institute provides detailed information on insuring a home-based business on its website at www.iii.org/inside.pl5?individuals=home=/index.html.

COMPREHENSIVE GENERAL LIABILITY

Comprehensive general liability is a single contract policy that provides insurance needed to cover liability for injuries or property damage sustained by the public. It covers accidents occurring on your premises or away from your premises as a result of business operations. It automatically covers certain hazards that do not now exist but that may develop during the life of the policy, and it contains fewer exclusions than individual policies. Comprehensive general liability insurance is owners', landlords', and tenants' (OL&T).

OL&T insurance is intended for risks primarily confined to a specific location. Coverage is provided for the payment of all sums that the insured may become legally obligated to pay due to bodily injury or property damage caused by an incident tied to the ownership and maintenance or use of the business's premises and the operations or business activities of the insured.

Generally, the property insured by basic property insurance includes the building and its contents. An important component of contents is inventory or supplies. Furniture and interior fixtures are also protected contents. Policies cover the property of others stored in the building as well, such as customers' clothing, if you have an alterations business.

Most policies do *not* cover pieces of property outside the building, such as signs or outdoor lighting. Other assets usually excluded are cash and securities, accounting and business records, and vehicles.

PRODUCTS LIABILITY

All manufacturers, wholesalers, retailers, restaurants, bottlers, and packaging firms—or any firm that has anything to do with a product that reaches the public—should have products liability insurance. This coverage is provided by the comprehensive general liability policy unless excluded.

Products coverage provides protection for bodily injury and property damage claims arising from the insured's products, or the claimant's reliance upon the guarantee or warranty you may have made for your product or service. The bodily injury or property damage must occur away from the premises owned by or rented to the insured and must occur after physical possession of the product has been relinquished by the insured.

CAUTION

In most states (find out if yours is one of them), a local store is liable for products claims merely because it sells the article, even if it is impossible for the store's owner to determine whether the article is defective or contains foreign matter. If you are both the manufacturer and the seller, products liability insurance is critical to protect you and your business.

An important feature of products liability is that it covers attorney fees and court costs. This is important to a small business because products liability cases can sometimes be very costly and drawn out, so even if you win, it could still cost you a lot to defend yourself. It can be difficult to get a qualified attorney to take on your case if you can't offer the attorney the guarantee of eventual payment that a products liability policy affords. When you consider people's current tendency to sue for almost everything and the tendency of the courts to decide in their favor, products liability insurance can be well worth the investment for a small business owner. The Insurance Information Institute provides detailed information on insuring a small business. Check out its website at www.iii.org/inside.pl5?individuals=home=/individuals/home/index.html.

BUSINESS OWNER'S POLICY (BOP)

Insurance companies usually offer a special combination type of policy called the business owner's policy (BOP). This policy is much like a typical homeowner's policy, covering most perils under one umbrella. Small businesses should seriously consider buying a BOP umbrella policy because it incorporates the most common types of small business coverage at a favorable price. Some kinds of small businesses, however, such as restaurants and auto shops, are not eligible for BOP policies.

The plan covers your business's property at your home or studio, on exhibition, and in transit. Loss or damage from fire, theft, flood, vandalism, and similar perils can be covered anywhere in the United States and Canada. The high-limit liability plans provide up to $1 million of broad protection. This coverage defends against products liability, bodily injury, property damage, and the business owner's personal and advertising injury. Landlords and show promoters may be named as additional insureds under this coverage.

A few years ago at an arts and craft show on the sidewalks of the main streets in Canandaigua, New York, many artisans learned the sad reality of not having insurance. A powerful wind- and rainstorm suddenly came up, so severe that it toppled canopies and even tossed them into the store windows of the surrounding businesses. The losses were enormous. Stained glass, pottery, and ceramics were smashed. Whole displays were tossed into the streets, and what the wind didn't ruin, the heavy rain did. The worst part was that many artisans at the show admitted that they had no insurance coverage whatsoever. Those who did have insurance could quickly recover their investments. For a list of insurance agents for your state, visit the National Association of Independent Insurance Adjusters website at www.naiia.com/.

HEALTH INSURANCE: KEY DECISION FACTORS FOR SMALL BUSINESS

Small businesses must consider many factors in selecting health insurance. Overall, many experts recommend a four-part approach:

1. Choose the basic kind of health services that you and/or your employees want.
2. Determine the level of benefits that you need.
3. Factor in how much the alternatives cost and how much your business can afford.
4. Identify a specific insurance company and health-care provider based on its quality and service.

Two different systems of health care exist. The first system is managed care. The major alternative is the fee-for-service plan, or indemnity plan.

MANAGED CARE

This system tries to manage health services for its customers in return for a set annual fee. Generally, the insurance carrier makes long-term contracts with doctors and hospitals to provide health care according to a predetermined fee plan.

Managed care is regarded as more oriented toward controlling health-care costs than are fee-for-service or indemnity plans. Because they charge a set annual fee, managed-care companies have an incentive to practice preventive health care, which is less expensive in the long run. However, because managed-care plans make deals with specified providers, patients cannot always use the doctor they want. In addition, the emphasis on cost control in managed care has, in a great number of cases, been shown to have compromised the quality of the care.

FEE-FOR-SERVICE PLANS, OR INDEMNITY PLANS

These plans pay doctors and hospitals for their services when performed, without an annual financial arrangement. Increasingly, some health insurers offer plans that combine aspects of fee-for-service and managed-care plans.

A fee-for-service (indemnity) plan is the traditional type of health insurance. It has become less common recently because it is often more expensive than managed-care plans. Many indemnity plans include some features to limit disbursements according to a schedule or to the normal amount charged for the service; however, these limitations have not been seen to be very effective in holding down costs to the business owner or the patient.

Fee-for-service plans generally do not restrict the choice of doctors to a specific list.

The payment alternatives, premium levels, benefits, and provisions of health insurance plans vary widely. As a business owner, you'll need to consider all of these factors in making your choice of a plan.

Special Provisions for Small Business

In the past, small businesses found it hard to buy health insurance because administrative costs and employees' poor health made it prohibitively expensive. Many major insurers and states have developed special programs for small business, usually defined as fewer than 50 employees. In some states, insurers are required to offer certain benefits and are prevented from canceling policies.

TIP

For more information on health insurance, check with the Health Insurance Association of America, telephone 202-824-1600, website at www.hiaa.org/.

Some trade associations, local chambers of commerce, or other types of small business groups offer group plans. Consider these special programs when choosing health and business insurance because the premiums and benefits offered are usually more cost-effective than other programs may be.

This overview of insurance is only to acquaint you with various types of insurance coverage available. Always seek the advice of a qualified insurance specialist before you make any decisions about the type of business insurance you need.

The 30-Second Recap

- Every business has different insurance needs, so it's important to evaluate your business's risks with the help of an insurance expert before you make your coverage decisions.
- A business owner's policy (BOP) is an umbrella policy that is usually the best type of insurance plan for a small business.

■ Most businesses that sell to consumers should have products liability as part of their insurance coverage.

■ You'll have to weigh many health insurance options carefully before you choose a plan for your business.

Selecting the Best Health Plan

If you've got employees, then you're going to need a good health plan. Choosing the right health plan is not an easy exercise. In this section, we'll discuss the most popular types of health plans you should consider for your business.

THE THREE TYPES OF HEALTH PLANS FOR YOUR EMPLOYEES

Nowadays, health insurance is considered to be a standard benefit offered to employees. But purchasing health insurance is a confusing and oftentimes expensive activity. If you plan to offer health insurance to your employees, your first step is to understand the three types of insurance available to you.

These three types of insurance are fee for service (indemnity), health maintenance organization (HMO), and preferred provider organization (PPO) plans. These plans are discussed later in this section.

The first type of health insurance is the traditional type, otherwise known as fee for service or *indemnity plans.* A typical fee-for-service plan is offered by one of the larger underwriters, such as Blue Cross, and acts as a traditional insurance plan. Basically, you pay a premium for each employee and their health insurance is covered with any doctor, for just about any problem. Almost always, there's a deductible involved.

Unfortunately, fee-for-service plans have some significant drawbacks. There are a lot of out-of-pocket expenses, and deductibles can be high. Typical plans cover only "reasonable and customary" medical expenses. This means that the insurance company determines how much things should cost, not the medical-care provider. So if your doctor charges you $150 for a procedure and the insurance company thinks he should charge you only $100, you may be stuck for the other 50 bucks!

For the employer, the typical fee-for-service plan tends to have the highest premiums of all choices. But then again, there's a much better choice of doctors for your employees, so you'll have to balance the pros with the cons.

PLAIN ENGLISH

Indemnity health insurance plans are also called "fee-for-service." These are the types of plans that primarily existed before the rise of HMOs and PPOs. With indemnity plans, the individual pays a predetermined percentage of the cost of health-care services, and the insurance company (or self-insured employer) pays the other percentage. Indemnity health plans offer individuals the freedom to choose their health-care professionals.

HMOs

Another type of health insurance is provided by *health maintenance organizations (HMOs)*. HMOs have become very popular during the past 20 years as overall health insurance costs have risen. An HMO is an organization that puts together a group of doctors, at prenegotiated rates, for its members to use. When you belong to an HMO plan, you must use a doctor from within the group if you want to get the expense covered by the plan. Using a doctor outside of the group means you'll have to pay the bill yourself.

PLAIN ENGLISH

A **health maintenance organization (HMO)** is a prepaid medical plan in which members agree to use a specific network of providers. The monthly fees remain the same, regardless of types or levels of services provided, Services are provided by physicians who are employed by, or under contract with, the HMO. HMOs vary in design.

An HMO does not provide nonemergency health-care reimbursement outside their network. By definition, an HMO wants to maintain the health of their members by periodic visits with their main doctor, rather than respond to health problems when they occur.

In an HMO, each employee has to assign him- or herself a primary care physician or PCP. The PCP acts as the gatekeeper for all medical work. He or she performs the standard medical checkups for you. The PCP has to approve visits to any other health-care professional. The idea is to keep the costs under control—your PCP may be able to treat you effectively before you see a more expensive specialist. Some aren't crazy with this type of system—for example, some HMOs require that you get approval from your PCP before even being admitted to a hospital.

The HMO is all about the network. If your employee's primary physician is already in the network, that's great. But if not, you may have a problem convincing your employee to switch. People get pretty close to their doctors, and asking them to change merely for the purpose of reducing your company health insurance rates is not an easy conversation to have!

HMOs sign up doctors and include them in their directories to attract new members. However, many doctors put a limit on the number of members from a particular HMO they intend to treat. Just because an employee's doctor is part of the organization doesn't mean he or she will be able to take your employees on as patients. This should be checked out by your employees in advance.

The financial stability of HMOs should be looked at during the evaluation stage. Many HMOs are public companies or make their financial information available. You can do credit checks at Moody's or Dun & Bradstreet to find out their true financial health. This should be done with any insurance you consider, not just health.

And some networks are better than others. If an employee needs a very specific procedure, such as a heart transplant or brain surgery, the best specialist might not be part of the network. Besides cost, choosing the right HMO with the widest available network is very important when selecting your health insurance plan.

Also be careful to see just what types of expenses your HMO covers. Some of them vary quite significantly. One HMO may cover certain prescription plans, ambulance service, or fertility costs whereas another may cover only a portion of these costs. Also consider things such as mental health, substance abuse, and psychological services. Are these covered? Do you have employees who may need these types of treatments?

PREFERRED PROVIDER ORGANIZATION/POINT OF SALE (PPO/POS)

A *preferred provider organization (PPO)* is pretty similar to an HMO. It's an organization of doctors and other health-care professionals who provide care to their member patients at prenegotiated rates. But the PPO combines the benefits of both the HMO and the traditional indemnity plan. If your employee's doctor is part of the organization, that's great—they'll have their expenses covered and pay the least amount. But if they want to go to a doctor outside the organization, they can do that, too, although their coverage will be significantly less.

PLAIN ENGLISH

A **preferred provider organization (PPO)** is an organization of hospitals and physicians who provide, for a set fee, services to insurance company clients. These providers are listed as preferred and the insured may select from any number of hospitals and physicians without being limited as with an HMO. Coverage is 100 percent, with a minimal copayment for each office visit or hospital stay. Contrast with HMOs.

Another attractive feature of the PPO plan is that most types of PPOs allow the member to go to other doctors without a referral from their primary care physician. A Point of Service plan is very similar to a PPO, except that visits outside the network still must be referred by the *primary-care physician*.

PLAIN ENGLISH

The **primary-care physician (PCP)** is a health-care professional (usually a physician) who is responsible for monitoring an individual's overall health-care needs. Typically, a PCP serves as a "quarterback" for an individual's medical care, referring the individual to more specialized physicians for specialist care.

But with the choice comes cost. It does sound great that an employee can go anywhere for treatment and not be confined to a specific network of health-care providers. But most PPO's penalize the member for doing this with higher deductibles and co-insurance premiums. Some PPOs also limit their out-of-network coverage to certain types of medical conditions. Others limit the maximum amount they'll pay out if an employee goes out of the network. Investigate this before signing on.

WHERE TO FIND THE HEALTH INSURERS

When it comes time to look for health insurance, you've got many options to choose from. Here are few sources to investigate:

■ **A local trade association.** Most business organizations or trade associations offer group health insurance policies at rates cheaper than if you negotiate the policy on your own. Because these organizations represent many more people than your single company, they can negotiate more attractive rates for their members. If you don't belong to a trade group, joining for the purposes of reduced health insurance premiums may be reason enough. Be aware that some of these groups charge member fees or require other financial contributions, so make sure your fees plus the health insurance premiums don't add up to more than what you would pay on your own. Also check out the insurance plan offered by the group before joining; it may not suit your company's needs.

- **The Internet.** There are plenty of online insurance companies ready and willing to take your money. Tread warily in this area. Just because some pop-up ad may be offering the cheapest rates available doesn't mean that the company behind the plan will be in business six months from now to reimburse for expenses. For a start, visit www. ehealthinsurance.com or www.ushealthquotes.com. The industry's trade group maintains a great website at www.hiaa.org where you can get up-to-the minute advice and facts on purchasing health insurance. There's also a great consumer guide for purchasing health insurance, which is maintained by Georgetown University. You can access this guide at www.healthinsuranceinfo.net. One other place to get great information is www.healthinsurance.org.

- **Referrals.** Another great way to look for health insurance is by asking other people. Most business owners offer some type of health insurance plans to their employees, so take an unofficial poll and see who's recommended.

- **Your insurance broker.** There's a very good chance that the broker who provides your company's general business and liability insurance also offers health insurance policies. If you like and trust your insurance broker, consider the policies he or she has to offer. You might be able to negotiate slightly lower rates by combining your policy with other plans.

WHAT IS THE COST OF HEALTH INSURANCE?

Health insurance is one of the fastest-rising costs of business today. In fact, health insurance costs have risen approximately 10 percent per year every year in the past decade. Both the government and the insurance industry are still trying to figure out how to maintain these costs. Unfortunately, small business people are stuck in the middle of this situation. There are some things you can do, however, to keep your costs as low as possible.

CHOOSE THE MOST AFFORDABLE PLAN

The rule of thumb is that traditional indemnity plans are the most expensive. These plans are like general insurance and cover for most medical expenses no matter who provides the health care. With an indemnity plan, your employees have the maximum choice, and with this come the highest premiums. In Foster Higgins's 2000 National Survey of Employer Sponsored Health Plans, a traditional health plan cost an average of $4,408 per employee per year.

HMOs are less expensive than the traditional plans, mostly because your employees are trading freedom of choice for lower overall premiums. The average yearly cost per employee for an HMO plan in 2000 was $3,713.

PPOs/SOPs are more expensive than HMO's. This is because an employee can use doctors from both within and outside their network, although for a penalty. In 2000, a PPO plan cost an employer an average of $4,032 per employee.

Do Your Research Beforehand

The Foster Higgins survey shows that HMOs and PPOs have become the most popular choices among small business owners, mainly because of their cost. Although cost is a very important factor, it should be considered among other factors when choosing a health plan for your company. Remember that this decision really impacts the lives of your employees and their families, so it should not be taken lightly!

When looking into a traditional indemnity plan, consider other factors rather than just the premium. Look at rates for both individual and families. Make sure the plan covers a broad range of services, such as prescription drugs and home care. Consider any medical conditions that your employees now have that may not be covered by the plan, or that require a waiting period (like pregnancy). Negotiate deductibles; it's possible by raising this amount you can reduce your annual premium payments. Confirm the co-insurance rate in advance so that there are no surprises down the road. Like any insurance policy, get in writing the total amount of any claim that will be covered. You or your employees don't want to be stuck with a large expenditure that exceeds an unknown cap on coverage.

PLAIN ENGLISH

Co-insurance is when you share the cost of insurance with the insurance company. Normally a policy will require that you cost share with them on the first $5,000 of medical claims.

Example: 80 percent/20 percent co-insurance: The insurance company would pay 80 percent of the first $5,000 of medical claims and you would pay 20 percent, after which the insurance company begins to pay the remainder per the terms of the policy.

Co-insurance can vary with different policies, so be sure you understand the terms of the plan in which you are interested.

HMOs may be cheaper, but they can come with a price. Find out exactly how the procedure works. Understand what happens if an employee wants to change doctors, how referrals are handled, and how easy it is to get appointments. Ask your employees to make sure their doctors not only participate in the plan, but accept new patients for reimbursement under the plan. Like the indemnity plan, confirm the limits of coverage with the insurer. Many HMOs cover only certain geographic areas, too. What if an employee travels and needs to see a doctor? Or worse than that, double-check that covered physicians and hospitals that are part of the network are also nearby to you and your people.

All of the previous factors should be considered for PPOs, too. Because a PPO allows your employees to go outside the network, however, there are other things you'll need to investigate. Find out how this process works and when your people will still need a referral. Understand the differences between a PPO and POS in case one of these plans better suits your employees' needs. Make sure you look at the difference in costs between doctors in and out of the network and gain very thorough understanding of what's covered and not covered with both options!

CONSIDER AN EMPLOYEE CO-PAY

Many small business owners just can't handle the cost of health insurance alone nowadays. One major way they've employed to keep their costs under control is to shift some of the burden onto their employees. It's not uncommon to see employees pay a portion of their health insurance premiums as part of the paycheck deductions. There are some tax incentives to do this, too, which are discussed shortly.

It's completely up to you to determine how much, if any, of the health insurance premiums should be shared by your employees. Some companies fully cover the employee's individual health insurance rate and then ask the employee to cover all or a portion of any additional premiums for their families. Other companies pick a flat percentage (like 20 percent or 50 percent) that they share. A few base their coverage on employee performance or bonus plans.

Making your employees share in the burden of health care serves two important purposes. Of course, it helps you reduce your overall health insurance costs. But in addition it makes everyone feel the pain of rising health-care costs and will hopefully contribute to popular support of some kind of solution in the future.

Your Health Insurance Premiums and the IRS

As long as your company is incorporated (or a partnership), you can fully deduct the cost of health insurance premiums you pay.

If you do provide health insurance to your employees, most experts recommend also setting up a Section 125 plan. Named after a section of the IRS code, this provision in the tax law allows employees to deduct their premiums from their pretax earnings so that they are taxed on the lower amount of earnings. This saves the employee taxes and will make you a hero.

There are two types of Section 125 plans that you should consider: the premium-only plan and flexible-spending accounts.

The Premium-Only Plan

In this plan, employees get to deduct health, dental, and life insurance premiums from their pretax earnings. There are no new benefits offered except for a higher take-home pay, and that's a good thing. And because the employee's gross pay is reduced by the amount of the premium, the company's share of his or her Social Security and Medicare taxes is also reduced.

Flexible-Spending Accounts

Many health-care plans don't reimburse for certain medical expenses, such as over-the-counter drugs or day care. Setting up a flexible-spending account allows the employee to still get a tax benefit from these expenditures.

With a flexible-spending account, the employee determines, at the beginning of the year, how much he or she is going to pay in health-care costs and puts this money aside in advance. The total amount is limited to $5,000 ($5,000 also for childcare). Although the amount is determined at the beginning of the year, it is deducted from the employee's paycheck in equal amounts throughout the year. The employee then has to submit receipts and get reimbursed by their employer. You, as the employer, have to administrate the employee's deductions with his or her reimbursed claims. There are outside companies who can help you administrate these. Employees should also know that any amounts not used by the end of the year are lost.

CAUTION

With a flexible-spending account, an unscrupulous employee may set aside the full $5,000 at the beginning of the year, submit receipts, and then leave early in the year. If the amount hasn't been funded by the employee's deductions, then you, the employer, are responsible for the rest.

DON'T FORGET DISABILITY INSURANCE!

Disability insurance covers a portion of an employee's salary when that employee is out on disability. There are both long- and short-term plans. The cost of this insurance is pretty low (a few dollars per employee) and well worth the expense. Remember that some employees, if disaster falls, may not have the means to support themselves and their families and could turn to you for help. A disability policy may be a lifesaver for both you and them! Most disability plans can be tacked on to your health insurance plan, so don't forget to consider this in your evaluation!

THE 30-SECOND RECAP

- Three types of health insurance plans are most popular with small businesses: traditional indemnity, health maintenance organizations (HMO), and preferred provider organizations (PPO).
- You can find health insurers on the web, through trade associations, and through referrals or your own insurance broker.
- Health insurance is expensive, with costs rising each year. Do extensive research before choosing your plan.
- A Section 125 plan reduces both yours and your employees' tax expense by allowing you to deduct certain health-care costs.

Ethics/Small Business Responsibility

Doing Well by Doing Good: Business Law and Ethics

The financial accounting and stock-trading scandals of the early 2000s revealed a high level of greed and self-dealing among senior managers of some companies. Enron, Global Crossing, Qwest, Computer Associates, and AOL were subject to criminal investigation. Executives at Arthur Andersen, WorldCom, Tyco, Adelphia Communications, and Imclone Systems were charged with crimes ranging from fraud to obstruction of justice. Merrill Lynch paid a $100 million fine to New York State for violations of securities law.

Moreover, scores of publicly held companies have had to restate their earnings over the past two years due to "aggressive" or improper accounting practices. Millions of investors collectively lost billions of dollars because they followed the recommendations of Wall Street analysts touting stocks that their own employers had a stake in (including stocks that they knew were worthless). The staggering levels of senior executive pay at some large companies—even when they perform poorly—and the tight link between politics and corporate contributions among members of both major political parties have further eroded people's trust in business, or at least "Big Business."

Of course, wrongdoing occurs in all institutions and professions, so business has not cornered the market on legal trouble and ethical lapses. Yet, given the scale of business wrongdoing in recent years, it's clearly time for every business-person to take time to understand his or her legal and ethical responsibilities.

This section aims to assist you in developing that understanding by providing an overview of the major legal and ethical issues in business.

SOCIETY, BUSINESS, AND THE LAW

Any society worthy of the name has laws. Many people believe laws form the very basis of society. Traditional tribal societies are governed by laws, and modern societies have extremely elaborate systems governing both criminal behavior and civil matters.

Society makes laws to govern people's behavior. The criminal code, the set of laws that define criminal behavior, simply forbids certain behavior. The civil code governs property rights and the rights of organizations and individuals. Each of us has a right to buy and own property, to enjoy using it, and to live without suffering because of someone else's negligent behavior. Similarly, each of us has an obligation to act responsibly, and that includes acting responsibly in our business dealings.

BUSINESS LAW

Business law governs the conduct of people and organizations engaged in business. Major areas of business law include the following:

- Antitrust
- Consumer protection
- Products liability
- Bankruptcy
- Business organization
- Contracts

- Real estate and insurance
- Employment
- Intellectual property
- Securities regulation
- *Uniform Commercial Code*
- Taxation

Here are some of the legal issues surrounding each of these areas.

ANTITRUST

The antitrust laws ensure that competition remains fair. The *monopolies* of the late 1800s and early 1900s in industries such as railroads, oil, and steel prompted the federal government to pass antitrust laws. Antitrust law prohibits companies from merging with one another or acquiring one another to form monopolies.

PLAIN ENGLISH

A **monopoly** exists when there is only one supplier of some product or service. The monopoly can usually charge whatever prices it wants to, because it has no competition.

Restraint of trade can include monopolistic practices and other attempts to limit competition in an industry or business. For instance, an agreement that "punishes" customers for doing business elsewhere would be an attempt to restrain trade.

In the late 1990s, several competitors of Microsoft filed a federal suit alleging unfair trade practices that effectively limited competition in the software market. For instance, among other practices they cited Microsoft's practice of bundling products—that is, packaging its Internet Explorer browser with its operating system and making retailers buy the whole bundle. This limited opportunities for other companies, such as Netscape, one of the companies that filed the suit, from selling Internet browsers.

The case was tried, and a federal judge found merit in the charges and ordered that Microsoft separate its operating system and applications software businesses. Microsoft is appealing the decision.

CONSUMER PROTECTION

Consumer protection laws are regulations regarding products, services, and credit practices. Some of these laws (such as the ban on cigarette advertising on television) are federal, whereas others (such as the "lemon laws" covering automobiles) are state law.

Consumer protection laws arise as the need demands. For example, in the 1970s many health clubs used hard-sell tactics to sign up people. So New York passed a law giving anyone who bought a health-club membership three days to reverse the decision without penalty.

Opponents of these laws believe that it is the buyer's responsibility to carefully inspect all purchases before buying (summed up in the saying *caveat emptor,* let the buyer beware), but regulatory authorities believe that the seller makes certain *implied warranties* about the products offered for sale. At the minimum, for example, the product should be safe to use.

PLAIN ENGLISH

Implied warranties are not explicitly stated by the seller but can reasonably be assumed by the buyer to exist. For instance, consumers should be able to assume that food is safe and that a car has working windshield wipers.

PRODUCTS LIABILITY

Products liability comes under consumer protection, yet there have recently been so many lawsuits in this area, with some resulting in awards against companies well into the millions of dollars, that it warrants separate mention.

Essentially, case law in this area says that a company cannot knowingly sell a product that it believes will be unsafe or harmful when it is used for its intended purpose. This logic underlies the investigations of the tobacco companies to discover when, if ever, management knew that smoking caused life-threatening diseases.

Most products liability suits seek to prove that the company either knowingly sold an unsafe product or that the outfit's negligence in manufacturing created a dangerous defect. Or the plaintiff—the party bringing the lawsuit against the defendant—tries to prove that the company should have issued warnings about the product's dangers.

Products liability suits are the reason for the warnings we see on everything from coffee-cup lids ("The beverage you are about to enjoy is very hot") to children's sleds ("Wear a helmet and use in an open area under adult supervision").

Many people believe products liability suits have gotten out of hand. They see a "victim culture" in the United States and believe juries are manipulated by attorneys. Defenders of the suits believe that safer products and useful warnings are the result.

BANKRUPTCY

The bankruptcy laws let a company that is having financial problems "seek protection" from the demands of creditors in order to either *reorganize* or *liquidate* the business.

You might hear about Chapter 11, as in, "If this doesn't work out, we're headed for Chapter 11." This refers to Chapter 11 of the bankruptcy code, the chapter of the code that regulates liquidation. Chapter 7 of the code regulates reorganizations.

PLAIN ENGLISH

The term **reorganization** more commonly refers to major changes in the way a company is structured. In connection with bankruptcy, it means a court-supervised procedure to reorganize the business while its creditors wait for payment. **Liquidation** means closing the company and selling its assets to pay creditors. The expression "10 cents on the dollar" refers to the fact that creditors usually wind up getting about 10 cents for each dollar they are owed.

BUSINESS ORGANIZATION

Laws govern the formation of businesses such as partnerships and corporations. A corporation is a "legal person," and this means it has certain rights, such as the right to purchase and own property, and responsibilities, such as paying taxes, just as a person does.

CONTRACTS

Contract law is complex and constantly evolving. Many people find it hard to understand how two parties who have agreed to a transaction can then spend more time and money on the details of the contract. However, the days when business was done "on a handshake" are gone.

TIP

In all your business (and personal) dealings, be very careful when you sign a contract. Many naïve people have unwittingly signed away valuable rights. Have an attorney, or at least a very knowledgeable person, review any contract that you are about to sign but do not fully understand.

A lot of the complexity of contracts comes from the terms and conditions that people (especially attorneys) put into them. These terms and conditions govern every aspect of the contract, such as "right to terminate" and so on.

Most lawsuits over contracts occur when one party fails to perform, or is seen as failing to perform, as agreed. This is called "breach of contract" and the usual remedy, if you cannot negotiate, is to sue the nonperforming party.

REAL ESTATE AND INSURANCE

Both real estate and insurance broadly come under contract law. However, these contracts can become extremely complex. For example, real estate transactions involving legal structures such as condominiums and cooperatives can be quite intricate. And insurance attorneys spend a lot of time, effort, and money deciding whether or not a major claim under an insurance policy is valid.

EMPLOYMENT

Employment laws regulate the hours and conditions under which people work and who can work. For example, the child-labor laws prohibit the hiring of children. The minimum wage sets a minimum level of hourly pay.

CAUTION

If you are a hiring authority or manage others, know your responsibilities under employment law. For example, it is illegal to ask certain questions in a job interview, such as those relating to age or childbearing intentions. In most companies, the human resources function can advise managers of their responsibilities in this area. But it is your responsibility to ask.

The most significant recent federal employment law was the *Americans with Disabilities Act (ADA)* of 1990. This law expanded the rights of disabled people in employment.

Employment laws, including those against racial, religious, age, and gender discrimination, impact most managers' day-to-day activities.

INTELLECTUAL PROPERTY

Intellectual property includes innovations, ideas, know-how, methods, processes, and other intangible elements of the business. Intellectual property rights are protected by copyrights, trademarks, and patents. These devices are key to protecting your business and to establishing ownership in the event that someone else tries to exploit these rights.

SECURITIES REGULATION

In the late 1800s and early 1900s, securities fraud was common. Bogus stocks and bonds, dishonest investment schemes, and various forms of market manipulation (running up the price of a stock) were common. The U.S. government realized that an honest, open, regulated securities market was essential to a capitalist economy, so it created the Securities and Exchange Commission (SEC).

The SEC has the ongoing job of policing all players in the financial markets. Among the most common and challenging situations the SEC faces are ...

- Insider trading, in which managers, board members, and other people who have information not available to the public buy or sell stocks on the basis of that information.

- Stock-price manipulation, such as "pump-and-dump" schemes in which a group of investors trade a stock among themselves to raise the price to artificially high levels and then sell it to unsuspecting investors attracted by the stock's rapid rise.

- Improper financial reporting by publicly held companies.

- Improper and illegal practices at brokerage firms, including overcharging customers, appropriating or "borrowing" funds from customers' accounts, "pushing" stocks that the firm wants to unload from its inventory, and allowing "good customers" to buy an initial public offering (IPO) early in the day so they can sell it later that day or soon thereafter when the price has skyrocketed.

Unfortunately, relatively few securities law violators go to jail. The March 18, 2002, *Fortune* reported that from 1992 to 2002, the SEC referred 609 cases to the Justice Department for possible prosecution. The Justice Department prosecuted about 335 of these cases and won guilty verdicts an impressive 76 percent of the time. But only 87 people spent any time in jail.

Also, when these white-collar criminals do land in jail, it is usually for a stay of one to two years in a minimum-security federal prison (known as "Club Fed").

UNIFORM COMMERCIAL CODE

The *Uniform Commercial Code,* or *UCC,* is a set of laws governing business transactions. Areas governed include sales of goods, commercial paper, bank deposits, shipping and delivery of goods, and so on. The *UCC* was prepared by the National Conference of Commissioners on Uniform State Laws and has been adopted by all 50 states except Louisiana, which has adopted most of it.

This body of law does what the name implies: It standardizes the laws that govern business transactions across all the states, which makes it easier to do business.

TAXATION

The federal tax code, as you probably know, is one of the lengthiest, most complex, and impenetrable documents ever created by political, legal, and accounting minds (and that's saying a lot). Major companies employ batteries of attorneys and accountants to interpret tax law and, if necessary, to defend the company's decisions in tax court, where differences with the IRS are decided (unless they are settled before going to court).

RULES AND REGULATIONS

In addition to all of these areas (and some not mentioned, such as maritime law, which governs the seas and shipping), businesses must cope with regulations issued by federal and state agencies.

Some of the more important federal agencies include ...

- The Food and Drug Administration (FDA), which regulates the quality of products for human consumption.
- The Environmental Protection Agency (EPA), which regulates air and water quality.
- The Federal Aviation Administration (FAA), which regulates air transportation.
- The Federal Reserve Board (the Fed), which regulates banks.
- The Equal Employment Opportunity Commission (EEOC), which enforces antidiscrimination laws.

Although all types of businesses are subject to the EEOC, a company's involvement with any particular agency depends on its business. Pharmaceutical companies such as Eli Lilly must deal with the FDA. American Airlines has to be concerned with the FAA. Merrill Lynch has the SEC to think about.

If you are in a large company in a regulated business, you'll become familiar with the major regulatory requirements and how they affect your job. But what about other managers and other laws? What do managers generally have to be concerned about in the law?

WHAT DOES ETHICS MEAN TO MANAGERS?

As a manager, it is not your responsibility to know the tiny details of the law in every area. Each legal area is its own field, employing attorneys focused on only that area. This specialization is necessary because the law is complex and constantly changing. In addition, most laws have an international aspect, which adds to the complexity.

Despite all this, your responsibilities as a manager are fairly straightforward. Here are some general guidelines, from one business person to another:

- Use common sense and think before you act. Most of us have learned the difference between right and wrong. For instance, if someone offers you a kickback if you'll do business with him, you don't need an attorney to tell you to refuse it and to take your business elsewhere.

- When in doubt about whether you need legal advice, ask for help. Your boss, legal department, or attorney can advise you, but only if you ask. It's wise to avoid legal difficulties rather than try to fix them later.

- Be very careful about what you sign. If a contract was drawn up by an attorney, have your attorney review it before you sign it.

- If the other party has an attorney, you should probably have one, too. If the other party brings an attorney to a transaction, you should have yours along.

- If you're ever actually accused of a crime, such as fraud, or something serious but not a crime, such as negligence, get an attorney. Say as little as possible (and nothing in a criminal case) until you get legal advice. Many innocent people have blurted something out that "sounded bad" or was misinterpreted and wound up in serious trouble.

Finally, conduct yourself as ethically as you possibly can on the job.

YOUR BUSINESS ETHICS

Ethics are moral guidelines that tell you right from wrong. Business ethics tell you what is right or wrong in a business situation, whereas professional ethics tell you the same thing regarding your profession. Ideally, there should be no conflict between your personal ethics and your business or professional ethics. However, ethical conflicts can arise when what might be best for the company is wrong morally or professionally.

Here's a real-life example. Your ethics probably tell you that child labor is wrong. Yet in some countries, children are put to work at a young age, and often in poor working conditions. They have no choice in the matter, and from our point of view are basically being exploited.

Suppose your company purchases well-made, inexpensive products from a foreign company that uses child labor in poor working conditions. The good quality and low price helps your company stay competitive. But is it right to purchase these products?

This is an ethical dilemma, particularly because no law is being broken. The foreign nation does not prohibit child labor, and the United States does not prohibit these imports. It may be legal, but is it right?

The child-labor situation has other complexities. Suppose you believe the purchase is wrong because children are being exploited, but the families of these children need their income for food and shelter. Is it still wrong? Under the circumstances, perhaps buying those products provides a *greater good*.

PLAIN ENGLISH

The **greater good** in a situation is the outcome that provides more benefit, at the expense of sacrificing an ethical standard or a smaller benefit to another party. For example, murder is wrong, but the state sanctions killing in war because the defense of our nation is the greater good.

Sometimes your professional or personal ethics may conflict with your business ethics. From the business standpoint, you are paid to further your employer's interests. But you also have professional and personal ethics to uphold. To minimize moral and psychological conflict, and to wind up consistently doing the right thing, it's best to work in a business—an industry and a company— that closely matches your own sense of ethics. It is also best to bring your own highest ethical standards to bear in your place of business.

Many people believe in having two sets of ethics, one for their business lives and one for their personal lives. They see business as a game in which honesty and fairness are relative terms and in which money made or lost is the only measure of value. A few of these people actually are honest and fair in their personal, as opposed to business, dealings. But people who behave unethically on the job have corrupted business and eroded the public's faith in business institutions.

Business sometimes does pose genuine ethical dilemmas. In those situations, each of us must do what our conscience tells us is right. This may well involve overcoming the "business reason" that we give ourselves or that someone else gives us for going against our conscience.

Every profession has an explicit or implicit code of ethics. When auditors at accounting firms such as Arthur Andersen overlooked improper accounting practices of clients such as Enron, they did so at least partly to protect the consulting revenues that their firms earned from these clients. Any senior manager aware of these auditors' actions could justify them by saying "Well, we need those consulting revenues."

However, accounting's professional standards state that audits must be conducted objectively and that certified financial statements must fairly reflect a company's condition. Those standards exist to help auditors overcome the kind of conflicts of interest that the consulting revenues posed. Those standards were ignored, however, which undermined investors' trust in financial statements and in the accounting profession.

HOT LEGAL AND ETHICAL TOPICS

You should be particularly aware of several "hot topics" that often come up in discussions of modern-day business ethics:

- **White-collar crime** is a fact of business life, so be on the lookout for it. Billions of dollars are lost annually due to fraud, embezzlement, theft of equipment and supplies, false insurance claims, bribery, kickbacks, and various schemes. Customers, suppliers, shareholders, and everyone else pays a price for this. If you learn of such activity, bring it to the attention of your company's chief of security or legal services.

- **Whistle-blowing** refers to going to the authorities or the media with proof that your company is engaged in wrongdoing. Some people see whistle-blowers as "squealers," whereas others see them as heroes. Extreme situations call for extreme measures, and whistle-blowing usually serves an important purpose.

- **Conflicts of interest** arise when you must play two conflicting roles in a situation. For example, if you are part owner of a company that could become a supplier to your current employer, you have a conflict of interest. How can you be objective regarding who should become the supplier when you stand to gain from the decision? When you face a conflict of interest, it's best to inform someone responsible about the situation or to relinquish one of your roles.

Most companies and agencies of the federal government, as well as most other levels of government, do not allow employees to accept gifts of any kind. A high-ranking U.S. government official returned a $79 pen he received in appreciation for a public-speaking engagement for which he was not paid.

Accepting gifts is prohibited because it could create a conflict of interest. Most companies also forbid giving gifts—for example, to customers or suppliers—for the same reason.

- **Fiduciary responsibilities** are typically those that an attorney, financial adviser, or executor of an estate have toward a client. In a fiduciary relationship, you must put your client's interests ahead of your own because the client has placed significant trust in you and your professional abilities. You must never harm the client's interests, must remove yourself from serving him or her if you judge yourself not fully competent, and must protect the client's rights at all costs.

- **Privacy** is the right of everyone. Many believe that our rights to privacy are being eroded by the capability of technology to capture and record personal information, and by government, corporate, and media intrusion into private matters.

- **Sexual harassment** is defined as unwanted repeated or aggressive sexual commentary or advances of a sexual nature toward another person. It is wrong, and it can amount to professional suicide.

TIP

You may have heard that the customer is always right. That's a good policy, but the fact is that the client is not always right. An attorney, accountant, financial adviser, or consultant must tell the client when he or she is wrong. The client relies on the professional's judgment, even if the client doesn't like it or disagrees.

- **Discrimination** based on race, religion, ethnicity, gender, age, marital status, or sexual preference is to be avoided on both legal and ethical grounds. Most of us, if we are honest with ourselves, understand that we all have prejudices to some degree. The goal is to be aware of them and not let them affect our behavior or relationships, especially on the job. In fact, many companies are seeing the benefits of developing a diverse staff, if only because the market is becoming more diverse and companies with diverse staffs will be best able to serve these markets.

- **Business and politics** have become linked in ways that distort the behavior and undermine the standing of both institutions. When legislators accept corporate campaign contributions and then sponsor and vote for bills that clearly benefit the contributors, the legislators and contributors erode trust in government and business. Trust is the foundation for the relationship between leaders and followers. So any "leadership crisis" we may be experiencing stems at least in part from self-dealing, cynical behavior by those in leadership positions in business and in both parties at all levels of government.

GOVERNING THE CORPORATION

Business scandals have moved the topic of *corporate governance* into the spotlight. The term corporate governance refers both to the policies by which a company operates and the system of controls and oversight that enables the company to operate according to those policies.

Policies are broad guidelines for behavior and decisions. For example, many companies once had a "no-layoffs" policy. (Few do today.) In tough times, they might have asked employees to take a pay cut, but they would not lay off anyone. Some companies' financial policies call for them to minimize their debt, whereas others believe in using debt as a large element in their financial structure. Some companies have a policy of paying as little tax as possible and use offshore tax havens (such as Bermuda) and other means to eliminate their taxes. Other companies have a policy of paying at least some tax as part of their obligation as corporate citizens.

PLAIN ENGLISH

Corporate governance refers both to a company's policies and to the system of controls that enables the organization to operate according to those policies. Ultimately, corporate governance is the responsibility of the board of directors, which oversees the company at the policy level. **Policies** are broad guides for acceptable behavior and decisions in specific areas, such as financial policies and human resources policies.

The ultimate authority over the corporation rests with the board of directors, who are elected by the shareholders. Therefore, ultimate responsibility for corporate governance rests with the board. That is why, when the scandals of the early 2000s were unfolding, many observers asked, "Where was the board of directors?" (The answer was often, "In management's back pocket.")

The board, which includes members of senior management (who are the "inside directors"), governs the corporation through two major means: quarterly meetings to discuss, review, and advise management on major developments and decisions; and various committees that oversee specific aspects of the organization.

Sound corporate governance demands that board meetings be well-informed, substantive debates about developments and decisions. Boards with outside directors who rubber-stamp every management decision are useless and do not represent the shareholders or other stakeholders effectively.

Good corporate governance also calls for board-level committees that can act forcefully. Typical oversight committees include the finance committee, which oversees major financial decisions; the audit committee, which oversees audits of the company's financial statements; the human resources committee, which reviews matters such as compensation policy and major layoffs; and the legal affairs committee, which deals with matters such as lawsuits.

Although it will take time for corporate governance in the United States to improve, it will certainly do so. Large shareholders, which include major pension funds, have the power to demand change, and they are demanding it. The erosion of investor confidence and the public's outrage over management abuses of power virtually guarantee that improvement will occur. But again, it will take time.

ACT WITH INTEGRITY

As a business owner, you have an obligation to your subordinates, peers, fellow shareholders, customers, and suppliers to act with integrity. You have the same obligation to the community and to society.

The word *integrity* has the same linguistic roots as the words *integrate* and *integral*. With various shades of meaning, all of these words indicate states of being whole and undivided. Thus, a manager with integrity does not have one set of ethics for business and another set for the rest of his life. Nor does he hold one set of ethics for all areas of his life, which he then betrays when he can profit by doing so.

Integrity comes from within the individual, from his conscience. Managers with integrity don't wonder whether or not they'll be caught violating the law or sound business ethics. They will catch themselves, and when they do, they will think less of themselves. Most importantly, they don't want to place themselves in that position in the first place.

The manager with integrity has one set of sound ethics based on honesty, fairness, and decency, and she applies them to all aspects of her life, including— make that especially—her business dealings.

Big businesses are often reviled by people outside business as being greedy, corrupt, and impersonal. But that can only be true to the extent that most people walk away from doing what we know to be fair and right. Millions and millions of businesspeople, the vast majority of whom never are covered by the media, have proven that you can do well by doing "good" in business.

THE 30-SECOND RECAP

■ Society makes laws to govern people's behavior. Business law governs business transactions, such as contracts, as well as issues such as monopolistic practices, employment, and taxes.

■ In the United States, laws can be created by legislatures, which write codes and statutes, and by courts, which create case law.

■ Key areas of the law for most managers to be concerned about include consumer protection, contracts, employment, and products liability.

■ As a manager you don't have to be a legal expert, but you must use your common sense, distinguish between right and wrong, and act with integrity. Also get legal advice when you need it, be careful what you sign, and use an attorney if the other party has one.

■ Although some managers see conflicts between business goals and ethical behavior, conducting business ethically is good from a business and financial perspective. A number of companies in the news (and executives under indictment) have proven this to be the case.

Consumer Rights and Your Responsibilities

We are all consumers, and most businesses want to do what is right for their customers. Most do. Some don't. The consumer protection laws are written for the minority of businesses that try to make a fast buck at the consumer's expense. No doubt you run a fair business, but even you can inadvertently violate a consumer protection law. This section alerts you to the major laws so that you can properly serve your customer as you intend—honestly.

ADVERTISING WITHOUT MISLEADING

Customers love quality at a bargain price, so you have to convince them that you provide both. Advertising is the means to do just that. Although you certainly do not intend to deceive any potential customer, it's possible that consumers may misconstrue your ad. This section discusses what the Federal Trade Commission (FTC) deems deceptive advertising, so you can avoid any possible claims that your ad campaign violates the law.

Although not all advertising comes within the authority of the FTC, many ads do, including the use of newspapers, electronic media, and the Internet. The FTC usually focuses on national advertising and leaves local deceptive ads to the state and local governments. The latter agencies usually follow the FTC guidelines.

DECEPTIVE ADVERTISING

The FTC requires advertising to be truthful and nondeceptive, fair, and accurate, with evidence to back up its claim.

An advertisement is deceptive if it is likely to mislead a reasonable consumer, contains a *material* misrepresentation, or omits material information. An advertisement is unfair if it causes or likely will cause significant consumer injury that the consumer could not reasonably avoid. Deception may occur when the ad claim takes on an appearance of authenticity—that is, makes specific and concrete claims.

PLAIN ENGLISH

Material refers to a fact of such important that it may reasonably influence a consumer's decision to buy or use a product.

The FTC focuses on the advertisement's effect on the consumer. The relevant questions it asks, and you should, too, about the ad are …

- Are consumers likely to reach false beliefs about the product or service?
- What are the consumer's expectations for the product or service after the ad?
- What would the typical consumer's response be to the ad?

The FTC looks at the ad from the perspective of the average consumer. For example, if an advertisement claims that it can kill numerous household germs, and then, in the fine print, lists dozens it does not affect, the ad is clearly deceptive.

An ad that misrepresents the product by implication is also deceptive. For example, an ad showing a wind-up toy dog strolling down a street implies that the toy dog is able to "walk" for a relatively long distance, such as a block or so. If the dog requires rewinding every 5 feet, you've created a deceptive ad.

Omitting important facts is also prohibited because what the ad doesn't say may be very misleading and deceptive. For example, an ad for a weight-reduction pill that guarantees a consumer will lose weight but fails to mention important side effects, such as vomiting and headaches, is likely to be deemed misleading.

If the advertisement makes any factual claims, such as a restaurant ad that states that a majority of food reviewers recommends the restaurant, there must be evidence to support the assertion. If the ad claims the scientific community supports the diet pill, there must be evidence of reliable studies to confirm the claim.

CAUTION

Never mislead or deceive with your advertising. Deceptive advertising may be the basis of a contract breach for misrepresentation or a tort action for fraud.

On the other hand, vague generalities and obvious exaggerations are not likely to mislead. For example, if you claim that your business serves customers better than any competitor in town, this is considered simple "puffing" and not deceptive advertising.

FTC IN ACTION

The FTC looks closely at claims about health and safety, as well as any claims that consumers have trouble evaluating for themselves. For example, an advertisement for a bicycle helmet may claim that the helmet protects against serious head injuries. That's a difficult concept for the average consumer to evaluate if something goes wrong. The FTC indicates that it will consider the following in acting against an advertisement:

- The scope of the advertising campaign
- The extent to which the ad represents a pattern of deception
- The extent of injury to the consumer's health, safety, or finances

The FTC will likely defer to state or local consumer protection agencies if the advertising is local. Often, a state attorney general has a consumer protection office, as do many municipalities. The Better Business Bureau can help resolve disputes, too. The FTC looks to the impact of the deception; the greater the potential for serious injury or widespread financial injury, the higher the priority for FTC action.

If the FTC receives a significant number of complaints about a deceptive or unfair advertisement, it will investigate and may issue a formal complaint to the alleged offender. If the company agrees to settle by modifying or withdrawing the ad, no further action may occur.

If there is no agreement, the FTC may conduct a hearing to determine whether the company violated the law. An administrative law judge conducts the hearing according to agency administrative rules.

If the FTC proves deceptive or unfair advertising, it may order the company to cease and desist, and may impose daily fines for future violations. It may order corrective advertising, in which the company must admit its earlier ad was misleading. The order may be reviewed or enforced through the federal courts.

YOUR ADS

Here's some positive advice on which most experts agree about creating advertising for your company:

- Be truthful; your ads must be factually accurate.
- Avoid the word *free* unless there are absolutely no strings attached.
- Double-check all pricing information.
- Don't mislead when you compare your product to those of your competitors.
- Have sufficient goods available to meet demands from the ad.
- Test the ad on some customers before you run it to be sure a term or description isn't open to easy misinterpretation.

DECEPTIVE SALES PRACTICES TO AVOID

States have enacted statutes that prohibit certain deceptive sales practices. A few of the violations include ...

- Bait-and-switch advertising.
- Claiming that a product or service is on sale or available when it isn't.
- Claiming a used product to be new.
- Claiming that a product requires replacement or repair when it doesn't.
- Claiming an endorsement of a product or service when none exists.

WHAT YOU SEE IS NOT WHAT YOU GET

Bait-and-switch advertising involves a company offering a very low price for an item to bring customers into the store, but then discouraging the customer from buying it or claiming that the item is unavailable. The low price is the bait, and the salesperson does the switch.

For example, Finest Furniture Company advertised a dining room table for $399. When the customer appeared in response to the ad, however, the salesperson, as instructed by the boss, criticized the advertised model as poorly made and pitched a more expensive $799 model. This is the classic bait-and-switch technique.

If you advertise or mark an item as "on sale," the sale price you set must be less than its usual price. Likewise, for any advertised item, you must have sufficient quantity in stock to meet a reasonably expected demand.

Sale Away!

If your company tags an item as on sale for $59.99 when the usual price is $55.00, this is a deceptive sales practice. If a company advertises VCR players for $111.11, but has only a few in stock (particularly if it then tries to switch customers to a higher-priced item), this, too, is a deceptive practice. Many of the consumer complaints to the FTC involve auto-repair shops billing customers for a new auto part when it's used, or making unwarranted repairs, all of which are deceptive practices.

Endorsing the Truth

If a company claims an endorsement, say from *Consumer Reports,* when there is none, it violates the law. It might be helpful to briefly review the FTC endorsement and testimonial guidelines. These are posted on the FTC website (www.ftc.gov). Product or service endorsements must reflect the honest opinions, findings, beliefs, or experience of the endorser. If the advertisement represents the endorser as using the product, the endorser must have been a bona fide user at the time the endorsement was made.

For example, Ima Smiley must use the toothpaste that she endorses. If an expert endorses the product, his or her qualifications must in fact give that person the expertise represented. For example, the endorser of an automobile's engineering designs should have engineering qualifications associated with cars, not a chemical engineering degree.

In sales, the biblical golden rule should apply. Treat your customers as you would want to be treated—and they will return.

Soliciting by Phone, Delivering by Mail

In addition to deceptive practice statutes, many states have laws restricting telemarketers' activities. These laws vary, so you need to contact your state consumer protection division. Federal law prohibits telephone solicitation using an automatic telephone dialing system or prerecorded message.

Many state laws permit a buyer who purchased merchandise at his or her residence to cancel the sale by written notification to the seller within three business days. For example, if Hal Homeowner buys a vacuum cleaner from a door-to-door salesman, Hal has three days to cancel the sale. If you receive unordered merchandise through the mail, you can refuse delivery or treat the unsolicited merchandise as a gift. For example, if you didn't order the multi-volume set of Lord Byron's *Complete Poems* but received one in your mail complete with a bill, you may either return or keep the unordered merchandise without cost to you. (However, keep in mind that you won't be able to do so if you're a member of a book or music club and simply fail to return the monthly selection slip.)

A company that sells over the telephone or takes mail-order sales must ship the product within the time stated or advertised, inform customers when the orders cannot be shipped on time, and issue a refund within a specified time when an order is cancelled.

CONSUMER SAFETY LAWS

Two federal agencies are responsible for the health and safety of many consumer products: the Consumer Product Safety Commission (CPSC) and the Food and Drug Administration (FDA).

PROTECTING CONSUMERS

The CPSC has comprehensive regulatory authority over about 15,000 consumer products, including toys, clothing, appliances, furniture, and playground and sports equipment. Regulations apply to any company that manufactures, imports, distributes, or sells any consumer product covered by its law.

The Consumer Product Safety Commission issues mandatory safety standards for some products (such as bicycles), bans certain products (such as lead-based paint), and helps develop standards for other products. CPSC maintains a clearinghouse of information on the risks associated with consumer products.

According to CPSC, small businesses must report to the CPSC when …

■ One of its products has a defect or creates a substantial risk of injury to the public.

■ One of the manufacturer's consumer products has been involved in three or more personal injury lawsuits in a two-year period.

■ Toys involve incidents of children choking on them.

TIP
CPSC has a small business ombudsman to assist you in answering questions about compliance with its laws. The CPSC website is www.cpsc.gov.

MEDICATION AND FOODSTUFF PROTECTION

The FDA protects consumers from purchasing and using adulterated or mis-branded food and drugs. The Food and Drug Administration regulates food additives and medical and other health devices. If your company is involved in any of these areas, it would be worthwhile to visit this agency's website at www.fda.gov. Federal and state laws regulate information provided on consumer product labels and packages. The statutes require accurate information about products and a warning of possible dangers from their use. For example, packaged-food labeling must include nutritional facts, and limit the use of such terms as *fresh* and *low fat*. The FDA, Agricultural Department, FTC, and Department of Health and Human Services are all involved in these areas, as are some state agencies. If your business includes packaging consumer goods, visit all these agencies' websites for more specific information.

CREDIT WHERE CREDIT IS DUE

Most businesses extend credit to their customers in one form or another. You need to know the consumer credit laws, which include the following:

- *Equal Credit Opportunity Act (ECOA)*
- *Fair Credit Reporting Act (FCRA)*
- *Truth in Lending Act*
- *Fair Credit Billing Act (FCBA)*
- *Electronic Fund Transfer Act (EFTA)*
- *Fair Debt Collection Practices Act (FDCPA)*

APPLYING FOR CREDIT

When a customer applies for credit, a business cannot discriminate on the basis of sex, race, marital status, religion, national origin, age, or receipt of public assistance. The *Equal Credit Opportunity Act (ECOA)* applies to any company that regularly extends credit, including retail and department stores. For example, the ABC store is violating the law if it requires married women to have their husband cosign any loan. The law doesn't prohibit you from refusing credit based on a customer's finances—you just can't discriminate based on nonfinancial factors.

TIP

Always notify your customers or potential employees if you use a credit report to deny them employment or take any other adverse action based on that report, as per the *FCRA*. You'll also need to provide the name and address of the reporting agency to your customers.

The *Fair Credit Reporting Act (FCRA)* is designed to ensure that consumer credit reporting companies furnish accurate and complete information. If you deny a customer credit because of a credit report, you must notify the customer of the name and address of the credit reporting agency.

Under the *FCRA,* the consumer has a right to receive a copy of his or her credit report from a credit reporting agency, to know who received the credit report in the last year (or two years if employment related), and to receive a free copy of the credit report if credit was denied on the basis of information in the report. Any consumer has the right to dispute the accuracy of the information in the report, and to add a summary explanation if the dispute is not satisfactorily resolved.

Full Disclosure

The *Truth in Lending Act* is primarily a credit disclosure law for personal loans and installment sales involving $25,000 or less. It also covers real estate mortgage loans. The purpose of the act is to allow consumers to comparison shop among lenders. If you extend credit to a consumer, you must conspicuously state the annual percentage rate (APR) of the loan and the total cost of the loan. For example, if a customer purchases an appliance on a retail installment contract, the agreement would state "10 percent APR, and total cost of payments for the life of loan is $1,100." The APR includes all the direct costs, including interest, and all indirect charges imposed for the credit offered, such as the cost of a credit report. A violation of the disclosure requirements may permit the consumer to sue for compensatory and punitive damages, as well as attorneys' fees.

Any loan that results in obtaining a second mortgage or refinance loan on a consumer's residence requires a three-business-day right to rescind. For example, a company that sells aluminum siding and obtains a second mortgage on the residence for the financing *must* allow this three-day rescission right.

Many consumer leases are also covered under amendments to *Truth in Lending.* The act regulates consumer leases involving a contractual obligation of $25,000 or less and the lease exceeds four months. Any advertisement and lease must disclose the total amount due, the number and amounts of lease payments, determination of residual value and realized value, and whether an extra charge is imposed at the end of the lease term. A new car lease is a typical application of the statute.

Laws that limit the rate of interest that can be charged are called usury statutes. State statutes may limit the rate of interest that can be charged on a loan or retail installment sale. Laws vary, so consult your state statutes.

Billing, Credit Cards, and the *EFTA*

Billing mistakes on credit card statements and electronic fund transfer accounts, including debit cards and ATMs, do occur. The *Fair Credit Billing Act (FCBA)* establishes a procedure for correcting those credit card billing mistakes. The credit card customer must notify the issuer (the credit card company, not the store from which he or she bought the item) within 60 days from the billing. The issuer is then obligated to investigate any alleged errors. If the error is confirmed, the charged item is deleted; however, if the issuer denies the error, the consumer may request documentation of the disputed transaction.

Credit card holders are liable for no more that $50 per card when unauthorized charges are made before the issuer is notified. A stolen credit card is the most typical example of limited liability. However, if a holder lends another person his or her credit card, and that person misuses it, the holder is liable for all charges.

The *Electronic Funds Transfer Act (EFTA)* covers automatic teller machines, point-of-sale (debit) cards, and electronic funds transfers. The consumer must promptly notify the issuer that the card is lost or stolen to minimize responsibility. If notice is given within two days, the liability is $50; over two days and up to 60 days, the liability is $500; over 60 days, the liability may be unlimited. If there are any errors on the EFT statement, the customer must report the error within 60 days, and after the timely reporting the issuer must investigate and report its conclusions to the customer.

Debt Collection

The *Fair Debt Collection Practices Act (FDCPA)* applies to debt collection companies and collection attorneys and prohibits certain abuses; they are liable for their misconduct. The act does not apply to creditors who are collecting their own accounts.

The act requires a collection agency to include a validation notice whenever it initially contacts a debtor for payment. The notice must state that the debtor has 30 days within which to dispute the debt and to request a written verification of the debt.

FDCPA specifically prohibits the collection agency from using the following tactics:

■ Contacting the debtor at his or her place of employment if the employer objects.

■ Contacting the debtor during inconvenient or unusual times

■ Contacting third parties other than the debtor's parents, spouse, or financial advisor

■ Harassing or intimidating the debtor, such as posing as a court official

■ Contacting the debtor after the debtor has notified the agency that he or she refuses to pay, except as to advise of a possible lawsuit

Again, a creditor is not covered by the act so long as the creditor does not use its own name.

HELPFUL SOURCES

Federal websites are very useful: Federal Trade Commission (www.ftc.gov); Consumer Product Safety Commission (www.cpsc.gov), Food and Drug Administration (www. fda.gov); Health and Human Services (www.hhs.gov); Small Business Administration, which has great links (www.sba.gov). Visit your state consumer protection website. Some local governments have a consumer affairs website. Consumer Union, the publisher of *Consumer Reports* magazine, has a website, both free and subscription (www. ConsumerReports.org).

THE 30-SECOND RECAP

■ A deceptive advertisement, according to the FTC, is one that is likely to mislead a reasonable consumer.

■ Federal law requires anyone who sells a product that has caused three or more serious personal injuries within two years to report this to the Consumer Product Safety Commission.

■ *Truth in Lending* requires installment sales retailers to notify the consumer of the annual percent rate (APR).

Growing Your Business Profitably

Techniques for Staying Ahead of the Competition

This section concentrates on ways to ensure that you're in touch with your market, as well as ways to avoid letting the competition eat up sales that you should have had. This section covers a variety of techniques that can help you stay ahead of the competition while you build your business.

Is Your Comfort Zone in a Rut?

Your personal comfort zone is where you're comfortable in what you're doing, in your business, your job, your life, and your experiences. It is having no feelings of risk or anxiety.

Feeling comfortable is a nice idea, but it could turn into being in a rut. You may be thinking, what's so bad about that? Well, maybe nothing—unless you're in business: If you're in business, it can be dangerous. While you lounge in your comfort zone, the competition will more than likely be leaving you in the dust.

Beware of the comfort zone! In our fast-paced, competitive world, complacency can severely limit your personal and professional growth and can be fatal to your business. You need to keep your edge, which is the unique character of your products or services. To do that, you have to keep your ideas fresh and be open to diversification and change. You also have to be profit-oriented and keep your eye on social trends and your market's taste in arts and crafts. Doesn't sound very comfortable, does it?

So how do you step out of the comfort zone? Try some simple things: Drive home a different way, shop at a different store, sleep on the other side of the bed, or design a new item. Make a conscious effort to experiment.

Here's the challenge to you: Make a list of 15 to 20 things that, if you could do them successfully, would help you feel more stimulated, energized, and productive—such as give a speech, write and publish a design, start an exercise program, meditate daily, teach a new class, feed a homeless person, volunteer, try a new product, learn to work in a new medium, sign up for a craft class, start a new project you've been meaning to get around to, and so on.

Choose one or two things from your list that you're willing to do within the next 30 days. Schedule them, and then go for it. Afterward, choose one or two more, and do it again. Make personal and professional growth a lifelong habit. Don't park in your comfort zone. It's bad for business; your competition *will* creep up on you.

TIP

Experiment with a new marketing method. Allow your anxiety level to increase, and allow the adrenaline in your body to make you sharp, creative, and quick. As we try new things, we gain confidence in our ability to survive and to implement new ideas.

KEEP CREATIVE THINKING ALIVE

A talk radio host told a story he swore he had read in the local newspaper. Whether or not it actually happened, the anecdote provides a great example of *thinking outside of the box*. It seems that a man was driving home one after-noon when he got a flat tire. He happened to pull over in front of the city's largest mental institution. The man noticed one of the patients watching him from behind the fence as he grabbed the jack out of his trunk.

The driver loosened each of the four lug nuts on the wheel and placed them inside the hubcap he had put on the ground. He put the spare tire on, but as he turned to grab the lug nuts, he kicked the hubcap and caused them all to roll into a sewer opening a few feet away. Dismayed, he screamed, "Oh no! Now what am I gonna do? I'm ruined. There's no way I can go anywhere now!"

A voice came from behind the mental institution's fence: "You still have four lug nuts on each of the other three wheels. Why not take one nut off of each one and put those three on the tire that you're changing. That should at least get you to a gas station or somewhere where you can get more lug nuts." The driver was relieved—and impressed. "Wow," he said, "that's amazing. How did you think of that?" The patient replied, "I may be crazy, but I'm not stupid."

Think about this story the next time you're faced with a challenge that seems insurmountable, or the next time you experience some type of creative block. *Don't focus on the problem area only.* Ask yourself, "What opportunities to remedy this situation are right here in front of me?" Look for a way over, under, around, or through the obstacle. Thinking outside of the box can keep you head and shoulders above the competition and in touch with your market.

BRAINSTORMING

Brainstorming can help you come up with scads of new ideas; it can help you decide which are the best ones. Here are a few tips to help you get into the brainstorming mode:

- Always have a small notebook and a pen or pencil with you and on your nightstand. If you're struck by an idea, you can quickly jot it down. Go window-shopping in gift shops and department stores— just take in the sights, or browse home décor and gift catalogs. New, unrelated ideas are often sparked in creative minds by being exposed to a multitude of products, colors, shapes, and styles. Write down anything that pops into your mind. When you reread your notes, you may discover that about 90 percent of your ideas are off-the-wall. Don't worry, that's normal. What's important is the other 10 percent, the ideas that are workable.

- If you're stuck for an idea, open a dictionary, randomly select a word, and then try to formulate ideas that incorporate the word. You'd be surprised how well this works. The concept is based on a simple but little-known truth: Freedom inhibits creativity. There's nothing like restriction to get you thinking.

- When you have a problem, define it. It could be, "We need a new product for the holiday season." When you write it out concisely, you'll probably find ideas positively spewing out of your head.

- If you can't think, go for a walk. A change of atmosphere is good for you, and gentle exercise helps shake up the brain cells.

- Exercise your brain. Like bodies, brains need exercise to keep fit. If you don't exercise your brain, it will get flabby and useless. Exercise your brain by reading a lot, talking to creative people, and disagreeing with people—arguing can be a terrific way to give your brain cells a workout. But note this: Arguing about fashion trends or politics is good for you; bickering over who should take out the trash is not. If you work alone, hop on the computer and network with some other artisans to get those creative ideas flowing.

TIP

Napoleon Hill, motivational speaker and author, said, "Whatever the mind can conceive and believe, it can achieve." Use brainstorming to jog your creativity and start new ideas flowing, and then follow through to achieve results.

Brainstorming can generate lots of ideas. It's most effective with a group of people and should be performed in a relaxed environment. But whether you brainstorm alone or in a group session, save all your notes; make it a practice to review them from time to time, and keep building on the list. You'll be amazed to find that looking at notes about your ideas weeks later can spark a whole new set of ideas. Continually generating new design ideas and marketing directions is the way to stay ahead of your competition.

THE CUSTOMER SERVICE EDGE

In looking at the competitive challenges of being in small business, we eliminated the possibility of competing with chain store prices. Many small business owners have figured out how to compete with their larger corporate customers. Customer relations is an area in which the business owner can build a loyal return customer base.

The truth is that no business is exempt from the occasional customer complaint, and as sales volume increases, the odds are good that so will the number of complaints. This is an inevitable part of doing business. Even if you're doing absolutely everything right, someone will complain. Accept the fact that it's impossible to please everyone, no matter what you do. What's important is how you handle troublesome customer matters.

TIP

When it comes to competing with chain stores, small business owners have a built-in competitive edge: They have unique and original product designs that chain stores do not, which gives them a market niche.

Remember that the customer is always right. Never be confrontational, and remain calm (you can let it all out later). One grumbling customer can do more harm to your business image than 10 totally satisfied ones will do good. Why? People love to gossip about the bad stuff; it's just human nature. Treat your customers with courtesy, solve their problems quickly, and turn every negative situation into a positive one. Give them the attention and responsiveness that a chain store can't provide, and you'll have an edge on the competition. Plan to outperform your competitors in every area of customer service.

PLAN FOR PROFITS

The secret to success in your business is to *think profit* in everything you do. Profits don't just keep happening. Continually evaluate every aspect of your business operation, and *plan for profits!*

- **Provide a variety of price ranges.** Use inexpensive items as attention-grabbers to stop traffic. This is particularly important when you sell at trade shows or malls. You want to have something to stop traffic at your booth. When you have the customer stopped, your chances are greatly improved that people will browse your full line and buy something.

CAUTION

Don't hang on to products or services that are slow sellers. Take them out of your line, or redesign them.

- **Be cost-effective.** Don't spend five hours producing an item that you can retail for only $30. Set a dollar amount for your labor, and factor it into every item that you make. Sell products that keep the time investment low and the profit margin high. Learn to group tasks to save time, not only in product production, but also in all your daily routine business tasks. Pay all the bills at once, enter all the orders together, and set aside a specific time to pack and ship orders or order more supplies.

- **Be impartial.** Don't be emotionally tied to your product or service. If a product or service is a slow seller or is not cost-effective, take it out of your line.

- **Follow market trends.** Stay updated on color trends, styles, themes, and lifestyle changes. Use these ideas to adapt your products to the hot-selling trends. Use your creative imagination to create new items or redesign some existing products or services. Remember, a small business has an advantage over a big business; it can usually react to market changes much faster and reap the rewards.

- **Have a hot seller.** Be prepared to ride the wave of a hot seller. Promote and feature your best-selling products. Look at what you can make in the way of compatible products to sell that will ride on the coattails of your sales leader.

- **Know your numbers.** Keep good records that can provide you with information to determine exactly where your actual profits come from. Review them to determine how to address unprofitable areas and then focus on the profit-making areas of your business. Sell in as many different markets as possible. This way, if one market is soft, you have alternative sales working to keep your income rolling in. Plan to make the time to evaluate all aspects of your business on a regular basis to guarantee a profitable, steady growth pattern.

TIP

Always be on the alert for new items to add to your line. Nothing remains a "hot seller" forever. Have new items worked into your line on a regular basis, or modify an existing product to the current selling trends.

WHAT ARE FADS AND TRENDS?

The latest styles, the hot new looks, new technology, or a new way of doing something … yes, they are as important to your product production as they are to the services you plan to offer.

WHAT'S THE DIFFERENCE BETWEEN A FAD AND A TREND?

A *fad* is fleeting—here today, gone tomorrow. It might be a new color, such as hot pink, or a garden bug, or a woodland critter. Most people don't want to decorate their entire house in hot pink or even live with it for the long term, but fads are fun touches for updating the home or for gift giving. They're an important part of your business.

A *trend* has staying power. Some trends start out as fads and then move on to become trends, or even classics. Fads and trends can very quickly create consumer demand, and your sales numbers will reflect this if you keep your line up to date.

TIP

A fad comes and goes; a trend has staying power. Some, but not all, trends—and even classics—started out as fads. The Slinky toy was a fad in the 1940's as well as hula hoops in the '50s and the Rubik's cube in the '70s. In the '80s and '90s, the trend in the toy industry was more toward electronics and toys tied to movies.

If you're an artisan, you need to be aware at all times of what is happening in the home décor and gift industries. If you're unable to attend trade shows, a quick and easy way to keep up with the latest news is to go to your local craft supply store and take a look at the newest pattern books. Really examine what's on the shelves and in the sales circulars. It's a way to take advantage of the trend research that's already been done by professional buyers. Study trade publications, find out what's new, and then continue monitoring products to see what has staying power and what's on the way out. It's important to keep checking, because trends—and even the classics—may evolve and change over time. Just look at how country décor has cleaned up its act: It's lighter, has less clutter, and has more of a contemporary edge. Use industry trends and forecasts to help you with design ideas.

THE COLOR STORY AND SOCIAL TRENDS

Color, and the direction it's taking, has always been a major factor in product design. CMG (Color Marketing Group) is a nonprofit organization made up of 1,600 color designers, founded in 1962 and based in Alexandria, Virginia. CMG members forecast *color directions* one to three years in advance for all major industries, manufactured products, and services for both consumer and commercial goods. CMG's forecasts serve as a guide for designers developing new colors for new and existing products.

CMG points to blue as an example of how color is influenced by social trends. Blue is both soothing and spiritual. It is also the favorite color of most Americans. In addition, blue is closely linked to symbols of our heritage and history, not to mention our favorite item of clothing. Blues have hit the marketplace in products ranging from dresses to dishes, but the clue to its lingering importance lies elsewhere. A variety of blues is now emerging in product categories where color longevity is valued. "Mass media and the Internet are changing the speed with which colors and trends move within our society, and around the world," says Sue Hannah, co-chairman of the Consumer Color Directions Committee. "A design launched in Tokyo today can be purchased in Des Moines tomorrow. It no longer takes years for a color trend to move from one continent to another."

With these important influences in mind, CMG members identified four color clusters that will be important to consumers during this next decade:

- **Techno-colors.** From gray to taupe to black and pure white, these colors are both from and for technology. Neutral colors are required for products that must work in widely differentiated environments.

- **Chromatic adrenaline colors.** These energetic hues will brighten color combinations and add punch to product lines.

- **Serenity colors.** These are colors influenced by consumers' desire for more balance and harmony in their lives. They are pale, soft, and reassuring; some come from nature, inspired mostly by water.

- **Mediterranean culture colors.** These are a group of rich, earthy, spice colors most often seen in textiles dyed with centuries-old natural methods.

DESIGNING TRENDS FORECAST

Forecasters of trends that will be influencing design in the new millennium point to the following:

- **Individualism.** People increasingly want to customize or personalize an object or their environment.

- **Simplicity.** People seek a more humanized way of living as a result of the recent incorporation of many new technologies into daily life. Softened, calm, and livable are strong themes surrounding the concept of simplicity, and they lead to forecasts for softer and lighter colors, as well as more neutralized color.

■ **Spirituality.** Lead the spirit, lead the eye. Approach life with optimism and hopefulness. We are more comfortable expressing ourselves through intuition and our spiritual sides.

■ **Water.** Cleansing and pure, water is a physical symbol of our themes of simplicity and spirituality. Water is the final evolution of nature's influence on the world's color palettes.

■ **Ethnic and cultural blending.** Interest in colors of various skin tones is evidence of increased acceptance of cultural blending resulting from increased globalization. For example, there was interest in all things Australian around the 2000 Olympics.

■ **Texture and finish.** Visual and actual texture, patterns, and finishes increase the perception of quality and value. For example, smooth and soft textures can complement or act as a counterbalance to coarse textures.

Fads, trends, colors, and textures are a vital part of what keeps designing new products fun and interesting—*and what keeps your customers coming back for more!*

PRODUCT LIFE CYCLE

All products and services go through a *life cycle.* They are the evolutionary four phases: infancy, growth, maturity, and decline. This starts from infancy (when it is developed) and moves to decline (when it is taken off the market). The perceived value and sales volume change throughout the life cycle. It's essential that you keep track of where your products or services are in their life cycle. It directly affects the amount of sales and income that you will receive during each phase, and it tells you when you need to update or cancel an item or create a new one.

■ **Phase 1.** In infancy, the product or service is first introduced to the market and needs time to build customer awareness and confidence.

■ **Phase 2.** Growth is the period in which sales are gradually building and competition usually starts to show up.

■ **Phase 3.** Maturity is the peak, the leveling-off period at which consumer demand has reached a saturation point in the market and competition is usually intense.

■ **Phase 4.** Decline happens when customer demand is gradually reduced because improved variations, new technology, or other factors make the product less desirable or obsolete.

The life cycle plays an important role. A few years ago, for example, "garden decorative" products were new to the gift industry and home décor market. The market seemed to be able to absorb every decorative bird house, yard sign, and stepping-stone produced. Today, however, buyers are selecting only the truly unique, distinctive items from this category because the market is maturing. In contrast, sales for home accessory categories are growing by leaps and bounds.

THE CHALLENGE OF CHANGE

Most new business owners often expect to devote a lot of time and effort to getting their businesses established. Then they plan to relax as the business "runs itself" and continues to grow. Maybe this was achievable in the past. It isn't today. Aggressive, innovative competitors and rapidly changing technology make it impossible to establish a system that will automatically meet all future challenges.

EXPECT CHANGE

Develop a "change is normal" attitude. Realize that you're never going to reach the point at which you know your business so well that you can stop learning or being innovative. Just when you think you've mastered operating it, something will change and disrupt your growth.

Make it a habit to look for changes that may be part of a developing trend. Then try to determine how this trend may impact the growth of your business. You can develop the best solution to a problem when you catch it early and take your time to carefully work out your response. There's nothing more difficult than trying to make good long-term business decisions while you're trying to rescue rapidly falling sales.

TAKE DEFENSIVE ACTION IN ADVANCE: DIVERSIFY

Diversification is your best defense against the impact of change. This applies in two major areas:

- The products or services you offer
- Your marketing activities

The primary reason that you want to offer a variety of related products or services to your customers is to maximize your income. But there's a second reason: Changing market conditions or an aggressive competitor can cause sales for a product or service to decline, often suddenly. The impact won't be devastating if a variety of other products or services continue to produce sales for you.

The same rule applies to marketing. You'll reach more prospects and generate more sales by using a variety of marketing methods than you will by using just one or two. This policy also protects you from suddenly losing a substantial volume of business because one of your marketing methods stopped producing results.

LOOK FOR OPPORTUNITY HIDDEN IN CHANGE

The challenge of change often forces you to discover a hidden opportunity that you can exploit to gain more business. Take Ron, for example, the owner of a small computer store near a fast-growing city in the Northeast. Two years ago, a large retail computer chain started building a new superstore nearby. Ron realized that he wasn't going to be able to compete with that store's prices and stay in business, so he set up a used computer equipment section in his store and started advertising that he would upgrade, refurbish, and buy or sell used equipment. Today most of Ron's income is generated by sales of used equipment. His total income has almost doubled, and he's even planning to expand his used equipment business to the Internet. It's an opportunity that Ron wouldn't have recognized without the challenge of competition.

TIP

Keep looking for and testing new marketing tools and some old ones that you haven't tried yet. Make it a habit to look for changes that may signal a developing trend, and then try to determine how the trend might impact the growth of your business.

The biggest challenge to business success today is change. Staying ahead of your competition is easy if you're aware of what you need to do and you then take the appropriate action.

THE 30-SECOND RECAP

- Always staying in your comfort zone can be very limiting. In our fast-paced competitive world, complacency can limit your personal growth and be fatal to your business.
- Think outside of the box to develop and maintain your creativity. Originality gives you a competitive edge.
- To stay ahead of the competition, expect change, and respond to it quickly and creatively.
- Being successful in business means skillfully weaving all the components of your business together in harmony, guided by your vision.

Charting a Course with Strategic Planning

All the activities and tools covered so far have to serve the larger needs of the company. All the things that finance, accounting, marketing, and sales do must be coordinated so that they work together smoothly.

This calls for a long-term strategic plan. You need a plan to give managers the framework for making good decisions. That plan must relate to the major goals of the whole company, and management's decisions must serve those goals.

This section explains long-range strategic planning, which is usually just called strategic planning. It tells you why you need a strategic plan and covers steps and techniques that will help you create one. (The business plan—a document that explains the operations, finances, and marketing goals of a small business or a business unit—is covered in Part 3.)

WHAT IS STRATEGIC PLANNING?

Strategic planning typically involves five steps:

1. Define the company's goals.
2. Analyze the company's environment.
3. Consider the company's resources.
4. Identify actions that will move the company toward its goals.
5. Implement the actions and monitor progress.

Through the rest of this section, each of these elements is explained.

DEFINE THE COMPANY'S GOALS

The company must have a large, unifying goal that will organize the thinking and activities of everyone in the outfit. The most widely accepted goal of a company is to maximize long-term *shareholder value*—that is, to improve the worth of the company.

PLAIN ENGLISH

Shareholder value is the investment of the owners of the company. The most common measure of this is the stock price multiplied by the number of shares of stock outstanding. The higher the stock's price, the higher the shareholder value.

Unfortunately, having the goal of maximizing shareholder value does not tell you *how* to maximize shareholder value. So most companies need one or more other strategic goals that will help them do that.

Your goals should help you direct the assessments of the environment and your resources. They can be broad ("to increase sales and operating profits by 10 percent") or more specific ("to increase European sales of the Mixmaster to $3 million next year").

Later, you may find that these goals are too low or too high. Or you may find that you can develop several specific goals that would support one overall goal. For instance, you might identify product lines that can increase sales and profits by more than 10 percent.

In setting a corporate goal you must …

- Define your business in the broadest terms possible.
- Make your goal measurable.
- Consider the basic sales-growth strategies.

Let's look at each of these guidelines.

DEFINE YOUR BUSINESS BROADLY

Many companies have gotten themselves in trouble by defining their business too narrowly. Management consultant Peter Drucker uses the example of the railroads to illustrate this. Before the development of air travel, the senior managers of railroads believed they were in the railroad business. If they had seen themselves in the transportation business instead, they would have been prepared to compete when airplanes came along.

Although it hardly guarantees success, looking at your business broadly will open your mind to possibilities you might otherwise miss. For example, if you are in training or consulting, think of yourself as being in the information business. This may open up possibilities in publishing and software. If you are in the restaurant business, think of it as food services or entertainment. You may find that corporate catering, cooking classes, or dinner theater are avenues of growth for you.

 TIP

Many companies fail because they are one-product firms. For long-term success, most companies need a "second act." WordPerfect was once the most popular word processing software around until Microsoft Word devoured the market. WordPerfect Corp had no second act to counter and eventually wound up selling out to Corel Corporation.

How Will You Know You Arrived?

To be "real," a goal must be measurable. Vague goals don't motivate people. Be precise. Define a goal in numerical terms, if possible. Useful measures include revenue and profit gains, number and size of accounts, market share in certain product and customer groups, and percentage of sales and profits in certain areas of the business. These goals are measurable. And if you fail to achieve them, at least you'll know how close you came.

Consider the Sales-Growth Strategies

The key strategic question that recurs every year is, "Where will growth come from?"

Thinking about your sales strategies as goals—for example, to sell new products to existing customers—will help you identify markets, customers, products, and price sensitivities as you assess the environment and your resources.

Analyze the Company's Environment

The company's environment includes the economy, market, competitive landscape, and regulatory and social climate. You have to analyze each of these aspects because threats and opportunities can emerge in any one of them. Most companies make a strategic plan every year or two because the environment changes, and as it does, so do the threats and opportunities.

Nonetheless, many companies have been blindsided by change—succumbing to competitors they failed to take seriously and missing opportunities that once stared them in the face.

Here are some examples of major threats and opportunities that have challenged various industries in the past 25 years:

- The U.S. auto industry faces an ongoing competitive threat from foreign automakers.
- The rise of microcomputers radically altered the market for mini-computers and mainframes.
- The tobacco industry faces serious regulatory and social challenges, as does health care, which also faces rising costs due to the aging of the population.

However, opportunities also abound, often imbedded in threats. The microcomputer brought tremendous opportunities to many companies of all kinds. Although foreign competitors pose threats, foreign nations have also become more robust export markets for U.S. goods. The entire "green revolution" has generated profits for companies that address environmental concerns.

The following sections look at the different parts of your environment that you need to continually monitor.

CUSTOMERS AND PROSPECTS

Any sales-growth strategies you suggest must take into account your customers' needs, satisfaction, price sensitivity, and alternative product choices. Be sure to get the views of the sales force on these issues. Market research and the business press can also be good sources of information on consumer preferences and habits.

COMPETITORS

You must closely monitor your competitors and—key point—your potential competitors by analyzing annual reports, reading announcements of personnel changes, examining new products, keeping up with acquisitions and alliances, and even speaking with former employees or current customers to gain insight into competitors' plans and operations. Again, your sales force can offer excellent insights into your competitors.

SUPPLIERS

Keep an eye on your suppliers because they can affect your future. If they plan to increase their prices or phase out a product, it could impact your outfit. Plan accordingly. Pay special attention to the financial condition of your major suppliers.

TIP

Keep abreast of any public company you compete with or do business with by asking for information as a potential investor. You can receive company announcements, quarterly and annual reports, and press releases.

To monitor suppliers, talk—and listen—to their salespeople and read the business press. Read the annual report of any supplier upon whom you depend heavily. Suppliers don't always warn customers of adverse changes. The sooner you know of any, the sooner you can respond.

REGULATORY AND SOCIAL CHANGE

The strategic-planning process *must* include an analysis of changes in regulations that affect your business. These changes are often driven by social change. Cigarettes are a good example of a product affected by both regulatory and social change. Since the 1960s, when television commercials for cigarettes were banned, the tobacco industry has seen increasing restrictions on its business.

Deregulation—the full or partial lifting of restrictions on business activity—can change the landscape, too. Deregulation of power generation, for example, has created an environment of change and competition in a business that had been stable and predictable.

PLAIN ENGLISH

Deregulation occurs when an industry that had been operating under close government restrictions sees those restrictions loosened or removed.

Your local, state, and federal representatives and your trade association can help you keep abreast of regulatory change. In large, publicly held companies, this is the job of the government affairs or legal staff.

ECONOMIC TRENDS

Depending on your business, the major economic factors you should consider might include interest rates; housing starts; consumer confidence; consumer spending; monetary and fiscal policies; and local, state, regional, and national (and perhaps international) growth trends.

Economic information, including news of the latest statistics and forecasts, is continually reported in the business press. Many large banks and investment firms make forecasts available to their customers. There are also consulting firms that sell economic forecasts and data, with DRI/WEFA and Economy.com among the most prominent.

ADD IT UP

After you assess the environment, you must examine each development you have identified and decide whether it is a threat or an opportunity. The following table shows how this kind of assessment might look for a U.S. auto manufacturer.

Development	Threat	Opportunity	Comment
Customers			
Larger vehicles falling out of favor	3		We get 60% of profits from mid- to large-size cars and SUVs.
Desire more comfort and performance in smaller cars	3	3	We can respond by repositioning our compacts.
Spending lower percentage of income on transportation	3		May hurt sales and profits. Stress economic benefits of our cars?

Development	Threat	Opportunity	Comment
		Competitors	
Several new competitive compact models	3		We must distinguish our lower-end models, perhaps by adding luxury features.
Lower-priced smaller cars added to Mercedes and BMW lines	3		We can deliver luxury in a small car at a much lower price.
		Suppliers	
Rising steel prices	3		Can we nail down low prices in contracts now?
Small firm has a new accident-prevention technology		3	Should we test it? Can we get an exclusive? At what cost?
		Economic	
Growth will slow next year	3		This will make it hard to match this year's sales level.
Rising interest rates ahead	3	3	Threat to sales volume, but can benefit our financing subsidiary.
		Regulatory/Social	
Environmental groups more visibly opposing large vehicles	3		Marketing must stress environmental friendliness.
Possibly higher gas prices		3	Could work in favor of our economy models.

As you see, some developments pose both a threat and an opportunity. This is often the case because changes in various areas actually open up opportunities while posing a threat. (Remember: The Chinese character for "crisis" combines the symbols for "threat" and "opportunity.")

CONSIDER THE COMPANY'S RESOURCES

Most companies do a decent, if incomplete, job of considering their resources.

In assessing your company's resources, you must consider the resources you need, as well as those you have. These needs are dictated by the company's goals and by the threats and opportunities in the environment. Your most important resources include the following:

- Product profitability and growth
- People
- Productive capacity
- Other resources

Let's examine each of these.

PROFITABILITY AND GROWTH

Regarding the profitability of current products, you must answer the questions: Which product lines and activities are making money? Which are not? How do we create more money-making ones? How do we phase out unprofitable ones?

Regarding growth, you must answer the questions: Which product lines and activities are growing the fastest? Which are stagnant or declining? How can we boost the growing products and eliminate the others?

A straight accounting analysis will tell you a lot about the profitability and growth of your company or products. This means that you need accurate numbers from your accountants that clearly identify revenues and costs.

 TIP

To protect themselves, some managers do not want their financial results to be very clear. They usually construct complicated systems, keep poor records, and argue about whose costs are whose. Senior management must insist that accounting work with department managers to develop clear, accurate, comparable numbers that fairly reflect their performance.

There is an excellent tool to help you evaluate the relative strength and profitability of your products or product lines: the growth-share matrix. The Boston Consulting Group (BCG) developed the growth-share matrix (or growth/market-share matrix) to help managers of multidivisional companies classify their subsidiaries. However, it also helps managers of a single company or division to classify products and product lines.

The classification system works along two dimensions: market growth and market share. Basically, growth is a measure of how much investment—that is, cash—the company or product requires. High growth requires lots of cash; low growth needs less cash. Market share is a measure of the company's or product's position in its market, which can range from dominant to weak. In general, the larger the market share, the more cash the company or product should be generating for the owners.

Here's how the growth-share matrix looks:

Market Growth	High	Star	?
	Low	Cash Cow	Dog
		High	Low
		Market Share	

Here's how to read the growth-share matrix:

- A star has high market share in a rapidly growing market. It needs a high level of investment, but it can generate lots of cash. That's why it's a star. To manage a star, invest whatever you can in it, because if you have a high share of a growing market you're going to make money.

- A cash cow has high market share in a slowly growing market. This kind of company or product should yield lots of cash, particularly if the market is large, yet requires relatively little investment. That's why it's called a cash cow. Invest only what you need to invest to keep a cash cow healthy. It should be a net source of cash.

- A question mark is a product in a high-growth market, but it has not achieved high share of that market. Like the star, it requires investment in order to expand capacity to win high share. The question is, if you make the investment in more capacity, will the product or division win high share? If you believe you can move it into the star area, you should invest in it. Otherwise, you shouldn't.

- A dog offers the worst of both worlds: low market share in a low-growth market. On the one hand, it does not require much investment. On the other hand, it's not going to generate much cash. It's a dog. A dog should be sold or phased out.

PEOPLE ARE THE COMPANY

At most companies, the resource assessment tends to be incomplete in the area of human resources. That's because the assets on the balance sheet are easier to inventory than the knowledge in people's heads. However, certain human resources can give a company a competitive edge that physical resources cannot.

In considering your resources, consider the skills, education, expertise, and experience of your employees. Consider knowledge they could apply to your business as well as what they are now applying.

Many companies with sophisticated human resources departments use a knowledge and skills inventory of their employees. A formal knowledge and skills inventory asks employees to list their skills, education, experience, and other characteristics, often for entry into a computerized database. This kind of inventory can help managers make sure they are making the most of their employees.

PRODUCTIVE CAPACITY

To determine your true productive capacity, you need to look beyond the fixed assets on your balance sheet. You need to understand everything about your equipment: downtime, maintenance requirements, ease or difficulty of operation, amount of training required, and the productivity of the machinery and of the people using it.

You must go to the machinery operators and their managers to get this information. These people have the information you need to assess productive capacity realistically.

OTHER RESOURCES

Other resources to consider are less tangible—and perhaps lie outside the company—but they can be important nonetheless. These include ...

- Patents, trademarks, and brands.
- Sales channels and distribution systems.
- Alliances or joint ventures with other companies.

Importantly, the potential to develop these kinds of resources can often point the way toward useful ways of acquiring resources that the outfit currently lacks. In fact, developing these resources is often among the action steps that fall out of a strategic plan.

ADD IT UP AGAIN

As you consider the company's resources, you must decide whether they are adequate to meeting the threats and capitalizing on the opportunities posed by the environment. The following table shows how this assessment might look for a U.S. auto manufacturer.

Resource	Strength	Weakness	Comment
Profitability & Growth			
Minivan and SUV lines are aging (cash cow).		3	Lines continue to be profitable but we haven't invested in them recently and we don't want to.
Midsize sedan line is in midsize market because we placed our bets on vans and SUVs.		3	Competitors have over-taken us losing ground (dog).
Our new high sports coupe has sold well.	3		We may be able to capital-ize on the performance of this key product strength to build a line of high-performance small (question mark) cars.
People			
Our dealer network has not been happy but remains committed to us.		3	We must improve dealer relations by helping them improve their profits.
Our U.S. workforce is aging as we have emphasized production in Mexico.		3	We cannot function without a solid, well-trained U.S. workforce.
Productive Capacity			
We have large amounts of capacity, but we have not updated it in some time.	3	3	This reflects our investment in minivan and SUV capacity, which we may need to retool for sedans.
Outsourcing has left us dependent on two major suppliers of key com-ponents.		3	This exposes us to price increases that can be dif-ficult to resist. We must bring some of this work back inside.

continues

continued

Resource	Strength	Weakness	Comment
Other Resources			
We have filed a number of patents that we haven't used or exploited in any way.	3		We must look into commercializing these inventions by applying them ourselves or licensing them to other companies.
Our financial structure remains strong.	3		Although we have new products, our reliance on cash cows has left us financially underinvested.

As with environmental developments, a resource can now and then represent both a strength and a weakness. Also, the preceding list represents a sample of resources to be considered. In reality, an automobile manufacturer would have many more resources to consider in every category, and perhaps several other categories as well.

What's SWOT?

From time to time you will hear the acronym SWOT, another example of MBA-ese. SWOT stands for an analysis of *strengths, weaknesses, opportunities,* and *threats.* Thus, SWOT also sums up the second step (analyze the company's environment) and the third step (consider the company's resources) of the strategic-planning process presented here.

That is, the product of Step 2, analyzing the environment, should be an assessment of the threats and opportunities the company faces in the marketplace. And the product of Step 3, considering the company's resources, should be an assessment of its strengths and weaknesses.

Although SWOT is widely discussed and used, it's only part of the strategic-planning story, which many managers forget. Many experts believe that a SWOT analysis works best when performed after the company sets at least a preliminary goal. Many experts also believe that it's best to analyze the environment (opportunities and threats) before you consider the company's resources (strengths and weaknesses). That way, you can evaluate the resources in light of the opportunities and threats you must address.

In sum, SWOT is an excellent mnemonic, but the process it represents must occur in context. Company goals provide that context. Also, if you literally follow the SWOT sequence and analyze strengths and weaknesses before identifying opportunities and threats, you are in a sense putting the cart before the horse.

That said, any strategic plan worthy of the name must include actions that will move the company toward its goals, our fourth step.

A staggering amount of information on goals, environmental developments, and resources can go into a strategic plan. Several software packages have been developed to assist the strategic planner. These range from cheap to pricey, and new packages and updates of existing packages are always being introduced. The key features to look for are the ability to handle various types of information—that is, text as well as columns of numbers—and to create alternative planning scenarios easily.

Alternative scenarios might include those based on assumptions of slow, medium, and fast economic growth. Or a resource assessment based on an optimistic, pessimistic, and best-guess levels of sales or market share. Software enables the planner to change the assumption and automatically generate new figures for any value tied to that assumption (such as equipment or number of people needed). In this way, the effects of different assumptions about the future can be considered more realistically.

IDENTIFY ACTIONS

On the basis of the information resulting from the first three steps, you should now be positioned to decide what action the company should take to move toward its goals. These actions must ...

- Neutralize or eliminate threats.
- Capitalize on opportunities.
- Exploit existing resources and develop or acquire needed resources.

Actions are the heart of the strategic plan. The result of this step should be the actual "To Do" items that operations, marketing, sales, finance, and other departments must undertake. Examples of useful action steps for key departments that would typically come out of a strategic plan include:

Marketing

Develop new products.

Develop a new marketing campaign.

Replace advertising agency.

Reposition existing products.

Identify new markets.

Develop new sales channels.

Sales

Explain price increase to customers.

Employ new sales tactics.

Restructure sales-force alignment.

Restructure sales territories.

Restructure sales compensation.

Improve customer service.

Finance

Secure debt financing.

Issue stock.

Refinance debt.

Adjust capital structure.

Improve financial controls.

Start a cost-cutting effort.

Secure international financing.

Production

Expand capacity.

Improve product quality.

Increase productivity.

Outsource production tasks.

Find new suppliers.

Improve inventory methods.

General Management/Human Resources

Expand certain areas of the organization.

Develop hiring or downsizing campaigns.

Increase use of independent contractors.

Form business alliances or joint ventures.

Merge with or acquire another company.

Of course, this list is not exhaustive, nor would all of these steps be taken at once.

Implement the Steps

If you are new to business, you may be surprised to learn that strategic plans are often created, presented to management, and even approved—but never implemented.

This occurs most often in companies with strategic-planning functions that are isolated from the company's real business and operating managers. These "ivory tower" planners are typically either too removed from the business to create a relevant plan or seen by operating managers as useless, or both.

To lessen the chances of this, you must get input from all managers before the plan is formulated. Then, after it is completed, you must tie their individual goals to the plan and tie their raises, bonuses, and promotions to those goals. Both of these tactics will make the plan much more relevant to them.

Also, certain management and leadership skills are essential to implementing strategic plans. For instance, managers must communicate the plan and its goals throughout the entire organization. Effective leaders link the strategic plan to the organizational vision. They focus people on the tasks that will get the plan implemented and hold them accountable for taking action and achieving the goals of the plan. They also ensure that the organization is aligned with the plan, and they take the time to coach and mentor people in the context of the plan.

Many strategic plans fail not because they're poor plans, but because they're poorly implemented. Implementation is the toughest step in the process, yet in a sense it lies outside strategic planning. That's because strategic planning is largely an analytical function, whereas implementing is a management function—getting things done through others.

Throughout the planning process, and especially when you are crafting the action steps, be sure that you can implement the plan. The plan is not an end in itself, but rather a tool to move the company toward its goals. It can do that only if the goals, analysis, and action steps are rooted in reality.

Strategic-Planning Guidelines

Although no part of strategic planning is easy, there are guidelines as well as tools and techniques that can help you in the process.

Set a Time Frame

The most common time frames for a strategic plan are one year and five years; that is, you have a plan for the coming year and for the coming five years. Most companies prepare the plan for the coming year in detail. Outfits vary in the detail they go into for the subsequent four years.

GET EVERYONE INVOLVED

A plan that originates with senior management and is then dictated to the troops is called a top-down plan. A bottom-up plan begins with input from the department managers, who may in turn get input from their employees.

Top-down and bottom-up represent two extremes. In reality, if senior managers try to impose a plan they develop unilaterally, they'll have trouble implementing it because they won't have buy-in from those who must implement the plan. On the other hand, if senior managers rely only on the input of department managers as the basis for the plan, they may miss a major development outside the day-to-day operations that are the main focus of the department managers. So a mix of the two approaches works best.

WHO NEEDS A PLAN?

Virtually every business of any size needs a strategic plan if it plans on being around for more than a year. Poor planning and lack of planning are repeatedly cited among the top reasons for business failure.

There is no valid excuse for not planning. Attempting to perform the basic managerial functions of organizing and controlling the company is difficult to impossible without a good plan. Planning brings the future into the present, so you can think about it more clearly and more productively than you can when it comes hurtling toward you. Remember: Proper planning prevents poor performance.

THE 30-SECOND RECAP

- A long-term strategic plan gives managers a framework for making good decisions that serve the long-term goals of the company. A strategic plan can ensure that day-to-day decisions and tactics move the company toward its major goals.

- A strategic plan should start with a goal, even if that goal will be modified as more information is gathered during the planning process.

- Because companies are affected by the business environment, you must assess the environment for threats and opportunities.

- Use Boston Consulting Group's growth-share matrix to examine your company's divisions (or products) for their growth rate and market share, and to assess current and future profitability.

- Be certain that the identified actions can be carried out by those who will be accountable for doing so. Align your incentives and communicate management's support of those who carry out the plan. Use management and leadership skills to implement the plan.

Keeping Productivity High

Have you ever given someone a job and heard him or her ask, "Do you want it done fast or do you want it done right?" Although you may not have liked hearing it, it's a good question. There is often a trade off between productivity and quality.

For a company, department, or other operation, productivity is usually measured by how fast something happens—how many units of product come off the assembly line per hour, how many hours it takes to build a car, how many tons of steel are produced by a mill in a year, how many customers a restaurant can serve per day. Productivity is about time and quantity: How long it takes to do how much.

Quality is measured by how well something is done. It's about how many defects occur, how many products break down, how many customers are satisfied rather than dissatisfied.

In this section, you learn about productivity and quality and ways of promoting them in your business.

WHAT IS PRODUCTIVITY?

Productivity is the amount of output created by a person, machine, or organization (or a nation). Output can be measured in dollars of value, units of product, number of customers served, kilowatts, or any another measure that makes sense for a business. The more output, the greater the productivity.

Productivity is really another way of saying efficiency. An efficient worker or machine produces more output than an inefficient one. An efficient use of funds produces a greater return than an inefficient one. This last point is key: Money itself must be put to the most productive uses available.

These elements—workers, machines, and money—are what economists call factors of production. It is management's job to make sure that each factor of production is used as efficiently as possible.

There is a wonderful saying in management: To manage it, you must measure it. Therefore, some ways of measuring and managing productivity are discussed in this section.

MEASURING PRODUCTIVITY

Productivity can be measured in various ways. Productivity as we are analyzing it here is not a total concept (as it is to an economist assessing a nation's productivity growth). Here we are concerned with productivity per worker or per machine. In a business, you increase productivity by increasing output per worker or per machine. If you increase the output of the business by simply adding more workers or equipment, you are not increasing productivity, but instead expanding your workforce or capacity. That may be desirable or necessary, but it is not increasing productivity.

MORE, MORE! FASTER, FASTER!

Everyone wants to increase productivity. There are several ways of doing this, including ...

- Improving worker skills and motivation.
- Improving the equipment.
- Improving production methods.

Each of these methods of increasing productivity involves an investment on the part of management. You must invest time, effort, and usually money to increase productivity. Why bother? Because the greater the productivity of an operation, the greater the financial returns it produces.

Let's look at each of these ways of increasing productivity.

TIP

However you measure productivity, be sure that you do measure it. In some businesses this can present challenges, but even an imperfect measure of productivity will enable you to manage it, provided you apply it consistently.

BOOSTING EMPLOYEE SKILLS AND MOTIVATION

To improve worker productivity, you generally must invest in workers. This can involve either hiring workers who have better skills, experience, and education, or training workers to become more productive.

To get higher productivity by investing in workers, you must invest in skills, experience, education, and training related to their jobs and day-to-day duties. Most companies with company-sponsored training or tuition-reimbursement plans for education use them only for courses that apply to the worker's current job. That's smart, because you don't want to be in the business of training and educating people so they can leave your company for a better position elsewhere.

TIP

In some situations, employees "take the training and run" or "take the experience and run" to another company. If you tend to pay low and hire young workers, you can be especially vulnerable to this.

A number of companies see high employee turnover as a way to control labor costs by constantly replacing experienced workers with less-experienced but cheaper ones. These firms tend not to invest much in training. But if you do invest in training, remember that you lose that investment when the employee leaves. So if you invest in training, try to limit your employee turnover.

Paying for Production

Another way to improve worker productivity is to provide incentives for them to be more productive. These incentives may be financial; perhaps you pay workers by the number of products they produce rather than the number of hours they work. Incentives can also be in the form of awards or special recognition, which tends to be less effective. You can offer productivity bonuses for individuals or teams, or provide awards or recognition on a team or individual basis.

Salespeople tend to be more productive when they have financial incentives. But you also saw that financial incentives, particularly straight commission, can cause trouble. For production workers, they can cause quality to suffer. If you send workers the message that quantity is the overriding goal, you can wind up with more product—and a lot more defects, breakdowns, and returns.

Another problem with paying for high production is that after a while it doesn't work. There are usually very real limitations on how much workers can produce. A worker can physically go only so fast. A machine can pop out only so many units. So unless the *limiting factor* in your operation is the speed at which employees work, you simply can't increase productivity significantly with financial incentives.

PLAIN ENGLISH

The **limiting factor** in a situation is the element that will stop the process, even when other factors are still operating. For example, the limiting factor in the distance a vehicle can travel is the amount of gasoline it can carry.

What's the Motivation?

Worker motivation is a major determinant of worker productivity. Motivating workers and teams calls for management and leadership skills.

To raise worker motivation to the highest possible levels, leaders must create and sustain a sense of mission in employees by building trust and sharing a vision of what the company could be. They must focus people on the right tasks (and have them stop performing unproductive tasks) and foster a sense of personal accountability in each employee. Effective leaders also coach their people to be more productive. Other tools for motivating people include mission statements (which set forth the corporate ideals), high expectations (which call on people to put forth their best efforts or leave the outfit), and participative management (which gives employees a greater role in setting and achieving goals).

There is no perfect way to increase and maintain motivation. But companies that truly excel do manage to create corporate cultures in which people are motivated to work very hard and to be very productive.

For a variety of reasons, after you have a skilled, educated, trained, well-paid, and motivated workforce, productivity comes down to managing well and requesting extraordinary time and effort from workers when the business demands extraordinary production.

Companies with the most productive workforces tend to be rapidly growing companies with strong leaders and clear goals. The rapid growth creates an external demand (from customers) for high productivity. The strong leader creates an internal demand for productivity and sets an example. The vision and the goals—for example, to be the biggest, the first, the best, or to reach a certain size by a certain time—bind everyone into a cohesive team. In this environment, unproductive people leave or are forced out.

Good examples include any number of firms that once experienced rapid growth with strong leaders and big goals. Several that come to mind include Digital Equipment, Apple Computer, Federal Express, and Starbucks. That kind of growth, unfortunately, does not last forever. So the challenge of managing to motivate people to stay highly productive never ends.

Improving Equipment

Perhaps the easiest, if not the cheapest, way to increase productivity is to give workers better equipment. There are several ways this investment can boost productivity:

- New equipment is often more productive simply because it runs better.
- New equipment (for example, an improved or higher-end model) often offers more productive capacity.

■ New equipment can often be run with fewer workers, thus enabling you to replace labor with capital.

■ New equipment can improve quality. (This is covered later in the section.)

TIP

Substituting capital for labor—that is, workers with machinery—is perhaps the oldest way of boosting productivity. In the long run, equipment is generally cheaper than employees. It requires less management and never gets sick or leaves for another employer. This substitution can, however, be tougher to achieve in service businesses than in manufacturing.

Returning to our earlier example, recall that the average worker can make 15 gewgaws an hour. That's worker productivity. Recall also that the average machine can make 45 gewgaws an hour. That's machine productivity. There were 5 machines in the shop, and each machine required 3 workers. The 15 workers operating the 5 machines produce 9,000 gewgaws per week, assuming a 40-hour week.

What would happen if we replace one of those five machines with a new one that requires only one worker and could produce 75 gewgaws per hour?

Productivity would increase. In fact, the 5 machines (which include the new one) could now produce a total of 9,000 gewgaws in a little more than 35 hours rather than 40 hours. This would allow you to reduce the workers' hours (thereby saving labor costs) while maintaining the same level of production.

Why?

Because in 35 hours, 4 machines producing 45 gewgaws an hour will make 6,300 gewgaws (= 4 × 35 × 45). And in 35 hours, 1 machine producing 75 gewgaws an hour will make 2,625 gewgaws (= 1 × 35 × 75). The total production of all the machines in 35 hours will be 8,925 (= 6,300 + 2,625).

Many service businesses have harnessed information technology, and the energy of their own customers, to raise their productivity. For example, when bank customers use ATMs, they enable the bank to reduce the number of tellers. When Federal Express enabled customers to track the status of their packages on the web, they also reduced the number of incoming phone calls employees had to field. Any company that enables customers to check the status of their accounts or troubleshoot their product problems on the web uses technology in the same way.

Ideally, this is a win-win strategy: It's more productive for the company and easier for the customer. However, reality often falls short of the ideal—for example, when customers can't reach a human receptionist or have no alternative to the technical manual on the website. Smart companies enable customers to serve themselves, but give them the option of being served.

That 8,925 is only 75 gewgaws short of 9,000. You can get to the 9,000 by keeping one additional worker on overtime for one hour to run the new machine for one extra hour and produce the final 75 gewgaws.

Again, thanks to this productivity increase, you can reduce your outfit's work week from 40 hours to 35 hours. This reduction will create significant savings on labor costs for your company. In fact, new and improved equipment can often kick an operation up to a completely new level.

IMPROVE THE PROCESSES

A final way to boost productivity is to examine the processes in your operation with an eye toward improving them. Process improvements are a major goal in *reengineering* a company.

PLAIN ENGLISH

Reengineering means analyzing a company or an operation, carefully deciding which activities the company should continue, abandon, or outsource, and then designing the most efficient way of doing this. The term *reengineering* has often been misused to refer to massive layoffs and redistribution of the same work to the remaining staff. This is not really reengineering.

Process improvements come from examining all the ways in which the work is performed and seeing how the tasks could be redesigned for greater efficiency, that is, for greater productivity. This can include examining and redesigning the type or the number of tasks performed by a single worker, the way work gets to the worker (for example, conveyor belts versus handoff from another worker), and the layout of the work area.

Improvements can be realized by training workers in new methods and in the use of new equipment. Thus, a process improvement can include both an investment in workers and an investment in equipment.

You can identify ways to improve work processes by interviewing the people actually doing the work. These interviews should be conducted by outside consultants who grant "amnesty" to workers who cite inefficiencies. That way, you'll get honest answers. The interviews should focus on identifying waste in all its forms, including wasted time, equipment, effort, materials, heat, and electricity. Focus especially on the time that people spend waiting for something or someone, working on a task that does not really require their skills, or tracking down information that should be readily available. When properly conducted, these interviews usually identify easy ways to save time and other resources and thus raise productivity.

Work studies are another way to understand your work processes. In a work study, some employees are asked to list all of the tasks they perform in an average week. Then, for about a month, they wear a beeper set to go off at random intervals. When the beeper goes off, they place a checkmark next to the task on the list that they were performing at the moment. (Few employees enjoy doing this, but dedicated people who realize that the work, and not their performance, is being studied will cooperate.)

Work studies break down processes and show how people actually spend their time. This enables management to eliminate waste by asking, "Why do we have people doing this?" Eliminating waste in a process is the surest way to increase the productivity of that process.

Studies conducted in supermarkets by Conway Management Company, a consulting firm, show that the average chain can increase its overall productivity by 20 to 30 percent by reducing wasted resources, including time, produce, baked goods, heat, and electricity. For instance, one chain had all stores constantly rearranging their produce displays to convey an image of freshness. This practice wasted employees' time, damaged produce (with added handling), and irritated customers, who couldn't find what they wanted because it was never in the same place. Why were the stores rearranging produce displays? Because they had always done it that way.

At another chain, a program of preventive maintenance—in which a part for a freezer is replaced on a schedule rather than waiting for it to break down—saved tens of thousands of dollars annually. The program reduced the time employees spent responding to crises, overtime pay for repair crews, and wasted food.

THE 30-SECOND RECAP

- Productivity is really another way of saying efficiency.
- To get higher productivity by investing in workers, you must invest in skills, experience, education, and training related to their jobs and day-to-day duties.
- Worker motivation is a major determinant of worker productivity.
- Perhaps the easiest, if not the cheapest, way to increase productivity is to give workers better equipment.

■ Process improvements come from examining all the ways in which the work is performed and seeing how the tasks could be redesigned for greater efficiency—that is, for greater productivity.

Quality Control Methodology for the Small Business Owner

We usually think of quality as goodness or excellence or superiority. In business it can mean these things, and often does. However, it is best to think of quality as a decision and a goal.

First, there's quality as a decision. You can have relatively low quality at a low price or relatively high quality at a high price. Customers know this, and so do companies. So a company has to decide what level of quality it wants to pursue.

TIP

Whatever the level of quality, it must be properly communicated to the employee. For example, in publishing, quality can be more about the deadline than anything else. Most editors would rather proofread a book three times than ship it on time because those editors believe in quality of content. However, if you are last to market when it comes to a hot topic or new release, you ultimately lose, meaning you didn't fulfill your quality goals of being first to market. When there is a mixed message about the level of quality, employees lack understanding, motivation, and so on.

That level of quality becomes the goal. For products, the goal is often best formulated in terms of the number of defects you can tolerate. These defects can be discovered by inspection or by the less-desirable means of merchandise returns, warranty claims, and breakdowns. In service businesses, the goal may be formulated by calculating the average waiting time for customers in a store or restaurant, customer satisfaction, and number of complaints.

The decision about quality flows from your company's business philosophy, image, costs, target markets, and prices, and its human, financial, and other resources. Here we focus on the pursuit of quality, after you have decided on a level of quality.

Quality Assurance

Quality assurance (also known as *quality control*) has several meanings. First, it can encompass all the activities that go into achieving the level of quality the company desires and customers demand. This could include everything from designing the product's specifications, to creating standards for suppliers of the materials used in the product, to various inspections done during manufacturing.

PLAIN ENGLISH

Quality assurance (or **quality control**) refers both to policies, programs, and efforts to minimize product defects and ensure a high degree of quality, and to the formal function that conducts these activities within a company.

Second, it refers to the final inspection performed before a product is shipped. Note that this inspection can be performed by a human being or through technology. For example, the manufacturing process can include running the product by a computerized scanner that is programmed to recognize any defects.

Third, quality control refers to mathematical tools involving statistics and probability that are applied in manufacturing for tasks such as sampling products and minimizing defects. For instance, in many situations it would be too costly to inspect every product. So an inspector may pull a mathematically determined sample of each hour's or each day's production and use the results of that inspection to measure the quality of the entire production run.

Finally, quality control can refer to the quality control department that inspects products and performs other activities associated with maintaining product quality. Most operations have someone responsible for a quality check, whereas major manufacturers have large departments dedicated to the task.

How to Control Quality

Over the past 20 years, towering stacks of books and more conferences than you could attend in a lifetime have been devoted to the issue of quality. The wake-up call for U.S. manufacturers was Japan's success in the U.S. auto market in the 1970s. Before then, U.S. manufacturers of autos—and of many other products—had grown complacent about quality. Some even designed their products for *planned obsolescence.*

PLAIN ENGLISH

Planned obsolescence refers to the tactic of withholding a feature from a product so you can introduce a "new and improved" product later, or repeatedly making cosmetic changes to a product so it constantly "goes out of style," or building the product so it breaks down at some future point and requires replacement. The product becomes obsolete, but you planned it that way.

Here are three practical steps in the quality control process:

- Developing quality standards
- Applying the quality standards
- Creating a corporate "culture of quality"

As you read about these steps, keep in mind that quality control has two basic purposes: first, to meet the customers' expectations and create satisfied customers; and second, to find cost-effective ways of fulfilling the first purpose.

DEVELOPING QUALITY STANDARDS

One big issue in quality control centers on the number or percentage of defects that are acceptable. Traditionally, manufacturers believed that because manufacturing processes are imperfect—machines go out of alignment, people get tired, mistakes are made—you cannot eliminate defects.

With this approach, quality control means deciding what number and what types of defects are acceptable. These decisions amount to your standards, which must factor in customer expectations. For example, you might say that defects that affect performance are not acceptable, but that small defects in appearance are. Or you may say that you are willing to discard only 2 percent of the production run for defects, and you ship the rest.

Of course, you have important decisions to make regarding the number and type of defects you will accept. Too many defects will result in poor quality. And the wrong type of defects—for instance, those affecting customer safety—can bankrupt the company in products liability claims.

WHAT ABOUT ZERO DEFECTS?

Quality consultant Philip Crosby has made the quest for zero defects his cause. This clearly goes against the traditional approach of deciding which defects to accept. Crosby believes that a policy of knowingly accepting any defects will lead to accepting too many. The standard should be zero defects, because to have a standard that accepts *any* defects is to tell employees that defects are okay. A common side-effect of accepting defects is a loss of focus on customer needs. After all, the customer wants zero defects.

Also underlying the zero-defects goal is the notion that it is easier to do something right the first time than to fix it later.

Nevertheless, perfection is a tough—and more to the point, expensive—goal to pursue. What's more, if you try to use it as a selling point, you may be going out on a limb. Customers may not believe it, and worse, it will amplify the impact of any defects or quality problems that do occur.

In the end, each company must define its own approach to quality standards.

WHAT ARE QUALITY STANDARDS?

Whether you accept some level of defects or shoot for zero, the way you define and measure standards will depend on your operation and industry. For most manufacturing operations, you will need standards in the following areas and of the following types:

Area	Type of Standard
Performance	Product fulfills its functions
	Product meets performance specifications
Appearance	Adherence to design specifications
	Uniformity of color
Workmanship	Smoothness of finish
	Tightness of joints and fittings
Content	Purity (for foods, drugs) and percentages of allowed content (for fat or other ingredients)
Safety	Resistance to fire or to breakage that would endanger the user

Management, marketing, engineering, operations, and the design team must all be involved in developing quality standards. The product must be as safe as the company can possibly make it. But beyond that, the standards must be developed with a sharp eye on costs, target market, and company image.

APPLYING QUALITY STANDARDS

Applying quality standards is traditionally the work of the quality control department. Most of us think of quality control as the department that inspects the final product to see whether or not it passes and is fit for shipment. However, you must apply quality standards more broadly than that.

You must apply quality standards in the purchasing function, in which the company decides which materials to buy and where to buy them. You must apply them in the receiving department, so that someone checks to see that materials shipped to the company meet the standards. You must apply them in operations, so that products are properly made at each step of production.

For most manufacturing processes, this constant quality control is more effective and less expensive than waiting until the product is completed before giving it a passing or failing grade.

Aside from applying quality standards to materials and products at various stages of production, quality control faces the task of discovering the reasons for variations in quality. Discovering defects is good, but preventing them is even better. So when quality-control people notice a pattern of standards not being met, they must learn why and try to fix it.

TIP

Good quality control can actually be more important to the company with a lower-quality, lower-priced strategy. There is less variation and fewer mistakes when you pay top dollar for labor and materials. With a low-cost, low-price strategy you have more chance of trouble as well as a smaller profit margin to absorb the costs of repairs, replacements, recalls, and warranty claims.

CREATING A CORPORATE "CULTURE OF QUALITY"

Some people think of quality as something that only applies to high-quality, high-priced products. However, quality control applies to every company, because the real issue is maintaining the desired level of quality—the level of quality that the customer wants and is willing to pay for.

For any company, when it comes to quality, the real management challenge is to create a culture of quality. In a culture of quality, every product and every customer is important. Every stage of production is important. In a culture of quality, every employee internalizes these ideas and works on quality.

How do you create a culture of quality?

It begins with the goals, strategies, and plans presented by management. It goes on to hiring, training, compensation, and promotion practices. It has to do with the marketing messages and sales stories you send to customers. It must permeate the customer service function. It affects purchasing, receiving, operations, and shipping. It extends to your suppliers and distribution channels. All of this amounts to *total quality management.*

PLAIN ENGLISH

The term **total quality management,** or TQM, refers to every area of the organization involved in creating quality. TQM means that everyone is responsible for quality. It also assumes that quality must be designed in and built in, rather than be something added at the last step of production. TQM was something of a "fad" in the 1990s, but became a permanent effort in some companies.

One excellent way to create a culture of quality is to have everyone in the company think of themselves as serving customers—even if they don't actually deal with "real" customers on a daily basis. Everyone has internal customers to serve. For example, the accounting function delivers reports to other managers, who are its internal customers. The marketing department has the sales department as its key internal customer. The purchasing department has operations as its internal customer. And so on.

Thus, the notions of customer service and customer satisfaction can be used as motivators and standards in every area and for every person in the outfit.

In a culture of quality, everyone works to high standards within the context of the company's costs and values. They hold themselves and they hold one another to these standards. Those who cannot or will not join the culture, or those who undermine the effort of the larger group, eventually either choose to leave or are forced out—if they even get into the company in the first place.

TOOLS FOR QUALITY CONTROL

In addition to the tasks of developing standards, applying standards, and creating a culture of quality, several tools can assist you in the quest for quality. These tools include the following:

- Supplier programs
- Quality circles
- Control charts
- Best practices and benchmarking

Let's talk briefly about each one.

SUPPLIER PROGRAMS

Various large manufacturers, including Ford Motor Company, have supplier programs that involve suppliers of materials and components in achieving and maintaining high quality. In a supplier program, the company issues strict specifications and works closely with suppliers to get the levels of quality it desires.

These programs often require the company to formally rate suppliers on their quality. The company will then, on the basis of these ratings, designate certain suppliers as "star suppliers" or a "prime source" and give them longer contracts or larger orders, or both, compared with other suppliers.

TIP

Supplier programs actually fall within the larger framework of supply-chain management. A company's supply chain includes its suppliers and the processes by which materials move from supplier to purchaser. Supply-chain management coordinates sales forecasts, production plans, inventory targets, costs, and quality between a company and its suppliers. This differs from the way companies used to purchase materials. Today companies and suppliers work together on common goals instead of constantly bargaining hard.

QUALITY CIRCLES

Quality circles are regular meetings of representatives from every part of the production function. In these meetings workers discuss quality problems, reasons for problems, and potential solutions. This is an effort by management to involve employees in maintaining quality and to educate them about the entire issue of quality.

Quality circles push both the responsibility and authority for quality down to those on the production line. This puts the tasks of identifying problems and creating solutions on the workers themselves. The result is greater worker involvement and cooperation and more pride in workmanship.

CONTROL CHARTS

A control chart shows the *control limits* for various dimensions of the product in a manufacturing process. These help us control the variations that occur in any manufacturing process and that affect product quality.

PLAIN ENGLISH

In a manufacturing process, **control limits** are the maximum acceptable deviations above and below a standard. The term **tolerance** refers to the maximum physical limits that the deviation from the standard could reach in a manufacturing process.

Suppose we are milling wooden 2 × 4s. Let's say that they are supposed to measure 1¾ inches (the thickness) by 3½ inches (the width) when they come off the saw at the mill. Our control chart might look like this.

Control Chart

Thickness	Specification and Control Limits	Width	Specification and Control Limits
$1\frac{13}{16}$"	Upper limit	$3\frac{7}{8}$"	Upper limit
$1\frac{3}{4}$"	Specification	$3\frac{1}{2}$"	Specification
$1\frac{11}{16}$"	Lower limit	$3\frac{5}{8}$"	Lower limit

This chart says that for the thickness of the piece of wood, the lower control limit is 1½, and the upper limit is $1\frac{13}{16}$. For the width, the lower limit is 3⅝, and the upper limit is 3⅞.

These limits are generally defined more tightly than the *tolerances*, which are the maximum potential physical deviation from the standard. For instance, in this case the mill may actually produce some 2 × 4s that measure 2¼ inches by 4 inches. That would define the upper tolerance. In common parlance, people often use the term *tolerance* to mean control limit, but technically they are distinct.

Referring to this chart—or better yet, incorporating it into an automated measurement process—will tell the production workers when the product is exceeding its control limits and thus moving toward substandard quality. Any pieces that were outside the limits would be recut, if possible, or discarded or sold as "seconds."

BEST PRACTICES AND BENCHMARKING

The term *best practices* refers to the most efficient and most effective way of structuring and conducting a business process. Best practices in product development, for example, indicate the use of cross-functional teams. Best practices in a certain type of electronics manufacturing may indicate the use of printed circuits rather than wiring.

Broadly, best practices means the best way of doing something. It means doing something in the way that those who do it best do it.

Benchmarking refers to a method of comparing your company's practices and performance with those of companies with the best practices that you want to employ. Benchmarking measures the results of best practices and describes how to get that performance in your processes.

For example, if another company can reduce the time it takes to develop a new product by using cross-functional teams or reduce the number of defects with the use of printed circuits, then you want to know the time they need to develop a new product or their number of defects. Those become the benchmarks, the targets you use in your business.

TIP

Employing best practices and benchmarking is not copying, or at least it shouldn't be. Instead, you must examine the logic and reasoning behind the practices and performance and then adapt the methods to your operation. Every company is different. Each has its own traditions, culture, and interactions. These "human factors" usually mean that simply trying to copy another company's practice rarely works.

One way to get benchmarking going in your company is to have a task force drawn from key areas of the outfit to investigate best practices in their respective areas. This "best practices task force" can represent their areas and draw on the experience of their people (some of whom may have worked at companies with best practices) and direct their people to do some investigating as well. Much of the research can be drawn from news stories and articles about other companies.

Finally, you actually adapt the best practice to your needs. You begin using cross-functional product-development teams, or start making printed circuits or getting a supplier to make them for you.

THE CHALLENGE OF GLOBAL COMPETITION

Until fairly recently, U.S. companies had the U.S. markets pretty much to themselves. In other countries, most companies had the domestic market to themselves. In today's global market, however, this is not the case.

When goods, services, money, people, and information can flow freely across national borders—the way they do across state lines in the United States—then competition occurs on a global scale. A company in Ohio or Oregon can see its markets seriously eroded by an outfit in Poland or Paraguay. And it can work the other way around, too.

Competition on a global scale means that productivity and quality are now the two most effective competitive weapons. A marketing strategy or promotional tactic may or may not translate well overseas. Sales methods and distribution channels vary widely from nation to nation. Accounting and financial tactics may or may not work under another nation's accounting policies or financial system.

However, cost, price, value, and satisfaction are universal. A focus on productivity enables a company to control its costs by making the most of its resources. A focus on quality enables a company to deliver the best possible products to its customers. A company that offers good quality at a reasonable price can compete in any environment.

THE 30-SECOND RECAP

- Productivity is usually measured by how efficiently something happens. It is about time and quantity: how long it takes to do how much.

- To compare productivity, dollars or units of output are the most common measures. You can calculate both the productivity of workers and of machinery.

- To increase productivity, you can improve worker productivity, improve production equipment, or improve production processes. Any of these moves involves an investment of time, effort, and (usually) money.

- Quality is measured by how well something is done. It's about how many defects occur, how many products break down, and how many customers are satisfied.

- To maintain or improve quality, you must develop quality standards, apply the quality standards, and, if at all possible, create a corporate "culture of quality."

- Specific tools that can help you achieve high quality include supplier programs, quality circles, control charts, and best practices and benchmarking.

Selling Your Business

Why Sell, Anyway?

The impetus to sell your company can come from any number of directions and at any time. The market could change, someone could pass away, an unsolicited company might offer to buy you, or the founders might simply get bored and want to do something different. Whatever the reason, selling is a big step that should not be taken lightly. Nevertheless, when it is time to sell, you want to be clear on your motivations, which better ensures that you get what you want out of the sale.

This section presents a number of reasons for selling your business; your situation might fit into one or several of the categories mentioned.

CLOSING UP SHOP COMPLETELY

It is very possible that you small business owners might decide that operating the business just isn't worth it anymore. That your motivation is no longer in competing and winning. That you would rather get out of what you are doing and do something different.

At this point you may decide that closing up shop completely is the simplest and most attractive answer. Well, this process is never simple. Trust me. It takes months to close even a small business. If your business has been around for any length of time at all and especially if you have employees, you will find this process more time- and emotion-consuming than anticipated.

TIP

Don't underestimate the complexity and the amount of time involved with completely closing your business. If you have achieved any level of business success at all, you will have vendors, customers, landlords, and employees who will require special attention. In addition, fully expect that you will grieve over the loss.

You should first evaluate your motivations:

- Are you simply tired and need a vacation? If so, take it while letting everyone know that business should continue as usual. But do take the time off. Recharge your emotional batteries before you make this major decision.

- Make sure that you are not reacting to having your pride hurt from the lack of success you had in selling your business. Contrary to how it might feel sometimes, you are not your business. Your professional and personal credibility is not tied to your business, and if you are closing due to a bruised ego, you should adjust your focus. There are many poor reasons to close, and this is one of the poorest.

■ Are you embarrassed to face your customers, vendors, and employees who participated in the unsuccessful sale process? If so, figure out a way to get over it and to get back to business. Once before you created a working, thriving business environment and you can do it again. But you have to take the first step. Do it.

■ Are you simply not having fun? Then look for ways to make it fun. Oddly enough, when you are ready to close the doors, you acquire an immense amount of freedom. After all, what can be worse than closing the doors? Why not take a few chances and have some fun? Perhaps the business needed a shakeup to move it to the next performance level.

This is an excellent time to take advantage of those business contacts you have cultivated over the years. Most likely you know some other business owner who has been through a similar situation. Talking with that person about how he or she reacted and handled the situation might help you determine the right next steps for you.

If you still decide that you want out, here are a few preparatory steps you can take:

1. Take an objective look around the company and see whether one of the employee buyout agreements (LBO, MBO, or ESOP) will provide a workable solution. Just because you have lost interest doesn't mean that the employees have. Why put the company to sleep if someone else wants to nurture it and make it grow? And you just might make more money in the process!

TIP

After you have determined the "fire-sale" value of your company, you might try talking to the previously interested buyers. For what may well be a substantially reduced price, one of these buyers might just take the whole company off your hands in a single purchase. This is faster for you, better for them, and it provides continuing employment for your employees.

2. If Step 1 does not present a viable option, review your assets and determine which you might want to keep for either personal or future business reasons. You will have to ask the other owners for similar feedback.

3. Determine which assets have liens attached to them along with the minimum sale price needed to cover the liens. It would really be a shame to sell your company and still owe money when finished.

4. Don't expect to get anywhere near what you paid for furniture, computers, and other operating equipment. That $250 desk might get you $50 in a sale, so adjust your expectations accordingly.

5. You might want to simplify the process by calling one of the liquidators in your area. These people come into your business, make a listing of everything that is for sale, and offer you one price for the whole lot. This is an easy approach, but you may find that their prices are substantially lower than you've typically been willing to accept.

6. Offer to sell equipment and other items to your employees. They might have had their eye on specific items for a long time, and this is a great way to give something to them at a reasonable price for both of you.

7. Talk to your vendors to see whether they are willing to take back any of your existing inventory items in exchange for a partial or full credit. You won't need it and they can probably sell it to someone else. Better to pay a smaller restocking fee than to eat the entire purchase amount.

8. Talk to your customers to see whether any of your products, services, and/or employees would be of interest to them. Your customers might get a great deal on something that they can use, and your employees might end up with an excellent job working for an appreciative employer. Once again, a win-win.

9. Expect that this process will take months, and even years, depending on the level of business complexity. This is never a quick fix, but if you decide it is right for you, so be it.

It is a strange feeling to walk out the door of your business for the last time, knowing that tomorrow you will not need to come in to answer the phones, talk to customers, or deal with vendors. It is also a freeing experience in that you can now move on to doing something different or even take some well-deserved time off.

THE TAX IMPLICATIONS OF LIQUIDATING

Liquidating assets has tax implications for the company and ultimately for you, depending on the specific company structure:

■ Assets sold by the company will have either a short-term or a long-term gain associated with them. And the gain will be based on the depreciated value of the asset, not its sale price, so careful record-keeping will help in this area.

■ Once completely liquidated, the remaining liquid assets will then be distributed to the shareholders, who will recognize either a gain or a loss depending on the basis of their shares.

TIP

Remember that you can move your business's legal address to the basement of your house and still keep a legal registration with the state. Liquidate the old business, keep the cash in the company, and let it sit (invested, naturally) for a while. You might need it as funding for your next venture.

■ Filings must be made with the state and the IRS to let them know that the company is no longer in business. It makes no sense to keep the company open, if not operational, because the longer it is a legal entity, the longer it is exposed to the potential of litigation. Why take that risk, even if it is a highly remote possibility?

■ If there is any possibility of going back into business, you might benefit from keeping the legal structure in place. Credit will be easier to obtain because the company has an established track record and the same Employer Information Number (EIN). Name recognition is on your side, even if associated with another business activity.

Different rules apply to sole proprietors, partnerships, S corporations, and C corporations. It is always best to check with your tax and legal professionals before making these final decisions. These are the general guidelines.

It's Valuable to Be on Top

Selling a hot company in a hot market is always better than the other way around. Let's face it: People want to associate with winners, and if your company is on a winning streak, people will be more likely to pay more for it.

Should financial markets alone determine whether you sell or not? Probably not. However, if you are going to sell, you and your shareholders are better served by selling while both the market and your company are in their best shape.

TIP

The best part of being on top is that you are not generally under any pressure to sell. If the timing and the offered deal are right, then sell. If not, then wait.

Determining when your company performance is at its peak is often a job for a fortuneteller, but you can do some simple trend analysis to see where your company stands.

Here are a few simple exercises you can perform to see where you stand with respect to the rest of your market, in particular, and the overall market, in general:

- Has your company shown a profit for the last five fiscal quarters? If so, you are immediately a viable financial investment.

- Are your historical net-income-before-tax results increasing over the prior five quarters, or are they erratic in nature? Financial markets like consistency, and the more consistent the income figures the better your company looks.

- Has your company been gaining market share with respect to other companies in your industry? If so, you look even better. If not, but your income continues to grow, it means the management is doing something right with respect to operations.

- Has your company recently obtained the rights to a patent, trademark, or other intellectual property item that has a long life and hot market potential? If so, selling now while the iron is hot may not be a bad idea. This is especially true if the technology is relatively unproven, such as might be the case with a new pharmaceutical drug where time may reveal unknown side effects related to taking the drug.

- Did your company just receive a major contract that extends over a number of years? This provides income consistency that is always attractive to a prospective buyer.

- Is your company in a hot market segment that is showing above-market-average stock price returns? If so, you might want to sell even if some other financial parameters are not in optimal condition. Remember that you are always competing with other investments, and if the other investments are not performing as well as your company's stock, it is still a solid investment.

Any one of these reasons, along with numerous others, might be reason to assume that your company is on a solid upswing. A combination of several simply makes the case even stronger.

The point is that you must do some research for yourself to determine the performance of your company with respect to the others in the industry.

TIP

Waiting until you start to see a downswing in your company's performance before you sell is generally not a good idea. Nobody knows for sure when an upswing will end, but everyone gets cold feet and more risk averse when things start to take a negative turn.

WHEN THE MARKET DROPS OFF

Playing the stock market is a lot like playing craps in Las Vegas. If you know the rules, you can even make money when the shooter (the person with the dice) is losing. You can make money when they win and when they lose. It may sound a little unethical or unrealistic, but it is true none the less.

The same is true with the stock market, but the opportunities for making money in a down (bear) market are fewer than those in an increasing (bull) market.

The good news for you business owners is that a well-run company is attractive in either a bear or a bull market. In a bull market, there is more money to go around, and there's a lot of optimism about the future, which generally allows you to command a higher price for your company. A bear market generally brings a less-optimistic view of the future and its earnings potential, and companies will generally sell for a lower price, unless the company is well run and/or has some particular strategic advantage. Somebody makes money in a bear market; it might as well be you and your shareholders.

TIP

Throwing good money after bad is never a sound financial policy, although it is one that many of us unwittingly practice. If your company really is precariously positioned when assessed against an extended market downturn, you must look at either selling the company or acquiring the resources needed to get through the slow times. Waiting, and doing nothing, will only push a questionable situation into a negative one that could cost you and your shareholders dearly.

What if you are not one of those prepared companies? Should you sell in a bear market? This good question can only be answered by knowing the specifics of your company. Here are a few things to consider when making this decision:

- How is your particular market segment affected by the bear market? If it is expected to suffer and customers expect to cut back on purchases, this does not bode well for your company's future sales.

- If your company has the cash or credit reserves to weather an extended downturn, and your competition does not, you might be the last company standing when the bull market returns. This could be great news.

- Suppose that your company has a large cash reserve on hand that is used up weathering the bear market. If the market downturn lasts longer than anticipated, you could put your company in a precarious position should you have to sell later.

- Selling a company with cash, receivables, and a good debt-equity ratio is much easier than the other way around.

By the way, having too much of your company's assets in cash and receivables makes you a takeover target; the purchasing company simply wants to get its hands on your current assets.

If you believe that an active market downturn might take your company with it, it is suggested that you move quickly and professionally toward selling your company. The earlier you sell, the more you will probably receive for your company. If things really get bad during the downturn, you are better off holding cash in your hand instead of stock in a company heading toward financial disaster.

WHEN TECHNOLOGY CHANGES

How would you have liked to be the owner of a horse and buggy manufacturing company on the day that the first Ford automobile drove down the street? Or how would you feel if you were the people at Western Electric who turned down Alexander Graham Bell when he offered to sell the patent rights to the telephone for $100,000?

Technology changes markets. And this has never been truer than today with the incredible impact of the Internet being felt in a more pronounced way every day.

Technological innovation rarely turns a market on its ear overnight, but it can do it over the span of a few years. If you are a company whose livelihood is jeopardized by the introduction of new technology from one of your competitors, you might look seriously at selling your company. Here are your basic choices when faced with this situation:

- You can develop your own technology that competes with that of this technologically advanced competitor. Advanced Micro Devices has done an excellent job in this area while competing with the Intel processors.

- You can band together with other affected companies to pool your resources in a defensive/offensive move against the new major threat. This might mean a merger or two, but the resulting consolidated company should be stronger and better able to weather the change.

- You can talk to the technologically advanced competitor and offer to sell strategic assets that will assist them in getting to market more quickly.

- Heck, you might even offer to buy the company that developed the new technology in the first place, and run the new product through your own distribution channels.

- Sometimes a lawsuit is filed against the new technology company with the underlying, and completely denied, intent of draining company resources. Distracting the newer company delays market penetration, and might even put the company out of business before it has a chance to do any substantial damage. This is called "legal blackmail," and it is commonly practiced when companies find themselves in a threatened circumstance.

One thing is sure: If you do not take some steps to protect yourself against major technological changes within your industry, you could end up like the guy watching the Ford roll down the street who figured it for a passing fancy. He probably wound up getting a job on the production line at Ford after bankrupting his buggy business.

I'M BORED—LET'S SELL

Boredom has caused the downfall and sale of more small businesses than most people want to admit. Entrepreneurs like new ground and challenges. When the challenges turn into routine business operation, most entrepreneurs will look for ways to spice things up. If they do not get themselves under control, they can spice up a good business into a crisis situation, which is what entrepreneurs deal with best. Do you see a pattern forming here?

TIP

Entrepreneurs who treat the sale of their company as another challenge might find the process rewarding and stimulating. Those who treat it like losing their little baby will probably get less for the sale, and they will probably suffer more emotional upset in the process.

If you are an entrepreneur whose business is doing well, you should first congratulate yourself for a job well done. Then look at the job you ended up with in your successful business. Some entrepreneurs have admitted that they would never have hired on to take the job they currently had, and the only reason they do it is that it is for their own company. They just don't like the daily administrative management of an established company, and they would like to get out to do something else.

If you are in this position and have convinced yourself that you need new challenges, you might be better served by selling your company before you do something that compromises its financial condition.

If you sell to a larger company, they may want you to take on a larger responsibility within the acquiring company, which could provide all of the excitement your little entrepreneurial heart desires.

If you merge with another company, you might be needed to manage the new merged entity, which, once again, could be fun and different.

Selling should provide you with enough financial resources to start another company, knowing that you will probably have to sign noncompete agreements as part of the sale of your first company.

Selling also should provide you with the freedom and money needed to do some of the personal things that you ignored when making your first company a success.

One entrepreneur sold his smaller company to a larger one that already had a national presence. He instantly moved the products produced by his smaller company to the national level simply by selling to a larger one that fit his strategic desires.

MANAGEMENT OR FAMILY SQUABBLES

This next topic is an unfortunate fact of life, but it happens frequently in closely held companies. People don't always get along, and the higher the personal stakes the riper the opportunity for personality conflict.

More than one happy relationship has broken up over money, and a successful, or even unsuccessful, business can cause personal friction between shareholders or owners.

If that friction starts to creep into the daily operation of the company, it can undo years worth of work in a short period of time.

CAUTION

If you are looking to purchase a family-owned/run business, spend some casual time with the family members themselves. These interactions can be complicated, and they will work substantially either for the benefit or for the detriment of the company. Either way, you inherit the family members and their relationships, after the purchase is finalized.

You might have expected that your children would run the business after you retired only to find out that they have no interest in the business, or that they are simply incompetent and would run it into the ground.

The death of an owner, a majority shareholder, or even your death will prompt the sale of a company. It might be to pay off the other partners in a partnership, or to divide up the deceased person's estate.

One member of a family-run business might want a newer house, or a new child might be on the way. Consequently, this family member might want to hold his or her portion of the family business as a liquid asset. This usually requires the sale of the corporation unless the other members decide to buy his or her share and have the financial resources to execute the purchase.

Family members have a power over other shareholders that is typically not possible in a conventional business environment. If you don't like a particular shareholder or officer in a publicly held corporation, so what? You don't have to spend Christmas with this person. You do with family members.

THE FINANCIAL STAKES ARE TOO HIGH

One area that most entrepreneurs rarely know about, or fully appreciate, is the impact a growing business will have on their personal financial picture. They want the business to grow, and they do everything in their power to make that happen. Then the creditors start to come into the picture and the entrepreneur's financial picture changes forever.

Any time a company obtains a loan for equipment, land, buildings, inventory purchases, expansion, or any of a number of other typical business needs, the lender almost always wants a personal guarantee from the primary stockholders that the loan will be repaid. Notice what just happened. The protection of your personal assets that was supposed to happen when you incorporated was just shot to pieces. The bank can now come after your personal assets if your corporation defaults on a loan.

When these loans are for a few thousand dollars, you rarely worry. When they grow to being hundreds of thousands—or millions—of dollars, things change.

Any of us can come up with a few thousand dollars, but there are very few people who could come up with several million.

For this reason alone, some entrepreneur/owners decide to sell their company. What was once fun now holds their personal assets, and the financial well-being of their family, at risk. Some owners simply decide to get out. Selling is a viable way to accomplish this goal, but make sure that you understand the reality of your situation when you decide to sell.

TIP

Most major creditors will want a personal loan guarantee from any corporation shareholders with more than a 20 to 40 percent ownership stake. Few people understand this de facto requirement when starting their own business, but they definitely understand it the first time that they obtain a major loan and never, never forget it after that.

Don't let your personal fears drive your decision, or you could end up with a purchase agreement that you later might regret. If your company is doing well, and from an objective viewpoint is performing financially in an attractive manner, you should seriously consider holding out until you get what the company is really worth. Just because you suddenly get nervous doesn't mean that your company is now a bad risk. You are just nervous. Take a deep breath, go on a few customer calls, and evaluate your most recent financial statements.

You might still decide to sell, but the desperation should not be there. If you still feel a sense of foreboding, then sell. Your intuition might just be telling you something that doesn't appear in financial statements.

THE 30-SECOND RECAP

- If you do not sell, expect to work extra hard at first convincing people that you are back in business to stay.
- Liquidating has tax implications that should be evaluated before hanging out the "For Sale" sign.
- ESOPs are a great way to create a winning situation for both you and your employees.
- It is usually better to sell when both your company performance and the overall market are at their best.
- A down market can spell opportunity for a well-run company that shows solid investment returns.
- Selling before reaching bottom allows you to keep more of what you worked for.

- Beware of family and management squabbles both as a buyer and as a seller.

- If you are bored, find a hobby; sell the company if you find yourself disrupting the operations to add spice to your entrepreneurial life.

Getting Ready to Sell Your Business

Shift your thinking to a clear understanding that selling your business won't happen overnight. And to sell your business for its maximum potential requires advance work on your part. The good news is that all of the advance work you do improves your daily operation, which is good news whether you sell or not. It often turns out that the prospect of selling motivates us to make the improvements we wanted to do anyway. This section runs through several highly recommended changes you can make to your business that will help it to sell at its maximum potential.

THE INITIAL PREPARATION

Selling a business, like most things in life, is almost always more complicated than anyone expects. Most experts will tell you to start preparing for the sale long before you actually decide to put it on the market.

Why? Simple. It takes time to get things set up in such a way that someone not familiar with your operation can see its intrinsic value.

Have you ever sold your house? If so, just before putting it on the market, you probably did all the things to the house that you had planned to do to while you were actually living in it. These might be putting on new siding, upgrading the windows, giving your bathrooms a facelift, adding that new roof, landscaping, and other things that make your house more attractive.

CAUTION

Financial people get concerned when they see business people make radical decisions on fundamental business areas such as selling a business or changing top management personnel. If you plan to sell your business, and not raise a lot of eyebrows, you must be adequately prepared to present your personal reasons for selling along with the financial aspects of the sale.

Many swear that they will make the changes (like the ones mentioned above) while still living in the house, so that they could be enjoyed. But they mostly wind up making the most expensive repairs at the end. Why? Because it improves the resale value of the home, allowing the seller to get the highest possible selling price for his home. It's hard to justify the time and expense required to make the changes while still living in the house.

The same logic often applies to your business, which makes little sense. Start early getting it ready for sale. Early can mean as much as two or three years before actually putting it up for sale. The earlier you start the more natural the changes will appear to a prospective buyer and the better your business will run—which is a good thing, whether the business sells or not.

MAKE SURE THE MONEY ADDS UP

The reason you and everyone else start a business is to make money. It doesn't mean that you don't like what you do; it just means that making money is a business fact of life.

As soon as you possibly can, you need to prepare valid financial statements that can stand up to close scrutiny by a trained accounting professional. It is never too early to get these statements accurate and financially consistent. Many experts recommend automating your accounting procedures from the start. You will have to automate eventually, so you might as well do it right from the beginning. At some point you will need financial statements for either your own management purposes or to work with financial colleagues, such as a bank or investor.

If you do not have financial statements that can be credibly reviewed by a prospective buyer's accountant, you have started out the sale process on shaky ground. After all, you are trying to convince someone else who is most likely not familiar with your business that owning your business is a solid financial decision. How can that person make this determination without comprehensive, consistent, and current financial statements?

To gain the confidence of prospective buyers, you must create a detailed review of your financial and accounting procedures and determine how your financial statements will look to someone who is not familiar with, or emotionally involved with, your business. If the statements make sense, you are probably in good shape. If the financial statements only raise more questions about the financial aspects of the company, you probably need changes to your financial reporting processes or the data itself needs careful evaluation.

If, after a close look, you find that your company is in great financial shape, congratulate yourself. If you find problems or just suspect that something is wrong (gut instinct), you need to engage an accountant to review your financials with an eye for finding any inconsistencies that might give rise to discrepancies (accounting errors) that might negatively impact your statements. If inconsistencies are not found, a further look at operations is required.

SYSTEMIZE YOUR PROCESSES

Have you ever talked to others about something that you cared about dearly and found that they just didn't care? Or perhaps they didn't understand? Or perhaps you were so close to the situation that you assumed they knew what you knew, which is almost never the case? You might not get more than one chance to convince a prospective buyer that purchasing your company is a solid investment. You need to "tell your story" to a prospective buyer. You want to remove as much uncertainty from the communication as you can.

Understanding what you have to sell is important or you cannot truly appreciate its value to an objective party. In addition, the buyer wants to understand what he or she is buying and your word about how things work just isn't enough. No offense meant.

As soon as you think you might want to sell your business, you should start looking at it as a *system*—that is, a process of everyday employee activities that have been created into a routine anyone on the outside can learn and follow.

Systems have *inputs* and *outputs*. Between the input and output is a process of some kind. If you are a manufacturing company, your inputs are typically raw materials and product specification information. Your output is typically a final product that meets that specification, which is then shipped to the customer. The process involves all of the work done to get the project from the input to the output.

PLAIN ENGLISH

System refers to a process of turning daily routines you or your employees "just know" how to do into specific procedures that someone else can learn and follow.

Input refers to the various items and/or skills required to make a process work properly.

Output refers to the final result of the process.

If you are a services company, your input is some type of work request from the customer. It may require some supplies and the labor of your skilled people. The output is the desired end result of work done by your company, which might be a clean building for a cleaning service or a report for a consulting company.

If your people "just know" how to do things and much of that "just knowing" is not documented, you are now selling a concept. There is nothing tangible you can show prospective buyers to convince them that you have been anything more than lucky. Consistently lucky, maybe, but lucky just the same. How does that buyer understand there is really a process in place—one that can be repeated? It is your job to help him or her get to that level of understanding.

So start looking at every aspect of your business for any possibility of its being systemized.

PROCEDURE MANUALS ARE SELLABLE

Systemizing also applies to the administrative aspects of your company. Assume that you have a two-week vacation policy that isn't written down, but everyone knows exists. This has worked well in the past and you fully intend to maintain this policy. How do you prove to a prospective buyer that this is your policy? You can tell them that this is your policy, but they must now verify the statement with employee interviews and reviews of past payroll records.

However, a better way to go is to simply include the specific details of your vacation policy in your corporate policy manual. Why? Because it is in print, it is published internally, and it is theoretically in the hands of your employees. This is no longer a thing that exists only in your head or in their minds. It's a policy that exists in the collective thinking of the organization. It simply makes it more real when written down.

TIP

People respond well to physical evidence that something exists. Telling someone that you follow specific procedures is one thing. Giving him or her a procedures manual shows that person it's for real.

Policies are those internal guidelines around which employees operate, almost like the "laws" of the company. They usually include guidelines for such things as vacation, sick leave, hours of operation, dress codes, antitheft, and other rules. A policies manual is a collection of all company policies that are used by employees for determining proper conduct under specific circumstances.

Procedures usually deal with operational topics, such as the creation of a final report, performing an audit, or testing a particular product. They often include detailed, step-by-step instructions for performing specific tasks. A procedures manual is a central location where procedures are stored so that employees can refer to them as required in the performance of their operational duties.

PLAIN ENGLISH

Policies are the internal laws around which employees operate, typically including guidelines for vacation, sick leave, and other rules.

Procedures deal with operational topics, such as the creation of a final report, performing an audit, or testing a particular product. They often include detailed, step-by-step instructions for performing specific tasks.

A word of caution is due at this point. Make sure that your procedures manual is current; otherwise it can do more harm than good. You need to talk the talk and walk the walk, meaning that you actually need to follow the procedures outlined in the manual. If the prospective buyers compare your actual procedures with those outlined in the book and find a discrepancy, you might wind up with a perceived integrity problem on your hands—which is probably the worst thing that could happen to you when selling your business. When they start to question the truth of what you say, the transaction almost always stalls, falls apart, or costs you something else as part of the negotiations. After all, would you completely trust someone who had already misrepresented the truth to you?

Automation provides an excellent foundation for establishing and following procedures. Accounting procedures can be built right into the software. Commercially available or custom-developed applications can be used for maintaining marketing communications and sales contact histories. Materials reporting (MRP) systems can be used to track *raw inventory, work in progress,* and *finished goods* that are ready to sell.

PLAIN ENGLISH

Raw inventory consists of asset items that were purchased so they can be combined to create a finished product. It includes items like screws, nuts, paper, ink, wire, and other basic materials.

Work in progress designates asset items that are in the process of being converted from raw materials into finished goods that can then be resold. This is sometimes called WIP by manufacturing folks.

Finished goods are items ready for sale to a customer. Notice that raw inventory, combined with some type of a process, creates finished goods.

Working with automation requires that you formalize your thinking and standardize your procedures. Only standardized procedures can be implemented by a computer, because it really cannot make any unpredicted, unanticipated decisions on its own. The good news is that it decreases the dependence on the human being. The bad news is that automation requires substantial amounts of time and/or money in the beginning, along with a sustaining, periodic investment to keep things current into the future.

FORMALIZE CUSTOMER AGREEMENTS

Handshake agreements work with many established customers. Some business people have closed deals for tens of thousands of dollars with large, established customers simply on the word of a key contact. However, one should always try to get it in writing as a precaution should something happen to that person or should the project not work out to everyone's satisfaction. But you may have long-term arrangements with customers that never involve a written contract simply because getting it in writing was not feasible, and you feel that the customer is a solid credit risk. This can happen when dealing with municipalities where the paperwork involved with a contract is complicated, and you know that a governmental agency will pay its bills.

When you sell your business, your customer relationships become one of your most prized assets. If those assets are not documented, the verification of those relationships becomes more difficult. For this reason, take a close look at creating a standardized agreement that you sign with your customers. This takes the guesswork out of your existing relationships, and it provides another level of confidence to prospective buyers.

You will benefit today from standardizing your agreements. It's easier for you to deal with customer agreement problems when everyone signs substantially the same agreement. When every agreement is an exercise in creativity, it makes it more difficult to keep them all straight. It also makes it more difficult for your sales people to sell, because your customers know that everything is negotiable if they can get to you.

CAUTION

Customers can react in strange ways when you try to formalize what has traditionally been an informal relationship. If it comes down to a choice between keeping the customer and formalizing the agreement, always keep the customer. An agreement without a customer is useless, whereas a customer without an agreement can still be a customer for years to come.

History shows that standardized terms and conditions, backed up by a written agreement, is the least disruptive, most productive process. And it will make it easier to sell your business later on.

LET YOUR BANK KNOW IN CONFIDENCE

Contrary to what you may think, your banker is not a penny-pinching adversary, but actually a potential ally. It is important that you let your banker know about major financial changes, especially if you have loans or other agreements that define what you can and cannot do with respect to business ownership.

The bank just wants to make sure that any outstanding loans it has made to you and your company will be repaid. New ownership adds a new risk into the banker's mind, and you should be prepared to minimize their perception of the risks. And the new owners might have to take over your financial obligations, including those to your bank, so it makes sense to involve them in your plans.

TIP

Your banker can be a potential ally. You are the president of your company, and you deal with your banker. This means that your banker also deals with other business presidents. He or she has also seen business plans from various companies just as he or she has seen yours. Do you see a pattern forming here?

You also want to ensure that your banker knows from the start that you and the business are not in financial trouble—unless you really are in trouble and think that the bank can help you out. The last thing you want is for the bank to call a loan when you are trying to make the company look as financially solvent as possible. Another thing to avoid is having your banker find out from a source other than you that your company is up for sale. They will wonder why you didn't tell them yourself, and you are once again on the defensive for what would otherwise be considered a sound business move on your part.

How much should you tell your banker? The answer: Only what they *need to know.* Your banker has a fiduciary responsibility first to the bank and secondly to you, which means that he or she will act first in the bank's best interest and secondly in your best interest. Your banker cannot ethically discuss your financial situation with anyone outside of the bank without your permission, so don't expect your banker to talk about your sale without you specifically authorizing him or her to do so, either verbally or in writing.

KEEP IT TO YOURSELF

Honesty may be the best policy, but providing information on a need-to-know basis is in a solid second place.

You and the other members of your staff who are directly involved with the sale of the company are the only ones who need to know about it. At some point, if your company is for sale for a long period of time, word will get out and you will have to address your employees. But that time is usually somewhere down the road, and not in the early stages of the sale process.

Letting even little items slip can cost you dearly while you are trying to sell the company. If employees think that the company is for sale because of financial problems, they may decide to start job hunting. If they succeed and leave your company, you have decreased the value of your company to a prospective buyer. If they succeed and your company does not sell, your daily operations have been hampered by their loss and for no real reason.

Finally, people might start assuming that you, a principle member of the company, are planning to leave the company. If they are there to work specifically for you, they might leave for any number of personal reasons that have nothing to do with business or money. And if the company, once again, does not sell, you have lost key employees and some credibility for no reason at all. Needless to say, all of these problems could be avoided if the sale is kept secret until finally completed.

BREAKING THE NEWS

In reality, no matter how secretive you are, the word eventually gets out. Secretaries type and copy documents that will be related to the sale. People will see changes around the company and speculate on your motivations. If you leave their minds to work in a vacuum, they could very well come up with disaster scenarios that are far worse than, or have nothing to do with, what is really going on. At some point, you are going to tell your employees something, and you should plan that strategy from the beginning.

CAUTION

If employees speculate that the potential buyer is someone for whom they would not work, they might start job hunting. Remember that you straddle the distance between the new buyer and your employees until the sale is completed.

When you do break the news, make sure you present it in a way that is beneficial to the employees, customers, and other owners. If they think you are being greedy, you might have a lot of resentful people on your hands. If they think their jobs are in jeopardy, they might jump ship. You must be sensitive to their side of the conversation and prepare your presentation so that it presents things in the most positive light for everyone involved.

Here are a few things to consider when finally relaying the information to employees, customers, and other owners:

- Remember to present the information in a way that is positive for those listening.
- If you have a gripe about the new owners, keep it to yourself. That is your problem, and it should not become your employees' problem.
- Let them know that their jobs are not in jeopardy, or that those who are caught in the reorganization will be given proper financial and personal consideration.
- Perhaps you are far enough along in the sale process that you can present the new owners. A favorable handoff from you to them is like gold to the new owners.
- Make sure that the new owners understand the impact of their statements on your employees. You know them better than the new owners do, and you might help them avoid mistakes during the transition period.
- Keep the details of your arrangement to yourself, and simply let them know that you are satisfied with the deal and that you are in no personal jeopardy. Your old employees might be more dedicated to you than you think, and you want to put their minds at ease with respect to your side of the sale.

Make Tomorrow Look Just Like Today

The most important thing that you must do in selling your company is also perhaps the most difficult. You must make tomorrow look just like today. Employees, customers, vendors, creditors, and other owners must not see a major disruption of standard business operations. If you are going nuts inside, don't display it at work. Get it out of your system with a friend, a family member, or by taking up kickboxing. Whatever it takes to keep the ship on course.

TIP

The stages of negotiations involved with selling your business should be kept to yourself and/or those on your core staff. Your emotional ups and downs, which will almost always happen as you progress through the sale stages, can ripple through the rest of the company. This is rarely a good thing, and it should be avoided. Keep it to yourself until it is time to let everyone else in on the details.

Remember that change is frightening to most people. The more perceived risk that they associate with your decisions, the more worried they will be that something will go wrong. As a result, they will be watching for any signs of change. Nobody ever complains about a positive change, such as a salary increase. Negative change, be it ever so slight, even something as seemingly minor as changing from a name-brand coffee to generic, can raise flags in people's minds, causing them anxiety and costing you the time and energy required to keep their fears under control.

Note that if your intention is keep "business as usual" after a sale becomes public knowledge, there is no real reason for people to get anxious. There is no guarantee that people won't still get anxious, but without real justification for their fears, most emotionally healthy people will also treat you in a "business as usual" way.

If your business is in turmoil, it will be less attractive to a prospective buyer. This makes your business more difficult to sell and will probably cost you money due to an uncertainty-induced sale price reduction. Risk/reward. The higher the perceived risk on the buyer's side, the more reward the buyer will want—which means a drop in sale price or the negotiation of less-favorable terms for you.

HELP THE BUYER WITH FINANCING

Once again, let's talk about your banker. Whoever buys your business will have to finance the purchase. If it is Bill Gates, congratulations. At least he should have the money to fund the purchase himself. However, there is only one Bill Gates, which means that your potential buyers will probably need to find ways to come up with some money.

Anyone providing credit to the buyer will primarily be interested in two things when evaluating the extension of credit: How solid is the business and how credible is the buyer?

Your current creditors already know your business. The fact that they have already lent you money means that they believed in you and your business at least once. You should involve them in the sale process and ask them whether they might consider providing credit to the new buyer. You might be doing your creditors, the buyer, and yourself a favor.

Be careful, however, when approaching your creditors to help your potential buyer; there may be a conflict of interest. They have an interest in seeing the company sold so that they can recover their existing loans, and they also want to ensure that the new buyer will properly repay existing debts that carry over with the sale. But, if they are providing credit to the new buyer, they want to see that the company does not wind up with so much debt that it becomes a financial risk. Make sure that you select creditors who won't try to squeeze you, but will work with you to find the best deal for all involved parties.

You probably already have creditor relationships that you have not used in part of your current operation. Determine which of these creditors would be open to funding a new, credible buyer. Then sell them on the future potential of your business. This lets them know your business reasons for wanting to sell and lays the groundwork for the new, creditworthy buyer.

The more attractive your business looks and the easier you make it to finance the sale, the more likely you are to sell in a reasonable time frame while also getting the price you want.

THE 30-SECOND RECAP

- Companies that have systems in place are less risky to buy and consequently easier to sell.

- Accounting processes and statements must be under control so that they present a consistent and accurate picture of your company's financial health.

- A procedure manual allows the buyer to have something more than your word on how things are done at your company.

- A seller should only reveal information to those people who have a "need-to-know"—until the word hits the street.

- When employees, creditors, vendors, and customers are about to find out about your intention to sell, you are best served by telling them the facts yourself.

- Helping your buyer find financiers can be very helpful to all parties involved—but be cautious about whom you approach.

Preparing Your Financials

Ultimately, any business venture comes down to an assessment of the financial situation. If your financial reports are not right, your credibility will be undermined along with the price you will receive for your company.

This section covers the financial aspects of selling your company. Advance preparation will make your financial statements and you look better. That translates into a quicker sale and higher sales dollars when the offers finally come.

THE FINANCIALS MUST SELL THEMSELVES

The ultimate goal of everything you create or do with respect to the sale of your company should be clearly targeted toward improving the likelihood of that sale happening. This is also true of any financial decisions you make during the period of the sale.

Most larger companies have dedicated finance and accounting departments, which typically have trained professionals who pride themselves on the precise accuracy of their accounting numbers.

TIP

You cannot take back any historical expenses, but you can control what you spend from this point forward.

However, you really can't make effective financial decisions if you don't know the current state of your finances. These departments should not dictate what happens in the company, but are an integral part of effectively, and profitably, running a company.

Whoever purchases your company must go over your financials with a magnifying glass, so they have to be correct. This cannot be emphasized enough. It is not just that your company will not sell if your financials are questionable, but the process will definitely be longer, harder, and will most likely cost you money with respect to the sale price.

Here are a few important points to understand when evaluating the current status of your financial reports:

- You have developed accounting procedures over the years that might be either documented or tacit. Those procedures are reflected in the financial statements.

- A listing of your current accounting and financial reporting procedures and policies is a good place to start. This list tells the reader how the numbers were prepared, which gives a basis of comparison against what would normally be expected.

■ If you are a publicly traded company, your historical financial reports are pretty well locked in by the information that you publicly disclosed. Changing these numbers at a later date is possibly illegal and certainly expensive.

■ Privately held, small companies usually take more liberties with their financial procedures and accounting, because they are the only ones, other than the IRS, to whom reporting must be done. This reporting is almost always prepared to minimize net income, which also minimizes taxes. (Recasting is discussed thoroughly in the next section.)

■ Obvious unusual items, like a negative liability account balance or a negative expense, will raise flags. If they are *really* supposed to be there, be ready to explain them. More likely, there is an accounting error somewhere that needs correction before you let others review the reports.

You must perform advance preparation to avoid future problems, instead of waiting until the problem finds you. An ounce of prevention may very well save you hours of dancing and unnecessary expenses finding a financial cure.

HISTORICAL INCOME AND NET WORTH REPORTS

Buyers purchase a company expecting some future performance levels. Determining the most likely future performance levels is often based on past performance. Therefore, although buyers purchase their version of the future, they often base their future expectations on past performance.

Assume that you have a friend who is consistently 30 minutes late. He or she asks to meet with you at 3 P.M. Will you push to arrive on time? We all will do our best, but if your past experience tells you that the other person will most likely *not* be there at 3, you might not worry as much about arriving on time.

The same overall impression is left with a trained financial person who reads a set of historical financial reports. They make assumptions about your past performance against which your future projections are compared. If the future doesn't track with the past, you had better have a story to tell regarding the discrepancy. Don't just count on being lucky, and don't just hope that they won't find it. More than likely, they will.

Therefore, the trick is to create the historical reports with as much positively oriented accuracy as possible and to then make a pro-forma projection of a reasonable future based on that past.

Should you have recent large changes to the financial condition of the company that cause the future projections to deviate substantially from the past, explain those changes in the financial report footnotes. Don't leave them unanswered, because the questions will come up, putting you on the defensive.

Track your company's historical information for the past three to five years. Only go for three years if years four and five add little to the picture or can seriously undermine your current state. Most businesspeople will discount those years anyway if the recent years show markedly better performance.

RECASTING FOR SMALL BUSINESSES

Small business owners have a special situation that must be addressed, especially if you are potentially selling to a publicly held company.

You manage your company to minimize net income, while obviously making a solid personal income. A publicly held company manages to maximize net income, which increases earnings, which increases the stock value when multiplied by the price-to-earning (PE) ratio.

Assume, for example, that the prospective buyer is a publicly held company that shows a 15 percent net income before tax (NIBT) on sales of $10 million. Also assume that this company has a stock price of $15. This means that every dollar of annually reported earnings, when divided by the total number of shares, increases the share price by $15. After all, isn't this what the PE ratio means?

This is the level of future performance that the investing public thinks is reasonable for this company, or they wouldn't purchase a stock with this particular set of earnings, price, and PE ratio.

Now assume that this company purchases your company, which you have specifically managed to show a loss of $100,000 for each of the last two years. Assume also that your company has annual sales of $2 million, or 20 percent of the parent (buying) company's total annual revenues. Your accounting approach minimizes your taxes, which was good as far as you were concerned. However, it is likely not good news for the buyers.

Notice that the income performance of the purchased company will decrease after the purchase. Here is why. A dollar in sales revenue for the purchased company returns a loss of 10 cents. Take a look at the numbers shown in the following situation. (Assume that no dividends are paid by either company and that the effect of taxes can be neglected, only to simplify the analysis.)

- The company's total projected revenues were previously $10 million, and are now $12 million after the purchase.

- The NIBT for the parent company used to be $1.5 million, or 15 percent of $10 million. It is now $1.4 million ($1.5 million – $100,000) or 14 percent.

- Notice that the earnings will drop, which now means that the amount of pro-rated earnings that can be multiplied by the PE ratio also drops, although the number of outstanding shares remains the same. The net effect is a drop in the stock price.

■ If the buying company's management is compensated based on stock performance, they just lost personal income because the stock price just dropped as a result of the acquisition.

■ Slick accounting and financial maneuvering on your part just put a huge boulder in the path of selling your company to a publicly held buyer.

This is an extreme example, because you cannot consistently operate your company at a loss or the IRS will want to chat with you. But the point should come across that diminishing your earnings, which is great for a small business, is not great for a publicly held company and therefore must be addressed.

Assume that you have paid yourself, or other family members, a higher salary than they would have normally received on the open market. These higher expense levels will disappear when the company is sold because the newer management will not have the emotional reason for helping them, or you, out in this same way. Assume that you have a car allowance for each of your managers, who also happen to be relatives. These expenses will likely also go away with the purchase. Perhaps you belong to a country club, where you transact business four days a week. These expenses will likely also not be paid by the buying company.

Notice that all of these expenses help you or your family out while decreasing net income, which ultimately decreases taxes. The buyer must be made aware of these discretionary expenses, and realize that they will not be incurred after the company is sold. In fact, taking them out of the past financial reporting might actually show that the company made a profit. This is *recasting* your financial statements.

PLAIN ENGLISH

Recasting is the process of removing unnecessary expenses from historical financial statements so that they more accurately reflect a realistic financial assessment of performance. It is often done by small companies to remove "special" expenses incurred to decrease net income and taxes.

TIP

Never forget that you cannot change the past, but you can shape the buyer's perception of the future. That is the point of recasting your financial statements.

Re-creating the past financial reports so that they do not include these non-transferred expenses recasts them in a light that the buyer can appreciate. Now the buyer can validly assess the value of your company based on a realistic set of financial numbers. Notice that if your recasted numbers show the company making a profit, or possibly even a NIBT, of higher than 15 percent, you are now adding to the share price instead of hurting it. Your company instantly became more attractive to the publicly held corporate buyer.

Take a look at the following figure to see how recasting your historical financial reports can turn a company that appears to be losing money into one that shows a positive NIBT. Assume that your salespeople (your brother and sister) get an 8 percent commission instead of the buying company's standard 5 percent; that you have an extra $215,000 in salaries that you pay your wife, mother, children, cousin, and other family members that would not transfer to the new owner; and that $25,000 in various general and administrative (G&A) expenses would not be needed, or approved, by the new owner's internal accounting policy.

Removing the impact of these expense numbers by adding them back into the NIBT number shown ($100,000) proves to the buyers that a more realistic assessment of their expected income is a positive $200,000 or 10 percent of sales. This may not match our sample buyer's goal of 15 percent, but it is a lot better than losing $100,000.

Is recasting starting to make sense to you? It should at this point.

TIP

It is okay to be a small business owner who aggressively, and legally, does everything possible to reduce the impact of taxes by reducing income. You just don't want your past financial manipulations to get in the way of the prospective buyer seeing the true financial value in your company.

CREATING PRO FORMA FINANCIAL REPORTS

Historical financial performance reporting is relatively cut and dried. Although it allows for some level of creativity, you are still working with past numbers that have already happened. The issue is not whether the numbers exist; the issue is where they should be reported.

Predicting the future is not as simple, and it is certainly open to interpretation. After all, no one can know what will happen in the future until it becomes the past. The point is that the future is open to interpretation and that buyers purchase the future. Bridging the gap between the past and the future is the role of the pro-forma financial statements.

PRO FORMA INCOME STATEMENT

YEAR	2004 (PURCHASE)	2004	2005	2006	2007
Sales and Cost of Goods Sold:					
Sales Revenues	2,000,000	2,300,000	2,645,000	3,041,750	3,498,013
Cost of Goods Sold	1,200,000	1,380,000	1,587,000	1,825,000	2,098,808
Gross Profit	800,000	920,000	1,058,000	1,216,700	1,399,205
Operating Expenses:					
Rent	65,000	68,900	73,034	77,416	82,061
Utilities	32,000	33,920	35,955	38,113	40,399
Depreciation	12,000	12,720	13,483	14,292	15,150
Salaries	565,000	598,900	634,834	672,924	713,299
General and Admin	66,000	69,960	74,158	78,607	83,323
Commissions	160,000	169,600	179,776	190,563	201,996
Total Operating Expenses	900,000	954,000	1,011,240	1,071,914	1,136,229
Net Income Before Tax (NIBT)	(100,000)	(34,000)	46,760	144,786	262,986
Recasting Adjustments:					
Adjust Commissions from 8& to 5%	60,000	63,600	67,416	71,461	75,749
Adjust Salaries to Post Purchase Levels	215,000	227,900	241,574	256,068	271,433
Adjust G&A for Misc. Expenses	25,000	26,500	28,090	28,775	31,562
Recasted NIBT Values	200,000	284,000	383,840	502,090	641,719
NIBT As a Percentage of Sales Revenues	10%	12%	15%	17%	18%
Estimated Annual Sales Growth	15%				
Estimated Operating Expense Increase	6%				

The preceding table displays two things:

1. Income performance in the year of sale, which is noted as such
2. Four years of estimated future income performance

It also shows the recasted NIBT for both current and future fiscal years. How you display the information is up to you; you can use this figure as a starting point.

Lawyers sometimes claim that pro forma statements are dangerous in that they can be interpreted as a "guarantee" of performance instead of as a best-guess estimate. But you want to be able to sell the future without some type of pro forma analysis. Leaving their creation up to the buyer takes it out of your hands and puts it into theirs. This is always a risky move when selling.

CPAs have an entire set of criteria that governs their involvement with prospective financial statements, which they classify as either forecasts or projections. Forecasts are appropriate for outside parties but require greater detail and disclosure. CPAs use standard language to explain that the forecasts may differ from actual results. You should definitely use a CPA to assist you in disseminating this important information. You may also want to talk to your counsel about disclaimers that can be added to protect you legally, but do provide this additional, highly valued buyer analysis.

The assumptions are of particular value in the prior figure and the way that those assumptions affect the buyer's perspective on the financial prospects for this company. Notice that the recasted NIBT number for 2004 shows NIBT as a percentage of sales equal to 10 percent. But look at what happens to these numbers when recasted for FY 2005 and beyond. See how the value starts at 12 percent and moves up to 18 percent by 2007?

TIP

Don't expect to create your own pro forma financial statements unless you have an accounting background. You are better served by having an accountant create them for you. They will be numerically consistent, and maybe even right, which is a lot to say about the future.

These higher values put the financial perspective on this company in a completely new light. Instead of this company being a drain on public stock price values, it now contributes earnings dollars due to the higher NIBT values. Each sales dollar now contributes more to the public stock price, via the PE ratio, than the current buying company's sales dollars.

It is common, at this point, to perform a discounted cash-flow analysis on the pro forma income statement values shown. This process provides insight into the present value of future cash flows, which helps to assess the value of the company as viewed from today.

It is common to create pro forma balance sheets and cash-flow statements. This is particularly true for companies that are concerned about the availability of cash to fund future growth. Growth is expensive, and high growth requires cash. The pro forma cash-flow statement provides these estimates.

ESTIMATING YOUR CUSTOMER VALUE

Customers are your most valued assets. Without them, there are no sales, which means no income or profits to you.

Many companies start taking their customers for granted. They stop making those unnecessary, but appreciated, thank you courtesy calls. They stop sending Christmas cards, stop soliciting them for new business, and stop thanking them for past business. In short, they start to treat their customers as if they will always be there.

John, the owner of a small manufacturing company, was one of those business managers who started taking his customers for granted. He focused so much internal company attention on creating the new products his customers wanted that he forgot to tell his customers what he was doing. When he was ready, some had already made plans to go with another vendor for those particular, and some other, needs. Now that hurt him, but it wasn't the customer's fault. He knew it was his.

John now works hard to retain his customers, and finds that he still goofs up. Customer service is very important, and it makes financial sense as well.

TIP

For every single customer complaint you hear about, there are many more out there you know nothing about. If you don't find out about them or if you manage them improperly, your buyers might disappear, which could cost you big-time money on the purchase price.

Every industry has its own set of marketing processes that must be followed. If you are in retail, your first major challenge is getting the consumer to try your store in the first place. If the experience goes well, they will likely come back. If not, you will be lucky to see them again, unless you offer something unique that is just not easily available elsewhere. It costs you advertising, promotion, and discount dollars to get them to come in. Getting them to come back is the least expensive part of the process, and the one most neglected.

If you are in a commercial industry, such as equipment sales, that has a regular equipment upgrade period, you can count on happy existing customers purchasing new equipment within a few years. Why would they go elsewhere if you have what they want, for a reasonable price, when they want it, and with minimal hassle to them?

Having been in business, you should have a number of repeat customers. You may want to perform this simple, yet interesting exercise:

1. Estimate the number of new customers you obtained last year. (For example, assume 20 new customers.)

2. Now estimate the number of expense dollars you spent that could be earmarked for "new customer generation" marketing and sales activities. (Assume that you spent $40,000 total on new customer generation activities.)

3. Divide the value obtained from Step 2 by the value obtained from Step 1. This provides you with a cost per new customer expense ratio. ($40,000 ÷ 200 = $200 per customer.)

Getting a new customer cost you $200. Keeping a new customer might only cost you a smile and a little attention.

TIP

A customer is also worth more than a single sale to your company. This customer represents a certain amount of money they will likely spend over the course of a year.

Kathy owns a software training business. It was typical for a customer to take several software classes over the course of a year. They might take both a beginning and an intermediate training class on a spreadsheet, word processing, and presentation graphic software package. This is a total of six classes at $200 each, or $1200 over the course of a year. In addition, every year they would take three more classes at $200 each, or $600 in sales revenue per customer.

Looking at a typical customer-related income stream for Kathy's business provides the following insight over a three-year period.

Projecting Customer Value	
Year 1 Revenues	$1,200
Year 2 Revenues	$600
Year 3 Revenues	$600
Three-Year Total Customer Revenues	$2,400

If we assume that Kathy's company has a NIBT of 10 percent, this particular customer yields $240 of net income over a three-year period, after all sales, operating, production, and fixed expenses are paid.

At this point, you might be wondering whether this number has any greater significance. The answer is "yes," for certain industries, such as health care, cable TV, vending machines, and others.

Many of these companies determine their value based on the number of customers they currently have. A dentist's office, for example, might show that it has 500 active customers. If it can show that its average revenue per customer is above the national average for dentists, that particular practice is worth more from a sales perspective.

TIP

The higher your customer retention rate, the higher the price you can expect to be placed on that particular customer's account. This is good news from a seller, and a business owner, standpoint.

The same is true for other recurring service industries, such as housecleaning or car detailing. If the business has a high repeat clientele, it costs less to keep those customers than it does to find new ones. If, on the other hand, you find high customer turnover when compared to the rest of that particular industry, you should expect your new customer sales expenses to be higher than the national average.

As an ongoing management tool, you want to clearly understand the average revenue you expect from each of your customers, and then keep those customers happy. It is always easier to keep a customer than it is to find him or her in the first place.

Projecting customer sales revenues into the future is a kind of pro forma exercise, and will also be based on historical trends and specific future customer agreements. A discounted cash-flow analysis can also be applied to these revenues.

EXPLAIN BOOK VALUE ASSUMPTIONS

Finally, a brief note should be added to your reported financial information explaining the assumptions on which the company's book value is determined. Remember that book value has nothing directly to do with the current market value of an asset. It is the purchase price minus the depreciation of an asset or the current remaining balance of a loan.

Understanding the methods used for calculating book value is important to the buyer. This company inherits the current, depreciated value of your assets if passed to the buyer as part of a company purchase. Book value is also used to determine the seller's gain in the event of an asset purchase. Therefore, book value determination methods are pertinent in most circumstances and to all parties involved.

Make sure that you explain the various book value assumptions, and you will avoid the questions that will inevitably come up later.

THE 30-SECOND RECAP

- Your financial statements and analyses must stand on their own, without explanation.

- Book value should be stated, even if not directly used as part of the purchase negotiations.

- Customers have an intrinsic and a financial value that can be estimated into the future.

- Pro forma financial statements are a best guess of the future, and they are well worth creating and providing, after first checking with legal counsel.

- Historical financial trends are often carried into the future as part of the pro forma statements.

Understanding the Tax Impacts When You Sell Your Company

Tax strategies, if handled properly, can increase the after-tax income seen by the seller while decreasing the purchase price paid by the buyer. Buyers and sellers may disagree about a lot of things, but both generally agree with giving as little money as possible to the IRS.

However, tax-avoidance strategies can be fraught with hidden dangers that could put the seller in the position of owning a lot of stock that does him or her no good at all. The seller's company and income source was sold to the purchaser, and he or she could be left with little of tangible value in return.

Nobody wants to be in this position. Work your way through this section and understand the various considerations involved with structuring a sale deal. This is not only good business, but also avoids unnecessary taxes.

INCOME ALWAYS BRINGS TAX CONSIDERATIONS

There is good news and bad news associated with making money. The good news is that you now have more money than you had before, which helps a great deal in making daily life a little more manageable. The bad news is that making money always means that paying taxes is not far behind.

There are various ways that money can be sheltered from the maximum tax bite, but you are almost always going to incur some type of tax bill when you sell a business and receive cash as part of the purchase. Even if your sale is an all-stock deal, you must still account for the increased (decreased) stock value as part of your, or the company's, tax return.

TIP

The tax impact of a transaction should always be in the back of your mind when evaluating any deal, but it should not determine the whole deal.

Structuring a deal that minimizes taxes at the expense of making as much as possible off the sale is winning a battle, but losing the war. Sure you paid less in taxes, but you also did not take home as much as possible from the sale of your company.

Your first concern should be with structuring a transaction that pays you what you want along with what you need, and then incorporates tax strategies. Complicated transactions like those associated with selling a business can be stalled if there is not a stake in the ground somewhere, determining a minimally reasonable offer.

This is your job as the owner/seller. You must define what constitutes a minimally acceptable deal. You can then put the tax guys to work trying to structure the deal so that both the seller and buyer benefit by meeting these deal criteria.

In general, taxes incurred from the sale will be minimized if a few simple strategies are used:

- Try to show as much of the sale as possible in the form of a capital gain to the seller, which should then qualify for a lower capital gains tax rate.

- Defer income to future years when the seller's tax rate might be lower, which would decrease the overall tax bite.

- Avoid double taxation to the selling company and its shareholders, which is achieved with the sale of an S corporation or with a non-taxable transfer to the purchasing company.

CAPITAL GAIN TAXES MINIMIZE THE BITE

Treating an asset as a long-term capital gain item allows you to take advantage of the IRS capital gain tax rate. For this reason, it is highly attractive to look at accepting payment for your company in such a way that the capital gain tax rate applies.

Here is the problem with this approach. The only ways to receive favorable capital gains tax treatment are to sell the company assets, to sell the company stock, or to merge the company and then subsequently sell the newly obtained stock.

TIP

The higher the tax bracket of the sellers, the more valuable the capital gain tax benefits become.

Here are some of the positive and negative aspects of selling company assets:

Positive Aspects

- The seller gets to choose which asset items are sold and which are kept.

- Sold asset items that have been owned for longer than the minimum 12-month capital gain holding period are eligible for lower capital gain tax treatment (individuals only—capital gain tax breaks are not available to corporations).

- The selling corporation continues its existence, which might be very good news if the intention of the sale is to move the company into another line of business where its established name would be of value.

- The selling corporation retains any favorable tax treatments it might have earned such as a carried-forward net operating loss, favorable unemployment or disability tax treatments, and others.

- The company is still an established company, with an established credit rating and financial relationships, making successful business continuance a more likely possibility.
- If the selling company is an S corporation, the capital gain tax benefits pass directly to the shareholders, except for cash, accounts receivable, and inventory sale proceeds, which are treated as income.
- The sellers get their money up front, without having to wait for a longer period of time.

Negative Aspects

- Paperwork must be managed for each sold asset including license transfers, warranty transfers, lien resolutions, and other miscellaneous areas.
- If you plan to sell the company, or shift it into another business area, you must still do something with the assets that are left over after the initial, large asset purchase/sale.
- Although the selling company receives capital gain treatment on the asset sale gains, the shareholders themselves do not. Double taxation is experienced when the proceeds from the asset sales are transferred to the shareholders themselves in the form of dividends or full liquidation.

TIP

Because the tax implications of any sale can have a substantial impact on the net cash you receive from the sale, most experts recommend that you review the transaction with an accountant before setting your expectations. The tax laws are incredibly complicated and so diverse that a professional is needed to assess your tax impact.

- The company still exists, which means that the selling owners must still deal with its operation, no matter how trivial it might become. This is a nuisance factor more than anything else, but it can become a liability should someone decide to go after the stripped corporation for something that happened in the past.
- If the assets have not been held for the 12-month minimum capital gain holding period, any gain on the sale of the asset will be taxed at an S corporation shareholder's regular income tax rate. (Regular corporations are not able to benefit from capital gain tax breaks.)

If only a percentage of outstanding shares is sold, the situation gets more complicated. There are only a few major items for consideration in this section. You must discuss the details of your particular situation with your tax professional.

Positive Aspects

■ Shareholders who sell capital gain-qualified shares will receive capital gain tax treatment on that gain.

■ The selling company still retains some ownership control over the daily operation of the company.

■ The selling company has an interest in seeing the purchased company succeed because it now has an investment in its future financial performance.

■ The purchasing company might be willing to give its stock to the shareholders of the purchased company, making the transaction tax-free to the selling company shareholders, at least until the shareholders sell the newly received stock. This decreases the cash outlay on the part of the purchasing company and decreases the tax impact on the sellers who receive stock.

 CAUTION

As soon as a publicly traded company becomes interested in buying your company, you should check out its historical stock performance. If it has a very low trading volume, you might have a hard time selling any stock that is included as part of the purchase agreement.

Negative Aspects

■ The prior owners now have a new set of owners, and probably board members, who must be dealt with.

■ No cash infusion was seen by the selling company, but its management hassle factor increased.

■ If the purchasing company acquired a majority of the shares, it might have the right to obtain a majority voting right on the board as well. This would transfer operational control to the purchasing company, even though the original founders/owners are still managing the company and may still have personally guaranteed company loans. This is a very precarious position for the previous owners.

■ The actual value of stock received will not be determined until a future date, when the stock is actually sold. If the purchasing company does well, having taken stock will be viewed as a great investment move. If its stock drops, taking stock instead of cash at the time of purchase will have a 20/20 hindsight regret associated with it.

Merging stocks is actually a simpler matter on almost all fronts because all assets transfer at their depreciated book values. All transactions are typically stock-for-stock transfers, which should have no tax consequences to the sellers, require minimal cash by the buyer, and minimize individual asset tracking/sale/negotiations. Remember that buyers may not want to fully acquire the company because they would also acquire all known, and unknown, liabilities along with all assets and goodwill. This reason alone is enough for many companies to never purchase another company outright.

LEAVING TOO MUCH IN THE COMPANY CAN BE RISKY

There is a natural tendency to take as much as possible in cash when selling your company. After all, what is more secure than cash?

For various reasons, buyers will often want to include some of their stock as part of the deal. These reasons might include a management motivation to keep the previous owners/managers interested in the performance of the new venture. They might include a financial motivation to minimize the amount of cash included in the purchase, making it less of an asset drain on the purchasing company. They might actually feel that the future value of the company stock is so positive that you are truly benefiting by owning the purchasing company's stock.

CAUTION

If the stock prices of the publicly traded company that is interested in buying your company have dropped over recent months, its stock might either be a bargain or still be on its way down. Only careful investigation will ensure that you know what you are getting into.

No matter the reason, the possibility of having stock presented as part of the deal is very real. The questions you will ask at that time are, should you take the stock and how much?

First, you want to ensure that you have a means for selling the received stock so that you can recoup some of your sale price when you choose.

Stock in a publicly traded company can usually be sold on the open market, but your stock might have restrictions on when and how it can be sold, especially if you become an officer in the purchasing company.

If there are any restrictions at all placed on how you can trade your acquired stock, the price of the stock should be discounted from its current market value. You don't know what the future holds for the market in general or for this stock in particular. Therefore, you want to protect yourself from future negative stock performance by acquiring the stock today at a discount that might be as much as 50 percent off the market price.

Think about this little financial trick if you feel yourself being wooed by the thought of major stock ownership. Assume for a moment that the acquiring company is trading at a price-to-earning (PE) ratio of 25, and your company has a PE ratio of 8, whether publicly or privately determined.

TIP

Check out the purchasing company's stock to determine whether it is worth owning on its own merits. If you yourself would not buy the stock outside of your purchase agreement, why would you want to acquire the stock as part of your own company's sale transaction? This would make no sense at all.

Notice that your company's earnings (sometimes called *accounting* or *paper profit*) will transfer to the purchasing company, which now will multiply the stock value by a factor of 25 instead of 8. If the executives on the purchasing side are compensated on stock price performance, this is a sound deal, especially if they can purchase your company with their stock, which is highly leveraged (as indicated by the 25 times multiplier).

PLAIN ENGLISH

Accounting or **paper profit** is profit that appears on the financial statements and that is the result of an administrative or accounting procedure or change, as opposed to one that results from an actual change in operation.

They haven't done a thing to functionally integrate the two companies, and have already shown an increase in stock price simply due to the earnings multiplier. As the buyer who is compensated based on stock price increases, this is a clever approach. As the seller, you want to make sure that you are compensated for allowing the buyer to take advantage of your lower PE ratio.

Taking a lot of stock as part of the transaction while not retaining any controlling interest in the purchasing company puts your future income and wealth in the hands of the purchasing company management. If they live up to your expectations, life is good. If not, you could find yourself, and your shareholders, holding worthless stock that cannot even be traded.

Finding the right mix of cash, loans, and stock that you should accept is a tough question, and one that is heavily dependent on the personality of the sellers. If you are a privately held company with all stock ownership in the hands of a few people, you can probably obtain a consensus about the right mix to accept. If it is just you, assess your own risk profile and accept the combination that is right for you.

If you have a large number of shareholders, you really have to take a more objective approach and determine the arrangement that optimizes shareholder wealth in today's dollars. This will likely require a discounted cash-flow analysis, so that you and the other board members are protected should future buyer performance not turn out as expected.)

WEIGHING WHAT YOU WANT AGAINST WHAT YOU NEED

Finally, don't finalize any sale transaction unless you get out of it what you yourself truly need. If you plan to leave the company after the sale, you want to make sure that you have adequate cash and/or income to cover your living expenses. If a large portion of that future cash is associated with a loan you provided the company, you probably want to reevaluate the deal. If the purchasing company ever defaults on the loan, your future income can be jeopardized along with what you thought might have been a comfortable early retirement.

TIP

Write down your bottom-line requirements before you get too far into the sale process details. The forest often gets lost in the trees, and you always want to make sure that your initial objectives are met once all details have worked themselves out.

If, on the other hand, you are motivated enough to want to keep working, you might be more willing to arrange the sale as a higher-risk/higher-potential-reward transaction. Your income is not jeopardized because you plan to continue working, and your higher-risk sale-transaction setup might just pay huge returns in a few years.

There is no "right" way to structure the deal. Knowing your bottom-line requirements helps you set a floor under which you are just not willing to go, unless your current company is in such bad shape that you just want to be out from under its weight.

LEAVING IT FOR YOUR HEIRS

If you are the owner of a closely held corporation, or sole proprietorship, and intend to leave it to your heirs, you should really talk with them about your plans. You just might find out that none of your heirs wants the company, and that they only want the proceeds that would come from its sale.

Should you pass away before the company is sold, its market value might be substantially reduced for any number of reasons:

- You will not be around to assist with the sale itself.
- You cannot be passed to the new owners as part of the transaction, making the overall transaction less valuable to the buyers.
- Nobody knows your business, or believes in your business, more than you do. That is worth something when selling.
- Any squabbling that might occur between heirs might force a quick sale as opposed to handling the sale in a solid, prepared manner as recommended in this book.
- Buyers look for good companies that are being sold as part of an estate resolution because this generally means highly motivated sellers and a lower price.
- If you died without having a will in place, your estate and business might be resolved in probate court, which most certainly is not what you want for your heirs.

For these reasons alone, you should take the time to plan the passage of your company to your heirs. It is difficult for an heir to deal with the loss of a loved one. It is even more difficult to see someone's wishes not fulfilled simply because he or she had not expressed them in writing or had not taken the time to plan appropriately while alive.

TIP

Your family members may not want to share in your dreams, and forcing your family into your vision will only cause personal hardship and will probably decrease the value of the business. An honest assessment might mean that you sell the company while you are still young enough to enjoy the sale proceeds. You can then have a good time while you are still healthy, leaving the balance to your spouse or children as part of your estate.

If you are holding on to the company so that it can be passed on to your family, do them a favor and talk honestly with them about their desires. You want what is best for them, and if what's best for them is not the company but its value in more liquid assets, plan accordingly. Nobody can handle that process more effectively than you can.

THE 30-SECOND RECAP

- Future stock value is riskier than current cash value.
- Set up either a succession plan or a sale plan to ensure that your heirs get the most from your estate.
- PE ratios should be considered when exchanging stock as part of the transaction.
- The right financial transaction structure will vary from one person to the next, so beware absolute "right" ways of doing things.
- Selling assets that you have held over 12 months allows personal capital gain tax benefits, which can reduce taxes by up to 50 percent.

Your Prospectus Looks Good

The sales prospectus, often called the marketing brochure or offering memorandum, outlines the important aspects of your company. It outlines them in such a way that the reader, and potential buyer, sees the company as a sound investment that is worth every penny of the asking price.

Taking the time to prepare a professional, accurate, and convincing prospectus is one of the most important things you will do when selling your company. Don't skimp here, because it will almost always cost you money in the end. This section will offer suggestions for building a strong sales prospectus.

THE COMPONENTS OF THE PROSPECTUS

The *prospectus* is a sales document. Period. The entire point is to move the buyer closer to accepting your asking price and to actually buying your company. You might not be there when the person reads the prospectus, meaning that it not only has to be accurate but also has to stand on its own merits. Think of it this way: When the reader, who is unfamiliar with your company, finishes reading the prospectus, will he or she feel motivated to buy your company? If so, you are on the right track. If not, the prospectus needs more work. It is just that simple.

PLAIN ENGLISH

A **prospectus** is a document that outlines the opportunity presented by a specific investment. Fundamentally, it is a sales document aimed at potential investors.

The more credible your prospectus, the better your company will appear, making your assertions more believable. A solidly built prospectus might very well reduce the buyer's due diligence requirements, decreasing the sale cycle, which more quickly sells your company.

Here are the common components of a prospectus. As always, don't feel constrained by this listing; just treat it as a starting point. Add any additional sections that are required to paint a complete, positive picture of your company to the reader.

Company Confidential Cover Sheet

1. Investment Summary
2. General Company Presentation
3. Overall Market Assessment
4. Sales and Marketing Overview
5. Special Assets, Processes, and Agreements
6. Key Management Personnel
7. Past Financial Performance
8. Projected Future Financial Performance
9. Ownership Structure
10. Asking Price and Financing
11. Conclusion

    Appendices (as needed)

INVESTMENT SUMMARY

Oddly enough, this section is usually written last. All of the information presented in the prospectus is designed to support this section. It is just what it sounds like—a summary of the investment opportunity outlined throughout the rest of the prospectus.

It should be no longer than two pages, with one page being the preferred length. Its job is to tease the reader into wanting to read the rest of the document. The details are in the various prospectus sections. The wrap-up is in the investment summary.

TIP

Keep the Investment Summary short and to the point. Spend a lot of time here making sure it delivers the message you intend: *Buy Me Now!*

The first paragraph will typically read something like this:

> ABC Company is a privately held corporation that manufactures specialty widgets. As the national widget market has decreased in overall sales dollars, ABC's sales have increased, allowing it to currently enjoy a 45 percent market share, up from 30 percent only three years ago.

The summary goes on to talk about the reason for selling, items that are for sale, time frame for the sale, and asking price, along with any specific financing requirements.

It should close with something like this:

> ABC is a well-run company with an excellent product mix and a dedicated professional staff and executive management team. An investment in ABC, as outlined in this prospectus, should provide an XX percent annual investment return, assuming no synergies exist with the purchasing company. Synergies should only enhance the return, making it even more attractive.

GENERAL COMPANY PRESENTATION

This is where you start your presentation about the company itself. Here are some basic points that must be contained in this section:

- How old is the company?
- How was it formed, by whom, and why has it been successful to date?
- The number of business locations, employees, and annual sales.
- What does the company sell and through what type of marketing channels? (Very general information only.)
- General information about proprietary technologies, intellectual property, processes, and any other unique attributes that make this company different.
- What its future looks like with respect to future marketing, product, service, or overall business plans (very general).
- Why the company is up for sale, presented in the most positive light possible.

This is simply an overview. The specific marketing, product, and financial sections will reveal the details.

OVERALL MARKET ASSESSMENT

This section covers the relationship between the company, the market in general, and its specific market in particular. Growth trends within the market, obtained by the company, or within the segment should all be presented over a three- to five-year historical perspective. Future market trends should also be included in this section.

SALES AND MARKETING OVERVIEW

The details of the company's products and/or services mix, marketing strategies, personnel, distribution channels, unique approaches, historical successes, and future goals should be presented in this area. It is also helpful to include competitive information so that industry comparisons can be drawn by the uninitiated reader. This is particularly helpful if you have been taking business away from your competition in recent years. Special customer arrangements/agreements should be included at this point. The general backgrounds of key marketing and sales personnel should be also included at this point.

A detailed analysis of customers, products, geographies, successes, and even struggles might be appropriate in this section. Every company has problems, and the buyer knows that, too. Revealing something significant yet not injurious might help to improve reception and credibility.

Finally, take a few moments to discuss the strategic focus of the company. Here might be a place to strut your stuff and to show them that you really know what you are talking about and that your success was not an accident.

SPECIAL ASSETS, PROCESSES, AND AGREEMENTS

This section contains information about any proprietary arrangements held by the company. These might include patents, trademarks, or copyrighted information. Special agreements with vendors, foreign countries, and key distributors should also be included here. Details regarding intellectual property, the scope of protection provided, length of protection, and other pertinent information should be included.

If special processes, which are personnel- or technique-dependent, are part of the company value mix, they should be presented here. After all, you want the information to convince the reader that you are offering a fair product for a fair price. If the processes or techniques are part of the value, it should be spelled out in such a way that the reader understands the value, as seen through your eyes.

TIP

Charts, graphs, tables, and pictures are great presentation tools. Get to know your computer graphics software packages if you don't know them already.

KEY MANAGEMENT PERSONNEL

The professional, educational, and pertinent personal background of key personnel should be presented in this section. The minimal people to include are the CEO, president, vice presidents, directors, key board members, key technology personnel, key operations personnel, influential staff consultants, investors, and other important personnel. Remember that you are often judged by the company you keep. By association, your company will be assessed by the people on its staff and board and by its investors.

Just because you are familiar with these people doesn't mean that their names have no clout in the industry. Make sure you start to look at these people, and yourself, as seen from an outsider's perspective. If someone has a patent, which might be old news to you, include it in his or her biography. This is interesting and impressive information to others. Make sure you don't reveal anything of a highly personal nature, but do include the information needed to convince the reader that these people are credible professionals, with excellent reputations, who have chosen to work here instead of elsewhere. That, in itself, says a lot about a company.

PAST FINANCIAL PERFORMANCE

This section adds financial meat to the skeleton presented in earlier sections. You have made claims about what made the company so great in the past, and this is where the numbers should confirm those assertions.

You should show financial statements for the last three to five years, with comparative financial statements provided for the last two years, including the current year to date.

Details about accounting procedures, such as cash or accrual accounting, should be revealed. If the company took special steps to orient the financial statements in one direction or another, that should also be stated. For example, a privately held company might perform its accounting functions so that income is minimized. This strategy would make the company's historical financial statements look poor to someone who manages to optimize income, which is typically done in a publicly held company. Explaining that this is part of the accounting strategy, instead of an accidental by-product, will improve the financial reception.

If there were special situations that caused radical drops or improvements in financial performance, also mention those at this point. Any credible financial person will find them anyway, so why not be up front about them, and show that you are not trying to hide something?

Projected Future Financial Performance

Predicting the future is always a tricky business. One entrepreneur described the forecasting process as "driving a car while looking in the rearview mirror." There is a lot of truth in this statement; you can really only look to past performance as a guide to the future, because the future is always changing.

Some legal people assert that future forecasts should not be included in any prospectus, because they might be construed as a commitment of future performance instead of a best guess. Checking with your legal counsel is always the right thing on a topic like this, and you should always make sure the reader knows that these are estimates, and not statements of fact. This seems obvious because you are talking about the future, but it is better to err on the safe side and include the disclaimers.

CAUTION

Check with your legal department before including future forecasts that might be construed as a commitment instead of a best-guesstimate.

By the way, it is certainly okay to correlate information from different sections. Suppose, for example, that the company currently has a 45 percent market share and that the market is growing at 10 percent per year. It is certainly reasonable to assert that company sales will grow by an estimated 4.5 percent (45 percent of 10 percent) over the next year, assuming that no market share was lost. These growth percentages can then be used to estimate future dollar-sales growth. The same might apply for manufacturing cost decreases that can be extrapolated into the future from the past along a specific volume curve. If sales increase, so does manufacturing volume; this should decrease production costs. All of these combined indicate increased sales and potentially increased gross margins as well.

Hopefully, you are getting the picture. This is a very important section of the prospectus. Some would contend, and with good justification, that it is the most important section. After all, the buyer is purchasing future performance projections, not past performance histories. Making the best possible financial case for the future is the best way to optimize your actual sale price.

Ownership Structure

This is usually a pretty dry section that presents who owns what, for how long, and in what percentages. Deadlines, covenants, and other financially related ownership issues are presented in this section. They are going to want to know who the partners are in a partnership, the shareholders are in a corporation, and any family members in a sole proprietorship.

Asking Price and Financing

Here is where you present your case for your asking price. You should have some justification for the asking price, whether you explicitly state it as part of this section or not. At least tell them the general procedure used to determine the price.

If special financing is being provided, or is required by the seller, spell it out in this section. For example, the sellers might be willing to offer a loan to the buyers. On the other hand, the board of directors might have determined that the company could only be merged, for tax reasons. Why waste time with a buyer who cannot, or will not, comply with your financial requirements?

TIP

You should already have financially qualified the buyer by this time. There is no reason to let the prospective buyer read the entire prospectus if he or she cannot comply with the basic financial arrangements. An unqualified buyer has "no need to know." Remember?

Finally, if you have already arranged financing for a solid buyer, also spell that out in this section. Anything that makes the workload lighter and makes you look more prepared is something that makes the purchase of your company more attractive.

Conclusion

This is the wrap-up section of the report. It often simply restates what was presented in the Investment Summary. It naturally should conclude that this is an excellent investment and that the buyer should move quickly to ensure that nobody else buys the company. This section is also written after all the other supporting sections are completed, although you really know what it will say before you start writing.

APPENDICES (AS NEEDED)

These sections might include product brochures, competitive information, Internet website information, samples, detailed biographies, and/or other pertinent information. Anything required to support the mid-report sections should be included in the appendices and referenced from the particular sections.

WHAT TO REVEAL?

There is still a natural inclination to keep information secret, even at this stage. It might be counterproductive at this point to keep information from a credible, qualified, and interested buyer.

After all, you should already have a nondisclosure agreement signed, should have met a few times talking about the various general details of your respective businesses, and should have generally given each other the *sniff test*. This is where you meet with each other and assess whether the other is a person with whom you want to, or are willing to, do business. Relationships that fail the sniff test often turn into untrusting, antagonistic relationships that become a resource, energy, and financial drain.

PLAIN ENGLISH

A **sniff test** is an unwritten, non-numeric, yet very real test that we all undergo and perform when negotiating something important. If the other person, or the situation, just doesn't "feel" right, it failed the test, which is never a good sign for future relations.

If you are sure that their interest is sincere, you really have to move forward by revealing this information. That is, unless you are lucky enough to have them simply offer you what you want based on your overall financial statements. This would be great news, but it doesn't happen very often. Don't plan on not having to reveal detailed information, and be happy if it is not a buyer requirement.

SELLING TO A COMPETITOR

You should be more on your guard if the buyer is a competitor rather than someone from another industry.

The "Specifically Vague" section is of paramount importance, and you will probably have this talent down to an art form by the time the competitive purchase is finalized. Always err on the side of caution when dealing with a competitor, but also know that your competition might also turn out to be your best buyer. After all, who would better appreciate your business and its industry-specific structure than a respected, and hopefully respectful, competitor? Just like a fine-art collector will pay premium prices for the right artwork, which he or she alone might recognize, a competitor might recognize things in your organization that others might miss or ignore. By the way, this can work either for you or against you.

Watch the Money, Not Your Ego

It is tempting to try to get as much as possible from the sale of your company. After all, this is your baby. This is particularly true for you entrepreneurs who conceived, started, financed, sweated, and dreamed your idea into the reality that you are now selling.

Others won't have your emotional attachment to the business. To them it is a business deal that either makes sense or doesn't. This is not to say that your passion for the business is without value. Just the opposite. Nobody can sell your business better than you can. You just want to be sure that you don't let your emotions get in the way of the business transactions.

People will find flaws with the business. That is a given. Nothing, no one, and no business is perfect. The buyer is there to get the most possible for the least money. The seller is there to get the most possible money for the sale. What you see as a benefit, the buyer might see as a detriment. So what? After the sale, the company won't be yours anyway. Letting go before the sale process begins is the best way to make sure that you transact the best financial deal for your company, which is not necessarily the best one for your ego.

CAUTION

An ego-inflated company valuation rarely turns into a dollar-inflated purchase price. Leave your ego at the door and sell the company for the maximum shareholder value.

Protecting Shareholder Interests

When all is said and done, the sale will be evaluated by your company shareholders and board of directors, based on whether it increases shareholder wealth. As the owner, you have a duty to maximize the investment return experienced by shareholders. As an owner who just sold his or her company, you want to get as much as you can for the sale, because it might be your retirement, play money, or funding for your next company.

At any rate, you really are best served when you serve the interests of your other owners and/or shareholders. Keep them in mind, and you will probably find yourself speaking not just on your own behalf, but on behalf of the others as well.

THE 30-SECOND RECAP

- The prospectus must be able to stand on its own.
- Show the prospectus only to sincere qualified, nondisclosure-covered buyers.
- Make sure that the prospectus presents a total, rational case that justifies your purchase price.
- Talk to legal counsel about revealing future projections.
- Sell the company, not your ego, and you will get a better return on your investment.

When It Is Better Not to Sell

This is every seller's worst nightmare: You do the preparation work. You prepare your finances. You work with several prospective buyers, and nobody makes you an offer. Or, even worse, the only offer you get is one that is so low you cannot justify selling. Now what do you do?

That is the focus of this section. This is a difficult topic because it really depends on the specifics of the situation and the emotional makeup of the people involved. However, there are options, and there is likely to be fallout resulting from the business not selling.

WHAT IF THEY OFFER TOO LITTLE?

It is sobering to have people tell you that your business is simply not worth what you think it's worth. An item is worth only what a buyer is willing to pay for it. Right? What do you do when the only offers you get are lower than you are willing to accept?

An obvious first answer is to drop the price. This is a particularly viable option if you have been told by the buyers that they would not make an offer because there was such a wide gap that any reasonable offer seemed ridiculous. Contrary to how mergers and acquisitions are portrayed on television, not everyone is a cutthroat waiting to gouge you. Some people may not make an offer, thinking that a substantially lower offer would simply be insulting.

- Is the price too high?
- What did your internal analysis tell you?
- Is it possible that the assumptions used on your present value analysis or in your future sales projections were so "rosy" that they bordered on unrealistic?
- Have the buyers moved on to other acquisitions, or do you think that they might still be interested?
- Would it cost you more than you are willing to give up to finally close the deal?

Whatever the reasons, they didn't buy. You may want to consider taking one or two of these prospective buyers to a very *private* lunch and have a long, detailed discussion about why they did not buy. Especially if one or two of them, in your opinion, should have bought not only for financial reasons but for strategic ones as well. Something in your assumptions was clearly inaccurate, and only feedback from buyers will help you pinpoint the problem.

Is it possible that you are not ready to sell? Perhaps you think that you are ready, but to the eyes of an objective observer, you might still be too possessive, causing them to think that the post-purchase period might be fraught with emotional baggage that is just not worth dealing with, from their perspective.

Although you always want to stress and sell the quality of your company and its various assets, you also have to offer them for a reasonable price.

THE LIABILITIES OF NOT SELLING

Assume for a moment that you take the company off the market. Now what? What kind of fallout should you expect? You can do this without major damage, but only by performing some kind of damage control with your employees, customers, and other owners.

All those who knew about the possibility of sale suffered some type of emotional fallout from the experience. They might have spent weeks obsessing about who their next boss would be, whether they would have a job after the sale, whether the division they work in will be closed down, or any number of other areas of potential concern.

At a minimum, you need to talk with the following:

- Major customers

- Major vendors
- Key employees
- Other investors

In short, you now have to evaluate your motivations and talk to the key people in your business life. They need to understand that you still care about the business and want it to remain successful. Any doubt about your motivations will turn into hesitancy on their part, which inevitably turns into less-favorable financial relationships for you. Risk and reward. Remember?

WHAT ABOUT YOUR CUSTOMERS?

Hopefully, most of your customers were not aware of your intention to sell. This would be good news and would minimize the fallout if the company does not sell. However, any prospective buyer of your business who was serious about the purchase probably talked with some of your key customers.

Customers may now start to wonder about your commitment to the business if it doesn't sell. After all, you had tried to sell and didn't. You gave them some reasons for wanting to sell, back in the early stages of putting the company on the market. Now what are your plans?

TIP

Most businesspeople will understand your wanting to sell, and that it didn't work out, as long as you are comfortable with the outcome and can present it in a credible way. Just as you would rehearse a speech or formal presentation, rehearse your failed-sale presentation to major vendors and customers. It might be the most important presentation you give in the precarious time just after taking the company off of the market. You don't have to reveal everything, but it needs to make business sense.

Expect some reticence on the part of your customers. You might even lose some of them. When you decide to take the company off of the market, you must go overboard in the service areas to make sure your customers accept that you are in business to stay and that your relationship with them will remain as positive as always. They will be looking for signs of negative change on your part, and you should work overtime to ensure them that their fears are unfounded—even if you are depressed or disappointed that the sale did not go through.

And don't use your customers as your therapist. Simply say something like,

"We just didn't find the right buyer, and I took it off the market so that we could get back to running our business." And leave it at that. Customers really don't need to know more than the basics. Besides, your actions will speak much louder than anything you can say at this point.

WHAT ABOUT VENDORS?

Vendors may change their credit relationship with you if they start to think that you are now in business for the short term instead of the long term, as they probably thought you were before you put the company up for sale.

You should expect some fallout if you tried to sell a smaller, privately owned business.

WHAT ABOUT YOUR EMPLOYEES?

Expect that you will have to do some damage control with your employees as well. They are probably relieved that the company didn't sell, but they will have the same concerns as your customers and vendors will. They might think that your loyalty to them has been placed in jeopardy, causing them to be less "company" oriented and more oriented toward protecting themselves.

If reorganization plans were floated as part of the sale process and your employees found out about it, you definitely will have to do damage control. These people are probably already looking for other jobs if they did not like the plan. Acting promptly and sincerely might keep some of the better ones around. However, if they feel that the trust between the company and themselves has been violated, you might have permanently disgruntled employees. If they are not as happy, but still able to perform their jobs in professional and c   nt ways, do the best you can to keep things upbeat and positive.

TIP

Just as the presentation to vendors and customers needs rehearsal, so does the presentation to your employees. If they don't believe you, you might lose them along with the prospects for selling the company.

Getting things back to normal and even throwing a company party to celebrate staying autonomous might not be a bad idea. You somehow need to convince them that the company and you are still in business and that their jobs are not in jeopardy. Otherwise, not selling may end up costing you more than the drop in price you would have needed to sell to a viable buyer would have. Now that would really hurt.

SELLING TO YOUR EMPLOYEES

Perhaps your best buyers already work for the company: your employees. You might find that the employees would be willing to purchase the company by any number of ways, including the following:

- Leveraged buyout (LBO)
- Management buyout (MBO)
- Employee stock option plan (ESOP)

These three plans really mean the same thing to you as the seller. The employees arrange to purchase your ownership shares in the company using the equity in the company as collateral for a loan or through shared contributions. The approach is still very valid, and you might be inclined to offer your employees a better price than you would a stranger. Especially because you now know that the strangers did not want to purchase the company for the price you wanted anyhow.

Notice that these options help to minimize the negative impact of the nonsale on the employees. Instead of the nonsale looking like bad news, it can now spell opportunity for them. You may want to approach this topic carefully. If you start down this road and it does not work out, you will definitely have bad feelings within the company.

There is one huge reason why you might consider selling to your employees, in the form of an ESOP, and offering them a discounted price at the same time. You don't pay federal taxes on money received as part of the ESOP purchase as long as your situation meets a few criteria:

- Your company cannot be publicly traded.
- You have held the stock for three years or more.
- You used the ESOP sale proceeds to buy securities in U.S. corporations.
- The corporations in which you purchase securities must use more than 50 percent of their assets in the active conduct of a trade or business, and a maximum of 25 percent of the company's gross income can come from passive investment income.
- You sold between 30 percent and 100 percent of outstanding shares

to the ESOP.

A few other comparatively rare criteria aren't listed here.

CAUTION

As the seller to an ESOP who then purchases other U.S. securities, you should be aware that the newly purchased U.S. securities will be subject to capital gain taxes when sold—the basis being the value of the shares at the time they were purchased.

If you think about this option, there are some very real incentives for you to work with your employees to make this happen. It not only benefits your employees, it also saves you tax money in the process. In fact, if you take a buyout from a third party instead of the ESOP, you will have to pay capital gain taxes on the money received, which will most likely be 20 percent. Dropping your price 10 percent and selling your shares to an ESOP allows your employees to purchase the company at a 10 percent discount and allows you to save 10 percent in taxes, and all is well.

There are other benefits associated with an ESOP purchase that improve ESOP dealings with banks that can offer ESOPs more attractive financing due to tax advantages that are passed on to the bank.

Maintaining an ESOP fund has administrative costs and hassles associated with it, but it might be worth it for both you and the employees.

Remember, too, that you can sell as little as 30 percent of your stock to an ESOP. This might make it attractive for you to sell 70 percent of your shares to an outside investor and the other 30 percent to the ESOP; that portion would, if reinvested as outlined earlier, be tax-free. In this way, you get the majority of your money up front while still providing the employees with an investment opportunity of their own.

You might find that selling to an ESOP is something to be pursued before selling to a separate company. Should your initial foray into selling the company not work out, don't forget about the ESOP and other employee purchase options.

DOING DAMAGE CONTROL ON WHAT WAS REVEALED

After you take the company off the market and get back to business as usual, you might start to regret the amount of information you revealed during the sale process. After all, if you talked with a competitor, you probably revealed processes and other information that they would not have otherwise known. You are now back competing with them, knowing that they know more about your operation than you know about theirs.

Forget it. You cannot undo what was done in the past, and it is easy to get caught up in trying to recapture something instead of simply moving on.

This doesn't mean that you shouldn't make appropriate adjustments to your operation based on this added level of exposure. You should be focusing on what you do, and doing it well. That is the best competitive weapon in your arsenal.

Don't forget that you also learned some things about them as part of the process. Perhaps you can use that information to your advantage. For example, you might know more about their financial operating models, which might help you when bidding competitively.

My point is this: Get back to business and forgive yourself for anything you might have done during the attempted sale process. It can't be undone, and carrying it with you into the future might be your undoing.

THE 30-SECOND RECAP

- When you're not selling, get feedback from your buyers as to why.
- Your larger customers will probably know about your intent to sell your business. If you do not sell your business, expect some reticence.
- Vendors may change their credit relationship with you if they start to think that you are now in business for the short term instead of the long term.
- There are many good reasons for selling to your employees.

Glossary

active listening A technique with origins in the field of psychotherapy that helps assure customers you're listening to them intently. Active listening means encouraging customers to talk freely by reflecting back to them the meaning of their communication, both verbal and nonverbal, in ways that promote further exploration and awareness. For example, "You're upset because our product doesn't seem to work properly when installed with your system."

agent An agent acts on behalf of his or her principal, and the principal is liable for his or her acts. A partner acts as an agent for the partnership when purchasing for the partnership.

angels Angels are independently wealthy businesspeople who are willing to invest in private companies for a piece of the action. Heaven-sent? Well, it depends on the terms they're offering in exchange for the money.

arm's-length government An arm's-length government organization is one that is primarily or partly funded by tax dollars but is outside the government system. Arm's-length organizations often have a board of directors and their own management structure.

basis of property Basis of property is usually the acquisition cost; for depreciable assets, such as equipment, the basis is reduced by depreciation. Basis is used to determine gain or loss on the sale of property by subtracting the basis from the sale price.

benchmark An operating measurement that defines the level of performance of any given practice or system. Benchmarks can help identify hidden opportunities to innovate and improve performance.

benchmarking An ongoing process of investigating and studying practices that produce exceptional results. Often the task of benchmarking involves the careful examination of the competitors' practices.

billable time Billable time refers to the time for which you will be directly compensated and is the financial bedrock of your practice.

brand equity The asset value associated with a particular trademarked name, such as Ford, Coca-Cola, Yahoo!, or Kleenex. Increasing the perceived market value of products bearing the brand name increases its brand equity.

bundle of rights   Picture the bundle of rights as a bundle of sticks with each stick representing a specific right you have in the property. If you sell a stick, the bundle gets smaller and you lose a right. Zoning laws and market conditions in an area will determine how big that bundle can be.

bylaws   Bylaws contain all provisions for managing the business and regulating the affairs of the corporation.

c-corporation   A corporation that is a completely separate entity from its owners and is taxed at the corporate level rather than the shareholder level.

cash surrender value   Cash surrender value is the amount of money you'd receive if you turned in your policy to the insurance company for cancellation.

closed-ended questions   With closed-ended questions, respondents choose from possible answers included on the questionnaire. Respondents answer open-ended questions in their own words.

common law   Common law is judge-made law, as contrasted with the contract law consisting of federal and state constitutions, statutes, and administrative agency regulations. Common law in your state may have developed over decades and is governed by the principle of precedent, or what courts have previously ruled on a legal question.

communication   From the Latin root *commune,* which means "something held in common." In the context of customer service, communication

is a process of sharing information with a customer in such a way that you understand what the customer is saying, and the customer understands you.

consensus   After deliberating on every viable alternative, all team members agree on a specific course of action. Although each member may not prefer the course of action, each supports it

consulting   Consulting is a process undertaken by a disinterested party with significant expertise and experience, and involves offering advice and problem solving to the client or customer using a well-defined consulting process.

contract assignment   Contract assignment means transferring a contract to a third party (assignee); for example, transferring your right to receive goods to another company.

contract manufacturer   A contract manufacturer produces products to the specifications of another company, which has designed the product and handles the marketing, sales, and distribution. This allows the entrepreneur to minimize his investment in productive plant and equipment.

contracts   When you are starting your business, consider contracts (large business and government) that are smaller in monetary value. The larger contracts are difficult to get until you have an established track record. Don't be afraid to start small.

corporation   A corporation is an artificial "person" (in the form of a business) that is chartered by the state to conduct business. The state also charters not-for-profit, or charitable, corporations.

customer   Any person or group who receives the work output (product or service) of another.

customer satisfaction   A survey construct that compares what actually takes place in a given situation with what a customer thought would happen. Typical customer responses include comments like, "What I received was not what I expected to receive"; "I can always count on your company to do what's right"; "Your product didn't do for me what your advertisements said it would." The purpose is to determine whether your product or service met your customer's expectations.

customer service   Meeting the needs and expectations of the customer as defined by the customer. A way of life that involves putting the customer first in every aspect of the business. It is characterized by an obsession to achieve complete customer satisfaction in each and every encounter. It is an obsession that is shared by everyone in the company from the chairman of the board on down.

customer-centered vision   A clear picture of how your business will serve the needs of customers in the future. According to Richard Whiteley of the Forum Corporation, such a vision is an ambitious, desirable future state that is connected to the customer and is better in some important way than the current state.

customer-centric   Anything that is centered entirely on the customer. The more "customer-centric" an organization becomes, the more it is aligned with the needs, wants, and desires of the customer.

customer-focused measurement
The comparison of customer expectations with actual company performance. For example, if customers expect deliveries within 24 hours of purchase, that number is compared with the actual delivery time and a determination is made of the number of times that the 24-hour expectation was actually met.

customer-focused standards   The internal regulations that govern how a job is done. Transactional standards deal with customer interaction and are often expressed in such guidelines as "Reassure the customer that the problem will be resolved" or "Be friendly and courteous." Outcome standards focus on outcomes: "The customer complaint can be considered resolved only when …"; "Twenty-four-hour delivery means that our product is actually in the hands of the customer within 24 hours."

due diligence   Due diligence refers to the process of discovering and understanding all aspects of the business and all the factors that could affect the prospects of the business. Due diligence must be undertaken by brokers representing securities for sale, managers, and investment bankers involved in a merger or acquisition, and anyone buying a business.

empathy   The ability to walk around in the shoes of a customer to know how he or she feels in them; it's the process of attempting to understand, from the customer's point of view, the thoughts and feelings he or she has about something of personal importance.

employee retention   An integrated process, not a series of isolated events or programs. The process of retention (keeping top-notch employees from going elsewhere) begins at the time of recruitment and is embedded in employment policies and practices that affect the employee throughout his or her career.

entrepreneur   An entrepreneur is a person who starts his or her own business. Being entrepreneurial is having the desire and ability to take risks, envision the future, and develop new business concepts and ideas or improve upon the business concepts of others.

equity   Equity in your home is the amount you'd be able to put in your pocket if you were to sell your house today after paying off any mortgages you already have on your home.

excellence in customer service   A way of doing business that involves going beyond the call of duty, stretching perceived limits, and empowering everyone in the organization to maintain the highest standards, pay attention to details, and go the extra mile. Take a lesson from Mother Goose: "Good, better, best; never rest till 'good' is 'better' and 'better' is 'best.'"

feasibility study   A feasibility study tests the many components of your business concept to see if it will work. There are plenty of great ideas out there, but getting them to actually work can be a different story. A feasibility study is something that you hire outside help to conduct. It can run you a few to many thousands of dollars, but is worth it if you aren't sure your concept will be a go for the consumer.

fiduciary   A fiduciary is a person who is bound to act with the utmost good faith in the management of property or affairs for the benefit of another. A partner is a fiduciary to the partnership.

flip   A flip is a real estate term for fixer-upper properties bought with the intention of renovating and then selling them to make a profit. A flip is a good way to start out in the B&B business, especially if you haven't found your dream B&B yet, or your resources are limited.

food cost   Food cost is one of the more important expenses to control if you are in the restaurant business. It is the cost of the ingredients that the restaurant pays. If you pay $1.25 for the ingredients that go into your chicken noodle casserole and you sell it for $3.99, your food cost is $1.25, or 31.3 percent.

frontline employees   Those who deal directly with the customer—the purchaser of the product or service.

functional skills   Skills that help people function effectively on the job. They include the ability to communicate, to listen, to lead, and to be flexible.

goal   A goal is an end that one strives to attain. Goals can help you achieve those small but important victories. Your goals should be realistic and quickly achievable.

goodwill   Goodwill is an intangible business asset that relates to the company's ability to generate income in excess of the normal rate of return for its physical assets due to superior management, marketing skill, and products.

historical society   A historical society is a committee of individuals who are concerned with preserving the historical integrity of a specific area. Since the 1960s, organizations concerned with historic preservation have tried to rehabilitate and revitalize urban neighborhoods and business districts, with much success. There are national and state historical registers of property all over the United States. Contact the local town hall for more information regarding historical districts and local societies.

holding company   A company that owns enough shares of stock in a particular company to have effective control over their disposition. A firm can be a holding company for several companies at once.

hot buttons   Those words, attitudes, phrases, or comments that cause us to react in an unhealthy and non-productive manner, usually with anger.

impossibility   The doctrine of impossibility, particularly regarding forces of nature, is often referred to as "acts of God."

insurance   Coverage by a contract binding a party to indemnify another against specified loss in return for premiums paid. Small business owners must be aware of a couple different types of insurance. Fire insurance is a must for any owner of property. Fire insurance protects the owner against the loss of the value of the investment up to the insured. Liability insurance is similar to fire insurance except it protects the owner against any claims of liability that may result at the property.

intellectual property   Capital assets owned by a company that are not tangible in nature, like equipment, but still have commercial value. Typically these properties involve legal protections, such as seen with patents, trademarks, and copyrights.

interpersonal skills   "People skills." Such skills are particularly important to consider when interviewing for frontline positions. Good interpersonal skills include the ability to respect others, to be empathetic and caring, to listen attentively and respond accordingly, and to maintain objectivity and refrain from emotionalism.

just cause   Just cause means good cause. The franchisor would be required to prove that the termination of the agreement was reasonable (based on just cause) due to franchisee misconduct, for instance.

letter of credit   A letter of credit is usually issued by a bank, agreeing to honor a draft and check of its customer.

limited partnership   A limited partnership is a partnership formed with two or more persons as co-owners, which means that it has one or more general partners and one or more limited partners.

mandatory success factors   The specific competencies and skills that are absolutely essential to successful job performance. They are determined by thoroughly analyzing the job and by providing profiles of the job and the ideal candidate.

market research   Market research is a systematic, objective collection and analysis of data about your target market, competition, and/or environment with the goal being increased understanding of them. Two types of market research are primary research, or original information gathered for a specific purpose; and secondary research, or information that already exists somewhere else.

moment of truth   A customer service term created by Jan Carlzon of Scandinavian Airlines. Carlzon defined a moment of truth as "an episode in which a customer comes in contact with any aspect of the company, however remote, and thereby has an opportunity to form an impression."

mortgage   A mortgage is placed on real estate for the property to serve as security for the payment of a debt. A financing statement records a debt against the personal property (collateral for a loan).

neighborhood revitalization zone   Many areas have implemented what is known as a neighborhood revitalization zone (NRZ). These zones comprise the people who live or own businesses in the area and enable them to make decisions that will determine the future of the neighborhood regarding its plan of development.

open-ended questions   Questions that can't be answered with a simple "yes" or "no." They often begin with phrases such as "Tell me about…" or "Describe what happened when …." The purpose of open questions is to obtain the information necessary to solve a customer problem by encouraging the customer to talk freely.

overhead time   Overhead time refers to the time you spend that is not directly compensated for by the client. It includes marketing, client meetings, and paperwork (like making sure your taxes are in order).

parent company   A company that owns the majority, or all, of the stock in another company. For example, a company that purchases all the stock in another company would be the purchased company's parent company.

participative management   A process in which managers and employees work together as peers to produce exceptional products and services that exceed customer expectations.

partnering   To partner with a customer means becoming so involved in the customer's business that you make your customer's success a matter of personal concern. Boeing, for example, not only works very closely with customers worldwide to design airplanes that accommodate their needs, it often goes the extra mile to help its customers run more efficient and productive airlines. Boeing will often lend its management expertise to customers who are experiencing growing pains. The result: Customers succeed and, as a result of their success, they buy more airplanes from Boeing.

partnership   A partnership is an association of two or more persons who will act as co-owners of a business for profit. Individuals or business entities may form partnerships.

perceived quality   A survey construct that attempts to compare the customer's perception of what happened with what the customer feels should have happened ideally. Customers express perceived quality with statements like, "Ideally, you should have …"; "When I booked my meeting at your five-star hotel, I expected …"; "I expected more from a company considered the best in the business." The purpose of the construct is to determine whether your product or service meets your customer's ideal expectations.

preferred stock   Preferred stock is stock that gives holders priority over the common shareholders in corporate dividends and liquidation. The corporation's articles of incorporation details all of the preferred shareholders' rights.

prevention-based management The supervision and control of those systems and processes designed to prevent customer dissatisfaction. It also concerns itself with the need for service recovery, which is the organization's attempt to make things right. Prevention-based management is proactive and attempts to identify problems before they affect customer perception.

proactive problem solving   Anticipating problems and obstacles associated with a particular task and solving them before they're actually encountered.

process owners   Employees, or groups of employees, who are responsible for a specific aspect of the finished product or service of an organization.

process skills   Process skills refer to the tools all consultants need and use to ensure that their advice and recommendations are as informed as possible. These tools include interpersonal communication, group facilitation, data gathering, and diagnostic skills.

pro forma   Pro forma financial statements project the values for the various accounts on the balance sheet, income statement, and cash-flow statement. Underlying pro forma statements are assumptions about future sales growth, financial requirements, and other factors. Therefore, the believability of the pro forma statements depends on the believability of the assumptions, which should be included as footnotes to the statements.

proxy   Proxy is the authority given by one person (for example, an LLC member) to another to serve as a substitute for a specified purpose, particularly voting.

qualitative research   Qualitative research relates the opinions and behaviors of the subjects in a market research study to the likelihood that specific products or services can be marketed to them. Quantitative research creates statistically valid market information that can be used in any number of ways.

quality of service   The customer's perception of the service that an organization provides. It is a perception that is reevaluated by the customer with each succeeding contact, wherever in the organization those contacts occur, from the executive level to the loading dock.

recovery   The process used by a company with its customer to rectify a mistake or solve a problem caused by the company. The goal of recovery is complete customer satisfaction.

S corporation   An S corporation or C corporation is a tax designation only. In an S corporation, the shareholders are taxed on the business income, whereas in a C corporation, the corporation itself is taxed.

saturation   Saturation is having more businesses in a particular locale than the available customer base can support.

segment   Segment means the "style" of a restaurant based on its prices, service, presentation, and atmosphere. Restaurant segments include casual dining, fast food, fine dining, concept dining, and many others. Each of these is considered its own segment in the restaurant industry.

self-management skills   Personal characteristics that help people do the job successfully. Included are such skills as creativity, honesty, competence, appearance, and helpfulness.

service   Any product-based interaction between a customer and a company. Service requires genuine concern for the customer by a representative of the organization who is technically capable of offering assistance. Service requires that the company representative possess both the desire and the ability to treat each individual's problem as unique, even though the representative may have dealt with the same problem on countless other occasions.

service delivery systems   The means, methods, and procedures used to provide a product or service to the public and to provide other customer assistance as deemed necessary by the customer.

service mark   This is similar to a trademark except related to a service procedure instead of a particular product. This term is commonly used by service organizations, such as consulting, accounting, and training companies.

shareholder wealth   The underlying value of a share of stock as determined by its assessed market value. Actions that increase market value increase shareholder wealth.

SIC code   The SIC code stands for Standard Industrial Classification. This is a standard system of coding businesses by numerical category, set up by the Small Business Administration (SBA).

slumlords   Whether you like it or not, most angry tenants, neighbors, and public officials have referred to landlords as slumlords. Don't be offended; to be a slumlord, you need a slum tenant. The truth is that responsible landlords well outnumber the irresponsible ones. A true slumlord is a person who buys a property, drains it of all potential rent, and then abandons it intentionally. This person is almost nonexistent.

start-up   A start-up is a new business created to bring a product or service to market. Most start-ups begin with one product or service, or an idea for one.

superintendent   Superintendent does not mean property manager. A superintendent is someone you hire to work for you, either as an employee or as an independent contractor, to do minor repair in and around the property. A superintendent does not need to be licensed as long as he or she stays within the scope of minor repair. A superintendent should not be handling any money, renting apartments, or signing leases associated with your property.

surety   A surety or guarantor is a person who agrees to be responsible for the debt of another.

sympathy   This occurs when one becomes so associated with another individual that he or she reacts or responds to a situation in much the same manner. Sympathy usually results from becoming so enmeshed with another person that objectivity and reason no longer play a functional role in problem solving.

synergy   The powerful force that occurs when two or more entities work together jointly. The total effect is greater than the sum of their individual effects when acting independently.

tender process   Large government contracts are awarded through the tender process. This involves submitting information (as requested by the client), such as price and basic project details.

trademark   A trademark is a word, name, or symbol used in commerce to identify a product. Pepsi and McDonald's are trademarked and cannot be used without the owner's permission. The franchisor's trademark is licensed to the franchisee for use during the period of the franchise agreement.

training An ongoing experience that has three primary objectives: to give employees a basic understanding of their job and a vision of the mission of the company, to provide the skills and tools necessary to perform the tasks of the job correctly and efficiently, and to keep people functioning at high levels throughout their careers.

triangular merger A merger involving the target company and a subsidiary corporation of the buyer's corporation.

unsecured loan An unsecured loan is one in which you don't have to put up your car or other property as collateral (security for the loan) that the lender can keep if you don't keep your promise to repay the loan on time.

vision statements Statements that briefly describe a company's commitment to customer service. They communicate, in a few well-chosen words, important company philosophy that undergirds practice.

voidable Voidable means a contract exists until the person disaffirms, whereas void means the contract cannot be enforced. A contract with a minor or mentally incapacitated person is voidable, unless that person has a guardian, in which case the contract is void.

Special Considerations for Different Types of Businesses

Depending on the type of business you decide to operate, there will be unique aspects you'll want to consider. Although many of the basic concepts for running a small business are the same, any restaurant owner or innkeeper will tell you there are issues that are only specific to their type of business. This appendix will discuss those distinct aspects you'll need to know to operate these and other kinds of small businesses including property management, bed and breakfasts, independent consulting, and retail stores.

Starting and Running a Restaurant Business

If you're reading this, then you have entertained thoughts of opening a restaurant with visions of raking in piles of cash and entertaining friends and neighbors, all while getting compliments for your delicious food and fabulous service. It's perhaps the most popular entrepreneurial dream of all—to own a restaurant. After all, restaurants are in nearly every village, town, and city in the world. Everyone eats. And besides, doesn't it look fun and easy? This section attempts to answer that question while giving you a realistic picture of starting and running a restaurant.

TABLE FOR ONE: IS THIS FOR ME?

Restaurant owners have owned sports teams, appeared on cooking shows on television, and led the local chamber of commerce. Restaurant success is relative, but in any town or city there are examples of those who have built thriving restaurants and wonderful lives. You've been in a restaurant. You know you can do it. Right?

Yes, you can.

But it may not be as easy as you think. Okay, the truth is that it won't be easy at all. You will certainly have to roll up your sleeves, and maybe the most important investment you'll make will be in a comfortable pair of shoes. But if you're in the restaurant business for the right reasons, all the hard work you're in for can be incredibly rewarding. Just remember, this is a different kind of life.

The best piece of advice is to examine your passions. If you're running from something (a bad job, a bad boss, etc.) rather than running to the restaurant business, then you need to reconsider. Restaurant ownership is not for the timid. The rewards certainly can be great, but the path is arduous.

This section is about risks and rewards and deciding whether the restaurant business is for you. There will be a gut check of pitfalls (for example, the dishwasher skipped a shift and you're elbow deep in pans after a 14-hour day) and rewards (Ray Kroc, who eventually owned the San Diego Padres baseball team, started McDonald's on less than $1,000).

CAUTION

Being a good cook, a great social host, or even a solid manager in a corporate environment does not guarantee your restaurant's success. Being able to point out the problems at the local restaurant is no guarantee of success either. A restaurant is your own show. Restaurants can have powerful profit-making potential if they're run extremely well, but they can also be a severe cash drain if they're run poorly.

WHY A RESTAURANT?

Something must have attracted you to the restaurant business. Was it the money, the lifestyle, the desire to serve others? All three are certainly draws, although the first two are a bit of a stretch as attractions—at least in the beginning. The truth is there probably won't be a lot of money at first, and as for lifestyle—well, let's clear up some tee time and regular dinner date issues. If you start a restaurant, you need to reconsider your social life. Sorry, but that is a fact. You'll hardly have any leisure time at all.

First, the money issues: If you are good at what you do, the restaurant business is a great place to make a healthy and substantial living, but huge profits don't often come quickly. As with any form of entrepreneurship, a long period of time, often many years and even decades, passes before a person hits it big. Many entrepreneurs never do. There are no guarantees. Thus, you'll need lots of patience.

Still, don't stop yourself from dreaming big and don't allow anyone else to stop you either. But understand that you have to do an awful lot of work before wonderful things can happen for you. Sometimes a new owner acts like he has reached the pinnacle of success by just opening a restaurant. He forgets that opening a restaurant isn't the objective; building a profitable restaurant is.

TIP

The 90/10 rule is a variation of the 80/20 rule, which states: Spend 80 percent of your time on the 20 percent most important things. The 90/10 rule is to spend 90 percent of your time on the 10 percent most important things. Starting a restaurant takes supreme effort and focus. To do it successfully, you must clear as much of your schedule as possible and stay focused on the task at hand.

CAUTION

As a restaurant owner, count on being "hands on." There are things you will be unable to avoid—washing dishes, mopping floors, unclogging toilets. And, oh, by the way, someone spilled a soda at table 27. Can you grab that?

As for lifestyle, owning a restaurant is more than a full-time job. When you start a restaurant, your free time becomes limited like never before. There is always more to do: organizing, ordering, cooking, cleaning, and on and on. And just because you have employees doesn't mean you'll be able to delegate everything. People can be unreliable. You will at times do every job in your restaurant, and often the times you have to do these jobs will be just when you want to leave for the day.

To be successful in the restaurant business, you have to enjoy serving people. Serving people is what a restaurant does, after all. People come to your place for food, but they won't come back if the service is bad. If serving others is something that is in your blood, you will be passionate about the restaurant business. And your customers will notice.

THERE ARE NO "TYPICAL" DAYS

Running a restaurant involves many twists and turns: staff turnover, broken equipment, slow moments, and mad rushes. The restaurant business is full of rapid change, and the restaurant owner must be able to perform many different tasks requiring a multitude of skills. A start-up operation requires that you do tasks such as check the previous day's receipts, prepare bank deposits, order products, do inventory, conduct operational checks, prepare food, build work schedules, greet customers, repair broken pieces of equipment, and more.

Very few fields require such a wide variety of skills and abilities as the restaurant business does. And the required skills change by the day, the hour, and even the minute. There is no schedule except for this: You're always on the go in the restaurant business.

You can count on a few things, though. Long hours, sore feet, and intense rushes seem to go hand in hand with a booming restaurant business. The alternative of short days, sitting around, and no rushes could spell disaster. Depending on your hours of operation and restaurant concept, you could be in for your fair share of late nights, early mornings, long weekends, and missed family gatherings.

So what is "typical" in the restaurant business? There is no typical.

WANTED: MANAGEMENT SKILLS

Somebody has to run this restaurant. Somebody has to manage these people. Somebody has to make all the decisions. Guess who that somebody is? After you've made the decision to become a restaurant owner, you need to be prepared to manage three core things: yourself, your people, and your business.

TIP

To learn about how a restaurant works and whether the lifestyle appeals to you, get a job on someone else's payroll. Although working for someone else is not the same as running your own place, the experience can be a great education.

YOURSELF

People who are great at leading themselves are usually great decision makers. Confidence garnered from knowledge makes it much easier to make smart decisions. Lack of data and information can cause you to make an uninformed, and therefore bad, decision. So use your head. Collect practical information and ask questions. Use your heart as well: See how you feel about your conclusions. Use the clock, too: After you have the required data, don't be afraid to take a 24-hour cooling-off period to make a quality decision. If you're still torn about your decision, don't ignore your feelings. They're telling you to go back and do more research.

Another part of managing yourself is being able to assess your talents and personality honestly. Do you like risk? That's a major test of this dream of yours, because your life becomes a risk when you take an entrepreneurial leap. An entrepreneur is able to endure and even enjoy risk as associated with a working business. Risk is part of the game. Winning strategies reduce risk.

YOUR PEOPLE

The restaurant business is a people business. The number of people it takes to create one positive dining experience can be mind-boggling.

The core of building any team or relationship begins and ends with trust. The word *trust* itself is also a helpful acronym for the elements necessary to build a successful team:

- **Truth.** Be truthful to yourself, your people, and your vision. If you always tell the truth, even when it would be easier to go another route, you will never have to remember what story to tell.

- **Respect.** To be successful in any business you must respect the people who work for you, the people who work with you, and the customer who pays you.

- **Understanding wants and needs.** Understanding the perspectives of others will help you. If you know the goals, wants, and needs of others, it will help you build a more substantial and long-term business relationship.

- **Solidifying team goals.** Goals are wonderful—team goals are powerful. If the team gets the opportunity to set their own goals and build action plans to achieve them together, you will see more team spirit and significantly better performance.

- **Touching hearts.** Leading people and engendering excitement within people begins by touching their hearts. It is not enough to merely understand. You must care.

YOUR BUSINESS

To manage your business, you need plans: business plans, financial plans, marketing plans, and operational plans. You cannot just wing it.

THE GREAT MONEY AND TIME QUESTIONS

Two of the most popular questions from people who want to start a restaurant are: "What are the financial requirements for starting a restaurant?" and "How long will it take to open a restaurant?"

These loaded questions are impossible to answer without knowing more details about the type of restaurant you're opening. Are you taking over a pre-existing establishment or opening a new one from scratch? Is the structure free-standing or is it in-line (a mall-type environment)? Do you want to lease or own the property? You get the idea. There are many questions to answer. If you pursue your dream wisely, it will be many months before you serve your first glass of water.

If you want to open a restaurant, you need to make the restaurant your passion. And if you invest the time into putting together a plan, you will find the money you need to fund that passion. If you are haphazard and vague about your goals, you will most likely struggle to find financing or be forced to fund your ill-conceived plan on your own.

If you proceed carefully and thoroughly, the financial requirements will become quite clear, and the hurdles of getting the necessary capital will be easier to navigate. Tons of capital resources are available, but investors always want to know your plan and how committed you are to that plan. Risking your own money is one way to demonstrate your level of commitment to other investors. If you are reluctant to risk your own money, not many people will risk theirs on you. But if the concept and business plan, born of your passion, work, the money will follow.

TIP

There are no rules about where start-up money must originate. There are many cases where little or no money comes out of the owner's pocket, and there are others where the entire show was self-financed. The only rule about investing is this: The successful owner always invests all of his or her passion.

PRELIMINARY START-UP COSTS

Starting a restaurant is clearly going to cost you lots of time doing research and planning. You will need to present to investors what you are specifically proposing and how much starting your restaurant is going to cost. Planning takes an immense amount of time, but you can keep most of the preliminary planning costs to a minimum.

A computer, which you might already have, is the tool of the trade during the planning stages. (If you don't have a computer, you can get one for a few hundred bucks or borrow one at the library for free.) Research data is easily accessible and mostly free. Business planning software and/or guidelines can cost you around $200 or can be accessed for free at the local library. Your office space can be your dining room table or even the food court in the mall. (Using the food court as an office is a great way to get you into the hustle and bustle of the restaurant business, not to mention the ideas it might spark during your concept design phases.)

As you can clearly see, the costs of initial planning are very small—unless you count the price of missing television.

Ask Questions

Being a restaurant owner takes an extreme amount of knowledge and interest in a wide variety of areas, so learn from the experts. Surround yourself with professional assistance every chance you get. Of course, take this advice with the understanding that defining who is an expert is difficult. An expert is very much in the eye of the beholder.

Engaging multiple experts with specific knowledge bases will enable you to get to the heart of many different areas quickly. Talk to bankers, lawyers, accountants, repairmen, vendors, chamber of commerce staff, teachers, professors, and more. Don't forget other entrepreneurs, especially restaurateurs. Talk to virtually anyone who has a level of expertise that may come in handy.

The best part of all this expert advice is that it does not have to come at an hourly rate. If you're great at networking and building lasting friendships, you can learn for free. The key, of course, is being prepared to pose the right questions to the right people.

Take stock of your motivation and pinpoint your focus. Make your questions specific and take notes. Then find the intestinal fortitude to pursue the answers. And consider this question: Are you asking the right questions or just getting the answers that you want to hear?

Here are a few of the right questions to ask an expert:

- What are the three most important keys to becoming a successful restaurant owner?
- What are some of the best educational resources for learning more about _____?
- Who is the best person you know at _____? Can you introduce me to him/her?
- How did you get started in your field?
- Would you mind if I called on you once in a while to ask for advice?

A Story About Service and Risk

A great restaurant story illustrates a good deal about service, investment, planning, and risk.

Joe owned a small Mexican-American eatery near Los Angeles. Once, a softball team that had never been in before came into his restaurant. They ordered 16 regular bean burritos, 1 bean burrito with no onions, and 17 sodas. Joe's team made the 16 regular bean burritos. He personally made the bean burrito with no onions and properly marked it.

Soon after receiving his food, the customer who had ordered the no-onion burrito came up to the counter stomping, spitting, and swearing, insisting that he did not get his no-onion burrito and that all the burritos had onions on them. Joe knew that the customer had received the correct order, but he was a bit intimidated by the customer's size and the number of his equally big buddies, not to mention the scene they were making.

Joe decided that for simplicity's sake and in the interest of avoiding bodily harm, he would not recognize the fact that they were either wrong, confused, or trying to cheat him (which he truly thought was the case). Instinctively, he asked the customer, "What can I do to make it right?" Immediately, Joe could sense that the customer's desire to fight went away, and he said, "I want a bean burrito with no onions for me and 16 more bean burritos for the rest of my team."

Joe immediately said, "Yes, sir. We are on it!" He then profusely apologized, handed the customer the entire order remade, smiled sheepishly, and thanked him for the opportunity to satisfy him and his team.

The customer, of course, strutted back to his table with his newfound wealth of burritos and the envy of all his teammates. Joe was simply happy to have all the commotion dissipate. Then a lady walked up to him and whispered that she had overheard the team jesting about "getting one over" on him regarding this whole burrito issue. Joe thanked her for her concerns, but told her that he wasn't worried about it and just wanted to make sure that each and every customer of his was satisfied to the best of his team's ability. She was shocked and in awe of his commitment to customer satisfaction.

When Joe did his follow-up visit with the ballplayers to ensure that they were happy, they admitted that they had taken advantage of him and that there really was no burrito issue. They thought it was hilarious that they each got two burritos for the price of one. Joe laughed along with them and praised them on their creativity and negotiating skills. They became even friendlier. Interestingly enough, the whole team eventually became regulars and stopped in after every softball game.

The whole bean burrito story became legendary conversation and a cornerstone of Joe's restaurant career. Those 17 extra bean burritos cost him about $4 in *food cost*, but they netted him thousands of dollars in sales. That's the restaurant business in a nutshell. You never know what kind of risk you may face, but if you do the right thing you've always got a good chance to reap tremendous rewards.

TIP

Don't worry about the very small percentage of people who may take advantage of you. Concentrate instead on the huge wins you can have by sticking to your business ideas and turning all situations into ways to build and/or start loyalty.

PLAIN ENGLISH

Food cost is one of the more important expenses to control if you are in the restaurant business. It is the cost of the ingredients that the restaurant pays. If you pay $1.25 for the ingredients that go into your Chicken Noodle Casserole and you sell it for $3.99, your food cost is $1.25, or 31.3 percent.

THE 30-SECOND RECAP

- The restaurant business is a different kind of life: long hours, long weeks, a fast pace one minute, a slow and relaxed pace the next. Expect to be on your feet all day and have lots of customer interaction.
- No two days in the restaurant business are exactly alike. Restaurant owners need to have a variety of skills, do many different tasks, and be able to adapt quickly.
- A good plan will go a long way in helping you find money and avoid pitfalls. Take the time to think it through.
- Being in charge means making lots of decisions.
- Your biggest investment will be your time.
- Risk brings reward.

Everybody Eats: The State of the Industry

It all started, as you might expect, in Paris.

A chef named Boulanger opened Champ d'Oiseau in Paris, France, in 1765. This was the first restaurant on record, and it came about because Boulanger had the audacity to try something new in the business world—serving food for profit at an outside establishment. Until then, chefs had worked for the wealthy, and everyone else cooked their own meals. But the concept of restaurants started to spread around 1789 when more chefs who were employed by the wealthy found themselves out of work and took to the idea of feeding the public for a price per meal. The French Revolution, it seems, spurred a revolution in how people ate.

By 1826, Union Oyster House was founded in Boston, and Delmonico's was founded in New York City in 1827. After World War I, the changing lifestyles of the American people (spurred especially by the invention of the automobile) prompted sweeping changes and growth in the restaurant industry.

In recent decades, many concept and industry changes have occurred as a result of the increasing importance of convenience in the mobile society. This section describes the current state of the restaurant industry, including the risks and threats to the business and the many opportunities that exist.

SOME RECENT HISTORY

By the mid-1980s, there was a variety of restaurants to cover every taste imaginable and a concept to fit every budget. Every corner had a restaurant, or so it seemed. That growth trend continues today. Approximately 13,000 to 17,000 new restaurants open in this country every year, and the concept designs and table fare continue to blossom.

People no longer go to restaurants simply to eat. They go to be entertained, to meet with clients, to build social relationships, to relax and unwind, and, yes, to save time.

The restaurant consumer has grown to have very high standards. Because of the large influx of unique and varied cuisine, the American palate has become both educated and critical. Our desire for great products and services at a fair price has become intense, and our loyalty to any one restaurant is liable to change. Restaurant owners and chefs have come to realize that they are no better than the last meal they served. There are too many dining choices for them to be complacent.

AN ABUNDANCE OF OPPORTUNITY

Whether you're planning to start a restaurant in New York City or Teardrop, Wyoming, you'll find plenty of opportunities. All of the great ideas have not been done quite yet. Even if your idea has been done before, you can always compete by outperforming the competition.

CAUTION

Eighty percent of new restaurants fail within three to five years.

There are many ways to break into the restaurant business. A variety of options allows you to choose something that fits your lifestyle and excites your passion. You need to believe in your idea, or you may as well burn your money. Each type of restaurant has its own client base and requires a unique set of skills to be successful.

Restaurants are typified by the kind of food they serve, their style of presentation, their atmosphere, and their price range. Some restaurants focus on a particular meal, such as breakfast or dinner, or offer only a portion of a meal, such as desserts or snack foods. Other restaurants specialize in a certain kind of food. The following list provides some common examples:

- Ethnic food (Mexican, Chinese, Italian, and so on)
- Chicken
- Barbeque
- Pizza
- Hamburgers
- Seafood
- Ice cream
- Sandwiches
- Hot dogs

Restaurants also differ in the way they serve the food. For example, a deli or a diner probably offers counter service. A pizza place may provide only take-out or delivery service. Steak house servers come to the customers' tables, and buffet restaurants let customers serve themselves.

Atmosphere differs greatly from restaurant to restaurant. A fast-food place is worlds away from a fine-dining establishment. A themed restaurant doesn't look the same as a truck stop. A restaurant's atmosphere attracts certain types of customers and affects the food prices. Coffee shop customers expect to pay less for their food than customers at a casual-dining restaurant, for example.

Evaluate your options. Do you want to be the hot dog king of your world, or would you be more content with a deli or a formal dining place serving seafood? Remember, it's your dream.

STRATEGIES FOR SUCCESS

The restaurant industry is thriving like never before. The reasons for this growth include the following:

- The concept of franchising
- The cultural changes of American society (for example, more air travel, longer commutes, more women in the workforce, and more entertainment opportunities)
- The growth of fast food or the quick service restaurant (QSR) *segment*

PLAIN ENGLISH

Segment means the "style" of a restaurant based on its prices, service, presentation, and atmosphere. Restaurant segments include casual dining, fast food, fine dining, concept dining, and many others. Each of these is considered its own segment in the restaurant industry.

- Easily accessible capital—more people are getting more money to open more businesses, especially restaurants, than ever before
- The American love affair with food, entertainment, and convenience

In America, we are surrounded by the abundance of opportunity that we call free enterprise, and the restaurant business is no exception. An early-morning person can choose a breakfast-oriented business. A late-night type can choose a dinner house with or without a bar. A chef can be a caterer. The choices are open to your imagination. You can invent a category. The opportunities to do what you want are great.

The flip side to this wealth of opportunity is that restaurants close down every day. The numbers are astonishing and rather sad because all of these owners thought they had a great idea. How can you avoid joining the statistics? Read on.

TIP

Here are the four big reasons restaurants fail:

- Lack of knowledge
- Poor planning
- Poor execution
- Undercapitalization

TIP

The restaurant business changes at the speed of light. Just when you think you know everything, something new comes into the picture. To be successful in this business, you must always continue to learn about it.

GET PAST THE CURSE OF IGNORANCE

What you don't know *can* hurt you. Every day that you don't learn means there is more you don't know, and a lack of specific industry knowledge and/or a lack of general business knowledge can quickly kill a restaurant. Complacency about the business will allow other, more aggressive owners to take advantage of what they know and exploit your weaknesses.

Learning is a required part of this job. Spend the necessary time gaining the required technical skills and absorbing as much information as you can about the industry. Then you can be comfortable knowing that you have approached your decision to enter this arena armed with a knowledge base and current information. Do the following to increase your restaurant knowledge:

- Conduct personal research on the restaurant industry. The National Restaurant Association, *Nations Restaurant News* (*NRN*), and your state Restaurant Association (you should become a member) are all wonderful places to conduct research.
- Read trade magazines and books: *Nations Restaurant News* (*NRN*), *QSR Magazine, Restaurants and Institutions,* and *Chain Leader. Restaurant Marketing Magazine* and many others are helpful resources as are restaurant-specific books and others that cover more broad-based concepts, such as accounting and marketing
- Attend industry seminars. There are multiple industry-specific trade shows and seminars every week in many places across the country.

Spend a few bucks and attend some of them. Many are free. Dates, location, and subject matter are listed in many of the industry magazines.

- Get information from vendors and suppliers. Pick up the phone book and call a few in your area. They have a vested interest in helping you be successful. You are the potential customer.

- Take useful industry-specific and general business classes. Register at the local college or university or sign up for some of the traveling classes listed in the newspaper.

- Know all you can about your customers and your competitors' customers. It is a people business, and knowing more about the people you deal with is critical.

- Conduct a *feasibility study* before buying or building a restaurant. Will your idea work?

PLAIN ENGLISH

A **feasibility study** tests the many components of your business concept to see if it will work. There are plenty of great ideas out there, but getting them to actually work can be a different story. A feasibility study is something that you hire outside help to conduct. It can run you a few to many thousands of dollars, but is worth it if you aren't sure your concept will be a go for the consumer.

- Seek guidance from reputable lawyers, accountants, and restaurant industry experts. It's back to the potential customer point. If they want your business, they will help you get started.

- Join local associations and network with other business owners and restaurant operators. Every city has many networking opportunities sponsored by the local chamber of commerce or other civic groups.

- Compare your performance to industry and segment averages and educate yourself on how others optimize performance.

When you dig into all of these resources, you will see all kinds of industry information pouring out. Look at it and compare, compare, and compare some more.

DON'T PLAN TO FAIL

People don't go into business planning to fail. However, plenty of people go into business failing to plan. A well-conceived and thought-out business plan is essential to making your business work and is a key ingredient to determining your restaurant's success or failure.

A business plan takes time, effort, analytical ability, and commitment. Your business plan will help you think through your ideas and refine areas of concern, as well as areas of strength, quickly and easily without the large cost of making a mistake later on. Your plan is meant to be a working document, which means that it is subject to change as your circumstances change. But it should still be solid enough to be used as a guide to business success and a refocusing tool when you get off your planned path. It will also help you immensely with your restaurant and business educational processes.

GET IT DONE

Poor execution is a bad meal, an unhappy employee, or a misplaced order. It is lost focus or what is facetiously called "that loving feeling."

Lost focus allows things to slide. For some reason or another, maybe personal issues, ego issues, forgetfulness, or who knows what, the simple tasks of running a restaurant move down the priority scale. Lost focus also happens when the owner becomes bored, disinterested, or unexcited by the prospect of owning a restaurant after all the work of the job is discovered. The owner forgets that running a restaurant is a career and comes to treat it like a hobby he or she is tired of.

At this point, the competition starts sniffing around. The complacent restaurant owner suddenly finds that the well of black ink has gone red while no one was watching. It's happened many times.

TIP

Competition can come in many forms, from a similar restaurant to a candy machine.

FIND SOME MONEY WITH GRIT, GOALS, AND GUTS

People say it takes money to make money. In the restaurant business, it takes money to buy forks, fire insurance, and cheese. Money is the blood of any business, and in the restaurant business lack of money can destroy your options and cause you to make bad decisions. Many poor decisions in the restaurant business come from being undercapitalized. Lack of money might tempt you to ...

- Select the cheaper of two sites.
- Skip legal and regulatory steps.
- Buy lower-quality products.

Plenty of other poor decisions are made in the restaurant world every day because of undercapitalization.

Investors are always looking for good ideas, but getting money for a business venture can be challenging. To be successful, you need grit, goals, and guts.

Grit is what keeps you asking for capital even when you have been rejected 37 times in a row for a business loan. Goals become more clearly defined when you write your business and financing plans, because without such planning, you can kiss virtually every capital resource good-bye. Guts are the intestinal fortitude to trust in your idea, your plan, and yourself.

 CAUTION

Restaurants on average are running 15 to 30 percent understaffed. It is the way of the restaurant world.

Hasty decisions about site selection have caused much pain for many restaurant companies, including Boston Market. Bad site decisions put a significant long-term strain on restaurant profitability, causing restaurants to raise prices to pay for overpriced property. These overpriced menus then resulted in declining customer bases and declining customer frequency, which resulted in lower sales. The effects of those decisions are still being felt today by many other restaurant owners and operators who followed their lead by selecting less-than-wonderful sites at significantly higher prices than the sites should have demanded.

RESTAURANT INDUSTRY CHALLENGES

Lions, and tigers, and bears, oh my! Well, maybe not, but even if you don't stray off of the yellow brick road (your business plan), there are plenty of challenges in the restaurant business.

TURNOVER

About 11 million people work in the restaurant industry in the United States, which makes the industry the second largest employer in the country behind the federal government. As you'll learn when you start your restaurant, these folks have a tendency to change jobs.

Turnover in the restaurant business has become a disease of astronomical proportions. Industry turnover averages run in excess of 200 percent for hourly employees and exceed 100 percent for salaried management. To put these numbers into perspective, if you have a projected staff level of 35 employees and a projected turnover of 200 percent, you will need to hire 70 employees in the next year to stay at 35. In this example, the average tenure of one of your restaurant employees is six months.

In addition, the shortage of qualified applicants is growing. Turnover has affected every segment of the industry and continues to be a driving force behind rising compensation levels, poor operations, and profit erosion.

MINIMUM WAGE LAWS

Minimum wage laws always affect the restaurant business. Where state and federal minimum wage levels are not the same, the higher of the two wage rates prevails. States such as Oregon, Washington, and California are leading the charge to increase the minimum wage well above the federal guidelines, and cities such as San Francisco are providing city-mandated living wage rates that increase the minimum allowable wage inside that city's limits even more. An increase of 50 cents in minimum wage can cost the average restaurant tens of thousands of dollars in lost profitability in a given year. This loss results in either a decrease in profits or an increase in menu prices to make up for the shortfall.

LEGAL ISSUES

The restaurant industry has become a legal minefield. Without the proper protection and knowledge, any restaurant owner can be destroyed both professionally and personally.

SITE SELECTION

Site selection changed forever in the early 1990s. Back then, the economy was strong, the restaurant industry was booming, cash was easy to get, and growth was running wild. Companies like Boston Market came along and scooped up sites at alarming rates and unbelievably high prices and forever changed the restaurant site selection landscape. Today, because of those past poor decisions when companies did not care about paying 30 percent to 100 percent more for a site than it was worth, finding a quality site at a fair price is much more challenging.

SATURATION

Saturation of any one market or specialty threatens the industry. The marketplace became inundated with restaurants that were poorly planned and restaurateurs who were inexperienced. In some parts of the country, the restaurant business became oversaturated and same-store sales started to decline.

PLAIN ENGLISH

Saturation is having more restaurants in a particular locale than the available customer base can support. Inexperienced restaurateurs open up poorly planned restaurants and customers spread their dollars around to try out the new dining experiences. For a short while—until the customer realizes a dining experience is not worthy of their repeat business (usually a six-month process)—the pieces of the consumer spending pie get split more ways. This causes the good restaurants to take a financial hit until the poorly run restaurants go out of business.

IF YOU ARE GREAT, YOU WILL SUCCEED

In a sense, however, the state of the restaurant industry is the same as it has always been. Change is always in the air, but the business is still serving food and catering to the American love of quality.

American restaurant owners know what customers expect. They do not expect a New York strip or a kung pao chicken dinner from McDonald's, so McDonald's doesn't try to deliver that. Customers want all-beef hamburgers, and McDonald's gives the customers what they want. Its success is tough to argue with. A customer who orders a filet mignon at a Morton's Famous Steakhouse wants a top-of-the-line piece of meat and is willing to pay for it.

Regardless of your restaurant's menu, category, or concept, if you are competing near the top of your segment with great products and services, you will always have a chance. Customers will frequent the restaurant that delivers the best products and services at the right price in a given market area. If Bill's restaurant is all that's available, that's the place people will spend their money. If they have two or three choices, they will spend their money at the place providing the best food and service at the fairest price. The restaurant business is a fun, competitive environment—if you're great.

The marketplace has plenty of room for new and innovative concepts as well. Our society has shown great interest in making a dining experience like a short vacation. If you have new products or services to bring to the market, you may very well find consumers who will buy. If you bring old products and services to the market, but deliver them in a new way, you may find a niche in today's competitive restaurant environment as well.

Although the restaurant business is difficult, new people are always stepping into the industry wanting to compete. Some want to compete with the big boys, some want to compete with the mom-and-pop places, some want to compete with new concepts, and some want to compete by improving on what has always been done, but they come in busloads ready to compete. The question that you must answer for yourself is: *Do you have what it takes to stand out from the crowd and succeed?*

THE 30-SECOND RECAP

- New restaurant concepts continue to blossom.
- Eighty percent of new restaurants fail in three to five years.
- Success comes with having the necessary knowledge, a good plan, the ability to execute well, and an ample supply of money.
- The best strategy is to be great at what you do.

Now that we've explored the ins and outs of running a restaurant, let's take a look at a very different kind of small business: property management.

What Is a Landlord?

According to the American Heritage Dictionary, *a landlord is a "person who owns and rents land, buildings, or dwelling units." In short, a landlord is the owner of rented property. This means that, unless you have people actually renting your property, you are not a landlord; you are simply a property owner. Sound strange? Think about it. A landlord is the person recognized by an occupant of a property as the owner of the property. Hence, no occupant means no landlord.*

Being a landlord means many things, and the perception of a landlord as the one who gets the rent every month has created a negative stigma. But don't let that scare you from entering the world of rental property investment. Rental property can be very profitable as an investment, and a certain satisfaction can be associated with supplying one of mankind's basic needs, housing.

This section gives you the facts you need to start down the road of property management. We look at a brief history of landlords, the pluses and minuses of owning rental property, the different type of landlords and various owner-ship theories.

A BRIEF HISTORY OF THE LANDLORD

Since the beginning of humankind, food, clothing, and shelter have been the primary needs for survival. The earliest *landlord* was probably a caveman who found a nice three-family cave with a view of a volcano. The first eviction probably had something to do with a club and a lot of hair-pulling. Many would still agree with that today.

PLAIN ENGLISH

Landlord, landlady, or landperson? The politically correct term should be, of course, **landperson.** The term **landlady** came into existence at the beginning of the nineteenth century when women were not a big part of the daily workforce. Many times, when a married couple lived in and owned rental property, the woman took care of the day-to-day activities at the property while her husband was at his job. The reputation of the landlady was usually one to be reckoned with because the "landlady" was no one to fool with.

The most recognized origins of the landlord and tenant relationship can be traced back to some political and military systems that became popular during the tenth and eleventh centuries, *seignorialism* and *feudalism.*

Seignorialism, or *manorialism* as it was known in England, was a political, economic, and social system that was devised in the fifth century. During the time of the Middle Ages in Europe, peasants, known as *serfs,* became legally bound to the land on which they lived and worked in servitude to the landowners, called *lords.* The serfs would give a portion of their crops, as well as other payments and taxes, as a form of rent payment to the lord in return for shelter, a small plot of ground, a share in the surrounding land and livestock, and protection from enemies.

Serfdom was different from slavery because serfs had the right to own property. Serfs also could not be sold and could purchase their freedom from their lords.

Feudalism was similar in some regards yet differed primarily because it existed only between members of nobility. In feudalism, a lord would grant a *fief,* which was usually land and labor, to a social peer who would become the lord's *vassal,* or servant, and in return the vassal would provide political and military services. The vassal would have to take an oath of allegiance as well as an oath of homage to the lord. These oaths acted as a contract between two individuals who held rights in the fief.

In both seignorialism and feudalism, you can easily see the development of the term *landlord.* In today's society, no one would be considered the lord of the land. Modern government, laws, and regulations dictate how property is to be used and governed by its owners. These early forms of government, however, impacted civilization and created what we know as the rental industry.

Being a landlord today is much different from what it used to be. The power associated with being a landlord and controlling property and tenants is still perceived as inherited, even though in reality that is not true. A landlord today needs to be able to wear many different hats. Rental property is a business and needs to be treated as such. A landlord must be a businessman and an investor who is skilled at locating property of value at a reasonable price; negotiating with lenders, tenants, contractors, and authorities; and working with contracts, office policies, tax issues, laws and legal issues, accounting techniques, construction, and maintenance. To be successful, a landlord must truly be a jack of many trades.

THE PLUSES AND MINUSES OF OWNING RENTAL PROPERTY

Owning rental property can be a profitable and interesting investment opportunity. Housing is still one of humankind's essential needs for survival and is therefore an excellent investment. It's kind of an investment in life.

In urban centers during the Industrial Revolution of the nineteenth century, the need for housing grew significantly in the United States. People were moving into cities like never before, attracted to the prospect of finding work. Many buildings were built to accommodate the need for shelter and privacy. Although investors purchased many, a great deal more were purchased for the owners to also live in. The idea of many people who purchased rental property was to put all of the profit made back into the building during the years that were work-productive for the owners. This way, the owners could fall back on a property that was free of a mortgage and could enjoy their golden years. It was a good plan and it worked.

Today many people buy investment property with the hope of someday reselling and making a profit on the return of sale. People also buy investment property to live in themselves, using the income either to live off of or to help pay for the house itself. Some people look at investment property as a career choice to provide a base income and support for their family. Others, unfortunately, seem to like the sense of power associated with owning rental property while taking advantage of all the other reasons mentioned.

ADVANTAGES OF OWNING OTHER PEOPLE'S HOMES

Money, money, money is the first thing people think of when they consider owning rental property. Most people can't believe that the owner of a rental property is doing anything but making money. It is reasonable to understand why people would feel this way. Put yourself in the shoes of a tenant for a minute. This person lives in a house that you own; it is his or her home but you still own it, and that takes money. The tenants never see real estate tax bills or, in many cases, water and sewer bills. They probably will never pay for repairs to the building; therefore, they never know what these things actually cost and that it takes money. The tenant will probably never pay for management services such as secretarial work, advertising, or legal council in regard to the property—and that takes money.

Income generated from rent can be quite considerable if a property is bought and managed correctly. The object, of course, is to keep expenses down while servicing the tenants, keeping the apartments rented, and maintaining the building so that rent received is maximized. There are other reasons for owning rental property; for instance, you may want to attempt to increase your net worth or take advantage of certain tax incentives. There is a sense of achievement in the world associated with property ownership, but remember to keep that ego in check. Many people obviously cannot afford their own homes (most tenants, for example), and many may resent the fact that you own their home.

CAUTION

This may be the only job in the world that you can't just quit. The responsibility and liability associated with the property are yours for as long as you own it. So if someday you get up in the morning and decide rental ownership is not for you, the reality is that you're still responsible until you either sell or transfer the title to someone else or file for bankruptcy and lose the investment.

DISADVANTAGES OF OWNING OTHER PEOPLE'S HOMES

Work, work, work is the first thing anyone who either owns or has owned a home, single or multi, will think of right after the money. Without question, property ownership is labor-intensive unless it is a piece of raw land and no one cares whether the grass is cut. But in any situation in which you own a property where someone else lives or will live, you can bet on spending some time and effort maintaining and improving the property. The more apartment units you own or are responsible for, the more work you can count on. The more units you own or manage, the more responsibility and liability you have to make sure the rental units and property are safe for residents and visitors. Work, work, work!

WHAT KIND OF LANDLORD WILL YOU BE?

There are a couple different types of landlords in this world. The two most notable names for describing rental owners are *owner-occupant* and *absentee.*

As you will see, the differences are quite evident in how the property is operated and in what the overall perception is from the community. Owner-occupant means that the owner of the property not only owns the property but also lives there. An absentee landlord is one who owns the property for investment purposes only, who does not live there, and whose presence is considered absent from the property daily. Both types of rental owners suffer many of the same challenges and reap the same rewards. Why you want to own rental property will determine which you become.

TIP

To prevent late-night emergency house calls, set up house rules in advance. Letting tenants know in advance when they can and cannot disturb you will help prevent future disputes.

THE OWNER-OCCUPANT: OPEN 24 HOURS

When the owner resides at the property, the property's condition usually benefits and appears to be better. A responsible property owner always picks up garbage or debris from the property when he or she sees it, but an owner who lives at the property will probably clean the property much more quickly and more routinely than one who does not live there. "In sight, in mind" is the basic concept here.

In the owner-occupant scenario, the landperson has constant knowledge of the day-to-day happenings at the property. If a tenant or someone at the property is creating a disturbance, the owner is more available to handle the problem than an absentee landlord would be. There is a huge benefit perceived by the community when an owner resides at the property. The chance for better property care combined with an ownership presence in the neighborhood helps ensure stability for residents in the surrounding area.

The flip side to living with your tenants is that, as the landlord, you are always available. Or at least that's how the tenants will perceive your time. Let's say it's 11:30 P.M., and Tenant B upstairs notices in her apartment an uninvited creature, which she promptly removes. Tenant B suspects that the creature has friends and that this might be a job for you. Tenant B could wait until the next day to alert you, her landlord, to the possible rodent problem, but why wait when the landlord is only steps away?

As an owner-occupant landlord, be aware that you are on call 24 hours a day. To the tenant, it's more a matter of convenience than an intention to invade your privacy. Make tenants aware that landlords have a life after work hours, too!

ABSENTEE BUT NOT FORGOTTEN

The absentee owner is a much more difficult scenario than the owner-occupant. The absentee owner most likely will not be at the property as much as an owner who lives there, and the daily maintenance of the property will suffer. The absentee owner is not as easily accessible to handle on-premises disturbances, which will annoy tenants and neighbors. Unless the absentee owner operates a management company, a management company may have to be hired to manage the daily activities of the property and to service the tenants. Unfortunately, the absentee owner has been the brunt of much criticism from many community organizations as the source of community problems when, in fact, society as a whole should be blamed.

CAUTION

Any person who sells or leases property for someone else must not only be licensed as a real estate sales agent but also affiliated with a licensed real estate broker. In other words, it is not enough to simply hold a sales license; an agent must also work for a broker.

OWNER-OCCUPANT VS. ABSENTEE: YOUR CHOICE

It may sound like the owner-occupant situation is the best. As previously mentioned, however, under those circumstances, the owner is working and on call 24 hours a day. The owner-occupant is very accessible to the tenants, which can be good unless the tenants misuse this privilege. It also is extremely difficult to treat rental property as a business when it is also your home. The personal relationship that exists between the tenant and you when you share a home can be very stressful for you to live with if the rent is late or the tenant violates your rules. Living with that kind of discomfort every day is not for everyone. As an absentee landlord, the pressure of keeping home separate from work doesn't exist.

The owner-occupant trend has been very popular in the United States. Years ago, most rental property was owner-occupant by necessity of the owner. Today, however, the federal government has instituted programs that boost owner-occupant ownership of rental property. These programs usually instruct and offer assistance to new owners regarding how to manage and operate rental property. These programs are expected to help stabilize the decline of troubled neighborhoods.

OWNERS VS. PROPERTY MANAGERS

Sometimes a rental owner will hire a property management company to manage the daily activities of the property. A management company is a specialized professional real estate service that, for a fee, can do the following:

- Rent or lease apartments
- Negotiate major and minor repairs
- Collect and disburse monies
- Service tenants
- Keep accounting records
- Evict tenants

Basically, as opposed to your own *superintendent*, an outside property management company can do just about everything discussed in this book. It has been said that an owner who manages his or her own property has a fool for a client. It might be a good idea to use this type of service if you do not possess the skills or tools associated with operating rental property. If you work another job that does not leave you the time and energy to invest in the property, or if the property is at a distant location and you find it hard to manage from that distance, you may want to hire a management company. If you needed the services of a lawyer or doctor, you would hire one, and the same regard should be given to this type of service. The real estate industry has many facets of expertise. Some companies deal with selling property, some develop, and some manage property.

PLAIN ENGLISH

Superintendent does not mean property manager. A superintendent is someone you hire to work for you, either as an employee or as an independent contractor, to do minor repair in and around the property. A superintendent does not need to be licensed as long as he or she stays within the scope of minor repair. A superintendent should not be handling any money, renting apartments, or signing leases associated with your property.

There is no special license requirement for buying and owning rental property, but there is a license requirement if you plan to manage property for anyone but yourself. Anyone who negotiates, charges, collects, and disburses the monies of others needs a license to do so. Therefore, before you hire a particular company for management services, make sure the company is licensed in accordance with the laws of the state in which the property is located. The license to operate this kind of service is generally called a real estate broker's license. A broker is the licensee or holder of the state license. He or she might have employees called salespeople or leasing agents either selling or renting property, and these people also have to be licensed in accordance with state laws.

The fee for property management is generally based on a percentage of income plus expenses. Some property managers have a repairperson on staff to correct minor problems at the property and can pass this savings on to you.

Try to hire the best you can. Your property manager represents you, and you don't want to be labeled a *slumlord* because of their efforts. Ask around and network with local landlords to find out who has the best reputation and best fits your needs. The management company should be familiar with properties like yours and should have the manpower to oversee its daily operation. This company must be easily reached both by you and your tenants in the event of an emergency. The company should be familiar with laws that govern your property to help protect you from liability. Remember, however, that it is your property, and you will still be the bottom line if something goes wrong, not the property manager. The property manager will probably not enter your property every day, but if it is managed correctly, he or she may not have to.

PLAIN ENGLISH

Whether you like it or not, most angry tenants, neighbors, and public officials have referred to landlords as **slumlords.** Don't be offended; to be a slumlord, you need a slum tenant. The truth is that responsible landlords well outnumber the irresponsible ones. A true slumlord is a person who buys a property, drains it of all potential rent, and then abandons it intentionally. This person is almost nonexistent.

OWNERSHIP THEORIES

There are some differences of opinion about why and how to operate investment property. These were touched on earlier in this section, but it's worth repeating and defining them again. The practice of these theories will affect not only your investment but also the neighborhoods surrounding your rental property.

One theory of operating rental property is to buy a property, rent it, and earn profits without ever putting any of the returns back into the property. This theory is called *short-term gain,* and it means to reap immediate rewards from profit from the property. This method used to be most common for small investors who were neither very handy around the property nor very good investors. The old idea was that you could purchase a rental building and never go there except to collect rents. Although the owner may have actually made quite a bit of money with the short-term method, the effects often were negative. Eventually, the building would suffer from disrepair, property value would plummet, and the neighborhood would suffer.

The theory of long-term ownership is better for the owner, the tenants, and the surrounding area of the property. Money made from profits is still the bottom line, but instead of simply draining all the profits from the property, some of the rental profit, through the use of good escrow techniques, is used to constantly make capital improvements to the property. This, in effect, helps maintain the property, increases its value, and benefits the surrounding neighborhood.

Real Estate 101

It is time for you to learn a little something about real estate. If you were planning to open a bakery, you would want to learn something about baking, and before you go out and purchase a car, you must learn how to drive. So why not learn a little something about the real estate business before making a sizable purchase like investment property?

There are different types of property and property ownership you should know about before becoming a landlord. Understanding these differences can help you in the long run. Your grade will be determined by whether you can successfully operate investment property. And you've got the rest of your life to study for that.

THE MANY CHARACTERISTICS OF REAL ESTATE

Real estate is made up of both physical and economic characteristics. As a landlord, you should be aware of these characteristics because understanding them will help you determine how the real estate market in a specific area will perform. This information is important to you not only while investigating property for purchase but also for the life of your ownership. Understanding the local real estate market will help you determine whether a property is rentable and at what price, as well as whether a property is saleable and at what price. This is all good stuff to know.

Here are the main physical characteristics that determine real estate property value:

- **Immobility.** Everything on top of land can be moved by actions of nature and people, but the geographic location of land will never change.

- **Lack of standardization.** No two pieces of land are exactly the same. Location, location, and location are the three big L's of real estate and possibly its biggest characteristic. Even two pieces of land right next to each other will be different because of their locations. The lack of standardization is what affects the value of real estate. Zoning restrictions and other encumbrances also add to the differences of real estate and affect the value of property.

- **Long life.** Land can have a life span of hundreds of years before a change is made in property lines or ownership.

- **Indestructibility.** Land is known to be durable and a relatively stable investment. Don't misunderstand us: Value can be destroyed, but the land will still remain.

THE ECO-DYNAMICS

When looking for real estate property, take note of these economic distinctions:

- **Scarcity.** Land in very desirable areas will become scarce or very valuable. There is, of course, plenty of land available that can be purchased for low prices, but land in specific areas and for specific uses often is insufficient and does not meet demand.

- **Fixed investment.** Most improvements to land, such as buildings, cannot be easily moved, and it may take 20 or 30 years to repay the investment, so the investment is known to be long lasting. As an investor, try to determine how long a property's usefulness will last before purchasing or improving it.

- **Location.** Just as location plays a physical role, it also affects the economic aspects of land. Desirability, climate, and population shifts can increase the value of land in one location, whereas the value of similar land in other areas may decline.

- **Improvements.** Land has the capability to be modified or improved. Buildings, fences, and other things added to the land directly impact its value.

THE MOST COMMON TYPES OF REAL ESTATE

There are different classifications for improved property: residential, commercial, industrial, farm, recreational, and government. *Improved property* simply means land that contains structures. Even though you may only be concerned with owning property that would meet one or two of these improved property classifications, you still should know what the other classifications represent:

- **Residential.** Residential property includes any type of structure designed for personal living. A wide range of properties is included in the residential categorization of property. In addition to single-family homes, there are apartments, town houses, row houses, condominiums, cooperatives, and mobile homes.

- **Commercial.** Commercial property represents any property designed for retail or wholesale services, financial services, office space, and shopping centers. Buildings with storefronts and apartment units are also considered commercial. Usually this type of property is acquired for investment purposes only.

- **Industrial.** Industrial property is improved land intended to be used for manufacturing and warehousing of industrial and consumer products. Factories, warehouses, and utility companies are just some examples of industrial property.

- **Farm.** Farm property, sometimes referred to as rural property, is usually used for agricultural purposes. Farmland, ranches, orchards, and pastures all fall under this classification.

- **Recreation.** Recreational property is improved land used for leisure activities and vacations. Mountain- or oceanside resorts, golf courses, and city parks are examples of recreational property. Many times, real estate developers will set aside land solely to be used for recreational purposes.

- **Government.** Government surplus land is property used and owned by the government. Much of this type of land is designated as public areas. The government, through its many agencies, owns approximately one third of all the land in the United States.

THE MOST COMMON TYPES OF RENTAL PROPERTY

With the exception of government land currently being used for some governmental capacity, all the other types of property have the potential of being purchased for investment purposes. And sometimes the government has been known to sell land that is no longer needed. Many industrial properties are rented as warehouse space for big industrial companies, just as there are instances in which farms and recreational property have been purchased by investors for rental income.

However, the most common types of real estate that are bought as investment property are residential and commercial properties. These categories of real estate start to take on new definitions when considered as rental real estate. Classifications technically remain the same; your local Uncle Sam figured out how to tax property differently based on the sizes and uses of properties.

Residential property is still classified as property designed for living in, but for it to be considered residential for tax purposes, there must be no more than four rental units in a building. So a five-family apartment house is still a residential property, but it is not taxed at a residential rate. Instead, this same five-family building is taxed at a commercial rate because it is now considered commercial property. And then there are zoning and mixed-use areas. Don't worry about that, though; just try to remember that this change in the definition of residential property relates only to tax issues. Residential property is considered one to four units regardless of whether the owner resides at the property.

There are also differences between residential and commercial property when it comes to operating these types of rental properties. You're probably thinking, what's the difference? Property is property, right? There are rules that deal not only with how to use property but also how to manage it. The Laundromat is handled much differently than the cottage at the lake. The law treats commercial property and residential property differently. Landlord and tenant responsibilities and liabilities will differ, as will eviction procedures and office policies. Remember, though, that landlords don't make the rules; they just try to live by them.

THE BUNDLE OF RIGHTS

Any professors who teach real estate know about the *bundle of rights*. The bundle of rights refers to the belief that, when you purchase real estate, you also purchase certain individual rights that are inherited with the ownership and use of the land and/or property.

PLAIN ENGLISH

Picture the **bundle of rights** as a bundle of sticks with each stick representing a specific right you have in the property. If you sell a stick, the bundle gets smaller and you lose a right. Zoning laws and market conditions in an area determine how big that bundle can be.

If you already own rental property, you might be wondering, "What rights?" It can be, and very often is, debated that property rights are fewer with each passing year. Regardless of personal opinion, the basic definition of real estate includes land, every interest and estate in land, and any permanent improvements on the land.

Real estate combines a physical element as well as the element of ownership. The land and everything permanently affixed to it are the physical portion. The ownership element refers to the nature, extent, amount, and quality of rights that a person or persons can possess in land. The basic concept of ownership is defined as the right to control, possess, enjoy, and dispose of property in a manner allowed by law. Some of the rights that relate to the physical aspects of the property may include mineral rights, air rights, and water rights. Other inherited rights of ownership are the rights to use, occupy, sell, and of course, rent.

WHO OWNS WHAT?

You think you're ready to take the plunge into the world of owning investment property? Well, before you find yourself up to your neck in shark-infested waters, you need to carefully plan how you will own your investment. You might be thinking, "What do you mean *how?*" There have been many before you who have not considered the extent of the liability associated with rental property, who did not plan accordingly, and who lost not only the investment but also much more.

So you thought you would just buy a rental property the same way you and your spouse bought your personal home. It is important for you as a new investor to recognize the different types of ownership that exist because selecting one or the other may award certain benefits and protection. A landlord today has a lot of liability, and the assets of the landlord need to be protected. Careful planning is necessary before investing in any venture, especially rental property. The same care should be taken before owning rental property as before investing in the stock market or starting a business. As a smart investor, you need to try to structure a plan that will successfully protect your assets from harsh liabilities and expensive taxes.

WHAT'S ALL THIS LIABILITY STUFF?

Along with the prestige of ownership comes the liability of ownership. Lawsuits are very popular in today's world, and a landlord must take the proper steps to insure and protect his or her investment. Remember that operating rental property is not just an investment but also a business. Accidents happen and the results can be damaging. The old "slip and fall" or unfortunate discoveries of environmental hazards such as lead paint are just a couple examples of an owner's liability. It's impossible to guarantee that no such hazard will occur or to watch over your property 24 hours a day. It also is not healthy to live in constant fear of these or other possible dangers. Therefore, you should examine and consider the different types of ownership and see if one will allow you to operate your property with peace of mind.

Choosing the Right Type of Ownership

The three main forms of business ownership are sole proprietorship, partnership, and corporation. As you will see in a moment, there are similarities and differences in each. The requirements to start each vary from state to state. Do your homework about each and consult with a licensed attorney or financial planner who specializes in this area to determine which form of ownership is right for you. These types of ownership are described in Chapter 1.

One type of ownership form is worth mentioning again here. It's the Limited Liability Company (LLC). LLCs have been used by rental property owners. An LLC is a combination of a corporation and a partnership. There are certain tax and legal advantages that make it a preferred choice of ownership. The LLC typically is taxed as a partnership, which means there is one level of taxation instead of the two that occur with close or C corporations. If the funds and operations are kept separate from personal assets and activities, limited liability can be achieved for its members.

The limited liability means the members of the LLC are responsible only up to the amount of their own contribution. In other words, if you put a property in an LLC and keep your home and other assets separate, only that property is attackable if your LLC is sued. Some investors place each property they purchase in a separate LLC; this way, each investment is protected separately. LLCs sometimes have as many investors as possible (but there can be a limit to the number of shareholders—check with your state regulations). The idea here not only is to reduce the amount of liability for each member but also to make it difficult for a plaintiff to find all the other partners to serve in a legal action. The more partners the better, and the more legal representation will be available.

One caution regarding the LLC is that laws differ from state to state. Because LLCs are a relatively new concept, laws and regulations are still developing in most states. So before you jump off your chair to create a corporation or an LLC, speak with an attorney and get professional help. Start-up is complicated and has special requirements, so you need assistance from someone qualified in corporate matters.

CAUTION

One of the biggest problems with using an LLC is operating within the rules of the LLC. One such rule is that you must use an attorney to represent the LLC in any legal matter. An LLC is a legal entity that exists by its own name, not yours, and therefore needs the services of a licensed attorney. You may be successful in doing the eviction yourself for the LLC, but if you get caught, opposing counsel can "pierce the corporate veil" (i.e., a court may disregard your immunity from liability for corporate acts and hold you personally responsible).

Checking Out the Neighborhood

Just about every town in America has rental property. Take a ride through the town in which you live, and you will find some. As you drive around, look for windows above storefronts for apartments; even the storefronts themselves are probably being rented. Count the number of mailboxes or electrical meters on a building; this sometimes indicates the presence of separate units.

Usually a town will have a section in which most of its rental housing stock is located and is most evident. Typically, the downtown area or the more urbanized areas will contain apartments. But even in rural areas and in small country towns there will be an apartment or two. Sometimes they are not easily recognizable. A basement apartment for the in-laws or a room over the garage for the college kid might not be so noticeable. However, it is impossible not to notice some rental property types; the large apartment complexes and big, multifamily homes seem to take on a look all their own. Of course, any property could be rented if an owner chooses. Single-family homes, mobile homes, condominiums, offices, retail stores, just about anything. Most of the property on Main Street, USA, is probably some form of rental property. The simple fact is landlords are everywhere.

WHERE SHOULD YOU BUY?

Anywhere you want to and can afford to. Determining where to buy should depend on what you want to buy and how much it costs. These are the questions you should ask yourself:

- How much do I want to invest?
- What kinds of property would I like to own?
- What kind of property can I handle?

If you are interested in owning apartments or commercial space to rent, you need to locate an area where there is either a demand for apartments and commercial space or a potential for demand. Supply and demand, the very basics you learned about in your college economics class, have an impact on how successful your rental property will be. For most people, the price of a property and their ability to hold on to the property will determine where they can buy.

Obviously, when there is a high demand for housing and a short supply of housing, the housing will be more expensive to buy. The same holds true for commercial real estate as well. As an investor, you need to research the area and the property to help determine what you should pay for it.

Consider the distance between where you live and the area in which you are considering buying. This is an important factor if you plan to own property that's a great distance from where you actually live or if you live very close. Rental property ownership is a very demanding business, and a rental property requires constant care. If you plan to own property a long distance from where you live, it will be very difficult for you to care for your property unless you hire a management company or a handyman to oversee daily repair and other business affairs. When you're a landlord, the emergency call in the middle of the night is inevitable. Whether the property is a great distance or just a few minutes away, the stress and anxiety associated with not being closer to the property can make the whole experience quite miserable.

On the other hand, if you live in very close proximity to the rental property, you also will become very accessible to tenant needs. This is good for the tenant, but not so good for you. If and when the emergency call comes, you will have the peace of mind of being close, but when calls come in at all hours that are not emergencies, the situation will become annoying and stressful. A tenant will usually not make a long-distance call just to complain about his or her rental unit unless it is a real emergency, but a local call is no big hardship for a tenant to make if he or she simply wants to complain. If you plan on being an absentee landlord who will run the property on your own, it might be smart to pick an area to own property that is close to where you live but still a toll call away.

CAUTION

Vacation property that you might plan to enjoy yourself, such as a time-share or summer rental in areas that are seasonal (14 weeks), can realistically expect 7 to 14 weeks of actual rent received depending on demand for the area.

TIP

Unless you are experienced with inspecting rental property, it might be wise for you to hire a private inspector to evaluate the property before you purchase it. Environmental concerns and structural hazards can prove quite costly.

A Sale Isn't Always a Bargain!

"Buy low and sell high" is the motto of the investor. No one ever wants to overpay for something he or she wants to own, and neither do you. The local real estate market will determine what property is selling for and what you can expect to pay for similar properties. In a hot real estate market in which property is in high demand and supply is low, it may be difficult to find a bargain. Not impossible, but certainly more difficult than finding bargains in areas where the demand is not as great. If you are interested in buying a two-family house in a specific, desirable area, affiliate yourself with a real estate agency familiar with that area and take a look at the agency listings to see which two-family houses are available and for how much.

Remember that just because someone is asking a certain price for a property doesn't mean the property is worth that price. Something is only worth what someone else is willing to pay for it. There are several ways to determine what people are paying for property in an area. You can pick up special publications such as the *Commercial Record,* a newspaper that lists actual sales and prices by the towns in which they occur. Town halls keep records of property transfers and prices for their respective areas. Real estate agents can tell you what prices certain properties in the area have sold for. You should be aware of some special considerations before purchasing a rental property. These considerations will help you determine whether the investment is a bargain.

Also beware of a property with a low price tag attached. The blue-light specials of this world should be researched and analyzed just as much as the higher-priced properties. Ask yourself why the property is so available, do a thorough inspection of the premises, and make sure you're not simply purchasing someone else's headache complete with costly environmental hazards and other such liabilities. We're not suggesting that you should not purchase this type of property; just be sure you know what you're getting into beforehand. We believe that, whatever you purchase and at whatever price, you should first carefully analyze the property and make sure it fits your investment needs.

LOCATING DISTRESSED PROPERTY

It's no big secret that the best deals are usually found in the wake of someone else's hardship. A distressed property is one that is either suffering or has suffered from some other underlying problem that is affecting the right of ownership. Although this is unfortunate, it does remain true that distressed property can sometimes be a real bargain.

Death, divorce, and destitution are the three Ds of finding distressed property. When a property owner is faced with some of these difficult life challenges, they can affect an owner's capability to still own the property; and these challenges often force the sale of the property, possibly well below market cost. Over the past 10 years, environmental concerns such as lead paint and asbestos, which are commonly found in buildings built prior to 1978, have forced many property owners who could not afford to correct these problems to lose their property. In some areas, high taxes combined with the high cost of daily repair have created negative returns from a property. When this happens, a mortgage payment might not be able to be satisfied, forcing either the sale or foreclosure of a property.

TIP

Foreclosed property can be purchased either directly from a lending institution or at an auction. Take special care when buying foreclosed property at auction. You might want to hire a lawyer or an agent to do a detailed title search of the property to be sure there are no liens, taxes due, or other encumbrances that could affect the ownership of the property.

CAUTION

The idea behind obtaining foreclosed property is to take advantage of reduced prices. This is not always possible, however, because sometimes the cost of recovery added to the value of the mortgage might be higher than the fair market value of the property.

Distressed property is not as difficult to find as it may sound. Property in great need of repair is a good indication that the property is experiencing problems. High grass, broken windows, and no sign of resident activity may indicate a property that has been abandoned. There are several ways to locate this type of property; you might find some while driving your car around town, or you can inquire about property at the town hall, where there is a wealth of information handy for finding distressed property. You can find out who the owner of record is for the property at the town hall and can contact this individual directly to see whether he or she wants to sell. Liens and foreclosure activity are a matter of public record available at the town hall. Many towns keep a list of empty or abandoned housing in the town area.

Legal ads in a newspaper will inform the public of estate and property auctions in the area where the paper circulates. Your lawyer or accountant might have a client who needs to liquidate a property due to financial troubles. You can contact local banks and ask to speak with someone in charge of the real estate owned (REO) department. A bank will have a list of property that has been foreclosed on by that bank. You can also contact mortgage companies for lists of property; some of these companies will also have foreclosed property available. This is sometimes the best way to locate and buy distressed property because the bank or mortgage company that wants to get rid of property may be willing to take back the paper on the loan with little money down just to quickly sell it. Contact the state in which you want to own property for a list of licensed banks and financial lenders in that state.

If you're dealing with a bank or a lending institution about a distressed property, the trick is to recoup their loss to them in return for a very low interest rate and a long term of fixed years with little to no money down. Would you pay 10 times the value for a property? The answer is "yes" if you had nothing to start with, if the terms were right, and if you could make money without putting any money down while owning it in an LLC without a personal signature. This may sound too good to be true, but when you deal with distressed property, many possibilities are available. Remember that a lender is a lender, not a property manager. The lender is probably not having much success operating the property.

In addition, many lenders will turn the property over to a VP in the office, someone who will now be working nights and weekends and will really want to dump the property and assist you in making a deal. If you find a property you like, make a cash offer; don't be afraid to offer a low price. You can always go up in price, but you can never come down. If you buy it right and refinance it right away for 100 percent of whatever you paid, you're ahead of the game. This is called "buying a property with mirrors."

SIGNS OF A GOOD NEIGHBORHOOD

The truth is that neighborhoods are all different, and beauty is in the eye of the beholder. What might seem like a bad neighborhood to one person may seem good to another.

The classic definition of a bad neighborhood is one with a high crime rate, deteriorated buildings, and declining property values. An impoverished neighborhood should not necessarily be considered a bad neighborhood. Unfortunately, it usually is by society's upper class simply because it may not appear the way these people feel it should. Deteriorated buildings and declining property values may be associated with poorer neighborhoods simply due to lack of revenue in the area. But it's the people who live in that area who will determine whether it's a good place to live. The best definition of a bad neighborhood is one that has lost its spirit and can't seem to get it back.

Nonetheless, while shopping for investment property, certain indicators will help you determine the value of not only a neighborhood's property but also the spirit of its people:

- **For Sale and For Rent signs.** If you see several For Sale signs in an area, it may indicate a stagnate market where property is not selling. The same may be true for rental units. If large numbers of people in an area are trying to sell and move out of the area, perhaps some other problems exist and will affect your success with owning rental property in the same area. When there is a demand shortage for housing and rental space, prices will have to be reduced to entice new investors, and rents will be low to appeal to new renters. If you are planning on purchasing property to resell for a profit, this type of area may not be the best suited for your purposes.

- **Vacancy rate.** Supply and demand directly affect a neighborhood. High vacancy rates mean no one wants to live there. This may be because of a multitude of reasons, but the bottom line is that vacancies will cost you money as a rental owner and will make operating the property effectively very difficult. You can check classified ads in local newspapers to see how many rental units are being advertised for rent, or you can check with the local town hall for vacancy statistics.

- **Taxes.** Local property taxes affect a neighborhood in many ways. High property taxes make it difficult for rental owners to turn a profit on their investment while maintaining the physical appearance of the property—especially when demand for such a property is low. The result is very often an unattractive property in the area. On the other hand, lower taxes help put money back into property while increasing the owners' profit.

- **Employment.** Look for industry and job opportunities in an area. Jobs mean employment and wages. The better the types of employment, the higher the wages and the greater the need for housing. Remember, the higher the demand, the higher the market rent will be and, hopefully, the higher the return on your investment. Unemployed areas as well as areas in which income is heavily subsidized by the government are usually more depressed economically and more deeply ridden with societal problems.

- **Crime.** Check with the local police department about police activity and crime rates in the area. High crime rates naturally negatively affect getting good renters to live there. Most people prefer to live in a safe community with low crime. (Many police departments keep records of crime activity by property locations.)

- **Housing and rehabilitation projects.** Look for new housing starts in the area. This indicates a demand for housing and healthy market activity. *Neighborhood revitalization zones* (NRZ) and rehab projects of older building stock, specifically by new investors, also indicates a healthy real estate market and a good rental market.

PLAIN ENGLISH

Many areas have implemented what is known as a **neighborhood revitalization zone (NRZ).** By definition, these zones comprise the people who live or own businesses in the area and enable them to make decisions that will determine the future of the neighborhood regarding its plan of development.

- **Revitalization.** Revitalization efforts usually indicate that an area has suffered or is suffering from some economic and social problems. Revitalization organizations have popped up all over the country, usually in specific urbanized areas, to try to solve problems they feel affect the area. The revitalization areas have been perceived as a good community development.

- **Schools.** School reputation is a big factor that new residents, whether owners or renters, consider before moving to an area. People want the best for their children, and a quality education in a safe school is always a priority.

- **Public services.** New residents often are attracted to an area based on the quality of services such as garbage pickup, snow removal, the quality of the town infrastructure, and the condition of roads and sidewalks. The more quality services for their tax dollar, the happier they will be.

938   Special Considerations for Different Types of Businesses

- **Parks and recreation.** New residents are attracted to areas with plenty of parks and recreational activities for children and adults.

The trick to locating a good neighborhood in which to purchase investment property is to find as many of these indicators as you can in an area and still be able to afford a property. Finding all these things in an area will seem like looking for nirvana. You should get to know an area before you purchase property in it. Make a list of what you feel are the good points in a neighborhood. Hopefully, they will outnumber the bad ones, will help you in your decision whether to purchase the property, and perhaps even will help you rent it.

Getting Ready to Buy

You have decided that rental property is a good investment because you know it's making money while you sleep. You have dreamed about that five-family building down the street that can be bought for a song, and if you hold on to it and collect rent while the property's value appreciates, you'll make all kinds of money. Sweet dreams, but beware of a nightmare on Elm Street!

A lot of investors have had sleepless nights because they didn't research the property correctly before marching blindly into a closing. Rental property ownership can be profitable, but the amount of return from the property depends heavily on the actual purchase price of the property. The location and type of property you consider buying will affect the price it can be bought for; and, of course, the trick to buying something right is to buy it for as low a price as possible.

WHAT DO YOU WANT TO BUY?

As a would-be investor, the first thing you should do before buying a property is decide what kind of property you are interested in buying. Will it be a two-family, three-family, four-family, or more? Perhaps you have your heart set on a single-family home to use as a vacation rental down by the shore or a cabin up in the woods. Will the building have commercial or other mixed uses? Whatever it is, you need to decide what to look for so that the property type will be easier to locate and research. You can always change your mind if you want!

CAUTION

One-, two-, three-, and four-family properties are usually considered residential and are taxed accordingly. Five-family and up or any property with retail or office space is usually taxed at a commercial rate.

The next thing you should decide is the property's physical location. Real estate markets are local by nature. A five-family house in one area can cost much less in another area even if the areas are close in proximity. Obviously, it is a good idea to purchase property in areas where the demand for such types of property is high. When there is a shortage of housing in an area, rents will probably be higher. Purchase prices will also usually be higher in these types of areas, but you never know—there might be a deal out there somewhere. In areas where demand is low, prices will be much lower and so will rents. It's important to note that just because rents might be higher in some areas doesn't necessarily mean there will be profit made from those properties. If a property can be purchased at or below market cost, or if the deal is structured correctly and the property is managed carefully and conservatively, a property has a chance to make money no matter where it is.

THIS PLACE IS BEAUTIFUL!

You have found the perfect property. It meets all the criteria that mean anything and everything to you. However, some reasons for purchasing a particular property may not be the right ones in the long haul. Remember that this is a business investment, not an investment in your ego!

Let's take a closer look at some popular reasons and why these reasons are not the best:

- **It's the right color.** The color of a house is not an important factor as an investment. Don't judge an investment by its color, even if you always wanted to own a white house with green shutters, and this is the one.

CAUTION

When studying to become a real estate agent, the first thing you learn is that the real estate market is a local market. The three most important things about a piece of real estate are its location, location, and location. Unlike stock market prices, which are not affected quite as easily, real estate prices can vary quite a bit from state to state, town to town, and street to street.

- **Its location reminds you of your youth.** Memory lane should be driven down in your mind, not in the creases of your wallet. Don't buy a house just because your best friend in high school used to live in it or some such similar nonsense.

- **It's what your spouse once wanted.** You once visited the house with your wife, and she said that someday she would love to own a house just like this one. Your spouse's emotional opinion is important, but not a prerequisite for purchase.

- **There is a swimming pool in the backyard.** Unless the property will benefit from a swimming pool, such as in a vacation area or where the climate is hot, you don't need it. A swimming pool is costly to maintain, and the liability associated with it is high.

- **It has beautiful, massive grounds.** To own land and become a land baron is a nice dream, but large yards with fancy landscaping can be extremely labor-intensive and expensive to upkeep.

- **It's a true antique according to the historical society.** The *historical society,* sometimes referred to by seasoned landlords as the "hysterical society," has rules that govern how a property is to look and be used. Understand that if you purchase property in a historical zone, you might be taking on partners you will not appreciate in time.

- **Your mother's friend told you it would make you lots of money.** Your mother's friend might mean well, but be sure he or she has a professional knowledge of real estate investment. Remember that the mentality of the general public is that all landlords make money; after all, look at the rent they collect.

- **Some of the apartments are empty, and you can renovate it your way without any intervention.** Vacant units translate into loss of revenue, and revenue is especially important at the time of purchase.

- **Your cousin's daughter lives at the property.** If there is a relative living at the property, you can say good-bye to that relationship. It won't be long before that side of the family stops talking to you.

PLAIN ENGLISH

A **historical society** is a committee of individuals who are concerned with preserving the historical integrity of a specific area. Since the 1960s, organizations concerned with historic preservation have tried to rehabilitate and revitalize urban neighborhoods and business districts, with much success. There are national and state historical registers of property all over the United States. Contact the local town hall for more information regarding historical districts and local societies.

■ **The price is right.** You know this to be true because you have been watching the For Sale ads in the paper, and you feel you have become quite good at determining the value of property. Do your homework, but include the actual prices listed in land records at the town hall. These are the prices that properties are actually selling for in that area. Also speak to your local banker and try to get a feel for what he or she thinks the value is; after all, the banker is going to be placing first mortgages on properties in the area and will not want to make a bad investment.

LET'S GET SERIOUS ABOUT RENTAL PROPERTY OWNERSHIP!

Now that we have explored some of the wrong reasons for purchasing property, let's look at some of the right ones:

■ You are making too much money at your business and your accountant thinks you need to be taking advantage of the IRS depreciation factors made available through property ownership.

■ You are planning for retirement and would like to someday sell a property for a profit and add to the nest egg.

■ You would like to set up a property account to act as a savings account for the college tuition for your children.

■ You simply want to earn some extra income.

■ You want to set up a portfolio of properties to create a net worth that is attractive to lenders so you can invest in a business venture and be able to borrow more money than you could based on your current income.

■ Research indicates that real estate market values are increasing, and you would like to cash in on the appreciation made available by holding on to a sound investment.

■ The business you are in does not provide a steady base income that is comfortable to your way of life.

■ If you purchase the building your business is located in, it might help reduce the overall cost of operating the business and enhance your profits.

■ By diversifying your investment portfolio to owning real estate, you have positioned yourself carefully in the world of investment by not placing all your apples in the same barrel.

■ You want to make money!

The one common denominator of all these reasons is money. We feel that, unless you or your organization has some special motive for owning investment property, the only reason to purchase rental property should be income oriented. Remember that by purchasing rental property, you are truly entering into a business, and everyone knows you should never mix business with pleasure!

EXPENSES? WHAT EXPENSES?

Yes, many expenses are incurred in operating property, especially when it's rental property. You'll need to determine these expenses before purchasing a property. The expense categories of the operating statement are important because they break down the various costs associated with the property. These costs are probably not much more than good estimates, and you should always portray these educated guesses to be kind of high. This is not a perfect world, nor is this form an exact science, and you are always better off preparing for the less-than-perfect situations. It is also important to note that many of these expenses can be offset if it is determined in the rental agreements with prospective tenants that the tenant pays for certain things like utilities or maintenance. Here's a breakdown of expenses:

- **Taxes** are the amount of money you will pay to the municipality in which the property is located. This amount is based on an assessed value of the property times a mill rate, and it is usually paid in two installments six months apart.

- **Insurance** is a necessary expense on a property. In the event that either the property is damaged or someone is injured on it and a claim is issued, an insurance company will pay the loss of the claim up to the amount insured. Contact an insurance agent for quotes associated with a specific type and location of building. It is important to note that multiple insurance policies might be required for the property, such as *fire insurance* and *liability insurance.*

PLAIN ENGLISH

Landlords must be aware of a couple different types of insurance. **Fire insurance** is a must for any owner of property. Fire insurance protects the owner against the loss of the value of the investment up to the insured. **Liability insurance** is similar to fire insurance except it protects the owner against any claims of liability that may result at the property.

■ **Electric** is the amount of money you will pay to illuminate the common areas of the building, such as hallways or stairways, and the outside grounds. Many times, apartments are rented that include utilities. This is a cost to the owner and must be estimated accordingly. This cost can be obtained from the seller's Schedule E of the 1040, or with the owner's permission you can call the electric company to get this information.

■ **Heat** is another utility that an owner sometimes will supply to a tenant as part of the rent. Again, careful estimates must be made when placing a value on this expense. This information is also available on a Schedule E, or you can call the company that supplies energy to the building for the cost of the last season.

■ **Hot water** is another possible cost for supplying a utility to the tenant. Hopefully, the tenants don't take long showers, or they might send your investment to the shower.

■ **Water,** unless stated otherwise, is the owner's responsibility for the entire building. The area's water company will have information regarding water usage and cost.

■ **Sewer,** unless there is a septic system on the property, is an expense you will probably have to pay (the cost associated with using the city sewer facilities). The cost of sewer usage can be a flat fee, or it can be based on water usage. This information can be obtained from either the service provider or the seller's 1040.

■ **Gas and/or propane** is an expense if you plan to supply utilities. This source of energy is very common and is used for heating hot water and cooking. Either the 1040 or the service provider can be used for heating estimates.

■ **Oil** is another source of energy used in some buildings, but not all.

■ **Wood** can be used for heating. However, most experts recommend not using this type of heat in apartment dwellings. The cost? Who can put a price on calloused hands and sweat?

■ **Snow** is an expense in areas that are likely to have it because removal of snow will be necessary. Unless stated otherwise in the agreement, snow removal is the owner's responsibility. It is common in commercial leasing to pass this cost on to the occupant. When the plowed area is shared by many, the cost is divided.

TIP

It is common in many older types of housing stock for the tenant to pay for the source of heat. This is because the buildings were usually designed that way, and most property owners would prefer not to pay this expense. Some landlords, however, prefer the added feature of paying the heating expense as a lure to attract tenants and fill vacancies. The landlord will try to adjust the rent to offset the expense. This works fine as long as the tenant doesn't misuse the heat in the apartment. In some instances, a landlord will regulate the heat from a controlled location to better protect against large heating expenses.

- **Elevators** can be an additional expense. If the building you are considering has one, the cost of servicing it could be yours.

- **Maintenance** is the cost of maintaining the building and property. One way to determine the maintenance cost of a property is to use a percentage such as 5 percent of gross income. The rule of thumb for most appraisers is to subtract the cost of vacancy from the gross income before using a percentage of gross income to arrive at a maintenance cost. The logic is that you will not experience maintenance on a vacant unit. The reality, however, is that there is a great deal of maintenance when preparing a vacant unit for rent.

- **Vacancy** is the cost associated with the loss of money you will experience from your yearly gross rental due to a unit not being occupied. To think that you will not have a vacant unit from time to time is not realistic. You might never experience vacancy, but you should still plan accordingly. You will have to research your area to find the figure that relates to that area. Many town planners, another department in the town hall, keep statistics on vacancy for the area. You might also be able to get this information from a local rental agency, which might even be able to assist you in renting.

- **Nonpayment** is the cost associated with the loss of money you will experience due to an occupant not paying the rent. From time to time, this unfortunate circumstance will occur, and you will need to factor in this loss.

- **Management** can be a cost if you seek assistance from someone else to oversee the day-to-day operation of the property. You should contact a management company in the area and find out what its fees are. Remember that the management service might include maintenance to the property, and you will need to separate the cost and include it in your maintenance figure.

- **Supplies** are materials needed to operate the property, such as construction or maintenance supplies.

- **Rubbish** is a cost when the owner must remove it. If the town in which the property is located supplies rubbish removal, the cost is included in the tax column. If the town does not have removal services, however, the property may require a dumpster. Contact a garbage-removal service in the area for prices.

- **Advertisement** is the cost associated with advertising the property for rent. If you have a vacancy, you most likely will incur some advertising expenses. The traditional For Rent sign may not satisfy the vacancy, and you will be forced to advertise in a local newspaper. Contact the area newspapers for advertising prices.

- **Legal** is a cost associated with obtaining the services of a lawyer, usually during an eviction or civil action.

TIP

Some owners have learned how to do evictions *pro se,* or without the services of a lawyer, to help eliminate this cost. For now, you should still factor in legal as an expense. Plus, you might need a lawyer's expertise in some other business associated with the property. Contact a lawyer in the area to see what the cost is for eviction work. Sheriff or marshal fees, process server fees, and court filing fees should also be included in this category of expenses.

- **Accounting** is the cost related to the services you may require to help keep track of all the money you will make or to have an accountant fill out the Schedule E of your 1040 tax return.

- **Landscaping** is the cost associated with keeping the grounds of the property well groomed.

- **Other** is any other expense that may be associated with ownership of the property such as occupancy permits or rental permits required in some areas.

CAUTION

Companies that perform inspections normally charge a flat fee for this type of service.

THE WALK-THROUGH: INSPECTING PROPERTY

Before you purchase a property, it is important for you to walk through it and inspect it. Make sure the property meets the requirements that are important to this kind of investment. Check both the physical and the mechanical aspects of the property to be sure everything is in satisfactory condition. Certified inspection services that do inspections of property are also available for hire. These inspectors are usually quite thorough and are very good at explaining any problems they find as well as offering good advice as to how to fix them. If you hire an inspector, remember to get a copy of the written report and don't be afraid to ask questions. After all, they are the experts, and you are paying for their time!

It is a good idea before you inspect to make a list of the physical and mechanical features of the property. Always start in the basement or mechanical room of the property and work your way up. Look for water damage, rotting materials, or environmental hazards. Locating such defects before purchasing may help in negotiating the price and relieving future headaches. Be sure to make a checklist of the following:

- Heating system
- Electrical service boxes
- Electrical wires
- Foundation
- Pipes
- Paint
- Fixtures
- Water
- Insulation
- Roof

The inspection is important. Make sure the property is everything you hoped it would be before purchasing so that there are few surprises with your new investment.

Putting new knowledge to the test is always a challenge. With investments, smart landlords always turn potential expenses and income into real numbers.

30-Second Recap

- You're not a landlord unless you have a tenant.
- There are advantages to owning rental property besides income from rents.
- An owner-occupant rental owner lives at the property he or she rents. An absentee owner of rental property does not live at the property he or she rents.
- Management companies supply the service of operating the rental property for a fee.
- Long-term ownership is a much healthier way of conducting a rental business than short-term theory attempts.
- Real estate has many physical and economic characteristics that affect its value.
- Before you invest in rental real estate, research the many different types of real estate ownership available to you.
- With the help of professionals, careful research, and financial planning, you can help deter possible claims against you for liability and maybe help protect your personal assets.
- Price and affordability are determining factors for where to purchase, as is your living proximity to the property.
- Tracking the market for real estate sales and rental rates in a given area will help you determine whether an area is desirable and whether the investment is profitable.
- Distressed property can sometimes be purchased at a real bargain.
- Don't purchase a rental property for sentimental reasons; examine your reasons for purchasing a particular rental property very carefully.
- Decide what type of property (one-family, two-family, three-family, or more) to buy before looking.
- Detail all possible expenses before purchasing to help determine a good or bad investment.
- Inspect the building and grounds before purchase so you know exactly what to expect.

Some property owners have the best tenants imaginable: themselves! They operate retail stores housed in the very same buildings that they own. Our next section will help prepare you to become the next Wal-Mart.

The Retail Store

Today, opening a retail store usually means operating seven days a week. Most stores are open six days from about 10 A.M. to 9 P.M., and on Sundays from noon to 5 or 6 P.M. But that's just half the story. There's the buying, receiving, merchandise pricing, stocking, completing paperwork, staffing, maintaining displays, and cleaning that goes on behind the scenes. Should this discourage you? Hopefully not. You should be alerted to the fact that running a store is a full-time-plus commitment, not one to be taken lightly. This section acquaints you with the basic factors you need to consider to make an informed decision about whether a hobby-related retail store is right for you.

THE STORE

The most successful merchants are those who enjoy the challenges that come with the retail trade: learning about their customers, finding out how to meet customer needs, creating something and seeing it succeed, and building a presence in the community. Profit motivation is important, but is only a part of the larger picture. Let's look at what makes a retail store work.

THE MARGIN

In retailing, you know that if you've paid $1 for an item that you've sold for $2, you have a 50 percent margin. Half of the sale pays for the product, the other half must pay for all the other costs of operating your business—plus profit. Because store prices range from full price to many variations of discount prices, the margin of markup is usually figured at what percentage of markup a store requires to satisfy its pricing strategy.

The margin is calculated by dividing the original cost into the amount of markup and then multiplying the result by 100. The amount of money that a business adds into a product's price, over and above the cost of the product, is expressed as a percentage. A candle costing $.05 to produce that has a markup of $.10 (meaning that the price to the consumer is $.15) has a 200 percent markup.

Some retailers operate successfully with margins as high as 55 percent or as low as 25 percent. Full-service, higher-cost retailers tend to operate at the high end of the margin scale; self-service, discount retailers operate at the low end.

INVENTORY TURNS

The second basic is the turn of your inventory. For example, all of a product for sale at your store was purchased at a wholesale cost of $50,000. Your store has an overall margin of 50 percent, meaning that when all the inventory has sold, $100,000 has run through the cash register. This is one inventory turn. Therefore, at five inventory turns, $500,000 is rung up.

Why are turns so important? Because a higher turn keeps your cash flow moving. But don't forget that with five turns, the first $250,000 is cost—the cost of inventory. Then you have to deduct all the overhead, wages, and taxes from the $250,000 left before you'll see a profit. Most experts agree that a healthy annual turn figure begins at four, although some retailers aren't happy unless they hit eight or more. What an average, well-managed retail store can expect in sales is usually four to six times its inventory turn.

TIP

To open a store, you have to have financial resources. A lot of would-be entrepreneurs choose to operate a home-based business first and then, by building the profits steadily with the help of lower overhead, they can eventually make the move to a retail store.

Opening a retail store requires a sizable investment in start-up costs and inventory, plus a big advertising budget, particularly in the beginning to build customer traffic. The smaller your store is and the less inventory it has in stock, the less potential income you'll have. Most major retailers acknowledge that about 70 percent of their annual business is made during the fall through holiday buying season. Poor holiday season sales can wipe out a small retailer without sufficient backup cash reserves.

You can boost your inventory turn by dealing with suppliers that can replace stock quickly. This means that you can avoid having a large supply of product that just sits there in your warehouse. That's considered dead money; it's not working for you. This is why it can often be worth paying a slightly higher price to a vendor that keeps your stock flowing and turning, instead of getting a big discount on a large supply of a product that will sit in your warehouse for months or maybe years. Smart buyers at retail stores try to keep only enough stock to get them through about a month. By using speedy suppliers, they can do it, and keep those important inventory turns high.

TECHNOLOGY IS THE ANSWER

A point-of-sale (POS) system integrates your cash register with your inventory database. Every time stock arrives from your suppliers, it's entered in the database. Then every customer purchase is tracked, and the items sold are deleted automatically from the database. True, a learning curve comes with a POS, but the advantages of having one can far outweigh the challenges.

The major advantages, in brief, are ...

■ **Inventory management.** A POS system gives you instantaneous information about your turns, which products are selling well, and which ones need help to get them moving.

■ **Customer database.** You can create a valuable self-maintaining customer database that tells you which customers are buying what products and when. You have the ability at your fingertips to develop promotions that can be targeted to exactly the right customers at exactly the right time.

■ **Savings of time and money.** When a POS system is up and running, most of your routine inventory tasks become automated, freeing you up to concentrate on other important functions that will bring customers to your store.

LOCATION, LOCATION, LOCATION

What real estate agents say is true: There really isn't anything more important than location. It's particularly true when you're looking for a location for your retail business. A poor location can kill your business, even if you do everything else absolutely right; a great location and doing everything right gives you a big head start toward achieving success. There are two main factors to consider when you're choosing a location:

■ **Demographics.** Who are your target customers? Which neighborhoods are filled with these potential customers? Which commercial areas cater to upscale shoppers, and which are for the budget-minded? If your target is the upscale customer, your store needs to be situated with other upscale retailers, and the same applies to attracting the cost-conscious.

■ **Traffic flow.** Traffic flow is the heart of any business, so the answer is simple: An arts-and-crafts products store must be in a location with heavy foot traffic. Drive-by traffic is not as important and can sometimes even be a detriment; people don't like to have to get in and out of heavy traffic. If the location has a good, steady, walk-by traffic flow, as many as four of every five people who walk past your store could be potential customers.

THE SALES TEAM

After location, people are what make a store work. The success secret of retailing is showing, or teaching, the customer. Retailers must take responsibility to ensure that the customer will enjoy and will successfully use the products they buy. If they don't, you won't be able to build a solid repeat business.

Because of the long hours that retail stores are required to stay open, you'll have to plan on enough employees to cover all the hours effectively, and have enough people capable of offering classes to teach customers how to use the products you sell. This is an important factor in building a loyal repeat customer base.

Gone are the days of putting products on the shelf and letting the customer figure out how to use them creatively. This means that you and the staff you select must be knowledgeable, trained in the products and their uses, able to communicate effectively, committed to customer service, and, most of all, able to put themselves in the customers' place and bring enthusiasm and empathy to their dealings with customers.

Managing your staff can be one of the most challenging areas of your business. Make certain that your staff members know what they're aiming for. Set the pace for their success and for great customer service:

- Require that every customer is welcomed with an open-ended greeting, which is nothing more than a simple, "Good morning," or "Good afternoon," giving the customer a chance to respond openly and in kind. "May I help you?" is not an open-ended greeting because the customer almost always replies, "No thanks, I'm just browsing."

- When customers seek help, make it part of the sales staff's job to ask enough questions to find out exactly what they want to know, or to do, and help them do it. If a salesperson can't locate a specific item that a customer asks for, make it his or her job to do the research necessary to find a substitute product or an alternative solution.

- Mandate that the staff members treat every customer with the same respect that they themselves would expect as customers.

Time spent training staff is always time well spent. Your customers need a great deal of support as they develop their creative skills, so a high level of staff expertise and flexibility is critical to the success of your store.

WHY RETAIL ARTS-AND-CRAFTS PRODUCTS?

According to a survey commissioned by the Hobby Industry Association, 80 percent of all families in the United States have at least one family member who enjoys making arts and crafts. The people who enjoy arts and crafts make for a tremendous potential market for any retailer. It's a market that offers great diversity—from independent specialty stores that focus on one niche area, such as ceramics, beading, needle crafts, or woodworking, to large, multicategory retailers.

CAN RETAIL BE PROFITABLE?

Retail can be profitable if you can juggle an extraordinary set of skills: a love of dealing with the public, the courage of a lion, the insight of a teacher, and the vision of a psychic, not to mention a lot of financial smarts and hard work. In addition to your love and knowledge of hobbies, you'll find that you'll need to develop a sophisticated range of business skills and retailing know-how. Some tips for making your retail store profitable are …

- **Define your customer.** First, you must know everything possible about the people you're trying to attract.

- **Supply the right product mix.** After you understand the demographics and interests of your target customers, then decide on the image of the store. Will it be focused on entertainment and creativity, or efficiency and bargain pricing? It's equally important to know the trends in your area and the interests that your customers have outside of their hobbies. These factors will influence your target customers' lifestyles and interests.

- **Determine value.** New retailers often mistake low pricing for "value." Experienced retailers understand that "value" for the customer is a complex mix of factors, and pricing is only part of it. Value is what will keep customers coming back, repeatedly—for instance:

  - **Convenience.** Are you conveniently located? Do you make it easy to buy? Do you make it easy to return merchandise?

  - **The right product mix.** Do you have the products that match your customers' interests?

  - **Selection.** Are you well stocked? Do you have all the related products on the shelf that a customer may need for a project?

  - **Display.** Do you show off your products with exciting, tempting display techniques that say "Buy me"?

■ **Timing.** Do you offer new ideas as they happen and keep your product mix current with the ever-changing trends?

■ **Service.** Will you do whatever is necessary to make certain that the customer will be successful with the products you sell? Will you offer classes? Are you prepared to answer any question?

If you focus on the items on this list, customers will pay a higher price for the privilege of doing business with you. If you don't offer much in the way of presentation, selection, or service, you'll need to offer convenience and efficiency, and be prepared to sell at a lower price.

RESEARCHING THE PRODUCT MIX

No matter what else you do right, what keeps customers returning to an arts-and-crafts store is an irresistible dynamic product mix, plus the activities associated with the products. Your goal has to be finding out what your potential customers can't resist.

To gather information and ideas that will help you create the best possible product mix, follow these tips:

1. Check with local community groups.

2. Visit all the stores within your market area that are related to your niche. Evaluate what their merchandising plans are. Look for areas that they're not serving or that they serve in only a limited fashion. Compare what you observe to the research material that you gathered on your target customer to try to determine the kinds of products that may be needed and wanted in your market area.

3. Learn what products are everyday staples that your customers will expect to see on the shelf all the time.

4. Find out what gift trends are popular in your area.

5. Pay attention to other related markets. Look for opportunities for crossover applications. The more you know about other markets, the better equipped you'll be to identify potential crossover opportunities.

STORE LAYOUT AND DESIGN

Being a creative person, you probably don't have to be told just how much a visually exciting, colorful retail environment can do to capture your customers' attention, or how that translates into sales.

Retail store layout and design is a huge subject, which we can only touch on here.

How Color Affects Your Displays

Depending on your target customer for a particular activity, using one color scheme versus another can be the difference between a display that sells and one that's ignored. If you're targeting children, for instance, you'll want to use the primary reds, blues, and yellows. If you're targeting an upscale customer, you may want to use colors that send an elegant signal, perhaps regal purples, rich earth tones, or dignified blues. Color isn't the only criterion for great displays. Don't forget about adding texture, composition, and the proper lighting and signs.

- Warm colors, such as red, yellow, orange, and pink, impress the eye and enhance the appearance of most merchandise. To the eye, they move items forward in a display.
- Cool colors, such as blue and green, appear calm and soothing. To the eye, they enlarge the display area.
- America's favorite colors are blue, red, green, white, pink, purple, and orange.
- Certain colors affect our emotions. When considering colors for your display themes, signs, and backgrounds, keep the following in mind.
  - **Red.** Powerful, exciting, the attention-grabber. It appeals to the emotions. It's more difficult, however, for the brain to process, and it has a negative connotation when associated with money.
  - **Yellow.** A dynamic color. It's associated with happiness and sunshine. Too much of it can be testy, though, so yellow should be used in moderation.
  - **Blue.** Soothing, tranquil, and calming. It's associated with water and is considered conservative. Blue is one of the least exciting colors, but it's one of the most popular ones in the U.S. market.
  - **Green.** Puts people at ease and has a positive connotation associated with money, the ecology, and nature. It was the color for the 1990s. It makes people feel secure and more creative.
  - **Orange.** Communicates informality and unisex style. It quickly catches the eye, so it works to call attention to something you want people to notice.

ARRANGING MERCHANDISE

Displaying your merchandise in a store is not as difficult as it may seem because there is a standard formula to follow. And what makes it easier is that it works for all types of products. The basic strategies for arranging merchandise are ...

- **In a vertical presentation.** Light down to dark, small down to large, warm down to cool

- **In a horizontal presentation.** From left to right, light to dark, warm to cool, small to large

TIP

Few people can walk past a mirror without "sneaking a peek," so include mirrors in your displays—behind a product or under a product—and you're guaranteed to stop traffic.

If you follow this basic formula, you'll be able to plan your merchandise layout in a logical and eye-pleasing manner.

STORE TRAFFIC FLOW

The placement of your shelving and display units will play a powerful role in determining what may or may not happen in your store. Rather than just using straight aisles, consider diagonal placements of display units and circular directions for traffic flow. This traffic flow circulates customers in subtle patterns that may lead them to discover areas of the store they may not have seen if the store had traditional straight aisles, predictably stocked.

With these ideas in mind, go shopping in a variety of stores, large and small. Pay attention to how they make use of color, texture, traffic patterns, displays, signs, and other things to project their image and boost sales. Store design is a profession in its own right. It may be worth the investment to hire a store design consultant to help you create an effective ambience that will translate into sales and repeat customers.

ADVERTISING AND PROMOTION

Advertising is essential to your survival. How else will the public know that you exist? Most retailers budget between 3 and 5 percent for advertising and marketing. A Yellow Pages ad is important. Beyond that, different retail markets usually require different methods of reaching potential customers.

Many successful retailers swear by direct mail and newsletters; others find that newspaper and radio advertising pays, whereas still others rely on cable television to reach their target audience.

OFFER CLASSES AND TRAINING

The majority of consumers who take classes make most of their purchases at the store where the class is offered. There's no question that seminars, workshops, and ongoing classes are proven business builders. They bring regular customers and new ones into the store and introduce people to new projects and products. A well-run activities and education program will help build your bottom line.

TARGETED PROMOTIONS

Attention-getting events are very effective. You could have a T-shirt or sweatshirt painting event, a family scrapbook night, a floral arranging event for every season, or an ornament-making contest, or you could even let your customers participate in creating the event. Have a suggestion box, and reward customers whose ideas are used with free supplies. Manufacturers will often help by providing a representative to meet with customers and put on demonstrations.

STAYING ON TOP

Becoming successful is just the beginning. Staying successful is the ongoing challenge. The arts-and-crafts industry is an ever-changing market. It's more important than ever that retailers stay current on trends and new products while watching for opportunities that may be just around the next corner. There's no secret to staying current other than to constantly be doing your market research. Spend time tracking your customers' interests, and survey them regularly to stay on top of any changes that may be in the wind.

TIP

Many very successful merchants will tell you that the most valuable information they get each year comes from sitting down and swapping ideas with noncompetitive peers at the trade shows.

ATTEND TRADE SHOWS

Where else but at a trade show can you find such a concentration of products and retail know-how? Most trade shows offer retailing seminars and training programs to boost your store's success—and don't forget the big benefits of networking and meeting new contacts to help you build your business. Sharing information and ideas can make or break your business.

Manufacturers and distributors clearly understand that if you're successful, they will be, too. Many vendors offer assistance and support for their customers.

As you can see, if you're thinking about opening a retail store, there's a lot to consider, and a lot of research to do before—and after—you take the plunge.

30-SECOND RECAP

- Margin and inventory turns are ways to determine the financial success of a retail store.
- Retail stores should be located close to the target customers' neighborhoods.
- Your product mix needs to satisfy the interests of your customers.
- The staff and educational programs you offer build good community relations and are key to the success of a retail hobby and arts and crafts store.

If you don't like the idea of selling products, you can always sell your knowledge. Many people become independent consultants and build a business around their own expertise. Our next section explores the ins and outs of the consulting profession.

The What, Who, and Why of a Mysterious Profession

If you were asked what a police officer does, you'd be able to give a coherent, informed answer. It's the same with other occupations, whether accountant, doctor, or janitor. Explaining what each of these occupations entails would be pretty easy. Not so with consulting. When someone says, "I'm a consultant," strange things happen. Tell an inquiring and sociable partygoer that you are a consultant and you're likely to see a look of puzzlement, usually followed by the question, "Yes, but what do you really do?"

The reality is that the word consultant *can mean almost anything. If you want to be a consultant (or if you are one already), you must be clear about the various meanings of the word, and what it means to be part of the consulting profession. That's what this section is about.*

What Is Consulting—What's in a Name?

What's in the name *consulting?* Not much, really. One consultant offers advice to high-powered executives of major companies, charges large fees, and does very little but advise. That person is known as a management consultant. Another offers help in redecorating houses and receives a much smaller fee. That person might be called an interior design consultant. An Internet web-design consultant might advise clients about how to create a top-quality website, and actually build that site for the client.

The range of fields in which you can specialize is huge. The services you offer are limited only by your imagination and what clients will pay for.

TIP

Whether you want to consult, or whether you are already working as a consultant, it's absolutely critical that you understand what your job entails—the roles you are expected to take on, your responsibilities, and your function.

Even though an exact definition of consulting is difficult to give, here is one that has worked well. *Consulting* is a process undertaken by a disinterested party with significant expertise and experience, and involves offering advice and problem solving to the client or customer using a well-defined consulting process.

Let's take a closer look at this definition, keeping in mind that a general definition of this type will be a bit vague.

First, what's a "disinterested party"? It's simple. A consultant (or disinterested party) is someone who has no vested interest in exactly how the client's problem is solved. Typically, the consultant is from outside the organization or the client's world and provides an objective approach to the client's problem.

This objectivity is very important and touches on the value of a consultant to the client. As a consultant, you will be expected to provide one or more of the following:

- A fresh look at the situation
- An unbiased view of the situation
- An innovative way to approach the problem

Second, what do "significant expertise and experience" involve? Anyone can call himself or herself a consultant, but that doesn't make the person one. A consultant brings to the client a significant body of skills, or *expertise,* in the field in which he or she works. And generally, the consultant also has a deep and broad range of experience related to the needs of the client.

For example, an Internet website consultant would need expertise in a number of areas. These might include knowledge about sound graphic design, ability to use web-development tools, and a broad understanding of how websites can contribute to business success for the client. And that's just scratching the surface.

In addition, a client would expect an Internet website consultant to have designed and implemented successful websites. That's the experience part.

In short, as a consultant you need to have enough expertise and experience to identify the client's problem and solve it, while at the same time inspiring confidence on the part of your client.

What Do Consultants Really Do?

Someone once characterized consultants as follows: "A consultant is like a seagull. He flies in, buzzes around crapping all over the place, then flies out leaving a royal mess in his wake."

Consultants may work as small business owners in that they work on their own or with associates. They may also work as regular employees for small or large consulting firms. This section focuses on consultants as small business owners.

Strictly speaking, that humorous definition would be fairly accurate, except one would hope that, upon flying out, the consultant would leave less mess than when he arrived.

Traditionally, consultants have been advice givers and not doers. But that view is a little too restrictive for us. Let's look at the different roles consultants can choose.

Consultants Who Advise

The advisory role is probably the classic one for consultants. Generally, a consultant is retained to achieve some goal the client wants to reach; that goal may be specific and defined up front, or it may be much more vague, requiring investigation and refinement.

For consultants who work solely in advisory mode, their involvement ends when they present their recommendation. That's it. They're done.

Here's an example. A government is considering whether it should build a new bridge to improve traffic patterns in the city. Not being traffic engineers, the politicians are obviously not able to assess the total impact of such a bridge. Neither do they and their employees have sufficient experience in building bridges to know whether building the bridge is a wise decision.

The solution, of course, is to hire a consultant to conduct a feasibility study. In this case the government contracts with an engineering consulting firm that is independent and has experience and expertise with bridges. The firm's mandate and goals are clear: to determine whether the bridge is cost-effective and worthwhile to build.

As far as the consulting firm is concerned, after the report and recommendations are presented to the client, the job is done. The firm doesn't actually build the bridge. If it's done its job well, it will have provided the government with the information and analysis necessary to make an informed decision.

TIP

There is no need to limit yourself to advising only, or doing only. Your role will depend on your skills and abilities. Whether you advise, do, or both, you must acquire whatever skills are needed to complete the task with a high level of expertise.

Most governments offer assistance in developing business plans for small businesses because new business helps support the community's growth. If you are thinking of starting a consulting business, find out what kinds of free services are available to you from government organizations.

In the bridge-building case the job is advisory, but let's look at another example—one closer to home. Let's say you are thinking about starting a consulting business. You think there is a market for the particular service you could provide, but you've never planned or actually run a business before. So you look for someone with expertise and experience in small business planning who can offer an unbiased and independent perspective.

You might hire an independent consultant to work with you to prepare a business and marketing plan. You might have specific questions you need answered; for example:

- Is there a market for my services?
- What services make sense to offer?
- How can I best market my consulting business?

In short, you want a professional business plan to guide you in building your new business.

The consultant you hire will answer your questions and help you develop a business plan to start and build your business. This person isn't going to run the business. He or she functions as an advisor to you. In some cases you might look to the consultant for ongoing advice, but generally, once the business plan is completed, the consultant will not be involved in the day-to-day decisions you must make as a businessperson.

CONSULTANTS WHO ADVISE AND DO

While the "pure" consulting role may be one of providing advice, the reality is that restricting yourself to advice giving may not be a good thing to do. Much depends on the field you work in. Sometimes it makes sense to both plan and advise, and then actually carry out the plan. Providing the work yourself may be more efficient for the client.

Let's look at some examples. Suppose you want a website related to your business. You have no web-development experience or skills, and except for some casual web surfing you don't know much about how it all works. Nor do you really want to invest the time in learning to develop the site yourself. So you find an individual who will advise you on the hows, whys, and wherefores of building and running a website. Part of what you want from your consultant is a sample of what your finished website will look like.

After that phase of the consulting process is complete, you have a much better idea of what your website can accomplish, where it can be hosted, and a lot of other critical information. But (and it's a big but), you still lack the skills to actually build and run the thing. As the client you have two options: Retain the original consultant to build and maintain the site for you, or hire someone new to build it consistent with the recommendations you received from the original consultant.

Which makes more sense? In this case (and in many others), it makes more sense to stay with the original consultant and have that person actually do it. After all, he or she developed the look, the feel, and the philosophy behind your site.

The point here is that "advising and doing" are often in the client's best interest. The one drawback is that there is some loss of objectivity on the consultant's part, because his or her initial recommendations can be tainted by the possibility of future work with the client.

Let's consider this job from the consultant's viewpoint. What are the advantages of "advice + doing"? First, there's a bigger money pot. The consultant gets paid for the advising and for the doing. Second, it's far more satisfying to be in at the start of a project, when you can plan it and then see it through to the results stage.

CAUTION

One of the worst things a consultant can do is claim to have sufficient skills to accomplish something when he or she does not. Learning on the job does a disservice to yourself and to the client.

There is something very important to consider here. You may have sufficient skills to advise on something but not sufficient skills to implement that advice. For example, if you are a graphic designer, you may be able to map out a "look" for a website but have no skills in coding to make that website come into existence. Likewise, you may be sensational at marketing strategy but lack the skills to implement that strategy on the Internet. There are ways around this deficiency—for example, subcontracting—but nevertheless it's an issue you need to be aware of.

Consultants Who Do

I've included consultants who "do" more to clarify an aspect of consulting rather than to suggest that you be "only a doer."

TIP

Here's something you probably haven't thought about. Consulting involves identifying client needs and figuring out how to meet those needs. Almost any job can include a consulting component, even if the job is focused on "doing." Consulting principles have even been applied to sales jobs. The term *consultative selling* means incorporating consulting principles into selling almost anything.

No matter what specific services or products you offer, using consulting principles and processes will increase the value of what you provide to clients. If you recognize this fact, you can treat everything you do as a consulting process. By clarifying customer needs and then, and only then, delivering solutions, you create higher levels of customer satisfaction.

Bottom line: Without including the consulting process in the project, there are very few situations in which you can just "do" while still pleasing your customer.

MONEY TREE?

Now that you know what consulting is, let's get to what you're probably really interested in—the money. What's the most common myth about consultants? Despite popular belief, most consultants aren't rich, and neither do most consultants charge the fees bandied about by those outside the industry. Yes, there are consultants who can charge $3,000 a day. But for every one of those, 20 or 30 other consultants are receiving fees in the $300-a-day range.

Think about it in terms of movie actors. For every Tom Cruise or Harrison Ford, who can command multimillion dollar fees for movies, hundreds of other actors are working for peanuts, hoping for a break—or, worse, waiting tables or standing in the unemployment line.

TIP

Realistic financial expectations are important for any new or growing business. Just because some consultants earn huge sums of money, don't count on being one of them. If you count on being a "consulting star" and this doesn't come to pass, you may end up bankrupt. Keep your financial expectations reasonable and on the low side.

Has the bubble burst for you? Good. Because there is no point in thinking about being a consultant unless you have a realistic and clear set of expectations about what you can expect to earn. Hopefully, you'll eventually command large fees. Just be prepared to struggle, at least for the first few years. Be prepared for the possibility that you can't "make it" financially as a consultant. Hope to make a comfortable living if you can cut it. Anything beyond that, consider it gravy.

SOME GOOD NEWS

If your hopes of millionairehood have been dashed, hold on a minute. There is some good news. Ready? The consulting sector is booming! Some have estimated that the consulting sector is growing globally at a rate of 16 percent a year. That figure may be a bit overly optimistic because it applies primarily to the consulting market with respect to services rendered to other businesses. Consulting to individuals (for example, decorating or fitness) will grow only as individuals have money to spend.

Consulting to business will continue to grow, provided that consultants offer services that are cost-effective and meet the needs of clients better than other alternatives.

There are a number of reasons for the boom, many of which have to do with the shifting economics of doing business. Hiring consultants to do the work has a built-in degree of efficiency and cost savings. No benefits are paid. A consultant can be hired without committing to long-term expenditures, whereas hiring a full-time employee involves an outlay for benefits. And companies often need help that is simply not available within the company, or perhaps is not worth keeping within the company on a permanent basis.

THE BAD NEWS

By now you may be thinking that reading this discussion of the financial side of consulting is like riding a roller coaster. Bad news, good news, and more bad news. Life's like that. Okay, here's the bad news. Although the consulting market is growing (more customers), tons more people are working in the consulting field. It's a heavily competitive business, not only in terms of fees charged, but also in terms of visibility, reputation, and skill.

It's likely that whatever field you choose as your specialization, there will already be a number of established consultants trying to do almost the identical work. A few of those will be direct competitors if they are geographically close to you, and there will be other competitors who aren't even in your geographic area.

The bottom line on earnings? You just might make it. Not only might you make it, but you might make it big. Or you might end up writing a book. But be prepared. This isn't a get-rich-quick profession, and for many, it may not even be a get-rich-slow profession.

WHY DO PEOPLE HIRE CONSULTANTS?

Knowing the reasons why people hire consultants is important. As a consultant, or for that matter as any small business owner, you need to understand your potential clients or customers. After all, if you don't have a clue as to why anyone would pay you for your expertise, then how can you define what you do? How can you market your abilities? You can't. So here are the major reasons why people hire consultants.

OBJECTIVITY

Some situations, particularly when they occur in large organizations or organizations somewhat political in nature, are best addressed by someone from outside the organization—someone who has no apparent bias and can be trusted to provide independent advice.

Let's consider an example. Acme Incorporated is facing an economic crunch. Its revenues are down and expenses up, and it needs to do something to remedy the situation or it will go under. The management of Acme has some ideas about what they should be doing to turn the company around, but they disagree about how to do it. They decide to hire an independent and expert consultant to come in, diagnose the present state of the company, and suggest actions the company can take.

TIP

It is critical that consultants take any steps they can to ensure their independence and an unbiased approach. The reason is simple: trust. Clients must be able to trust the advice of the consultant.

Let's assume that the consultant suggests a number of actions. One of those suggestions involves laying off 15 percent of the staff, a controversial and painful process in any company. Now here's the advantage of using a consultant. Because the recommendation comes from an independent and unbiased individual, it somewhat insulates management from accusations of bias. Also, the use of an independent consultant may make it easier to get all of senior management to support what will be a painful decision.

Here's a simpler example. Husband and wife want to redecorate their home. They disagree on a number of issues. Rather than struggle with those issues, they hire an interior decorating consultant to make some suggestions and draw up sketches. That way, they'll have an objective opinion to draw upon.

FRESH VIEWPOINT

It's very easy for people to get stuck thinking about things in the same old ways. This happens to everyone. Consultants are thus often hired to offer a fresh viewpoint. Coming from outside the situation, it's likely that the consultant's perceptions will provide a new way of looking at the problem. This input helps companies innovate and come up with new ideas to solve old problems.

LACK OF IN-HOUSE EXPERTISE

One very obvious reason why people hire consultants is that the person hiring lacks the knowledge, skills, and experience needed to solve a set of problems and is not interested or able to learn those skills. The obvious solution is to seek out someone who already has those abilities.

TIP

Understanding why clients might hire you (and what they hope to gain) is absolutely critical if you are to market yourself effectively. Prove that you can deliver what the client needs, and you'll get the contract.

COST-EFFECTIVENESS

Despite some of the jokes about consultants and alleged huge fees collected by consultants, clients hire a consultant with the idea that the consultant will "add more value" than the cost incurred. In other words, it may be cheaper to hire someone outside than to address problems in other ways.

COMPLETELY LOST

Sometimes you will encounter clients who are completely lost. They know they need "something better" than what they have, but they don't know what that "something" is and they don't really know what "better" should mean. So, being completely lost, they look for a consultant to lead them out of the wilderness. By the way, these are the toughest consulting situations, but also the most rewarding if you succeed.

EXPERT CREDIBILITY

Consultants are occasionally hired because advice coming from an outside expert tends to be treated with more respect than the same advice provided from within a company. If you think about it, this preference is rather silly, but it's a reality you can benefit from if you develop a track record as an expert or if your company has a high-profile reputation in the community in which you work.

It is possible that you might be hired as an expert who will confirm your client's course of action. Your confirmation validates the existing ideas of the person hiring you. This is fine except when those ideas are really bad ones.

Beware of feeling pressured to provide that expert validation when your judgment says you should go in another direction.

How Do Consultants Spend Their Time?

Exactly how do consultants spend their time? An independent consultant (someone who owns the business in a one-person shop) is going to spend a major portion of his or her time hunting for business and dealing with prospective clients. In other words, this person is going to be marketing himself or herself.

Marketing means developing promotional material, calling prospective clients, taking part in associations where prospective clients may be found, networking, and so on.

Expect that during the first few years of running a consulting practice you will spend a good amount of your time in overhead activities. These are activities that take up time, don't actually get you paid, but must be done.

The idea is that this *overhead time* will diminish and your *billable time* will increase. Billable time refers to the time for which you get paid (even if you aren't charging by the hour). It's what puts bread on the table. No billable time? No money. No money? No business, and it's back to finding a "real" job.

PLAIN ENGLISH

Overhead time refers to the time you spend that is not directly compensated for by the client. It includes marketing, client meetings, and paperwork (like making sure your taxes are in order). **Billable time** refers to the time for which you will be directly compensated and is the financial bedrock of your practice.

Let's talk about that billable time. What kinds of things might you expect to get paid for, keeping in mind that the field in which you consult will determine where your time goes?

Your billable time includes activities you undertake to meet the goals set out in the consulting agreement. It might involve client meetings, data collection, and meeting with other members of the client's organization. It will also involve reporting your advice and opinions in written and/or oral form. Above all, though (and surprisingly), you are really paid to think and to draw on your expertise. Always keep this in mind.

As a final comment on the subject of time, if you dream of a job in which you get to do really neat stuff and don't have to do all the junk jobs you hate (like paperwork, selling, and so on), beginning a consulting business is not the way to go. It's not very romantic, and you are going to work harder for yourself than you would ever work as a salaried person for an employer.

MORE ABOUT THE MARKET, MORE ABOUT THE BUSINESS

Despite being told that you're unlikely to make a fortune as a consultant, some of you are still reading this book. That shows stick-to-itiveness and a number of other prime qualities that will stand you in good stead when you practice as a consultant. For those of you who have given up, good luck. You wouldn't have made it anyway.

Because you're hanging in here, you're interested in learning about who might pay you to consult (your possible markets) and the various fields in which you can consult. Knowing the possible markets and deciding on your consulting areas are very important considerations, because the first steps in entering the consulting profession involve deciding where your expertise lies, what kinds of things people will actually pay you to do, and who might pay you to do these things.

Let's begin with an overview of the major consulting markets, examining the pros and cons of each of them. Each market is discussed in more detail, including the kinds of services you might offer there. It's not possible to exhaust all the possibilities, but the idea is to stimulate your thinking about your skills and abilities, and how you might be able to sell them.

TIP

The consulting markets you choose to target for your practice will depend on your particular expertise, the marketplaces in your locale, and your familiarity with each sector.

FOUR MAJOR CONSULTING MARKETS

The consulting market can be divided into four primary areas, or sectors. Each sector operates somewhat differently from the others. For example, getting hired by a government is quite different from getting hired by an individual. Working with small business requires a different perspective than working with a government agency does. There are also advantages and disadvantages associated with the various sectors.

GOVERNMENT

If you are familiar with the government context, you already know that delivery of consulting services to government should be a prime focus of your business. Here are the reasons why:

■ No matter where you live, you will have governments and potential government clients.

- Governments often "outsource," or hire consultants on both short- and long-term assignments.
- Government contracts can be very lucrative (but not always).
- Finding decision makers is easier than in other sectors because listings of government staff and management are available to the public. This fact makes marketing easier.
- If you establish a reputation as an expert in government issues and environment, word of mouth becomes very helpful.

A couple of cautions. There is a perception that governments squander money and that government is a gravy train for consultants. That may be true in some cases, but it is mostly incorrect. Don't target government markets simply because you believe they're an easy ride. They aren't.

Consider also that you should have experience working in government if you want to succeed in the government market. Governmental decision makers believe (and rightly so) that the government context is different from other contexts, and they will usually ask you about your experience in working with and helping governments. If you don't have any, your credibility drops. That means not getting hired.

When considering the government market, take a look at all levels and facets of the sector. It's bigger than you might think. Look at all organizations funded in whole or in part by government funds. These include …

- City and town governments.
- State and provincial governments.
- Federal governments.
- *Arm's-length government* organizations.
- Educational organizations.

PLAIN ENGLISH

An **arm's-length government** organization is one that is primarily or partly funded by tax dollars but is outside the government system. Arm's-length organizations often have a board of directors and their own management structure.

Rather than thinking about governments in a traditional narrow way, think about this potential market in a broad way: Any organization that is funded in whole or in part with taxpayers' dollars falls under the government umbrella.

LARGE BUSINESSES

Large businesses and corporations can be lucrative sources for consulting contracts. In this category are multinational companies and other companies that most of us would consider huge in revenue and employee numbers.

TIP

When you are starting your business, consider contracts (large business and government) that are smaller in monetary value. The larger contracts are difficult to get until you have an established track record. Don't be afraid to start small.

Do these organizations hire consultants from outside? Yes, indeed. And contracts with large corporations can be quite large.

As with government, the more experience you have with respect to large corporations and how they work, the better placed you will be to grab contracts. And if you understand the specific industry of the potential customer, that's an immediate plus.

You should know that in both government and large business sectors, competition for the larger contracts is often fierce.

SMALL BUSINESSES

Small businesses constitute a large sector of the consulting market. Small businesses are defined as ranging from one or two people (just like you) up to hundreds of employees.

Did you know that small businesses are considered the backbone of our economy? This market includes literally millions of potential clients. What's interesting is that many small businesses that could benefit from consulting services don't realize their own needs and are less likely to know where to get help.

Although specializing in consulting work for small business has some advantages—primarily stemming from less competition for contracts—the marketing costs to reach small business decision makers can be higher. Contracts will generally be smaller, depending on the size and resources of the small business customer.

If you already have a reputation within the small business community in your area, this may well be a good place to start your consulting business.

INDIVIDUALS

The last sector of the consulting market is perhaps the most challenging: that of individuals. Just plain folks like yourself. Typically, you'd provide some form of personal service to people in need of that service. For example, a personal fitness trainer consults with individuals to tailor a fitness program for the customer, and may also supervise workouts. An investment consultant works with individuals to develop a financial or retirement plan and to provide advice.

Consulting to individuals is like retailing in that you work with a number of individuals, whereas in consulting to large corporations you work with a smaller number of customers. However, consulting to individuals means you need to have a larger number of customers, because your fees and contracts are going to be much smaller.

Therefore, unless you are well established in marketing to individuals, much of your time will be spent in continual marketing, and word of mouth can be helpful in this sector.

DIFFERENCES AMONG THE FOUR SECTORS

To help you understand your potential clients, the following table sums up some important differences among the four consulting sectors. The upcoming discussions further expand these differences, detailing issues like marketing and the pros and cons of each sector.

Differences Among Consulting Sectors

	Government	Corporate	Small Business	Individuals
Red tape level	Usually high	Also can be high	Low	None
Contract size	From low to high	From low to high	From moderate to low	Low
Difficult to get paid?	No	No	Higher chance of problems	Higher chance of problems
Moves quickly	Decisions and projects move slowly	Tend to be slow, but often faster than government	The smaller the business, the faster it tends to move	Fast—get the agreement done and get to work
Ease of contacting decision makers	Very easy	Difficult	Difficult	Depends on marketing

continues

Differences Among Consulting Sectors *continued*

	Government	Corporate	Small Business	Individuals
Requires formal proposals?	Often yes and may be extensive	Often yes and may be extensive	Unlikely, and may be shorter	Not usually
Formal qualifications a factor? (e.g., important academic degrees)	Possibly	Possibly	Less important	Not usually

GOVERNMENT CONTRACTS

What's it like to provide services to governments and other publicly funded organizations? Well, it can be lucrative and it can be exceedingly frustrating. Here's why.

Consulting to government is unique in almost every respect. Don't assume you have an understanding of government processes simply by virtue of being a citizen. To succeed in government consulting, you have to understand government from the inside. When dealing with government staff, listen and learn; make sure you understand any specific constraints and requirements associated with working with your government clients.

Because governments have a responsibility to ensure that the public's money is spent effectively (hard to believe, but it's true), the process of getting a government organization to make decisions or sign a contract can be lengthy and annoying. For example, any specific potential project may require getting the approval of a large number of decision makers—a process that slows things down. It also means that your "done deal" consulting arrangement can be shot down by any one of the decision makers involved.

There's another thing you should know. Governments need to be seen as awarding contracts in a fair way. Hence they use a process called *tendering*. This means you may be asked to write a tender, or detailed proposal, and compete with other consulting vendors. Proposals and tenders are often tedious to develop, and carry no guarantee of getting the job.

PLAIN ENGLISH

Large government contracts are awarded through the **tender** process. This involves submitting information (as requested by the client), such as price and basic project details.

Luckily, small projects often do not involve tendering. Most government organizations have a money figure that serves as a cutoff for the tendering process. If the money figure is under the cutoff point, you don't need to do complex tendering. Over that amount, and you will be required to do so. The exact cutoff point will vary from organization to organization, but the important thing to remember is that it is a whole lot easier to get small government contracts than large ones.

GETTING GOVERNMENT CONTRACTS

There are two basic ways to obtain government contracts. The first is through a *request for proposal,* often abbreviated as *RFP.*

Most governments publish requests for proposals for specific projects. Generally, the RFP contains basic information and explains the format in which to submit your proposal; this format must be followed exactly. You then submit your proposal and wait until a decision has been made, or until you are asked to present your proposal to decision makers in person. The proposal tends to be long and drawn out. Sometimes no one is hired if budgets change or political factors intervene. The second way to obtain government contracts is less formal, involving much more face-to-face contact. These are called *relationship-based contracts.* Contracts received this way tend to be smaller in value.

Typically, in relationship-based contracting, you'd market to individual decision makers in government organizations, and you would develop more personal relationships with those people. For example, if you were in the human resources consulting business, you'd want to build relationships with the human resources department managers or executives.

In relationship-based contracting, you receive the contract because you …

- Are in the right place at the right time.
- Have created confidence in your abilities over time.
- Are the first to come to mind when a need arises.

Here is the fundamental difference between formal approaches, such as RFPs, and relationship-based contracting. With formal processes your first contact with the customer is through a paper process, and the decision to hire you is slow and delayed. With relationship-based contracts, the decision to hire you often has already been made (at least tentatively) from the time a potential client contacts you about a possible project.

GOVERNMENT MARKETING ISSUES

One of the most challenging tasks for any consultant involves finding and communicating with the people who have the power to hire. How do you find the right people to talk to in any organization?

Finding the decision makers becomes much less of an issue with government, and the reason is simple. Government organizations generally list their employees, managers, and decision makers in directories (both on paper and on the Internet). Directories are available to the public; not only are names listed, but job titles also. To someone familiar with government and how decisions are made, it's a simple matter to identify the key decision makers and contact them to begin creating a positive profile.

HELPFUL QUALIFICATIONS TO HAVE FOR GOVERNMENT CONTRACTS

Ae there any special qualifications needed to consult with government organizatrions? It's hard to generalize, but the following qualifications are good to have:

- An understanding of how government works
- A previous track record working with government
- A university degree or professional certification
- A reputation as an expert on government *and* an expert in the area of practice you specialize in

PROS AND CONS OF GOVERNMENT CONTRACTS

Here are a few of the positives about working with the government:

- You'll get paid. You don't have to worry about deadbeat governments.
- There's a possibility of large contracts that can sustain you for a long time.
- Access to government officials (potential clients) is relatively easy.
- Once you develop a profile as an expert who serves government, word of mouth makes marketing easier.

And of course, here are a few of the negatives you'll encounter in the government environment:

- Approvals are typically slow.
- Payments are slow. (You'll get it, but it takes a while.)
- Doing business with government clients often requires large volumes of paperwork.

LARGE BUSINESSES (CORPORATION) CONTRACTS

Of the four major consulting sectors, businesses that fall into the "large business" sector are probably the most difficult to characterize or describe. They can be all over the board in terms of who and how they hire. Often they resemble government organizations in that they may be inflexible and slow to react, but there are many exceptions to this.

The major difference between working with governments compared with large businesses is that governments rarely, if ever, violate their own rules regarding hiring consultants. Large businesses, on the other hand, make their own rules, and they can alter them or make exceptions. It's easier to negotiate with large businesses for this reason. Don't assume that client rules are etched in stone.

Although large businesses may need to comply with some regulations regarding who and how they hire consultants, they can generally make up their own rules. Hence, you will find companies that will hire on the basis of the say-so of a single decision maker, as well as companies that must have a large number of people involved in hiring. Some large businesses may require formal proposals and client meetings before contracting, whereas others may not. Some may need or want fancy contracts, and others may work on a handshake basis, very informally.

A definite advantage of consulting for corporations is that they have the resources to contract with you at a rate higher than you might receive working for small businesses or individuals. If you work for a large corporation, and provided everything goes as planned, you will likely get paid without having to chase your money.

GETTING CORPORATE CONTRACTS

Because corporations make their own rules about how they hire consultants, you will find both formal and informal processes for hiring. Some corporations are easy to deal with. Others will be more like government bureaucracies.

In general, personal relationships become more important as organizations give more flexibility and authority to their individual decision makers (managers and executives). Even in the corporate world, a good percentage of consulting contracts are awarded because the consultant keeps his or her name and expertise in the minds (and hearts) of prospective clients.

It's not unheard of for a consulting project to emerge out of casual conversation between a potential client and a consultant, and for that project to end up in a request for proposal written specifically for the consultant involved in that discussion. When this happens, you want to be "that consultant," because you'll have the inside track.

CORPORATE MARKETING ISSUES

Dealing with large corporations involves a major marketing challenge. Unlike government organizations, which publish directories that make it relatively easy to identify key decision makers, corporations don't do that. You probably won't have access to the corporate executive and management directories, because they aren't available to outsiders.

In marketing to government, it's rather easy to send out 1,000 promotional letters and brochures targeted to government decision makers. It isn't so easy to do so for corporate organizations. Often the only way you can figure out who you need to contact at a potential corporation is to call and ask. Even that's no guarantee, because you have to ask the right questions of the right people—not an easy feat.

TIP

Don't assume that because you have made one contact with a potential customer, you have marketed to them. You haven't. Marketing requires consistent contact over time to develop a positive reputation and profile with prospective clients.

There's a balancing force, however. Corporate decision makers tend to join professional organizations more often than their government counterparts do. For example, you aren't likely to find government personnel actively involved in the local chamber of commerce, but you will almost certainly find corporate representation there. Or, for example, if you provide financial services, you are more likely to find corporate decision makers at financial association gatherings than you are to find government financial personnel. Thus, you'll find that networking through associations (wherever corporate businesspeople gather to learn or socialize) becomes very important for this sector.

Advertising in trade publications may also work well for corporations, because decision makers may be more likely to read trade material and pay attention to ads in those publications.

HELPFUL QUALIFICATIONS TO HAVE FOR CORPORATE CONTRACTS

Are there special qualifications necessary for corporate contracting? It's hard to generalize on this one. Corporations are usually more likely to hire you if you have a background in and demonstrated experience working in their business area. Are they a lot more likely to hire based on that background? Probably not. Certainly it's less important in this sector than in the government sector. For example, suppose you are a human resources consultant who works with companies to help them hire the best new employees. Provided you are expert in that particular area, you can offer the same service to an insurance company or a manufacturing company. The actual business doesn't matter much.

Are academic degrees or professional certifications good to have? Yes, but they are likely going to weigh less in the decision to hire you than they would in the government sphere. If you have them, you put yourself one step ahead of those who don't.

Bottom line: You need to know your stuff and prove to your potential client that you can do the job the client needs.

Pros and Cons of Corporate Contracts

A few of the positives related to working with larger companies and corporations are …

- You'll likely get paid without having to dun deadbeat clients.
- The possibility of large contracts is enticing. You need score only a few major contracts to live.
- Although you can't count on corporations being more flexible than governments in their consultant hiring processes, they often are.

And what about the negatives? There aren't a lot of negatives here, although the situation is affected by whether the particular client is flexible or is bound by rule after rule:

- There is a potential for some corporations to be slow moving, particularly if they are bureaucratic and highly controlled by executives at the top.
- Competition is heavy.

Small Business Contracts

There are literally millions of small businesses, ranging from small mom-and-pop outfits to companies that employ 100 or 200 people. And of course the range of business types is huge. No matter if you are in a city the size of New York or a very small town, small businesses will be there, which means a significant local market for your services.

The huge size of the small business market seems to make it a prime focus for consultants—a market of considerable value. It may also be the case that this market is one of the more underdeveloped sectors and is overlooked by consultants.

Definitely consider this market, but pay special attention to the marketing needs and the challenges of small business contracts.

GETTING SMALL BUSINESS CONTRACTS

Getting a small business contract is, in fact, the chief challenge of this sector. Small-business consulting contracts tend to be small because of the relatively limited resources that small businesses have. Of course, this factor depends on the size of the client company. The mom-and-pop store may be in dire need of marketing or personnel help from consultants but probably won't have the money to pay a consultant any significant fee.

At the larger end of the small business spectrum, resources may be less of a concern. A company with 100 employees is going to be able to contract for services over a longer time and for a more lucrative fee level.

TIP

How can you contact small business owners? Apart from carrying out the usual advertising and marketing approaches, become a member of your chamber of commerce. Find out whether any organizations in your area offer free help to businesses, and offer to volunteer. Volunteering, even though it's free, often helps you break into a new area.

The other factor to consider is that small businesses are less likely to hire a consultant proactively. They are less likely to understand what consultants can offer them and are less likely to know where to go for consulting help if they recognize the need. They are also accustomed to doing everything themselves. As a consultant to small business, you will probably not be invited to consult with them. Marketing, then, becomes paramount.

So what does this mean in terms of getting small business contracts? You'll find that contracts with small businesses come largely from personal contacts and networking. And that fact has profound implications for how you market.

SMALL BUSINESS MARKETING ISSUES

It's hard to generalize about marketing to small business, because much depends on the size of the business and the nature of its business. However, your marketing thrust must emphasize two things. The first involves educating small business owners about how you can help them succeed in their businesses. The second involves establishing personal relationships that inspire confidence and trust on the part of your potential customers, who are not accustomed to asking outsiders for help.

You'll find that marketing tactics useful for government and corporations (for example, Internet initiatives, fancy brochures) are going to be less important and that personal contact (for example, telephone calls, involvement in chambers of commerce and other networking venues) will be more important.

HELPFUL QUALIFICATIONS TO HAVE FOR SMALL BUSINESS CONTRACTS

With respect to really small businesses, academic qualifications are unlikely to be important. What will be important is an understanding of the concerns of small businesses and of the kinds of people who own and operate them. Of course, experience in the particular business (for example, retailing, manufacturing, restauranting) is also important.

PROS AND CONS OF SMALL BUSINESS CONTRACTS

The pros of working with small businesses can be summarized as follows:

- Numerous small businesses are to be found in your local market, regardless of where you live.
- There is usually less red tape to deal with.
- This market is an underexploited one for consultants.
- The competition from other consultants is less.

Most consultants tend to underexplore the small business market because of certain difficulties associated with this sector. Here are the cons of working with small businesses:

- Contracts are smaller due to fewer resources.
- Small businesses tend to lack an understanding of the value of external consultants.
- This sector is difficult to market to. You have to market one small business at a time, often on a one-to-one basis.
- You may encounter difficulty in collecting fees.

PERSONAL SERVICE (INDIVIDUAL) CONTRACTS

The fourth market sector is individuals. Obviously, individuals don't purchase the same kinds of consulting services that companies purchase. This market does, however, purchase services related to finance and investment, employment, health, and the home.

If your areas of expertise match these services, consider this market.

Contracting with Individuals

Contracting with individuals is relatively straightforward, and in many cases business can be done on the basis of verbal agreement or a simple contract. You don't need the approval of a dozen people to put together a contract, and you will be dealing directly with the recipient of the services. In some ways it's simpler to do business in this sector than in any of the other ones.

On the other hand, your contracts will be very small, and your market will be limited to individuals wealthy enough to purchase your services. Although at first glance the individual market seems huge, it is smaller than you think.

Finally, individuals are used to doing things themselves. For example, if you offer interior design services, you will be competing with other interior design experts and also with those homeowners who are handy at doing such things on their own.

Some services marketed to individuals can serve as springboards to providing services to companies. For example, if you do individual financial counseling, your clients may be able to give you an entrée into their respective companies, where you could deliver group training on the same subject.

Marketing to individuals is a mass-marketing process. Because most of us aren't expert in this process, you might want to consider working with a marketing or advertising specialist to devise a marketing plan.

Personal Service Marketing Issues

Because fees from individuals are going to be smaller than those from the business and government sectors, you need a lot of customers, and that means extensive volume-based marketing. You need to make yourself visible to as many potential clients as possible while paying special attention to individual customer satisfaction. Word of mouth is very important in this sector.

Your advertising options are more numerous in this market, because your potential clients are likely to pay attention to ads placed in mass media (radio, television, newspapers, and magazines), but less likely to be reachable through the Internet, professional publications, and organizations.

Helpful Qualifications to Have for Personal Service Contracts

Perhaps the most important qualification associated with working with individuals and providing personal services to them is a true enjoyment of working with people one on one. After all, that's what you are going to be doing. Not everyone likes this kind of interaction, which can be more personal than the interactions you may have with corporate staff.

When you enjoy working with individuals, you are more likely to be seen by your clients as interested in them as human beings, and that's critical to the personal services relationship.

Generally, you have to be a good conversationalist, and know how to draw people out of their shells so you can get the information you need to help them. Conversational skills, such as asking questions in a gentle way and encouraging people to talk, are useful.

Apart from that you also need whatever certifications or licenses are required by law to work in your chosen field, and sufficient credentials and experience to convince your clients that you are worthy of their business.

PROS AND CONS OF PERSONAL SERVICE CONTRACTS

Working directly with individuals can be very satisfying, particularly if you work with the same customers over time. In some cases you may form friendships with your customers. The following are some other pros and cons to consider:

- This market is satisfying to work with.
- The potential clients are numerous (but the market for your services may be smaller than you think).
- Contracting hassles are few, and there is little red tape.
- There is a much higher probability of difficulty in collecting your fee.
- Contracts are typically small, thus requiring you to have a large client base.
- Sustained and sophisticated marketing is necessary to reach a large number of potential clients.

POSSIBLE AREAS OF SPECIALIZATION

Now that you have a clear idea of the various markets available to you, it's time to find out what areas of specialization exist in the consulting world. Because there are hundreds if not thousands available, it's impossible to list them all, so this section must confine itself to just a few major areas of specialization. Hopefully, this discussion will stimulate your thinking about where your skills and expertise might lead you in the consulting world.

MANAGEMENT AND BUSINESS

Management consulting and consulting in business are prime areas of practice for consultants. The markets are significant, and businesses have money to pay consultants. Consider the following as potential consulting areas, but keep in mind that you must match your expertise and background with the consulting areas:

- Providing training and development
- Designing marketing and business plans
- Helping organizations turn around financially
- Providing help with, or offering human resource services in, the areas of recruiting and hiring, application of regulations, and payroll
- Facilitating internal development such as strategic planning sessions or team building
- Diagnosing organizational problems
- Creating policies and procedures
- Implementing and planning ad programs in various media

TIP

Don't box yourself in too rigidly regarding your specializations. You know more than you think. For example, you might see yourself as a human resources expert, but you may also have skills unconnected with this job that are marketable—writing, training, and interviewing skills. Don't forget to consider those skills.

TECHNOLOGY/COMPUTERS

Technology and computer-related consulting is a growing area, and one that is likely to continue to be exceedingly lucrative. This is due partly to a move to "outsource" various technology projects, enlisting the help of programmers and designers on an as-needed basis. In fact, almost everything companies do related to technology and computers can be hired out to consultants.

Here are some examples of jobs that can be hired out to consultants:

- Computer programming of every sort
- Internet website design and implementation
- System design advice and planning
- Hardware installation and maintenance
- Computer and network security
- Internet marketing and search engine optimization

FINANCIAL SERVICES

Financial services and advice are areas in which consultants are in demand. Many of these services are offered specifically to individuals (for example, financial and retirement planning, investment advice), but companies use consultants in financial specializations as well.

Some examples of financial services are as follows:

- Investment and retirement planning
- Advising on taxation issues, which can include filing tax returns on the client's behalf
- Personal finance and debt counseling, including things like developing household budgets and debt consolidation
- Providing computer support and installation for financial record-keeping

PERSONAL AND HOME-RELATED SERVICES

The areas of personal and home-related specializations usually involve offering services directly to individuals rather than to businesses. Examples include the following:

- House inspections
- Relocation assistance and advice
- Food services (catering, menu planning)
- Job-search advice and assistance
- Editorial assistance
- Fitness and health advice and services
- Interior design and landscaping

OTHER PROFESSIONS

Finally, most professional activities can be undertaken on a consulting or freelance basis, for example:

- Consulting engineers (to conduct feasibility studies)
- Architectural services
- Clerical and administrative tasks (for example, stenography, language translation, dictation)

PREREQUISITES FOR SUCCESS

As you consider a career as an independent consultant, you need to know what elements are essential for success. And, boy, there are a lot of things you need to know, a lot of skills you must have, and a certain outlook you need to cultivate.

Ideally, you will have many of these elements before you hang out your consultant shingle, but it's not necessary to have absolutely everything. You are going to learn as you go. However, the more resources and skills you bring to the table from the start, the more likely you will reduce your number of growing pains, mistakes, and hard economic times.

If you are a practicing consultant, this section is also important to you. It's an opportunity to begin a self-assessment to identify any gaps in knowledge, skills, and attitudes you may have. And we all have them.

This section covers the basic elements you need for success.

SPECIALTY-RELATED SKILLS AND KNOWLEDGE

Specialty-related skills and knowledge refer to those basic and advanced skills and knowledge that are required in your chosen field, and that are needed by you to provide expert advice to clients and to be seen as credible by prospective clients.

It's difficult to tell exactly what skills and knowledge this entails, because obviously your needs depend on the field in which you want to practice. However, you'd better know your field well and what it requires before you market yourself as a consultant.

Regardless of whether or not you know your field, try to identify four or five consultants who work in your field. Find several consultants who work in your geographic area, but also track down one or two who work outside your area. This provides some balance.

Explain that you are considering starting a consulting business in this particular field and that you would like 15 to 20 minutes of their time to ask them some questions. When they agree, make sure you ask the following two questions:

- What skills and knowledge have you found most valuable in running a successful consulting business in your field?
- Before I start a new consultancy, are there any absolutely essential things that I need to know and understand to have a good chance of success?

If you are wondering whether potential competitors will be willing to help you, don't worry about it. Even though you may find a few consultants who guard their secrets, those really aren't the ones you want to talk to and learn from. The majority of consultants (provided they have the time) will be glad, even honored, to give advice, and that advice can be golden.

Listen carefully. Ask in humility.

This picking of consultants' brains allows you to get some other perspectives on your business, something we all need.

Although consultants are generally honest people and will give you the "straight goods" on most questions, there's one area in which you will likely get inaccurate information. Probably every consultant on the planet is going to exaggerate his or her own success, for good reason. If a consultant is known to be struggling, clients hear about it and shy away. So take statements about the great success of small consulting businesses with a grain of salt. The consultants aren't being dishonest so much as protecting their businesses.

When discussing specialty-related skills and knowledge, you must consider two significant questions: How broad should your knowledge be and how deep should it be? The answers will be the topics of the next two sections.

BREADTH OF KNOWLEDGE AND SKILLS

What is *breadth of knowledge?* Breadth of knowledge refers to the number of different areas in which you have expertise. Let's say you're a financial consultant. You need a wide range of skills and knowledge so you can provide your clients with high-quality advice and service. For example, you might have significant expertise in the following areas:

- Tax laws
- Stock market investment strategies
- Retirement plans and funds
- Mutual funds

Every time you learn something new, you increase your breadth of knowledge. The broader the range of things you know, the better off you are. Why is that?

Because consultants sell their knowledge; the more you have, the more you can offer to your clients. Keep in mind that clients looking for consulting advice want someone who has more knowledge in *more* areas than they themselves have.

There's another reason why breadth is important. Our world is complex, and giving good advice requires that you look at a number of interrelated factors. Let's look at the tale of two financial consultants.

Our first financial consultant, Fred, knows a great deal about tax laws, mutual funds, and stock market investment strategies. However, he isn't familiar with retirement plans and regulations. Jane, our second financial consultant, has a wider range of expertise. She's got all the areas of expertise that Fred has, and more. Now which consultant do you think is going to be more successful over time? All things being equal, Jane's got the upper hand, because she's able to offer more complete advice—advice that takes into account more options and possibilities.

The bottom line on breadth of knowledge and skills is that you need to know way more than you might think. And you must strive to increase your breadth of knowledge throughout your career as a professional consultant.

DEPTH OF KNOWLEDGE AND SKILLS

If breadth of knowledge is about how many relevant skills and how much information you have at your disposal, *depth of knowledge* is about how well you know each area. You can know a lot of things superficially, but that kind of shallow knowledge isn't what clients are paying you for. You have to have depth to your knowledge.

To use another financial consultant example, imagine a financial consultant who knows just some of the tax laws relevant to financial planning. Would you take advice from that person? Maybe initially, but as soon as you got dinged for a big tax bill, you would be telling that consultant sayonara. You'd also tell your friends not to hire the person.

Make sense? You don't want to be a consultant who can offer only inferior service because the breadth and the depth of your knowledge falls short of excellent.

As a final point on both depth and breadth of knowledge, consider that you can't ever know exactly how deep and how broad your knowledge and skills must be. However, the market and your clients will often give you important clues:

- ■ Keep in mind that you have gaps in breadth and depth of knowledge and be aware of situations in which they interfere with providing great consulting services. Identify them and address them.

- ■ Be a continuous learner. It's essential that you commit to learning constantly. Think of what you learn as your knowledge inventory. The more you have to offer and sell, the more likely you will succeed.

PROCESS SKILLS—TOOLS OF THE TRADE

Suppose you have 20 years of experience in your consulting area, but no actual experience as a consultant. Is that enough? Absolutely not. Consultants require a number of other skills and expertise in the consulting process. These are called *process skills.*

Process skills are those skills that help you identify client needs and wants, build relationships of trust with your clients, and ensure that you offer each client exactly what the client needs.

PLAIN ENGLISH

Process skills refer to the tools all consultants need and use to ensure that their advice and recommendations are as informed as possible. These tools include interpersonal communication, group facilitation, data gathering, and diagnostic skills.

The process of determining what your client needs (and delivering it) is what sets apart the consultant from a salaried employee in the same field. An employee is often told what to do by a manager or boss. It's expected that the employee will do what he or she is told to do.

Not so with a consultant. Although your client may have an idea of what she wants you to do, it's your professional responsibility to assess whether what the client wants is what the client needs. And the two are often not the same.

Your process skills enable you to make that assessment. Let's look at the essential process skills.

INTERVIEWING SKILLS

To succeed as a consultant, you need to build trusting relationships with your clients. You also need to get the information necessary to make judgments and offer advice that fits the individual customer. You can't make use of your specialized knowledge if you don't understand the client's situation.

To complicate matters, clients are not always able to provide this information without guidance. It's your role to provide that guidance through the interview process, by asking questions, helping the client clarify his or her needs, and conducting discussions that will elicit the information you need without being confrontational or alienating your client.

GROUP SKILLS

Unless your client involves only one person, you are going to be working with a group of people. Groups can be as small as two (for example, a husband and wife) or as large as several hundred people (for example, employees at a large corporation).

TIP

A consultant ill-prepared to deal with group dynamics and the anger, resistance, and confrontation that can occur in group meetings is likely to crash and burn, first temporarily, then permanently. Difficult situations will occur, and your skill in dealing with them constructively will determine failure or success.

Groups skills refer to the tools and techniques a consultant uses to obtain information from groups, but they also include the following:

- Creating an atmosphere so group members feel comfortable speaking and participating
- Dealing with group disagreements
- Using techniques to keep group discussions on track and positive
- Employing public speaking skills

Not only do you need these skills during the consulting project, they are also absolutely essential in the front-end phase: getting the contract. That's because the process of getting a contract often involves interacting with a group of decision makers to convince them they should hire you.

DATA COLLECTION AND OBSERVATION SKILLS

Suppose a client contacts you with this complaint: My staff turnover is high. Every year we lose about 50 percent of staff, and it's killing us to hire and train new people every year.

A poor soon-to-crash-and-burn consultant may take a quick look around and tell the client to increase salaries. But a good consultant avoids the quick and easy answer and instead investigates. The first question that must be answered is, "What is causing the turnover?" Without knowing this, it's impossible to suggest informed solutions. The consultant needs to collect data and make observations regarding the work environment.

The skills needed to get the pertinent information or data on which to base recommendations are known as *data collection and observation skills*.

Consultants have a wide range of tools they can draw upon to collect data. The more tools you can use and the more expert you are (there's that breadth and depth thing again), the more likely you will hit the mark with your advice. Here are a few of those tools:

- One-on-one interviewing
- Small-group discussions (facilitation)
- Small- and large-scale surveys
- Direct observation of how people work, behave, and interact

INTERPRETATIVE, DIAGNOSTIC, AND LOGIC SKILLS

No question that getting information is absolutely critical to providing a great consulting service. However, information on its own is not enough. You must interpret the information to provide an accurate diagnosis. That requires diagnostic and logic skills.

What do these skills comprise? Giving a complete list is difficult, but here are the major abilities:

- Delaying judgment until all available data have been considered
- Weeding out the relevant from the irrelevant
- Using different sets of data to confirm or disconfirm a tentative diagnosis
- Applying statistical techniques to large quantities of data
- Putting your personal biases on hold
- Knowing when to follow your gut feeling

CAUTION

A common consultant error involves developing a "pet way" of seeing things, and then seeing every consulting project in terms of that one way. For example, a team-development consultant might tend to see all problems as related to faulty teams. A human resources consultant might look at exactly the same information and see the problem as one of hiring the wrong people. Be aware of your pet ways. Recognize that you need to be flexible.

NEGOTIATION SKILLS

Consultants are always negotiating. You negotiate a contract, a time span, and fees. If you are involved in the implementation of a solution, you negotiate how the implementation should be carried out—who is responsible for what, when, and how it should occur, for example.

PROJECT MANAGEMENT AND TIME MANAGEMENT

Finally, consultants need the ability to manage their time and to complete projects on schedule and on budget. Although most of us think we are fairly organized and systematic in our personal lives, consulting tends to highlight any project- and time-management flaws.

These flaws become apparent because a successful consultant juggles several projects and tasks at once, and it seems that everything needs to be done yesterday. The consultant's task is to make sure that if something really needed to be done yesterday, it was done yesterday.

Project and time management thus require the ability to prioritize tasks, develop plans of action that make sense, and maximize personal productivity. Wasted time and missed deadlines mean lost money (and lost future contracts).

EXPERIENCE AND CONTACTS

The more experience you have in your chosen field and the more contacts you have, the more likely you are to start your consulting practice and quickly generate revenue. In addition, extensive experience and contacts help you do the job well.

EXPERIENCE AND GETTING THE JOB

Think about a time when you worked for someone else. Can you recall when you were asked to do something new, something you didn't know too much about? If you're like most people, you learned on the job and hopefully completed the task successfully. When you work for someone else, you have some leeway to learn as you go and still get paid.

When someone hires a consultant, he or she wants a consultant who will walk in the door with the experience and skills required to do the job. That's why experience is so important. The client will want to know whether you've done "this" before. Where have you done it? In the client's sector? With what level of success?

The client will avoid hiring someone who needs to learn on the job or whom the client sees as inexperienced. That's one reason why a consultant who has worked in his or her chosen field for an extensive period of time is likely to be more successful, as compared with, say, a recent university graduate having limited experience.

If there's something to be learned here, it's that you should choose areas of practice in which you actually have significant experience. This is not just "book learning."

EXPERIENCE AND DOING THE JOB

The more experience you have in your field, the more likely you are to complete your consulting assignment so that the customer is delighted with the results. Experience helps you in diagnosing and in suggesting solutions that have track records. Experience also enhances your credibility in the eyes of the people you must have as partners in the project.

TIP

The greater your experience, the greater your ability to identify patterns and situations you have seen before. For example, experience in working with groups helps you identify the early warning signs that sometimes appear in group dynamics—signs that indicate problems under the surface.

If a single piece of advice fits here, it's that you must be very careful not to accept assignments way beyond your experience levels. However, do accept assignments that stretch you and give you new experience to use in future projects. In other words, take moderate risks, always trying to ensure you will succeed and please your client.

CONTACTS KEEP YOU ALIVE

Contacts are your lifeline in the consulting business. Let's say you are a fitness fanatic. You even have a degree in physical education, and you've been working as a phys. ed. teacher. You're tired of the school system and want to do what you love—help adults become healthier and physically fit. So you quit your teaching job and become a "fitness consultant," offering to develop and supervise personal fitness plans for individual clients.

You're going to be in big trouble. You may be fit and skilled and have all the knowledge you need, but if you don't have the contacts in the field (both practitioners and potential customers), how do you let people know you can help them?

Well, you market. You place ads. And you struggle.

Now suppose you plan ahead and develop important contacts before you leap into the business. You might instruct at a fitness gym as a contract employee, join local fitness professional associations, and so on. The situation has now changed immensely. Because you've taken the time to develop some contacts, you at least have some easily accessible sources for potential clients when you do hang out your shingle.

It doesn't matter which field you work in. Your initial contacts in the field are going to allow you to generate income much more quickly than if you had no contacts. They will tide you over until your other marketing techniques kick in and start generating business.

Contacts aren't important only at start-up. They are also important when you've been in business for a while. They help generate income during tough times when business is slack. Keep in mind that many consulting assignments come as a result of word of mouth rather than aggressive sales and marketing. Your contacts are your livelihood. Cultivate them before you start your business, and continue to expand your contacts whenever possible.

PERSONAL QUALITIES

Okay, you've got breadth and depth in the knowledge and skills in your chosen practice area. You have a good grasp of the process skills specific to consulting (but you continue to learn). You have experience and contacts. Is that it? No. Successful consultants tend to have certain personal qualities that stand them in good stead in a tough, competitive industry. What are those personal characteristics?

WILLINGNESS TO TAKE RISKS

Just making the decision to commit to a consulting business, with its potentially unstable income and hours, requires risk taking. But beyond that, you need to be comfortable with taking risks, making mistakes, and having to pay the price when things go wrong. The success or failure of your business is almost entirely up to you. You are responsible for it. If you are uncomfortable living with risk and errors, running your own consulting business is not going to work for you. There is no net to fall into.

TIP

Don't underestimate the importance of the fit between your attitudes and values and the realities of the consulting business. Do a realistic assessment of yourself and what you want from your life, and compare it to the life you anticipate as a consultant.

Apart from your attitude about risk, you need to have the resources to recover when things go wrong. If you are flat broke and have to provide food for your children, you can't afford the risk if your consulting endeavor fails. That kind of pressure causes bad decisions, and bad decisions cause failed businesses.

ABILITY TO TOLERATE INSECURITY

Can you live with the idea of having your professional and financial life "ride the roller coaster"? If you can't, you'd better choose another profession. You will have lean times and good times. You'll have elated times and depressed times. Above all, you will rarely know whether the next six months will be lean or good. Until you are well established, there is no security except that which you generate.

DESIRE TO LEARN CONTINUOUSLY

One key to successful consulting is to slowly and cautiously add more services and expertise to your "inventory." That requires continuous learning of new things.

Learning in an ongoing way is also critical because most consulting projects are going to put you face to face with situations or contexts in which you must learn (and learn fast) to succeed.

Your curiosity and desire to learn will be essential for long-term success.

STRONG INTERPERSONAL SKILLS

No matter what your field of expertise, your most important set of skills and knowledge has to do with people. The essence of consulting is about communicating, generating trust, and getting information from people who don't even know they have it. You must have the necessary interpersonal skills to know when to press, to be aggressive, to just listen, and much more. And above all, you need to get along well with people. That includes being comfortable with conflict and being able to deal with it when it occurs.

PEOPLE ORIENTATION

There are a large number of people working in the technical areas (notably computers and Internet specialties) who have huge amounts of technical skill. Some of them are people-oriented. Others would just as soon be left alone to fiddle on their computers and would prefer not to talk to anyone at all.

A solitary personality in an employee who is relied upon for his or her technical wizardry will be tolerated, but this kind of personality will not work if you want to run your own consulting business. No matter how technical your field, if you don't like working with people, and lack the required people skills, you'll have an uphill battle in the consulting business.

TIP

Whether you realize it or not, your spouse is an important part of your consulting business. Spouses offer valuable support. They are also asked to tolerate the uncertainties of your business, including the need to travel. Include your spouse in decision making.

STRONG SUPPORT SYSTEM IN PLACE

Running your own consulting business can be an isolating endeavor. You'll do a lot of your work (for example, thinking and analysis) on your own. To counteract the possibility of becoming socially and professionally isolated, you need a good support system. A support system involves people whom you can meet, talk to, consult for advice, or even just complain to about life.

And speaking of support systems, let's not understate the importance of a spouse who is supportive of your endeavors and who can live with the insecurity and ambiguity of your new career.

COMMITMENT TO PERSONAL AND PROFESSIONAL INTEGRITY

For some reason our society seems to undervalue qualities such as integrity, ethical behavior, and a commitment to honesty. Remember this: Your consulting lifeblood is your reputation. Your reputation is built on your integrity, honesty, and ethics. If you aren't prepared to set the highest standards for yourself, your customers and prospective customers will find out. Cut corners to make a few bucks, and eventually you won't have any clients.

In consulting, integrity is much more than a nicety. Honesty isn't optional. Your integrity and honesty have profound implications on your bottom line.

Accepting a consulting contract for which you are ill-prepared is an action lacking in integrity. Making promises you can't possibly keep to a client is a dishonest action. Don't kid yourself. Do these things at your own risk. Your reputation is your lifeblood. Protect it even if you must turn down a project.

WORKING "WITH" PEOPLE

Some people work best when they work *for* someone else. They are most comfortable being told what to do. Some people work best when they feel *above* others in authority or skill. Others like to work *with* people, as relatively equal partners. Working "with" means respecting and valuing the abilities and perceptions of your partners (that is, your customers). It means not appearing to place yourself above them, and not waiting for them to tell you what to do. Consulting requires that you deal with your clients as partners in a process.

Business Acumen

Finally we come to the last set of prerequisites. You need to know how to run a business and you should have the required skills to do so, or else make sure you have access to people who have the skills you lack.

You can't hire someone to exercise good business judgment in your stead. Neither can you rely on someone else to make decisions based on sound ethics and principles. You can hire other people to handle some of the business procedures in which you lack the expertise.

The following sections provide a quick list of the skills you need to succeed in business.

TIP

You might consider hiring a marketing expert (or consultant) to help you develop a marketing plan for your business. This type of investment can really pay off and is particularly useful at start-up because it will help you learn about marketing and get your business off the ground. Make sure the person you hire is familiar with your target market and area of specialization.

Marketing Skills

During the first year, you will be spending a good deal of your time figuring out how to market to your potential clients. That means you have to know something about sales and the marketing process, and about the various options you have at your disposal (for example, brochures, cold contacts, networking, associations, advertising, Internet presence).

Don't worry if you don't yet have this knowledge, but do commit to acquiring it as soon as possible. You will learn much as you go along.

Networking Skills

Networking is often part of the marketing process, but it's also an important aid in keeping your sanity and growing your support network. There is an art to it. You have to balance your "sales needs" with the need to establish free and equal relationships with other people. For example, if you use networking as a way to push your services down other people's throats, you soon won't have anyone to talk to. Nobody likes a pushy, self-centered networker.

Think about whom you should be networked with and then decide how to go about it. To increase sales, you need to network with people who are in positions to hire you or advise people who can hire you. Don't make the mistake of confusing networking with other consultants with networking with potential clients. Both are important but address different goals.

FINANCIAL MANAGEMENT SKILLS

Have trouble balancing your checkbook? Ever been late filing or paying taxes? Hate paperwork? Not good. Even though managing your company's finances is a tedious and sometimes burdensome task for which you don't get paid, it must be done. Luckily, some or much of this task can be offloaded to others (accountants and tax preparers). Decide now whether you want to do it yourself (be realistic here) or have someone else help you out.

COMPUTER SKILLS

Computer skills are even more important than you'd think. Being able to use computers efficiently to create documents, prepare marketing copy, and communicate with clients (via computer, fax, or Internet) is essential.

Which computer skills are absolutely essential? The ability to use a word processor package, the know-how to send and receive e-mail, the ability to browse the Internet to accomplish simple tasks, and the ability to use a basic financial management or accounting package are musts. Also useful is the ability to use web development tools and a desktop publishing program.

Perhaps it's occurred to you that you may not be able to afford someone to handle and create correspondence, operate your customer database, or computerize your billing and accounts receivable. If you don't have the skills to undertake these tasks yourself, consider enrolling in local community college classes to acquire them. If you are well capitalized, you might be able to employ someone else to do those things—but likely not, at least in the early days of your business.

The more you can do on your computer, the faster you can work. And the less you need to rely on paid help.

Oh yes. You *can* type, right?

WRITTEN COMMUNICATION SKILLS

Written communication skills are a definite must for consulting with organizations of any size, although they are less important if you are consulting to individuals. You need to be able to write prose that is easy to understand, clear, and precise. You also need to be able to create documents quickly. If it takes you a week to draft a five-page report, you are in trouble.

Your written communication skills are important in getting contracts (both in the marketing stages and in the contracting stage) and completing such documents as consulting project reports to your clients. At minimum, your clients are going to expect something on paper that summarizes your advice. Some projects may require the submission of major reports and also interim reports done during the life of the project.

Presentation Skills

Presentation skills relate to your ability to speak in public to (usually) a group of people. There are some people who would rather have teeth pulled than speak to a group of people. So are these skills essential? Yes, unless you work only with individuals.

When is it likely you'll have to do group presentations? Often, this is something you'll have to do right up front. Corporate clients in particular may ask you to speak to a group of people about what you can offer. Next, it won't be uncommon for you to have to speak to a group of people during a contract, either to report on progress, to present interim advice, or simply to get information from them. Finally, you will want the opportunity (yes, opportunity) to speak to clients to present your advice in ways that will encourage them to use and implement it.

Proposal-Writing Skills

Finally, if you plan on working for clients who may require you to respond to requests for proposals or who want fairly detailed plans about how you can help them, you need to develop skills in writing proposals. For some consultants, especially those who consult to government and corporations, these skills are essential. The ability to give proposal reviewers exactly what they want and little more is invaluable. A combination of writing skills, such as concise phrasing and document organization, along with a knack for understanding what proposal reviewers are looking for, will help you compete for contracts.

For others, such as those who consult mainly to individuals, they may be irrelevant.

The 30-Second Recap

- Have realistic expectations regarding finance and revenue.
- Begin thinking about the consulting roles you want to undertake and for which you are qualified.

■ Now that you know the main reasons why people hire consultants, start thinking about how you can mobilize your expertise to meet the needs of potential clients.

■ Consulting is not a romantic profession. Evaluate whether you are prepared to spend a lot of time doing very boring and uninteresting things.

■ Don't rule out any particular sector or market. Consider the pros and cons of each.

■ Your ability to market to particular sectors should be a major determinant of where you focus your practice. Evaluate where your contacts and network will be most useful.

■ Practicing in an area where you are already known and have a positive reputation is a good idea.

■ When deciding which areas you want to specialize in, consider the market conditions—both in your geographical area and beyond—your expertise, and your ability to market in that area. All are important.

■ Assess your knowledge and skills in your specialty areas in terms of breadth and depth.

■ Pay special attention to identifying where you may need to develop your consulting process skills.

■ Before making an irrevocable decision to start a consulting business, be clear about the challenges involved and examine your own values and attitudes. Is this something you will *really* enjoy?

■ Begin thinking about the business skills you may lack and consider filling in the gaps or deciding where you can find the expertise you lack.

Maybe you prefer to spend your time surrounded by strangers ... 24 hours a day! Running a bed-and-breakfast might be for you. The next section explores this type of business.

Running a Bed-and-Breakfast

Think you're ready to start your own bed-and-breakfast? This section gives you some things to consider in advance.

OPEN, SEZ ME!

This is it. The dream of opening your own bed-and-breakfast could come true very soon. Running a bed-and-breakfast may be the best adventure of your life, and, as in any new adventure, you'll encounter pitfalls, triumphs, and a lot of "in betweeners."

Before you dive into the B&B way of life, you need to be armed with the best advice first. Hear everyone and listen to no one. The lifestyle is rewarding, demanding, and a great way to earn extra income. Keep in mind, however, that it also is completely different from anything you've ever experienced. First, take the test: Find out whether your personality and abilities will give you a good shot at running a successful B&B—and enjoying it. If you decide to plunge in, this book will prepare you for the many challenges you'll encounter in planning, setting up, and running your very own bed-and-breakfast.

THE TRADITION OF WELCOMING STRANGERS

In the United States, the B&B business is relatively new. In other parts of the world, particularly Europe, the industry is centuries old. As you might have guessed, the business of charging strangers to sleep in your house has been a way to make a few extra nickels, francs, or marks for a long time. Pre–twenty-first-century travelers didn't have Best Westerns to check in to, so they had to rely on strangers to give them a bed for the night and to send them off with a hot meal in the morning.

Guests would pay cash or trade something for their night's lodging and breakfast, sometimes choosing stops because they were known for their excellent rolls or comfortable beds.

It wasn't long before the casual services homeowners offered to travelers grew into a business, and throughout North America the bed-and-breakfast became an alternative to the commercial hotel.

DO YOU HAVE WHAT IT TAKES?

As a host, you'll need to have the right balance of charm, generosity, humor, and professionalism. As an employer, you'll be striving for a positive working environment for your staff and efficiency without micromanagement. As an owner, you'll need to anticipate and plan for every aspect of the business, from marketing to taxes.

Your skills as a host, employer, and owner are not all it takes to make it as a B&B owner; you need emotional and mental strength, too. If you have a short fuse or you lack the natural tendency to look after the needs of others, it might not be the right business for you, or you might need to do some work in these areas.

You, or you and your partner if there are two of you in the enterprise, need to know how to instantly put your guests at ease. A good B&B host radiates an easygoing nature and genuine charm. We're not talking an Eddie Haskel, "Boy, ma'am, you sure do look lovely today" kind of charm. You need to truly like—and be interested in—people. If you're not fond of dealing with strangers, your guests will pick up on it right away; the worst thing you can do is to make them feel like intruders! But don't despair: It is possible to bump up your charm quotient.

Before you start picking out carpet and hanging numbers on guest rooms, find some time to analyze yourself in every way. In addition to being personable and confident, a good host is efficient, accommodating, energetic, humble, observant, humorous, and able to troubleshoot with the best of them.

Just think, owning a B&B means that you'll run a business out of your home. No more boss, no more lousy commute, no more 9 to 5! That's all true. You'll be your own boss, which can be great—and also a great responsibility. The commute certainly is a short one if your B&B is the home you live in. And if you think you won't be working 9 A.M. to 5 P.M. anymore, you're right— prepare for a 9 A.M. to 9 A.M. workload (translation: 24 hours a day)!

Now is the time—before you knock down walls and buy pillows—to decide whether this business is for you. Running a B&B is not a job; it's a lifestyle. You'll start going to the grocery store at 2:00 P.M. on Tuesdays because it's the best time to miss the crowds. Your Sunday morning routine of reading the paper and taking the dog for a walk now will move to Monday evening, during your manager's shift. You'll learn to buy your favorite Gap jeans online instead of wasting time at the mall. These might seem like small adjustments now, but they'll become big sacrifices if you're not fond of changing routines.

When imagining what your life will be like as the innkeeper, do yourself a favor and consider how every part of your life will be affected. Take into account your daily routine, your evenings, your family's routine, your vacations, and your weekends. Make sure your trade-offs will not undermine your happiness. If you're determined to make this lifestyle change, you will find ways to compensate for whatever you have to give up.

CAUTION

Knowing your own strengths and not-such-strengths before you open a B&B can save you a lot of grief. Taking the test that follows is a good start.

THIS IS A TEST; THIS IS ONLY A TEST

Cheat on this test and you'll be cheating on—that's right—yourself. If you plan to co-own your B&B, have your partner take this test, too, and then match up the scores. You might discover (or confirm) that one person will make a better host, whereas the other has better organizational skills. Be honest in your answers and then keep reading to find out how to improve your score.

1. **Social misfit?** Your partner drags you kicking and screaming to a boring but swanky corporate party. During the evening, your partner gets into an involved conversation with the company's head cheese. You ...

    a. Sit in the corner and sulk.

    b. Talk to the office clown.

    c. Walk over to the bar and get plastered.

    d. Find an outsider like yourself to talk with.

    How you did: You probably didn't pick **a** or **c** because you knew those were the "wrong" answers (although some of us have, at one time or another, sulked in a corner or drunk our sorrows away). If you picked "talk to the office clown," it shows that you're social, but you won't go out of your way to make conversation. Talking with an outsider shows that you have no problems conversing with a total stranger. When your guests first stay with you they will be, after all, just strangers.

2. **Persistence potential.** Your B&B has been up and running for two months now. All that time you've been trying, unsuccessfully, to get a particular travel writer to swing your way. You ...

    a. Give it a rest and maybe try again next month.

    b. Call your mom.

    c. Keep calling the writer, even if you get voicemail every time.

    d. Send a clever package—maybe a picture of a toothbrush with the words, "Now that you've packed, we'll take care of the rest" on your business card, tucked inside a brochure.

How you did: You might have chosen **c,** but if someone won't talk to you or get back to you, take the hint. Don't take it personally, but do stop calling. If you chose **a,** you're closer than you think to giving up altogether. Choosing **b** definitely is a sign of giving up. Probably **d** was an obvious answer, but stop and think about why this option can work so well. You haven't spent tons of money, you're not being a pest, and you've made yourself and the business stand out in an unusual way. Not getting what you want can be frustrating, especially when it comes to the success of your business. Persistence will always pay off, especially if your tactics are understated but you still get your point across. Being persistent doesn't mean you need to be pesky. If one game plan doesn't work, figure out why and switch to something else.

3. **Time-management technique.** Your last set of guests just checked in for the day. You have a spare hour so you decide to …

    a. Organize your messy kitchen, starting with the cereal.

    b. Call your mom.

    c. Write out the breakfast menu for the coming week and make a shopping list.

    d. Go out food shopping.

How you did: Guests just checked in, so **d** is not a good choice; **c** is okay, but it won't take the full hour; and **a** is ambitious, but the kitchen's condition might be making you crazy and slowing you down as well. If you think you can plan the menu, write the list, and give Ma a ring, good for you. If you can organize the kitchen and call Mommy, you'll be destined for B&B greatness. (Remember to tell her about your clever idea of sending a package to the travel writer. She'll be so proud!)

4. **Crisis control.** On a particularly crazy day, a staff member shows up an hour late, just when guests are eating a sit-down meal. At the same time, a guest calls to say there's no soap in the bathroom. While you're on the phone, you notice that your tardy employee is gabbing with another staffer who is trying to get things done. You …

    a. Quickly apologize to the guest about the soap and offer to send someone up right away. When you get off the phone, you speak to the tardy employee in private.

b. Take care of the tardy employee right away because the guests who are eating breakfast need tending to while you're on the phone.

c. Take orange marmalade and scrawl the words "get back to work" on the kitchen counter.

d. Ignore your employees, finish your phone conversation, and then tend to the dining area yourself.

How you did: Although **c** will get the job done, your employees will receive it as a very hostile act; choosing **d** means you need to work on confrontation; if you chose **b,** you will have insulted the guest on the phone and been seen as unprofessional. Taking each situation as it's presented to you usually works best. Choosing **a** means being gracious and responsive to the angered guest on the phone and handling your tardy employee in private. This is not just a test of how well you handle your employees or your guests. Handling everyday situations quickly and correctly will make your B&B run smoothly. Think of yourself as the wizard behind the curtain (or in the kitchen). All your guests are Dorothys who can never know your behind-the-scenes secrets. To accomplish this, you need to make fast decisions that keep the show rolling.

5. **Confrontation cool.** At check-out guests inform you that they had not received towel service that day nor did they sleep very well either night because of noise from a nearby room. They demand a full refund. You …

a. Give them sincere apologies. You then gently point out that, if you'd been informed of the problems the day before, you could have done such and such about them. You offer them a discount, but not a full refund.

b. Buckle, and give them a full refund. After all, you need returning guests.

c. Show them the door. Who needs guests like that?!

d. Apologize over and over and over again. Tell them you'll do anything to satisfy them except give them any type of refund on the bill.

How you did: Choosing **c** feels bad all around; you feel as if you've failed somehow (even if you haven't). The **b** choice feels all wrong. You want guests to return, but do you want these guests to return?

Choosing **d** is a wishy-washy way to handle this situation. Trying to get the guests to leave without making any amends at all could develop into a riotous situation. The **a** choice lets your guests know that you would have taken care of the problem. Offering a compromise enables you to stand your ground while letting them feel as if they've won. Situations such as this are tricky. You want your guests to be happy, but you can't give in to every request, either. You won't have (if all goes well) every guest asking for a full refund, but it will happen.

6. **Team spirit.** A staff member is out sick and your other employee is struggling to ready four guest rooms in two hours, before all guests check in. You're busy paying bills and answering the phone, which has been ringing off the hook. You ...

   a. Keep doing what you're doing.
   b. Put the bills down, let the machine get the phone, and help your staff.
   c. Put the bills down, take the phone with you, and help your staff.
   d. Decide to go to the store to get away from the madness.

How you did: If you chose **a** or **d,** those rooms will not be ready when guests arrive. The choice between **b** and **c** is tricky; it's up to you and how you like to operate. If you don't want to miss any calls or have to return any, take the phone with you. If you know that answering the phone will distract you too much from the work at hand, let the machine take care of it. If you have staff helping you out, remember that they are helping you out. Having hands-on, go-getting blood in your veins is the only way to run a B&B. You or your partner as well as your manager will need to approach the daily work this way so that nothing suffers.

7. **Flexibility fitness.** Potential guests who've visited your website call for a one-night, midweek stay during a normally slow period. They inquire about a corporate rate. You ...

   a. Tell them you're closed midweek, thinking you don't want to be bothered for one night at a lower rate.
   b. Tell them you can't speak English.

    c. Tell them you're not equipped to handle business travelers and mention that there's a Ramada Inn nearby.

    d. Ask them how much they're looking to spend and what services, if any, they need.

How you did: There are two tricks to this question. First, how flexible are you willing to be to get a room filled? The second, more understated, consideration is, are you asking the right questions? Maybe the potential guests actually are three travelers looking for three rooms. If you chose **d,** be sure to mention a range of rates to get a better sense of what the guests need. Also find out exactly what they need in business services. If these guests request the use of a fax machine and you don't have one, **c** is a good choice, and also can be the best one if you really don't want to be bothered for one night during the week. You'll just resent their being there, especially if it's not worth it financially. The important thing is to be flexible when you get the call, find out what the situation is, and then choose how you'll handle the caller.

8. Funny bone factor. A guest calls down from the room to say there's an emergency. You rush up to find the guest grasping onto the cord of an air conditioner that's dangling from the window—above your car! You and the guest try to get the AC up but, when it looks ready to give way, you get the idea of moving your car. You run down, start the car, and get it out of the way—just as the AC comes crashing down. Not a scratch on the car, just the busted air conditioner. You …

    a. Charge the guest for the replacement value of the AC and for opening the window in the first place.

    b. Joke with the guest that there are easier ways to get cool, such as turning on the AC instead of taking it out of the window. Then, strike a deal.

    c. Give the guest a piece of your mind.

    d. Clean up the mess, move your car, and then give the guest the silent treatment until he or she leaves.

How you did: If you can't laugh at some situations, you'll be a very rigid and stressed-out host. We chose the "dangling air conditioner" scenario because, believe it or not, we've heard this story from several innkeepers! Most guests will feel very silly in a situation like this and will, let's hope, offer to pay for the AC. If they don't, we'd be inclined to choose **b**—make a joke of it and strike a deal with the embarrassed guest. If the guest is arrogant, shoot for most or all of the replacement value. Worse things than this can happen, and you, too, will have an air conditioner story to tell.

Hosting 101: Improve Your Score

Assessing what you're good at—and not so good at—is tough. A lot of the questions we asked made you react to situations based on your personality. There isn't, and shouldn't be, a set of rules that each host must follow. Everyone is different (a very good thing), and each B&B will provide a different atmosphere based on, well, you.

Do you find it easy to talk to anyone or only to people in similar situations, or people of your age or race? Are you nervous or self-conscious, and is that obvious to other people? Do they just smile and move quietly away, or are they engaged and put at ease by you? These are all things that can be improved upon.

Start by making conversation with total strangers and pay attention to how they react to you. The more people you talk to, the easier this will get. If you're lacking in the confidence category, this is something that needs to change right away. Don't be intimidated by a person's blank stare or sharp comment. If you have the confidence to break the ice with people, they'll respond in a positive way. If they don't, laugh it off and move on. The important thing is that you make the effort, and by doing that, you're well on your way to becoming a charming and genuine host.

If you need to manage your time better, put yourself to the test. Work a typical day and keep a time log of what you did. When you look at it at the end of the day, you'll find holes or places where you could have been doing something more productive. The following day, schedule in projects that you know can be completed in the time you allow. Have several projects waiting in the wings in case you need to switch to something that can be completed in a shorter time period.

TIP

Managing your day is not always easy, especially when unexpected situations pop up. If you have a good handle on how long projects actually take and when you can get them done, each day will become smoother than the one before.

There are certain skills, such as being flexible, managing your time, and dealing well with conflict, that are must-have skills. If you've discovered through our test that you need work in some of these areas, do the work. Put yourself in situations that require those skills. If you're low on people skills, start talking to strangers. If you give up on things, take on a project that you know will require persistence to complete. If you're used to being in a management position, volunteer for a hands-on community project to get a feel for being part of a team.

TIP

If we had the space, we could ask you a gazillion more questions that would help you assess your capabilities. With a friend or your partner, try thinking up situations on your own to test your responses. Some suggested areas are your enjoyment of providing services to others, acceptance of all types of people, handling of finances, everyday stamina, how well you take care of yourself, and how honest you are with yourself when things aren't going right.

Any steps you take to improve on your skills will be of help. Just having an awareness of your innkeeping capabilities is enough to put you ahead.

COMMON MISCONCEPTIONS

If you're like most people who have come to this life decision, some good experiences at B&Bs have sparked a dreamy notion of B&B ownership. The key here is that you had those good times as a B&B guest. If running a B&B were like staying at a B&B, everyone would be doing it! There are a lot of misconceptions about being a B&B owner, such as …

■ **Working at home is bliss.** Working at home definitely can be great. Advantages such as a short commute and no required dress code have more and more people looking for ways to work from home. If these are your main reasons for owning a B&B, however, think twice before making the decision. "I work at home" would be the last way a B&B owner would describe how he or she makes a living. It would be more like "I own my own bed-and-breakfast." Owning your own B&B is a career, not a part-time job. Even if you plan to run a very small operation, make sure you head into this new career with a professional head on your shoulders.

- **I'll own a B&B when I retire.** To retire means to "withdraw," "retreat," or "go away from." In other words, to stop working! If you've worked hard at your current job for 40 years and then decided to "relax" by owning a B&B, you're in for a rough ride. A lot of people assume that cleaning, cooking, and "mingling" with guests are light duty. After all, you do it for your family or yourself, why not do it for a few extra people who will pay you? Again, keep in mind that this is a business, not a cocktail party (although opening a B&B is a great reason to have one!).

- **People will be lined up outside my door.** Well, maybe if you bought an existing operation that kept excellent books, or found the spectacular location that was crying out for lodgers. Otherwise, nearly all new B&Bs can expect a slow start, mostly because no one will know you exist for a while. Although you'll be itching for income, growing gradually and working out the day-to-day kinks will give you a good foundation for the future.

- **This friend of my uncle's cousin's sister opened a B&B six months ago and already makes a ton of dough.** It is possible to make good money in this business; but be prepared to not see a major profit in the first year or even few years. Let's hope you get lucky and have 100 percent occupancy in your first year—but that's rare. Your best advertisement is word of mouth and, because your first few months will see a limited number of guests, the word can be spread only so far. Plus you'll dish out a fair amount of clams for start-up expenses, which will eat into your profit for the first year and beyond.

- **After the house is renovated and decorated, my job will be done.** Having your property ready for business will be one of your most gratifying accomplishments, primarily because you'll feel a sense of completion. As you joyfully suck down eggnog at your open house, though, don't allow yourself to think that your work is done. Your newly renovated house is the start of your newly renovated life. The preparation is over, now on to the adventure!

- **The neighbors will love having a B&B next door!** Don't count your chickens (unless you're on a farm, silly). Neighbors might not welcome 5, 10, or 20 cars coming and going at all hours. They might have had a quiet existence until you showed up, and they'd probably like to keep it that way. Talk to your neighbors before you move ahead with the business. Tell them about your plans for construction (if any) and for keeping them happy (building a fence or creating a different parking area). Try to involve them in the process and listen to their suggestions. However, be careful to not let them push you around. Property lines get fuzzy when someone decides to make improvements.

MORE THAN MAKING BEDS AND BREAKFAST

Starting up a B&B is exciting and anxiety inducing at the same time. Before you have heartburn trouble or sweaty palms, do all you can to prepare yourself mentally and physically for the experience.

Running a B&B is more than just making beds and serving breakfast, because it requires you to be much more than housecleaner and chef. The roles you take on and the challenges you must meet will stretch from one end of your patience to the other. The only way to prepare for this undertaking is to do your homework. Find out about this business from those who've been there. Get to know the process of start-up, and watch out for the challenges to come.

FINDING OUT THE REAL DEAL FIRSTHAND

It's one thing to imagine Grandma's apple pie and quite another to have a slice. Take time out to learn about the B&B business firsthand from owners and managers. It's the only way to get a real taste for the everyday life of an innkeeper!

- **Level one: Start by sleeping around.** Try to visit a few B&Bs of different sizes. If you can, stay in at least one that's in a completely different part of the country. By staying at a few B&Bs, you'll get a different perspective from each experience and a better sense of what makes you comfortable in a B&B.

- **Level two: Go back to school.** There are many conferences, seminars, and courses you can take related to this business. If you plan to operate a 23-room inn and restaurant, consider taking some heavy courses in hotel management, accounting, and food preparation. Even if your B&B is smaller, it certainly won't hurt to sign up for a few weekend seminars. You may find that the interaction between people who are going through start-up and those who've been in the business for years is worth the experience.

TIP

When you call to make reservations, it's not a good idea to let the innkeepers know why you're planning a visit. When you visit, if hosts seem receptive, broach this in the middle or near the end of your stay. Observe closely, but be unobtrusive. When you're there, talk casually with the owners about how they got into the business, tricks they've learned, and odd guests they've had. Take notes about what you like and don't like about the rooms, the policies, breakfast, and how the innkeepers interact with other guests.

■ **Level three: Get out there.** Getting some experience will really put you ahead in your own business. Even if you can find only part-time work at a hotel, it will help. If you already have management experience look for work as an inn-sitter. Some B&B owners want to take a vacation or even take a few afternoons a week off. By doing some inn-sitting you can gain priceless familiarity with the day-to-day life of owning a B&B.

As an innkeeper, the best investment you can make is in yourself. Do all you can to fill your noggin with as much information and work experience as possible, and you'll soon be on your way to success and peace of mind.

THE BEST DECISION YOU EVER MAKE

We hope you come to feel that opening up your home to paying strangers is well worth the time and trouble. Running a B&B can be a great experience. If you enjoy hosting and entertaining in your home, that's a good start. If you're willing to take the baggage that comes with hosting every day, such as endless cleaning and cooking, that's even better.

Although you won't know until you're in the business if this is the life for you, you can start preparing now for the adjustments. Get ready to find strength and perseverance that you didn't know was in you! Your world will now revolve around your B&B business. If you run that business with professionalism, smarts, and a lot of laughs, you'll learn to love the way of life that goes with it. Only then will you decide that this was the best decision you ever made.

Big Things in Small(er) Packages

The trend toward B&Bs began about 15 to 20 years ago. You might even remember the first time you said, "What's a B-n-B?" Now most everyone

knows what B&B means (and that it's not "bed & brothel"), or at least thinks
they know. The classic definition of a cute old couple in a cute old farmhouse
with cute lace curtains, home-baked biscuits, and decorative ducks definitely
has changed. There are still very nice country-style B&Bs out there, but they
are no longer the only option. What started as a trend has turned into a
steadily growing industry. And all in about a decade!

B&B vs. Inn: What's in a Name?

What's the difference between a B&B and an inn? Good question. Here's
another good one: Does it matter which term you use? Not really. Although
there are some basic guidelines for the distinctions between B&B, inn, B&B
inn, guesthouse, homestay, manor, house, mansion, lodge, and plantation, the
terms differ in meaning from place to place anyway.

The most important part of your business's name will be what you add to
"Inn," "B&B," "Lodge," or the like. Spend some time on this and come up
with something that represents you as the owner, the area you're located in, or
the house itself. Pick something catchy, historical, or quaint. If the house was
built before 1900, find something from the past to use in the name. A lot of
houses built in the eighteenth century use the year of construction in their
names, such as "The 1776 Hale House."

Sam and Richard Corcoran of Old Mystic, Connecticut, have the hottest spot
in town. When they started up their B&B four years ago, they wanted a name
that would "eliminate people looking for Aunt Tilly's Tea Room and would
ensure that our guests have a sense of humor." Richard was a heating engineer
for 30 years; the B&B is painted flaming red, and has five fireplaces and gar-
goyles as the main décor. All of these factors led to naming the B&B "Hell's
Blazes." Sam and Richard say the name alone attracts business. "If you don't
have an interesting name, you won't stick out. You have to have a gimmick to
give you an edge."

Here are some of the common distinctions among types of B&Bs and their
counterparts:

- **Bed-and-breakfast.** Because of its designation, this type of establishment must provide some kind of meal in the morning. Typically,
  a true B&B will serve a full breakfast or something close to one.
  B&Bs that do not serve hot breakfasts usually will have buffet-style
  fare with a wide range of muffins, bagels, breads, cereal, toasting
  waffles, and fruit. The majority of them have an area set off for
  breakfast. Some B&Bs have a dining area with an outdoor patio, but

all have some kind of area conducive to sitting down for a spell to enjoy morning coffee. B&Bs usually are smaller than inns, and average about 3 to 6 rooms, although some have as many as 15 rooms or even more. The owners of B&Bs typically live on the premises, which is not always the case with other types of houses. Amenities in B&Bs have been minimal in the past, but that is changing as more of them are adding such extras as whirlpool tubs and other special facilities to their rooms. (See "All the Rage," later in this section.)

TIP

Some owners wisely describe the type of B&B they have in its name by adding, for example, Farm, Tavern, Beach House, Château, or even Maison if the house has a French theme. Some houses that are linked to a second business reflect it in names such as "Inn and Golf Course" or "B&B and Antiques."

- **Inn.** Like B&Bs, a lot of inns offer a full breakfast. The major distinction of most inns—and this is the classic definition—is that they usually operate as a full-service restaurant for guests and nonguests. Inns also tend to be larger than B&Bs, with six or more guest rooms. There are, however, many smaller inns that do not have restaurants but use the term *inn* because they don't offer a full breakfast (or any breakfast) and don't want to give guests the false hope of full morning fare. As you can see, anything goes in the name game!

- **B&B inn (or inn B&B).** Some use both "B&B" and "Inn" in their names. What for? Hard to tell. Some want to be known as an inn and also want to make it clear that breakfast is included in the room rate. Maybe others just couldn't choose between the two terms!

- **Guesthouse.** B&B and guesthouse are almost interchangeable except that breakfast is not expected in a guesthouse. It sometimes is served but it is rarely a full breakfast. Guesthouse is more commonly used in some parts of the country, such as in the South, whereas in New England, for example, owners are more inclined toward B&B or inn. Old Bates-type motels (remember *Psycho*), built from the 1950s through the 1970s, have become another recent trend among fixer-uppers. Some restore the rooms with kitschy décor from the period.

- **Homestay.** A homestay typically is the most casual of all types of establishments. Usually three rooms are the most you'll find in a homestay. They rarely have private baths for any of the rooms, but breakfast usually is included in the rate. Homestay owners usually live on the property, renting rooms within the family quarters (hence the name) but reserving most of the space for the family. Because homestays are born of a need for extra cash, few have state licenses or signs out front. Breakfast is not necessarily served and most guests are passersby who need a place to crash for the night and find the homestay by asking around.

- **Manor, house, mansion, lodge, homestead, ranch, or plantation.** These are some of the more typical designations used for special types of houses or houses set in special locations. Manor and mansion can be interchangeable, but sometimes *manor* is used for a house that is not quite big enough to be considered a mansion. When *house* or *homestead* is used, it usually refers to a historic period or past owner; the "Captain Morgan House," for example. Lodges typically are set in the mountains and have a distinctly woodsy décor. Plantation B&Bs usually are found in the South, and owners have restored or kept up their original charm. Some ranch B&Bs are extensions of operating ranches, created for supplemental income.

INSIGHTS INTO A BOOMING INDUSTRY

People from all walks of life—from cell phone salespeople to kindergarten teachers, and computer geeks to travel agents—are leaving their commuting jobs and starting up B&Bs. Those with experience in the service and hotel industry are learning from the bigwigs and then applying their knowledge to their own business. It's a smart way to go, especially as the outside world and B&B owners start to take the profession more seriously. Guests now are expecting more service at B&Bs, or at least more hotel-like amenities, such as TV/VCRs with remotes and small bottles of high-quality shampoo, and they're getting it, particularly in touristy and bustling areas where there's more competition among B&Bs for guests who increasingly pass up hotels for cozier lodgings at the "little guy."

Boutique guesthouses are fast becoming a popular trend among investors. These properties have a distinct character based on what they were originally; a property could have been something as unique as a prison, as common as a bank, or have simply been a hotel that went on to operate as a rooming house in the late 1800s or early 1900s. Owners have restored the original structures but updated the amenities, and they typically offer pampering guest service.

Utilizing all manner of unlikely buildings, *boutique hotels* tend to have 50 or more rooms and are filling a gap in the expanding hotel market here and abroad. These often quirky, sometimes trend-setting properties are springing up all over the place, even in big cities where there simply is not enough space to build conventional hotels.

B&B Owners: A Growing Breed

More and more potential B&B owners are considering this lifestyle change for two main reasons. First, the industry has grown because of exposure through the Internet and because people are traveling more than ever. As B&B owners look to sell, they've been able to use the Internet as a marketing tool to reach investors they might not have found otherwise. In addition, the increasing number of travelers who stay in B&Bs gain insight into B&B life or, at least, what they imagine B&B life is like, and are drawn to it.

Second, more people who are making money in other fields are looking for either a lifestyle change or an investment property to use as a tax shelter. This growing breed of B&B owners looking for a piece of the B&B lifestyle has created a lot of turnover in the business. Some find out that they bit off more in workload than they could chew, and others fix up and sell B&Bs to make a profit.

CAUTION

Because of the Internet, B&B for sale properties are easier to find. Many folks are lured into this laid-back lifestyle before doing much research or taking an innkeeper's seminar. Consequently, buyers go into this new venture ill-prepared.

According to the Professional Association of Innkeepers International (PAII) in the 1998 B&B/Country Inn Industry Study, "An overwhelming majority of innkeepers are part of a couple, although for many only one part of the couple is full time at the inn." Also according to PAII, the average age range for innkeepers is "30 to 65+ years old with a heavy cluster in the 40 to 55 range."

So you're not retired—you're not even part of a couple—can you own a B&B? Of course! Although it's true that couples own a good portion of B&Bs, singles are starting to get into the mix, too. As the industry has grown from a mom-and-pop operation, more and more singles are moving from their respective fields into the B&B business.

TIP

Get any kind of work experience at a B&B before opening up your own. Then there will be no surprises. Go and do the work. See whether you enjoy it before you pour heart and soul into something you may not like at all!

Michael MacIntyre, co-owner and innkeeper of The Brass Key in Province-town, Massachusetts, has some insights into why older rather than younger innkeepers are more typical. "I see the average B&B owner as being between 40 and 65 years old. I think it's due to the fact that this population has already gone through the first phase of the typical work environment. They no longer want to work for others. They also have more money put away to invest in a B&B. Young people don't normally have the resources and life experiences that the older age bracket has."

The biggest attraction for a lot of future B&B owners is the ability to work at home. Most haven't done enough research, and don't realize just how much work they'll be doing at home when they run a B&B. Buying this book is a good start; so is attending seminars and classes, and talking to other B&B owners.

Best Areas to Raise the Roof

Location, location, location. Learning a few things from your brothers and sisters in the real estate business will serve you well. If you live in Boonie-town, USA, where very few people pass by in any season or for any reason, you might want to reconsider your location. If you live in Boonietown but there's a reason for people to come your way, however, such as great hiking, you might have a reason to be in the business there.

TIP

The chamber of commerce can give you the scoop on the scope of tourist business in the area you're looking at. If it's near urban life, find out what city B&Bs and boutique hotels are offering and create an alternative!

Most B&Bs are found in coastal areas, in the mountains, near lakes, by rivers, and in other vacation areas. One of the biggest trends in location, however, is big cities. A lot of B&Bs are cropping up in New York City, Boston, Seattle, San Francisco, and other urban locations. Wherever you decide to locate your B&B, first find out how other businesses are doing. Get to know the area by talking with owners of lodging houses, restaurants, gift shops, and bookstores, and anyone else who can give you insight into the economy and your business prospects.

TIP

Always remember location, location, location, but don't forget supply and demand. Opening a bed and breakfast in a popular tourist spot may be a good idea, but if there's already a glut of inn space then you may have a lot of empty rooms!

If your B&B is near a college, vacation spot, cultural or historical area, convention center (or any place that attracts people!), you're already a step ahead. B&Bs that are a little farther out of reach can be a tougher sell.

Location also is one of the biggest determinants in how much you can charge. If you're in a remote location and not directly in the path of a "hot" destination, it might be difficult to get as high a rate as B&Bs closer to the action. Adding amenities and services, though, will allow you to bump up your rates and be competitive with B&Bs in central locations.

WHEN TRAFFIC IS A GOOD THING

There's no doubt that B&Bs on a main street have an advantage. Even if you're in a small town, you might not get a lot of drop-ins, but people will know you're there. Relatives and friends who visit your town for weddings and special events will more likely be referred to your B&B than to those at a distance. Even if someone doesn't know you or what your B&B is like, the fact that you're on a main drag makes you stick out … "Hey, isn't there a B&B on Suchensuch Street? Let's drive by and get the name."

TIP

Keep in mind that although guests will appreciate the convenience of reaching your house, once inside they won't want to be reminded of the traffic outside. Consider putting landscaping buffers in strategic places to minimize noise. Also talk with a knowledgeable heating engineer or handyman about adding extra insulation.

If you're close to a commercial district but off a direct route, find ways to reach business travelers such as offering a 10 percent discount to area businesses that book clients with you.

TRAPPING TOURISTS

To *visit* is a pretty light word for what most tourists do on vacation. Most out-of-towners like to immerse themselves in the areas they've chosen as getaways. In your brochure and when you talk with callers, use your area hot spots to advantage ("only a five-minute drive from the world's largest ball of wool" or "within walking distance of shops, restaurants, and museums").

If your B&B is near a touristy or vacation spot but not in the heart of it all, use both of those factors as sell points. "Close to downtown on a quiet, residential street" will sound like the best of both worlds to most tourists.

OFF THE MAIN ROAD

B&Bs located off the beaten-down path are starting to pop up all over the place. Have you ever been driving through a highly residential area, spotted a B&B, and thought, what is that doing out here? A big reason is that, when location isn't a strength, B&B owners are offering a lot more on the inside. Even though your neighborhood B&B might seem a little out of place at first, neighbors might come to be thankful for it after they've placed relatives in your comfortable home for the holidays instead of their overcrowded one.

If your B&B's address is Nowheresville, think about investing in big and small amenities that will keep guests going out of their way to get to you.

CAUTION

Beware of the urge to exaggerate! When describing your location, it might be tempting to sweeten up the reality: Don't stretch truths. If your property is 30 driving minutes outside a city, don't tout it as "close to downtown"!

When describing your B&B, highlight the attributes of its being in the boonies by using a phrase such as "getaway retreat" or "private and peaceful." If you're somewhat near an urban area, try to stay away from using language such as "far from the hustle and bustle." Most guests will want the option of going into town, so it's wise to play up everything that your location offers.

If you're really out there, you'll more than likely draw a different clientele by offering a lot of unusual amenities and services. Reserving hot air balloon rides or setting up day hikes will help your establishment become somewhat of a destination in itself.

Though some guests may be contented to hang around the house, others will prefer to hover above it!

Your guests also would be looking for a home-cooked breakfast. If you serve only a continental breakfast and it's a haul to the nearest breakfast spot, your empty-stomached guests might be grumpy for the rest of the day. Having top-notch services and an outstanding breakfast will help keep them extra-happy and coming back for more getaways.

TIP

Some owners promote the fact that there are no phones in the room, the television is well hidden, and the newspaper is a day late.

NEAR AN EVENT CENTER OR COLLEGE

Being close to the bustle of a college, boarding school, convention center, or anything that draws crowds is a great plus. Count on being booked for parents' weekends or the great annual Spoon Hangers Convention.

TIP

Leave your business cards and brochures where people congregate such as on high-traffic college bulletin boards, brochure racks at convention centers, hospitals, nursing homes, food stores, and fitness centers. Make connections with people who can really spread the word for you. If the people aren't coming to you, go get them!

Keep on top of what events are happening when so that you can get your highest rates during these times. Pay attention to how the incoming crowds will affect other businesses, too. If Stan's Bistro, the best restaurant in town, always books early, don't wait until 4:00 P.M. to make reservations for your guests. Develop a good relationship with the best restaurants in town and soon you might find that they're saving tables for you.

GROWING PAINS

We've all had growing pains; so do growing industries. Many newer B&Bs and inns and other types of small lodging have become just a little bit sleeker, leaving older ones to fall by the wayside. Some new B&Bs fail, too, when owners eager to jump into a growing industry take a big leap before looking both ways. It's a good idea to talk to people who've given up a B&B, if they'll talk to you. Why not learn from their mistakes? Listen closely to their advice, but don't let it dishearten you. Just because they couldn't make it work doesn't mean you can't!

THE B&B APPEAL

A couple of decades ago, those travelers who frequented B&Bs were mostly looking for a quaint getaway. They knew what to expect: minimal amenities, a quiet house, a shared bath, and morning chatter with the host over home-baked biscuits and tea. These guests expected to travel a bit out of their way, but would do so for lower room rates or relaxed ambiance.

Times do change mighty fast and, although some of these experiences still exist, the industry is growing up. As it grows, B&Bs become more sophisticated. Gone from most of them are lace doilies under candy dishes and pictures of Grandma's kids in the hallways. Gone are the days of hosts eating breakfast with guests and telling stories of the "Guest of Christmas Past." The biggest trend among new ownerships is a movement into more hotel-like guest services. Guests might opt for your B&B over a Holiday Inn, but they'll still look for those little bottles of shampoo and big white towels.

We're not saying that the charm and quaint appeal of B&Bs has been tossed aside. Absolutely not! It's okay to be nostalgic; those were good times. Some of those good times still exist, especially in B&Bs run by the same owner for many years. Your guests will stay with you in hopes of having a more personal experience. They're looking to you and your B&B for the comfortable and relaxed atmosphere that they know hotels can't offer. It's the combination of these two worlds—a charming atmosphere with more amenities and services—that has broadened the B&B's appeal and brought the industry into a new era.

You've Got ... Personality

Guests will choose your place over the Holiday Inn because they want a different experience. Do you know what a major part of that experience is? You!

You are an extension of your business and your business is an extension of you. In larger inns (25 rooms or more), guests don't anticipate having much—if any—contact with the owners, although they still expect employees to be more charming and personable than hotel staff. The smaller the establishment, the more the guests look forward to making a personal connection with you and your troupe. This doesn't mean that guests expect, or even want, a host who follows them around or spends the evening with them, but before guests walk through your door, they'll assume that you have an easygoing, charming nature and that you'll want to make their stay memorable. That is exactly what they should find! As the lodging industry grows and changes, the factor that continues to distinguish the B&B from the more commercial establishment is—again—you. If hosting is not your cup of tea (or your partner's), you have some work ahead of you.

All the Rage

Some trends such as platform shoes and the Smiley Face tend to float in and out like, well, platform shoes and Smiley Faces. The B&B and country-style inn, however, is a trend that began about 15 years ago and is now a booming industry. The current industry-wide emphasis on guest services seems to be less of a trend and more of a response to a general change in the lifestyle of B&B clientele.

Although the contemporary B&B retains much of its traditional warmth and charm (due in great part to the host), guests expect more in the way of room amenities. Some of the "extras" that guests are looking for are a phone with voicemail; TV/VCR; mini-fridge with freezer for ice; iron/ironing board; alarm clock/CD player; hair dryer, bathrobes, shampoo, soap, and lotion; and control of heat and air conditioning. Most guests don't expect bigger attractions such as a whirlpool tub, small kitchen, fireplace, or deck or patio access, but those perks do appeal to those who are willing to pay more.

It's important when taking a reservation to tell guests as much as possible about the amenities in each room. Put your best feature forward when you get a sense of what your future guest is looking for in a room.

CAUTION

Watch out for white lie fever! You sometimes might feel the urge to "enhance" your description of a room or of your B&B with a little more, shall we say, glitter? Don't do it! If the "poolside room" turns out to be a third-floor room above a small, barely visible pool, you just lost a returning guest. Don't coat your descriptions in spice unless you have the rack to back it up with.

Other expectations guests might have are services such as a fax machine and phone lines with data ports, popular in B&Bs that service a lot of business travelers. For vacationers, it's becoming more common to provide concierge-type services such as making reservations for meals and tours. B&Bs looking to pamper their guests will offer bath salts for their whirlpool tubs, and full turn-down service.

In whatever direction you decide to take your B&B, remember that you are not limited in your choices. Guests will be pleasantly surprised by even the smallest touches that reflect you and the personality of your house.

THE B&B GUEST

There are some classic traits of the typical B&B guest. Does this mean that all your guests will either be fun-loving honeymooners or sweet old couples? Not by a long shot. You'll encounter a wide range of interesting and not-so-interesting folk from around the world. Major segments of the B&B guest market, however, do fall into categories. Here are some of them from a recent study (adjusted for inflation) created by YBR Marketing and the Professional Association of Innkeepers International:

- 77 percent of guests are middle-aged (age 25 to 54).
- 92.8 percent attended college and/or graduate school.
- 47.9 percent will pay you from their household income of $75,000 or more.
- Approximately $90.00 is the average amount that guests spend for a night's lodging.

Your typical guest will vary according to your type of operation and location. If you're near a college town, expect a lot of middle-aged parents and traveling speakers. A B&B in a touristy town, particularly by the ocean, will see all types. Historical areas typically draw older folk or historians. Convention center areas fill up fast, so if you're near one expect to see a lot of suits at your breakfast table.

WHAT IT'S REALLY LIKE

Think about the office worker bee, the standard nine-to-fiver. Maybe you are one: You go to work, do your thing, pack up, and go home. The day is done until it starts up again tomorrow. Even if you really like your job, we're sure you'll agree that there's a lot of satisfaction in leaving it at day's end.

Since the Industrial Revolution, we've been programmed to think that professional careers exist only outside the home. How many of you have had a parent say when you were a teenager, "Go out and get a job"? "Staying in" to generate income is just not seen as hard work. Ironically, running a B&B in your home is some of the hardest work around.

You've no doubt considered that operating a B&B will be different. One minute you'll be taking a reservation over the phone, the next minute you're solving a plumbing problem. Just when you start cleaning up after a guest who checked out late, in walks an arriving guest who is two hours early. Sit down and eat that sandwich? Not a chance.

We don't want to scare you off from owning a bed and breakfast. What we are suggesting is that you follow your own path. Some people have an image of what a B&B should look like and how it should operate but, in reality, no two B&Bs are the same. Heed the advice and suggestions of other owners and draw on what you've learned from them when you have choices to make and problems to solve. The best thing you can do for yourself and for a successful B&B is to learn as much as you can about the business and then apply it to your own situation. Whatever happens with your new business will be your own unique experience—as it should be!

STAYING POSITIVE AT THE GET-GO

No matter what you're told about something you have yet to experience, it will always be different from what you imagine. Sometimes knowing this can provide peace, but keeping your spirits up during a transition to an unknown world can be difficult. Not impossible, but difficult.

Staying positive is easy when you're looking for a B&B property or going over plans to renovate your house with the architect. Picking out colors for your rooms and buying linens also are cheerful tasks. But when you become doubtful of your abilities as a host or you stress over making the mortgage payments, you might start to lose your Pollyanna attitude. The best way to stay positive during the lengthy and challenging process of starting a B&B is to keep your feelings in check. Your first day, your first week, maybe even your first month might really, really stink. It's possible, and it happens. Just remember that you're new to this business. You won't get everything right the first time even though you will place those demands on yourself. If you keep plugging away and attacking each day with humility and a fierce, Rocky-style attitude, you'll make it.

DEALING WITH THE WORK-AT-HOME WAY

Making the adjustment to working at home might appear easy; it's the reason a lot of people go into the B&B business. Working out of your home, how-ever, can be a huge adjustment. Your contact with the outside world ceases, and people tend to think that because you don't go out to work, you're not working. Your best friend calls to see whether you can tape *Oprah* while she's "at work." Your partner, who works outside the home, asks you to run errands because he or she thinks you don't have much to do. On checking out, a guest asks, "So, is this *all* you do?" It's difficult to get others to understand that what you're doing at home is working.

TIP

It's easy to become frustrated when people don't understand what it takes to run your business. Don't give in to anger: Firmly and with good humor bring them into the program. If you take your profession seriously, everyone else will, too.

Tell your best friend that you wish you had time to watch television, never mind figure out the VCR. Tell your partner that you can do one errand while you're out shopping for the B&B, and that any more than that will interfere with your business—*your source of income.* And last but not least, say this to the know-it-all guest: "No, I have other jobs, too. I'm also a cook, house-cleaner, plumber, decorator, manager, receptionist, and host. I just don't leave my home to do those jobs." And don't forget to smile and crack a joke. After all, taking *any* job too seriously wouldn't be much fun!

Say Good-Bye to Saturday Night

If you've said to yourself, "Oh, I barely do anything on Saturday nights any-way. How bad can it be?" you're about to find out. The only way you won't mind giving up your Saturday nights is if you understand the real trade-off. You're not making an even swap from "nothing to do" to "something to do." You'll be staying home on Saturday nights because you have to. A house full of guests, especially if they stay in on a rainy night, means work for you.

If you like dining out, catching a movie, or cutting a rug or two at your favorite club, imagine what it will be like without these escapes. You might not have to completely erase these pleasures from your life, but they might be limited. You'll need to find ways to compensate for them or, during slow times, go out during the week. Even if you can afford to hire a manager to take your place when you're out, it will be a long while before you feel comfortable leaving the house in someone else's hands.

Owning a B&B can be a real catch-22. As owner, you run the business, but most of the time it ends up running you! There are ways to keep your sanity, and pencil in some private time. Just make sure that you can live without your Saturday nights.

Considering Family Members

As the owner of a B&B, having the support of your family is not only nice, it's necessary. If you have a wife, husband, or partner, whether or not he or she pitches in, you'll need this person's full support. If you have school-age kids, let them know what will change around the house and how they'll need to lend a hand.

Involve everyone in the process. Sit down with household family members and discuss all possible changes such as routines, meals, and even simple chores. For instance, running the washing machine at midnight won't be an option anymore if the laundry room is right below a guest room.

If you already give your kids allowances or incentives for doing chores around the house, consider bumping up their duties in exchange for better perks. Try not to Cinderella them; just see if they can pitch in enough, for example, to let your housecleaner leave two hours early on Tuesdays and Thursdays.

TIP

Make sure you listen to the family's concerns after the business gets underway, too. No one will know exactly how things will change until it actually happens. As long as you talk about the adjustments and smooth out the kinks that come along with new territory, you'll be able to get through it.

WHAT YOU'LL GAIN BESIDES INCOME

Aside from shooting for a profit (keep your fingers crossed), there are other great advantages to owning a B&B:

■ **Become the host with the most.** Hosting can be very satisfying, especially if your guests think you're doing it right! If you have a lot of fun entertaining in your home and would enjoy doing it a lot—a whole heck of a lot—you will gain a lot of pride in your new career. If you haven't had a lot of experience hosting in your own home, what's stopping you? Have a couple of dinner parties for family and friends. It will give you a taste of both sides of hosting: the feel-good side of preparing a meal for other people and the unglamorous side of behind-the-scenes preparation and cleanup.

■ **Top executive status.** Owning your own business can be very rewarding. If you've ever worked for someone else, you'll particularly love being your own boss! If you also enjoy the challenges and responsibility of being the head cheese, this business is for you.

■ **You can work in your slippers.** Well, not in front of the guests, but working at home can be a comfortable way to spend your day. Although every perk has its downside, this one is especially two-sided. When you work at home, there's nowhere else to go at the end of your day! Keeping comfortable private quarters will help you to enjoy working at home because it will provide an escape from the business itself.

CAUTION

Watch out for the urge to turn rooms in your private quarters into guest rooms in hope of earning more income. Determine whether the extra money is really worth it; don't sacrifice the sanity of private relaxation for a few extra bucks a week. You might end up missing your privacy so much that you bag the business altogether.

- **Live in your dream house.** Many innkeepers would not be able to afford their homes if they didn't rent out rooms for the extra income. You might not become wealthy in this business, but having a B&B can afford you a better lifestyle.
- **Shortest commute in town.** For those who live at their B&Bs, being able to avoid traffic and long drive times is a real plus. If you plan to own a B&B that is farther than 10 to 15 minutes away from your home, consider it carefully. Some hindrances are that you'll need to hire someone to be at the property 24 hours a day, and you'll spend most of your days and nights at the B&B anyway!
- **Gimme a break, Uncle Sam!** If your B&B is run out of your home, you can get tax breaks on the house, food, and supplies.

You probably have even more personal reasons for choosing the B&B way of life. Before you dive in, be sure to take time out to make a list of all the conceivable advantages and disadvantages of it. If your cons outweigh your pros and you still decide to move forward, at least you know what you're diving into.

A Day in the Life

The following example is not typical of every B&B but it's a close shot at what a day in the life of an owner can be like. This scenario is based on one person running a six-room B&B, without staff or much help from a partner, who works outside the home.

6:00 A.M.: Alarm sounds, hit snooze bar and mentally prepare for the morning.

6:10 A.M.: Get up, take three-minute shower (full house of early risers). Wake up partner (two-minute shower allowed); get dressed.

6:30 A.M.: Start preparing breakfast items for cooking or baking; double-check eating areas to make sure all is in place from setup the night before; have juice and cereal.

7:00 A.M.: Prepare coffee and hot water for tea for early risers; continue working on breakfast.

7:23 A.M.: Pack up, as prearranged, muffins, fruit, and coffee for business travelers in suites 5 and 6 who are checking out at 7:30.

7:50 A.M.: Check out business travelers who are running late, and give them the best, quickest directions to their next destination.

8:00 A.M.: Guests start filing down for full breakfast (served buffet style).

8:15 A.M.: Serve breakfast and apologize for the wait (due to late check-out of business travelers).

8:27 A.M.: Phone rings, couple needs room for the weekend. Ask if you can arrange to call in 10 minutes.

8:31 A.M.: Return to dining area to check on guests and refill coffee.

8:40 A.M.: Return call and complete sale.

8:56 A.M.: When last guest files out, clean up eating area and kitchen; load dishwasher, but don't run it (in case of any late showers).

9:15 A.M.: Clean suites 5 and 6.

TIP

To make guests happy without losing your sanity, don't promise anything you can't deliver in normal routines. Be sure that in your service plan you anticipate, meet, and exceed the normal guests' needs, so they won't be calling you after hours. Have high-quality tea, hot water, soft drinks, fruits, cheeses, and snacks available for them to help themselves. Provide dining information and offer to take care of their dining needs in the morning so it's all done for them by evening.

10:30 A.M.: Take a phone reservation; send out reservation confirmation; organize office; hang around desk for 11:00 A.M. check-outs for rooms 2 and 4; and check e-mail.

11:30 A.M.: Make dinner reservations as requested by guests in rooms 1 and 3 during breakfast; leave messages on guests' voicemails confirming reservations were made; run the dishwasher.

11:50 A.M.: Drink a protein shake and glance at the newspaper.

12:00 P.M.: Start cleaning rooms 2 and 4.

1:30 P.M.: Start a load of laundry.

1:40 P.M.: Change towels and tidy up rooms 1 and 3.

2:17 P.M.: Greet arriving guests, get remaining balance of payment, give tour of house, answer questions, and show them to room 4.

2:50 P.M.: Put first load of laundry into dryer and start a second.

3:00 P.M.: Eat a late lunch of …

3:05 P.M.: Answer more questions from newly arrived guests.

3:15 P.M.: … tuna salad; unload dishwasher.

3:30 P.M.: Clean common sitting areas and bathroom; start on third load of laundry; fold first set; call cable company.

4:30 P.M.: More laundry; run to store for a few breakfast items.

4:55 P.M.: Greet guests returning from their day out on the town; give them directions to restaurants; chill wine in your fridge for room 1 to drink later that evening.

5:20 P.M.: Sweep front steps; tidy outside common areas. (This includes stomping down unearthed lawn created by pesky mole family.)

6:00 P.M.: Finish laundry; stock linen closets.

6:20 P.M.: Set up common areas for evening time: low lights, candles, fireplace, classical music.

6:30 P.M.: Greet guests checking in very late for room 2.

7:00 P.M.: Greet partner who came home an hour ago.

7:05 P.M.: Make late dinner reservations for room 2; call room 2 to confirm reservation was made.

7:10 P.M.: Deliver fax that arrived for room 3.

7:15 P.M.: Meet room 2 guests in the hallway. (They've decided to order in instead.)

7:20 P.M.: Cancel dinner reservation and bring take-out menus up to room 2.

7:30 P.M.: Prepare tray with plates, napkins, silverware, glasses, and chocolates for room 2.

7:40 P.M.: Sit down to eat lovely dinner prepared by partner (wishful thinking?).

7:50 P.M.: Answer door, take tray and delivery person to room 2, and then show delivery person out.

8:00 P.M.: Finish dinner; do dishes.

8:20 P.M.: Put feet up and have a cup of tea.

8:40 P.M.: Write out some bills; check e-mail.

9:27 P.M.: Check breakfast areas for next morning meal: refill condiments; set up buffet; make muffin mix for next day and put in fridge.

10:11 P.M.: Write out notes for next day's schedule.

10:30 P.M.: Watch evening news.

11:00 P.M.: Close down common room.

11:20 P.M.: Hit the sack.

Phew! And that's a slow day!

You've probably noticed in our "day in the life" example that running a B&B is a combination of repetitive action (things such as laundry are endless) and surprises (guests changing their minds). A lot of days, running a B&B is just full of repetitiveness.

Totally Devoted to You

It's 10:30 P.M. You finally have some spare time to yourself. Do you write out bills, check your e-mail, file paperwork, or call it a day? Demanding as this business is, you'll learn that setting aside time for yourself can be just as demanding.

Finding Time and How Much You'll Need

Finding time for yourself sounds very passive, as if time is just hanging out there in space waiting to be caught. You'll need to make that time for yourself and your family. If you wait to stumble into some empty time, you'll be waiting an eternity.

TIP

Taking time out to relax is not only good for your psyche, it's good for business. The best host is calm, well rested, and happy. If you can't take a vacation, section off bits of time every day just for yourself. Part of the charm of your B&B is you. If you're cranky to your guests, it won't matter how charming your décor looks.

Determining how much time you'll need to make for yourself is a bit tricky. When you first start out you can expect to be consumed by the work. In part, this is a really good thing. Squeeze as much work out of yourself as you can while your enthusiasm is off the charts.

Be careful, though, to not go overboard. Burning out in the first few months is common. As you'll need that explosive enthusiasm to last you for more than the first few months, try not to trade in all your free time to work on the business. Stay alert to how this extra work affects you mentally and physically. Do you have to have someone drag you out of bed in the morning? Are you snapping at your 12-year-old? Do you find yourself fading in and out of concentration?

Everyone needs different amounts of personal time to keep them going. You might discover that running a B&B affords you more time than you thought. On the other hand, if you find that personal time is slipping away from you, take steps to get it back. Hire staff, if you can afford it, or shut down the business for two days during your off season. You might lose some income initially, but you'll be better prepared to stay in business for the long haul.

TIP

If you give guests access to the kitchen, make sure that your own quarters are closed off from this area. Guests won't know where they're going and could wander into your private rooms. This also will cut down on late-night noise creeping into your quarters (usually guests in search of ice).

BALANCING YOUR LIFE

Now that your work and home are in one place, you'll need to make some mental and physical adjustments. Melding work into your home life requires a great deal of organization. It also forces you to think and live differently from when you worked outside the home.

Physically, you need to arrange business and personal affairs as separate entities. Paperwork should be kept in different files, family food is separate from your guests', and your living quarters in the house are kept private for you and your family.

CAUTION

Do not assume you will be happy doing everything yourself for very long. You will burn out. Develop and implement a concept that sets you up as a business, one that you will continue to grow as the years go on. This means staffing, computer systems, renovation and marketing growth.

Mentally separating your business from your personal life is a bigger challenge. Turning the day off at night is difficult because if you live on the premises, you don't get to actually leave your place of work. Removing yourself from the house is a good way to mentally shift gears. When you do have some time to yourself, go to the gym or have lunch with friends. If you can't get out of the house, do your best to leave business out of your private quarters. Set a cut-off time in the evenings after which you and your partner do not discuss the business. Everyone needs downtime. Whether you physically or mentally get away from work, either tactic will help you stay sharp during your workday.

30-Second Recap

- Before you plunge ahead and open a bed-and-breakfast, find out whether you have the personal characteristics and abilities you need to be successful at it.

- Owning a B&B is not only a career change; it's a lifestyle change. Explore the effects that changing your way of life will have on you and yours.

- There are many common misconceptions about owning a B&B. Do your homework before you make your decision.

- The best way to prepare for life as an innkeeper is to visit B&Bs, take courses, go to seminars, and gain work experience.

- The delineation between a B&B, an inn, and other similar terms has blurred. Choosing a name for your B&B is important, but don't get too hung up on labels.

- A decade ago the B&B was a trend. Now it's a booming industry with changes in ownership, style, and guest services.

- Location is important to your success. If your house exists in a remote area, be sure to offer something that guests can't get in busier towns.

- The B&B tradition of a welcoming and an affable host is what continues to lure travelers to B&Bs.

- Running a B&B requires that you alter your thinking (and that of others) about working inside the home.

- It's essential that you prepare yourself and your live-in family members for a change in lifestyle.

- A day in the life of a B&B owner is made up of repetitiveness sprinkled with surprises.

- When you live and work at home, making separate time for yourself and your family will keep you balanced and refreshed.

Contract Basics

Contracts That Are Binding

Contracts are the fuel for your business. Most contracts are oral, though some are written, and most contracts are performed, though some are breached. You need to prepare contracts that clearly state both parties' intent, without unduly cluttering the contract with verbose legalese. This section is intended to help you do just that.

IN SEARCH OF A SOLID CONTRACT

A contract is a promise or set of promises for the breach of which the law gives a remedy, or the performance of which the law in some way recognizes a duty. Actually, most of us know a contract when we see one, mainly because it says "contract" or "agreement" right on it. However, I'm not sure that we always know a contract when we hear one. Oral contracts are usually no less binding than written ones, but their precise terms may be much more elusive.

The essence of each contract involves certain rights and duties. The contract rights (benefits) for one party correspond to the duties (obligations) of the other party. For example, Purchase Company promises in a contract to pay Seller Company $100,000 (duty), and Purchase would receive the deed to Seller's real estate (right). Conversely, Seller agreed to convey the deed to Purchaser (duty) and will receive his or her payment (right). Each contract you enter can be viewed as rights or benefits you receive and duties or obligations you must perform.

Contracts are either bilateral or unilateral. Bilateral contracts involve an exchange of promises of future performance. For example, Purchaser and Seller exchanged promises: Purchaser to pay $100,000, and Seller to convey the deed to the property at a date set in the future. Most contracts are bilateral.

However, if one party makes a contract offer, and the other party accepts by immediately performing the contract, then this is a unilateral contract. Suppose, for example, that Ms. Customer orders 100 widgets from Supplier Company, who ships the order in response to her contract offer; they've just made a unilateral contract.

How does all this matter to your business? Contract law requires you to ask two questions:

1. Do we have a contract?
2. What are the terms of the contract?

Neither question is as simple as it appears, and answers to either may have an important impact on your business. Contracts are not made to be broken, but some are breached; you need to know your rights.

Contract law has two sources: *Uniform Commercial Code,* Article 2, for sales of goods, and *common law* for all contracts not involving sales of goods, such as employment, insurance, and real estate. The differences are discussed in this appendix.

PLAIN ENGLISH

Common law is judge-made law, as contrasted with the **contract law,** which consists of federal and state constitutions, statutes, and administrative agency regulations. Common law in your state may have developed over decades and is governed by the principle of precedent, or what courts have previously ruled on a legal question.

FORMING A SOLID CONTRACT

Every contract your business enters into requires four elements for its legal existence:

1. Offer
2. Acceptance
3. Consent
4. Consideration

In addition, the parties to the contract must have the legal capacity to enter into the contract, and the contract has to be to legal. Also, a few contracts—real estate contracts and sales of goods worth $500 or more—must be in writing to be enforceable. This writing requirement is called the Statute of Frauds. Let's take a look at what goes into the creation of a contract.

OFFER

You (the offeror) make an offer to another company (the offeree) to enter into a contract, and the offer specifies the proposed contract terms. If the offeree accepts the offer, a contract is formed. If the offeree rejects the proposal outright, no contract is formed. If the offeree suggests different terms, he or she creates a new offer. Only when both parties agree is a contract formed.

The offer by the offeror should ...

- Convey the offer to a specific offeree (Company B).
- Have a definite subject matter (10 pounds of cotton).
- Set a time for acceptance (by 1 P.M., April 1, 2005).

If you send a purchase order to a supplier, or conversely, a customer comes into your store and orders your merchandise, either conveys the offer to the other party. The offeror intends to make a contract.

The terms of the offer must be sufficient to form an enforceable contract; too vague or ambiguous an offer may not be sufficiently clear to be accepted and have identifiable terms.

ACCEPTANCE

The offeror should establish a deadline for the offeree to accept, preferably in writing. If the offeree doesn't accept the terms within the time limit, there is no contract. An acceptance that materially varies from the offer also is considered a rejection. However, a minor variation in the terms such as an alteration of just a few days for the time of performance may result in a contract if it involves the sale of goods. Therefore, you may want your offer to contain a requirement that acceptance must be according to all the terms of the contract.

TIP

Write your contracts in plain, good English. You can use a form contract as a starting point, but too many contain unnecessary legalese. Say what you intend. A simple list of offeror and offeree rights and duties will usually suffice.

You may revoke your offer at any time before the offeree accepts. However, if you are a merchant selling goods and provide the customer with a firm offer, which is a written promise to keep the offer open for a specified period, you cannot revoke before that time has expired. Suppose, for example, that you make a written offer to sell a riding lawnmower for $1,500 and you include in the offer your promise to keep the offer open for two days. You then cannot revoke the offer before the two days are up. Another exception is referred to as detrimental reliance. For example, you told a prospective employee that if she moved to your city at her expense, you would hire her; you have made a nonrevocable offer if she relies on your offer to move to your city; if you end up not hiring her, she can sue you for her expenses and lost salary.

If you are the offeree, make sure that you understand all the offeror's terms. If you don't understand a term, have the offeror clarify it and amend the written offer to reflect the clarification. Don't sign a contract that doesn't contain all the important terms of the contract, because if it's not in the contract the court may refuse to enforce it. This is particularly true if this so-called external term contradicts a term in the written agreement, or if the contract contains a zipper clause that specifically states that the parties agree there are no terms outside the agreement.

TIP

A prospective buyer could enter into an option contract with a seller to make the offer irrevocable for the period of the option. For example, the prospective buyer could give the seller $5,000 to keep the seller's offer to sell Blackacre open for 30 days. In essence, the option contract buys time.

An acceptance may be conditional; therefore, the contract would exist only if the stated condition occurred. For example, if you are buying a building, you would want to condition your purchase upon evidence that the seller owned the property free of liens (as shown by title insurance) and satisfactory evidence of the building's structural soundness. After you receive evidence that the seller has removed the conditions, you can proceed to contract.

CONSENT

Each contracting party must consent to the agreement voluntarily. You may pay more for a good or service than you want, but if you weren't forced or defrauded, then your agreement was consensual. In a lawsuit, a party may ask the court to be excused from performance because of a lack of consent, which means the party may seek to prove one of four charges:

- **Duress** means that one coerced another into signing the contract. In fact, an act may be legal in itself, but so overcomes the other party's free will to amount to duress. For example, if a boss tells an employee that he will fire her if she doesn't sell her house to him, this is duress, even though he may be able to fire her under employment at-will. In most business transactions, this would be difficult to prove, unless one party is so strong that it can literally cram down the contract on the small party. In that instance, the court may not enforce a completely unfair and one-sided contract, but these are rare cases.

■ **Undue influence** means that one party uses a dominant position of trust to unfairly persuade the other party to enter into a one-sided contract. For example, if an attorney persuaded a client to sell him property at a very advantageous price, this misconduct may amount to undue influence because the client is apt to trust that the attorney (whom the client hired and pays) will act in the client's best interest. However, it takes proof that a buyer completely dominated a seller in order for a court to determine that selling an item at a very low price came about through undue influence.

■ **Misrepresentation** is the most common of claims. One party misrepresents material facts that then become the major inducement for the other party to contract. If the misrepresentation is intentional, then it is fraud. For example, you contract with Bill Builder to add on to your store after Builder claims to have built several additions like yours. However, Builder had never built any addition before and thus has materially misrepresented his skills. The misrepresentation would permit the innocent party to rescind the contract.

■ **Mutual material mistake of fact** involves both parties making a false assumption about a material term in the contract. For example, both the buyer and the seller believe that the land is suitable for growing crops, but later both discover that the land was polluted prior to the contract and all the topsoil must be removed. The basis of the contract was the assumption that the land could grow crops, which was a mutual material mistake.

If the party proves duress, undue influence, or misrepresentation, the court may refuse to enforce the contract and may award damages to the injured party. If the party proves mutual material mistake of fact, the contract may be annulled. Please read the section on contract remedies later in this section.

CONSIDERATION

A contract requires consideration, which is a legal term for a bargained-for exchange of benefits between the parties. Courts usually do not examine the adequacy of the consideration, only its existence. The focus is on the exchange of something of value, not whether the buyer paid too much or the seller got too little from the contract.

However, consideration can exist without the bargained-for exchange under certain limited circumstances. Specifically, a contract without consideration is valid if the contract involves the other party's reliance on your promise for the following:

- **Charitable pledge.** If you pledge $10,000 to a local charity for a building project, which it undertakes in reliance on your promise, you are contractually bound even though you haven't received any tangible benefit for the contribution.

- **Contract guarantee.** If a parent or spouse guarantees a contract in writing, the guarantee is enforceable even though the guarantor received nothing of value.

- **Promissory estoppel.** Promissory estoppel protects a party who spends money or gives up time or energy relying on the other party's promise. Courts won't allow the promissor to later claim lack of consideration as a way to void the contract. For example, a franchisor promises to grant you a franchise to sell hamburgers if you buy a building and pay the franchisor for training. In this case, the franchisor requested that you change your financial position in reliance on its promise of a job. If the franchisor claims it received no benefit from your conduct, thus no consideration, you respond by asserting promissory estoppel. (The franchisor is stopped from denying the existence of consideration.)

A unilateral, or one-party, mistake generally cannot excuse performance, unless the mistake was so obvious to the other party that it would be unfair to enforce the contract, such as a typographical error that obviously understates the price by 50 percent. The court can reform the contract to reflect what terms the parties intended.

CAPACITY AND LEGALITY

Any party to a contract must be of legal age—18—and have the mental capacity to understand his or her contractual rights and duties. Any minor can disaffirm (avoid) the contract within a reasonable time after becoming age 18 by returning the consideration received. For example, if you sold a motorcycle to a minor, the minor buyer can return the cycle in the same condition as purchased and receive his or her money back. A person who lacks mental capacity can likewise disaffirm the contract personally or through his or her guardian, and thus the contract is *voidable*.

An illegal bargain involves a contract term or performance that is criminal, a civil wrong such as fraud, or against public policy. The subject matter of the contract may be illegal, such as the sale of marijuana, or the purpose may be illegal, such as hiring a goon to attack another performer or creating a price-fixing agreement in violation of the federal antitrust laws.

PLAIN ENGLISH

Voidable means the contract exists until the person disaffirms, whereas void means the contract cannot be enforced. A contract with a minor or mentally incapacitated person is voidable, unless that person has a guardian, in which case the contract is void.

An illegal contract is unenforceable. However, if a term of the contract is illegal but can be separated from the rest of the contract without materially changing the contract, the contract itself, minus the illegal provision, may be enforceable. For example, if the contract violates the state usury law (illegal rate of interest), the court may be able to amend this to a legal rate and otherwise enforce the contract.

STATUTE OF FRAUDS WRITING REQUIREMENT

The Statute of Frauds has nothing to do with fraud. Instead it is a requirement that certain contracts have to be in writing if you want to enforce them. For business contracts, these terms include ...

- Contracts for the sale of land.
- Broker commission contracts.
- Contracts that cannot be fully performed within one year.
- Suretyship or guarantee contracts.
- Contracts for the sale of goods worth $500 or more.

For instance, a contract that requires producing a television program for two years cannot be fully performed within one, and must be in writing to be enforceable. However, some contracts with a stated period of over one year may not come within the Statute of Frauds, such as a two-year insurance contract for fire coverage, because the property may be destroyed within one year.

A *suretyship* or *guaranty* requires a written document to hold the surety or guarantor liable. For example, if you sell a car to a young person with little credit history, you will want to have the parents sign a written guarantee that they will pay if their child does not. You may also want them to cosign the promissory note for the loan or a sale on credit.

PLAIN ENGLISH

A **surety** or **guarantor** is a person who agrees to be responsible for the debt of another.

The Statute of Frauds requires a writing, that it contain enough terms to indicate that it's a contract, and that it be signed by the person against whom the contract is being enforced.

The writing can be handwritten or typed; a faxed document with a signature and an e-mail document with a digital signature would be considered a "writing." The document must have enough terms to show that it is a contract, such as the names of the parties and the services to be performed or goods sold. The defendant in a lawsuit may assert that the contract did not comply with the Statute. Then it's up to the plaintiff to show that the defendant's signature or its equivalent appears on the writing. If the defendant receives a memo confirming the oral contract and did not object within 10 days, however, the court will waive the signature requirement.

TIP

Always put it in writing. If you have an oral order for goods costing $500 or more, fax or mail the written confirmation with the details of the order. If the buyer does not object within 10 days, you have an enforceable contract.

Further, if you specially manufacture the goods for the party who orders them, the court may also waive the writing requirement. For example, if you made business cards to order for a customer, complete with the customer's logo and address, and the customer refuses to accept delivery because you had no written contract, you can enforce the contract. If a customer has accepted part of any shipment, the Statute of Frauds applies only to the part not yet accepted.

INTERPRETING THE VAGUE AND AMBIGUOUS

Too often our contract terms are not clearly expressed or are capable of having more than one meaning. This fault may land you in court and require a judge to interpret what you probably meant at the time you formed the contract. Read Strunk and White's *The Elements of Style* (Macmillan, 1973), a handy little book that emphasizes clarity. Then write your contract according to its principles, or insist your lawyer do so.

If the court or an arbitrator must interpret your contract, he or she will hear evidence as to what you and the other party intended. However, that testimony may be colored by the self-interest required to win the case. Or to put it tersely, the other party may lie.

The court may use one of several methods to interpret what the parties intended, including the following:

- **Plain meaning of ordinary words within the context of the entire contract.** This first approach is often referred to as the "dictionary interpretation." Almost literally, the court goes to the dictionary to ascertain what the term means. This approach may be more applicable when contracts are written in plain English, but may be less helpful if the contract is poorly written. Nonetheless, you need to know that a court may take you at your word, at least as it's commonly understood.

- **Performance of the term under this or past contracts.** The court may look to performance under this contract or under past contracts to interpret a term. Said another way, actions speak louder than words. For example, if you are halfway through the current contract and have accepted a discount for each payment made within 10 days, you really have indicated to the other party that the discount exists, even if not expressed well, or at all, on paper. Likewise, if you have a new contract, and past practice under similar contracts required you to pick up the goods at the seller's place of business, the term *delivery* will continue to mean that you'll pick up the goods at the seller's business—unless your new contract expressly requires delivery at your business location.

- **Trade usage.** Trade usage recognizes that businesses in a specialized area of commerce use special terms among themselves. The court will recognize this usage.

TIP

Make sure you're clear on your terms every time you sign a contract. Review each contract renewal. Compare the expressed terms with each party's practice. If you do not want to continue the same way, clearly express the change in the new contract.

- ■ **Gap fillers.** The *Uniform Commercial Code (UCC) for Sales* has a provision for absent terms, or gap fillers, for contracts where none of the foregoing methods apply. For example, if the parties haven't expressly indicated price or implied one, the *UCC* gap filler states that price is the reasonable value at the delivery location. Likewise, if the parties haven't indicated a delivery location, the *UCC* specifies that delivery will be at the seller's place of business or where the goods are located.

- ■ **Construed against the party writing the contract.** Finally, the court may construe the contract against the party who drafted it and created the vague or ambiguous term. This is particularly appropriate when the contract is a standard form and the party drafting it insists upon its wording.

ON TIME AND IT WORKS

If your company sells cars, carpet, or canned carrots, each sale involves certain warranties. Any contract, whether with a consumer or supplier, requires both parties to fully perform the contract according to its terms, and the failure to do so may result in a lawsuit.

CAUTION

If you make a written contract offer, read the acceptance of its terms by the offeree because he or she might add terms. These additional terms may be enforceable if you do not timely reject them (or if they materially alter the contract). You could insist in your offer that your contract must be accepted without alteration.

WARRANTIES

Contracts for the sale of goods may contain express warranties and become part of the bargain between the seller and buyer. The express warranty may be created by a description of the goods in the contract or by a sample or model. Most expensive products, such as cars, riding mowers, and computers, have a written express warranty detailing the expected quality of the product. Some products contain a simple warranty, such as "100 percent cotton" or "will not shrink if washed according to instructions." A written warranty is not required, but if given cannot be disclaimed by language such as *as is* or *no warranties.* Once given, the express warranty exists.

In addition, the federal *Magnuson-Moss Act* creates certain warranty rights for consumers. For any consumer product costing $15 or more, the act requires consumers to be informed of ...

- Who is entitled to warranty protection.
- Which parts of the product are warranted.
- What can be done to correct a defect in the product.
- When the warranty becomes effective.
- From whom the consumer can obtain warranty performance.

The act does permit a disclaimer of consequential damage for the defective product that damages a consumer's other property. For example, a defective coffeepot may explode and damage a nearby toaster; the damage to the toaster was consequential and liability disclaimed by the coffeepot manufacturer.

Defective products that harm persons or damage property may breach an express or implied warranty; the manufacturer may also be liable under negligence or products liability.

If you sell consumer goods, your buyers also receive an implied warranty of merchantability that the goods sold are of at least average quality and fit for ordinary usage, are adequately packaged and labeled, and conform to any promise made on the label. Many consumer product recalls involve defects, such as metal in margarine, loose engine bolts, and baby swings that collapse. The contract includes this implied warranty, and the consumer can sue for a defect, unless there is an effective disclaimer.

Sometimes the implied warranty can be disclaimed if the seller conspicuously does so—for example, by putting a disclaimer in boldface print and using the phrase *as is* or *seller disclaims warranty of merchantability.* Courts construe such disclaimers narrowly and usually will not enforce the disclaimer when personal injury results from the defect.

If a seller knows that the buyer is relying on the seller's expertise to select goods appropriate for the buyer's requirement, there may be an implied warranty of "fitness for a particular purpose." For example, if you own a ski shop and a novice skier relies on you to select the appropriate skis for his or her size and skill, by your selection alone and by implication, you are warranting that the skis are fit for the customer's intended use. Courts in some states are reluctant to allow the seller to disclaim this warranty.

TIP

Despite the implied warranty of good title, if you are buying equipment that carries a substantial price tag, always do a search with your secretary of state *UCC* file for any financing statements (liens) against the equipment. If any are filed, the creditor who filed has a claim against the property.

In addition to any warranties of quality, the *UCC* requires from the seller an implied warranty of good title to the goods sold and that there are no liens or security interests against the goods.

PERFORMANCE BY THE PARTIES

Contracting parties are required to follow the terms of their agreement. Of course, they may amend the original contract. Any amendment may require additional consideration by the party seeking the change, such as additional money or additional services. Under the *UCC* sale of goods, however, the modification may be valid even without additional consideration if requested in good faith, such as if a seller delays delivery because his or her supplier failed to get the goods delivered on time. Under the *UCC*, the seller is obligated to timely deliver goods that conform to the terms of the contract. Unless the contract indicates otherwise, the goods are to be delivered in a single lot, and title passes when delivery occurs. The buyer is then required to accept and pay for goods that conform to the terms of the contract. The buyer has the right to inspect the goods before acceptance and reject nonconforming goods. However, if the buyer fails to inspect the goods in a timely manner or if he or she uses the goods, the courts may deem that behavior is acceptance under the *UCC*. If the buyer rejects nonconforming goods, the buyer must give timely notice of the rejection and specify the particular defects. Thereafter the buyer must follow the seller's reasonable instructions as to the disposition of the rejected goods.

The buyer may revoke acceptance if the seller assured the buyer that the defects would be fixed, or the defect was difficult to discover.

If one party has not fully performed, there is a contract breach, unless the buyer permits the breach (as buyer would if he or she accepted late delivery of goods). Remedies for a contract breach are discussed later in this section.

TIP

If the other party to your contract indicates he or she might not perform, the *UCC* permits you to demand assurance of performance. You send a letter to the other party requesting a definite assurance (promise) that the other party will timely perform. If the other party repudiates the contract or fails to respond to your request, you can treat this as a contract breach.

THIRD-PARTY PERFORMANCE

A contract may involve performance by a third party, which is called contract delegation, better known as subcontracting. Some contract performance is typically delegated; construction companies frequently subcontract to others. Contracting parties may delegate part or all of the performance unless one of these conditions exist:

- The contract specifically prohibits delegation.
- Delegation materially affects the other party's expectations.

Whereas delegation is expected in construction contracts, it may not be in other areas of business, particularly in personal service contracts or where the manufacturer's expertise is expected. For example, if you hire a carpenter to remodel, you would not want me as a substitute carpenter. If you contract with Eli Lilly to supply your medication, you don't want the company to delegate production to some fly-by-night drug manufacturer. If the proposed delegation substantially alters the bargain, neither party is allowed to delegate.

EXCUSING PERFORMANCE

Sometimes contract performance, or at least timely performance, may be excused by the law. One of the traditional excuses is the doctrine of impossibility. Impossibility involves some force of nature, such as a tornado that destroys the seller's manufacturing plant or a fire that destroys a building ready to be sold. In some cases, impossibility may only excuse timely performance—that is, only postpone the date—such as when a severe snowstorm delays delivery.

The law may excuse performance that is impractical, but requires evidence that ...

- The nonperforming party was not at fault.
- An event has occurred that the parties had not contemplated when they made the contract.
- The nonperforming party did not agree to assume the risk of the occurrence.

For example, a builder agrees to construct a high-rise building, and substantial subsurface testing showed only minor impediments. However, after construction began, the soil proved nearly impossible to hold the high-rise and the project had to be abandoned. Contract performance may be excused because of the unforeseen difficulty rendering the project impractical to complete.

In addition, the parties may have agreed upon conditions affecting performance that change after both parties sign the contract. The occurrence may increase or decrease a party's duties, or terminate the contract. For example, a franchise contract may require the franchisee to pay a higher fee as the gross sales increase, or an employment contract may permit termination if the employee discloses trade secrets to a competitor.

DRAFTING CHECKLIST

You may want to draft your own contracts, and then have your attorney review the draft. Most contracts contain the following:

- **Parties.** The parties to the contract must be identified: ABC Corporation, an Indiana corporation (seller), and Able LLC, an Indiana limited liability company (buyer).
- **Recitals.** In this section the parties indicate their intent to contract and the general purpose of the contract. The seller intends to sell pickup trucks to the buyer.
- **Consideration.** This section specifies the subject matter of the contract, what the parties are exchanging. For example, the seller shall deliver 10 #222 pickup trucks to the buyer for the sum of $225,000.
- **Conditions.** Either party may state conditions of contract performance. One such condition might be that the buyer has to provide a valid *letter of credit* to the seller before the seller ships the first installment.

PLAIN ENGLISH

A **letter of credit** is usually issued by a bank, agreeing to honor a draft and check of its customer.

- **Performance.** This section may provide the details of performance, such as delivery by lots, delivery time and location, and payment. For example, "seller will deliver five pickup trucks on April 1, 2005, and five to be delivered on May 1, 2005, at buyer's place of business, and with payment after inspection but no later than 10 days from delivery."

- **Term.** The contract may involve a specified period, such as "Seller will provide warranty service on pickup trucks for a period of one year from date of last delivery, after which the contract terminates."

- **Assignment and delegation.** If the parties want to exclude *assignment* or delegation, they should specify that condition; otherwise the law may permit either if there is no material effect by assignment or delegation.

PLAIN ENGLISH

Contract assignment means transferring a contract to a third party (assignee); for example, transferring your right to receive goods to another company.

- **Remedies.** The parties should indicate what constitutes a breach, such as nonpayment or late delivery of defective trucks. The method of computing damages may be included. Certainly, there should be a provision for payment of attorney fees to the nonbreaching party; otherwise, each party pays its own fees.

- **Integration.** This section specifies that all the terms of the parties' contract are included in the written agreement. If you have any oral or written promises made by the other party, make sure you write them into the final written agreement; otherwise, the integration clause will exclude them.

- **Severablity.** If one section of the contract is declared by the court to be unenforceable, the rest of the contract shall remain and be enforceable.

- **Signature.** If either contracting party is an entity, such as a corporation, the person is signing the contract on its behalf, such as Jan Jones, as president, ABC Corporation.

REMEDIES FOR BREACH OF CONTRACT

A party may breach the contract if it fails to perform its end of the bargain. If its performance is incomplete, defective, or repudiated, the nonbreaching party may sue for the contract breach.

A contract party may cancel a contract if the other party fails or refuses to perform, or may sue for a contract breach and request money damages or other forms of relief. The goal of contract remedies is to place the nonbreaching party in as good a condition as the party would be in if the contract had been properly performed.

Money Damages

Money damages are the most typical remedy sought. Courts calculate damages by estimating how much money it would take to make the nonbreaching party whole—in essence, substituting money for performance.

The measure of damages could be the cost to complete the contract—for example, if you contract to have your lawn landscaped for $5,000 and pay in advance, but the landscaper fails to plant some bushes worth $500 that you have paid for, the damages are $500 in your favor.

TIP

Punitive damages—damages in excess of what it would cost to make the nonbreaching party whole—are usually available only when the breaching party has committed fraud.

The court could also calculate damages based upon your lost profit. Let's say someone hired you as a caterer to furnish a party with food, but your client backed out at the last minute. In addition to paying you for your time and expenses, a court may also demand that the client pay you $1,000 for the profit you would have made had you been allowed to perform.

Consequential damages—damages to make up for a loss that extends beyond the immediate contract—may be awarded in certain contract breaches, often as a result of nontimely performance. If time is important, you must tell the other party prior to performance of the possible consequences, such as the need for additional expenses or lost revenue. For example, you contract for construction of your retail store and the builder promises completion on a certain date. If you inform the builder (preferably in writing) that you will lose approximately $5,000 in sales for each day that you are not open, you have set the stage for consequential damages if the construction is not completed on time.

Equity Remedies

Under certain special circumstances, money damages may not provide an adequate remedy for the nonbreaching party. In such cases, the court awards what is known as equity. Equity may permit the three following outcomes:

- **Rescission.** Rescission allows the court to cancel the contract because of unjust benefit or harm to one party. Grounds for rescission may include misrepresentation, mutual mistake, duress, undue influence, or incapacity. For example, you contract to buy shelving for your store, but the seller misrepresented its load-carrying capacity and so you can't use it. You can sue for rescission and get your money back.

■ **Reformation.** Reformation permits the court to change the contract to reflect what the parties intended but did not adequately express in the written contract, or to modify an illegal term in the contract. For example, you intended to buy 100 reams of typing paper, which was what the seller intended to sell; however, due to an unnoticed typo the contract read 1,000 reams. The court can reform the contract to read what you intended. (But don't count on court intervention, so read and understand what you sign.)

■ **Specific performance.** Specific performance may be available when the other party refuses to close a sale for real estate or for unique goods, including antiques and collectibles. In this case, the court can order the breaching party to specifically perform their duties under the contract.

YOUR AGENT MAY BIND YOU TO A CONTRACT

You may have an employee who has the authority to contract on behalf of your business. For example, your office manager has the authority to order office supplies, and your company buyer has authority to purchase goods for sale at your retail stores. These employees are agents for your company.

Your company will be bound to any contract your agent agrees to if the agent acts within his or her express authority. For example, if you authorize your office manager to buy up to $500 of supplies with ABC Company, you are obligated to pay for the order within those parameters.

Your company may also be liable for any contract your agent agrees to if the agent acts within his or her apparent authority. In other words, your conduct may lead a seller to believe that your agent has the authority to contract, when, in fact, the agent has no such authority, or has exceeded his or her express authority. For example, your office manager has $500 express authority and has bought from ABC Company for several months. On one occasion, however, your manager orders $600 in supplies. Even though your manager's $100 over the limit, you may be bound because it was reasonable for ABC to assume your manager has the authority to purchase and did so within his or her authority.

THE 30-SECOND RECAP

- Important contracts should be in writing and contain all the terms agreed upon between the parties.

- A contract requires consideration, which is a legal term for a bargained-for exchange of benefits between the parties. Courts usually do not examine the adequacy of the consideration, only its existence.

- Contracts should be written in clear, precise English.

- Courts may award money damages for a breach, require the party to perform the contract, or rescind or reform the contract.

Basic Business Forms

The forms in this section are useful starting points for any businessperson. Each state has its own body of law, so no form can be completely applicable for each state. Likewise, laws change. Consult an attorney after preparing a draft of your legal document.

General legal forms are available from several sources. On the web, for example, you can find forms at www.lectlaw.com and www.ilrg.com. Or you can buy *Quicken Business Lawyer 2003,* which is a collection of legal forms on disc. Your state also may have business entity forms, such as articles of incorporation, on its website.

In the meantime, here are some basic forms to get you started:

- Partnership agreement
- Shareholder agreement
- Limited liability articles of organization
- Lease
- Agreement to sell business
- Installment promissory note
- Estate planning information
- Last will and testament

The following sections present each of these.

PARTNERSHIP AGREEMENT

This partnership agreement form is for a small number of active partners. The development of real estate is used as an example of a partnership "purpose." The form contains the basic terms and can be used as a checklist to determine what terms your partners agree to. Mark up the form as a tentative agreement, and then submit it to your attorney for final drafting.

General Partnership Agreement
of
ABC Property Associates

This General Partnership Agreement (the Agreement) is made and entered into this _____ day of _____, 20__, by and among the persons who have executed this Agreement on the signature page hereof and all other persons who hereafter become a party hereto by executing an addendum to this Agreement (referred to collectively as the "Partners" and each individually as a "Partner").

Recitals

WHEREAS, the parties hereto desire to form a partnership (the Partnership) to purchase, develop, and lease certain real property located in Any County, Any State (the Property);

NOW, THEREFORE, in consideration of the mutual covenants herein contained and intending to be legally bound hereby, the Partners hereby agree as follows:

Name, Place of Business, and Purpose

1.1   The activities and business of the Partnership shall be conducted under the name of ABC PROPERTY ASSOCIATES.

1.2   The principal office of the Partnership shall be 123 America Drive, Any County, Any State, or at such other places within or without the state as the Partners may determine.

1.3   The purpose of the Partnership shall be to acquire, develop, lease, own, and sell the Property; to enter into agreements of purchase, lease, and sale and other undertakings as may be related to the Property; to obtain such loans, make such arrangements or rearrangements as may be necessary or desirable in carrying out any or all of the foregoing purposes; and to carry on such activities as may be necessary or incidental to the foregoing purposes.

Term of the Partnership

2.1.   The term of the Partnership shall begin on the date hereof and shall continue until terminated as specifically provided in this Agreement.

Contributions to the Partnership

3.1.   The partners shall make cash contributions from time to time to the capital of the Partnership in accordance with the respective percentages set forth in Section 4.3.

3.2.   If any Partner makes a disproportionate advance of any funds to or for the account of the Partnership in excess of his or her percentage interest in the Partnership, such advance, in the absence of a written agreement of the Partners to the contrary, shall be considered a loan to the Partnership and shall not result in an increase in the percentage interest of such Partner in the Partnership.

3.3   A capital account shall be maintained for each Partner, reflecting his or her capital contributions, allocation of net income or losses, withdrawals, and all other appropriate adjustments.

Profits and Losses and Drawings by the Partners

4.1.   The net income and losses of the Partnership shall be determined in accordance with the cash receipts and disbursements method of accounting used by the Partnership for federal income tax purposes.

4.2.   Drawings of income shall be made by each Partner from Partnership funds in such amounts and at such times as all Partners shall agree upon.

4.3.   The net income or losses of the Partnership shall be allocable to the Partners in the proportions set forth here:

James Bond	25%
Karen Kute	25%
Diane Dont	30%
Suzanne Swift	20%

Partnership Property

5.1.   All right, title, and interest to real or personal property acquired by the Partnership, including all improvements placed or located on such property, and all rents, issues, and profits arising therefrom, shall be owned by the Partnership.

Fiscal Matters

6.1.   Proper and complete books and records shall be kept with reference to all Partnership transactions and property, and each Partner shall at all reasonable times during business hours have access thereto. The books shall be kept by a cash receipts and disbursement method of accounting. The books and records of the Partnership shall be reviewed annually at the expense of the Partnership by an accountant selected by the Partnership, who shall prepare and deliver to the Partnership, for filing, appropriate partnership income tax returns and such other information as may be necessary to enable each Partner to file his or her personal federal, state, and local tax returns.

Management of the Partnership

7.1.   All material Partnership decisions, including, without limitation, those specified in Section 7.2., shall be made jointly unless such authority is otherwise delegated by one Partner to the others in a particular instance.

7.2. No Partner, without the consent of the other Partners, may:

  (i) Do any act in contravention of this Agreement;

 (ii) Do any act that would make it impossible to carry on the business of the Partnership;

(iii) Affiliate, employ, or terminate professional or nonprofessional personnel of the Partnership;

 (iv) Possess Partnership property or assign the right of the Partnership or the Partners in specific Partnership property for other than a Partnership purpose;

  (v) Make, execute, or deliver any general assignment for the benefit of creditors;

 (vi) Assign, transfer, pledge, compromise, or release any claim of the Partnership except for full payment;

(vii) Make, execute, or deliver any deed, long-term lease, or contract to sell all or substantially all the Partnership property;

(viii) Make, execute, or deliver for the Partnership any note, bond, mortgage, deed of trust, guaranty, indemnity bond, or surety bond if such document creates any personal liability for any Partner other than that personal liability to which the Partner may have agreed in writing;

 (ix) Make any expenditures or disbursement in excess of $_____;

  (x) Borrow monies to the extent such borrowing would cause the aggregate amount of indebtedness to exceed $_____; and

 (xi) Purchase or acquire real property.

7.3. An account or accounts in the name of the Partnership may be maintained in such bank or banks as the Partnership may select from time to time, and checks drawn thereon may be signed on behalf of the Partnership by any two Partners, except as provided in Section 7.2(ix).

7.4. No salaries or other compensation shall be paid to the Partners.

Dissolution and Liquidation

8.1. The Partnership shall be dissolved upon the occurrence of any of the following:

  (a) The mutual consent of the Partners; or

  (b) The sale, abandonment, or disposal by the Partnership of all or substantially all of its assets; or (**c**) The entry of a final judgment, order, or decree of a court of competent jurisdiction adjudicating the Partnership to be a bankrupt; or

(**d**) The bankruptcy of a Partner; or

(**e**) The death of a Partner.

8.2.   Upon the dissolution of the Partnership, the Partner charged with winding up the Partnership affairs shall proceed to liquidate its assets, wind up its affairs, and apply and distribute the proceeds, after debts and expenses and subject to reasonable reserves, to the Partners or their personal representatives in cash according to their respective percentage interests in the Partnership.

Miscellaneous

9.1.   All notices, statements, or other documents required or contemplated by this Agreement shall be in writing and shall either be personally delivered to the person entitled thereto or mailed, postage prepaid, to such person at his or her last known mailing address.

9.2.   This Agreement shall be interpreted and construed in accordance with the laws of the State of Any State.

9.3.   The Partners agree that they will execute any further documents or instruments and perform any acts that are or may become necessary to effectuate and to carry on the Partnership created by this Agreement.

9.4.   This Agreement may be executed in any number of counterparts, each of which may be executed by one or more of the Partners, and all such counterparts when executed and delivered shall together constitute one and the same instrument.

IN WITNESS WHEREOF, the parties hereto have executed this Agreement on the day and year first above written.

Partners:

_____

_____

_____

_____

SHAREHOLDER AGREEMENT

The shareholder agreement is a form for a corporation with a few active shareholders. The shareholders agree to name specific shareholders as directors and officers. They limit the right to transfer the stock by giving the first option to buy to the existing shareholders. There is a mandatory purchase of a deceased shareholder's stock. Mark up the agreement, then submit it to your attorney for redrafting.

Shareholder Agreement

AGREEMENT made _____, 20__, by and between _____ Corporation having its principal office at _____, City of _____, State of _____, hereinafter sometimes referred to as the corporation; _____, residing at _____ City of _____, State of _____; _____, residing at _____ City of _____, State of _____; _____, residing at _____ City of _____, State of _____, each of the foregoing being the owner this day of one-third the outstanding shares of the corporation, and together being the owners of all the outstanding shares of said corporation.

WHEREAS the parties desire to promote their mutual interests and the interest of the corporation by making provision to avoid future differences.

NOW, THEREFORE, it is mutually agreed as follows:

1. Each of the undersigned shareholders agrees that so long as [he/she] shall remain a shareholder [he/she] will vote [his/her] respective shares in the above-mentioned corporation for each of the following as a director so long as the said director-designee remains a shareholder of the corporation:

(1) _____

(2) _____

(3) _____

Any of the foregoing directors who ceases to be a shareholder of the corporation shall simultaneously with the transfer or surrender of [his/her] shares submit to the corporation [his/her] written resignation as a director.

2. For the best interest of the corporation, _____ Corporation and the undersigned shareholders agree to have each of the following appointed and elected an officer of the corporation so long as the said office-designee remains a shareholder and proves faithful, efficient, and competent:

For President:

_____

For Secretary:

_____

For Treasurer:

_____

Any one of the foregoing officers who ceases to be a shareholder of the corporation shall simultaneously with the transfer or surrender of [his/her] shares submit to the corporation [his/her] written resignation as an officer.

3. All parties hereto further agree that each of the aforesaid officers, so long as [he/she] remains a shareholder and proves faithful, efficient, and competent, shall continue to be employed in the additional posts presently occupied by [him/her]; inactivity because of age or ill health shall not be construed incompetence. Any one of the foregoing employees who ceases to be a shareholder of the corporation shall simultaneously with the transfer or surrender of [his/her] shares submit to the corporation [his/her] written resignation as an employee.

4. Each of the undersigned employees agrees that [he/she] will devote [his/her] best efforts to enhance and develop the best interests of the corporation. Salary shall serve as compensation for services both as officer and employee.

5(a). Each of the undersigned shareholders agrees that [he/she] will not transfer, assign, sell, pledge, hypothecate, or otherwise dispose of, the shares owned by [him/her] or them, or the certificates representing the same, unless such shares shall have been first offered to the corporation at a price per share to be computed pro rata on the basis of the value hereinafter provided in subparagraph 5(c) hereof for a one-third interest in the corporation, as revised from time to time as therein provided. Such offer shall be made in writing and remain standing for a period of thirty (30) days. In the event the offeree wishes to accept the offer, it must agree in writing to purchase the entire block of shares offered and shall simultaneously make a down payment in cash of thirty (30) per cent of the purchase price. The balance of the purchase price shall be payable on the same terms as are prescribed in subparagraph 5(d) hereof for all payments after the initial payment on purchase of the interest of a deceased shareholder. In the event the offeree shall not signify its intention to purchase said shares within such thirty (30) day period, then the offeror shall be authorized to otherwise sell or dispose of his stock, which stock shall thereafter be freely transferable and no longer subject to the provisions and limitations of this agreement. The provisions of this paragraph shall not bar a transfer, assignment, bequest, or sale of shares of stock by one of the undersigned to a member of [his/her] immediate family who shall take, however, subject to all the limitations of this agreement as if he or she were a party hereto.

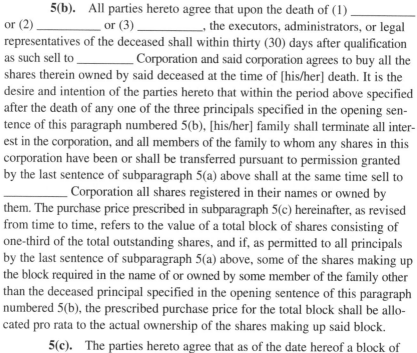

5(b).   All parties hereto agree that upon the death of (1) _____ or (2) _____ or (3) _____, the executors, administrators, or legal representatives of the deceased shall within thirty (30) days after qualification as such sell to _____ Corporation and said corporation agrees to buy all the shares therein owned by said deceased at the time of [his/her] death. It is the desire and intention of the parties hereto that within the period above specified after the death of any one of the three principals specified in the opening sentence of this paragraph numbered 5(b), [his/her] family shall terminate all interest in the corporation, and all members of the family to whom any shares in this corporation have been or shall be transferred pursuant to permission granted by the last sentence of subparagraph 5(a) above shall at the same time sell to _____ Corporation all shares registered in their names or owned by them. The purchase price prescribed in subparagraph 5(c) hereinafter, as revised from time to time, refers to the value of a total block of shares consisting of one-third of the total outstanding shares, and if, as permitted to all principals by the last sentence of subparagraph 5(a) above, some of the shares making up the block required in the name of or owned by some member of the family other than the deceased principal specified in the opening sentence of this paragraph numbered 5(b), the prescribed purchase price for the total block shall be allocated pro rata to the actual ownership of the shares making up said block.

5(c).   The parties hereto agree that as of the date hereof a block of shares representing a one-third interest in the corporation has a value of $ _____. It is the intention of the parties to revise this figure on April 30, July 21, and October 31 of every year, and the last figure agreed upon in writing by the parties hereto prior to an *inter-vivos* offer as set forth in subparagraph 5(a) or 5(b) or before the death of one of the three individuals set forth in subparagraph 5(b) shall be conclusive as to the value of said block for purpose of this agreement. The parties hereto have included in their initial figure and intend to include in future revisions thereof an allowance for goodwill.

5(d).   The purchase price shall be paid as follows: <u>Thirty (30%)</u> per cent in cash within <u>30</u> days after qualification of the legal representatives of the deceased shareholder. One-quarter of the unpaid balance shall be paid *twelve* months thereafter; and a similar sum shall be paid every *six* months thereafter until the shares have been fully paid for; interest at the rate of _____ % on the installment being paid shall be paid with every installment. The obligation to make the *four (4)* installment payments shall be evidence by negotiable, promissory notes signed by the corporation, as maker, and endorsed by all surviving signatories to this agreement, as accommodation endorsers. Time is declared to be of the essence for such payments. The promissory notes shall provide that the maker shall have the right to prepay the whole or any part thereof without premium or penalty.

If on the occurrence of the contingencies above specified, the corporation is unable lawfully to pay the full purchase price, then such funds as are available shall be used to purchase part of the shares offered, and the corporation and its shareholders shall promptly take action to the extent necessary to make funds available for purchase of the remaining shares. If the funds shall be insufficient within the period of time hereinabove prescribed to make payments for the entire block of shares offered for sale, the parties hereto agree that then and in that event, a special joint directors' and shareholders' meeting shall be called for the purpose of dissolving the corporation, and each of the parties hereto agrees that at such meeting he or she will vote to dissolve the corporation. In lieu of voting dissolution, as above provided, the shareholders other than the offeror shall have the privilege of purchasing said shares as individuals, in proportion to their then ownership of outstanding shares.

5(e).   The last principal to survive shall be free to dispose of as [he/she] pleases the shares owned by [him/her], free from any of the restrictions imposed by this agreement.

6.   Each share certificate of the Corporation shall bear the following legend in conspicuous type:

Transfer or pledge of the shares represented by this certificate is restricted under a shareholder's agreement dated _____, 20__. A copy of the agreement, which affects also other rights of the holder of these shares, is on file at the office of the Corporation.

7.   Should at any time any dispute arise between any one or more of the parties hereto with respect to his or her or their rights, obligations, duties, and requirements under and by virtue of the provisions of this agreement, except as to the valuation of stock, said dispute, except as aforesaid, shall be referred to, and consent and approval of each of the parties hereto is expressly given to refer said dispute for determination to the American Arbitration Association, whose determination and/or decision shall be final and binding upon the parties hereto, and there shall be no appeal from said decision.

8.   The corporation is authorized to enter into this agreement by virtue of a resolution adopted at a special joint meeting of the shareholders and directors held on _____, 20__.

9.   This agreement or any of its provisions may at any time be changed, modified, or canceled by mutual consent of all the undersigned, their heirs, executors, administrators, legal representatives, or assigns, but unless and until so changed, modified, or canceled, this agreement shall be binding upon the parties, and their heirs, executors, administrators, legal representatives and assigns, any or all of whom shall execute and deliver all necessary documents required to carry out the terms of this agreement.

10. In the event that any provision of this agreement shall be ruled invalid or unenforceable by a court of competent jurisdiction, it is the intent of the parties hereto that the balance of the agreement shall be enforced as if said invalid or unenforceable provision has not been included in this agreement.

IN WITNESS WHEREOF, the individual parties hereto hereunto set their hands and seals, and the corporation has caused this agreement to be signed by its duly authorized officers and its corporate seal affixed.

_____ Corporation

Attest by:

_____

President

_____

Secretary

_____

_____

Shareholders

LIMITED LIABILITY ARTICLES

File this limited liability company articles of organization, or your state's own equivalent form, with your state's secretary of state. The form may be simplified in some states by just including the basic information in articles 1 through 6. You must have an operating agreement, but you don't have to file it. Your attorney should draft your operating agreement. That form is not included here because state laws on limited liability corporations vary considerably, unlike partnership agreements, which are governed by fairly uniform laws in the various states.

Articles of Organization
of

_____

The undersigned, acting as organizer (Organizer), hereby forms a limited liability company under the _____ Act of the State of _____ (the Act) and does hereby adopt as the Articles of Organization of such limited liability company the following:

Article 1. Name. The name of the limited liability company shall be _____, LLC (the Company).

Article 2. Duration. The period of the Company's duration shall be perpetual until the Company is dissolved in accordance with the Operating Agreement of the Company or the Act.

Article 3. Purpose. The Company shall have unlimited power to engage in and do any lawful act concerning any or all lawful businesses for which limited liability companies may be organized according to the laws of the State of _____ including all powers and purposes now and hereafter permitted by law to a limited liability company.

Article 4. Registered Office and Registered Agent.

(a) The street address of the registered office of the Company in_____ is _____, _____, _____.

(b) The name of the registered agent of the Company at the above registered office is _____.

Article 5. Continuation of Business of the Company. Upon the resignation, expulsion, bankruptcy, or dissolution of a Member or occurrence of any other event that terminates the continued membership of a Member in the Company, or if any Member transfers all or a portion of its Interest in the Company, the Company shall be immediately dissolved, unless the business of the Company is continued by the remaining Members in accordance with Section 6.1 of the Company's Operating Agreement.

Article 6. Management. The Company is to be managed by its Members as provided in the Operating Agreement of the Company.

Article 7. Indemnification of Members, Organizers, and Managers.

(a) To the greatest extent not inconsistent with the laws and public policies of Indiana, the Company shall indemnify any Member, Organizer, or Manager, if the Company has a Manager or Managers (any such Member, Organizer, or Manager, and including any responsible officers, partners, shareholders, directors, or managers of any such Member, Organizer, or Manager that is an Entity, hereinafter being referred to individually and collectively as the indemnified person) made a party to any proceeding because such person is or was a Member, Organizer, or Manager as a matter of right, against all liability incurred by such person in connection with any proceeding; provided that it shall be determined in the specific case in accordance with paragraph (d) of this Article that indemnification of such person is permissible in the circumstances because the person has met the standard of conduct for indemnification set forth in paragraph (c) of this Article. The Company shall pay for or reimburse the reasonable expenses incurred by a Member, Organizer, or Manager in connection with any such proceeding in advance of final disposition thereof if (i) the person furnishes the Company a written affirmation of the person's good faith belief that the person has met the standard of conduct for indemnification described in paragraph (c) of this Article, (ii) the person furnishes the Company a written undertaking, executed personally or on such person's behalf, to repay the advance if it is ultimately determined that such individual did not meet such standard of conduct, and (iii) a determination is made in accordance with paragraph (d) that based upon facts then known to those making the determination, indemnification would not be precluded under this Article. The undertaking described in subparagraph (a)(ii) above must be a general obligation of the person, subject to such reasonable limitations as the Company may permit, but need not be secured and may be accepted without reference to financial ability to make repayment. The Company shall indemnify a Member, Organizer, or Manager who is wholly successful, on the merits or otherwise, in the defense of any such proceeding, as a matter of right, against reasonable expenses incurred by the person in connection with the proceeding without the requirement of a determination as set forth in paragraph (c) of this Article. Upon demand by a Member, Organizer, or Manager for indemnification or advancement of expenses, as the case may be, the Company shall expeditiously determine whether the Member, Organizer, or Manager is entitled thereto in accordance with this Article. The indemnification and advancement of expenses provided for under this Article shall be applicable to any proceeding arising from acts or omissions occurring before or after the adoption of this Article.

(b) The Company shall have the power, but not the obligation, to indemnify any person who is or was an employee or agent of the Company to the same extent as if such person was a Member, Organizer, or Manager.

(c) Indemnification of a person is permissible under this Article only if (i) such person conducted himself, herself, or itself in good faith, (ii) such person reasonably believed that the person's conduct was in or at least not opposed to the Company's best interest, and (iii) in the case of any criminal proceeding, such person had no reasonable cause to believe the person's conduct was unlawful. Indemnification is not permissible against liability to the extent such liability is the result of willful misconduct, recklessness, or any improperly obtained financial or other benefit to which the person was not legally entitled. The termination of a proceeding by judgment, order, settlement, conviction or upon a plea of *nolo contendere* or its equivalent is not, of itself, determinative that the individual did not meet the standard of conduct described in this paragraph (c).

(d) A determination as to whether indemnification or advancement of expenses is permissible shall be made by any one of the following procedures:

    (i) By the Members by a majority vote consisting of Members not at the time parties to the proceeding; or

(ii) By special legal counsel selected by the Members in the manner prescribed in subparagraph (d)(i) above.

(e)   A Member, Organizer, or Manager of the Company who is a party to a
proceeding may apply for indemnification from the Company to the court, if
any, conducting the proceeding or to another court of competent jurisdiction.
On receipt of an application, the court, after giving notice the court considers
necessary, may order indemnification if it determines:

(i) In a proceeding in which the Member, Organizer, or Manager is
wholly successful, on the merits or otherwise, the Member, Organizer,
or Manager is entitled to indemnification under this Article, in which
case the court shall order the Company to pay the individual his or
her reasonable expenses incurred to obtain such court ordered
indemnification; or

(ii) The person is fairly and reasonably entitled to indemnification in
view of all the relevant circumstances, whether or not the person met
the standard of conduct set forth in paragraph (c) of this Article.

(f)   Indemnification shall also be provided for a person's conduct with respect
to an employee benefit plan if the person reasonably believed the person's
conduct to be in the interests of the participants in and beneficiaries of the
plan.

(g)   Nothing contained in this Article shall limit or preclude the exercise or
be deemed exclusive of any right under the law, by contract or otherwise,
relating to indemnification of or advancement of expenses to any person who
is or was a Member, Organizer, or Manager of the Company or is or was serving at the Company's request as a director, officer, partner, manager, trustee,
employee, or agent of another foreign or domestic company, partnership,
association, limited liability company, corporation, joint venture, trust,
employee benefit plan, or other enterprise, whether for-profit or not. Nothing
contained in this Article shall limit the ability of the Company to otherwise
indemnify or advance expenses to any person. It is the intent of this Article to
provide indemnification to Members, Organizers, and Managers to the fullest
extent now and hereafter permitted by the law consistent with the terms and
conditions of this Article. Indemnification shall be provided in accordance
with this Article irrespective of the nature of the legal or equitable theory
upon which a claim is made including without limitation negligence, breach
of duty, mismanagement, waste, breach of contract, breach of warranty, strict
liability, violation of federal or state securities law, violation of the Employee
Retirement Income Security Act of 1974, as amended, or violation of any
other state or federal law.

(h)   For purposes of this Article:

 (i)   The term *expenses* includes all direct and indirect costs (including without limitation counsel fees, retainers, court costs, transcripts, fees of experts, witness fees, travel expenses, duplicating costs, printing and binding costs, telephone charges, postage, delivery service fees, and all other disbursements or out-of-pocket expenses) actually incurred in connection with the investigation, defense, settlement, or appeal of a proceeding or establishment or enforcing a right to indemnification under this Article, applicable law or otherwise.

 (ii)   The term *liability* means the obligation to pay a judgment, settlement, penalty, fine, excise tax (including an excise tax assessed with respect to an employee benefit plan), or reasonable expenses incurred with respect to a proceeding.

 (iii)   The term *party* includes a person who was, is, or is threatened to be made, a named defendant or respondent in a proceeding.

 (iv)   The term *proceeding* means any threatened, pending, or completed action, suit or proceeding, whether civil, criminal, administrative, or investigative and whether formal or informal.

 (v)   The Company may purchase and maintain insurance for its benefit, the benefit of any person who is entitled to indemnification under this Article, or both, against any liability asserted against or incurred by such person in any capacity or arising out of such person's service with the Company, whether or not the Company would have the power to indemnify such person against such liability.

Article 8. Definitions. Terms used but not defined in these Articles of Organization shall have the meanings set forth in the Act.

Dated: _____

   _____
   Organizer

LEASE

This is a basic lease form for a small office or retail store. Use the form as a checklist of terms to go over with your prospective tenant, and then have your attorney draft the final form.

Lease

THIS LEASE, entered into by

_____, (hereinafter referred

to as Landlord) and _____,

(hereinafter referred to as Tenant),

WITNESSETH THAT Landlord and Tenant, in consideration of their mutual undertakings, agree as follows: Landlord hereby leases to Tenant and Tenant hereby leases from Landlord:

[Legal description attached]

common address:

_____

(hereinafter referred to as Leased Premises) and all appurtenances thereto for a term of _____, commencing on _____, 20___, and ending on _____, 20__, unless sooner terminated, and Tenant without demand or notice shall pay a monthly rental of

_____

($_____), payable on or before the first day of each month in advance, at the address of the landlord set forth in this Lease, or such other address as Landlord by notice shall direct, all upon the following covenants, terms, and conditions:

1. USE, COMPLIANCE WITH LAWS. The Leased Premises shall be used by Tenant only for the purpose of a residence. Tenant shall keep the Leased Premises in a clean and orderly manner. Tenant may not use the Leased Premises in a manner that would violate law or create a nuisance.

2. SURRENDER AND HOLDOVER. Upon the expiration or sooner termination of this Lease, Tenant shall surrender to Landlord the Leased Premises, together with all other property affixed to the Leased Premises broom clean and in the same order and condition in which Tenant received them, the effects of ordinary wear, acts of God, and casualty excepted. Tenant shall remove all of its personal property prior to the termination of this Lease; any property left shall be deemed abandoned and may be kept or disposed of by the Landlord. If Tenant shall remain in possession after the term of this Lease expires, with the consent of the Landlord, then Tenant shall be lessee from month to month and subject to all the terms of this Lease.

3. ASSIGNMENT AND SUBLETTING. Tenant may not assign or sublet the Lease or Leased Premises without the written consent of Landlord.

4. ALTERATIONS AND MAINTENANCE OF LEASED PREMISES. Tenant may not make any substantial additions or alterations without the written consent of the Landlord. Tenant shall maintain the Leased Premises in the same order and condition in which Tenant received the premises. A List of Landlord improvements to be made, if any, are attached and made a part of this Lease; otherwise, Tenant leases premises in "as is" condition.

5. DESTRUCTION. If the Leased Premises should be damaged or destroyed by fire or other cause and not habitable, then either party may cancel this Lease by giving written notice to the other party.

6. TENANT'S PERSONAL PROPERTY. Landlord is not liable for the loss or destruction of Tenant's personal property.

7. INSURANCE. Tenant shall maintain a liability insurance policy for injuries on the premises in the amount of _____ Dollars ($ _____). Tenant may maintain a contents policy on Tenant's personal property.

8. CONDEMNATION. If the Leased Premises is condemned by any legally constituted authority, or if a conveyance or other acquisition in lieu of such condemnation is made, then this Lease shall terminate as of the date of possession required by the condemnor. All compensation paid in connection with the condemnation shall belong to the Landlord.

9. MECHANIC'S LIENS. Tenant may not permit any mechanic's liens to be filed against Leased Premises; however, if any mechanic's lien is filed, Tenant shall promptly obtain a release.

10. INDEMNIFICATION AND RELEASE. Regardless of whether separate, several, joint or concurrent liability may be imposed upon the Landlord, Tenant shall indemnify and hold harmless Landlord from and against all damages, claims, and liability arising from or connected with Tenant's control or use of the Leased Premises, including without limitation, any damage, or injury to person or property. This indemnification shall include Landlord's attorney fees in connection with any such claim. Tenant does hereby release Landlord for any accident, damage, or injury caused to person or property on or about the Leased Premises.

11. UTILITIES. Tenant shall pay all utilities, including but not limited to heat, electricity, water, sewer, and telephone.

12. DEFAULT. Any violation of this Lease for a period in excess of five (5) days, or the filing of bankruptcy or other similar creditor action against Tenant, shall be deemed a default. Upon the occurrence of any default, the Landlord may, at its option, in addition to any other remedy or right it has hereunder or by law, (1) re-enter the premises, without demand or notice, and resume possession without being liable for trespass or for any damages and without terminating the Lease, (2) terminate this Lease at any time upon the date specified in the notice to Tenant, and Tenant's liability for damages shall survive such termination, (3) without terminating the Lease, relet the Leased Premises without the same being deemed an acceptance of a surrender of this Lease nor a waiver of Landlord's rights herein.

A late fee of _____Dollars ($_____) shall be paid by Tenant if Tenant is _____ (_____) days late in payment of the rent.

13. ADVANCES AND INTEREST. If a default occurs, and Landlord exercises its option to cure the default by paying a sum of money, then such sum shall be due from Tenant to Landlord immediately, and shall bear a rate of interest of ten percent (10%) until paid.

14. ATTORNEY FEES. Each party shall pay the other party's reasonable legal costs and attorney's fees incurred in successfully enforcing the terms of this Lease against the other party.

15. ACCESS BY LANDLORD TO LEASED PREMISES. Landlord, agents, and prospective lessees, purchasers, or mortgagees shall be permitted to inspect and examine the Leased Premises at all reasonable times and Landlord to make repairs not made by Tenant.

16. QUIET ENJOYMENT. If Tenant shall perform all of the covenants and agreements herein provided, Tenant shall have peaceable and quiet enjoyment of possession of the Leased Premises without any manner of hindrance from Landlord or any parties lawfully claiming under Landlord.

17. OTHER TERMS.

_____

_____

_____

_____

_____

_____

_____

18. GENERAL AGREEMENT. This Lease shall extend to and be binding upon the heirs, personal representatives, successors, and assigns of the parties. All notices to be given to the parties hereunder shall be deemed sufficiently given when in writing and actually served or deposited in first-class U.S. mail, postage prepaid:

if Landlord

_____

if Tenant

_____

IN WITNESS WHEREOF, Landlord and Tenant have executed this Lease on
_____, 20___.

LANDLORD _____

TENANT   _____

AGREEMENT TO SELL BUSINESS

This is a basic form to buy/sell a small business. Because businesses vary
greatly, use this form as a checklist of terms to consider, and then submit the
marked-up copy to your attorney for final drafting.

Agreement to Sell Business

Agreement made this _____ day of _____, 20__ by and
between _____ and
_____ (doing business as _____)
of _____ (hereinafter referred to
as "Seller") and _____ (hereinafter referred
to as the "Buyer").

Whereas the Seller desires to sell and the Buyer desires to buy the
business of a certain _____ now being operated at
_____ and known as _____
and all assets thereof as contained in Schedule "A" attached hereto, the parties
hereto agree and covenant as follows:

1. The total purchase price for all fixtures, furnishings, and equipment is
$_____ Dollars payable as follows: (a) $_____ paid in cash;
certified or bank checks, as a deposit upon execution of this Agreement, to
be held by _____. (b) $_____ additional to
be paid in cash, certified or bank checks, at the time of passing papers.
(c) $_____ to be paid by a note of the Buyer to the Seller, bearing interest
at the rate of _____ percent per annum with an option of the Buyer to prepay
the entire outstanding obligation without penalty. Said note shall be secured
by a chattel mortgage and financing statement covering the property to be
sold hereunder, together with any and all other property acquired during the
term of said note and placed in or within the premises known as

_____, _____.

2. The property to be sold hereunder shall be conveyed by a standard form
Bill of Sale, duly executed by the Seller.

3. The Seller promises and agrees to convey good, clear, and marketable
title to all the property to be sold hereunder, the same to be free and clear of
all liens and encumbrances. Full possession of said property will be delivered
in the same condition that it is now, reasonable wear and tear expected.

4. Consummation of the sale, with payment by the Buyer of the balance of the down payment and the delivery by the Seller of a Bill of Sale, will take place on or before _____, 20__.

5. The Seller may use the purchase money, or any portion thereof, to clear any encumbrances on the property transferred and in the event that documents reflecting discharge of said encumbrances are not available at the time of sale, the money needed to effectuate such discharges shall be held by the attorneys of the Buyer and Seller in escrow pending the discharges.

6. Until the delivery of the Bill of Sale, the Seller shall maintain insurance on said property in the amount that is presently insured.

7. Operating expenses of _____ including but not limited to rent, taxes, payroll, and water shall be apportioned as of the date of the passing of papers and the net amount thereof shall be added to or deducted from, as the case may be, the proceeds due from the Buyer at the time of delivery of the Bill of Sale.

8. If the Buyer fails to fulfill his or her obligations herein, all deposits made hereunder by the Buyer shall be retained by the Seller as liquidated damages.

9. The Seller promises and agrees not to engage in the same type of business as the one being sold for_____ years from the time of passing, within a _____ radius of _____.

10. The Seller agrees that this Agreement is contingent upon the following conditions: (a) Buyer obtaining a Lease on the said premises or that the existing Lease be assigned in writing to the Buyer. (b) Buyer obtaining the approval from the proper authorities of the transfer of all necessary licenses to the Buyer. (c) The premises shall be in the same condition, reasonable wear and tear expected, on the date of passing as they are currently in.

11. All of the terms, representations and warranties shall survive the closing. This Agreement shall bind and inure to the benefit of the Seller and Buyer and their respective heirs, executors, administrators, successors, and assigns.

12. If this Agreement shall contain any term or provision that shall be invalid or against public policy or if the application of same is invalid or against public policy, then the remainder of this Agreement shall not be affected thereby and shall remain in full force and effect.

IN WITNESS WHEREOF, the parties hereto have caused this instrument to be executed in triplicate on the day and year first above written.

SELLER:

_____

BUYER:

_____

Installment Promissory Note

This installment promissory note is for a loan that you'll repay over a relatively short period of time. The loan is not secured by a mortgage or collateral in this note. State laws vary, so have your attorney review this form before the debtor signs.

Installment Promissory Note

$_____ Final Installment Due Date: _____

For value received, the undersigned promises to pay to the order of _____ the sum of _____
($_____), at the payee's residence or at such other place as the holder hereof may direct in writing, with interest upon the unpaid principal balance at the rate of _____ percent (__%) per annum from the date of this instrument until maturity, and _____ percent (__%) per annum after maturity until paid, with attorneys' fees and costs of collection and without relief from valuation and appraisement laws, payment of the principal and interest to be made as follows:

On or before the _____ of each month, beginning _____ maker shall make principal and interest payment of _____; the final installment shall be due and payable on or before _____.

In event of default in payment of any of said installments when due, the entire unpaid balance of principal and interest shall become due and payable immediately, without notice, at the election of the holder hereof.

No delay or omission on the part of the holder hereof in the exercise of any right or remedy shall operate as a waiver thereof, and no single or partial exercise by the holder hereof of any right or remedy shall preclude other or further exercise thereof or of any other right or remedy.

This note (may) (may not) [delete one] be assigned or negotiated without the written consent of the maker.

This note and all extensions or renewals hereof are not secured by any property.

Signed and delivered at _____, _____ this _____ day of _____, 20___.

_____ as President of ABC, Inc.

Estate Planning Information

Fill out this form before visiting your attorney for estate planning. Keep a copy and update it periodically so that your heirs will know what property you own at your death.

Estate Planning Information Sheet

Name _____ Birth _____

SS# _____

Name of Spouse _____ Birth _____

SS# _____

Residence Address
_____

Names of Children
_____

Age _____ Marital Status _____ Number of Children _____

ASSETS

Real Estate (Residence and Other Land)

Description	Present Value	Purchase Price	Mortgage	How Owned
_____	_____	_____	_____	_____
_____	_____	_____	_____	_____
_____	_____	_____	_____	_____

Business Interests (Sole Proprietor, Partnership, Corporation)

Form of Business	Value of Interest	Who Owns
_____	_____	_____
_____	_____	_____

Accounts (Bank, Brokerage, Certificates of Deposit)

Type of Account	Account Name	Value	Who Owns
_____	_____	_____	_____
_____	_____	_____	_____
_____	_____	_____	_____

Stocks and Bonds

Stocks/Bonds Company	Market Value	Cost	Who Owns

Motor Vehicles

Make	Model	Year	Value	Who Owns

Miscellaneous Personal Property (Household Goods, Sporting Equipment, Jewelry, Art, etc.)

Type of Property	Value	Who Owns

Life Insurance

Insurance Company	Face Value	Cash Value	Insured	Owner	Beneficiary

Retirement Benefits (401(k), Pension/Profit Sharing, IRA, Keogh, etc.)

Type of Plan	Owner	Beneficiary	Value to Date
_____	_____	_____	_____
_____	_____	_____	_____
_____	_____	_____	_____

Other Assets (Including Possible Inheritances)

Type of Asset	Owner	Value
_____	_____	_____
_____	_____	_____
_____	_____	_____

Total Assets $ _____

Liabilities

Type of Liability	Amount	Who Owes
_____	_____	_____
_____	_____	_____
_____	_____	_____

Total Liabilities $_____

Total Assets minus Total Liabilities equals Net Worth $_____

LAST WILL AND TESTAMENT

This is a basic last will and testament for a married person with children who wants to leave his or her property to the spouse and then the children. The will may be modified to add to the "specific devises," such as "I devise 100 shares of XYZ stock to my daughter, Sarah Hiatt." Use the form as a tentative draft of your will, and then submit it to your attorney for the final draft and signing.

Last Will and Testament
of

_____

I,_____, of _____,
_____, being of sound and disposing mind and memory, do make, publish, and declare this to be my Last Will and Testament, and I hereby revoke all Wills and Codicils heretofore made by me.

I. Identification, Definitions, Comments

A. I am married to _____. I have _____ children:
_____.

B. A beneficiary must survive me by thirty (30) days to be entitled to receive a devise.

C. "Issue" is to be construed as lawful lineal descendants, and include adopted persons. Issue shall receive any devise by representation, not per capita.

II. Debts, Expenses, Encumbrances, Taxes

A. I direct that my enforceable debts, expenses of my last illness, and funeral and administrative expenses of my estate shall be paid by my personal representative from my residuary estate. In his or her discretion, my personal representative may continue to pay any installment obligations incurred by me during my lifetime on an installment basis or may prepay any or all of such obligations in whole or in part, and my personal representative may, in his or her discretion, distribute any asset encumbered by such an obligation subject to the obligation.

B. I direct that all inheritance, estate, and succession taxes (including interest and penalties thereon) payable by reason of my death shall be paid out of and be charged generally against my residuary estate without reimbursement from any person.

III. Specific Devises

I devise all my personal effects and household goods, such as jewelry, clothing, furniture, furnishings, silver, books, pictures, motor and recreation vehicles to _____. If he (or she) does not survive me, I devise said property, in equal shares, to _____. If a child does not survive me, then his or her share devolves to the deceased child's issue, or if none survive me, then the share devolves, equally, to the surviving children.

IV. Residuary Estate

I devise my residuary estate to _____. If he (or she) does not survive me, I devise my residuary estate, in equal shares, to _____ _____. If a child does not survive me, then his or her share devolves to the deceased child's issue, or if none survive me, then the share devolves, equally, to the surviving children.

V. Personal Representative

I hereby appoint _____as personal representative. If he (or she) cannot serve, I appoint _____ as co-personal representatives. I authorize unsupervised administration of my estate. I request that the personal representative serve without bond, or if a bond is required, that a minimum bond be required. My personal representative shall have all powers enumerated and granted to personal representatives under the _____ Code, and any other power that may be granted by law, to be exercised without the necessity of Court approval, as my personal representative determines to be in the best interest of the estate.

VI. Guardian

I appoint _____as guardian of the person and property of each of my minor children. If _____ cannot serve as guardian, I appoint _____ as alternate guardian. I request that no bond be required for the guardian; however, if such a bond is required, then I request that such bond be nominal in amount.

VI. Miscellaneous

If my spouse and I executed Wills at approximately the same time, this Last Will and Testament is not made pursuant to any contract or agreement with my spouse.

I have signed this Last Will and Testament in the presence of the undersigned witnesses on this _____ day of _____, 20___.

Signature _____

Printed Name _____

The foregoing instrument, consisting of two typewritten pages, this included, was at _____, _____, this _____ day of _____, 20__, signed, sealed, published, and declared by _____ to be her (or his) Last Will and Testament, in our presence, and we, at her (or his) request and in her (or his) presence and in the presence of each other, have hereunto subscribed our names as attesting witnesses.

_____ residing at _____

_____ residing at _____

Recommended Reading and Websites for the Small Business Owner

One great thing about living in the twenty-first century is that there is no shortage of helpful resources for the small business owner. In fact, there's so much out there it's hard to figure out what's useful and what should be avoided. We've compiled here a listing of excellent books and websites that every small business owner should have on his or her reading list.

Books

The following books, in the editor's humble opinion, should rest on every small business owner's bookshelf.

- Beckwith, Harry. *Invisible Touch: Four Keys to Modern Marketing*, Warner Books, 2000

  Harry Beckwith's Invisible Touch *is a must read for any small business owner who wants to better market his or her products.*

- Carnegie, Dale. *How to Win Friends and Influence People*, Pocket Books, 1990

  This classic will never grow old. Originally published in 1937, Dale Carnegie's advice still rings true decades later.

- Collins, Jim. *Good to Great*, HarperCollins, 2001

  A recent hit—all about how certain well-known companies make themselves better and better.

- Covey, Stephen R. *The Seven Habits of Highly Effective People*, Simon & Schuster, 1990

  This best-selling book explains what separates leaders from the rest of the pack.

■ Dawson, Roger. *The Secret of Power Negotiating, Second Edition*, Career Press, 2000

  Everything in life is a negotiation. Roger Dawson is the master.

■ Drucker, Peter. *Managing for Results*, HarperBusiness, 1993

  Management guru Drucker is read by top CEOs and small business owners around the world. This is one of his best.

■ Ernst & Young. *The Ernst & Young Tax Guide 2004*, John Wiley & Sons, 2003

  An excellent resource for the tax laws affecting both individuals and businesses alike.

■ Gerber, Michael. *The E-Myth Revisited*, Harper Business, 1995

  Why do most small businesses never grow beyond a certain point? Michael Gerber's book explains.

■ Godin, Seth. *Purple Cow—Transform Your Business by Being Remarkable*, Portfolio, 2003

  An excellent little book about making yourself unique.

■ Hopkins, Tom. *How to Master the Art of Selling*, Warner Books, 1988

  One of the most recommended sales books of all time and a must read for small business owners and their sales teams.

■ Locke, Christopher. *Cluetrain Manifesto—The End of Business As Usual*, Perseus Publishing, 2001

  A book about the power of the Internet and what it means to you.

■ Paulson, Edward. *The Complete Idiot's Guide to Starting Your Own Business*, Third Edition. Alpha Books, 2000.

  The standard book for anyone thinking of starting his or her own venture.

■ Peters, Tom. *In Search of Excellence*, Warner Books, 1988

  A groundbreaking classic that studies the best of the best in corporate America and what makes them so successful.

- Strunk, William Jr. *Elements of Style,* Fourth Edition, Pearson Higher Education, 2000

  This book tells you everything you need to know about writing.

- Ziglar, Zig. *Zig Ziglar's Secrets of Closing the Sale*, Fleming H. Revell, 2003

  This book is rivaled only by Zig Ziglar's public presentations. Read it and see him.

WEBSITES

If you haven't saved these websites on your Favorites list, you should book-mark them now!

Business Week **(www.businessweek.com/smallbiz/).** This popular magazine's online edition has interesting articles of particular interest to the small business owner.

Business.com **(www.business.com).** A great business-to-business search engine.

CEO Express (www.ceoexpress.com). A home page created with meticulous care for the CEO of any company—big or small.

Dictionary (www.dictionary.reference.com). Combines a dictionary, the-saurus, a translator, and other tools for the writer.

Entrepreneur Magazine **(www.entrepreneur.com).** A great website contain-ing articles, advice, and important information directly targeted at small busi-nesses and start-ups.

Forbes Magazine **(www.forbes.com).** One of the leading business sites from one of the leading business magazines.

Google (www.google.com). The granddaddy of search engines.

GovSpot (www.govspot.com). A portal for every government website—federal, state, and local. An excellent research tool for laws and data.

Hoovers (www.hoovers.com/free/). An excellent service that provides finan-cial and credit information on thousands of small and large companies.

Inc. Magazine **(www.inc.com).** A website devoted to small business, from the magazine devoted to the same.

Internal Revenue Service (www.irs.gov). The place to go for all things related to taxes, especially downloading forms.

KnowX (www.knowx.com). Need to run a credit check on a customer? Or see if a prospective employee has a prior criminal record? Go no further.

Microsoft bCentral (www.bcentral.com). Setting up a storefront? Need to manage your contacts online? bCentral is a great place to start.

Microsoft Expedia (www.expedia.com). The number-one travel site on the web, and for good reason. Expedia has great bargains and a very easy system for booking your travel.

Quicken for Small Business (http://www.quicken.com/small_business/). More helpful advice from the people who make the world's leading small business accounting and personal financial software.

Small Business Administration (www.sba.gov). The SBA guarantees millions of dollars in loans to small businesses every year. Find out how to qualify here.

Uncle Fed's Tax Board (www.unclefed.com/). Better than the IRS's own site, this user-friendly service helps its viewers find the right forms *and* fill them out correctly.

Wall Street Journal **(www.wsj.com).** The definitive business paper also has one of the strongest paid online reader communities, too.

Index

F